16th edition

ATKINSON & HILGARD'S
INTRODUCTION
TO PSYCHOLOGY

CENGAGE

Australia • Br... ...n • United Kingdom • United States

Susan Nolen-Hoeksema

Barbara L. Fredrickson

Geoffrey R. Loftus

Christel Lutz

Atkinson & Hilgard's Introduction to Psychology, 16th Edition
Susan Nolen-Hoeksema, Barbara L. Fredrickson, Geoffey R. Loftus and Christel Lutz

Publisher: Andrew Ashwin

Commissioning Editor: Annabel Ainscow

Editorial Assistants: Ana Arede & Jenny Grene

Senior Production Editor: Alison Burt

Senior Manufacturing Buyer: Eyvett Davis

Marketing Manager: Vicky Fielding

Typesetter: MPS Limited

Cover design: Adam Renvoize

Text design: Design Deluxe

For product information and technology assistance, contact **emea.info@cengage.com**.

For permission to use material from this text or product, and for permission queries, email **emea.permissions@cengage.com**.

British Library Cataloguing-in-Publication Data
A catalogue record for this book is available from the British Library.

ISBN: 978-1-4080-8902-6

Cengage Learning EMEA
Cheriton House, North Way, Andover, Hampshire, SP10 5BE, United Kingdom

Cengage Learning products are represented in Canada by Nelson Education Ltd.

For your lifelong learning solutions, visit **www.cengage.co.uk**

Purchase your next print book, e-book or e-chapter at **www.cengagebrain.com**

Printed in China by RR Donnelley
1 2 3 4 5 6 7 8 9 10 – 16 15 14

BRIEF CONTENTS

1 The Nature of Psychology 2

2 Biological Foundations of Psychology 32

3 Psychological Development 66

4 Sensory Processes 100

5 Perception 144

6 Consciousness 194

7 Learning and Conditioning 224

8 Memory 258

9 Language and Thought 304

10 Motivation 342

11 Emotion 376

12 Intelligence 412

13 Personality 434

14 Stress, Health, and Coping 470

15 Psychological Disorders 496

16 Treatment of Mental Health Problems 536

17 Social Influence 556

18 Social Cognition 596

Appendix: Statistical Methods and Measurement 630

Glossary 640

References 660

Name Index 716

Subject Index 717

Credits Page 722

DEDICATION

This 16th Edition of the work is dedicated to the memory of Susan Nolen-Hoeksema who died unexpectedly in January 2013, and to her surviving family – her husband, Richard Nolen-Hoeksema, and her son, Michael Nolen-Hoeksema.

CONTENTS

Cutting edge research xv
Seeing both sides xvi
Preface xviii
Walkthrough tour xxii
About the Authors xxiv

1 THE NATURE OF PSYCHOLOGY 2

The Scope of Psychology 5
  Interim Summary 7
  Critical Thinking Questions 7

The Historical Origins of Psychology 7
  Nature–nurture debate 8
  The beginnings of scientific psychology 8
  Structuralism and functionalism 9
  Behaviorism 9
  Gestalt psychology 9
  Psychoanalysis 10
  Later developments in twentieth-century psychology 11
  Interim Summary 11
  Critical Thinking Questions 11

Contemporary Psychological Perspectives 12
  The biological perspective 12
  The behavioral perspective 13
  The cognitive perspective 13
  The psychoanalytic perspective 14
  The subjectivist perspective 14
  Relationships between psychological and biological perspectives 15
  Major subfields of psychology 16
  Interim Summary 17
  Critical Thinking Questions 17

How Psychological Research is Done 19
  Generating hypotheses 19
  Experiments 19
  Correlation 21
  Observation 23
  Literature reviews 24
  Ethics of psychological research 24
  Interim Summary 25
  Critical Thinking Questions 25

2 BIOLOGICAL FOUNDATIONS OF PSYCHOLOGY 32

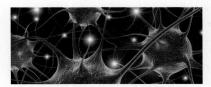

The Study of the Biological Bases of Psychology 34
  Interim Summary 35
  Critical Thinking Questions 35

Neurons, the Building Blocks of the Nervous System 36
  Action potentials 37
  Neural coding and synaptic transmission 39
  Interim Summary 40
  Critical Thinking Questions 41
  Neurotransmitters 41
  Interim Summary 42
  Critical Thinking Questions 42

The Organization of the Brain 42
  The hindbrain 42
  The midbrain 43
  The forebrain 43
  Mapping the brain 47
  Asymmetries in the brain 48

The Autonomic Nervous System 52
  Interim Summary 54
  Critical Thinking Questions 54

The Endocrine System 54
    Interim Summary 55
    Critical Thinking Questions 55

Evolution, Genes, and Behavior 55
    Evolution of behavior 56
    Chromosomes and genes 56
    Genetic studies of behavior 58
    Interim Summary 62
    Critical Thinking Questions 62

3 PSYCHOLOGICAL DEVELOPMENT 66

Nature Versus Nurture 68
    Stages of development 70
    Interim Summary 71
    Critical Thinking Questions 71

Capacities of the Newborn 71
    Vision 71
    Hearing 72
    Taste and smell 73
    Learning and memory 73
    Interim Summary 75
    Critical Thinking Questions 75

Cognitive Development in Childhood 75
    Piaget's stage theory 75
    A critique of Piaget's theory 78
    Alternatives to Piaget's theory 79
    Theory of mind 82
    The development of moral judgment 83
    Interim Summary 85
    Critical Thinking Questions 85

Personality and Social Development 86
    Temperament 86
    Early social behavior 87
    Attachment 89
    Self-concept 92
    Interim Summary 93
    Critical Thinking Questions 93

Adolescent Development 93
    Biological development 93
    Social relationships in adolescence 95
    Interim Summary 98
    Critical Thinking Questions 98

4 SENSORY PROCESSES 100

Characteristics of Sensory Modalities 102
    Threshold sensitivity 102
    Suprathreshold sensation 105
    Signal detection theory 106
    Sensory coding 108
    Interim Summary 110
    Critical Thinking Questions 111

Vision 111
    Light and vision 111
    The visual system 111
    Seeing light 113
    Seeing patterns 115
    Seeing color 116
    Sensation and perception: A preview 121
    Interim Summary 122
    Critical Thinking Questions 122

Audition 123
    Sound waves 123
    The auditory system 124
    Hearing sound intensity 125
    Hearing pitch 126
    Interim Summary 129
    Critical Thinking Questions 129

Other Senses 129
    Olfaction 129
    Gustation 131
    Pressure and temperature 132
    Pain 133
    Interim Summary 140
    Critical Thinking Questions 140

5 PERCEPTION 144

What is the Use of Perception? 147
Processing and using incoming sensory information 147
Five functions of perception 147
Interim Summary 148

Attention 148
Selective attention 148
Auditory attention 149
Attention, perception, and memory 150
Costs and benefits of selectively attending to stimuli 150
Interim Summary 151
Critical Thinking Questions 151

Localization 151
Separation of objects 151
Perceiving distance 155
Perceiving motion 157
Interim Summary 159
Critical Thinking Questions 159

Recognition 159
Global-to-local processing 159
The binding problem: Pre-attentive and attentive processes 161
Determining what an object is 162
Later stages of recognition: Network models 163
Recognizing natural objects and top-down processing 165
Special processing of socially relevant stimuli: Face recognition 168
Failure of recognition 169
Interim Summary 170
Critical Thinking Questions 170

Abstraction 170
Exact to abstract 171
The advantages of abstraction: Required storage and processing speed 171
Interim Summary 173
Critical Thinking Questions 173

Perceptual Constancies 173
The nature of constancies 174
Color and brightness constancy 174
Shape constancy 175
Size constancy 176
Illusions 176
Constancies in all sensory modalities 178
interim summary 178
Critical Thinking Questions 179

Divisions of Labor In The Brain 179
The neural basis of attention 179
The visual cortex 180
Recognition versus localization systems 181
Interim Summary 183
Critical Thinking Questions 183

Perceptual Development 183
Discrimination by infants 183
Controlled stimulation 185
Interim Summary 189
Critical Thinking Question 189

6 CONSCIOUSNESS 194

Aspects of Consciousness 196
Consciousness 196
Preconscious memories 197
The unconscious 197
Automaticity and dissociation 198
Interim Summary 199
Critical Thinking Questions 199

Sleep and Dreams 199
Stages of sleep 200
Sleep theory 202
Sleep-wake disorders 202
Dreams 204
Interim Summary 206
Critical Thinking Questions 206

Meditation 206
Interim Summary 208
Critical Thinking Questions 208

Hypnosis 208
Induction of hypnosis 208
Hypnotic suggestions 209
Interim Summary 210
Critical Thinking Questions 210

Psychoactive Drugs 210
Depressants 211
Illicit drugs 214
Opiates 215
Stimulants 216
Interim Summary 217
Critical Thinking Questions 220

7 LEARNING AND CONDITIONING 224

Perspectives on Learning 226
Interim Summary 227
Critical Thinking Questions 227

Classical Conditioning 227
Pavlov's experiments 227
Cognitive factors 231
Biological constraints 232
Interim Summary 233
Critical Thinking Questions 233

Instrumental Conditioning 234
Skinner's experiments 234
Cognitive factors 241
Biological constraints 242
Interim Summary 242
Critical Thinking Questions 242

Learning and Cognition 242
Observational learning 243
Prior beliefs 244
Interim Summary 246
Critical Thinking Questions 246

Learning and the Brain 246
Habituation and sensitization 246
Classical conditioning 247
Cellular basis of learning 248
Interim Summary 250
Critical Thinking Questions 250

Learning and Motivation 251
Arousal 251
From incentives to goals 251
Intrinsic motivation and learning 251
Interim Summary 254
Critical Thinking Questions 254

8 MEMORY 258

Three Important Distinctions 260
Three stages of memory 260
Three memory stores 261
Different memories for different kinds of information 261
Interim Summary 262
Critical Thinking Question 262

Sensory Memory 262
Sperling's experiments: The partial-report experiment 262
Visible persistence: The temporal integration experiment 263
Partial report, visible persistence, and a theory that integrates them 263
Interim Summary 264
Critical Thinking Questions 265

Working Memory 265
Encoding 265
Current conceptions of working memory 266
Storage 268
Retrieval 269
Working memory and thought 270
Transfer from working memory to long-term memory 270
Division of brain labor between working memory and long-term memory 272
Interim Summary 272
Critical Thinking Questions 273

Long-Term Memory 273
Encoding 273
Retrieval cues 274
Forgetting: Loss of information from storage 277
Interactions between encoding and retrieval 277
Emotional factors in forgetting 278
Interim Summary 280
Critical Thinking Question 280

Implicit Memory 280
Memory in amnesia 280
A variety of memory systems 283
Implicit memory in normal individuals 284
Interim Summary 285
Critical Thinking Questions 285

Constructive Memory 285
  Piaget's childhood memory 286
  Constructive processes at the time of memory
    encoding 286
  Post-event memory reconstruction 287
  Constructive memory and the legal system 290
  Memory errors and normal memory 293
  Interim Summary 293
  Critical Thinking Questions 294

Improving Memory 294
  Chunking and memory span 294
  Imagery and encoding 295
  Elaboration and encoding 295
  Context and retrieval 296
  Organization 296
  Practicing retrieval 297
  Interim Summary 300
  Critical Thinking Questions 300

9 LANGUAGE AND THOUGHT 304

Language and Communication 306
  Properties of language 306
  Language structure 306
  Effects of context on comprehension and production 309
  The neural basis of language 309
  Interim Summary 311
  Critical Thinking Questions 311

The Development of Language 311
  Milestones 311
  Language acquisition 313
  Interim Summary 316
  Critical Thinking Questions 317

**Concepts and Categorization: The Building Blocks of
Thought** 317
  Functions of concepts 317
  Prototypes 318
  Hierarchies of concepts 320
  Different categorization processes 320
  Acquiring concepts 321
  The neural basis of concepts and categorization 322
  Interim Summary 323
  Critical Thinking Questions 324

Reasoning and Decision-Making 324
  Deductive reasoning 324
  Inductive reasoning 325
  The neural basis of reasoning 328
  Interim Summary 329
  Critical Thinking Questions 330

Thought in Action: Problem-Solving 330
  Problem-solving strategies 330
  Representing the problem 331
  Imaginal thought 332
  Experts versus novices 335
  Automaticity 336
  Interim Summary 337
  Critical Thinking Questions 337

10 MOTIVATION 342

Drives and Homeostasis 345
  Body temperature and homeostasis 345
  Thirst as a homeostatic process 346
  Interim Summary 347
  Critical Thinking Questions 347

Incentive Motivation and Reward 347
  Drug addiction 349
  Interim Summary 351
  Critical Thinking Questions 352

Hunger, Eating, and Eating Disorders 352
  Interactions between homeostasis and incentives 352
  Physiological hunger cues 354
  Integration of hunger signals 354
  Obesity 356
  Anorexia and bulimia 359
  Interim Summary 362
  Critical Thinking Questions 363

Gender and Sexuality 363
  Early sexual development 363
  Hormones versus environment 364
  Adult sexuality 365
  Sexual orientation 369
  Interim Summary 373
  Critical Thinking Questions 373

11 EMOTION 376

Components of Emotion 378
   Interim Summary 380
   Critical Thinking Questions 380

Cognitive Appraisal and Emotion 380
   Discovery of appraisals 380
   Themes and dimensions of appraisals 382
   Conscious and unconscious appraisals 384
   Appraisals in the brain 384
   Interim Summary 385
   Critical Thinking Questions 385

Subjective Experiences and Emotion 385
   Feelings modify attention and learning 386
   Feelings modify evaluations and judgments 386

Thought–Action Tendencies and Emotion 387
   Interim Summary 388
   Critical Thinking Questions 388

Bodily Changes and Emotion 388
   Intensity of emotions 389
   Differentiation of emotions 390
   Interim Summary 392
   Critical Thinking Questions 393

Facial Muscle Movements and Emotion 393
   Communication of emotion through facial muscle
     movements 393
   The facial feedback hypothesis 395
   Interim Summary 395
   Critical Thinking Questions 395

Responses to Emotion: Emotion Regulation 395
   Interim Summary 397
   Critical Thinking Questions 397

Emotions, Gender, and Culture 397
   Gender differences 398
   Cultural differences 399
   Interim Summary 400
   Critical Thinking Questions 401

Positive Psychology 401
   Positive emotions and longevity 401
   Positive emotions build personal resources 403
   Interim Summary 408
   Critical Thinking Question 409

12 INTELLIGENCE 412

Assessment of Intellectual Abilities 414
   Early intelligence tests 414
   The Stanford-Binet Intelligence Scale 414
   The Wechsler Intelligence Scales 415
   Interim Summary 416
   Critical Thinking Questions 417

**Contemporary Theories: Many or Few
Intelligences?** 417
   Gardner's theory of multiple intelligences 418
   Anderson's theory of intelligence and cognitive
     development 419
   Sternberg's triarchic theory 420
   Interim Summary 421
   Critical Thinking Questions 421

Genetics and Intelligence 421
   Heritability 422
   Interim Summary 424
   Critical Thinking Questions 425

Emotional Intelligence 425
   Interim Summary 426
   Critical Thinking Questions 426

General Learning Disability 426
   Causes of general learning disability 427
   Treatments for general learning disability 428
   Interim Summary 429
   Critical Thinking Questions 432

13 PERSONALITY 434

Conceptualizing and Measuring Personality 437
   How many traits? 437
   Personality inventories 438
   Interim Summary 440
   Critical Thinking Questions 441

The Psychoanalytic Approach 441
Defense mechanisms 442
Personality development 444
Modifications of Freud's theories 444
Projective tests 445
Problems with projective tests 447
A psychoanalytic portrait of human nature 447
An evaluation of the psychoanalytic approach 447
Interim Summary 449
Critical Thinking Questions 449

The Behaviorist Approach 449
Social learning and conditioning 450
A behaviorist portrait of human behavior 450
An evaluation of the behaviorist approach 451
Interim Summary 451
Critical Thinking Questions 451

The Cognitive Approach 451
Social-learning theory 451
Kelly's personal construct theory 453
Self-schemas 453
A cognitive portrait of human nature 454
An evaluation of the cognitive approach 454
Interim Summary 455
Critical Thinking Questions 455

The Humanistic Approach 455
Carl Rogers 455
Abraham Maslow 457
A humanistic portrait of human nature 458
An evaluation of the humanistic approach 458
Interim Summary 459
Critical Thinking Questions 459

The Evolutionary Approach 459
An evolutionary portrait of human nature 460
An evaluation of the evolutionary approach 462
Interim Summary 462
Critical Thinking Questions 462

The Genetics of Personality 463
Interactions between personality and environment 463
Interim Summary 467
Critical Thinking Questions 467

14 STRESS, HEALTH, AND COPING 470

Interim Summary 474
Critical Thinking Questions 474

Physiological Reactions to Stress 474
Interim Summary 476

Stress and Physical Health 476
Coronary heart disease 477
The immune system 478
Health-related behaviors 480
Interim Summary 481
Critical Thinking Questions 481

Stress and Psychological Health 481
Interim Summary 484
Critical Thinking Questions 484

Appraisals, Coping, and Health 485
Appraisals 485
Coping 487
Interim Summary 490
Critical Thinking Questions 490

Managing Stress 490
Behavioral techniques 490
Cognitive techniques 491
Modifying type A behavior 491
Interim Summary 494
Critical Thinking Questions 494

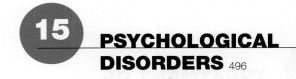

15 PSYCHOLOGICAL DISORDERS 496

Defining Abnormality 498
Deviation from cultural norms 498
Unusualness 499
Maladaptive behavior 499
Personal distress 499
Classifying mental health problems 500
Perspectives on mental health problems 502
Interim Summary 502
Critical Thinking Questions 502

Anxiety Disorders 503
Panic disorders 503
Understanding panic disorder and agoraphobia 504
Phobias 506
Understanding phobias 507
Obsessive-compulsive disorder 508
Understanding obsessive-compulsive disorder 509
Interim Summary 510
Critical Thinking Questions 511

Depression and Bipolar Disorders 511
   Depression 511
   Bipolar disorder 512
   Understanding mood disorders 513
   Interim Summary 518
   Critical Thinking Questions 518

Schizophrenia 518
   Characteristics of schizophrenia 518
   Behavioral symptoms and withdrawal from reality 520
   Culture and the progression of schizophrenia 521
   Understanding schizophrenia 521
   Interim Summary 523
   Critical Thinking Questions 524

Personality Disorders 524
   Antisocial personality disorder 524
   Understanding antisocial personality disorder 525
   Borderline personality disorder 526
   Understanding borderline personality disorder 527
   Interim Summary 528
   Critical Thinking Questions 528

Autism spectrum disorder 528
   Diagnosis of autism spectrum disorder 528
   Understanding autism spectrum disorder 532
   Interim Summary 533
   Critical Thinking Questions 533

16

TREATMENT OF MENTAL HEALTH PROBLEMS 536

Historical Background 538
   Interim Summary 541
   Critical Thinking Questions 541

Techniques of Psychotherapy 541
   Behavior therapies 541
   Systematic desensitization and in vivo exposure 542
   Cognitive-behavior therapies 544
   Psychodynamic therapies 545
   Humanistic therapies 546
   Interim Summary 548
   Critical Thinking Questions 548

Biological Therapies 548
   Psychotherapeutic drugs 548
   Electroconvulsive therapy 549
   Combining biological and psychological therapies 550
   Interim Summary 550
   Critical Thinking Questions 550

Enhancing Mental Health 551
   Interim Summary 554
   Critical Thinking Questions 554

17

SOCIAL INFLUENCE 556

The Presence of Others 559
   Social facilitation and social inhibition 559
   Deindividuation 561
   Bystander effects 562
   Interim Summary 565
   Critical Thinking Questions 565

Compliance and Obedience 566
   Conformity to a majority 566
   Minority influence 570
   Obedience to authority 571
   Interim Summary 578
   Critical Thinking Questions 578

Internalization 578
   Self-justification 578
   Reference groups and identification 582
   Interim Summary 584
   Critical Thinking Questions 584

Group Interactions 584
   Institutional norms 585
   Group decision-making 586
   Interim Summary 589
   Critical Thinking Questions 592

Recap: Social Psychological Views of the Seemingly Inexplicable 592
   Critical Thinking Questions 592

18 SOCIAL COGNITION 596

Impression Formation 598
    Stereotypes 598
    Individuation 604
    Attributions 607
    Interim Summary 609
    Critical Thinking Questions 610

Attitudes 611
    Persuasive communication 611
    Attitudes and behavior 614
    Interim Summary 616
    Critical Thinking Questions 616

Interpersonal Attraction 616
    Liking and attraction 617
    Loving and mating 620
    Interim Summary 623
    Critical Thinking Questions 626

Recap: a Tale of Two Modes of Social Cognition 626
    Critical Thinking Questions 626

Appendix: Statistical Methods and Measurement 630
Glossary 640
References 660
Name Index 716
Subject Index 717
Credits Page 722

CUTTING EDGE RESEARCH

1 Twenty-First-Century Psychology 17
Barbara L. Fredrickson, University of North Carolina, Chapel Hill

2 What Happens in the Brains of Expert Athletes? 52
Aidan Moran, University College Dublin

3 Adolescents and the Internet 94
Susan Nolen-Hoeksema, Yale University

4 Where in the Brain Are Illusions? 127
Scott Murray, University of Washington

5 Distraction via Virtual Reality Diminishes Severe Pain 152
Hunter Hoffman, University of Washington

6 Pictures of Consciousness? 207
Susan Nolen-Hoeksema, Yale University

7 Do Singing Mice Provide Insights into the Evolution of Human Speech? 245
Julia Fischer, German Primate Center

8 How Metacognition can be Used to Improve Student Performance 284
Phil Higham, University of Southampton

9 Evolutionary Research into the Nature of Language 329
Gareth Davies, University of the Highlands and Islands

10 Environment-Related Human Needs and Urban Planning 350
Dr Majken Bieniok, Humbolt University, Berlin

11 Emotions Change Gene Expression in Immune Cells 392
Barbara L. Fredrickson, University of North Carolina, Chapel Hill

12 Strengths-Based Approaches to Intellectual Difficulties 421
Israel Berger, Sydney Medical School, University of Sydney

13 Finding the Self in the Brain 461
Susan Nolen-Hoeksema, Yale University

14 Using New Media to Improve People's Health 489
Susan Nolen-Hoeksema, Yale University

15 Understanding Suicide 516
Susan Nolen-Hoeksema, Yale University

16 Mindfulness for Mental Health Problems 547
Meg Barker, Senior Lecturer in Psychology, The Open University

17 The Collapse of Compassion 566
C. Daryl Cameron, University of Iowa

18 Embodied Social Cognition 610
Barbara L. Fredrickson, University of North Carolina, Chapel Hill

SEEING BOTH SIDES

1 ARE WE NATURALLY SELFISH? 26

→ *We are naturally selfish* by George C. Williams, State University of New York, Stony Brook

→ *We are not naturally selfish* by Frans B. M. de Waal, Emory University

2 TO LOCALIZE OR NOT TO LOCALIZE: THAT'S THE QUESTION 60

→ *To localize* by Annick Ledebt, VU University, Amsterdam

→ *To not localize* by John Stins, VU University, Amsterdam

3 HOW INSTRUMENTAL ARE PARENTS IN THE DEVELOPMENT OF THEIR CHILDREN? 96

→ *Parents have no lasting influence on the personality or intelligence of their children* by Judith Rich Harris, award-winning psychologist and author (*The Nurture Assumption, No Two Alike*)

→ *Parents are instrumental in the development of their children* by Jerome Kagan, Harvard University

4 SHOULD OPIOIDS BE USED FOR TREATING CHRONIC PAIN? 136

→ *Opioids are an appropriate treatment for chronic pain* by Robert N. Jamison, Harvard Medical School

→ *Why opioids should be less frequently used for treating people with chronic pain* by Dennis C. Turk, University of Washington School of Medicine

5 IS PERCEPTUAL DEVELOPMENT AN INNATE OR SOCIALLY ACQUIRED PROCESS? 186

→ *Perceptual development is an intrinsic process* by Elizabeth S. Spelke, Massachusetts Institute of Technology

→ *Perceptual development is an activity-dependent process* by Mark Johnson, University of London

6 DOES BRAIN DEATH MEAN DEATH? 218

→ *Cellular death following brain death* by Israel Berger, Sydney Medical School, University of Sydney

→ *Understanding and defining what death really is* by Matthew Georgiades, Sydney Medical School, University of Sydney

7 WHAT ARE THE BASES OF SOCIAL LEARNING? 252

→ *Social learning cannot be explained by associative learning* by Juan Carlos Gómez, School of Psychology, University of St. Andrews

→ *Learning, not instinct, determines behavior: social or otherwise* by Phil Reed, Swansea University

8 ARE REPRESSED MEMORIES VALID? 298

→ *Recovered memories or false memories?* by Kathy Pezdek, Clairmont College

→ *Repressed memories: a dangerous belief?* by Elizabeth F. Loftus, University of California, Irvine

9 DO PEOPLE WHO SPEAK DIFFERENT LANGUAGES THINK DIFFERENTLY? 338

→ *The role of language in mind* by Stephen C. Levinson and Asifa Majid, Max-Planck-Institute for Psycholinguistics, Nijmegen

→ *How is language related to thought?* by Anna Papafragou, University of Delaware

10 DO THE BRAINS OF ADDICTS REVEAL DISORDERS WITH REWARD OR WITH ANTI-REWARD? 370

→ *The case for disorders with reward* by Kent Berridge, University of Michigan

→ *The case for problems with anti-reward* by George F. Koob, The Scripps Research Institute, California, USA

11 What Is the Underlying Structure of Emotions? 404

➜ *Psychological constructionist approaches to emotion* by Kristen A. Lindquist, University of North Carolina, Chapel Hill and Lisa F. Barrett, Northeastern University

➜ *An argument for discrete emotions* by Robert W. Levenson, University of California–Berkeley

12 How Important Is Emotional Intelligence? 430

➜ *Emotional intelligence is important* by Marc A. Brackett and Peter Salovey, Yale University

➜ *A critique of emotional intelligence* by Chockalingam Viswesvaran, Florida International University

13 Is Freud's Influence on Psychology Still Alive? 464

➜ *Freud's influence on psychology is alive and vibrant* by Joel Weinberger, Adelphi University, Long Island, New York

➜ *Freud is a dead weight on psychology* by John F. Kihlstrom, University of California, Berkeley

14 Are there Universal or Distinct Reactions to Coping with Stress? 492

➜ *There are universal coping reactions present across populations* by Roslyn Thomas, Webster University, Geneva

➜ *There are distinct reactions for populations under extreme stress* by Erik Mansager, Webster University, Geneva

15 Is Attention Deficit Hyperactivity Disorder (ADHD) Overdiagnosed? 530

➜ *ADHD is overdiagnosed* by Caryn L. Carlson, The University of Texas at Austin

➜ *ADHD is neither overdiagnosed nor overtreated* by William Pelham, SUNY Buffalo

16 Is Alcoholics Anonymous (AA) an Effective Intervention for Alcohol Misuse? 552

➜ *Alcoholics anonymous: an evidence-based resource* by Keith Humphreys, Veterans Affairs Palo Alto Health Care System and Department of Psychiatry and Behavioral Sciences, Stanford University

➜ *Alcoholics anonymous is not the only way* by G. Alan Marlatt, University of Washington

17 Are the Effects of Affirmative Action Positive or Negative? 590

➜ *Negative aspects of affirmative action* by Madeline E. Heilman, New York University

➜ *The benefits of affirmative action* by Faye J. Crosby, University of California, Santa Cruz

18 Should We Trust Automatic Thinking? 624

➜ *Yes, we should trust automatic thinking* by Ap Dijksterhuis, Radboud University Nijmegen

➜ *No, we should not trust automatic thinking* by B. Keith Payne, University of North Carolina, Chapel Hill

PREFACE

INTRODUCTION

This 16th Edition of *Atkinson & Hilgard's Introduction to Psychology* includes several welcome developments to the text since the publication of the 15th Edition in 2009. Firstly, the author team has been expanded, and for the first time includes authors from outside North America, bringing a fresh international perspective to the textbook. The established author team of Susan Nolen-Hoeksema, Barbara L. Fredrickson, and Geoffrey R. Loftus has been joined by Christel Lutz (University of Utrecht), who have helped to add a fresh European influence, and create a truly transatlantic introductory textbook for undergraduate psychology students wherever they are studying.

APPROACH

For those familiar with the content, style and approach of *Atkinson & Hilgard*, which was first published in 1953, this new edition is the next step in the rich history of the book. As a book with an established reputation on both sides of the Atlantic, the introduction of European coauthors has coincided with a move to broaden the international horizons of the text. Our aim is to increase the relevance and accessibility of *Atkinson & Hilgard* to the many lecturers and students who use the book outside of North America without diluting the appeal to our longstanding American readership.

As with previous editions we continue to cover classic landmark research while also investigating contemporary cutting edge research. The classic studies that are the foundation of psychology are critical for students to understand and appreciate. We continue to cover these studies, emphasizing their impact on the field and on our daily lives. We also acknowledge the tremendous amount of innovative work that is being done in contemporary psychology. In the 16th Edition, we cover the most promising new work in psychology, including developments in cognitive neuroscience and research on the brain and behavior, creative applications of basic research in sensation and perception, the 'new wave' of research on emotion, intelligence, genetic, and evolutionary theories of personality, positive psychology, and social psychological perspectives on culture. The result is a comprehensive and exciting overview combining the best of the old and the best of the new in psychology.

WHAT'S NEW?

Each chapter has been carefully revised with the help of critical review input from specialists in each chapter topic, in order to ensure that each chapter is thoroughly up-to-date and contains a careful blend of coverage drawing from notable trends in psychology from North America, Europe, and beyond. The recent changes from DSM-IV-TR to DSM-5 have been taken account of.

Over 350 new references have been added since the 15th Edition, including a mix of very recent research, and broader coverage of relevant studies in each topic area. The teaching of psychology is constantly evolving and careful attention has been paid to ensure that this edition covers the needs of introductory psychology courses, at undergraduate level, as they are being taught in 2013.

The *Seeing Both Sides* features, which present divergent perspectives on specific topics, have been preserved in the 16th Edition and can be found towards the end of each chapter. Most have been revised by existing authors, or have been replaced by new debates reflecting current hot topics of debate. We thank the wide range of highly regarded international contributors who have shared their own research-driven perspectives with us throughout this edition.

The *Cutting Edge Research* features have also even been revised to include new topics, such as how emotional habits alter gene expression, and embodied social cognition, and existing features have been updated to reflect how different areas of research have evolved in recent years.

All other student-friendly learning features that underpinned the previous edition have been retained and updated to match the new content of the 16th Edition. Each subsection of each chapter opens with *Learning Objectives* and concludes with an *Interim Summary* and *Critical Thinking Questions* allowing readers to break down their study of content into digestible chunks.

REVIEWER ACKNOWLEDGMENTS

The publishers and authors would like to thank the following academics for providing in-depth review feedback which has helped to shape this new edition:

Mohammad	Adnan Alghorani	Associate Professor of Psychology, United Arab Emirates University, UAE
Kimmo	Alho	Professor of Psychology, University of Helsinki, Finland
Reem	AL-Sabah	Assistant Professor, Psychology, Kuwait University, Kuwait
Y. Gavriel	Ansara	Academic Tutor, Department of Psychology, University of Surrey, UK
Josephine	Arasa	Assistant Professor of Psychology, United States International University, Kenya
Dr Chris	Barnes	Lecturer in Psychology, University of Derby, UK
Avi	Besser	Professor of Psychology, Sapir Academic College, Israel
Sinead	Bracken	Psychology Lecturer, Athlone Institute of Technology, UK
Chris	Chandler	Principal Psychology Lecturer, London Metropolitan University, UK
Maurizio	Codispoti	Associate Professor, Psychology, University of Bologna, Italy
Ihsan	Dag	Professor, Psychology, Hacettepe University, Turkey
Gareth	Davies	Lecturer, Psychology, University of the Highlands and Islands, UK
Boele	de raad	Emeritus Professor of Psychology, University of Groningen, The Netherlands
Susanne	Ehrlich	Senior Lecturer, Psychology, London Metropolitan University, UK
Ian	Fairholm	Teaching Fellow & Deputy Director of Undergraduate Studies in Psychology, University of Bath, UK
Alexandra	Freund	Professor of Psychology, Dept. of Psychology, University of Zurich, Switzerland
Kerry	Greer	Psychology Lecturer, Mary Immaculate College, Ireland, UK
Aldis	Gudmundsdottir	Psychology Lecturer, Hamrahlid College, Iceland
Ran	Hassin	Professor of Psychology, The Hebrew University, Israel
Kenneth	Holmqvist	Professor of Psychology, Lund University, Sweden
Merima	Homarac	Psychology Lecturer, United World College, Mostar
Odilo	Huber	Psychology Lecturer, University of Fribourg, Switzerland
Dr. Daniel	Kahn	Psychology Lecturer, Bar Ilan University, Israel
Peter	Karlsson	Psychology Lecturer, Halmstad University, Sweden
Shaul	Kimhi	Professor of Psychology, Tel Hai College, Israel
Jurek	Kirakowski	Senior Lecturer in Psychology, University College Cork, UK
Svein	Larsen	Professor of Psychology, University of Bergen, Norway
Lilac	Lev Ari	Psychology Lecturer, Ruppin Academic Center, Israel
Elaine	Luti	Adjunct Professor of Psychology, John Cabot University, Italy
Dr Anne	Manyande	Programme Leader for Psychology, University of West London, UK
Jennifer	Meehan	Psychology Lecturer, Liverpool John Moores University, UK
Maggie	Moremi	Psychology Lecturer, University of Limpopo, South Africa
Julita	Naviaitiene	Psychology Lecturer, Vilnius Pedagogical University, Lithuania
Dr Lisa	Oakley	Psychology Lecturer, Manchester Metropolitan University, UK
Brigid	O'Hea	Psychology Lecturer, Tralee Institute of Technology, Ireland, UK
Gert-Jan	Pepping	Psychology Lecturer, University of Groningen, The Netherlands
Oliver	Robinson	Senior Lecturer in Psychology, University of Greenwich, UK
Dr R	Sanders	Senior Lecturer in Psychology, York St John University, UK
Brian	Schiff	Associate Professor of Psychology, The American University of Paris, France
Mark	Sergeant	Senior Lecturer in Psychology, Nottingham Trent University, UK
Roma	Simulioniene	Associate Professor of Psychology, Klaipeda University, Lithuania
Benjamin	Spicher	Lecturer in Psychology, Zentrum für Testentwicklung, Switzerland
Lievens	Stefaan	Professor of Psychology, University Ghent, Belgium
John	Stins	VU University, Amsterdam, The Netherlands
Sabrina	Tahboub-Schulte	Assistant Professor of Psychology, American University of Sharjah, UAE

Ros	Thomas	Head of Psychology and Counseling Dept, Webster University, Geneva, Switzerland
Mladenka	Tkalcic	Professor of Psychology, University of Rijeka, Croatia
Joseph	Tzelgov	Professor of Psychology, Ben Gurion University, Israel
Catherine	Ward	Senior Lecturer in Psychology, University of Capetown, South Africa
Wim	Waterink	Associate Professor of Psychology, Open University of the Netherlands
Klaas	Wijma	Professor of Psychology, Linköping University, Sweden
Ilene	Winckler	Professor of Psychology, Touro College Berlin, Germany

We would also like to recognize the following academics who contributed to the development of previous editions of the text through review feedback:

James Ackil, Western Illinois University; Cynthia Allen, Westchester Community College; Eileen Astor-Stetson, Bloomsburg University; Gordon D. Atlas, Alfred University; Raymond R. Baird, University of Texas, San Antonio; Jeff Baker, The University of Texas Medical Branch; Ted A. Barker, Okaloosa-Walton Community College, N. Jay Bean, Vassar College; A. G. Beese, University of Leeds; Charles Behling, University of Michigan; John B. Best, Eastern Illinois University; Randolph Blake, Vanderbilt University; Terry Blumenthal, Wake Forest University; Richard W. Bowen, Loyola University; Thomas Brothen, University of Minnesota; James P. Buchanan, University of Scranton; James F. Calhoun, University of Georgia; Rose Capdevila, University College Northampton; Charles S. Carver, University of Miami; Avshalom Caspi, University of Wisconsin; Janice Chapman, Bossier Parrish Community College; Paul Chara, Loras College; Stephen Clark, Vassar College; Stanley Coren, University of British Columbia; Daniel Cervone, University of Illinois at Chicago; Edward Deci, University of Rochester; G. William Domhoff, University of California, Santa Cruz; Richard Eglfaer, Sam Houston State University; Gilles Einstein, Furman University; Judith Erickson, University of Minnesota; G. William Farthing, University of Maine; Mary Ann Fischer, Indiana University Northwest; William Rick Fry, Youngstown State University; Karl Gegenfurtner, Justin-Liebig-Universitat; Richard Gist, Johnson County Community College; W. B. Perry Goodwin, Santa Clara University; Carla Grayson, University of Michigan; Bill Graziano, Texas A&M University; Paul Greene, Iona College; Sandra Grossmann, Clackamas Community College; Charla Hall, Southeastern Oklahoma State University, David T. Hall, Baton Rouge Community College; Andrew Hill, University of Leeds; Elizabeth Hillstrom, Wheaton College; Stefan Hofmann, Boston University; David Holmes, University of Kansas; William L. Hoover, Suffolk County Community College; Ralph Hupka, California State University; Addie Johnson, Utrecht University; Fred A. Johnson, University of the District of Columbia; Wesley P. Jordan, St. Mary's College of Maryland; Grace Kannady, Kansas City Kansas Community College; Richard A. Kasschau, University of Houston; Richard Keefe, Scottsdale Community College; Charles Ksir,

University of Wyoming; Cantey Land, Vassar College; Joan Lauer, Indiana University/Purdue University; David Leiser, Bengurion University of the Negev; Elissa M. Lewis, Southwest Missouri State University; Marc A. Lindberg, Marshall University; Emma Lou Linn, St. Edwards University; Richard Lippa, California State University, Fullerton; Daniel Lord, University of Alaska, Anchorage; Joseph Lowman, University of North Carolina; James V. Lupo, Creighton University; Traci Mann, University of California, Los Angeles; Michael Martin, University of Kansas; Douglas Matheson, University of the Pacific; Fred Maxwell, Southwest Missouri State University; Mary Benson McMullen, Indiana University; Steven E. Meier, University of Idaho; Chandra Mehrotra, College of Saint Scholastica; Sheryll Mennicke, University of Minnesota; Mitchell M. Metzger, Penn State University–Shenango; Thomas Miller, University of Minnesota; Thomas Miller, University of Oklahoma; Jannay Morrow, Vassar College; Dean Murakami, American River College; Gregory L. Murphy, University of Illinois at Urbana-Champaign; Frank Muscarella, Barry University; David Neufeldt, Hutchinson Community College; Gayle Norbury, University of Wisconsin–Milwaukee; Michael O'Hara, University of Iowa; Paul V. Olczak, SUNY, Geneseo; Carrol Perrino, Morgan State University; Jacqueline B. Persons, Oakland, California; David Pitlenger, Marietta College; Shane Pitts, Birmingham-Southern College; Steve Platt, Northern Michigan University; Mark Plonsky, University of Wisconsin–Stevens Point; Tom Posey, Murray State University; Janet Proctor, Purdue University; David Raskin, University of Utah; Erin Rasmussen, College of Charleston; Cheryl A. Rickabaugh, University of Redlands; Steven Robbins, Haverford College; Tim Robinson, Gustavus Adolphus College; Irvin Rock, University of California, Berkeley; Brian H. Ross, University of Illinois at Urbana-Champaign; Jack Rossman, Macalister College; Alex Rothman, University of Minnesota; Gene Sackett, University of Washington; D. Kim Sawrey, University of North Carolina, Wilmington; Harold Schiffman, Duke University; J. Anthony Shelton, Liverpool John Moores University; Robert Smith, George Mason University; Steven Smith, Texas A&M University; C.R. Snyder, University of Kansas; Joan Stanton, Wheaton College; Tim Strauman, University of Wisconsin, Madison; Elaine K. Thompson, Georgian Court College; Francine Tougas, University of Ottawa; Lynne S. Trench, Birmingham-Southern

College; Stuart Valins, SUNY, Stonybrook; Frank Vattano, Colorado State University; Ann L. Weber, University of North Carolina at Asheville; Paul J. Wellman, Texas A&M University; and Carsh Wilturner, Green River College; Lance Workman, University of Glamorgan

ACKNOWLEDGMENTS

The late Susan Nolen-Hoeksema wished to acknowledge the invaluable assistance of Frank Keil and Edward Watkins.

Barbara L. Fredrickson wishes to acknowledge her doctoral student Elise Rice for her assistance in preparing updates to this edition, and C. Daryl Cameron, who wrote the Cutting Edge Research section for Chapter 17. She also wishes to acknowledge former mentors Neil Lutsky, Laura Carstensen and Robert Levenson, for drawing her into psychological science, and the Psychology faculty at Stanford University and the faculty of the 1989–1992 NIMH post-doctoral training program on Emotions Research for their indelible influences on her intellectual growth.

Geoffrey R. Loftus wishes to acknowledge the contributions of Julie Anne Séguin and Sarah Wyler who both played a major role in the rewriting of the Sensory Process chapter (Chapter 4), the Perception chapter (Chapter 5) and the Memory chapter (Chapter 8).

Christel Lutz wishes to acknowledge her students at University College Utrecht for making teaching such a pleasure, and Willem Albert Wagenaar, Nico Frijda, Saul Sternberg, Jack Nachmias, Paul Rozin, Jeffrey Goldstein, Lonia Jakubowska, Jocelyn Ballantyne, Julie Gros Louis, Jesse Snedeker and Julia Fischer for being inspiring mentors, colleagues and friends.

Each chapter begins with a **brief example**, directly showing how themes from each chapter manifest themselves in the real world.

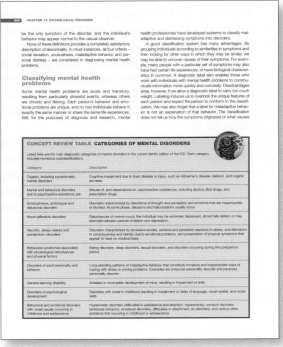

Concept Review Tables explain psychological concepts in simple tabular form.

Interim Summaries and Critical Thinking Questions conclude each section, summing up key points and offering questions to test your understanding of chapter content.

Cutting Edge Research boxes focus on research developments at the forefront of each chapter topic.

Seeing Both Sides essays take a single issue related to each chapter and explore contrasting areas of debate, emphasizing the range of perspectives that exist in every area of psychology.

CORE CONCEPTS

law of effect	biological perspective	variable
over justification effect	behavioral perspective	independent variable
validity	cognitive perspective	dependent variable
psychology	psychoanalytic perspective	experimental groups
prosopagnosia	subjectivist perspective	control group
fundamental attribution error	naive realism	random assignment
childhood amnesia	reductionism	multivariate experiment
obese	biological psychologists	measurement
cathartic effect	cognitive psychologists	statistics
aggression	developmental psychologists	mean
physiology	social psychologists	statistical significance
nature–nurture debate	personality psychologists	correlation coefficient
nature view	clinical psychologists	positively correlated
nurture view	counseling psychologists	negatively correlated
tabula rasa	school psychologists	recognition test
associationist psychology	educational psychologists	test
attention	organizational psychologists	direct observation
introspection	engineering psychologists	survey method
structuralism	cognitive neuroscience	social desirability effects
functionalism	affective neuroscience	case history
behaviorism	social neuroscience	literature review
Gestalt	evolutionary psychology	narrative review
psychoanalysis	cultural psychology	meta-analysis
unconscious	neuroplasticity	minimal risk
free association	phenotypic plasticity	informed consent
information-processing models	hypothesis	debriefing
psychological perspective	theory	right to privacy
psi (Ψ)	scientific	anxiety
eclectic approach	experiments	cues

Core Concept lists aggregate important terms from each chapter and definitions of these can be found in the glossary.

CHAPTER SUMMARY

1 The basic unit of the nervous system is a specialized type of cell called a neuron. Projecting from the cell body of a neuron are short branches called dendrites and a slender tubelike extension called the axon. Stimulation of the dendrites and cell body leads to a neural impulse that travels down the length of the axon. Sensory neurons transmit signals from sense organs to the brain and spinal cord; motor neurons transmit signals from the brain and spinal cord to muscles and glands. A nerve is a bundle of elongated axons belonging to hundreds or thousands of neurons.

2 A stimulus moves along a neuron as an electro chemical impulse that travels from the dendrites to the end of the axon. This traveling impulse, or action potential, is caused by depolarization, an electrochemical process in which the voltage difference across cell mechanisms is changed at successive points along the neuron.

3 Once started, an action potential travels down the axon to many small swellings at the end of the axon called terminal buttons. These terminal buttons release chemical substances called neurotransmitters, which are responsible for transferring the signal from one neuron to an adjacent one. The neurotransmitters diffuse across the synapse, a small gap between the juncture of the two neurons, and bind to receptors in the cell membrane of the receiving neuron. Some neurotransmitters have an excitatory effect, and others have an inhibitory effect. If the excitatory effects on the receiving neuron become large relative to the inhibitory effects, depolarization occurs, and the neuron fires an all-or-none impulse.

4 There are many different kinds of neurotransmitter–receptor interactions, and they help explain a range of psychological phenomena. The most important neurotransmitters include acetylcholine, norepinephrine, dopamine, serotonin, gamma-aminobutyric acid (GABA), and glutamate.

5 The nervous system is divided into the central nervous system (CNS) (the brain and spinal cord) and the peripheral nervous system (the nerves connecting the brain and spinal cord to other parts of the body). Subdivisions of the peripheral nervous system (PNS) are the somatic system (which carries messages to and from the sense receptors, muscles, and the surface of the body) and the autonomic system (which connects with the internal organs and glands).

6 The human brain is composed of three functional divisions: the central core, the limbic system, and the cerebral cortex. The central core includes the medulla, which is responsible for respiration and postural reflexes; the cerebellum, which is concerned with motor co-ordination; the thalamus, a relay station for incoming sensory information; and the hypothalamus, which is important in emotion and in maintaining homeostasis. The reticular formation, which crosses through several of the other central core structures, controls the organism's state of arousal and consciousness.

7 The limbic system controls some of the instinctive behaviors regulated by the hypothalamus, such as feeding, attacking, fleeing, and mating. It also plays an important role in emotion and memory.

8 The cerebral cortex is divided into two cerebral hemispheres. The convoluted surface of these hemispheres, the cerebral cortex, plays a critical role in higher mental processes such as thinking, learning, and decision-making. Certain areas of the cerebral cortex are associated with specific sensory inputs or control of specific movements. The remainder of the cerebral cortex consists of association areas concerned with memory, thought, and language.

9 Techniques have been developed to obtain detailed pictures of the human brain without causing the patient undue distress or damage. They include computerized axial tomography (CAT or CT), magnetic resonance imaging (MRI), and positron emission tomography (PET).

10 When the corpus callosum (the band of nerve fibers connecting the two cerebral hemispheres) is severed, significant differences in the functioning of the two hemispheres can be observed. The left hemisphere is skilled in language and mathematical abilities. The right hemisphere can understand some language but cannot communicate through speech. Instead, it has a highly developed spatial and pattern sense.

11 The term aphasia is used to describe language deficits caused by brain damage. People with damage to Broca's area have difficulty enunciating words correctly and speak in a slow, labored way. People with damage to Wernicke's area can hear words but do not know their meaning.

Chapter Summaries condense the key points from each chapter.

WALKTHROUGH TOUR

ABOUT THE AUTHORS

Susan Nolen-Hoeksema, Ph.D. who died unexpectedly in January 2013 was Professor of Psychology at Yale University. She received her B.A. in psychology from Yale University and her Ph.D. in clinical psychology from University of Pennsylvania. Nolen-Hoeksema's research focuses on women's greater rates of depression compared to men and on the effects of rumination in depression. In addition to her peer-reviewed journal articles, she has published 12 books, including scholarly books, textbooks and books for lay audiences. Nolen-Hoeksema has won three major teaching awards and several awards for her research, including the David Shakow Early Career Award from the American Psychological Association (APA), the Leadership Award from the Committee on Women of the APA, and a Research Career Award from the National Institute for Mental Health.

Barbara L. Fredrickson, Ph.D. is Kenan Distinguished Professor at the University of North Carolina at Chapel Hill, with appointments in Psychology and the Kenan-Flagler School of Business. She received her B.A. in psychology from Carleton College and her Ph.D. from Stanford University. Fredrickson's research centers on emotions, especially positive emotions and their links to health and well-being. She has shared her research findings with scientists and students of psychology through scores of peer-reviewed journal articles and also with a general audience through her books, *Positivity* (2009, Crown) and Love 2.0 (2013, Penguin). Her research and teaching have been recognized with several honors and awards, including the American Psychological Association's Templeton Prize in Positive Psychology, and the Society for Experimental Social Psychology's Career Trajectory Award.

Geoffrey R. Loftus received his B.A. from Brown University, and Ph.D. from Stanford University. He has been professor at the University of Washington in Seattle since 1973, as well as visiting professor at MIT. He served as editor of Memory & Cognition, associate editor of Cognitive Psychology, and editorial-board member of various other journals. He has authored numerous books, book chapters, and articles.

His research concerns human perception and memory, as well as mathematics, statistics, scientific methodology, urban design, and video games. He has testified as an expert witness in approximately 250 civil and criminal legal cases.

Christel Lutz, Ph.D. is a lecturer in Psychology at University College Utrecht, the Netherlands. She received her MSc. in physics from Utrecht University and her Ph.D. in experimental cognitive psychology from the University of Pennsylvania, where she taught courses in perception and cognitive psychology. She is a fellow in the Department of Social Sciences at University College Utrecht, and has developed courses in experimental psychology and the psychology of human motivation. Her current research focuses on learning and motivation, and on the intellectual development of college students.

CONTRIBUTORS

An extensive number of contributors have invaluably assisted with the new edition, including editing chapters and contributing to the Cutting Edge Research and Seeing Both Sides features.

DIGITAL SUPPORT RESOURCES

Dedicated Instructor Resources

To discover the dedicated instructor online
support resources accompanying this textbook,
instructors should register here for access:
http://login.cengage.com

Resources include:

- Instructor's Manual containing a range of additional
  material for every chapter of the text
- PowerPoint slides for use in teaching, complementing
  the content and coverage of each chapter
- ExamView Testbank

Instructor access

Instructors can access CourseMate by registering at
http://login.cengage.com or by speaking to their local
Cengage Learning EMEA representative.

Instructor resources

Instructors can use the integrated Engagement Tracker in CourseMate to track students'
preparation and engagement. The tracking tool can be used to monitor progress of the class as
a whole, or for individual students.

Student access

Log In & Learn In 4 Easy Steps

1. To register a product using the access code printed on the inside front-cover of the book
   please go to: **http://login.cengagebrain.com**
2. Register as a new user or log in as an existing user if you already have an account with
   Cengage Learning or CengageBrain.com
3. Follow the online prompts
4. If your instructor has provided you with a course key, you will be prompted to enter this after
   opening your digital purchase from your CengageBrain account homepage.

Student resources

CourseMate offers a range of interactive learning tools tailored to the sixteenth edition of
Atkinson & Hilgard's Introduction to Psychology including:

- Multiple Choice Questions and Quizzes
- Critical Thinking Questions
- Practice Essay Questions
- Videos
- Glossary, Flashcards, and More

THE NATURE OF PSYCHOLOGY

LEARNING OBJECTIVES

After reading this chapter you should be able to:

- Understand the scope of scientific psychology.
- Understand differing historical perspectives on the topics within psychology.
- Know five contemporary perspectives within psychology.
- Be familiar with seven major subfields within contemporary psychology.
- Know four cutting-edge interdisciplinary approaches in psychology.

Define psychology.

Give examples of psychological research.

Identify key ideas and debates that shaped the history of psychology.

Give examples of five different perspectives within contemporary psychology.

Explain how psychologists use the scientific method to uncover knowledge.

State the principles that guide the ethical conduct of psychological research.

CHAPTER OUTLINE

THE SCOPE OF PSYCHOLOGY

THE HISTORICAL ORIGINS OF PSYCHOLOGY

Nature–nurture debate

The beginnings of scientific psychology

Structuralism and functionalism

Behaviorism

Gestalt psychology

Psychoanalysis

Later developments in twentieth-century psychology

CONTEMPORARY PSYCHOLOGICAL PERSPECTIVES

The biological perspective

The behavioral perspective

The cognitive perspective

The psychoanalytic perspective

The subjectivist perspective

Relationships between psychological and biological perspectives

Major subfields of psychology

CUTTING EDGE RESEARCH: TWENTY-FIRST–CENTURY PSYCHOLOGY

Reading opens the door to education and advancement. What's the best way to encourage kids to read? One American chain of pizza restaurants believes it has the answer: reward kids for reading. Kids' teachers set monthly reading goals – in terms of books or pages read – and give them Pizza Award Certificates when they reach the goals. The kid who brings a certificate to a local participating restaurant gets a free pizza. Parents and teachers say the program works – it gets their kids to read more. Through this program, for nearly 20 years kids have been earning pizzas for reading across the USA.

But is this program PC? Is it 'psychologically correct'? Let's see what the research says. You might already be aware of one of the fundamental tenets of learning theory: when a reward follows a behavior, that behavior is strengthened. In Chapter 7, you'll see that this powerful influence of rewards is termed the **law of effect**. When kids are rewarded with pizzas for reading, they read more. Seems like a great success, right?

Consider other outcomes – like how kids feel about reading and whether they continue to read once the pizza program ends. Dozens of psychology experiments, many conducted in school classrooms, have addressed these questions. In one classic experiment (Greene *et al.*, 1976), psychologists had teachers introduce several new mathematics games to their students and then for 2 weeks simply observe how much time they spent playing them. In the third week, kids in some classrooms were rewarded for playing these same mathematics games, and kids in other classrooms were not. As expected, the rewards increased the amount of time kids played the games: the law of effect held. But what happened several weeks later, when the rewards were discontinued? Those who had received rewards suddenly lost interest in the mathematics games and spent hardly any time on them. By contrast, those who were never rewarded continued to play them regularly.

This experiment demonstrates how rewards sometimes backfire and undermine kids' intrinsic interest in activities like reading and mathematics. When people see that their behavior is caused by some external, situational factor – like a free pizza – they discount any internal, personal factors – like their own enjoyment of the activity. So when kids ask themselves why they read, they'll say it's for the pizza. And when there's no more pizza to be had, they'll see no particular reason to read. Even though they enjoyed reading, the rewards loomed larger. This undermining influence of rewards is the **over justification effect** – going overboard and explaining one's own behavior with too much emphasis on salient situational causes and not enough emphasis on personal causes.

Getting kids to read for external reasons – like for free pizzas – can lead them to discount the contribution of any internal reasons for reading – like their own interest. This overjustification effect explains why rewarding desired behaviors sometimes backfires.

HOW PSYCHOLOGICAL RESEARCH IS DONE

Generating hypotheses

Experiments

Correlation

Observation

Literature reviews

Ethics of psychological research

SEEING BOTH SIDES: ARE WE NATURALLY SELFISH?

You might be thinking that grades in college, or university, are also rewards for learning. Do they backfire in the same way as receiving pizza for reading? Not exactly. One important difference is that the grade you get in a college course depends on how well you perform. Research has shown that performance-contingent rewards are less likely to undermine interest – and at times can even increase interest – because they tell you that you are good at an activity (Tang & Hall, 1995). Even so, a focus on grades can sometimes overshadow the sheer interest you might have in a subject. It's useful to remind yourself that two reasons to study coursework can exist side by side: to get a good grade and to enjoy the material. It can be 'both–and,' not 'either–or.'

Luckily, most students find psychology fascinating. We do, too, and we do our best to convey this fascination to you in the pages of this book. Psychology interests people because it asks questions that touch virtually every aspect of our lives: how does the way your parents raised you affect the way you'll raise your own children? What is the best treatment for substance use disorder? Can a man care for an infant as capably as a woman can? Can you remember a traumatic experience in more detail under hypnosis? How should a nuclear power plant be designed to minimize human error? What effects does prolonged stress have on the immune system? Is psychotherapy more effective than drugs in treating depression? Psychologists are conducting research to find answers to these and many other questions.

Psychology also affects our lives through its influence on laws and public policy. Psychological theories and research have influenced laws dealing with discrimination, capital punishment, courtroom practices, pornography, sexual behavior, and personal responsibility for actions. For example, in the USA so-called lie-detector tests are not admissible as evidence in a court of law because psychological research has shown them to be unacceptably inaccurate.

Because psychology affects so many aspects of our lives, even people who do not intend to specialize in it need to know something about this dynamic field. An introductory course in psychology should give you a better understanding of why people think, feel, and act as they do, as well as insights into your own attitudes and reactions.

This course will also help you evaluate the many claims made in the name of psychology. Everyone has seen newspaper headlines like these:

→ New Form of Psychotherapy Facilitates Recovery of Repressed Memories

→ Anxiety Controlled by Self-Regulation of Brain Waves

→ Proof of Mental Telepathy Found

→ Spacing Out for a Bit Can Boost Your Memory

→ Want to Feel Healthier and Happier?: Cut Back on Lying

→ Sweet Drink May Boost Exam Performance

→ Transcendental Meditation Extends Life Expectancy

→ Appearance Concerns Take Mental Toll

How can we decide whether to believe these claims? You need to know two things to evaluate the **validity** of psychological claims. First, you need to know what psychological facts are already firmly established. If the new claim is not compatible with those facts, you should be cautious. Second, you need to have the knowledge to determine whether the arguments that support the new claim meet the standards of scientific evidence. If they do not, again you have reason for skepticism. This book aims to meet both needs. First, it reviews the current state of knowledge in psychology. It presents the most important findings in the field so that you know the established facts. Second, it examines the nature of research – how a psychologist designs a research program that can provide strong evidence for or against a hypothesis – so that you know the kind of evidence needed to back up a new claim.

In this chapter, we begin by considering the kinds of topics that are studied in psychology. After a brief review of psychology's historical origins, we discuss the perspectives that psychologists adopt in investigating these topics. Then we describe the research methods of psychological investigation, including the ethical guidelines that have been proposed for such research.

THE SCOPE OF PSYCHOLOGY

Psychology can be defined as the scientific study of behavior and mental processes. An astonishing variety of topics fit this definition, as can be seen in the brief examples presented next. (All of these topics are discussed in more detail at various points in this book.)

Brain damage and face recognition

It is no surprise that when people suffer brain damage, their behavior is affected. What is surprising is that damage in a specific part of the brain may change a person's behavior in one way but not in any other ways. In some cases, for example, people are unable to recognize familiar faces as a result of damage to a particular region on the right side of the brain – yet they can do just about everything else normally: a condition called **prosopagnosia**. A famous example of this condition was described by neurologist Oliver Sacks (1985) in his book *The Man Who Mistook His Wife for a Hat*. In another case, a man with prosopagnosia complained to a waiter that someone was staring at him, only to be informed that he was looking in a mirror! Such cases tell us a lot about the way the normal brain works. They indicate that some psychological functions – like face recognition – are localized in particular parts of the brain.

Attributing traits to people

Suppose that in a crowded department store a person soliciting for a charity approaches a customer and implores her to make a contribution. The woman donates a small sum to the charity. Would you think the woman was generous, or would you think she had been pressured into making the donation because so many people were watching her? Experiments designed to study situations like this have shown that most people consider the woman generous, even though the situational pressures were so great that just about everybody would behave similarly. When explaining the behavior of others, people tend to overestimate the causal effect of personality traits and underestimate those of situational factors – a mistake social psychologists call the **fundamental attribution error** (see Figure 1.1). If we contrast the fundamental attribution error with the over justification effect (discussed in the context of earning pizzas for reading), we begin to see some important distinctions between how we judge others and how we judge ourselves. When making sense of our own behavior, we often overestimate – not underestimate – situational causes.

Childhood amnesia

Most adults can recall events from their early years, but only back to a certain point. Almost no one can accurately recall events from the first 3 years of life, a phenomenon called **childhood amnesia**. Consider a significant event like the birth of a sibling. If the birth occurred after you were three years old,

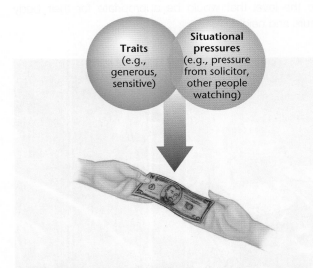

FIGURE 1.1 **Trait Attribution.** *In deciding whether another person's substantial donation to charity is caused by the giver's traits or by the situation, we are biased towards believing that a trait was the critical factor. This illustrates the fundamental attribution error.*

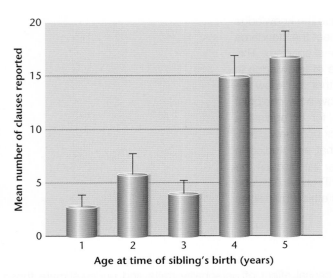

FIGURE 1.2 **The Boundaries of Childhood Amnesia.** *The mean number of clauses spoken by participants during free recall when asked to describe what they remember about the birth of a sibling, as a function of participant's age at the time of birth.*

you may have some memory of it. But if the birth occurred before age three, you probably remember very little about it, if anything at all (see Figure 1.2). Childhood amnesia is particularly striking because our first 3 years are so rich in experience: we develop from helpless newborns to crawling, babbling infants to walking, talking children. But these remarkable transitions leave few traces in our memories.

Obesity

Nearly a quarter of UK adults and more than a third of adults in the USA are **obese**; their weight is 30 per cent or more above the level that would be appropriate for their body structure and height.

Psychologists are interested in what causes people to eat too much. Among the possible causes they have studied are genetic factors and environmental influences, such as a tendency to overeat in the presence of certain stimuli.

This is compared to 10 per cent of the adult population in the Netherlands and a tiny 3 per cent of Japanese adults. Obesity is dangerous. It increases vulnerability to diabetes, high blood pressure, heart disease, and even some forms of cancer. Psychologists are interested in what factors lead people to eat too much. One factor seems to be a history of deprivation. If rats are first deprived of food, then allowed to eat until they return to their normal weight, and finally allowed to eat as much as they want, they eat more than rats that have no history of deprivation.

Effects of media violence on children's aggression

The question of whether watching violence on television causes children to be more aggressive has long been controversial. Although many observers believe that televised violence affects children's behavior, others suggest that watching violence has a **cathartic effect**. It may actually reduce **aggression** by allowing children to express it vicariously and 'get it out of their system.' But research does not support the cathartic effect view. A recent prospective study of 430 children aged seven to 11, found that both boys' and girls' likelihood of being physically aggressive is appreciably higher when their exposure to media violence is high. (See Figure 1.3.)

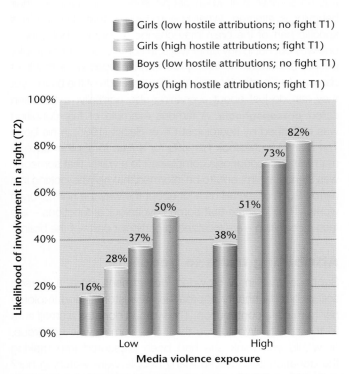

FIGURE 1.3 **The Relationship Between Childhood Media Violence Exposure and Adult Aggression.** *A classic study shows that preferences for viewing violent TV programs by boys and girls at age 9 (T1) is related to aggressive behavior as rated by peers at age 19 (T2).*

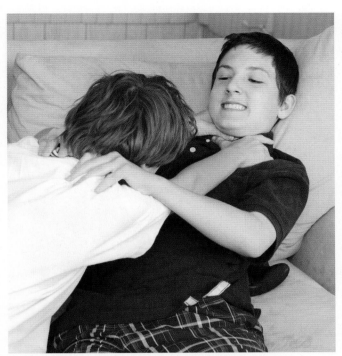

Psychological studies provide evidence that violent television programming may have harmful effects on young viewers.

INTERIM SUMMARY

➡ Psychology touches on many aspects of our lives and influences laws and public policy.

➡ To evaluate new claims made about psychology, you need to know (1) what psychological facts are already firmly established and (2) the standards for scientific evidence.

➡ Psychology is the scientific study of behavior and mental processes.

➡ The scope of psychology is broad, covering topics such as face recognition, social judgments, memory, obesity, violence, and many more.

CRITICAL THINKING QUESTIONS

1 Review the newspaper headlines about psychology listed on page 4. Find an article in the newspaper or on the Internet that covers psychological findings. Do you believe what the news account claims? Why or why not?

2 How do you know when to trust a news article? What more would you need to know to accept as fact the psychological claim you located?

THE HISTORICAL ORIGINS OF PSYCHOLOGY

The roots of psychology can be traced to the great philosophers of ancient Greece. The most famous of them, Socrates, Plato, and Aristotle, posed fundamental questions about mental life: what is consciousness? Are people inherently rational or irrational? Is there really such a thing as free choice? These questions, and many similar ones, are as important today as they were thousands of years ago. They deal with the nature of the mind and mental processes, which are the key elements of the cognitive perspective in psychology.

Other psychological questions deal with the nature of the body and human behavior, and they have an equally long history. Hippocrates, often called the 'father of medicine', lived around the same time as Socrates. He was deeply interested in **physiology**, the study of the functions of the living organism and its parts. He made many important observations about how the brain controls various organs of the body. These observations set the stage for what became the biological perspective in psychology.

The ancient Greek philosopher Socrates posed fundamental questions about mental life. Many of these questions are as important today as they were in Socrates' time.

Nature–nurture debate

One of the earliest debates about human psychology is still raging today. This **nature–nurture debate** centers on the question of whether human capabilities are inborn or acquired through experience. The **nature view** holds that human beings enter the world with an inborn store of knowledge and understanding of reality. Early philosophers believed that this knowledge and understanding could be accessed through careful reasoning and introspection. In the seventeenth century, Descartes supported the nature view by arguing that some ideas (such as God, the self, geometric axioms, perfection, and infinity) are innate. Descartes is also notable for his conception of the body as a machine that can be studied much as other machines are studied. This is the root of modern information-processing perspectives on the mind, discussed later in this chapter.

The **nurture view** holds that knowledge is acquired through experiences and interactions with the world. Although some of the early Greek philosophers held this opinion, it is most strongly associated with the seventeenth-century English philosopher John Locke. According to Locke, at birth the human mind is a **tabula rasa**, a blank slate on which experience 'writes' knowledge and understanding as the individual matures. This perspective gave birth to **associationist psychology**. Association-ists denied that there were inborn ideas or capabilities. Instead, they argued that the mind is filled with ideas that enter by way of the senses and then become associated through principles such as similarity and contrast. Current research on memory and learning is related to early association theory.

The classic nature–nurture debate has become much more nuanced in recent decades. Although some psychologists still argue that human thought and behavior result primarily from biology or primarily from experience, most psychologists take a more integrated approach. They acknowledge that biological processes (such as heredity or processes in the brain) affect thoughts, feelings, and behavior, but say that experience leaves its mark, too. So the current question is not whether nature *or* nurture shapes human psychology but rather how nature *and* nurture combine to do so (Plomin & Asbury, 2005). The nature–nurture issue comes up at numerous points in later chapters.

The beginnings of scientific psychology

Although philosophers and scholars continued to be interested in the functioning of both the mind and the body through the centuries, scientific psychology is usually considered to have begun in the late nineteenth century, when Wilhelm Wundt established the first psychological

Wilhelm Wundt.

Wilhelm Wundt established the first psychological laboratory at the University of Leipzig.

laboratory at the University of Leipzig in Germany in 1879. The impetus for the establishment of Wundt's lab was the belief that mind and behavior, like planets or chemicals or human organs, could be the subject of scientific analysis. Wundt's own research was concerned primarily with the senses, especially vision, but he and his co-workers also studied **attention**, emotion, and memory.

Wundt relied on introspection to study mental pro-cesses. **Introspection** refers to observing and recording the nature of one's own perceptions, thoughts, and feel-ings. Examples of introspection include people's reports of how heavy they perceive an object to be and how bright a flash of light seems to be. The introspective method was inherited from philosophy, but Wundt added a new dimension to the concept. Pure self-observation was not sufficient: it had to be supplemented by experiments. Wundt's experiments systematically varied some physical dimension of a stimulus, such as its intensity, and used the introspective method to determine how these physical changes modified the participant's conscious experience of the stimulus.

The reliance on introspection, particularly for very rapid mental events, proved unworkable. Even after extensive training, different people produced very different introspec-tions about simple sensory experiences, and few conclu-sions could be drawn from these differences. As a result, introspection is not a central part of the current cognitive perspective. And, as we will see, some psychologists' reactions to introspection played a role in the development of other modern perspectives.

Structuralism and functionalism

During the nineteenth century, chemistry and physics made great advances by analyzing complex compounds (molecules) into their elements (atoms). These successes encouraged psychologists to look for the mental elements that combined to create more complex experiences. Just as chemists analyzed water into hydrogen and oxygen, perhaps psychologists could analyze the taste of lemonade (perception) into elements such as sweet, bitter, and cold (sensations). The leading proponent of this approach in the USA was E. B. Titchener, a Cornell University psychologist who had been trained by Wundt. Titchener introduced the term **structuralism** – the analysis of mental structures – to describe this branch of psychology.

But some psychologists opposed the purely analytic nature of structuralism. William James, a distinguished psychologist at Harvard University, felt that analyzing the elements of consciousness was less important than understanding its fluid, personal nature. His approach was named **functionalism**, studying how the mind works to enable an organism to adapt to and function in its environment.

Nineteenth-century psychologists' interest in adaptation stemmed from the publication of Charles Darwin's theory of evolution. Some argued that consciousness had evolved only because it served some purpose in guiding the individual's activities. To find out how an organism adapts to its environment, functionalists said that psychologists must observe actual behavior. However, both structuralists and functionalists still regarded psychology as the science of conscious experience.

Behaviorism

Structuralism and functionalism played important roles in the early development of twentieth-century psychology. Because each viewpoint provided a systematic approach to the field, they were considered competing schools of psychology. By 1920, however, both were being displaced by three newer schools: behaviorism, Gestalt psychology, and psychoanalysis.

Of the three, **behaviorism** had the greatest influence on scientific psychology in North America. Its founder, John B. Watson, reacted against the view that conscious experience was the province of psychology. Watson made no assertions about consciousness when he studied the behavior of animals and infants. He decided not only that animal psychology and child psychology could stand on their own as sciences but also that they set a pattern that adult psychology might follow.

For psychology to be a science, Watson believed, psychological data must be open to public inspection like the data of any other science. Behavior is public; consciousness is private. Science should deal only with public facts. Because psychologists were growing impatient with introspection, the new behaviorism caught on rapidly, and many younger psychologists in the USA called themselves 'behaviorists.' (The Russian physiologist Ivan Pavlov's research on the conditioned response was regarded as an important area of behavioral research, but it was Watson who was responsible for behaviorism's widespread influence.)

Watson, and others ascribing to behaviorism, like the famous Harvard psychologist, B. F. Skinner, argued that nearly all behavior is a result of conditioning and the environment shapes behavior by reinforcing specific habits. For example, giving children sweets to stop them from whining reinforces (rewards) the habit of whining. The conditioned response was viewed as the smallest unit of behavior, from which more complicated behaviors could be created. All types of complex behavior patterns coming from special training or education were regarded as nothing more than an interlinked fabric of conditioned responses.

Behaviorists tended to discuss psychological phenomena in terms of stimuli and responses, giving rise to the term *stimulus–response (S–R) psychology*. Note, however, that S–R psychology itself is not a theory or perspective but a set of terms that can be used to communicate psychological information. S–R terminology is still sometimes used in psychology today.

Gestalt psychology

About 1912, at the same time that behaviorism was catching on in the USA, Gestalt psychology was appearing in Germany. **Gestalt** is a German word meaning 'form' or 'configuration,' which referred to the approach taken by Max Wertheimer and his colleagues Kurt Koffka and Wolfgang Köhler, all of whom eventually emigrated to the USA.

The Gestalt psychologists' primary interest was perception, and they believed that perceptual experiences depend on the patterns formed by stimuli and on the organization of experience. What we actually see is related to the background against which an object appears, as well as to other aspects of the overall pattern of stimulation (see Chapter 5). The whole is different from the sum of its parts, because the whole depends on the relationships among the parts. For example, when we look at Figure 1.4, we see it as a single large triangle – as a single form or Gestalt – rather than as three small angles.

William James, John B. Watson, and Sigmund Freud were key figures in the early history of psychology. James developed the approach known as functionalism, Watson was the founder of behaviorism, and Freud originated the theory and method of psychoanalysis.

FIGURE 1.4 **A Gestalt Image.** *When we look at the three angles of an equilateral triangle, we see a single large triangle rather than three small angles.*

Among the key interests of Gestalt psychologists were the perception of motion, how people judge size, and the appearance of colors under changes in illumination. These interests led them to a number of perception-centered interpretations of learning, memory, and problem-solving that helped lay the groundwork for current research in cognitive psychology.

The Gestalt psychologists also influenced key founders of modern social psychology – including Kurt Lewin, Solomon Asch, and Fritz Heider – who expanded on Gestalt principles to understand interpersonal phenomena (Jones, 1998). For instance, Asch (1946) extended the Gestalt notion that people see wholes rather than isolated parts from the simple case of object perception to the more complex case of person perception (Taylor, 1998). Plus, they saw the process of imposing meaning and structure on incoming stimuli as automatic and outside conscious awareness, a Gestalt view that continues to influence contemporary research on social cognition to this day (see Chapter 18; Moskowitz *et al.*, 1999).

Psychoanalysis

Psychoanalysis is both a theory of personality and a method of psychotherapy originated by Sigmund Freud around the turn of the twentieth century.

At the center of Freud's theory is the concept of the **unconscious** – the thoughts, attitudes, impulses, wishes, motivations, and emotions of which we are unaware. Freud believed that childhood's unacceptable (forbidden or punished) wishes are driven out of conscious awareness and become part of the unconscious, where they continue to influence our thoughts, feelings, and actions. Unconscious thoughts are expressed in dreams, slips of the tongue, and physical mannerisms. During therapy with patients, Freud used the method of **free association**, in which the patient was instructed to say whatever comes to mind as a way of bringing unconscious wishes into awareness. The analysis of dreams served the same purpose.

In classical Freudian theory, the motivations behind unconscious wishes almost always involved sex or aggression. For this reason, Freud's theory was not widely accepted when it was first proposed. Contemporary psychologists do not accept Freud's theory in its entirety, but they tend to agree that people's ideas, goals, and motives can at times operate outside conscious awareness.

Later developments in twentieth-century psychology

Despite the important contributions of Gestalt psychology and psychoanalysis, until World War II psychology was dominated by behaviorism, particularly in the USA. After the war, interest in psychology increased. Sophisticated instruments and electronic equipment became available, and a wider range of problems could be examined. It became evident that earlier theoretical approaches were too restrictive.

This viewpoint was strengthened by the development of computers in the 1950s. Computers were able to perform tasks – such as playing chess and proving mathematical theorems – that previously could be done only by human beings. They offered psychologists a powerful tool for theorizing about psychological processes. In a series of papers published in the late 1950s, Herbert Simon (who was later awarded a Nobel Prize) and his colleagues described how psychological phenomena could be simulated with a computer. Many psychological issues were recast in terms of information-processing models, which viewed human beings as processors of information and provided a more dynamic approach to psychology than behaviorism. Similarly, the information-processing approach made it possible to formulate more precisely some of the ideas of Gestalt psychology and psychoanalysis. Earlier ideas about the nature of the mind could be expressed in concrete terms and checked against actual data. For example, we can think of the operation of memory as analogous to the way a computer stores and retrieves information. Just as a computer can transfer information from temporary storage in its internal memory chips (RAM) to more permanent storage on the hard drive, so, too, our working memory can act as a way station to long-term memory (Atkinson & Shiffrin, 1971a; Raaijmakers & Shiffrin, 1992).

Another important influence on psychology in the 1950s was the development of modern linguistics. Linguists began to theorize about the mental structures required to comprehend and speak a language. A pioneer in this area was Noam Chomsky, whose book *Syntactic Structures*, published in 1957, stimulated the first significant psychological analyses of language and the emergence of the field of psycholinguistics.

At the same time, important advances were occurring in neuropsychology. Discoveries about the brain and nervous system revealed clear relationships between neurological events and mental processes. In recent decades, advances in biomedical technology have enabled rapid progress in research on these relationships. In 1981 Roger Sperry was awarded a Nobel Prize for demonstrating the links between specific regions of the brain and particular thought and behavioral processes, which we discuss in Chapter 2.

The development of information-processing models, psycholinguistics, and neuropsychology in the second half of the twentieth century produced what has been called the 'cognitive revolution' in psychology, which transformed nearly all areas of the field. Although the principal concern of this new emphasis on cognitive processes was the scientific analysis of mental processes and structures, cognitive approaches are not exclusively concerned with thought and knowledge. As illustrated throughout this book, this approach has been expanded to many other areas of psychology, including perception, motivation, emotion, clinical psychology, personality, and social psychology. Two decades after the cognitive revolution, came another revolution of sorts, a renewed emphasis on the scientific study of emotions, termed affective science.

In sum, during the twentieth century the focus of psychology came full circle. After rejecting conscious experience as ill-suited to scientific investigation and turning to the study of overt, observable behavior, psychologists are once again theorizing about covert aspects of the mind, such as thoughts and emotions, this time with new and more powerful tools.

INTERIM SUMMARY

→ The roots of psychology can be traced to the fourth and fifth centuries BC. One of the earliest debates about human psychology focused on the question of whether human capabilities are inborn or acquired through experience (the nature–nurture debate).

→ Scientific psychology was born in the late nineteenth century with the idea that mind and behavior could be the subject of scientific analysis. The first experimental laboratory in psychology was established by Wilhelm Wundt at the University of Leipzig in 1879.

→ Among the early 'schools' of psychology in the twentieth century were structuralism, functionalism, behaviorism, Gestalt psychology, and psychoanalysis.

→ Later developments in twentieth-century psychology included information-processing theory, psycholinguistics, and neuropsychology, foundations of the cognitive revolution in psychology

CRITICAL THINKING QUESTIONS

1 What assumptions about human nature underlie the various historical approaches to psychology?

2 Considering these underlying assumptions, which of the historical approaches are compatible with one another? Which are incompatible?

CONTEMPORARY PSYCHOLOGICAL PERSPECTIVES

What is a **psychological perspective**? Basically, it is an approach, a way of looking at topics within psychology. Any topic in psychology can be approached from different perspectives. Indeed, this is true of any action a person takes. Suppose that, following an insult, you punch someone in the face. From a biological perspective, we can describe this act as involving certain brain areas and as the firing of nerves that activate the muscles that move your arm. From a behavioral perspective, we can describe the act without reference to anything within your body; rather, the insult is a stimulus to which you respond by punching, a learned response that has been rewarded in the past. A cognitive perspective on this action would focus on the mental processes involved in producing the behavior, and we might explain your punch in terms of your goals and plans: your goal is to defend your honor, and aggressive behavior is part of your plan for achieving that goal. From a psychoanalytic perspective, your action could be described as an expression of an unconscious aggressive instinct. And finally, from a subjectivist perspective, your aggressive act can be understood as a reaction to interpreting the person's utterance as a personal insult.

Despite the many possible ways to describe any psychological act, these five perspectives represent the major approaches to the contemporary study of psychology (see Figure 1.5). Because these five perspectives are discussed throughout the book, here we provide only a brief description of some main points for each of them. Keep in mind that these approaches need not be mutually exclusive; rather, they may focus on different aspects of the same complex phenomenon. In fact, understanding many psychological topics requires an **eclectic approach** that spans multiple perspectives.

The biological perspective

The human brain contains well over 10 billion nerve cells and an almost infinite number of interconnections between them. It may be the most complex structure in the universe. In principle, all psychological events can be related to the activity of the brain and nervous system. The biological approach to the study of human beings and other species attempts to relate overt behavior to electrical and chemical events taking place inside the body. Research from the **biological perspective** seeks to specify the neurobiological processes that underlie behavior and mental processes. The biological approach to depression, for example, tries to understand this disorder in terms of abnormal changes in levels of neurotransmitters, which are chemicals produced in the brain that make communication between nerve cells possible.

We can use one of the problems described earlier to illustrate this perspective. The study of face recognition in patients with brain damage indicates that particular regions of the brain are specialized for face recognition. The human brain is divided into right and left hemispheres, and the regions devoted to face recognition seem to be located mainly in the right hemisphere. There is considerable hemispheric specialization in

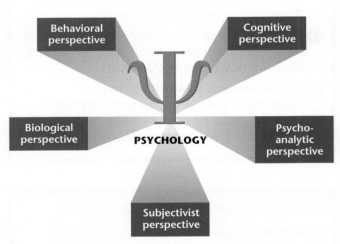

FIGURE 1.5 Perspectives in Psychology. *The analysis of psychological phenomena can be approached from several perspectives. Each offers a somewhat different account of why individuals act as they do, and each can make a contribution to our conception of the total person. The Greek letter psi (Ψ) is sometimes used as an abbreviation for psychology.*

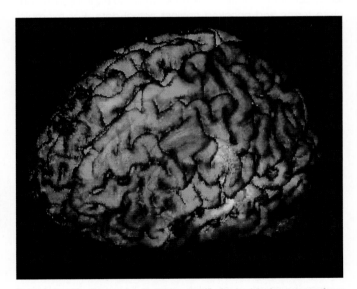

By imaging the human brain during psychological tasks, researchers learn which brain structures underlie the targeted phenomena. Here we see a three-dimensional representation of the human brain while listening to speech obtained through functional MRI (magnetic resonance imaging). Red indicates the greatest areas of activation, whereas yellow indicates areas of moderate activation. The neural activity is located in Wernicke's area of the brain. This approach illustrates a biological perspective on psychology.

humans. In most right-handed people, for example, the left hemisphere is specialized for understanding language, and the right hemisphere is specialized for interpreting spatial relations.

The biological perspective has also assisted in the study of memory. It emphasizes the importance of certain brain structures, including the hippocampus, which is involved in consolidating memories. Childhood amnesia may be partly due to an immature hippocampus, a structure that is not fully developed until a year or two after birth.

The behavioral perspective

As described in our brief review of the history of psychology, the **behavioral perspective** focuses on observable stimuli and responses and regards nearly all behavior as a result of conditioning and reinforcement. For example, a behavioral analysis of your social life might focus on which people you interact with (the social stimuli), the kinds of responses you make to them (rewarding, punishing, or neutral), the kinds of responses they in turn make to you (rewarding, punishing, or neutral), and how the responses sustain or disrupt the interaction.

We can use our sample problems to further illustrate this approach. With regard to obesity, some people may overeat (a specific response) only in the presence of specific stimuli (such as watching television), and learning to avoid these stimuli is part of many weight-control programs. With regard to aggression, children are more likely to express aggressive responses, such as hitting another child, when such responses are rewarded (the other child withdraws) than when their responses are punished (the other child counterattacks).

Historically, the strict behavioral approach did not consider the individual's mental processes at all, and behaviorists usually do not conjecture about the mental processes that intervene between the stimulus and the response. Nevertheless, psychologists other than strict behaviorists often record what people say about their conscious experiences (a verbal self-report) and draw inferences about their mental activity from these subjective data. Although few psychologists today would define themselves as strict behaviorists, many modern developments in psychology have evolved from the work of the earlier behaviorists (Malone, 2003; Skinner, 1981).

The cognitive perspective

The contemporary cognitive perspective is in part a return to the cognitive roots of psychology and in part a reaction to the narrowness of behaviorism, which tended to neglect complex human activities like reasoning, planning, decision-making, and communication. Like the nineteenth-century version, the contemporary **cognitive perspective** is concerned with mental processes such as perceiving, remembering, reasoning, deciding, and problem-solving. Unlike the nineteenth-century version, however, the contemporary cognitive approach is not based on introspection. Instead, it assumes that (1) only by studying mental processes can we fully understand what organisms do, and (2) we can study mental processes in an objective fashion by focusing on specific behaviors (just as behaviorists do) but interpreting them in terms of underlying mental processes. In making these interpretations, cognitive psychologists have often relied on an analogy between the mind and a computer. Incoming information is processed in various ways: it is selected, compared, and combined with other information already in memory, transformed, rearranged, and so on.

Consider the phenomenon of childhood amnesia described at the beginning of the chapter. Perhaps we cannot remember events from the first few years of life because of a major developmental change in the way we organize our experience in memory.

If the aggressive child has her way and the other child yields the toy then the aggressive behavior will be rewarded and the child will be more likely to behave aggressively in the future. This exemplifies a behavioral perspective on psychology.

Events that happen early in childhood usually are not remembered. This little boy probably will not remember the events surrounding the birth of his baby brother. An explanation that illustrates the cognitive perspective on psychology emphasizes the important role that language plays in organizing memories.

Such changes may be particularly pronounced at about age three, when our language abilities increase immensely, and language offers us a new way of organizing our memories.

The psychoanalytic perspective

Sigmund Freud developed the psychoanalytic conception of human behavior in Europe at about the same time that behaviorism was evolving in the USA. In some respects, psychoanalysis was a blend of the nineteenth-century versions of cognition and physiology. In particular, Freud combined cognitive notions of consciousness, perception, and memory with ideas about biologically based instincts to forge a bold new theory of human behavior.

The basic assumption of the **psychoanalytic perspective** is that behavior stems from unconscious processes, meaning beliefs, fears, and desires that a person is unaware of but that nonetheless influence behavior. Freud believed that many of the impulses that are forbidden or punished by parents and society during childhood are derived from innate instincts. Because each of us is born with these impulses, they exert a pervasive influence that must be dealt with in some manner. Forbidding them merely forces them out of awareness into the unconscious. They do not disappear, however. They may manifest themselves as emotional problems and symptoms of mental illness or as socially approved behavior such as artistic and literary activity. For example, if you feel a lot of anger toward your father but you cannot afford to alienate him, your anger may become unconscious, perhaps expressed in a dream about him being hurt in an atrocious accident.

Freud believed that we are driven by the same basic instincts as animals (primarily hunger, sex, and aggression)

Many aspects of the psychoanalytical setting have not changed much since Freud's day. The patient comes to daily sessions at pre-arranged times and lies on the couch while the analyst sits in a chair just behind the couch.

and that we are continually struggling against a society that stresses the control of these impulses. The psychoanalytic perspective suggests new ways of looking at some of the problems described at the beginning of the chapter. For example, Freud claimed that aggressive behavior stems from an innate instinct. Although this proposal is not widely accepted in human psychology, it is in agreement with the views of some biologists and psychologists who study aggression in animals.

The subjectivist perspective

The **subjectivist perspective** contends that human behavior is a function of the perceived world, not the objective world. Like the cognitive approach, the subjectivist perspective drew from the Gestalt tradition and reacted against the narrowness of behaviorism. Although allied with cognitive psychology, subjectivism has been most pervasive within social and personality psychology. To understand human social behavior, this view holds, we must grasp the person's own 'definition of the situation,' which is expected to vary by culture, personal history, and current motivational state. This perspective, then, is the most open to cultural and individual differences and to the effects of motivation and emotion.

In one sense, the idea that people actively construct their own subjective realities calls for introspective methods. Even so, subjectivists do not rely exclusively on subjective self-reports because they also assume that people fail to see their subjective realities as personal constructions. This **naïve realism** refers to people's tendency to take their constructed, subjective realities to be faithful renderings of an objective world. Therefore, a subjectivist approach also involves systematic observation of judgments and behaviors. A subjectivist perspective is illustrated by a classic early study that found that people reliably overestimate the physical size of valuable coins, more so than for coins of lower value. This tendency is exaggerated among poor children (Bruner & Goodman, 1947; note that coins in general probably seemed much more valuable in the 1940s!).

Consider again the problem of trait attribution. The study of how people make sense of other people's actions – in the example mentioned earlier – donating money to charity – emerged from a subjectivist emphasis on how situations are defined by the people in them (Heider, 1958). One contemporary explanation for the pervasive tendency to attribute other people's actions to their personality traits suggests that, because Western cultures have long emphasized personal agency, Westerners often fail to see the influence of situations (Nisbett *et al.*, 2001; see Chapter 18). Likewise, a subjectivist view of the link between media violence and aggression suggests that habitual consumption of violent media instills and strengthens aggressive schemas and scripts, which are later used to define subsequent interpersonal encounters (Anderson & Bushman, 2001).

Is this woman generous? Westerners have a strong tendency to say, 'Yes, she is,' making a trait attribution for her behavior. An emphasis on how people perceive and interpret their social world characterizes the subjectivist perspective.

CONCEPT REVIEW TABLE
FIVE PERSPECTIVES
WITHIN PSYCHOLOGY

Biological perspective	An orientation toward understanding the neurobiological processes that underlie behavior and mental processes.
Behavioral perspective	An orientation toward understanding observable behavior in terms of conditioning and reinforcement.
Cognitive perspective	An orientation toward understanding mental processes such as perceiving, remembering, reasoning, deciding, and problem-solving and their relationship to behavior.
Psychoanalytic perspective	An orientation toward understanding behavior in terms of unconscious motives stemming from sexual and aggressive impulses.
Subjectivist perspective	An orientation toward understanding behavior and mental processes in terms of the subjective realities people actively construct.

Relationships between psychological and biological perspectives

The behaviorist, cognitive, psychoanalytic, and subjectivist perspectives all rely on concepts that are purely psychological (such as perception, the unconscious, and attributions). Although these perspectives sometimes offer different explanations for the same phenomenon, those explanations are always psychological in nature. The biological perspective is different. In addition to using psychological concepts, it employs concepts (such as neurotransmitters and hormones) drawn from physiology and other branches of biology.

There is a way, though, in which the biological perspective makes direct contact with the psychological perspectives. Biologically oriented researchers attempt to explain psychological concepts and principles in terms of their biological counterparts. For example, researchers might attempt to explain the normal ability to recognize faces solely in terms of neurons and their interconnections in a certain region of the brain. Such attempts are termed reductionism because they involve reducing psychological notions to biological ones. Throughout this book, we present examples of successful reductionism – situations in which what was once understood at only the psychological level is now understood at least in part at the biological level.

If reductionism can be successful, why bother with psychological explanations at all? Is psychology just something to do until the biologists figure everything out? The answer is clearly no.

First, psychological findings, concepts, and principles direct biological researchers in their work. Given that the brain contains billions of brain cells and countless interconnections between these cells, biological researchers cannot hope to find something of interest by arbitrarily selecting some brain cells to study. Rather, they must have a way of directing their efforts to relevant groups of brain cells. Psychological findings can supply this direction. For example, psychological research indicates that our ability to discriminate among spoken words and our ability to discriminate among spatial positions obey different principles. So, biological psychologists might look in different regions of the brain for the neural basis of these two kinds of discrimination capacities (the left hemisphere for word discrimination and the right hemisphere for spatial-position discrimination). As another example, if psychological research indicates that learning a motor skill is a slow process that is hard to undo, biological psychologists can direct their attention to brain processes that are relatively slow but permanently alter connections between neurons (Churchland & Sejnowski, 1988).

Second, our biology always acts in concert with our past circumstances and current environment. For example, obesity can be the result of (1) a genetic predisposition to gain weight (a biological factor), (2) learning bad eating habits (a psychological factor), or (3) a reaction to cultural pressures toward extreme thinness (a sociocultural factor). The biologist can seek to understand the first factor, but it is still up to the psychologist to explore and explain the past experiences and current circumstances that influence a person's eating habits.

Nevertheless, the push for reductionism goes on at an ever-increasing rate. For many topics in psychology, we now have both psychological explanations and knowledge about how the relevant psychological concepts are implemented or executed in the brain (for example, what particular parts of the brain are involved and how they are interconnected). This kind of biological knowledge typically falls short of total reductionism, but it is still very important. Memory researchers, for example, have long distinguished between working memory and long-term memory (which are psychological notions), but now they also know something about how these two kinds of memory are actually coded differently in the brain. So, for many of the topics discussed in this book, we review what is known at the biological level as well as at the psychological level.

Indeed, a central theme of this book – and of contemporary psychology in general – is that psychological phenomena can be understood at both the psychological and biological levels. The biological analysis shows us how the psychological notions can be implemented in the brain. Both levels of analysis are clearly needed (although for some topics, including many dealing with social interactions, biological analyses have only just begun).

Major subfields of psychology

So far, we have gained a general understanding of the nature of psychology by looking at its topics and perspectives. We can further our understanding by looking at what different kinds of psychologists do and at emerging fields of emphasis in twenty-first-century psychology (see the Cutting Edge Research feature).

About half the people who have advanced degrees in psychology work in colleges and universities. In addition to teaching, they may devote much of their time to research or counseling. Other psychologists work in schools, hospitals or clinics, research institutes, government agencies, or business and industry. Still others are in private practice and offer their services to the public for a fee. We now turn to a brief description of some of the subfields of psychology.

Biological psychology

Biological psychologists (also referred to as physiological psychologists and behavioral neuroscientists) look for the relationship between biological processes and behavior.

Cognitive psychology

Cognitive psychologists are concerned with people's internal mental processes, such as problem-solving, memory, and language and thought.

Developmental psychology

Developmental psychologists are concerned with human development and the factors that shape behavior from birth to old age. They might study a specific ability, such as how language develops in children, or a particular period of life, such as infancy.

Social and personality psychology

These two subfields overlap. **Social psychologists** are interested in how people perceive and interpret their social world and how their beliefs, emotions, and behaviors are influenced by the real or imagined presence of others. They are also concerned with the behavior of groups and with social relationships between and among people. **Personality psychologists** study the thoughts, emotions, and behaviors that define an individual's personal style of interacting with the world. Accordingly, they are interested in differences between individuals, and they also attempt to synthesize all the psychological processes into an integrated account of the total person (Swann & Seyle, 2005).

Clinical and counseling psychology

Clinical psychologists are the largest group of psychologists. They apply psychological principles to the diagnosis and treatment of emotional and behavioral problems, including mental illness, drug addiction, and marital and family conflict. **Counseling psychologists** perform many of the same functions as clinical psychologists, although they often deal with less serious problems. They frequently work with high school or university students.

School and educational psychology

Because serious emotional problems often make their first appearance in the early grades, many elementary schools employ psychologists whose training combines courses in child development, education, and clinical psychology. These **school psychologists** work with children to evaluate learning and emotional problems. In contrast, **educational psychologists** are specialists in learning and teaching. They may work in schools, but more often they work in a university's school of education, where they do research on teaching methods and help train teachers.

Organizational and engineering psychology

Organizational psychologists (sometimes called *industrial psychologists*) typically work for a company. They are concerned with selecting people who are most suitable for particular jobs or designing structures that facilitate collaboration and teamwork. **Engineering psychologists** (sometimes called *human factors engineers*) try to improve the relationship between people and machines. For instance, they improve human–machine interaction by designing machines with the most efficient placement of gauges and controls, which leads to better performance, safety, and comfort.

→ Many new areas of inquiry, including cognitive neuroscience (as well as affective neuroscience and social cognitive neuroscience), evolutionary psychology, cultural psychology, and positive psychology, span traditional subfields and disciplines.

INTERIM SUMMARY

→ The study of psychology can be approached from several perspectives. Five contemporary perspectives are the biological perspective, the behavioral perspective, the cognitive perspective, the psychoanalytic perspective, and the subjectivist perspective.

→ The biological perspective differs from the other perspectives in that its principles are partly drawn from biology. Biological researchers often attempt to explain psychological principles in terms of biological ones; this is known as reductionism.

→ Among the major subfields of psychology are biological psychology, cognitive psychology, developmental psychology, social and personality psychology, clinical and counseling psychology, school and educational psychology, and organizational and engineering psychology.

CRITICAL THINKING QUESTIONS

1 Consider the question, 'What are the determinants of an individual's sexual orientation?' How would the different perspectives outlined in this chapter approach this question?

2 Many of the new approaches to twenty-first-century psychology (described in the Cutting Edge Research box) integrate divergent perspectives or fill prior gaps in the field. What other new advances might be on the horizon in twenty-first-century psychology? That is, what other opportunities for integrating perspectives and filling gaps do you predict?

CUTTING EDGE RESEARCH TWENTY-FIRST-CENTURY PSYCHOLOGY

Barbara L. Fredrickson, University of North Carolina, Chapel Hill

Increasingly, psychologists span multiple subfields in their research and also stretch beyond psychology to forge collaborations with researchers in other disciplines. These cross-area and interdisciplinary approaches have gained considerable momentum since the start of the twenty-first century and promise to be very important in the decades to come. Of particular interest are cognitive neuroscience, evolutionary psychology, cultural psychology, and behavioral epigenetics. Here we briefly describe each of these approaches, with examples of the kinds of research being done in each field.

Cognitive neuroscience

Cognitive neuroscience focuses on cognitive processes and relies heavily on the methods and findings of neuroscience (the branch of biology that deals with the brain and nervous system). In essence, cognitive neuroscience attempts to learn how mental activities are executed in the brain. The key idea is that cognitive psychology provides hypotheses about specific cognitive capacities – such as recognizing faces – and neuroscience supplies proposals about how these specific functions might be executed in the brain.

What is particularly distinctive about cognitive neuroscience is its reliance on new techniques for studying the brains of normal participants (as opposed to brain-damaged ones) while they are performing a cognitive task. These neuroimaging or brain-scanning techniques create visual images of a brain in action, with an indication of which regions of the brain show the most neural activity during a particular task. An example is the study of how people remember information for brief or long periods. When people are asked to remember information for a few seconds, neuroimaging results show increases in neural activity in regions in the front of the brain. When they are asked to remember information for a long period, there is increased activity in an entirely different region, one closer to the middle of the brain. Thus, different mechanisms seem to be used for the short-term and long-term storage of information (Squire & Wixted, 2011).

The connection between psychology and neuroscience is not limited to cognitive psychology. Psychologists have also initiated affective neuroscience (Lindquist et al., 2012) to discover how emotional phenomena are executed in the brain, as well as social neuroscience (Singer, 2012) to discover how stereotyping, attitudes, person perception, motor mimicry, and empathy are executed in the brain.

►

Evolutionary psychology

Evolutionary psychology is concerned with the biological origins of psychological mechanisms. In addition to psychology and biology, the other disciplines involved in this approach include anthropology and psychiatry. The key idea behind evolutionary psychology is that, like biological mechanisms (e.g., the ability to develop calluses), psychological mechanisms must have evolved over millions of years through a process of natural selection. As such, **evolutionary psychology** holds that psychological mechanisms have a genetic basis, which in the past increased our ancestors' chances of surviving and reproducing. To illustrate, consider a liking for sweets. Such a preference can be thought of as a psychological mechanism, and it has a genetic basis. Moreover, we have this preference because it increased our ancestors' chances of survival: the fruit that tasted the sweetest had the highest calorific value, so by eating it they increased the chances of continued survival of the relevant genes (Rozin *et al*., 2009).

An evolutionary perspective can affect the study of psychological issues in several ways (Ploeger, 2008). Certain topics are of particular importance because of their link to survival or successful reproduction. Such topics include how we select our mates and how we think and behave when experiencing particular emotions (Buss, 2009). An evolutionary perspective can also provide new insights into familiar topics. Concerning obesity, we noted earlier that a history of deprivation can lead to overeating in the future. Evolutionary psychology provides an interpretation of this puzzling phenomenon. Until comparatively recently in human history, people experienced deprivation only when food was scarce. An adaptive mechanism for dealing with scarcity is overeating when food is available. So, evolution may have favored individuals with a tendency to overeat following deprivation.

Cultural psychology

Scientific psychology in the West has often assumed that people in all cultures have exactly the same psychological processes. Increasingly, this assumption is being challenged by proponents of cultural psychology, an interdisciplinary movement of psychologists, anthropologists, sociologists, and other social scientists. **Cultural psychology** is concerned with how the culture in which an individual lives – its traditions, language, and worldview – influences that person's mental representations as well as their psychological and neural processes.

Here is an example. In the West – North America and much of western and northern Europe – we think of ourselves as separate and autonomous agents with unique abilities and traits. In contrast, many cultures in the East – including those of India, China, and Japan – emphasize the interrelationships among people rather than their individuality (Markus & Kitayama, 2010). Moreover, Easterners tend to pay more attention to social situations than Westerners do. These differences lead Easterners to explain the behavior of another person differently than do Westerners. Rather than explaining a piece of behavior solely in terms of a person's traits, Easterners also explain it in terms of the social situation in which it occurred (Varnum *et al*., 2010). This has profound implications for trait attribution, one of the sample problems discussed at the beginning of the chapter. These differences between East and West in explaining behavior can also have educational implications. Because of their emphasis on collectivism rather than individualism, Asian students tend to study together more than American students. Such group study may be a useful technique, and it may be part of the reason why Asian students outperform their American counterparts in math. In addition, when an American student is having difficulty in math, both the student and the teacher tend to attribute the difficulty to the student's individual abilities. When a comparable case arises in a Japanese school, student and teacher are more likely to look to the situation – the student–teacher interaction in the instructional context – for an explanation of the poor performance.

Behavioral epigenetics

Whereas evolutionary psychology holds that many human traits and behaviors represent adaptations to the environment that were shaped incrementally over millennia through the process of natural selection and handed down to us by our human ancestors, behavioral epigenetics spotlights the biological mechanisms through which our own traits and behaviors can adapt to shifts in environments and experiences within and throughout our own lifespan. A central tenet of this perspective is that the neural structures and genetic phenotypes (observable characteristics) that shape human traits and behaviors are not fixed or set in stone or DNA. Instead they are characterized by considerable plasticity, meaning that structural aspects of our biology can and do change in response to our experiences. **Neuroplasticity** refers to how experiences can produce changes in brain structure, whereas **phenotypic plasticity** refers to how experiences can change in gene expression at cellular levels throughout our body and brain.

One example of a behavioral epigenetics approach comes from the study of human memory. For decades, psychologists have distinguished short-term from long-term memory, with the former operating over the span of minutes, and the latter over the span of days, weeks, or years. Recent evidence suggests that the transition of information from short- to long-term memory involves changes in gene expression that yield synaptic growth in the brain (Bailey & Kandel, 2004). A second example comes from the study of the biology of stress. For decades, we've known that stress triggers the release of cortisol and other biochemicals. New breakthroughs in behavioral epigenetics now tells us that these biochemicals lead to changes in gene expression within the human immune system, which helps explain why so many diseases and chronic health conditions are triggered or worsened by stress (Cole, 2009). The broader message from behavioral epigenetics is that human growth and change throughout the lifespan is undergirded by cellular and synaptic changes which in turn support those new changes.

HOW PSYCHOLOGICAL RESEARCH IS DONE

Now that we have some idea of the topics psychologists study and their perspectives, we can consider the research strategies they use to investigate them. In general, doing research involves two steps: (1) generating a scientific hypothesis, and (2) testing that hypothesis.

Generating hypotheses

The first step in any research project is to generate a hypothesis – a statement that can be tested – about the topic of interest. Regarding childhood amnesia, for example, we might generate the hypothesis that people can retrieve more memories of their early life if they are back in the same place where the incidents originally occurred. How does a researcher arrive at such a hypothesis? There is no single answer. An astute observer of naturally occurring situations may have an advantage in coming up with hypotheses. For example, you might have noticed that you can remember more about your high school years when you are back home, which could generate such a hypothesis. It also helps to be very familiar with the relevant scientific literature – previously published books and articles about the topic of interest.

The most important source for scientific hypotheses, however, is often a scientific theory, an interrelated set of propositions about a particular phenomenon. For example, one theory of sexual motivation proposes a genetic predisposition toward heterosexuality or homosexuality. This leads to the testable scientific hypothesis that pairs of identical twins – who have identical genes – should be more likely to have the same sexual orientation than pairs of fraternal twins, who share only about half their genes. A competing theory emphasizes childhood events as the source of an individual's sexual orientation and generates a competing set of hypotheses that can also be tested. As we will see throughout this book, testing hypotheses derived from competing theories is one of the most powerful ways of advancing scientific knowledge.

The term scientific means that the research methods used to collect the data are (1) unbiased (do not favor one hypothesis over another), and (2) reliable (other qualified people can repeat the observations and obtain the same results). The methods considered in this section have these two characteristics. Although some are better suited to certain perspectives than to others, each method can be used with each perspective.

Experiments

The most powerful scientific method is the experiment. Experiments provide the strongest tests of hypotheses about cause and effect. The investigator carefully controls conditions – often in a laboratory – and takes measurements in order to discover the causal relationships among variables.

CONCEPT REVIEW TABLE
TERMINOLOGY OF EXPERIMENTAL RESEARCH

Hypothesis	A statement about cause and effect that can be tested.
Experiment	A well-controlled test of a hypothesis about cause and effect.
Variable	Something that can occur with different values and can be measured.
Independent variable	A variable that represents the hypothesized 'cause' that is precisely controlled by the experimenter and independent of what the participant does.
Dependent variable	A variable that represents the hypothesized 'effect' whose values ultimately depend on the value of the independent variable.
Experimental group	A group in which the hypothesized cause is present.
Control group	A group in which the hypothesized cause is absent.
Random assignment	A system for assigning participants to experimental and control groups so that each participant has an equal chance of being assigned to any group.
Measurement	A system for assigning numbers to different values of variables.
Statistics	Mathematical techniques for determining the certainty with which a sample of data can be used to draw generalizations or inferences.

A variable is something that can occur with different values (see Concept Review Table: Terminology of experimental research). For example, an experiment might explore whether the amount of sleep causes memory changes (Does recall of childhood events decrease with lack of sleep?). If an experiment shows that memory performance changes systematically with hours of sleep, an orderly causal relationship between these two variables has been found.

The ability to exercise precise control over a variable distinguishes the experimental method from other methods of scientific observation. For example, if the hypothesis is that individuals will perform better on a math problem if they are offered more money for a good performance, the experimenter might randomly assign participants to one of three conditions: one group is told that they will be paid $10 if they perform well, the second group is promised $5, and the third group is not offered any money. The experimenter then measures and compares the performance of all three groups to see if, in fact, more money (the hypothesized cause) produces better performance (the hypothesized effect).

In this experiment, the amount of money offered is the independent variable because it is a variable that is independent of what the participant does. In fact, the **independent variable** is under the complete control of the experimenter, who creates it and controls its variation. In an experiment, the independent variable represents the hypothesized 'cause.' The hypothesized 'effect' in an experiment is the **dependent variable** because it is hypothesized to depend on the value of the independent variable. In this experiment, the dependent variable is performance on the math problems. The experimenter manipulates the independent variable and observes the dependent variable to learn the outcome of the experiment. The dependent variable is almost always some measure of the participants' behavior. The phrase 'is a function of' is often used to express the dependence of one variable on another. For this experiment, we could say that the participants' performance on the math problems is a function of the amount of money offered. The groups that are paid money would be the **experimental groups**, or groups in which the hypothesized cause is present. The group that was not paid would be the **control group**, the group in which the hypothesized cause is absent. In general, a control group serves as a baseline against which experimental groups can be compared.

One important feature of the experiment just described is random assignment of participants to groups or conditions. **Random assignment** means that each participant has an equal probability of being placed in any group. Without random assignment, the experimenter cannot be certain that something other than the independent variable might have produced the results. For example, an experimenter should never let participants choose which group they would like to be in. Although most participants might choose to be in the highest-paid group, those who are made nervous by pressure might choose to be in a 'casual' group that was not paid. In any case, the problem is that the groups would now contain different kinds of people, and the differences in their personalities, rather than the amount of money offered, serves as an alternative explanation for why one group might do better than another. Or suppose that an experimenter runs all the paid groups first and runs the no-payment control group afterward. This introduces a host of potential problems, sometimes called experimental confounds. Perhaps performance varies as a function of the time of day (morning, afternoon, or evening); maybe those who participate later in the experiment are closer in time to their final exams than earlier participants. In addition to these uncontrolled variables, many others of which the experimenter is unaware might bias the results. All such problems are resolved by randomly assigning participants to conditions. Only with random assignment can we be certain that all extraneous variables – such as participant personality, time of day, or time of semester – are evenly represented across conditions and therefore are unlikely to introduce bias. Random assignment is one of the most important ingredients of an experiment.

The experimental method can be used outside the laboratory as well. For example, in research on obesity, the effects of different methods of weight control can be investigated by trying these methods on separate but similar groups of obese individuals. The experimental method is a matter of logic, not location. Still, most experiments take place in laboratories, chiefly because a laboratory setting allows researchers to measure behavior more precisely and control the variables more completely. And again, it is often random assignment that is at issue: if two obesity clinics use different methods and achieve different results, we cannot conclude with confidence that the different methods are responsible because the clinics might attract different kinds of people to their programs or have different staff cultures and expectations.

The experiments described so far examine the effect of one independent variable on one dependent variable. Limiting an investigation to only one independent variable, however, is too restrictive for some problems. **Multivariate experiments** – experiments manipulating several independent variables at once – are common in psychological research. In the hypothetical study in which participants were offered different amounts of money for solving math problems, the experimenter might also vary the level of difficulty of the problems. Now there would be six groups of participants, each combining one of three different amounts of money with one of two levels of difficulty (easy versus difficult).

Measurement

Psychologists using the experimental method often have to make statements about amounts or quantities. Sometimes variables can be measured by physical means, such as hours of sleep deprivation or dosage of a drug. At other times, variables have to be scaled in a manner that places them in some sort of order. In rating a patient's feelings of aggression, for example, a psychotherapist might use a 5-point scale ranging from *never* through *rarely*, *sometimes*, and *often* to *always*. For purposes of precise communication, experiments require some form of **measurement**, a system for assigning numbers to variables.

Experiments usually involve making measurements on many participants, not just one. The results therefore are data in the form of a set of numbers that can be summarized and interpreted. To accomplish this task, the experimenter needs to use **statistics**, the mathematical discipline that deals with sampling data from a population of individuals and then drawing inferences about the population from those data. Statistics plays an important role not only in experimental research but in other methods as well. The most common statistic is the **mean**, which is simply the technical term for an arithmetic average, the sum of a set of scores divided by the number of scores in the set. In studies with one experimental group and one control group, there are two means to be compared: a mean for the scores of the participants in the experimental group and a mean for the scores of the participants in the control group. The difference between these two means is, of course, what interests the experimenters. If the difference between the means is large, it can be accepted at face value. But what if the difference is small? What if the measures used are subject to error? What if a few extreme cases are producing the difference? Statisticians have solved these problems by developing tests for determining the significance of a difference. A psychologist who says that the difference between the experimental group and the control group has **statistical significance** means that a statistical test has been applied to the data and the observed difference is unlikely to have arisen by chance or because of a few extreme cases.

Correlation

Not all problems can be easily studied by using the experimental method. In many situations the investigator has no control over which participants go in which conditions. For example, if we want to test the hypothesis that people with anorexia are more sensitive to changes in taste than normal-weight people, we cannot select a group of normal-weight participants and require half of them to become anorexic! Rather, we select people who are already anorexic or already of normal weight and see if they also differ in taste sensitivity. More generally, we can use the correlational method to determine whether some variable that is not under our control is associated – or correlated – with another variable of interest.

In the example just given, there were only two values of the weight variable: anorexic and normal. It is more common to have many values of each variable and to determine the degree to which values on one variable are related to values on another. This is done by using a descriptive statistic called the **correlation coefficient**, an estimate of the degree to which two variables are related. The correlation coefficient, symbolized by r, is expressed as a number between -1.00 and $+1.00$. A perfect relationship – which is rare – is indicated by 1.00 (1.00 if the relationship is positive and -1.00 if the relationship is negative). No relationship at all is indicated by a correlation close to zero. As r goes from 0 to 1.00 (or from 0 to -1.00), the strength of the relationship increases.

A correlation can be either + or –. The sign of the correlation indicates whether the two variables are **positively correlated**, meaning that the values of the two variables either increase together or decrease together, or **negatively correlated**, meaning that as the value of one variable increases, the value of the other decreases. Suppose that the number of times a student is absent from class correlates -0.40 with the final course grade (the more absences, the lower the grade). On the other hand, the correlation between the number of classes attended and the course grade would be $+0.40$. The strength of the relationship is the same, but the sign indicates whether we are looking at classes missed or classes attended.

To get a clearer picture of a correlation coefficient, consider the hypothetical study presented in Figure 1.6. As shown in Figure 1.6a, the study involves patients with brain damage leading to problems in face recognition (prosopagnosia). What is of interest is whether the degree of deficit, or error, in face recognition increases with the amount of brain tissue that is damaged. Each point on the graph in Figure 1.6a represents the percentage of errors made by one patient on a test of face recognition. For example, a patient who had only 10 per cent brain damage made 15 per cent errors on the face-**recognition test**, but a patient who had 55 per cent brain damage made 75 per cent errors. If errors in face recognition *always* increased along with the amount of brain damage, the points in the graph would consistently increase in moving from left to right; if the points had all fallen on the diagonal line in the figure, the correlation would have been r 1.0 – a perfect correlation. A couple of points fall on either side of the line though, so the correlation is about 0.90. Such a high correlation indicates a very strong relationship between amount of the brain damage and errors in face recognition. In Figure 1.6a, the correlation is positive because more errors are associated with more brain damage.

If, instead of focusing on errors, we plot the percentage of correct responses on the face recognition test, we end up with the diagram in Figure 1.6b. Now the correlation is negative – about -0.90 – because *fewer* correct responses are associated with *more* brain damage. The diagonal line in Figure 1.6b is simply the inverse of the one in Figure 1.6a.

Finally, consider the diagram in Figure 1.6c. Here we have graphed errors on the face recognition test as a function of the patients' height. Of course, there is no reason to expect a relationship between height and face recognition, and the graph shows that there is none. The points neither consistently increase nor consistently decrease in moving from left to right but rather bounce around a horizontal line. The correlation is 0.

In psychological research, a correlation coefficient of 0.60 or more is considered quite high. Correlations in the range from 0.20 to 0.60 are of practical and theoretical value and are useful in making predictions. Correlations between 0 and 0.20 must be judged with caution and are only minimally useful in making predictions.

Tests

The familiar use of the correlational method involves tests that measure aptitudes, achievement, or other psychological traits, such as the test of face recognition just discussed. A **test** presents a uniform situation to a group of people who vary in a particular trait (such as brain damage, math ability, manual dexterity, or aggression). The variation in scores on the test can be correlated with variations on another variable. For example, people's scores on a test of math ability can

a) Positive correlation

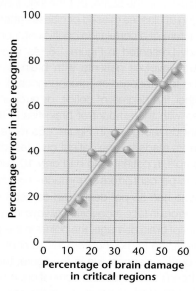

The patients are ordered along the horizontal axis with respect to the amount of brain damage, with the patient represented by the leftmost point having the least brain damage (10%) and the patient represented by the rightmost point having the most brain damage (55%). Each point on the graph represents a single patient's score on a test of face recognition. The correlation is a positive 0.90.

b) Negative correlation

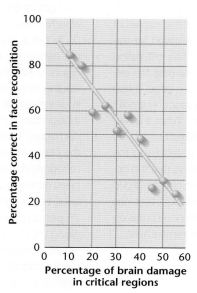

The same data are depicted, but we now focus on the percentage of correct responses (rather than errors). Now the correlation is a negative 0.90.

c) Zero correlation

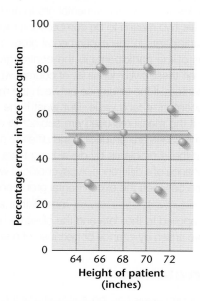

The patients' performance on the face recognition test is graphed as a function of their height. Now the correlation is 0.

FIGURE 1.6 Scatter Diagrams Illustrating Correlations. *These hypothesized data are based on ten patients, all of whom have some damage in regions of the brain known to be involved in face recognition.*

be correlated with their subsequent grades in a college math course. If the correlation is high, then the test score may be used to determine which of a new group of students should be placed in advanced sections of the course.

Correlation and causation

There is an important distinction between experimental and correlational studies. In a typical experimental study, one variable (the independent variable) is systematically manipulated to determine its causal effect on some other variable (the dependent variable). Such cause-and-effect relationships cannot be inferred from correlational studies.

For instance, studies have shown that the more TV violence a young boy watches, the more aggressive he is. But does watching violent TV cause the aggression, or do more aggressive boys choose to watch more violent TV? If all we have is a correlation, we cannot say which variable is cause and which is effect. As noted earlier in the chapter, however, other studies do demonstrate a causal relationship between watching violent TV and behaving aggressively.

Experimenters had control over the independent variable and used random assignment of participants to conditions.

Two variables can also be correlated when neither is the cause of the other. For example, many years before careful medical experiments demonstrated that cigarette smoking causes cancer, a correlation between smoking and lung cancer was shown. That is, it was already known that people who smoked were more likely to contract cancer. But – as the tobacco companies rushed to point out – this correlation left open the possibility that some third cause was responsible. For example, if people who live in smoggy urban areas are more likely to smoke than people who live in rural areas with cleaner air, then air pollution rather than smoking could cause higher cancer rates in smokers.

In short, when two variables are correlated, variation in one of them may possibly be the cause of variation in the other. Indeed, correlation is a prerequisite for causation. But, without further experiments, no such conclusion is justified from correlational studies, because correlation does not necessarily imply causation.

Observation

Direct observation

In the early stages of research, the most efficient way of making progress toward an explanation may be **direct observation** – to simply observe the phenomenon under study as it occurs naturally. Careful observation of animal and human behavior is the starting point for a great deal of research in psychology. For example, observation of primates in their native environment may tell us things about their social organization that will help in later laboratory investigations. Video recordings of newborn babies reveal details of their activity shortly after birth and the types of stimuli to which they respond. However, investigators observing naturally occurring behavior must be trained to observe and record events accurately so that their own biases do not influence what they report.

Observational methods may be used in a laboratory if the problem being studied is partly biological. For example, in their classic study of the physiological aspects of human sexuality, William Masters and Virginia Johnson (1966) developed techniques for directly observing sexual responses in the laboratory. The data included (1) observations of behavior, (2) recordings of physiological changes, and (3) responses to questions about the participants' sensations before, during, and after sexual stimulation. Although the researchers agreed that human sexuality has many dimensions besides the biological one, their observations of the anatomical and physiological aspects of sexual response have been very helpful in understanding the nature of human sexuality, as well as in solving sexual problems.

Field studies can often tell us more about social behavior than experimental studies can. Professor Shirley Strum has been observing the same troop of baboons in Kenya for more than 20 years, identifying individual animals, and making daily recordings of their behaviors and social interactions. Her data have provided remarkable information about the mental abilities of baboons and the role of friendships in their social system.

The survey method

Some problems that are difficult to study by direct observation may be studied by indirect observation through the use of questionnaires or interviews. Rather than observe people engaging in a particular behavior, such as exercising regularly, researchers using the **survey method** simply ask people if they engage in the behavior of interest. The survey method is more open to bias than direct observation, however. Of particular concern are **social desirability effects**, which occur when some people try to present themselves in a favorable light (for example, by saying that they exercise more than they actually do). Still, the survey method has produced many important results. For example, before Masters and Johnson conducted their research on the human sexual response, most of the available information on how people behave sexually (as opposed to how laws, religion, or society said they should behave) came from extensive surveys conducted by Alfred Kinsey and his associates 20 years earlier. Information from thousands of interviews was analyzed, resulting in the publication of two pioneering works: *Sexual Behavior in the Human Male* (Kinsey, Pomeroy, & Martin, 1948) and *Sexual Behavior in the Human Female* (Kinsey *et al.*, 1953).

Surveys have also been used to discover people's political opinions, product preferences, health care needs, and so on. Gallup polls and the government census are among the most familiar surveys in the USA for example. An adequate survey requires presenting a carefully pretested questionnaire to a sample of people who have been selected by methods designed to ensure that they are representative of the larger population being studied.

Case histories

Still another form of indirect observation is to obtain a **case history**, which is a partial biography of a particular individual. This involves asking people to recall relevant experiences from their past. For example, if the research is concerned with the childhood antecedents of adult depression, the researcher might begin by asking questions about earlier life events. These case histories are biographies designed for scientific use, and they are important sources of data for psychologists who are studying individuals.

A major limitation of case histories is that they rely on a person's memories and reconstructions of earlier events, which are frequently distorted or incomplete. Sometimes other data can be used to corroborate information obtained in a case history. For example, written records, such as death certificates, can be used to check on specific dates, or relatives of the person being interviewed can be asked to report their own memories of the relevant events. Even so, their limitations make case histories less useful for testing a theory or hypothesis than for suggesting hypotheses that can then be tested in more rigorous ways or checked with a larger sample of participants. In this way, scientists use the case history in much the same way that a therapist or physician might when trying to formulate a diagnosis and treatment for a particular individual.

Literature reviews

One final way in which psychological research is done is by conducting literature reviews. A **literature review** is a scholarly summary of the existing body of research on a given topic. Because the field of psychology grows at a fast pace, an up-to-date literature review is an indispensable tool for assessing patterns within the accumulating scientific evidence for a particular psychological hypothesis or theory.

Literature reviews come in two forms. One form is a **narrative review**, in which authors use words to describe studies previously conducted and discuss the strength of the available psychological evidence. University students enrolled in upper-level psychology courses often write narrative reviews of a chosen topic for term papers. Another type of review, which has become increasingly popular, is a **meta-analysis**, in which authors use statistical techniques to combine and draw conclusions about a group of studies previously conducted on a particular topic or that used a particular method. In any given experiment, as we have seen, participants are treated as 'cases,' with each participant contributing his or her own unique data, which are then summarized statistically. In a meta-analysis, by contrast, individual studies are treated as 'cases,' with each study contributing its own unique summary data, which are then further summarized at a higher – or *meta* – level of analysis. As you might imagine, meta-analyses have the potential to be more systematic and evenhanded than narrative reviews. Throughout this book, we often rely on meta-analyses to describe the state of the evidence for psychological theories and hypotheses.

Ethics of psychological research

Because psychologists study living beings, they need to be sensitive to ethical issues that can arise in the conduct of research. Accordingly, the American Psychological Association (APA) and its counterparts in Canada, Great Britain, and other countries, have established guidelines for the treatment of both human participants and animal subjects. In the USA for instance, federal regulations require any institution that conducts federally funded research to establish an internal review board, which reviews proposed studies to ensure that participants will be treated properly.

Research with humans

The first principle governing the ethical treatment of human participants is **minimal risk**. In most cases, the risks anticipated in the research should be no greater than those ordinarily encountered in daily life. Obviously, a person should not be exposed to physical harm or injury, but deciding how much psychological stress is ethically justified in a research project is not always so clear-cut. In everyday life, of course,

people may be impolite, lie, or make other people anxious. Under what circumstances is it ethically justifiable for a researcher to treat a participant in such ways to meet the goals of a research project? These are the kinds of questions that review boards consider on a case-by-case basis.

The second principle governing the ethical treatment of human participants is **informed consent**. Participants must be told ahead of time about any aspects of the study that could influence their willingness to co-operate and, after this disclosure, they must enter the study voluntarily and be permitted to withdraw from it at any time they desire without penalty. Like the principle of minimal risk, informed consent is not always easy to implement. In particular, informed consent is sometimes at odds with another common requirement of research: that participants be unaware of the hypotheses being tested in a study. If a researcher plans to compare participants who learn lists of familiar words with participants who learn lists of unfamiliar words, no ethical problem arises by simply telling participants ahead of time that they will be learning lists of words: they do not need to know how the words vary from one participant to another. Nor are any serious ethical issues raised if participants are given a surprise quiz they did not expect. But what if the researcher wants to compare participants who learn words while in a neutral mood with participants who learn words while they are angry or embarrassed? Clearly the research would not yield valid conclusions if participants had to be told ahead of time that they would be intentionally angered (by being treated rudely) or embarrassed (by being led to believe that they had accidentally broken a piece of equipment). Accordingly, the guidelines specify that if such a study is permitted to proceed at all, participants must be debriefed about it as soon as possible afterwards. During **debriefing**, the reasons for keeping them in ignorance – or deceiving them – about the procedures must be explained, and any residual emotional reactions must

Survey researchers ask individuals or, as in this case, a father and daughter about their attitudes and behavior. For survey results to be valid, the respondents must be representative of the larger population being studied.

be dealt with so that participants leave with their dignity intact and their appreciation for the research enhanced. The review board must be convinced that the debriefing procedures are adequate to this task.

A third principle of ethical research is the **right to privacy**. Information about a person acquired during a study must be kept confidential and not made available to others without the research participant's consent. A common practice is to separate the names and other information used to identify participants from the data collected in the study. The data are then identified only by code or case numbers. In that way, no one other than the experimenter has access to how any particular participant responded. Another common practice is to report only aggregated data – for example, data averaged across all participants in the same group or condition. This further protects the privacy of individual research participants.

Even if all of these ethical conditions are met, the researcher must still weigh the costs of the study – not the economic costs but the costs in human terms – against the potential benefits. Is it really necessary to conduct a study in which participants will be deceived or embarrassed? Only if the researcher and the review board are reasonably certain that the study can uncover worthwhile information – either practical or theoretical – can the research proceed.

Research with animals

Another area in which ethical standards must be observed is research with animals. About 7 per cent of psychological studies employ animals, 95 per cent of which are rats, mice, and birds. Psychologists conduct research with animals for two main reasons. One is that animal behavior can itself be interesting and worthy of study. A second is that animal systems can provide models for human systems, and so research on animals can produce knowledge that might be impossible or unethical to obtain from humans. Animal research has in fact played a pivotal role in understanding and treating psychological problems such as **anxiety**, stress, aggression, depression, drug abuse, eating disorders, hypertension, and Alzheimer's disease (Carroll & Overmier, 2001). Although debate continues about whether and what kind of research with animals is ethical, in the USA most psychologists (80%) and most psychology majors (72%) support the use of animals in research (Plous, 1996a, 1996b). Amid this wide support, concerns remain about the small subset of animal studies that involve painful or harmful procedures. To address these concerns, both federal and American Psychological Association (APA) guidelines require that any painful or harmful procedures imposed on animals must be thoroughly justified in terms of the knowledge to be gained from the study. APA guidelines also underscore that researchers have a moral obligation to treat animals humanely and to minimize their pain and suffering. Specific rules about the living conditions and maintenance of laboratory animals govern how this moral obligation is to be met.

Aside from these specific guidelines, a central principle of research ethics is that those who participate in psychology studies should be considered full partners in the research enterprise. Some of the research discussed in this text was conducted before the ethical guidelines just described were formulated and would not be permitted by most review boards today.

INTERIM SUMMARY

● Doing psychological research involves generating a hypothesis and then testing it by using a scientific method. Core concepts necessary for understanding psychology experiments include independent and dependent variables, experimental and control groups, random assignment, and measurement and statistics.

● When experiments are not feasible, the correlational method may be used to determine whether one naturally occurring variable is associated with another. The degree of association between two variables is measured by the correlation coefficient, r, which can be positive (up to $+1.00$) or negative (down to -1.00), depending on whether one variable increases with another ($+$) or one variable decreases as the other increases ($-$).

● Another way of conducting research is to use the observational method, either through direct observation, indirect survey methods, or case histories.

● A final way of conducting research is by literature review, either narrative reviews or statistical meta-analyses.

● The basic ethical principles governing the ethical treatment of human participants are minimal risk, informed consent, and the right to privacy. Any painful or harmful procedures imposed upon animals must be thoroughly justified in terms of the knowledge to be gained from the study.

CRITICAL THINKING QUESTIONS

1 Figure 1.3 displays the results of a classic study showing that preference for viewing violent TV programs by boys at age 9 is related to aggressive behavior at age 19. Why does this study fail to demonstrate that watching violence on TV makes boys more aggressive? What kind of evidence would be needed to make such an argument?

2 Suppose a researcher finds a correlation of 0.50 between symptoms of disordered eating and a preoccupation with physical appearance. What can the researcher conclude? What might explain the observed relationship? Can you formulate a hypothesis about cause and effect? How could you test that hypothesis?

SEEING BOTH SIDES
ARE WE NATURALLY SELFISH?

WE ARE NATURALLY SELFISH

George C. Williams, State University of New York,
Stony Brook

Yes we are selfish, in a special biological sense, but an important one that should be borne in mind in discussing human affairs, ethical philosophy, and related topics (Williams, 1996: Chapters 3 and 9). We are selfish in the special way that our genes demand. They are maximally selfish because, if they were not, they would not exist. The genes that get passed on through many generations are those that are best at getting themselves passed on. To do this they must be better than any alternatives at making bodies, human or otherwise, that transmit genes more profusely than other members of their population. Individuals can win this genetic contest mainly by surviving to maturity and then competing successfully for the resources (food, nest sites, mates, etc.) needed for their own reproduction.

In this sense we are necessarily selfish, but this need not imply that we are never expected to be unselfish in the sense in which this term is normally understood. Individuals can and often do assist others in gaining resources and avoiding losses or dangers. For a biological understanding of such behavior, the important observations lie in the circumstances in which the apparent benevolence occurs. The most obvious example of helpful behavior is that performed by parents for their own offspring. Its obvious explanation is that parents would not successfully transmit their genes if they did not help their own young in special ways: mammalian mothers must nurse their babies; birds must bring food to their nestlings; a plant must pack an optimum quantity of nutrients into each of its seeds. Yet this kind of provisioning is never a generalized helpfulness of adults toward the young. There are always mechanisms at work by which parents can usually identify their own offspring and confine their helpfulness to them alone.

If all reproduction is sexual and mates are seldom closely related to each other, each offspring has half of each parent's genes. From a parent's perspective, a son or daughter is genetically half as important as itself, and an offspring's reproduction is half as important as its own, for getting genes transmitted. Yet the same kind of partial genetic identity is true of all relatives, not just offspring. It may serve the genetic selfishness of an individual to behave helpfully toward relatives in general, not merely offspring. Such behavior arises from what is termed kin selection, natural selection for the adaptive use of cues that indicate degrees and probabilities of relationship. To whatever extent there is evidence of genealogical connections, an individual is expected to favor relatives over non-relatives and close relatives (parents, offspring, siblings) over more distant ones.

A male bird whose mate laid eggs in his nest can be favored in evolution if he incubates the eggs and feeds the later hatchlings. But what about possible cuckoldry? Can he really be sure that his mate was not inseminated by a neighboring male so that one or more of those eggs are not actually his own offspring? Extra-pair mating by female birds, with or without consent, does happen in many species. Males in such species are especially watchful of their mates' behavior and diligent in chasing rival males from their territories. It is expected that males, in species in which an average of 10 per cent of the eggs are fertilized by rivals, will be less conscientious toward their nestlings than in species in which cuckoldry never happens. Kin selection is one factor that causes what looks like unselfish behavior. Reciprocation between unrelated individuals, with immediate or likely future profit to each participant, is another. So is that which is caused by the selfish deception or manipulation of another's kin-selected or other altruistic or co-operative instincts. Female birds, like males, cannot be certain that nestlings are their own, because egg dumping (Sayler, 1992), the laying of an egg in another bird's nest while its owner is briefly away feeding, happens in many species. One female gains genetically by exploiting the parental instincts of another. The species in which deception and manipulation are most extensively developed is our own, by virtue of our language capability. Henry V, according to Shakespeare, addressed his army as 'We band of brothers.' Feminist leaders speak of the 'sisterhood.' Deception and manipulation of others' emotions can, of course, be for either a worthy or an unworthy cause.

George C. Williams

SEEING BOTH SIDES
ARE WE NATURALLY SELFISH?

WE ARE NOT NATURALLY SELFISH

Frans B. M. de Waal, Emory University

'How selfish soever man may be supposed, there are evidently some principles in his nature, which interest him in the fortune of others, and render their happiness necessary to him, though he derives nothing from it, except the pleasure of seeing it.'

Adam Smith, 1759

When Mr. Lenny Skutnik dove into the icy Potomac River in Washington, DC, in 1982, to rescue a plane-crash victim, or when Dutch civilians sheltered Jewish families during World War II, life-threatening risks were taken on behalf of complete strangers. Similarly, Binti Jua, a lowland gorilla at Chicago's Brookfield Zoo, rescued an unconscious boy who had fallen into her enclosure, following a chain of actions no one had taught her.

Such examples make a deep impression mainly because they benefit members of our own species. But in my work on the evolution of empathy and morality, I have found evidence so rich of animals caring for one another and responding to each other's distress that I am convinced that survival depends not only on strength in combat but also at times on co-operation and kindness (de Waal, 1996). For example, it is common among chimpanzees that a bystander approaches the victim of an attack to gently wrap an arm around his or her shoulder.

Despite these caring tendencies, humans and other animals are routinely depicted by biologists as complete egoists. The reason is theoretical: all behavior is supposed to have evolved to serve the actor's own interests. It is logical to assume that genes that fail to benefit their carrier are at a disadvantage in the process of natural selection. But is it correct to call an animal selfish simply because its behavior evolved for its own good?

The process by which a behavior came to exist over millions of years of evolution is irrelevant when considering why an animal here and now acts in a particular way. Animals only see the immediate consequences of their actions, and even those are not always clear to them. We may think that a spider builds a web to catch flies, but this is true only at the functional level. There is no evidence that spiders have any idea what webs are for. In other words, a behavior's purpose says nothing about its underlying motives.

Only recently has the concept of 'selfishness' been robbed of its vernacular meaning and applied outside the psychological domain. Even though the term is now seen by some as synonymous with self-serving, selfishness implies the intention to serve oneself, hence knowledge of what one stands to gain from a particular behavior. A vine may serve its own interests by overgrowing a tree, but since plants lack intentions and knowledge, they cannot be selfish except in a meaningless, metaphorical sense. For the same reason, it is impossible for genes to be selfish.

Charles Darwin never confused adaptation with individual goals, and endorsed altruistic motives. In this he was inspired by Adam Smith, the moral philosopher and father of economics. It says a great deal about the distinction between self-serving actions and selfish motives that Smith, known for his emphasis on self-interest as the guiding principle of economics, also wrote about the universal human capacity of sympathy.

The origins of this inclination are no mystery. All species that rely on co-operation show group loyalty and helping tendencies. These tendencies evolved in the context of a close-knit social life in which they benefited relatives and companions able to repay the favor. The impulse to help was, therefore, never totally without survival value to the ones showing the impulse. But the impulse became divorced from the consequences that shaped its evolution, permitting its expression even when pay-offs were unlikely, such as when strangers were the beneficiaries.

To call all behavior selfish is like describing all life on earth as converted sun energy. Both statements have some general value but offer little help in explaining the diversity we see around us. Some animals survive through ruthless competition, others through mutual aid. A framework that fails to distinguish the contrasting mind-sets involved may be of use to the evolutionary biologist: it has no place in psychology.

Chimpanzees are known to 'console' one another – the behavior seems a form of empathy without tangible benefit to the performer. Such 'consolations' have as yet not been reported for other animals.

CHAPTER SUMMARY

1 Psychology is the scientific study of behavior and mental processes.

2 The roots of psychology can be traced to the fourth and fifth centuries BC. The Greek philosophers Socrates, Plato, and Aristotle posed fundamental questions about the mind, and Hippocrates, the 'father of medicine,' made many important observations about how the brain controlled other organs. One of the earliest debates about human psychology focused on the question of whether human capabilities are inborn (the nature view) or acquired through experience (the nurture view).

3 Scientific psychology was born in the late nineteenth century with the idea that mind and behavior could be the subject of scientific analysis. The first experimental laboratory in psychology was established by Wilhelm Wundt at the University of Leipzig in 1879.

4 Among the early 'schools' of psychology in the twentieth century were structuralism (the analysis of mental structures), functionalism (studying how the mind works so that an organism can adapt to and function in its environment), behaviorism (the study of behavior without reference to consciousness), Gestalt psychology (which focuses on the patterns formed by stimuli and on the organization of experience), and psychoanalysis (which emphasizes the role of unconscious processes in personality development and motivation).

5 Later developments in twentieth-century psychology included information-processing theory, psycholinguistics, and neuropsychology.

6 The study of psychology can be approached from several perspectives. The biological perspective relates actions to events taking place inside the body, particularly the brain and nervous system. The behavioral perspective considers only external activities that can be observed and measured. The cognitive perspective is concerned with mental processes, such as perceiving, remembering, reasoning, deciding, and problem-solving, and with relating these processes to behavior. The psychoanalytic perspective emphasizes unconscious motives stemming from sexual and aggressive impulses. The subjectivist perspective focuses on how people actively construct and interpret their social worlds, which is expected to vary by culture, personal history, and current motivational state. A particular topic often can be analyzed from more than one of these perspectives.

7 The biological perspective differs from the other viewpoints in that its principles are partly drawn from biology. Often, biological researchers attempt to explain psychological principles in terms of biological ones; this is known as reductionism. Behavioral phenomena are increasingly being understood at both the biological and psychological levels.

8 Among the major subfields of psychology are biological psychology, cognitive psychology, developmental psychology, social and personality psychology, clinical and counseling psychology, school and educational psychology, and industrial and engineering psychology. Many new areas of inquiry gaining momentum in twenty-first-century psychology span traditional subfields and disciplines. These new areas include cognitive neuroscience (as well as affective and social cognitive neuroscience), evolutionary psychology, cultural psychology, and behavioral epigenetics.

9 Doing psychological research involves generating a hypothesis and then testing it by using a scientific method. When applicable, the experimental method is preferred because it seeks to control all variables except the ones being studied and can thus test hypotheses about cause and effect. The independent variable is the one that is manipulated by the experimenter; the dependent variable (usually some measure of the participant's behavior) is the one being studied to determine whether it is affected by changes in the independent variable. In a simple experimental design, the experimenter manipulates one independent variable and observes its effect on one dependent variable. An essential element of experimental design is the random assignment of participants to experimental and control groups.

10 In many experiments the independent variable is something that is either present or absent. The simplest experimental design includes an experimental group (with the hypothesized cause present for one group of participants) and a control group (with the hypothesized cause absent for another group of participants). If the manipulation of the independent variable results in a statistically significant difference in the dependent variable between the experimental and control groups, we know that the experimental condition had a reliable effect, and the difference is not due to chance factors or a few extreme cases.

11 In situations in which experiments are not feasible, the correlational method may be used. This method determines whether a naturally occurring difference is associated with another difference of interest. The degree of correlation between two variables is measured by the correlation coefficient, r, a number between $+1.00$ and -1.00. The absence of any relationship is indicated by 0; a perfect relationship is indicated by 1. As r goes from 0 to 1, the strength of the relationship increases. The correlation coefficient can be positive or negative, depending on whether one variable increases with another $(+)$ or one variable decreases as the other increases $(-)$.

12 Another way of conducting research is to use the observational method, in which one observes the phenomenon of interest. Researchers must be trained to observe and record behavior accurately. Phenomena that are difficult to observe directly may be observed indirectly by means of surveys (questionnaires and interviews) or by reconstructing a case history.

13 The basic ethical principles governing the ethical treatment of human participants are minimal risk, informed consent, and the right to privacy. Any painful or harmful procedures imposed upon animals must be thoroughly justified in terms of the knowledge to be gained from the study.

CORE CONCEPTS

law of effect	biological perspective	variable
over justification effect	behavioral perspective	independent variable
validity	cognitive perspective	dependent variable
psychology	psychoanalytic perspective	experimental groups
prosopagnosia	subjectivist perspective	control group
fundamental attribution error	naïve realism	random assignment
childhood amnesia	reductionism	multivariate experiment
obese	biological psychologists	measurement
cathartic effect	cognitive psychologists	statistics
aggression	developmental psychologists	mean
physiology	social psychologists	statistical significance
nature–nurture debate	personality psychologists	correlation coefficient
nature view	clinical psychologists	positively correlated
nurture view	counseling psychologists	negatively correlated
tabula rasa	school psychologists	recognition test
associationist psychology	educational psychologists	test
attention	organizational psychologists	direct observation
introspection	engineering psychologists	survey method
structuralism	cognitive neuroscience	social desirability effects
functionalism	affective neuroscience	case history
behaviorism	social neuroscience	literature review
Gestalt	evolutionary psychology	narrative review
psychoanalysis	cultural psychology	meta-analysis
unconscious	neuroplasticity	minimal risk
free association	phenotypic plasticity	informed consent
information-processing models	hypothesis	debriefing
psychological perspective	theory	right to privacy
psi (Ψ)	scientific	anxiety
eclectic approach	experiments	cues

DIGITAL SUPPORT RESOURCE

Students should use the unique access code included in the front of the book to access the digital support resources which accompany the new edition. These include:

- Multiple Choice Questions and Quizzes
- Critical Thinking Questions
- Practice Essay Questions

- Videos
- Glossary, Flashcards, and more

2

BIOLOGICAL FOUNDATIONS OF PSYCHOLOGY

LEARNING OBJECTIVES
After reading this chapter you should be able to:

Understand the organization and the physiology of the human brain.

Have learned the research methods used to study the brain.

Be able to consider evolutionary arguments.

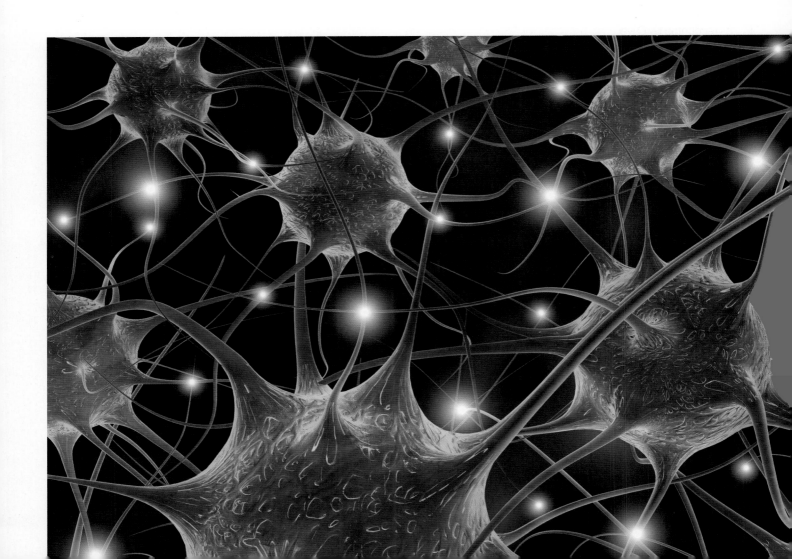

CHAPTER OUTLINE

THE STUDY OF THE BIOLOGICAL
BASES OF PSYCHOLOGY

NEURONS, THE BUILDING BLOCKS OF
THE NERVOUS SYSTEM
Action potentials
Neural coding and synaptic transmission
Neurotransmitters

THE ORGANIZATION OF THE BRAIN
The hindbrain
The midbrain
The forebrain
Mapping the brain
Asymmetries in the brain

CUTTING EDGE RESEARCH: WHAT
HAPPENS IN THE BRAINS OF EXPERT
ATHLETES?

THE AUTONOMIC NERVOUS SYSTEM

THE ENDOCRINE SYSTEM

EVOLUTION, GENES, AND BEHAVIOR
Evolution of behavior
Chromosomes and genes
Genetic studies of behavior

SEEING BOTH SIDES: TO LOCALIZE
OR NOT TO LOCALIZE: THAT'S THE
QUESTION

Imagine waking up one morning to discover that your sense of smell has intensified to such a degree that all other perceptual experiences pale in comparison. You soon discover that you can tell all your friends and acquaintances apart by just their body odor and that you can find your way in your home town by the smell of the familiar shops and street corners. Excitement takes hold of you. You realize you are shivering with emotion, a yearning to take in the smell of everything and everyone that surrounds you, and a desire to touch it all as well. And although you are aware that your desires are not sexual, you resist these temptations when you are in the company of others – it would seem inappropriate to behave that way.

These were actually the experiences of a young medical student named Stephen D., as recounted by Oliver Sacks in the story 'The Dog Beneath the Skin' in his famous book *The Man Who Mistook His Wife for a Hat*. Oliver Sacks is a neurologist whose writings of case histories have inspired many students of the human brain. Stephen, we are told, is a regular user of cocaine, PCP, and amphetamines. One night he has a very lively dream in which he is a dog and his world is rich with inspiring odors. He awakens to discover that his sense of smell has actually changed dramatically. And Stephen feels emotionally different. His longing to smell and touch everything comes with a sense of melancholia, a desire to return to a long-forgotten place. His thinking also seems to change. He enjoys the immediacy of every experience deeply and discovers that he is finding it more difficult than before to reflect on his experiences and think abstractly. After 3 weeks Stephen's symptoms disappear and everything returns to normal, to his relief and regret.

Olfaction is the term used for our sense of smell. Hyperosmia (the increased ability to smell), as well as anosmia (the inability to smell), can be the consequence of brain injury or infection, or caused by the use of certain medications. These changes in olfactory sensations have a remarkable impact on the emotional experiences of the patients. How can this be explained? Olfactory information is transmitted to a few different places in the brain, through multiple pathways. One pathway involves areas that are responsible for the perception and discrimination of odors, and damage to these areas results in the inability to discriminate odors. Another pathway involves brain areas that are responsible for emotional and motivational aspects of behavior. This latter pathway sets the olfactory system apart from the other sensory systems: the emotional experience that accompanies the sensation of an odor is quite literally experienced *more* directly than the emotion that might result from a visual or auditory experience.

We will see that many aspects of human behavior can be understood by taking a look at our biology. For example: exploring the consequences of certain brain injuries teaches us how the brain represents our experiences and behaviors. Similarly, the effects of medications or recreational drugs illustrate the role neurotransmitters play as the chemical messengers of the nervous system. In this chapter we will take a look at the nervous system, its building blocks and organization, as well as its evolutionary history.

THE STUDY OF THE BIOLOGICAL BASES OF PSYCHOLOGY

The introduction illustrates that our perceptions, experiences and behaviors are based on the activation of our nervous system, and that an understanding of its functioning is important for the study of psychology. If this idea strikes you as mechanistic, as if to reduce a human being to some type of biological machine, you are not the first to have this response. The French philosopher René Descartes (1596–1650) proposed that all animal and human action was a mechanical response to an external stimulus: a reaction of a complex system consisting of tubes containing fluids and switching gears (Descartes, 1662). But Descartes was well aware of the fact that denial of the existence of a human soul would have theological implications that would offend the Church and make his theory unacceptable. He was careful to leave room for the human soul and proposed that it is our soul that chooses a particular response from among a set of possible responses. It affords us our flexibility, so that we can have different responses to the same stimulus. Descartes' mind-body dualism proposes that the mind (or soul) exists separately from the physical body, and that both can influence each other.

In this chapter, you will be introduced to our current understanding of our biological foundation. It will not be a story about a system of tubes and gears, but rather about the nervous system. This physical system consists of biological cells (neurons) that communicate with one another biochemically. You might find it quite difficult to think of oneself in terms of a neural system: your unique human experiences (love, fear, bewilderment) seem impossible to reduce to something as prosaic as that. However, you might also find it quite stimulating. If the human experience is awe-inspiring, then the biological system that makes it possible for us to have these experiences must be rather complex and fascinating itself. Our brain might very well be the single most complex object that we know about.

The study of the biological basis of our behavior involves considerations about its evolution. An important concept in evolutionary biology is that of pre-adaptation introduced by Ernst Mayr. An example is the evolution of a voicing system: mouth, teeth and tongue gained a new function in producing sounds (and later, the pronunciation of language), even though they clearly evolved initially for eating. Mayr's idea was that many evolutionary 'novelties' are the result of a process by which an existing system is co-opted, which means that it allows for the development of a new function (Mayr, 1960). A similar mechanism is often proposed to explain the development of specific human abilities. Two compelling examples are the development of moral disgust and the development of our response to social exclusion.

Paul Rozin, an American psychologist who likes to refer to himself as 'Dr Disgust,' proposes that moral disgust could

develop because of the existence of a distaste and disgust system created by evolution to protect us from ingesting poisonous food (Rozin et al., 2000). The 'disgust face' was mentioned already by Darwin, who described the gape, the tongue extension, the nose wrinkle, and the dropping of the mouth corners as a response that would prevent food from entering the mouth, or encourage its discharge. Nausea, the physiological state that might accompany disgust, has a similar function, as does the associated response of increased salivation. We know that the disgust response is associated with brain activation in the right prefrontal area as well as the basal ganglia. Rozin proposes that disgust, which started its evolutionary life as response to avoid harm to the body, ultimately evolved to become a mechanism for avoiding harm to the soul. Moral offenses (such as sexual offenses or war atrocities) elicit an emotional response that is similar to the basic disgust response. Exactly which behaviors are considered morally disgusting differs to some degree across different cultures, so that learning what is morally offensive and disgusting is part of an individual's socialization.

Another human response that can be understood from within a model of pre-adaptation is our response to being socially excluded. For human beings it is important to be part of a social group because such connections provide safety. It has been shown that social exclusion poses a threat to an individual's health (Uchino et al., 1996). Research has also shown that human beings respond to social exclusion by becoming indifferent and apparently numb to emotional pain (DeWall & Baumeister, 2006). We may understand this if we realize that the evolution of a system of social interaction might have co-opted an evolutionarily older system: the system that allowed for responses to *physical* pain. A healthy reaction to a painful stimulus sometimes is to (defensively) increase the **pain threshold**, meaning that pain sensitivity is reduced. According to the pre-adaptation model, the physiological system that responds to physical pain evolved to take on the function of responding to social pain. This leads to the prediction that social exclusion should influence how an individual responds to physical pain. This prediction was tested experimentally by Nathan DeWall and Roy Baumeister (DeWall & Baumeister, 2006). The experimenters threatened half of their subjects with the prospect of a lonely future, whereas control subjects were told that they would have meaningful and lasting relationships. Subjects were made to believe that the experimenters based their predictions on the results of a personality test. In reality, subjects were randomly assigned to one of the two conditions. The researchers hypothesized that the physical **pain thresholds** of the subjects in the 'future alone' condition should be higher, and this is exactly what they found. Subjects in this condition also had higher physical **pain tolerance** (the ability to withstand pain) than subjects in the control condition. These results suggest that the emotional numbness reported by ostracized people might be part of a defensive response generated by a common physiological system that is responsible for physical as well as emotional pain. Further support for this comes from studies showing that certain areas in the brain are activated by distress associated with physical pain as well as with social exclusion (Eisenberger *et al.*, 2003).

We have seen that some human behaviors (the response to morally offensive behavior and to social exclusion) can be studied, and by taking the evolutionary history of our nervous system into account. At this point, it is important to introduce some basic terminology (see Figure 2.1). The term **nervous system** refers to *all* neural tissue. This system is divided into the central nervous system (CNS) and the peripheral nervous system (PNS). The **central nervous system** includes the **brain** (the part of the nervous system that resides in the skull) and the **spinal cord**. The **peripheral nervous system** includes the remainder of the neural tissue in the rest of the body. **Afferent nerves** carry signals from the body to the CNS, whereas **efferent nerves** carry signals from the CNS to the body.

The PNS consists of the **somatic system**, which carries messages to and from the sense receptors, muscles, and the surface of the body (for conscious sensory functions and voluntary motor functions), and the **autonomic system**, which connects with the internal organs and glands (for automatic and involuntary functions, such as the beating of the heart). The *sensory nerves* of the somatic system transmit information about external stimulation from the skin, muscles, and joints to the CNS. That is how we become aware of pain, pressure, and temperature variations. The *motor nerves* of the somatic system carry impulses from the CNS to the muscles, where they initiate action. All the muscles we use in voluntary movements, as well as involuntary adjustments in posture and balance, are controlled by these nerves. The nerves of the autonomic system run to and from the internal organs, regulating processes such as respiration, heart rate, and digestion.

In this chapter we will study these systems in detail by taking a look at specific parts of the nervous system (in particular: the brain and the autonomic system), as well as the *endocrine system* (the system of glands in charge of hormone secretion). The final section of this chapter concerns evolutionary biology and its relevance for the study of human behavior. We will start with the basic building blocks of the nervous system (*neurons*), and their communication system.

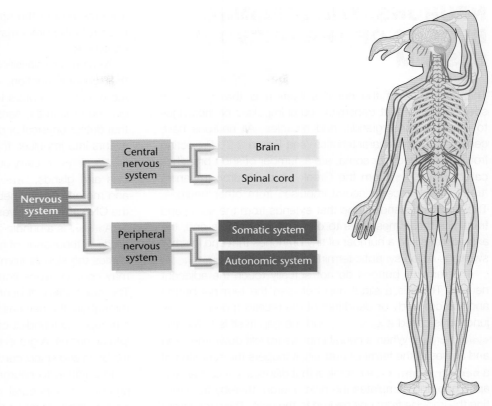

FIGURE 2.1 The Organization of the Nervous System. *In these diagrams of the human nervous system, the central nervous system (brain and spinal cord) is shown in blue and the peripheral nervous system shows the somatic in red and the autonomic in green.*

INTERIM SUMMARY

➲ Some human functions (such as moral disgust and our response to social exclusion) may have developed through a process of pre-adaptation, by co-opting existing systems (in these cases, the systems for physical disgust and physical pain).

➲ The nervous system is divided into the CNS and the PNS. The CNS includes the brain and the spinal cord. The PNS includes the somatic system and the autonomic system.

CRITICAL THINKING QUESTIONS

1 Can you think of another human function that might have developed by co-opting an existing function?

2 Most contemporary psychologists would claim that it is important to study how the nervous system works. Why do you think they say that? And do you agree?

NEURONS, THE BUILDING BLOCKS OF THE NERVOUS SYSTEM

The basic unit of the nervous system is the **neuron**, a specialized cell that transmits neural impulses or messages to other neurons, glands, and muscles. All neurons have certain common characteristics (see Figure 2.2). Projecting from the cell body, or soma, are a number of short branches called **dendrites** (from the Greek word dendron, meaning 'tree'), which receive neural impulses from other neurons. The **axon** is a slender tube that extends from the soma and transmits these messages to other neurons. At its end, the axon divides into a number of tiny branches that end in small swellings called synaptic terminals or **terminal buttons**.

The terminal buttons do not actually touch the adjacent neuron. There is a slight gap between the terminal button and the cell body or dendrites of the receiving neuron. This junction is called a **synapse**, and the gap itself is called the **synaptic gap**. When a neural impulse travels down the axon and arrives at the terminal buttons, it triggers the secretion of a **neurotransmitter**, a chemical that diffuses across the synaptic gap and stimulates the next neuron, thereby transmitting the impulse from one neuron to the next. The axons from a great many neurons form synapses on the dendrites and cell body of a single neuron. In this way, the post-synaptic (receiving) neuron integrates information from multiple pre-synaptic neurons.

Although all neurons have these general features, they vary greatly in size and shape (see Figure 2.3). A neuron in the spinal cord may have an axon up to a meter long, running from the end of the spine to the muscles of the big toe; a neuron in the brain may cover only a few thousandths of a centimeter.

Neurons are classified into three categories, depending on their general function. **Sensory neurons** transmit impulses received by receptors to the CNS. The **receptors** are specialized cells in the sense organs, muscles, skin, and joints, that detect physical or chemical changes and translate these events into impulses that travel along the sensory neurons. **Motor neurons** carry outgoing signals from the CNS to muscles and glands. **Interneurons** connect sensory (afferent) and motor (efferent) neurons. Interneurons are found only in the CNS and in the eyes.

A **nerve** is a bundle of elongated axons belonging to hundreds or thousands of neurons. For example, the optic nerve carries the signals from the eye to the brain. A single nerve may contain axons from both sensory and motor neurons. The cell bodies of neurons are generally grouped together throughout the nervous system. In the brain and spinal cord, a group of cell bodies of neurons is referred to as a **nucleus** (plural: nuclei). A group of neuronal cell bodies found outside the brain and spinal cord is called a **ganglion** (plural: ganglia).

In addition to neurons, the nervous system has a large number of nonneural cells, called **glial cells**, which are interspersed among neurons. These glial cells greatly outnumber neurons and take up more than half the volume of the brain. Glial cells were long thought just to provide a support system for the neurons. The name glia, derived from the Greek word for 'glue,' suggests one of these functions: to hold neurons in place. Glial cells also provide insulation between cells. In addition, they provide nutrients to the neurons and appear to 'keep house' in the brain by gathering

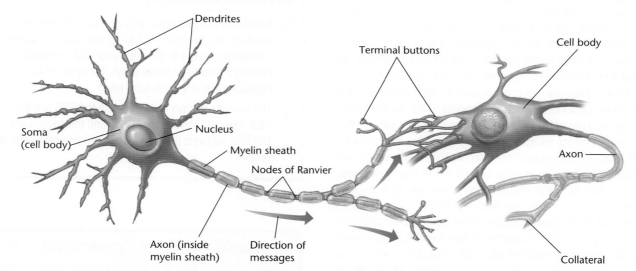

FIGURE 2.2 Diagram of a Neuron and Synapses at the Cell Body. *Arrows indicate the direction of the nerve impulse. Some axons are branched; the branches are called collaterals. The axons of many neurons are covered with an insulating myelin sheath that helps increase the speed of the nerve impulse. Many different axons, each of which branches repeatedly, synapse on the dendrites and cell body of a single neuron. Each branch of an axon ends in terminal buttons that contain neurotransmitters. When released, neurotransmitters transmit the nerve impulse across the synapse to the dendrites or cell body of the receiving cell.*

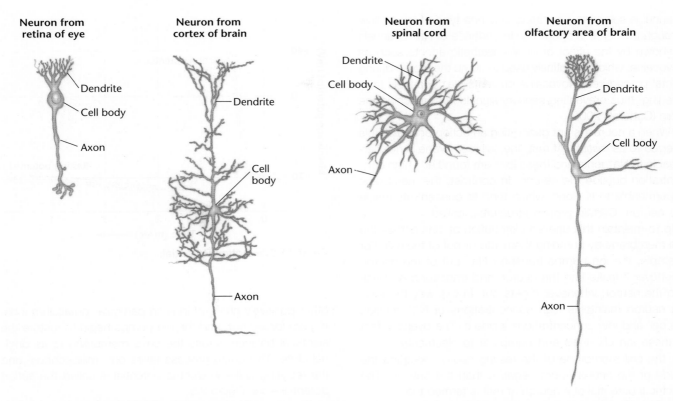

FIGURE 2.3 Shapes and Relative Sizes of Neurons. *The axon of a spinal cord neuron (not shown in its entirety in the figure) may be about a meter long.*

waste products, thereby maintaining the signaling capacity of neurons (Haydon, 2001). Recent evidence shows that glial cells have functions other than 'just' supportive ones. For example: glial cells are essential during embryonic development, providing tracks for new neurons to migrate along (Allen & Barres, 2009). Glial cells have even been shown to be actively involved in the transmission of neural signals (Gourine *et al.*, 2010).

Action potentials

One important term left unexplained thus far is the *neural impulse*. Information moves along a neuron in the form of a neural impulse called an **action potential** – an electrochemical impulse that travels from the cell body down to the end of the axon. Each action potential is the result of movements by electrically charged molecules, known as **ions**, in and out of the neuron. The key to understanding the generation of the action potential lies in appreciating that neurons are normally very selective about what ions can flow in and out of the cell. That is, the cell membrane of the neuron (including its axon) is semi-permeable, which means that some ions can pass through the cell membrane easily and others are not allowed to pass through except when special passageways in the membrane are open. These passageways, called **ion channels**, are doughnut-shaped protein molecules that form pores across the cell membrane

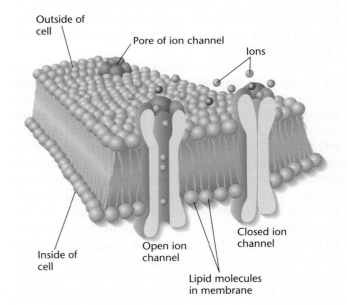

FIGURE 2.4 Ion Channels. *Ions such as sodium (Na^+) potassium (K^+), and Chloride (Cl^-) pass through the cell membranes via doughnut-shaped protein molecules called ion channels.*

(see Figure 2.4). These proteins regulate the flow of ions such as sodium (Na^+), potassium (K^+), and chloride (Cl^-) in and out of the neuron. (You may be more familiar with the terms *natrium* for Na^+, and *kalium* for K^+.) Each ion channel is selective, permitting only one type of ion to flow through it when it is open. The importance of Na⁺ channels is shown by the effect of local anesthetic agents such as novocaine, which is routinely used to numb the mouth during dental procedures. Novocaine prevents Na⁺ channels from opening, thus preventing sensory signals from reaching the brain (Catterall, 2000).

When a neuron is not generating an action potential, it is referred to as *resting*. At rest, the cell membrane is not permeable to Na⁺ ions, and these ions are found at a high concentration outside the neuron. In contrast, the membrane is permeable to K⁺ ions, which tend to concentrate inside the neuron. Certain protein structures, called **ion pumps**, help to maintain this uneven distribution of ions across the cell membrane by pumping them into or out of the cell. For example, the ion pumps transport Na⁺ out of the neuron whenever it leaks into the neuron and transports K⁺ back into the neuron whenever it gets out. In this way the resting neuron maintains high concentrations of Na⁺ outside the cell and low concentrations inside it. The overall effect of these ion channels and pumps is to electrically **polarize** the cell membrane of the resting neuron, keeping the *inside* of the neuron *more negative* than the outside. The electrical potential of a neuron at rest is termed the **resting potential**. For most neurons, the resting potential is around −70 millivolts (mV). The resting potential of a neuron is similar to the charge held by a battery; both neurons and batteries use electrochemical gradients to store energy. The neuron's energy can be used to generate action potentials. How does this happen?

The electric potential across a neuron's cell membrane will change if it is stimulated by other neurons. This stimulation is caused by the action of neurotransmitters that are released by the pre-synaptic neuron, and received by the post-synaptic neuron. If the change in electric potential is very small, nothing dramatic will happen. For example, if the potential is raised to about −60 mV or so, the neuron's ion pumps will quickly restore the resting potential of −70 mV. However, if the change in electric potential is large enough, a different set of events occurs. For most neurons, −55 mV constitutes the **excitation threshold**: if the electric potential is raised above this value, the cell membrane becomes temporarily unstable, resulting in an action potential. In other words: the initial depolarization caused by external stimulation raises the potential above threshold. This leads to a cascade of events resulting in a temporary reversal (called **depolarization**) of the potential across the membrane. First, voltage-sensing Na⁺ channels located on the axon suddenly open so that Na⁺ ions can now cross the membrane *into* the cell. These positively charged sodium ions will flood into the cell because opposite charges attract one another and the inside of the cell is negatively charged. Now the inside of that area of the axon becomes positive relative to the outside, going up to about +40 mV or so. Next, some

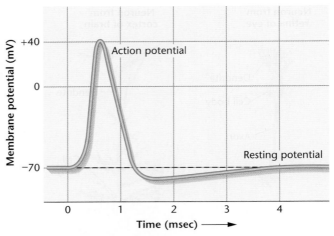

FIGURE 2.5 Action Potential.

other positively charged ions (in particular potassium ions, K⁺) are forced out, and the ion pumps begin to restore the electrical balance across the cell's membrane to its original state. This entire process takes only milliseconds, and the resulting spike in electric potential is called the *action potential* – see Figure 2.5

The action potential will propagate itself down the axon, in the direction of the terminal buttons. This is because neighboring Na⁺ channels sense the depolarization and open, causing the adjacent area of the axon to depolarize in turn. This process repeats itself down the length of the axon (see Figure 2.6). The reason that an action potential travels only in one direction and not backwards, is the result of a **refractory period**: after it has generated a 'spike,' the membrane cannot do so again for about one millisecond.

The speed of the action potential as it travels down the axon can vary from about 1 to 120 meters per second. The speed is affected by whether the axon is covered with a **myelin sheath**. This sheath consists of specialized glial cells that wrap themselves around the axon, one after another, with small gaps between them (refer back to Figure 2.2). These tiny gaps are called **nodes of Ranvier**, named after the French anatomist. The insulation provided by the myelin sheath allows for **saltatory conduction**, in which the nerve impulse jumps from one node of Ranvier to the next. This greatly increases the speed of transmission of the action potential down the axon. (Saltatory comes from the Latin word *saltare*, which means 'to leap.') The myelin sheath is particularly prevalent where rapid transmission of the action potential is critical – for example, along axons that stimulate skeletal muscles. In multiple sclerosis (MS), a disorder in which symptoms first become evident between the ages of 16 and 30, the immune system attacks and destroys the body's own myelin sheaths, producing severe motor nerve dysfunction.

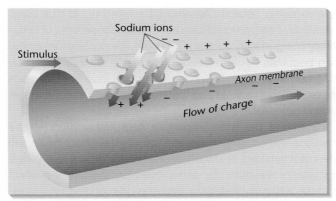

a) During an action potential, sodium gates in the neuron membrane open and sodium ions enter the axon, bringing a positive charge with them.

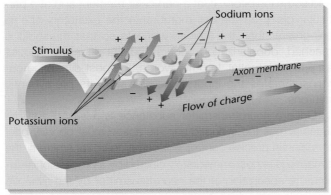

b) After an action potential occurs at one point along the axon, the sodium gates close at that point and open at the next point along the axon. When the sodium gates close, potassium gates open and potassium ions flow out of the axon, carrying a positive charge with them.

FIGURE 2.6 Action Potential Propagating Along the Axon.

Neural coding and synaptic transmission

It is important to realize that, in terms of neural communication, firing off an action potential is *all* a neuron can do. The neuron fires an action potential in a single, brief pulse and then becomes inactive for a few thousandths of a second. It can only be triggered if the stimulation by pre-synaptic neurons reaches the threshold level. Thus, in response to any given synaptic input, a neuron either fires an action potential or it does not, and *if* it fires an action potential, the potential is always the same size. This is referred to as the **all-or-none law**. You can think of neuronal action potentials as the binary signals (0's and 1's) computers use to implement software instructions. Neurons are either firing an action potential (1) or not (0). Once initiated, the action potential travels down the axon to its many axon terminals.

But how can the nervous system code for (that is, represent) the complexity of our experiences, if the basic unit of communication is so very simple? Each 'coding question'

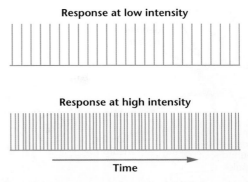

FIGURE 2.7 Response of a Single Neuron to a Stimulus Presented at Low and High Intensity. *Each 'spike' is an action potential generated in response to the stimulus. For most neurons, the maximum rate of response is about 1000 action potentials per second.*

has a different answer, revealing the complexity of the nervous system itself. But there are some basic principles. For example, imagine listening to a sound and noticing that it is becoming louder. This change in intensity is coded for at the level of the response of single neurons. Even though a neuron can only fire off action potentials, the frequency of its firing *can* change. In other words: a single neuron might respond to a particular sound with a response rate of 200 action potentials per second, and increase its response rate to 800 action potentials per second as the sound increases in intensity. This kind of frequency coding is depicted in Figure 2.7.

Another way for the nervous system to reflect something as simple as an increase in the intensity of a stimulus is by involving a greater population of neurons in the response. Population coding can be powerful, because the synchronization (or lack thereof) in the response of the individual neurons often contains meaning as well. The consideration of coding questions reveals that the true power of the nervous system lies in the complexity of the *connections* between individual neurons.

As mentioned earlier, neurons do not connect directly at a synapse, and the signal must travel across a slight gap (see Figure 2.8). When an action potential moves down the axon and arrives at the terminal buttons, it stimulates synaptic vesicles in the terminal buttons. The synaptic vesicles are small spherical structures that contain neurotransmitters. When they are stimulated, they discharge the neurotransmitters into the synapse. The neurotransmitters diffuse from the pre-synaptic neuron across the synaptic gap and bind to receptors, which are proteins lodged in the dendritic membrane of the post-synaptic neuron.

The neurotransmitter and the receptor site fit together like the pieces of a jigsaw puzzle or a key and its lock. This **lock-and-key action** causes a change in the permeability of ion channels in the receiving neuron. The effect of this change might be either excitatory or inhibitory. An **excitatory** effect allows positively charged ions (such as Na^+) to enter the

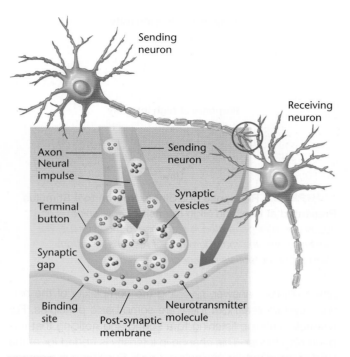

Sending neuron

Receiving neuron

Axon
Neural impulse

Sending neuron

Terminal button

Synaptic vesicles

Synaptic gap

Binding site

Post-synaptic membrane

Neurotransmitter molecule

FIGURE 2.8 Release of Neurotransmitters into a Synaptic Gap. *The neurotransmitter is carried into the pre-synaptic vesicles, which fuse with the membrane and release their contents into the synaptic gap. The neurotransmitters diffuse across the gap and combine with receptor molecules in the post-synaptic membrane.*

post-synaptic neuron, which depolarizes as a result (so that the inside is more positively charged than it was before). This makes the post-synaptic neuron *more likely* to reach its excitation threshold and thus more likely to generate an action potential. The change in permeability of the ion channels in the receiving neuron can also be **inhibitory**. In that case, positively charged ions (such as K^+) leave the neuron, or negatively charged ions (such as Cl^-) enter. The post-synaptic neuron becomes **hyperpolarized** (the inside is more negatively charged than before). Consequently, it is *less likely* to reach its excitation threshold and therefore less likely to generate an action potential.

Some of the most important neurotransmitters in our nervous system are described below. The effect of certain neurotransmitters is always excitatory, for others is it always inhibitory. However, for some neurotransmitters the effect can be *either* excitatory *or* inhibitory, depending on the receptor molecules in place.

Any particular neuron may receive input from many pre-synaptic neurons. Some of this input might be excitatory, and some inhibitory. If (at a particular moment and at a particular place on the cell membrane) the excitatory effects are greater than the inhibitory effects so that threshold is reached, depolarization occurs and the neuron produces an action potential. In other words, the post-synaptic neuron *summates* the input it receives from its pre-synaptic neurons.

Once a neurotransmitter substance is released and diffuses across the synaptic gap, its action must be very brief to maintain precise control. For some neurotransmitters, the synapse is almost immediately cleared by a process of **reuptake**: re-absorption of the neurotransmitter by the synaptic terminals from which it was released. Reuptake cuts off the action of the neurotransmitter and spares the axon terminals from having to manufacture more of the substance. For other neurotransmitters, the effect is terminated by **degradation**: enzymes in the synaptic gap chemically break up the neurotransmitter and make it inactive.

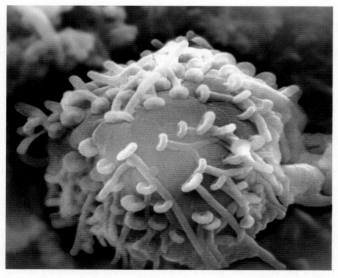

An electron micrograph of a neuron densely packed with synapses.

INTERIM SUMMARY

➔ The basic unit of the nervous system is the neuron.

➔ Neurons receive chemical signals on branches called dendrites and transmit electrochemical potentials down a tubelike extension called the axon.

➔ Chemical neurotransmitters are released at synapses and carry messages between two neurons. Neurotransmitters exert their action by binding to receptors.

➔ When a neuron is depolarized above its excitation threshold, it generates an all-or-none action potential. This action potential moves down the axon and initiates the release of neurotransmitters at the terminal buttons.

CRITICAL THINKING QUESTIONS

1 Only about a tenth of the cells in your brain are neurons (the rest are glial cells). Does this mean that you use only 10 per cent of your brain when you think? What else might this fact mean?

2 Local anesthetics, such as those used by dentists, work by blocking Na$^+$ gates in the neurons near the point of injection. Of course, dentists and physicians typically inject them in a part of the body near the source of pain. What do you think such a drug would do if it was injected into the brain? Would it still block pain or would its effect be different?

Neurotransmitters

More than a hundred different neurotransmitters have been identified, and more are likely to be discovered (Kandel *et al.,* 2000). Some neurotransmitters can bind to more than one type of receptor and cause different effects on different types of receptors. Certain neurotransmitters are excitatory at some sites and inhibitory at other sites because different receptor molecules are involved. In this chapter we cannot discuss all of the neurotransmitters in the nervous system. Instead, we will focus on a few that influence behavior.

Acetylcholine

Acetylcholine is present at many synapses throughout the nervous system. It is usually excitatory, but it can also be inhibitory, depending on the type of receptor molecule in the membrane of the receiving neuron. Acetylcholine is particularly prevalent in an area of the forebrain called the hippocampus, which plays a key role in the formation of new memories (Eichenbaum, 2000). This neurotransmitter plays a prominent role in Alzheimer's disease, a devastating memory disorder. Neurons in the forebrain that produce acetylcholine tend to degenerate in Alzheimer's patients. The less acetylcholine is produced, the more serious the memory loss.

Acetylcholine is also released at every synapse between a motor neuron axon and a skeletal muscle fiber, causing the muscle contraction. Certain drugs that affect acetylcholine can produce muscle paralysis. For example, *botulinum toxin*, which forms from bacteria in improperly canned foods, blocks the release of acetylcholine and can cause death by paralyzing the muscles used in breathing. Some nerve gases developed for warfare, as well as many pesticides, cause paralysis by destroying the enzyme that degrades acetylcholine once the neuron has fired. When the degradation process fails, there is an uncontrolled buildup of acetylcholine and normal synaptic transmission becomes impossible.

Norepinephrine

Norepinephrine (or noradrenaline) is produced mainly by neurons in the brainstem, causing alertness and arousal. Any drug that causes norepinephrine to increase or decrease in the brain is correlated with an increase or decrease in the individual's mood level. *Cocaine* and *amphetamines* prolong the action of norepinephrine by slowing down its reuptake. Because of this delay, the receiving neurons are activated for a longer period, which causes these drugs' stimulating psychological effects. In contrast, *lithium* speeds up the reuptake of norepinephrine, causing a person's mood level to be depressed.

Dopamine

Dopamine is chemically very similar to norepinephrine. It is involved in the regulation of motivation and emotional pleasure. In recent years, addiction researchers have shown that dopamine is involved especially in regulating the *incentive salience* of a reward (Schultz, 2002) – in other words: how much we *want* something (see also Chapter 10). Too much dopamine in some areas of the brain may cause schizophrenia, and too little in other areas may lead to Parkinson's disease. Drugs used to treat schizophrenia, such as *chlorpromazine* or *clozapine*, block the receptors for dopamine. In contrast, *L-dopa*, a drug commonly prescribed to treat Parkinson's disease, increases dopamine in the brain.

Serotonin

Like norepinephrine, **serotonin** plays an important role in mood regulation. For example, low levels of serotonin have been associated with feelings of depression. Serotonin reuptake inhibitors are antidepressants that increase serotonin levels in the brain by blocking its uptake. *Prozac*, *Zoloft*, and *Paxil*, drugs that are commonly prescribed to treat depression, are serotonin reuptake inhibitors. Because serotonin is also important in the regulation of sleep and appetite, it is also used to treat the eating disorder bulimia. Interestingly, the hallucinogenic drug *lysergic acid diethylamide* (LSD) induces its effects by binding to serotonin receptors in the brain.

Glutamate

The excitatory neurotransmitter glutamate is present in more neurons of the central nervous system than any other transmitter. Glutamate is excitatory because it depolarizes neurons upon which it is released. Of the three or more subtypes of glutamate receptors, one in particular, the NMDA receptor, is thought to affect learning and memory (Madden, 2002). It is named for the chemical (N-methyl-D-aspartate) that is used to detect it. Disruptions in glutamate neurotransmission have been implicated in schizophrenia.

GABA

Another prominent amino acid neurotransmitter is gamma-aminobutyric acid (GABA). This substance is a major inhibitory transmitter; in fact, most synapses in the brain use

GABA. The drug *picrotoxin*, which blocks GABA receptors, produces convulsions because muscle movement cannot be controlled by the brain without GABA's inhibiting influence. The tranquilizing effects of certain antianxiety drugs, the *benzodiazepines*, are a result of GABA's inhibitory action.

INTERIM SUMMARY

➡ The most important neurotransmitters include acetylcholine, norepinephrine, dopamine, serotonin, glutamate, and gamma-aminobutyric acid (GABA).

➡ Many neurotransmitters can have either excitatory or inhibitory effects on neurons, depending on the type of post-synaptic receptor they bind to.

CONCEPT REVIEW TABLE
NEUROTRANSMITTERS AND THEIR FUNCTIONS

Neurotransmitter	Function
Acetylcholine	Involved in memory and attention as well as in muscle control. Decreases associated with Alzheimer's disease.
Norepinephrine	Involved in arousal. Stimulants increase its effect. Low levels contribute to depression.
Dopamine	Involved in motivation. Mediates the effects of natural rewards (food and sex, for example) as well as recreational drugs.
Serotonin	Involved in mood regulation. Drugs that increase serotonin levels alleviate depression and anxiety.
Glutamate	Major excitatory neurotransmitter in brain. Involved in learning and memory.
GABA	Major inhibitory neurotransmitter in brain. Anti-anxiety drugs enhance the activity of GABA.

CRITICAL THINKING QUESTIONS

1 There are many different neurotransmitter systems in the brain. Identify two advantages and two disadvantages of the fact that there are multiple neurotransmitters, rather than just one or two.

2 Alzheimer's disease cannot be cured through the intake of a neurotransmitter. Why might that be?

THE ORGANIZATION OF THE BRAIN

One way to conceive of the organization of the brain is in terms of *function*. The Canadian investigator Paul MacLean (MacLean, 1973) proposed that we can think of the human brain as three concentric layers, which each developed as a result of evolutionary changes: (1) the **central core**, which regulates our most primitive behaviors, (2) the **limbic system**, which controls our emotions, and (3) the **cerebral cortex**, which regulates our higher intellectual processes.

A more common approach to describing the structure of the brain is one that divides the brain into three main regions based on *location* (see Figures 2.9 and 2.10): (1) the **hindbrain**, which includes all the structures located in the hind ('posterior') part of the brain, closest to the spinal cord, (2) the **midbrain**, located in the middle of the brain, and (3) the **forebrain**, which includes the structures located in the front ('anterior') part of the brain.

The hindbrain

The hindbrain sits on top of the spinal cord, and it is crucial for basic life functions.

Medulla

The first slight enlargement of the spinal cord as it enters the skull is the **medulla**, a narrow structure that controls breathing and some reflexes that help maintain upright posture.

Pons

Above the medulla is the **pons**, which is important for the control of attentiveness, as well as the timing of sleep. At this point, the major nerve tracts coming up from the spinal cord cross over so that the right side of the brain is connected to the left side of the body, and the left side of the brain is connected to the right side of the body.

Reticular formation

A network of neural circuits that extends from the lower brainstem up to the thalamus in the forebrain, and traversing some of the other central core structures, is called the **reticular formation**. This network of neurons acts to control arousal. When an electric current of a certain voltage is sent through electrodes implanted in the reticular formation of a cat or dog, the animal goes to sleep; stimulation by a current with a more rapidly changing waveform awakens the sleeping animal. The reticular formation also plays a role in our ability to focus attention on particular stimuli. All of the sense receptors have nerve fibers that feed into the reticular system, which appears to act as a filter. It allows some sensory messages to pass to the cerebral cortex (that is, to conscious awareness) while blocking others.

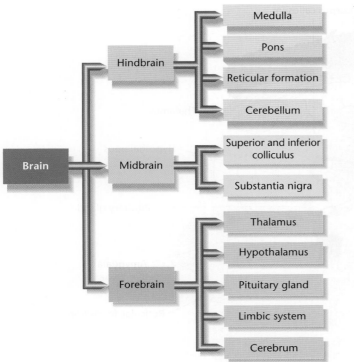

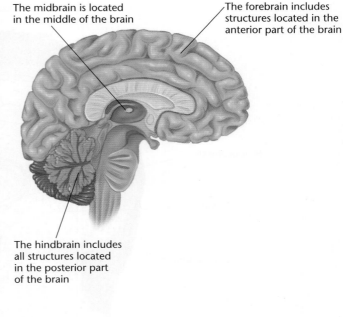

The midbrain is located in the middle of the brain

The forebrain includes structures located in the anterior part of the brain

The hindbrain includes all structures located in the posterior part of the brain

FIGURE 2.9 Organization of the Brain.

Cerebellum

Attached to the rear of the brainstem slightly above the medulla is a convoluted structure called the **cerebellum** (Latin for 'little brain'), which is concerned primarily with the co-ordination and timing of movement. Specific movements may be initiated at higher levels, but the co-ordination of those movements depends on the cerebellum. Damage to the cerebellum results in jerky movements. In addition to co-ordinating movement, the cerebellum is involved in learning new motor responses (Boyden *et al.*, 2004).

The midbrain

The midbrain is relatively small in humans. It is found just above the pons, and surrounded by the forebrain.

Superior and inferior colliculus

The midbrain contains two small structures (the **superior colliculus and the inferior colliculus**) that are important for relaying sensory information to the brain, and for movement control (including eye movements).

Substantia nigra

Another important midbrain structure is the **substantia nigra**, a crucial part of the dopamine-containing pathway (also referred to as the 'reward-pathway'). It is the substantia nigra that deteriorates in Parkinson's disease.

The forebrain

In humans the forebrain is relatively large, and covers the midbrain and parts of the hindbrain (see Figure 2.10). A large part of it, the cerebral cortex, is especially more highly developed in humans than in any other organism. The outer layer of the brain is called the cerebral cortex (or simply cortex) from the Latin word for 'bark.' Below, we will see that this is the most important region of the brain for many psychological functions. The other structures in the forebrain (the thalamus, the hypothalamus, and the areas comprising the limbic system) are found just underneath the cortex and are therefore called *subcortical* structures.

Thalamus

Located just above the midbrain inside the cerebral hemispheres are two egg-shaped groups of nerve cell nuclei, the **thalamus**. It acts as a sensory relay station, directing incoming information from the sense receptors (such as vision and hearing) to the cerebral cortex.

Hypothalamus

The **hypothalamus** is a much smaller structure located just below the thalamus. Centers in the hypothalamus regulate eating, drinking, and sexual behavior. The hypothalamus is involved in maintaining homeostasis by exerting control over the autonomic nervous system (discussed later). **Homeostasis** is a term that refers to the level of functioning that is characteristic

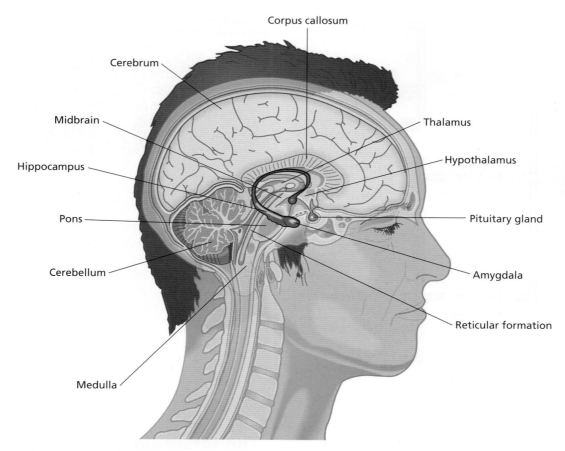

FIGURE 2.10 The Main Structures of the Human Brain.

of a healthy organism, such as normal body temperature, heart rate, and blood pressure. When an organism is under stress, homeostasis is disturbed, and processes are set into motion to correct this lack of equilibrium. For example, if we are too warm, we perspire, and if we are too cool, we shiver. Both processes tend to restore normal temperature and are controlled by the hypothalamus. The hypothalamus also has an important role in the sensation of emotions and in our response to stress-producing situations. Mild electrical stimulation of certain areas in the hypothalamus produces feelings of pleasure; stimulation of adjacent regions produces unpleasant sensations.

Pituitary gland

The **pituitary gland** is the most important part of a system of glands called the *endocrine system* (to be discussed later). Through its influence on the pituitary gland, which lies just below it, the hypothalamus controls the endocrine system and thus the production of hormones.

Limbic system

Around the central core of the brain and closely interconnected with the hypothalamus is the **limbic system**, a set of structures that impose additional control over some of the instinctive behaviors regulated by the central core. Animals

that have only rudimentary limbic systems, such as fish and reptiles, carry out activities such as feeding, attacking, fleeing, and mating by means of stereotyped behaviors. In mammals, the limbic system seems to inhibit some of these instinctive patterns and allow the organism to be more flexible and better able to adapt to changes in the environment.

One part of the limbic system, the **hippocampus**, has a special role in memory. This role was discovered in the 1950s, when patients had the structure surgically removed to treat their epilepsy. Upon recovery from such an operation, patients readily recognize old friends and recall earlier experiences, and they can read and perform skills learned earlier in life. However, they cannot remember events occurring after the operation. For example, they do not recognize a new person with whom they may have spent many hours earlier in the day.

The limbic system is also involved in emotional behavior. The **amygdala**, an almond-shaped subcortical structure is critical in the formation of emotional memories, especially those involving fear responses (see also Chapter 7, Fear conditioning). As early as the 1930s, researchers reported that monkeys with damage to the amygdala exhibit marked reduction in fear (Klüver & Bucy, 1937). Humans with such damage are unable to recognize **facial expressions** of fear or learn new fear responses (Bechara *et al.*, 1995). The amygdala is not itself a memory site, but through its widespread connections to the rest of the brain it modulates the strength of memories: the more emotionally relevant an event, the more active the amygdala is while it occurs – and the stronger the subsequent memory (Paré *et al.*, 2002). More recently, the amygdala has been shown to play a role in social behavior: the size of the amygdala is correlated with the size and complexity of one's social network (Bickart *et al.*, 2011).

Cerebral cortex

Each of the sensory systems sends information to specific areas of the cerebral cortex. Motor responses, or movements of body parts, are controlled by specific areas of the cortex. The rest of the cortex, which is neither sensory nor motor, consists of *association areas*. These areas occupy the largest portion of the human cortex and are concerned with memory, thought, and language. The cortex of the preserved brain appears gray because its surface consists largely of nerve cell bodies and unmyelinated fibers – hence the term gray matter (see Figure 2.11). More towards the inside, it consists of mostly myelinated axons and appears white (also called white matter).

The cortex is composed of two hemispheres on the left and right sides of the brain that are connected by the **corpus callosum**. They are basically symmetrical, with a deep division (the **longitudinal fissure**) between them. We therefore refer to the left and right **hemispheres**. Each hemisphere is divided into four **lobes**: the **frontal**, **parietal**, **occipital**, and **temporal lobes**. These are large regions of the cerebral cortex that perform diverse functions. The frontal lobe is separated from the parietal lobe by the **central fissure**, a groove that runs from near the top of the head sideways to the ears. The division between the parietal lobe and the occipital lobe

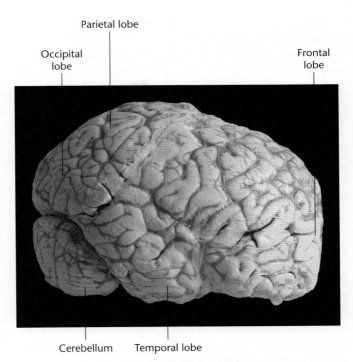

FIGURE 2.11 Photograph of Human Brain.

is less clear-cut. For our purposes, we can say that the parietal lobe is at the top of the brain behind the central fissure and that the occipital lobe is at the rear of the brain. A deep fissure at the side of the brain, the **lateral fissure**, sets off the temporal lobe (see Figure 2.12a).

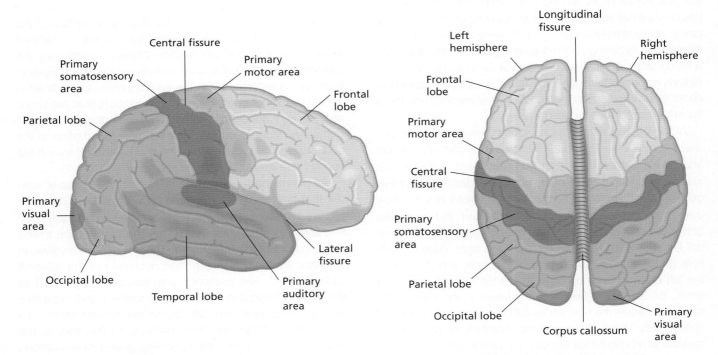

FIGURE 2.12A Cerebral Cortex (Lateral View).

FIGURE 2.12B Cerebral Cortex (Superior View).

The **primary motor area**, just in front of the central fissure, controls voluntary movements of the body. When motor cortex is injured, movement is impaired. The name of Canadian neurosurgeon Wilder Penfield is associated with the method to 'map' the human brain using electrical stimulation. In the 1940s Penfield stimulated the cortex of his patients while he was performing surgery to cure epilepsy (Penfield & Jasper, 1954). He observed which parts of the body would move if he stimulated specific areas of the motor cortex. The motor homunculus shows that certain areas on the body are associated with relatively large areas on the cortex – the hands for example. Our hands can make very precise movements. Other parts of the body, like the legs, make far less finely controlled movements and have proportionally smaller parts of cortex associated with them. The body is represented on the motor cortex in approximately upside-down form. For example, movements of the toes are controlled from an area near the top of the head, but tongue and mouth movements are controlled from near the bottom of the motor area. Movements on the right side of the body are governed by the motor cortex of the left hemisphere; the right hemisphere governs movements on the left side.

In the parietal lobe, separated from the motor area by the central fissure, lies an area that is responsible for sensory experiences: the **primary somatosensory area**. When this area is stimulated electrically, it produces a sensory experience somewhere on the opposite side of the body. Heat, cold, touch, pain, and the sense of body movement are represented here. In general, the amount of somatosensory area associated with a particular part of the body is related to its sensitivity and use. This can be seen in the sensory homunculus depicted in Chapter 4. We also see this kind of representation in other animals. For example, among four-footed mammals, the dog has only a small amount of cortical tissue representing its forepaws, whereas the raccoon – which makes extensive use of its forepaws in exploring and manipulating its environment – has a much larger cortical area to control its forepaws, including regions for separate fingers. The rat, which learns a great deal about its environment by means of its sensitive whiskers, has a separate cortical area for each whisker.

At the back of each occipital lobe in the cortex is the **primary visual area**. Figure 2.13 shows the optic nerve fibers and neural pathways leading from each eye to the **visual cortex**. Notice that some of the optic fibers from the right eye go to the right cerebral hemisphere, whereas others cross over at a junction called the **optic chiasm** and go to the opposite hemisphere; the same arrangement holds true for the left eye. Specifically, fibers from the right sides of both eyes go to the right hemisphere of the brain, and fibers from the left sides of both eyes go to the left hemisphere. As a result, the left visual field is represented in the right hemisphere, whereas the right visual field is represented in the left hemisphere. This fact is sometimes helpful in pinpointing the location of a brain tumor or other abnormalities.

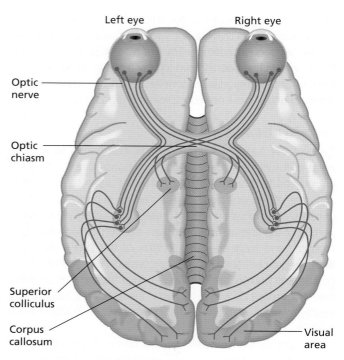

FIGURE 2.13 Visual Pathways. *Nerve fibers from the inner, or nasal, half of the retina cross over at the optic chiasm and go to opposite sides of the brain. Nerve fibers from the outer, or temporal, half of the retina remain on the same side of the brain. Thus, stimuli falling on the right side of each retina are transmitted to the right hemisphere, and stimuli falling on the left side of each retina are transmitted to the left hemisphere. Also note that some of the input from the eyes is sent directly to the superior colliculus, for eye movement control.*

The **primary auditory area**, located on the surface of the temporal lobe at the side of each hemisphere, is involved in the analysis of complex auditory signals – particularly the temporal patterning of sound, as in human speech. Input to both ears is represented in the auditory areas on both sides of the cortex, but connections to the opposite side are stronger. The right ear sends information to both the right and left primary auditory areas, but it sends more information to the auditory area on the left side of the brain. Similarly, the left ear sends more information to the right side.

As mentioned earlier, the areas of the cerebral cortex that are not directly concerned with sensory or motor processes are **association areas**. The *frontal association areas* (or prefrontal cortex) are the parts of the frontal lobes in front of the motor area. These areas are involved in memory, thinking, planning, and decision-making (Miller & Cohen, 2001). The prefrontal area has been described as the brain's 'executive' because it monitors and organizes thought processes and selects certain actions while it inhibits others. Individuals with damage to this area of the brain indeed have difficulties planning goal-directed actions and paying attention. In addition, they can show decreased sensitivity to the social and moral consequences of their actions (Koenigs *et al*., 2007).

The *posterior association areas* are located near primary sensory areas and consist of sub-areas that serve a particular sense. For example, the lower portion of the temporal lobe is related to visual perception. Damage to this area causes deficiencies in the ability to recognize different forms. Though the patient can 'see' the form and trace its outline, they cannot identify the shape or distinguish it from a different form (Gallant *et al*., 2000).

Mapping the brain

Researchers rely on multiple methods to study the function of different structures in the brain. Most of the more sophisticated methods described here have become available only in the last decades and can obtain detailed pictures of the living human brain without causing the patient or subject distress or damage.

Brain damage and selective lesions

One of the ways to study brain function is to study the effects of *brain damage*. Unfortunately, brain damage can occur in a number of ways: individuals can suffer a traumatic injury to the brain (in car accidents or through gunshot wounds, for example), or suffer from a condition which leaves the brain damaged (a tumor, epilepsy, or vascular or degenerative disease). The results of neuropsychological tests to establish the deficits, in combination with post-mortem dissection of the brain have provided much information about the relationship between brain structure and function.

Researchers can also *lesion* the brain – that is, cause localized damage with the purpose of studying its functional consequence. Obviously, the vast majority of such lesion studies are carried out in animals. Researchers can surgically remove brain tissue, or damage it using other methods (relying on electricity, temperature, or chemicals).

Brain stimulation

Instead of destroying brain tissue, researchers can also stimulate certain brain regions – again with the purpose of studying the consequence. Stimulation may be done chemically, by inserting a small tube into the brain and injecting chemicals (neurotransmitters, for example). Electrical stimulation is done by inserting or implanting an electrode with which to stimulate a certain region of the brain.

A newer technique, called *transcranial magnetic stimulation* (TMS) involves the use of a magnetic field produced by a magnetic coil held over the subject's head. This method allows researchers to increase or decrease the activation of specific areas of the brain, near the surface area of the skull. A great advantage of this method is that it is painless and non-invasive.

Electrical recording

A third general method of studying brain function is to 'listen' to the brain – that is, to monitor and record the electrical activity of neurons while the brain is active. This can be done using *electroencephalograms* (EEGs). Electrodes are placed on the scalp, and the electrical activity of large groups of neurons is amplified, recorded, and made visible. The EEG signal can also be used to study so-called **event-related potentials (ERPs)**, when electrical activity is recorded in response to a specific event, such as a stimulus or a motor response.

More detailed study of the electrical activity of neurons is afforded *by single-cell recordings*, in which researchers study the activity of individual neurons by probing them with small microelectrodes. This way, they can discover what stimulus or behavior triggers that cell's activity.

Structural brain imaging

Certain modern neuro imaging techniques allow researchers to create images of the living brain. The first two that we will discuss are CT (or CAT) and MRI scans, which have in common that they provide us with a *structural* image of the entire brain, which can be used to scan for tumors and other types of structural abnormalities.

Computerized axial tomography (CT or CAT) scans the brain using multiple computer enhanced X-ray photographs taken from different angles. Relative to MRI, CT scans are inexpensive.

Magnetic resonance imaging (MRI) techniques provide us with more expensive but also more precise scans of the entire brain. The MRI produces magnetic pulses which cause a temporary response in the molecules of the brain tissue, resulting in the release of energy which gets picked up by the scanner. This signal is converted to high-resolution images of the brain.

Functional brain imaging

The two last techniques to be discussed here, PET and fMRI, provide us with *functional* images of the brain which allow researchers to study localized brain activity while research subjects are carrying out specific tasks. The development of these methods has greatly advanced the field of neuropsychology because it means that we can directly correlate mental activity with brain activity.

Positron emission tomography (PET) scans measure brain activity using a radioactive tracer mixed with glucose. Brain activity can be measured this way, because active brain tissue requires more glucose, resulting in more radioactivity in active brain regions.

Functional magnetic resonance imaging (fMRI) relies on the fact that oxygenated blood floods to brain areas that are active. The magnetic changes that result from this process are recorded by the MRI scanner. The resulting images of the active brain are more precise than those produced by

PET, because it can measure changes in brain activity across much smaller time periods.

Asymmetries in the brain

At first glance, the two halves of the brain look like mirror images. But when brains are measured during autopsies, the left hemisphere is almost always larger than the right hemisphere. The right hemisphere also contains many long neural fibers that connect widely separated areas of the brain, whereas the left hemisphere has many shorter fibers that provide large numbers of interconnections within a limited area (Hellige, 1993).

Magnetic resonance imaging (MRI) techniques provide us with more expensive but also more precise scans of the entire brain.

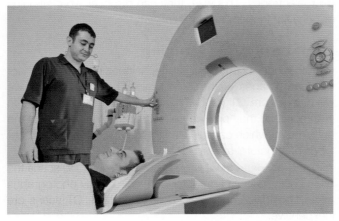

PET scans in a human subject illustrating that different areas of the brain are involved in different modes of word processing.

Language

Much of our information about brain mechanisms for language comes from observations of patients with brain damage. The damage may be due to tumors, penetrating head wounds, or the rupture of blood vessels. The term **aphasia** is used to describe language deficits caused by brain damage. As early as 1861, the French physician Paul Broca examined the brain of a deceased patient who had suffered speech loss. He found damage in an area of the left hemisphere just above the lateral fissure in the frontal lobe (see Figure 2.14). This region, now known as **Broca's area**, is involved in speech production. People with damage to Broca's area suffer from *expressive aphasia*: they have difficulty enunciating words correctly and speak in a slow, labored way. Their speech often makes sense, but it includes only key words. Nouns are generally expressed in the singular, and adjectives, adverbs, articles, and conjunctions are likely to be omitted. However, these individuals have no difficulty understanding either spoken or written language. Destruction of the equivalent region in the right hemisphere usually does not result in speech impairment. The areas involved in understanding speech and being able to write and understand written words are also usually located in the left hemisphere. A stroke that damages the left hemisphere is more likely to produce language impairment than one with damage confined to the right hemisphere. Not all people have left-hemisphere speech centers; some left-handed individuals have right-hemisphere speech centers.

In 1874 a German investigator, Carl Wernicke, reported that damage to another site in the cortex – also in the left hemisphere but in the temporal lobe – is linked to a language disorder called *receptive aphasia*. People with damage in this location, known as **Wernicke's area** (see Figure 2.15), are unable to comprehend words: they can hear words, but they do not know their meaning. They can produce strings of words without difficulty and with proper articulation, but they make errors in usage and their speech tends to be meaningless. Analyzing defects, Wernicke developed a model to explain how the brain functions in producing and understanding language. Although his model is more than 100 years old, its general features still appear to be correct. Norman Geschwind built on these ideas in developing a theory that has come to be known as the *Wernicke–Geschwind model*

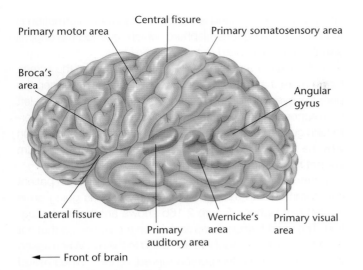

Primary motor area

Central fissure

Primary somatosensory area

Broca's area

Angular gyrus

Lateral fissure

Wernicke's area

Primary visual area

Primary auditory area

← Front of brain

FIGURE 2.14 Specialization of Function of the Left Cortex. *A major part of the cortex is involved in generating movements and analyzing sensory inputs. These areas (which include motor, somatosensory, visual, auditory, and olfactory areas) are present on both sides of the brain. Other functions are located on only one side of the brain. For example, Broca's area and Wernicke's area are involved in the production and understanding of language, and the angular gyrus helps in matching the visual form of a word with its auditory form; these functions are found on the left side of the human brain.*

(Geschwind, 1979). According to this model, Broca's area stores articulatory codes, which specify the sequence of muscle actions required to pronounce a word. When these codes are transmitted to the motor area, they activate the muscles of the lips, tongue, and larynx in the proper sequence and produce a spoken word. Wernicke's area, by contrast, is where auditory codes and the meanings of words are stored. For a word to be spoken, its auditory code must be activated in Wernicke's area and transmitted to Broca's area, where it activates the corresponding articulatory code. In turn, the articulatory code is transmitted to the motor area to activate the muscles that produce the spoken word.

To understand a word spoken by someone else, it must be transmitted from the auditory area to Wernicke's area. There the spoken form of the word is matched with its auditory code, which in turn activates the word's meaning. When a written word is presented, it is first registered in the visual area and then relayed to the *angular gyrus* (see Figure 2.14), which associates the visual form of the word with its auditory code in Wernicke's area; once the word's auditory code has been found, so has its meaning. Thus, the meanings of words are stored along with their acoustical codes in Wernicke's area. Broca's area stores articulatory codes, and the angular gyrus matches the written form of a word to its auditory code. Neither of these areas, however, stores information about word meaning. The meaning of a word is retrieved only when its acoustical code is activated in Wernicke's area.

The Wernicke-Geschwind model explains many of the language deficits aphasics show. Damage that is limited to Broca's area disrupts speech production but has less effect on the comprehension of spoken or written language. Damage to Wernicke's area disrupts all aspects of language comprehension, but the person can still articulate words properly (even though the output is meaningless) because Broca's area is intact. The model also correctly predicts that individuals with damage in the angular gyrus are not able to read but have no difficulty speaking or comprehending speech. Finally, if damage is restricted to the auditory area, a person can read and speak normally but cannot comprehend speech.

Split-brain research

Although the left hemisphere's role in language has been known for some time, only recently has it been possible to investigate what each hemisphere can do on its own. In a normal individual, the brain functions as an integrated whole. Information in one hemisphere is immediately transferred to the other via a broad band of connecting nerve fibers, the corpus callosum (see Figure 2.15). This connecting bridge is a problem in some forms of epilepsy because a seizure starting in one hemisphere may cross over and trigger a massive response in neurons in the other hemisphere. To try to prevent such generalized seizures, neurosurgeons have surgically severed the corpus callosum in individuals with severe epilepsy. These split-brain patients have yielded important insights into the functions of the left and right hemispheres.

To understand what happens when the corpus callosum is severed, please take a look at Figure 2.15. We have seen that the motor nerves cross over as they leave the brain, so that the left cerebral hemisphere controls the right side of the body, and the right hemisphere controls the left. We noted also that the speech production area (Broca's area) is located in the left hemisphere. Consider also that when the eyes are fixated directly ahead, images to the left of the fixation point go through both eyes to the right side of the brain, and images to the right of the fixation point go to the left side of the brain. Each hemisphere therefore has a view of the half of the visual field in which 'its' hand normally functions; for example, the left hemisphere sees the right hand in the right visual field. In the normal brain, stimuli entering one hemisphere are rapidly communicated to the other, and the brain functions as a unit. Now, given these three facts about the brain, let us take a look at what happens when the corpus callosum is severed – leaving a split brain – and the two hemispheres cannot communicate with each other.

Roger Sperry, who pioneered work in this field, was awarded the Nobel Prize in 1981. In one of Sperry's test situations, a person who has undergone split-brain surgery is seated in front of a screen that hides his hands from view (see

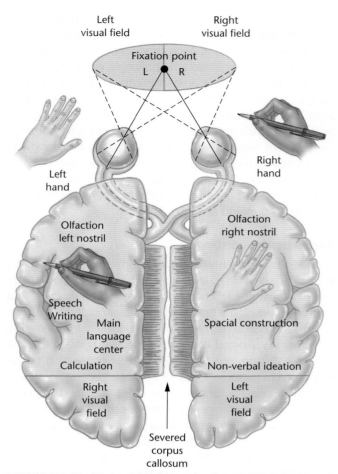

FIGURE 2.15 Sensory Inputs to the Two Hemispheres.
With the eyes fixated straight ahead, stimuli to the left of the fixation point go to the right cerebral hemisphere, and stimuli to the right go to the left hemisphere. The left hemisphere controls movements of the right hand, and the right hemisphere controls the left hand. Hearing is largely crossed in its input, but some sound representation goes to the hemisphere on the same side as the ear that registered it. The left hemisphere controls written and spoken language and mathematical calculations. The right hemisphere can understand only simple language; its main ability seems to involve spatial construction and pattern sense.

Figure 2.16a). His gaze is fixed on a spot at the center of the screen. The word *nut* is flashed on the left side of the screen for a tenth of a second. Remember that this visual signal goes to the right side of the brain, which controls the left side of the body. With his left hand, the person can easily pick up a nut from a pile of objects hidden from view. But he cannot tell the experimenter what word flashed on the screen because speech is controlled by the left hemisphere and the visual image of 'nut' was not transmitted to that hemisphere. When questioned, he seems unaware of what his left hand is doing. Because the sensory input from the left hand goes to the right hemisphere, the left hemisphere receives no information

about what the left hand is feeling or doing. All information is fed back to the right hemisphere, which received the original visual input of the word *nut*.

In this experiment the word must be flashed on the screen for no more than a tenth of a second. If it remains longer, the person's eyes move, and the word is also projected to the left hemisphere. When people can move their eyes freely, information goes to both cerebral hemispheres; this is one reason why the deficiencies caused by severing the corpus callosum are not readily apparent in a person's daily activities.

Further experiments demonstrate that a split-brain patient can communicate through speech only what is going on in the left hemisphere. Figure 2.16b shows another test situation. The word *hatband* was flashed on the screen so that *hat* went to the right hemisphere and *band* to the left. When asked what word he saw, the person replied, 'band.' When asked what kind of band, he made all sorts of guesses – 'rubber band,' 'rock band,' 'band of robbers,' and so forth – and said 'hatband' only by chance. Tests with other compound words (such as *keycase* and *suitcase*) have shown similar results. What the right hemisphere perceives is not transferred to the conscious awareness of the left hemisphere. With the corpus callosum severed, each hemisphere seems oblivious to the experiences of the other.

If split-brain patients are blindfolded and a familiar object (such as a comb, toothbrush, or keycase) is placed in the left hand, they appear to know what it is and can demonstrate its use by appropriate gestures. But they cannot express this knowledge in speech. If asked what is going on while they are manipulating the object, they have no idea as long as any sensory input from the object to the left (speaking) hemisphere is blocked. But if the patient's right hand inadvertently touches the object or the object makes a characteristic sound (like the jingling of a keycase), the speaking hemisphere immediately gives the correct answer. Although the right hemisphere cannot produce speech, it does have some linguistic capabilities. It recognized the meaning of the word *nut* in our first example, and it can produce writing. In the experiment illustrated in Figure 2.16c, split-brain patients are first shown a list of common objects, such as a cup, a knife, a book, and a glass. This list is displayed long enough for the words to be projected to both hemispheres. Next, the list is removed, and one of the words (for example, *book*) is flashed briefly on the left side of the screen so that it goes to the right hemisphere. When patients are asked to write what they saw, the left hand begins writing the word *book*. If asked what the left hand has written, they have no idea and guess any of the words on the original list. They know that they have written something because they feel the writing movements through their body. But because there is no communication between the right hemisphere that saw and wrote the word and the left hemisphere that controls speech, they cannot tell you what they wrote (Sperry, 1968, 1970; see also Gazzaniga, 1985; Hellige, 1990).

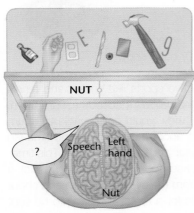

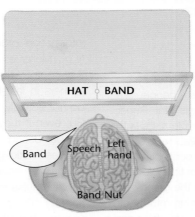

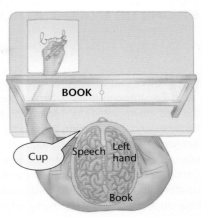

a) A split-brain patient correctly retrieves an object by touch with the left hand when its name is flashed to the right hemisphere, but he cannot name the object or describe what he has done.

b) The word 'hatband' is flashed so that 'hat' goes to the right cerebral hemisphere and 'band' goes to the left hemisphere. The patient reports that he sees the word 'band' but has no idea what kind of band.

c) A list of common objects (including 'book' and 'cup') is initially shown to both hemispheres. One word from the list ('book') is then projected to the right hemisphere. When given the command to do so, the left hand begins writing the word 'book,' but when questioned, the patient does not know what his left hand has written and guesses 'cup.'

FIGURE 2.16 Testing the Abilities of the Two Hemispheres.

Hemispheric specialization

Studies with split-brain patients indicate that the two hemispheres function differently. The left hemisphere governs our ability to express ourselves in language. It can perform complicated logical activities and is skilled in mathematical computations. The right hemisphere can comprehend only very simple language. It can, for example, respond to simple nouns by selecting objects such as a nut or a comb, but it cannot comprehend more abstract linguistic forms. If it is presented with simple commands like 'wink,' 'nod,' 'shake head,' or 'smile,' it seldom responds.

The right hemisphere, however, has a highly developed spatial and pattern sense. It is superior to the left hemisphere in constructing geometric and perspective drawings. It can assemble colored blocks to match a complex design much more effectively than the left hemisphere can. When split-brain patients are asked to use the right hand to assemble blocks to match a design shown in a picture, they make numerous mistakes. Sometimes they have trouble keeping the left hand from automatically correcting the right hand's mistakes.

Studies with normal individuals tend to confirm the different specializations of the two hemispheres. For example, verbal information (such as words or nonsense syllables) can be identified faster and more accurately when flashed briefly to the left hemisphere (that is, in the right visual field) than to the right hemisphere. In contrast, identification of faces, facial expressions of emotion, line slopes, or dot locations occurs more quickly when these are flashed to the right hemisphere

(Hellige, 1990). Also, studies using EEGs indicate that electrical activity from the left hemisphere increases during a verbal task, whereas during a spatial task, electrical activity increases in the right hemisphere (Kosslyn, 1988; Springer & Deutsch, 1989).

This discussion does not mean that the two hemispheres work independently. Just the opposite is true. The hemispheres differ in their specializations, but they continually integrate their activities. It is this interaction that enables mental processes that are greater than and different from each hemisphere's special contribution. As one researcher describes it:

> These differences are seen in the contrasting contributions each hemisphere makes to all cognitive activities. When a person reads a story, the right hemisphere may play a special role in decoding visual information, maintaining an integrated story structure, appreciating humor and emotional content, deriving meaning from past associations and understanding metaphor. At the same time, the left hemisphere plays a special role in understanding syntax, translating written words into their phonetic representations and deriving meaning from complex relations among word concepts and syntax. But there is no activity in which only one hemisphere is involved or to which only one hemisphere makes a contribution.

(Levy, 1985, p. 44)

CUTTING EDGE RESEARCH WHAT HAPPENS IN THE BRAINS OF EXPERT ATHLETES?

Aidan Moran, University College Dublin

Whether out of envy or admiration, we marvel at the breathtaking feats of expert performers – people, like the golf champion Rory McIlroy or the tennis star Roger Federer, who can perform apparently impossible skills with remarkable consistency and precision. These feats raise some obvious questions. For example, how can expert golfers hit the ball accurately to targets within a few feet of the hole from positions that are over 200 yards away from the green? Or how do top tennis players manage to hit winning returns off balls that are served at them at speeds (of up to 150 miles per hour) that preclude the possibility of accurate visual tracking?

Attracted by these mysteries of the mind, cognitive researchers have developed a new field of inter disciplinary inquiry – the study of 'expertise' or the growth of specialist knowledge and skills as a result of sustained and effortful practice in a specific domain of human achievement such as sport or music. Within this field, expertise in sport has become a hot topic in neuroscience (e.g., Yarrow *et al.*, 2009), sport psychology (e.g., Williams & Ford, 2008) and popular science (e.g., Syed, 2010). To understand why this is so, let's explore three key developments in this field.

First, research on expertise reveals the extraordinary power of practice. Indeed, it seems that there is no such thing as a difficult task – only an unpracticed one (Moran, 2012). But what type of practice works best? According to longitudinal studies by Ericsson *et al.* (1993), the key to developing expertise is 'deliberate practice' – a form of training in which learners strive purposefully and single-mindedly to improve their skills under the guidance of specialist instructors. To give you a flavor of what this type of practice entails, consider how Anders Ericsson, the man who coined this term, explains it: 'When most people practice, they focus on things they can do effortlessly. Expert practice is different. It entails considerable, specific, and sustained efforts to do something you can't do well – or even at all' (cited in Syed, 2010, pp. 73–74).

The second breakthrough in expertise research occurred with the discovery that *knowledge* – or rather, anticipation – can help people to circumvent the limits of human information processing. Experiments (e.g., Müller *et al.*, 2010) have shown that contrary to popular wisdom, expert performers in fast-ball, reactive sports like cricket and tennis do *not* actually 'watch the ball' as it speeds toward them. But even if they did so, they would not be able to return the ball because there is about a 200 millisecond time-lag between noticing a stimulus and responding to it. This time-lag arises because it takes about 100 milliseconds for a nerve impulse to travel from the eye to the brain and about another 100 milliseconds for a motor message to be sent from the brain back to the muscles. So, strange as it may seem, expert cricket batsmen and tennis players manage to overcome this hard-wired delay in human information processing. According to expertise researchers, countless hours of deliberate practice enable expert cricket batsmen to use early signals ('advance cues') from their opponents' body position and/or limb movements to anticipate the type of delivery, trajectory and likely destination of speeding balls directed at them.

The third important development in this field concerns the search for neuroscientific mechanisms that underlie athletic expertise. One line of inquiry (see review by Cooke, in press) shows that expert performers in aiming sports (e.g., rifle shooting) show significant cardiac deceleration immediately before executing their shots. As yet, however, it is not clear what is happening in the minds of these performers as they prepare to shoot. Another line of inquiry in this area comes from neuroimaging studies on the differences between expert and novice athletes' brain networks. For example, Wang *et al.* (2013) showed that the brains of world-class gymnasts showed greater activation in the attentional and motor regions than did those of less proficient counterparts. Finally, exciting progress is being made in understanding the brain regions used by expert athletes when they 'see' and 'feel' their skills in their imagination (a process known as motor imagery; see Moran *et al.*, 2012) before actually performing them.

THE AUTONOMIC NERVOUS SYSTEM

We noted earlier that the peripheral nervous system has two divisions. The *somatic system* controls the skeletal muscles and receives information from the skin, muscles, and various sensory receptors. The *autonomic system* is a system of nerves outside the brain and spinal cord. It controls the glands and the smooth muscles, including the heart, the blood vessels, and the lining of the stomach and intestines. (These muscles are called 'smooth' because that is how they look under a microscope – skeletal muscles, in contrast, have a striped appearance.) The autonomic nervous system (ANS) derives its name from the fact that many of the activities it controls, such as digestion and circulation, are autonomous, or self-regulating, and continue even when a person is asleep or unconscious. ANS activity is controlled by the nervous system, in particular by the *hypothalamus*.

The autonomic nervous system has two divisions, sympathetic and parasympathetic, whose actions are often antagonistic (reciprocal). The **sympathetic nervous system** typically is active during times of intense arousal, and the **parasympathetic nervous system** is associated with rest. Typically, the sympathetic division will be activated during 'emergencies,' preparing the body for a response (often referred to as 'fight or flight'). The parasympathetic division will restore the body afterwards. Figure 2.17 shows the contrasting effects of the two systems on some organs. The balance between these two systems maintains the normal (homeostatic) state of the body – somewhere between extreme excitement and vegetative placidity.

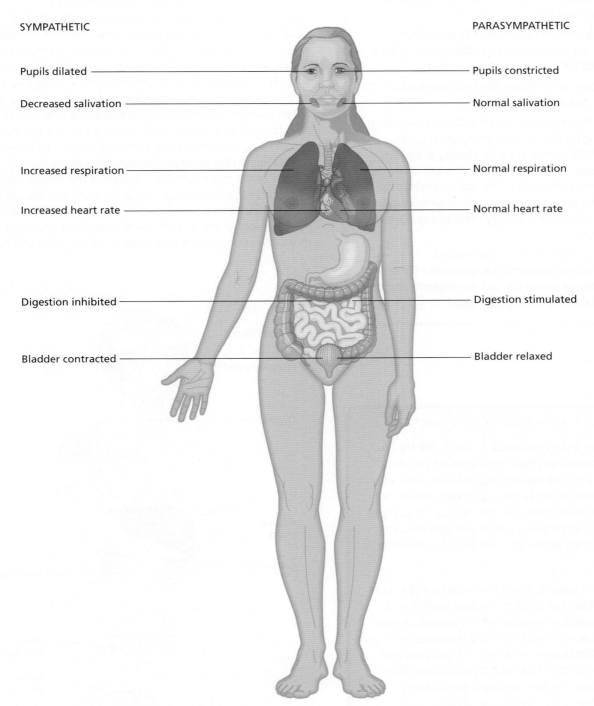

SYMPATHETIC

Pupils dilated

Decreased salivation

Increased respiration

Increased heart rate

Digestion inhibited

Bladder contracted

PARASYMPATHETIC

Pupils constricted

Normal salivation

Normal respiration

Normal heart rate

Digestion stimulated

Bladder relaxed

FIGURE 2.17 The Autonomic Nervous System. *The sympathetic division mobilizes the body for an active response; the parasympathetic division restores the body and conserves its resources.*

INTERIM SUMMARY

➔ The nervous system is divided into the CNS (the brain and spinal cord) and the PNS (the nerves connecting the brain and spinal cord to other parts of the body). Subdivisions of the PNS are the somatic system (which carries messages to and from the sense receptors, muscles, and the surface of the body) and the autonomic system (which connects with the internal organs and glands).

➔ The human brain is composed of three functional divisions: the central core, the limbic system, and the cerebral cortex.

➔ Anatomically, we divide the brain into the hindbrain, the midbrain, and the forebrain.

➔ Severing the corpus callosum (the band of nerve fibers connecting the two cerebral hemispheres) causes significant differences in the functioning of the two hemispheres. The left hemisphere is skilled in language and mathematical abilities. The right hemisphere can understand some language but cannot communicate through speech; it has a highly developed spatial and pattern sense.

➔ The ANS consists of the sympathetic and parasympathetic divisions. The sympathetic division is active during excitement, and the parasympathetic system is dominant during quiescence.

CRITICAL THINKING QUESTIONS

1 Why is your brain symmetrical (meaning that the left and right sides look alike)? You have a left and right motor cortex, a left and right hippocampus, a left and right cerebellum, and so on. In each case, the left side is a mirror image of the right side (just as, for example, your left eye is a mirror image of your right eye). Can you think of any reason why your brain is symmetrical in this way?

2 In split-brain patients, whose corpus callosum has been cut, the left and right sides of the brain seem to work independently after the operation. For example, a word shown to one side may be read and responded to without the other side knowing what the word was. Does such a person have two minds, each capable of knowing different things, or does the patient still have only one mind?

THE ENDOCRINE SYSTEM

We can think of the nervous system as controlling the fast-changing activities of the body by directly activating muscles and glands. Glands are organs located throughout the body that secrete special substances, such as sweat, milk, or a particular hormone. The **endocrine system** acts more slowly, indirectly affecting the activities of cell groups throughout the body. It does so by means of **hormones**: chemicals secreted by the endocrine glands into the bloodstream and transported to other parts of the body, where they have specific effects on cells that recognize their message (see Figure 2.18). Hormones act in various ways on cells of different types. Each target cell is equipped with receptors that recognize only the hormone molecules that act on that cell. The receptors pull those molecules out of the bloodstream and into the cell. Some endocrine glands are activated by the nervous system, and others are activated by changes in the internal chemical state of the body.

One of the major endocrine glands is the pituitary gland. This gland is partly an outgrowth of the brain and lies just below the hypothalamus (refer back to Figure 2.10). The pituitary has been called the 'master gland' because it produces the most different hormones and controls the secretion activity of

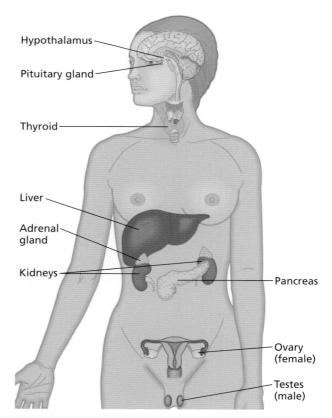

FIGURE 2.18 Major Endocrine Glands and Hypothalamus.

other endocrine glands. One of the pituitary hormones, growth hormone, has the crucial job of controlling the body's growth. Dwarfism is caused by too little of this hormone, and gigantism is caused by too much of it. Other hormones released by the pituitary trigger the action of other endocrine glands, such as the thyroid, the sex glands, and the outer layer of the adrenal gland. Courtship, mating, and reproductive behavior in many animals are based on a complex interaction between nervous system activity and the influence of the pituitary on the sex glands.

The relationship between the pituitary gland and the hypothalamus illustrates the complex interactions. In response to stress (fear, anxiety, pain, emotional events, and so forth), certain neurons in the hypothalamus secrete corticotropin-releasing factor (CRF), which is carried to the pituitary through a channel-like structure. CRF stimulates the pituitary to release adrenocorticotropic hormone (ACTH), the body's major stress hormone. ACTH, in turn, is carried by the bloodstream to the adrenal glands and other organs, causing the release of some 30 hormones, each of which plays a role in the body's adjustment to emergency situations. For example, the cellular demand for glucose increases in a state of emergency, and cortisol, an adrenal hormone that is released under stress, promotes liberation of glucose from fat stores in the body. Interestingly, cortisol has effects on cognitive function as well. At low levels, it enhances memory, but at high levels it causes memory impairments and neuronal death.

The adrenal glands play an important role in determining a person's mood, energy level, and ability to cope with stress. The inner core of the adrenal gland secretes epinephrine and norepinephrine (also known as adrenaline and noradrenaline). Epinephrine prepares the organism for an emergency. In conjunction with the sympathetic division of the autonomic nervous system, it affects the smooth muscles and sweat glands. It also constricts the blood vessels in the stomach and intestines and makes the heart beat faster. Norepinephrine also prepares the organism for emergency action. It stimulates the pituitary to release a hormone that acts on the outer layer of the adrenal glands; this hormone, in turn, stimulates the liver to increase the blood sugar level to give the body the energy required for quick action.

The hormones of the endocrine system and the neurotransmitters of neurons perform similar functions: they both carry messages between cells. A neurotransmitter carries messages between adjacent neurons, and its effects are highly localized. In contrast, a hormone may travel a long distance through the body and act in various ways on many different types of cells. Despite these differences, some of these chemical messengers serve both functions. Epinephrine and norepinephrine, for example, act as neurotransmitters when they are released by neurons and as hormones when they are released by the adrenal gland.

INTERIM SUMMARY

➔ The endocrine glands secrete hormones into the bloodstream that travel through the body, acting in various ways on cells of different types.

➔ The pituitary gland controls the secretion activity of other endocrine glands.

CRITICAL THINKING QUESTIONS

1 When hormones are released into the bloodstream, they can reach every cell in the body. How then do hormones exert selective actions on certain bodily tissues? Can you think of analogies with synaptic transmission in the brain?

2 During winter, your furnace heats the air inside your house, and the thermostat detects when the indoor air temperature reaches the level you set. How might this principle be used in the endocrine system to maintain levels of hormones in the bloodstream? What master gland might serve as the endocrine system's 'thermostat'?

EVOLUTION, GENES, AND BEHAVIOR

To fully understand the biological foundations of psychology, we need to know something about evolutionary and genetic influences as well. Biological organisms have evolved over millions of years, and environmental factors have played an important role in shaping the organization and function of their nervous systems. Natural selection, the process described by Charles Darwin to account for evolutionary change, plays an essential role in shaping both behavior and brain. Darwin's principle of natural selection states that it is those variations on inheritable traits that most contribute to an organism's survival that are passed on to the next generation. The field of behavior genetics combines the methods of genetics and psychology to study the inheritance of behavioral characteristics (Plomin et al., 1994). We know that many physical characteristics – height, bone structure, hair and eye color, and the like – are inherited. Behavioral geneticists are interested in the degree to which psychological characteristics, including mental ability, temperament, and emotional stability, are transmitted from parent to offspring (Bouchard, 1984, 1995). Researchers led by Robert Plomin of London's Institute of Psychiatry have identified chromosomal markers that contribute to intelligence (Fisher *et al.*, 1999). However, such findings are not conclusive. As we will see in this section, environmental conditions have a lot to do with the way a particular genetic factor is expressed in an individual as he or she matures.

Evolution of behavior

Any examination of behavior must include not only *proximate* causes of the behavior, such as the firing of spinal motor neurons that drives the knee jerk reflex, but also *ultimate* causes. **Ultimate causes** of behavior explain behavior in its evolutionary context. Whereas **proximate causes** explain *how* a behavior is generated, ultimate causes help us to understand *why* a behavior exists in the first place – that is, why it evolved by natural selection. Consider, for example, male aggression. In both humans and other mammals, males are typically more aggressive than females (Buss & Shackelford, 1997), particularly in same-sex social interactions. In mammals whose sexual reproduction is seasonally regulated, intermale (male to male) aggression is particularly pronounced during the breeding season. In red deer and elephant seals, for example, males attempt to control small groups of females ('harems') for mating and behave aggressively toward other males that attempt to mate with these females.

The proximate causes of aggressive behavior are reasonably well understood. For example, circulating levels of the gonadal steroid, testosterone, are correlated with aggressive behavior, and damage to subcortical brain structures can reduce or potentiate aggressive behavior in animals. Recent evidence indicates serotonin is important in aggressive behavior (Nelson & Chiavegatto, 2001), and olfactory cues, at least in rodents, appear to mediate male aggression (Stowers *et al.*, 2002). Moreover, social context powerfully modulates the nature and pattern of aggressive behavior. During the breeding season, male red deer and elephant seals display to and attack other males that approach them but do not attack sexually receptive females.

But why do aggressive behavior and the neural and hormonal systems underlying this behavior exist at all? What are the ultimate causes of aggressive behavior? From an evolutionary or functional point of view, aggressive behavior in breeding males is **adaptive**. It confers reproductive success, and reproductive success promotes the perpetuation of genes that control aggressive behavior. In red deer, aggressive males are more likely to secure and mate with receptive females and thereby increase the proportion of males in subsequent generations that carry genes for aggressiveness. Unaggressive male red deer are less likely to secure mates, and their genes become poorly represented in the population. This does not mean that male aggression is 'good' from an ethical or moral point of view. Rather, the behavior is adaptive in an evolutionary context.

Aggressive behavior is said to be sexually selected because it is invoked by competition for mating opportunities. **Sexual selection**, a special case of natural selection, yields traits that promote reproductive success in the sex with the greater potential reproductive rate. In deer, the female reproductive rate is limited by gestation and nursing, but the male reproductive rate is limited only by available females. In some birds, the male reproductive rate is slower than that in females because the males brood over the nest to hatch the eggs while the females seek other males with which they mate. In this case, female birds show greater aggression than males. In either case, any trait that confers an advantage in securing mates will be selected for in the sex with the greatest reproductive potential. These traits are not limited to behavioral proclivities such as aggression but include physical traits such as body size and coloration.

Chromosomes and genes

Natural selection operates on **genes**, which are segments of deoxyribonucleic acid (DNA) molecules that form the fundamental hereditary unit. The genes we receive from our parents and transmit to our offspring are carried by **chromosomes**, structures in the nucleus of each cell in the body. Most body cells contain 46 chromosomes. At conception, the human being receives 23 chromosomes from the father's sperm and 23 chromosomes from the mother's ovum. These 46 chromosomes form 23 pairs, which are duplicated each time the cells divide (see Figure 2.19). As shown in Figure 2.20, the DNA molecule looks like a twisted ladder or a double-stranded helix (spiral).

Each gene gives coded instructions to the cell, directing it to perform a specific function (usually to manufacture a particular protein). Although all cells in the body carry the same genes, each cell is specialized because only 5 per cent to 10 per cent of the genes in any given cell are active. In the process of developing from a fertilized egg, each cell switches on some genes and switches off all others. When 'nerve genes' are active, for example, a cell develops as a neuron because the genes are directing the cell to make the products that allow it to perform neural functions (which would not be possible if irrelevant genes, such as 'muscle genes,' were not switched off).

Genes, like chromosomes, exist in pairs. One gene of each pair comes from the sperm chromosomes, and one gene comes from the ovum chromosomes. Thus, a child receives only half of each parent's total genes. The total number of genes in each human chromosome is about a thousand, perhaps higher. Because the number of genes is so high, two human beings, even siblings, are extremely unlikely to inherit exactly the same set of genes. The only exception is identical twins, who, because they developed from the same fertilized egg, have exactly the same genes.

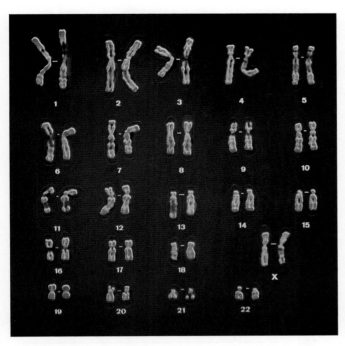

FIGURE 2.19 Chromosomes. *This photo (greatly enlarged) shows the 46 chromosomes of a normal human female. In a human male, pairs 1 through 22 would be the same as those in the female, but pair 23 would be XY rather than XX.*

Dominant and recessive genes

Either gene of a gene pair can be *dominant* or *recessive*. When both members of a gene pair are dominant, the individual manifests the form of the trait specified by these dominant genes. When one gene is dominant and the other recessive, the dominant gene again determines the form of the trait. Only if the genes contributed by both parents are recessive is the recessive form of the trait expressed. In the case of the genes determining eye color, for example, blue is recessive and brown is dominant. Thus, a blue-eyed child may have two blue-eyed parents, one blue-eyed parent and one brown-eyed parent (who carries a recessive gene for blue eyes), or two brown-eyed parents (each of whom carries a recessive gene for blue eyes). A brown-eyed child, in contrast, never has two blue-eyed parents. Some other characteristics that are carried by recessive genes are baldness, albinism (lack of pigment in the skin), hemophilia (a disorder that impairs blood clotting), and susceptibility to poison ivy.

Most human characteristics are not determined by the actions of a single gene pair, but there are some striking exceptions in which a single gene has enormous importance. Of special interest from a psychological viewpoint are diseases like phenylketonuria (PKU) and Huntington's disease (HD), both of which involve deterioration of the nervous system and associated behavioral and cognitive problems. Geneticists have identified the genes that cause both of these disorders.

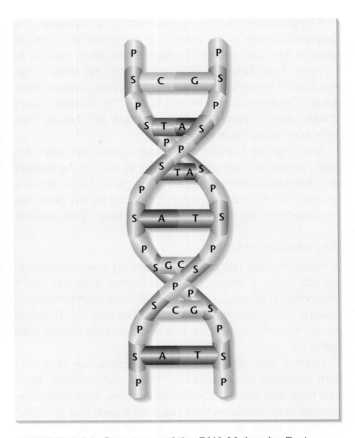

FIGURE 2.20 Structures of the DNA Molecule. *Each strand of the molecule is made up of an alternating sequence of sugar (S) and phosphate (P); the rungs of the twisted ladder are made up of four bases (A, G, T, C). The double nature of the helix and the restriction on base pairings make possible the self-replication of DNA. In the process of cell division, the two strands of the DNA molecule come apart, with the base pairs separating, and one member of each base pair remains attached to each strand. Each strand then forms a new complementary strand using excess bases available in the cell. An A attached to a strand attracts a T, and so forth. By this process, two identical molecules of DNA come to exist where previously there was one.*

PKU results from the action of a recessive gene inherited from both parents. The infant cannot digest phenylalanine (an amino acid found in protein-rich foods such as milk, eggs, and cheese), which then builds up in the body, poisons the nervous system, and causes irreversible brain damage. Children with PKU are severely retarded and usually die before reaching age 30. If the PKU disorder is discovered at birth and the infant is immediately placed on a diet that controls the level of phenylalanine, the chances of survival with good health and intelligence are fairly high. Until the PKU gene was located, the disorder could not be diagnosed until an infant was at least 3-weeks old.

A single dominant gene causes Huntington's disease. The long-term course of the disease is degeneration of certain areas in the brain and progressive deterioration over 10 to 15 years. Individuals with HD gradually lose the ability to talk and control their movements, and they show marked deterioration in memory and mental ability. The disease usually strikes when a person is 30 to 40 years old; before then, there is no evidence of the disease.

Now that the Huntington's disease gene has been isolated, geneticists can test individuals at risk for the disease and determine whether they carry the gene. As yet, there is no cure for HD, but the protein produced by the gene has been identified and may provide a key to treating the disease.

Sex-linked genes

A normal female has two similar-looking chromosomes in pair 23, called X chromosomes. A normal male has one X chromosome in pair 23 and one that looks slightly different, called a Y chromosome (refer back to Figure 2.19). Thus, the normal female chromosome pair is XX, and the normal male pair is XY.

Women, who have two X chromosomes, are protected from recessive traits carried on the X chromosome. Men, who have only one X chromosome and one Y chromosome, express more recessive traits because a gene that is carried on one of these chromosomes will not be countered by a dominant gene on the other. Genetically determined characteristics and disorders that are linked to the twenty-third chromosome pair are called **sex-linked traits**. For example, color blindness is a recessive sex-linked trait. A male is color-blind if the X chromosome he received from his mother carries the gene for color blindness. Females are less likely to be color-blind, because a color-blind female has to have both a color-blind father and a mother who is either color-blind or carries a recessive gene for color blindness.

Genetic studies of behavior

Single genes determine some traits, but many genes combine to determine most human characteristics; they are **polygenic**. Traits such as intelligence, height, and emotionality do not fall into distinct categories but show continuous variation. Most people are neither dull nor bright. Intelligence is distributed over a broad range, with most individuals located near the middle. Sometimes a specific genetic defect can result in mental retardation, but in most cases a large number of genes influence the factors underlying the different abilities that determine a person's intellectual potential. Of course, as we will discuss shortly, what happens to this genetic potential depends on environmental conditions (Plomin *et al.*, 1994).

Selective breeding

One method of studying the inheritance of particular traits in animals is selective breeding. In **selective breeding**, animals

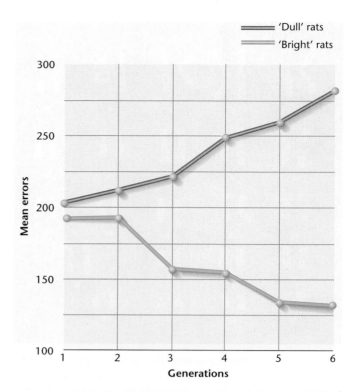

FIGURE 2.21 Inheritance of Maze Learning in Rats. *Mean error scores of 'bright' (green line) and 'dull' (purple line) rats selectively bred for maze-running ability.*

that are high or low in a certain behavioral or physical trait are mated with each other. For example, in an early study of the inheritance of learning ability in rats, females that did poorly in learning to run a maze were mated with males that did poorly, and females that did well were mated with males that did well. The offspring of these matings were tested on the same maze. After a few rodent generations, 'bright' and 'dull' strains of rats were produced (see Figure 2.21). Such breeding may not necessarily yield more or less intelligent animals, however. A less fearful animal, for example, would be expected to perform better in the maze because it would be more likely to explore the apparatus.

Selective breeding has been used to demonstrate the inheritance of a number of behavioral characteristics. Dogs have been bred to be excitable or lethargic; chickens, to be aggressive and sexually active; fruit flies, to be more or less attracted to light; and mice, to be more or less attracted to alcohol. If a trait is influenced by heredity, changing it through selective breeding should be possible. If selective breeding does not alter a trait, we assume that the trait is dependent primarily on environmental factors (Plomin, 1989).

Twin studies

Because breeding experiments with human beings are obviously unethical, we must look instead at similarities in behavior among individuals who are related. Certain traits

Identical twins are referred to as monozygotic because they develop from a single fertilized egg. Fraternal or dizygotic twins develop from different egg cells and therefore are no more similar genetically than ordinary siblings.

often run in families. But family members not only are linked genetically but also share the same environment. If musical talent 'runs in the family,' we do not know whether inherited ability or parental emphasis on music is the primary influence. Sons of alcoholic fathers are more likely than others to develop alcoholism. Do genetic tendencies or environmental conditions play the major role? In an effort to answer questions of this sort, psychologists have turned to studies of twins, especially twins who have been adopted and raised in separate environments.

Identical twins develop from a single fertilized egg and therefore share exactly the same genes – they are referred to as **monozygotic** because they come from a single zygote, or fertilized egg. Fraternal twins develop from different egg cells and are no more alike genetically than ordinary siblings – they are referred to as **dizygotic** because they come from two zygotes. Studies that compare identical and fraternal twins help sort out the influences of environment and heredity. Identical twins are more similar in intelligence than fraternal twins, even when they are separated at birth and reared in different homes (see Chapter 13). Identical twins are also more similar than fraternal twins in some personality characteristics and in susceptibility to schizophrenia (see Chapter 15). A recent study shows that the amount of gray matter in the brain, as measured with MRI, is more correlated in identical twins than in fraternal twins, and it is also correlated with intelligence (Thompson *et al.*, 2001). That is, smarter individuals have more gray matter in their brains, and the amount of gray matter appears to be strongly related to genetic factors (Plomin & Kosslyn, 2001).

One surprising finding from studies of adopted children suggests that genetic influences may become stronger as

people age. The psychological traits of young children are not particularly similar to those of either their biological parents or their adoptive parents. As they grow older, we might expect them to become more like their adoptive parents in traits such as general cognitive ability and verbal ability and less like their biological parents. Contrary to this expectation, as adopted children approach age 16, they become more similar to their biological parents than to their adopted parents in these traits (Plomin *et al.*, 1997), suggesting an emerging role of genetic influences.

Molecular genetics of behavior

In recent years, some researchers have suggested that certain human traits, such as some aspects of personality, are influenced by specific genes, which are thought to affect particular neurotransmitter receptors (Zuckerman, 1995). In most studies of this sort, family members who have a certain psychological trait are identified and compared with family members who lack that trait. Using techniques of molecular genetics, the researchers attempt to find genes or chromosome segments that are correlated with the presence of the trait under study. For example, a combination of traits referred to as 'novelty seeking' (that is, a tendency to be impulsive, exploratory, and quick-tempered, as measured by scores on personality scales) has been linked to a gene that controls the D4 receptor for dopamine (Benjamin *et al.*, 1996).

Occasionally this type of analysis has been applied to very specific behavioral traits. As mentioned earlier, sons of alcoholic fathers are more likely to be alcoholics themselves than are people chosen at random.

TO LOCALIZE OR NOT TO LOCALIZE: THAT'S THE QUESTION

TO LOCALIZE

Annick Ledebt, VU University, Amsterdam

The notion that different psychological and motor functions take place in the brain is nowadays well established and is no longer questioned anymore. As a matter of fact, the passionate discussions that took place in the eighteenth and nineteenth century revolved around where in the material body, and/or in the immaterial soul, the origin of feeling, personality and mental faculties was located. In the nineteenth century, the phrenology movement (grounded by Franz Jozef Gall) spread the idea that personality traits (e.g., 'feeling of property,' and 'vanity') and intellectual faculties (e.g. 'the memory of facts,' and 'the faculty of imitation') were localized in different areas at the surface of the brain. These areas in turn were thought to protrude from the skull, so that examination of the surface of the skull allowed assessing how well developed certain faculties were. Although phrenology is now considered a pseudoscience, it had some merit, at that time, in shifting the attention toward the claim that psychological functions like emotions are located in the brain and not in the heart. While the phrenologists considered the brain from its structure visible from the skull, looking inside the brain afforded another perspective on the functioning of this organ. In the late nineteenth century, the careful descriptions of the symptoms of several patients with various sorts of brain damage by Paul Broca and Carl Wernicke shed new light on the localization of functions in the brain. The patient described by Broca suffered from a language deficit ('aphasia') characterized by the inability to produce any other word than 'tan'. Surprisingly, his ability to understand language seemed to be intact. After autopsy, Broca found that the left inferior frontal lobe had been damaged and inferred that language production was probably localized there. Shortly after these findings, Wernicke described another patient with specific language comprehension problems, but who could still produce speech. This patient had a lesion in the posterior superior temporal gyrus. Other descriptions of both types of aphasias soon followed and confirmed these seminal findings. To explain the coupling between the comprehension of speech and the production of speech, Wernicke anticipated the presence of a direct connection between the temporal area that he had identified, and Broca's frontal area.

The attempts to couple specific functions to specific areas in the brain are still guided by the anatomy of the brain but are also increasingly taking into account the knowledge of the online functioning brain using various brain imaging techniques such as PET, MEG, fMRI, and the related diffusion tensor MRI tractography. These techniques allow assessing the complexity of the brain's activity in a living individual with or without brain lesions. The demonstration of the involvement of a specific brain area for a specific function is thus not only dependent on the description of patients with brain damage, but is nowadays also based on the activity of intact brains of individuals, when they are engaged in a particular task. With respect to language, there is now evidence that in addition to the localization of speech comprehension and speech production within the temporal and frontal lobe, additional parts of the left hemisphere (e.g. the inferior parietal lobe) are involved in language. These different brain areas are connected with each other within a network with a direct pathway between Wernicke's and Broca's areas and an indirect pathway connecting these two areas with the inferior parietal lobe (Catani *et al.*, 2005). Contemporary connectionist accounts of language integrated the earlier findings of two cortical language areas into a more complex network with parallel distributed processing that involves distributed groups of neurons rather than localized centers. The main idea of this connectionist account is that, within Broca's and Wernicke's areas, different sub-specialized cortical regions are connected by subsets of fiber bundles. One can therefore argue that the localization of language as put forward by the pioneer neuroscientists as Broca and Wernicke was not abandoned, but was rather transformed into a more fine-grained model of localized areas related through multiple parallel interconnections. Important nodes of neurons subserving different aspect of a function seem to be grouped in the brain within areas that appear now to have more blurred limits and that appear to be more flexible (i.e., plasticity of the brain tissue) than previously thought. Different aspects of a function such as language might be distributed along a complex network but the different nodes that compose a given network seem to be preferentially situated at specific locations of the brain. Lesions occurring at different locations of the network therefore result in different problems which supports the older localization idea. In the case of language function one of the different basic abilities such as naming (the ability to identify an object, color, or other aspect using an appropriate word), repetition (the ability to repeat words and sentences), or hearing comprehension (the ability to understand spoken language) might be impaired due to brain damage, with little or no loss of function in the other abilities. These specific impairments are related to focal lesions affecting specific locations of the linguistic network, which argues against a linguistic network in which localization of these specific abilities is completely absent.

This example from the neuropsychology of language serves to illustrate that the search for localization of functions has to take into account recent findings about the complex connectivity in the brain, and acknowledge that it is relevant to consider that specific cortical (and subcortical) locations are specialized in a given process. Nevertheless, the specialization of the elements of a network are not fixed forever and functioning of the network is under the constant influence of learning (Friederici *et al.*, 2011) and brain damage.

TO LOCALIZE OR NOT TO LOCALIZE: THAT'S THE QUESTION

TO NOT LOCALIZE

John Stins, VU University, Amsterdam

Brain imaging techniques such as PET and fMRI provide a spectacular window into the workings of the living human brain. By systematically manipulating environmental conditions and recording the resulting brain activity, it should be possible – in principle – to draw up a 'map' of the brain. Each region or sector within this map is devoted to a specific function, such as language, reasoning, face recognition, and so on. The idea that brain areas perform specialized psychological functions originated from studies of brain damage. Famous case studies, such as Phineas Cage, Broca's patient Tan, and H, provide compelling evidence of the specialized and localized nature of the brain. This theory is known as functional specialization, and has large intuitive appeal; after all, different parts of your body (e.g., hands, kidneys, eyes) perform highly different functions. Why shouldn't the brain be anatomically organized likewise?

A number of researchers have started to question the idea of functional specialization, and instead emphasize that a hallmark of the brain is its high connectivity. According to some estimates, the human brain consists of a staggering 10^{15} connections. The study of brain connectivity takes as its starting point the ongoing and highly flexible functional interactions between various parts of the brain, that are often spatially quite separate. There is emerging recognition that it is precisely this pattern of neural interaction across disparate areas that gives rise to our thoughts, feelings, and conscious experiences. This view has led to novel perspectives on healthy neurocognitive functioning, and on psychiatric and neurologic syndromes.

The study of brain connectivity is a rapidly increasing field of research, where psychologists, neuroscientists and mathematicians team up and study how global communication within the brain gives rise to our thoughts, feelings, and behaviors. But this new approach comes at a cost; it is far from obvious how to come up with an operational measure of brain connectivity. A popular approach is to simplify the problem, and to model the brain as a large collection of nodes that are connected with each other via so-called 'edges,' resulting in a highly interconnected network of information pathways. The anatomical (hard-wired) connectivity which characterizes the brain (the white matter) can give rise to rapid information exchange between distant nodes. When two or more nodes across the network display correlated behavior during a task one speaks of functional connectivity. A branch of mathematics called graph theory is employed to characterize various properties of this network, such as its overall connectivity, the existence of '*hubs*' (nodes that

form many connections with other nodes, and that are thus essential to overall network functioning), and whether subsets of nodes form clusters or modules of high local connectivity. Note that functional connectivity is not static; it can change according to task demands and environmental circumstances and it can change as a result of learning or pathology.

As an example of the power of this approach, van den Heuvel *et al.* (2009) measured whole brain resting state fMRI activity in 19 individuals. Each brain was then modeled as a network consisting of 9500 so-called voxels (nodes) and their interactions (the edges). It was found that the efficiency of this network was strongly predictive of IQ, as measured afterwards. In other words, intellectual performance was related to how efficient multiple brain regions communicate and integrate information. What is even more remarkable was that this association was observed when the brain was idle, i.e., not engaged in any particular task.

As another example, network theory has been highly successful in quantifying states of consciousness. A review by Jin and Chung (2012) described a set of studies that investigated changes in consciousness due to anesthesia or due to brain injury leading to disorders of consciousness such as coma or vegetative state. One of the findings was that disorders of consciousness are marked by a global reduction in overall connectivity and a disconnection between selected brain regions. The review demonstrates that connectivity analysis might help to unravel the neural correlate of consciousness.

Connectivity analysis has also been employed to study the global brain organization in psychiatric syndromes. Alexander-Bloch *et al.* (2010) studied connectivity in a group of children with childhood-onset schizophrenia (COS). The analysis revealed that the brain network in COS was not very effective for local communication, whereas global communication was apparently superior. The findings raise the intriguing possibility that the fragmentation of the mind in schizophrenia is a very real phenomenon, and is reflected in the way the brain network as a whole is configured.

Studies of functional brain connectivity make no assumptions regarding the underlying neural architecture. Although it is not denied that the brain may consist of a number of functional modules that each perform a specialized task, it is also acknowledged that the brain is very flexible and in a constant state of flux. By focusing on how various parts of the brain form coalitions and co-operate, researchers hope to move beyond the idea of functional specialization, which has dominated cognitive neuroscience, and to solve some old puzzles on how the brain performs its tasks using an exciting new approach.

When they drink alcohol, sons of alcoholics also tend to release more endorphin (the natural opiate neurotransmitter related to reward) than other people (Gianoulakis *et al.*, 1996), suggesting a possible biological predisposition toward alcoholism.

But these analyses can sometimes be misleading and must be viewed with caution. For example, it was once claimed that a gene for the D2 dopamine receptor occurred only in severe alcoholics and thus was a genetic basis for alcoholism. More recent studies of this gene, however, indicate that it also occurs in individuals who pursue many other types of pleasure and may be linked to drug abuse, obesity, compulsive gambling, and other forms of 'unrestrained behavior' (Blum *et al.*, 1996). Our understanding of the role of this gene, and of its relationship to behavior, clearly has changed in the years since its discovery and may change again as further evidence emerges. Such studies highlight the need to await further confirmation before concluding that the genetic basis for behavior of any kind has been identified. In several cases, what appeared at first to be a clear genetic explanation was later found to be spurious.

Environmental influences on gene action

The inherited potential with which an individual enters the world is very much influenced by the environment the infant encounters. One example is diabetes. The tendency to develop diabetes is hereditary, although the exact method of transmission is unknown. In diabetes, the pancreas does not produce enough insulin to burn carbohydrates and thus provide energy for the body. Scientists assume that genes determine the production of insulin. But people who carry the genetic potential for diabetes do not always develop the disease. If one identical twin has diabetes, the other twin develops the disorder in only about half the cases. Not all of the environmental factors that contribute to diabetes are known, but one variable that is fairly well established is obesity. An overweight person requires more insulin to metabolize carbohydrates than a thin person does. Consequently, an individual who carries the genes for diabetes is more likely to develop the disorder if he or she is overweight.

Schizophrenia presents a similar situation. As we will see in Chapter 15, substantial evidence suggests that this disorder has a hereditary component. If one identical twin is schizophrenic, chances are high that the other twin will exhibit some signs of mental disturbance. But whether or not the other twin develops full-blown schizophrenia depends on a number of environmental factors. Genes may predispose a person to schizophrenia, but the environment in which he or she grows up shapes the actual outcome.

INTERIM SUMMARY

➔ Chromosomes and genes, segments of DNA molecules that store genetic information, transmit an individual's hereditary potential.

➔ Behavior depends on the interaction between heredity and environment: an individual's genes set the limits of his or her potential, but what happens to that potential depends on the environment in which he or she grows up.

CRITICAL THINKING QUESTIONS

1 Every year seems to bring the discovery of a new gene for alcoholism or for substance use disorder, schizophrenia, sexual orientation, impulsiveness, or some other complex psychological trait. But it often turns out after further studies that the gene is related to the trait in some people but not in everyone. And often the gene also turns out to be related to other behavioral traits in addition to the one to which it was originally linked. Can you think of any reasons why genes might affect psychological traits in this way? In other words, why is there not a perfect one-to-one match between the presence of a gene and the strength of a particular psychological trait?

2 Genes have an important influence on brain and behavior. But are genes responsible for everything? Can you think of examples of behavior that is not genetically programmed? How is this behavior transmitted across generations?

CHAPTER SUMMARY

1 The basic unit of the nervous system is a specialized type of cell called a neuron. Projecting from the cell body of a neuron are short branches called dendrites and a slender tubelike extension called the axon. Stimulation of the dendrites and cell body leads to a neural impulse that travels down the length of the axon. Sensory neurons transmit signals from sense organs to the brain and spinal cord; motor neurons transmit signals from the brain and spinal cord to muscles and glands. A nerve is a bundle of elongated axons belonging to hundreds or thousands of neurons.

2 A stimulus moves along a neuron as an electro chemical impulse that travels from the dendrites to the end of the axon. This traveling impulse, or action potential, is caused by depolarization, an electrochemical process in which the voltage difference across cell mechanisms is changed at successive points along the neuron.

3 Once started, an action potential travels down the axon to many small swellings at the end of the axon called terminal buttons. These terminal buttons release chemical substances called neurotransmitters, which are responsible for transferring the signal from one neuron to an adjacent one. The neurotransmitters diffuse across the synapse, a small gap between the juncture of the two neurons, and bind to receptors in the cell membrane of the receiving neuron. Some neurotransmitters have an excitatory effect, and others have an inhibitory effect. If the excitatory effects on the receiving neuron become large relative to the inhibitory effects, depolarization occurs, and the neuron fires an all-or-none impulse.

4 There are many different kinds of neurotransmitter–receptor interactions, and they help explain a range of psychological phenomena. The most important neurotransmitters include acetylcholine, norepinephrine, dopamine, serotonin, gamma-aminobutyric acid (GABA), and glutamate.

5 The nervous system is divided into the central nervous system (CNS) (the brain and spinal cord) and the peripheral nervous system (the nerves connecting the brain and spinal cord to other parts of the body). Subdivisions of the peripheral nervous system (PNS) are the somatic system (which carries messages to and from the sense receptors, muscles, and the surface of the body) and the autonomic system (which connects with the internal organs and glands).

6 The human brain is composed of three functional divisions: the central core, the limbic system, and the cerebral cortex. The central core includes the medulla, which is responsible for respiration and postural reflexes; the cerebellum, which is concerned with motor co-ordination; the thalamus, a relay station for incoming sensory information; and the hypothalamus, which is important in emotion and in maintaining homeostasis. The reticular formation, which crosses through several of the other central core structures, controls the organism's state of arousal and consciousness.

7 The limbic system controls some of the instinctive behaviors regulated by the hypothalamus, such as feeding, attacking, fleeing, and mating. It also plays an important role in emotion and memory.

8 The cerebral cortex is divided into two cerebral hemispheres. The convoluted surface of these hemispheres, the cerebral cortex, plays a critical role in higher mental processes such as thinking, learning, and decision-making. Certain areas of the cerebral cortex are associated with specific sensory inputs or control of specific movements. The remainder of the cerebral cortex consists of association areas concerned with memory, thought, and language.

9 Techniques have been developed to obtain detailed pictures of the human brain without causing the patient undue distress or damage. They include computerized axial tomography (CAT or CT), magnetic resonance imaging (MRI), and positron emission tomography (PET).

10 When the corpus callosum (the band of nerve fibers connecting the two cerebral hemispheres) is severed, significant differences in the functioning of the two hemispheres can be observed. The left hemisphere is skilled in language and mathematical abilities. The right hemisphere can understand some language but cannot communicate through speech. Instead, it has a highly developed spatial and pattern sense.

11 The term *aphasia* is used to describe language deficits caused by brain damage. People with damage to Broca's area have difficulty enunciating words correctly and speak in a slow, labored way. People with damage to Wernicke's area can hear words but do not know their meaning.

12 The autonomic nervous system (ANS) has sympathetic and parasympathetic divisions. Because it controls the action of the smooth muscles and the glands, the autonomic system is particularly important in emotional reactions. The sympathetic division is active during excitement, and the parasympathetic system is dominant during quiescence.

13 The endocrine glands secrete hormones into the bloodstream that travel through the body, acting in various ways on cells of different types. The pituitary has been called the 'master gland' because it controls the secretion activity of other endocrine glands. The adrenal glands are important in determining mood, energy level, and ability to cope with stress.

14 An individual's hereditary potential, which is transmitted by the chromosomes and genes, influences his or her psychological and physical characteristics. Genes are segments of DNA molecules, which store genetic information. Some genes are dominant, some recessive, and some sex-linked. Most human characteristics are polygenic; that is, they are determined by many genes acting together rather than by a single gene pair.

15 Selective breeding (mating animals that are high or low in a certain trait) is one method of studying the influence of heredity. Another means of sorting out the effects of environment and heredity is twin studies, in which the characteristics of identical twins (who share the same heredity) are compared with those of fraternal twins (who are no more alike genetically than ordinary siblings). Behavior depends on the interaction between heredity and environment: an individual's genes set the limits of his or her potential, but what happens to that potential depends on the environment in which he or she grows up.

CORE CONCEPTS

PCP	receptor	excitatory
olfactory system	motor neuron	inhibitory
pain threshold	interneuron	hyperpolarized
pain tolerance	nerve	reuptake
nervous system	nucleus	degradation
brain	ganglion	serotonin
spinal cord	glial cell	central core
central nervous system	action potential	limbic system
peripheral nervous system	ion	cerebral cortex
afferent nerves	ion channel	hindbrain
efferent nerves	ion pump	midbrain
somatic system	polarized	forebrain
autonomic system	resting potential	medulla
neuron	excitation threshold	pons
dendrites	depolarized	reticular formation
axon	refractory period	cerebellum
terminal buttons	myelin sheath	superior and inferior colliculus
synapse	nodes of Ranvier	substantia nigra
synaptic gap	saltatory conduction	thalamus
neurotransmitter	all-or-none law	hypothalamus
sensory neuron	lock-and-key action	homeostasis

pituitary gland

limbic system

hippocampus

amygdala

facial expressions

corpus callosum

longitudinal fissure

hemispheres

lobes

frontal lobe

parietal lobe

occipital lobe

temporal lobe

central fissure

lateral fissure

primary motor area

primary somatosensory area

primary visual area

visual cortex

optic chiasm

primary auditory area

association areas

event-related potentials (ERPs)

computerized axial tomography (CAT or CT)

magnetic resonance imaging (MRI)

positron emission tomography (PET)

functional magnetic resonance imaging (fMRI)

aphasia

Broca's area

Wernicke's area

sympathetic nervous system

parasympathetic nervous system

endocrine system

hormones

natural selection

behavior genetics

ultimate cause

proximate cause

adaptive

sexual selection

genes

chromosomes

sex-linked trait

polygenic

selective breeding

monozygotic

dizygotic

MEG (Magnetoencephalography)

DIGITAL SUPPORT RESOURCES

Students should use the unique access code included in the front of the book to access the digital support resources which accompany the new edition. These include:

- Multiple Choice Questions and Quizzes
- Critical Thinking Questions
- Practice Essay Questions
- Videos
- Glossary, Flashcards, and More

3 PSYCHOLOGICAL DEVELOPMENT

LEARNING OBJECTIVES

After reading this chapter you should be able to:

Understand how heredity and environment interact to determine human development. Be able to define the concept of maturation and show how it relates to this interaction, using motor development as an example.

Be familiar with what psychologists mean by developmental stages and by the related concepts of critical and sensitive periods.

Be able to describe the capacities of the newborn and the procedures used to assess these capacities.

Know the sequence of Piaget's stages of cognitive development and the major events that characterize each stage. Be familiar with some difficulties with Piaget's theory and with alternative views, including the recent work on children's theory of mind.

Be able to describe Kohlberg's work on moral reasoning and its three levels.

Be familiar with characteristics of personality development and early social behavior, including the research on attachment in animals, a model for categorizing types of attachment in human babies, and research on effects of day care.

Be familiar with some aspects of the physiology of puberty and with psychological effects of this period on various dimensions of the adolescent including body image, mood, and others.

It is parents' night at the beginning of the school year at the local primary school. Mrs Vohland, the teacher for the first year students, has given the parents of her new class a short presentation of the kinds of activities they will be doing over the academic year. The parents are milling around the room, looking at their children's artwork, and getting to know each other. A few parents approach Mrs Vohland to introduce themselves or thank her for her presentation. One intense-looking father named Philip walks up to Mrs Vohland and begins to ask her a series of pointed questions about her goals for the children. When will they learn to read? Will they have mastered addition and subtraction by the end of the year? Will his son be able to write short paragraphs by the end of the year? Mrs Vohland tries to explain that Grade 1 is for developing the building blocks of reading, arithmetic, and writing. Some children will be very advanced by the end of the year, and some will not, because children develop at different paces. Philip is not satisfied with her answer, though, and informs Mrs Vohland that his son has tested as 'bright' and he expects him to have accomplished all these goals by the end of the year.

When Philip finally lets her go, Mrs Vohland takes a deep breath and begins to tidy her desk. Another father, Sam, approaches. He also looks a bit intense, and Mrs Vohland braces herself for another onslaught of questions. Sam begins by saying that he is concerned about his son, who apparently has also been labeled as 'bright' by some early intelligence tests. Sam's concerns, however, are quite different from Philip's. 'I just want him to have a normal childhood. He's only six and the hard work will come later. I want him to have fun and to enjoy school. I'm worried you might push him too hard because he's supposedly smart.'

Parents, obviously, can have very different expectations for their children. Particularly with a first child, these expectations are often based on their own personal experiences as a child, or what they've read in the media or heard from friends. In addition, children vary greatly in their pace of development. In this chapter, we describe the progress of 'typical' development, but keep in mind the variations across children, families, and cultures.

Of all mammals, human beings require the longest period of maturation and learning before they are self-sufficient. A lemur (a primitive primate) can move about

CHAPTER OUTLINE

NATURE VERSUS NURTURE

Stages of development

CAPACITIES OF THE NEWBORN

Vision

Hearing

Taste and smell

Learning and memory

COGNITIVE DEVELOPMENT IN CHILDHOOD

Piaget's stage theory

A critique of Piaget's theory

Alternatives to Piaget's theory

Theory of mind

The development of moral judgment

PERSONALITY AND SOCIAL DEVELOPMENT

Temperament

Early social behavior

Attachment

Self-concept

ADOLESCENT DEVELOPMENT

Biological development

Social relationships in adolescence

CUTTING EDGE RESEARCH:

ADOLESCENTS AND THE INTERNET

SEEING BOTH SIDES: HOW

INSTRUMENTAL ARE PARENTS IN THE

DEVELOPMENT OF THEIR CHILDREN?

on its own shortly after birth and is soon able to fend for itself. An infant monkey is dependent on its mother for several months, a chimpanzee for several years. But even a chimpanzee – one of our closest relatives – will be a functioning adult member of its species long before a human of the same age.

Developmental psychologists are concerned with how and why different aspects of human functioning develop and change across the life span. They focus on physical development, such as changes in height and weight and the acquisition of motor skills; cognitive development, such as changes in thought processes, memory, and language abilities; and personality and social development, such as changes in self-concept and interpersonal relationships. The development of particular psychological abilities and functions is treated in more detail in later chapters. In this chapter we provide a general overview of psychological development and consider two central questions: (1) How do biological factors interact with events in the child's environment to determine the course of development? and (2) Is development best understood as a gradual, continuous process of change or as a series of abrupt, qualitatively distinct stages?

NATURE VERSUS NURTURE

The question of whether nature (i.e., biological factors) or nurture (i.e., environmental factors) is more important in determining the course of human development has been debated for centuries. The seventeenth-century British philosopher John Locke rejected the prevailing notion that babies were miniature adults who arrived in the world fully equipped with abilities and knowledge and simply had to grow for these inherited characteristics to appear. On the contrary, Locke believed that the mind of a newborn infant is a *tabula rasa* (Latin for 'blank slate'). What gets written on this slate is what the baby experiences – what he or she sees, hears, tastes, smells, and feels. According to Locke, all knowledge comes to us through our senses. It is provided entirely by experience; there is no built-in knowledge.

Charles Darwin's theory of evolution (1859), which emphasizes the biological basis of human development, led many theorists to emphasize heredity. Darwin argued that through natural selection, the process by which organisms that can adapt to environmental conditions are then able to reproduce and pass on their genes to subsequent generations, certain abilities become built into the genetic code. This suggests that many abilities that develop in humans are biologically based rather than purely products of learning.

With the rise of behaviorism in the twentieth century, however, the environmentalist position once again dominated. Behaviorists like John B. Watson and B. F. Skinner argued that human nature is completely malleable: early training can turn a child into any kind of adult, regardless of his or her heredity. Watson (1930, p. 104) stated this argument in its most extreme form:

Give me a dozen healthy infants, well-formed, and my own specified world to bring them up in, and I'll guarantee to take any one at random and train him to be any type of specialist I might select – doctor, lawyer, artist, merchant-chief, and, yes, even beggar-man and thief, regardless of his talents, penchants, tendencies, abilities, vocations, and race of his ancestors.

Today most psychologists agree not only that both nature and nurture play important roles but also that they interact continuously to guide development. The newborn infant has an estimated 100 billion neurons in his or her brain but relatively few connections between them. The connections between neurons develop rapidly after birth, and the infant brain triples in weight in the first 3 years after birth (DiPietro, 2001). Brain development is heavily influenced both by genetic factors and by the stimulation or deprivation a child receives from the environment in the early years.

Infants appear to be born, however, with the capacity to take in certain inputs from the environment and learn certain skills or concepts especially easily or quickly. The acquisition of language provides a good example (Chomsky, 1986). Parents often try to teach their children specific words: 'This is a *ball*. Can you say *ball*?' But they do not spend much time directly teaching their children grammatically correct sentences. Yet, when children do begin speaking in sentences, their sentences reflect some knowledge of grammatical rules, and it's clear they are not simply imitating sentences they have been taught. For example, one of the first sentences uttered by the son of one of this textbook's authors was 'I do it myself!' – his parents had definitely not been teaching him this particular sentence! Children seem equipped with the capacity to learn the complex structures of language by simply being exposed to everyday language.

Still, even forms of development that seem to be determined by innate biological timetables can be affected by environmental events. At the moment of conception, a remarkable number of personal characteristics are already determined by the genetic structure of the fertilized ovum. Our genes program our growing cells so that we develop into a person rather than a fish or a chimpanzee. They determine our sex, the color of our skin, eyes, and hair, and our overall body size, among other things. These genetically determined characteristics are expressed through the process of **maturation** – an innately determined sequence of growth and change that is relatively independent of external events. The human fetus develops according to a fairly fixed schedule, and foetal behavior, such as turning and kicking, also follows an orderly sequence that depends on the stage of growth. However, if the uterine environment is seriously abnormal in some way, maturational processes can be disrupted. For example, if the mother contracts rubella during the first 3 months of pregnancy (when the fetus's basic organ systems are developing according to the genetically programed schedule), the infant may be born deaf, blind, or brain-damaged, depending on which organ system was in a critical stage of development at the time of infection. Maternal malnutrition, smoking, and consumption of alcohol and drugs are other environmental factors that can affect the normal maturation of the fetus.

Motor development after birth also illustrates the interaction between genetically programmed maturation and environmental influences. Virtually all children go through the same sequence of motor behaviors in the same order: rolling over, sitting without support, standing while holding onto furniture, crawling, and then walking (see Figure 3.1). But they go through the sequence at different rates, and developmental psychologists have long wondered about the importance of learning and experience in such differences. Although early studies suggested that learning did not play a role (Dennis & Dennis, 1940; Gesell & Thompson, 1929; McGraw, 1935/1975), later studies indicated that practice or extra stimulation can accelerate the appearance of motor behaviors to some extent. For example, newborn infants have a stepping reflex. If they are held in an upright position with their feet touching a solid surface, their legs make stepping movements that are similar to walking. In some cultures, such as the Kipsigis people of rural Kenya, parents actively teach their infants how to sit up, stand, and walk, and these babies reach these developmental milestones 3 to 5 weeks earlier than American babies (Cole & Cole, 2001). In contrast, among the Ache, a nomadic people from eastern Paraguay, children get little experience with locomotion on their own because the forest they live in is so dense. These children begin walking almost a full year later than children in the USA or Europe (although they catch up to, and probably surpass, them in motor skills by mid-childhood).

The development of speech provides another example of the interaction between genetically determined characteristics and experience. In the course of normal development, all human infants exposed to some language input learn to speak, but not until they have attained a certain level of neurological development. With

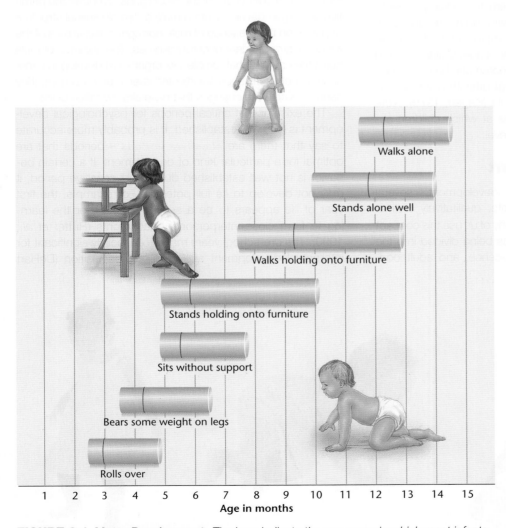

FIGURE 3.1 Motor Development. *The bars indicate the age range in which most infants develop behavior indicated.*

Walks alone

Stands alone well

Walks holding onto furniture

Stands holding onto furniture

Sits without support

Bears some weight on legs

Rolls over

1 2 3 4 5 6 7 8 9 10 11 12 13 14 15
Age in months

Because the terrain in which they live is so densely forested, infants in the Ache people of Paraguay reach developmental milestones almost a year after those in the West.

rare exceptions, infants less than a year old cannot speak in sentences. But children reared in an environment where people talk to them and reward them for making speech-like sounds talk earlier than children who do not receive such attention. For example, children in middle-class European homes begin to talk at about one year of age. Children reared in San Marcos, a remote village in Guatemala, have little verbal interaction with adults and do not utter their first words until they are more than two years old (Kagan, 1979). Note that the environment affects the rate at which children acquire the skills, not the ultimate skill level.

Stages of development

In explaining the sequence of development, several psychologists have proposed discrete, qualitatively distinct steps or **stages of development**. Many of us use this concept informally. We think of the life span as being divided into the stages of infancy, childhood, adolescence, and adulthood.

Parents might say that their adolescent is going through a 'rebellious stage.' Developmental psychologists, however, have a more precise concept in mind: the concept of stages implies that behaviors at a given stage are organized around a dominant theme or a coherent set of characteristics, behaviors at one stage are qualitatively different from behaviors at earlier or later stages, and all children go through the same stages in the same order. Environmental factors may speed up or slow down development, but the order of the stages does not vary. A child cannot enter a later stage without going through an earlier one first. As we will see later in the chapter, however, not all psychologists agree that development proceeds according to a fixed sequence of qualitatively distinct stages.

Closely related to the concept of stages is the idea of **critical periods** in human development – crucial time periods in a person's life when specific events occur if development is to proceed normally. Critical periods have been identified for some aspects of physical development in the human fetus. For example, the period 6 to 7 weeks after conception is critical for normal development of the sex organs. Whether the primitive sex organ develops into a male or female sexual structure depends on the presence of male hormones, regardless of the XX or XY arrangement of chromosomes. The absence of male hormones means that female sex organs will develop in either case. If male hormones are injected later in development, they cannot reverse the changes that have already taken place.

The existence of critical periods for psychological development is less well established. It is probably more accurate to say that there are **sensitive periods** – periods that are optimal for a particular kind of development. If a certain behavior is not well established during this sensitive period, it may not develop to its full potential. For example, the first year of life appears to be a sensitive period for the learning to form close interpersonal attachments (Rutter *et al.*, 1990). The pre-school years may be especially significant for intellectual development and language acquisition (DeHart

Virtually all children go through the same sequence of motor behaviors in the same order, but they go through the sequence at different rates.

et al., 2000). Children who have not had enough exposure to language before age six or seven may fail to acquire it altogether (Goldin-Meadow, 1982). The experiences of children during such sensitive periods may shape their future course of development in a manner that will be difficult to change later.

INTERIM SUMMARY

➜ A central question in developmental psychology is: how does nature (biological factors) interact with nurture (environmental experiences) to determine the course of development?

➜ Some developmental psychologists believe that development occurs in a sequence of periods in which (1) behaviors at a given stage are organized around a dominant theme or a coherent set of characteristics, (2) behaviors at one stage are qualitatively different from behaviors at earlier or later stages, and (3) all children go through the same stages in the same order.

➜ An individual's genetic heritage is expressed through the process of maturation: innately determined sequences of growth or other changes in the body that are relatively independent of the environment.

➜ Critical or sensitive periods are times during development when specific experiences must occur for psychological development to proceed normally.

CRITICAL THINKING QUESTIONS

1 Why do you think some parents are very concerned that their children develop basic skills faster than other children the same age? What effect do you think this has on the child's development?

2 Some theorists have claimed that there are sensitive periods for the development of attachments between an infant and his or her caregiver. What would the implications of such sensitive periods be, if they do exist?

CAPACITIES OF THE NEWBORN

At the end of the nineteenth century, psychologist William James suggested that the newborn child experiences the world as a 'buzzing, blooming confusion,' an idea that was still prevalent as late as the 1960s. We now know that newborn infants enter the world with all of their sensory systems functioning and are well prepared to learn about their new environment.

Because babies cannot explain what they are doing or tell us what they are thinking, developmental psychologists have had to design some ingenious procedures to study the capacities of infants. The basic method is to change the baby's environment in some way and observe the responses. For example, an investigator might present a tone or a flashing light and see if there is a change in heart rate or if the baby turns its head or sucks more vigorously on a nipple. This would suggest that the baby noticed the change. Researchers often use babies' looking behavior as a measure of their discrimination or interest – for instance, the researcher might present two stimuli at the same time to determine whether infants look longer at one than at the other. If they do, it indicates that they can tell the stimuli apart and perhaps that they prefer one over the other. Another method researchers use is the violation-of-expectation paradigm, in which infants are shown events that would be expected or unexpected to an adult (e.g., an object resting on a surface or an object floating in mid-air); infants often look longer at unexpected outcomes (researchers often say infants are 'surprised'), and this method can be used to uncover whether their understanding of aspects of how the world works is continuous with that of adults. In this section we describe some research findings on infant capacities, beginning with studies of infants' vision.

Vision

Newborns have poor visual acuity, their ability to change focus is limited, and they are very nearsighted. The computer-manipulated picture in Figure 3.2 shows how a mother's face may look to an infant. By 7 or 8 months of age, infants' visual acuity is close to that of adults (Keil, in press). Newborns spend a lot of time actively looking about. They scan the world in an organized way and pause when their eyes encounter an object or some change in their **visual field**, which is the full scope of what they can see. They are particularly attracted to areas of high contrast, such as the edges of an object. Instead of scanning the entire object, as an adult would, they keep looking at areas that have the most edges. They also prefer complex patterns over plain ones and patterns with curved lines over patterns with straight lines.

There is some evidence that newborns have a **facial preference** – an inborn, unlearned preference for faces. Newborns prefer to look at a normal face more than a scrambled or blank face, and even prefer to look at happy faces over fearful faces (Farroni *et al.*, 2007). The brains of newborns may come prepared to orient toward faces and obtain information from faces (Johnson & Morton, 1991). Newborns do not come equipped to perceive faces exactly as older children and adults do, however, and a great deal of learning about faces happens in the early days and months of life. For example, although newborns prefer normal faces over scrambled ones (see Figure 3.3),

FIGURE 3.2 **Visual Acuity.** *The newborn's poor visual acuity meakes the mother's face look fuzzy (left) rather than clear (right) even when viewed from close up.*

FIGURE 3.3 **Normal versus Scrambled Faces.** *Infants as young as three months show a preference for a normally configured face and a face with the features scrambled. Such preferences may be present at birth.*

they do not prefer normal faces over highly distorted ones in which the eyes are set so far apart the face appears rabbit-like. In contrast, 3 month-olds show a clear preference for normal faces over distorted ones (Bhatt *et al.*, 2005). In addition, newborns do not show a preference for faces of their own culture or race, but by 3 months of age, infants clearly prefer to look at faces of race they see most often in their environment (Bar-Haim *et al.*, 2006; Kelly *et al.*, 2009). Thus, newborns seem to come equipped to perceive the basic features of faces and to learn very rapidly about the faces they frequently see.

Hearing

Even fetuses 26 to 28 weeks old move in response to a sharp sound. Newborn infants turn their heads toward the source of a sound. Interestingly, the head-turning response disappears at about 6 weeks and does not re-emerge until 3 or 4 months, at which time the infants also search with their eyes for the source of the sound. By 4 months, infants reach toward the source of a sound in the dark, which helps young infants to learn what objects go with what sounds (Keil, in press).

Infants seem to learn particularly rapidly about the sounds made in human speech, and this learning may begin in the womb. Newborns show a preference for their mothers' voice over a stranger's, and even show a preference for stories their mothers read aloud in the last weeks of pregnancy over novel stories (DeCasper *et al.*, 1994). Newborns also show a preference for speech over acoustically similar non-speech sounds (Vouloumanos & Werker, 2007). While in the womb, infants are probably perceiving the low frequency sounds of their mothers' voices. They are also picking up on the distinctive qualities of their mother's language: newborns of French mothers can distinguish between recordings of a woman speaking French and Russian, while newborns whose mother is neither French nor Russian cannot discriminate the two recordings (Mehler *et al*., 1988). It seems it is the particular rhythms of a language that infants are discerning. Newborns will not distinguish between their own language and other languages that are similar in rhythm, such as Dutch and English, but will distinguish between languages with different rhythms, such as Japanese and Polish (Ramus, 2002).

Across cultures, adults speak to young infants quite differently from how they speak to older children and adults, using a higher pitch to the voice, different contours to sentences (e.g., 'helllllloooo, little baby' with the 'hello' starting at a high pitch then declining in pitch and the 'l' and 'o' drawn out), and longer pauses between sentences. This style of speech, often referred to as babytalk or motherese, seems to be just what a baby wants and needs. Infants in the first months of life prefer motherese over normal speech, even when presented by a stranger, and motherese helps infants detect the boundaries between words (Cooper *et al*., 1997; Fernald, 1985; Thiessen *et al*., 2005). Infants as young as 6 months are also able to discriminate between intonations of voice indicating approval and disapproval, and smile more in response to approval intonations over disapproval intonations, even when presented in a language different from their own (Fernald, 1993). Thus, infants seem to be able to extract important meanings from the speech around them, and are especially attentive to the kind of speech most frequently directed at them.

Taste and smell

Infants can discriminate between tastes shortly after birth. They prefer sweet-tasting liquids over liquids that are salty, bitter, sour, or bland. The characteristic response of the newborn to a sweet liquid is a relaxed expression resembling a slight smile, sometimes accompanied by lip-licking. A sour solution produces pursed lips and a wrinkled nose. In response to a bitter solution, the baby opens its mouth with the corners turned down and sticks out its tongue in what appears to be an expression of disgust.

Newborns can also discriminate among odors. They turn their heads toward a sweet smell, and heart rate and respiration slow down; these are indicators of attention. Noxious odors, such as those of ammonia or rotten eggs, cause them to turn their heads away; their heart rate and respiration accelerate, indicating distress. Infants are able to discriminate among even subtle differences in smells. After nursing for only a few days, an infant will consistently turn its head toward a pad saturated with its mother's milk in preference to one saturated with another mother's milk (Russell, 1976). Only breast-fed babies show this ability to recognize the mother's odor (Cernoch

Infants show their likes and dislikes for certain tastes at a very young age using universal facial expressions, such as the expression for disgust.

& Porter, 1985). When bottle-fed babies are given a choice between the smell of their familiar formula and that of a lactating breast, they choose the breast (Porter *et al*., 1992). There seems to be an innate preference for the odor of breast milk. In general, the ability to distinguish among smells has a clear adaptive value: it helps infants avoid noxious substances and thereby increases their chances of survival.

Learning and memory

It was once thought that infants could neither learn nor remember, but this is not the case. Evidence for early learning and remembering comes from several classic studies. In one, infants only a few hours old learned to turn their heads right or left, depending on whether they heard a buzzer or a tone. To taste a sweet liquid, the baby had to turn to the right when a tone sounded and to the left when a buzzer sounded. At first, the babies behaved randomly, discovering the association between the sounds and the tastes by accident. After only

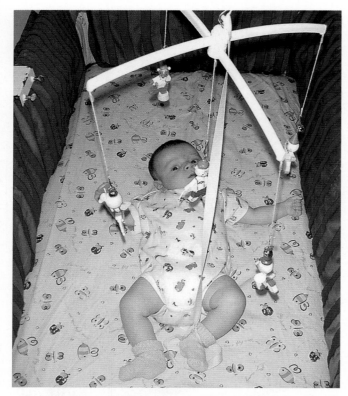

FIGURE 3.4 **A Study of Infant Memory.** *A study showed that three-month-old infants could easily learn to move a mobile by pulling on a ribbon attached to their leg; the infants remembered this new behavior when tested in the same situation 8 days later.*

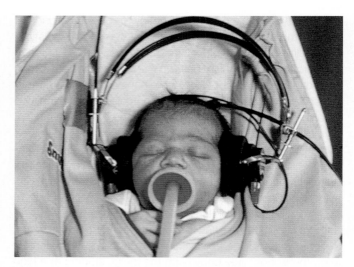

FIGURE 3.5 **Preference for Sounds.** *A newborn can indicate a preference for certain sounds – such as the mother's voice – by sucking more vigorously on a nipple when it causes the preferred sounds to be played through earphones.*

a few trials, the babies had learned the contingencies and were performing without error – turning to the right when the tone sounded and to the left when the buzzer sounded. The experimenter then reversed the situation so that the infant had to turn the opposite way when either the buzzer or the tone sounded. The babies mastered this new task quickly (Siqueland & Lipsitt, 1966).

By the time they are 3 months old, infants have good memories. When a mobile over an infant's crib was attached to one of the baby's limbs by a ribbon, 3-month-old infants quickly discovered which arm or leg would move the mobile and moved that limb more often. When the infants were placed in the same situation 8 days later, they remembered which arm or leg to move (Rovee-Collier, 1999) (see Figure 3.4).

More startling is evidence that infants remember sensations they experienced before birth, while still in the mother's uterus. Newborn infants can distinguish the sound of the human voice from other sounds. They also prefer the human voice over other sounds. A few days after birth, infants can learn to suck on an artificial nipple in order to turn on recorded speech or vocal music, and they suck more vigorously to hear speech sounds than to hear non-speech sounds or instrumental music (Butterfield & Siperstein, 1972). They also

prefer heartbeat sounds and female voices over male voices, and they prefer their mother's voice to other women's voices. But they do not prefer their father's voice to other men's voices (Brazelton, 1978; DeCasper & Fifer, 1980; DeCasper & Prescott, 1984) (see Figure 3.5).

These preferences appear to stem from the infant's prenatal experience with sounds. For example, the mother's voice is more audible than the father's in the uterus, which would appear to explain why a newborn infant prefers her voice over others (Richards *et al.*, 1992). Perhaps most surprising is evidence that the fetus may actually be learning to discriminate among some of the sounds of individual words. In an extraordinary experiment, pregnant women read aloud passages from children's stories each day during the last 6 weeks of pregnancy. For example, some women read the first 28 paragraphs of the Dr Seuss book *The Cat in the Hat*. Others read the last 28 paragraphs of the same story, but with the main nouns changed so that it was about the 'dog in the fog' instead of the 'cat in the hat.' By the time the infants were born, they had heard one of the selected stories for a total of about three hours.

Two or 3 days after the infants were born, they were permitted to suck on a special pacifier wired to record sucking rates (like the apparatus shown in Figure 3.5). Sucking on the pacifier turned on a tape recording of either their mother's voice or an unfamiliar woman's voice reading aloud either the story the infants had heard before birth or the story they had not heard previously. As in previous experiments, the infants showed by their sucking rates that they preferred their mother's voice to the stranger's. The startling finding, however, was that they also preferred the familiar story over the unfamiliar one – even when the two stories were read by the stranger (DeCasper & Spence, 1986).

In sum, the research we have described challenges the view of the newborn as experiencing the world as 'buzzing, blooming confusion,' as well as the view that the child enters the world as a 'blank slate.' Clearly, the infant enters the world well prepared to perceive and learn, but very early experience also shapes what infants learn.

INTERIM SUMMARY

➡ Early theorists believed that all sensory preferences and abilities had to be learned, but research over the past several decades has established that infants are born with their sensory systems intact and prepared to learn about the world.

➡ Newborns have poor vision and cannot see as well as an adult until about age two.

➡ Some theorists thought infants were born with a preference for faces, but research suggests infants are not attracted to faces per se but to stimulus characteristics such as curved lines, high contrast, edges, movement, and complexity – all of which faces possess.

➡ Even newborns pay attention to sounds, and they seem to be born with perceptual mechanisms that are already tuned to the properties of human speech that will help them learn language.

➡ Infants can discriminate between different tastes and odors shortly after birth. They seem to show a preference for the taste and odor of breast milk.

➡ Infants can learn from the moment they are born and show good memories by 3 months of age.

CRITICAL THINKING QUESTIONS

1 What do you think the evidence regarding infants' memories says about claims that adults can remember events from their first year of life?

2 Can an infant's environment be too stimulating? What might be the effects of an overly stimulating environment?

COGNITIVE DEVELOPMENT IN CHILDHOOD

One of the most amazing developments in childhood is the growth in children's ability to think and reason, referred to as cognitive development. How contemporary psychologists describe these changes has been profoundly influenced by the Swiss psychologist Jean Piaget (1896–1980). Prior to Piaget, psychological thinking about children's cognitive development was dominated by two perspectives, the biological-maturation, which emphasized the 'nature' component of development, and the environmental-learning perspective, which emphasized 'nurture.' In contrast, Piaget focused on the interaction between children's naturally maturing abilities and their interactions with the environment. In this section we outline Piaget's stage theory of development and then turn to a critique of that theory and to some more recent approaches. We also discuss the work of Lev Vygotsky, a Russian psychologist whose ideas about cognitive development, originally published in the 1930s, have attracted renewed interest in recent years.

Piaget's stage theory

Partly as a result of his observations of his own children, Piaget became interested in the relationship between the child's naturally maturing abilities and his or her interactions with the environment. He saw the child as an active participant in this process, rather than as a passive recipient of biological development or external stimuli. He viewed children as 'inquiring scientists' who experiment with objects and events in their environment to see what will happen. ('What does it feel like to suck on the teddy bear's ear?' 'What happens if I push my dish off the edge of the table?') The results of these 'experiments' are used to construct schemas – theories about how the physical and social worlds operate. Upon encountering a novel object or event, the child attempts to assimilate it – understand it in terms of a pre-existing schema. Piaget argued that if the new experience does not fit the existing schema, the child, like any good scientist, will engage in accommodation, modifying a schema to fit new information, thereby extending the child's theory of the world (Piaget & Inhelder, 1969). For example, if a boy's schema for firefighter is a male adult who wears a big, bulky uniform, but he sees a picture of a woman in a firefighter's uniform, he may first refuse to believe that women can be firefighters. To assimilate this new information with his existing schema of firefighters, he may argue that the woman in the picture must be playing 'dress-up.' Upon further evidence of women firefighters, however, the boy may engage in accommodation of his schema for firefighters, accepting that firefighters can be women, too.

Piaget's first job as a postgraduate student in psychology was as an intelligence tester for Alfred Binet, the inventor of the IQ test (see Chapter 12). In the course of this work, he began wondering why children made the kinds of errors they did. What distinguished their reasoning from that of adults? He observed his own children closely as they played, presenting them with simple scientific and moral problems and asking them to explain how they arrived at their answers. Piaget's observations convinced him that children's ability to think and reason progresses through a series of qualitatively

CONCEPT REVIEW TABLE
PIAGET'S STAGES OF COGNITIVE DEVELOPMENT

The ages given are averages. They may vary considerably depending on intelligence, cultural background, and socioeconomic factors, but the order of the progression is assumed to be the same for all children. Piaget has described more detailed phases within each stage; only a general characterization of each stage is given here.

Stage	Characterization
1. Sensorimotor (birth–2 years)	Differentiates self from objects Recognizes self as agent of action and begins to act intentionally; for example, pulls a string to set a mobile in motion or shakes a rattle to make a noise
2. Preoperational (2–7 years)	Learns to use language and to represent objects by images and words Thinking is still egocentric: has difficulty taking the viewpoint of others Classifies objects by a single feature; for example, groups together all the red blocks regardless of shape or all the square blocks regardless of color
3. Concrete operational (7–11 years)	Can think logically about objects and events Achieves conservation of number (age six), mass (age seven), and weight (age nine) Classifies objects according to several features and can order them in series along a single dimension, such as size
4. Formal operational (11 years and up)	Can think logically about abstract propositions and test hypotheses systematically Becomes concerned with the hypothetical, the future, and ideological problems

distinct stages. He divided cognitive development into four major stages, each of which has a number of substages. The major stages are the sensorimotor stage, the preoperational stage, the stage of concrete operations, and the stage of formal operations (see Concept Review Table).

The sensorimotor stage

Piaget designated the first 2 years of life as the **sensorimotor stage**, when infants are busy discovering the relationships between their actions and the consequences of those actions. They discover, for example, how far they have to reach to grasp an object. In this way they begin to develop a concept of themselves as separate from the external world.

An important aspect of understanding that they are separate from the external world is understanding that the world is composed of objects, which continue to exist even when they are not in plain sight. This concept is known as **object permanence**. If a cloth is placed over a toy that an 8-month-old is reaching for, the infant immediately stops reaching and appears to lose interest in the toy. The baby seems neither surprised nor upset, makes no attempt to search for the toy, and acts as if the toy had ceased to exist (see Figure 3.6).

FIGURE 3.6 **Object Permanence.** *When the toy is hidden by a screen, the infant acts as if the toy no longer exists. From this observation, Piaget concluded that the infant had not yet acquired the concept of object permanence.*

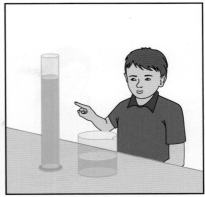

FIGURE 3.7 **The Concept of Conservation.** *A four-year-old acknowledges that the two short, wide glasses contain the same amount of liquid. However, when the contents of one glass are poured into a tall, thin glass, he says that it contains more liquid. Not until he is several years older will he state that the two different-shaped glasses contain the same amount of liquid.*

In contrast, a 10-month-old will actively search for an object that has been hidden under a cloth or behind a screen. The older baby, having attained the concept of object permanence, seems to realize that the object exists, even though it is out of sight. But even at this age, search is limited. The infant who has had repeated success in retrieving a toy hidden in a particular place will continue to look for it in that spot even after watching an adult conceal it in a new location. Not until about one year of age will a child consistently look for an object where it was last seen, regardless of what happened on previous trials.

The preoperational stage

By about one to two years of age, children have begun to use symbols. Words can represent things or groups of things, and one object can represent another. At this point, children become able to engage in pretense. A 3 year old may treat a stick as a horse and ride it around the room, a block of wood can become a car, and one doll can become a father and another a baby. But although three and four year olds can think in symbolic terms, their words and images are not yet organized in a logical manner. During this **preoperational stage** of cognitive development, the child does not yet comprehend certain rules or operations. An **operation** is a mental routine for logically separating, combining, and otherwise transforming information. For example, if water is poured from a tall, narrow glass into a short, wide one, adults know that the amount of water has not changed because they can reverse the transformation in their minds. They can imagine pouring the water from the short glass back into the tall glass, thereby arriving at the original state. In the preoperational stage of cognitive development, a child might say the shorter glass contains less water because the understanding of reversibility and other mental operations is absent or weak. As a result, according to Piaget, preoperational children have not yet attained **conservation**, the understanding that the

amount of a substance remains the same (is conserved) even when its form is changed (see Figure 3.7).

Piaget believed that preoperational thinking is dominated by visual impressions. For instance, a change in the visual appearance of a ball of clay influences the child more than less obvious but more essential qualities, such as mass or weight. This reliance on visual impressions is illustrated by an experiment on the conservation of number. If two rows of counters are matched one for one against each other, young children will say, correctly, that the rows have the same number of counters (see Figure 3.8). If the counters in one row are brought closer together to form a cluster, 5 year olds say that there are now more counters in the straight row even though no counters have been removed. The visual impression of a long row of counters overrides the numerical equality that was obvious when the counters appeared in matching rows. In contrast, 7 year olds assume that if the number of objects was equal before, it must remain equal. At this age, numerical equality has become more significant than visual impression.

Another key characteristic of preoperational children, according to Piaget, is **egocentrism**. Preoperational children are unaware of perspectives other than their own – they believe that everyone else perceives the environment the same way they do (Piaget, 1950a). To demonstrate this, Piaget created the 'three-mountain problem.' A child is allowed to walk around a table on which are arranged three mountains of different heights. Then the child stands on one side of the table while a doll is placed on the table at various locations (and therefore has a different view of the three mountains than the child). The child is asked to choose a photograph that shows what the doll is seeing. Before the age of six or seven, most children choose the photograph that illustrates their own perspective on the three mountains (Piaget & Inhelder, 1948/1956).

Piaget believed that egocentrism explains the rigidity of preoperational thought. Because young children cannot

FIGURE 3.8 Conservation of Number. *When two rows of ten counters are evenly spaced, most children report that they contain the same amount. When one row is then spread out into a larger space, children under age six or seven say that the original row contains fewer counters.*

appreciate points of view other than their own, they cannot revise their schemas to take into account changes in the environment. This is why they are unable to reverse operations or conserve quantity.

Operational stages

Between the ages of seven and 12, children master the various conservation concepts and begin to perform other logical manipulations. They can place objects in order on the basis of a dimension such as height or weight. They can also form a mental representation of a series of actions. Five year olds can find their way to a friend's house but cannot direct you there or trace the route with paper and pencil. They can find their own way because they know that they have to turn at certain places, but they have no overall picture of the route. In contrast, 8 year olds can readily draw a map of the route. Piaget calls this period the **concrete operational stage**: although children are using abstract terms, they are doing so only in relation to concrete objects – objects to which they have direct sensory access.

At about the age of 11 or 12, children arrive at adult modes of thinking. In the **formal operational stage**, the child is able to reason in purely symbolic terms. In one test for formal operational thinking, the child tries to discover what determines how long a pendulum will swing back and forth (its period of oscillation). Given a length of string suspended from a hook and several weights that can be attached to the lower end, the child can vary the length of the string, change the attached weight, and alter the height from which the bob is released. Children who are still in the concrete operational stage experiment by changing some of the variables but not in a systematic way. Average adolescents, however, set up a series of hypotheses and test them systematically. They reason that if a particular variable (weight) affects the period of oscillation, the effect will appear only if they change one variable and hold all others constant. If this variable seems

to have no effect on how long the pendulum swings, they rule it out and try another. Considering all the possibilities – working out the consequences for each hypothesis and confirming or denying these consequences – is the essence of formal operational thought.

A critique of Piaget's theory

Piaget's theory was a major intellectual achievement that revolutionized the way we think about children's cognitive development. However, new, more sophisticated methods of testing the intellectual functioning of infants and preschool children reveal that Piaget underestimated their abilities. Many of the tasks designed to test stage theories actually require several skills, such as attention, memory, verbal ability, and specific factual knowledge. Children may have the ability being tested but be unable to perform the task because they lack one of the other required skills.

Take the example of object permanence. As we saw earlier, when infants younger than 8 months are shown a toy that is then hidden or covered while they watch, they act as if the toy no longer exists and do not attempt to search for it. Note, however, that successful performance on this test requires children not only to understand that the object still exists but also to remember where the object was hidden, and to show through some physical action that they are searching for it. Because Piaget believed that early cognitive development depends on sensorimotor activities, he did not consider the possibility that the infant might know that the object still exists but be unable to show this knowledge through searching behavior.

In a study designed to test this possibility, children were not required to actively search for the hidden object. As shown in the far left section of Figure 3.9, the apparatus was a screen hinged at one edge to the top of a table. At first the screen lay flat on the table. As the infant watched, the screen was slowly rotated away from the infant through

a) Habituation event
Infants are shown a rotating screen until they no longer attend to it.

b) Test events
In these test events, a box is placed where it can be hidden by the screen. The infants then see either a possible event (the screen rotates until it would hit the box and then returns to its starting position) or an impossible event (the screen appears to pass right through the box). Infants attend more to the impossible event, indicating that they realize that the hidden box still exists.

FIGURE 3.9 Testing Object Permanence.

a complete 180-degree arc until it was again flat on the table. The screen was then rotated in the opposite direction, toward the infant.

When the infants were first shown the rotating screen, they looked at it for almost a full minute, but after repeated trials they lost interest and turned their attention elsewhere. At that point a brightly painted box appeared on the table beyond the hinge, where it would be hidden as the screen moved into its upright position. (The infant was actually seeing a reflected image of a box, not the actual box.) As shown in Figure 3.9, the infants were then shown either a possible event or an impossible event. One group of infants saw the screen rotate from its starting position until it reached the point where it should bump against the box. At that point the screen stopped and then moved back to its starting position. The other group saw the screen rotate to the upright position but then continue to rotate all the way to the other side of the 180-degree arc, just as though no box was in the way. The investigators reasoned that if the infants thought the box still existed even when the screen hid it, they would be surprised when it seemed to pass through the box – an impossible event. The infants would then look at the screen longer than they would when the screen seemed to bump into the box before returning to its starting point. This is exactly what happened. Even though the impossible event was perceptually identical to an event that they had seen repeatedly and lost interest in, the infants found it more interesting than a physically possible event that they had never seen before – the screen stopping halfway through the arc and then reversing direction (Baillargeon *et al.*, 1985).

Because the infants in this experiment were only four-and-a-half months old, they displayed object permanence 4 to 5 months earlier than Piaget's theory predicts. Replications of this study have found that some infants as young as three-and-a-half months display object permanence (Baillargeon, 1987; Baillargeon & DeVos, 1991).

Other experiments using Piaget's conservation tasks have also yielded evidence that children's mental capacities develop earlier than he thought. In one study of number conservation, two sets of toys were lined up in one-to-one correspondence (as in Figure 3.8). The experimenter then said, 'These are your soldiers and these are my soldiers. What's more, my soldiers, your soldiers, or are they both the same?' After the child answered this question correctly, the experimenter spread out one of the rows of toys and repeated the question. As Piaget and others had previously reported, five-year-old children failed to conserve, stating that the spread-out row contained more soldiers. But then the investigator introduced a second set of conditions. Instead of describing the toys as individual soldiers, she said, 'This is my army and this is your army. What's more, my army, your army, or are they both the same?' With this simple change of wording, most of the children were able to conserve, judging the two 'armies' to be the same size, even when one of them was spread out. When children are prompted to interpret the display as an aggregate or collection rather than as a set of individual items, their judgments of equality are less likely to be influenced by irrelevant perceptual transformations (Markman, 1979).

Other research has identified more factors that can influence the development of concrete operational thought. For example, the experience of going to school seems to promote mastery of Piagetian tasks (Artman & Cahan, 1993). This and other evidence suggest that concrete operational reasoning may not be a universal stage of development that emerges during middle childhood but, instead, a product of the cultural setting, schooling, and the specific wording of questions and instructions.

Alternatives to Piaget's theory

Developmental psychologists generally agree that these kinds of findings show that Piaget underestimated children's abilities, and his theory has been challenged on many grounds. However, there is no consensus on the best alternative to pursue. Some psychologists favor information-processing approaches, and others have pursued knowledge-acquisition and sociocultural approaches.

Information-processing approaches

We have already noted that many of the experiments challenging Piaget's views were inspired by investigators who view cognitive development as the acquisition of several separate **information-processing skills** – specific skills at gathering and analyzing information from the environment. Accordingly, they think that the standard Piagetian tasks fail to separate these skills from the skill that the task is supposed to assess. But they disagree among themselves about exactly how their views challenge Piaget's theory. For example, they disagree on the important question of whether development is best understood as a series of qualitatively distinct stages or as a continuous process of change. Some think that the entire notion of stages should be abandoned (Klahr, 1982). In their view, the separate skills develop smoothly and continuously rather than in a series of discrete stages. But other information-processing theorists think that gradual changes in information-processing skills do in fact lead to discontinuous, stagelike changes in children's thinking (Case & Okamoto, 1996). These theorists are sometimes referred to as neo-Piagetians. Other neo-Piagetians agree that there are genuine stages but only within more narrow domains of knowledge. For example, a child's language skills, mathematical understanding, social reasoning, and so forth may all develop in a stagelike fashion, but each domain proceeds at its own pace relatively independently of the others (Mandler, 1983).

Knowledge-acquisition approaches

Some developmental psychologists think that after infancy, children and adults have essentially the same cognitive processes and capacities and that the primary difference between them is the adult's more extensive knowledge base. By **knowledge** they mean not just a larger collection of facts but a deeper understanding of how facts in a particular domain are organized. An example of a knowledge-acquisition approach is Siegler's (1996) *overlapping waves theory* of cognitive development, which suggests that children have access to multiple ways of solving problems at any one time but with age and experience, some strategies become more frequent while others become less frequent.

The distinction between facts and the organization of facts is shown in a study that compared a group of ten-year-old chess experts competing in a tournament with a group of college students who were chess amateurs. When asked to memorize and recall lists of random numbers, the college students easily outperformed the 10 year olds. But when tested on their ability to recall actual positions of the chess pieces on the board, the ten-year-old chess experts did better than the

Studies of young chess experts suggest their greater store of knowledge about chess allows them to process information about appropriate moves more efficiently, giving them the upper hand in competitions with older but less expert chess players.

18-year-old chess amateurs (Chi, 1978). The relevant difference between the two groups is not different stages of cognitive development or different information-processing abilities, but domain-specific knowledge. Because the 10 year olds had a deeper grasp of the underlying structure of chess, they could organize and reconstruct the arrangements from memory by 'chunking' the separate pieces of information into larger meaningful units (for example, a king-side attack by white) and eliminating from consideration implausible placements of the pieces. (We discuss experts versus amateur problem solvers in Chapter 9.)

Increasing knowledge of the world, rather than a qualitative shift in cognitive development, may also account for children's increasing ability to solve Piaget's conservation tasks as they grow older. For example, a child who does not know that mass or number is the critical feature that defines 'more clay' or 'more sandwiches' is likely to judge that the quantity has changed when only its visual appearance has changed. An older child may simply have learned the essential defining feature of 'more.' If this hypothesis is correct, children who fail to show conservation in one domain may show conservation in another, depending on their understanding of the domain. For example, in a study kindergarten children were told about a series of 'operations' that doctors or scientists had performed. Some operations altered an animal so that it looked like a different animal; other operations altered an animal so that it looked like a plant (see Figure 3.10). Children were told that:

> The doctors took a horse [shows child picture of horse] and did an operation that put black and white stripes all over its body. They cut off its mane and braided its tail. They trained it to stop neighing like a horse, and they trained it to eat wild grass instead of oats and hay. They also trained it to live

FIGURE 3.10 Early Testing of Conservation. *Children are told that doctors or scientists operated on an animal until it looked like a different animal (horse to zebra) or until it looked like a plant (hedgehog to cactus). Children who say that the animal is 'really' the new animal or plant are failing to show conservation; children who say that the animal is still 'really' the original animal are showing conservation.*

in the wilds in Africa instead of in a stable. When they were all done, the animal looked just like this [shows picture of zebra]. When they were finished, was this animal a horse or a zebra?

(Keil, 1989, p. 307)

When asked about operations that transformed one kind of animal into another, a majority of the children failed to conserve. About 65 per cent agreed that the horse had been genuinely changed into a zebra. But when faced with the transformation of an animal into a plant, only about 25 per cent agreed that a porcupine had been genuinely changed into a cactus (Keil, 1989). Studies like these demonstrate that in some domains preoperational children can ignore dramatic changes in visual appearance because they have learned that an invisible but essential defining feature of the object has remained unchanged.

Sociocultural approaches

Although Piaget emphasized the child's interactions with the environment, the environment he had in mind was the immediate physical environment. The social and cultural context plays virtually no role in Piaget's theory. Yet much of what children must learn is the particular ways their culture views reality, what roles different people – and different sexes – are expected to play, and what rules and norms govern social relationships in their particular culture. In these areas there are no universally valid facts or correct views of reality. According to those who take a **sociocultural approach** to development, the child should be seen not as a physical scientist seeking 'true' knowledge but as a newcomer to a culture who seeks to become a native by learning how to look at social reality through the lens of that culture (Rogoff, 2000).

Culture can influence children's development in several ways (Keil, in press):

→ By providing the opportunity for specific activities: children learn by observation, experience, or at least hearing about an activity, for example, because water is scarce in the desert, children of the Kung of the Kalahari Desert are unlikely to learn about conservation by pouring water from one glass to another, but children growing up in Seattle or Paris are unlikely to learn how to find water-bearing roots in the desert.

→ By determining the frequency of certain activities: for example, traditional dancing is important in Balinese culture, so children growing up in Bali become skilled dancers, but Norwegian children become expert skiers or skaters.

→ By how they relate to different activities: for example, in cultures in which making pottery is important, children associate molding clay with interaction with their parents and perhaps with selling pots in the market. In cultures where making pottery is not important, children may view molding clay only as a nursery school pastime.

→ By controlling the child's role in the activity: in many cultures, meat is obtained in a supermarket, and children (and their parents) play no role in trapping, killing, and preparing the animal from which the meat comes. In other cultures, children learn from a young age how to hunt, kill, and prepare animals for family meals.

The origins of this view of cognitive development can be seen in the work of the Russian scholar Lev Vygotsky (1934/1986). Vygotsky believed that we develop understanding and expertise primarily through what might be described as apprenticeship – we are guided by more knowledgeable individuals, who help us understand more and more about our world and develop new skills. He also distinguished between two levels of cognitive development: the child's actual level of development, as expressed in problem-solving ability, and the child's level of potential development, which is determined by the kind of problem-solving the child can do when guided by an adult or a more knowledgeable peer. According to Vygotsky, we need to know both the actual and potential levels of development in a particular child to fully understand that child's level of cognitive development and provide appropriate instruction.

Because language is the primary means by which humans exchange social meanings, Vygotsky viewed language development as central to cognitive development. In fact, he regarded language acquisition as the most important aspect of children's development (Blanck, 1990). Language plays an important role in developing new skills and knowledge. As adults and peers help children master new tasks, the communication between them becomes part of the children's thinking. The children then use their language ability to guide their own actions as they practice the new skill. What Piaget referred to as egocentric speech Vygotsky considered an essential component of cognitive development: children speak to themselves to give themselves guidance and direction. This kind of self-instruction is termed private speech. You can observe this process in a child who gives herself instructions about how to perform a task, such as tying her shoes, that she previously heard from an adult (Berk, 1997).

Theory of mind

As adults, we behave and think in ways that reflect our understanding that other people have minds – they think, they have expectations and beliefs, they have their own assumptions, and so on. Much of our behavior toward other people is based on our understanding of what they are thinking. For example, we have a date to meet a friend for coffee at 2 p.m. but realize that the meeting we are in is not going to be finished until 2:30 p.m. Knowing the friend expects us to be at the coffee house at 2 p.m., we take a break from the meeting to call our friend and tell her we are going to be late. We also occasionally reflect on our own thinking process by, for example, evaluating what we think about a situation or wondering how we could have been mistaken in a belief. This thinking about thinking is referred to as **metacognition**.

Humans have some capacity for understanding that other people have minds from a very early age. By 6 to 9 months, infants are generally capable of sharing experiences about objects or events with others by following the visual gaze of those other people (Bakeman & Adamson, 1984; Scaife & Bruner, 1975). For example, if a caregiver says, 'see the toy over there' while looking or pointing at a toy across the room, an infant will follow the caregiver's gaze or point to the toy. This is referred to as **joint attention** (Bruner, 1975), and this capacity is critical to the development of social communication and language. The development of joint attention seems to be the product of both the development of specific areas of the brain and repeated exposure to events such as the one just described in which other people share with the infant a reference to an object, event or person (Mundy & Jarrold, 2010).

From this foundation of the development of joint attention, children develop knowledge about basic mental states, such as desires, percepts, beliefs, knowledge, thoughts,

Studies suggest that by pointing to attract the adult's attention, the child may be aware that the adult's mind works differently from her own.

intentions, and feelings. This knowledge is often referred to as **theory of mind**. The sophistication of children's theory of mind develops gradually over the first years of life, however. The following study is typical in research on theory of mind and illustrates the basic developmental finding (Flavell, 1999).

An experimenter shows a five-year-old child a candy box with pictures of candy on it and asks her what she thinks is in it. 'Candy,' she replies. Then the child gets to look inside and discovers to her surprise that it actually contains crayons, not candy. The experimenter then asks her what another child who had not yet seen inside the box would think it contained. 'Candy,' the child answers, amused at the deception. The experimenter then tries the same procedure with a 3 year old. The response to the initial question is the expected 'Candy,' but the response to the second is surprising – a confident 'Crayons.' Even more surprising is that in response to further questioning, the 3 year old claims that she had initially thought that there were crayons in the box and had even said that there were.

The basic interpretation of these results of the *false belief task* is that pre-schoolers do not yet fully comprehend that other people have minds and thoughts different from their own, and therefore do not understand that people can have beliefs different from their own or different from reality.

How does this understanding develop? Bartsch and Wellman (1995) argue that the developmental sequence has three steps. First, about age two, children have an elementary conception of simple desires, emotions, and perceptual experiences. They understand that people can have wants and fears, and can see and feel things, but they do not understand that people mentally represent both objects and their own desires and beliefs. Second, at about age three, children begin to talk about beliefs and thoughts as well as desires, and they seem to understand that beliefs can be false as well as true and can differ from one person to another. Yet, they still continue to explain their own actions and others' actions by appealing to desires rather than beliefs. Finally, at about age four, children begin to understand that people's thoughts and beliefs affect their behaviors and that people can have beliefs that simply do not reflect reality. By age five, most children, all over the world, pass false belief tasks (Callaghan *et al.*, 2005).

The building blocks for this understanding of others' minds are in place even earlier than two years of age, however (Tomasello, Carpenter, & Liszkowski, 2007). A good example is a 1 year old's use of pointing to direct the attention of an adult. Such behavior suggests that the infant knows the adult's mind is different from her own and that by pointing, she can direct the adult's attention to an interesting object. Evidence that pointing is used intentionally to direct the mind (attention) of an adult comes from experiments in which adults ignored an infant's pointing at an object like a puppet – such behavior on the part of the adult results in annoyance by the infant and repeated attempts to direct the adult's attention (Liszkowski *et al.*, 2004). Other work using the 'looking'

paradigms described earlier shows that even infants have some understanding that other people can have false beliefs (Onishi & Baillargeon, 2005; Luo, 2011). Once again, early research may have underestimated the capabilities of very young children by requiring them to perform complex tasks to show what they know.

One of the most interesting applications of research on theory of mind is the study of **autism spectrum disorder**, as defined by DSM-5. This is a serious disorder in which children can seem unresponsive to others and tend to have significant problems in communicating with others (see Chapter 15). Simon Baron-Cohen (Baron-Cohen & Wheelwright, 2004) has suggested that children with an autism spectrum disorder lack a fundamental theory of mind, which robs them of the ability to understand others' feelings, desires, and beliefs. As a result, people can seem like any other object to an autistic child. This contributes to the autistic child's apparent lack of interest in others and retreat into an inner world. Author Temple Grandin, who has an autism spectrum disorder but has still achieved much in her life, describes it this way:

> **Social interactions that come naturally to most people can be daunting for people with autism. As a child, I was like an animal that had no instincts to guide me; I just had to learn by trial and error. I was always observing, trying to work out the best way to behave, but I never fit in. I had to think about every social interaction. When other students swooned over the Beatles, I called their reaction an ISP – interesting sociological phenomenon. I was a scientist trying to figure out the ways of the natives. I wanted to participate, but did not know how.**

(Grandin, 1995, p. 132)

The development of moral judgment

In addition to studying the development of children's thought, Piaget was interested in how children develop **moral judgment**, children's understanding of moral rules and social conventions. He believed that children's overall level of cognitive development determined their moral judgment. On the basis of observations he made of children of different ages playing games with rules, such as marbles, he proposed that children's understanding of rules develops in a series of four stages (Piaget, 1932/1965). The first stage emerges at the beginning of the preoperational period. Children at this stage engage in 'parallel play,' in which each child follows a private set of idiosyncratic rules. For example, a child might sort marbles of different colors into groups or roll all the big ones across the room, followed by all the small ones. These 'rules' give the child's play some regularity, but they are frequently changed and serve no collective purpose such as co-operation or competition.

Beginning about age five, the child develops a sense of obligation to follow rules, treating them as absolute moral imperatives handed down by some authority such as God or the child's parents. Rules are permanent, sacred, and not subject to modification. Obeying them to the letter is more important than any human reason for changing them. For example, children at this stage reject the suggestion that the position of the starting line in the marble game might be changed to accommodate younger children who might want to play.

At this stage, children judge an act more by its consequences than by the intentions behind it. Piaget told children several pairs of stories. In one pair, a boy broke a teacup while trying to steal some jam when his mother was not home; another boy, who was doing nothing wrong, accidentally broke a whole trayful of teacups. 'Which boy is naughtier?' Piaget asked. Preoperational children tended to judge as naughtier the person in the stories who did the most damage, regardless of the intentions or motivation behind the act.

In Piaget's third stage of moral development, the child begins to appreciate that some rules are social conventions – co-operative agreements that can be arbitrarily changed if everyone agrees. Children's moral realism also declines: when making moral judgments, children in this stage give weight to subjective considerations such as a person's intentions, and they see **punishment** as a human choice rather than as inevitable, divine retribution.

The beginning of the formal operational stage coincides with the fourth and final stage in children's understanding of moral rules. Youngsters show an interest in generating rules to deal even with situations they have never encountered. This stage is marked by an ideological mode of moral reasoning, which addresses wider social issues rather than just personal and interpersonal situations.

The American psychologist Lawrence Kohlberg extended Piaget's work on moral reasoning to adolescence and adulthood (Kohlberg, 1969, 1966). He looked for universal stages in the development of moral judgments by presenting research participants with moral dilemmas in the form of stories. In one story, a man whose dying wife needs a drug he cannot afford pleads with a pharmacist to let him buy the drug at a cheaper price. When the pharmacist refuses, the man decides to steal the drug. Participants are asked to discuss the man's action.

By analyzing answers to several such dilemmas, Kohlberg arrived at six developmental stages of moral judgment, which he grouped into three levels: **preconventional**, **conventional**, and **postconventional** (see Concept Review Table). The answers are scored on the basis of the reasons given for the decision, not on the basis of whether the action is judged to be right or wrong. For example, agreeing that the man should have stolen the drug because 'If you let your wife die, you'll get in trouble' or disagreeing because 'If you steal the drug, you'll be caught and sent to jail' are both scored at Level I, or

CONCEPT REVIEW TABLE STAGES OF MORAL REASONING

Kohlberg believed that moral judgment develops with age according to these stages.

Level I	Preconventional morality
Stage 1	Punishment orientation (Obeys rules to avoid punishment)
Stage 2	Reward orientation (Conforms to obtain rewards, to have favors returned)
Level II	Conventional morality
Stage 3	Good-boy/good-girl orientation (Conforms to avoid disapproval of others)
Stage 4	Authority orientation (Upholds laws and social rules to avoid censure of authorities and feelings of guilt about not 'doing one's duty')
Level III	Postconventional morality
Stage 5	Social-contract orientation (Actions guided by principles commonly agreed on as essential to the public welfare; principles upheld to retain respect of peers and, thus, self-respect)
Stage 6	Ethical principle orientation (Actions guided by self-chosen ethical principles, which usually value justice, dignity, and equality; principles upheld to avoid self-condemnation)

preconventional. In both instances, the man's actions are evaluated as right or wrong on the basis of anticipated punishment.

Kohlberg believed that all children are at Level I until about age ten, when they begin to evaluate actions in terms of other people's opinions, which characterizes the conventional level. Most youngsters can reason at this level by age 13. Following Piaget, Kohlberg argued that only individuals who have achieved formal operational thought are capable of the abstract thinking that is necessary for Level III, postconventional morality, in which actions are evaluated in terms of higher-order ethical principles. The highest stage, Stage 6, requires the ability to formulate abstract ethical principles and uphold them in order to avoid self-condemnation.

Kohlberg reported that fewer than 10 per cent of his adult participants showed the kind of 'clear-principled' Stage 6 thinking that is exemplified by the following response of a 16 year old to the story described earlier: 'By the law of society [the man] was wrong. But by the law of nature or of God the druggist was wrong and the husband was justified. Human life is above financial gain. Regardless of who was dying, if it was a total stranger, man has a duty to save him from dying' (Kohlberg, 1969, p. 244). Before he died, Kohlberg eliminated Stage 6 from his theory; Level III is now sometimes simply referred to as high-stage principled reasoning.

Kohlberg presented evidence for this sequence of stages in children from several cultures, including the USA Mexico, Taiwan, and Turkey (Colby et al., 1983; Nisan & Kohlberg, 1982). On the other hand, there is evidence that people use different rules for different situations and that the stages are not sequential (Kurtines & Greif, 1974). The theory has also been criticized as male centered because it places a masculine style of abstract reasoning based on justice and rights higher on the moral scale than a feminine style of reasoning based on caring and concern for the integrity and continuation of relationships (Gilligan, 1982).

Moreover, both Piaget's and Kohlberg's research has been criticized as having grossly underestimated the moral reasoning capabilities of young children by relying too heavily on verbal abilities. Modern research shows that even infants make judgments about the actions of others as 'good' or 'bad' – in other words, they make moral judgments – and they prefer 'good' actors over 'bad' actors. For example, one set of experiments showed six-month- and ten-month-old infants scenes of a 'helper' object (a figure with eyes and nose) assisting a ball to climb a hill and a 'hinderer' object (a different shaped figure with eyes and nose) push the ball down the hill. Then they were presented a plate with both the helper and hinderer object and allowed to choose which one they wanted. Infants at both six and ten months of age overwhelmingly chose the helper object over the hinderer object (Hamlin et al., 2007).

Other research shows that infants show distress at another's pain and anger at agents inflicting pain, and toddlers will help other people with no expectation of reward (see review by Wynn, 2008). Such evidence has led some theorists to argue that humans are evolutionarily prepared to be altruistic, even to those who are not their kin, or who cannot reciprocate in some way (Warneken & Tomasello, 2009).

INTERIM SUMMARY

➔ Piaget's theory describes stages in cognitive development. They proceed from the sensorimotor stage (in which an important discovery is object permanence), through the preoperational stage (when symbols begin to be used) and the concrete operational stage (when conservation concepts develop), to the formal operational stage (when hypotheses are tested systematically in problem-solving).

➔ New methods of testing reveal that Piaget's theory underestimates children's abilities, and several alternative approaches have been proposed.

➔ Information-processing approaches view cognitive development as reflecting the gradual development of processes such as attention and memory.

➔ Other theorists emphasize increases in domain-specific knowledge.

➔ Still others, including Vygotsky, focus on the influence of the social and cultural context.

➔ Research on theory of mind is concerned with children's understanding that other people have beliefs and expectations that can be different from their own and different from reality.

➔ Piaget believed that children's understanding of moral rules and judgments develops along with their cognitive abilities. Kohlberg extended Piaget's work to include adolescence and adulthood. He proposed three levels of moral judgment: preconventional, conventional, and postconventional.

➔ More recent research shows that even infants engage in moral judgments and show altruism toward others.

CRITICAL THINKING QUESTIONS

1 What does Piaget's theory suggest about the likely success of academic programs for elementary school children that attempt to 'accelerate' children's cognitive development? What do newer theories of cognitive development suggest about these programs?

2 What level of moral reasoning seems to be implied by campaigns designed to discourage young people from using drugs or being sexually active? Can you think of campaign themes that would appeal to a higher stage of moral reasoning?

PERSONALITY AND SOCIAL DEVELOPMENT

Soon after Christine brought baby Mike home from the hospital, she noticed that he seemed different from her first child, Maggie, at the same age. Maggie had been an easy baby to deal with – Christine's mother and sisters had been amazed at how quickly she fell into a regular sleeping and eating schedule, and how easily she adapted to changes. It seemed she could fall asleep anywhere, and she didn't seem to mind being passed around from relative to relative at the family's large, noisy holiday gatherings. Mike wasn't really difficult to deal with, but it took a bit more time and patience to get him on a regular schedule. Every new experience, from his first bath to his first taste of strained peas, met with mild but clear protest from Mike. But Christine soon discovered that if she soothed him, kept trying, and gave him a little time, he eventually adjusted to each new thing (adapted from DeHart *et al.*, 2000, p. 213).

Like Christine, parents are often surprised that their second child has a very different personality from their first. As early as the first weeks of life, infants show individual differences in activity level, responsiveness to changes in their environment, and irritability. One infant cries a lot; another cries very little. One endures diapering or bathing without much fuss; another kicks and thrashes. One is responsive to every sound; another is oblivious to all but the loudest noises. Infants even differ in 'cuddliness': some seem to enjoy being cuddled and mold themselves to the person holding them; others stiffen and squirm (Rothbart & Bates, 1998). The term **temperament** is used to refer to such mood-related personality characteristics.

Temperament

The observation that temperamental differences arise early in life challenges the traditional view that all of an infant's behaviors are shaped by their environment. Parents of a fussy baby, for example, tend to blame themselves for their infant's difficulties. But research with newborns has shown that many temperamental differences are inborn and that the relationship between parent and infant is reciprocal – in other words, the infant's behavior also shapes the parent's response. An infant who is easily soothed, who snuggles and stops crying when picked up, increases the parent's feelings of competence and attachment. An infant who stiffens and continues to cry, despite efforts to comfort it, makes the parent feel inadequate and rejected. The more responsive a baby is to the stimulation provided by the parent (snuggling and quieting when held, attending alertly when talked to or played with), the easier it is for parent and child to establish a loving bond.

A pioneering study of temperament began in the 1950s with a group of 140 middle- and upper-class American infants.

Fussy child.

The initial data were gathered through interviews with parents and were later supplemented by interviews with teachers and by scores on tests administered to the children. The infants were scored on nine traits, which were later combined to define three broad temperament types. Infants who were playful, were regular in their sleeping and eating patterns, and adapted readily to new situations were classified as having an **easy temperament** (about 40 percent of the sample). Infants who were irritable, had irregular sleeping and eating patterns, and responded intensely and negatively to new situations were classified as having a **difficult temperament** (about 10 percent of the sample). Infants who were relatively inactive, tended to withdraw from new situations in a mild way, and required more time than easy infants to adapt to new situations were classified as having a **slow to warm up temperament** (about 15 percent of the sample). The remaining 35 per cent of the infants were not rated high or low on any of the defining dimensions (Thomas *et al.*, 1963).

Of the original sample, 133 individuals were followed into adult life and again assessed on temperament and psychological adjustment. The results provide mixed evidence for the continuity of temperament. On the one hand, temperament scores across the first 5 years of these children's lives showed significant correlations: children with 'difficult' temperaments were more likely than 'easy' children to have school problems later on. Adult measures of both temperament and adjustment were also significantly correlated with measures of childhood temperament obtained at ages three, four, and five. On the other hand, all the correlations were low (about 0.3), and when considered separately, most of the nine traits measured showed little or no continuity across time (Chess & Thomas, 1984; Thomas & Chess, 1986, 1977).

This early research on the stability of temperament was criticized on several methodological grounds. It relied heavily on parents' reports of their infants' temperaments, and there is reason to believe that parents can be biased in their judgments, either rating their baby more positively or negatively than observers rate the baby. Later research, using both parents' reports and direct observation of children's behavior, suggests that the stability of temperamental characteristics shown in the early infant years is low. That is, a child's temperament at 2 months of age doesn't resemble very closely that child's temperament at age five years. But assessments of temperament made once a child is at least in the toddler years do predict the child's emotional and behavioral characteristics later in life (Rothbart & Bates, 1998). In one study, 79 children were categorized at 21 months as either extremely inhibited or uninhibited. At age 13, those who had been categorized as inhibited at 21 months of age scored significantly lower on a test of externalizing, delinquent behavior and aggressive behavior (Schwartz et al., 1996). Other research has found that the tendency to approach or avoid unfamiliar events, which is an aspect of temperament, remains moderately stable over time (Kagan & Snidman, 1991). There is evidence that temperament is at least somewhat influenced by heredity. Several studies show more similarity in temperament between identical twins than between fraternal twins (Rothbart & Bates, 1998). This greater similarity between identical twins than fraternal twins suggests that genes play a role in temperament, because identical twins share the same genetic makeup, but fraternal twins are no more alike genetically than any other two siblings.

Researchers emphasize that continuity or discontinuity of temperament is a function of the interaction between the child's genotype (inherited characteristics) and the environment. In particular, they believe that the key to healthy development is a good fit between the child's temperament and the home environment. When parents of a difficult child provide a happy, stable home life, the child's negative, difficult behaviors decline with age (Belsky et al., 1991). Thomas and Chess cite the case of Carl, who displayed a very difficult temperament from the first few months of life through age five. Because Carl's father took delight in his son's 'lusty' temperament and allowed for his initial negative reactions to new situations, Carl flourished and became increasingly 'easy.' At age 23 he was

clearly classified into the 'easy' temperament group. Nevertheless, Carl's original temperament often emerged briefly when his life circumstances changed. For example, when he started piano lessons in late childhood, he showed an intense negative response, followed by slow adaptability and eventual positive, zestful involvement. A similar pattern emerged when he entered college (Thomas & Chess, 1986).

Strong evidence for an interaction between genes and environment in producing a child's temperament comes from a study of twins raised apart since early in life (Plomin, 1994). Identical twins raised apart showed some similarity in their tendencies to be inhibited and to show negative emotions, which could be considered aspects of temperament. Yet, the similarity of these twins raised apart was significantly less than the similarity of identical twins raised together, suggesting that environment does play a role.

Early social behavior

Within minutes of birth, babies can imitate gross facial expressions of adults, suggesting they enter the world ready for social interaction (Meltzoff & Decety, 2003). By 5 months of age, the average child smiles at the sight of its mother's or father's face. Delighted with this response, parents go to great lengths to encourage it. Indeed, the infant's ability to smile at such an early age may have evolved precisely because it strengthened the parent–child bond (Goldstein, 1987). Parents interpret these smiles to mean that the infant recognizes and loves them, and this encourages them to be even more affectionate and stimulating in response. A mutually reinforcing system of social interaction is thus established and maintained.

The infant's ability to smile may contribute to a mutually reinforcing system of social interaction with its primary caregivers.

Infants all over the world begin to smile at about the same age, suggesting that maturation plays an important role in determining the onset of smiling. Blind babies also smile at about the same age as sighted infants, indicating that smiling is an innate response (Eibl-Eibesfeldt, 1970).

By their third or fourth month, infants show that they recognize and prefer familiar members of the household by smiling or cooing more when seeing these familiar faces or hearing their voices, but they are still fairly receptive to strangers. At about 7 or 8 months, however, many infants, like the ones depicted in Figure 3.11 begin to show wariness or distress at the approach of a stranger and protest strongly when left in an unfamiliar setting or with an unfamiliar person. Parents are often disconcerted when their formerly gregarious infant, who had always happily welcomed the attentions of a babysitter, now cries inconsolably when they prepare to leave – and continues to cry for some time after they have left. Although not all infants show this stranger anxiety, the number of infants who do increases dramatically from about 8 months of age until the end of the first year. Similarly, distress over separation from the parent reaches a peak between 14 and 18 months and then gradually declines. By the time they are three years old, most children are secure enough in their parents' absence to interact comfortably with other children and adults.

The waxing and waning of these two fears appears to be only slightly influenced by conditions of child rearing. The same general pattern has been observed among American children reared entirely at home and among those attending a day care center. Research by Kagan *et al.*, (1978) showed that although the percentage of children who cry when their mother leaves the room varies in different cultures, the age-related pattern of onset and decline is very similar.

How do we explain the systematic timing of these fears? Two factors seem to be important in both their onset and their decline. One is the growth of memory capacity. During the second half of the first year, infants become better able to remember past events and to compare past and present. This makes it possible for the baby to detect, and sometimes fear, unusual or unpredictable events. The emergence of stranger anxiety coincides with the emergence of fear of a variety of stimuli that are unusual or unexpected. A weird-looking mask or a jack-in-the-box that brings smiles to a 4 month old often causes an 8 month old to look apprehensive and distressed. As children learn that strangers and unusual objects are not generally harmful, such fears gradually diminish.

Memory development is probably also involved in **separation anxiety**, the child's distress when a caretaker is not nearby. The infant cannot 'miss' the parent unless he or she can recall that parent's presence a minute earlier and compare it with the parent's absence now. When the parent leaves the room, the infant is aware that something is amiss, and this can lead to distress. As the child's memory of past instances of separation improves, the child becomes better able to anticipate the return of the absent parent, and anxiety declines. Kagan, Kearsley, & Zelazo wrote about this in 1978,

FIGURE 3.11 Children's Stress at Mother's Departure. *Even though the percentages of children who cry when their mothers leave the room varies from one culture to another, the age-related pattern of onset and decline of such distress is similar across cultures.*

and the findings were that though the percentages of children who cry when their mothers leave the room varies from one culture to another (they studied African Bushmen, Guatemalan Indians, Israeli Kibbutz, and Antigua in Guetemala), the age-related pattern of onsert and decline of such distress is similar across cultures.

The second factor is the growth of **autonomy**, the child's independence from caretakers. One year olds are still highly dependent on the care of adults, but children two or three years old can head for the snack plate or toy shelf on their own. They can also use language to communicate their wants and feelings. Dependence on caregivers in general and on familiar caregivers in particular decreases, and the parent's presence becomes less critical for the child.

Attachment

The term **attachment** is used to describe an infant's tendency to seek closeness to particular people and to feel more secure in their presence. Psychologists at first theorized that attachment to the mother developed because she was the source of food, one of the infant's most basic needs. But some facts did not fit. For example, ducklings and baby chicks feed themselves from birth, yet they still follow their mothers about and spend a great deal of time with them. The comfort they derive from the mother's presence cannot come from her role in feeding. A well-known series of experiments with monkeys also showed that there is more to mother–infant attachment than nutritional needs (Harlow & Harlow, 1969).

Infant monkeys were separated from their mothers shortly after birth and placed with two artificial 'mothers' constructed of wire mesh with wooden heads. The torso of one mother was bare wire; the other was covered with foam rubber and terry cloth, making it cuddly and easy to cling to (see Figure 3.12). Either mother could be equipped to provide milk by means of a bottle attached to its chest.

The experiment sought to determine whether the young monkey would cling to the mother that was always the source of food. The results were clear-cut: no matter which mother provided food, the infant monkey spent its time clinging to the terry-cloth mother. This purely passive but soft-contact mother was a source of security. For example, the obvious fear of the infant monkey placed in a strange environment was allayed if the infant could make contact with the cloth mother. While holding on to the cloth mother with one hand or foot, the monkey was willing to explore objects that were otherwise too terrifying to approach.

Although contact with a cuddly, artificial mother provides an important aspect of 'mothering,' it is not enough for satisfactory development. Infant monkeys raised with artificial mothers and isolated from other monkeys during the first 6 months of life showed bizarre behavior in adulthood. They rarely engaged in normal interaction with other monkeys later on (either cowering in fear or showing abnormally aggressive

FIGURE 3.12 **A Monkey's Response to an Artificial Mother.** *Although it is fed via a wire mother, the infant spends more time with the terry-cloth mother. The terry-cloth mother provides a safe base from which to explore strange objects.*

behavior), and their sexual responses were inappropriate. When female monkeys that had been deprived of early social contact were successfully mated (after considerable effort), they made poor mothers, tending to neglect or abuse their first-born infants – although they became better mothers with their later children. Note, however, that these monkeys were deprived of all social contact. Monkeys with artificial mothers do fine as adults if they are allowed to interact with their peers during the first 6 months.

Although generalizing from research on monkeys to human development requires care, there is evidence that the human infant's attachment to the primary caregiver serves the same functions. Most of the work on attachment in human infants originated with the psychoanalyst John Bowlby in the 1950s and 1960s. Bowlby became interested in attachment while watching the behaviors of infants and young children who were in residential nurseries and hospital wards and therefore separated from their mothers. His research convinced him that a child's failure to form a secure attachment to one or more persons in the early years is related to an inability to develop close personal relationships in adulthood (Bowlby, 1973).

Mary Ainsworth, one of Bowlby's associates, made extensive observations of children and their mothers in Uganda and the USA and then developed a laboratory

TABLE 3.1 EPISODES IN THE STRANGE SITUATION PROCEDURE

1. A mother and her child enter the room. The mother places the baby on the floor, surrounded by toys, and goes to sit at the opposite end of the room.
2. A female stranger enters the room, sits quietly for a minute, converses with the mother for a minute, and then attempts to engage the baby in play with a toy.
3. The mother leaves the room unobtrusively. If the baby is not upset, the stranger returns to sitting quietly. If the baby is upset, the stranger tries to soothe him or her.
4. The mother returns and engages the baby in play while the stranger slips out of the room.
5. The mother leaves again, this time leaving the baby alone in the room.
6. The stranger returns. If the baby is upset, the stranger tries to comfort him or her.
7. The mother returns and the stranger slips out of the room.

procedure for assessing the security of a child's attachments from about 12 to 18 months of age (Ainsworth *et al.*, 1978). This procedure, called the **strange situation**, is a series of episodes in which a child is observed as the primary caregiver leaves and returns to the room (see Table 3.1). Throughout this sequence, the baby is observed through a one-way mirror and several observations are recorded: the baby's activity level and play involvement, crying and other distress signs, proximity to and attempts to gain the attention of the mother, proximity to and willingness to interact with the stranger, and so on. On the basis of their behaviors, babies are categorized into one of the following three groups:

Securely attached. Regardless of whether they are upset at the mother's departures (episodes 3 and 5), babies who are classified as securely attached seek to interact with her when she returns. Some are content simply to acknowledge her return from a distance while continuing to play with the toys. Others seek physical contact with her. Still others are completely preoccupied with the mother throughout the entire session, showing intense distress when she leaves. The majority of babies fall into this category.

Insecurely attached: avoidant. These babies avoid interacting with the mother during the reunion episodes. Some ignore her almost entirely; others display mixed attempts to interact and avoid interacting. Avoidant babies may pay little attention to the mother when she is in the room and often do not seem distressed when she leaves. If they are distressed, they are as easily comforted by the stranger as by the mother.

Insecurely attached: ambivalent. Babies are classified as ambivalent if they show resistance to the mother during the reunion episodes. They simultaneously seek and resist physical contact. For example, they may cry to be picked up and then squirm angrily to get down. Some act very passive, crying for the mother when she returns but not crawling toward her, and then showing resistance when she approaches.

Because some babies did not seem to fit any of these categories, studies have included a fourth category, **disorganized** (Main & Solomon, 1986). Babies in this category often show contradictory behaviors. For example, they may approach the mother while taking care not to look at her, approach her and then show dazed avoidance, or suddenly cry out after having settled down. Some seem disoriented, appear emotionless, or look depressed. Babies who are maltreated or whose parents are being treated for mental disorders are more likely to fall into this category.

Parenting styles

In attempting to account for differences in attachment among babies, researchers have directed most of their attention to the behavior of the primary caregiver, usually the mother. The main finding is that a caregiver's **sensitive responsiveness** to the baby's needs produces secure attachment. Mothers of securely attached babies usually respond promptly when the baby cries and behave affectionately when they pick up the baby. They also tailor their responses to the baby's needs (Clarke-Stewart, 1973). In feeding, for example, they use an infant's signals to determine when to begin and end feeding, and they attend to the baby's food preferences. In contrast, mothers of babies who are insecurely attached respond according to their own needs or moods rather than according to signals from the baby. For example, they respond to the baby's cries for attention when they feel like cuddling the baby but ignore such cries at other times (Stayton, 1973).

Not all developmental psychologists agree that the caregiver's responsiveness is the major cause of an infant's attachment behaviors. They call attention to the baby's own inborn temperament (Campos *et al.*, 1983; Kagan, 1984). Perhaps the temperaments that make some babies 'easy' also make them more securely attached than do the temperaments of 'difficult' babies. And, as noted earlier, a parent's response to a child is often itself a function of the child's own behavior. For example, mothers of difficult babies tend to spend less time playing with them (Green *et al.*, 1983). Attachment patterns may reflect this interaction between a baby's temperament and the parents' responsiveness.

In reply, attachment theorists point to evidence that supports the 'sensitive responsiveness' hypothesis. For example, in the first year of life, an infant's crying changes much more than the mother's responsiveness to the crying does. Moreover, the mother's responsiveness over a 3-month period predicts the infant's crying over the next 3 months significantly better than the infant's crying predicts the mother's subsequent responsiveness to crying. In short, the mother appears to influence the infant's crying more than the infant influences the mother's responsiveness to crying (Bell & Ainsworth, 1972). In general, the mother's behavior

Attachment patterns reflect a baby's temperament and a parent's responsiveness.

appears to be the most important factor in establishing a secure or insecure attachment (Isabella & Belsky, 1991).

Other research may resolve this debate. Recall that the attachment classification is based not on the baby's distress when the mother leaves but on how the baby reacts when she returns. It appears that an infant's temperament predicts the former but not the latter (Frodi & Thompson, 1985; Vaughn et al., 1989). Babies with easy temperaments typically are not distressed when the mother leaves. When she returns, they tend to greet her happily – showing secure attachment – or show the avoidant type of insecure attachment. Babies with difficult temperaments typically are distressed when the mother leaves. When she returns, they tend to seek her out and cling to her – showing secure attachment – or show the ambivalent type of insecure attachment (Belsky & Rovine, 1987). Children's overall reaction to the departure and return of their primary caregiver is a function of both the caregiver's responsiveness to the child and the child's temperament.

Later development

A baby's attachment classification remains quite stable when re-tested several years later – unless the family experiences major changes in life circumstances (Main & Cassidy, 1988; Thompson et al., 1982). Stressful life changes are likely to affect parental responsiveness to the baby, which, in turn, affects the baby's feelings of security.

Early attachment patterns also appear to be related to how children cope with new experiences. In one study, 2 year olds were given a series of problems requiring the use of tools. Some of the problems were within the child's capacity; others were quite difficult. Children who had been rated as securely attached at 12 months approached the problems with enthusiasm and persistence. When they encountered difficulties, they seldom cried or became angry. Rather, they sought help from adults. Children who had earlier been rated as insecurely attached behaved quite differently. They easily became frustrated and angry, seldom asked for help, tended to ignore or reject directions from adults, and quickly gave up trying to solve the problems (Matas et al., 1978).

These and similar studies suggest that children who are securely attached by the time they enter their second year are better equipped to cope with new experiences. However, we cannot be certain that the quality of children's early attachments is directly responsible for their later competence in problem-solving. Parents who are responsive to their children's needs in infancy probably continue to provide effective parenting during early childhood – encouraging autonomy and efforts to cope with new experiences, yet ready with help when needed. A child's competence may therefore reflect the current state of the parent–child relationship rather than the relationship that existed 2 years earlier. Moreover, children's temperament – which, as we saw earlier, affects their behavior in the strange situation procedure – might also influence their competence as preschoolers.

Cultural differences in attachment classifications

Although Ainsworth conducted some research in Uganda, the majority of her work was in middle-class American samples. Subsequent research suggested there is wide variation in the percentages of children classified into the traditional attachment categories based on their responses to the strange situation paradigm (see Table 3.2). For example, the majority of German infants were categorized as having either an avoidant or anxious attachment style, and much larger percentages of Japanese and Israeli infants were categorized as having the anxious attachment style compared to American, Dutch, Swedish, or British infants (Thompson, 1998).

These cultural differences may arise because the strange situation task is an inappropriate indicator of the quality of the relationship between mother and child in many cultures (Keil, in press). For example, Japanese infants typically are not separated from their mothers much at all in their early years, thus the forced separation created by the strange situation may be particularly frightening to them, leading them to be classified as 'insecure: anxious.' In contrast, some German children are encouraged to be independent from their mothers at an early age; their responses to the strange situation may have suggested they were 'insecure: avoidant' when they were really demonstrating their familiarity with independence. This is not to say that there are not differences in interpersonal styles

TABLE 3.2

The percentages of attachment styles as measured by the Strange Situation, varies dramatically across different cultures. Percentages do not add up to 100 because attachment styles could not be reliably coded for some infants or were coded as Type D.

	Avoidant	Secure	Anxious
Sweden	21.57%	74.51%	3.92%
Israel	8.43%	56.63%	33.73%
Great Britain	22.22%	75.00%	2.78%
Japan	0.00%	68.33%	31.67%
Germany	48.9%	32.65%	12.24%
Netherlands	34.15%	5.85%	0.00%
USA	21.70%	66.04%	12.26%

across cultures. Rather, results from the strange situation must be understood within the cultural milieu of the child, and not misinterpreted to conclude that some cultures are better at raising secure children than others.

Self-concept

If you stealthily put a red smudge on the forehead of an 18-month-old child without her realizing it, then put her in front of a mirror, she will reach up and touch the mark on her head (Gallup, 1998). This rudimentary test, called the *mirror test*, indicates that children this young have some sense that the image in the mirror is themselves, and that it is different from what they usually look like. Prior to about 18 months, children in the mirror test will either not reach up and touch the mark on their own head or will try to touch the mark on the 'other child's' head in the mirror.

Children's **self-concepts** grow steadily through development, and encompass many different aspects of self (Harter,

Children's self-concepts develop as they grow.

1998; Neisser, 1988). These may include a sense of their bodies in space and a sense of the self as continuous in time ('I am who I am, yesterday and today'). Children develop a sense of themselves as social agents interacting with others and a sense of the self in the broader social and cultural context, including their roles in relation to others. Finally, as we discussed somewhat in the section on 'theory of mind; children have a sense of the self as a private entity that others do not have direct access to.

Self-esteem

One aspect of the self that has been studied extensively in children is **self-esteem**, which we might define as the value-laden sense of self (Harter, 1998). Children's self-esteem generally shows several patterns of change from preschool into the adolescent years. Preschoolers tend to have extremely positive views of themselves that are sometimes comically unrealistic. A 3 year old may boast that he is the bravest, fastest, smartest kid around! This extreme self-optimism may be adaptive for the young child, giving him confidence to persist even in the face of frequent failures.

Children in the early school years tend to be positive, but not as unrealistically positive as preschoolers. They may compare themselves to others, but more often compare themselves to their younger selves, commenting on how much taller, stronger, or bigger they now are (Ruble & Frey, 1991). They may become discouraged if they fail at tasks (Lewis *et al.*, 1992), but failures usually do not have a persistent effect on their general sense of self.

In middle childhood (roughly ages 8–12), children engage in considerably more comparisons of themselves and their skills to other children, and these social comparisons begin to influence the children's self-esteem (Frey & Ruble, 1990). For example, a child may notice that she can't kick the ball as far as her soccer team-mates, or run as fast, and conclude that she is not as good an athlete as others. Children's self-esteem is often domain-specific; they will tell you they are not a good athlete, but they are good at math, for example. But although children may differentiate between their abilities in different domains, they are beginning to make trait-attributions for themselves, for example, believing they will never be good at athletics, but they will continue to be good at math.

Finally, in adolescence and young adulthood, social comparison becomes key to self-esteem. Young people care deeply about how they compare to others, and what others think of them. These social comparisons and evaluations can have profound effects on how positively they think of themselves (although young people differ greatly in how susceptible they are to these evaluations). Their sense of self becomes complex, and they increasingly think of themselves in terms of enduring traits and dispositions. Moreover, in many societies, young people must begin making life choices based on their own, and others; evaluations of their talents and capabilities.

Peers are increasingly important to self-concept in adolescence.

INTERIM SUMMARY

➜ Some early social behaviors, such as smiling, reflect innate responses that appear at about the same time in all infants, including blind infants. The emergence of many later social behaviors – including wariness of strangers and distress over separation from primary caregivers – appears to depend on the child's developing cognitive skills.

➜ An infant's tendency to seek closeness to particular people and to feel more secure in their presence is called attachment. Attachment can be assessed in a procedure called the strange situation, a series of episodes in which a child is observed as the primary caregiver leaves and returns to the room.

➜ Securely attached infants seek to interact with a caretaker who returns from an absence.

➜ Insecurely attached: avoidant infants avoid a caretaker returning from an absence.

➜ Insecurely attached: ambivalent infants show resistance to a caretaker returning from an absence.

➜ Disorganized infants show contradictory behaviors (sometimes avoidant, sometimes approaching) to a caretaker returning from an absence.

➜ A caregiver's sensitive responsiveness to a baby's needs has important influences on the security of the attachment. The baby's temperament also plays a role.

➜ There are cultural differences in the percentage of babies classified in various attachment categories. These differences may indicate that the strange situation paradigm is not an appropriate test of attachment across cultures.

➜ Children's self-concepts grow throughout development, from a generally positive sense of the self to a more complex, domain-specific sense of one's enduring traits and capabilities.

CRITICAL THINKING QUESTIONS

1 Some psychologists have suggested that our childhood attachment styles can influence the kinds of romantic relationships we form as adults. What forms might the attachment styles discussed in this chapter assume in an adult romantic relationship? Can you relate your own adult 'attachment styles' to your childhood attachment style, or to features of your childhood environment?

2 Would your parents have characterized your infant personality as easy, difficult, or slow to warm up? Which aspects of your current personality seem to be primarily a reflection of your inborn temperament, which aspects seem to reflect the way you were raised, and which aspects seem to reflect a blend or interaction between nature and nurture?

ADOLESCENT DEVELOPMENT

Adolescence refers to the period of transition from childhood to adulthood. It extends roughly from age 12 to the late teens, when physical growth is nearly complete. During this period, the young person becomes sexually mature and establishes an identity as an individual apart from the family.

Biological development

Puberty, the period of sexual maturation that transforms a child into a biologically mature adult capable of sexual reproduction, takes place over a period of 3 or 4 years. It starts with a period of very rapid physical growth (the so-called **adolescent growth spurt**) accompanied by gradual development of the reproductive organs and secondary sex characteristics (breast development in girls, beard growth in boys, and the appearance of pubic hair in both sexes).

There is wide variation in the age at which puberty begins and the rate at which it progresses. Some girls attain **menarche**, the first menstrual period, before age 11, others as late as 17, and the average age is about 12 years. Boys, on average, experience their growth spurt and mature about 2 years later than girls. The wide variation in the timing of puberty is strikingly apparent in classrooms of young adolescents. Some of the girls look like mature women with fully developed breasts and rounded hips; others still have the size and shape of little girls. Some of the boys are gangly adolescents; others look much as they did at the age of nine or ten. (See the discussion of hormonal changes at puberty in Chapter 10.)

The brain undergoes a great deal of development and change in adolescence. In early adolescence the areas of the brain involved in emotion, reward, and motivation (e.g., the amygdala and ventral striatum) become more reactive to

CUTTING EDGE RESEARCH ADOLESCENTS AND THE INTERNET

Susan Nolen-Hoeksema, Yale University

The Internet is a fixture in the lives of adolescents in many nations. Between 85 and 98 per cent of teenagers in the UK and the USA use the Internet, and over half log on daily, surfing the web, trading emails, and creating their own websites (Lenhart *et al.*, 2005). The most frequent use of the Internet among teens is communicating with friends (Gross, 2004). Through emails, text messages, and social networking sites, teens communicate with friends they way they formerly did by phone, sharing personal information and gossip. Given the prevalence of Internet use among today's youth, researchers have begun to assess whether adolescents' Internet use is good or bad for their development and well-being.

One of the greatest fears for parents is that their Internet-surfing teens will become victims of online sexual predators. Sexual solicitation and harassment are not rare experiences for teens. One study of over 1500 adolescents in the U.S. found that one in four had experienced at least one unwanted sexual solicitation or harassment over the Internet in the last year (Mitchell *et al.*, 2007). The youths who had been victimized were more depressed, anxious, and afraid than those who had not been victimized. Some youths engage in risky behaviors that increase their risk of victimization. A study of teenagers in New Zealand found that one-third had given out personal information on the Internet, and one-quarter had actually met in person with someone they had met on the Internet (Berson & Berson, 2005).

Another concern is that some troubled teens use the Internet to facilitate their maladaptive behaviors. For example, one study found over 400 message boards for 'self-injurors,' people who engage in cutting, burning, and otherwise harming themselves (Whitlock *et al.*, 2006). The vast majority of visitors to these sites were teenage girls. On the one hand, these sites provided these girls with an opportunity to talk about their behaviors and their feelings with supportive others. Many girls who engage in self-injury are depressed and isolated, hiding their self-injury from their parents and friends, but desperate to talk to someone. These message boards provide social support and encouragement to seek professional help. On the other hand, these message boards also may normalize self-injury, making it seem common and acceptable, thereby reinforcing the behaviors. Some boards even provide 'how to' instructions on self-injury, and on hiding self-injuries from others. Similar concerns have been raised about message boards for people with eating disorders, which normalize the behavior and provide 'training' as to how to successfully engage in bingeing (compulsive and uncontrollable eating of large amounts of food), purging, and self-starvation.

There are also many benefits to Internet use for teens, however. Researchers gave a group of African-American teens home access to the Internet, and found that those who used the Internet more showed increases in standardized academic test scores over a 16-month period (Jackson *et al.*, 2007). The authors speculate that engagement on the Internet provided youths with opportunities to improve reading skills, and generally increased their motivation to learn. Internet-based programs are also providing health interventions to people who might not otherwise have access to them. A weight-loss program called Hipteens included exercises for overweight teen girls to evaluate their food intake, plan dietary changes, recognize triggers for eating, and communicate with personal counselors (Williamson *et al.*, 2007). The adolescents who participated in the program lost significantly more body fat over the first six months than a control group of adolescents who did not participate in the program. As adolescents' use of the web-based program declined beyond the initial six months, however, they tended to gain back the weight.

Thus, it seems that the Internet can be both a danger and detriment in teens' lives, and a benefit and force for positive change. Supervision by parents of their adolescents' Internet use is an important safeguard to increase the good, and protect against the bad that the Internet can bring.

---

emotional and social stimuli, and to rewards (Ernst *et al.*, 2006; Guyer *et al.*, 2008). This, along with pubertal hormonal changes, may account for greater fluctuations in daily emotional states, more extreme emotional experiences (both positive and negative), and stronger biases towards emotional stimuli in young adolescents compared with children and adults (Larson & Richards, 1994; Quevedo *et al.*, 2009; Silk *et al.*, 2009).

In contrast, frontal areas of the brain involved in cognitive control of impulses and behaviors develop later in adolescence (Casey *et al.*, 2010). These frontal regions of the brain continue to develop into young adulthood, reorganizing through synaptic pruning over an extended period of time (Durston & Casey, 2006).

As a result of the disjunction in timing of development of the emotional and cognitive control areas of the brain, adolescence has been characterized as a period of 'all gas and no breaks' or as 'starting the engines with an unskilled driver' (Dahl, 2004; Steinberg, 2008). Adolescents are greatly oriented and reactive to the emotional and social environment, and hypersensitive to rewarding stimuli, while not yet having well-developed control over their emotions, desires, and behaviors. One consequence is that adolescents tend to engage in significantly more risk-taking behaviors than children or adults (Steinberg, 2008). Indeed, the rate of accidents, violence, suicide and risky sexual and health behaviors all increase dramatically in adolescence (Ozer *et al.*, 2002).

Social relationships in adolescence

Peers become extremely important in adolescence. During adolescence, time spent with peers and friends increases and elevated positive moods are experienced in these contexts. In contrast, time spent with parents decreases and is characterized by more negative affect (Larson & Richards, 1991). Peers are highly influential on adolescents' behavior. For example, in a simulated driving game, adolescents' risk-taking behavior increases when same-age peers are in the room compared to no peers, and this increase is greater for adolescents than for children or adults (Gardner & Steinberg, 2008).

Parents often report a lot of storm and stress in their relationships with their adolescents, and here the research largely backs up the common lore (Steinberg & Morris, 2001). Bickering and squabbling between parents and their offspring increase in adolescence, and there is a decline in how close parents and adolescents feel to each other (Larson & Richards, 1991). Adolescents typically pull away from their parents in an attempt to forge their own individual identities, and many parents are distressed by this withdrawal (Silverberg & Steinberg, 1990). In most families, however, the period of increased conflict in early adolescence is followed by the establishment of a new parent–adolescent relationship that is less volatile and more egalitarian. Parents who remain authoritative – warm and supportive but firm and clear about rules and their enforcement – tend to have adolescents who come through the adolescent years with the least enduring problems (Steinberg & Morris, 2001). In contrast, adolescents whose parents are authoritarian (with rigid rules and little obvious warmth in their dealings with their children) or overly permissive tend to encounter more emotional and behavioral problems (Baumrind, 1980).

The psychoanalyst Erik Erikson believed that the major task confronting the adolescent is to develop a sense of identity, to find answers to the questions 'Who am I?' and 'Where am I going?' Although Erikson coined the term **identity crisis** to refer to this active process of self-definition, he believed that it is an integral part of healthy psychosocial development. Similarly, most developmental psychologists believe that adolescence should be a period of role experimentation for young people to explore various behaviors, interests, and ideologies. Many beliefs, roles, and ways of behaving may be tried on, modified, or discarded in an attempt to shape an integrated concept of the self.

Adolescents try to synthesize these values and appraisals into a consistent picture. If parents, teachers, and peers project consistent values, the search for identity is easier. In a simple society in which adult models are few and social roles are limited, the task of forming an identity is relatively easy. In complex societies, it is a difficult task for many adolescents. They are faced with an almost infinite array of possibilities regarding how to behave and what to do in life. As a result, there are large differences among adolescents in how the development of

In most families, conflict between teens and parents is short-lived.

their identity proceeds. Moreover, any particular adolescent's identity may be at different stages of development in different areas of life (for example, sexual, occupational, and ideological).

Ideally, the identity crisis should be resolved by the early or mid-twenties so that the individual can move on to other life tasks. When the process is successful, the individual is said to have achieved an identity – a coherent sense of sexual identity, vocational direction, and ideological worldview. Until the identity crisis is resolved, the individual has no consistent sense of self or set of internal standards for evaluating his or her self-worth in major areas of life. Erikson called this unsuccessful outcome **identity confusion**.

More contemporary research has focused on the development of self-concept from the perspective of cognitive theories, rather than based on Erikson's stages of identity development. As adolescents mature cognitively, they develop more abstract characterizations of themselves. They begin to view themselves more in terms of personal beliefs and standards and less according to social comparisons (Harter, 1998). Adolescents' self-concepts vary across different situations, so that they see themselves differently when they are with parents than when they are with peers (Harter, 1998). They often engage in behaviors that do not represent how they really see themselves, especially among classmates or in romantic relationships.

In early adolescence, self-esteem is somewhat unstable but becomes more stable during later adolescence (Harter, 1998). African–American adolescents tend to have higher self-esteem than white adolescents (Gray-Little & Hafdahl, 2000), and males have higher self-esteem than females (Kling et al., 1999). Not surprisingly, however, across both genders and most ethnic groups, higher self-esteem is related to parental approval, peer support, adjustment, and success in school (DuBois et al., 1998).

During adolescence and early adulthood, many minority youth struggle with their ethnic identity, and their resolution of this struggle can come in many forms (Phinney & Alipuria, 1990; Sellers et al., 1998). Some minority youth assimilate into the majority culture by rejecting their own culture. Some live in the majority culture but feel estranged.

SEEING BOTH SIDES

HOW INSTRUMENTAL ARE PARENTS IN THE DEVELOPMENT OF THEIR CHILDREN?

PARENTS HAVE NO LASTING INFLUENCE ON THE PERSONALITY OR INTELLIGENCE OF THEIR CHILDREN.

Judith Rich Harris, award-winning psychologist and author
(The Nurture Assumption, No Two Alike)

Your parents took care of you when you were little. They taught you many things. They play leading roles in your memories of childhood. Nevertheless, your parents may have had no lasting impact on your personality or intelligence or on the way you behave when they're not around.

Hard to believe? Try to put aside your gut reaction for a moment and consider the evidence. Consider, for example, studies designed to separate the effects of genes from those of the home environment by examining pairs of people who are or are not biologically related, and who did or did not grow up in the same home (Plomin *et al.*, 2012). Such studies have shown that having similar genes makes people more alike, but that sharing a childhood home environment does not. Unless they are biologically related, people who grew up in the same home are not noticeably more alike in personality or intelligence than two people picked at random from the same population. Almost all the similarities between brothers or sisters reared together are due to the genes they have in common. If they are adoptive siblings, they are no more alike than adoptees reared in different homes. On average, an adopted child reared by agreeable parents is no nicer than one reared by grouches. One reared by parents who love books is no smarter, as an adult, than one reared by parents who love soap operas (Harris, 1995, 2009).

These findings don't fit conventional views of child development but they are backed up by a variety of other observations. For example, the only child does not, on average, differ in personality from children who have to vie with their siblings for parental attention (Falbo, 2012). Behavioral differences between boys and girls did not diminish when parents began to try to treat their sons and daughters alike (Serbin *et al.*, 1993). Children who speak Korean or Spanish at home but English with their peers end up as English speakers. The language learned outside the home takes precedence over the one their parents taught them – and, unlike their parents, they speak it without a foreign accent (Harris, 2006).

But what about the evidence that dysfunctional parents tend to have dysfunctional offspring, and that children who are treated with affection tend to turn out better than children who are treated harshly? The trouble with this evidence is that it comes from studies that provide no way to distinguish genetic from environmental influences, or causes from effects. Are the offspring's problems due to the unfavorable environment provided by the parents or to personality characteristics inherited from them? Do the hugs cause the child to develop a pleasant personality, or does her pleasant personality make her parents want to hug her? Research using appropriate methods has shown that the problems are at least partly inherited and that the child's pleasant personality evokes the hugs (Reiss, 2005).

Some developmental psychologists have tried to explain away the findings that puzzle them by claiming that parents do have important effects but it's difficult to measure them. The difficulty is blamed on the fact that the outcome of a given style of parenting depends upon the child's genetic makeup (Collins *et al.*, 2000). Undoubtedly, some individuals are genetically more vulnerable than others (Caspi *et al.*, 2011), but this can't account for the negative results of the studies I described above (Harris, 2006). Nor can it account for the fact that reared-together identical twins often differ in personality and in mental health problems. Identical twins have the same genes and thus should react similarly to parental treatment, but pairs reared in the same home – treated very much alike by their parents – are no more alike in personality than those separated at birth. Nor are they *less* alike (Bouchard & McGue, 2003).

There is no question that parents influence the way their children behave at home. The problem is that the way children behave at home is not a good predictor of how they'll behave in the classroom or playground. When researchers discover that children behave differently in different social contexts, they usually assume that the way children behave with their parents is somehow more important or long-lasting than the way they behave elsewhere. But the children who speak Korean or Spanish at home and English outside the home use English as their primary language in adulthood. A boy whose cries evoke sympathy when he hurts himself at home learns not to cry when he hurts himself on the playground, and as an adult he seldom cries. A child who is dominated by her older sibling at home is no more likely than a firstborn to allow herself to be dominated by her peers (Abramovitch *et al.*, 1986). Children learn separately how to behave at home and outside the home, and it's their outside-the-home behavior they bring with them to adulthood. This makes sense, since they are not destined to spend their adult lives in their parents' house.

The notion that children are in a great hurry to grow up and that they see their own world as a pale imitation of the adult world is an adult-o-centric one. A child's goal is not to be like her mother or his father: it's to be a successful child. Children have their own agenda; they are not putty in their parents' hands. They have to learn how to get along in the world outside the home, and out there the rules are different.

Judith Rich Harris

HOW INSTRUMENTAL ARE PARENTS IN THE DEVELOPMENT OF THEIR CHILDREN?

PARENTS ARE INSTRUMENTAL IN THE DEVELOPMENT OF THEIR CHILDREN

Jerome Kagan, Harvard University

The development of the skills, values, and social behaviors that facilitate a child's adaptation to his or her society requires an orchestration of a number of relatively independent conditions. The most important are: (1) inherited temperamental biases, (2) the social class, ethnic, and religious affiliations of the child's family, which become bases for later identifications, (3) social relationships with siblings and peers, (4) historical era and the culture in which childhood and adolescence are spent, and (5) the behaviors and personality of the parents.

The parents' influences assume two different forms. The first refers to their direct interactions with their child, including the behaviors they reward or punish, the skills they praise, and the actions that their children interpret either as signs of affection implying that they are valued, or signs of indifference or neglect which are interpreted as rejection or hostility. Parents who talk or read to their children typically produce adolescents with the largest vocabularies, the highest intelligence scores, and the best grades (Raikes *et al.*, 2006). Parents who reason with their children while making requests for obedience typically have more civil children (Kagan, 1998). The power of the family is seen in a study of over 1000 children from ten different American cities who were raised only at home or had surrogate care for varied amounts of time each week. The family had the most important influence on the older child's personality, cognitive skills, and character (NICHD Early Childcare Research Network, 2004). Even children who were orphaned, or made homeless by war, were able to regain intellectual and social skills they did not develop during their early privation, if they were adopted before age 4 by nurturant, accepting families (Rathbun *et al.*, 1958).

Culture and historical period can bias the child to construct different interpretations of the same behaviors. Almost all children of Puritan parents growing up in seventeenth-century New England were punished harshly, but most interpreted these practices as motivated by the parents' desire for them to develop good character. As a result, the undesirable consequences of harsh punishment that would occur in contemporary New England did not occur in the seventeenth century. Chinese parents centuries ago used to bind the feet of their young daughters in order to make them attractive to future suitors. Although this was extremely painful and compromised their ability to walk, most girls accepted this burden because they believed it served their interests. The same conclusion would not be arrived at today. The important principle is that it is the child's interpretation of the parents' behaviors, not the actual behaviors, that is critical for development.

Children are also influenced by their parents' personality characteristics and behaviors that are not necessarily direct interactions with the child. Children arrive at conclusions about themselves, often incorrect, because they assume that since they are biological offspring, they probably possess some psychological qualities of their parents. This emotionally charged belief, called *identification*, is the basis for pride in and loyalty to one's family, on the one hand, or shame over undesirable parental characteristics, including alcoholism, criminality, or unemployment, on the other. If children perceive their parent as affectionate, fair, and talented, they are likely to assume that they, too, possess desirable traits and, as a result, feel more confident than they are entitled to given the objective evidence. Children who perceive a parent as rejecting, unfair in doling out punishment, or without talent feel ashamed because they assume that they may possess some of the same undesirable characteristics (Kagan, 1998).

By the sixth or seventh birthday, children have begun to identify with the social class of their family. Children from affluent, middle-class families come to believe that they have a greater sense of agency and more privilege than children from economically disadvantaged families. The latter are apt to perceive their relative deprivation of material advantage as implying some compromise in their sense of psychological potency. This belief is usually supported by parental actions and communications implying that life is difficult and their children face serious obstacles as they plan their lives. As a result, the social class of rearing in North America and Europe is the best predictor of IQ scores, grades in school, criminality, future occupation, and a variety of illnesses (Werner & Smith, 1982; Johnson *et al.*, 1990).

The dramatic advances in the neurosciences and genetics, disseminated by the media, have persuaded many Americans and Europeans that genes are the more important cause of the intellectual and emotional profiles of adolescents. However, this claim is exaggerated. The evidence reveals that the family remains an important cause of variation in many psychological traits, especially values, academic talents, and attitude toward authority, more important than any gene discovered thus far. The current attraction to genetic determinism is popular because it removes some of the blame from the family for undesirable outcomes in their children.

Most societies, ancient and modern, believe that the family has a significant influence on children, but it is often difficult to measure. A commentator who denies parental influence resembles someone who decides on a foggy morning that the trees have disappeared because they cannot see them.

Jerome Kagan

Some reject the majority culture and focus only on their own culture. And some try to find a balance between the majority culture and their own culture, a resolution sometimes referred to as biculturalism.

INTERIM SUMMARY

➔ Puberty has significant effects on an adolescent's body image, self-esteem, moods, and relationships; but most adolescents make it through this period without major turmoil.

➔ According to Erikson's theory, forming a personal sense of identity is the major task of the adolescent period.

CRITICAL THINKING QUESTIONS

1   Can you identify how and when your religious, sexual, occupational, and political identities have developed and changed over your adolescence?

2   What experiences might influence the development of a minority youth's ethnic identity? For example, what experiences might lead a youth to develop a bicultural identity, and what experiences might lead a youth to reject majority culture?

CHAPTER SUMMARY

1 Some developmental psychologists believe that development occurs in a sequence of periods in which (a) behaviors at a given stage are organized around a dominant theme or a coherent set of characteristics, (b) behaviors at one stage are qualitatively different from behaviors at earlier or later stages, and (c) all children go through the same stages in the same order. Critical or sensitive periods are times during development when specific experiences must occur for psychological development to proceed normally.

2 Early theorists believed that all sensory preferences and abilities had to be learned, but research over the last several decades has established that infants are born with their sensory systems intact and prepared to learn about the world.

3 Newborns have poor vision and cannot see as well as an adult until about age two. Some theorists thought infants were born with a preference for faces, but research suggests infants are not attracted to faces per se but to stimulus characteristics such as curved lines, high contrast, edges, movement, and complexity – all of which possess faces. Even newborns pay attention to sounds. They seem to be born with perceptual mechanisms that are already tuned to the properties of human speech that will help them learn language. Infants can discriminate between different tastes and odors shortly after birth. They seem to prefer the taste and odor of breast milk. Infants can learn from the moment they are born and show good memories by 3 months of age.

4 Piaget's theory describes stages in cognitive development. These proceed from the sensorimotor stage (in which an important discovery is object permanence),

through the preoperational stage (when symbols begin to be used) and the concrete operational stage (when conservation concepts develop), to the formal operational stage (when hypotheses are tested systematically in problem-solving). New methods of testing reveal that Piaget's theory underestimates children's abilities, and several alternative approaches have been proposed.

5 Information-processing approaches view cognitive development as reflecting the gradual development of processes such as attention and memory. Other theorists emphasize increases in domain-specific knowledge. Still others, including Vygotsky, focus on the influence of the social and cultural context. More recent research in children's cognitive development focuses on children's theory of mind, or understanding that other people have beliefs and expectations that can be different from their own and different from reality.

6 Piaget believed that children's understanding of moral rules and judgments develops along with their cognitive abilities. Kohlberg extended Piaget's work to include adolescence and adulthood. He proposed three levels of moral judgment: preconventional, conventional, and postconventional.

7 An infant's tendency to seek closeness to particular people and to feel more secure in their presence is called *attachment*. Attachment can be assessed in a procedure called the *strange situation*, a series of episodes in which a child is observed as the primary caregiver leaves and returns to the room. Securely attached infants seek to interact with a caretaker who returns from an absence. Insecurely attached:

avoidant infants avoid a caretaker who returns from an absence. Insecurely attached: ambivalent infants show resistance to a caretaker who returns from an absence. Disorganized infants show contradictory behaviors (sometimes avoidant, sometimes approaching) to a caretaker who returns from an absence.

8 A caregiver's sensitive responsiveness to a baby's needs has important influences on attachment. The baby's temperament also plays a role. Cultural differences in the percentage of children classified in different attachment categories may indicate that the strange situation paradigm is an inappropriate test of attachment in some cultures.

9 Puberty has significant effects on an adolescent's body image, self-esteem, moods, and relationships, but most adolescents make it through this period without major turmoil.

10 According to Erikson's theory, forming a personal sense of identity is the major task of the adolescent period. 'Identity crisis' is Erikson's phrase to describe the active period of self-definition characteristic of adolescence. Identity confusion is the unsuccessful outcome of identity crisis in which the adolescent has no consistent sense of self or set of internal standards for evaluating his or her self-worth in major areas of life.

CORE CONCEPTS

maturation	knowledge	separation anxiety
stages of development	sociocultural approach	autonomy
critical periods	metacognition	attachment
sensitive periods	joint attention	strange situation
visual field	theory of mind	securely attached
facial preference	autism spectrum disorder	insecurely attached: avoidant
schema	moral judgment	insecurely attached: ambivalent
accommodation	punishment	disorganized
sensorimotor stage	preconventional level of moral development	sensitive responsiveness
object permanence		self-concepts
preoperational stage	conventional level of moral development	self-esteem
operation		adolescence
conservation	postconventional level of moral development	puberty
egocentrism		adolescent growth spurt
concrete operational stage	temperament	menarche
formal operational stage	easy temperament	identity crisis
information-processing skills	difficult temperament	identity confusion
	slow to warm up temperament	

DIGITAL SUPPORT RESOURCES

Students should use the unique access code included in the front of the book to access the digital support resources which accompany the new edition. These include:

- Multiple Choice Questions and Quizzes
- Critical Thinking Questions
- Practice Essay Questions
- Videos
- Glossary, Flashcards, and more

4

SENSORY PROCESSES

Explain how sensations are experienced on a psychological and a biological level.

Describe the role of sensitivity, intensity, and magnitude of above threshold stimuli for the different sensory modalities.

Understand that signals are present in background noise and that they may be missed when present (misses) and may be detected when not present (false alarms).

Learn what signal transduction is and how it plays a role in the five senses.

Understand to what extent signal transduction in vision is similar to signal transduction in hearing, and understand how they are different.

Explain how the different facets of the visual sensory system contribute to the two theories of color vision and to visual acuity.

Imagine yourself sitting late at night in a deserted church. Although the image is one of profound serenity, there is in reality an enormous amount of information impinging on you from the world: light from the altar, dim though it may seem, is entering your eyes. The sounds of the city, soft though they may seem, are entering your ears. The pew you're sitting in is pushing up on your body; the smell of incense is wafting into your nose; and the taste of the wine you just drank still lingers in your mouth.

And this is just the environmental information that you're aware of! In addition, there's lots more information that you're unaware of. The microwave transmitter on the hill behind you, the radio station on the other side of town, and the mobile phone of a talkative passer-by outside are all issuing various sorts of electromagnetic radiation that, while enveloping you, aren't touching your consciousness. Across the street a dog owner blows his dog whistle, sending a high-frequency shriek that, while very salient to the dog (and to any bats in the vicinity), is inaudible to you. Likewise, there are particles in the air and in your mouth, and subtle pressures on your skin that constitute information, yet do not register.

Even in the calmest of circumstances the world is constantly providing us with a vast informational tapestry. We need to assimilate and interpret at least some of this information in order to appropriately interact with the world. This need raises two considerations. First, which aspects of the environmental information register with our senses and which don't? For example, why do we see electromagnetic radiation in the form of green light, but not electromagnetic radiation in the form of X-rays or radio waves? Second, how do the sense organs work such that they efficiently acquire the information that is acquirable?

The first question, while fascinating, is largely beyond the scope of this book, but is best understood from an evolutionary perspective. Canadian psychologist and linguist Steven Pinker's classic *How the Mind Works* (1997) provides a superb description of this perspective. A brief answer to the question of why we see only the forms of electromagnetic radiation that we do would go like this: to operate and survive in our world, we need to know about *objects* – what they are and where they are – and so we've evolved to use that part of the electromagnetic spectrum that best accomplishes this goal. With some forms of electromagnetic radiation – short-wave radiation like X-rays or gamma rays, for example – most objects are invisible, that is, the radiation passes right through them rather than reflecting off them to our eyes. Other forms of radiation – long-wave radiation like radio waves, for example – would reflect off the objects to our eyes, but in a manner that would be so blurred as to be useless in any practical sense.

Our senses are our input systems. From them we acquire data about the world around us. This information constitutes the most immediate means (although, as we shall see, not the only means) by which we determine the character of the environment within which we exist and behave. In this chapter we discuss some of the major properties of the senses. Some of the research we review deals with psychological phenomena; other studies deal with the biological bases of these phenomena.

At both the biological and psychological levels of analysis, a distinction is often made between **sensation** and perception. At the psychological level, sensations

CHAPTER OUTLINE

CHARACTERISTICS OF SENSORY MODALITIES
Threshold sensitivity
Suprathreshold sensation
Signal detection theory
Sensory coding

VISION
Light and vision
The visual system
Seeing light
Seeing patterns
Seeing color
Sensation and perception: A preview

AUDITION
Sound waves
The auditory system
Hearing sound intensity
Hearing pitch

CUTTING EDGE RESEARCH: WHERE IN THE BRAIN ARE ILLUSIONS?

OTHER SENSES
Olfaction
Gustation
Pressure and temperature
Pain

SEEING BOTH SIDES: SHOULD OPIOIDS BE USED FOR TREATING CHRONIC PAIN?

are fundamental, raw experiences associated with stimuli (for example, sense of sight may register a large red object), while **perception** involves the integration and meaningful interpretation of these raw sensory experiences ('It's a fire engine'). At the biological level, sensory processes involve the sense organs and the neural pathways that emanate from them, which are concerned with the initial stages of acquiring stimulus information. Perceptual processes involve higher levels of the cortex, which are known to be more related to meaning. This chapter concerns sensation, while Chapter 5 concerns perception.

The distinction between sensation and perception is somewhat arbitrary. Psychological and biological events that occur early in the processing of a stimulus can sometimes affect interpretation of the stimulus. Moreover, from the perspective of the nervous system, there is no sharp break between the initial uptake of stimulus information by the sense organs and the brain's subsequent use of that information to ascribe meaning. In fact, one of the most important features of the brain is that, in addition to taking in sensory information, it is constantly sending messages from its highest levels back to the earliest stages of sensory processing. These **back projections** actually modify the way sensory input is processed (Damasio, 1994; Zeki, 1993).

This chapter is organized around the different senses: vision, hearing, smell, taste, and touch; the latter includes pressure, temperature, and pain. In everyday life, several senses are often involved in any given act – we see a peach, feel its texture, taste and smell it as we bite into it, and hear the sounds of our chewing. Moreover, many sensory judgments are more accurate when multiple senses are employed; for instance, people are more accurate at judging the direction from which a sound is coming when they are able to use their eyes to 'target' the approximate location than when they use their ears alone (Spence & Driver, 1994). For purposes of analysis, however, we consider the senses one at a time. Before beginning our analysis of individual senses, or sensory modalities, we will discuss some properties that are common to all senses.

CHARACTERISTICS OF SENSORY MODALITIES

Any sensory system has the task of acquiring some form of information from the environment and *transducing* it into some form of neural representation in the brain. The mechanisms that operate in any sensory modality incorporate at least two processes: (1) Data acquisition – mostly from the environment but also from memory – and (2) transduction, in which that information is converted to a neural representation. Thus understanding of the workings of a sensory system entails two steps: first understand what are the *relevant dimensions* of a particular form of environmental information and then to understand how that dimension is translated by the sensory organ into a neural representation. The dimensions corresponding to any given form of information can be roughly divided into 'intensity' and 'everything else.'

Threshold sensitivity

It is important to single out intensity because it is common to all forms of information, although it takes different forms for different kinds of information. For example, for light, intensity

corresponds to the number of incoming photons per second, while for sound intensity corresponds to the amplitude of sound pressure waves.

It is entirely intuitive that the more intense some stimulus is, the more strongly it will affect the relevant sense organ: a high-amplitude light will affect the visual system more than a dimmer light; a high-volume sound will affect the **auditory system** more than a soft sound, and so on. This intuitively obvious observation is important but not surprising: it is analogous to the equally intuitive observation that a dropped apple will fall downward. In other words, it is a scientific starting point. So just as Newton (supposedly) began from the dropped-apple observation to develop a detailed and quantitative theory of gravity, sensory psychologists have long sought to detail and quantify the relation between physical stimulus intensity and the resulting sensation magnitude. In what follows, we will describe some of the results of this endeavor.

Absolute thresholds: Detecting minimum intensities

A basic way of assessing the sensitivity of a sensory modality is to determine the **absolute threshold**: the minimum magnitude of a stimulus that can be reliably discriminated

TABLE 4.1 MINIMUM STIMULI

Approximate minimum stimuli for various senses.

Sense	Minimum stimulus
Vision	A candle flame seen at 30 miles (48.28 kilometers) on a dark, clear night
Hearing	The tick of a clock at 20 feet (6.10 meters) under quiet conditions
Taste	One teaspoon of sugar in 2 gallons (7.57 liters) of water
Smell	One drop of perfume diffused into the entire volume of six rooms
Touch	The wing of a fly falling on your cheek from a distance of 1 centimeter

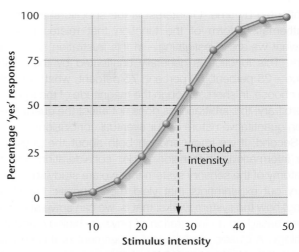

FIGURE 4.1 **Psychopysical Function for a Detection Experiment.** *Plotted on the vertical axis is the percentage of times the participant responds, 'Yes, I detect the stimulus'; on the horizontal axis is the measure of the magnitude of the physical stimulus. Such a graph may be obtained for any stimulus dimension to which an individual is sensitive.*

from no stimulus at all – for example, the weakest light that can be reliably discriminated from darkness. One of the most striking aspects of our sensory modalities is that they are extremely sensitive to the presence of, or a change in, an object or event. Some indication of this sensitivity is given in Table 4.1. For five of the senses, we have provided an estimate of the minimal stimulus that they can detect. What is most noticeable about these minimums is how low they are – that is, how sensitive the corresponding sensory modality is.

These values were determined using what are called **psychophysical procedures**, which are experimental techniques for measuring the relation between the physical magnitude of some stimulus (e.g., the physical intensity of a light) and the resulting psychological response (how bright the light appears to be). In one commonly used psychophysical procedure, the experimenter first selects a set of stimuli whose magnitudes vary around the threshold (for example, a set of dim lights whose intensities vary from invisible to barely visible). Over a series of what are referred to as **trials**, the stimuli are presented one at a time in random order, and the observer is instructed to say 'yes' if the stimulus appears to be present and 'no' if it does not. Each stimulus is presented many times, and the percentage of 'yes' responses is determined for each stimulus magnitude.

Figure 4.1 depicts hypothetical data that result from this kind of experiment: a graph showing that the percentage of 'yes' responses rises smoothly as stimulus intensity (defined here in terms of hypothetical 'units') increases. When performance is characterized by such a graph, psychologists have agreed to define the absolute threshold as the value of the stimulus at which it is detected 50 per cent of the time. For the data displayed in Figure 4.1, the stimulus is detected 50 per cent of the time when the stimulus's intensity is about 28 units; thus 28 units is defined to be absolute threshold.

At first glance, this definition of 'threshold' may seem vague and unscientific. Why 50 per cent? Why not 75 per cent or 28 per cent? Any value would seem arbitrary. There are two answers to this question.

The first, which is generally true, is that establishing a threshold is generally only a first step in some experiment. As an example, suppose one is interested in **dark adaptation**, i.e., in establishing how sensitivity is affected by the amount of time that an observer has spent in the dark. One would then plot (as indeed we do later in this chapter) how threshold

Our sensory modalities are extremely sensitive in detecting the presence of an object – even the faint light of a candle in a distant window. On a clear night, a candle flame can be seen from 30 miles away!

is affected by time. Of interest is the specific shape and/or mathematical form of the function that relates threshold to what we are investigating – in this illustration, time in the dark. This function is generally unaffected by the specific value – 28 percent, 50 percent, 75 percent, whatever – that we choose. In short, although the magnitude of the threshold is arbitrary, this arbitrariness does not affect the qualitative or even quantitative nature of our eventual conclusions.

Second, if we know enough both about the physics of the informational dimension under consideration and the anatomy of the sensory system that we are studying, we can carry out experiments that yield more specific knowledge about how the system works; that is, we can arrive at conclusions based on an integration of physics, biology, and psychology. A classic, and elegant experiment of this sort was reported by Hecht et al. (1942) of Columbia University in the USA, who endeavored to determine the absolute threshold for vision and in the process, demonstrated that human vision is virtually as sensitive as is physically possible. As every graduate of elementary physics knows, the smallest unit of light energy is a **photon**. Hecht and his colleagues showed that a person can detect a flash of light that contains only 100 photons. This is impressive in and of itself; on a typical day, many billions of photons are entering your eye every second. What is even more impressive is that Hecht and his colleagues went on to show that only seven of these 100 photons actually contact the critical molecules in the eye that are responsible for translating light into the nerve impulses that correspond to vision (the rest are absorbed by other parts of the eye) and furthermore that each of these seven photons affects a different neural receptor on the retina. The critical receptive unit of the eye (a particular molecule within the receptor), therefore, is sensitive to a single photon. This is what it means to say that 'human vision is as sensitive as is physically possible.'

Difference thresholds: Detecting changes in intensity

Absolute thresholds may be determined by how much stimulus intensity must be raised from zero in order to be distinguishable from zero. More generally, we can ask: by how much must stimulus intensity be raised from some arbitrary level (called a **standard**) in order that the new, higher level be distinguishable from the base level? This is a measurement of change detection. In a typical change-detection study, observers are presented with a pair of stimuli. One of them is the standard – it is the one to which other stimuli are compared. The others are called comparison stimuli. On each presentation of the pair, observers are asked to respond to the comparison stimulus with 'more' or 'less.' What is being measured is the **difference threshold** or **just noticeable difference (jnd)**, the minimum difference in stimulus magnitude necessary to tell two stimuli apart.

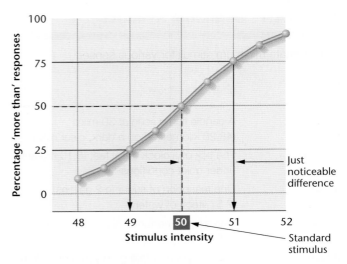

FIGURE 4.2 Results from an Experiement on Change Detection. *Plotted on the vertical axis is the percentage of times the participant responds, 'Yes, I detect more than the standard'; on the horizontal axis is the measure of the magnitude of the physical stimulus. The standard stimulus in this example is in the center of the range of stimuli. Such a graph may be obtained for any stimulus dimension for which an individual is sensitive to differences.*

To illustrate, imagine measuring the visual system's sensitivity to changes in the brightness of a light. Typical results are shown in Figure 4.2. In this experiment the standard (a 50-watt bulb) was presented along with each comparison stimulus (ranging from 47 watts to 53 watts, in 1-watt steps) dozens of times. We have plotted the percentage of times in which each comparison stimulus was judged to be 'brighter' than the standard. In order to determine the jnd, two points are estimated, one at 75 per cent and the other at 25 per cent on the 'percentage brighter' axis. Psychologists have agreed that half of this distance in stimulus intensity units will be considered to be the just noticeable difference. In this case, then, the estimated jnd is $(51-49)/2 = 1$ watt. If an individual's sensitivity to change is high, meaning that he or she can notice tiny differences between stimuli, the estimated value of the jnd will be small. On the other hand, if sensitivity is not as high, the estimated jnd's will be larger.

This relationship between stimulus intensity and sensitivity was first studied about a century-and-a-half ago, by two German scientists: Ernst Heinrich Weber, a physiologist, and Gustav Fechner, a physicist. Their seminal finding was that the larger the value of the standard stimulus, the less sensitive the sensory system is to changes in intensity. Under a wide range of circumstances, the relation can be described as follows: *the intensity by which the standard must be increased in order for the change to be noticed is proportional to the intensity of the standard.* For example, take a room containing 25 candles. If in order for you to detect a change in lighting, two extra candles need to be lit – that is, 8 per cent more – then a room

TABLE 4.2 JUST NOTICEABLE DIFFERENCES (JND) FOR VARIOUS SENSORY QUALITIES

(expressed as the percentage change required for reliable change detection)

Quality	Just noticeable difference (jnd)
Light intensity	8%
Sound intensity	5%
Sound frequency	1%
Odor concentration	15%
Salt concentration	20%
Lifted weights	2%
Electric shock	1%

containing 100 candles would require an additional 8 candles (8% × 100 = 8) for you to be able to detect the change in lighting. This proportional relation has come to be known as the Weber–Fechner law, and the constant of proportionality (8 percent in our candle example) is referred to as the **Weber fraction**. Table 4.2 shows some typical jnd's for different sensory qualities, expressed in terms of the Weber fraction.

Table 4.2 shows, among other things, that we are generally more sensitive to changes in light and sound – that is, we can detect a smaller increase – than is the case with taste and smell. These values can be used to predict how much a stimulus will need to be changed from any level of intensity in order for people to notice the changes reliably. For example, if a theater manager wished to produce a subtle but noticeable change in the level of lighting on a stage, he or she might increase the lighting level by 10 per cent. This would mean a 10-watt increase if a 100-watt bulb was being used to begin with, but it would mean a 1000-watt increase if 10 000 watts were already flooding the stage. Similarly, if a soft-drink manufacturer wanted to produce a beverage that tasted notably sweeter than a competitor they could employ the Weber fraction for sweetness for this purpose. This leads to a final important point regarding psychophysical procedures: they often have direct and useful applications to the real world. For instance, Twinkies (a popular American snack cake) include the ingredients sodium stearol lactylate, polysorbate 60, and calcium sulphate. It is unlikely that these substances taste good; however, if the manufacturer is careful to keep the intensities below the absolute taste threshold, they can be added as preservatives without fear of degrading the taste.

Suprathreshold sensation

Knowledge of sensory thresholds in vision and other sensory modalities is important in understanding the fundamentals of how sense organs are designed – for example, the knowledge that a molecule of light-sensitive pigment in the eye responds to a single photon of light is an important clue in understanding how the light-sensitive pigments work. However, quite obviously, most of our everyday visual behavior takes place in the context of above-threshold or **suprathreshold conditions**. Beginning with Weber and Fechner in the mid-nineteenth century, scientists have been investigating the relation between suprathreshold stimulus intensities and corresponding sensory magnitudes by presenting stimuli of various intensities to humans and attempting to measure the magnitude of the humans' responses to them.

Imagine yourself in the following experiment. You sit in a dimly lit room looking at a screen. On each of a series of trials, a small spot of light appears on the screen. The spot differs in physical intensity from one trial to the next. Your job is to assign a number on each trial that reflects how intense that trial's light spot appears to you. So to a very dim light you might assign a '1' while to a very bright light, you might assign '100.' Figure 4.3 shows typical data from such an experiment.

In the mid-twentieth century, the American psychologist S.S. Stevens carried out an intensive investigation of suprathreshold sensation using this kind of experiment. To interpret his data, Stevens derived a law, bearing his name, from two assumptions. The first assumption is that the Weber–Fechner law, described above, is correct; that is, a jnd above some standard stimulus is some fixed percentage of the standard. The second assumption is that psychological intensity is appropriately measured in units of jnd's (just as distance is appropriately measured in meters or weight is appropriately

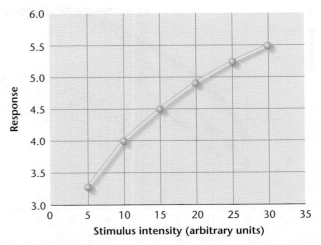

FIGURE 4.3 **Psychophysical Data from a Magnitude-Estimation Experiment.** *Plotted on the vertical axis is the average magnitude estimate given by the observer; on the horizontal axis is the measure of the magnitude of the physical stimulus. Such a graph may be obtained for any stimulus dimension the observer can perceive.*

measured in grams). This means, for example, that the difference between four and seven jnd's (i.e., three jnd's) would to an observer be the same as the difference between ten and 13 jnd's (also three). We will skip the mathematical derivations and go straight to the bottom line: Stevens' law, implied by these assumptions, is that perceived psychological magnitude (Ψ) is a **power function** of physical magnitude (Φ). By this is meant that the relation between Ψ and Φ is (basically), $\Psi = \Phi^r$ where r is an **exponent** unique to each sensory modality. The function shown in Figure 4.3 is a power function with an exponent of 0.5 (which means that Ψ is equal to the *square root* of Φ).

Stevens and others have reported literally thousands of experiments in support of the proposition that the relation between physical and psychological intensity is a power function. It is of some interest to measure the value of the exponent for various sensory dimensions. You may have noticed that a power function is quite different depending on whether r, the exponent, is less than or greater than 1.0. As illustrated in Figure 4.4, a power function with a less-than-1 exponent, such as that corresponding to loudness, is concave down; that is, increasing levels of physical intensity lead to progressively smaller increases in sensation. In contrast, a power function with a greater-than-1 exponent, such as

that corresponding to electric shock, is concave up; that is, increasing levels of physical intensity lead to progressively greater increases in sensation. The exact reasons why the exponents differ among the sensory modalities is not known. It is interesting to note, however, that relatively benign sensory modalities such as light intensities have less-than-1 exponents, while relatively harmful sensory modalities such as electric shock have greater-than-1 exponents. This configuration probably serves adaptive purposes. For relatively 'benign' modalities such as light intensity, the relation between physical intensity and the psychological response simply conveys useful information that may or may not be immediately relevant: for instance, a loud train whistle, bespeaking a nearby train, signals a greater need to be cautious than a softer whistle indicating that the train is far away. However, a modality like pain signals the need for immediate action, and it would make sense to make it as obvious to the perceiver as possible that such action should be taken because bodily harm is likely: if your finger accidentally comes in contact with a red-hot coal, it is important that this highly pain-evoking stimulus produce a very high response; otherwise loss of life or limb could result!

Signal detection theory

At first glance, it may appear as if a sensory system's job is a simple one: if something important is there – say a malignant tumor in a lung – then register its presence via the sensory information that it provides so that the observer can take appropriate action, such as consider possible treatments.

In reality, however, life is not that simple because, as any communications engineer will tell you, information of any sort consists of both **signal** and **noise**. Do not be confused by the term 'noise,' which in common language refers to the auditory domain only (as in 'There's an awful lot of unpleasant noise coming from that party across the street!'). In the world of science, 'signal' refers to the important relevant part of the information, while 'noise' refers to the unimportant and irrelevant part of the information. As we shall demonstrate below in the visual modality, noise occurs as part of any kind of information. Critically, in any modality, the task of the detector is to separate out the signal which it wants from the noise which can obscure and disguise it.

To illustrate this problem in a real-life context we will describe an American medical malpractice lawsuit. A radiologist, Dr A, examined a chest X-ray of a patient, Mr P, during a routine medical exam. Sadly, there was a small but cancerous tumor in Mr P's chest, undetected by Dr A that, 3 years later, had grown substantially and resulted in Mr P's death. Mr P's family filed the lawsuit against Dr A, asserting that the tumor had been detectable in the original X-ray and that Dr A should have detected it. During the ensuing trial Mr P's family called upon another radiologist, Dr B, as an expert witness. As part of his preparation, Dr B first viewed

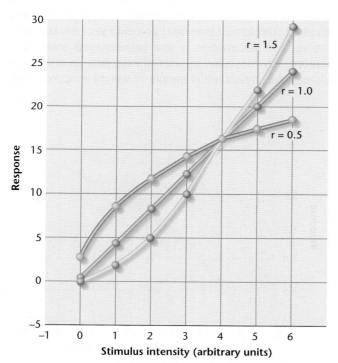

FIGURE 4.4 Psychophysical Data from a Magnitude-Estimation Experiment. *Here different curves are shown for different sensory modalities that entail different exponents. An exponent less than 1.0 produces a concave-down curve, an exponent of 1.0 produces a linear curve, and an exponent greater than 1.0 produces a concave-up curve.*

recent X-rays, taken just before Mr P's death, in which the tumor, large and ominous at that point, was clearly visible. Dr B then viewed the original X-ray – the one seen by Dr A – and easily 'detected' the then-smaller tumor that Dr A had missed. Dr B's conclusion was that, because he, Dr B, was able to detect the tumor in the original X-ray, Dr A should have also detected it, and Dr A, in missing it, was therefore negligent.

This case raises several interesting issues in the domain of sensation and perception. One, roughly characterized as 'hindsight is 20/20,' will be discussed in the next chapter. In this chapter however, we will focus on another issue, which is the distinction between **sensation** and **bias**. To understand this distinction, let's consider generally the task of a radiologist viewing an X-ray trying to determine whether it is normal, or whether it shows the presence of a tumor. In scientific language, this task is, as we've just noted, one of trying to detect a signal embedded in noise. This concept is illustrated in Figure 4.5. There are three panels in the figure, each of which has the same background, which consists of random-visual noise. Suppose that your task was to decide whether there was a small black generally diamond-shaped blob embedded somewhere in this noise. This task is strongly analogous to the radiologist's task of finding a poorly defined tumor in an X-ray.

Consider first the left panel of Figure 4.5. As indicated, there is, in this panel, only noise (we know this is true because we created it that way). Would you indicate that the signal was present? Well there's not much evidence for the small diamond (as indeed there shouldn't be since actually there isn't one). There is, however, a random collection of noise over at the right, indicated by the arrow in the left panel that maybe *could* be the sought-after signal, and perhaps you might incorrectly choose it – or maybe you'd correctly decide that there's only noise. In the middle panel, a weak signal is present, also indicated by an arrow. In this case, you might correctly choose it, or may still feel that it's only noise

and incorrectly claim there to be only noise. Finally, the right panel shows a strong signal, which you would probably correctly detect as a signal.

Hits and false alarms

Now suppose that you are given a whole series of stimuli like the ones in Figure 4.5. Some, like the left panel, contain only noise while others, like the right panel, contain noise plus signal. Your task is to say 'yes' to those containing signal and 'no' to those containing only noise. Of importance is the fact that it is not possible to carry out this task perfectly. To see why this is, look at the left panel of Figure 4.5, which contains only noise. You might, upon inspecting it, think it contains a signal – for instance, the area indicated by the arrow, which resembles the kind of black blob that you are seeking. So you might reasonably respond 'yes' to it, in which case you would be incorrect. If you did this, you would make an error that is referred to as a **false alarm**.

In the kind of signal-detection experiment that we have just described, we could measure the proportion of noise-only trials that result in an incorrect 'yes response.' This proportion is referred to as the false-alarm rate. We can also measure the proportion of noise-plus-signal trials that result in a correct 'yes' response. Such responses are referred to as hits, and the proportion of hits is referred to as the **hit rate**.

We now have a powerful tool to investigate the sensitivity of some sense organ. We know that if no signal is there to be detected, the observer says 'yes' anyway with some probability equal to the false-alarm rate. So we infer that the observer does detect a signal only under those conditions that the hit rate exceeds the false-alarm rate. If the hit rate exceeds the false-alarm rate by a lot, we infer that sensitivity is high. If the hit rate exceeds the false-alarm rate by only a little, we infer that sensitivity is low. If the hit rate equals the false-alarm rate, we infer the sensitivity is zero.

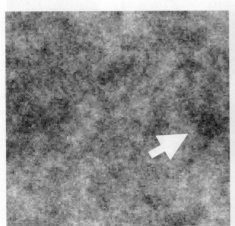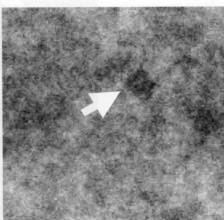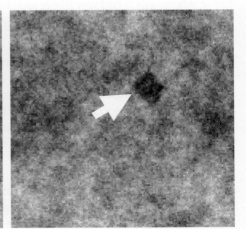

FIGURE 4.5 Examples of Signals Embedded in Noise. *Each panel shows a background of random noise. In the left panel, there is no signal, although the small blob indicated by the arrow may look like a signal. In the middle panel, there is a low signal added, indicated by the arrow. In the right panel, the signal is strong and obvious.*

Sensitivity and bias

Notice something interesting here. An observer is at liberty to choose what his or her false-alarm rate will be. Imagine two hypothetical observers, Charlotte and Linda, who are equally good at detecting signals, but who differ in an important way. In particular, Charlotte is a 'conservative' observer – that is, Charlotte requires a lot of evidence to claim that a signal is present. Charlotte will say 'yes' infrequently which means that she will have a low false-alarm rate, but also a low hit rate. Suppose in contrast that Linda is a 'liberal' observer – she will claim 'signal' given the slightest shred of evidence for a signal. Linda, in other words, will say 'yes' frequently which will endow her with a high false-alarm rate, but also with a high hit rate.

The most useful characteristic of a signal-detection analysis is that it allows separation of **bias** (referred to as β) and **sensitivity** (referred to as d', pronounced 'dee-prime'). In our Charlotte–Linda example, Charlotte and Linda would be determined to have equal sensitivities, even though they have quite different bias values.

Let's conclude this discussion by going back to the medical-malpractice lawsuit that we described earlier. Notice that there are two observers: Dr A and Dr B. The suit alleges that Dr A has poor sensitivity – poor ability to detect a tumor – compared to Dr B and it is for this reason (essentially) that Dr A is alleged to have been negligent. However, we can now see that this conclusion doesn't necessarily follow from the fact that Dr A didn't detect the original tumor while Dr B did detect it. It is equally plausible that Dr B simply had more of a bias to say 'yes I detect a tumor' than did Dr A. This explanation actually makes a good deal of sense. Psychologists have discovered that, in a signal-detection situation, a number of factors influence bias, including **expectation**: reasonably enough, the greater the observer's expectation that a signal will be present, the greater is the observer's bias to respond 'yes.' And, of course, Dr B had good reason to expect the presence of a tumor, whereas Dr A had very little reason to expect it.

Sensory coding

Each sensory system has two fundamental problems that it has to solve: first, how to translate incoming physical information, for example light, to an initial neural representation and second how to encode various features of the physical information (e.g., intensity, hue) to a corresponding neural representation. In this section we will address these questions of **sensory coding**.

The first problem is addressed by the use of specialized cells in the sense organs called receptors. For instance, the receptors for vision, to which we briefly alluded earlier, are located in a thin layer of tissue on the inside of the eye. Each visual receptor contains a chemical that reacts to light, which in turn triggers a series of steps that results in a neural impulse. The receptors for audition are fine hair cells located deep in the ear; vibrations in the air bend these hair cells, thus creating a neural impulse. Similar descriptions apply to the other sensory modalities.

A receptor is a specialized kind of nerve cell or neuron (see Chapter 2); when it is activated, it passes its electrical signal to connecting neurons. The signal travels until it reaches its receiving area in the cortex, with different sensory modalities sending signals to different receiving areas. Somewhere in the brain the electrical signal results in the conscious sensory experience that, for example, underlies responses in a psychophysical experiment. Thus, when we experience a touch, the experience is occurring in our brain, not in our skin. One demonstration of this comes from the Canadian brain surgeon Wilder Penfield. During brain surgeries on awake patients he electrically stimulated the surface of a region of the parietal lobe called the primary somatic sensory cortex with an electrode; patients reported feeling a tingling sensation in a specific location on their bodies (Penfield & Rasmussen, 1950). As he moved his electrode along this strip of cortex the patients felt the tingling move along their bodies. This allowed Penfield to map out how sensory input from various body parts was distributed along the sensory cortex. The map of sensory representations is called the homunculus, which is Latin for 'little man.' The size of the area of somatic sensory cortex responsible for processing information from

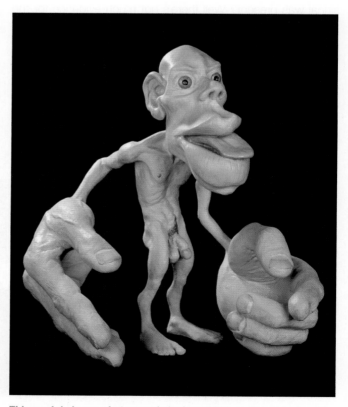

This model shows what a man's body would look like if each part grew in proportion to the area of the cortex of the brain concerned with its sensory perception.

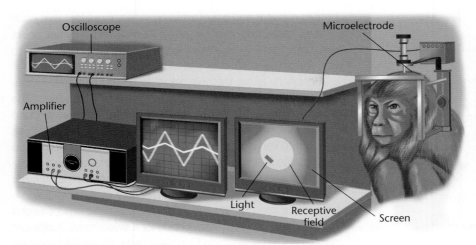

FIGURE 4.6 Single-Cell Recording.
An anesthetized monkey is placed in a device that holds its head in a fixed position. A stimulus, often a flashing or moving bar of light, is projected onto the screen. A microelectrode implanted in the visual system of the monkey monitors activity from a single neuron, and this activity is amplified and displayed on an oscilloscope.

each part of the body is proportional to the amount of sensory neurons in that body part. Thus, input from the more sensitive areas of the body such as the lips and fingers occupy larger areas of the homunculus than less sensitive areas such as the elbow.

In normal life, the electrical impulses in the brain that mediate the experience of touch are themselves caused by electrical impulses in touch receptors located in the skin. Penfield apparently stimulated the brain regions where those impulses are received and converted into touch experiences. Similarly, our experience of a bitter taste occurs in our brain, not in our tongue, but the brain impulses that mediate the taste experience are themselves caused by electrical impulses in taste receptors on the tongue. In this way our receptors play a major role in relating external events to conscious experience. Numerous aspects of our conscious perceptions are caused by specific neural events that occur in the receptors.

Coding of intensity and quality

Our sensory systems evolved to pick up information about objects and events in the world. What kind of information do we need to know about an event such as a brief flash of a bright red light? Clearly, it would be useful to know its intensity (bright), quality (red), duration (brief), location, and time of onset. Each of our sensory systems provides some information about these various attributes, although most research has focused on the attributes of intensity and quality.

When we see a bright red color patch, we experience the quality of redness at an intense level; when we hear a faint, high-pitched tone, we experience the quality of the pitch at a non-intense level. The receptors and their neural pathways to the brain must therefore code both intensity and quality. How do they do this? Researchers who study these coding processes need a way of determining which specific neurons are activated by which specific stimuli. The usual means is to record the electrical activity of single cells in the receptors

and neural pathways to the brain while some subject (which, in the case of single-cell recording, is generally an animal such as a cat or a monkey) is presented with various inputs or stimuli. By such means, one can determine exactly which attributes of a stimulus a particular neuron is responsive to.

A typical single-cell recording experiment is illustrated in Figure 4.6. This is a vision experiment, but the procedure is similar for studying other senses. Before the experiment, the animal (in this case a monkey) has undergone a surgical procedure in which thin wires are inserted into selected areas of its visual cortex. The thin wires are microelectrodes, insulated except at their tips, that can be used to record electrical activity of the neurons they are in contact with. They cause no pain, and the monkey moves around and lives quite normally. During the experiment, the monkey is placed in a testing apparatus and the microelectrodes are connected to recording and amplifying devices. The monkey is then exposed to various visual stimuli on a computer-controlled monitor. For each stimulus, the researcher can determine which neurons respond to it by observing which microelectrodes produce sustained outputs. This is an example of distributive or spatial coding, where a specific stimulus activates an area or a specific neuron in the brain. Most neurons emit a series of nerve impulses that appear on a second computer screen in whatever format the experimenter wishes. Even in the absence of a signal (i.e., even in a noise-only situation), many cells will respond at a slow rate. If a signal to which the neuron is sensitive is presented, the cells respond faster. This is the most fundamental neural correlate of the signal-detection situation that we described above.

With the aid of single-cell recordings, researchers have learned a good deal about how sensory systems code intensity and quality. The primary means for coding the intensity of a stimulus is via the number of neural impulses in each unit of time, that is, the rate of neural impulses. We can illustrate this point with the sense of touch. If someone lightly touches

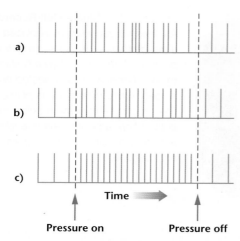

FIGURE 4.7 Coding Intensity. *Responses of a nerve fiber from the skin to (a) soft, (b) medium, and (c) strong pressure applied to the fiber's receptor. Increasing the stimulus strength increases both the rate and the regularity of nerve firing in this fiber.*

your arm, a series of electrical impulses are generated in a nerve fiber. If the pressure is increased, the impulses remain the same in size but increase in number per unit of time (see Figure 4.7). The same is true for other sensory modalities. In general, the greater the intensity of the stimulus, the higher the neural firing rate; and in turn, the greater the firing rate, the greater the perceived magnitude of the stimulus.

The intensity of a stimulus can also be coded by other means. One alternative is coding by the **temporal pattern** of the electrical impulses. At low intensities, nerve impulses are further apart in time, and the length of time between impulses is variable. At high intensities, though, the time between impulses may be more regular (see Figure 4.7). Another alternative is coding by number of neurons activated: the more intense the stimulus, the more neurons are activated.

Coding the quality of a stimulus is a more complex matter. The key idea behind coding quality was proposed by German physiologist Johannes Müller in 1825. Müller suggested that the brain can distinguish between information from different sensory modalities – such as lights and sounds – because they involve different sensory nerves (some nerves lead to visual experiences, others to auditory experiences, and so on). Müller's idea of specific nerve energies received support from subsequent research demonstrating that neural pathways originating in different receptors terminate in different areas of the cortex (e.g. visual signals travel to the visual cortex in the occipital lobes and signals from the ears travel to the auditory cortex in the temporal lobes). It is now generally agreed that the brain codes the qualitative differences between sensory modalities according to the specific neural pathways involved.

But what about the distinguishing qualities within a sense? How do we tell red from green or sweet from sour? It is likely that, again, the coding is based on the specific neurons involved. To illustrate, there is evidence that we distinguish

between sweet and sour tastes by virtue of the fact that each kind of taste has its own nerve fibers. Thus, sweet fibers respond primarily to sweet tastes, sour fibers primarily to sour tastes, and ditto for salty fibers and bitter fibers.

Specificity is not the only plausible coding principle. A sensory system may also use the pattern of neural firing to code the quality of a sensation. While a particular nerve fiber may respond maximally to a sweet taste, it may respond to other tastes as well, but to varying degrees. As another example of distributive coding, one fiber may respond best to sweet tastes, less to bitter tastes, and even less to salty tastes; a sweet-tasting stimulus would thus lead to activity in a large number of fibers, with some firing more than others, and this particular pattern of neural activity would be the system's code for a sweet taste. A different pattern would be the code for a bitter taste. As we will see when we discuss the senses in detail, both specificity and patterning are used in coding the quality of a stimulus.

INTERIM SUMMARY

➲ The senses include the four traditional ones of seeing, hearing, smell, and taste, plus three 'touch' sensations, pressure and temperature, and pain, plus the body senses.

➲ Sensations are psychological experiences associated with simple stimuli, that have not, as yet, been endowed with meaning.

➲ For each sense, two kinds of threshold sensitivity can be defined: absolute threshold (the minimum amount of stimulus energy reliably registers on the sensory organ) and difference threshold (the minimum difference between two stimuli that can be reliably distinguished by the sensory organ).

➲ The **psychophysical function** is the relation between stimulus intensity and the magnitude of sensation for above-threshold ('suprathreshold') stimuli.

➲ Sensation is often viewed as the process of detecting a signal that is embedded in noise. In some cases, a signal may be falsely 'detected' even when only noise is present – a false alarm. Correctly detecting a signal that is present is a hit. The difference between hits and false alarms is a measure of the magnitude of the stimulus's effect on the sensory organ. The use of signal-detection theory allows the process of detecting a stimulus to be separated into two numbers, one representing the observer's sensitivity to the signal and the other representing the observer's bias to respond to 'signal present.'

➲ Every sensory modality must recode or transduce the physical energy engendered from a stimulus into neural impulses. The nature of such coding, unique to each sensory modality, must encode stimulus intensity, along with various qualitative characteristics of the stimulus.

VISION

Humans are generally credited with the following senses: (a) vision, (b) audition, (c) smell, (d) taste, (e) touch (or the skin senses), and (f) the body senses (which are responsible for sensing the position of the head relative to the trunk, for example). Since the body senses do not always give rise to conscious sensations of intensity and quality, we will focus on them less than the better understood senses of vision and hearing.

Only vision, audition, and smell are capable of obtaining information that is at a distance from us, and of this group, vision is the most finely tuned in humans. In this section we first consider the nature of the stimulus energy to which vision is sensitive; next we describe the visual system, with particular emphasis on how its receptors carry out the transduction process; and then we consider how the visual modality processes information about intensity and quality.

Light and vision

Each sense responds to a particular form of physical energy, and for vision the physical stimulus is light. Light is a form of electromagnetic energy, energy that emanates from the sun and the rest of the universe and constantly bathes our planet. Electromagnetic energy is best conceptualized as traveling in waves, with wavelengths (the distance from one crest of a wave to the next) varying tremendously from the shortest cosmic rays (4-trillionths of a centimeter) to the longest radio waves (several kilometers). Our eyes are sensitive to only a tiny portion of this continuum: wavelengths of approximately 400 to 700 nanometers, where a nanometer is a billionth of a meter. Visible electromagnetic energy – light – therefore makes up only a very small part of electromagnetic energy.

The visual system

The human visual system consists of the eyes, several parts of the brain, and the pathways connecting them. Go back to Figure 2.13 (visual pathways figure) for a simplified illustration of the visual system and notice in particular that (assuming you're looking straight ahead) the right half of the visual world is initially processed by the left side of the brain and vice-versa.

The first stage in vision is, of course, the eye, which contains two systems: one for forming the image and the other for transducing the image into electrical impulses. The critical parts of these systems are illustrated in Figure 4.8.

An analogy is often made between an eye and a camera. While this analogy is misleading for many aspects of the visual system, it is appropriate for the image-forming system, whose function is to focus light reflected from an object so as to form an image of the object on the retina, which is a thin layer of

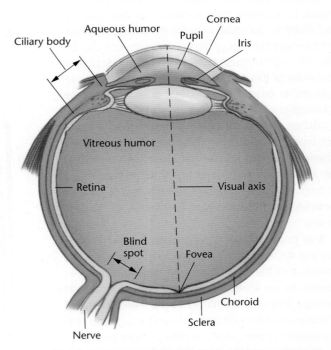

FIGURE 4.8 Top View of the Right Eye. *Light entering the eye on its way to the retina passes through the cornea, the aqueous humor, the lens, and the vitreous humor. The amount of light entering the eye is regulated by the size of the pupil, a small hole toward the front of the eye formed by the iris. The iris consists of a ring of muscles that can contract or relax, thereby controlling pupil size. The iris gives the eyes their characteristic color (blue, brown, and so forth).*

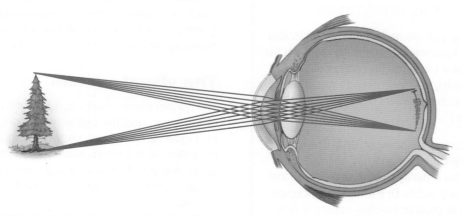

FIGURE 4.9 Image Formation in the Eye. *Some of the light from an object enters the eye, where it forms an image on the retina. Both the cornea and the lens bend the light rays, as would a lens in a telescope. Based purely on optical considerations we can infer that the retinal image is inverted.*

tissue at the back of the eyeball (see Figure 4.9). The image-forming system itself consists of the cornea, the **pupil**, and the lens. The cornea is the transparent front surface of the eye: light enters here, and rays are bent inward by it to begin the formation of the image. The lens completes the process of focusing the light on the retina (see Figure 4.9). To focus on objects at different distances, the lens changes shape. It becomes more spherical for near objects and flatter for far ones. In some eyes, the lens does not become flat enough to bring far objects into focus, although it focuses well on near objects; people with eyes of this type are said to be myopic (nearsighted). In other eyes, the lens does not become spherical enough to focus on near objects, although it focuses well on far objects; people with eyes of this type are said to be hyperopic (farsighted). As otherwise normal people get older (into their 40s) the lens loses much of its ability to change shape or focus at all. Such optical defects can of course, generally be corrected with eyeglasses or contact lenses.

The pupil, the third component of the image-forming system, is a circular opening between the cornea and the lens whose diameter varies in response to the level of light present. It is largest in dim light and smallest in bright light, thereby helping to ensure that enough light passes through the lens to maintain image quality at different light levels.

All of these components focus the image on the retina. There the transduction system takes over. This system begins with various types of neural receptors which are spread over the retina, somewhat analogously to the way in which photodetectors are spread over the imaging surface of a digital camera. There are two types of receptor cells, **rods** and **cones**, so-called because of their distinctive

shapes, shown in Figure 4.10. The two kinds of receptors are specialized for different purposes. Rods are specialized for seeing at night; they operate at low intensities and lead to low-resolution, colorless sensations. Cones are specialized for seeing during the day; they respond to high intensities and

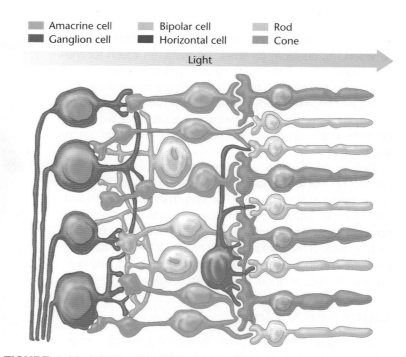

FIGURE 4.10 A Schematic Picture of the Retina. *This is a schematic drawing of the retina based on an examination with an electron microscope. The bipolar cells receive signals from one or more receptors and transmit those signals to the ganglion cells, whose axons form the optic nerve. Note that there are several types of bipolar and ganglion cells. There are also sideways or lateral connections in the retina. Neurons called horizontal cells make lateral connections at a level near the receptors; neurons called amacrine cells make lateral connections at a level near the ganglion cells.*

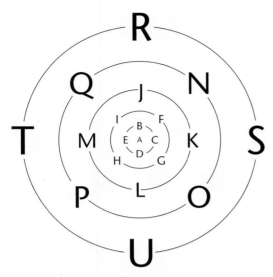

FIGURE 4.11 Visual Acuity Decreases in the Periphery.
Letter sizes have been scaled so that when the central A is looked at directly, all the other letters are approximately equally easy to read.

receptors means higher resolution, as, analogously, a computer monitor set to more pixels per screen (e.g., one set to 1600 × 1200) has a higher resolution than when it is set to fewer pixels per screen (e.g., 640 × 480). The high-density fovea is therefore the highest-resolution region of the fovea, the part that is best at seeing details. To get a sense of how your perception of detail changes as an image is moved away from your fovea, look at Figure 4.11 and keep your eyes trained on the central letter (A). The sizes of the surrounding letters have been adjusted so that they are all approximately equal in visibility. Note that in order to achieve equal visibility, the letters on the outer circle must be about ten times larger than the central letter.

Given that light reflected from an object has made contact with a receptor cell, how does the receptor transduce the light into electrical impulses? The rods and cones contain chemicals, called photopigments, that absorb light. Absorption of light by the photopigments starts a process that eventuates in a neural impulse. Once this **transduction** step is completed, the electrical impulses must make their way to the brain via connecting neurons. The responses of the rods and cones are first transmitted to bipolar cells and from there to other neurons called ganglion cells of which there are several types (refer to Figure 4.10). The long axons of the ganglion cells extend out of the eye to form the optic nerve to the brain. Between the optic nerve and the visual cortex, there is a structure called the lateral geniculate nucleus (LGN) through which all visual information must pass before reaching the visual cortex. It is here that primary visual information is organized using neural coding. Distributive coding is used by the LGN to help map and differentiate the visual signals. The LGN is layered in a retinotopic map that is reproduced in the visual cortex. At the place where the optic nerve leaves the eye, there are no receptors; we are therefore blind to a stimulus in this region (see Figure 4.12). We do not notice this hole in our visual field – known as the blind spot – because the brain automatically fills it in (Ramachandran & Gregory, 1991).

result in high-resolution sensations that include color. The retina also contains a network of other neurons, along with support cells and blood vessels.

When we want to see the details of an object, we routinely move our eyes so that the object is projected onto a small region at the center of the retina called the **fovea**. The reason we do this has to do with the distribution of receptors across the retina. In the fovea, the receptors are plentiful and closely packed; outside the fovea, on the periphery of the retina, there are fewer receptors. More closely packed

a)

b)

FIGURE 4.12 Locating Your Blind Spot. *(a) With your right eye closed, stare at the cross in the upper right-hand corner. Put the book about a foot from your eye and move it forward and back. When the blue circle on the left disappears, it is projected onto the blind spot. (b) Without moving the book and with your right eye still closed, stare at the cross in the lower right-hand corner. When the white space falls in the blind spot, the blue line appears to be continuous. This phenomenon helps us understand why we are not ordinarily aware of the blind spot. In effect, the visual system fills in the parts of the visual field that we are not sensitive to; thus, they appear to be a part of the surrounding field.*

Seeing light

Sensitivity

Our sensitivity to light is determined by the rods and cones. There are three critical differences between rods and cones that explain a number of phenomena involving perceived intensity, or brightness. The first difference is that rods and cones are activated under different levels of light. In broad daylight or in a well-lit room, only the cones are

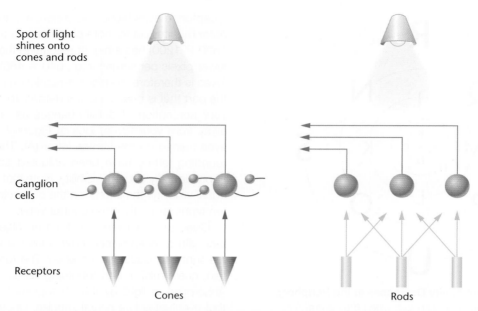

Spot of light shines onto cones and rods

Ganglion cells

Receptors

Cones

Rods

FIGURE 4.13 How Cones and Rods Connect to Ganglion Cells. *This diagram shows a single spot of light shining onto a cone and a rod. To simplify matters, we have omitted several other types of cells located between receptors and ganglion cells. Arrows represent a signal to increase neuronal firing. Dots represent a signal to decrease neuronal firing. The long arrows emanating from the ganglion cells are axons that become part of the optic nerve.*

active; the rods send no meaningful neural signals. On the other hand, at night under a quarter moon or in a dimly lit room, only the rods are active.

A second difference is that cones and rods are specialized for different tasks. This can be seen in the way they are connected to ganglion cells, as illustrated in Figure 4.13. The left side of the figure shows three adjacent cones, each of which is connected to a single ganglion cell. This means that if a cone receives light it will increase the activity of its corresponding ganglion cell. Each ganglion cell is connected to its nearest neighbor by a connection that decreases the activity of that neighboring cell; it is also connected to the visual area of the brain by a long axon. Together these axons form the optic nerve. The right side of the figure shows three adjacent rods, each of which is connected to three ganglion cells. Here, however, there are no connections among ganglion cells that decrease neural activity.

To understand the implications of these wiring differences, suppose that a single spot of light was presented to either the cones or the rods. When it was presented to the cones, only one of the ganglion cells, corresponding to the location of the spot, would respond. However, when a spot of light was presented only to the rods, it would cause up to three ganglion cells to increase their activity. This combined activity would help ensure that the signal reached the brain, but it would also mean that there would be considerable uncertainty about the exact location of the spot of light. Thus, the connections among ganglion cells associated with cones help ensure detailed form perception under well-lit conditions, whereas the convergence

of many rods on a single ganglion cell helps ensure sensitivity to light under low lighting conditions. Thus you can do tasks requiring high resolution, such as reading fine print, only in reasonably well lit conditions in which the cones are active.

A third difference is that rods and cones are concentrated in different locations on the retina. The fovea contains many cones but no rods. The periphery, on the other hand, is rich in rods but has relatively few cones. We have already seen one consequence of the smaller number of cones in the periphery (see Figure 4.11). A consequence of the distribution of rods can be seen when viewing stars at night. You may have noticed that in order to see a dim star as clearly as possible it is necessary to look slightly to one side of the star. This ensures that the maximum possible number of rods are activated by the light from the star.

Dark adaptation

Imagine yourself entering a dark movie theater from a bright street. At first you can see hardly anything in the dim light reflected from the screen. However, in a few minutes you are able to see well enough to find a seat. Eventually you are able to recognize faces in the dim light. This change in your ability to see in the dark is referred to as **dark adaptation**: as you spend time in the dark, two processes occur that account for it. One, which we've already mentioned, is that the eye's pupil changes size – it enlarges when the surrounding environment becomes dark. More importantly, there are photochemical changes in the receptors that increase the receptors' sensitivity to light.

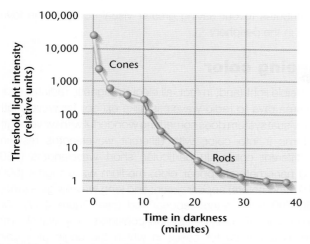

FIGURE 4.14 The Course of Dark Adaptation. *Subjects look at a bright light until the retina has become light adapted. When the subjects are then placed in darkness, they become increasingly sensitive to light, and their absolute thresholds decrease. This is called light adaptation. The graph shows the threshold at different times after the adapting light has been turned off. The green data points correspond to threshold flashes whose color could be seen; the purple data point correspond to flashes that appeared white regardless of the wavelength. Note the sharp break in the curve at about 10 minutes; this is called the rod-cone break. A variety of tests show that the first part of the curve is due to cone vision and the second part to rod vision. (Data are approximate, from various determinations.)*

Figure 4.14 shows a **dark-adaptation curve**: it shows how the absolute threshold decreases with the length of time the person is in darkness. The curve has two limbs. The upper limb reflects adaptation of the cones, which takes place quite rapidly – cones are fully adapted within about 5 minutes. While the cones are adapting, the rods are also adapting, but more slowly. Eventually, the rod adaptation 'catches up' with the already-complete cone adaptation, but the rods then continue to adapt for an additional 25 minutes or so which accounts for the second limb of the dark-adaptation curve.

Seeing patterns

Visual acuity refers to the eye's ability to resolve details. There are several ways of measuring visual acuity, but the most common measure is the familiar eye chart found in optometrists' offices. This chart was devised by Dutch ophthalmologist Herman Snellen in 1862. **Snellen acuity** is measured relative to a viewer who does not need to wear glasses. Thus, an acuity of 20/20 indicates that the viewer is able to identify letters at a distance of 20 meters that a typical viewer can read at that distance. An acuity of 20/100 would mean that the viewer can only read letters at 20 meters that are large enough for a typical viewer to read

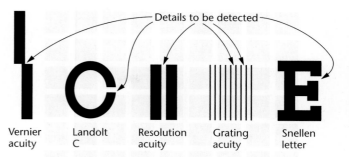

FIGURE 4.15 Some Typical Forms Used in Tests of Visual Acuity. *Arrows point to the details to be discriminated in each case.*

at a distance of 100 meters. In this case, visual acuity is less than normal.

There are a number of reasons why the Snellen chart is not always the best way to measure acuity. First, the method is not good for young children or other people who do not know how to read. Second, the method is designed to test acuity only for objects seen at a distance (e.g., 10 meters); it does not measure acuity for reading and other tasks involving near distances. Third, the method does not distinguish between **spatial acuity** (the ability to see differences in form) and **contrast acuity** (the ability to see differences in brightness). Figure 4.15 presents examples of typical forms used in tests of visual acuity, with arrows pointing to the critical detail to be detected. Notice that each detail is merely a region of the field where there is a change in brightness from light to dark (Coren *et al.*, 1999).

The sensory experience associated with viewing a pattern is determined by the way visual neurons register information about light and dark. The most primitive element of a visual pattern is the edge, or contour, the region where there is a transition from light to dark or vice versa. One of the earliest influences on the registration of edges occurs because of the way ganglion cells in the retina interact (see Figure 4.13). The effects of these interactions can be observed by viewing a pattern known as the Hermann grid, shown in Figure 4.16. You can see gray smudges at the intersections of the white spaces separating the black squares. A disconcerting aspect of this experience is that the very intersection you are gazing at does not appear to be filled with a gray smudge; only intersections that you are not currently gazing at give the illusion of the gray smudge.

This illusion is the direct result of the connections producing decreased activity among the neighbors of active ganglion cells. For example, a ganglion cell that is centered on one of the white intersections of the grid will be receiving signals that decrease its rate of firing from neighboring ganglion cells on four sides, a phenomenon known as lateral inhibition (that is, the cells centered in the white spaces are inhibited by the dark squares above, below, to the right, and to the left of the intersection). A ganglion cell that is centered on one of

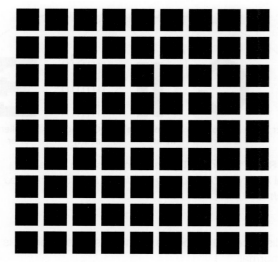

FIGURE 4.16 **The Hermann Grid.** *The gray smudges seen at the white intersections are illusionary. They are seen by your eye and brain but are not on the page. To convince yourself that they are not really there, move your eyes to the different intersections. You will note that there is never a gray smudge at the intersection you are looking at directly. They appear only in intersections that fall on your peripheral visual field.*

the white rows or columns, on the other hand, will be receiving signals that decrease its rate of firing from neighboring cells on only two sides. As a result, the intersections appear darker than the white rows or columns, reflecting the larger number of signals to decrease the rate of firing being received by ganglion cells centered there. The purpose of lateral inhibition is to enhance edge detection by darkening one side of the edge and lightening the other (e.g., Mach Bands).

But why do the smudges appear only off to the side, not at the intersection you are looking at directly? This happens because the range over which the signals are sent is much smaller at the fovea than in the periphery. This arrangement contributes to our having greater visual acuity at the fovea than in the periphery.

Seeing color

All visible light (and, in fact, all electromagnetic radiation from gamma rays to radio waves) is alike except for wavelength. Our visual system does something wonderful with wavelength: it turns it into color, with different wavelengths resulting in different colors. In particular, short wavelengths (450–500 nanometers) appear blue; medium wavelengths (500–570 nanometers) appear green; and long wavelengths (about 650–780 nanometers) appear red (see Figure 4.17). Our discussion of color perception considers only wavelength. This is adequate for cases in which the origin of a color sensation is an object that emits light, such as the sun or a light bulb. Usually, however, the origin of a color sensation is an object that reflects light when it is illuminated by a light source. In these cases, our perception of the object's color is determined partly by the wavelengths that the object reflects and partly by other factors. One such factor is the surrounding context of colors. A rich variety of other colors in the spatial neighborhood of an object makes it possible for the viewer to see the correct color of an object even when the wavelengths reaching the eye from that object do not faithfully record the object's characteristic color (Land, 1986). Your ability to see your favorite blue jacket as navy despite wide variations in the ambient lighting is called **color constancy**. We will discuss this topic more fully in Chapter 5.

Color appearance

Seeing color is a subjective experience in the sense that 'color' is a construction of the brain based on an analysis of wavelengths of light. However, it is also objective in that any two viewers with the same kinds of color receptors (cones) appear to construct 'color' in the same way. The most

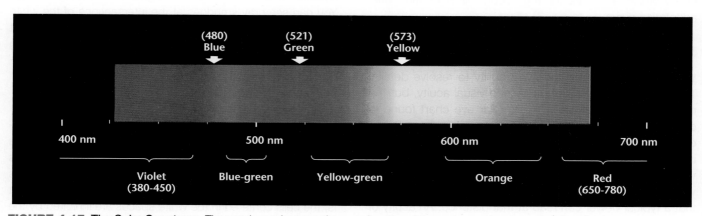

FIGURE 4.17 **The Solar Spectrum.** *The numbers given are the wavelengths of the various colors in nanometers (nm).*

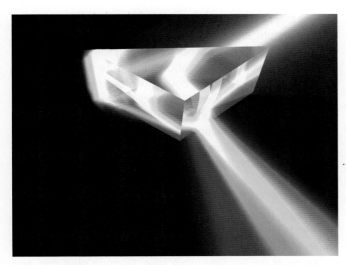

A prism breaks up light into different wavelengths. Short wavelengths appear blue, medium wavelengths green, and long wavelengths red.

common way of referring to the various color experiences of a typical viewer is to organize them on three dimensions: hue, brightness, and saturation. **Hue** refers to the quality best described by the color's name, such as red or greenish-yellow. **Brightness** refers to how much light appears to be reflected from a colored surface, with white being the brightest possible color and black the dimmest. **Saturation** refers to the purity of the color, in that a fully saturated color, such as crimson, appears to contain no gray, while an unsaturated color, such as pink, appears to be a mixture of red and white. American artist Albert Munsell proposed a scheme for specifying colored surfaces by assigning them one of ten hue names and two numbers, one indicating saturation and the other brightness. The colors in the **Munsell system** are represented by the color solid (see Figure 4.18). (The key characteristics of color and sound are summarized in the Concept Review Table.)

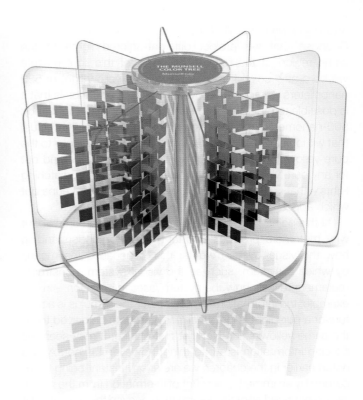

FIGURE 4.18 **The Color Solid.** *The three dimensions of color can be represented on a double cone. Hue is represented by points around the circumference, saturation by points along the radius, and brightness by points on the vertical axis. A vertical slice taken from the color solid will show differences in the saturation and lightness of a single hue.*

Given a means of describing colors, we can ask how many colors we are capable of seeing. Within the 400–700 nanometer range to which humans are sensitive, we can discriminate among 150 hues, suggesting that we can distinguish among about 150 wavelengths. This means that, on average, we can discriminate between two wavelengths that are only two nanometers apart; that is, the jnd for wavelengths is two nanometers. Given that each of the 150 discriminable colors can have many different values of lightness and saturation, the estimated number of colors among which we can discriminate is over 7 million! Moreover, according to estimates by the National Bureau of Standards, we have names for about 7 500 of these colors. These numbers give some indication of the importance of color to our lives (Coren *et al.*, 1999).

Color mixture

The most important fact for understanding how the visual system constructs color is that all the hues among which we can discriminate can be generated by mixing together only three basic colors. This was demonstrated many years

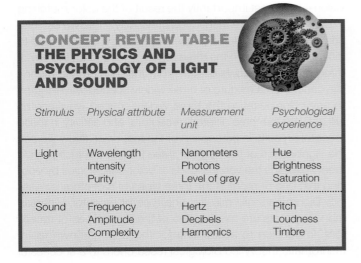

CONCEPT REVIEW TABLE
THE PHYSICS AND PSYCHOLOGY OF LIGHT AND SOUND

Stimulus	Physical attribute	Measurement unit	Psychological experience
Light	Wavelength	Nanometers	Hue
	Intensity	Photons	Brightness
	Purity	Level of gray	Saturation
Sound	Frequency	Hertz	Pitch
	Amplitude	Decibels	Loudness
	Complexity	Harmonics	Timbre

ago using what is called the **color-matching experiment**. Suppose that we project different-colored lights to the same region of the retina. The result of this light mixture will be a new color. For example, a pure yellow light of 580 nanometers will appear yellow. Of critical importance is that it is possible to create a mixture of a 650-nanometer light (red), 500-nanometer light (green) and 450-nanometer light (blue) that will look identical – and we literally mean *identical* – to the pure yellow light. This matching process can be carried out for any pure visible light whatsoever. A pair of such matching lights – that is, two lights with different physical makeups but which appear to be identical – are called **metamers**.

At this point, we will make a few general comments about why metamers provide important clues for understanding how the visual system works: this is because the means by which a system, such as the visual system, constructs metamers reveals how the system *loses information* – in our example, the information about whether the stimulus is a mixture or a pure light is lost when they are both perceived to be the same yellow color. Now, at first glance, it may seem as if losing information is a bad thing; however it is not. As we noted earlier in the chapter, we are at any instant being bombarded by an immense amount of information from the world. We do not need all of this information or even the majority of it to survive and flourish in the environment. This means that we must eliminate much of the incoming information from the environment or we would constantly be overwhelmed by information overload. It is this information-elimination process that creates metamers. As we shall see below the fact that three, and exactly three, primary colors are needed to match – that is, to form a metamer of – any arbitrary color provides an important clue about how the visual system is constructed.

Implication of the matching-by-three-primaries law

Before describing the value of this clue we note two implications. First, this arrangement for color mixing has important practical uses. A good example is that color reproduction in television or photography relies on the fact that a wide range of colors can be produced by mixing only three primary colors. For example, if you examine your television screen with a magnifying glass you will find that it is composed of tiny dots of only three colors (blue, green, and red). Additive color mixture occurs because the dots are so close together that their images on your retina overlap. (See Figure 4.19 for a way of representing color mixtures.)

A second implication has to do with our understanding of color deficiencies. While most people can match a wide range of colors with a mixture of three primaries, others can match a wide range of colors by using mixtures of only two primaries. Such people, referred to as **dichromats**, have deficient color vision, as they confuse some colors that people with normal vision (trichromats) can distinguish among. But dichromats

can still see color. Not so for monochromats, who are unable to discriminate among different wavelengths at all. Monochromats are truly color-blind. (Screening for color blindness is done with tests like that shown in Figure 4.20, a simpler procedure than conducting color mixture experiments.) Most color deficiencies are genetic in origin. As noted in Chapter 2, color blindness occurs much more frequently in males (2 percent) than in females (0.03 percent), because the critical genes for this condition are recessive genes located on the X chromosome (Nathans, 1987).

Theories of color vision

Two major theories of color vision have been suggested. The first was proposed by English physicist Thomas Young in 1807, long before scientists even knew about the existence of cones. Fifty years later, German physician and physicist Hermann von Helmholtz further developed Young's theory. According to the Young–Helmholtz or **trichromatic theory**, even though we can discriminate among many different colors, there are only three types of receptors for color. We now know that these are the cones. Each type of cone is sensitive to a wide range of wavelengths but is most responsive within a narrower region. As shown in Figure 4.21, the short-wavelength cone is most sensitive to short wavelengths (blues), the medium-wavelength cone is most sensitive to medium wavelengths (greens and yellows), and the long-wavelength cone is most sensitive to long wavelengths (reds). The joint action of these three receptors determines the sensation of color. That is, a light of a particular wavelength stimulates the three receptors to different degrees, and the specific ratios of activity in the three receptors leads to the sensation of a specific color. Hence, with regard to our earlier discussion of coding quality, the trichromatic theory holds that the quality of color is coded by the pattern of activity of three receptors rather than by specific receptors for each of a multitude of colors.

The trichromatic theory explains the facts about color vision – and most importantly the result of the color-matching experiment – that we mentioned previously. First, we can discriminate among different wavelengths because they lead to different responses in the three receptors. Second, the law of three primaries follows directly from the trichromatic theory. We can match a mixture of three widely spaced wavelengths to any color because the three widely spaced wavelengths will activate the three different receptors, and activity in these receptors results in perception of the test color. (Now we see the significance of the number three.) Third, the trichromatic theory explains the various kinds of color deficiencies by positing that one or more of the three types of receptors is missing: Dichromats are missing one type of receptor, whereas monochromats are missing two of the three types of receptors. In addition to accounting for these long-known facts, trichromatic theory led biological researchers to a successful

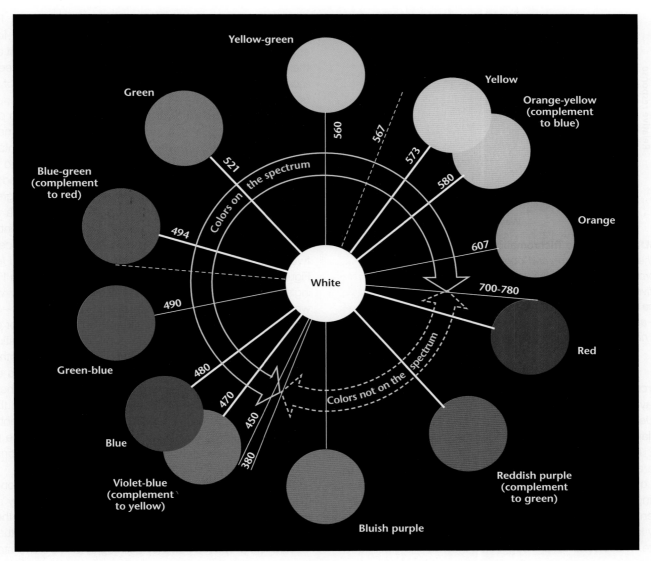

FIGURE 4.19 The Color Circle. *A simple way to represent color mixture is by means of the color circle. The spectral colors (colors corresponding to wavelengths in our region of sensitivity) are represented by points around the circumference of the circle. The two ends of the spectrum do not meet; the space between them corresponds to the non-spectral reds and purples, which can be produced by mixtures of long and short wavelengths. The inside of the circle represents mixtures of lights. Lights toward the center of the circle are less saturated (or whiter); white is at the very center. Mixtures of any two lights lie along the straight line joining the two points. When this line goes through the center of the circle, the lights, when mixed in proper proportions, will look white. Such pairs of colors are called complementary colors.*

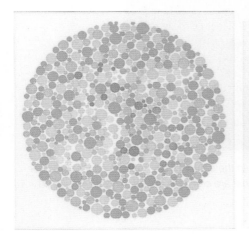

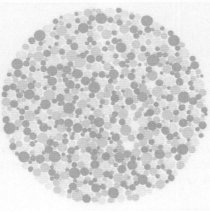

FIGURE 4.20 Testing for Color Blindness. *Two plates used in color blindness tests. In the left plate, individuals with certain kinds of red-green blindness see only the number 5; others see only the number 7; still others, no number at all. Similarly, in the right plate, people with normal vision see the number 15, whereas those with red-green blindness see no number at all.*

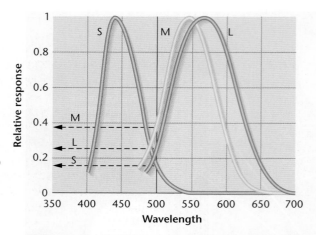

FIGURE 4.21 The Trichromatic Theory. *Response curves for the short-, medium-, and long-wave receptors proposed by trichromatic theory. These curves enable us to determine the relative response of each receptor to light of any wavelength. In the example shown here, the response of each receptor to a 500-nanometer light is determined by drawing a line up from 500 nanometers and noting where this line intersects each curve.*

search for the three kinds of cones that are familiar to us today.

Despite its successes, the trichromatic theory cannot explain some well-established findings about color perception. In 1878, German physiologist Ewald Hering observed that all colors may be described as consisting of one or two of the following sensations: red, green, yellow, and blue. Hering also noted that nothing is perceived to be reddish-green or yellowish-blue; rather, a mixture of red and green may look yellow, and a mixture of yellow and blue may look white. These observations suggested that red and green form an opponent pair, as do yellow and blue, and that the colors

in an opponent pair cannot be perceived simultaneously. Further support for the notion of opponent pairs comes from studies in which an observer first stares at a colored light and then looks at a neutral surface. The observer reports seeing a color on the neutral surface that is the complement of the original one (see Figure 4.22).

These phenomenological observations led Hering to propose an alternative theory of color vision called opponent-color theory. Hering believed that the visual system contains two types of color-sensitive units. One type responds to red or green, the other to blue or yellow. Each unit responds in opposite ways to its two opponent colors. The red-green unit, for example, increases its response rate when a red is presented and decreases it when a green is presented. Because a unit cannot respond in two ways at once, if two opponent colors are presented, white is perceived (see Figure 4.22). **Opponent-color theory** is able to explain Hering's observations about color. The theory accounts for why we see the hues that we do. We perceive a single hue – red or green or yellow or blue – whenever only one type of opponent unit is out of balance, and we perceive combinations of hues when both types of units are out of balance. Nothing is perceived as red-green or as yellow-blue because a unit cannot respond in two ways at once. Moreover, the theory explains why people who first view a colored light and then stare at a neutral surface report seeing the complementary color; if the person first stares at red, for example, the red component of the unit will become fatigued, and consequently, the green component will come into play.

We therefore have two theories of color vision – trichromatic and opponent-color – in which each theory can explain some facts but not others. For decades the two theories were viewed as competing with each other, but eventually, researchers proposed that they be integrated into a two-stage theory in which the three types of receptors identified by the

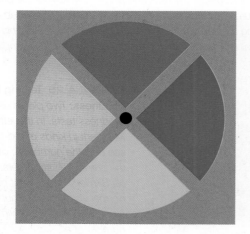

FIGURE 4.22 Complementary Afterimages. *Look steadily for about a minute at the dot in the center of the colors, and then transfer your gaze to the dot in the gray field at the right. You should see a blurry image with colors that are complementary to the original. The blue, red, green, and yellow are replaced by yellow, green, red, and blue.*

trichromatic theory feed into the color-opponent units at a higher level in the visual system (Hurvich & Jameson, 1974). This view suggests that there should be neurons in the visual system that function as color-opponent units and operate on visual information after the retina (which contains the three kinds of receptors of trichromatic theory). And in fact such color-opponent neurons have been discovered in the thalamus, a neural waystation between the retina and the visual cortex (DeValois & Jacobs, 1984). These cells are spontaneously active, increasing their activity rate in response to one range of wavelengths and decreasing it in response to another. Thus, some cells at a higher level in the visual system fire more rapidly if the retina is stimulated by a blue light and less rapidly when the retina is exposed to a yellow light; such cells seem to constitute the biological basis of the blue-yellow opponent pair. A summary neural wiring diagram that shows how the trichromatic and opponent-process theories may be related is presented in Figure 4.23.

This research on color vision is a striking example of successful interaction between psychological and biological approaches to a problem. Trichromatic theory suggested that there must be three kinds of color receptors, and subsequent biological research established that there were three kinds of cones in the retina. Opponent-color theory said that there

must be other kinds of units in the visual system, and biological researchers subsequently found opponent-color cells in the thalamus. Moreover, successful integration of the two theories required that the trichromatic cells feed into the opponent-color ones, and this, too, was confirmed by subsequent biological research. Thus, on several occasions outstanding work at the psychological level pointed the way for biological discoveries. It is no wonder that many scientists have taken the analysis of color vision as a prototype for the analysis of other sensory systems.

Sensation and perception: A preview

In this chapter we have been focusing on raw sensory input – light waves, in the instance of vision – and how that sensory input is transformed into neural patterns. In the next chapter, we will focus on perception – how the raw sensory input is transformed to knowledge about the structure of the world. In this section, we will briefly describe some recent research that bridges the gap between the two.

The research begins with a prosaic question: How does the distance between an observer and an object affect the ability of the observer to perceive the object? Suppose you are standing on a street corner in Times Square watching the people milling to and fro. As a particular person walks toward you, you are increasingly able to see what she looks like. At some distance you can tell she's a woman. Then you can tell that she has a narrow face. Then you can tell that she has rather large lips. And so on. As she moves closer and closer, you can make out more and more details about her appearance.

Enough is known about the workings of the visual system for us to know fairly precisely why this happens. Both the optics of the eye and the neurology of the rest of the system causes the representation of an image to be slightly out of focus (this is not unique to the visual system; it is true of any optical device). The further away from you is an object, like the person you're looking at, the smaller is that person's image on your retina, and the greater the degree to which the out-of-focusness degrades larger details. Recent research (Loftus & Harley, 2005) has quantified these general ideas and in particular demonstrated that seeing an object – a face in this research – from a particular distance is equivalent, from the visual system's perspective, to *blurring* the object by a particular amount. Furthermore, the work allowed an exact specification of how much blurring corresponds to any particular distance. Figure 4.24 shows an example: a picture of Anne Hathaway, shrunk (left panels) or blurred (right panels) to demonstrate the loss of visual information when she's seen from approximately 13 meters away (top panels) or 52 meters away (bottom panels). This research, and the findings from it, provide an example of using what's known about the fundamental manner in which the visual system acquires

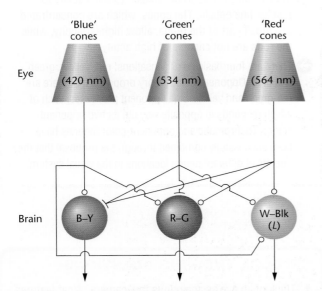

FIGURE 4.23 How the Trichromatic and Opponent-Process Theories May Be Related. *This diagram shows three types of receptors connected to produce opponent-process neural responses at a later stage in processing. The numbers in the cones indicate wavelengths of maximum sensitivity. The lines with arrows represent connections that increase activity; the lines with dots represent connections that decrease activity. Note that this is only a small part of the whole system. Another set of opponent-process units has the reverse arrangement of increasing and decreasing connections.*

FIGURE 4.24 Effects of Distance. *Two theoretically equivalent representations of Anne Hathaway's face viewed from 13 meters (top panels) and 52 meters (lower panels): resizing (left panels) and filtering (right panels). The left panels are valid if viewed from 50 cm away.*

and treats basic information (i.e., what's known about sensation) to demonstrate in a clear and intuitive manner what is the effect of a particular variable – distance – on the resulting *perception*. As we shall see in the next chapter, this knowledge not only is useful in practical settings (e.g., demonstrating to a jury in a criminal trial how well a witness could have seen a criminal from a particular distance) but also provides a scientific tool to investigate other perceptual phenomena.

INTERIM SUMMARY

- The stimulus for vision is light, which is electromagnetic radiation in the range from 400 to 700 nanometers.

- The transduction system for vision consists of visual receptors in the retina at the back of the eye. The visual receptors broadly consist of rods and cones. There are three subtypes of cones, each subtype maximally sensitive to a different wavelength.

- Different wavelengths of light lead to sensations of different colors. Color vision is understood via the trichromatic theory, which holds that perception of color is based on the activity of three types of cone receptors. The rods are insensitive to color and to fine details; however rods are capable of detecting very small amounts of light and are used for seeing under conditions of low illumination.

- Visual acuity refers to the visual system's ability to resolve fine details. The cones, which are concentrated in a small part of the retina, allow highest-acuity, while the rods are not capable of high acuity.

- There are four basic color sensations: red, yellow, green, and blue. Opponent-color theory proposes that there are red-green and yellow-blue opponent processes, each of which responds in opposite ways to its two opponent colors. Trichromatic and opponent-color theories have been successfully combined through the proposal that they operate at different neural locations in the visual system.

CRITICAL THINKING QUESTIONS

1 Think of an eye as analogous to a camera. What features of the eye correspond to which features of a camera?

2 Pilots preparing for flying at night often wear red goggles for an hour or so prior to their flight. Why do you suppose that they would do this?

3 From an evolutionary standpoint, can you think of reasons why some animals' eyes consist almost entirely of rods, other animals' eyes have only cones, and those of others, such as humans, have both cones and rods?

AUDITION

Along with vision, audition (hearing) is our major means of obtaining information about the environment. For most of us, it is the primary channel of communication as well as the vehicle for music. As we will see, it all comes about because small changes in sound pressure can move a membrane in our inner ear back and forth.

Our discussion of audition follows the same plan as our discussion of vision. We first consider the nature of the physical stimulus to which audition is sensitive; then describe the auditory system, with particular emphasis on how the receptors carry out the transduction process; and finally consider how the auditory system codes the intensity of sound and its quality.

Prolonged exposure to loud noises can cause permanent hearing loss. This is why airport workers always wear ear protectors.

Sound waves

Sound originates from the motion or vibration of an object, as when the wind rushes through the branches of a tree. When something moves, the molecules of air in front of it are pushed together. These molecules push other molecules and then return to their original position. In this way, a wave of pressure changes (a sound wave) is transmitted through the air, even though the individual air molecules do not travel far. This wave is analogous to the ripples set up by throwing a stone into a pond.

A sound wave may be described by a graph of air pressure as a function of time. A pressure-versus-time graph of one type of sound is shown in Figure 4.25. The graph depicts a sine wave, familiar to anyone who has taken trigonometry. Sounds that correspond to sine waves are called pure tones. An important dimension of a pure tone is the tone's **frequency**, which is the number of cycles per second (or **hertz**), at which the molecules move back and forth (see Figure 4.25). Frequency is the basis of our perception of **pitch**, which is one of the most noticeable qualities of a sound. High-frequency tones take the form of high-frequency sine waves (like the 5000 hertz sine wave shown in the top panel of Figure 4.25) while lower-frequency tones take the form of low-frequency sound waves (such as the 500 cycle/sec sine wave shown in the bottom panel of Figure 4.25). Sine waves are important in the analysis of audition because, as proved by the French mathematician Fourier, any complex sound can be decomposed into pure tones; that is, any complex sound can be represented as a weighted sum of a series of different-frequency sine waves.

A second aspect of a pure tone is its **amplitude**, which is the pressure difference between the peak and the trough in

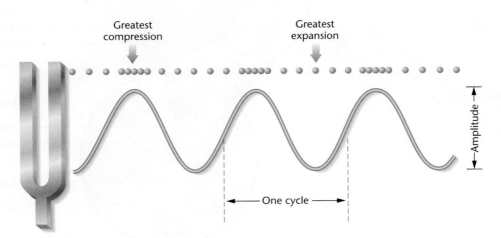

FIGURE 4.25 A Pure Tone. *As the tuning fork vibrates, it produces a pure tone, which is made up of successive aircompression waves that form a sine-wave pattern. The amplitude of the wave corresponds to the wave's intensity, while the number of waves per second is its frequency. Using a technique called Fourier analysis, any arbitrary sound wave can be decomposed into the sum of sine waves of different frequencies and intensities.*

a pressure-versus-time graph (see Figure 4.25). Amplitude underlies our sensation of **loudness**. Sound amplitude is usually specified in decibels which is a type of logarithmic scale; an increase of 10 decibels corresponds to a 10-fold increase in amplitude above the sound's threshold; 20 decibels, a 100-fold increase; 30 decibels, a 1000-fold increase; and so forth. For example, a soft whisper in a quiet library is approximately 30 decibels, a noisy restaurant may have a level of 70 decibels, a rock concert may be near 120 decibels, and a jet taking off may be over 140 decibels. Consistent exposure to sound levels at or above 100 decibels is associated with permanent hearing loss.

A final aspect of sound is **timbre**, which refers to our experience of the complexity of a sound. Almost none of the sounds we hear every day are as simple as the pure tones we have been discussing. (The exceptions are tuning forks and some electronic instruments.) Sounds produced by acoustical instruments, automobiles, the human voice, other animals, and waterfalls are characterized by complex patterns of sound pressure. The difference in timbre is, for example, what makes a middle-C produced by a violin sound different from a middle C produced by a trombone.

Musical instruments produce complex patterns of sound pressure. They are referred to as the sound's timbre.

The auditory system

The auditory system consists of the ears, parts of the brain, and the various connecting neural pathways. Our primary concern will be with the ears: this includes not just the appendages on the sides of the head, but the entire hearing organ, most of which lies within the skull (see Figure 4.26).

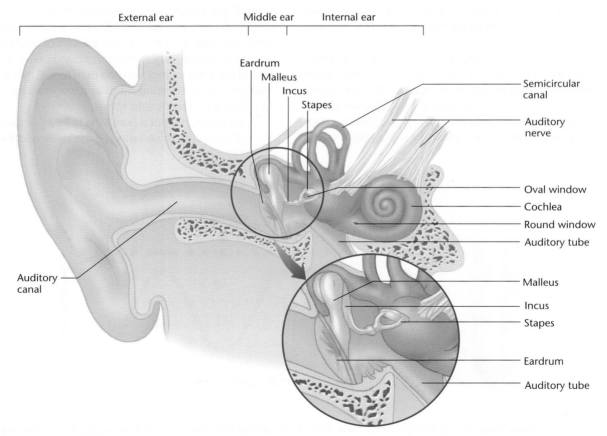

FIGURE 4.26 A Cross-Section of the Ear. *This drawing shows the overall structure of the ear. The inner ear includes the cochlea, which contains the auditory receptors, and the vestibular apparatus (semicircular canals and vestibular sacs), which is the sense organ for our sense of balance and body motion.*

Like the eye, the ear contains two systems. One system amplifies and transmits the sound to the receptors, whereupon the other system takes over and transduces the sound into neural impulses. The transmission system involves the **outer ear**, which consists of the external ear (or pinna) along with the auditory canal, and the **middle ear**, which consists of the eardrum and a chain of three bones called the malleus, incus, and stapes. The transduction system is housed in a part of the inner ear called the cochlea, which contains the receptors for sound.

Let us take a more detailed look at the transmission system (see Figure 4.27). The outer ear aids in the collection of sound,

funneling it through the auditory canal to a taut membrane, the **eardrum**. The eardrum, the outermost part of the middle ear, is caused to vibrate by sound waves funneled to it through the **auditory canal**. The middle ear's job is to transmit these vibrations of the eardrum across an air-filled cavity to another membrane, the **oval window**, which is the gateway to the inner ear and the receptors. The middle ear accomplishes this transmission by means of a mechanical bridge consisting of three small bones called the **malleus**, **incus**, and **stapes**. The vibrations of the eardrum move the first bone, which then moves the second, which in turn moves the third, which results in vibrations of the oval window. This mechanical arrangement not only transmits the sound wave but greatly amplifies it as well.

Now consider the transduction system. The **cochlea** is a coiled tube of bone. It is divided into sections of fluid by membranes, one of which, the **basilar membrane**, supports the auditory receptors (Figure 4.27). The receptors are called **hair cells** because they have hairlike structures that extend into the fluid. Pressure at the oval window (which connects the middle and inner ear) leads to pressure changes in the cochlear fluid, which in turn causes the basilar membrane to vibrate, resulting in a bending of the hair cells and an electrical impulse. Through this complex process, a sound wave is, at last, transduced into an electrical impulse. The neurons that synapse with the hair cells have long axons that form part of the auditory nerve. Most of these auditory neurons connect to single hair cells. There are about 31 000 auditory neurons in the auditory nerve, many fewer than the 1 million neurons in the optic nerve (Yost & Nielson, 1985). The auditory pathway from each ear goes to both sides of the brain and has synapses in several nuclei before reaching the auditory cortex located in the temporal lobe.

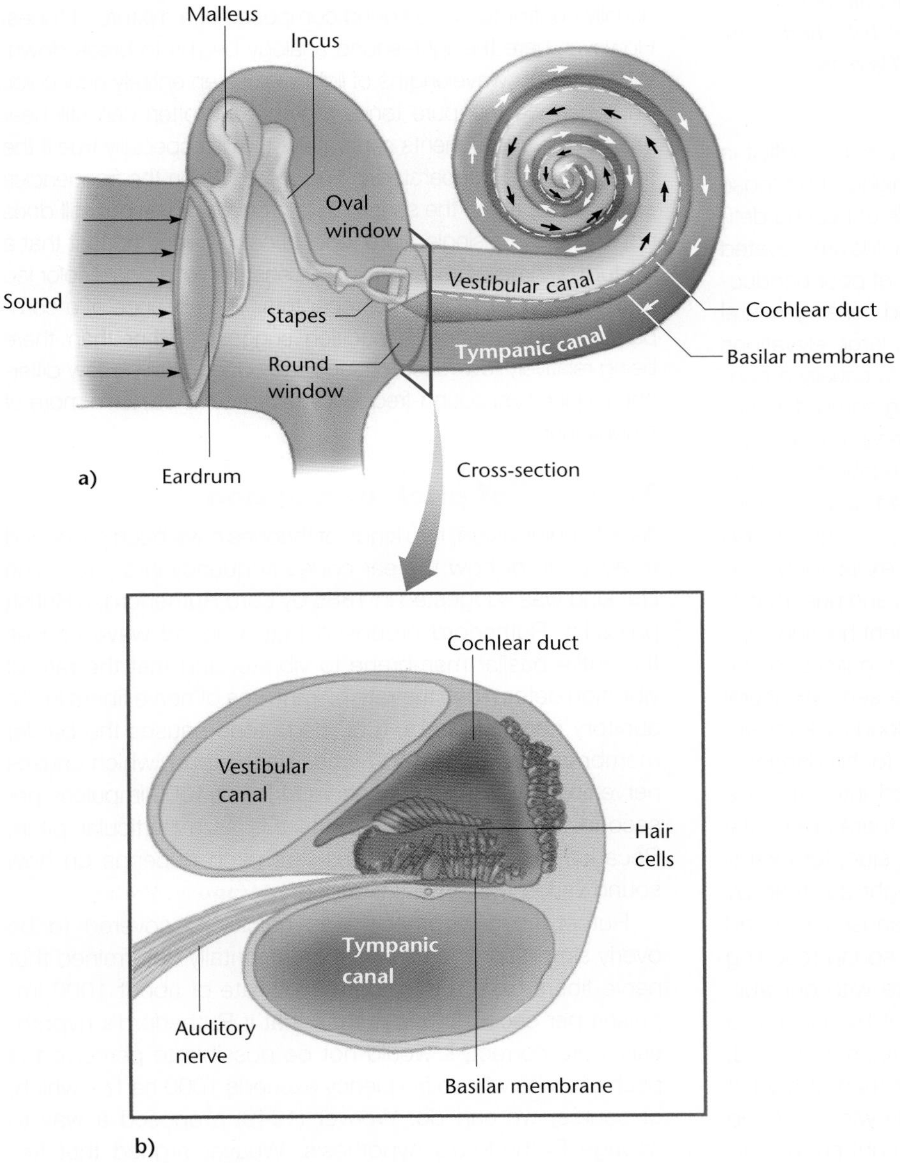

FIGURE 4.27 **A Schematic Diagram of the Middle and Inner Ear.** *(a) Movement of the fluid within the cochlea deforms the basilar membrane and stimulates the hair cells that serve as the auditory receptors. (b) A cross-section of the cochlea showing the basilar membrane and the hair cell receptors.*

Hearing sound intensity

Recall that our vision is more sensitive to some wavelengths than to others. A similar phenomenon occurs in audition. We are more sensitive to sounds of intermediate frequency than we are to sounds near either end of our frequency range. This is illustrated in Figure 4.28, which shows the absolute threshold for sound intensity

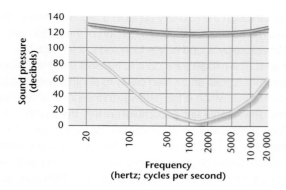

FIGURE 4.28 Absolute Threshold for Hearing. *The lower curve shows the absolute intensity threshold at different frequencies. Sensitivity is greatest in the vicinity of 1000 hertz. The upper curve describes the threshold for pain. (Data are approximate, from various determinations.)*

as a function of frequency. Many people have some deficit in hearing and consequently have a threshold higher than those shown in the figure. There are two basic kinds of hearing deficits. In one kind, called conduction loss, thresholds are elevated roughly equally at all frequencies as the result of poor conduction in the middle ear. In the other kind, called sensory-neural loss, the threshold elevation is unequal, with large elevations occurring at higher frequencies. This pattern is usually a consequence of inner-ear damage, often involving some destruction of the hair cells, which are unable to regenerate. Sensory neural loss occurs in many older people and explains why the elderly often have trouble hearing high-pitched sounds. Sensory neural loss is not limited to the elderly, though. It also occurs in young people who are exposed to excessively loud sound. Rock musicians, airport-runway crews, and pneumatic-drill operators commonly suffer major, permanent hearing loss. For example, Pete Townshend, the well-known guitarist of the 1960s rock group The Who, suffered severe sensory neural loss because of his continuous exposure to loud rock music; since then he has alerted many young people to this danger.

It is natural to assume that the perceived intensity of a sound is the same at both ears, but in fact there are subtle differences. A sound originating on our right side, for example, will be heard as more intense by our right ear than by our left ear. This happens because our head causes a 'sound shadow' that decreases the intensity of the sound reaching the far ear. This difference does not interfere with our ability to hear, however; we take advantage of it by using it to localize where the sound is coming from. It is as if we said, 'If the sound is more intense at my right ear than at my left ear, it must be coming from my right side.' Likewise, a sound originating on the right side will arrive at the right ear a split-second before it reaches the left ear (and vice versa for a sound originating on the left). We also take advantage of this difference to localize the sound ('If the sound arrived at my right ear first, it must be coming from the right').

Hearing pitch

As we have noted, one of the primary psychological qualities of a sound is its **pitch**, which is a sensation based on the frequency of a sound. As frequency increases, so does pitch. Young adults can detect pure tone frequencies between 20 and 20 000 hertz, with the jnd being less than 1 hertz at 100 hertz and increasing to 100 hertz at 10 000 hertz.

With sound, as with light, we rarely have opportunities to hear pure sensory stimuli. Recall that for the visual system we usually see mixtures of wavelengths rather than a pure stimulus – a light consisting of only one wavelength (an exception would be the light emitted by a laser). A similar situation characterizes the auditory system. We rarely hear a pure tone; instead, we are usually confronted by a sound composed of a mixture of tones. However, here the light–sound analogy begins to break down. When we mix wavelengths of light we see an entirely new color, but when we mix pure tones together we often can still hear each of the components separately. This is especially true if the tones are widely separated in frequency. When the frequencies are close together, the sensation is more complex but still does not sound like a single, pure tone. In color vision, the fact that a mixture of three lights results in the sensation of a single color led to the idea of three types of receptors. The absence of a comparable phenomenon in audition suggests rather than there being relatively few receptors specialized for relatively few different frequencies, sound-frequency receptors must form more of a continuum.

Theories of pitch perception

As with color vision, two kinds of theories have been proposed to account for how the ear codes frequency into pitch. The first kind was suggested in 1886 by Lord Rutherford, a British physicist. Rutherford proposed that a sound wave causes the entire basilar membrane to vibrate, and that the rate of vibration determines the rate of impulses of nerve fibers in the auditory nerve. Thus, a 1000-hertz tone causes the basilar membrane to vibrate 1000 times per second, which causes nerve fibers in the auditory nerve to fire at 1000 impulses per second, and the brain interprets this as a particular pitch. Because this theory proposes that pitch depends on how sound varies with time, it is called a **temporal theory**.

Rutherford's hypothesis was quickly discovered to be overly simplistic when it was experimentally determined that nerve fibers have a maximum firing rate of about 1000 impulses per second. This means that if Rutherford's hypothesis were correct, it would not be possible to perceive the pitch of tones whose frequency exceeds 1000 hertz – which, of course, we *can* do. Weaver (1949) proposed a way to salvage Rutherford's hypothesis. Weaver argued that frequencies over 1000 hertz could be coded by different groups of nerve fibers, each group firing at a slightly different pace. If one group of neurons is firing at 1000 impulses per second, for example, and then 1 millisecond later a second group of neurons begins firing at 1000 impulses per second, the combined rate of impulses per second for the two groups will be 2000 impulses per second. This version of temporal theory received support from the discovery that the pattern of nerve impulses in the auditory nerve follows the waveform of the stimulus tone even though individual cells do not respond on every cycle of the wave (Rose *et al.*, 1967).

While clever, this hypothesis is still insufficient: the ability of nerve fibers to follow the waveform breaks down at about 4000 hertz – yet we can hear pitch at much higher frequencies. This implies that there must be another means of coding the quality of pitch, at least for high frequencies. The second kind of theory of pitch perception deals with this question. It dates back to 1683, when the French anatomist Joseph Guichard Duverney proposed that frequency is coded into pitch mechanically by **resonance** (Green & Wier, 1984). To appreciate this proposal, it is helpful to first consider an example of resonance. When a tuning fork is struck near a piano, the piano string that is tuned to the frequency of the fork will begin to vibrate. To say that the ear works the same way is to say that the ear contains a structure similar to a stringed instrument, with different parts tuned to different frequencies, so that when a frequency is presented to the ear the corresponding part of the structure vibrates. This idea

proved to be roughly correct; the structure turned out to be the basilar membrane.

In the 1800s the ubiquitous Hermann von Helmholtz (remember him from color-vision theory?) developed this hypothesis further, eventually proposing the **place theory** of pitch perception, which holds that each specific place along the basilar membrane will lead to a particular pitch sensation. The fact that there are many such places on the membrane is consistent with there being many different receptors for pitch. Note that place theory does not imply that we hear with our basilar membrane; rather, the places on the membrane that vibrate most determine which neural fibers are activated, and that determines the pitch we hear. This is an example of a sensory modality coding quality according to the specific nerves involved.

How the basilar membrane actually moves was not established until the 1940s, when the Hungarian-born biophysicist Georg von Békésy measured its movement through small holes drilled in the cochleas of guinea pigs and human cadavers. von Békésy's findings required a modification of place theory: rather than behaving like a piano with separate strings, the basilar membrane behaves more like a bed sheet being shaken at one end. Specifically, von Békésy showed that the whole membrane moves for most frequencies, but that the place of maximum movement depends on the

CUTTING EDGE RESEARCH WHERE IN THE BRAIN ARE ILLUSIONS?

Scott Murray, University of Washington

Context has a dramatic effect on how we perceive object size. For example, in the picture illustrated, the two spheres are exactly the same physical size – they occupy the same size on the page (check it out!) and therefore occupy the same amount of space on the retina. However, we cannot help but perceive the sphere at the back of the hallway as being larger than the sphere at the front of the hallway. As we shall see in more detail in Chapter 5, illusion makes perfect sense for a visual system that has evolved to interpret a three-dimensional (3-D) world. The depth cues in the image give rise to a difference in perceived distance between the two spheres, and our visual system takes this into account when arriving at an estimate of object size. This example is a powerful illustration of how identical input at the retina can be transformed into very different perceptions depending on the 3-D information present in an image.

One important question is where in the visual system the 3-D information provided by the pictured hallway exerts its influence on the sensory representations of the spheres. Since the 3-D information is quite complex, this integration might occur at late stages of the visual system that are specialized for processing 3-D information and object recognition. Or, it could happen much earlier – the 3-D

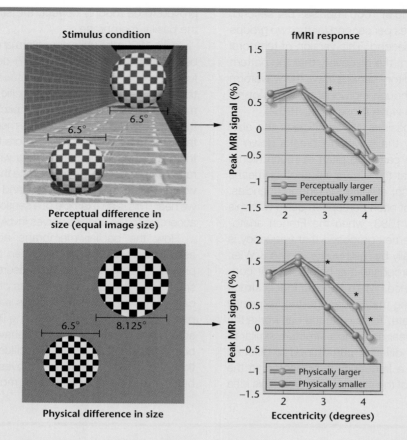

Stimulus condition

6.5° 6.5°

Perceptual difference in size (equal image size)

fMRI response

Peak MRI signal (%)

* *

- Perceptually larger
- Perceptually smaller

2 3 4

6.5° 8.125°

Physical difference in size

Peak MRI signal (%)

* * *

- Physically larger
- Physically smaller

2 3 4

Eccentricity (degrees)

information could be used to change our perceptions as soon as the image of the spheres enters the brain. Indeed, there is a strong sense in which we 'can't make the illusion go away,' which suggests that the representations of the spheres are altered at very early stages of the visual system.

To test this we used a brain imaging technique called fMRI to measure the amount of cortex that is activated by the front and back spheres. The early visual system is retinotopically organized, meaning that nearby positions on the retina project to nearby positions in visual cortex. The result is a 'map' of visual space – an object projecting an image on the retina literally activates a contiguous region of cortex. Using fMRI we measured whether the map is smaller when people are looking at the front sphere as compared to the back sphere.

We found that in 'primary visual cortex' (or V1) – the very first area of our cortex to receive information from the eyes – that the maps for the front and back spheres are different. The front sphere activated a smaller area of cortex than the back sphere. This is shown in the second picture. The top row shows that the map extends further for the perceptually larger back sphere than for the perceptually smaller front sphere. The graphs look very similar when we used a stimulus that did not have 3-D context but had a real difference in size that matched the size illusion, as is shown in the bottom row.

Why would the visual system change the maps in the early visual cortex? Size is an important cue for recognizing objects. For example, object size can quickly help you discriminate

between a golf ball, baseball, and volleyball. But in order for your recognition system to be able to use object size, 3-D information must be taken into account. For example, a golf ball held close to your eye can produce a larger visual image than a volleyball that is far away. Our fMRI research indicates that distance information is taken into account early, presumably so that we can obtain an accurate estimation of object size for recognition.

Our research has been followed up by several other research groups that have shown a number of exciting new developments. For example, Schindel and Arnold (2010) show that human orientation discrimination improves with an *apparent* increase in the size of an object. This implies that we are able to see fine details better on the 'far' versus the 'near' object even though their retinal images are equivalent. In addition, Schwarzkopf *et al.*, (2011) showed a surprising relationship between the size of V1 – which, for unknown reasons, varies considerably between individuals– and the magnitude of the size illusion. People with smaller V1s have a larger size illusion, a finding that further supports the role of V1 in size perception.

Our research, along with these recent findings, help explain why illusions such as the ball example above are so powerful – the differences in image size between the two spheres seem very real. By showing that there are differences in the maps in the very earliest stages of the visual system – for our brains, at least – these differences are real.

specific frequency sounded. High frequencies cause vibration at the near end of the basilar membrane; as frequency increases, the vibration pattern moves toward the oval window (von Békésy, 1960). For this and other research on audition, von Békésy received a Nobel Prize in 1961.

Like temporal theories, place theories explain many pitch-perception phenomena, but not all. A major difficulty for place theory arises with low-frequency tones. With frequencies below 50 hertz, all parts of the basilar membrane vibrate about equally. This means that all the receptors are equally activated, which implies that we have no way of discriminating between different frequencies that are below 50 hertz. In fact, though, we can discern frequencies as low as 20 hertz. Hence, place theories have problems explaining our perception of low-frequency tones, while temporal theories have problems dealing with high-frequency tones. This led to the idea that pitch depends on both place and temporal pattern, with temporal theory explaining our perception of low frequencies and place theory explaining our perception of high frequencies. It is not clear, however, where one mechanism leaves off and the other takes over. Indeed, it is possible that frequencies between 1000 and 5000 hertz are handled by both mechanisms (Coren *et al.*, 1999).

INTERIM SUMMARY

➡ The stimulus for hearing is a wave of air-pressure changes (a sound wave).

➡ Sound waves are transduced by the outer and middle ear, causing the basilar membrane to vibrate, which results in a bending of the hair cells that produces a neural impulse.

➡ Sound intensity is determined by the magnitude of the sound wave, i.e., the difference between a wave's minimum and maximum pressure.

➡ Pitch, the most striking quality of sound, is determined by the frequency of the sound wave. There are two theories of pitch perception: temporal theories, and place theories. These theories are not mutually exclusive. Temporal theory explains perception of low frequencies, and place theory accounts for perception of high frequencies.

CRITICAL THINKING QUESTIONS

1 Consider the relation between the eye and the ear. Each organ is made up of various components that perform various functions. What are the correspondences between the eye components and the ear components in terms of the functions they perform?

---

2 Why do you suppose that it is high-frequency sounds that are heard poorly by older adults?

OTHER SENSES

Senses other than vision and audition lack the richness of patterning and organization that have led sight and hearing to be called the 'higher senses.' Still, these other senses are vitally important. Smell, for example, is one of the most primitive and most important of the senses. This is probably related to the fact that smell has a more direct route to the brain than any other sense. The receptors, which are in the nasal cavity, are connected to the brain without synapses. Moreover, unlike the receptors for vision and audition, the receptors for smell are exposed directly to the environment – they are right there in the nasal cavity with no protective shield in front of them. (In contrast, the receptors for vision are behind the cornea, and those for audition are protected by the outer and middle ear.) Since smell is clearly an important sensory modality, we begin our discussion of the other senses with smell, also termed **olfaction**.

Olfaction

Olfaction aids in the survival of our species: it is needed for the detection of spoiled food or escaping gas, and loss of the sense of smell can lead to a dulled appetite. Smell is even more essential for the survival of many other animals. Not surprisingly, then, a larger area of the cortex is devoted to smell in other species than in our own. In fish, the olfactory cortex makes up almost all of the cerebral hemispheres; in dogs, about one-third; in humans, only about one-twentieth. These variations are related to differences in sensitivity to smell. Taking advantage of the superior smell capability of dogs, law enforcement agencies around the world train them to check unopened packages for contraband – such as drugs – and trained police dogs can sniff out hidden explosives.

Because smell is so well developed in other species, it is often used as a means of communication. Insects and some other animals secrete **pheromones**, chemicals that float through the air to be sniffed by other members of the species. For example, a female moth can release a pheromone so powerful that males are drawn to her from a distance of several kilometers. It is clear that the male moth responds only to the pheromone and not to the sight of the female; the male will be attracted to a female in a wire container even though she is blocked from view, but not to a female that is clearly visible in a glass container from which the scent cannot escape. (The fascinating novel *Perfume* by Patrick Suskind deals with a man who, although born with absolutely no odor of his own, was exquisitely sensitive to all odors of the world. To others he seemed to have 'extrasensory' powers, since he could, for example, predict the imminent arrival of an unseen person by his or her odor.)

Ants carry away a dead ant from the nest due to its smell.

Insects use smell to communicate death as well as 'love.' After an ant dies, the chemicals formed from its decomposing body stimulate other ants to carry the corpse to a refuse heap outside the nest. If a living ant is experimentally doused with the decomposition chemicals, it is carried off by other ants to the refuse heap. When it returns to the nest, it is carried out again. Such premature attempts at burial continue until the 'smell of death' has worn off (Wilson, 1963).

Do humans have a vestige of this primitive communication system? Experiments indicate that we can use smell at least to tell ourselves from other people and to distinguish males from females. In one study, observers wore undershirts for 24 hours without showering or using deodorant. The undershirts were collected by the experimenter, who then presented each observer with three shirts to smell. One was the observer's own shirt, while the other two belonged to other people: one was a male's, and the other was a female's. Based only on odor,

most observers could identify their own shirt and tell which of the other shirts had been worn by a male or a female (Russell, 1976; Schleidt *et al.*, 1981). Other studies suggest that we may communicate subtler matters by means of odor. Women who live or work together seem to communicate their stage in the menstrual cycle by means of smell, and over time this results in a tendency for their menstrual cycles to begin at the same time (McClintock, 1971; Preti *et al.*, 1986; Russell *et al.*, 1980; Weller & Weller, 1993). However, it is important to remember that these are effects on physiological functioning, not behavior. Although menstrual regularity is associated with healthy reproductive functioning and fertility, it does not have a direct influence on human behavior. Indeed, many researchers now believe that the behavioral effects of pheromones on humans are likely to be indirect, since social and learning factors influence our behavior more than they do that of other mammals (Coren *et al.*, 1999).

The olfactory system

The volatile molecules given off by a substance are the stimulus for smell. The molecules leave the substance, travel through the air, and enter the nasal passage (see Figure 4.29). The molecules must also be soluble in fat, because the receptors for smell are covered with a fatlike substance.

The olfactory system consists of the receptors in the nasal passage, certain regions of the brain, and interconnecting neural pathways. The receptors for smell are located high in the nasal cavity. When the cilia (hairlike structures) of these receptors come into contact with volatile molecules, an electrical impulse results; this is the transduction process. This impulse travels along nerve fibers to the **olfactory bulb**, a region of the brain that lies just below the frontal lobes. The olfactory bulb in turn is connected to the **olfactory cortex** on

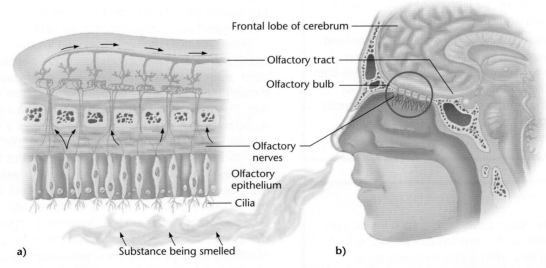

FIGURE 4.29 Olfactory Receptors. *(a) Detail of a receptor interspersed among numerous supporting cells. (b) The placement of the olfactory receptors in the nasal cavity.*

the inside of the temporal lobes. (Interestingly, there is a direct connection between the olfactory bulb and the part of the cortex known to be involved in the formation of long-term memories; perhaps this is related to the Proustian idea that a distinctive smell can be a powerful aid in retrieving an old memory.)

Sensing intensity and quality

Human sensitivity to smell intensity depends greatly on the substance involved. Absolute thresholds can be as low as 1 part per 50 billion parts of air. Still, as noted earlier, we are far less sensitive to smell than other species. Dogs, for example, can detect substances in concentrations 100 times lower than those that can be detected by humans (Marshall *et al.*, 1981). Our relative lack of sensitivity is not due to our having less sensitive olfactory receptors. Rather, we just have fewer of them by about a factor of 100: roughly 10 million receptors for humans versus 1 billion for dogs.

Although we rely less on smell than do other species, we are capable of sensing many different qualities of odor. Estimates vary, but a healthy person appears to be able to distinguish among 10000 to 40000 different odors, with women generally doing better than men (Cain, 1988). Professional perfumers and whiskey blenders can probably do even better – discriminating among perhaps 100000 odors (Dobb, 1989). Moreover, we know something about how the olfactory system codes the quality of odors at the biological level. The situation is most unlike the coding of color in vision, for which three kinds of receptors suffice. In olfaction, many kinds of receptors seem to be involved; an estimate of 1000 kinds of olfactory receptors is not unreasonable (Buck & Axel, 1991). Rather than coding a specific odor, each kind of receptor may respond to many different odors (Matthews, 1972). So quality may be partly coded by the pattern of neural activity, even in this receptor-rich sensory modality.

Gustation

Gustation, or the sense of taste, gets credit for a lot of experiences that it does not provide. We say that a meal 'tastes' good, but when our ability to smell is eliminated by a bad cold, food seems to lack taste and we may have trouble telling red wine from vinegar. Still, taste is a sense in its own right. Even with a bad cold, we can tell salted from unsalted food.

In what follows, we will refer to the taste of particular substances, but note that the substance being tasted is not the only factor that determines its taste. Our genetic makeup and experience also affect taste. For example, people vary in their sensitivity to the bitter taste in caffeine and saccharin, and this difference appears to be genetically determined (Bartoshuk, 1979). The role of experience is illustrated by Indians living in the Karnataka province of India, who eat many sour foods and experience citric acid and quinine (the bitter taste of tonic water) as pleasant tasting. Most Westerners experience the opposite sensations. This particular difference seems to be a matter of experience, for Indians raised in Western countries find citric acid and quinine unpleasant tasting (Moskowitz *et al.*, 1975).

Humans vary in their sensitivity to different tastes. Some people, like this tea taster, are able to discriminate among very subtle differences in the tastes of particular substances.

Dogs are far more sensitive to smells than humans, and for this reason they were used in the aftermath of the World Trade Center disaster for the search-and-rescue operation and bomb detection.

The gustatory system

The stimulus for taste is a substance that is soluble in saliva. The gustatory system includes receptors that are located on the tongue as well as on the throat and roof of the mouth; the system also includes parts of the brain and interconnecting neural pathways. In what follows, we focus on the receptors on the tongue. These **taste receptors** occur in clusters, called taste buds, on the bumps of the tongue and around the mouth. At the ends of the taste buds are short, hairlike structures that extend outward and make contact with the solutions in the mouth. The contact results in an electrical impulse; this is the transduction process. The electrical impulse then travels to the brain.

Sensing intensity and quality

Sensitivity to different taste stimuli varies from place to place on the tongue. While any substance can be detected at almost any place on the tongue (except the center), different tastes are best detected in different regions. Sensitivity to salty and sweet substances is best near the front of the tongue; sensitivity to sour substances along the sides; and sensitivity to bitter substances is best on the soft palate (see Figure 4.30). In the center of the tongue is a region that is insensitive to taste (the place to put an unpleasant pill). While absolute thresholds for taste are generally very low, jnds for intensity are relatively high (Weber's constant is often about 0.2). This means that if you are increasing the amount of spice in a dish, you usually must add more than 20 per cent or you will not taste the difference.

Recent research suggests that 'tongue maps,' such as the one in Figure 4.30, may be oversimplified in that they suggest that if the nerves leading to a particular region were cut, all sensation would be lost. However, this does not occur because taste nerves inhibit one another. Damaging one nerve abolishes its ability to inhibit others; thus, if you cut the nerves to a particular region, you also reduce the inhibitory effect, and the result is that there is little change in the everyday experience of taste (Bartoshuk, 1993).

There is an agreed-upon vocabulary for describing tastes. Any taste can be described as one or a combination of the four basic taste qualities: sweet, sour, salty, and bitter (McBurney, 1978). These four tastes are best revealed in sucrose (sweet), hydrochloric acid (sour), sodium chloride (salty), and quinine (bitter). When people are asked to describe the tastes of various substances in terms of just the four basic tastes, they have no trouble doing this. Even if they are given the option of using additional qualities of their own choice, they tend to stay with the four basic tastes (Goldstein, 1989).

The gustatory system codes taste in terms of both the specific nerve fibers activated and the pattern of activation across nerve fibers. There appear to be four types of nerve fibers, corresponding to the four basic tastes. While each fiber responds somewhat to all four basic tastes, it responds best to just one of them. Hence, it makes sense to talk of 'salty fibers' whose activity signals saltiness to the brain. Thus, there is a remarkable correspondence between our subjective experience of taste and its neural coding. Nonetheless, our taste experiences may be influenced not only by receptor activation, but also by peoples' expectations regarding the foods that they eat. For instance, Plassmann *et al.* (2008) asked participants to taste the identical wine, marked as costing either $10 or $90. Participants perceived the 'more expensive wine' as tasting better. Although one might tend to simply interpret this as a bias effect, electrophysiological measures indicated that areas of the brain associated with pleasure were more activated by the 'more expensive' wine, producing a shift in taste experience. Similar results were reported in the domain of olfaction by Rachel Herz (2003). She randomly labeled perfumes as naturally or artificially scented. Participants consistently rated the products labeled as natural to be better smelling, regardless of whether the product itself was natural or artificial. Examples like this show that although receptor activation may provide the dominant information resulting in sensory experience, cognitive factors may also contribute. As will be seen in the next chapter, our conscious experiences of the world are often the result of a complex process of 'give and take' between patterns of sensory activation and expectations.

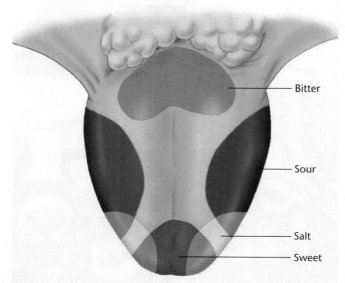

FIGURE 4.30 Taste Areas. *Although any substance can be detected anywhere on the tongue – except in the center – different areas are maximally sensitive to different tastes. The area labeled 'sweet' for example, is most sensitive to sweet tastes.*

Bitter

Sour

Salt

Sweet

Pressure and temperature

Traditionally, touch was thought to be a single sense. Today, it is considered to include three distinct skin senses: one responding to pressure, another to temperature, and the third to pain. This section briefly considers pressure and temperature, and the next discusses pain.

Pressure

The stimulus for sensed pressure is physical pressure on the skin. Although we are not aware of steady pressure on the entire body (such as air pressure), we can discriminate among variations in pressure over the surface of the body. Some parts of the body are more sensitive than others at sensing the intensity of pressure: The lips, nose, and cheek are the most sensitive, while the big toe is least sensitive. These differences are closely related to the number of receptors that respond to the stimulus at each of these locations. In sensitive regions, we can detect a force as small as 5 milligrams applied to a small area. However, like other sensory systems, the pressure system shows profound adaptation effects. If you hold a friend's hand for several minutes without moving, you will become insensitive to its pressure and cease to feel it.

When we are actively exploring the environment through touch, the motor senses contribute to our experience. Through active touch alone we can readily identify familiar objects, using it to recognize coins, keys, and other small objects that we keep in our pockets and purses (Klatzky *et al.*, 1985).

Temperature

The stimulus for temperature is the temperature of our skin. The receptors are neurons just under the skin. In the transduction stage, cold receptors generate a neural impulse when there is a decrease in skin temperature, while warm receptors generate an impulse when there is an increase in skin temperature (Duclauz & Kenshalo, 1980; Hensel, 1973). Hence, different qualities of temperature can be coded primarily by the specific receptors activated. However, this specificity of neural reaction has its limits. Cold receptors respond not only to low temperatures but also to very high temperatures (above 45 degrees centigrade or 113 degrees Fahrenheit). Consequently, a very hot stimulus will activate both warm and cold receptors, as you may have experienced when you accidentally plunged your foot into a very hot bath.

Because maintaining body temperature is crucial to survival, it is important that we be able to sense small changes in our skin temperature. When the skin is at its normal temperature, we can detect a warming of only 0.4 degrees centigrade and a cooling of just 0.15 degrees centigrade (Kenshalo *et al.*, 1961). Our temperature sense adapts completely to moderate changes in temperature, so that after a few minutes the stimulus feels neither cool nor warm. This adaptation explains the strong differences of opinion about the temperature of a swimming pool between those who have been in it for a while and those who are first dangling a foot in it.

After being in a swimming pool for a while, our temperature sense adapts to the change in temperature. However, when first dangling a foot into the water, we can detect the cooler temperature.

Pain

Of all our senses, none captures our attention like pain. We may sometimes take a blasé view of the other senses, but it is hard to ignore pain. Yet for all the discomfort it causes, we would be at risk if we had no sense of pain. It would be difficult for children to learn not to touch a hot stove, or to stop chewing their tongues. In fact, some people are born with a rare genetic disorder that makes them insensitive to pain, and they typically die young, owing to tissue deterioration resulting from wounds that could have been avoided if they had been able to feel pain.

The pain system

Any stimulus that is intense enough to cause tissue damage is a stimulus for pain. It may be pressure, temperature, electric shock, or chemical irritants. Such a stimulus causes the release of chemical substances in the skin, which in turn stimulate distinct high-threshold receptors (the transduction stage). These receptors are neurons with specialized free nerve endings, and researchers have identified several types (Brown & Deffenbacher, 1979). With regard to variations in the quality of pain, perhaps the most important distinction is between the kind of pain we feel immediately upon suffering an injury, called **phasic pain**, and the kind we experience after the injury has occurred, called **tonic pain**. Phasic pain is typically a sharp, immediate pain that is brief in duration (that is, it rapidly rises and falls in intensity), whereas tonic pain is typically dull and long-lasting.

To illustrate, if you sprain your ankle, you immediately feel a sharp undulating pain (phasic pain), but after a while you start to feel the steady pain caused by the swelling (tonic pain). The two kinds of pain are mediated by two distinct neural pathways, and these pathways eventually reach different parts of the cortex (Melzack, 1990).

Non-stimulus determinants of pain

More than any other sensation, the intensity and quality of pain are influenced by factors other than the immediate stimulus. These factors include the person's culture, expectations, and previous experience. The striking influence of culture is illustrated by the fact that some non-Western societies engage in rituals that seem unbearably painful to Westerners. A case in point is the hook-swinging ceremony practiced in some parts of India:

> The ceremony derives from an ancient practice in which a member of a social group is chosen to represent the power of the gods. The role of the chosen man (or 'celebrant') is to bless the children and crops in a series of neighboring villages during a particular period of the year. What is remarkable about the ritual is that steel hooks, which are attached by strong ropes to the top of a special cart, are shoved under his skin and muscles on both sides of his back [see Figure 4.31]. The cart is then moved from village to village. Usually the man hangs on to the ropes as the cart is moved about. But at the climax of the ceremony in each village, he swings free, hanging only from the hooks embedded in his back, to bless the children and

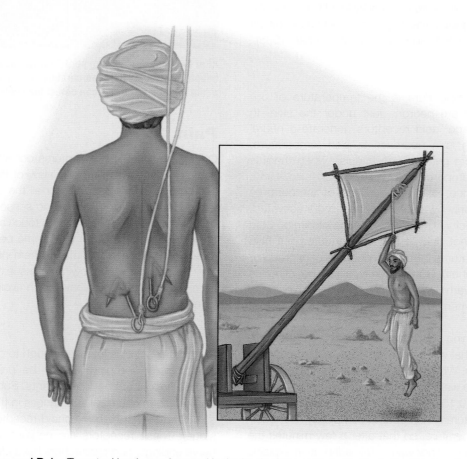

FIGURE 4.31 Culture and Pain. *Two steel hooks are inserted in the back of the celebrant in the Indian hook-swinging ceremony. Right: The celebrant hangs onto the ropes as a cart takes him from village to village. As he blesses the village children and crops, he swings freely suspended by the hooks in his back.*

crops. Astonishingly, there is no evidence that the man is in pain during the ritual; rather, he appears to be in a 'state of exaltation.' When the hooks are later removed, wounds heal rapidly without any medical treatment other than the application of wood ash. Two weeks later the marks on his back are scarcely visible.

(Melzak, 1973)

Clearly, pain is as much a matter of mind as of sensory receptors.

Phenomena like the one just described have led to the gate control theory of pain (Melzack & Wall, 1982, 1988). According to this theory, the sensation of pain requires not only that pain receptors on the skin be active but also that a 'neural gate' in the spinal cord be open and allow the signals from the pain receptors to pass to the brain (the gate closes when critical fibers in the spinal cord are activated). Because the neural gate can be closed by signals sent down from the cortex, the perceived intensity of pain can be reduced by the person's mental state, as in the hook-swinging ceremony. What exactly is the 'neural gate'? It appears to involve a region of the midbrain called the periaqueductal gray, or PAG for short; neurons in the PAG are connected to other neurons that inhibit cells that would normally carry the pain signals arising in the pain receptors. So when the PAG neurons are active, the gate is closed; when the PAG neurons are not active, the gate is open.

Interestingly, the PAG appears to be the main place where strong painkillers such as morphine affect neural processing. Morphine is known to increase neural activity in the PAG, which, as we have just seen, should result in a closing of the neural gate. Hence, the well-known analgesic effects of morphine fit with the gate control theory. Moreover, our body produces certain chemicals, called endorphins, that act like morphine to reduce pain, and these chemicals, too, are believed to create their effect by acting on the PAG in such a way as to close the neural gate.

There are other striking phenomena that fit with gate control theory. One is stimulation-produced analgesia, in which stimulation of the PAG acts like an anesthetic. One can perform abdominal surgery on a rat using only PAG stimulation as the anesthetic, with the rat showing no sign of experiencing pain (Reynolds, 1969). A milder version of this phenomenon is familiar to all of us: rubbing a hurt area relieves pain, presumably because pressure stimulation is closing the neural gate. A phenomenon related to stimulation-produced analgesia is the reduction in pain resulting from acupuncture, a healing procedure developed in China in which needles are inserted into the skin at critical points. Twirling these needles has been reported to eliminate pain entirely, making it possible to perform major surgery on a conscious patient (see

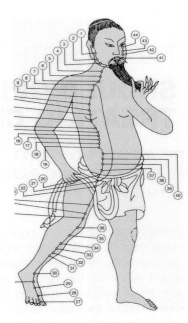

FIGURE 4.32 A Typical Acupuncture Chart. *The numbers indicate sites at which needles can be inserted and then either twisted, electrified, or heated. An impressive analgesia results in many cases.*

Figure 4.32). Presumably, the needles stimulate nerve fibers that lead to a closing of the pain gate.

At the psychological level, then, we have evidence that drugs, cultural beliefs, and various non-standard medicinal practices can dramatically reduce pain. However, all of these factors may stem from a single biological process. Here, then, is a case in which research at the biological level may actually unify findings at the psychological level.

The interplay between the psychological and biological research on pain is typical of the successful interaction between these two approaches to sensation. As we commented at the beginning of the chapter, in perhaps no other area of psychology have the biological and psychological approaches worked so well together. Again and again we have seen that neural events occurring in receptors can explain phenomena occurring at the psychological level. Thus, in discussing vision we showed how variations in sensitivity and acuity – which are psychological phenomena – can be understood as the direct consequence of how different kinds of receptors (rods versus cones) connect to ganglion cells. Also with regard to vision, we pointed out how psychological theories of color vision led to discoveries at the biological level (for example, three kinds of cone receptors). In the case of audition, the place theory of frequency perception was initially a psychological theory, and it led to research in the physiology of the basilar membrane. If ever anyone needed justification for intertwining psychological and biological research, the study of sensation provides it.

SEEING BOTH SIDES
SHOULD OPIOIDS BE USED FOR TREATING CHRONIC PAIN?

OPIOIDS ARE AN APPROPRIATE TREATMENT FOR CHRONIC PAIN

Robert N. Jamison, Harvard Medical School

Pain is a serious problem in the USA and throughout the rest of the world. About a third of the American population, or more than 100 million people, are severely affected by pain according to a recent report by the Institute of Medicine (2011). Chronic pain affects more than diabetes, cancer, and heart disease combined and is the major reason people visit their primary care physicians. Chronic pain can affect all aspects of your life, interfering with sleep, employment, socializing with others, and daily activities and places a devastating toll on overall quality of life. Persons who have chronic pain (defined as pain that lasts longer than 3 months) frequently report emotional distress, sexual problems, and decreased energy. Chronic pain accounts for about a quarter of all emergency room visits and annual missed work days, and, when direct and indirect costs are considered, imposes a greater economic burden than any other disease, with estimates of annual costs of up to $630 billion for medical expenses and lost productivity (Institute of Medicine, 2011). Chronic pain has remained a stubborn, debilitating problem for untold millions of individuals who continue to suffer due to poor response to therapy or limited access to care.

Despite medical advances in treating pain, opioids remain the most potent class of medications available to treat pain (McCarber & Billington, 2006). Yet many physicians and healthcare professionals are reluctant to support the use of opioid medication for patients with chronic pain because of concerns about adverse effects, tolerance, diversion, and addiction. Some clinicians worry that regular use of prescription opioid analgesics will contribute to dependence and impaired cognition, and may lead to the eventual use of other street drugs like heroin. For the vast majority of those individuals prescribed opioids for pain, however, these fears have been unfounded. Researchers and clinicians cite the relatively low incidence of abuse and addiction among patients with chronic pain. They suggest that the potential for increased functioning and improved quality of life significantly outweighs the minimal risk of abuse. Investigators have also suggested that chronic opioid therapy may decrease the cost of rehabilitation programs for pain patients while improving outcome. Although recent evidence suggests that non-medical use of opioids has become a major problem in the USA in part because of the increased availability of these

drugs, legitimate concerns have been expressed from those with clear pain pathology about greater sanctions on opioid prescriptions to manage their pain. With increasing numbers of individuals who are living longer come a greater number of physical symptoms, including chronic pain. There has been a tendency among some providers, however, to undertreat chronic pain for fear that any use of opioids will lead to abuse and addiction, even among those who have metastatic disease such as cancer.

Although most individuals do not misuse opioids, protocols to assist clinicians in assessing risk and monitoring aberrant drug-related behavior (validated self-report questionnaires, improved toxicology screening, regular implementation of opioid agreements, and motivational counseling) have been increasingly adopted and have been shown to decrease the risk of opioid misuse and to increase compliance (Butler *et al.*, 2007). My colleagues and I recently conducted a controlled trial to investigate the benefits of a number of strategies to reduce opioid abuse among chronic pain patients, including risk assessment screening, careful monitoring with periodic urine screens, compliance check lists, and education including motivational counseling (Jamison *et al.*, 2010). The results of our controlled trial suggested that back pain patients taking opioids for pain who were determined to be low risk for opioid misuse tended to show improvements in pain and function and to have few incidents of aberrant drug-related behavior based on self- and physician-report measures and urine toxicology screens. Most importantly, we found that those who were classified to be high risk for opioid abuse based on past behavior and family history and who were exposed to interventions to help maintain medication compliance also showed the same low levels of aberrant drug-related behavior compared with a control group without exposure to these interventions. This suggested to us that interventions to avoid misuse can be effective even among those who may present with risk factors. Thus, when risk of potential opioid misuse exists, careful monitoring, support and supervision have been shown to further enhance safety and improve the risk/benefit ratio (Savage *et al.*, 2008).

Another concern raised about long-term use of opioids is hyperalgesia (heightened pain sensitivity). Although the literature suggests that this phenomenon exists among rodents, the evidence is less clear among humans. In a recent well-controlled large clinical trial, patients with chronic back pain who had been taking either no opioids or high doses of opioids for over 6 months were assessed on measures of pain, mood, and activity interference and were given sensitivity tests using quantitative sensory testing of touch, pressure, heat, and cold. No evidence was found of opioid-induced hyperalgesia among those on high-dose opioid therapy. Rather, opioid risk categorization, anxiety, and 'catastrophizing' were the best predictors of hypersensitivity regardless of whether the subjects were taking opioids or not (Edwards *et al.*, 2011).

The future holds promise for the treatment of chronic pain with tamper- and abuse-resistant opioid formulas designed to help to combat the divergence of opioids into the hands of others who may want the medication just for their euphoric properties. We remain hopeful that other treatments using different delivery systems will also be discovered to help those who suffer needlessly from back pain, headaches, arthritis, and pain associated with the residual treatment of cancer and other chronic diseases. In the meantime, further education is needed to eradicate prejudices about the use of opioids for pain. The myth that all those who request opioid medication for their chronic pain are drug abusers should be challenged. We know that, when used responsively and intelligently, opioids can help to significantly diminish pain. There is still a wide gap of knowledge that exists regarding the use of opioids in clinical practice for chronic pain. While all medications have associated risk factors (including overuse of non-narcotic analgesic alternatives such as non-steroidal antiiflamatories – NSAIDS) the argument that long-term opioid therapy does not achieve the goals of treatment goes beyond the available data. There are clear individual differences in response to opioid therapy that future genome research will help us to sort out in identifying markers of those who benefit the most from long-term use of opioids. Although this debate is important, care must be taken to avoid returning to opioid phobia that has undermined rational pain management approaches in the past. Opioids have been and will continue to be an important part of pain management in the future. The goal is to improve the quality of life of the millions of people who continue to live each day in severe pain. The World Health Organization has declared than many persons with pain have a drug problem – they do not have access to the medication that will help their pain the most. The undertreatment of pain continues to be a needless tragedy and when used responsibly, opioids can be an appropriate treatment for many who experience debilitating chronic pain.

Robert N. Jamison

SEEING BOTH SIDES
SHOULD OPIOIDS BE USED FOR TREATING CHRONIC PAIN?

WHY OPIOIDS SHOULD BE LESS FREQUENTLY USED FOR TREATING PEOPLE WITH CHRONIC PAIN

Dennis C. Turk, University of Washington School of Medicine

Perhaps the earliest mention of the use of opioids for treating pain was contained in the Ebers papyrus dating back to the fourth century BC where opium is recommended by the goddess Isis as a treatment for the god Ra's headaches. Since then there has been little question as to the effectiveness of opioids for the treatment of acute pain – such as that following surgery. The long-term use of opioids, even for pain associated with cancer, has been much more controversial and has swung from common use, to resistance, and back again. In the 1960s and 1970s, two trends challenged the thinking about the medical use of opioids.

Behavioral scientist Wilbert Fordyce (1976) suggested that it is impossible to know how much pain someone experiences – there is no pain thermometer – other than by what the person tells you verbally or demonstrates by behaviors. He suggested that these 'pain behaviors' (overt expressions of pain, distess, and suffering such as moaning, limping, and grimacing) were observable and a source of communication. As such, these behaviors were capable of being responded to by others, including family members and physicians. Fordyce also suggested that opioids could serve as a negative reinforcement for pain behaviors. That is, if the patient took opioid medication as is commonly prescribed, 'as needed,' the pain behaviors might increase in order to obtain the pain-relieving and mood-elevating (positive reinforcing) effects of the medication themselves. Fordyce suggested that prescribing medication, if deemed essential, on a round-the-clock schedule would reduce the reinforcing effects of these medications.

Dennis Turk and Akiko Okifuji (1997) showed that physicians were more likely to prescribe the chronic use of opioids if the patients were depressed, complained that pain impacted their lives greatly, and displayed a large number of pain behaviors even though there were no differences in either actual physical pathology detected or reported pain severity. Thus, the opioids appeared to be prescribed in response to emotional distress, not specifically for pain or the presence of objective physical pathology. The reinforcing properties of the opioids could thereby maintain the patients' complaints and even their experience of pain.

The second development that challenged the use of opioids for chronic pain was the social movement in the 1970s to combat drug abuse –'Just say no,' Unfortunately, the campaign to reduce the inappropriate use of drugs was extended into clinical areas. Thus, even appropriate uses of opioids were influenced by concerns about misuse and abuse.

Fears of addiction, tolerance, and adverse side-effects became prominent and not unfounded (Ballantyne & LaForge, 2007). For example, recent data indicate that prescription opioids account for more overdose deaths than heroin and cocaine combined (Paulozzi et al., 2011). In 2010, 4.8 per cent of the US population aged > 12 (~14.4 million) used opioids non medically (SAMHSA, 2010).

Addiction is often confused with physical dependence. Addiction refers to a behavioral pattern characterized by overwhelming involvement with the use of a drug, securing of its supply, and tendency to relapse despite physical, psychological, and social harm to the user. Physical dependence develops with continued use of many drugs as the body becomes tolerant to the effects, not just opiods. Physical dependence is a pharmacological property of a drug characterized by the occurrence of withdrawal following abrupt discontinuation of the substance or administration of a drug antagonist and does not imply an aberrant psychological state or behavior. One concern with the use of opiods is that with long-term use, patients will require escalating doses of the medication to obtain the same level of pain relief. At times it is difficult to distinguish the need for increased dosage due to tolerance or progression of a disease process that might be increasing the pain severity.

There is a growing body of research, primarily on animals, indicating prolonged use of opioids sensitizes peripheral nerves leading to reduction in the threshold for perceiving pain – 'hyperalgesia' (Angst & Clark, 2006; Chang et al., 2007). Paradoxically, prolonged use of opioids appears to *lower* thresholds for pain producing a need for higher dosages of the drug to produce the same analgesic affect.

Beginning In the mid-1980s, psychologist Ronald Melzack (1990), and physicians Russell Portenoy and Kathleen Foley (1986) began to question the generalization from the illicit to the medical use of opioids. They suggested that if the use of opioids produced symptomatic improvement in chronic pain patients, long-term use might be a reasonable treatment and the failure to treat pain sufferers with appropriate and available opioids would be unethical. These influential authors had an significant impact on prescribing opioids for patients with chronic pain. Such that opioids are now the most commonly prescribed class of medications in the USA. More than 3 per cent of the US adults currently receive long-term opioid therapy for chronic pain unrelated to cancer (Dunn *et al.*, 2010). Currently, the USA constitutes 4.6 per cent of the world's population but consumes over 80 per cent of the global opioid supply (McLellan & Turner, 2010). A number of studies have evaluated the effectiveness of long-term use of opioids in the treatment of chronic pain. The results of these studies report approximately 30 per cent reduction in pain in less than 40 per cent of patients (Kalso *et al.*, 2004; Furlan *et al.*, 2006; Chou *et al.*, 2009). Even when pain is reduced, studies have found little support to indicate that the benefits of opioids are accompanied by significant improvement in physical functioning and reductions in emotional distress. Moreover, some studies have reported that both pain severity and physical functioning improve following *withdrawal* from opioids (Flor *et al.*, 1992).

'Long-term' opioid use should be used in quotas as the average duration of the published, double-blind, randomized controlled studies for the treatment of chronic pain with opioids is less than 5 weeks (Chou *et al.*, 2003). Moreover, the sizes of the samples included in these studies are small and the rates of dropouts are high, averaging around 30 per cent (Noble *et al.*, 2008).

Finally, although many of the studies report significant reductions in pain severity without serious problems, some have noted particular problems with abuse and intolerable side-effects (e.g., persistent constipation, depletion of sex hormones, neurotoxicity). Urine toxicology screening for opioid misuse suggest that as many as 45 per cent of patients treated with opioids for chronic pain are not taking the medication as prescribed and consume a range of illicit substances in addition to opioids (Wasan *et al.*, 2007). Also troubling is the rapidly increasing number of cases of non-medical uses (i.e., taken for the mood-elevating effect and not to treat physical pain) of prescription opioids and deaths that are associated with abuse correlated with the greater availability of these medications (SAMHSA, 2004).

The results of the available studies raise serious concerns about the long-term use of opioids: (1) the actual benefits reported are rather modest and there are no cures associated with long-term use of opioids, (2) few studies have shown any improvement in the patients' physical or psychological functioning, (3) adverse side-effects can be substantial, (4) studies have reported significant problems with misuse, abuse, and diversion of the drugs, and (5) the outcomes of clinics specializing in the treatment of patients with chronic pain have demonstrated reduction of pain associated with reduction of opioids. The central question is not whether chronic pain patients should ever be treated with opioids but, rather, what are the characteristics of patients who are able to reduce pain and improve physical and psychological functioning without significant problems accompanying long-term use? At the present time it seems premature to recommend that opioids be used on a long-term basis for a significant number of patients with chronic pain unrelated to cancer although there is no question that some are able to benefit without significant aberrant behaviors.

Dennis C. Turk

INTERIM SUMMARY

➔ The stimuli for smell are the molecules given off by a substance, which travel through the air and activate olfactory receptors located high in the nasal cavity.

➔ The stimulus for taste is a substance that is soluble in saliva; many of the receptors occur in clusters on the tongue (taste buds).

➔ Two of the skin senses are pressure and temperature. Sensitivity to pressure is greatest at the lips, nose, and cheeks, and least at the big toe. We are highly sensitive to temperature and are able to detect a change of less than 1 degree centigrade. We code different kinds of temperatures primarily by whether hot or cold receptors are activated.

➔ Any stimulus that is intense enough to cause tissue damage is a stimulus for pain. Phasic pain is typically brief and rapidly rises and falls in intensity; tonic pain is typically long-lasting and steady. Sensitivity to pain is greatly influenced by factors other than the noxious stimulus, including expectations and cultural beliefs.

CRITICAL THINKING QUESTIONS

1 Some people have described sensory experiences that cross over between two sensory systems. Called synesthesia, this apparently can occur both through natural causes and under the influence of a psychoactive drug. For example, people have reported being able to see the 'color' of music, or being able to hear the 'tunes' associated with different smells. On the basis of what you know about sensory coding, can you think of what might cause such experiences?

2 How would your life change if you did not have a sense of pain? How would it change if you did not have a sense of smell? Which do you think would be worse, and why?

CHAPTER SUMMARY

1 At the psychological level, sensations are experiences associated with simple stimuli. At the biological level, sensory processes involve the sense organs and connecting neural pathways, and are concerned with the initial stages of acquiring stimulus information. The senses include vision; audition (hearing); olfaction (smell); gustation (taste); the skin senses, which include pressure, temperature, and pain; and the body senses.

2 One property that can be used to describe all senses is sensitivity. Sensitivity to stimulus intensity is measured by the absolute threshold, which is the minimum amount of stimulus energy that can be reliably detected. Sensitivity to a change in intensity is measured by the difference threshold or jnd, the minimum difference between two stimuli that can be reliably detected. The amount of change needed for detection to occur increases with the intensity of the stimulus and is approximately proportional to it (the Weber–Fechner law).

3 Another property of great interest is the relation between stimulus intensity and the magnitude of sensation for above-threshold stimuli. This relation is captured in Stevens' power law which states that perceived stimulus magnitude is a power function of physical stimulus magnitude. The exponent of the power function differs for different sensory modalities; for most, like sound intensity, the exponent is less than 1.0, which means that the function relating perceived to physical intensity is concave down. For others, like pain intensity, the exponent is greater than 1.0, which means that the function relating perceived to physical intensity is concave up.

4 Sensation is often viewed as the process of detecting a signal that is embedded in noise. In some cases, a signal may be 'detected' even when only noise is present; this is referred to as a false alarm, while correctly detecting a signal that is present is called a hit. The use of signal detection theory allows the process of detecting a stimulus to be decomposed into two separate numbers: one representing the observer's sensitivity to the signal and the other representing the observer's bias to respond 'signal present.' Signal-detection theory is not only useful as a fundamental scientific tool, but has important practical applications, such as evaluating the performance of a radiologist trying to detect abnormalities in noisy X-rays.

5 Every sense modality must recode or transduce its physical energy into neural impulses. This transduction process is accomplished by the receptors. The receptors and connecting neural pathways code the intensity of a stimulus primarily by the rate of neural impulses and their patterns; they code the quality of a stimulus according to the specific nerve fibers involved and their pattern of activity.

6 The stimulus for vision is light, which is electromagnetic radiation in the range from 400 to 700 nanometers. Each eye contains a system for forming the image (including the cornea, pupil, and lens) and a system for transducing the image into electrical impulses. The transduction system is in the retina, which contains the visual receptors, that is, the rods and cones.

7 Cones operate at high light intensities, lead to sensations of color, and are found mainly in the center (or fovea) of the retina; rods operate at low intensities, lead to colorless sensations, and are found mainly in the periphery of the retina. Our sensitivity to the intensity of light is mediated by certain characteristics of the rods and cones. Of particular importance is the fact that rods connect to a larger number of ganglion cells than do cones. Because of this difference in connectivity, visual sensitivity is greater when it is based on rods than when it is based on cones, but visual acuity is greater when it is based on cones than when it is based on rods.

8 Different wavelengths of light lead to sensations of different colors. The appropriate mixture of three lights of widely separated wavelengths can be made to match almost any color of light. This fact and others led to the development of trichromatic theory, which holds that perception of color is based on the activity of three types of receptors (cones), each of which is most sensitive to wavelengths in a different region of the spectrum.

9 There are four basic color sensations: red, yellow, green, and blue. Mixtures of these make up our experiences of color, except that we do not see reddish-greens and yellowish-blues. This can be explained by the opponent-color theory, which proposes that there are red-green and yellow-blue opponent processes, each of which responds in opposite ways to its two opponent colors. Trichromatic and opponent-color theories have been successfully combined through the proposal that they operate at different neural locations in the visual system.

10 The stimulus for audition (hearing) is a wave of pressure changes (a sound wave). The ear includes the outer ear (the external ear and the auditory canal); the middle ear (the eardrum and a chain of bones); and the inner ear. The inner ear includes the cochlea, a coiled tube that contains the basilar membrane, which supports the hair cells that serve as the receptors for sound. Sound waves transmitted by the outer and middle ear cause the basilar membrane to vibrate, resulting in a bending of the hair cells that produces a neural impulse.

11 Pitch, the most striking quality of sound, increases with the frequency of the sound wave. The fact that we can hear the pitches of two different tones sounded simultaneously suggests that there may be many receptors, which respond to different frequencies. Temporal theories of pitch perception postulate that the pitch heard depends on the temporal pattern of neural responses in the auditory system, which itself is determined by the temporal pattern of the sound wave. Place theories postulate that each frequency stimulates a particular place along the basilar membrane more than it stimulates other places, and that the place where the maximum movement occurs determines which pitch is heard. There is room for both theories, as temporal theory explains perception of low frequencies while place theory accounts for perception of high frequencies.

12 Olfaction (smell) is even more important to non-human species than to humans. Many species use specialized odors (pheromones) for communication, and humans seem to possess a vestige of this system. The stimuli for smell are the molecules given off by a substance. The molecules travel through the air and activate olfactory receptors located high in the nasal cavity. There are many kinds of receptors (on the order of 1 000). A normal person can discriminate among 10 000 to 40 000 different odors, with women generally doing better than men.

13 Gustation (taste) is affected not only by the substance being tasted but also by genetic makeup and experience. The stimulus for taste is a substance that is soluble in saliva; many of the receptors occur in clusters on the tongue (taste buds). Sensitivity varies from one place to another on the tongue. Any taste can be described as one or a combination of the four basic taste qualities: sweet, sour, salty, and bitter. Different qualities of taste are coded partly in terms of the specific nerve fibers activated – different fibers respond best to one of the four taste sensations – and partly in terms of the pattern of fibers activated.

 Two of the skin senses are pressure and temperature. Sensitivity to pressure is greatest at the lips, nose, and cheeks, and least at the big toe. We are very sensitive to temperature, being able to detect a change of less than 1 degree centigrade. We code different kinds of temperatures primarily by whether hot or cold receptors are activated.

15 Any stimulus that is intense enough to cause tissue damage is a stimulus for pain. There are two distinct kinds of pain, which are mediated by different neural pathways. Phasic pain is typically brief and rapidly rises and falls in intensity; tonic pain is typically long-lasting and steady. Sensitivity to pain is greatly influenced by factors other than the noxious stimulus, including expectations and cultural beliefs. These factors seem to exert their influence by opening or closing a neural gate in the spinal cord and midbrain; pain is felt only when pain receptors are activated and the gate is open.

CORE CONCEPTS

sensations	psychophysical function	loudness
perception	retina	timbre
back projections	pupil	outer ear
auditory system	rods and cones	middle ear
absolute threshold	fovea	eardrum
psychophysical procedures	transduction	auditory canal
trials	dark adaptation	oval window
dark adaptation	dark adaptation curve	malleus, incus, and stapes (of the ear)
dark adaptation curve	visual acuity	cochlea
photon	Snellen acuity	basilar membrane
standard	spatial acuity	hair cells
difference threshold	contrast acuity	pitch
just noticeable difference (jnd)	color constancy	temporal theory
Weber fraction	hue	resonance
suprathreshold conditions	brightness	place theory
power function	saturation	olfaction
exponent	Munsell system	pheromones
signal detection theory	color-matching experiment	olfactory bulb
signal versus noise	metamers	olfactory cortex
sensation versus bias	dichromatism	taste receptors
false alarm	trichromatic theory	phasic pain
hit rate	Opponent-color theory	tonic pain
sensitivity and bias	frequency (of a tone)	gate control theory of pain
expectation	hertz	periaqueductal gray
sensory coding	pitch	
temporal pattern	amplitude (of a tone)	

DIGITAL SUPPORT RESOURCES

Students should use the unique access code included in the front of the book to access the digital support resources which accompany the new edition. These include:

- Multiple Choice Questions and Quizzes
- Critical Thinking Questions
- Practice Essay Questions

- Videos
- Glossary, Flashcards, and More

5 PERCEPTION

LEARNING OBJECTIVES

After reading this chapter you should be able to:

Describe the role, benefits, and costs of selective attention in perception.

Understand the principles of object separation, distance perception, and motion perception.

Explain how object features are bound together and the involvement of pre-attentive and attentive processes.

Learn what the difference is between bottom-up and top-down processing.

Learn why abstraction is important.

Explain how the perceptual system achieves and maintains constancy, and how this can cause illusions.

Briefly describe the neural underpinnings of attention, recognition, and localization.

On a warm Saturday some years ago, two young men – we'll call them Alex and Simon – left their homes for a day's hunting trip. As they walked along an abandoned road, their conversation touched on various hunting-related topics, but mostly they talked about bears. Alex had seen a bear the previous weekend, and both men were apprehensive about these dangerous creatures. They knew that their hunting rifles were powerful, but they were well aware that bears were equally powerful. The hunters maintained a constant vigil.

It was almost midnight by the time Alex and Simon retraced their path along the road bound for home. There was no moon; the forest was quiet and dark. The two hunters were tired from their day's efforts. As they rounded a curve, they suddenly became aware of a low growling sound which they perceived to come from a large, dimly illuminated animal quivering slowly but ominously in the middle of the road, about 50 meters away. Terrified, they raised their rifles and fired. The growling noise and the quivering abruptly ceased. An instant later an unmistakably human scream pierced the night. The hunters' relief at having killed the bear was replaced by confusion and dismay as they realized that the bear wasn't a bear at all. It was a tent in which had dwelt two campers. One of the campers now lay dead from a bullet wound, while the other knelt above him, wailing in horror.

Investigation carried out in the aftermath of this terrible event revealed that Simon's bullets had passed harmlessly through the tent; it was one of the bullets from Alex's gun that killed the camper. Accordingly, Alex went to trial, accused of negligent homicide. The tragedy of the killing was mirrored in the courtroom by Alex's overwhelming sorrow about what had happened. There was one critical fact, however, about which both Alex and Simon were certain: they had perceived a bear, not a tent that night. 'We never would have shot if we had had any idea that it wasn't a bear,' they both swore. The prosecutor dismissed these assertions as ridiculous and desperate lies: the bullet-riddled tent itself was placed in the center of

How could the defendant have possibly mistaken this yellow tent for a furry brown bear?

CHAPTER OUTLINE

WHAT IS THE USE OF PERCEPTION?

Processing and using incoming sensory information

Five functions of perception

ATTENTION

Selective attention

Auditory attention

Attention, perception, and memory

Costs and benefits of selectively attending to stimuli

LOCALIZATION

Separation of objects

Perceiving distance

Perceiving motion

CUTTING EDGE RESEARCH:

DISTRACTION VIA VIRTUAL REALITY

DIMINISHES SEVERE PAIN

RECOGNITION

Global-to-local processing

The binding problem: Pre-attentive and attentive processes

Determining what an object is

Later stages of recognition: Network models

Recognizing natural objects and top-down processing

Special processing of socially relevant stimuli: Face recognition

Failure of recognition

ABSTRACTION

Exact to abstract

The advantages of abstraction: Required storage and processing speed

PERCEPTUAL CONSTANCIES

The nature of constancies

Color and brightness constancy

Shape constancy

Size constancy

Illusions

Constancies in all sensory modalities

DIVISIONS OF LABOR IN THE BRAIN

The neural basis of attention

The visual cortex

Recognition versus localization systems

PERCEPTUAL DEVELOPMENT

Discrimination by infants

Controlled stimulation

SEEING BOTH SIDES: IS PERCEPTUAL
DEVELOPMENT AN INNATE OR
SOCIALLY ACQUIRED PROCESS?

the courtroom and the prosecutors asked the jury, 'How could the defendant have possibly mistaken this rectangular yellow tent for a furry brown bear?'

How indeed? On the face of it, the prosecution's question seems quite reasonable. There, sitting in the courtroom, for all to behold, was a big yellow tent, appearing not at all similar to a bear. However, a half-century's research on perception – visual perception in this instance – suggests that under the circumstances, it wasn't at all unreasonable for Simon and Alex to have perceived the tent to be a bear. In this chapter we will elaborate on why this is so, demonstrating in the process how the raw sensations that we discussed in Chapter 4 become translated into the perceptions that are directly responsible for our behavior.

To get a feel for what we mean by this, let's start with a couple of demonstrations. Look first at the left panel of Figure 5.1. Do you recognize an object? If you are like most people (and have not seen this demonstration previously), your answer would be, 'No,' Now look at the right panel of Figure 5.1. What does it say? Again if you're normal and haven't seen this demonstration before, you probably read, 'I LOVE PARIS IN THE SPRINGTIME.' In both cases you had **perceptions** that were somehow derived from the basic, objective stimulus (i.e., the light that entered your eyes and fell on your retina). You perceived meaningless black-and-white blobs in one instance and a common cliché in the other. In both instances, however, there are interesting and systematic disconnects between the raw data and the ensuing perception. Does that 'I love Paris' statement really say what you thought it did? Look at it again, this time reading it very slowly and word-by-word. You will see that it actually says, 'I love Paris in *the the* Springtime.' What about those meaningless blobs in the left panel of Figure 5.1? Look at the picture and return here when you've done so. Are you back? The left panel of Figure 5.1 is no longer meaningless, is it? Indeed, if you are like most people, it is difficult for you to believe that it ever *was* meaningless. The stimulus entering your eyes is identical to what it was before, but the perception is entirely different: the black-and-white blobs are now organized into a meaningful object.

These demonstrations are designed to convince you that while information may enter our senses in bits and pieces, that is not how we perceive the world. We perceive a world of objects and people, a world that gracefully presents us with integrated wholes, rather than chaotically bombarding us with piecemeal sensations. Only under unusual circumstances, or when we are drawing or painting, do we notice the individual features and parts of stimuli. However, most of the time we experience things in their entirety; we see three-dimensional objects, hear words and music, taste and smell the frying fish and chips, and feel a hand on our arm.

I
LOVE
PARIS IN THE
THE SPRINGTIME

FIGURE 5.1 Raw Data and the Resulting Perception. *Left panel: Do you see a meaningful object? (Look at Figure 5.38 later in the chapter if you need help.) Right panel: What does the phrase say?*

WHAT IS THE USE OF PERCEPTION?

Any living organism must solve an unending series of problems presented to it by the environment within which it dwells. The complexity of the problems and associated sophistication of the solutions depend on the nature and complexity of the organism. If you are a daffodil, for example, the problems you must deal with are relatively simple. You must figure out where your roots should go on the basis of the soil structure you're planted in, determining in the process, the soil's texture, along with the distribution within the soil of moisture and nutrients. Additionally you must determine which way to orient yourself on the basis of where the sun is.

But that's about it for daffodils. Humans, it won't surprise you to hear, are quite a bit more complex. With respect to perception, the most important differences between daffodils and humans are these: first a human is *mobile*: the vast majority of us must make our way through the environment, determining in the process, the potential routes that we could take and the obstacles that must be surmounted for each route. Second, a human *manipulates objects*: we turn the steering wheel on a car, sign our names with a pen, and kick a ball toward the goal. Third, a human makes decisions on the basis of **symbols** such as written or spoken words or hieroglyphics. Fourth, a human makes and executes complex *plans* to deal with sudden unexpected events: upon glimpsing a sinister form in a dark alley, we evaluate our options and cross to the other side of the street where we can seek safety in the crowd that has gathered there.

Processing and using incoming sensory information

How do we do this? One possibility is that the information from the environment – in the case of vision, the environment's two-dimensional representation on our retina – is all that is really necessary to live a normal life. The American J.J. Gibson offered a **theory of ecological optics**, which specified just that. According to Gibson, the vast richness of optical information from the world – the change in texture with distance, the shifting of objects' images relative to one another as one walks by them, and so on – is sufficient to solve all vision-related problems that the world presents us.

Although ingenious, sophisticated, and useful, Gibson's theory has been rejected by most perception scientists as insufficient. Instead, it is argued, humans require a continually updated image or a **model of the environment** within our brains, and it is then based on that model that humans perceive, make decisions, and behave. Two ingredients are necessary to formulate and maintain such a model. The first is some means of acquiring raw information about the environment. In Chapter 4, we discussed how our sense organs are used to accomplish this.

But acquiring raw information is not sufficient to build a model, any more than acquiring a stack of wood is sufficient to build a house. In addition, we need a means of organizing all this raw information into some kind of coherent structure.

Such organization is not simple. Most basically, perception of the world involves solving what is referred to as the *many-to-one problem*. Illustrated in vision, this problem boils down to the mathematical necessity that many configurations of objects in the environment all give rise to the same representation on the retina. Later in this chapter we will have quite a bit more to say about this. For the moment, to illustrate, think of seeing a pine tree in the distance. A 2-meter-high tree seen from a distance of 100 meters would produce the same-size retinal image as a 4-meter-high tree seen from a distance of 200 meters (as would an infinite number of other height–distance combinations). The many-to-one problem entails deciding, based on the one retinal image, which of the infinite possible size–distance configurations gives rise to the retinal image. The visual system must solve this problem by using other information – both information already stored in the brain (e.g., these trees are Christmas trees which are generally 2-meter rather than 4-meter trees) and additional visual cues (e.g., the person standing next to the tree is about the same height as the tree).

More generally, making inferences from the sensory data back to the state of the environment that gave rise to the data requires *assumptions* about how the world is put together – birds are usually to be found above horses, stoves are usually to be found near refrigerators, a scene is usually illuminated by a single kind of light source, and so on. Thus, perception is the use of such assumptions to integrate incoming sensory information into a model of the world, based upon which we make decisions and take action. Usually this process works pretty efficiently and, for example, a yellow tent in the environment produces a model – a perception – of a yellow tent in our mind. Sometimes it doesn't work so well: a yellow tent in the environment produces the perception of a bear in our mind, and we shoot it. Generally speaking, each sensory modality – seeing, hearing, and so on – has both a sense organ involved in acquiring the raw information from the environment and a more central system in the brain for transforming this information into organized percepts.

Five functions of perception

Perception is sufficiently complex that any classification of it must be somewhat arbitrary. For organizational purposes, however, it is useful to divide perceptual issues into five categories. First, via the process of *attention*, a decision must be made about *which* incoming information is to be further processed, and which is to be discarded (should I be eavesdropping on the conversation on my left which seems to be about my spouse or the conversation on my right which seems to involve cricket scores?). Second, the system must be able to determine *where* objects of interest are (is that potentially dangerous object at arm's length, on my left, hundreds of meters straight ahead, or where?). Third, the perceptual system must be able to determine *which* objects are out there (is that a tent or a bear that I'm looking at?). Fourth, the system must be able to *abstract* the critical features of a recognized object (a couch that has wrinkles and bumps in it would be reasonably perceived and described as 'rectangular' even though its shape isn't a perfect rectangle). This abstraction ability is closely related to the fifth category of perceptual issues, that of perceptual constancy: the perceptual system must maintain certain inherent features of objects (e.g., a door's inherent rectangular shape) even when the door's angle to you is such that it forms a trapezoid on your retina.

In the next five sections, we will discuss these five issues: attention, localization, recognition, abstraction, and constancy. We will then discuss some of the biological correlates of these perceptual processes. Finally, we consider the development of perception. Throughout the chapter we focus primarily on visual perception because this is the area that has been most investigated. Keep in mind, though, that the goals of localization, recognition, and constancy apply to all sensory modalities. With regard to recognition, for example, we can use our hearing to recognize a Mozart sonata, our sense of smell to recognize fish and chips, our sense of touch to recognize our keys in our trouser pocket, and our body senses to recognize that we are upright in a dark room.

INTERIM SUMMARY

➲ The study of perception deals with the question of how organisms process and organize incoming raw sensory information in order to (1) form a coherent representation or model of the world within which the organism dwells, and (2) use that representation to solve naturally occurring problems, such as navigating, grasping, and planning.

➲ Five major functions of the perceptual system are: (1) determining which part of the sensory environment to attend to, (2) localizing, or determining *where* objects are, (3) recognizing, or determining *what* objects are, (4) *abstracting* the critical information from objects, and (5) keeping the appearance of objects *constant*, even though their retinal images are changing. Another area of study is how our perceptual capacities develop.

ATTENTION

We began the previous chapter, Sensory Processes, by underscoring that at any given instant our sense organs are being bombarded with a vast amount of information from the environment. As you sit reading, stop for a moment and

attend to the various stimuli that are reaching you. There is, in your visual field, more than just the pages of this book. Perhaps your left shoe is feeling a little tight. What sounds do you hear? What odors are there in the air?

Meanwhile the human bombardee is generally engaged in trying to *accomplish some task*. This task could be as simple as drinking a cup of coffee or as complex as doing brain surgery, or something in between like trying to digest the information in this book. Whatever the task, however, only a tiny portion of the incoming stream of information is relevant to it; the vast majority is irrelevant. This state of affairs implies that the sensory systems and the brain must have some means of *screening* the incoming information – allowing people to select only the information relevant to the task at hand for perceptual processing, and to ignore the irrelevant information. If such a screening process did not exist, the irrelevant information would overwhelm the relevant information, and we would never get anything done.

The ability to selectively attend only to a small subset of all of the information in the environment is the topic of this section. This seemingly simple ability is now widely believed to involve three separate sets of processes that are anatomically distinct in the brain (e.g., Fan *et al*., 2002). One is responsible for keeping us alert. For example, an air-traffic controller needs to remain alert in order to remain aware of the various aircraft that she is responsible for; failure of this system might lead to a disastrous attentional lapse. A second system is responsible for orienting processing resources to task-relevant information (e.g., focusing on the voice so that we can understand what is being said), and the third, sometimes referred to as the 'executive,' decides whether we want to continue attending to the information or instead switch attention to other information (e.g., 'This person is talking about chloroplasts – I have no interest in chloroplasts'). The point is that rather than being a single process, attention is best thought of as involving multiple interacting processes. We describe these processes in more detail below.

Selective attention

How exactly do we direct our attention to objects of interest? The simplest means is by physically reorienting our sensory receptors. For vision, this means moving our eyes until the object of interest falls on the fovea which, you will recall from Chapter 4, is the most sensitive region of the retina – the region designed to process visual detail.

Eye movements

Studies of visual attention often involve observing an observer looking at a picture or scene. If we watch the person's eyes, it is evident that they are not stationary. Instead visual scanning takes the form of brief periods during which the eyes are relatively stationary, called eye fixations, separated by quick jumps of the eye called saccades. Each

FIGURE 5.2 Eye Movements in Viewing a Picture. *Next to the picture of the girl is a record of the eye movements made by an individual inspecting the picture.*

fixation lasts approximately 300 milliseconds (about a third of a second) while saccades are very fast (on the order of 20 milliseconds). It is during the fixation periods that visual information is acquired from the environment; vision is essentially suppressed during saccades.

By monitoring a person's eye fixation pattern over a scene, we can gain considerable insight about the sequencing of the person's visual attention. There are a number of techniques for recording eye movements but all of them eventually produce a millisecond-to-millisecond computer record of where on the scene is the gaze. Such a record can be used, among other things, to reproduce the scene itself along with the sequence of fixations on it, as shown in Figure 5.2. Generally speaking, the points on which the eyes fixate are not random, but rather are the areas of the scene that contain the most information. The exact definition of 'information' is beyond the scope of this book, but in this context it refers roughly to those areas that are most likely to distinguish the scene being viewed from any other similar scene. For example, as shown in Figure 5.2, a person looking at a face makes many fixations on the eyes, nose, and mouth – those features that most efficiently distinguish one face from another. Loftus and Mackworth (1978) demonstrated the relation between fixations and pictorial information. Participants were presented a picture containing an object that was either unusual or not unusual within some background context. For instance, one observer might be shown a picture of a farmyard with a tractor in the middle of it, while another observer would see the same farmyard picture but with an octopus rather than the tractor. Eye fixations were directed earlier and more frequently to the unusual object (the octopus) than to the normal object (the tractor). For control purposes, a separate observer would see a picture with an octopus in an underwater scene

and another observer would see a picture of a tractor in the same underwater scene; here the tractor would be the unusual object and the octopus would be the normal object.

Weapon focus

A useful practical application of this kind of eye movement research concerns what is referred to as **weapon focus**: victims of armed crimes are often able to very accurately describe what the weapon looked like, but seem to know relatively little about other aspects of the scene, such as the appearance of the person who was wielding the weapon, suggesting that attention was primarily focused on the weapon. Laboratory studies have generally confirmed this anecdotal evidence (see Steblay, 1992). Loftus *et al.*, (1987) recorded eye movements while observers looked at a slide sequence, one of which showed a person handling a critical object which was either benign (a cheque book) or threatening (a knife). They found that more eye fixations occurred on the critical object compared to the rest of the scene when the object was threatening than when it was benign; correspondingly, observers were less able to recognize other aspects of the scene, such as the face of the person holding the object, when they had viewed a threatening compared to a benign object.

It's important to note that the laboratory studies undoubtedly underestimate the attention-demanding power of a weapon compared to the real-life situations that they are meant to explore. In both the real-life and the laboratory situations, a weapon is unusual and would be expected to draw attention on that basis, as described above. However, the real-life situation has the added component that the weapon constitutes crucial environmental information relevant to what becomes the threatened individual's immediate task: that of survival.

Directed attention without eye movements

Although we normally attend to what our eyes are pointed at, we can also selectively attend to a visual stimulus without moving our eyes. In experiments that demonstrate this, observers have to detect when an object occurs. On each trial, the person stares at a blank field, then sees a brief *cue* directing them to attend either to the left or to the right. An object is then presented either in the location indicated by the cue or in the opposite location. The interval between the cue and object is too brief for observers to move their eyes, yet they can detect the object faster when it occurs in the cued location than elsewhere. Presumably, they are attending to the cued location even though they cannot move their eyes there (Posner & Raichle, 1994).

Auditory attention

Attention is multimodal; that is, attention can move within a modality (e.g., from one visual stimulus to another) or

Although we may hear a number of conversations around us, as at a cocktail party, we remember very little of what we do not attend to. This is known as selective listening.

between modalities (we have all had the experience of shifting our attention from watching the road while driving to listen to the person who just called our cell phone). Much of the original research on attention was done on auditory attention (e.g., Cherry, 1953). A real-life analogue of Cherry's work is a crowded party. The sounds of many voices bombard our ears. However, we can use purely mental means to selectively attend to the desired message. Some of the cues that we use to do this are the direction the sound is coming from, the speaker's lip movements, and the particular characteristics of the speaker's voice (pitch and intonation). Even in the absence of any of these cues, we can (though with difficulty) select one of two messages to follow on the basis of its meaning.

Attention, perception, and memory

With some caveats to be described in Chapter 8, a general rule has emerged about the relation between attention and later memory: we are consciously unaware of, and remember little, if anything, about non-attended information. In the auditory domain, a procedure known as **shadowing** is used to demonstrate this. The observer wears stereo earphones; however, entirely different messages are played to the two different ears. The person is asked to repeat (or 'shadow') one of the messages as it is heard. After a few minutes the messages are turned off and the listener is asked about the unshadowed message. The listener's report of the message is usually limited to the physical characteristics of the sound in the unshadowed ear – whether the voice was high or low, male or female, and so forth; he or she can say almost nothing about the content of the message and, indeed, does not even notice when the language changes from English to French and then back again (Moray, 1969). Loftus (1972) reports an analogous finding in vision. He showed two pictures, side-by-side, but asked the observer to look at only

one of them (and monitored the observer's eye movements to ensure compliance). The finding was that later memory was considerable for the attended picture, but was nil for the unattended picture.

The fact that we can report so little about auditory messages that we do not attend to initially led researchers to the idea that non-attended stimuli are filtered out completely (Broadbent, 1958). However, there is now considerable evidence that our perceptual system processes non-attended stimuli to some extent (in vision as well as audition), even though those stimuli rarely reach consciousness. One piece of evidence for partial processing of non-attended stimuli is that we are very likely to hear the sound of our own name, even when it is spoken softly in a non-attended conversation. This could not happen if the entire non-attended message were lost at lower levels of the perceptual system. Hence, lack of attention does not block messages entirely; rather, it attenuates them, much like a volume control that is turned down but not off (Treisman, 1969).

Costs and benefits of selectively attending to stimuli

As the previous section indicates, one cost of selectively attending to information is that observers are often oblivious to other, potentially important, stimuli in the environment. For example, Simons and Chabris (1999) showed participants a film of several students passing a basketball to one another; the observers' task was to count the total number of passes. During the film a person dressed in a gorilla suit slowly walked right through the middle of the scene. Because participants attended to the basketball almost nobody noticed the gorilla! This **inattention blindness** is closely related to **change blindness**, which is the failure of people to notice even large-scale changes to scenes. An interesting case of this was demonstrated by Simons and Levin (1998) on the campus of Cornell University, New York State. In each trial of their experiment a student stopped a pedestrian to ask directions to a building. While the pedestrian responded, two people carrying an opaque door walked between the two people, temporarily blocking the pedestrian's view of the student; during this time the student switched places with one of the door carriers. Subjects noticed less than half of the time that they were now talking to a completely different person! Manipulations that drew attention to the speaker's face substantially reduced this change-blindness effect.

That people can switch attention between sets of information has been put to interesting use by medical science in surgery for cataracts, which occur when the lens of the eye becomes cloudy so that it no longer adequately transmits light. The typical procedure is to remove the cloudy lens, replacing it with a clear artificial one. However, unlike a natural lens which can adjust its thickness to focus on objects at varying distances, artificial lenses are usually rigid. As a result, people who receive them can clearly see objects that are 3 feet away and further, but need special glasses to focus on close objects and to read. New artificial lenses have been developed that consist in a set of numerous concentric rings, where alternating rings focus on close and far objects. As a result, two images are simultaneously projected onto the retina – one in which near objects are in focus and far ones are blurry, and a second where far but not near objects are in focus. Research indicates that patients who receive these lenses can selectively attend to one image or the other, and are unaware of the non-attended image. Thus a single fixed lens can provide clear perception for objects both near and far (e.g., Brydon, 2003).

INTERIM SUMMARY

➔ Selective attention is the process by which we select some stimuli for further processing while ignoring others. In vision, the primary means of directing our attention are eye movements. Most eye fixations are on the more informative, i.e., unusual, parts of a scene.

➔ Selective attention also occurs in audition. Usually we are able to selectively listen by using cues such as the direction from which the sound is coming and the voice characteristics of the speaker.

➔ For the most part, we can only remember what we attend to. Our ability to selectively attend is mediated by processes that occur in the early stages of recognition as well as by processes that occur only after the message's meaning has been determined.

➔ By not attending to – i.e., ignoring – large parts of the environment, we lose the ability to remember much about those parts of the environment. However, such selective attention pares down the amount of necessary information processing to the point where it is manageable by the brain.

CRITICAL THINKING QUESTIONS

1 It seems quite clear that attention can be monitored by watching where a person looks. Suppose that you hypothesize that selective visual attention could go from one place to another in the environment even with the eyes held still. How would you test this hypothesis?

2 How does selective attention aid perception under everyday circumstances? What would be the consequences of driving a car in a city where no one had the ability to attend selectively? What kinds of accidents might occur more frequently than occur now? Would any kinds of accidents be apt to occur *less* frequently?

LOCALIZATION

Earlier, we described various problems that humans must solve for which localization of information is relevant. The most important of such problems are (1) navigating our way around the often cluttered environment (think about what is required just to make your way from your bed to your kitchen sink without running into anything), and (2) grasping an object (to smoothly guide your fingers in the quest of picking up your pen, you must know accurately where the pen is to begin with).

To know where the objects in our environment are, the first thing that we have to do is separate the objects from one another and from the background. Then the perceptual system can determine the position of the objects in a three-dimensional world, including their distance from us and their patterns of movement. In this section we discuss each of these perceptual abilities in turn.

Separation of objects

The image projected on our retina is a mosaic of varying brightnesses and colors. Somehow our perceptual system organizes that mosaic into a set of discrete objects projected against a background. This kind of organization was of great concern to Gestalt psychologists. (Recall from Chapter 1 that Gestalt psychology was an approach to psychology that began in Germany early in the twentieth century.) The Gestalt psychologists emphasized the importance of perceiving whole objects or forms, and proposed a number of principles to explain how we organize objects.

Figure and ground

The most elementary form of perceptual organization is that in a stimulus with two or more distinct regions, we usually see part of it as a figure and the rest as ground (or background). The regions seen as a figure contain the objects of interest – they appear more solid than the ground and appear in front of it. Figure 5.3a shows that figure–ground organization can be ambiguous. When you look at this pattern you might see a pair of silhouette faces gazing at each other, or you might see an ornate vase. The vase appears white against a black ground, whereas the faces are black against a white ground. Notice that as you look at Figure 5.3b for a few moments, the two pattern

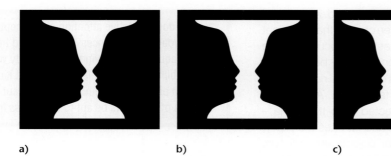

a)   b)   c)

FIGURE 5.3 **Reversible Figure and Ground.** *Three patterns in which either a white vase or a pair of black faces can be seen. Note that it is impossible to see both organizations at the same time, even though you know that both are possible percepts. When the white area is smaller (a), the vase is more likely to be seen; when the black area is smaller (c), the faces are more likely to be seen.*

organizations alternate in consciousness, demonstrating that the organization into figure and ground is in your mind, not in the stimulus. Notice, also, that the faces and the vase never appear together. You 'know' that both are possible, but you cannot 'see' both at the same time. Generally speaking, the smaller an area or a shape, the more likely it is to be seen as figure. This is demonstrated by comparing Figures 5.3a, b, and c. It is easier to see the vase when the white area is smaller, and it is easier to see the faces when the black area is smaller (Weisstein & Wong, 1986). These figure–ground principles are not restricted to simple stimuli. As shown in Figure 5.4, they apply to quite complex pictures as well.

It should be noted that, while vision is the most salient source of figure–ground relations, we can also perceive figure–ground relations in other senses. For example, we may hear the song of a bird against a background of outdoor noises, or the melody played by a violin against the harmonies of the rest of the orchestra.

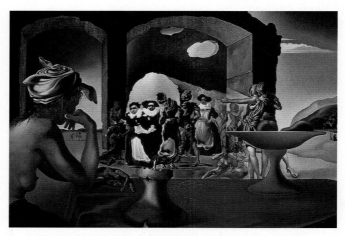

FIGURE 5.4 **The Slave Market with a Disappearing Bust of Voltaire.** *A reversible figure is in the center of this painting by Salvador Dali (1940). Two nuns standing in an archway reverse to form a bust of Voltaire.*

CUTTING EDGE RESEARCH DISTRACTION VIA VIRTUAL REALITY DIMINISHES SEVERE PAIN

Hunter Hoffman, University of Washington

While racing to rescue an ambushed US military patrol humvee convoy in Afghanistan, young Lt Sam Brown was badly burned when a terrorist's roadside bomb exploded up into his own Army vehicle. Deep third degree flash burns to his face, chest, arms and hands covered over 30 per cent of his body, and required skin transplants/grafting.

Although opioid and ketamine painkillers helped reduce his pain as he lay motionless in his hospital bed, they were much less effective during wound-care procedures. While having his wounds cleaned, Sam, like most burn patients, experienced severe to excruciating pain as well as numerous unpleasant side-effects from the drugs, and was concerned about becoming dependent on narcotic pain meds. In response, his doctor suggested he try a new non-drug pain distraction

technique, virtual reality SnowWorld, to help reduce excessive pain from his combat-related burn injury (Maani *et al.*, 2011, see story about Sam Brown in the February 2012 issue of GQ Magazine, http://gqm.ag/xqNcyy and related NBC news story search for 'Rock Center SnowWorld'). The patient benefitted, and in an unrelated twist, married his nurse.

In 1996, Dr Hunter Hoffman, a cognitive psychologist from the University of Washington's Human Interface Technology Laboratory and Dr David Patterson from Seattle's Harborview Hospital Burn Center co-originated a new psychological pain control technique – one that relied on diverted attention in a virtual-reality (VR) setting – to supplement the usual drugs.

Diverting attention is particularly useful with burn pain. The reason for this is that pain perception has a strong psychological component. As described in Chapter 4, pain,

▶

like any sensory input, consists of a specific signal, in this case, a train of nerve impulses from pain receptors in the skin. However, as we discuss in this chapter, perception, which is the interpretation of sensory input, is not entirely determined by the sensory input. This potential disconnect between sensation and perception is particularly salient with pain: the same incoming pain signal can be interpreted as painful or not painful, depending on what the patient is thinking and doing, and what task they are performing.

To explore what happens in someone's brain when they experience virtual reality analgesia, the researchers designed a unique magnet-friendly fiberoptic photonic VR goggle system so subjects could have the illusion of going inside SnowWorld while scientists measured their brain activity. Since fMRI brain scanners measure *changes* in brain activity, Hoffman *et al.* (2004) attached a small medical hotplate to the foot of healthy volunteers, which delivered 30 seconds of pain plus 30 seconds of no pain, six times. Participants reported feeling strong pain when the hotplate was hot, and their brains showed increased activity in five brain areas of the brain associated with pain perception. Interestingly, when these participants went into SnowWorld, they reported large reductions in pain even when the hotplate was on, and the amount of pain-related brain activity dropped 50 to 97 per cent in all five brain 'regions of interest.' In other words, fMRI brain scans provided objective evidence that VR reduces pain, and early clues to how VR reduces pain (see Hoffman, 2004). In a followup laboratory fMRI brain scan study, VR alone reduced pain as much as morphine alone, and the two techniques combined was most effective at reducing pain and pain-related brain activity (Hoffman *et al.*, 2007).

These results can be interpreted within the context of what is known as a *gate control theory* of pain. The idea here is that higher order thought processes such as attentional distraction, can initiate feedback signals from the cortex to the spinal cord, thereby inhibiting the intensity of incoming pain signals. In other words, in addition to influencing the way patients *interpret* incoming pain signals, distraction may actually reduce the intensity of the incoming pain signals, like a volume control that is turned down.

The problem with burn patients is that, unable to rise from their beds during wound care, they are not generally able to interact with any sort of interesting, attention-attracting real-world environment during wound care, and have no clear task. Enter VR, which allows the patient to enter any world imaginable without physically going anywhere. A VR computer set up in the hospital room sends video output to two miniature computer screens positioned in front of the patient's eyes using a specially designed helmet. Motion sensors track the patient's head position and feed this information into the computer. When the patient moves his or her head (e.g., looks up), the computer updates the artificial environment accordingly (e.g., changing the image from a virtual river to a virtual sky). These real-time changes in sensory input, in response to patients' actions, afford the illusion of actually being in the computer-generated environment. In principle, a person's perception within VR can perfectly mimic the perception of a person within the real world (as spectacularly envisioned by the science-fiction writer, Neil Stephenson in his novel, *Snow Crash*).

An incoming pain signal requires conscious attention to be perceived as pain. But being drawn into another world – one of virtual reality – drains a substantial amount of attentional resources, leaving less available to process pain signals. Since humans are overwhelmingly visually dominant, the vast majority of information enters through their eyes, bringing the information to the visual cortex. A huge 20 per cent or more of the human brain is visual cortex. When in VR, patients' eyes are no longer able to see the real world. The helmet blocks their view. Instead of pointing their eyes to look at their open burn wounds, when in VR, eye fixations dart around looking at various objects in the virtual world displayed via the VR helmet, as patients explore the 3-D canyon and search for targets to shoot with snowballs. As a result, the attentional 'spotlight' that would normally be focused on the pain is lured instead into the virtual world. For many patients undergoing VR treatment, their pain – particularly the normally excruciating pain associated with the care and cleansing of their wounds – becomes little more than an annoyance, distracting them from their primary goal of exploring and interacting with the virtual world (Wender *et al.*, 2009).

In a preliminary case study (Hoffman *et al.*, 2000b), two patients with severe burns went into a VR environment consisting of a virtual kitchen complete with countertops, a window looking out at a partly cloudy sky, cabinets, and doors. Patients could perform actions – pick up a teapot, plate, toaster, plant, or frying pan – by inserting their cyberhand into the virtual object, and clicking a grasp button on their 3-D mouse. Each patient could pick up a virtual wiggly legged spider or eat a virtual chocolate bar that possessed solidity, weight, and taste, created via a mixed-reality force feedback technique developed by Hoffman.

The VR treatments showed a great deal of promise with these two initial patients. Patient 1 had five staples removed from a burn skin graft while playing Nintendo (a control condition), and six staples removed from the same skin graft while in VR. He reported dramatic reductions in pain in the VR compared to the Nintendo condition. Patient 2, even with more severe and extensive burns, showed the same pattern.

Hoffman *et al.*, (2000a) have found additional support that VR reduces burn pain. Twelve severely burned patients reported substantial pain reduction during physical therapy when in VR compared to conventional treatment. In addition to distracting the patients, VR can likely be used to motivate patients to perform necessary but normally very painful stretching motions, using behavioral reinforcement techniques. For example, while playing in a VR game they could get virtual fuel for their virtual jet by gripping and ungripping their healing hand ten times. Preliminary results from a study currently underway at Shriners Hospital for Children in Galveston (Hoffman *et al.*, 2012) recently found that VR reduced pain during a passive range of motion skin stretching exercises in children with large severe burn wounds. VR reduced patients' pain for 20-minute physical therapy sessions, 10 days in a row, with no reduction in analgesic effectiveness. Many patients report having fun during wound care and physical therapy, when allowed to use virtual reality. In addition, the military study in which Lt Sam Brown participated found that VR was most effective for patients with the highest pain (I.e., those who needed additional pain control the most).

With funding from the the National Institutes of Health, Scandinavian Design, and the Paul Allen Family Foundation, Hoffman and worldbuilder Ari Hollander have developed a more attention-grabbing virtual environment specifically designed for treating pain (selected into the 2006 Smithsonian Cooper-Hewitt National Museum of Design Triennial). Patients fly through an icy canyon with a river and frigid waterfall, and they shoot snowballs at snowmen, igloos, penguins and woolly mammoths (with animated impacts, sound effects, and soothing background music provided by Paul Simon). The technology for these advances in pain reduction are proceeding apace with the psychological advances. Hoffman, Jeff Magula, and Eric Seibel have recently completed a custom optic fiber VR helmet that uses photons instead of electrons, so burn patients can get VR while sitting in the water-filled scrubtanks (Hoffman *et al.*, 2008). They also recently developed a pair of articulated robot-arm mounted helmet-less VR goggles for patients unable to wear conventional helmets (Maani *et al.*, 2011).

A new company (http://www.kickstarter.com/projects/1523379957/oculus-rift-step-into-the-game) has recently announced they are developing wide field of view VR goggles to sell to video gamer players (consumers) at less than the 1/35th of the current price, making VR pain distraction technology much more widely accessible.

Hoffman, Patterson, Sharar, and colleagues are optimistic that virtual reality can provide a much needed psychological pain control technique that could prove valuable for treating other pain populations in addition to burn pain (e.g., combat-related blunt force trauma injuries, cancer procedures, emergency room 'ERVR,' dental pain, and physical therapy during recovery from knee surgery). Their project nicely demonstrates the growing interdisciplinary alliance between research in psychology on the one hand and real-world problems in medicine on the other. Further details about the work can be found at http://www.vrpain.com.

Grouping of objects

We see not only objects against a ground, but we see them in a particular *grouping* as well. Even simple patterns of dots fall into groups when we look at them. To illustrate this, begin by looking at the matrix of dots shown in Figure 5.5a. These dots are equally spaced up and down, so they can be seen as being organized in rows or columns, or even as lying along diagonal paths. This is, therefore, an ambiguous pattern that follows similar principles to those illustrated in Figures 5.3 and 5.4. Only one organization is seen at a time, and at intervals this organization will spontaneously switch to another.

The Gestalt psychologists proposed a number of determinants of grouping for these kinds of dot patterns. For instance, if the vertical distance between dots is reduced, as in Figure 5.5b, columns will most likely be seen. This is grouping by proximity. If instead of varying the dot distances we vary the color shape of the elements, we can organize the dots on the basis of similarity (Figures 5.5c and d). If we move the dots to form two intersecting wave lines of dots, we are grouping by good continuation (Figure 5.5e), and if we enclose a space using lines of dots, we will tend to see grouping by closure (Figure 5.5f). Note that in this last case we see a diamond positioned between two vertical lines, even though the pattern could be two familiar letters stacked on each other (W on M) or even facing each other (K and a mirror-image K). This illustrates the powerful nature of the Gestalt grouping determinants. These determinants serve to create the most stable, consistent, and simple forms possible within a given pattern.

Modern research on visual grouping has shown that the Gestalt determinants have a strong influence on perception. For example, in one series of studies, visual targets that were part of larger visual groupings based on proximity were much harder to detect than the same targets seen as standing outside the group (Banks & Prinzmetal, 1976; Prinzmetal, 1981). In another set of studies, targets that were dissimilar to non-targets in color and shape were easier to find than targets that were more similar (Treisman, 1986). Even the similarity among the various non-targets has an important effect: targets are easier to find as the similarity of non-targets increases, allowing the target to 'pop out' as a figure distinct from the background (Duncan & Humphreys, 1989). Finally, there are reliable illusions associated with the Gestalt determinants, such that people judge distances among the elements within perceptual groups to be smaller than the same distances when they are between elements in different groups (Coren & Girgus, 1980; Enns & Girgus, 1985). All of

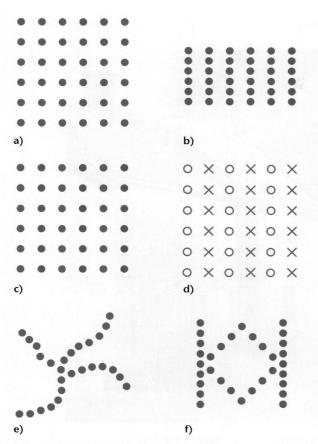

FIGURE 5.5 Gestalt Determinants of Grouping. *(a) Equally spaced dots can be seen as rows, columns, or even diagonals. (b) Grouping into columns by proximity. (c) Grouping into columns by color similarity. (d) Grouping into columns by shape similarity. (e) Grouping by good continuation. (f) Grouping by closure.*

these results show that visual grouping plays a large role in the way we organize our visual experience.

Although perceptual grouping has been studied mainly in visual perception, the same determinants of grouping appear in audition. Many demonstrations of this come from researchers who study music perception. Proximity in time clearly operates in audition. For example, four drumbeats with a pause between the second and third beats will be heard as two pairs. Similarly, sets of notes that are close together in time will be grouped together (as in the DUH-DUH-DUH-DUMMM opening of Beethoven's 5th Symphony). Notes that are proximal in pitch will also be grouped together. Music often involves counterpoint, where two melodies occur simultaneously. Listeners can shift attention between melodies so that the attended melody becomes the figure and the non-attended one becomes the ground. Often this is possible because the two melodies are in different octaves, so that notes within a melody are close to one another in pitch and notes between melodies are not. Similarity and closure are also known to play important roles in hearing tones and more complex stimuli (Bregman, 1990).

Perceiving distance

To know where an object is, we must know its distance or depth. Although perceiving an object's depth seems effortless, it is actually a remarkable achievement because we have no direct access to the depth dimension, thereby leading to one form of the many-to-one problem that we discussed earlier. A retina is a two-dimensional surface onto which a three-dimensional world is projected. The retina therefore directly reflects height and width, but depth information is lost and must somehow be reconstructed on the basis of subtle pieces of information known collectively as **depth cues**. Depth cues can be classified as binocular or monocular.

Binocular cues

Why are we and other animals equipped with two eyes rather than with just one? There are two reasons. Some animals, for example fishes, have eyes on either side of their head, which allows them to see a very large percentage of the world around them without moving their heads or their bodies. Other animals, for example humans, have two eyes in the front of their heads, both pointing in the same direction. Humans can see less of the world at any given instant than fishes, but they can use their two eyes to perceive depth. (Try covering one eye, and then sit as a passenger in a car driving in stop-and-go traffic. It's a scary experience, because you have much less sense than you normally would of how close you are to cars and other objects in front of you.)

The two eyes' ability to jointly infer depth comes about because the eyes are separated in the head, which means that each eye has a slightly different view of the same scene. You can easily demonstrate this by holding your right index finger close to your face and examining it first with only one eye open and then with only the other eye open. The term **binocular disparity** is used to refer to the difference in the views seen by each eye. The disparity is largest for objects that are seen at close range and becomes smaller as the object recedes into the distance. Beyond 3 to 4 meters, the difference in the views seen by each eye is so small that binocular disparity loses its effectiveness as a cue for depth. However, for many everyday tasks, such as reaching for objects and navigating around obstacles, the difference in the views seen by each eye is a powerful cue for depth.

In humans and other animals with binocular vision, the visual part of the brain uses binocular disparity to assign objects to various locations in space, depending on how far apart the two images of an object are when compared. If the images of an object are in the same place in the two views, the brain assumes that this is the location on which both eyes are fixating. If the difference between the images is large, as it is for the two views of your finger held close to your face, the brain concludes that the object is much closer.

In addition to helping us see depth in the everyday world, binocular disparity can be used to fool the eye into seeing

Height in field   Interposition

Shading/shadows   Perspective   Relative size

FIGURE 5.6 Monocular Distance Cues in a Picture. *Artists use cues such as shading/shadows, perspective, relative size, and height, to portray depth on a two-dimensional surface. All of these same cues are present in a photograph of a natural scene and are also present in the retinal image of the eye.*

depth when none is really present. One way this is achieved is by using a device called a stereoscope, which displays a slightly different photograph to each eye. In Victorian times these devices were proudly displayed in the sitting rooms of middle-class homes, much as high-definition TV sets might be today. Yet the stereoscope is not just a curious antique. The same principle of binocular disparity is used today in special effects 3-D movies for which viewers must wear glasses with colored or light-polarizing filters that selectively allow one image to arrive at one eye and a slightly different image to arrive to the other.

Monocular cues

As indicated, the use of binocular cues is limited to objects that are relatively close. What about objects that are further away like distant clouds, cityscapes, or mountains? Here, binocular cues are relatively ineffective and other cues, known as monocular cues, must be used, and the task of the visual system is not straightforward. Essentially, the system has to make use of a hodge-podge of available information in the environment in order to come to a conclusion, much as a detective must use a hodge-podge of available evidence about a

murder to figure out who the murderer is. Figure 5.6 illustrates five monocular cues; these plus one other are as follows:

1 **Relative size.** If an image contains an array of similar objects that differ in size, the viewer interprets the smaller objects as being further away.

2 **Interposition.** If one object is positioned so that it obstructs the view of the other, the viewer perceives the overlapping object as being nearer.

3 **Relative height.** Among similar objects, those that appear closer to the horizon are perceived as being further away.

4 Perspective. When parallel lines in a scene appear to converge in the image, they are perceived as vanishing in the distance.

5 **Shading and shadows.** Whenever a surface in a scene is blocked from receiving direct light, a shadow is cast. If that shadow falls on a part of the same object that is blocking the light, it is called an attached shadow or simply shading. If it falls on another surface that does not belong to the object casting the shadow, it is called a cast shadow. Both kinds of shadows are important cues

to depth in the scene, giving us information about object shapes, distances between objects, and where the light source is in a scene (Coren *et al.*, 1999).

6 Motion. Have you ever noticed that if you are moving quickly – perhaps on a fast-moving train – nearby objects seem to move quickly in the opposite direction while more distant objects move more slowly (though still in the opposite direction)? Extremely distant objects, such as the moon, appear not to move at all. The difference in the speeds with which these objects appear to move provides a cue to their distance from us and is termed motion parallax.

Perceiving motion

This last monocular cue, motion, brings us to the next main topic involving localization. If we are to move around our environment effectively, we need to know not only the locations of stationary objects but also the trajectories of moving ones. We need to know, for example, that the car coming toward us from a block away will not yet have arrived at the intersection by the time we have finished crossing the street. We must, that is, be able to perceive motion.

Stroboscopic motion

What causes us to perceive motion? The simplest idea is that we perceive that an object is in motion whenever its image moves across our retina. This answer turns out to be that simple, though, for we can see motion even when nothing moves on our retina. This phenomenon, which is shown in Figure 5.7, was demonstrated in 1912 by Wertheimer in his studies of stroboscopic motion. Stroboscopic motion is produced most simply by flashing a light in darkness and then,

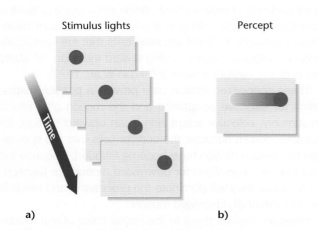

FIGURE 5.7 Stroboscopic Motion. *The sequence of still frames in (a), shown at the appropriate intervals, results in the percept shown in (b). The illusion of continuous motion resulting from successively viewed still pictures is the basis of motion in movies, video, and television.*

a few milliseconds later, flashing another light near the location of the first light. The light will seem to move from one place to the other in a way that is indistinguishable from real motion.

Wertheimer's demonstration of stroboscopic is not just an idle academic exercise; the phenomenon is crucial to a great deal of present-day visual-display technology. A prime example is movies, wherein the motion we perceive is **stroboscopic motion**. A movie is, as most people realize, simply a series of still photographs (or 'frames'), each one slightly different from the preceding one. Thus, as the frames are successively displayed on the screen, the discrete frame-to-frame differences in, say, the position of Daniel Craig's hand during an action sequence in a James Bond film, are perceived as motion – stroboscopic motion to be sure, but motion which is perceived pretty much exactly as normal, continuous motion.

Real motion

Of course, our visual system is also sensitive to real motion – that is, movement of an object through all intermediate points in space. However, the analysis of such motion under everyday conditions is amazingly complex. Some paths of motion on the retina must be attributed to movements of the eye over a stationary scene (as occurs when we are reading). Other motion paths must be attributed to moving objects (as when a bird enters our visual field). Moreover, some objects whose retinal images are stationary must be seen to be moving (as when we follow the flying bird with our eyes), while some objects whose retinal images are moving must be seen as stationary (as when the stationary background traces motion across the retina because our eyes are pursuing a flying bird).

It therefore is not surprising that our analysis of motion is highly relative. We are much better at detecting motion when we can see an object against a structured background (**relative motion**) than when the background is a uniform color and only the moving object can be seen (absolute motion). Certain patterns of relative movement can even serve as powerful cues to the shape and identity of three-dimensional objects. For example, researchers have found that the motion displays illustrated in Figure 5.8 are sufficient to enable viewers to easily identify the activity of a human figure, even though it consists of only 12 (or even fewer) points of light moving relative to one another (Johansson *et al.*, 1980). In other studies using these displays, viewers were able to identify their friends and even tell whether the model was male or female after seeing only the lights attached to the ankles (Cutting, 1986).

Another important phenomenon in the study of real motion is **selective adaptation**. This is a loss in sensitivity to motion that occurs when we view motion; the adaptation is selective in that we lose sensitivity to the motion viewed and to similar motions, but not to motion that differs significantly in direction or speed. If we look at upward-moving stripes, for example, we lose sensitivity to upward motion, but our ability to see downward motion is not affected (Sekuler, 1975). As

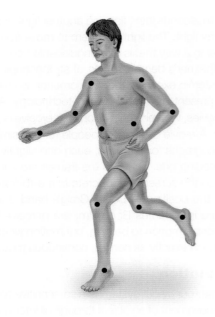

Time

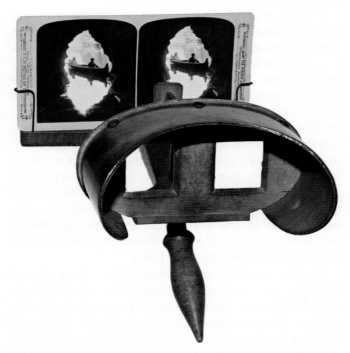

a) This is an example of the types of displays used by investigators to study patterns of humans in motion. Positions of lights affixed to individuals are indicated.

b) A sequence of movement positions made by a dancing couple.

FIGURE 5.8 Patterns of Human Motion.

with other types of adaptation, we do not usually notice the loss of sensitivity, but we do notice the after-effect produced by adaptation. If we view a waterfall for a few minutes and then look at the cliff beside it, the cliff will appear to move

The Holmes–Bates stereoscope, invented by Oliver Wendell Holmes in 1861 and manufactured by Joseph Bates, creates a vivid perception of depth.

upward. Most motions will produce such after-effects, always in the opposite direction from the original motion.

How does the brain implement the perception of real motion? Some aspects of real motion are coded by specific cells in the visual cortex. These cells respond to some motions and not to others, and each cell responds best to one direction and speed of motion. The best evidence for the existence of such cells comes from studies with animals in which the experimenter records the responses of single cells in the visual cortex while the animal is shown stimuli with different patterns of motion. Such single-cell recording studies have found cortical cells that are tuned to particular directions of movement. There are even cells that are specifically tuned to detect an object moving toward the head, an ability that is clearly useful for survival (Regan *et al.*, 1979).

These specialized motion cells provide a possible explanation for selective adaptation and the motion after-effect. Presumably, selective adaptation to an upward motion, for example, occurs because the cortical cells that are specialized for upward motion have become fatigued. Because the cells that are specialized for downward motion are functioning as usual, they will dominate the processing and result in the after-effect of downward motion.

However, there is more to the neural basis of real motion than the activation of specific cells. We can see motion when we track a luminous object moving in darkness (such as an airplane at night). Because our eyes follow the object, the image is almost motionless on the retina, yet we perceive a smooth, continuous motion. Why? The answer seems to be that information about how our eyes are moving is sent from motor regions in the front of the brain to the visual cortex and influences the motion we see. In essence, the motor system is informing the visual system that it is responsible for the lack of regular motion on the retina, and the visual system then corrects for this lack. In more normal viewing situations, there are both eye movements and large retinal-image movements. The visual system must combine these two sources of information to determine the perceived motion. You can demonstrate a consequence of this arrangement by gently pushing up on your eyeball through your lid. You'll note that the world appears to move. This is because the world is moving across your retina, but the normal signals from the motor regions are absent; the only way the brain can interpret it is if the world itself is moving.

To control the ball and avoid being tackled, soccer players must be able to perceive motion accurately.

RECOGNITION

The perceptual system needs to determine not only where relevant objects are in the scene, but also *what* they are. This is the process of recognition. Ideally, if a cat crosses our path, we should be able to recognize it as a cat, not as a skunk or a hula hoop. Similarly, if a benign tent is in front of us, we should be able to recognize it as a benign tent, not as a dangerous bear. (It is, however, noteworthy that from an evolutionary perspective, we would be better off misperceiving a tent for a bear than a bear for a tent. Our visual system has probably evolved in such a way that it is biased to perceive objects as dangerous even if sometimes they are not.)

Recognizing an object, in turn, entails several problems. First, we have to acquire fundamental or **primitive features** of information from the environment and assemble them properly. For example, if we acquire the information that there's something red and something green and a circle and a square we must somehow figure out that it's the circle that's red and the square that's green, not vice-versa. Second, we have to figure out what the objects we're seeing actually are. In the simple example we've just described, we somehow have to figure out that it's a square there to begin with. A more complex task would be to figure out that the combination of lines, angles, and shapes that we're looking at constitutes a human face, and a yet more complex task would be to figure out that the face belongs to a particular person, like Queen Elizabeth.

In what follows, we will discuss these various functions of recognition. We'll start by talking about *global-to-local processing*: the means by which a scene aids in the perception of individual objects within the scene. We will then move on to the **binding problem**: how activity in different parts of the brain, corresponding to different primitives such as color and shape, are combined into a coherent perception of an object. Next, we'll talk about how we actually recognize what an object *is*.

Global-to-local processing

Look at the object in Figure 5.9 (left panel). What is it? It could be a loaf of bread or it could be a mailbox. How is the

---

INTERIM SUMMARY

➜ To localize objects, we must first separate them and then organize them into groups.

➜ Localization involves determining an object's position in the up–down and left–right dimensions. This is relatively easy because the required information is part of our retinal image. Localizing an object also requires that we know its distance from us. This form of perception, known as depth perception, is not so easy because it's not available in the retinal image. We have a variety of depth cues, both monocular and binocular, that allow us to do this.

➜ Localizing an object sometimes requires that we know the direction in which an object is moving. This can be done either with real motion or with stroboscopic motion.

CRITICAL THINKING QUESTIONS

1 Imagine what your visual experience might be like if you suddenly became unable to see motion; in other words, suppose you saw things happening like a slide show rather than like a movie. How does motion perception contribute to your experience of a coherent world, and in what ways would the world become incoherent without a perception of motion?

2 Rank all the distance-perception cues from most important to least important. The main part of your answer should be to describe why you believe some distance-perception cues to be more or less important than others. This, of course, requires a *definition* on your part of what it means for a distance-perception cue to be 'important.'

In the early stages of recognition, the perceptual system uses information on the retina to describe the object in terms of primitive components like lines and edges. In later stages, the system compares this description to those of various categories of objects stored in the visual memory, such as 'dogs.'

visual system to disambiguate these two possibilities? One of the most powerful tools used by the perceptual system to solve this and other similar problems is to use the context (the scene) within which the object is embedded to make inferences about what the object is. That is, the system can start by carrying out *global processing* – understanding what the scene is – followed by *local processing* – using knowledge about the scene to assist in identifying individual objects. Thus, if the system determined that the scene was of a street, the object would be interpreted as a mailbox, while if the system determined that the scene was of a kitchen, the object would be interpreted as a loaf of bread (see Figure 5.9, middle and right panels).

The logic of this process is articulated by Tom Sanocki (1993), who notes that objects in the world can appear in an infinite number of orientations, sizes, shapes, colors, and so on, and point out that, accordingly: 'If during object identification, the perceptual system considered such factors for an unconstrained set of alternatives, the enormous number of combinations of stimulus features and feature-object mappings would create a combinatorial explosion' (p. 878). Sanocki notes that an obvious means of reducing what would be an otherwise impossible information-processing task is to use early (global) information to constrain the interpretation of later information.

A number of lines of research have determined that, indeed, exactly this kind of process occurs. For example, Schyns and Oliva (1994) showed *composite pictures* of naturalistic scenes. Composite pictures are 'double exposures' of two unrelated pictures, for example a skyline and a street. One of the scenes comprising the composite (say the skyline) contained only global information whereas the other (the street) contained only local information. These composites were then shown either briefly (e.g., around 10 milliseconds) or for longer (e.g., around 100 milliseconds) and the observers were asked what they had seen. For short exposures, observers reported seeing the scene containing

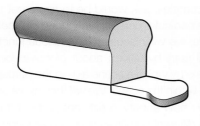

FIGURE 5.9 **Global and Local Processing.** *Is the image in the left panel a mailbox or a loaf of bread? It can be interpreted differently in different contextual settings.*

only global information (the skyline in this example) while at the longer exposures, observers reported seeing the scene containing only local information (the street). This provides evidence that the visual system tends to acquire global information first, followed by local information.

The binding problem: Pre-attentive and attentive processes

In our earlier discussion of attention, we learned that attention is the process by which we select what of the vast amount of incoming information is processed and eventually perceived consciously. Attention has also been conceptualized as having the role of binding together different features of an incoming stimulus. An excellent illustration of what we mean by this is known as an **illusory conjunction**. Suppose an observer is shown very briefly (e.g., a twentieth of a second) a stimulus such as the one in Figure 5.10 – a small red circle, a large green square, and a medium-size blue triangle – and asked to report what they saw. The observer is typically able to report the three shapes and the three colors – but often incorrectly reports which color went with which shape, e.g., the observer might report that the square was green, not red. Thus the conjunction of shape (square) and color (red) is what is perceived, but it is illusory. People often experience a

rough analogy of this phenomenon while reading: they might conjoin part of one word on one line of text, e.g., the 'liver' from 'delivery' with part of another word on a different line, e.g., the 'pool' from 'cesspool' and perceive that they see the word 'Liverpool' in the text – thereby misconjoining the primitive features of shape and location.

Feature integration theory

Illusory conjunctions suggest that information from the visual world is pre-attentively encoded along separate dimensions – in the example, shape and color are encoded separately – and then integrated in a subsequent *attentive* processing stage. This idea is, indeed, at the heart of **feature-integration theory**, initially proposed by English-born cognitive psychologist Anne Treisman (Treisman, 1986, 1992) who is now at Princeton University. The general idea is that in a first, pre-attentive stage, primitive features such as shape and color are perceived while in the second, *attentive* stage, focused attention is used to properly 'glue' the features together into an integrated whole. Illusory conjunctions occur when stimulus duration is sufficient for the primitives to be obtained, but not sufficient for the longer, attentional gluing stage.

A standard experimental procedure for distinguishing primitive features from 'glued-together' features is a **visual search task** in which the observer's task is to determine whether some target object is present in a cluttered display. A typical visual search task is shown in Figure 5.11 where the task is to find a green 'L.' In the left panel of Figure 5.11, the task is simple; the green L 'pops out' from the collection of red T's and red L's. In the right panel, however, the task of finding the same green L is considerably more difficult when the background is a collection of red L's and green T's. The reason, according to feature integration theory, is that color is a primitive feature: in the left panel, you can simply scan the information all at once; what is red and what is green

FIGURE 5.10 Illusory Conjunction. *When images are flashed briefly, observers often miscombine shape and color. This is known as illusory conjunction.*

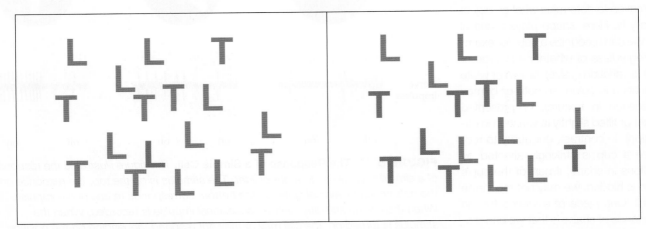

FIGURE 5.11 A Visual Search Task. *Find the green L. This is an easy task in the left panel, where pop-out takes place, but a difficult task in the right panel, where each stimulus requires focal attention.*

will perceptually separate and the presence of the one green object – the target green L – will be apparent. In the right panel, in contrast, you cannot distinguish the target from the background on the basis of the primitive attribute of color; you must attend to each letter, using the attentive stage to bind together the color and the shape, before you can determine whether that letter is or is not the target.

Problems with feature integration theory

Feature integration theory has enjoyed a great deal of support over the past couple of decades. In recent times, however, it has come under attack from the perspective of both theoretical parsimony and biological plausibility. The major problem is that, using visual search and related procedures, scientists have unveiled too many presumed 'primitives' to be realistic. A particularly lucid description of the problems with the theory is provided by Di Lollo *et al.* (2001). They go on to describe an alternative, **dynamic control theory**, whose central premise is that, 'instead of an early, hard-wired system sensitive to a small number of visual primitives, there is a malleable system whose components can be quickly reconfigured to perform different tasks at different times, much as the internal pattern of connectivity in a computer is rearranged dynamically by enabling and disabling myriad gates under program control' (p. 11). This basically means that the system rearranges itself for different tasks – as opposed to there being many subsystems for each possible task.

Determining what an object is

Attentive versus pre-attentive processing is concerned with the problem of determining which visual characteristics belong to the same object. A second problem is that of using the resulting information to determine what an object actually *is*. Here, *shape* plays a critical role. We can recognize a cup, for example, regardless of whether it is large or small (a variation in size), brown or white (a variation in color), smooth or bumpy (a variation in texture), or presented upright or tilted slightly (a variation in orientation). In contrast, our ability to recognize a cup is strikingly affected by variations in shape; if part of the cup's shape is hidden, we may not recognize it at all. One piece of evidence for the importance of shape is that we can recognize many objects about as well from simple line drawings, which preserve only the shapes of the objects, as from

detailed color photographs, which preserve many other attributes of the objects as well (Biederman & Ju, 1988).

Here also, visual processing can be divided into earlier and later stages. In early stages, the visual system uses information on the retina, particularly variations in intensity, to describe the object in terms of primitive components like lines, edges, and angles. The system uses these components to construct a description of the object. In later stages, the system compares this description to those of various categories of objects stored in visual memory and selects the best match. To recognize a particular object as the letter B, for example, is to say that the object's shape matches that of B's better than it matches that of other letters.

Feature detectors in the cortex

Much of what is known about the primitive features of object perception comes from biological studies of other species (such as cats and monkeys) using single-cell recordings in the visual cortex. These studies examine the sensitivity of specific cortical neurons when different stimuli are presented to the regions of the retina associated with those neurons; such a retinal region is called a receptive field.

These single-cell studies were pioneered by Canadian David Hubel and Swede Torsten Wiesel who, in 1981, won a Nobel Prize for their work. Hubel and Wiesel identified three types of cells in the visual cortex that can be distinguished by the features to which they respond. **Simple cells** respond when the eye is exposed to a line stimulus (such as a thin bar or straight edge between a dark and a light region) at a particular orientation and position within its receptive field. Figure 5.12 illustrates how a simple cell

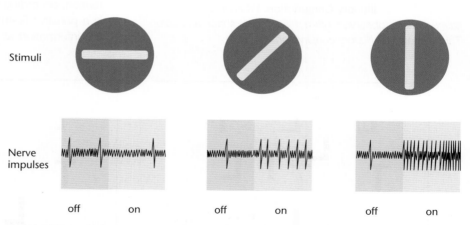

FIGURE 5.12 The Response of a Simple Cell. *This figure illustrates the response of a simple cortical cell to a bar of light. The stimulus is on the top, the response on the bottom; each vertical spike on the bottom corresponds to one nerve impulse. When there is no stimulus, only an occasional impulse is recorded. When the stimulus is turned on, the cell may or may not respond, depending on the position and orientation of the light bar. For this cell, a horizontal bar produces no change in response, a bar at 45 degrees produces a small change, and a vertical bar produces a very large change.*

will respond to a vertical bar and to bars tilted away from the vertical. The largest response is obtained for a vertical bar, and the response decreases as the orientation varies from the optimal one. Other simple cells are tuned to other orientations and positions. A **complex cell** also responds to a bar or edge in a particular orientation, but it does not require that the stimulus be at a particular place within its receptive field. It will respond continuously as the stimulus is moved across that field. **Hypercomplex cells** require not only that the stimulus be in a particular orientation, but also that it be of a particular length. If a stimulus is extended beyond the optimal length, the response will decrease and may cease entirely. Since Hubel and Wiesel's initial reports, investigators have found cells that respond to shape features other than single bars and edges; for example, there are hypercomplex cells that respond to corners or angles of a specific length (DeValois & DeValois, 1980; Shapley & Lennie, 1985).

All of the cells described above are referred to as feature detectors. Because the edges, bars, corners, and angles to which these detectors respond can be used to approximate many shapes, the feature detectors might be thought of as the building blocks of shape perception. As we will see later, though, this proposal seems to be truer of simple shapes like letters than of complex shapes like those of tables and tigers.

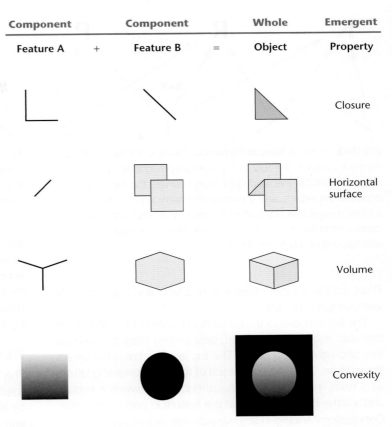

Component		Component		Whole	Emergent
Feature A	+	Feature B	=	Object	Property
					Closure
					Horizontal surface
					Volume
					Convexity

FIGURE 5.13 Relationships Between Features. *When simple two-dimensional features such as lines, angles, and shapes are combined, the resulting pattern is highly dependent on the spatial relations between the component features. In addition, new features are created. These emergent features have a perceptual reality, even though they involve complex spatial relations.*

Relations among features

There is more to a description of a shape than just its features: the relations among features must also be specified. The importance of such relations is illustrated in Figure 5.13 where it is evident that, for example, the features of a right angle and a diagonal line must be combined in a specific way to result in a triangle; likewise, a Y-intersection and a hexagon must be specifically aligned to result in the drawing of a cube. It was these kinds of relations between features that Gestalt psychologists had in mind when they emphasized that 'the whole is different from the sum of its parts.'

One way in which the whole is different is that it creates new perceptual features that cannot be understood by simply examining the component parts. Figure 5.13 shows four such **emergent features**. These emerge from very specific spatial relations among more elementary features, but nevertheless often behave just like simpler features in perceptual tasks such as target detection and visual search (Enns & Resnick, 1990; Enns & Prinzmetal, 1984; He & Nakayama, 1992). Thus, the visual system performs many sophisticated analyses of shape before the results of these analyses are made available to consciousness.

Later stages of recognition: Network models

Now that we have some idea of how an object's shape is described, we can consider how that description is matched to shape descriptions stored in memory to find the best match – that is to decide what an object is.

Simple networks

Much of the research on the matching stage has used simple patterns, specifically handwritten or printed letters or words. Figure 5.14 illustrates a proposal about how we store shape descriptions of letters. The basic idea is that letters are described in terms of certain features, and that knowledge about what features go with what letter is contained in a network of connections. Such proposals are referred to as **connectionist models**. These models are appealing because it is easy to conceive that the brain's array of interconnected neurons can be organized into networks.

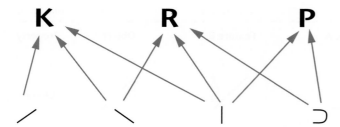

FIGURE 5.14 A Simple Network. *The bottom level of the network contains the features (ascending diagonal, descending diagonal, vertical line, and right-facing curve), the top level contains the letters, and a connection between a feature and a letter means that the feature is part of the letter. Because the connections are excitatory, when a feature is activated, the activation spreads to the letter.*

Thus, connectionism offers a bridge between psychological and biological models.

The bottom level of the network in Figure 5.14 contains the features: ascending diagonal, descending diagonal, vertical line, and right-facing curve. The top level contains the letters themselves. We will refer to each of these features and letters as a node in the network. A connection between a feature and a letter node means that the feature is part of the letter. Connections ending in arrowheads are **excitatory connections**: if the feature is activated, the activation spreads to the letter (in a manner analogous to the way electrical impulses spread in a network of neurons).

To see how this network can be used to recognize (or match) a letter, consider what happens when the letter K is presented. It will activate the features of ascending diagonal, descending diagonal, and vertical line. All three of these features will activate the node for K, while two of them – the descending diagonal and vertical line – will activate the node for R; and one of them – the vertical line – will activate the node for P. Only the K node has all of its features activated, and consequently it will be selected as the best match.

This model is too simple to account for many aspects of recognition, however. Consider what happens when the letter R is presented. It activates the features of descending diagonal, vertical line, and right-facing curve. Now the nodes for both R and P have all their features activated, and the model has no way of deciding which of the two categories provides a better match. What the model needs to know is that the presence of a descending diagonal means that the letter cannot be a P. This kind of negative knowledge is included in the **augmented network** in Figure 5.15, which has everything the preceding one had, plus **inhibitory connections** (symbolized by solid circles at their ends) between features and letters that do not contain those features. When a feature is connected to a letter by an inhibitory connection,

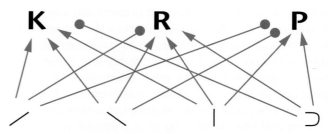

FIGURE 5.15 An Augmented Network. *The network contains inhibitory connections between features and letters that do not contain these features, as well as excitatory connections.*

activating the feature decreases activation of the letter. Thus, when R is presented to the network in Figure 5.15, the descending diagonal inhibits the P node, thereby decreasing its overall level of activation; now the R node will receive the most activation and, consequently, will be selected as the best match.

Networks with feedback

The basic idea behind the model we just considered – that a letter must be described by the features it lacks as well as by the features it contains – does not explain a pervasive and interesting finding: a letter is easier to perceive when it is presented as part of a word than when it is presented alone. For example, as shown in Figure 5.16, if observers are briefly presented with either the single letter K or the word WORK, they are more accurate in identifying whether a K or D was present when the display contained a word than when it contained only a letter.

To account for this result, our network of feature-letter connections has to be altered in a few ways. First, we have to add a level of words to our network, and along with it excitatory and inhibitory connections that go from letters to words, as shown in Figure 5.17. In addition, we have to add excitatory connections that go from words down to letters; these **top-down feedback connections** explain why a letter is more perceptible when presented briefly in a word than when presented briefly alone. When R is presented alone, for example, the features of vertical line, descending diagonal, and right-facing curve are activated, and this activation spreads to the node for R. Because the letter was presented very briefly, not all the features may have been fully activated, and the activation culminating at the R node may not be sufficient for recognition to occur. In contrast, when R is presented in RED, there is activation not only from the features of R to the R node, but also from the features of E and D to their nodes; all of these partially activated letters then partially activate the RED node, which in turn feeds back activation to its letters via its top-down connections.

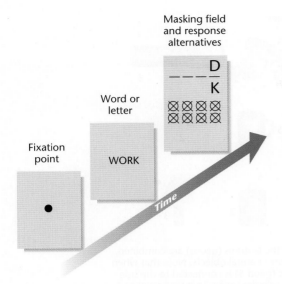

FIGURE 5.16 Perception of Letters and Words. *This figure illustrates the sequence of events in an experiment that compares the perceptibility of a letter presented alone or in the context of a word. First, participants saw a fixation point, followed by a word or a single letter, which was present for only a few milliseconds. Then the experimenter presented a stimulus that contained a visual mask in the positions where the letters had been, plus two response alternatives. The task was to decide which of the two alternatives occurred in the word or letter presented earlier.*

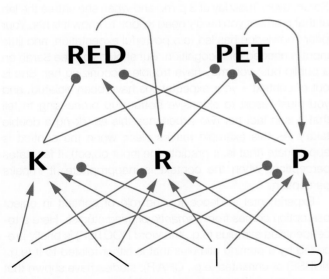

FIGURE 5.17 A Network with Top-Down Activation. *The network contains excitatory and inhibitory connections between letters and words (as well as between features and letters), and some of the excitatory connections go from words to letters.*

The upshot is that there is an additional source of activation for R when it is presented in a word – namely, activation coming from the word – and this is why it is easier to recognize a letter in a word than when it is presented alone. Many other findings about letter and word patterns have been shown to be consistent with this connectionist model (McClelland & Rumelhart, 1981). Models like these have also been used successfully in machines designed to read handwriting and recognize speech (Coren *et al.*, 1999).

Recognizing natural objects and top-down processing

We know quite a bit about the recognition of letters and words, but what about more natural objects – animals, plants, people, furniture, and clothing? In this section we examine how we recognize such objects.

Features of natural objects

The shape features of natural objects are more complex than lines and curves, and more like simple geometric forms. These features must be such that they can combine to form the shape of any recognizable object (just as lines and curves can combine to form any letter). The features of objects must also be such that they can be determined or constructed from more primitive features, such as lines and curves, because, as noted earlier, primitive features are the only information available to the system in the early stages of recognition.

Recognition-by-components is a popular though controversial theory of **object recognition**, first proposed by Irving Biederman (1987). It suggests that the features of objects include a number of geometric forms, such as cylinders, cones, blocks, and wedges, as illustrated in Figure 5.18a. Biederman argues that a set of 36 such features, referred to as **geons** (short for 'geometric ions') combined according to a small set of spatial relations, is sufficient to describe the shapes of all objects that people can possibly recognize. To appreciate this point, as shown in Figure 5.18b you can form an object by combining any two geons – and the number of possible such two-geons objects is 36 × 36 = 1296; likewise, the number of possible three-geon objects is 36 × 36 × 36 = 46 656. Thus, two or three geons are sufficient to create almost 50 000 objects, and we have yet to consider objects made up of four or more geons. Moreover, geons like those in Figure 5.18a can be distinguished solely in terms of primitive features. For example, geon 2 in Figure 5.18a (the cube) differs from geon 3 (the cylinder) in that the cube has straight edges but the cylinder has curved edges; straight and curved edges are primitive features.

Evidence that geons are features comes from experiments in which observers try to recognize briefly presented objects. The general finding is that recognition of an object is good

a) Geons

b) Objects

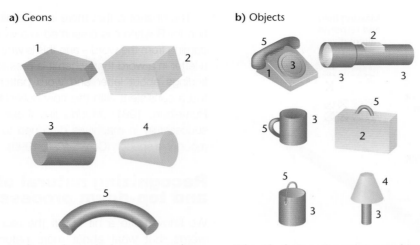

Wedges, cubes, cylinders, cones, and arcs may be features of complex objects.

When the features (geons) are combined, they form natural objects. Note that when the arc (geon 5) is connected to the side of the cylinder (geon 3), it forms a cup; when connected to the top of the cylinder, it forms a pail.

FIGURE 5.18 A Possible Set of Features (Geons) for Natural Objects.

to the extent that the geons of the object are perceptible. In one study, part of the shape of an object was deleted in such a way that the deletion either interfered with recovering the geons (see the right column of Figure 5.19) or did not (see the middle column). Recognition of the objects was much better when there was no interference with the geons.

As usual, the description of an object includes not just its features but also the relations among them. This is evident in Figure 5.18b. When the arc is connected to the side of the cylinder, it forms a cup; when it is connected to the top of the cylinder, it forms a pail. Once the description of an object's shape is constructed, it is compared to an array of geon descriptions stored in memory to find the best match. This matching process between the description of an object's shape and the descriptions stored in memory resembles the process described earlier for letters and words (Hummel & Biederman, 1992).

The importance of context

A key distinction in perception, to which we have previously alluded, is that between **bottom-up** and **top-down processes**. Bottom-up processes are driven solely by the input – the raw, sensory data – whereas top-down processes are driven by a person's knowledge, experience, attention, and expectations. To illustrate, recognizing the shape of an object solely on the basis of its geon description involves only bottom-up processes; one starts with primitive features of the input, determines the geon configuration of the input, and then makes this description available to shape descriptions stored in memory. In contrast, recognizing that the object is a lamp partly on the basis of its being on a night table next to

a bed involves some top-down processes; other information is used besides the input regarding shape. While most of the processes considered thus far in this chapter are bottom-up ones, top-down processes also play a major role in object perception.

Top-down processes, in the form of expectations, underlie the powerful effects of context on our perception of objects and people. You expect to see your chemistry lab partner, Sarah, every Tuesday at 3 p.m., and when she enters the lab at that moment you hardly need to look to know it is her. Your prior knowledge has led to a powerful expectation, and little input is needed for recognition. But should you see Sarah on a public bus, you may have trouble recognizing her. She is out of context – your expectations have been violated, and you must resort to extensive bottom-up processing to tell that it is in fact her (we experience this as 'doing a double take'). As this example makes clear, when the context is appropriate (that is, it predicts the input object), it facilitates perception; when the context is inappropriate, it impairs perception.

Experimental evidence for the role of context in object perception comes from *semantic priming* studies. Here a to-be-identified stimulus (e.g., the word DOCTOR) is briefly preceded by a priming stimulus that is either related to it (e.g., NURSE) or unrelated (e.g., CHAIR); studies have shown that both pictures and words are identified more quickly and remembered more accurately when they are preceded by related rather than unrelated primes (e.g., Palmer, 1975; Reinitz et al., 1989).

The effects of context are particularly striking when the stimulus object is ambiguous – that is, can be perceived

FIGURE 5.19 Object Recognition and Geon Recovery.
Items used in experiments on object recognition. The left column shows the original intact versions of the objects. The middle column shows versions of the objects in which regions have been deleted, but the geons are still recoverable. The right column shows versions of the objects in which regions have been deleted and the geons are not recoverable. Recognition is better for the middle versions than for the rightmost versions.

FIGURE 5.20 An Ambiguous Stimulus. *An ambiguous drawing that can be seen as either a young woman or as an old woman. Most people see the young woman first. The young woman is turning away and we see the left side of her face. Her chin is the old woman's nose and her necklace is the old woman's mouth.*

in more than one way. An ambiguous figure is presented in Figure 5.20; it can be perceived either as an old woman or as a young woman. If you have been looking at unambiguous pictures that resemble the young woman in the figure (that is, if young women are the context), you will tend to see the young woman first in the ambiguous picture. This effect of temporal context is illustrated with another set of pictures in Figure 5.21. Look at the pictures as you would at a comic strip, from left to right and top to bottom. The pictures in the middle of the series are ambiguous. If you view the figures in the sequence just suggested, you will tend to see the ambiguous pictures as a man's face. If you view the figures in the opposite order, you will tend to see the ambiguous pictures as a young woman.

Context effects and top-down processing also occur with letters and words, and play a major role in reading. Both the number of eye fixations we make on text and the durations of these fixations are greatly influenced by how much we know about the text – and, hence, by the amount of top-down

processing we can invoke. When the material is unfamiliar, there is little top-down processing. In such cases we tend to fixate on every word, except for function words like 'a,' 'of,' 'the,' and so on. As the material becomes more familiar, we can bring our prior knowledge to bear on it, and our fixations become shorter and more widely spaced (Just & Carpenter, 1980; Rayner, 1978).

Top-down processing occurs even in the absence of context if the input is sufficiently sparse or degraded. Suppose that at a friend's flat, you enter her dark kitchen and see a smallish black object in the corner. You think the object could be your friend's cat, but the perceptual input is too degraded to convince you of this, so you think of a particular feature of the cat, such as its tail, and selectively attend to the region of the object that is likely to contain that feature if it is indeed a cat (Kosslyn & Koenig, 1992). This processing is top-down, because you have used specific knowledge – the fact that cats have tails – to generate an expectation, which is then combined with the visual input. Situations like this are common in everyday life. Sometimes, however, the input is very degraded and the expectations we form are way off the mark, as when we finally realize that our would-be cat in the kitchen is really our friend's purse.

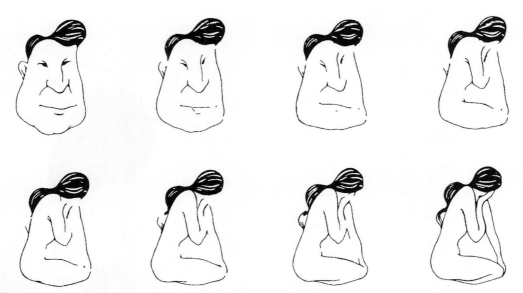

FIGURE 5.21 Effects of Temporal Context. *What you see here depends on the order in which you view the pictures. If you start at the beginning and work forward, the middle pictures will appear to be a young woman. In other words, your initial perception perseveres.*

One reason that top-down processing is useful is because it constrains the set of objects that are likely to occur in a given setting. For instance, we do not mistake a loaf of bread in a kitchen as a mailbox because we know that bread and not mailboxes tend to occur in kitchens. Similarly, individuals more accurately identify spoken words when they can see the speaker's lips than when they can't see them, because we have learned that specific lip movements constrain the set of sounds that the speaker can produce (e.g., Sams *et al.*, 1991). However, these same top-down processes can sometimes produce perceptual illusions such that our perceptions are distorted by our expectations. One interesting example, called the **McGurk effect** (McGurk & MacDonald, 1976) results from conflicting auditory and visual information. In particular, an observer watches a video of a speaker in which the speaker's lips form the sound, 'ga-ga,' while the simultaneous soundtrack provides speech that is normally perceived as 'ba-ba.' These sources of information are in conflict because we have learned that it is not possible to produce the sound 'ba' without closing one's lips; however, because the video portrays the speaker mouthing 'ga' his lips never close. The conjunction of these conflicting sources of information, surprisingly, produces the perception of 'da-da.' Thus, the speaker integrates the visual and auditory information with an entirely unexpected, 'illusory' result.

Perceptual distortions resulting from top-down processes may sometimes lead to tragedy. In 1996 New York City police chased an African man named Amadou Diallo to his doorway. Thinking that the police were asking him for identification he took his wallet from his pocket and was instantly killed in a barrage of bullets from police officers who apparently thought that he had drawn a gun. Motivated by this and similar tragedies, psychologists have developed video-game-like procedures to investigate such misperceptions. In a typical experiment people are told to shoot individuals on the screen who draw guns, but not individuals who brandish harmless objects. Studies have repeatedly shown that stereotypes strongly influence performance in this task; participants are more likely to shoot people with dark skin than to shoot light-skinned people when they quickly draw harmless objects (e.g., Correll *et al.*, 2002; Dasgupta *et al.*, 2000). These simulations have been helpful in training police officers to avoid these potential biases.

Special processing of socially relevant stimuli: Face recognition

As the Diallo case demonstrates, social factors can influence perception. In fact, evidence suggests that people have developed perceptual processes that are specialized for processing socially relevant stimuli. Nowhere is this truer than in recognizing faces. It is of the utmost social importance to be able to recognize kin, and to distinguish friend from foe. In addition, faces tend to be similar to one another. While other types of objects, such as houses, can differ in terms of the number and location of features (e.g., houses can have doors and windows in diverse places) faces all contain eyes, a nose, and a mouth in the same general pattern. The social importance of faces, combined with inherent recognition difficulties resulting from their similarity to one another, has

The US President Barack Obama.

apparently led to the development of special recognition processes that are employed for faces but not for objects. Three types of evidence are often cited as evidence for special face processing. First, **prosopagnosia** is a syndrome that can arise following brain injury, in which a person is completely unable to identify faces but retains the ability to recognize objects. Second, the **inversion effect** (Yin, 1969, 1970) is the name given to the finding that faces but not objects are extremely hard to recognize when they are presented upside-down, such as the photograph above. Finally, object recognition and face recognition appear to have different developmental trajectories. Childrens' abilities to recognize objects tends to increase steadily with age; however, there is evidence that for many children face recognition ability actually declines temporarily during early adolescence. A popular theory to account for these face-object differences is that while objects are recognized on the basis of their component parts, faces are recognized on the basis of the overall pattern (or configuration) that the parts form (e.g., Farah *et al.*, 1995). By this explanation, prosopagnosics retain the ability to perceptually process parts but not configurations (e.g., Sergent, 1984), and inversion obscures parts less than it obscures the overall pattern that the parts form (Rock, 1988).

Failure of recognition

Recognizing an object is usually so automatic and effortless that we take it for granted. But the process sometimes breaks down. We have already seen that in normal people recognition can fail in simple situations (as with illusory conjunctions) and in more complex situations (as when a tent is mistaken for a bear). Recognition also fails routinely in people who have suffered from certain kinds of brain damage (due to accidents or diseases such as strokes). The general term for such breakdowns or disorders in recognition is **agnosia**.

Of particular interest is a type of agnosia called **associative agnosia**. This is a syndrome in which patients with damage to temporal lobe regions of the cortex have difficulty recognizing objects only when they are presented visually. For example, the patient may be unable to name a comb when presented with a picture of it, but can name it when allowed to touch it. The deficit is exemplified by the following case:

> **For the first 3 weeks in the hospital the patient could not identify common objects presented visually and did not know what was on his plate until he tasted it. He identified objects immediately on touching them [but] when shown a stethoscope, he described it as 'a long cord with a round thing at the end', and asked if it could be a watch. He identified a can opener as 'could be a key'. Asked to name a cigarette lighter, he said, 'I don't know'. He said he was 'not sure' when shown a toothbrush. Asked to identify a comb, he said, 'I don't know'. For a pipe, he said, 'some type of utensil, I'm not sure'. Shown a key, he said, 'I don't know what that is; perhaps a file or a tool of some sort'.**
>
> **(Reubens & Benson, 1971)**

What aspects of object recognition have broken down in associative agnosia? Since these patients often do well on visual tasks other than recognition – such as drawing objects or determining whether two pictured objects match – the breakdown is likely to be in the later stages of recognition, in which the input object is matched to stored object descriptions. One possibility is that the stored object descriptions have been lost or obscured in some way (Damasio, 1985).

Some patients with associative agnosia have problems recognizing certain categories but not others. These category-specific deficits are of considerable interest because they may tell us something new about how normal recognition works. The most frequent category-specific deficit is prosopagnosia, the loss of the ability to recognize faces. This deficit is typically the result of injury to the extrastriate visual cortex of the right hemisphere (sometimes accompanied by damage in homologous regions of the left hemisphere), although there are reports of patients born with prosopagnosia. The condition is illustrated by the following case:

> He could not identify his medical attendants. 'You must be a doctor because of your white coat, but I don't know which one you are. I'll know if you speak'. He failed to identify his wife during visiting hours…. He failed to identify pictures of Churchill, Hitler, and Marilyn Monroe. When confronted with such portraits he would proceed deductively, searching for the 'critical' detail which would yield the answer.
>
> (Pallis, 1955)

A second kind of category deficit is loss of the ability to recognize words, called pure alexia (typically accompanied by damage in the left occipital lobe). Patients with this deficit typically have no difficulty recognizing natural objects or faces. They can even identify individual letters. What they cannot do is recognize visually presented words. When presented with a word, they attempt to read it letter by letter. It can take as long as 10 seconds for them to recognize a common word, with the amount of time needed increasing with the number of letters in the word (Bub *et al.*, 1989).

Other types of category-specific deficits involve impairment in the ability to recognize living things such as animals, plants, and foods. In rare cases patients are unable to recognize non-living things such as household tools (Warrington & Shallice, 1984).

Some of the suggested explanations of category-specific deficits have implications for normal recognition. One hypothesis is that the normal recognition system is organized around different classes of objects – one subsystem for faces, another for words, a third for animals, and so on – and these subsystems are localized in different regions of the brain. If a patient suffers only restricted brain damage, he or she may show a loss of one subsystem but not others. Damage in a specific part of the right hemisphere, for example, might disrupt the face-recognition subsystem but leave the other subsystems intact (Damasio, 1990; Farah, 1990).

INTERIM SUMMARY

➔ Recognizing an object requires that the various features associated with the object (such as shapes and colors) be correctly bound together, a process that requires attention.

➔ Recognition of a particular object is aided by first acquiring 'global' aspects of the scene; for example quickly understanding that you are looking at a kitchen helps in recognizing an ambiguous object as a loaf of bread rather than a mailbox.

➔ Recognizing an object entails binding together various features of an object such as its shape and its color. The features themselves are acquired via pre-attentive processes, while 'gluing' them together requires attention.

➔ There are known kinds of cells in the visual cortex that are sensitive to various kinds of stimulus features such as orientation and position within the visual field.

➔ Recognition of visual stimuli can be mimicked by a connectionist model or network.

➔ Bottom-up recognition processes are driven solely by the input, whereas top-down recognition processes are driven by a person's knowledge and expectations. The shape features of natural objects are more complex than lines; they are similar to simple geometric forms such as cylinders, cones, blocks, and wedges. A particular set of such forms is a geon.

➔ Face recognition may be special, i.e., different in important respects from recognition of other objects.

CRITICAL THINKING QUESTIONS

1 At the beginning of this chapter we described a tent that was tragically mistaken for a bear. Why do you think this misperception happened? What could the hunters have done to have avoided the misperception?

2 Do you think there is a fundamental difference between recognizing a natural object, such as an eagle, and recognizing an artificial object such as a stop sign? Give reasons for your answers.

ABSTRACTION

The *physical description* of an object is a listing of all the information necessary to completely reproduce the object. Many stimuli studied in the scientific laboratory – patches of light, squares, single letters – are relatively simple and their physical descriptions are likewise simple. However, the physical description of most real-life objects is enormously complicated. Look at Cate Blanchett pictured on the next page. The visual detail that exists within it seems almost infinite. As you look closer and closer at her skin, for example, small blemishes and irregularities become apparent. Each individual hair on her head is positioned just so. The shadowing across her features, while subtle, is complex. To write a complete description of her

Australian actress Cate Blanchett.

Exact to abstract

However, in real life, these limitations don't usually present a problem because you don't need all that much detail to solve the problems assigned to you by the world. For instance, in the Cate Blanchett example, you would only need as much detail as is necessary to (1) recognize her face to begin with, and (2) determine from her expression what kind of mood she is in (caricaturists know this quite well; with a few deft strokes of their pen, they can capture the likeness and expression of a person with remarkable clarity). This situation is not, of course, unique to faces. Whether you are looking at a hairpin or a pencil sharpener or an armchair or anything else, you rarely if ever need to know all the infinite visual detail. Rather, you only need to know enough to carry out whatever task is requiring you to perceive the object to begin with.

The advantages of abstraction: Required storage and processing speed

To get a feel for this, look at the two drawings in Figure 5.22. Both were created using a computer drawing program. The face on the left was drawn freehand, while the one on the right was drawn as a 'copy' of the one on the left, using nothing but the drawing program's oval and line tools. Clearly the left-hand original contains considerably more detail; however both give the same impression – of a slightly bewildered looking individual.

When these two versions of the face were saved as files, the original, freehand version required 30 720 bytes of memory, while the 'abstracted' version required only 902 bytes – a saving of about 97 per cent! Clearly it is more efficient in many respects to perceive and encode in

face, in other words, would take an extremely long time. Really the only way you could do it would be by creating a bitmap of her face, and, even then, the completeness of the description would be limited by the bitmap's resolution.

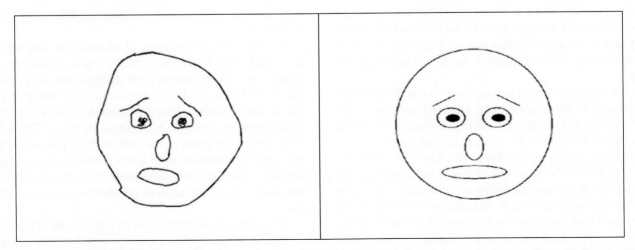

FIGURE 5.22 The Process of Abstraction. *Two versions of the same sad face. The one on the left was drawn freehand, and the one on the right was drawn with 'abstracting' tools such as ovals and lines. The left face takes up considerably more disk space than the right, which illustrates one of the virtues of abstracting for any visual-processing device, including biological visual systems.*

Reproduced figure	Verbal labels	Stimulus figures	Verbal labels	Reproduced figure

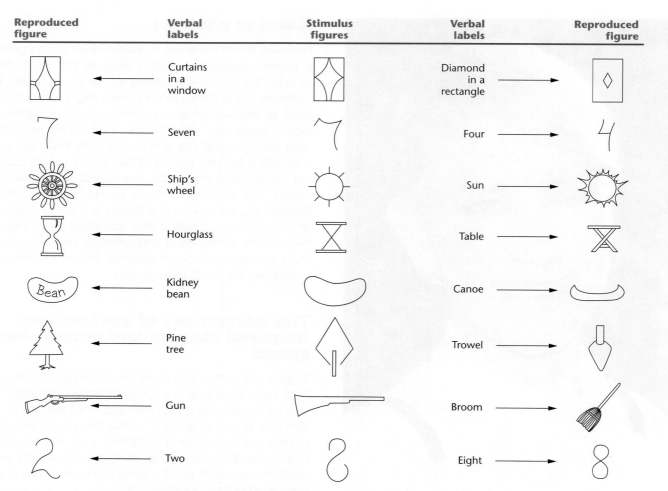

FIGURE 5.23 **Verbal Labels and Abstraction.** *Carmichael et al. (1932) showed people the kind of ambiguous stimuli shown in the middle panel. Observers were given one of the two verbal labels shown in the second and fourth columns. The subjects' later reconstructions of what they had seen conformed to the verbal label, as shown in the first and fifth columns. This experiment indicates that subjects remember not what they literally saw but rather abstract the fundamental information from it.*

memory an **abstraction** of the object rather than an exact representation of the object itself. As we noted earlier, object recognition is well conceptualized as the construction of objects using a 'drawing program' where the primitives are geons.

A nice example of how perception of a real-life object is schematized in this manner was reported by Carmichael *et al.*, (1932), who presented ambiguous stimuli such as those shown in Figure 5.23, middle column, labeled 'Stimulus Figures,' along with a *label* that told the observers what they were looking at. For instance, while viewing the stimulus in the top middle column, some observers were told that they were looking at 'curtains in a window' while others were told that they were looking at 'a diamond in a rectangle.' The observers were later asked to reproduce what they had seen. Examples are shown in the left and right columns of Figure 5.23. As you can see, what the subjects perceived and stored in memory corresponded

very strongly to what they considered themselves to be looking at.

A different demonstration of abstraction was reported by Intraub and Richardson (1989). Here, observers were shown pictures of objects such as those shown in the top panels of Figure 5.24. The general finding was that when the observers later redrew the pictures, they expanded the boundaries, as shown in the bottom panels of Figure 5.24. The conclusion again is that, rather than perceiving, storing, and later remembering a more-or-less literal image of what they had seen, the observers abstracted the important information (here the object's context as well as the object itself).

The notion of abstraction harks back to our discussion in Chapter 4 of *color metamers*. You'll recall that color metamers are different physical stimuli (for instance a pure yellow light on the one hand and a red-green mixture on the other) that lead to the exact same color perception. In this instance, the

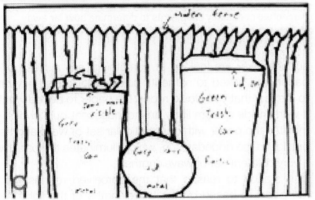

FIGURE 5.24 Boundary Extension and Abstraction. *Subjects tend to remember having seen a greater expanse of a scene than was shown to them in a photograph. For example, when drawing the close-up view in panel A from memory, the subject's drawing (panel C) contained extended boundaries. Another subject, shown a wider-angle view of the same scene (panel B), also drew the scene with extended boundaries (panel D).*

visual system is throwing away the information corresponding to the physical difference between the stimuli. Abstraction entails much the same thing: the information corresponding to the exact physical description (the 'bitmap') of the stimulus is lost; what is retained is the critical information that is needed.

INTERIM SUMMARY

➔ Abstraction is the process of converting the raw sensory information acquired by the sense organs (for example, patterns of straight and curved lines) into abstract categories that are pre-stored in memory (for example, letters or words).

➔ Abstracted information takes less space and is therefore faster to work with than raw information. A useful analogy is between a bitmapped computer image of a face versus an abstracted image of the same face that is made up of preformed structures such as ovals and lines.

CRITICAL THINKING QUESTIONS

1 In what way is the behavior of a visual artist influenced by color and shape constancy? Can you think of ways in which perceptual constancies actually make the artist's task more difficult than it would be without constancy?

2 In Chapter 4 we talked about metamers. Can you see a relation between metamers and the process of abstraction? What is it?

PERCEPTUAL CONSTANCIES

You walk into a movie and discover, somewhat to your annoyance, that because all the seats in the middle section of the theater are taken, you are forced to sit far over on the left side. As the movie begins, however, you forget about your seating locale and just lose yourself in the movie's plot, its characters, and its stunning special effects. All visual aspects of the movie appear to be entirely normal – and yet they're not. Because you're sitting off to the side, at an angle to the screen, the image of the movie screen on your retina is not a rectangle; rather it's a trapezoid, and all the visual images you see on the screen are analogously distorted. And yet this doesn't really bother you; you see everything as normal. How can this be? In this section we will describe a truly remarkable ability of the perceptual systems, termed the maintenance of **constancy**.

The nature of constancies

To understand the idea of constancies, it is important to first understand the relation and distinction between the inherent physical characteristics of an object and the information available to our perceptual systems about these objects. A movie screen, for example, is rectangular; that's a physical characteristic of it. But the image of it on our retina can be rectangular or trapezoidal depending on the angle from which you view it. A black cat seen in bright light is objectively lighter (it reflects more light to you) than a white cat in dim light; yet somehow in any kind of light, we maintain the perception that the black cat is actually black, while the white cat is actually white. An elephant seen from far away projects a smaller image on our retina than a gopher seen from close up; yet somehow, no matter what the distance, we maintain the perception that the elephant is larger than the gopher. In general, what we perceive is – and this almost sounds like magic – a perception of what an object is actually like rather than a perception based solely on the 'objective' physical information that arrives from the environment.

Although constancy is not perfect, it is a salient aspect of visual experience and it should be; otherwise the world would be one where sometimes elephants are smaller than mice and where Denzel Washington is sometimes lighter colored than Brad Pitt, depending on the particular situation. If the shape and color of an object changed every time either we or it moved, the description of the object that we construct in the early stages of recognition would also change, and recognition would become an impossible task.

Color and brightness constancy

Suppose I tell you that I am thinking of two numbers whose product is 36, and I ask you to tell me what the two original numbers are. Your reasonable response would be that you don't have enough information to answer: the numbers I'm thinking of could be 2 and 18, or 6 and 6, or any of an infinite number of other pairs.

Impossible though this task seems, it is, in a very real sense, what the visual system does when it maintains lightness and color constancy. To see what we mean by this,

Perceptual constancy enables us to determine how far away objects are.

suppose you are looking at something, say a piece of red paper, and asked to name its color. Color constancy refers to the fact that you would report the paper to be red whether it were inside a room lit by an incandescent bulb, which illuminates the paper with one particular set of wavelengths, or outside in the noonday sun, which illuminates the paper with a very different set of wavelengths.

It stands to reason that the perceived redness of the red paper is based on the wavelengths of the light that is reflected off the paper reaching your eyes. We will call these the **available wavelengths**. Let's now consider the physics of where these available wavelengths come from. It's a two-step process. First, the paper is illuminated by some light source which could be, among many other things, an incandescent bulb inside, or the sun outside. We will call the wavelengths provided by the source the **source wavelengths**. Second, the red paper itself reflects some wavelengths more than others (in particular it reflects mostly wavelengths corresponding to red and less of other wavelengths). We will call this property of the paper the **reflectance characteristic**. Now in every real, mathematical sense, the available wavelengths reaching your eyes are the *products* of the source wavelengths and the reflectance characteristic. Realizing this puts us in a position to define color constancy, which is the ability of the visual system to perceive the reflectance characteristic – an inherent property of the object – no matter what the source wavelengths. It is in this sense, therefore that the visual system is presented with a product – the available wavelengths – and somehow figures out one of the factors, namely the reflectance characteristic. The incandescent bulb and the sun provide very different source wavelengths and – because the reflectance characteristic of the red paper doesn't change – very different available wavelengths reach the eye. Yet somehow, the visual system is able to divide the source wavelengths out of the available wavelengths to arrive at the correct reflectance characteristic in both cases. This is analogous to your somehow figuring out that the first number I'm thinking of (analogous to the source wavelengths) is 12 which means that the other number (analogous to the reflectance characteristic) must be 36 / 12 or 3.

Brightness constancy is similar to color constancy, and refers to the fact that the perceived lightness of a particular object changes very little, if at all, even when the intensity of the source, and thus the amount of light

The Adelson Checkerboard.

reflected off the object, changes dramatically. Thus, a black velvet shirt can look just as black in sunlight as in shadow, even though it reflects thousands of times more light when it is directly illuminated by the sun. A dramatic example of this finding is shown in the left-hand checkerboard picture above: the squares labeled A and B are, astonishingly, exactly the same level of gray. We have demonstrated this in the right-hand version which is identical except that the two squares have been connected by gray bars. Your visual system is responding, though, not to the physical data arriving at your eyes, but rather to the data plus the visual system's inferences about the grau level of the square: it 'corrects' for the shadow being cast on Square B with a resulting perception of a white square that is as white as any of the other white portions of the board!

How does the visual system manage to do these tricks? A clue comes about by examining the circumstances under which constancy *fails*. Suppose that the black shirt is put behind an opaque black screen and you view the shirt through a peephole in the screen. The screen reduces what you see through the opening to just the actual light reflected from the shirt, independent of its surroundings. Now, when it is illuminated, the shirt looks white because the light that reaches your eye through the hole is more intense than the light from the screen itself.

This demonstration underscores the fact that when we perceive objects in natural settings, rather than through peepholes, many other objects are usually visible. Color and brightness constancy depend on the relations among the intensities of light reflected from the different objects; essentially by using our past knowledge of object colors in general, our visual system is able to correct for the effect of the source illumination (both the source intensity and the source wavelengths) and arrive at the brightness and the color of the objects being seen (Gilchrist, 1988; Land, 1977; Maloney & Wandell, 1986).

Shape constancy

We have provided an example of shape constancy in describing the non-effect of sitting to one side of a movie theater. Another is illustrated in Figure 5.25. When a door swings toward us, the shape of its image on the retina goes through a series of changes. The door's rectangular shape produces a trapezoidal image, with the edge toward us wider than the hinged edge; then the trapezoid grows thinner, until finally all that is projected on the retina is a vertical bar the thickness of the door. Nevertheless, we perceive an unchanging door swinging open. The fact that the perceived shape is constant while the retinal image changes is an example of shape constancy.

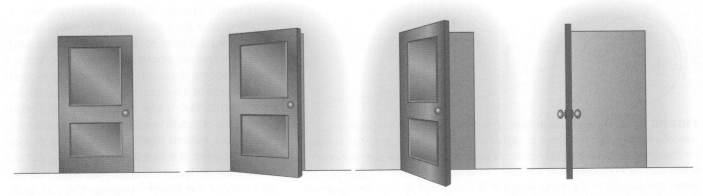

FIGURE 5.25 Shape Constancy. *The various retinal images produced by an opening door are quite different, yet we perceive a door of constant rectangular shape.*

Size constancy

The most thoroughly studied of all the perceptual constancies is size constancy: an object's perceived size remains relatively constant no matter how far away it is. As an object moves further away from us, we generally do not see it as decreasing in size. Hold a quarter 1 foot in front of you and then move it out to arm's length. Does it appear to get smaller? Not noticeably. Yet, as shown in Figure 5.26, the retinal image of the quarter when it is 24 inches away is only about half the size of its retinal image when it is 12 inches away.

Dependence on depth cues

The example of the moving quarter indicates that when we perceive the size of an object, we consider something in addition to the size of the retinal image. That additional something is the perceived distance of the object. As long ago as 1881, Swiss ophthalmologist Emmert was able to show that size judgments depend on distance. Emmert used an ingenious method that involved judging the size of afterimages.

Observers were first asked to fixate on the center of an image for about a minute (see Figure 5.27 for an example of such an image). Then they looked at a white screen and saw an afterimage of what they had just seen. Their task was to judge the size of the afterimage; the independent variable was how far away the screen was. Because the retinal size of the afterimage was the same regardless of the distance of the screen, any variations in judgments of the size of the afterimage had to be due to its perceived distance. When the screen was far away, the afterimage looked large; when the screen was near, the afterimage looked small. Emmert's experiment is so easy to do that you can perform it on yourself.

On the basis of such experiments, Emmert proposed that the perceived size of an object increases with both the retinal size of the object and the perceived distance of the object. This is known as the size–distance invariance principle. It explains size constancy as follows: when the distance to an object

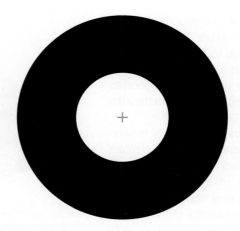

FIGURE 5.27 Emmert's Experiment. *Hold the book at normal reading distance under good light. Fixate on the cross in the center of the figure for about a minute, and then look at a distant wall. You will see an afterimage of the two circles that appears larger than the stimulus. Then look at a piece of paper held close to your eyes. The afterimage will appear smaller than the stimulus. If the afterimage fades, blinking can sometimes restore it.*

increases, the object's retinal size decreases, but if distance cues are present, perceived distance will increase. Hence, the perceived size will remain approximately constant. To illustrate: when a person walks away from you, the size of her image on your retina becomes smaller but her perceived distance becomes larger; these two changes cancel each other out, and your perception of her size remains relatively constant.

Illusions

Walk into the Haunted House at Disneyland. As you nervously make your way down the first corridor, you see mask-like faces staring at you from the walls. As you move past them, the masks appear to physically swivel, ever gazing at you. Although disconcerted, you marvel at this effect, figuring that the masks must somehow be mounted on little motors that are sensitive to your approach and movement.

However, in reality the masks are stationary; it is only in your perception that they move. If you somehow managed to turn on the lights and inspect the masks closely, an oddity would immediately become apparent: you are actually looking at the inside of the mask rather than the outside, as is normal. But, under the poor viewing conditions of the Haunted House, you don't realize this. Your visual system makes the assumption that you are looking at a face from the outside, just as you usually do, but, if this is so, it turns out that the geometry of the situation requires that you must perceive the face to be rotating as you shift position relative to it. (This is an easy demonstration

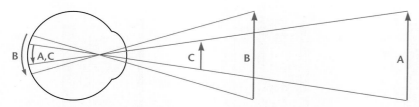

FIGURE 5.26 Retinal Image Size. *This figure illustrates the geometric relationship between the physical size of an object and the size of its image on the retina. Arrows A and B represent objects of the same size, but one is twice as far from the eye as the other. As a result, the retinal image of A is about half the size of the retinal image of B. The object represented by arrow C is smaller than that of A, but its location closer to the eye causes it to produce a retinal image the same size as A.*

that you can do for yourself. Go to a costume store and find a cheap mask – one that just goes on the front of your face, not the pull-it-down-over-your-head type. Have a friend hold the mask up across the room so that the inside of the mask is facing you. Particularly if you cover one eye, you will perceive the face as coming out at you rather than going in from you as is actually the case. Once you have that perception, you will find that as you shift back and forth, the mask will appear to rotate.)

The perceived-to-be-rotating mask is an example of an **illusion**: your perception of something differs systematically from physical reality. The mask illusion, like many illusions, arises because of the visual system's attempts to maintain constancy – in this case its assumption that a face is, like most faces, being viewed from the outside rather than from the inside.

Constancies and illusions

We have noted that the various constancies serve an important purpose: they allow us to perceive fundamental characteristics of the world around us even when the information arriving at our sense organs (our retinas in the examples we've discussed) change dramatically as a result of different source wavelengths, different source intensities, different distances from the object or different viewing angles. For better or for worse, however, these constancies also lead to numerous optical illusions, as in the mask illusion that we have just described.

The moon illusion

The size–distance principle is fundamental to understanding a number of size illusions. An example is the moon illusion: when the moon is near the horizon, it looks as much as 50 per cent larger than when it is high in the sky, even though, in fact, the moon's retinal image is a tiny bit larger when it is directly overhead, because it is a little bit closer when directly overhead than when on the horizon (just as, for example, an

The moon looks much larger when it is near the horizon than when it is high in the sky, even though in both locations its retinal image is the same size.

airplane is closer when it is directly overhead than when you first see it on the horizon).

One explanation for the moon illusion is this (see Reed, 1984; Loftus, 1985). Think about a normal flying object like an airplane that approaches you from the horizon. As we just mentioned, the geometry of the situation is that the airplane's retinal image gets larger as it moves from the horizon to the zenith. Because an airplane is relatively close to the earth, the degree to which the retinal image gets larger is quite dramatic. Size constancy, however, compensates for this change in retinal image size in the usual fashion such that the airplane *appears* to remain the same physical size throughout its ascendance.

Qualitatively, there is no difference between an airplane and the moon. The moon's retinal image size also (surprisingly!) increases as the moon ascends from horizon to zenith. The difference between the moon and the airplane is quantitative: the moon, unlike close-to-earth objects like airplanes that we are used to, is so far away that the change in its visual image is miniscule. However, our visual system still insists on constancy: as the moon approaches zenith, the visual system 'believes' that its retinal image size *should be increasing quite a lot*, just as an airplane's does. The moon's failure to increase its retinal image size in this expected manner is 'explained' by the visual system perceiving the moon's physical size to decrease; hence the moon illusion.

Another way of looking at the moon illusion is that the perceived distance to the horizon is judged to be greater than the distance to the zenith. However, because the visual angle remains almost constant as the moon rises from horizon to zenith, the visual system must conclude that the moon itself is larger at the distant horizon compared to the nearer zenith (Kaufman & Rock, 1989). One way to reduce the effectiveness of the depth cues that indicate that the horizon moon is far away is to view the moon upside down. This can be done by placing your back to the moon, bending over, and viewing it through your legs. If you have a photo of the moon on the horizon, it can be done by simply turning the picture upside down (Coren, 1992).

The Ames room illusion

Another size illusion is created by the Ames room (named after its inventor, Adelbert Ames). Figure 5.28 shows how the Ames room looks to an observer seeing it through a peephole. When the boy is in the left-hand corner of the room (see the photograph on the left), he appears much smaller than when he is in the right-hand corner (see the photograph on the right). Yet it is the same boy in both pictures! Here we have a case in which size constancy has broken down. Why? The reason lies in the construction of the room. Although the room looks like a normal rectangular room to an observer seeing it through the peephole, it is actually shaped so that its left corner is almost twice as far away as its right corner

FIGURE 5.28 The Ames Room. *A view of how the Ames room looks to an observer viewing it through the peephole. The sizes of the boy and the girl depend on which one is in the left-hand corner of the room and which one is in the right-hand corner. The room is designed to wreak havoc with our perceptions. Because of the perceived shape of the room, the relative sizes of the boy and the girl seem impossibly different.*

(see the diagram in Figure 5.29). Hence, the boy on the left is much further away than the one on the right, and consequently projects a smaller retinal image. We do not correct for this difference in distance, though, because the lines in the room lead us to believe that we are looking at a normal room and therefore assume that both boys are the same distance from us. Again the visual system's only interpretation of the boy subtending a smaller angle, but being no further away is that the boy is smaller. In essence, our assumption that the room is normal blocks our application of the size–distance invariance

principle, and consequently size constancy breaks down.

The 'Ames-room effect,' shown in Figures 5.28 and 5.29, was used to great advantage by the movie director, Peter Jackson, in his *Lord of the Rings* trilogy. These movies involved different classes of beings (e.g., Hobbits, Dwarves, Elves, and Humans) who, in keeping with J. R. R. Tolkien's original books, needed to appear to be very different sizes (e.g., Hobbits are only about half as tall as humans) even though the different beings were played by actors of similar heights. In part these effects were achieved by computer-graphics techniques, but for the most part they were achieved by illusion. For example, Aragorn, a human, would be filmed apparently walking along-side Frodo, a Hobbit. However, during the filming Viggo Mortensen playing Aragorn would be in the foreground, close to the camera, while Elijah Wood playing Frodo would actually be in the background, approximately twice as far from the camera as Mortensen.

Constancies in all sensory modalities

Although all the examples of constancy that we have described are visual, constancies also occur in the other senses. For example, a person will hear the same tune even if the frequencies of all its notes are doubled. Whatever the sensory modality, constancies depend on relations between features of the stimulus – between retinal size and distance in the case of size constancy, between the intensity of two adjacent regions in the case of lightness constancy, and so forth.

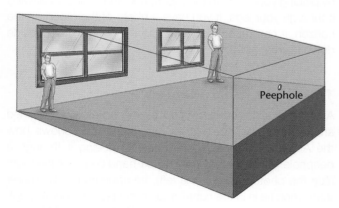

Peephole

FIGURE 5.29 The True Shape of the Ames Room. *This figure shows the true shape of the Ames room. The boy on the left is actually almost twice as far away as the boy on the right. However, this difference in distance is not detected when the room is viewed through the peephole.*

INTERIM SUMMARY

➔ Another major function of the perceptual system is to achieve perceptual constancy – to keep the appearance of objects the same in spite of large variations in the initial representations of the stimuli received by the sense organs that are engendered by various environmental factors.

➔ Color and brightness constancy entail perceiving the actual color and brightness of a stimulus even when the actual information arriving at the eye varies in color makeup (because of the color makeup of the ambient lighting) and in brightness (because of the level of ambient illumination).

➔ Size constancy entails perceiving the actual size of a stimulus even when the actual size of the object's image on the retina varies because of the object's distance.

➡ Intrinsically, constancies entail 'illusion' in the sense that by a constancy's very nature, perception differs systematically from the physical nature of the stimulus. It logically follows, and is empirically true, that many visual illusions may be explained by the various constancies.

➡ Constancies occur in all sensory modalities.

➡ Various kinds of perceptual illusions can be explained by the perceptual system's insistence on maintaining constancies.

➡ Although visual constancies are the most salient, constancies exist in all sensory modalities.

CRITICAL THINKING QUESTIONS

1 Do you think that the moon illusion would be more pronounced if the moon were seen rising over a flat, featureless plane or if it were seen rising behind a city skyline? Suppose that you were on a boat approaching the city. Would the moon illusion be more pronounced if you were closer to the city or further from the city?

2 In what way is the behavior of a visual artist influenced by color and shape constancy? Can you think of ways in which perceptual constancies actually make the artist's task more difficult than it would be without constancy?

DIVISIONS OF LABOR IN THE BRAIN

In the past decade a great deal has been learned about the neural processes underlying perception. We have already touched upon some of this knowledge. In this section, we will describe a bit more of what has been discovered. We will begin by talking about the neural basis of attention, and then we will turn to the visual cortex – which is a crucial waystation for incoming visual information.

The neural basis of attention

Recent years have produced major breakthroughs in our understanding of the neural basis of attention, particularly visual attention. The research of interest has concerned two major questions: (1) What brain structures mediate the psychological act of selecting an object to attend to? and (2) How does the subsequent neural processing differ for attended and non-attended stimuli? Let's consider each of these questions in turn.

Three brain systems in attention

As previously described, there is evidence for three separate but interacting attentional systems. One functions to keep us alert. Numerous brain imaging studies have shown that when people are given tasks that require them to maintain attention on a task there is increased activity in the parietal and frontal regions of the right hemisphere of the brain. These areas are associated with the neuro-transmitter norepinephrine, which is associated with arousal (Coull et al., 1996). Two additional brain systems seem to mediate selective attention. The first is responsible for orienting attention to a stimulus. This system represents the perceptual features of an object, such as its location in space, its shape, and its color, and is responsible for selecting one object among many on the basis of the features associated with that object. This is sometimes referred to as the **posterior system** because the brain structures involved – the parietal and temporal cortex, along with some subcortical structures – are mostly located in the back of the brain (though recent research indicates a role of frontal cortex in attentional orienting). The second system, designed to control when and how these features will be used for selection, is sometimes referred to as the **anterior system** because the structures involved – the frontal cortex and a subcortical structure – are located in the front of the brain. In short, we can select an object for attention by focusing on its location, its shape, or its color. Although the actual selection of these features will occur in the posterior part of the brain, the selection process will be guided by the anterior part of the brain. Because of this function, some researchers refer to the anterior system as the 'chief executive officer' or CEO of selective attention.

Some critical findings regarding the posterior system come from PET scans of humans while they are engaged in selective-attention tasks. When observers are instructed to shift their attention from one location to another, the cortical areas that show the greatest increase in blood flow – and, hence, neural activity – are the parietal lobes of both hemispheres (Corbetta et al., 1993). Moreover, when people with brain damage in these regions are tested on attentional tasks, they have great difficulty shifting attention from one location to another (Posner, 1988). Hence, the regions that are active when a normal brain accomplishes the task turn out to be the same areas that are damaged when a patient cannot do the task. Moreover, when single-cell recording studies are done with non-human primates, cells in the same brain regions are found to be active when attention must be switched from one location to the next (Wurtz et al., 1980). Taken together, these findings strongly indicate that activity in parietal regions of the brain mediates attending to locations. There is comparable evidence for the involvement of temporal regions in attending to the color and shape of objects (Moran & Desimone, 1985).

Neural processing on attended objects

Once an object has been selected for attention, what changes in neural processing occur? Consider an experiment in which a set of colored geometric objects is presented and the observer is instructed to attend only to the red ones and to indicate when a triangle is presented. The anterior system will direct the posterior system to focus on color, but what else changes in the neural processing of each stimulus? The answer is that the regions of the visual cortex that process color become more active than they would be if the observer were not selectively attending to color. More generally, the regions of the brain that are relevant to the attribute being attended to (be it color, shape, texture, motion, and so forth) will show amplified activity (Posner & Dehaene, 1994). There is also some evidence that brain regions that are relevant to unattended attributes will be inhibited (La Berge, 1995; Posner & Raichle, 1994).

Some of the best evidence for this amplification of attributes that are attended to again comes from PET studies. In one experiment (Corbetta *et al.*, 1991), observers whose brains were being scanned viewed moving objects of varying color and form. In one condition, the individuals were instructed to detect changes among the objects in motion, while in other conditions they were instructed to detect changes among the objects in color or shape; hence, motion is the attribute attended to in the first condition, color or shape in the other conditions. As shown in Figure 5.30, even though the physical stimuli were identical in all the conditions, posterior cortical areas known to be involved in the processing of motion were found to be more active in the first condition, whereas areas involved in color or shape processing were more active in the other conditions. Attention, then, amplifies what is relevant, not only psychologically but biologically as well.

The visual cortex

At a general level, the part of the brain that is concerned with vision – the visual cortex – operates according to the principle of division of labor: different regions of the visual cortex are specialized to carry out different perceptual functions (Kosslyn & Koenig, 1992; Zeki, 1993). There are over 100 million neurons in the cortex that are sensitive to visual input. Everything we know about them and the way they function has been learned through a small number of techniques. In studies involving animals, what we know is based largely on research in which electrical impulses are recorded (using microelectrodes) from single cells, as discussed in Chapter 4. Modern techniques for conducting such research owe much to the pioneering work of Hubel and Wiesel, mentioned earlier.

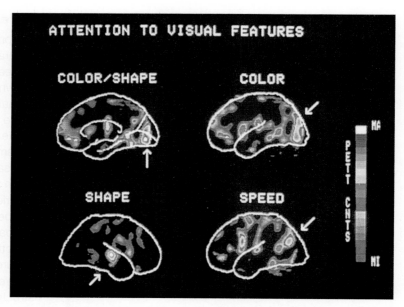

FIGURE 5.30 PET Images Reveal Differences in Cortical Activity. *The image on the top right is from the condition in which participants attended to changes in color, whereas the images in the bottom row are from the conditions in which individuals attended to changes in shape or speed.*

In studies involving humans, much of what we know comes from 'natural experiments' – that is, cases of brain injury and disease that cast light on how visual behaviors relate to specific regions of the brain. Researchers in this area include neurologists (medical doctors who specialize in the brain) and neuropsychologists (psychologists who specialize in treating and studying patients with brain injury). An excellent introduction to this area is presented in Oliver Sacks's (1985) *The Man Who Mistook His Wife for a Hat*.

Today the most exciting discoveries about the human brain are being made by taking pictures of the brain without surgery. This field is called brain imaging and includes techniques such as event related potentials (ERPs), positron emission tomography (PET), and functional magnetic resonance imaging (fMRI).

The most important region of the brain for visual processing is the area known as the primary visual cortex, or V1. Its location at the back, or posterior, part of the brain is shown in Figure 5.31. This is the first location in the cerebral cortex to which neurons sending signals from the eye are connected. All the other visually sensitive regions of the cortex (more than 30 such locations have been identified) are connected to the eyes through V1.

As has so often been the case, the function of V1 was discovered long before the development of modern recording or imaging techniques. It first became obvious when physicians examined patients who had suffered localized head injuries through accident or war. As shown in Figure 5.32, tissue damage (technically referred to as a lesion) to a

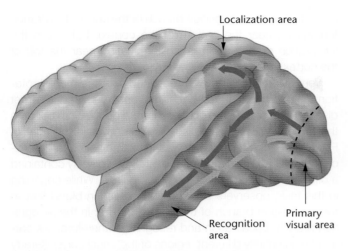

Localization area

Primary
visual area

Recognition
area

FIGURE 5.31 Two Cortical Visual Systems. *The arrows going from the back of the brain toward the top depict the localization system; the arrows going from the back toward the bottom of the brain depict the recognition system.*

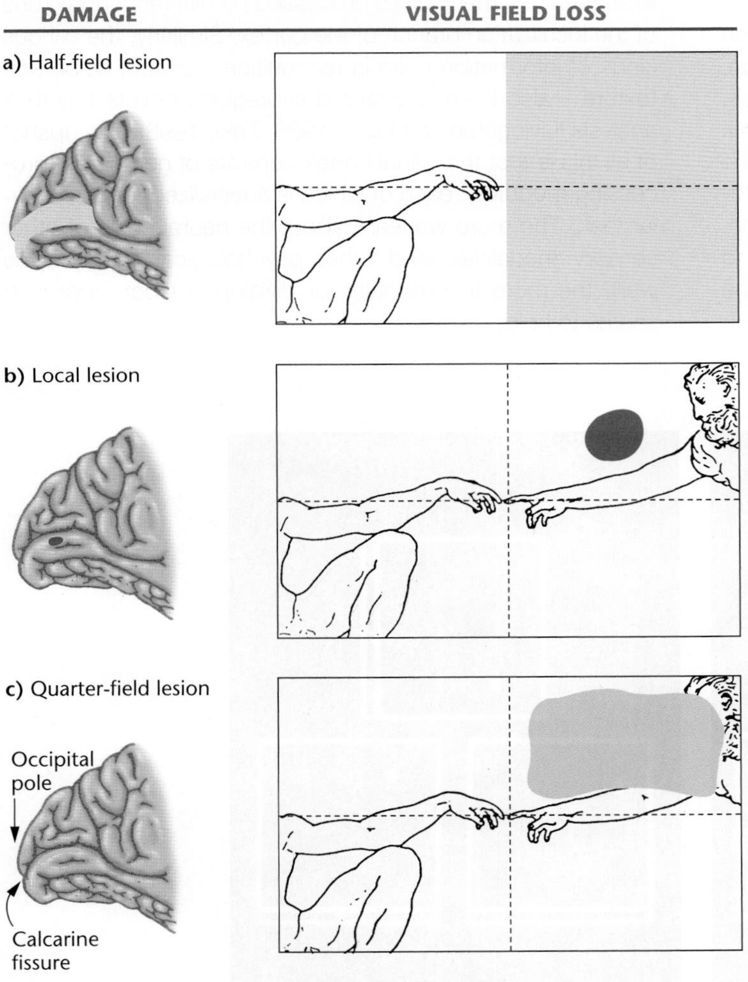

DAMAGE	VISUAL FIELD LOSS
a) Half-field lesion	
b) Local lesion	
c) Quarter-field lesion	

Occipital
pole

Calcarine
fissure

FIGURE 5.32 The Visual Consequences of Various Kinds of Lesions in the Primary Visual Cortex (V1). *The 'map' of the visual field is upside down and mirror reversed.*

specific part of V1 was linked to blindness in very specific parts of the visual field (technically, a scotoma). Note that this form of blindness is not caused by damage to the eyes or the optic nerve; it is entirely cortical (pertaining to the cortex) in origin. For example, the very center of the visual field – the fovea – will suffer a scotoma if a lesion occurs at the extreme rear of V1. Scotomas in more peripheral portions of the visual field are caused by lesions further forward in V1. It is as though a map of the visual field has been stretched over the back of the cortex, with its center directly over the rearmost part of the cortex.

Neurons in the primary visual cortex are sensitive to many features contained in a visual image, such as brightness, color, orientation, and motion. However, one of the most important features of these neurons is that they are each responsible for analyzing only a very tiny region of the image. In the foveal part of the image, this can be as small as less than 1 millimeter seen at arm's length. These neurons also communicate with one another only in very small regions. The benefit of this arrangement is that the entire visual field can be analyzed simultaneously and in great detail. What is missing from this analysis, however, is the ability to co-ordinate information that is not close together in the image – that is, to see the 'forest' in addition to the 'trees.'

To accomplish this task, cortical neurons send information from V1 to the many other regions of the brain that analyze visual information. Each of these regions specializes in a particular task, such as analyzing color, motion, shape, and location. These more specialized regions are also in constant contact with V1, so that the neural communication between regions is better thought of as a conversation than as a command (Damasio, 1990; Zeki, 1993). One of the most important divisions of labor in visual analysis by the brain is between localization and recognition, to which we now turn.

Recognition versus localization systems

The idea that localization and recognition are qualitatively different tasks is supported by research findings showing that they are carried out by different regions of the visual cortex. *Recognition* of objects depends on a branch of the visual system that includes the primary visual cortex and a region near the bottom of the cerebral cortex. In contrast, as shown in Figure 5.31, *localization* of objects depends on a branch of the visual system that includes the primary visual cortex and a region of the cortex near the top of the brain. Studies with non-human primates show that if the recognition branch of an animal's visual system is impaired, the animal can still perform tasks that require it to perceive spatial relations between objects (one in front of the other, for example) but cannot perform tasks that require discriminating between the actual objects – for example, tasks that require discriminating a cube from a cylinder. If the location branch is impaired, the animal can perform tasks that require it to distinguish a cube from a cylinder, but it cannot perform tasks that require it to know where the objects are in relation to each other (Mishkin *et al.*, 1983). Similar results have been reported in humans who have suffered parietal-lobe damage, e.g., Phan *et al.*, (2000).

More recent research has used brain imaging to document the existence of separate object and location systems in the human brain. One widely used technique is PET (discussed in Chapter 2). A observer first has a radioactive tracer injected into her bloodstream and then is placed in a PET scanner while she performs various tasks. The scanner measures increases in radioactivity in various brain regions, which indicate increases in blood flow to those regions. The regions that show the most increase in blood flow are the ones that mediate performance of the task.

In one such study, observers performed two tasks, one a test of face recognition, which depends on the brain region for object recognition, and the other a test of mental rotation, which requires localization. In the face-recognition task, observers saw a target picture with two test faces beneath it during each trial. One of the test faces was the face of the person depicted by the target, except for changes in orientation and lighting; the other was the face of a different person. As shown in the left of Figure 5.33, the observer's task was to decide which test face was the same as the target. While the observer was engaging in this task, there was an increase in

blood flow in the recognition branch of the cortex (the branch terminating near the bottom of the cortex), but not in the localization branch (the branch terminating near the top of the cortex).

Very different results were obtained with the mental rotation task. In this task, on each trial, observers saw a target display of a dot at some distance from a double line; beneath the target were two test displays. As shown in the right of Figure 5.33, one test display was the same as the target, except that it had been rotated; the other test display contained a different configuration of the dot and lines. While engaging in this task, observers showed an increase in blood flow in the localization branch of the cortex, but not in the recognition branch. Localization and recognition, therefore, are carried out in entirely different regions of the visual cortex (Grady *et al.*, 1992; Haxby *et al.*, 1990).

The division of labor in the visual cortex does not end with the split between localization and recognition. Rather, the different kinds of information that are used in localization – eye movements, motion analysis, and depth perception, for example – are themselves processed by different subregions of the localization branch of the cortex. Similarly, the various kinds of information used in recognition – shape, color, and texture – also have specialized subregions devoted to their analysis (Livingstone & Hubel, 1988; Zeki, 1993). The upshot of all this is that the visual cortex consists of numerous 'processing modules,' each of which is specialized for a particular task. The more we learn about the neural basis of other sensory modalities (and other psychological functions as well), the more this modular, or division-of-labor, approach seems to hold.

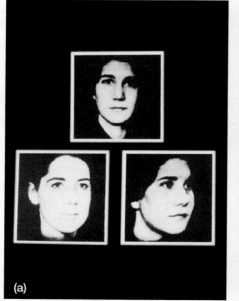
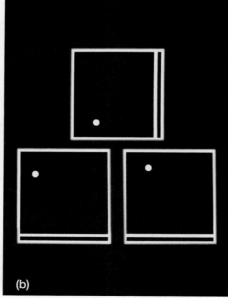

(a)   (b)

FIGURE 5.33 Recognition and Localization Tasks. *Sample items from the face-matching (left) and dot-location (right) matching tasks.*

CRITICAL THINKING QUESTIONS

1 Why do you think the brain seems to solve many problems by dividing the work among specialized regions? What advantages may be gained by this approach? What problems might be caused by this division of labor?

2 Some people are skeptical about the value of studying perception and behavior from a biological perspective. Given what you have learned about vision and visually guided behavior, how would you argue against such skeptics?

PERCEPTUAL DEVELOPMENT

An age-old question about perception is whether our abilities to perceive are learned or innate – the familiar nature-versus-nurture problem. Contemporary psychologists no longer believe that this is an 'either-or' question. No one doubts that both genetics and learning influence perception; rather, the goal is to pinpoint the contribution of each and to spell out their interactions. For the modern researcher, the question 'Must we learn to perceive?' has given way to more specific questions: (a) What discriminatory capacities do infants have (which tells us something about inborn capacities), and how does this capacity change with age under normal rearing conditions? (b) If animals are reared under conditions that restrict what they can learn (referred to as **controlled stimulation**), what effects does this have on their later discriminatory capacity? (c) What effects does

rearing under controlled conditions have on perceptual-motor co-ordination? We will address each of these issues in turn.

Discrimination by infants

Perhaps the most direct way to find out what human perceptual capacities are inborn is to see what capacities an infant has. At first, you might think that this research should consider only newborns, because if a capacity is inborn it should be present from the first day of life. This idea turns out to be too simple, though. Some inborn capacities, such as perception of form, can appear only after other more basic capacities, such as the ability to register details, have developed. Other inborn capacities may require that there be some kind of environmental input for a certain length of time in order for the capacity to mature. Thus, the study of inborn capacities traces perceptual development from the first minute of life through the early years of childhood.

Methods of studying infants

It is hard for us to know what an infant perceives because it cannot talk or follow instructions, and has a fairly limited set of behaviors. To study infant perception, a researcher needs to find a form of behavior through which an infant indicates what it can discriminate. As shown in Figure 5.34, one such behavior is an infant's tendency to look at some objects more than at others; psychologists make use of this behavior in a technique known as the **preferential looking method** (Teller, 1979). Two stimuli are presented to the infant side by side. The experimenter, who is hidden from the infant's view, looks through a partition behind the stimuli and, by watching the infant's eyes, measures the amount of time that the infant looks at each stimulus. (Usually the experimenter uses a television camera to record the infant's viewing pattern.) During the experiment the positions of the stimuli are switched randomly. If an infant consistently looks at one stimulus more than at the other, the experimenter

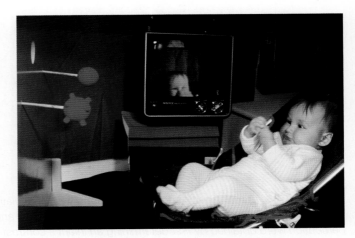

FIGURE 5.34 Testing the Visual Preferences of an infant.

concludes that the infant can tell them apart – that is, discriminate between them.

A related technique is called the **habituation method** (Frantz, 1966; Horowitz, 1974). It takes advantage of the fact that although infants look directly at novel objects, they soon become bored with the same object – that is, they habituate. Suppose that an object is presented for a while and then replaced by a new object. To the extent that the second object is perceived as identical or highly similar to the first one, the infant should spend little time looking at it; conversely, to the extent that the second object is perceived as substantially different from the first one, the infant should spend a lot of time staring at it. By these means, an experimenter can determine whether two physical displays look the same to an infant.

Using these techniques, psychologists have studied a variety of perceptual capacities in infants. Some of these capacities are needed to perceive forms, and hence are used in the task of recognition; others, particularly depth perception, are involved in the task of localization; and still others are involved in the task of keeping the appearance of perceived objects constant.

Perceiving forms

To be able to perceive an object, a person must first be able to discriminate one part of it from another, an ability referred to as visual acuity. Acuity is often assessed by varying both the contrast in a pattern (the difference in brightness between dark and light regions) and the spatial frequency of the pattern (the number of times a pattern is repeated within a given area). For any particular level of contrast there are always some spatial frequencies that cannot be resolved by the visual system because they are too fine. At the other extreme, there are other spatial frequencies that cannot be seen because they change over too large an area.

The method typically used in studying acuity in infants is preferential looking, with a pattern of stripes as one stimulus

and a uniform gray field as the other. Initially the stripes are relatively wide, and the infant prefers to look at the pattern rather than at the uniform field. Then the researcher decreases the width of the stripes until the infant no longer shows a preference. Presumably at this point the infant can no longer discriminate a stripe from its surroundings, so that the pattern of stripes no longer has perceptible parts and looks like a uniform field. When first studied at about 1 month of age, infants can see some patterns, but their acuity is very low. Acuity increases rapidly over the first 6 months of life; then it increases more slowly, reaching adult levels between one and two years of age (Courage & Adams, 1990a, 1990b; Teller & Movshon, 1986).

What do studies like this tell us about the infant's perceptual world? At 1 month, infants can distinguish among relatively large objects but cannot distinguish fine details. Such vision is sufficient to perceive some general characteristics of an object, including some of the features of a face (which create something like a pattern of dark and light stripes). Figure 5.35 uses the results of acuity experiments to simulate what 1-, 2-, and 3-month-old infants see when viewing a woman's face from a distance of 6 inches. At 1 month, acuity is so poor that it is difficult to perceive facial expressions (and indeed newborns look mostly at the outside contours of a face). By 3 months, acuity has improved to the point where an infant can decipher facial expressions. No wonder that infants 3 so much more socially responsive at three months than at 1 month.

Being able to discriminate dark from light edges is essential for seeing forms, but what about other aspects of object recognition? Our sensitivity to some of the shape features of objects is manifested very early in life. When presented with a triangle, even a 3-day-old infant will direct its eye movements toward the edges and vertices rather than looking randomly over the form (Salapatek, 1975). Also, infants find some shapes more interesting than others. As noted in Chapter 3, they tend to look more at forms that resemble human faces, a tendency that appears to be based on a

FIGURE 5.35 Visual Acuity and Contrast Sensitivity. *Simulations of what one-, two-, and three-month-old infants see when they look at a woman's face from a distance of about 6 inches and a photograph of what an adult sees. The simulations of infant perception were obtained by first determining an infant's contrast sensitivity and then applying this contrast-sensitivity function to the photograph.*

preference to attend to objects with more visual complexity in the upper portion of the object (Macchi Cassia *et al.*, 2004). By 3 months an infant can recognize something about the mother's face, even in a photograph, as revealed by an infant's preference to look at a photograph of the mother rather than one of an unfamiliar woman (Barrera & Maurer, 1981a).

Perceiving depth

Depth perception begins to appear at about 3 months but is not fully established until about 6 months. Thus, at around 4 months infants will begin to reach for the nearer of two objects, where nearness is signaled by binocular disparity (Granrud, 1986). A month or two later they will begin to reach for objects that are apparently nearer on the basis of monocular depth cues such as relative size, linear perspective, and shading cues (Coren *et al.*, 1999).

Further evidence of the development of monocular depth perception comes from studies using what is called a 'visual cliff,' illustrated in Figure 5.36. This consists of a board placed across a sheet of glass, with a surface of patterned material located directly under the glass on the shallow side and at a distance of a few feet below the glass on the deep side. (The appearance of depth in Figure 5.36 – the 'cliff'– is created by an abrupt change in the texture gradient.) An infant who is old enough to crawl (six–seven months) is placed on the board; a patch is placed over one eye to

FIGURE 5.36 The Visual Cliff. *The 'visual cliff' is an apparatus used to show that babies and young animals are able to see depth by the time they are able to move about. The apparatus consists of two surfaces, both displaying the same checkerboard pattern and covered by a sheet of thick glass. One surface is directly under the glass; the other is several fee below it. When placed on the center board between the deep side and the shallow side, the baby refuses to cross to the deep side but will readily move off the board onto the shallow side.*

eliminate binocular depth cues. When the mother calls or beckons from the shallow side, the infant will consistently crawl toward her; but when the mother beckons from the deep side, the infant will not cross the 'cliff.' Thus, when an infant is old enough to crawl, depth perception is relatively well developed.

Perceiving constancies

Like the perception of form and depth, the perceptual constancies start to develop in the first few months of life. This is particularly true of shape and size constancy (Kellman, 1984). Consider an experiment on size constancy that used the habituation method. Four-month-old infants were first shown one teddy bear for a while and then shown a second one. The second bear was either (a) identical in physical size to the original one, but presented at a different distance so that it produced a different-sized retinal image, or (b) different in physical size from the original bear. If the infants had developed size constancy, they should perceive bear 'a' (same physical size) as identical to the one they saw originally, and hence spend little time looking at it compared to the amount of time spent looking at bear 'b' (which was actually bigger than the original). And this is exactly what happened (Granrud, 1986).

Controlled stimulation

We turn now to the question of how specific experiences affect perceptual capacities. To answer this question, researchers have systematically varied the kind of perceptual experiences a young organism has, and then looked at the effects of this experience on subsequent perceptual performance.

Absence of stimulation

The earliest experiments on controlled stimulation sought to determine the effects of rearing an animal in the total absence of visual stimulation. The experimenters kept animals in the dark for several months after birth, until they were mature enough for visual testing. The idea behind these experiments was that if animals have to learn to perceive, they would be unable to perceive when first exposed to the light. The results turned out as expected: chimpanzees that were reared in darkness for their first 16 months could detect light but could not discriminate among patterns (Riesen, 1947). However, subsequent studies showed that prolonged rearing in the dark does more than prevent learning; it causes deterioration of neurons in various parts of the visual system. It turns out that a certain amount of light stimulation is necessary to maintain the visual system. Without any light stimulation, nerve cells in the retina and visual cortex begin to atrophy (Binns & Salt, 1997; Movshon & van Sluyters, 1981).

Although these findings do not tell us much about the role of learning in perceptual development, they are important in

SEEING BOTH SIDES
IS PERCEPTUAL DEVELOPMENT AN INNATE OR SOCIALLY ACQUIRED PROCESS?

PERCEPTUAL DEVELOPMENT IS AN INTRINSIC PROCESS

Elizabeth S. Spelke, Massachusetts Institute of Technology

Human beings have a striking capacity to learn from one another. This capacity already is evident in the one-year-old child, who can learn the meaning of a new word by observing just a few occasions of its use and who can learn the functions of a new object simply by watching another person act on it. The rapid and extensive learning that occurs in early childhood suggests that much of what humans come to know and believe is shaped by our encounters with other things and people. But is our very ability to perceive things and people itself the result of learning? Or, does perception originate in intrinsically generated growth processes and develop in relative independence of one's encounters with things perceived?

For two millennia, most of the thinkers who have pondered this question have favored the view that humans learn to perceive, and that the course of development proceeds from meaningless, unstructured sensations to meaningful, structured perceptions. Research on human infants nevertheless provides evidence against this view. For example, we now know that newborn infants perceive depth and use depth information as adults do, to apprehend the true sizes and shapes of objects. Newborn infants divide the speech stream into the same kinds of sound patterns as do adults, focusing in particular on the set of sound contrasts used by human languages. Newborn infants distinguish human faces from other patterns and orient to faces preferentially. Finally, newborn infants are sensitive to many of the features of objects that adults use to distinguish one thing from another, and they appear to combine featural information in the same kinds of ways as do adults.

How does perception change after the newborn period? With development, infants have been found to perceive depth, objects, and faces with increasing precision. Infants also come to focus on the speech contrasts that are relevant to their own language in preference to speech contrasts relevant to other languages. (Interestingly, this focus appears to result more from a decline in sensitivity to foreign language contrasts than from an increase in sensitivity to native language contrasts.) Finally, infants become sensitive to new sources of information about the environment, such as stereoscopic information for depth, configural information for object boundaries, and new reference frames for locating objects and events. These developments bring greater precision and richness to infants' perceptual experience, but they do not change the infant's world from a meaningless flow of sensation to a meaningful, structured environment.

The findings from studies of human infants gain further support from studies of perceptual development in other animals. Since the pioneering work of Gibson and Walk, we have known that depth perception develops without visual experience in every animal tested: innate capacities for perceiving depth allow newborn goats to avoid falling off cliffs, and they allow dark-reared rats and cats to avoid bumping into approaching surfaces. More recent studies reveal that newborn chicks perceive the boundaries of objects much as human adults do, and they even represent the continued existence of objects that are hidden. Studies of animals' developing brains reveal that both genes and intrinsically structured neural activity are crucial to the development of normally functioning perceptual systems, but encounters with the objects of perception — external things and events — play a much lesser role. As with human infants, normal visual experience enriches and attunes young animals' perceptual systems, and abnormal visual experience may greatly perturb their functioning. Like human infants, however, other animals do not need visual experience to transform their perceptual world from a flow of unstructured sensations into a structured visual layout.

In sum, perception shows considerable structure at birth and continuity over development. This continuity may help to explain why young human infants are so adept at learning from other people. Consider an infant who watches an adult twist a lid off a jar while saying, 'Let's open it,' If the infant could not perceive the lid and jar as distinct movable and manipulable objects, she would not be able to make sense of the adult's action. If she could not perceive the sounds that distinguish 'open' from other words, she could not begin to learn about this distinctive utterance. And if she could not perceive the person as an agent in some way like herself, then watching the person's action and listening to his speech would reveal nothing about what the infant herself could learn to do or say. Infants' prodigious abilities to learn, therefore, may depend critically on equally prodigious, unlearned abilities to perceive.

SEEING BOTH SIDES

IS PERCEPTUAL DEVELOPMENT AN INNATE OR SOCIALLY ACQUIRED PROCESS?

PERCEPTUAL DEVELOPMENT IS AN ACTIVITY-DEPENDENT PROCESS

Mark Johnson, University of London

Most developmental scientists now agree that both nature and nurture are essential for the normal development of perception. However, there is still much dispute about the extent to which either nature or nurture is the more important factor. Points of view on this issue are more than just philosophical musings; they affect the kinds of research programs that are undertaken. Since the 1980s a major thrust in developmental psychology has centered on identifying and delineating aspects of perceptual and cognitive function that can be termed innately specified core knowledge (Spelke & Kinzler, 2007). Core knowledge is contrasted with learning mechanisms engaged by visual experience. I argue here that this line of thinking fails to reflect the fact that the most interesting phenomena in development involve interactions between acquired and intrinsic processes, and that common mechanisms of brain adaptation may underlie the two processes. I propose that perceptual development is better characterized as an activity-dependent process involving complex and subtle interactions at many levels, and that the infant actively seeks out the experience it needs for its own further brain development.

To begin to illustrate my point, let's consider neurobiological work on the prenatal development of the visual cortex in another species, rodents. The neurons studied in these experiments are those involved in binocular vision. Experiments show that the prenatal tuning of these neurons arises through their response to internally generated waves of electrical activity from the main inputs to the visual cortex, the lateral geniculate nucleus and eye (Katz & Shatz, 1996). In other words, the response properties of these visual cortical neurons are shaped by a kind of 'virtual environment' generated by cells elsewhere in the brain and eye. Although the term *innate* can be stretched to cover this example of development, we could equally well describe this process as the cortical cells learning from the input provided by their cousins in the LGN and eye. Further, after birth the same cortical neurons continue to be tuned in the same way, except that now their input also reflects the structure of the world outside the infant. Thus, when we examine development in detail, it becomes harder to argue that 'innate knowledge' is fundamentally different from learning.

Another example of the role of activity-dependent processes in perceptual development comes from the ability to detect and recognize faces. Because regions of the adult human cortex are specialized for processing faces, some have argued that this ability is innate. However, experiments with infants reveal a more complex story (Johnson, 2005). The tendency for newborns to look more toward faces turns out to be based on a very primitive reflex-like system that may be triggered by a stimulus as simple as three high-contrast blobs in the approximate locations of the eyes and mouth. This simple attention bias, together with a sensitivity to the human voice, is sufficient to ensure that newborns look much more at faces than at other objects and patterns over the first weeks of life. One consequence of this is that developing brain circuits on the visual recognition pathway of the cortex get more input related to faces and thus are shaped by experience with this special type of visual stimulus. We can now study this process by using new brain-imaging methods. Such studies have shown that the brains of young children show less localized and less specialized processing of faces in the cortex than do the brains of adults. It is not until around ten years old that children start to show the same patterns of brain specialization for processing faces as adults, by which time they have had as much as 10 000 hours of experience of human faces.

Another example comes from the study of infants' eye movements to visual targets. Although newborns are capable of some primitive reflexive eye movements, only much later in the first year can they make most of the kinds of complex and accurate saccades (fast movement of the eyes) seen in adults. One view is that the very limited ability present in newborns is just sufficient to allow them to practice and develop new brain circuits for the more complex integration of visual and motor information necessary for adult-like eye movements. And practice they do! Even by 4 months, babies have already made more than 3 million eye movements. Once again, it appears that infants actively contribute to their own subsequent development.

These considerations should also make us skeptical about claims made for innate perceptual abilities based on experiments with babies that are several months old. In fact, when the same experiments were done with younger infants, quite different results have sometimes been obtained, suggesting dramatic changes in perceptual abilities over the first few weeks and months after birth (Haith, 1998).

Infants are not passively shaped by either their genes or their environment. Rather, perceptual development is an activity-dependent process in which, during postnatal life, the infant plays an active role in generating the experience it needs for its own subsequent brain development.

Mark Johnson

themselves. They reveal that when an animal is deprived of visual stimulation from birth, the longer the period of deprivation, the greater the deficits. Adult cats, on the other hand, can have a patch over one eye for a long period without losing vision in that eye. These observations led to the idea that there is a critical period for the development of inborn visual capacities. (A critical period is a stage in development during which the organism is optimally ready to acquire certain abilities.) Lack of stimulation during a critical period for vision can permanently impair the visual system (Cynader *et al.*, 1980).

Limited stimulation

Researchers no longer deprive animals of stimulation for a long time; instead, they study the effects of rearing animals that receive stimuli in both eyes, but only certain kinds of stimuli. For example, researchers have raised kittens in an environment in which they see only vertical stripes or only horizontal stripes. The kittens become blind to stripes in the orientation – horizontal or vertical – that they do not experience. Single-cell recording studies show that many cells in the visual cortex of a 'horizontally reared' cat respond to horizontal stimuli and none responds to vertical stimuli, whereas the opposite pattern is found in the visual cortex of a 'vertically reared' cat (Blake, 1981; Movshon & van Sluyters, 1981). This blindness seems to be caused by the degeneration of cells in the visual cortex.

Of course, researchers do not deprive humans of normal visual stimulation, but sometimes this happens naturally or as a consequence of medical treatment. For example, after eye surgery the eye that was operated on is usually covered with a patch. If this happens to a child in the first year of life, the acuity of the patched eye is reduced (Awaya *et al.*, 1973). This suggests that there is a critical period early in the development of the human visual system similar to that in animals; if stimulation is restricted during this period, the system will not develop normally. The critical period is much longer in humans than in animals. It may last as long as 8 years, but the greatest vulnerability occurs during the first 2 years of life (Aslin & Banks, 1978).

None of these facts indicates that we have to learn to perceive. Rather, the facts show that certain kinds of stimulation are essential for the maintenance and development of perceptual capacities that are present at birth. But this does not mean that learning has no effect on perception. For evidence of such effects, we need only consider our ability to recognize common objects. The fact that we can recognize a familiar object more readily than an unfamiliar one – a dog versus an aardvark, for example – must certainly be due to learning. If we had been reared in an environment rich in aardvarks and sparse in dogs, we could have recognized the aardvark more readily than the dog.

Active perception

When it comes to co-ordinating perceptions with motor responses, learning plays a major role. The evidence for

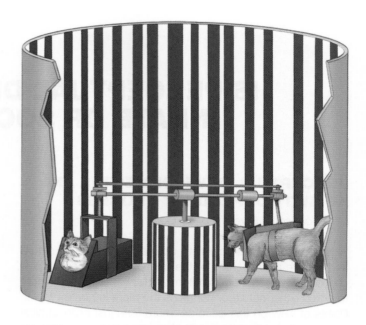

FIGURE 5.37 **The Importance of Self-Produced Movements.** *Both kittens received roughly the same visual stimulation, but only the active kitten had this stimulation produced by its own movement.*

this comes from studies in which observers receive normal stimulation but are prevented from making normal responses to that stimulation. Under such conditions, perceptual-motor co-ordination does not develop.

For example, in one classic study, two kittens that had been reared in darkness had their first visual experience in the 'kitten carousel' illustrated in Figure 5.37. As the active kitten walked, it moved the passive kitten riding in the carousel. Although both kittens received roughly the same visual stimulation, only the active kitten had this stimulation produced by its own movement. And only the active kitten successfully learned sensory-motor co-ordination; for example, when picked up and moved toward an object, only the active kitten learned to put out its paws to ward off a collision.

Similar results have been obtained with humans. In some experiments, people wear prism goggles that distort the directions of objects. Immediately after putting on these goggles, they temporarily have trouble reaching for objects and often bump into things. If they move about and attempt to perform motor tasks while wearing the goggles, they learn to co-ordinate their movements with the actual location of objects rather than with their apparent locations. On the other hand, if a person is pushed in a wheelchair he or she does not adapt to the goggles. Apparently, self-produced movement is essential to prism adaptation (Held, 1965).

In sum, the evidence indicates that we are born with considerable perceptual capacities. The natural development of some of these capacities may require years of normal input

FIGURE 5.38 Meaningful Objects Help Our Perceptions.
After looking at this picture, look back at the left panel of Figure 5.1 at the beginning of the chapter. Now what do you see?

from the environment. But there clearly are learning effects on perception as well; these are particularly striking when perception must be co-ordinated with motor behavior.

This chapter, like the preceding one, includes many examples of the interplay between psychological and biological approaches. Throughout the chapter we have encountered cases in which specific psychological functions are implemented by specific cells or brain regions. We have seen that specialized cells are used to perceive motion and that separate parts of the brain are used to register the visual features of location, shape, and color. Still other

regions of the brain are involved in determining which of these features will be used to control behaviors and actions. These and other examples illustrate how significant the findings of biological research can be in the study of psychological processes.

INTERIM SUMMARY

➡ Research on perceptual development is concerned with the extent to which perceptual capacities are inborn and the extent to which they are learned through experience.

➡ To determine inborn capacities, researchers study the discrimination capacities of infants with methods such as preferential looking and habituation. Perceptual constancies begin to develop as early as 6 months.

➡ Animals raised in darkness suffer permanent visual impairment, and animals raised with a patch over one eye become blind in that eye, suggesting a critical period early in life when lack of normal stimulation produces deficiency in an innate perceptual capacity.

CRITICAL THINKING QUESTION

1 Do you think that in general infants are more or less able to perceive the world than their parents think they are?

CHAPTER SUMMARY

1 The study of perception deals with the question of how organisms process and organize incoming raw, sensory information in order to (a) form a coherent representation or model of the world within which the organism dwells, and (b) use that representation to solve naturally occurring problems, such as navigating, grasping, and planning.

2 Five major functions of the perceptual system are: (a) Determining which part of the sensory environment to attend to, (b) localizing, or determining *where* objects are, (c) recognizing, or determining *what* objects are, (d) *abstracting* the critical information from objects, and (e) keeping appearance of objects *constant*, even though their retinal images are changing. Another area of study is how our perceptual capacities develop.

3 Selective attention is the process by which we select some stimuli for further processing while ignoring others. In vision, the primary means of directing our attention are eye movements. Most eye fixations are on the more informative parts of a scene. Selective attention also occurs in audition. Usually we are able to selectively listen by using cues such as the direction from which the sound is coming and the voice characteristics of the speaker. Our ability to selectively attend is mediated by processes that occur in the early stages of recognition as well as by processes that occur only after the message's meaning has been determined.

4 To localize objects we must first separate them from one another and then organize them into groups. These processes were first studied by Gestalt psychologists, who proposed several principles of organization. One such principle is that we organize a stimulus into regions corresponding to figure and ground. Other principles concern the bases that we use to group objects together, including proximity, closure, similarity, good continuation, and closure.

5 Localizing an object requires that we know its distance from us. This form of perception, known as depth perception, is usually thought to be based on depth cues. Monocular depth cues include relative size, interposition, relative height, linear perspective, shading, and motion parallax. A binocular depth cue is binocular disparity, which results from the fact that any object produces slightly different images on the two retinas.

6 Localizing an object sometimes requires that we know the direction in which an object is moving. Motion perception can be produced in the absence of an object moving across our retina. One example of this phenomenon is stroboscopic motion, in which a rapid series of still images induces apparent movement; another example is induced motion, in which movement of a large object induces apparent movement of a smaller stationary object. Perception of real motion (movement of a real object through space) is implemented by specific cells in the visual system, as indicated by single-cell recordings and experiments on selective adaptation.

7 Recognizing an object requires that the various features associated with the object (e.g., shapes, colors) be correctly bound together. It is generally believed that attention is required for this binding process; when such binding fails, an illusory conjunction – the incorrect conjunction of two or more features of different objects – may occur.

8 Recognizing an object amounts to assigning it to a category and is based mainly on the shape of the object. In early stages of recognition, the visual system uses retinal information to describe the object in terms of features like lines and angles; neurons that detect such features (feature detectors) have been found in the visual cortex. In later stages of recognition, the system matches the description of the object with shape descriptions stored in memory to find the best match.

9 Matching can be explained by a connectionist model or network. The bottom level of the network contains features and the next level contains letters; an excitatory connection between a feature and a letter means that the feature is part of a letter, while an inhibitory connection means that the feature is not part of the letter. When a letter is presented, it activates some features in the network, which pass their activation or inhibition up to letters; the letter that receives the most activation is the best match to the input. The network can be expanded to include a level of words and to explain why a letter is easier to recognize when presented in a word than when presented alone.

10 The shape features of natural objects are more complex than lines; they are similar to simple geometric forms such as cylinders, cones, blocks, and wedges. A limited set of such forms may be sufficient in combination to describe the shapes of all objects that people can recognize.

11 Research indicates that face recognition involves processes separate from object recognition. Object recognition depends on processing features, and face recognition depends in part on processing overall configuration.

12 Bottom-up recognition processes are driven solely by the input, whereas top-down recognition processes are driven by a person's knowledge and expectations. Top-down processes underlie context effects in perception: the context sets up a perceptual expectation, and when this expectation is satisfied, less input information than usual is needed for recognition.

13 Another major function of the perceptual system is to achieve perceptual constancy – that is, to keep the appearance of objects the same in spite of large changes in the stimuli received by the sense organs. Lightness constancy refers to the fact that an object appears equally light regardless of how much light it reflects, and color constancy means that an object looks roughly the same color regardless of the light source illuminating it. In both cases, constancy depends on relations between the object and elements of the background. Two other well-known perceptual constancies are shape and location constancy.

14 Size constancy refers to the fact that an object's apparent size remains relatively constant no matter how far away it is. The perceived size of an object increases with both the retinal size of the object and the perceived distance of the object, in accordance with the size–distance invariance principle. Thus, as an object moves away from the perceiver, the size of its retinal image decreases but the perceived distance increases, and the two changes cancel each other out, resulting in constancy. This principle can be used to explain certain kinds of perceptual illusions.

15 Three separate brain systems seem to mediate the psychological act of selecting an object to attend to. In the posterior system, objects are selected on the basis of location, shape, or color. The anterior system is responsible for guiding this process, depending on the goals of the viewer. PET studies further show that once an object has been selected, activity is amplified in the posterior regions of the brain that are relevant to the attribute being attended to.

16 The visual cortex operates according to the principle of division of labor. Localization and recognition are carried out by different regions of the brain, with localization mediated by a region near the top of the cortex and recognition by a region near the bottom of the cortex. Recognition processes are further subdivided into separate modules: for example, color, shape, and texture.

17 Research on perceptual development is concerned with the extent to which perceptual capacities are inborn and the extent to which they are learned through experience. To determine inborn capacities, researchers study the discrimination capacities of infants using methods such as preferential looking and habituation. Acuity, which is critical to recognition, increases rapidly during the first 6 months of life and then increases more slowly. Depth perception begins to appear at about 3 months but is not fully established until about 6 months. Perceptual constancies begin to develop as early as 6 months.

18 Animals raised in darkness suffer permanent visual impairment, and animals raised with a patch over one eye become blind in that eye. Adult animals do not lose vision even when deprived of stimulation for long periods. These results suggest that there is a critical period early in life during which lack of normal stimulation produces deficiency in an innate perceptual capacity. If stimulation early in life is controlled in such a way that certain kinds of stimuli are absent, both animals and people become insensitive to the stimuli of which they have been deprived; again, this effect does not have much to do with learning. Perceptual-motor co-ordination must be learned, however. Both animals and people require self-produced movement to develop normal co-ordination.

CORE CONCEPTS

perception	selective adaptation	bottom-up versus top-down processes
symbol	selective attention	McGurk effect
theory of ecological optics	primitive features	prosopagnosia
model of the environment	binding problem	inversion effect
perceptual constancy	illusory conjunction	agnosia
eye fixations	feature-integration theory	associative agnosia
saccade	visual search task	abstraction
weapon focus	dynamic control theory	constancy
shadowing	simple cell	available wavelengths
inattention blindness	complex cell	source wavelengths
charge blindness	hypercomplex cell	reflectance characteristic
depth cues	emergent features	illusion
binocular disparity	connectionist models	posterior system
Relative size	excitatory connections	anterior system
Interposition	augmented network	controlled stimulation
Relative height	inhibitory connections	preferential looking method
Shading and shadows	top-down feedback connections	habituation method
stroboscopic motion	object recognition	
relative motion	geons	

DIGITAL SUPPORT RESOURCES

Students should use the unique access code included in the front of the book to access the digital support resources which accompany the new edition. These include:

- Multiple Choice Questions and Quizzes
- Critical Thinking Questions
- Practice Essay Questions

- Videos
- Glossary, Flashcards, and More

6 CONSCIOUSNESS

LEARNING OBJECTIVES

After reading this chapter you should be able to:

Define consciousness in terms of its function in monitoring information and controlling our actions.

Know what is meant by the terms preconscious memories and the unconscious. Be familiar with the phenomena of automaticity and of dissociation.

Discuss in some detail sleep schedules, stages of sleep, REM and NREM sleep, and sleep disorders.

Describe Freud's perspective on the purpose of dreams.

Define meditation and describe the consequences of meditation training.

Veronica was sitting in a restaurant with her friend Gina, listening to Gina's recounting of a party she went to the night before. For a while, Veronica was interested in what Gina was saying, but as Gina went on and on about what a mutual acquaintance of theirs was wearing, Veronica lost interest, looked down at her watch, and then let her mind begin to drift. Suddenly, Gina said sharply, 'Veronica! You haven't heard a word I've said!' Indeed, Veronica had not heard what Gina had said, and when she looked down at her watch, she was stunned to see that 10 minutes had passed.

Sound like a familiar experience? If so, you are in good company. One survey of a random sample of adults found that more than 80 per cent acknowledged they had had the experience of missing part of a conversation because their mind 'wandered' (Ross, 1997). Similarly, several people acknowledged not being sure whether they had done something or only thought about it (73 per cent of the sample), remembering the past so vividly that they seemed to be reliving it (60 per cent), not being sure if they remembered an event or it was just a dream (55 per cent), and driving a car and realizing that they didn't remember part of the trip (48 per cent).

These experiences might be referred to as altered states of consciousness. To most psychologists, an altered state of consciousness exists whenever there is a change from an ordinary pattern of mental functioning to a state that seems different to the person experiencing the change. Although this definition is not very precise, it reflects the fact that states of consciousness are personal and therefore highly subjective. Altered states of consciousness can vary from the distraction of a vivid daydream to the confusion and perceptual distortion caused by drug intoxication. In this chapter, we will look at some altered states of consciousness that are experienced by everyone (sleep and dreams), as well as some that result from special circumstances (meditation, hypnosis, and the use of drugs).

CHAPTER OUTLINE

ASPECTS OF CONSCIOUSNESS

Consciousness

Preconscious memories

The unconscious

Automaticity and dissociation

SLEEP AND DREAMS

Stages of sleep

Sleep theory

Sleep-wake disorders

Dreams

MEDITATION

CUTTING EDGE RESEARCH: PICTURES OF CONSCIOUSNESS?

HYPNOSIS

Induction of hypnosis

Hypnotic suggestions

PSYCHOACTIVE DRUGS

Depressants

Illicit drugs

Opiates

Stimulants

SEEING BOTH SIDES: DOES BRAIN DEATH MEAN DEATH?

When we concentrate, we are unaware of background stimuli. This ability to select stimuli to focus on enables us to avoid information overload.

ASPECTS OF CONSCIOUSNESS

Discussions about the nature of conscious experience and the functions of consciousness will appear throughout this book as we consider perception, memory, language, problem-solving, and other topics. What is consciousness? Philosophers such as René Descartes focused on the subjective experience of the mind ('I think therefore I am') in defining consciousness. The early psychologists defined *psychology* as 'the study of mind and consciousness.' Willhelm Wundt used the introspective method, along with controlled experiments, to study consciousness in the nineteenth century in Germany.

As noted in Chapter 1, both introspection as a method for investigation and consciousness as a topic for investigation fell from favor with the rise of behaviorism in the early 1900s. John Watson and his followers believed that if psychology was to become a science, its data must be objective and measurable. Behavior could be publicly observed, and various responses could be objectively measured. In contrast, an individual's private experiences might be revealed through introspection but could not be directly observed by others or objectively measured. If psychology dealt with overt behavior, it would be dealing with public events rather than private events, which are observable only to the person experiencing them.

Behaviorism did not require as radical a change as its pronouncements seemed to imply. The behaviorists themselves dealt with private events when their research required them to do so. They accepted verbal responses as a substitute for introspection when the participant's own experiences were studied. What participants said was objective, regardless of the underlying subjective condition. Still, many psychologists continued to believe that when people said they experienced a series of colored afterimages after staring at a bright light, they probably did see colors in succession. That is, their words were not the whole story. While behaviorists could deal with many phenomena in terms of verbal responses, their preoccupation with observable behavior caused them to neglect interesting psychological problems (such as dreaming, meditation, and hypnosis) because the subjective aspects made those topics irrelevant to them.

By the 1960s, psychologists began to recognize that various aspects of consciousness are too pervasive and important to be neglected. This does not mean that psychology must again be defined exclusively as the study of consciousness; it means only that it cannot afford to neglect consciousness. Confining psychology to the study of observable behavior is too limiting. If we can theorize about the nature of consciousness, and that theory leads to testable predictions about behavior, then such theorizing is a valuable contribution to understanding how the mind works.

Consciousness

Many textbooks define **consciousness** as the individual's current awareness of external and internal stimuli – that is, of events in the environment and of his or her own bodily sensations, memories, and thoughts. We are conscious not only when we monitor our environment (internal and external) but also when we seek to control ourselves and our environment. In short, consciousness involves (1) monitoring ourselves and our environment so that we are aware of memories, thoughts and perceptual experiences, and (2) controlling ourselves and our environment so that we are able to initiate and end behaviors and thoughts (Kihlstrom, 2007).

Monitoring

Knowing what is going on around us is critical to survival and flourishing. Our sensory systems (i.e., hearing, seeing, feeling, tasting) lead to awareness of what is going on in our surroundings as well as within our own bodies. However, we could not possibly attend to all of the stimuli that impinge on our senses without experiencing information overload. Our consciousness, therefore, focuses on some stimuli and ignores others. Often what grabs our attention is change. While concentrating on this paragraph, for example, you are probably unaware of numerous background stimuli. But should there be a change – the lights dim, the air begins to smell smoky, or the noise of the air conditioner ceases – you would suddenly be aware of such stimuli. Our attention also gives priority to events or conditions that are important to survival. If we are hungry, it is difficult for us to concentrate on studying; if we experience a sudden pain, we push all other thoughts out of consciousness until we do something to make the pain go away.

Controlling

Consciousness not only monitors ongoing behavior but plays a role in directing and controlling that behavior as well by planning, initiating, and guiding our actions. Whether the plan is simple and readily completed (such as meeting a friend for lunch) or complex and long-range (such as preparing for a career), our actions must be guided and arranged to co-ordinate with events around us. In planning, events that have not yet occurred can be represented in consciousness as future possibilities. We may envision alternative 'scenarios,' make choices, and initiate the appropriate activities.

Not all actions are guided by conscious decisions, nor are the solutions to all problems carried out at a conscious level. One of the tenets of modern psychology is that mental events involve both conscious and non-conscious processes and that many decisions and actions are conducted entirely outside of consciousness. This certainly happens with motor behaviors that are well-learned. A batsman successfully hitting a ball does this in approximately 80 milliseconds, far too fast for him to be conscious of the sequence of behaviors required to strike the ball. When you are working on a complex problem, the solution may occur out of the blue without your being aware that you have been thinking about it. And once you have the solution, you may be unable to offer an introspective account of how you reached the solution. Decision-making and problem-solving often occur at a non-conscious level.

Preconscious memories

We cannot focus on everything that is going on around us at any given time, nor can we keep in mind our entire store of knowledge and memories of past events. At any given moment, we can focus attention on only a few stimuli. We ignore, select, and reject all the time, so that the contents of consciousness are continually changing. Nevertheless, objects or events that are not the focus of attention can still have some influence on consciousness. For example, you

may not be aware of hearing a clock strike the hour. But after a few strokes you become alert, and then you can go back and count the strokes that you did not know you heard. Another example of peripheral attention (or non-conscious monitoring) occurs when you are standing in a queue (Farthing, 1992). You are talking with a friend as you wait, ignoring other voices and general noise, when the sound of your own name in another conversation catches your attention. Clearly, you would not have detected your name in the other conversation if you had not, in some sense, been monitoring that conversation. You were not consciously aware of the other conversation until a special signal drew your attention to it. A considerable body of research indicates that we register and evaluate stimuli that we do not consciously perceive (Bargh, 2007). These stimuli are said to influence us subconsciously, or to operate at a non-conscious level of awareness.

Many memories and thoughts that are not part of your consciousness at this moment can be brought to consciousness when needed. At this moment, you may not be conscious of your vacation last summer, but the memories are accessible if you wish to retrieve them, and then they become part of your consciousness. The term **preconscious memories** is used to refer to memories that are accessible to consciousness. They include specific memories of personal events as well as the information accumulated over a lifetime, such as your knowledge of the meaning of words, the layout of the streets of a city, or the location of a particular country. They also include knowledge about learned skills like the procedures involved in driving a car or the sequence of steps in tying a shoelace. These procedures, once mastered, generally operate outside conscious awareness, but when our attention is called to them, we are capable of describing the steps involved.

The unconscious

One of the earliest theories of consciousness – and one that has been subject to considerable criticism over the years – is the psychoanalytic theory of Sigmund Freud. Freud and his followers believed that there is a portion of the mind, the **unconscious**, that contains some memories, impulses, and desires that are not accessible to consciousness. Freud believed that some emotionally painful memories and wishes are repressed – that is, diverted to the unconscious, where they may continue to influence our actions even though we are not aware of them. Repressed thoughts and impulses cannot enter our consciousness, but they can affect us in indirect or disguised ways – through dreams, irrational behaviors, mannerisms, and slips of the tongue. The term **Freudian slip** is commonly used to refer to unintentional remarks that are assumed to reveal hidden impulses. Saying, 'I'm sad you're better' when you intended to say, 'I'm glad you're better' is an example of such a slip.

Most psychologists accept the idea that there are memories and mental processes that are inaccessible to introspection and accordingly may be described as unconscious. However, many would argue that Freud placed undue emphasis on the emotional aspects of the unconscious and not enough on other aspects. They would include in the unconscious a large array of mental processes that we depend on constantly in our everyday lives but to which we have no conscious access (Bargh, 2007). For example, during perception, the viewer may be aware of two objects in the environment but have no awareness of the mental calculations that she performed almost instantaneously to determine that one is closer or larger than the other (see Chapter 5). Although we have conscious access to the outcome of these mental processes – we are aware of the size and distance of the object – we have no conscious access to their operations.

Even complex goals that we think we consciously choose, such as the goals to perform well on academic tasks or to be co-operative with others, can be influenced subtle cues from the environment. In one set of experiments, participants first completed a puzzle in which they searched for words embedded in a 10 × 10 matrix of letters (Bargh *et al.*, 2001). Participants were randomly assigned to a condition in which all the words in the matrix were neutral (carpet, river, shampoo) or to a condition in which half of the words pertained to high performance goals (win, compete, succeed). Then they completed three more word-search puzzles in which all the words they searched for were neutral (they were types of bugs, colors, or foods). The participants primed with high

achievement words in the first puzzle performed significantly better on the subsequent puzzles than did the participants who initially completed the neutral word puzzle.

In another study, participants first completed a 'psycholinguistic task' in which they unscrambled letters to make words. Half the participants were randomly assigned to receive scrambles of neutral words, and half were assigned to receive scrambles of words pertinent to co-operation (helpful, co-operative, fair). Then all participants played a game in which they played the role of a fisherman on a lake with a stock of 100 fish. They played several rounds of the game in which they always won 15 fish. They were told it was critical to keep the lake stocked with at least 70 fish, which could be accomplished by throwing some of their own fish back in the lake to replenish it, or relying on the other fishermen on the lake to do the replenishment. The participants who had been primed with co-operation goals in the initial 'psycholinguistic task' co-operated more by throwing more of their own fish back into the lake. It is important to note that in neither the achievement study nor the co-operation study were participants aware of the links between the initial tasks they had completed and their achievement or co-operation behavior. Instead, the simple cue of an achievement or co-operation goal in a seemingly unrelated task primed these goals and affected the participants' behaviors in the subsequent tests.

Automaticity and dissociation

An important function of consciousness is control of our actions. However, as we noted earlier, some activities are practiced so often that they become habitual or automatic. Learning to drive a car requires intense concentration at first. We have to concentrate on co-ordinating the different actions (shifting gears, releasing the clutch, accelerating, steering, and so forth) and can scarcely think about anything else. However, once the movements become automatic, we can carry on a conversation or admire the scenery without being conscious of driving – unless a potential danger quickly draws our attention to the operation of the car. This habituation of responses that initially required conscious attention is termed **automaticity**.

Skills like driving a car or riding a bike, once they are well learned, no longer require our attention. They become automatic and allow a relatively uncluttered consciousness to focus on other matters. Such automatic processes may have negative consequences on occasion – for example, when a driver cannot remember landmarks passed along the way. The more automatic an action becomes, the less it requires conscious control. Another example is the skilled pianist who carries on a conversation with a bystander while performing a familiar piece. The pianist is exercising control over two activities – playing and talking – but does not think about the music unless a wrong key is hit, alerting her attention to it and temporarily disrupting the conversation. You can undoubtedly think of other examples of well-learned, automatic activities that require little conscious control. One way of interpreting this is to say that the control is still there (we can focus on automatic processes if we want to) but has been dissociated from consciousness. The French psychiatrist Pierre Janet (1889) originated the concept of **dissociation**, in which under certain conditions some thoughts and actions become split off, or dissociated, from the rest of consciousness and function outside of awareness.

When faced with a stressful situation, we may temporarily put it out of our minds in order to function effectively; when bored, we may lapse into reverie or daydreams. These are mild examples of dissociation that involve dissociating one part of consciousness from another. More extreme examples of dissociation are demonstrated by cases of **dissociative identity disorder**, or multiple personality, a rare psychological disorder.

INTERIM SUMMARY

➜ A person's perceptions, thoughts, and feelings at any given moment constitute that person's consciousness.

➜ An altered state of consciousness is said to exist when mental functioning seems changed or out of the ordinary to the person experiencing the state. Some altered states of consciousness, such as sleep and dreams, are experienced by everyone; others result from special circumstances, such as meditation, hypnosis, or drug use.

➜ The functions of consciousness are (1) monitoring ourselves and our environment so that we are aware of what is happening within our bodies and in our surroundings, and (2) controlling our actions so that they are co-ordinated with events in the outside world. Not all events that influence consciousness are at the center of our awareness at a given moment. Memories of personal events and accumulated knowledge, which are accessible but are not currently part of a person's consciousness, are called preconscious memories. Events that affect behavior, even though we are not aware of perceiving them, influence us subconsciously.

➜ According to psychoanalytic theory, some emotionally painful memories and impulses are not available to consciousness because they have been repressed – that is, diverted to the unconscious. Unconscious thoughts and impulses influence our behavior even though they reach consciousness only in indirect ways – through dreams, irrational behavior, and slips of the tongue.

➜ The notion of automaticity refers to the habituation of responses that initially required conscious attention, such as driving a car.

CRITICAL THINKING QUESTIONS

1 Many amateur pianists memorize a piece for a recital by playing it over and over again until they can play it automatically, without paying attention to it. Unfortunately, they still often get stuck or forget parts of it during the actual recital. In contrast, some professional pianists deliberately memorize the music away from the piano, so that their 'mind, not just their fingers' knows the piece. What does this imply about automatic processes and the controlling function of consciousness?

2 Freud argued that certain desires or thoughts remain in the unconscious because making them conscious arouses anxiety in the individual. What might be some other reasons that certain desires or thoughts might remain out of conscious awareness to us?

SLEEP AND DREAMS

We begin our discussion of consciousness with a state that seems to be its opposite: sleep. But, although sleep might seem to have little in common with wakefulness, there are similarities between the two states. The phenomenon of dreaming indicates that we think while we sleep, although the type of thinking we do in dreams differs in various ways from the type we do while awake. We form memories while sleeping, as we know from the fact that we can remember dreams. Sleep is not entirely quiescent: some people walk in their sleep. People who are asleep are not entirely insensitive to their environment: parents are awakened by their baby's cry. Nor is sleep entirely planless: some people can decide to wake at a given time and do so. In this section we explore several facets of sleep and dreaming.

Stages of sleep

Some people are readily roused from sleep; others are hard to wake. Research begun in the 1930s (Loomis, Harvey, & Hobart, 1937) has produced sensitive techniques for measuring the depth of sleep and determining when dreams are occurring. This research uses devices that measure electrical changes on the scalp associated with spontaneous brain activity during sleep, as well as eye movements that occur during dreaming. The graphic recording of the electrical changes, or brain waves, is called an *electroencephalogram,* or EEG (see Figures 6.1 and 6.2). The EEG measures the rapidly fluctuating electrical potential of thousands of neurons lying on the surface of the cortex under the electrode. It is a rather crude measure of cortical activity, but it has proved very useful in sleep research.

Analysis of the patterns of brain waves suggests that there are five stages of sleep: four differing depths of sleep and a fifth stage, known as rapid eye movement (or REM) sleep. When a person closes his or her eyes and relaxes, the brain waves characteristically show a regular pattern of 8 to 12 hertz (cycles per second); these are known as alpha waves. As the individual drifts into Stage 1 sleep, the brain waves become less regular and are reduced in amplitude. Stage 2 is characterized by the appearance of spindles – short runs of rhythmical responses of 12 to 16 hertz – and an occasional sharp rise and fall in the amplitude of the whole EEG (referred to as a K-complex). The still deeper Stages 3 and 4 are characterized by slow waves (1 to 2 hertz), which are known as delta waves. Generally, it is hard to wake the sleeper during Stages 3 and 4, although

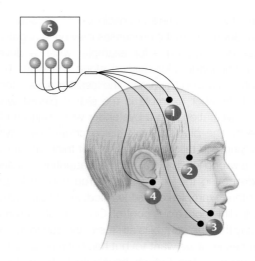

1 Electrodes on the scalp record the patterns of brain waves.

2 Electrodes near the person's eyes record eye movement.

3 Electrodes on the chin record tension and electrical activity in the muscles.

4 A neutral electrode on the ear completes the circuit through amplifiers.

5 Amplifiers produce graphical records of the various patterns.

FIGURE 6.1 Arrangement of Electrodes for Recording the Electrophysiology of Sleep. *This diagram shows the way electrodes are attached to the person's head and face in a typical sleep experiment.*

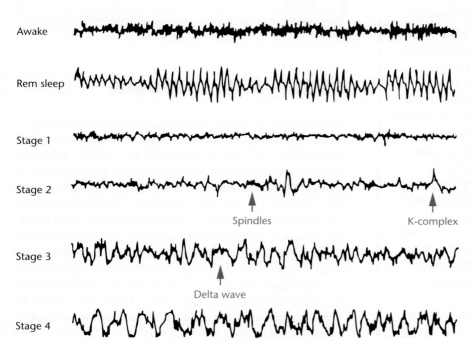

FIGURE 6.2 Electrophysiological Activity During Sleep. *This figure represents EEG recordings during wakefulness and during the various stages of sleep. The Awake Stage (relaxed with eyes closed) is characterized by alpha waves (8–12 hertz). Stage 1 is basically a transition from wakefulness to the deeper stages of sleep. Stage 2 is defined by the presence of sleep spindles (brief bursts of 12–16 hertz waves) and K-complexes (a sharp rise and fall in the brainwave pattern). Stages 3 and 4 are marked by the presence of delta waves (1–2 hertz), and the only difference between these two stages is the amount of delta waves found. Stage 3 is scored when 20% to 50% of the record contains delta waves, and Stage 4 when the percentage of delta waves is 50% or more.*

he or she can be aroused by something personal, such as a familiar name or a child crying. A more impersonal disturbance, such as a loud sound, may be ignored.

Succession of sleep stages

After an adult has been asleep for an hour or so, another change occurs. The EEG becomes very active (even more so than when the person is awake), but the person does not wake up. The electrodes placed near the person's eyes detect rapid eye movements so pronounced that one can even watch the sleeper's eyes move around beneath the closed eyelids. This highly active stage is known as **REM sleep**; the other four sleep stages are known as **non-REM (or NREM) sleep**.

These various stages of sleep alternate throughout the night. Sleep begins with the NREM stages and has several sleep cycles, each containing some REM and some NREM sleep. Figure 6.3 illustrates a typical night's sleep for a young adult. As you can see, the person goes from wakefulness into a deep sleep (Stage 4) very rapidly. After about 70 minutes, Stage 3 recurs briefly, immediately followed by the first REM period of the night. Notice that the deeper stages (3 and 4) occurred during the first part of the night, whereas most REM sleep occurred in the last part. This is the typical pattern: the deeper stages tend to disappear in the second half of the night as REM becomes more prominent. There are usually four or five distinct REM periods over the course of an 8-hour night, with an occasional brief awakening as morning arrives.

The pattern of the sleep cycles varies with age. Newborn infants, for instance, spend about half their sleeping time in REM sleep. This proportion drops to 20 per cent to 25 per cent of total sleep time by age five and remains fairly constant until old age, when it drops to 18 per cent or less. Older people tend to experience less Stage 3 and 4 sleep (sometimes these stages disappear) and more frequent and longer night-time awakenings. A natural kind of insomnia seems to set in as people grow older (Liu & Ancoli-Israel, 2006).

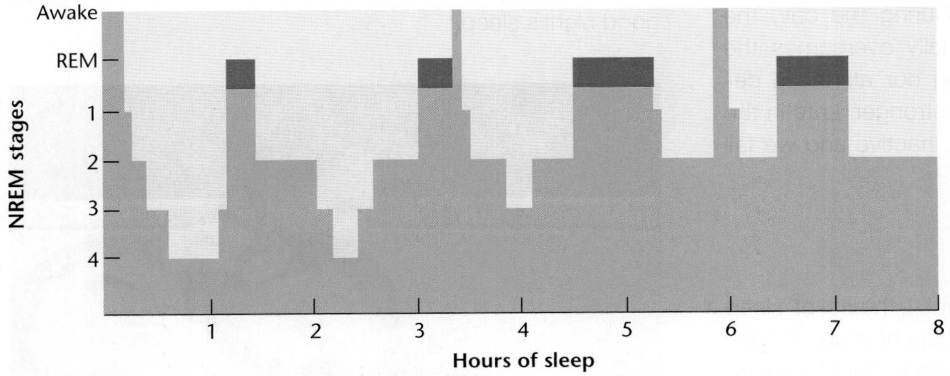

REM and NREM compared

During NREM sleep, eye movements are virtually absent, heart and breathing rates decrease markedly, the muscles are relaxed, and the brain's metabolic rate decreases 25 to 30 per cent compared with wakefulness. In contrast, during REM sleep, very rapid eye movements occur in bursts lasting 10 to 20 seconds, the heart rate increases, and the brain's metabolic rate increases somewhat compared with wakefulness. Further, during REM sleep we are almost completely paralyzed – only the heart, diaphragm, eye muscles, and smooth muscles (such as the muscles of the intestines and blood vessels) are spared. To summarize, NREM sleep is characterized by a very relaxed body, whereas REM sleep is characterized by a brain that appears to be wide awake in a virtually paralyzed body.

Physiological evidence indicates that in REM sleep the brain is largely isolated from its sensory and motor channels. Stimuli from other parts of the body are blocked from entering the brain, and there are no motor outputs. Nevertheless, the brain is still very active, spontaneously driven by the discharge of giant neurons that originate in the brain stem. These neurons extend into parts of the brain that control eye movements and motor activities. During REM sleep, the brain registers the fact that the neurons normally involved in walking and seeing are activated, even though the body itself is doing neither of these things (Stoerig, 2007). In addition, during REM sleep, the areas of the brain involved in the processing of emotional memories show significant increases in activation (Maquet, 2000).

About 80 per cent of sleepers who are awakened during REM sleep report having a dream, but when awakened during NREM sleep they report a dream only about 50 per cent of the time (Stoerig, 2007). The dreams reported when a person is roused from REM sleep tend to be visually vivid with emotional and illogical features, and the visual cortex becomes very active, reflecting the visual nature of dreams. They represent the type of experience we typically associate with the word *dream*. The longer the period of REM sleep before arousal, the longer and more elaborate the reported dream. In contrast, NREM dreams are neither as visual nor as emotionally charged as REM dreams, and they are more

FIGURE 6.3 **The Succession of Sleep Stages.** *This graph provides an example of the sequence and duration of sleep stages during a typical night. The individual went successively through Stages 1 to 4 during the first hour of sleep. He then moved back through Stage 3 to REM sleep. Thereafter, he cycled between NREM and REM periods, with two brief awakenings at about 3.5 and 6 hours of sleep.*

directly related to what is happening in the person's waking life. As indicated by the types of dreams we report and the frequency of reporting a dream, mental activity is different in REM and NREM periods.

Sleep theory

Why are we awake at certain times and asleep at others? Two leading sleep researchers, Dale Edgar and William Dement (1992), have proposed an **opponent-process model of sleep and wakefulness**. According to this model, the brain possesses two opponent processes that govern the tendency to fall asleep or remain awake. They are the homeostatic sleep drive and the clock-dependent alerting process.

The **homeostatic sleep drive** is a physiological process that strives to obtain the amount of sleep required for a stable level of daytime alertness. It is active throughout the night, but it also operates during the daytime. Throughout the day, the need to sleep is continuously building. If we have slept too little the previous night, the tendency to fall asleep during the day will be significant.

The **clock-dependent alerting process** is the process in the brain that arouses us at a particular time each day. It is controlled by the so-called biological clock, which consists of two tiny neural structures located in the center of the brain. This 'clock' controls a series of psychological and physiological changes, including rhythms of alertness, that are termed **circadian rhythms** because they occur approximately every 24 hours (the term comes from the Latin words *circa*, meaning 'around,' and *dies*, 'day'). The biological clock is affected by exposure to light: daylight signals it to stop the secretion of **melatonin**, a hormone that induces sleep.

The two opponent processes – homeostatic sleep drive and the clock-dependent alerting process – interact to produce our daily cycle of sleep and wakefulness. Whether we are asleep or awake at any given time depends on the relative strength of the two processes. During the day, the clock-dependent alerting process usually overcomes the drive for sleep, but during the evening our alertness decreases as the urge to sleep becomes stronger. Late in the evening, the biological clock becomes inactive and we fall asleep.

Sleep-wake disorders

Young adults need an average of about 9 hours of sleep each day, yet most get only about 7.5 hours or fewer per day (National Sleep Foundation, 2009). Similarly, most middle-aged adults need 7 or 8 hours of sleep each day but most get fewer than 7 hours. The effects of sleep deprivation are cumulative: a person builds up an increasing 'sleep debt' for every 24-hour period in which he or she does not get adequate sleep (Wolfson, 2001). Sleepiness during the daytime is not the only consequence of sleep deprivation. Consider the following statistics:

→ People who sleep fewer than 6 hours per night have a 70 per cent higher mortality rate than those who sleep at least 7 or 8 hours per night (Ikehara *et al.,* 2009; Kryger *et al.,* 1994).

→ Sleeping only 5 hours per night for two nights in a row significantly reduces performance on math problems and creative thinking tasks; so skipping sleep to study significantly impairs your ability to do well in exams (Wolfson, 2010). On the other hand, sleep plays a causal role in memory formation so studying before you go to bed – while going to bed early enough to get a sufficient amount of sleep – can improve retention of information

→ Over half of automobile drivers admit to having driven when drowsy at least once in the past year, and 28 per cent say they have fallen asleep at the wheel. Almost 20 per cent of serious automobile injuries are due to driver sleepiness (National Sleep Foundation, 2009).

→ The nuclear accidents at Chernobyl and Three Mile Island occurred in the early morning hours, when night-shift workers were fatigued and missed, or were confused by, warning signals on their control panels (Mitler & Miller, 1995).

Sleep researchers have demonstrated that alertness significantly increases when people who normally get 8 hours of sleep get an additional 2 hours of sleep. Although most people can operate satisfactorily on 8 hours of sleep, they are not at their best. Moreover, they lack a safety margin to make up for the times when they get less than that amount of sleep. The loss of as little as an hour of sleep increases the likelihood of inattentiveness, mistakes, illness, and accidents (Wolfson & Armitage, 2008). Even if you cannot arrange to get 10 hours of sleep a night, you can avoid excessive sleep debt by getting 8 or 9 hours of restful sleep. Table 6.1 suggests techniques that can be used to ensure a good night's sleep.

Sleep deprivation is a common cause of underperformance among students.

TABLE 6.1 ADVICE FOR A GOOD NIGHT'S SLEEP

There is considerable agreement among researchers and clinicians on how to avoid sleep problems. These recommendations are summarized in the table; some are based on actual research, and others are simply the best judgments of experts in the field.

Regular sleep schedule Establish a regular schedule of going to bed and getting up. Set your alarm for a specific time every morning and get up at that time no matter how little you may have slept. Be consistent about naps. Take a nap every afternoon or not at all; when you take a nap only occasionally, you probably will not sleep well that night. Waking up late on weekends can also disrupt your sleep cycle.

Alcohol and caffeine Having a stiff drink of alcohol before going to bed may put you to sleep, but it disturbs the sleep cycle and can cause you to wake up early the next day. In addition, stay away from caffeinated drinks like coffee or cola for several hours before bedtime. Caffeine works as a stimulant even on those people who claim they are not affected by it, and the body needs 4 to 5 hours to halve the amount of caffeine in the bloodstream at any one time. If you must drink something before bedtime, try milk; there is evidence to support the folklore that a glass of warm milk at bedtime induces sleep.

Eating before bedtime Don't eat heavily before going to bed, since your digestive system will have to do several hours of work. If you must eat something before bedtime, have a light snack.

Exercise Regular exercise will help you sleep better, but don't engage in a strenuous workout just before going to bed.

Sleeping pills Be careful about using sleeping pills. All of the various kinds tend to disrupt the sleep cycle, and long-term use inevitably leads to insomnia. Even on nights before exams, avoid using a sleeping pill. One bad night of sleep tends not to affect performance the next day, but hangover from a sleeping pill may.

Relax Avoid stressful thoughts before bedtime and engage in soothing activities that help you relax. Try to follow the same routine every night before going to bed; it might involve taking a warm bath or listening to soft music for a few minutes. Find a room temperature at which you are comfortable and maintain it throughout the night.

When all fails If you are in bed and have trouble falling asleep, don't get up. Stay in bed and try to relax. But if that fails and you become tense, then get up for a brief time and do something restful that reduces anxiety. Doing push-ups or some other form of exercise to wear yourself out is not a good idea.

Some people encounter significant difficulties with sleep even when they try to get adequate sleep. When sleep problems lead to chronic impairment in daily functioning, a person may be diagnosed with a **sleep disorder**. We consider some common sleep disorders in this section.

Insomnia

The term **insomnia** refers to chronic difficulty initiating or maintaining sleep, or sleep that does not restore energy and alertness. Whether or not a person has insomnia is a largely subjective matter. Many people who complain of insomnia are found to have perfectly normal sleep when they are studied in a sleep laboratory, whereas others who do not complain of insomnia have detectable sleep disturbances (Carney, Berry, & Geyer, 2004). This does not mean that insomnia is not a real condition, only that subjective reports of sleeplessness do not always correlate well with more objective measures.

Up to 50 per cent of adults report they have had insomnia at some time in their lives, often during times of stress (Wolfson, 2001). Chronic insomnia affects 10 to 15 per cent of adults, and is more frequent in women than men, and in older adults than younger adults (Wolfson, 2001; Zhang & Wing, 2006).

Narcolepsy and apnea

Two relatively rare but severe sleep disorders are narcolepsy and apnea. DSM-5 has been updated regarding Sleep-Wake Disorders. It now distinguishes narcolepsy – now known to be associated with hypocretin deficiency – from other forms of hypersomnolence (hypersomnolence disorder). A person with **narcolepsy** has recurring, irresistible attacks of drowsiness and may fall asleep at any time – while writing a letter, driving a car, or carrying on a conversation. If a student falls asleep while a professor is lecturing, that may be perfectly normal, but a professor who falls asleep while lecturing may be suffering from narcolepsy. Such episodes can occur several times a day in severe cases and last from a few seconds to 30 minutes. Narcoleptics have difficulty keeping jobs and driving because of their daytime sleepiness. Narcolepsy most often starts in adolescence and is quite rare.

Essentially, narcolepsy is the intrusion of REM episodes into daytime hours. During attacks, victims go quickly into a REM state, so rapidly, in fact, that they may lose muscle control and collapse before they can lie down. Moreover, many report experiencing hallucinations during an attack as reality is replaced by vivid REM dreams. Narcolepsy runs in families, and there is evidence that a specific gene or combination

In an experiment by noted sleep researcher William Dement, a narcoleptic dog suddenly falls asleep. About 1 in 1000 humans suffers from this debilitating sleep disorder.

of genes makes an individual susceptible to the disorder (Carney *et al.*, 2004).

In **apnea** the individual stops breathing whilst asleep, and the DSM-5 has now identified different types, including obstructive sleep apnea hypopnea and central sleep apnea. There are two reasons for apnea attacks. One reason is that the brain fails to send a 'breathe' signal to the diaphragm and other breathing muscles, thus causing breathing to stop. The other reason is that muscles at the top of the throat become too relaxed, allowing the windpipe to partially close and thereby forcing the breathing muscles to pull harder on incoming air, which causes the airway to completely collapse. During an apnea episode, the oxygen level of the blood drops dramatically, leading to the secretion of emergency hormones. This reaction causes the sleeper to awaken in order to begin breathing again.

Most people have a few apnea episodes each night, but people with severe sleep problems may have several hundred episodes per night. With each one, they wake up to resume breathing, but these arousals are so brief that the person generally is unaware of them. The result is that people who suffer from apnea can spend 12 or more hours in bed each night and still be so sleepy the next day that they cannot function and may even fall asleep in the middle of a conversation (Vandeputte & de Weerd, 2003). Sleep apnea is common among older men. Sleeping pills, which make arousal more difficult, lengthen periods of apnea (during which the brain is deprived of oxygen) and may prove fatal.

Dreams

Dreaming is an altered state of consciousness in which picture stories are constructed based on memories and current concerns, emotions, fantasies, and images. Although many people do not recall their dreams in the morning, evidence from studies of REM sleep suggests that nonrecallers often do as much dreaming as recallers. What happens on awakening seems to be a crucial factor in dream recall. Unless a distraction-free waking period occurs shortly after dreaming, the memory of the dream is not consolidated – that is, the dream cannot be stored in memory (Cohen & Wolfe, 1973).

Other researchers argue that a person's motivation to recall dreams and interest in dreams is a good predictor of ability to recall dreams (see Schredl, 2007). If upon awakening we make an effort to remember what we were dreaming at the time, some of the dream content will be recalled at a later time. Otherwise, the dream will fade quickly. We may know that we have had a dream but will be unable to remember its content.

Some dreams seem almost instantaneous. The alarm clock rings, and we awaken to complex memories of a fire breaking out and fire engines arriving with their sirens blasting. Because the alarm is still ringing, we assume that the sound must have produced the dream. Research suggests, however, that a ringing alarm clock or other sound merely reinstates a complete scene from earlier memories or dreams. This experience has its parallel during wakefulness, when a single cue may tap a rich memory.

Some people have **lucid dreams**, in which events seem so normal (lacking the bizarre and illogical character of most dreams) that the dreamers feel as if they are awake and conscious. Lucid dreamers report doing various 'experiments' within their dreams to determine whether they are awake or dreaming. They also report an occasional 'false awakening' within a dream. For example, one lucid dreamer discovered that he was dreaming and decided to call a taxicab as an indication of his control over events. When he reached into his pocket to see if he had some change to pay the driver, he thought that he woke up. He then found the coins scattered about the bed. At this point he really awoke and found himself lying in a different position, and, of course, without any coins (Brown, 1936). Note, however, that relatively few people achieve lucidity with any regularity (LaBerge, 2007).

Dreams with disturbing content are usually referred to as *nightmares*. Occasional nightmares are fairly common, with about 85 per cent of people reporting they had a nightmare in the last year (Levin & Nielsen, 2007). Between 8 and 25 per cent of people have nightmares monthly, a figure that is very similar across cultures. Weekly nightmares are reported by 2 to 6 per cent of people across cultures, and can constitute a mental health problem (Levin & Nielsen, 2007).

Theories of dreaming

One of the earliest theories of the function of dreams was suggested by Sigmund Freud, who proposed that dreams provide a 'royal road to a knowledge of the unconscious activities of the mind.' He believed that dreams are a disguised attempt at wish fulfillment. By this he meant that the dream touches on wishes, needs, or ideas that the individual finds unacceptable and have been repressed to the unconscious (for example, sexual longings for the parent of the opposite sex). These wishes and ideas are the latent content of the dream. Freud used the metaphor of a censor to explain the conversion of latent content into manifest content (the characters and events that make up the actual narrative of the dream). In effect, Freud said, the censor protects the sleeper, enabling him or her to express repressed impulses symbolically while avoiding the guilt or anxiety that would occur if they were to appear consciously in undisguised form.

According to Freud, the transformation of latent content into manifest content is done by 'dream work,' whose function is to code and disguise material in the unconscious in such a way that it can reach consciousness. However, sometimes dream work fails, and the resulting anxiety awakens the dreamer. The dream essentially expresses the fulfillment of wishes or needs that are too painful or guilt-inducing to be acknowledged consciously (Freud, 1933).

Subsequent research challenged several aspects of Freud's theory. After surveying dozens of studies of dreaming, Fisher and Greenberg (1977, 1996) concluded there is good evidence that the content of dreams has psychological meaning, but there is none that supports Freud's distinction between manifest and latent content. Although most psychologists would agree with Freud's general conclusion that dreams focus on emotional concerns, they question the concept of 'dream work' and the idea that dreams represent wish fulfillment.

Since Freud's time, a variety of theories have been advanced to explain the role of sleep and dreams. Evans (1984), for example, views sleep, particularly REM sleep, as a period when the brain disengages from the external world and uses this 'offline' time to sift through the information that was input during the day and to incorporate it into memory (see also Crick & Mitchinson, 1983). We are not consciously aware of the processing that occurs during REM sleep. During dreaming, however, the brain comes back online for a brief time, and the conscious mind observes a small sample of the modification and reorganization of information that is taking place. The brain attempts to interpret this information the same way it would interpret stimuli coming from the outside world, giving rise to the kinds of pseudo-events that characterize dreams. According to Evans, dreams are nothing more than a small subset of the vast amount of information that is being scanned and sorted during REM sleep, a momentary glimpse by the conscious mind that we remember if we awaken.

Analysis of dreams shows that their emotional content varies widely and includes nightmares and terrors, social dreams with significant others that arouse happiness, dreams of loss of a loved one that engender intense sadness, and bizarre dreams that arouse confusion and strangeness (Businck & Kuiken, 1996; Kuiken & Sikora, 1993). Dream content may reflect personal conflicts, but dreams do not necessarily function to resolve those conflicts (Levin & Nielsen, 2007). Dreams often contain elements related to events of the previous day, but not full memories of episodes in the day (Nielsen & Stenstrom, 2005). Rather, fragments of events during the day may be included, such as a stranger in the dream who

We all like to have good dreams, but it is generally very difficult to control the content of our dreams.

looks like the dreamer's mother. In addition, there are more negative than positive emotions in dreams. Overall, dreams cannot be viewed as simple extensions of the previous day's activities.

INTERIM SUMMARY

→ Patterns of brain waves show four stages (depths) of sleep, plus a fifth stage characterized by rapid eye movements (REMs). These stages alternate throughout the night. Dreams occur more often during REM sleep than during the other four stages (NREM sleep).

→ The opponent-process model of sleep proposes that two opposing processes – the homeostatic sleep drive and the clock-dependent alerting process – interact to determine our tendency to fall asleep or remain awake. Whether we are asleep or awake at any given time depends on the relative forces exerted by the two processes.

→ There are a variety of sleep disorders, including sleep deprivation, insomnia, narcolepsy, and apnea.

→ Freud attributed psychological causes to dreams, distinguished between their manifest and latent content, and suggested that dreams are wishes in disguise.

→ Other theories see dreaming as a reflection of the information processing that the brain is doing while asleep.

CRITICAL THINKING QUESTIONS

1 How might dream theories explain instances when people appear to have dreamed of an event they were not expecting before it actually happens?

2 What personality characteristics do you think might be related to the tendency to remember your dreams?

MEDITATION

Meditation refers to achieving an altered state of consciousness by performing certain rituals and exercises, such as controlling and regulating breathing, sharply restricting one's field of attention, eliminating external stimuli, assuming yogic body positions, and forming mental images of an event or symbol. The result is a pleasant, mildly altered subjective state in which the individual feels mentally and physically relaxed. After extensive practice, some individuals may have mystical experiences in which they lose self-awareness

The rituals of meditation include regulating breathing, restricting one's field of attention, eliminating external stimuli, and forming mental images of an event or symbol. Traditional forms of meditation follow the practices of yoga.

and gain a sense of being involved in a wider consciousness, however defined. The belief that such meditative techniques may cause a change in consciousness goes back to ancient times and is represented in every major world religion. Buddhists, Hindus, Sufi Muslims, Jews, and Christians all have literature describing rituals that induce meditative states.

Traditional forms of meditation follow the practices of yoga, a system of thought based on the Hindu religion, or Zen, which is derived from Chinese and Japanese Buddhism. Two common meditation techniques are opening-up meditation, in which the person clears his or her mind in order to receive new experiences, and concentrative meditation, in which the benefits are obtained by actively attending to some object, word, or idea. The following is a typical description of opening-up meditation:

This approach begins with the resolve to do nothing, to think nothing, to make no effort of

CUTTING EDGE RESEARCH PICTURES OF CONSCIOUSNESS?

Susan Nolen-Hoeksema, Yale University

As neuroimaging techniques have become more sophisticated, researchers have been intrigued at the possibility that these techniques could shed light on the nature of consciousness, and what brain structures control various aspects of consciousness. Thus, functional magnetic resonance imagery (fMRI), electroencephalograms (EEG), and positron emission tomography (PET) are all being used to image the brain of people in various forms of consciousness, including people sleeping, people in a coma, and people who have recently learned how to meditate.

For example, in one study, 16 brain injury patients in a completely vegetative state were given the instructions to imagine squeezing their right hand into a fist then relaxing it, or to wiggle all the toes on both feet then relax them (Cruse *et al.,* 2011). In three of 16 patients, EEG readings indicated activity in motor areas of the brain consistent with the behavior the patients were instructed to imagine. This was despite the fact that none of these three patients showed any behavioral responses to the imagery task. Similarly, fMRI studies find that about 17 per cent of completely vegetative patients show brain activity consistent with instructions to engage in some motor behavior (Monti *et al.,* 2010; Owen *et al.,* 2006). Such findings raise the possibility that neuroimaging techniques may be used to more accurately diagnose whether brain injured individuals are truly lacking any consciousness or not.

Other researchers have been interested in the differences in brain structure and functioning between everyday people and those who are expert at achieving altered state of consciousness. Specifically, these researchers have been using neuroimaging techniques to understand the effects of long-time practice of meditation on brain functioning (see Lutz *et al.,* 2007). The participants in these studies have been experienced Buddhist meditators (with over 10 000 hours of cumulative meditation practice) and newly trained novice meditators. In one study (Brefczynski *et al.,* 2004), participants performed a focused attention meditation in which the mind is focused singularly and unwaveringly on an individual object (a white dot on the screen). Magnetic resonance imagery showed that both the experts and the novices showed increased activation in areas of the brain associated with attention during the meditation phase of the study, as compared to a rest phase. However, the experts showed even greater activity in these attention areas than the experts while meditating. In contrast, the novices showed greater activity than the experts in areas of the brain associated with detecting errors, possibly because they were having more difficulty maintaining their concentration and thus diverting their attention away from the white dot more often.

In another study, these researchers had Buddhist practitioners and novices engage in a form of meditation in which they were to generate an unconditional feeling of lovingkindness and compassion. Neuroimaging showed that while in this state, both the experts and novices showed increased activity in areas of the brain associated with positive emotions and the planning of movements, but the experts showed greater activity in these areas than the novices. The researchers interpreted these data as suggesting that a conscious state of lovingkindness toward others involves both emotional processing and an inclination to act on these feelings.

These studies raise intriguing questions about how practicing certain states of consciousness, as in mediation, can actually change the functioning of the brain. They also raise hope that training certain mental activities may help to generate new or altered activity in the brain, which could prove therapeutic for individuals with brain damage or deficiencies. Do these studies tell us anything, however, about the nature of consciousness? One impediment to understanding consciousness is the fact that we still must rely on individuals' self-report to determine what is, or is not, going through their mind. Thus, although sophisticated neuroimaging techniques can give us pictures of the activity associated with consciousness, they can't give us a direct lens on consciousness itself.

one's own, to relax completely and let go of one's mind and body... stepping out of the stream of ever-changing ideas and feelings which your mind is in, watch the onrush of the stream. Refuse to be submerged in the current. Changing the metaphor... watch your ideas, feelings, and wishes fly across the firmament like a flock of birds. Let them fly freely. Just keep a watch. Don't let the birds carry you off into the clouds.

(Chauduri, 1965, pp. 30–31)

Here is a corresponding statement for concentrative meditation:

The purpose of these sessions is to learn about concentration. Your aim is to concentrate on the blue vase. By concentration I do not mean analyzing the different parts of the vase, but rather, trying to see the vase as it exists in itself, without any connections to other things. Exclude all other thoughts or feelings or sounds or body sensations.

(Deikman, 1963, p. 330)

After a few sessions of concentrative meditation, people typically report a number of effects: an altered, more intense perception of the vase; some time shortening, particularly in retrospect; conflicting perceptions, as if the vase fills the visual field and does not fill it; decreasing effectiveness of external stimuli (less distraction and eventually less conscious registration); and an impression of the meditative state as pleasant and rewarding.

In one experimental study of individuals who underwent an 8-week training in meditation practices, experimenters found that trainees (compared to a wait-list control group) reported reductions in anxiety and other negative affect, increases in activity in areas of the brain associated with positive affect, and enhanced immune system functioning (Davidson *et al.,* 2003). Meditation training is increasingly being incorporated into interventions for people with stress-related disorders (see Chapter 14). Some researchers argue that the benefits of meditation come largely from relaxation of the body. Other researchers suggest that the psycho-logical benefits of meditation may be due to learning to put aside repetitive and troubling thoughts (see Holzel *et al.,* 2011).

INTERIM SUMMARY

➡ Meditation represents an effort to alter consciousness by following planned rituals or exercises such as those of yoga or Zen.

➡ The result is a somewhat mystical state in which the individual is extremely relaxed and feels divorced from the outside world.

CRITICAL THINKING QUESTIONS

1 People who make a daily practice of meditating often say they are calmer and better able to respond to stress throughout the day as a result of meditating. If this is true, what might account for these effects?

2 There is some evidence that meditation can improve physical health. What might be the mechanisms for these effects, if true?

HYPNOSIS

Of all the altered states of consciousness discussed in this chapter, none has raised more questions than hypnosis. Once associated with the occult, hypnosis has become the subject of scientific investigation (see Kihlstrom, 2007).

As in all fields of psychological investigation, uncertainties remain, but by now many facts have been established. In this section we explore what is known about this controversial phenomenon.

Induction of hypnosis

In hypnosis, a willing and co-operative individual (the only kind that can be hypnotized under most circumstances) relinquishes some control over his or her behavior to the hypnotist and accepts some distortion of reality. The hypnotist uses a variety of methods to induce this condition. For example, the person may be asked to concentrate on a small target (such as a thumbtack on the wall) while gradually becoming relaxed. The hypnotist may suggest that the person is becoming sleepy because, like sleep, hypnosis is a relaxed state in which a person is out of touch with ordinary environmental demands. But sleep is only a metaphor. The person is told that he or she will not really go to sleep but will continue to listen to the hypnotist. The following changes are characteristic of the hypnotized state:

➔ Planfulness ceases. A deeply hypnotized individual does not like to initiate activity and would rather wait for the hypnotist to suggest something to do.

➔ Attention becomes more selective than usual. A person who is told to listen only to the hypnotist's voice will ignore any other voices in the room.

➔ Enriched fantasy is readily evoked. People may find themselves enjoying experiences at places that are distant in time and space.

➔ Reality testing is reduced and reality distortion accepted. A person may uncritically accept hallucinated experiences (for example, conversing with an imagined person who is believed to be sitting in a nearby chair) and will not check to determine whether that person is real.

➔ Suggestibility is increased. An individual must accept suggestions in order to be hypnotized at all, but whether suggestibility is increased under hypnosis is a matter of some dispute. Careful studies have found some increase in suggestibility following hypnotic induction, though less than is commonly supposed (Wegner, 2002).

➔ Posthypnotic amnesia is often present. When instructed to do so, an individual who is highly responsive to hypnotism will forget all or most of what took place during the hypnotic session. When a prearranged release signal is given, the memories are restored.

Not all individuals are equally responsive to hypnosis, as Figure 6.4 indicates. Roughly 5 to 10 per cent of the popu-lation cannot be hypnotized even by a skilled hypnotist, and

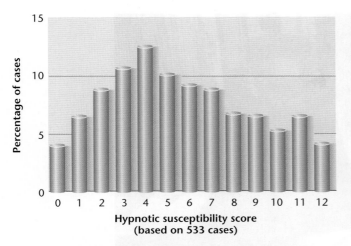

FIGURE 6.4 Individual Differencse in Hypnotizabilty.
Participants were hypnotized, then given 12 different hypnotic suggestions. Their response to each suggestion was scored as present or absent, and the present responses were totaled for each participant to yield a score ranging from 0 (no responses) to 12 (responded to all). Most individuals fell in the middle ranges.

the remainder show varying degrees of susceptibility. However, a person who is hypnotized on one occasion probably will be equally susceptible on another occasion (Kihlstrom, 2007).

Hypnotic suggestions

Suggestions given to a hypnotized individual can result in a variety of behaviors and experiences. The person's motor control may be affected, new memories may be lost or old ones re-experienced, and current perceptions may be radically altered.

Control of movement

Many hypnotized individuals respond to direct suggestion with involuntary movement. For example, if a person stands with arms outstretched and hands facing each other and the hypnotist suggests that the person's hands are attracted to each other, the hands will soon begin to move together, and the person will feel propelled by some external force. Direct suggestion can also inhibit movement. If a suggestible individual is told that an arm is stiff (like a bar of iron or an arm in a splint) and then is asked to bend the arm, it will not bend, or more effort than usual will be needed to make it bend.

A **posthypnotic response** occurs when people who have been roused from hypnosis respond with movement to a prearranged signal by the hypnotist. Even if the suggestion has been forgotten, they will feel a compulsion to carry out the behavior. They may try to justify such behavior as rational, even though the urge to perform it is impulsive. For example,

a young man searching for a rational explanation of why he opened a window when the hypnotist took off her glasses (the prearranged signal) remarked that the room felt a little stuffy.

Posthypnotic amnesia

At the suggestion of the hypnotist, events occurring during hypnosis may be 'forgotten' until a signal from the hypnotist enables the individual to recall them. This is called **posthypnotic amnesia**. People differ widely in their susceptibility to posthypnotic amnesia, as Figure 6.5 shows. The items to be recalled in this study were ten actions that the participants performed while hypnotized. A few participants forgot none or only one or two items; most participants forgot four or five items. However, a sizable number of participants forgot all ten items. Many studies of posthypnotic amnesia have shown similar results. The group of participants with the higher recall is larger and presumably represents the average hypnotic responders; the participants who forgot all ten items have been described as 'hypnotic virtuosos.'

Differences in recall between the two groups do not appear to be related to differences in memory capacity: once the amnesia is canceled at a prearranged signal from the hypnotist, highly amnesic participants remember as many items as those who are less amnesic. Some researchers have suggested that hypnosis temporarily interferes with the person's ability to retrieve a particular item from memory but does not affect actual memory storage (Kihlstrom, 2007).

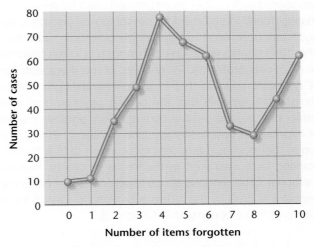

FIGURE 6.5 The Distribution of Posthypnotic Amnesia.
Individuals performed ten actions while hypnotized and were then given posthypnotic amnesia instructions. When asked what occurred during hypnosis, these individuals varied in the number of actions they failed to recall: The level of forgetting for a given individual ranged from none to ten items. The experiment involved 491 people, and the graph plots the number of people at each level of forgetting. The plot shows a bimodal distribution for posthypnotic amnesia, with peaks at four and ten items forgotten.

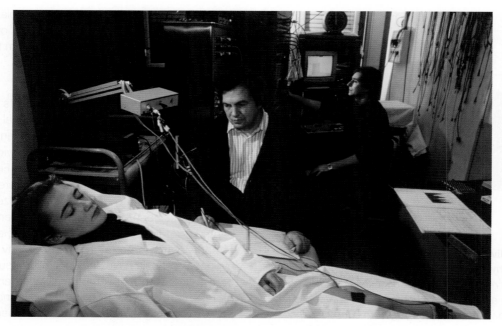

Hypnosis is used to treat a number of physiological and psychological disorders.

Hypnosis as therapy

Hypnosis is used to treat a number of physiological and psychological disorders (see reviews by Lynn *et al.*, 2000; Pinnell & Covino, 2000). In medicine, hypnosis has been used to reduce anxiety related to medical and dental procedures, asthma, gastrointestinal diseases, and the nausea associated with cancer treatment and used for general pain management. In treatment for psychological disorders, hypnosis has been used to help people overcome addictions. The most controversial use of hypnosis is in the treatment of emotional problems. Proponents of the therapeutic use of hypnosis suggest that it allows therapists to uncover repressed memories that are behind psychological problems, but several researchers caution against the use of hypnosis in psychotherapy (see Kihlstrom, 2007). They argue that hypnosis amounts to no more than a therapist planting false memories in the minds of clients, including memories of horrendous abuse experiences that never happened. We discuss the rather substantial evidence for the claims of these opponents in Chapter 8.

> → Characteristic hypnotic responses include enhanced or diminished control over movements, distortion of memory through posthypnotic amnesia, and **positive hallucinations** and **negative hallucinations**.
>
> → Reduction of pain is one of the beneficial uses of hypnosis.

CRITICAL THINKING QUESTIONS

1 Do you think you would be a good hypnotic subject or not? Why?

2 If it is true that hypnosis only plants false ideas in the minds of suggestible people, does this mean the phenomenon of hypnosis is not real?

PSYCHOACTIVE DRUGS

In addition to meditation and hypnosis, drugs can be used to alter a person's state of consciousness. Since ancient times, people have used drugs to stimulate or relax, to bring on sleep or prevent it, to enhance ordinary perceptions, or to produce hallucinations. The word *drug* can be used to refer to any substance (other than food) that chemically alters the functioning of an organism. The term **psychoactive drugs** refers to drugs that affect behavior, consciousness, and/or mood. These drugs include not only illegal 'street' drugs

INTERIM SUMMARY

→ Hypnosis is a responsive state in which individuals focus their attention on the hypnotist and his or her suggestions.

→ Some people are more readily hypnotized than others, although most people show some susceptibility.

such as heroin and marijuana but also legal drugs such as tranquilizers and stimulants. Familiar, widely used drugs such as alcohol, nicotine, and caffeine are also included in this category.

Whether a particular drug is legal or not does not reflect the risks and dangers associated with the drug. For example, caffeine (coffee) is totally accepted in almost all cultures, and its use is unregulated; nicotine (tobacco) is minimally regulated in most cultures; alcohol is legal in most cultures but highly regulated in some; and marijuana is legal in some cultures but illegal in others. Yet it could be argued that of all these substances nicotine is the most harmful, because it is responsible for hundreds of thousands of deaths each year. We could well ask whether nicotine would even be made a legal drug if someone tried to introduce it today.

Table 6.2 lists and classifies the psychoactive drugs that are most frequently used and abused. Caffeine and nicotine are also listed in the table. Although both substances are stimulants and can have adverse effects on health, they do not significantly alter consciousness and hence are not discussed in this section.

Much substance use by adolescents and young adults is experimental. Typically, young people try alcohol or marijuana and maybe even try heroin or cocaine a few times but do not use them chronically or continue to use them as they grow older. Some substances, however, have such powerful reinforcing effects on the brain that many people who try these substances,

TABLE 6.2 PSYCHOACTIVE DRUGS THAT ARE COMMONLY USED AND ABUSED

Only a few examples of each class of drug are given. The generic name (for example, psilocybin) or the brand name (Xanax for alprazolam; Seconal for secobarbital) is used, depending on which is more familiar.

Depressants (Sedatives)	Stimulants
Alcohol (ethanol)	Amphetamines
Barbiturates	Benzedrine
Nembutal	Dexedrine
Seconal	Methedrine
Minor tranquilizers	Cocaine
Miltown	Nicotine
Xanax	Caffeine
Valium	Hallucinogens
Inhalants	LSD
Paint thinner	Mescaline
Glue	Psilocybin
Opiates (Narcotics)	PCP (Phencyclidine)
Opium and its derivatives	Cannabis
Codeine	Marijuana
Heroin	Hashish
Morphine	
Methadone	

even experimentally, find themselves craving more of the substance and have a difficult time resisting taking the substance. In addition, some people have a greater vulnerability to becoming 'hooked' psychologically or physically on substances, so even a little experimentation may be dangerous for them.

The drugs listed in Table 6.2 are assumed to affect behavior and consciousness because they act on the brain in specific biochemical ways. With repeated use, an individual can become dependent on any of them. It should be explained here that DSM-5 does not separate the diagnoses of substance abuse and dependence as in DSM-IV. Rather, criteria are provided for substance use disorder, accompanied by criteria for intoxication, withdrawal, substance/medication-induced disorders, and unspecified substance-induced disorders, where relevant. What was referred to pre-DSM-5 as drug **dependence** has three key characteristics: (1) tolerance – with continued use, the individual must take more and more of the drug to achieve the same effect; (2) withdrawal – if use of the drug is discontinued, the person experiences unpleasant physical and psychological reactions; and (3) compulsive use – the individual takes more of the drug than intended, tries to control his or her drug use but fails, and spends a great deal of time trying to obtain the drug.

The degree to which tolerance develops and the severity of **withdrawal symptoms** vary from one drug to another. Tolerance for opiates, for example, develops fairly quickly, and heavy users can tolerate a dosage that would be lethal to a non-user. In contrast, marijuana smokers seldom build up much tolerance. Withdrawal symptoms are common and easily observed following heavy and sustained use of alcohol, opiates, and sedatives. They are common, but less apparent, for stimulants, and non-existent after repeated use of **hallucinogens** (Brick, 2008).

Although tolerance and withdrawal are the primary characteristics of substance dependence, they are not necessary for a diagnosis. A person who shows a pattern of compulsive use without any signs of tolerance or withdrawal, as some marijuana users do, would still be considered as dependent.

Referred to pre-DSM-5 as **drug misuse** means continued use of a drug, despite serious consequences, by a person who is not dependent on it (that is, shows no symptoms of tolerance, withdrawal, or compulsive craving). For example, someone whose over-indulgence in alcohol results in repeated accidents, absence from work, or marital problems (without signs of dependence) is said to misuse alcohol.

In this section we look at several types of psychoactive drugs and the effects they may have on those who use them.

Depressants

Depressants are drugs that depress the CNS. They include tranquilizers, barbiturates (sleeping pills), inhalants (volatile solvents and aerosols), and ethyl alcohol. Of these, the most frequently used and abused is alcohol, and we will focus on it here.

Alcohol is the depressant drug most often used.

Alcohol and its effects

People in most societies consume alcohol in some form. Alcohol can be produced by fermenting a wide variety of materials: grains such as rye, wheat, and corn; fruits such as grapes, apples, and plums; and vegetables such as potatoes. Through the process of distillation, the alcoholic content of a fermented beverage can be increased to obtain 'spirits' such as whiskey or rum.

The alcohol used in beverages is called ethanol and consists of relatively small molecules that are easily and quickly absorbed into the body. Once a drink is swallowed, it enters the stomach and small intestine, where there is a heavy concentration of small blood vessels. These give the ethanol molecules ready access to the blood. Once they enter the bloodstream, they are rapidly carried throughout the body and to all of its organs. Although the alcohol is fairly evenly distributed through the whole body, its effects are likely to be felt most immediately in the brain because a substantial portion of the blood that the heart pumps at any given time goes to the brain and the fatty tissue in the brain absorbs alcohol very well.

Measuring the amount of alcohol in the air we exhale (as in a breathalyzer) gives a reliable index of the amount of alcohol in the blood. Consequently, it is easy to determine the relationship between blood alcohol concentration (BAC) and behavior. At concentrations of 0.03 per cent to 0.05 per cent in the blood (30 to 50 milligrams of alcohol per 100 milliliters of blood), alcohol produces light-headedness, relaxation,

and release of inhibitions. People say things that they might not ordinarily say and tend to become more sociable and expansive. Self-confidence may increase, but motor reactions begin to slow. In combination, these effects make it dangerous to drive after drinking.

At a BAC of 0.10 per cent, sensory and motor functions become noticeably impaired. Speech becomes slurred, and people have difficulty co-ordinating their movements. Some people become angry and aggressive; others grow silent and morose. At a level of 0.20 per cent the drinker is seriously incapacitated, and a level above 0.40 per cent may cause death.

How much does a person have to drink to achieve these different BACs? The relationship between BAC and alcohol intake is not a simple one. It depends on a person's sex, body weight, and speed of consumption. Age, individual metabolism, and experience with drinking are also factors. Although the effects of alcohol intake on BAC vary a great deal, the average effects are shown in Figure 6.6. It is not true that beer or wine is less likely to make someone drunk than spirits. A small beer or glass of wine or a nip of whiskey have about the same alcohol content and about the same effect.

Alcohol usage

Many young adults view drinking as an integral part of social life. It promotes conviviality, eases tension, releases inhibitions, and generally adds to the fun. Nevertheless, social drinking can create problems in terms of lost work time, poor performance 'the morning after,' and arguments or accidents while intoxicated. Clearly the most serious problem is accidents: unintentional alcohol-related injuries due to car

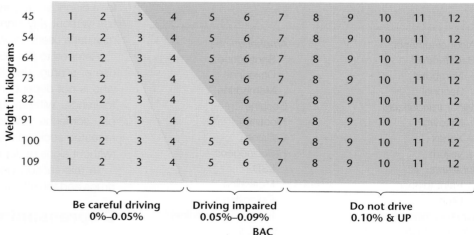

Drinks in a two-hour period
(One small beer or glass of wine or one nip of spirits)

Weight in kilograms												
45	1	2	3	4	5	6	7	8	9	10	11	12
54	1	2	3	4	5	6	7	8	9	10	11	12
64	1	2	3	4	5	6	7	8	9	10	11	12
73	1	2	3	4	5	6	7	8	9	10	11	12
82	1	2	3	4	5	6	7	8	9	10	11	12
91	1	2	3	4	5	6	7	8	9	10	11	12
100	1	2	3	4	5	6	7	8	9	10	11	12
109	1	2	3	4	5	6	7	8	9	10	11	12

Be careful driving
0%–0.05%

Driving impaired
0.05%–0.09%

Do not drive
0.10% & UP

BAC

FIGURE 6.6 BAC and Alcohol Intake. *Approximate values of blood-alcohol concentration as a function of alcohol consumption in a 2-hour period. For example, if you weigh 82 kilos and had four beers in 2 hours, your BAC would be between 0.05% and 0.09%, and your driving ability would be seriously impaired.*

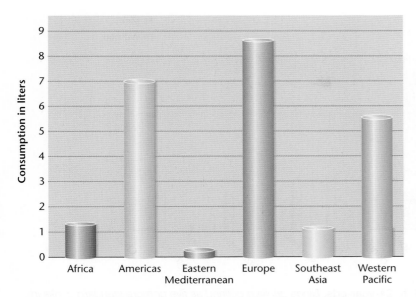

FIGURE 6.7 **Consumption of Pure Alcohol in Various Regions of the World.** *Cultures vary greatly in their consumption of alcohol. (Southeast Asia includes India and neighboring countries. Western Pacific includes Australia, China, Japan, and the Pacific Rim Countries.).*

accidents, drowning, burns, poisoning, and falls account for approximately 600 000 deaths per year internationally (WHO, 2005). In addition, more than half of all murderers and their victims are believed to be intoxicated with alcohol at the time of the murder, and people who commit suicide often do so when under the influence of alcohol. The consumption of alcohol varies greatly across nations and cultures (see Figure 6.7). Globally, 46 per cent of all men and 73 per cent of all women abstain from alcohol; most of these people are concentrated in a belt stretching from Northern Africa, over the Eastern Mediterranean, South Central Asia and Southeast Asia to the islands of Indonesia (WHO, 2010). In other areas of the world, such as Europe, less than 20 per cent of the population abstains from alcohol.

Heavy or prolonged drinking can lead to serious health problems. High blood pressure, stroke, ulcers, cancers of the mouth, throat, and stomach, cirrhosis of the liver, and depression are some of the conditions associated with regular use of substantial amounts of alcohol. The Russian Federation and the surrounding countries, which show a high overall intake of alcohol and detrimental drinking patterns, have the highest level of adverse health effects associated with alcohol (Rehm *et al.*, 2009). Latin America is another region with a relatively high level of negative health due to alcohol. The least alcohol-related harm is found in Africa, the Eastern Mediterranean, and the southern part of Asia, especially in regions with predominantly Muslim individuals.

Alcohol not only affects the drinker; when pregnant women drink, the fetus is exposed to the alcohol and a number of negative effects can result. Pregnant women who drink heavily are twice as likely to suffer repeated miscarriages and to produce low-birth-weight babies. A condition called **fetal alcohol syndrome** is characterized by mental retardation and multiple deformities of the infant's face and mouth, caused by the mother's drinking during pregnancy. The amount of alcohol needed to produce this syndrome is unclear, but as little as a few alcoholic drinks a week is thought to be detrimental (Streissguth *et al.*, 1999).

Gender and age differences in alcohol disorders

Across all nations, men are more likely than women to drink, and to have problems due to alcohol consumption (Wilsnack *et al.*, 2009). The gender gap in alcohol use is much greater among men and women who subscribe to traditional gender roles, which condone drinking for men but not for women (Huselid & Cooper, 1992).

Binge drinking may be especially damaging to health and safety. Binge drinking is defined somewhat differently across cultures and studies, but a common definition is five or more drinks in one sitting for men, four or more for women (because it takes less alcohol for women to achieve a high BAC). Binge-drinking on university campuses is common. One study found that 44 per cent of university students reported binge drinking in the last month, compared to 39 per cent of 18- to 22-year olds who were not in college (SAMHSA, 2005; Wechsler & Nelson, 2008). Lost study time, missed classes, injuries, unprotected sex, and trouble with police are some of the problems reported by students who engage in binge-drinking. Internationally, there appears to be a pattern among young people toward binge drinking and drinking to intoxication (WHO, 2005). Figure 6.8 shows patterns of binge drinking for 18–24-year-olds in various countries.

Elderly people are less likely than others to misuse or be dependent on alcohol, probably for several reasons. First, with age, the liver metabolizes alcohol at a slower rate, and the lower percentage of body water increases the absorption of alcohol. As a result, older people can become intoxicated faster and experience the negative effects of alcohol more severely and quickly. Second, as people grow older, they may become more mature in their choices, including the choice about drinking alcohol to excess. Third, older people have grown up under stronger prohibitions against alcohol use and abuse and in a society with more stigma associated with alcoholism, leading them to curtail their use of alcohol more than younger people do. Finally, people who have used alcohol excessively for many years may die from alcohol-related diseases before they reach old age.

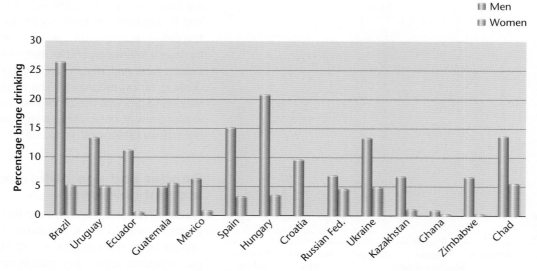

FIGURE 6.8 Differencs in Binge Drinking among 18- to 24-year-ods. *Binge drinking defined as five or more standard drinks in one sitting at least once per week.*

Illicit drugs

Illicit drugs are drugs that have significant psychological effects and that are legally restricted or prohibited in many nations. Examples include opiates, such as heroin, stimulants, such as cocaine, hallucinogens, and cannabis. The United Nations estimates that over 185 million people worldwide are users of illicit drugs, with cannabis being the most frequently used drug (see Figure 6.9; WHO, 2008). Half of all drug seizures worldwide involve cannabis, and about 2.5 per cent of the world population consumes cannabis annually.

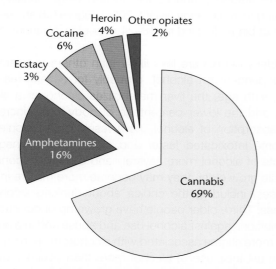

FIGURE 6.9 Percentage of Illicit Drug Users Reporting Use of Various Drugs in the Last Year. *Cannabis is the most frequently used illicit drug.*

Cannabis

Cannabis is a psychoactive substance that creates a high feeling, cognitive and motor impairments, and sometimes hallucinations. The cannabis plant has been harvested since ancient times for its psychoactive effects. The dried leaves and flowers are used to produce **marijuana**, and the solidified resin of the plant is called **hashish**. Marijuana and hashish are usually smoked but may also be taken orally, mixed with tea or food. The active ingredient in both substances is THC (tetrahydrocannabinol). Taken orally in small doses (5–10 milligrams), THC produces a mild high; larger doses (30–70 milligrams) produce severe and longer-lasting reactions that resemble those of hallucinogenic drugs. As with alcohol, the reaction often has two stages: a period of stimulation and euphoria, followed by a period of tranquility and sleep.

When marijuana is smoked, THC is rapidly absorbed by the rich blood supply of the lungs. Blood from the lungs goes directly to the heart and then to the brain, causing a high within minutes. However, THC also accumulates in other organs, such as the liver, kidneys, spleen, and testes. The amount of THC reaching the body varies according to how the user smokes: a cigarette allows for the transfer of 10 to 20 per cent of the THC in the marijuana, whereas a pipe allows about 40 to 50 per cent to transfer. A water pipe, or bong, traps the smoke until it is inhaled and therefore is a highly efficient means of transferring THC. Once in the brain, the THC binds to cannabinoid receptors, which are especially numerous in the hippocampus. Because the hippocampus is involved in the formation of new memories, it is not surprising that marijuana use inhibits memory formation (Pope *et al.*, 2001).

Regular users of marijuana report a number of sensory and perceptual changes: a general euphoria and sense of well-being, some distortions of space and time, and changes in social perception. Not all marijuana experiences are pleasant. Sixteen per cent of regular users report anxiety, fearfulness, and confusion as a 'usual occurrence,' and about one-third report that they occasionally experience such symptoms as acute panic, hallucinations, and unpleasant distortions in body image. Individuals who use marijuana regularly (daily or almost daily) often report both physical and mental lethargy, and about a third show mild forms of depression, anxiety, or irritability (Ruiz *et al.,* 2007). Marijuana smoke contains even larger amounts of known carcinogens than tobacco (but marijuana users tend to smoke less than cigarette smokers, and their total intake of these substances is lower).

Marijuana use interferes with performance on complex tasks. Motor co-ordination is significantly impaired by low to moderate doses, and reaction time for car braking and the ability to negotiate a twisting road course are adversely affected. These findings make it clear that driving under the influence of the drug is dangerous. The number of car accidents related to marijuana use is difficult to determine because, unlike alcohol, THC declines rapidly in the blood, quickly going to the fatty tissues and organs of the body. A blood analysis performed 2 hours after a heavy dose of marijuana may show no signs of THC, even though an observer would judge the person to be clearly impaired. The effects of marijuana may persist long after the subjective feelings of euphoria or sleepiness have passed. A study of aircraft pilots using a simulated flight-landing task found that performance was significantly impaired as much as 24 hours after smoking one marijuana cigarette containing 9 milligrams of THC – despite the fact that the pilots reported no awareness of any after-effects on their alertness or performance (Yesavage *et al.,* 1985). These findings have led to concern about marijuana use by people whose jobs affect public safety.

Marijuana has two clear effects on memory. First, it makes short-term memory more susceptible to interference. People under the influence of marijuana may lose the thread of a conversation or forget what they are saying in the middle of a sentence because of momentary distractions. Second, marijuana disrupts learning by interfering with the transfer of new information from short-term to long-term memory. These findings suggest that it is not a good idea to study while under the influence of marijuana; later recall of the material will be poor.

Opiates

Opium and its derivatives, collectively known as **opiates**, are drugs that diminish physical sensation and the capacity to respond to stimuli by depressing the CNS. (These drugs are commonly called *narcotics*, but *opiates* is a more accurate term; the term *narcotics* is not well defined and covers a variety of illegal drugs.) Opiates are used in medical settings to reduce pain, but their ability to alter mood and reduce anxiety has led to widespread illegal consumption. Opium, which is the air-dried juice of the opium poppy, contains a number of chemical substances, including morphine and codeine. Codeine, a common ingredient in prescription painkillers and cough suppressants, is relatively mild in its effects (at least at low doses). Morphine and its derivative, heroin, are much more potent. Most illegal opiate use involves heroin because it is more concentrated and can be concealed and smuggled more easily than morphine.

All opiate drugs bind to the same molecules in the brain, known as opiate receptors. The differences among these drugs depend on how quickly they reach the receptors and how much it takes to activate them – that is, their potency. The rate at which opiates enter the body depends on how they are taken. When opiates are smoked or injected, they reach peak levels in the brain within minutes. The faster this occurs, the greater the danger of death by overdose. Drugs that are 'snorted' are absorbed more slowly because they must pass through the mucous membranes of the nose to the blood vessels beneath.

Heroin usage

Heroin is an opiate that can be injected, smoked, or inhaled. At first it produces a sense of well-being. Experienced users report a special thrill, or 'rush,' within a minute or two after an intravenous injection. Some describe this sensation as intensely pleasurable, similar to an orgasm. Young people who sniff heroin report that they forget everything that troubles them. Following this, the user feels 'fixed,' or gratified, and has no awareness of hunger, pain, or sexual urges. The person may be alternately waking and drowsing while comfortably watching television or reading a book. Unlike a person who is intoxicated by alcohol, a heroin user can readily produce skilled responses to tests of agility and intelligence and seldom becomes aggressive or assaultive.

The changes in consciousness produced by heroin are not very striking; there are no exciting visual experiences or feelings of being transported elsewhere. It is the change in mood – the feeling of euphoria and reduced anxiety – that prompts people to start using the drug. However, heroin is very addictive; even a brief period of usage can create physical dependence. After a person has been smoking or 'sniffing' (inhaling) heroin for a while, tolerance builds up, and this method no longer produces the desired effect. In an attempt to recreate the original high, the individual may progress to intravenous drug use and then to 'mainlining' (injecting into a vein). Once the user starts mainlining, stronger and stronger doses are required to produce the high, and the physical discomforts of withdrawal from the drug become intense (chills, sweating, stomach cramps, vomiting, headaches). Additional motivation to continue using the drug stems from the need to avoid physical pain and discomfort.

The hazards of heroin use are many; the average age at death for frequent users is 40 (Hser *et al.,* 1993). Death is caused by suffocation resulting from depression of the brain's respiratory center. Death from an overdose is always a possibility because the concentration of street heroin fluctuates widely, and the user can never be sure of the potency of the powder in a newly purchased supply. Heroin use is generally associated with a serious deterioration of personal and social life. Because maintaining the habit is costly, the user often becomes involved in illegal activities to acquire money to purchase the drug.

Additional dangers of heroin use include HIV, hepatitis C, and other infections associated with unsterile injections. Sharing needles used to inject drugs is an extremely easy way to be infected with HIV; blood from an infected person can be trapped in the needle or syringe and injected directly into the bloodstream of the next person who uses the needle. Sharing of needles and syringes by people who inject drugs is a primary means by which HIV is spreading today.

Opioid receptors

In the 1970s, researchers made a major breakthrough in understanding opiate dependence with the discovery that opiates act on very specific neuroreceptor sites in the brain. Neurotransmitters travel across the synaptic junction between two neurons and bind to neuroreceptors, triggering activity in the receiving neuron (see Chapter 2). The molecular shape of the opiates resembles that of a group of neurotransmitters called *endorphins*. Endorphins bind to opioid receptors, producing sensations of pleasure as well as reducing discomfort. Heroin and morphine relieve pain by binding to opioid receptors that are unfilled (see Figure 6.10). Repeated heroin use causes a drop in endorphin production; the body then needs more heroin to fill the unoccupied opioid receptors in order to reduce pain. The person experiences painful withdrawal symptoms when heroin is discontinued because many opioid receptors are left unfilled. In essence, the heroin has replaced the body's own natural opiates (Ruiz *et al.,* 2007).

These findings have led to the development of drugs that operate by modulating the opioid receptors. These drugs are of two basic types: agonists and antagonists. **Agonists** bind to the opioid receptors to produce a feeling of pleasure and thereby reduce the craving for opiates, but they cause less psychological and physiological impairment than the opiates. **Antagonists** also lock onto the opioid receptors but in a way that does not activate them; the drug serves to 'block' the receptors so that the opiates cannot gain access to them. Antagonists produce no feeling of pleasure and the craving is not satisfied (see Figure 6.10).

Methadone is the best-known agonist drug used in treating heroin-dependent individuals. It is addictive in its own right, but it produces less psychological impairment than heroin and has few disruptive physical effects. When taken orally in low doses, it suppresses the craving for heroin and prevents withdrawal symptoms. **Naltrexone**, an antagonist drug, blocks the action of heroin because it has a greater affinity for the opioid receptors than does heroin itself. Naltrexone is often used in hospital emergency rooms to reverse the effects of a heroin overdose, but it has not proved generally effective as a treatment for heroin dependence. Interestingly, naltrexone does reduce the craving for alcohol. Alcohol causes the release of endorphins, and naltrexone, by blocking opioid receptors, reduces the pleasurable effects of alcohol and hence the desire for it.

Stimulants

In contrast to depressants and opiates, **stimulants** are drugs that increase alertness and general arousal. They increase the

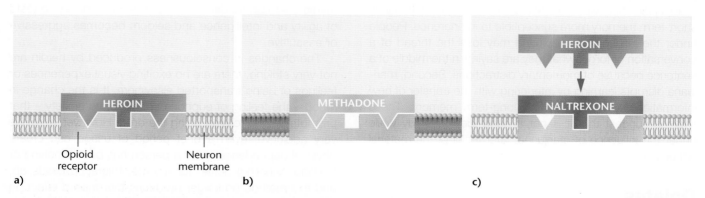

FIGURE 6.10 Drug Abuse Medications. *Methadone and naltrexone block the effects of heroine by binding to the same neuronal receptors that heroin binds to.*

amount of monoamine neurotransmitters (norepinephrine, epinephrine, dopamine, and serotonin) in the synapse. The effects resemble what would happen if every one of the neurons that released a monoamine fired at once. The result is to arouse the body both physically, by increasing heart rate and blood pressure, and mentally, causing the person to become hyperalert.

Amphetamines

Amphetamines are powerful stimulants; they are sold under such trade names as Methedrine, Dexedrine, and Benzedrine and known colloquially as 'speed,' 'uppers,' and 'bennies.' The immediate effects of consuming such drugs are an increase in alertness and a decrease in feelings of fatigue and boredom. Strenuous activities that require endurance seem easier after taking amphetamines. As with other drugs, the ability of amphetamines to alter mood and increase self-confidence is the principal reason for their use. People also use them to stay awake.

Low doses that are taken for limited periods to overcome fatigue (for example, when driving at night) seem to be relatively safe. However, as the stimulating effects of amphetamines wear off, there is a period when the user feels depressed, irritable, and fatigued and may be tempted to take more of the drug. Tolerance develops quickly, and the user needs increasingly larger doses to produce the desired effect. Because high doses can have dangerous side-effects – agitation, confusion, heart palpitations, and elevated blood pressure – medications containing amphetamines should be used with caution. When tolerance develops to the point at which oral doses are no longer effective, many users inject amphetamines into a vein. Large intravenous doses produce an immediate pleasant experience (a 'flash' or 'rush'). This sensation is followed by irritability and discomfort, which can be overcome only by an additional injection. If this sequence is repeated every few hours over a period of days, it will end in a 'crash,' a deep sleep followed by a period of lethargy and depression. The amphetamine abuser may seek relief from this discomfort by turning to alcohol or heroin.

Long-term amphetamine use is accompanied by drastic deterioration of physical and mental health. The user may develop symptoms that are indistinguishable from those of acute schizophrenia (see Chapter 15), including persecutory delusions (the false belief that people are persecuting you or out to get you) and visual or auditory hallucinations. The delusions may lead to unprovoked violence. For example, during an epidemic of amphetamine use in Japan in the early 1950s (when amphetamines were sold without prescription and advertised for 'elimination of drowsiness and repletion of the spirit'), 50 per cent of the murders that occurred in a 2-month period were related to amphetamine abuse (Hemmi, 1969).

Cocaine

Like other stimulants, cocaine, or 'coke,' a substance obtained from the dried leaves of the coca plant, increases energy and self-confidence; it makes the user feel witty and hyperalert. Early in the twentieth century, cocaine was widely used and easy to obtain. In fact, it was an ingredient in the original recipe of Coca-Cola. Its use then declined, but in the 1980s and 1990s its popularity increased, even though it is now illegal in most countries.

Cocaine can be inhaled or 'snorted,' or made into a solution and injected directly into a vein. It can also be converted into a flammable compound, 'crack,' which is smoked. One of the earliest studies of the effects of cocaine was conducted by Freud (1885). In an account of his own use of cocaine, he was at first highly favorable to the drug and encouraged its use. However, he changed his mind about the drug after using it to treat a friend, with disastrous results. The friend developed severe dependence on the drug, demanded ever-larger dosages, and was debilitated until his eventual death.

Despite earlier reports to the contrary, and as Freud soon discovered, cocaine is highly addictive. In fact, it has become more addictive and dangerous with the emergence of crack. Tolerance develops with repeated use, and withdrawal effects, although not as dramatic as those associated with opiates, do occur. The restless irritability that follows the euphoric high becomes, with repeated use, a feeling of depressed anguish. The down is as bad as the up was good and can be alleviated only by more cocaine (see Figure 6.11).

Heavy cocaine users can experience the same abnormal symptoms as people who use amphetamines heavily. A common visual hallucination is flashes of light ('snow lights') or moving lights. Less common – but more disturbing – is the feeling that bugs ('cocaine bugs') are crawling under one's skin. The hallucination may be so strong that the individual will use a knife to cut out the bugs. These experiences occur because cocaine is causing the sensory neurons to fire spontaneously.

INTERIM SUMMARY

➔ Psychoactive drugs have long been used to alter consciousness and mood.

➔ Repeated use of any of these drugs can result in problems. Formerly these were commonly divided into "drug dependence" and "drug misuse." However, DSM-5 does not separate the diagnoses of substance abuse and dependence as in DSM-IV, criteria are provided for substance use disorder, accompanied by criteria for intoxication, withdrawal, substance/ medication-induced disorders, and unspecified substance-induced disorders, where relevant.

SEEING BOTH SIDES
DOES BRAIN DEATH MEAN DEATH?

CELLULAR DEATH FOLLOWING BRAIN DEATH

Israel Berger, Sydney Medical School,
University of Sydney

Brain (or brain stem) death occurs when the brain becomes so damaged that it dies. Damage most commonly occurs due to trauma or lack of oxygen. Brain death is a permanent condition and can be diagnosed through the use of physical neurological examination and specialized tests, including electroencephalography (EEG). Clear criteria exist for the diagnosis of brain death, although some countries, states, or hospitals use more stringent criteria than others (see, for example, American Academy of Neurology, 1995; Academy for Medical Royal Colleges, 2008; Massachusetts General Hospital, 2011; Puswella *et al.,* 2004; see also Wijdicks, 2012).

First, it must be determined that the patient is not suffering from a reversible unconscious state, such as overdose, hypothermia, or hypoglycemia. Usually, two physicians must perform a neurological evaluation of the patient separated by a period of time (however, current criteria may mean that one examination is sufficient, and a second examination may negatively impact organ donation, Lustbader *et al.,* 2011). Typical criteria include:

No spontaneous movement and no movement in respose to painful stimuli (spinal reflexes do not preclude the diagnosis of brain death). No seizures or other involuntary movements. Cranial nerve reflexes such as papillary response to light, corneal reflexes, gagging and coughing with suction, and caloric response (movement of the eyes in response to stimulation of the ear canal) must be absent. Respiration is absent after ventilation has been given as 100 percent oxygen and 100 percent oxygen is given through a mask. Blood gases are continually assessed and the patient is observed for breathing efforts.

Further confirmatory tests may also be used:

Flat (isoelectric) EEG at multiple points. Absence of flow in the intracranial arteries or small peaks during heartbeats measured using transcranial Doppler. EEG using somatosensory evoked potentials reveal an absence of response on certain waves (N20/P22). Intracranial pressure is sustained and elevated. Cranial radionuclide angiography and contrast angiography demonstrate no cerebral blood flow, in which case the brain cannot function, and death can be determined by this test alone.

Although there have been misdiagnoses of brain death, further investigation has revealed that the criteria had not been applied properly (e.g., van Norman, 1999). These errors have led to a popular belief that brain death is equivalent to deep comas such as those that may occur during hypothermia, hypoglycemia, barbiturate, or other sedative overdose, alcohol poisoning, or trauma. A coma is a protective state during which the brain heals itself, and some form of consciousness may be restored at some point. Even in states such as anencephaly, a birth defect in which the forebrain is missing, what parts of the brain exist are alive, and the child can usually breathe spontaneously. In brain death, the cells have died and do not heal, making spontaneous respiration impossible.

If the braindead person is on a ventilator, the heart may continue to beat for some time due to the effect of oxygen on the cardiac muscle. However, the cells in the rest of the body begin to die (cellular death), leading to changes in the cardiovascular, endocrine, immune, and pulmonary systems, build-up of toxins, and eventual death of the body (somatic or systemic death) (Bugge, 2009; see also Cobb *et al.,* 1996, on mechanisms of cell death). Cardiac and systemic death usually occurs within hours or days of brain death but can occasionally take longer (Jennet *et al.,* 1981). Death is a process, not an event; the exact point at which death is confirmed has been debated for centuries (Bondeson, 2001). Brain death is a sign of death, and reliable criteria have been developed to identify it.

SEEING BOTH SIDES

DOES BRAIN DEATH MEAN DEATH?

UNDERSTANDING AND DEFINING WHAT DEATH REALLY IS

Matthew Georgiades, Sydney Medical School, University of Sydney

Since death is the cessation of life, any conceptualization of death necessarily involves a clear understanding of life. Living cells are able to obtain and/or synthesize nutrients and molecules necessary for their survival. These nutrients and molecules are used to synthesize proteins and macromolecules necessary for the carrying out of physiological functions, for the maintenance of homeostasis, for the provision of energy in the form of ATP to sustain life, and for the replication of life in cell division.

We know that when life has ceased then death has occurred, but it is quite difficult to elucidate the boundaries between life and death. Prior to the development of life-sustaining therapies like cardiopulmonary resuscitation (CPR), defibrillation, and tracheal positive pressure ventilation (TPPV) the conception of death was simple since cessation of any of the three interdependent vital functions (circulation, respiration, and brain function) would lead to cessation of the other two, and, hence, death (Bernat, 2013). More recently, the criterion of brain death for determination of death has been proposed and asserts that irreversible cessation of brain-stem functions is sufficient for the declaration of death (see American Medical Association, 1981; American Academy of Neurology, 1995; Wijdicks, 2003; and Academy for Medical Royal Colleges, 2008 for discussion of criteria for the determination of death).

The criterion of brain death seems to make sense in the declaration of death since without function of centers in the brainstem then breathing, circulation, temperature regulation and other vital processes do not occur. In this sense, the lack of brain stem function contributes to death since it leads to cessation of normal homeostatic mechanisms, breathing, and circulation that maintain life. However, within our modern context and with consideration of life support therapies it is clear that death involves a significant systemic component that is not immediate, but is a gradual and physiological process.

In addition, many have argued that brain death is not sufficient for the determination of death for the organism as a whole. These arguments are formed on the basis of the knowledge that the spinal cord also has a role in integrating the functions of the organism, thus undermining the brain-centerd concept of death (Shewmon, 2004). Evidence for these arguments is also taken from the cases of patients diagnosed as brain dead but whose circulation and organ function were maintained for months or longer (Bernat, 2013; for discussion and presentation of these arguments see also Shewmon, 1998; Shewmon, 2004; and Miller, 2009). When respiration and circulation cease, the cells of the body lose access to oxygen and other substances essential to their function and survival. Without oxygen, the process of oxidative phosphorylation cannot continue, and as a result energy stores in the form of ATP become depleted. Now many of the enzymes and proteins necessary for the cell's functioning do not have the necessary energy source to continue their reactions. Pumps that rely on ATP to maintain the fine balance of concentration gradients either side of the cell membrane cease to function. The loss of fine control of the cellular environment further disrupts the functioning of sensitive proteins and as salts build up inside the cell, water rushes in causing swelling and ultimately, rupture of the cells. As cells die, organ function ceases, leading to systemic death. (For a more detailed description of cellular death see the recommended pathology or physiology textbooks: Kumar *et al.*, 2009; and Silverthorn, 2012).

It is clear that brain function is essential for the regulation and maintenance of life in an organism as a whole. However, with support from life-sustaining therapies, life can be prolonged irrespective of brain function. Systemic death is a gradual, physiological process of cell death in the organism which will ultimately result in overall death. The point at which we decide to declare someone as dead has significant implications legally, economically (life support is expensive), medically (since organs can be donated from the deceased to promote life in the living), morally, and ethically.

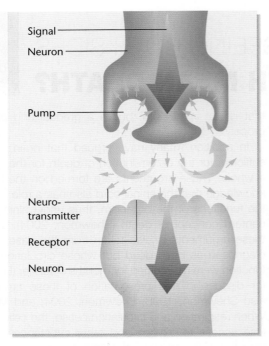

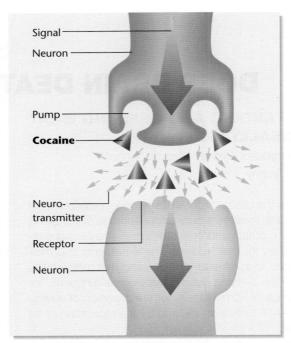

a) A nerve impulse causes the release of neurotransmitters that carry the signal across the synapse to a receiving neuron. Some of the neurotransmitters are then reabsorbed into the originating neuron (reuptake process), while the rest are broken up chemically and made inactive (degradation process). These processes are discussed in Chapter 2.

b) Research findings indicate that cocaine blocks the reuptake process for three neurotransmitters (dopamine, serotonin, and norepinephrine) that are involved in the regulation of mood.

FIGURE 6.11 Molecular Effects of Cocaine.

→ Cannabis, such as marijuana and hashish, creates a high feeling, cognitive and motor impairments, and, in some people, hallucinations.

→ Depressant drugs, such as alcohol, tranquilizers, and inhalants, depress the CNS. The most commonly used depressant is alcohol.

→ Opiates, such as heroin and morphine, reduce perceptions of pain and induce euphoria, followed by a sense of drowsiness. Severe intoxication can lead to respiratory difficulties, unconsciousness, and coma.

→ Stimulants, such as amphetamines and cocaine, activate those parts of the brain that register reward or pleasure, and they produce euphoria, energy, and a sense of self-esteem. Withdrawal from stimulants can cause depression, restlessness, and dangerous physiological symptoms.

CRITICAL THINKING QUESTIONS

1 Laws that criminalize some psychoactive drugs (marijuana, cocaine) but not others (alcohol, tobacco) do not seem well matched to the drugs' actual dangers. If you were to redesign your country's drug policies from scratch, basing them only on current scientific knowledge, which drugs would you want to discourage most vigorously (or criminalize)? Which drugs would you worry about least?

2 It has been demonstrated that the ancient Asian medical practice of acupuncture, in which needles are inserted into the skin at different 'acupuncture points,' stimulates the brain's production of endorphins. How might this explain why acupuncture seems to help people overcome dependence on heroin?

CHAPTER SUMMARY

1 A person's perceptions, thoughts, and feelings at any given moment constitute that person's consciousness. An altered state of consciousness is said to exist when mental functioning seems changed or out of the ordinary to the person experiencing the state. Some altered states of consciousness, such as sleep and dreams, are experienced by everyone; others result from special circumstances such as meditation, hypnosis, or the use of drugs.

2 The functions of consciousness are (a) monitoring ourselves and our environment so that we are aware of what is happening within our bodies and in our surroundings, and (b) controlling our actions so that they are co-ordinated with events in the outside world. Not all events that influence consciousness are at the center of our awareness at a given moment. Memories of personal events and accumulated knowledge, which are accessible but not currently part of one's consciousness, are called *preconscious memories*. Events that affect behavior, even though we are not aware of perceiving them, influence us subconsciously.

3 According to psychoanalytic theory, some emotionally painful memories and impulses are not available to consciousness because they have been repressed – that is, diverted to the unconscious. Unconscious thoughts and impulses influence our behavior even though they reach consciousness only in indirect ways – through dreams, irrational behavior, and slips of the tongue.

4 The notion of automaticity refers to the habituation of responses that initially required conscious attention, such as driving a car.

5 Sleep, an altered state of consciousness, is of interest because of the rhythms evident in sleep schedules and in the depth of sleep. These rhythms are studied with the aid of the electroencephalogram (EEG). Patterns of brainwaves show four stages (depths) of sleep, plus a fifth stage characterized by rapid eye movements (REMs). These stages alternate throughout the night. Dreams occur more often during REM sleep than during the other four stages (NREM sleep).

6 The opponent-process model of sleep proposes that two opposing processes – the homeostatic sleep drive and the clock-dependent alerting process – interact to determine our tendency to fall asleep or remain awake. Whether we are asleep or awake at any given time depends on the relative forces exerted by the two processes. There are a variety of sleep disorders, including sleep deprivation, insomnia, narcolepsy, and apnea.

7 Freud attributed psychological causes to dreams, distinguishing between their manifest and latent content and suggesting that dreams are wishes in disguise. Other theories see dreaming as a reflection of the information processing that the brain is doing while asleep. Recently some theorists have concluded that dreaming is a cognitive process that reflects the individual's conceptions, concerns, and emotional preoccupations.

8 Meditation represents an effort to alter consciousness by following planned rituals or exercises such as those of yoga or Zen. The result is a somewhat mystical state in which the individual is extremely relaxed and feels divorced from the outside world.

9 Hypnosis is a responsive state in which individuals focus their attention on the hypnotist and his or her suggestions. Some people are more readily hypnotized than others, although most people show some susceptibility. Characteristic hypnotic responses include enhanced or diminished control over movements, distortion of memory through posthypnotic

amnesia, and positive and negative hallucinations. Reduction of pain is one of the beneficial uses of hypnosis.

10 Psychoactive drugs have long been used to alter consciousness and mood. They include depressants, such as alcohol, tranquilizers, and inhalants; cannabis, such as marijuana and hashish; opiates, such as heroin and morphine; stimulants, such as amphetamines and cocaine.

CORE CONCEPTS

altered states of consciousness	sleep disorder	drug misuse (pre-DSM-5)
consciousness	insomnia	depressants
preconscious memories	narcolepsy	fetal alcohol syndrome
unconscious	apnea	illicit drugs
Freudian slip	dreaming	cannabis
automaticity	lucid dream	marijuana
dissociation	meditation	hashish
dissociative identity disorder	hypnosis	opiates
REM sleep	posthypnotic response	heroin
non-REM sleep (or NREM)	posthypnotic amnesia	agonists
opponent-process model of sleep and wakefulness	positive hallucinations	antagonists
	negative hallucinations	methadone
homeostatic sleep drive	psychoactive drugs	naltrexone
clock-dependent alerting process	drug dependence (pre-DSM-5)	stimulants
circadian rhythms	withdrawal symptoms	amphetamines
melatonin	hallucinogens	cocaine

DIGITAL SUPPORT RESOURCES

Students should use the unique access code included in the front of the book to access the digital support resources which accompany the new edition. These include:

- Multiple Choice Questions and Quizzes
- Critical Thinking Questions
- Practice Essay Questions

- Videos
- Glossary, Flashcards, and More

7

LEARNING AND CONDITIONING

LEARNING OBJECTIVES

After reading this chapter you should be able to:

Understand the history of the study of animal and human learning.

Know the different types of conditioning and the way in which they are studied.

Understand the brain physiology underlying learning processes.

Know the topics of cognition and motivation, as they interact with learning.

I f you have ever experienced a panic attack, you know that it is a terrifying experience: your heart is racing, you feel out of breath and perhaps even faint, and you are convinced that something terrible will happen. A panic attack can be thought of as an overreaction to a real or perceived threat in the environment (see Chapter 15). The symptoms are the result of the excitation of the sympathetic division of the autonomic nervous system (recall the 'fight-or-flight' response discussed in Chapter 2). Panic attacks are not at all uncommon, especially during times of stress: up to 40 per cent of young adults have occasional panic attacks (see Chapter 15).

Far fewer individuals develop a panic disorder – in these cases the attacks are frequent and the intense worry about them interferes with everyday life. Research has shown that an effective form of treatment for panic disorders is **cognitive behavior therapy** (see Chapter 16). This is a treatment method that involves procedures to change maladaptive cognitions and beliefs. Cognitive behavior therapy has its roots in **behavior therapy**, a general term referring to treatment methods based on the principles of learning and conditioning. The effectiveness of these forms of therapy suggests that some of the behaviors involved in panic disorders seem to be *learned* responses, which may be unlearned in the therapy.

Learning and conditioning are the topics of this chapter. We will engage in a systematic analysis of learning that will give you insight into how experience alters behavior. **Learning** is defined as a relatively permanent change in behavior that occurs as a result of experience. Behavior changes that are due to maturation or to temporary conditions (such as fatigue or drug-induced states) are not included.

Not all cases of learning are the same, though. There are two basic kinds of learning: non-associative learning and associative learning. **Non-associative learning** involves learning about a single stimulus, and it includes habituation and sensitization. **Habituation** is a type of non-associative learning that is characterized by a decreased behavioral response to an innocuous stimulus. For example, the sound of a horn might startle you when you first hear it. But if the horn toots repeatedly, your startle response will progressively decrease. In contrast, **sensitization** is a type of non-associative learning whereby there is an increase in a behavioral response to an intense stimulus. Sensitization typically occurs when noxious or fearful stimuli are presented to an organism. For example, the startle response to a horn is greatly enhanced if you enter a dark alley right before the loud sound. Habituation and sensitization are typically relatively short-lived, lasting for minutes to hours. Both types of learning are exceptionally important for determining what an organism attends to in the world. Indeed, the fact that non-associative learning can be demonstrated in all animals, ranging from single-celled organisms to humans, is a testament to the

CHAPTER OUTLINE

PERSPECTIVES ON LEARNING

CLASSICAL CONDITIONING

Pavlov's experiments

Cognitive factors

Biological constraints

INSTRUMENTAL CONDITIONING

Skinner's experiments

Cognitive factors

Biological constraints

LEARNING AND COGNITION

Observational learning

Prior beliefs

CUTTING EDGE RESEARCH: DO SINGING MICE PROVIDE INSIGHTS INTO THE EVOLUTION OF HUMAN SPEECH?

LEARNING AND THE BRAIN

Habituation and sensitization

Classical conditioning

Cellular basis of learning

LEARNING AND MOTIVATION

Arousal

From incentives to goals

Intrinsic motivation and learning

SEEING BOTH SIDES: WHAT ARE THE BASES OF SOCIAL LEARNING?

importance of this form of learning. We will revisit non-associative learning in the section on the brain and learning.

Associative learning is much more complicated than non-associative learning, because it involves learning relationships among events. It includes classical conditioning and instrumental conditioning. Classical and instrumental conditioning both involve forming associations – that is, learning that certain events go together. These forms of learning will be discussed in detail in this chapter. In classical conditioning, an organism learns that one event follows another. For example, a baby learns that the sight of a breast will be followed by the taste of milk. In instrumental conditioning, an organism learns that a response it makes will be followed by a particular consequence. For example, a young child learns that striking a sibling will be followed by disapproval from his or her parents.

This chapter will also cover a more complex form of learning: observational learning. For other forms of complex learning in humans, the role of memory and cognition are crucial – these are the topics of Chapters 8 and 9; social learning is addressed in more detail in Chapter 13. We will also take a look at the neural basis of learning, referring back to concepts introduced in Chapter 2. Lastly, the importance of motivation for learning is briefly discussed – you will see that the topic of motivation is further explored in Chapter 10.

PERSPECTIVES ON LEARNING

Recall from Chapter 1 that three of the most important perspectives on psychology are the behaviorist, cognitive, and biological perspectives. The study of learning has involved all three of these perspectives.

Most of the early work on learning, particularly on conditioning, was done from a behaviorist perspective. During the early decades of the last century, especially in North America, this approach to the study of behavior took psychology by storm. The most important 'spokesman' for behaviorism was the American John Watson. A brief article he published in 1913, titled 'Psychology as the Behaviorist Views it,' is referred to as 'the behavioristic manifesto.' His ideas were formulated in response to the writings by some of the 'founding fathers' of psychology, William James, E. B. Titchener, and Wilhelm Wundt. William James was interested in topics such as consciousness and emotion whereas Titchener devoted his research to the study of mental structures. The German Wilhelm Wundt, as we saw in Chapter 1, was the first to establish a laboratory dedicated to the study of psychology. His method of inquiry was that of introspection. In Watson's opinion, the methods of psychology were too subjective. Watson also argued that the subject matter of psychological research should not be consciousness, but rather *behavior*. He was inspired by animal studies carried out by Ivan Pavlov, a Russian scientist. Watson believed that such experiments gave psychologists a scientific method of inquiry: objective and replicable.

For early behaviorists the focus was on external stimuli and observable responses, in keeping with the behavioristic

dictum that behavior is better understood in terms of external causes than mental ones. The behaviorists' approach to learning included other key assumptions as well. One was that simple associations of the classical or instrumental kind are the basic building blocks of *all* learning processes, regardless of what is being learned or who is doing the learning – a rat learning to run a maze or a child mastering arithmetic (Skinner, 1971, 1938). They argued that something as complex as acquiring a language is presumably a matter of learning many associations (Staats, 1968). These views led behaviorists to focus on how the behaviors of nonhuman organisms, particularly rats and pigeons, are influenced by rewards and punishments in simple laboratory situations.

The findings and phenomena uncovered in this work continue to form the basis for much of what we know about associative learning. But as we will see, the behavioristic assumptions have had to be modified in light of subsequent work. To understand conditioning and complex learning, it turns out that we will have to consider what the organism *knows* about the relations between stimuli and response (even if the organism is a rat or a pigeon). This brings in the cognitive perspective. Moreover, it now appears that no single set of laws underlies learning in all situations and by all organisms. In particular, different mechanisms of learning seem to be involved in different species, which brings in the biological perspective.

The discoveries described in this chapter set the stage for the 'cognitive revolution' in psychology, an intellectual movement in the 1950s championed by Jerome Bruner and others, who rejected the constraints of behaviorism (Bruner, 1997). They believed that mental representations are not only *important* topics in psychology, but that they *can* and *should* be studied using the scientific method. As described in

Chapter 1, this movement was strengthened by the development of computers in the second half of the last century. New technology allowed researchers (for example, Nobel Prize winner Herbert Simon) to simulate cognitive processes, ushering in a view of human beings as processors of information – rather than organisms that are simply conditioned to respond to external events.

It remains invaluable to study the work done by behaviorists. Their experimental paradigms and discoveries have laid the foundation for much of the research into human behavior that has been carried out since.

INTERIM SUMMARY

➔ Learning is a relatively permanent change in behavior that is the result of experience.

➔ There are four basic kinds of learning: (1) habituation and sensitization, (2) classical conditioning, (3) instrumental conditioning, and (4) complex learning.

CRITICAL THINKING QUESTIONS

1 The ubiquity of learning questions whether any behavior is innate. Indeed, one could make the argument that all behavior is learned. Do you agree with this view? Why or why not?

2 Several paradigms of thought have influenced the design and interpretation of learning experiments. For example, behaviorists have focused on observable changes in behavior that occur with experience, and cognitive scientists study the architecture of mental representations that yield learned behavior. Why are these different approaches important? How has the emergence of biopsychology influenced the study of learning?

CLASSICAL CONDITIONING

Ivan Pavlov, a Russian physiologist who had already received the Nobel Prize for his research on digestion, made an important discovery in the early years of the twentieth century. For his research, he was measuring dogs' salivation in response to food – any dog will salivate when food is placed in its mouth. But Pavlov noticed that the dogs in his laboratory began to salivate at the mere *sight* of a food dish. It occurred to him that the dogs had perhaps learned to associate the sight of the dish with the taste of the food, and he decided to see whether a dog could be taught to associate food with other stimuli, such as a light or a tone. The elegant experiments that Pavlov designed to study this question have contributed much to our understanding of one of the most basic processes of learning: classical conditioning (often referred to as 'Pavlovian conditioning'). **Classical conditioning** is a learning process in which a previously neutral stimulus becomes associated with another stimulus through repeated pairing with that stimulus. The food dish was originally a *neutral* stimulus: it did not lead to a salivation response. However, the food itself *does* cause salivation when it is placed in the mouth of the dog. After food and a food dish are presented together ('paired') repeatedly, the mere sight of the food dish is enough to cause a salivation response. The dog has learned that two events (the sight of a food dish, and the taste of food in the mouth) are *associated*.

You will be introduced to the vocabulary of classical conditioning through a presentation of Pavlov's initial findings. Over the years, many psychologists have devised interesting variations of Pavlov's experiments – we will also discuss some of these important and more recent discoveries.

Pavlov's experiments

In Pavlov's basic experiment, a tube is attached to the dog's salivary gland so that the flow of salivation can be measured. Then the dog is placed in front of a pan into which meat powder can be delivered automatically. The dog is hungry and when meat powder is delivered, salivation is registered. This salivation is an **unconditioned response (UR)**: an unlearned response elicited by the taste of the food. By the same token, the food itself is termed the **unconditioned stimulus (US)**: a stimulus that automatically elicits a response without prior conditioning. The researcher can also turn on a light in a window in front of the dog. This event is called a **neutral stimulus (NS)** because it does not cause salivation – although it may of course lead to other responses by the dog (such as tail wagging, jumping, and barking). Next, the researcher will repeatedly pair the presentation of the food with the light.

Pavlov and assistants.

First the light is turned on, then some meat powder is delivered and the light is turned off. This is called the *conditioning* phase of the experiment. After a number of such paired presentations, the dog will salivate in response to the light even if no meat powder is delivered. This teaches us that the dog has learned that the two events (food and light) are associated – the light has become a **conditioned stimulus (CS)**, causing a **conditioned response (CR)**. Figure 7.1 illustrates the different phases of Pavlov's conditioning experiment. In variations on this experiment, Pavlov used a tone (or other stimuli) instead of a light, and found similar results in each case.

In a classical conditioning experiment, the researcher capitalizes on the existence of a specific unconditioned response, typically a reflex – in our basic example the salivation. Such responses are part of the natural behavioral repertoire of the animal or human under study (for example: the eye blink in response to a puff of air on the eye, or a knee jerk reflex in response to a tap on the knee).

In Pavlov's experiments, the form of the conditioned response often mimicked the form of the unconditioned response – in our basic example it was salivation in both cases. In most cases, however, it is a bit more complicated than that. Note that, in our example, you might consider the salivation in response to the light (the CR) to be *anticipatory*: the dog salivates in response to the light, because it has learned that the light *precedes* the food. This anticipatory nature of the conditioned response explains why in some cases it takes on quite a different form from the unconditioned response. In this way, classical conditioning can help to explain the complex response humans have to the repeated intake of specific drugs.

Drug tolerance

When a drug is taken repeatedly its effect decreases. This is called **drug tolerance**. In other words, increased doses are required to produce the same effects that were initially produced with smaller doses. Research has shown that classical conditioning contributes to drug tolerance. These insights are important, not in the last place because drug tolerance is important in drug addiction.

Habitual coffee drinkers will develop a degree of tolerance to caffeine: with repeated intake, the effect of the caffeine (which is to raise blood pressure) is attenuated. Even though the coffee *originally* resulted in an increased blood pressure, it no longer does so after the coffee-drinking habit has formed. But when these same habitual coffee drinkers are given caffeine intravenously (injected directly into a vein), the original effect of the caffeine returns (Corti *et al.*, 2002). It appears that drug tolerance is greater when the drug is taken under the usual circumstances. This effect is called the 'situational specificity of drug tolerance,' and it can be explained by classical conditioning.

The intake of a drug will trigger a *compensatory response* of the body – recall our discussion of *homeostasis* in Chapter 2. When caffeine (the unconditioned stimulus, US) is consumed and blood pressure is raised (the unconditioned response, UR), the body responds to restore homeostasis by bringing the blood pressure back down to its normal level. It turns out that when someone habitually drinks a cup of coffee, this compensatory response (the conditioned response, CR) will be elicited by cues related to the habitual caffeine intake (the conditioned stimulus, CS) – the smell of the coffee, for example. Classical conditioning explains how the body learned to respond to the situational cues (the CS) that are associated with regular caffeine intake, simply because of their repeated pairing with the caffeine intake (the US). In this way, classical conditioning explains how tolerance develops: the body's

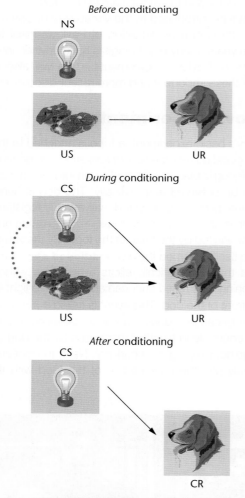

Before conditioning
NS

US   UR

During conditioning
CS

US   UR

After conditioning
CS

CR

FIGURE 7.1 **A Diagram of Classical Conditioning.** *Before conditioning, the unconditioned stimulus (US) causes the unconditioned response (UR) – this does not have to be learned. The neutral stimulus (NS) does not lead to a response. During conditioning, the unconditioned stimulus (US) and the conditioned stimulus (CS) are paired, and their association is learned. After conditioning, the conditioned stimulus (CS) causes the conditioned response (CR). In this example, both UR and CR are salivation.*

compensatory response (the CR) clearly contributes to tolerance for the drug. Another example is that of *alcohol tolerance*. Imagine someone who habitually drinks a few beers. It has been found that this person will show greater tolerance to the alcohol in a beer (the usual drink), than when the same amount of alcohol is consumed in another drink (Remington *et al.,* 1997).

So, when a habitual user takes a drug under unusual circumstances (for example an injection of caffeine or alcohol in an unusual beverage), tolerance to the drug is reduced because the conditioned compensatory response is not triggered. This analysis explains the perplexing finding that most deaths due to an 'overdose' of a recreational drug (such as heroin or cocaine) are in fact *not* the result of an actual *overdose* (Siegel, 2001). It has been reported that, in most of these cases, the habitual user of the drug took *no more* than their normal dose of the drug – but rather, took it under unusual circumstances (for example, by injecting in a different part of the body, or in a different room than normally). The unusual circumstances deprived the user of the life-saving compensatory response, thereby reducing tolerance to the drug and making it lethal.

Acquisition

We will return to Pavlov's original experiments to introduce a few more important aspects of learning through classical conditioning. Each paired presentation of the CS (light) followed by the US (food) is called a reinforced trial. Repeated pairings of the CS and the US strengthen the association between the two, as illustrated by the increase in the magnitude of the CR (the salivation response) in the left panel of Figure 7.2. This is the **acquisition** stage of the experiment,

and the figure represents the **learning curve**. The largest change in the magnitude of the CR happens in the earliest conditioning trials, and there is little change in the CR later on.

Extinction

If the US is subsequently omitted, the CR will gradually diminish, as illustrated by the middle panel of Figure 7.2. As you see, after about ten trials or so there is no salivation in response to the light, if it is not followed by food. **Extinction** represents learning that the CS no longer predicts the US.

Spontaneous recovery

When the experimenter allows the dog to rest for a certain period, and then presents again *only* the light, the (extinguished) salivation response reappears – see right panel of Figure 7.2. This is called **spontaneous recovery**: no reinforced trials are needed, and the CS again leads to a CR. As you can see, the recovered CR is weaker than it was after acquisition. With repeated presentation of the CS alone, the CR will again diminish. Spontaneous recovery reflects that the association between the CS and the US that was originally learned, does not simply disappear during extinction. Rather, extinction seems to involve the formation of a *new* association (between CS and *no* US). The spontaneous recovery of the CR means that the dog 'remembers' that the light *used* to predict food – even though the response itself was completely extinguished.

Extinction can also be undone by reinforcing the original association through repeated pairing of the CS and the US, as it was originally done during acquisition. The re-learning curve would be steeper than the learning curve presented in

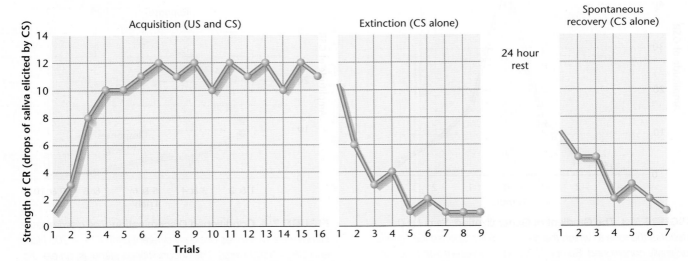

FIGURE 7.2 Acquisition and Extinction of a Conditioned Response. *The curve in the panel on the left depicts the acquisition phase of an experiment. Drops of saliva in response to the CS (before the onset of the US) are plotted on the vertical axis; the number of trials is plotted on the horizontal axis. After 16 acquisition trials, the experimenter switched to extinction; the results are presented in the panel in the middle. The panel on the right shows spontaneous recovery of the response after a 24 hour rest period.*

the left panel of Figure 7.2 (re-learning an association is faster than originally learning it). This suggests again that the association between the CS and the US was not forgotten, even though the CR was extinguished. Consider again the example of our habitual coffee drinker: the smell of coffee (the CS) causes the compensatory response to decrease blood pressure (the CR). This compensatory response will eventually be extinguished if the coffee drinker switches to decaffeinated coffee, which constitutes the presentation of the CS *in the absence* of the US (the caffeine). But when this person switches back to drinking regular coffee, the body will respond by quickly re-learning the old association.

Stimulus generalization

Pavlov noticed that the dogs that had been trained to have a conditioned response to a certain tone, would show the same response to a tone that was slightly higher or lower in pitch. This is called **response generalization**: the more similar the new stimuli are to the original CS, the more likely they are to evoke the same response. Suppose that a person is conditioned to have a mild emotional reaction to the sound of a tuning fork producing a tone of middle C. This emotional reaction can be measured by the galvanic skin response, or GSR, which is a change in the electrical activity of the skin that occurs during emotional stress. That person will show a change in GSR in response to higher or lower tones without further conditioning (see Figure 7.3).

Stimulus generalization accounts in part for a human or animal's ability to react to novel stimuli that are similar to familiar ones – an ability that is clearly adaptive. Organisms might not be exposed to exactly the same stimulus very often, but similar stimuli are likely to predict similar events.

Stimulus discrimination

A process that is complementary to generalization is discrimination. Stimulus generalization is a reaction to similarities, and **stimulus discrimination** is a reaction to differences. Conditioned discrimination is brought about through differential conditioning, as shown in Figure 7.4. Instead of just one tone during conditioning, now there are two. The low-pitched tone, CS_1, is always followed by a mild forefinger shock, and the high-pitched tone, CS_2, is not. Initially, participants show a GSR to both tones. During the course of conditioning, however, the amplitude of the conditioned response to CS_1 gradually increases while the amplitude of the response to CS_2 decreases. Through this process of *differential reinforcement*, participants are conditioned to discriminate between the two tones. It is important to note that the presentation of CS_2 leads to a suppression of the response (lowered GSR). This is because its presentation contains information for the subject, namely that *no shock* will follow. Most of the examples of conditioning we discussed thus far were examples of **excitatory conditioning**, in which case the CS leads to an increase in the probability

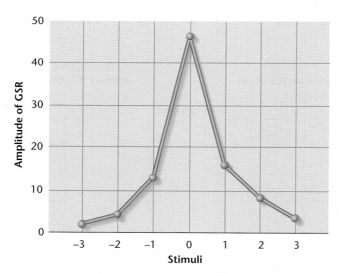

FIGURE 7.3 The Gradient of Generalization. *Stimulus 0 denotes the tone to which the galvanic skin response (GSR) was originally conditioned. Stimuli 1, 2, and 3 represent test tones of increasingly higher pitch; stimuli-1, -2, and -3 represent tones of increasingly lower pitch. Note that the amount of generalization decreases as the difference between the test tone and the training tone increases.*

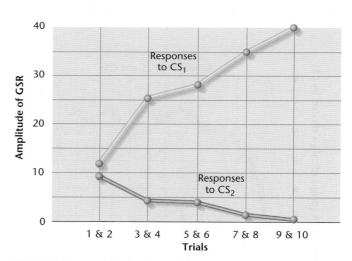

FIGURE 7.4 Conditioned Discrimination. *The discriminative stimuli were two tones of clearly different pitch (CS_1 = 700 Hertz and CS_2 = 3500 Hertz). The unconditioned stimulus, an electric shock applied to the left forefinger, occurred only on trials when CS_1 was presented. The strength of the conditioned response, in this case the GSR, gradually increased following CS_1 and extinguished following CS_2.*

or magnitude of a certain response. But differential reinforcement teaches us that another possible consequence of classical conditioning is a decrease in the probability or magnitude of a behavioral response – this is **inhibitory conditioning**.

Generalization and discrimination occur frequently in everyday life. A young child who has learned to associate the sight of her pet dog with playfulness may initially approach all dogs. Eventually, through discrimination, the child may expect playfulness only from dogs that look like hers. The sight of a threatening dog has come to inhibit the child's response to approaching dogs.

Second-order conditioning

Once a dog has been conditioned to salivate in response to a light, it is possible to condition the dog to salivate in response to another stimulus (for example, a tone), simply by repeatedly pairing the light and the tone. This is called **second-order conditioning**. In other words, once the light has taken on the role of a conditioned stimulus, it acquires the power of an unconditioned stimulus. If the dog is now put in a situation in which it is exposed to a tone (CS_2) followed by the light (CS_1), the tone alone will eventually elicit the conditioned response – even though it was never paired with food. During this conditioning there must also be trials that reinforce the association between the light and the food; otherwise, the originally conditioned association will be extinguished.

The existence of second-order conditioning greatly increases the scope of classical conditioning. Especially in humans, most conditioned responses are established through second-order conditioning. The original US is usually a biologically significant stimulus, such as food, pain or nausea. All that is needed for conditioning to occur is the pairing of that stimulus with another. Consider the plight of cancer patients who are undergoing chemotherapy to stop the growth of their tumors. Chemotherapy involves injecting toxic substances (the US) into the patient, who as a result often becomes nauseated (the UR). Young cancer patients are often given ice cream before the chemotherapy session. The ice cream is intended to lighten the child's distress about the treatment, but unfortunately it becomes associated with it. The ice cream can take on the role of a CS and cause nausea by itself (Bernstein, 1978, 1999). If the child is then repeatedly presented with other stimuli, such as certain toys, followed by ice cream, the patient may start to experience unpleasant feelings in response to the toys alone. This would be a consequence of second-order conditioning, since the toys were never directly paired with treatment or nausea.

Conditioning and fear

Classical conditioning also plays a role in emotional responses like fear. Suppose that a rat in an enclosed compartment is periodically subjected to electric shock. Just before the shock occurs, a tone sounds. After repeated pairings of the tone (the CS) and the shock (the US), the tone alone will produce reactions in the rat that indicate fear, including freezing and crouching. In addition, its blood pressure increases. The rat has been conditioned to be fearful when exposed to what was previously a neutral stimulus. Humans, too, can be conditioned to be fearful (Jacobs & Nadel, 1985; Watson & Rayner, 1920). Indeed, classical conditioning of fear seems to be at the root of several anxiety disorders, such as post-traumatic stress disorder and panic disorder (Bouton *et al.* 2001).

We have seen repeatedly that a CS leads to a CR, precisely because it *predicts* the occurrence of a certain US. Predictability it is also important for emotional reactions. If a particular CS reliably predicts that pain is coming, the *absence* of that CS predicts that pain is *not* coming so that the organism can relax. The CS has become a 'danger' signal, and its absence a 'safety' signal. When such signals are erratic, the emotional toll on the organism can be devastating. When rats have a reliable predictor that shock is coming, they respond with fear only when the danger signal is present; if they have no reliable predictor, they appear to be continually anxious and may even develop ulcers (Seligman, 1975). There are clear parallels to human emotionality. If a dentist gives a child a danger signal by saying that a procedure will hurt, the child will be fearful until the procedure is over. In contrast, if the dentist always tells a child that it won't hurt, when in fact it sometimes does, the child has no danger or safety signals and may become terribly anxious whenever in the dentist's office. As adults, many of us have experienced the anxiety of being in a situation where something disagreeable is likely to happen but no warnings exist for us to predict it. Unpleasant events are, by definition, unpleasant, but unpredictable unpleasant events are downright intolerable (see also Chapter 14).

Cognitive factors

Pavlov and others believed that it was enough for conditioning to occur if the CS and the US were **temporally contiguous** – that is, the CS and the US occur close together in time. Pavlov was careful not to make any claims about the organism's cognitive understanding of relationships between stimuli; such internal events were considered not to be observable. From our previous discussion, however, it would seem that conditioning occurs if the CS *predicts* the US. In such cases, we say that the US is **contingent** on the CS (the US is more likely to occur when the CS is presented, than when it is not presented). Some researchers indeed argued that the critical factor behind classical conditioning is what the animal knows (Bolles, 1972; Tolman, 1932). In this cognitive view, classical conditioning gives an organism new knowledge about the relationship between two stimuli: given the CS, the organism has learned to expect the US (Rescorla, 1968).

In a series of important and elegantly designed experiments, Rescorla (1968) contrasted contiguity and contingency. He was able to show that the CS must be a reliable predictor of the US. Mere temporal contiguity is *not* enough for conditioning to occur. The procedure for one of these experiments is called Rescorla's Experiment. There are two groups of rats, group A and B. The number of temporally contiguous pairings of tone and shock was the same in both groups. So, if *temporal contiguity* determines conditioning, both groups of rats should show equal amounts of conditioning. What was different, however, was the contingency of the shock on the tone: for group A all shocks were preceded by tones, whereas for group B shocks were equally likely in the presence and absence of the tone. Therefore, the tone was highly predictive of the shock for group A, but it had no predictive power for group B. So, if *contingency* determines conditioning, we would expect only group A to exhibit conditioning. And this is exactly what Rescorla found: only the rats in group A developed a conditioned fear response. In other groups in the experiment, the strength of the conditioning was directly related to the predictive value of the CS in signaling the occurrence of the US. Subsequent experiments supported the conclusion that the predictive relationship between the CS and the US is more important than either temporal contiguity or the frequency with which the CS and US are paired (Rescorla, 1972).

Biological constraints

Early behaviorists assumed that the laws of learning were the same for all species. Moreover, they assumed that any CS could be associated with *any* US through classical conditioning.

This doctrine places these early behaviorists firmly on the *nurture* side of the nature–nurture debate: what an organism learns, depends entirely on its experiences with the environment. Others, however, had emphasized the biological function

of the learning process: it allows the organism to adapt and survive. Early ethologists (for example, European Nobel Prize winners Konrad Lorentz, Nikolaas Tinbergen, and Karl von Frisch) made discoveries that revealed powerful *biological predispositions* in human and animal behavior (Tinbergen, 1951).

Ethologists, like behaviorists, are concerned with the behavior of animals, but place greater emphasis on evolution and genetics – and they study the behavior of animals in their natural environment. This perspective on learning draws attention to the fact that exactly *what* an organism needs to learn depends on its evolutionary history – to some extent animals are 'pre-programmed' to learn particular things in particular ways.

Consider the example of a **learned taste aversion**. Many of us have had the experience of becoming ill after eating a certain food, and would not want to eat that particular food ever again. Garb and Stunkard (1974) found that over one-third of people have had at least one such experience. Typically, a novel food was eaten and the person got ill (nausea and vomiting) within a few hours. Learned taste aversions at first seem typical instances of classical conditioning: the taste of the food has become associated with the illness. However, upon closer inspection, the conditioning does not entirely comply with the rules of classical conditioning. First of all, most taste aversions occur after just one bad experience with the food – no repeated pairings are necessary. Second, the CS–US interval is usually very long: the illness (the US) occurs a few hours after the ingestion of the food (the CS). From an evolutionary perspective, it is very easy to see what is adaptive about the ability of an organism to be able to learn to avoid particular foods in a single trial: the organism will avoid food that is potentially harmful. The existence of learned taste aversions shows that organisms are very selective in what they are able to learn: certain associations are learned very readily, while others may never be learned.

Garcia and Koelling (1966) carried out a series of controlled experiments that reveal the importance of biological predispositions in learning. One of their experiments is illustrated in Table 7.1. In the first stage of the experiment, an experimental group of rats is allowed to lick at a tube that

TABLE 7.1   AN EXPERIMENT ON CONSTRAINTS AND TASTE AVERSION

The design of an experiment showing that taste is a better signal for sickness than shock, whereas light-plus-sound is a better signal for shock than sickness.

Condition	Conditioned stimuli (CS)	Unconditioned stimulus (US)	Result
Poison	Sweet taste; light + click	Lithium chloride	Taste : suppression of drinking Light + click : no suppression of drinking
Shock	Sweet taste; light + click	Footshock	Taste : no suppression Light + click : suppression of drinking

contains a flavored solution. Each time the rat licks the tube, a click and a light are presented. The rat experiences three stimuli simultaneously – the taste of the solution, as well as the light and the click. In the second stage of the experiment, rats in the experimental group are mildly poisoned with lithium chloride. Which stimuli – the sweet taste or the light-plus-click – will become associated with feeling sick? To answer this question, in the third and final stage, rats in the experimental group are again presented with the tube. Sometimes the solution in the tube has the same flavor as before but there is no light or click, and at other times the solution has no flavor but the light and click are presented. The animals avoid the solution when they experience the taste, but not when the light-plus-click is presented. Therefore, the rats have associated only taste with feeling sick. These results cannot be attributed to taste being a more potent CS than light-plus-click, as shown by the control condition of the experiment, which is shown at the bottom of Table 7.1. In the second stage, instead of being mildly poisoned, the rat is shocked. In the final stage, the animal avoids the solution only when the light-plus-click is presented, not when it experiences the taste alone (Garcia & Koelling, 1966).

So, taste is a better signal for sickness than for shock, and light-plus-click is a better signal for shock than for sickness. Why does this selectivity of association exist? It does not fit with the early behaviorist idea that equally potent stimuli can be substituted for one another. Because taste and light-plus-click can both be effective conditioned stimuli, and being sick and being shocked are both effective unconditioned stimuli, it should have been possible for either CS to become associated with either US. On the other hand, selectivity of association fits perfectly with the ethological perspective and its emphasis on an animal's evolutionary adaptation to its environment. In their natural habitat, rats rely on taste to select their food. Consequently, there may be a genetically determined relationship between taste and intestinal reactions that fosters an association between taste and sickness but not between light and sickness. Moreover, in a rat's natural environment, pain resulting from external factors like cold or injury is invariably due to external stimuli. As a result, there may be a built-in relationship between external stimuli and 'external pain,' which fosters an association between light and shock but not one between taste and shock.

If rats learn to associate taste with sickness because it fits with their natural means of selecting food, another species with a different means of selecting food might have trouble learning to associate taste with sickness. This is exactly what happens. Birds naturally select their food on the basis of looks rather than taste, and they readily learn to associate a light with sickness but not to associate a taste with sickness (Wilcoxin *et al.,* 1971). Here, then, is a perfect example of different species learning the same thing – what causes sickness – by different means. In short, if we want to know what may be conditioned to what, we cannot consider the CS and US in isolation. Rather, we must focus on the two in combination and consider how well that combination reflects built-in relationships. This conclusion differs considerably from the assumption that the laws of learning are the same for all species and situations. In fact, several theorists have explored classical conditioning by using a behavior systems approach that considers the evolutionary history of the behaviors under study (Fanselow, 1994; Domjan, 2005). One example of conditioning with ecologically relevant stimuli in human subjects is the observation that food taste (the CS) becomes associated with caloric repletion (the sense of being satisfied, the US). These conditioned preferences depend on how hungry the subject is (see Domjan, 2005).

INTERIM SUMMARY

- In classical conditioning, a conditioned stimulus (CS) that consistently precedes an unconditioned stimulus (US) comes to serve as a signal for the US and will elicit a conditioned response (CR) that often resembles the unconditioned response (UR).
- For classical conditioning to occur, the CS must be a reliable predictor of the US; that is, there must be a higher probability that the US will occur when the CS has been presented than when it has not.
- The ability of stimuli to become associated in a classical conditioning experiment is constrained by biology and evolution.

CRITICAL THINKING QUESTIONS

1 In classical conditioning, it is generally believed that associations between the CS and US, rather than the CS and UR, are the essence of conditioning. Can you think of an experiment that might differentiate these possibilities?

2 Some anxiety disorders in humans may be mediated by classical conditioning. For example, patients with panic disorder often experience panic attacks in situations that they have experienced before. Further, panic attacks can be precipitated when bodily sensations reminiscent of panic, such as increases in heart rate, occur during exercise. Can you describe the onset of panic attacks in terms of classical conditioning? What are the CS, US, CR, and UR?

INSTRUMENTAL CONDITIONING

In classical conditioning, the conditioned response is a response that was part of the animal's natural repertoire – like salivation. But how do dogs learn *new* 'tricks,' like rolling over and playing dead? If you have ever trained a dog to perform such tricks, you know that it involves rewarding the dog whenever it does what you want it to do. Initially, you will reward the dog for approximating the desired behavior, but eventually you will only reward it if it performs the entire trick. In **instrumental conditioning**, certain behaviors are learned because they *operate on* the environment. Your dog learns that performing the trick results in food: the behavior is *instrumental* in producing a certain change in the environment. If we think of the dog as having food as a goal, instrumental conditioning amounts to learning that a particular behavior (called the '*response*' – in this case rolling over) leads to a particular goal (Rescorla, 1987). Classical conditioning involves learning the relationship between events; instrumental conditioning (also called '*operant conditioning*') involves learning the relationship between responses and their outcomes.

In this section, we will review the findings of B. F. Skinner, an American psychologist who contributed much to our understanding of instrumental conditioning. By the 1950s, Skinner was the leading proponent of behaviorism in the USA. As before, we will also discuss more recent discoveries and insights.

The study of instrumental conditioning did not begin with Skinner's work. E. L. Thorndike carried out a series of important experiments at the turn of the twentieth century (Thorndike, 1898). He was inspired by the writings of Charles Darwin, which contained many anecdotes about animals revealing seemingly intelligent and insightful behavior. But Thorndike felt that controlled experiments should be carried out to study animal intelligence. From his experiments, Thorndike concluded that animals, unlike humans, do not learn by developing some **insight** (an understanding of the situation,

leading to the solution of a problem) – rather, they learn through trial-and-error. In a typical experiment, a hungry cat is placed in a cage whose door is held fast by a simple latch, and a piece of fish is placed just outside the cage. Initially, the cat tries to reach the food by extending its paws through the bars. When this fails, the cat moves about the cage, engaging in a variety of behaviors. At some point it inadvertently hits the latch, frees itself, and eats the fish. Researchers then place the cat back in its cage and put a new piece of fish outside. The cat goes through roughly the same set of behaviors until once more it happens to hit the latch. The procedure is repeated again and again. Over a number of trials, the cat eliminates many of its irrelevant behaviors, and eventually it opens the latch and frees itself as soon as it is placed in the cage. The cat has learned to open the latch to obtain food.

It may sound as if the cat is acting intelligently, but Thorndike argued that there is little 'intelligence' operating here. There is no moment in time when the cat seems to have an insight about the solution to its problem. Instead, the cat's performance improves gradually over a series of trials. The cat appears to be engaging in **trial-and-error learning**, and when a reward immediately follows one of those behaviors, the learning of that action is strengthened. Thorndike referred to this strengthening as the **law of effect**. He argued that in instrumental learning, the law of effect selects from a set of random responses only those that are followed by positive consequences.

Skinner's experiments

Skinner's method of studying instrumental conditioning was simpler than Thorndike's: he studied only one response at a time. In a Skinnerian experiment, a hungry animal – usually a rat or a pigeon – is placed in a box like the one shown in Figure 7.5, which is called an *operant chamber* (also referred to as a *Skinner box*). The inside of the box is bare except for a protruding bar with a food dish beneath it. A small light above the bar can be turned on at the experimenter's discretion. Left alone in the box, the rat moves about, exploring. Occasionally it inspects the bar and presses it. The rate at which the rat first presses the bar is the *baseline level*.

Acquisition and extinction

After establishing the baseline level, the experimenter activates a food magazine located outside the box. Now, every time the rat presses the bar, a small food pellet is released into the dish. The rat eats the food pellet and soon presses the bar again. The food reinforces bar pressing, and the rate of pressing increases dramatically. If the food magazine is disconnected and pressing the bar no longer delivers food, the rate of bar pressing diminishes. An instrumental response that is not reinforced undergoes extinction, just as a classically conditioned response does.

B. F. Skinner was a pioneer in the study of instrumental conditioning.

FIGURE 7.5 Apparatus for Instrumental Conditioning. *This photograph shows an operant chamber (often called a 'Skinner box') with a magazine for delivering food pellets. The computer is used to control the experiment and record the rat's responses.*

Instrumental conditioning increases the likelihood of a response by following the behavior with a reinforcer (often something like food or water). Because the bar is always present in the Skinner box, the rat can respond to it as frequently or as infrequently as it chooses. The organism's

rate of response is therefore a useful measure of the instrumental learning; the more frequently the response occurs during a given time interval, the greater the learning.

Reinforcement versus punishment

In instrumental conditioning, an environmental event that follows behavior produces either an increase or a decrease in the probability of that behavior. **Reinforcement** refers to the process whereby the delivery of an stimulus *increases* the probability of a behavior. Reinforcement can be done by giving an appetitive stimulus (**positive reinforcement**) or by the removal of an aversive stimulus (**negative reinforcement**). In other words, there may be either a *positive* or a *negative* contingency between the behavior and reinforcement. A positive contingency means that something is given: for example, bar pressing is followed by food. A negative contingency means that something is taken away: for example, bar pressing terminates or prevents shock. *Punishment* is the converse of reinforcement: it *decreases* the probability of a behavior, and consists of the delivery of an aversive stimulus (**positive punishment**, or simply 'punishment') or the removal of an appetitive stimulus (**negative punishment** or 'omission training'). Again, note that there may be either a positive contingency between the behavior and punishment (bar pressing is followed by shock) or a negative contingency (bar pressing terminates or prevents food delivery). (See the Concept Review Table.)

Although rats and pigeons have been the favored experimental subjects, instrumental conditioning applies to many species, including our own. Indeed, instrumental conditioning has a good deal to tell us about child rearing. A particularly illuminating example is the following case. A young boy had

CONCEPT REVIEW TABLE TYPES OF REINFORCEMENT AND PUNISHMENT

Type	Definition	Effect	Example
Positive reinforcement	Delivery of a pleasant or appetitive stimulus following a behavioral response	Increases the frequency of the behavioral response	If studying is followed by a high grade on an exam, then the incidence of studying before exams will increase
Negative reinforcement	Removal of an unpleasant or aversive stimulus following a behavioral response	Increases the frequency of the behavioral response	If leaving a study area removes you from a noisy classmate, then the time you spend away from the study area will increase
Positive punishment ('Punishment')	Delivery of an unpleasant or aversive stimulus following a behavioral response	Decreases the frequency of the behavioral response	If your professor embarrasses you for asking a question in class, then the likelihood you will ask questions in class will decrease
Negative punishment ('Omission training')	Removal of a pleasant or appetitive stimulus following a behavioral response	Decreases the frequency of the behavioral response	If your girlfriend or boyfriend withholds affection whenever you watch TV, the time you spend in front of the TV will decrease

temper tantrums if he did not get enough attention from his parents, especially at bedtime. Because the parents eventually responded to the tantrums, their attention probably reinforced the boy's behavior. To eliminate the tantrums, the parents were advised to go through the normal bedtime ritual and then ignore the child's protests, painful though that might be. If the reinforcer (attention) was withheld, the behavior should be extinguished – which is just what happened. The time the child spent crying at bedtime decreased from 45 minutes to not at all over a period of only 7 days (Williams, 1959). This is an example of omission training because withholding something the boy wanted (parental attention) decreased the behavioral response (bedtime crying).

Shaping

Suppose that you want to use instrumental conditioning to teach your dog a trick – for instance, to get the mail from the slot in your front door. You cannot wait until the dog does this naturally and then reinforce it, because you may wait forever. When the desired behavior is truly novel, you have to condition it by taking advantage of natural variations in the animal's actions. To train a dog to get the mail, you can give the animal a food reinforcer each time it approaches the door, requiring it to move closer and closer to the mail for each reinforcer until finally the dog grabs the mail. This technique, called **shaping**, is reinforcing only variations in response that deviate in the direction desired by the experimenter. Animals can be taught elaborate tricks and routines by means of shaping. Two psychologists and their staff trained thousands of animals of many species for television shows, commercials, and county fairs (Breland & Breland, 1966). One popular show featured 'Priscilla, the Fastidious Pig.' Priscilla turned on the TV set, ate breakfast at a table, picked up dirty clothes and put them in a hamper, vacuumed the floor, picked out her favorite food, and took part in a quiz program by answering questions from the audience by flashing lights that indicated yes or no. She was not an unusually bright pig; in fact, because pigs grow so fast, a new 'Priscilla' was trained every 3 to 5 months. The ingenuity was not the pig's but the experimenters,' who used instrumental conditioning and shaped the pig's behavior to produce the desired result. Shaping has been used to train pigeons to locate people lost at sea (see Figure 7.6), and porpoises to retrieve underwater equipment.

Importantly, the Brelands' work also indicated that not *all* behaviors could be shaped. For example, they had great difficulty training raccoons to drop coins into a piggy bank to receive a food reward. Rather than drop the coins in the bank to obtain a food reinforcer, the raccoons would rub them together incessantly, drop them in the bank, pull them out again, and continue rubbing them together. This behavior, of course, resembles the behavior that raccoons normally display to natural food items. The behavioral predisposition of the raccoon to vigorously manipulate an object associated with food made it difficult to shape a novel response. The phenomenon of animals resorting to biologically natural behaviors is called *instinctive drift*. It reveals that instrumental conditioning, like classical conditioning, operates under biological constraints.

Conditioned reinforcers

Most of the reinforcers we have discussed are called *primary* because they satisfy basic drives. If instrumental conditioning

Pigeon sitting

Pigeon pecking key

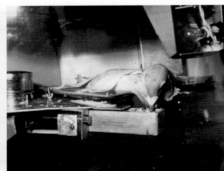
Pigeon rewarded

FIGURE 7.6 **Search and Rescue by Pigeons.** *The Coast Guard has used pigeons to search for people lost at sea. Shaping methods are used to train the pigeons to spot the color orange, the international color for life jackets. Three pigeons are strapped into a Plexiglas chamber attached to the underside of a helicopter. The chamber is divided into thirds so that each bird faces in a different direction. When a pigeon spots an orange object, or any other object, it pecks a key that buzzes the pilot. The pilot then heads in the direction indicated by the bird that responded. Pigeons are better suited than people for the task of spotting distant objects at sea. They can stare over the water for a long time without suffering eye fatigue, they have excellent color vision, and they can focus on a 60- to 80-degree area, whereas a person can focus only on a 2- to 3-degree area.*

occurred only with primary reinforcers, it would not occur very often because primary reinforcers are not that common. However, virtually any stimulus can become a *secondary* or **conditioned reinforcer**, which is a stimulus that has been consistently paired with a primary reinforcer. Conditioned reinforcers greatly increase the generality of instrumental conditioning. A minor variation in the typical instrumental conditioning experiment illustrates how conditioned reinforcement works. When a rat in a Skinner box presses a lever, a tone sounds momentarily and is followed shortly by delivery of food (the food is a primary reinforcer; the tone will become a conditioned reinforcer). After the animal has been conditioned in this way, the experimenter begins the extinction process, so that when the rat presses the lever, neither the tone nor the food occurs. In time, the animal ceases to press the lever. Then the tone is reconnected but not the food magazine. When the animal discovers that pressing the lever turns on the tone, its rate of pressing increases markedly, overcoming the extinction even though no food is delivered. The tone has acquired a reinforcing quality of its own through classical conditioning. Because the tone was reliably paired with food, it came to signal food. Secondary reinforcers apply to human behavior as well: our lives abound with conditioned reinforcers. Two of the most prevalent are money and praise. Mere praise can sustain many activities without even the promise of a primary reinforcer. And money is a powerful reinforcer because it has been paired so frequently with so many primary reinforcers – we can buy food, drink, and comfort, to mention just a few of the obvious things. Recent research shows exactly how intertwined the two reinforcers money and food are. Briers *et al.* (2006) showed that hunger affects donation behavior negatively: hungry subjects donated less money to a charity than did subjects who were not hungry. The inverse was also shown: when the researchers increased subjects' desire for money (by asking them to fantasize about winning the lottery), their

consumption of candy went up. This symmetric relation between food and money in driving their subjects' behavior suggests that money may have become a primary reinforcer for humans.

Generalization and discrimination

Again, what was true for classical conditioning holds for instrumental conditioning as well: organisms generalize what they have learned, and generalization can be curbed by discrimination training. If a young child is reinforced by her parents for petting the family dog, she will soon generalize this petting response to other dogs. Because this can be dangerous (the neighbors might have a vicious watchdog), the child's parents may provide some discrimination training so that she is reinforced when she pets the family dog but not the neighbor's.

Discrimination training will be effective to the extent that there is a discriminative stimulus (or a set of them) that clearly distinguishes cases in which the response should be made from those in which it should be suppressed. Our young child will have an easier time learning which dog to pet if her parents can point to an aspect of dogs that signals friendliness (a wagging tail, for example). In general, a discriminative stimulus will be useful to the extent that its presence predicts that a response will be followed by reinforcement and its absence predicts that the response will not be followed by reinforcement (or vice versa). Just as in classical conditioning, the predictive power of a stimulus seems to be critical to conditioning.

Schedules of reinforcement

In real life, not every instance of a behavior is reinforced. For example, hard work is sometimes followed by praise, but often it goes unacknowledged. If instrumental conditioning occurred only with continuous reinforcement, it might play a limited role in our lives. Once a behavior is established, however, it can be maintained when it is reinforced only a fraction of the time. This phenomenon, *partial reinforcement*, can be illustrated in the laboratory by a pigeon that learns to peck at a key for food. Once this instrumental response is established, the pigeon continues to peck at a high rate, even if it receives only occasional reinforcement. In some cases, pigeons that were rewarded with food an average of once every 5 minutes (12 times an hour) pecked at the key as often as 6000 times per hour – 500 pecks per pellet of food received!

Moreover, extinction following the maintenance of a response on partial reinforcement is much slower than extinction following the maintenance of a response on continuous reinforcement. Extinction of pecking in pigeons reinforced every 5 minutes takes days, whereas pigeons reinforced continuously extinguish in a matter of minutes. This phenomenon is known as the *partial-reinforcement effect*. It makes intuitive

Praise is an effective reinforcer for many people.

CONCEPT REVIEW TABLE SCHEDULES OF REINFORCEMENT

	Ratio schedules	Interval schedules
Fixed	Fixed ratio (FR): Reinforcement is provided after a fixed number of responses	Fixed interval (FI): Reinforcement is provided after a certain amount of time has elapsed since the last reinforcement
Variable	Variable ratio (VR): Reinforcement is provided after a certain number of responses, with the number varying unpredictably	Variable interval (VI): Reinforcement is provided after a certain amount of time has elapsed since the last reinforcement, with the duration of the interval varying unpredictably

sense because there is less difference between extinction and maintenance when reinforcement during maintenance is only partial.

When reinforcement occurs only some of the time, we need to know exactly how it is scheduled – after every third response? After every 5 seconds? It turns out that the schedule of reinforcement determines the pattern of responding. There are four basic schedules of reinforcement (see the Concept Review Table).

Some schedules are called **ratio schedules**, because reinforcement depends on the number of responses the organism makes. It's like being a factory worker who gets paid per piece of work finished. The ratio can be either fixed or variable. On a **fixed ratio schedule** (called an FR schedule), the number of responses that have to be made is fixed at a particular value. If the number is 5 (FR 5), 5 responses are required for reinforcement; if it is 50 (FR 50), 50 responses are required; and so on. In general, the higher the ratio, the higher the rate at which the organism responds, particularly when the organism is initially trained on a relatively low ratio (say, FR 5) and then is continuously shifted to progressively higher ratios, culminating, say, in FR 100. It is as if our factory worker initially got $5 for every 5 hems sewn, but then times got tough and he needed to do 100 hems to get $5. But perhaps the most distinctive aspect about behavior under an FR schedule is the pause in responding right after the reinforcement occurs (see Figure 7.7). It is hard for the factory worker to start on a new set of hems right after he has just finished enough to obtain a reward.

On a **variable ratio schedule** (a VR schedule), the organism is still reinforced only after making a certain number of responses, but that number varies unpredictably. In a VR 5 schedule, the number of responses needed for reinforcement may sometimes be 1, at other times 10, with an average of 5. Unlike the behavior that occurs under FR schedules, there are no pauses when the organism is operating under a VR schedule (see Figure 7.7), presumably because the organism has no way of detecting how far it is from a reinforcement. A good example of a VR schedule in everyday life is the operation of a slot machine. The number of responses (plays)

Gamblers who play the slot machines are reinforced with payoffs on a variable ratio schedule. Such a schedule can generate very high rates of responding.

needed for reinforcement (payoff) keeps varying, and the operator has no way of predicting when reinforcement will occur. Of a schedules of reinforcment, VR schedules can generate the highest rates of responding. Gamblers playing at a slot machine ('fruit machine') are reinforced on a VR schedule. This feature contributes to the 'addictiveness' of the game (Griffiths, 1993).

Other schedules of reinforcement are called **interval schedules**, because under these schedules reinforcement is available only after a certain time interval has elapsed (and the animal makes a response). Again, the schedule can be either fixed or variable. On a **fixed interval schedule** (an FI schedule), the organism is reinforced for its first response after a certain amount of time has passed since its last reinforcement. On an FI 2 (minutes) schedule, for example, reinforcement is available only when 2 minutes have elapsed since the last reinforced response; responses made during that 2-minute interval have no effect. One distinctive aspect of responding on an FI schedule is a pause that occurs immediately after reinforcement (see Figure 7.7). This post-reinforcement pause can be even longer than the one that occurs under FR schedules. Another distinctive aspect

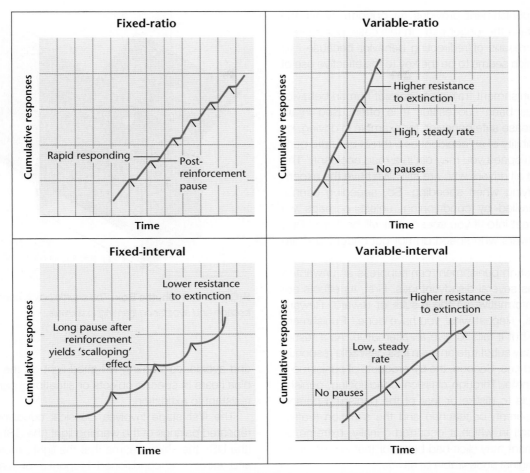

FIGURE 7.7 **Typical Patterns of Responding on the Four Basic Schedules of Reinforcement.** *Each curve plots an animal's cumulative number of responses as a function of time; the slope of the curve thus indicates the animal's rate of responding. The short tick marks on each line indicate the moment reinforcement occurred. In the curve for the FR schedule, note the horizontal segments, which correspond to pauses (they show no increase in the cumulative number of responses). In the curve for the FI schedule, note again that the horizontal segments correspond to pauses.*

of responding on an FI schedule is an increase in the rate of responding as the end of the interval approaches, producing a pattern often described as a scallop (see again Figure 7.7). A good example of an FI schedule in everyday life is mail delivery, which comes just once a day (FI 24 hours) or in some places twice a day (FI 12 hours). Right after your mail is delivered, you would not check it again, but as the end of the mail-delivery interval approaches, you will start checking again.

On a **variable interval schedule** (a VI schedule), reinforcement still depends on a certain interval having elapsed, but the interval's duration varies unpredictably. In a VI 10 (minute) schedule, for example, sometimes the critical interval is 2 minutes, sometimes 20 minutes, and so on, with an average of 10 minutes. Unlike the variations in responding under an FI schedule, organisms tend to respond at a uniform high rate when the schedule is a VI schedule (see Figure 7.7). For an example of a VI schedule in everyday life,

consider redialing a telephone number after hearing a busy signal. To receive reinforcement (getting your call through), you have to wait some time interval after your last response (dialing), but the length of that interval is unpredictable.

Aversive conditioning

Negative or aversive events, such as a shock or a painful noise, are often used in instrumental conditioning. In punishment training, a response is followed by an aversive stimulus or event, which results in the response being weakened or suppressed on subsequent occasions. It can effectively eliminate an undesirable response if it is consistent and delivered immediately after the undesired response – especially if an alternative response is rewarded. Rats that have learned to take the shorter of two paths in a maze to reach food will quickly switch to the longer one if they are shocked when taking the shorter path. The temporary suppression produced by punishment provides an opportunity for the rat to learn to take the longer path. In this case, punishment is an effective means of redirecting behavior because it is informative, which seems to be the key to the effective use of punishment.

Applying punishment training to correct human behavior has not always been successful. It is often used in an attempt to increase safe behavior, for example in driving, by using the possibility of an accident as a threat or future punishment: 'If you speed you may die in a road accident.' The problem is that all drivers who are still alive have the experience of *not* dying when speeding. So, speeding cannot really be controlled by conditioning, unless perhaps we change the threat into 'If you speed, you will be fined.' But, again, most drivers who speed do not get caught and are not fined.

So, even though punishment can suppress an unwanted response, it has several disadvantages. First, its effects are often not as informative as the results of reward. Reward essentially says, 'Repeat what you have done.' Punishment says, 'Stop it!' but it fails to give an alternative. As a result, the organism may substitute an even less desirable response for the punished one. Second, the by-products of punishment can be unfortunate. Through classical conditioning, punishment often leads to dislike or fear of the punishing person (traffic police, parent, or teacher) and the situation (traffic, home, or school) in which it occurred. Finally, extreme or painful punishment may elicit bad behavior that is more serious than the original undesirable behavior.

Escape and avoidance behavior

We have seen that punishment training can sometimes work to inhibit unwanted behaviors. But aversive events can also be used in the learning of new responses. Organisms can learn to make a response that terminates an ongoing aversive event (for example, we may leave a room if there is a painfully loud noise there): this is called **escape learning**. Often, escape learning is followed by **avoidance learning**; the organism learns to make a certain response to prevent an aversive event from even starting (for example, avoiding a certain room if it was associated with a loud noise in the past). To study escape and avoidance learning in animals, psychologists have used a device called a *shuttle box* (see Figure 7.8). The shuttle box consists of two compartments divided by a barrier. On each trial, the animal is placed in one of the compartments. At some point a warning light is flashed, and 5 seconds later the floor of that compartment is electrified. To get away from the shock, the animal must jump over the barrier into the other compartment. Initially, the rat jumps over the barrier only when the shock starts – this is escape learning. With practice, it learns to jump upon seeing the warning light, thereby avoiding the shock entirely – this is avoidance learning. An analysis of the two stages of escape

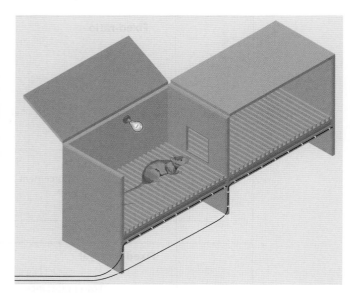

FIGURE 7.8 Shuttle Box. *The shuttle box is used to study escape and avoidance learning in animals.*

and avoidance learning will shed light on the fact that phobias (fears of specific objects or situations) can be extremely resistant to extinction.

The first stage involves classical conditioning. Through repeated pairings of the warning light (the CS) and the shock (the US), the animal learns that the light predicts the shock, and exhibits a conditioned response of fear (the CR) in response to the light alone.

The avoidance learning seems to present a puzzle: we know that a CR will extinguish if the CS is presented in the absence of the US. And that seems to be the case here: once the animal has learned to avoid being shocked (by escaping on time), the CS is no longer followed by the US (the shock). So, why doesn't the CR extinguish? What reinforces the animal for jumping over the barrier? You might say that it is the absence of the shock, but that is a non-event. The solution to this puzzle – and the second stage of our analysis – involves instrumental conditioning. The animal has learned that jumping over the barrier removes an aversive event, namely the conditioned fear itself (see Figure 7.9). Therefore, what first appears to be a non-event is actually fear, and the avoidance behavior is reinforced because it reduces this fear (Mowrer, 1947; Rescorla & Solomon, 1967).

Consider someone who has developed a particular fear – let's say, test anxiety – because of past experiences, such as failure on tests. The CR (fear) can be reduced by avoiding having to take the test, for example by sleeping through the alarm, or by asking for a later test date. The successful reduction of the aversive stimulus (the conditioned fear response) reinforces the avoidance behavior, and will strengthen it in the future. And though it may lead to

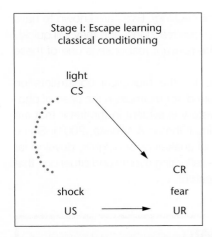
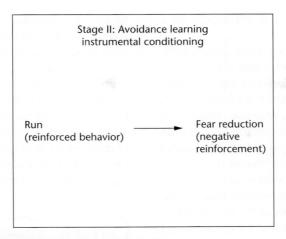

FIGURE 7.9 Two-stage Analysis of Escape and Avoidance Learning.

temporary relief, the consequences of such avoidance behavior are clearly detrimental in the long run. But what to do, when test anxiety is a real problem? Students who suffer from test anxiety will have to be convinced that their fear response is a learned reaction to past events, which can and will be unlearned with repeated experiences of successful test-taking. See Chapter 15 for further discussion of anxiety disorders and phobias.

Cognitive factors

Cognitive factors play an important role in instrumental conditioning, just as they do in classical conditioning. It is useful to view the organism in an instrumental conditioning situation as acquiring new *knowledge* about relationships between responses and reinforcers. As with classical conditioning, we want to know what factor is critical for instrumental conditioning to occur. Again, one of the options is temporal contiguity: an instrumental response is conditioned whenever it is immediately followed by reinforcement (Skinner, 1948). A more cognitive option, closely related to predictability, is that of *control*: an instrumental response is conditioned only when the organism interprets the reinforcement as being controlled by its response.

Important experiments by Maier and Seligman (1976) provide support for the control view. Their basic experiment has two stages. In the first stage, some dogs learn that whether they receive a shock or not depends on (is controlled by) their own behavior, while other dogs learn that they have no control over the shock. Think of the dogs as being tested in pairs. Both members of a pair are in a harness that restricts their movements, and occasionally the pair receives an electric shock. One member of the pair, the 'control' dog, can turn off the shock by pushing a nearby panel with its nose; the other member of the pair, the 'yoked' dog, cannot exercise any control over the shock. Whenever the control dog is shocked, so is the yoked dog, and whenever the control dog turns off

the shock, the yoked dog's shock is also terminated. The control and yoked dogs therefore receive the same amount of electrical shocks.

To find out what the dogs learned in the first stage of the experiment, a second stage is needed. In this stage, the experimenter places both dogs in a shuttle box. On each trial a tone is first sounded, indicating that the compartment the animal currently occupies is about to be subjected to an electric shock. To avoid the shock, the dog must learn to jump the barrier into the other compartment when it hears the warning tone. Control dogs learn this response rapidly – as we saw before in avoidance learning in rats. The yoked dogs are another story. Initially, the yoked dogs make no movement across the barrier, and as trials progress, their behavior becomes increasingly passive, finally lapsing into utter helplessness. Why? Because during the first stage the yoked dogs learned that shocks were not under their control. This non-control made avoidance learning in the second stage impossible. In other words: during the first stage of the experiment the animals had learned that they were *helpless*, and this 'discovery' prevents them from learning to avoid shock later on, even when they could. The phenomenon of **learned helplessness** has important implications. It supports the notion that instrumental conditioning occurs only when the organism perceives reinforcement as being under its control (Seligman, 1975). (See Chapter 15 for a detailed discussion of learned helplessness, control, and stress.)

We can also talk about these findings in terms of contingencies. We can say that instrumental conditioning occurs only when the organism perceives a contingency between its responses and reinforcement. In the first stage of the preceding study, the relevant contingency is between pushing a panel and the absence of shock. Perceiving this contingency amounts to determining that the likelihood of avoiding shock is greater when the panel is pushed than when it is not. Dogs that do not perceive this contingency in the first stage of the study appear not to look for any contingency in the second stage. This contingency approach makes it clear that the results of research on instrumental conditioning fit with the findings about the importance of predictability in classical conditioning: knowing that a CS predicts a US can be interpreted as showing that the organism has detected a contingency between the two stimuli. In both classical and instrumental conditioning, what the organism seems to learn is a contingency between two events: in classical conditioning, a behavior is contingent on a particular stimulus; in instrumental conditioning, a behavior is contingent on a particular response.

Our own ability to learn contingencies develops very early. In a study of 3-month-old infants, each infant was lying in a crib with its head on a pillow (Watson, 1967). Beneath each pillow was a switch that closed whenever the infant turned its head. For infants in the control group, whenever they turned their heads and closed the switch, a mobile on the opposite side of the crib was activated. For these infants, there was a contingency between head turning and the mobile moving – the mobile was more likely to move with a head turn than without. These infants quickly learned to turn their heads, and they reacted to the moving mobile with signs of enjoyment (they smiled and cooed). The situation is quite different for infants in the non-control group. For these infants, the mobile was made to move roughly as often as it did for infants in the control group, but whether it moved or not was not under their control: there was no contingency between head turns and the mobile movements. These infants did *not* learn to turn their heads more frequently, and after a while they showed no signs of enjoying the moving mobile at all. The mobile appears to have gained its reinforcing character when its movement could be controlled and lost it when its movement could not be controlled. Interestingly, people sometimes suffer from what has been termed an 'illusion of control': they believe that they have control over the outcome of a chance event. Langer (1975) describes gamblers who believe that their winnings in a game are the result of their skill, whereas they think of their losses as chance events. This illusion probably leads gamblers to behave extremely risky (Thompson, 1999).

Biological constraints

As with classical conditioning, biology imposes constraints on what may be learned through instrumental conditioning. The instinctive drift discussed under the 'shaping' section above is one example of that. Consider pigeons in two experimental situations: reward learning, in which the animal acquires a response that is reinforced by food, and escape learning, in which the animal acquires a response that is reinforced by the termination of shock. In the case of reward, pigeons learn much faster if the required response is pecking a key than if it is flapping their wings. In the case of escape, the opposite is true: pigeons learn faster if the required response is wing flapping than if it is pecking (Bolles, 1970). These seem inconsistent with the assumption that the same laws of learning apply to all situations, but they make sense from an ethological perspective. The reward case with the pigeons involved eating, and pecking (but not wing flapping) is part of the birds' natural eating activities. A biologically determined connection between pecking and eating is reasonable. Similarly, the escape case involved a danger situation, and the pigeon's natural reactions to danger include

flapping its wings (but not pecking). Birds are known to have a small repertoire of defensive reactions, and they will quickly learn to escape only if the relevant response is one of these natural reactions.

In humans, evidence for the biological constraints on learning has also been found, for example in the case of phobias. Our evolutionary history is evident in the fears that are readily learned by humans (Öhman & Mineka, 2001). Some phobias, such as a fear of snakes or of heights, develop far more easily than others – reflecting events and situations that were threats for our ancestors.

INTERIM SUMMARY

→ In instrumental conditioning, animals learn that their behavior has consequences. For example, a rat may learn to press a lever to obtain food reinforcement. The rate of response is a useful measure of response strength. The rate and pattern of responding during instrumental conditioning is determined by schedules of reinforcement.

→ Reinforcers increase the probability of a response, whereas punishers decrease the probability of behavioral responses. Reinforcers and punishers can be arranged in either positive or negative contingencies with a particular behavior.

CRITICAL THINKING QUESTIONS

1 Suppose that you are taking care of an 8 year old who won't make his bed and, in fact, doesn't seem to know how to begin the task. How might you use instrumental conditioning techniques to teach him to make his bed?

2 Sometimes a person may be fearful of a neutral object, such as loose buttons, but not know why. How could you explain this phenomenon in terms of principles presented in this chapter?

LEARNING AND COGNITION

This is a famous quote by Watson: 'Give me a dozen healthy infants, well-formed, and my own specified world to bring them up in and I'll guarantee to take any one at random and train him to become any type of specialist I might select – doctor, lawyer, artist, merchant-chief and yes, even beggar-man and thief, regardless of his talents, penchants, tendencies, abilities, vocations, and race of his ancestors' (1930,

p. 104). The doctrine of early behaviorists can be summarized as follows: to predict human behavior – to control it, even – we need to know only the situation that the human reacts to. And to study the mechanics of learning, it suffices to study simple animals. Since the assumption is that learning results only from experience (with stimulus–response relationships, and with the consequence of responses), there is no reason to study or assume 'higher mental processes.'

We have seen that the empirical approach to the study of behavior had a considerable impact on the history of psychology, especially in the USA. We have also seen that many of the experiments that were carried out by behaviorists later in the century revealed the importance of cognition. Recall the experiments by Rescorla, showing that not all stimulus–response relationships are learned equally easily (contingency matters), as well as the experiments by Seligman, showing that reinforcers can lose their 'power' if the organism perceives no control over them. These results highlight the importance of cognitions held by the animals.

But the basic behaviorist doctrine actually never went unchallenged. Already in the 1930s, Edward C. Tolman, an American psychologist, described findings showing latent learning in simple animals: he was able to show that animals were learning, while their behavior did not change in a corresponding way (Tolman & Honzik, 1930). In a typical study, rats would learn to run a complicated maze. One group of rats was rewarded with food for finding their way through the maze: these rats improved gradually in solving the maze, over the course of a number of days. A second group was not rewarded initially, and consequently showed little improvement in solving the maze. However, when a reward was introduced for this second group of rats, their performance almost instantly caught up with the performance of the first group. This showed that the second group of rats had 'latent knowledge' of the maze, which was only expressed behaviorally once the food was introduced. Tolman concluded that a rat running through a complex maze was not learning a sequence of right- and left-turning responses, but rather was developing a cognitive map – a mental representation of the layout of the maze (Tolman, 1932). And more importantly: that this learning occurs even when the animal is not reinforced.

Observational learning

Humans, too, learn many things without immediately being reinforced for the behavior. Consider how you learned to give a presentation in class: when you prepared for it, you probably considered how others go about giving a lecture, and you might have even picked up a book for some advice on how to structure your presentation. Clearly, you did not learn how to give a successful presentation through simple conditioning, which would involve randomly trying out many possible behaviors and repeating only those that were rewarded with a good grade. Rather, you learned through imitation and observational learning: you copied the behavior of others, whose behavior you observed to be successful.

Important research on observational learning was carried out by Albert Bandura. Early on, Bandura emphasized that observational learning occurs through the principles of operant conditioning (Bandura & Walters, 1963): models inform us about the consequences of our behaviors. Models often are actual persons whose behaviors we observe, but they can also be more abstract (for example, the written instructions found in a book). Reinforcement in many cases is 'vicarious': the imitator expects to be reinforced just like the model was.

One of Bandura's early studies concerned the observational learning of aggressive behavior in young children (Bandura et al., 1961), the 'Bobo doll study.' A Bobo doll is an inflatable toy with a heavy base that ensures that the doll springs back up when it is pushed over. One group of children was shown adult models behaving aggressively towards a Bobo doll (see Figure 7.10). Another group of children was exposed to adult models behaving non-aggressively. Afterwards, the children were led into a room in which they could play with many different toys. The first group of children was shown to display more aggressive behavior towards the Bobo doll than the second group of children. Bandura later showed that the effects are very similar if the children are exposed to aggressive behavior by models presented in film sequences on a TV screen (Bandura et al., 1963). For this reason, Bandura's work is often cited in discussions concerning the effects of television violence on aggressive behavior in children. Increased aggressive tendency after exposure to violent media content has been reported – both in the short term in laboratory studies (see, for example, Anderson et al., 2003a) as well as over the lifetime, in longitudinal studies (Huesman et al., 2003). More recently, studies focusing on the aggressive content in video games have shown similar effects (Anderson, 2004).

In his later work, Bandura emphasized the cognitive abilities that are necessary for observational learning to occur (Bandura, 1977, 2001). The learner must be able to (1) pay attention to the model's behavior and observe its consequences, (2) remember what was observed, (3) be able to reproduce the behavior, and (4) be motivated to do so. In other words: observational learning involves the ability to imagine and anticipate – thoughts and intentions are essential. Recent evidence suggests that mirror neurons play a role in observational learning. Mirror neurons are active when a subject observes someone else perform a behavior, but even more active when that behavior is carried out with a certain purpose or in a meaningful context (Catteano & Rizzolatti, 2009). In other words: mirror neurons are involved in understanding others' actions and intentions.

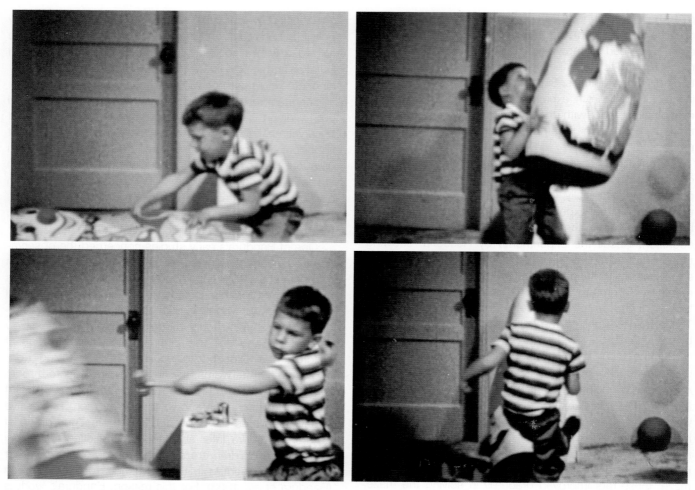

FIGURE 7.10 Bandura's 'Bobo Doll Study.' *Bandura showed that children learned to behave aggressively towards a Bobo doll toy, after watching a model behave similarly.*

Most of Bandura's work focuses on the importance of cognition in social learning in humans. In his view, humans are agents of their own experiences, not 'undergoers' (Bandura, 2001). His theory on social learning is further discussed in Chapter 13. For now, it suffices to say that Bandura's 'agentic perspective' draws our attention to the fact that cognitions motivate actions, and that a sense of self-efficacy (an individual's belief in their own effectiveness) is essential for complex and social learning. If you believe that you are simply incapable of giving a good presentation in class, you are unlikely to motivate yourself to plan and anticipate the effects of the decisions you make regarding that talk.

Prior beliefs

Humans and animals alike are very sensitive to learning relationships between stimuli, as we have seen. When relationships between stimuli or events are less than perfectly predictable, humans can even estimate the degree of objective relationships between stimuli (Wasserman, 1990). This has been shown with experimental tasks that were novel to

the subjects, and that did not concern stimuli about which the subjects had any prior beliefs. But when similar experiments are carried out using stimuli about which the subjects do hold prior beliefs, the situation changes in an interesting way: such studies show that prior beliefs can constrain what the subjects learn. This again indicates that learning involves processes in addition to those that form associations between inputs.

In such studies, a different pair of stimuli – for example, a picture and a word – is presented on each trial, and the participant's task is to learn the relationship between the members of the pairs. Subjects might detect, for example, that certain pictures are more likely to appear alongside certain words. Some striking evidence for the role of prior beliefs comes from cases in which there is no objective association between the pairs of stimuli, but participants nevertheless detect such a relationship. The relationships they reported were ones that they probably believed before participating in the experiment – for example: that large eyes are associated with suspiciousness or that a large mouth is associated with a desire to be taken care of by others. These nonexistent but

CUTTING EDGE RESEARCH DO SINGING MICE PROVIDE INSIGHTS INTO THE EVOLUTION OF HUMAN SPEECH?

Julia Fischer, German Primate Center

Human language is the foundation for the expression of thoughts and concepts, the formation of societal institutions, and the emergence of cumulative culture. Language can be characterized in terms of its symbolic and syntactic nature. Both symbolism and syntax are based on conventionalization, and thus the ability to learn (Fitch, 2010). Thus, spoken language requires the capacity for vocal production and auditory comprehension learning. Somewhat surprisingly, comparative studies revealed that within the primate order, vocal production learning is restricted to humans. Monkeys and apes, in contrast, lack the ability to vocally imitate, and they do not rely on auditory input to develop their species-specific communication sounds (Hammerschmidt & Fischer, 2008).

As humans are the only primates that have direct volitional control over their sound production, this raised the question which genes might be involved in the reorganization of the brain that enabled humans to talk. One candidate gene in this context is FOXP2. Intriguingly, analyses of the evolution of the FOXP2 gene identified two amino acid substitutions that became fixed in the human lineage after its separation from the chimpanzee (Enard *et al.,* 2002). There are now a number of studies that investigated the effects of variation in the FOXP2 alleles on vocal production in mice models (reviewed in Fischer & Hammerschmidt, 2012; Graham & Fisher, 2012). Mice pups emit ultrasonic isolation calls when separated from their littermates, while male and female adult mice produce long bouts of vocalizations, termed 'songs' when confronted with intruders or in the mating context. Mice with two non-functional FOXP2 alleles exhibit severe developmental deficits and die around 3 weeks after birth. Not surprisingly, they also produce fewer calls. More interesting was the question whether mice carrying the human version of the FOXP2 gene would experience a gain of function, and perhaps produce more elaborate calls. Their calls, however, revealed only subtle differences in call structure compared to their wild-type littermates. More importantly, mice carrying the human variant had lower dopamine concentrations in the brain and an increased synaptic plasticity in the striatum, indicating that the humanized FOXP2 allele affects the basal ganglia, which are involved in motor learning. Thus, the FOXP2 protein probably plays a role in motor planning and motor learning in general. It should also be noted that FOXP2 is a transcription factor that affects the function of many genes and is involved, for instance, in the development of the lungs, heart, and other organs (Graham & Fisher 2012).

Recent studies raised the question whether mice are suitable models to study the evolution of vocal learning. Just as their non-human primate cousins, mice do not need to learn their songs from conspecifics. Deaf mice, for instance, show no differences in call structure or occurrence from their hearing littermates (Hammerschmidt *et al.,* 2012). Irrespective of this restriction, mice USVs have shown to be highly informative in studies of the genetic foundations of social behaviour, specifically autism spectrum disorder, where mice models for autism spectrum disorder produce fewer calls in social contexts. Thus, while their contribution to the evolution of vocal learning might be limited, they may provide important insights into the genetic foundations of social behaviour (Fischer & Hammerschmidt, 2012).

---

plausible relationships detected by the subjects are referred to as *spurious associations* (Chapman & Chapman, 1969). The fact that humans are prone to detect associations or even causal relationships between events when in fact there are none, can also be explained from an evolutionary perspective. Statistical analyses show that in circumstances where the probability that two events are really associated is weak, it can sometimes be advantageous to assume that a relationship does exist (Foster & Kokko, 2009). Superstitious behavior might be adaptive! Some authors even argue that this insight holds the key to explaining the evolution of religious behavior in humans (Hood, 2009).

Even when there is an objective association to be learned, prior beliefs affect what subjects actually learn. This was shown in studies similar to the one described above (Jennings *et al.,* 1982). On each of a set of trials, participants were presented with two measures of an individual's honesty taken from two completely different situations. For example, one measure might have been how often a young boy copied another student's homework in school, and the second an indication of how often that same boy was dishonest at home. Most people believe (erroneously) that two measures of the same trait (such as honesty) will always be highly correlated. This is the critical prior belief. In fact, the objective relationship between the two measures of honesty varied across different conditions of the experiment, sometimes being quite low. The participants' task was to estimate the strength of this relationship by choosing a number between 0 (which indicated no relation) and 100 (a perfect relation). The results showed that participants consistently overestimated the strength of the relationship. Their prior belief that an honest person is honest in all situations led them to see more than was there.

The results of these studies are reminiscent of what we called top-down processing in perception (see Chapter 5), in which perceivers combine their expectations of what they are likely to see with the actual input to yield a final percept. In top-down processing in learning, the learner combines prior belief about an associative relationship with the objective input about that relationship to yield a final estimate of the strength of that relationship.

The importance of prior beliefs in human learning strengthens the case for a cognitive approach to learning. The research also has a connection to the ethological approach to learning. Just as rats and pigeons may be constrained to learning only associations that evolution has prepared them for, so we humans seem to be constrained to learn associations that our prior beliefs have prepared us for. Without prior constraints of some sort, perhaps there would simply be too many potential associations to consider, and associative learning would be chaotic, if not impossible.

INTERIM SUMMARY

➡ According to the cognitive perspective, the crux of learning is an organism's ability to represent aspects of the world mentally and then operate on these mental representations rather than on the world itself.

➡ Learning through imitation and observation happens as a result of vicarious reinforcement: by observing a model's behavior, the imitator expects to be reinforced just like the model was.

➡ When learning relationships between stimuli that are not perfectly predictive, people often invoke prior beliefs.

CRITICAL THINKING QUESTIONS

1 Do you believe that there are differences between how we learn facts and how we learn motor skills? If so, what are some of those differences?

2 When a rat learns to swim for a food reward in a T-shaped maze, it will remember the location of the reward (say, in the left arm of the T) if the maze is drained and the rat is allowed to run for the food. What does this tell you about the nature of the learning that has occurred?

LEARNING AND THE BRAIN

The transition from behaviorism to a more cognitive approach to the study of learning was also stimulated by ideas concerning the brain. The Canadian researcher Donald Hebb

contributed much to early theories about learning and the brain; his ideas have been very influential in the field of behavioral neuroscience.

We have seen that early behaviorists focused on the study of observable events, rather than on mental processes. Hebb saw humans as biological organisms and the product of evolution. He believed that mental processes should be regarded as processes that involve the nervous system and the brain – and that learning is a process that involves *changes in neural activity*. Moreover, he believed that it was possible to speculate about these processes in a meaningful way – a clear departure from the influential ideas of behaviorism at that time. Hebb formulated ideas about learning and the brain, that were inferences based on observations (Hebb, 1966).

Hebb's main contribution to the study of learning concerns his ideas about possible neurological changes underlying learning. Hebb hypothesized that if input from neuron A repeatedly increases the firing rate of neuron B, then the connection between neurons A and B will grow stronger (Hebb, 1958). In other words: repetition of the same response leads to permanent changes at the synapses between neurons. This idea is known as the **Hebbian learning rule**. At Hebb's time, this notion was a theoretical speculation. Current knowledge of the biochemistry underlying neurological changes has confirmed Hebb's ideas, as we will see.

In this section we will discuss **neural plasticity**: the ability of the neural system to change in response to experience. To appreciate these ideas, you need to recall from Chapter 2 the basic structure of a neural connection and how it transmits an impulse. An impulse is transmitted from one neuron to another by the axon of the sending neuron. Because the axons are separated by the synaptic gap, the sender's axon secretes a neurotransmitter, which diffuses across the synaptic gap and stimulates the receiving neuron. The key ideas regarding learning are (1) that a change in the synapse is the neural basis of learning, and (2) that the effect of this change is to make the synapse more (or less) efficient.

Habituation and sensitization

To understand the neural basis of complex psychological phenomena, it is best to examine simple forms of learning and memory. Perhaps the most elementary form of learning is non-associative learning. Habituation and sensitization are examples of this type of learning. During habituation, a behavioral response, such as orienting to an unfamiliar sound, decreases over successive presentations of that stimulus. During sensitization, a behavioral response increases during presentations of intense stimuli, such as very loud noises. In both cases, learned changes in behavior can persist for hours to days.

To study these learning processes at the neural level, a team of researchers led by Nobel Prize winner Eric Kandel chose to work with an organism with a very simple nervous system: the marine slug, *Aplysia californica* (Kandel *et al.*, 1991). *Aplysia* has proven to be an excellent experimental model for studying non-associative learning, because it has a simple and accessible nervous system. Learning in *Aplysia* has been studied by measuring the gill withdrawal reflex, which can be elicited by gentle mechanical stimulation of the gill or surrounding tissue. The gill withdrawal reflex is a defensive response that protects the fragile gill from injury.

When the gill is lightly stimulated with a water jet, the gill is withdrawn. However, repeated stimulation of the gill produces weaker and weaker withdrawal responses. Researchers have shown that this habituation learning is accompanied by a decrease in the amount of neurotransmitter secreted by gill sensory neurons onto a motor neuron that controls gill withdrawal (Figure 7.11).

The gill withdrawal reflex also exhibits sensitization. If an intense stimulus, such as an electric shock to the tail or head is administered, then the light touch to the gill will elicit a much larger withdrawal response. Like habituation, sensitization learning involves a change in synaptic transmission between sensory and motor neurons that control the gill. In this case, the intense stimulus causes an increase in the amount of neurotransmitter secreted by the sensory neuron. This increase depends on the activation of interneurons that release serotonin onto the gill sensory neurons. These findings provide relatively direct evidence that elementary learning is mediated by synaptic changes at the neuronal level.

Classical conditioning

What about associative learning? Do synaptic changes like the ones just described mediate classical conditioning? Indeed, researchers have proposed a neural model of classical conditioning in *Aplysia* that is remarkably similar to that for sensitization (Hawkins & Kandel, 1984). Incredible progress has also been made in understanding the neural mechanisms of classical conditioning in mammals, including

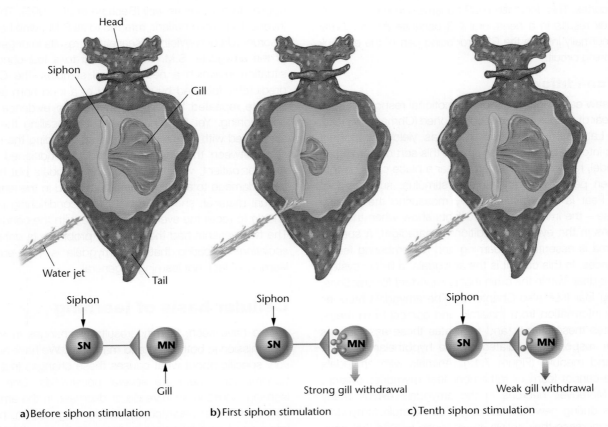

a) Before siphon stimulation   **b)** First siphon stimulation   **c)** Tenth siphon stimulation

FIGURE 7.11 Habituation in *Aplysia californical.* *(a) Before mechanical stimulation of the siphon, the gill is extended. (b) When water is squirted on the siphon for the first time during habituation training, the gill withdraws vigorously. A simple circuit involving siphon sensory neurons (SN) that form excitatory synaptic contacts onto motor neurons (MN) mediates gill withdrawal. (c) After the tenth siphon stimulus, the magnitude of gill withdrawal is small. The gill withdrawal response has habituated. Habituation is mediated by a decrease in pre-synaptic neurotransmitter release at the SN-MN synapse.*

humans. Two experimental models have been used with great success: eyeblink conditioning and fear conditioning.

Eyeblink conditioning

When a stimulus, such as an air puff (the US), is directed at the eye, it elicits a reflexive blink. This unconditional eyeblink response can be conditioned if a CS, such as a tone, precedes the puff. After training, the CS will come to elicit eyeblink CRs even when the air puff is not presented.

Detailed mapping studies in rabbits by Richard Thompson and colleagues have revealed the neural circuitry in this form of classical conditioning (Thompson & Krupa, 1994). The essential site of synaptic plasticity appears to reside in the cerebellum. Animals with cerebellar lesions cannot learn or remember the conditioned eyeblink (although they show normal eyeblink URs). Eyeblink conditioning is associated with changes in synaptic transmission in the cerebellum. This change is called **long-term depression** (LTD) and is associated with a long-lasting decrease ('depression') in synaptic transmission at synapses in the cerebellar cortex. This decrease in CS transmission in the cerebellar cortex results in a behavioral CR because the cerebellar cortex normally inhibits the CR-producing part of the eyeblink conditioning circuit.

Fear conditioning

As we saw earlier in this chapter, emotional responses such as the fear of snakes are easily conditioned (Öhman & Mineka, 2001). Laboratory work with rats has yielded important insights into the brain mechanisms of this sort of learning. In this model, rats are conditioned to fear a place or a cue that has been paired with an aversive stimulus, such as foot shock. Fear is often assessed by measuring the freezing response – the immobility that rodents show when they are afraid. As in the eyeblink conditioning paradigm, a specific brain area is essential for learning and remembering fearful experiences. In this case it is the amygdala, a limbic system structure deep within the brain that is important for emotions, including fear (see also Chapter 2). The amygdala receives sensory information from thalamic and cortical brain areas, associates these stimuli, and translates these associations into fear responses mediated by the hypothalamus, midbrain, and medulla (Figure 7.12). Animals with amygdala damage cannot learn or remember fear memories (Maren, 2001). Moreover, neurons in the amygdala exhibit many changes during new fear learning. For example, amygdala neurons increase their activity in response to CSs that have been associated with aversive UCSs. It appears that learning in the amygdala is mediated by **long-term potentiation** (LTP), which is a persistent increase in synaptic transmission in pathways that send CS information to the amygdala (Rogan & LeDoux, 1996).

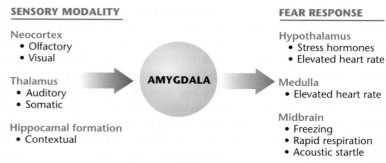

FIGURE 7.12 Neural Circuit for Classical Fear Conditiong. *The amygdala receives sensory information from many sensory areas, including the thalamus, neocortex, and hippocampus. The amygdala associates this information during fear conditioning and then generates fear CRs by projecting to brain areas, such as the midbrain, hypothalamus, and medulla, that mediate a number of different fear responses.*

Hence, in both eyeblink conditioning and fear conditioning, changes in synaptic transmission in defined brain areas are responsible for the behavioral changes that accompany associative learning.

Another study shows that what holds for other mammals applies to humans as well (Bechara *et al.*, 1995). This study involved a human patient, referred to as S.M., who had a rare disorder (Urbach–Wiethe disease) that results in degeneration of the amygdala. S.M. was exposed to a fear-conditioning situation in which a neutral visual stimulus (the CS) was predictably followed by the sound of a loud horn (the US). Despite repeated trials, S.M. showed no evidence of fear conditioning. Yet S.M. had no trouble recalling the events associated with the fear conditioning, including the relationship between the conditioned and unconditioned stimuli. Another patient, who had a normal amygdala but had suffered damage to a brain structure involved in the learning of factual material, showed normal fear conditioning but was unable to recall the events associated with the conditioning. The two patients had the opposite problems (a *double dissociation*) indicating that the amygdala is involved in the learning of fear, not learning in general.

Cellular basis of learning

As we have seen, learning results in changes in synaptic transmission in both slugs and mammals. We have not been very specific about what causes these changes in synaptic transmission. There are several possibilities. One is that learning results in an increase or decrease in the amount of neurotransmitter secreted by the sending neuron, perhaps because of an increase or decrease in the number of axon terminals that secrete the neurotransmitter (as we saw with sensitization and habituation in the *Aplysia*). Alternatively, there may be no change in the amount of neurotransmitter sent, but there may be a change in the number of post-synaptic receptors. Other possibilities are that the synapse could change in size or that entirely new synapses could be established. All of these changes are examples of **synaptic plasticity**: changes in the morphology (form and structure) and/or physiology of synapses involved in learning and memory. Indeed, learning may also be accompanied by the growth of new neurons (Gould *et al.*, 1999; van Praag *et al.*, 1999).

A critical advance in understanding the cellular basis of memory was made when the synapses in certain brain areas were studied (Berger, 1984; Bliss & Lømo, 1973). For example, rapid electrical stimulation of synapses in the hippocampus causes an enhancement in the magnitude of synaptic responses that lasts for days or even weeks (Figure 7.13). This long-term potentiation requires a special

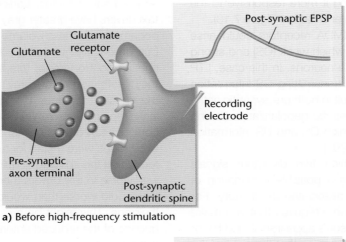

a) Before high-frequency stimulation

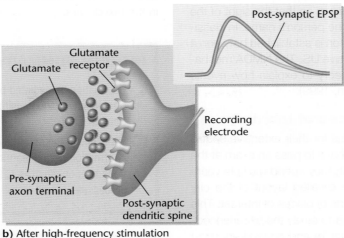

b) After high-frequency stimulation

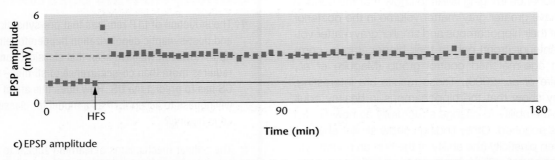

c) EPSP amplitude

FIGURE 7.13 Long-term Potentiation in the Hippocampus. *(a) Before high-frequency stimulation (HFS), pre-synaptic glutamate release activates post-synaptic glutamate receptors to produce an excitatory post-synaptic potential (EPSP). (b) After high-frequency stimulation of the pre-synaptic neuron, the post-synaptic EPSP is greatly increased in amplitude. This increase is due to an enhancement of pre-synaptic neurotransmitter release and an increase in the number of post-synaptic glutamate receptors. (c) Graph illustrating the amplitude of the EPSP before and after HFS. Long-term potentiation is indicated by the persistent increase in EPSP amplitude.*

type of neurotransmitter receptor, the NMDA receptor (Malinow *et al.,* 1994; Zalutsky & Nicoll, 1990). The NMDA receptor is unlike other receptors, in that two conditions must be satisfied for the receptor to open. First, pre-synaptic glutamate must bind to the NMDA receptor. Second, the post-synaptic membrane in which the receptor resides must be strongly depolarized. Once opened, the NMDA receptor allows a very large number of calcium ions to flow into the neuron. That influx of ions appears to cause a long-term change in the membrane of the neuron, making it more responsive to the initial signal when it recurs at a later time (see Figure 7.13).

Interestingly, activation of NMDA receptors could arise during classical conditioning, in which weak (CS) and strong (US) inputs converge onto single neurons. In this case, LTP would be induced at synapses transmitting CS information because conditioning would result in both pre-synaptic activity (during the CS) and post-synaptic depolarization (during the US) in the neurons upon which CS and US information converge (Maren & Fanselow, 1996).

Such a mechanism, in which two divergent signals strengthen a synapse, provides a possible explanation of how separate events become associated in memory. For example, learning someone's name requires that you make an association between the person's appearance and his or her name. LTP strengthens synapses so that the sight of the person will prompt you to recall the person's name. In classical fear conditioning, an association is established between a relatively neutral CS and an aversive US. The NMDA mechanism thus offers an intriguing theory to explain how events are associated in memory (Maren, 1999).

Structural consequences of learning

Taxi drivers in London are famous for their extensive spatial memory. All London taxi drivers have to pass an exam at the Public Carriage Office. To pass it, they spend multiple years acquiring 'The Knowledge': the detailed layout of the city with 25 000 streets and thousands of places of interest. This makes them excellent candidates to study the experienced-based plasticity in the brain. Maguire and co-workers used magnetic resonance imaging (MRI) to show that the London taxi drivers have greater gray matter volume in the posterior (back) part of their hippocampus and smaller gray matter volume in the anterior (front) part of their hippocampus, compared to an age-matched control group (Maguire *et al.,* 2000; Maguire *et al.,* 2003). These results are interesting, because they show that the hippocampus in healthy adult humans has the ability to change structurally as new spatial knowledge is acquired. Other findings show similar environmentally driven plasticity (the ability of the human neural system to change structurally in response to specific demands). For example: Draginski *et al.* (2004) showed structural changes in the brains of subjects who trained their juggling skills. Musicians also show an increase in gray matter volume in motor and auditory areas, associated with time spent

practicing and practice intensity (Gaser and Schlaugh, 2003). Maguire and her co-workers directly compared London taxi drivers to a control group who also spend all day driving in busy London: London bus drivers (Maguire *et al.,* 2006). The two groups of subjects were similar on many dimensions (driving experience, stress levels, age, handedness, education, IQ) but differed in one important way: whereas taxi drivers navigate the city freely (relying on their superior memory of the city's layout), bus drivers use only a constrained set of routes. Earlier MRI findings were replicated: taxi drivers have greater gray matter volume in posterior hippocampus and less volume in anterior hippocampus than bus drivers (Maguire *et al.,* 2006). Because of the carefully chosen control group, this finding lends further support to the hypothesis that the gray matter differences are a result of the specific demands placed on spatial memory. Interestingly, the study also revealed that there might be a price that London's taxi drivers pay for acquiring 'The Knowledge.' The two groups were tested for functional differences, and it was found that the ability to acquire new visuo-spatial information was worse in taxi drivers than in bus drivers. In fact, the taxi drivers did worse than would be expected for healthy men their age. This might be a cognitive trade-off, and a consequence of the reduced anterior hippocampus volume found in the taxi drivers.

INTERIM SUMMARY

➜ Habituation is mediated by a decrease in synaptic transmission, and sensitization by an increase in transmission.

➜ Synapses in the mammalian brain are involved in storing information during learning. Increases in synaptic transmission, such as LTP, are part of these learning processes.

CRITICAL THINKING QUESTIONS

1 The induction of LTP requires that pre-synaptic activity and post-synaptic depolarization happen together in time. However, we have seen that classical conditioning requires more than co-occurrence of stimuli – the CS has to predict the US. How does this affect your willingness to accept LTP as a model for classical conditioning?

2 The cellular mechanisms of learning appear to be similar in a wide range of animal species. For example, learning in the sea slug and the rat are mediated by changes in synaptic transmission. Why are these learning mechanisms so similar?

LEARNING AND MOTIVATION

Coming to the end of this chapter on learning, you may be surprised to have read preciously little about the kind of learning you are engaging in at this very moment: studying. We have focused instead on very basic learning processes. However, psychology does have much to say about the kind of processes involved in the *how* and the *why* of complex learning. Most of this will be covered in the next couple of chapters in this book: the 'how' of complex human learning is described in Chapters 8 and 9, which address memory and cognition, respectively. Questions regarding the 'why' of certain behaviors will be addressed in Chapter 10, which concerns motivation. In this section, we will briefly review some of the most relevant theories that tie concepts from the field of motivation to the study of complex human learning.

Learning is more enjoyable and more effective when you are intrinsically motivated.

Arousal

We have already discussed some of Hebb's work on the neural underpinnings of learning. Hebb also formulated an arousal theory of motivation. This aspect of his work was also instrumental in 'closing the gap' between the behavioral and the physiological approaches to learning. **Arousal** has both a physiological and a psychological dimension. Physiologically, the term refers to the level of alertness of an organism. Psychologically, the term refers to the tension that can accompany different levels of arousal, ranging from calmness to anxiety. In Hebb's view, arousal is an important motivational concept (Hebb, 1955). He proposed that any organism is motivated to maintain that level of arousal which is appropriate for the behavior it is engaged in. Hebb's insights were based on the **Yerkes–Dodson law** (Yerkes & Dodson, 1908), which relates performance to arousal. This law states that most tasks are best performed at intermediate levels of physiological arousal. Since very complex tasks have enough arousal associated with them, they drive the individual to seek out calmness. Very simple tasks, on the other hand, can become boring at low levels of arousal. According to Hebb, the bored individual will seek out other activities or novel stimuli to increase arousal. Others have even argued that the **exploratory behavior** of humans (our desire to discover and learn novel things) is the result of a desire for stimulation, which can be explained by arousal theory (Berlyne, 1966).

From incentives to goals

The history of the study of motivation mirrors what we saw in the history of the study of learning. Early theorists focused on **incentives**: a behavior is motivated by its expected reward – for example: a hungry animal is driven to eat because that will reduce the hunger it experiences (Hull, 1943). Hebb (1966), Tolman (1951), as well as others at the time, pointed out that many human behaviors cannot be motivated by the expectation of an immediate reward. Consider again the example of studying: you are probably motivated to study this book partly because you would like to do well in the course and attain your degree. Your desire to graduate is a long-term goal that motivates your current behavior – an example of complex *goal-oriented behavior*. It is clear that cognition plays a role in our ability to anticipate the long-term consequences of current behavior.

Some of the most complex human behavior can be said to arise from our psychological needs, and have to do with intellectual and emotional aspects of our functioning – our needs for social belonging and self-esteem, for example. The study of human emotion (the topic of Chapter 11) is closely linked to the study of motivation.

Intrinsic motivation and learning

In a cognitive approach to the study of motivation, the emphasis is on the individual's understanding and interpretation of their own actions: why do we think we do things? In other words: what do we *attribute* our own motivations to? Ask yourself why you are studying this chapter, right now. Is it because you are interested in the material, and comprehending it gives you a sense of competence and pride? If so, you are **intrinsically motivated** by these feelings. Or perhaps you are studying because you think it is necessary in order to do well on your exam and get a good grade in your course. If that is the case, you are **extrinsically motivated** by the external rewards that you anticipate.

Research has shown that intrinsically motivated individuals are more persistent at a task, that their memory of complex concepts is better, and that they handle complex material in cognitively more creative ways (Deci *et al.*, 1999).

SEEING BOTH SIDES
WHAT ARE THE BASES OF SOCIAL LEARNING?

SOCIAL LEARNING CANNOT BE EXPLAINED BY ASSOCIATIVE LEARNING

Juan Carlos Gómez, School of Psychology, University of St. Andrews

Social learning is a complex affair relying upon a plurality of cognitive and motivational mechanisms in which associative learning plays only a limited role. I will illustrate this claim with the case of *gaze following* – looking in the same direction as others to identify their objects of attention, a key social cognitive skill that develops during the first year of life, but not through associative learning. This was dramatically, albeit unwittingly, demonstrated by Corkum and Moore (1998) in an experiment with 8–9-month-old infants who had not yet acquired gaze following. They wanted to demonstrate that gaze following is acquired through selectively reinforced associations. Thus, they arranged for a group of children to consistently find a reward when they looked in the same direction as an adult, whereas a second group found the reward in the direction opposite to the adult's attention. If gaze following is learned through simple association, this group of children should have learned to look in the direction *opposite to* the adult. However, they were completely unable to learn this reverse, unnatural contingency. In contrast, children in the normal contingency group immediately learned to follow the gaze of the adult. Even more importantly, children in the reverse contingency group spontaneously learned to follow gaze in the natural direction, despite being rewarded for the opposite! Gaze direction is not just an arbitrary stimulus: there seems to be something intrinsically directional in gaze that tightly constraints what can be learned and how it is learned.

Recent claims that infant gaze following can be explained by associative learning (e.g., Paulus, 2011) confuse outcomes with processes of learning. Gaze following may indeed lead to coding a type of 'association' (a relation) between an agent and an object, but the underlying process is not associative learning. For example, Paulus showed 14-month-old infants a person looking at one of two objects. When the infants later saw the same person looking midway between the objects, they still looked more at the previously attended Object 1, whereas if the objects were shown without the person present, they attended more to the previously neglected Object 2. Paulus concludes that the infants had formed an association between the stimulus 'Person' and the stimulus 'Object 1,' such that seeing the 'Person' automatically primed their attention to the associated 'Object 1.'

However, the very essence of gaze following – how infants' attention can go from an agent's gaze to a particular object with which no physical connection exists – remains unexplained and is taken for granted by this model. Why should infants link another person's gaze to a particular object in the first place, if no physical 'line of gaze' associates them? As the earlier experiment by Corkum and Moore (1998) demonstrated, this is not a learned association. Moreover, in another condition of Paulus' experiment, when an agent looked at Object 1 four times without doing anything else, and then the agent started a grasping action, infants did not anticipate she would act upon Object 1. In contrast, infants who just once saw the agent grasping Object 1 instead of just looking at it, anticipated that she would again grasp Object 1. The simple association model fails to explain why the gaze-established associative prime between Agent and Object 1 fails to operate in the action trial: if the presence of the agent automatically primes associative attention to Object 1, infants should still show a preference to look first at this object. These results are better explained by a model positing that infants code *intentional relations* between agents and objects (e.g., Gómez, 2008). Because the agent repeatedly failed to act upon the object she was looking at, infants learned that the agent was not likely to act upon that object.

That social learning does not occur by simple associative learning also explains the difficulty in teaching children with autism basic social skills like gaze following. Children with autism can be good at associative learning (it is used to teach them adaptive behaviors, such as dressing, or extinguish undesirable habits, such as self-injury). In an experiment, children with autism easily learned the meaning of an invented word broadcast from a loudspeaker when they touched a particular toy. However, typical children failed to learn word meanings with this method – they need the social context of a person *looking at* the named object to learn word meanings through gaze following (Baron-Cohen *et al.*, 1997). Children with autism frequently seem to engage in pure associative learning, and this may lead to insufficient or maladaptive social learning (e.g., learning the wrong meaning of words coincidentally uttered while they were handling an object). They are good at detecting simple and straightforward physical contingencies, but they have difficulty dealing with the imperfect, context-dependent, contingencies of social interaction. For this, specific social cognitive adaptations that go beyond simple associative learning are needed. The case of autism dramatically illustrates the limitations of associative learning in explaining the complexity of social learning and cognition.

SEEING BOTH SIDES

SEEING BOTH SIDES
WHAT ARE THE BASES OF SOCIAL LEARNING?

LEARNING, NOT INSTINCT, DETERMINES BEHAVIOUR: SOCIAL OR OTHERWISE

Phil Reed, Swansea University

In the early twentieth century, a great debate raged between those who believed that behavior is best explained by learning (e.g., behavioral psychologists, such as Watson), and those who believed that behavior is best accounted for by inherited instincts (e.g., 'instinct psychologists,' such as McDougall). This debate remains central to understanding the great theories in psychology. At the height of this debate, Holt (1931, p. 4) famously commented on 'instinct psychology': 'Man is impelled to action, it is said, by his instincts... if he twiddles his thumbs, it is the thumb-twiddling instinct; if he does not twiddle his thumbs, it is the thumb-not-twiddling instinct. Thus, everything is explained by magic – word magic.' This statement remains relevant now to explain flaws in contemporary views of social learning which rely on notions such as instinct or innate drives.

By reducing the argument for instinct to an absurdity, Holt highlighted three problems. First, the circular nature of the explanation offered; it merely re-describes the observed behavior as if it were a theory about that behavior: why does she twiddle her thumbs? Because she has a 'thumb-twiddling' instinct! How do you know she has a 'thumb-twiddling' instinct? Because she twiddles her thumbs! This argument has been central to many critiques of cognitive psychology. Second, the naïve view of the phenomenon to be explained; i.e. assuming that a complex set of behaviors can be characterized as a single entity, which can be explained by reference to a small set of constructs (instinct). If 'thumb twiddling' were replaced by 'social learning,' the assumption that there is one entity called 'social learning,' that can be explained by reference to a very small number of instincts, certainly seems overly simplistic. Finally, instinct theories do not offer explanations of where and how such instincts arise.

Tomasello (1999) suggests that social learning underlies human cultural evolution, allowing a cumulative growth in knowledge not apparent in other species. Other species are claimed not to engage in the kinds of social learning that enable this incremental cultural learning to occur, rather each generation has to acquire knowledge afresh (Kummer & Goodall, 1985). He suggests that some innate mechanism, highly developed in humans, helps drive critical processes such as: joint attention, language learning, and cultural learning (Tomasello, 2003). This mechanism has been termed

an 'interactional instinct' (Lee *et al.,* 2009), and this labeling reveals the true nature of this form of theorizing: this is 1920s 'instinct psychology' reborn, as if a century of progress in empirical findings in learning theory had not occurred!

Social learning is regarded as having two major forms (Whiten & Ham, 1992). 'Non-imitative social learning' occurs when the presence of another facilitates the acquisition of knowledge, but not necessarily the specifics of an observed behavior. Whereas, in 'true imitation' an observer learns to exactly copy the actions of a model. Learning theory supplies explanations of both forms across the species: non-imitative social learning is explained by classical conditioning (Mineka & Cook, 1988); and true imitation is explained by discriminated operant learning (learning when certain actions will have particular consequences; Miller & Dollard, 1941). Both forms can be shown to occur in non-humans, and to relate to cultural transmission. The availability of such explanations, and the supporting evidence, suggests there is little need to argue for special social learning instincts in humans.

There are many examples of non-imitative social learning in non-humans, which illustrate the application of classical conditioning (see Olsson & Phelps, 2007). A seminal example relates to the way in which rats learn food preferences, and how this learning spreads throughout a colony. Galef (1996) presented rats with another rat, together with a novel food (typically avoided by rats), and found that an observer subsequently ate the food more readily than a rat presented with the food in the absence of another rat. Similarly, Mineka and Cook (1988) demonstrated that laboratory-reared monkeys learned to fear snakes when exposed to wild monkeys showing fear of snakes. These examples can be explained by the observer learning the relationship between a stimulus and an outcome through classical conditioning. Importantly, this form of learning produces changes in 'cultural practice,' which is neither based on true imitation, nor restricted to humans.

It has been argued that true imitation is uniquely human due to the highly cognitively demanding 'cross-model matching' required to match an observer's visual representation of a behavior to the kinesthetic senses of their own movements (Tomasello, 1996). However, Heyes and Dawson (1990) have shown that, when a rat was placed in a cage, opposite another rat pushing a bar, either right or left, to earn food, then, when later exposed to the bar, the observer rat would press in the same direction as the demonstrator rat. As the observer was moved 180 degrees before being exposed to the bar, this meant that it must have learned to press in the same direction as the demonstrator, and not in the direction that it witnessed the bar moving across its own visual field; the observer rat had learned about the specific actions of another rat. However, Mitchell *et al.* (1999) found that observer rats may detect odor on the side of a bar that demonstrators had pushed, suggesting that the observers were not encoding the visual representation of the other rats. This does not mean that true imitation cannot occur, but that it may not occur in a visual medium for largely non-visual species. Similarly, Reed *et al.* (1996) noted that imitation only occurred in rats who had been socially reared, not in those reared in isolation, suggesting that imitation needs to be learned in a social environment (see Baer *et al.,* 1967).

In summary, learning theory argues that an 'imitative instinct' is an empty explanatory concept, and there is ample evidence that social learning can occur in many species, certainly in its non-imitative (classically conditioned) form, as well as in its imitative (instrumentally conditioned) form, and that both types of social learning can produce cultural transmission.

This suggests that studying is not only more fun, but also more effective when you are intrinsically motivated. According to some researchers, the attribution of motives to intrinsic causes results in a feeling that one is in control of one's own actions, that one is self-determined (Deci & Ryan, 1985). When external rewards become important, they take away from our sense of self-determination. Persistence is reduced, and – especially for difficult tasks – the individual will be more easily discouraged. These ideas are closely related to ideas expressed by Bandura; we saw earlier that he emphasized the importance of self-efficacy.

There is experimental evidence showing that external rewards can harm intrinsic motivation. One early example is research with children that was carried out by Lepper and Green (1975). One group of children was solving puzzles, expecting no reward. The other group of children were told that they would be allowed to play with certain toys, if they worked on the puzzles first. At a later time, both groups were allowed to play with the puzzles spontaneously (neither group expecting a reward). More of the children who had initially not expected a reward, chose to work with the puzzles spontaneously. This type of research has been repeated many times, confirming the detrimental effects of external rewards for persistence and performance on a task that was initially intrinsically motivating (Deci *et al.,* 1999). When rewards are introduced, it seems that 'play becomes work': the individual attributes their own engagement with the task to the anticipated external reward, rather than to the inherent satisfaction associated with it. This effect is called the **overjustification effect**: the external reward becomes the justification for performing the task – a cognitive interpretation of the situation that reduces the intrinsic motivation.

Let's assume for the moment that you are intrinsically motivated to study your psychology textbook – as of course we hope you are. The research shows that your intrinsic motivation might suffer once you realize that effective studying also holds the promise of an external reward: the good grade. And that would be a pity! Motivation researchers point to the importance of self-determination and self-efficacy, as we have seen. This means that – besides studying – you should try to protect your intrinsic motivation. Spend some time actively asking yourself what interests you about the material. How does it relate to questions that you ask yourself, and to other topics that interest you? And also realize that grades are not only external rewards. Grades also provide information about your level of achievement. A good grade tells you that you have mastered something, and a poor grade – especially when there is also some meaningful feedback – informs you about what might have been lacking in your preparation. Reinterpreting the meaning of a grade in this way (from external reward to a source of information) is an active way to increase your own sense of control.

INTERIM SUMMARY

➔ In humans, complex learning can be thought of as goal-oriented behavior arising from our psychological needs for self-determination and achievement.

➔ Intrinsically motivated individuals are more persistent at a task than extrinsically motivated individuals.

➔ External rewards can be detrimental to intrinsic motivation.

CRITICAL THINKING QUESTIONS

1 Use the Yerkes-Dodson law to explain why a student who usually gives good presentations is likely to give an even better presentation when there is a large audience present. And why is the opposite the case for a student who usually gives weak presentations?

2 Besides grades, what other external rewards do you anticipate to receive if you study hard? And how might you reinterpret these rewards to prevent them from harming your intrinsic motivation?

CHAPTER SUMMARY

1 Learning may be defined as a relatively permanent change in behavior that is the result of practice. There are four basic kinds of learning: (a) habituation, in which an organism learns to ignore a familiar and inconsequential stimulus, (b) classical conditioning, in which an organism learns that one stimulus follows another, (c) instrumental conditioning, in which an organism learns that a particular response leads to a particular consequence, and (d) complex learning, in which learning involves more than the formation of associations.

2 Early research on learning was done from a behaviorist perspective. It often assumed that behavior is better understood in terms of external causes than internal ones, that simple associations are the building blocks of all learning, and that the laws of learning are the same for different species and different situations. These assumptions have been modified in light of subsequent work. The contemporary analysis of learning includes cognitive factors and biological constraints, as well as behaviorist principles.

3 In Pavlov's experiments, if a conditioned stimulus (CS) consistently precedes an unconditioned stimulus (US), the CS comes to serve as a signal for the US and will elicit a conditioned response (CR) that often resembles the unconditioned response (UR). Stimuli that are similar to the CS also elicit the CR to some extent, although discrimination training can curb such generalization. These phenomena occur in organisms as diverse as flatworms and humans.

4 Cognitive factors also play a role in conditioning. For classical conditioning to occur, the CS must be a reliable predictor of the US; that is, there must be a higher probability that the US will occur when the CS has been presented than when it has not.

5 According to ethologists, what an animal learns is constrained by its genetically determined 'behavioral blueprint.' Evidence for such constraints on classical conditioning comes from studies of taste aversion. Although rats readily learn to associate the feeling of being sick with the taste of a solution, they cannot learn to associate sickness with a light. Conversely, birds can learn to associate light and sickness but not taste and sickness.

6 Instrumental conditioning deals with situations in which the response operates on the environment rather than being elicited by an unconditioned stimulus. The earliest systematic studies were performed by Thorndike, who showed that animals engage in trial-and-error behavior and that any behavior that is followed by reinforcement is strengthened; this is known as the law of effect.

7 In Skinner's experiments, typically a rat or pigeon learns to make a simple response, such as pressing a lever, to obtain reinforcement. The rate of response is a useful measure of response strength. Shaping is a training procedure that is used when the desired response is novel; it involves reinforcing only variations in response that deviate in the direction desired by the experimenter.

8 A number of phenomena can increase the generality of instrumental conditioning. One is conditioned reinforcement, in which a stimulus associated with a reinforcer acquires its own reinforcing properties. Other relevant phenomena are generalization and discrimination; organisms generalize responses to similar situations, although this generalization can be brought under the control of a discriminative stimulus. Finally, there are schedules of reinforcement. Once a behavior is established, it can be maintained when it is reinforced only part of the time. Exactly when the reinforcement comes is determined by its schedule; the basic types of reinforcement schedules are fixed ratio, variable ratio, fixed interval, and variable interval schedules.

9 There are three kinds of aversive conditioning. In punishment, a response is followed by an aversive event, which results in the response being suppressed. In escape, an organism learns to make a response in order to terminate an ongoing aversive event. In avoidance, an organism learns to make a response to prevent the aversive event from even starting.

10 Cognitive factors play a role in instrumental conditioning. For instrumental conditioning to occur, the organism must believe that reinforcement is at least partly under its control; that is, it must perceive a contingency between its responses and the reinforcement. Biological constraints are also a factor in instrumental conditioning. There are constraints on what reinforcers can be associated with what responses. With pigeons, when the reinforcement is food, learning is faster if the response is pecking a key rather than flapping the wings, but when the reinforcement is termination of shock, learning is faster when the response is wing flapping rather than pecking a key.

11 According to the cognitive perspective, the crux of learning is an organism's ability to represent aspects of the world mentally and then operate on these mental representations rather than on the world itself. In complex learning, the mental representations depict more than associations, and the mental operations may constitute a strategy. Studies of complex learning in animals indicate that rats can develop a cognitive map of their environment, as well as acquire abstract concepts such as cause.

12 Learning through imitation and observation happens as a result of vicarious reinforcement: by observing a model's behavior, the imitator expects to be reinforced just like the model was. Humans learn many complex and social behaviors through observational learning.

13 When learning relationships between stimuli that are not perfectly predictive, people often invoke prior beliefs. This can lead to the detection of relationships that are not objectively present (spurious associations). When the relationship is objectively present, having a prior belief about it can lead to overestimating its predictive strength; when an objective relationship conflicts with a prior belief, the learner may favor the prior belief. These effects demonstrate top-down processing in learning.

14 The neural mechanisms of non-associative forms of learning have been studied in invertebrate slugs. Habituation is mediated by a decrease in synaptic transmission, and sensitization by an increase in transmission. Regression and growth, respectively, of synapses are also involved in these types of learning.

15 Synapses in the mammalian brain take part in storing information during learning. The cerebellum is particularly important for motor conditioning, and the amygdala is essential for emotional conditioning. Increases in synaptic transmission, termed long-term potentiation, are involved in these learning processes.

16 Intrinsically motivated individuals are more persistent at a task than individuals motivated by an external reward. Experiments show that adding external rewards can lead to overjustification of the behavior. As a consequence, the individual attributes his or her engagement with the task to the external rewards. This is damaging to intrinsic motivation, as well as to performance. Complex tasks are best accomplished if the individual perceives a sense of control and self-determination.

CORE CONCEPTS

cognitive behavior therapy	drug tolerance	instrumental conditioning
behavior therapy	acquisition	insight
learning	learning curve	trial-and-error learning
non-associative learning	extinction	law of effect
habituation	spontaneous recovery	reinforcement
sensitization	response generalization	positive and negative reinforcement
associative learning	stimulus discrimination	positive and negative punishment
classical conditioning	excitatory conditioning	shaping
unconditioned response	inhibitory conditioning	conditioned reinforcer
unconditioned stimulus	second-order conditioning	ratio schedule
neutral stimulus	temporal contiguity	fixed and variable ratio schedule
conditioned stimulus	contingency	interval schedule
conditioned response	learned taste aversion	fixed and variable interval schedule

escape learning	self-efficacy	Yerkes-Dodson law
avoidance learning	Hebbian learning rule	exploratory behavior
learned helplessness	neural plasticity	incentive
latent learning	long-term depression (LTD)	intrinsic motivation
cognitive map	long-term potentiation (LTP)	extrinsic motivation
observational learning	synaptic plasticity	overjustification effect
vicarious	arousal	

DIGITAL SUPPORT RESOURCES

Students should use the unique access code included in the front of the book to access the digital support resources which accompany the new edition. These include:

- Multiple Choice Questions and Quizzes
- Critical Thinking Questions
- Practice Essay Questions
- Videos
- Glossary, Flashcards, and More

8 MEMORY

In December 1986, a man named Ronald Cotton went on trial, accused of brutally raping a university student named Jennifer Thompson. From the witness stand, Ms Thompson testified that during her ordeal, which occurred in the night-time darkness of her apartment bedroom, she intently studied the rapist's face. In a newspaper column, written 15 years later, she stated that, 'I looked at his hairline; I looked for scars, for tattoos, for anything that would help me identify him.' Based on what she presumed to be the resulting very strong memory of her attacker's appearance, she confidently identified Mr Cotton as the man who raped her. Based on Ms Thompson's identification, Mr Cotton, despite a strong alibi for the night in question, was convicted and sentenced by the judge to serve life plus 54 years.

On the face of it, it would seem that the jury did the right thing in convicting Mr Cotton: alibi or no, Ms Thompson's identification was pretty convincing. She described, as recounted above, the vivid memory she had formed of her attacker's appearance; she eventually picked Mr Cotton out of a collection of police photos; she picked him again out of a police lineup; and her trial testimony left the jury with no doubt that she believed she had picked the right man. As she later wrote, 'I knew this was the man. I was completely confident. I was sure.... If there was the possibility of a death sentence, I wanted him to die. I wanted to flip the switch.'

As the years passed, Ronald Cotton appealed his conviction from his jail cell, always maintaining his innocence. Eventually, another man, a prison inmate, Bobby Poole, was discovered to have boasted to his cellmates about having committed the rape for which Mr Cotton had been convicted. As a precaution, Jennifer Thompson was shown Mr. Poole and asked about the possibility that he, not Mr Cotton, could have been her attacker. Ms. Thompson stuck to her guns, proclaiming confidently, 'I have never seen this man [Bobby Poole] in my life. I have no idea who he is.'

But Jennifer Thompson was wrong, both in her identification of Ronald Cotton and in her rejection of Bobby Poole as the man who raped her. After serving 11 years in prison, Mr Cotton was exonerated of the crime by the emerging science of DNA matching; moreover, the same evidence confirmed that Bobby Poole was indeed the rapist. Jennifer Thompson, finally convinced of her false memory, but profoundly shocked by it, became a strong advocate of extreme caution when convicting a defendant solely on the basis of someone's memory.

In their landmark book *Actual Innocence*, Barry Scheck, Peter Newfeld, and Jim Dwyer described the Innocence Project, a program devoted to using DNA evidence as a means of exonerating the falsely accused. In their accounts of dozens of other plights similar to that of Ronald Cotton, the authors note that, 'In a study of DNA exonerations, by the Innocence Project, 84% of the wrongful convictions rested, at least in part, on mistaken identification by an eyewitness or victim,' and they go on to point out that, dramatic as these results are, they only confirm a century of social science research and judicial fact finding. It is, in large part, this research with which we are concerned in this chapter. Our memories are usually more or less correct – if they weren't, we'd have a tough go of it through life. However, they are incorrect more often than we might think, and sometimes the consequences of incorrect memories are dramatic.

CHAPTER OUTLINE

THREE IMPORTANT DISTINCTIONS

Three stages of memory

Three memory stores

Different memories for different kinds of information

SENSORY MEMORY

Sperling's experiments: The partial-report experiment

Visible persistence: The temporal integration experiment

Partial report, visible persistence, and a theory that integrates them

WORKING MEMORY

Encoding

Current conceptions of working memory

Storage

Retrieval

Working memory and thought

Transfer from working memory to long-term memory

Division of brain labor between working memory and long-term memory

LONG-TERM MEMORY

Encoding

Retrieval cues

Forgetting: Loss of information from storage

Interactions between encoding and retrieval

Emotional factors in forgetting

IMPLICIT MEMORY

Memory in amnesia

A variety of memory systems

Implicit memory in normal individuals

CUTTING EDGE RESEARCH:

HOW METACOGNITION CAN BE

USED TO IMPROVE STUDENT

PERFORMANCE

CONSTRUCTIVE MEMORY

Piaget's childhood memory

Constructive processes at the time of memory encoding

Post-event memory reconstruction

Constructive memory and the legal system

Memory errors and normal memory

IMPROVING MEMORY

Chunking and memory span

Imagery and encoding

Elaboration and encoding

Context and retrieval

Organization

Practicing retrieval

SEEING BOTH SIDES: ARE REPRESSED MEMORIES VALID?

A moment's thought should convince you that the memory is the most critical mental facility we possess with regard to our ability to operate as humans. We make almost all decisions based on memory of one sort or another. Even a person deprived of the sensory input that most of us take for granted – for instance a blind and deaf person like Helen Keller – is entirely capable of living a superbly fulfilling life. In contrast, as is attested by anyone who knows a person ravaged by Alzheimer's disease, even with normal sensory input, lack of memory is profoundly debilitating.

It is not surprising, therefore, that memory is the focus of a great amount of research, both in psychology and in the biological sciences; and in this chapter we describe a small portion of that research. To appreciate the scientific study of memory, however, we need to understand how researchers divide the field into manageable units.

THREE IMPORTANT DISTINCTIONS

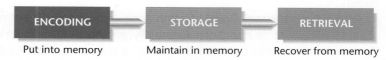

FIGURE 8.1 **Three Stages of Memory.** *Theories of memory attribute forgetting to a failure at one or more of these stages.*

Psychologists today make three major distinctions about memory. The first concerns three stages of memory: encoding, storage, and retrieval. The second deals with different memories for storing information for short and long periods. The third distinction is about different memories being used to store different kinds of information (for example, one system for facts and another for skills). For each of these distinctions, there is evidence that the entities being distinguished – say, working versus long-term memory – are mediated in part by different structures in the brain.

Three stages of memory

Suppose that you are introduced to another student and told that her name is Barbara Cohn. That afternoon you see her again and say something like, 'You're Barbara Cohn. We met this morning.' Clearly, you have remembered her name. But how exactly did you remember it?

This memory feat can be divided into three stages (see Figure 8.1). First, when you were introduced, you somehow entered Barbara Cohn's name into memory; this is the **encoding stage**. You transformed a physical input (sound waves) corresponding to her spoken name into the kind of code or representation that memory accepts, and you 'placed' that representation in memory; you likewise transformed another physical input, the pattern of light corresponding to her face, into a memory for her face; and you connected the two representations. Second, you retained – or stored – the information corresponding to her name and her face during the time between the two meetings; this is the **storage stage**. Third, based on the stored representation of her face, you recognized her in the afternoon as someone you had met in the morning and, based on this recognition, you recovered her name from storage at the time of your second meeting. All of this is the **retrieval stage**.

Memory can fail at any of these three stages. Had you been unable to recall Barbara's name at the second meeting, this could have reflected a failure in encoding (you didn't properly store her face to begin with), in storage (you forgot her name somewhere along the way), or retrieval (you hadn't connected her name to her face in such a way that you could conjure up one from the other). Much of the current research on memory attempts to specify the mental operations that occur at each of the three stages of memory and explain how these operations can go awry and result in memory failure.

Memory has three stages. The first stage, encoding, consists of placing a fact in memory. This occurs when we study. The second stage is storage, when the fact is retained in memory. The third stage, retrieval, occurs when the fact is recovered from storage – for example, when we take an exam.

A number of recent studies suggest that the different stages of memory are mediated by different structures in the brain. The most striking evidence comes from brain-scanning studies. These experiments involve two parts. In Part 1, which focuses on encoding, participants study a set of verbal items – for example, pairs consisting of a category and uncommon instance of that category (furniture–sideboard). In Part 2, which focuses on retrieval, participants have to recognize or recall the items when cued with the category name. In both parts, measures of brain activity are recorded using positron emission tomography (PET) while participants are engaged in their task. The most striking finding is that during encoding most of the activated brain regions are in the left hemisphere, whereas during retrieval most of the activated brain areas are in the right hemisphere (Shallice *et al.*, 1994; Tulving *et al.*, 1994).

Three memory stores

The three stages of memory do not operate the same way in all situations. Memory processes differ between situations that require us to store material (1) for less than a second, (2) for a matter of seconds, and (3) for longer intervals ranging from minutes to years.

The Atkinson–Shiffrin theory

A classic basis for the distinction between different memories corresponding to different time intervals was formalized by Richard Atkinson and Richard Shiffrin in 1968. The basic tenets of this theory were as follows:

1 Information arriving from the environment is first placed into what was termed **sensory store**, which has the following characteristics (see Massaro & Loftus, 1996). First it is large – the sensory store pertaining to a given sense organ contains all the information impinging on that sense organ from the environment. Second, it is transient. Information from sensory store decays over a time period; the rate of decay ranges from a few tenths of a second for visual sensory store to a few seconds for auditory sensory store. Third, that small portion of information in sensory store that was attended to (see Chapter 5) was transferred out of sensory store into the next major component of the system, **short-term memory**.

2 Short-term memory has the following characteristics. First, it can be roughly identified with *consciousness*; information in short-term memory is information that you are conscious of. Second, information in short-term memory is readily accessible; it can be used as the foundation of making decisions or carrying out tasks in times on the order of seconds or less. Third, all else being equal, information in short-term memory will decay – be forgotten – over a period of approximately 20 seconds. Fourth, information can be prevented from decaying if it is **rehearsed**, that is, repeated over and over (see Sperling, 1967), Fifth, information that is rehearsed or that undergoes other forms of processing, collectively known as **elaboration** (for example, being transformed into a suitable visual image) is transferred from short-term memory into the third repository of information, **long-term store**.

3 Long-term store is, as the name implies, the large repository of information in which all information that is generally available to us is maintained. Long-term store has the following characteristics. First, information enters it via various kinds of elaborative processes, from short-term memory. Second, the size of long-term store is, as far as is known, unlimited. Third, information is acquired from long-term store via the process of retrieval (discussed briefly above) and placed back into short-term memory where it can be manipulated and used to carry out the task at hand.

Different memories for different kinds of information

Until about three decades ago, psychologists generally assumed that the same memory system was used for all kinds of memories. For example, the same long-term memory was presumably used to store both one's recollection of a grandmother's funeral and the skills one needs to ride a bike. More recent evidence indicates that this assumption is wrong. In particular, we seem to use a different long-term memory for storing facts (such as who had lunch with us yesterday) than we do for retaining skills (such as how to ride a bicycle). The evidence for this difference, as usual, includes both psychological and biological findings; these are considered later in the chapter.

English singer, songwriter and multi-instrumentalist Chris Martin in concert. Recent evidence indicates that we use a different long-term memory for storing skills, like the ability to play the piano, than we do for retaining facts.

The kind of memory situation that we understand best is **explicit memory**, in which a person *consciously recollects an event in the past, where this recollection is experienced as occurring in a particular time and place*. In contrast, **implicit memory** is one in which a person *unconsciously remembers information of various sorts* – for example, information required to carry out some physical task such as kicking a football.

INTERIM SUMMARY

➡ There are three stages of memory: encoding, storage, and retrieval. There is increasing biological evidence for these distinctions. Recent brain-scanning studies of long-term memory indicate that most of the brain regions activated during encoding are in the left hemisphere and that most of the regions activated during retrieval are in the right hemisphere.

➡ There are three kinds of memory that differ in terms of their temporal characteristics: sensory memory lasts over a few hundred milliseconds; short-term store (now called *working memory*) operates over seconds; long-term store operates over times ranging from minutes to years.

➡ Explicit memory is conscious, and implicit memory is unconscious.

CRITICAL THINKING QUESTION

1 Suppose that a friend complained to you, 'I have a terrible memory.' What questions might you ask in view of what you've just learned about memory in this section?

SENSORY MEMORY

The information initially acquired from the environment via the sense organs is placed into a short-lasting memory store called **sensory memory**. We have briefly described sensory memory: it holds a large amount of information, it holds a fairly faithful representation of the sensory information that enters the sense organ, and it is short-lasting. When you have the dramatic experience of seeing an otherwise dark world briefly lit up by a lightning flash, you are experiencing the sensory memory corresponding to vision, called iconic memory.

There are probably sensory memories corresponding to all sensory modalities, but, as with sensation and perception, those that have been studied most extensively are the ones corresponding to vision (iconic memory) and to audition (echoic memory). For purposes of brevity we will, in what follows, concentrate on the most-studied sensory memory, iconic memory.

Sperling's experiments: The partial-report experiment

In 1960, George Sperling published a seminal paper based on his Harvard doctoral dissertation. Sperling began with the observation that when people were briefly presented with a large amount of information – say 12 digits arranged as three rows of four columns per row – they typically could only report about four or five of the digits. This amount, known as the **span of apprehension**, had been known for almost a century and was assumed to represent the maximum amount of information a person could acquire from such an informational array. However, people had two intuitions that indicated that things were not quite so simple. The first was that they were able to see more than they could report but that they quickly forgot it: 'By the time we are able to write down four or five digits,' they complained, 'we can't remember the rest of the display any more.' The second intuition was that the image of the display appeared to *persist* longer than the display itself. Both these intuitions are easy to demonstrate: go into a pitch-dark closet with a book; open the book to a random page, and fire a flash with a camera (the picture doesn't matter, just the flash). You will find that you can 'see' much of the text in the book, but you won't be able to report much of it. Moreover, although the flash lasts only microseconds, your image of the book will appear to last in the order of half a second.

Sperling tested these intuitions using an ingenious experimental procedure called a **partial-report procedure** which is demonstrated in Figure 8.2. An array of letters was flashed to observers for a brief period – about a twentieth of a second. The number of letters in the array was varied and the letters were arranged in rows (left panel of Figure 8.2). There were two report conditions. In the standard, *whole-report*

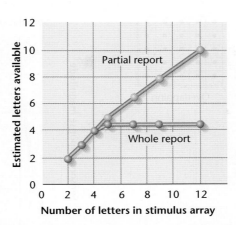

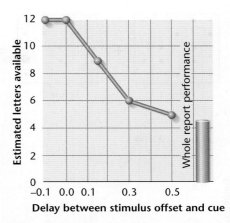

FIGURE 8.2 **The Partial-Report Experiment.** *The left panel shows the stimulus configuration: three rows of four letters per row. A high, medium, or low tone (cue) signals the observer to report the top, middle, or bottom row. The middle and right panels show data from this kind of experiment. The middle panel shows that as the number of letters in the display increases,* whole-report performance *levels off at 4.5 letters; however, partial-report performance continues to increase, thereby demonstrating the basic existence of a large-capacity sensory memory. The right panel shows that as the delay between the array's offset and the signaling tone increases, partial-report performance declines, reflecting the rapid decay of sensory memory. The bar at the far right of the right panel graph represents whole-report performance – about 4.5 letters.*

condition, the observer simply reported as many letters as possible. In the *partial-report* condition the observer had to report only one of the rows of letters. An auditory cue presented immediately after the array told the observer which row was to be reported: a high tone indicated the top row, a medium tone indicated the middle row, and a low tone indicated the bottom row. In the partial-report condition, Sperling estimated how many letters the observer had available by multiplying the average numbers of letters the observer was able to report from the indicated row by the number of rows. Thus, for example, if the observer could report three letters from the indicated row, the inference was that he or she must have had three letters available from each of the three rows (since he or she didn't know which row to report until after the array was physically gone) or 3 × 3 = 9 letters in all. The middle panel of Figure 8.2 shows the results of this experiment. As the number of letters in the array increased, the number of reported letters leveled out at about 4.5 for the whole-report condition – simply a replication of past results. However, in the partial-report condition, the number of letters reported continued to rise with the number of letters presented, thereby implying that the observers' first intuition was correct: they had more letters available than they were able to report in the traditional whole-report condition.

In a second experiment Sperling kept the number of letters in the array constant – 12 in our example – but varied the delay between the offset of the letter array and the auditory row-indicating cue, using a partial-report procedure. As can be seen in the right panel of Figure 8.2, the results were dramatic: as cue delay interval increased, the estimated number of letters available dropped with cue interval up to around 300 ms. The implication is that iconic memory fades away over a period of about a third of a second.

Visible persistence: The temporal integration experiment

Soon after Sperling's seminal work, came a series of experiments demonstrating the essentially visual aspects of iconic memory. These experiments are best exemplified by a paradigm invented and described by Di Lollo (Di Lollo, 1980; Di Lollo *et al.*, 2001). In this paradigm, 24 dots are presented in 24 of the 25 squares of an imaginary 5 × 5 array, as shown in Figure 8.3a, and the observer's task is to report the location of the missing dot. Even when the array is shown briefly, the missing dot's location can be easily reported; however, the trick is that the 24-dot stimulus was presented as two 'frames' of 12 dots per frame, separated in time. Figure 8.3b shows the result of this experiment: when the time between the two frames was brief, the missing dot location could be reported with high probability; however, performance declined precipitously as the inter-frame interval increased up to about 150 milliseconds. The interpretation was that as the first frame's iconic memory decreased over time, the first frame became less visible and could be less easily integrated with the image of the second frame.

Partial report, visible persistence, and a theory that integrates them

Initially, the partial-report paradigm and the temporal integration paradigm were thought to measure pretty much the same thing. It soon became clear, however, that these two aspects of iconic memory – that part that allowed information to be extracted and that part that was visible – had somewhat different characteristics (Coltheart, 1980) which meant that the two tasks were not simply two measures of the same

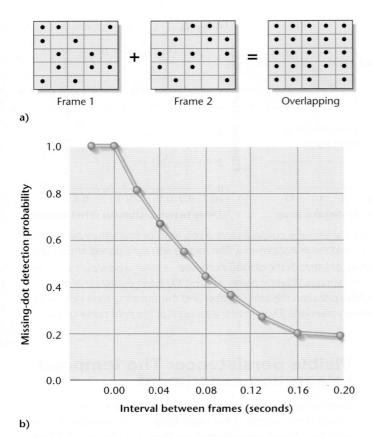

a)

b)

FIGURE 8.3 The Temporal-Integration Task. *(a) The stimulus configuration. Two frames of 12 dots per frame form, when overlapping, a 5 × 5 array of dots with one dot missing. (b) Data from this kind of experiment are plotted. As the interval between the two frames increases, performance declines, demonstrating the quick decline of the visible persistence necessary to visually integrate the two frames.*

thing. Busey and Loftus (1994) proposed a theory designed to integrate both paradigms as well as to integrate work on sensation and perception with work on memory. The mathematics of this theory are beyond the scope of this introductory text; however the basics of it are as follows:

1 A briefly presented visual stimulus (e.g., an array of letters or an array of dots or the world lit up by a lightning flash) triggers what is called a **sensory response** in the nervous system. This response can be conceptualized as the magnitude of nervous activity, whose general time course is shown in Figure 8.4: response magnitude rises with the onset of the stimulus, continues to rise for a short time following the offset of the stimulus, and then decays to zero.

2 The amount of information acquired from the stimulus (which, for example, can be used as a basis for responding in Sperling's experiments) is related to the area under the sensory-response function.

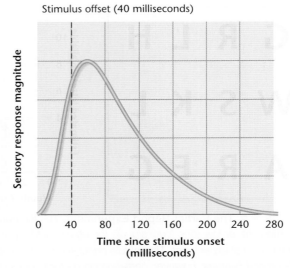

FIGURE 8.4 Sensory Response Magnitude. *A sensory response function generated by a stimulus presented for 40 milliseconds. The magnitude of the assumed neural response is plotted as a function of time since the onset of the stimulus. The area under the curve determines information acquired from the stimulus, and the height of the curve at any given point largely determines how visible the stimulus is.*

3 The visibility of the stimulus is related to the rate at which the observer is acquiring information from the stimulus.

This last point, equating visibility to information-acquisition rate, is not quite so odd as it might seem at first glance. Have you ever had the experience of daydreaming while driving a car and then suddenly realizing that you had not been conscious of any of the scenery that you were passing? This is tantamount to saying that your conscious awareness of the passing scenery – that is, its visibility – depends on the degree to which you were acquiring information from it: no information acquisition, no visibility.

INTERIM SUMMARY

➔ Sensory memory, first explored in detail by George Sperling, has a very large capacity but decays in a very short time. Information within sensory memory that is attended to is transferred to the next memory, working memory.

➔ Visible persistence is information that maintains a persisting, conscious, visual representation over a period of several tenths of a second.

➔ A sensory response function is a concept that allows integration of sensory memory and visible persistence.

WORKING MEMORY

As noted earlier, sensory memory contains an enormous amount of quickly decaying information. Only information that is attended to is transferred from sensory memory to the next memory store. Atkinson and Shiffrin referred to this memory store as short-term memory. Experiments demonstrate that a short-term memory system exists that is separate from both the sensory stores and long-term memory (e.g., Brown, 1958; Peterson & Peterson, 1959). In this section we first discuss classic findings about how information is encoded, stored, and retrieved from short-term memory. We then discuss the contemporary view of short-term memory as a 'workspace' for performing mental computations on information that is relevant to the task at hand so that we may perform tasks effectively. Theorists who take this view use the term **working memory** to refer to the short-term memory, to highlight its role in thinking rather than as simply a storage space.

Encoding

To encode information into working memory, we must attend to it. Since we are selective about what we attend to (see Chapter 5), our working memory will contain only what has been selected. This means that much of what we are exposed to never even enters working memory and, of course, will not be available for later retrieval. Indeed, many 'memory problems' are really lapses in attention. For example, if you bought some groceries and someone later asked you the color of the checkout clerk's eyes, you might be unable to answer, not because of a failure of memory but because you had not paid attention to the clerk's eyes in the first place. This phenomenon is nicely illustrated by a cartoon on page 266.

Phonological coding

When information is encoded into memory, it is entered in a certain code or representation. For example, when you look up a telephone number and retain it until you have dialed it, in what form do you represent the digits? Is the representation visual – a mental picture of the digits? Is it phonological – the sounds of the names of the digits? Research indicates that we can use both of these possibilities to encode information into working memory, although we favor a phonological code when we are trying to keep the information active through rehearsal – that is, by repeating an item over and over. Rehearsal is a particularly popular strategy when the information consists of verbal items such as digits, letters, or words. So in trying to remember a telephone number, we are most likely to encode the number as the sounds of the digit names and to rehearse these sounds to ourselves until we have dialed the number.

In a classic experiment that provided evidence for a phonological code, researchers briefly showed participants a list of six consonants (for example, RLBKSJ); when the letters were removed, they had to write all six letters in order. Although the entire procedure took only a second or two, participants occasionally made errors. When they did, the incorrect letter tended to be similar in sound to the correct one. For the list mentioned, a participant might have written RLTKSJ, replacing the B with the similar-sounding T (Conrad, 1964). This finding supports the hypothesis that the participants encoded each letter phonologically (for example, 'bee' for B), sometimes lost part of this code (only the 'ee' part of the sound remained), and then responded with a letter ('tee') that was consistent with the remaining part of the code. This hypothesis also explains why it is more difficult to recall the items in order when they are acoustically similar (for example, TBCGVE) than when they are acoustically distinct (RLTKSJ).

Visual coding

If need be, we can also maintain verbal items in a visual form. Experiments indicate that while we can use a visual code for verbal material, the code fades quickly. When a person must store non-verbal items (such as pictures that are difficult to describe and therefore difficult to rehearse phonologically), the visual code becomes more important. For example, imagine the task of fitting several pieces of luggage into the back of one's car. An effective strategy might be to encode a short-term representation of each bag, and to then imagine its placement in the car to determine whether it would fit. People are quite variable in their abilities to make such mental images. While most of us can maintain some kind of visual image in working memory, a few people are able to maintain images that are almost photographic in clarity. This ability occurs mainly in children. Such children can look briefly at a picture and, when it is removed, still experience the image before their eyes. They can maintain the image for as long as several minutes and, when questioned, provide a wealth of detail, such as the number of stripes on a cat's tail

(see Figure 8.5). Such children seem to be reading the details directly from an eidetic (or photographic) image (Haber, 1969). Eidetic imagery is very rare, though. Some studies with children indicate that only about 5 per cent report visual images that are long-lasting and possess sharp detail.

Moreover, when the criteria for possessing true photographic imagery are made more stringent – for example, being able to read an imaged page of text as easily from the bottom up as from the top down – the frequency of eidetic imagery becomes minuscule, even among children (Haber, 1979). The visual code in working memory, then, is something short of a photograph. This makes complete sense when we think back about how the retina of the eye is organized (Chapter 4). The high-resolution central fovea allows detailed perception only of the central area of the scene; the periphery is progressively lower-resolution. So even if the brain were able to 'take a photograph' of a scene as perceived while the eyes were steady, the result would be a picture that, while clear and focused at the center, became progressively blurrier toward the periphery.

Current conceptions of working memory

The existence of both phonological and visual codes led researchers to argue that working memory consists of several

FIGURE 8.5 Testing for Eidetic Images. *An observer looking at this photo of a tabby cat for 30 seconds would see several things. But if the picture were then removed, what they could recall about the picture (such as the whiteness of the cat's tummy or the number of stripes on his tail) would be their eidetic image.*

When you look up a telephone number and retain it until you have dialled it, do you retain it visually, phonologically, or semantically?

Mental rotation stimuli.

distinct workspaces or buffers. One system (referred to as the **phonological loop**) is for storing and operating upon information in an acoustic code. Information in this system may be rapidly forgotten but may be maintained indefinitely through the process of rehearsal. A second is referred to as the **visual-spatial sketchpad**, which holds and operates upon visual or spatial information (Baddeley, 1986). For example, look at the mental rotation stimuli picture opposite. Try to figure out whether each object in the left panel does or does not match each of the right-panel counterparts, that is, whether the two objects are identical or are mirror-images of one another. Most people make this determination by first making a mental image of one object, and then mentally rotating it so that it is in the same spatial orientation as the comparison object. This task illustrates many of the attributes of working memory. First, the visual information is not only being stored for the short term – it is also being actively operated upon in order to perform some ongoing real-world task. Second, the visual information is being held for the short term, and will be replaced by different information as soon as the person is done with the task. Finally, note that you are aware of the information while it is present in working memory. As will be discussed later, the contents of working memory constitute much of what we are currently conscious of (some people have gone so far as to equate working memory and consciousness, e.g., Baddeley & Andrade, 2000).

Various types of evidence indicate that the phonological loop and the visual-spatial sketchpad are mediated by different brain structures. For instance, Warrington and Shallice (1969) reported a patient who, following a brain injury, could repeat back only two or three consecutive digits presented to him (normal individuals can repeat back about seven digits). However, this same individual performed normally on

visual-spatial working memory tasks such as the mental rotations task described. This pattern suggests that the patient had suffered damage to his phonological loop, but not to his visual-spatial sketchpad. Brain imaging experiments further support separate working memory components. In one experiment, on every trial participants saw a sequence of letters in which both the identity and the position of the letter varied from one item to another (see Figure 8.6). On some trials, participants had to attend only to the identity of the letters; their task was to determine whether each letter presented was identical to the one presented three back in the sequence. On other trials, participants had to attend only to the position of the letters; their task was to determine whether each letter's position was identical to the position of the letter presented three back in the sequence (see Figure 8.6). Thus, the actual stimuli were identical in all cases; what varied was whether the participants were storing verbal information (the identities of the letters) or spatial information (the positions of

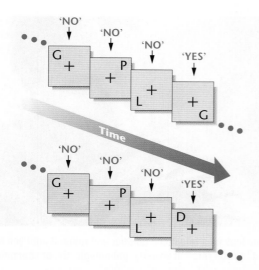

FIGURE 8.6 An Experiment on Acoustic and Visual Buffers. *Participants had to decide whether each item was identical to the one three back in the sequence. The top half of the figure shows a typical sequence of events in which participants had to attend only to the identity of the letters, along with the responses required for each item. The bottom half of the figure shows the trial events when individuals had to attend only to the position of the letters, along with the responses required for each item.*

the letters). Presumably, the verbal information was being kept in the phonological loop and the spatial information in the visual-spatial sketchpad.

On both the identity and the spatial trials, PET measures of brain activity were recorded. The results indicated that the two buffers are in different hemispheres. On trials in which participants had to store verbal information (acoustic buffer), most of the brain activity was in the left hemisphere; on trials in which participants had to store spatial information (visual-spatial buffer), most of the brain activity was in the right hemisphere. The two buffers seem to be distinct systems (Smith *et al.*, 1996). This finding is not very surprising, considering the brain's tendency toward hemispheric specialization, as discussed in Chapter 2.

How do the phonological loop and the visual-spatial sketchpad interact with one another? British psychologists Baddeley and Hitch (1974) proposed that both of these systems are controlled by another 'master' system called the *executive*. This system controls the other two systems by deciding what information will be encoded into them (that is, it directs attention), and what operations will be performed on that information. Because the other two systems are under the control of the executive they are sometimes referred to as 'slave systems.' Finally, Baddeley (2000) recently acknowledged the need to propose an additional component of working memory, called the *episodic buffer*. An important function of this subsystem is to *bind* or associate different aspects of a memory. For instance, the phonological loop may store a person's name, and the

visual-spatial sketchpad her face – but the episodic buffer would associate the two so that the name and face 'go together.'

Storage

Perhaps the most striking fact about working memory is that its capacity is very limited. For the phonological loop, the limit is seven items, give or take two (7 ± 2). Some people store as few as five items; others can retain as many as nine. It may seem strange to give such an exact number to cover all people when it is clear that individuals differ greatly in memory ability. These differences, however, are due primarily to long-term memory. For working memory, most normal adults have a capacity of 7 ± 2. This constancy has been known since the earliest days of experimental psychology. German psychologist Hermann Ebbinghaus, who began the experimental study of memory in 1885, reported results showing that his own limit was seven items. Some 70 years later, American cognitive psychologist George Miller (1956) was so struck by the consistency of this finding that he referred to it as the 'magic number seven.' It was later shown that the limit holds in non-Western cultures as well as Western ones (Yu *et al.*, 1985).

Psychologists determined this number by showing people various sequences of unrelated items (digits, letters, or words) and asking them to recall the items in order. The items are presented rapidly, and the individual does not have time to relate them to information stored in long-term memory; hence, the number of items recalled reflects only the storage capacity of the individual's working memory. On the initial trials, participants have to recall just a few items – say, three or four digits – which they can easily do. In subsequent trials, the number of digits increases until the experimenter determines the participant's **memory span** – the maximum number of items (almost always between five and nine) that the participant can recall in perfect order. This task is so simple that you can easily try it yourself. The next time you come across a list of names (a directory in a business or university building, for example), read through the list once and then look away and see how many names you can recall in order. It will probably be between five and nine.

Chunking

As just noted, the memory-span procedure discourages individuals from connecting the items to be remembered to information in long-term memory. When such connections are possible, performance on the memory-span task can change substantially. To illustrate this change, suppose that you were presented with the letter string SRUOYYLERECNIS. Because your memory span is 7 ± 2, you would probably be unable to repeat the entire letter sequence since it contains 14 letters. If, however, you noticed that these letters spell the phrase SINCERELY YOURS in reverse order, your task would become easier. By using this knowledge, you have decreased the number of items that must be held in working memory from 14 to two (the two words). But where did this spelling knowledge come from? From long-term memory, where knowledge about words is stored. Thus, you can use long-term memory to perform what is known as **chunking**, or recoding new material into larger, more meaningful units and storing those units in working memory. Such units are called chunks, and the capacity of working memory is best expressed as 7 ± 2 chunks (Miller, 1956). Chunking can occur with numbers as well. The string 106614921918 is beyond our capacity, but 1066 – 1492 – 1918 is well within it, or it is if you are knowledgeable about European history. The general principle is that we can boost our working memory by regrouping sequences of letters and digits into units that can be found in long-term memory (Bower & Springston, 1970).

Forgetting

We may be able to hold on to seven items briefly, but in most cases they will soon be forgotten. Forgetting occurs either because the items 'decay' over time or because they are displaced by new items.

Information in working memory may simply decay as time passes. We may think of the representation of an item as a trace that fades within a matter of seconds. One of the best pieces of evidence for this hypothesis is that our working memory span holds fewer words when the words take longer to say; for example, the span is less for long words such as 'harpoon' and 'cyclone' than for shorter words such as 'cat' and 'pen' (try saying the words to yourself to see the difference in duration). Presumably this effect arises because as the words are presented we say them to ourselves, and the longer it takes to do this, the more likely it is that some of the words' traces will have faded before they can be recalled (Baddeley *et al.,* 1975).

The other major cause of forgetting in working memory is the displacement of old items by new ones. The notion of displacement fits with the idea that working memory has a fixed capacity. Being in working memory may correspond to being in a state of activation. The more items we try to keep active, the less activation there is for any one of them. Perhaps only about seven items can be simultaneously maintained at a level of activation that permits all of them to be recalled. Once seven items are active, the activation given to a new item will be taken away from items that were presented earlier; consequently, those items may fall below the critical level of activation needed for recall (Anderson, 1983).

Retrieval

Let us continue to think of the contents of working memory as being active in consciousness. Intuition suggests that access to this information is immediate. You do not have to dig for it; it is right there. Retrieval, then, should not depend on the number of items in consciousness. But in this case intuition is wrong.

Research has shown that the more items there are in working memory, the slower retrieval becomes. Most of the evidence for this comes from a type of experiment introduced by Sternberg (1966). On each trial of the experiment, a participant is shown a set of digits, called the memory list, that he or she must temporarily maintain in working memory. It is easy for the participant to do so because the memory list contains between one and six digits. The memory list is then removed from view and a probe digit is presented. The participant must decide whether the probe was on the memory list. For example, if the memory list is 3 6 1 and the probe is 6, the participant should respond 'yes'; given the same memory list and a probe of 2, the participant should respond 'no.' Participants rarely make an error on this task; what is of interest, however, is the decision time, which is the elapsed time between the onset of the probe and the participant's pressing of a 'yes' or a 'no' button. Figure 8.7 presents data from such an experiment, indicating that decision time increases directly with the length of the memory list. What is remarkable about these decision times is that they fall along a straight line. This means that each additional item in working memory adds a fixed amount of time to the retrieval process – approximately 40 milliseconds, or one-twenty-fifth of a second. The same results are found when the items are letters, words, auditory tones, or pictures of people's faces (Sternberg, 1975).

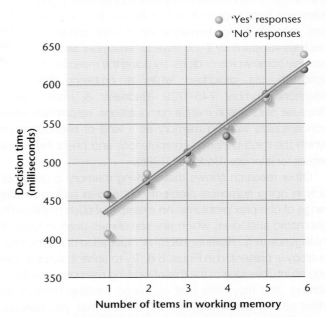

FIGURE 8.7 Retrieval as a Search Process. *Decision times increase in direct proportion to the number of items in short-term memory. Green circles represent yes reponses; purple circles, no responses. The times for both types of decision fall along a straight line. Because the decision times are so fast, they must be measured with equipment that permits accuracy in milliseconds (thousandths of a second).*

The most straightforward interpretation of these results is that retrieval requires a search of working memory in which the items are examined one at a time. This search presumably operates at a rate of 40 milliseconds per item, which is too fast for people to be aware of it (Sternberg, 1966). However, thinking of working memory as a state of activation leads to a different interpretation of the results. Retrieval of an item in working memory may depend on the activation of that item reaching a critical level. That is, one decides that a probe is in working memory if it is above a critical level of activation, and the more items there are in working memory, the less activation there is for any one of them (Monsell, 1979). Such **activation models** have been shown to accurately predict many aspects of retrieval from working memory (McElree & Dosher, 1989).

Working memory and thought

Working memory plays an important role in thought. When consciously trying to solve a problem, we often use working memory to store parts of the problem as well as information accessed from long-term memory that is relevant to the problem. To illustrate, consider what it takes to multiply 35 by 8 in your head. You need working memory to store the given numbers (35 and 8), the nature of the operation required (multiplication), and arithmetic facts such as $8 \times 5 = 40$ and $8 \times 3 = 24$. Not surprisingly, performance on mental arithmetic declines substantially if you have to remember simultaneously some words or digits; try doing the mental multiplication just described while remembering the telephone number 745-1739 (Baddeley & Hitch, 1974). Because of its role in mental computations, researchers often conceptualize working memory as a kind of blackboard on which the mind performs computations and posts the partial results for later use (Baddeley, 1986).

Other research shows that working memory is used not only in doing numerical problems but also in solving a wide range of complex problems. An example of such problems is geometric analogies, which are sometimes used in tests of intelligence (e.g., Ravens, 1965). An illustration of a geometric analogy is presented in Figure 8.8. Try to solve it; this will give you an intuitive idea of the role of working memory in problem solving. You may note that you need working memory to store (a) the similarities and differences that you observe among the forms in a row, and (b) the rules that you come up with to account for these similarities and differences and that you then use to select the correct answer. It turns out that the larger one's working memory, the better one does on problems like these (even though there is relatively little variation in capacities of working memory within the population). Moreover, when computers are programmed to simulate people

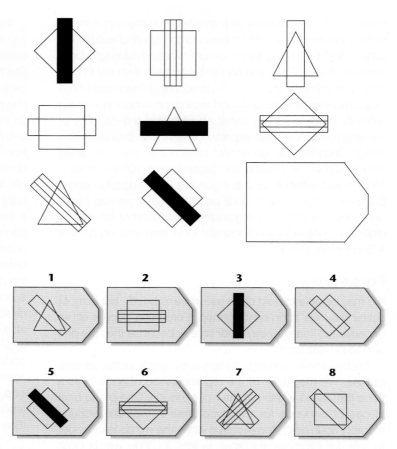

FIGURE 8.8 Illustration of a Geometric Analogy. *The task is to inspect the forms in the top matrix in which the bottom right entry is missing, and to determine which of the eight alternatives given below is the missing entry. To do this, you have to look across each row and determine the rules that specify how the forms vary, and then do the same thing for each column.*

solving problems such as the one in Figure 8.8, one of the most important determinants of how well the program does is the size of the working memory created by the programmer. There seems to be little doubt that part of the difficulty of many complex problems is the load they place on working memory (Carpenter *et al.*, 1990).

Working memory is also crucial for language processes like following a conversation or reading a text. When reading for understanding, often we must consciously relate new sentences to some prior material in the text. This relating of new to old seems to occur in working memory because people who have more working-memory capacity score higher than others on reading comprehension tests (Daneman & Carpenter, 1980; Just & Carpenter, 1992).

Transfer from working memory to long-term memory

From what we have seen so far, working memory serves two important functions: it stores material that is needed for

"Can we hurry up and get to the test? My short-term memory is better than my long-term memory."

Short-term memory.

short periods, and it serves as a work space for mental computations. Another possible function is serving as a way station to long-term memory. That is, information may reside in working memory while it is being encoded or transferred into long-term memory (Atkinson & Shiffrin, 1971a, 1971b; Raaijmakers & Shiffrin, 1992). While there are a number of different ways to implement the transfer, one way that has been the subject of considerable research is rehearsal, the conscious repetition of information in working memory. Rehearsal apparently not only maintains the item in working memory but also can cause it to be transferred to long-term memory. Thus, the term 'maintenance rehearsal' is used to refer to active efforts to hold information in working memory; 'elaborative rehearsal' refers to efforts to encode information in long-term memory.

Some of the best evidence for the 'way-station' function of working memory comes from experiments on free recall. In a free-recall experiment, participants first see a list of perhaps 40 unrelated words that are presented one at a time. After all the words have been presented, participants must immediately recall them in any order (hence the designation 'free'). The results from such an experiment are shown in Figure 8.9. The chance of correctly recalling a word is graphed as a function of the word's position in the list. The part of the curve to the left in the graph is for the first few words presented, and the part to the right is for the last few words presented.

Presumably, at the time of recall the last few words presented are still likely to be in working memory, whereas the remaining words are in long-term memory. Hence, we would expect recall of the last few words to be high because

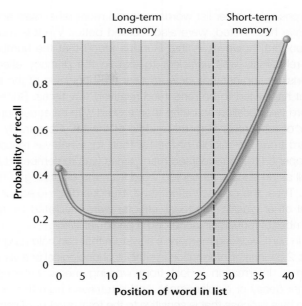

FIGURE 8.9 Results of a Free Recall Experiment. *The probability of recall varies with an item's position in a list, with the probability being highest for the last five or so positions, next highest for the first few positions, and lowest for the intermediate positions. Recall of the last few items is based on short-term memory, whereas recall of the remaining items is based on long-term memory.*

items in working memory can be retrieved easily. Figure 8.9 shows that this is indeed the case; it is called the *recency effect*. But recall for the first words presented is also quite good; this is called the *primacy effect*. Why does the primacy effect occur? This is where rehearsal enters the picture. When the first words were presented, they were entered into working memory and rehearsed. Since there was little else in working memory, they were rehearsed often and therefore were likely to be transferred to long-term memory. As more items were presented, working memory quickly filled up and the opportunity to rehearse and transfer any given item to long-term memory decreased. So only the first few items presented enjoyed the extra opportunity for transfer, which is why they were later recalled so well from long-term memory.

A classic demonstration of this explanation was provided by the American psychologist, Dewey Rundus, in 1971. Rundus carried out a free-recall experiment in which subjects were required to *rehearse* the words they were learning, that is, they were asked to speak the words aloud as the list was being presented. Which of the list words the subjects spoke at any moment was up to them as long as they included only list words. Rundus recorded the words as they were being spoken; thus he eventually had, for each word in each list, (1) the number of times it was rehearsed, and (2) its probability of being recalled. Rundus discovered that, not surprisingly, earlier list words received more rehearsals and, as we have noted, were also recalled better. What is more important, however, is that Rundus found that the number of rehearsals was *sufficient* to explain the primacy effect. Consider, for instance, a word near the beginning of the list that happened to be rehearsed relatively few times. Such a word was recalled no better than a word with an equal number of rehearsals from the middle of the list. Conversely, a word from the middle of the list that, for whatever reason, happened to be rehearsed many times was remembered as well as an equally rehearsed word from the beginning of the list. Thus, the primacy effect (and, Rundus discovered, several other classic free-recall effects) were mediated by the number of rehearsals accorded a particular word.

In sum, working memory is a system that can hold roughly 7 ± 2 chunks of information in either a phonological or a visual format. Information is lost from working memory through either decay or displacement, and is retrieved from this system by a process that is sensitive to the total number of items being kept active at any given time. Lastly, working memory is used to store and process information that is needed during problem solving, and therefore is critical for thought.

Division of brain labor between working memory and long-term memory

It has been known for some time that working memory and long-term memory are implemented by somewhat different brain structures. In particular, the hippocampus, a structure located near the middle of the brain beneath the cortex, is critical for long-term memory but not for working memory. Much of the relevant evidence comes from experiments with monkeys and other non-human species. In some experiments, one group of monkeys is first subjected to damage to the hippocampus and the surrounding cortex, and a second group is subjected to damage in a completely different region, the front of the cortex. Both groups of monkeys then have to perform a delayed-response task. On each trial, first one stimulus (such as a square) is presented and then, after a delay, a second stimulus (such as a triangle) is presented; the animal has to respond only when the second stimulus differs from the first. How well the animal performs on this task depends on the kind of brain damage it has suffered and the length of the delay between the two stimuli.

When the delay is long (15 seconds or more), animals with damage to the hippocampus perform poorly, but those with damage in the front of the cortex perform relatively normally. Because a long delay between stimuli requires long-term memory for storage of the first stimulus, these results fit with the idea that the hippocampus is critical for long-term memory. When the delay between the two stimuli is short (just a few seconds), the opposite results occur: now animals with damage in the front of the cortex perform poorly and

those with hippocampal damage perform relatively normally. Because a short delay between stimuli requires working memory for storage of the first stimulus, these results indicate that regions in the frontal cortex are involved in working memory. Hence, different regions of the brain are involved in working memory and long-term memory (Goldman-Rakic, 1987; Zola-Morgan & Squire, 1985).

What evidence is there for this distinction in humans? Patients who happen to have suffered damage in certain brain regions provide an 'experiment of nature.' Specifically, some patients have suffered damage to the hippocampus and surrounding cortex, and consequently show a severe memory loss; because the hippocampus is located in the middle of the temporal lobe, these patients are said to have medial-temporal lobe amnesia. Such patients have profound difficulty remembering material for long intervals but rarely have any trouble remembering material for a few seconds. Thus, a patient with medial-temporal lobe amnesia may be unable to recognize their doctor when they enter the room – even though the patient has seen this doctor every day for years – yet will have no trouble repeating the physician's name when they are reintroduced (Milner *et al.,* 1968). Such a patient has a severe impairment in long-term memory but a normal working memory.

Other patients, however, show the opposite problem. They cannot correctly repeat a string of even three words, yet they are relatively normal when tested on their long-term memory for words. Such patients have an impaired working memory but an intact long-term memory. And their brain damage is never in the medial temporal lobe (Shallice, 1988). Thus, for humans as well as for other mammals, working memory and long-term memory are mediated by different brain structures.

Recent research using brain-scanning techniques has revealed that neurons in the **prefrontal lobes**, just behind the forehead, hold information for short-term use, such as a telephone number that is about to be dialed. These neurons appear to act like a computer's random access memory (RAM) chips, which hold data temporarily for current use and switch quickly to other data as needed. These cells are also able to draw information from other regions of the brain and retain it as long as it is needed for a specific task (Goldman-Rakic, cited in Goleman, 1995).

INTERIM SUMMARY

➔ Information in working memory tends to be encoded acoustically, although we can also use a visual code.

➔ Working memory is conceptualized as being divided into an 'auditory' part, the phonological loop, and a 'visual' part, the visual-spatial sketchpad.

- The auditory storage capacity is limited to 7 ± 2 chunks. The amount of information in working memory can be increased by increasing the amount of information in each chunk, e.g., by chunking sequences of letters into meaningful units like words.
- Retrieval from working memory slows down as the number of items in working memory increases.
- Working memory is used in solving various kinds of problems, such as mental arithmetic, geometric analogies, and answering questions about text.
- Working memory acts as a buffer from which information may be transferred to long-term memory.
- Experiments with the hippocampus and surrounding brain areas support a qualitative distinction between working memory and long-term memory.

CRITICAL THINKING QUESTIONS

1 Why do you think that phonological encoding is such a major part of how working memory is organized?

2 How might an increase in the size of your working memory affect your performance on a standardized test of comprehension like the SAT? Try to explain how underlying comprehension processes might be affected.

LONG-TERM MEMORY

Long-term memory is involved when information has to be retained for intervals as brief as a few minutes (such as a point made earlier in a conversation) or as long as a lifetime (such as an adult's childhood memories). In experiments on long-term memory, psychologists have generally studied forgetting over intervals of minutes, hours, or weeks, but a few studies have involved years or even decades. Experiments that use intervals of years often involve the recall of personal experience (called autobiographical memory) rather than the recall of laboratory materials. In what follows, studies using both kinds of material are intermixed because they seem to reflect many of the same principles.

Our discussion of long-term memory will again distinguish among the three stages of memory – encoding, storage, and retrieval – but this time there are two complications. First, unlike the situation with working memory, important interactions between encoding and retrieval occur in long-term memory. In view of these interactions, we will consider some aspects of retrieval in our discussion of encoding and present

a separate discussion of interactions between encoding and retrieval. The other complication is that it is often difficult to know whether forgetting from long-term memory is due to a loss from storage or to a failure in retrieval. To deal with this problem, we will delay our discussion of storage until after we have considered retrieval so that we have a clearer idea of what constitutes good evidence for a storage loss.

Encoding
Encoding meaning

For verbal material, the dominant long-term memory representation is neither acoustic nor visual; instead, it is based on the meanings of the items. Encoding items according to their meaning occurs even when the items are isolated words, but it is more striking when they are sentences. Several minutes after hearing a sentence, most of what you can recall or recognize is the sentence's meaning. Suppose that you heard the sentence, 'The author sent the committee a long letter.' The evidence indicates that two minutes later you would do no better than chance in telling whether you had heard that sentence or one that has the same meaning: 'A long letter was sent to the committee by the author' (Sachs, 1967).

Encoding of meaning is pervasive in everyday memory situations. When people report on complex social or political situations, they may misremember many of the specifics (who said what to whom, when something was said, who else was there) yet can accurately describe the basic situation. Thus, in the Watergate scandal of the early 1970s that led to the downfall of American President Nixon, the chief government witness (John Dean) was subsequently shown to have made many mistakes about what was said in particular situations, yet his overall testimony is generally thought to accurately describe the events that occurred (Neisser, 1982).

Although meaning may be the dominant way of representing verbal material in long-term memory, we sometimes code other aspects as well. We can, for example, memorize poems and recite them word for word. In such cases we have coded not only the meaning of the poem but the exact words themselves. We can also use a phonological code in long-term memory. When you get a telephone call and the other party says 'Hello,' you often recognize the voice. In a case like this, you must have coded the sound of that person's voice in long-term memory. Visual impressions, tastes, and smells are also coded in long-term memory. Thus, long-term memory has a preferred code for verbal material (namely, meaning), but other codes can be used as well.

Adding meaningful connections

Often the items that we need to remember are meaningful but the connections between them are not. In such cases memory can be improved by creating real or artificial links between the items. For example, people who are learning to read music must remember that the five lines in printed music are referred to as EGBDF; although the symbols themselves are meaningful (they refer to notes on a keyboard), their order seems arbitrary. What many learners do is convert the symbols into the sentence 'Every Good Boy Does Fine'; the first letter of each word names each symbol, and the relationships between the words in the sentence supply meaningful connections between the symbols. These connections aid memory because they provide retrieval paths between the words: once the word 'Good' has been retrieved, for example, there is a path or connection to 'Boy,' the next word that must be recalled.

One of the best ways to add connections is to elaborate on the meaning of the material while encoding it. The more deeply or elaborately one encodes the meaning, the better the resulting memory will be (Craik & Tulving, 1975). Thus, if you have to remember a point made in a textbook, you will recall it better if you concentrate on its meaning rather than on the exact words. And the more deeply and thoroughly you expand on its meaning, the better you will recall it.

An experiment by Bradshaw and Anderson (1982) illustrates some of these points. Participants read facts about famous people that they would later have to recall, such as 'At a critical point in his life, Mozart made a journey from Munich to Paris.' Some facts were elaborated according to either their causes or their consequences, as in 'Mozart wanted to leave Munich to avoid a romantic entanglement.' Other facts were presented alone. Later the participants were tested on their memory of just the facts (not the elaborations). Participants recalled more facts that had been given elaborations than facts that had been presented alone. Presumably, in adding the cause (or consequence) to their memory representation, they set up a retrieval path from the cause to the target fact in the following manner:

→ Mozart journeyed from Munich to Paris.
→ Mozart wanted to avoid a romantic entanglement in Munich.

At the time of recall, participants could either retrieve the target fact directly or retrieve it indirectly by following the path from its cause. Even if they forgot the target fact, they could infer it if they retrieved the cause.

Results like these establish an intimate connection between understanding and memory. The better we understand some material, the more connections we see between its parts. Because these connections can serve as retrieval links, the better we understand items and the more we remember.

Retrieval cues

Many cases of forgetting from long-term memory result from loss of access to the information rather than from loss of the information itself. That is, poor memory often reflects a retrieval failure rather than a storage failure. (Note that this is

When we forget information in long-term memory, it doesn't mean that the information itself is lost. We may be able to retrieve the information if something reminds us of it. This is one reason why families maintain photograph albums.

unlike working memory, in which forgetting is a result of decay or displacement and retrieval is thought to be relatively error free.) Trying to retrieve an item from long-term memory is like trying to find a book in a large library. Failure to find the book does not necessarily mean that it is not there; you may be looking in the wrong place, or the book may simply be misfiled.

Evidence for retrieval failures

Our everyday experience provides considerable evidence for retrieval failures. At some point all of us have been unable to recall a fact or experience, only to have it come to mind later. How many times have you taken an exam and not been able to recall a specific name, only to remember it later? Another example is the 'tip-of-the-tongue' phenomenon, in which a particular word or name lies tantalizingly outside our ability to recall it (Brown & McNeill, 1966). We may feel quite tormented until a search of memory (dredging up and then discarding words that are close but not quite right) finally retrieves the correct word.

A more striking example of retrieval failure occurs when a person undergoing psychotherapy retrieves a memory that had previously been forgotten. Although we lack firm evidence for such occurrences, they suggest that some seemingly forgotten memories are not lost but merely difficult to get at.

For stronger evidence that retrieval failures can cause forgetting, consider the following experiment. Participants were asked to memorize a long list of words. Some of the words were names of animals, such as dog, cat, horse; some were names of fruit, such as apple, orange, pear; some were names of furniture; and so on (see Table 8.1). At the time of recall, the participants were divided into two groups. One group was supplied with retrieval cues such as 'animal,' 'fruit,' and so on; the other group, the control group, was not.

TABLE 8.1 EXAMPLES FROM A STUDY OF RETRIEVAL FAILURES

Participants who were not given the retrieval cues recalled fewer words from the memorized list than other participants who were given the cues. This finding shows that problems at the retrieval stage of long-term memory are responsible for some memory failures.

List to be memorized

dog	cotton	oil
cat	wool	gas
horse	silk	coal
cow	rayon	wood
apple	blue	doctor
orange	red	lawyer
pear	green	teacher
banana	yellow	dentist
chair	knife	football
table	spoon	baseball
bed	fork	basketball
sofa	pan	
knife	hammer	shirt
gun	saw	socks
rifle	nails	pants
bomb	screwdriver	shoes

Retrieval

animals	cloth	fuels
fruit	color	professions
furniture	utensils	sports
weapons	tools	clothing

The group that was given the retrieval cues recalled more words than the control group. In a subsequent test, when both groups were given the retrieval cues, they recalled the same number of words. Hence, the initial difference in recall between the two groups must have been due to retrieval failures.

In sum, the better the retrieval cues available, the better our memory. This principle explains why we usually do better on a recognition test of memory than on a **recall test**. In a recognition test, we are asked whether we have seen a particular item before (for example, 'Was Bessie Smith one of the people you met at the wedding?'). The test item itself is an excellent retrieval cue for our memory of that item. In contrast, in a recall test, we have to produce the memorized items using minimal retrieval cues (for example, 'Recall the name of the woman you met at the party'). Since the retrieval cues in a recognition test are generally more useful than those in a recall test, performance is usually better on

recognition tests (such as multiple-choice exams) than on recall tests (such as essay exams; Tulving, 1974).

Interference

Among the factors that can impair retrieval, the most important is interference. If we associate different items with the same cue, when we try to use that cue to retrieve one of the items (the target item), the other items may become active and interfere with our recovery of the target. For example, if your friend Dan moves and you finally learn his new telephone number, you will find it difficult to retrieve the old number. Why? Because you are using the cue 'Dan's telephone number' to retrieve the old number, but instead this cue activates the new number, which interferes with recovery of the old one. (This is referred to as retroactive interference.) Or suppose that your reserved space in a parking garage, which you have used for a year, is changed. At first you may find it difficult to retrieve your new parking location from memory. Why? Because you are trying to learn to associate your new location with the cue 'my parking place,' but this cue retrieves the old location, which interferes with the learning of the new one (proactive interference). In both examples, the power of retrieval cues ('Dan's telephone number' or 'my parking place') to activate particular target items decreases with the number of other items associated with those cues. The more items are associated with a cue, the more overloaded it becomes and the less effective it is in aiding retrieval.

Interference can operate at various levels, including the level of whole facts. In one experiment, participants first learned to associate various facts with the names of professions. For example, they learned the following associations:

The banker

1 was asked to address the crowd

2 broke the bottle, and

3 did not delay the trip.

The lawyer

1 realized that the seam was split, and

2 painted an old barn.

The occupational names 'banker' and 'lawyer' were the retrieval cues. Since 'banker' was associated with three facts and 'lawyer' was associated with just two, 'banker' should have been less useful than 'lawyer' in retrieving any of its associated facts ('banker' was the more overloaded cue). When participants were later given a recognition test, they did take longer to recognize any one of the facts learned about the banker than any one of those learned about the lawyer. In this study, then, interference slowed the speed of retrieval. Many other experiments show that interference can lead to a complete retrieval failure if the target items are weak or the interference is strong (Anderson, 1983). Indeed, it has

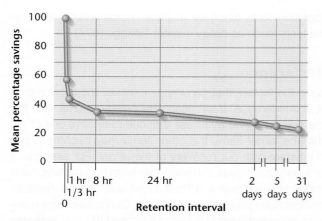

FIGURE 8.10 **Forgetting as a Function of Time.** *A forgetting curve graphs the decline in recall as a function of time. This graph was one of the first forgetting graphs ever.*

long been thought that interference is a major reason why forgetting from long-term memory increases with time: the relevant retrieval cues become more and more overloaded with time (see Figure 8.10).

Models of retrieval

In attempting to explain interference effects, researchers have developed a variety of models of retrieval. As with retrieval from short-term memory, some models of long-term-memory retrieval are based on a search process whereas others are based on an activation process.

The interference effects in the banker–lawyer experiment fit nicely with the idea that retrieval from long-term memory may be thought of as a search process (e.g., Raaijmakers & Shiffrin, 1981). To illustrate, consider how the sentence 'The banker broke the bottle' might be recognized (see Figure 8.11). The term 'banker' accesses its representation in memory, which localizes the search to the relevant part of long-term memory. There, three paths need to be searched to verify that 'broke the bottle' was one of the facts learned about the banker. In contrast, if the test sentence is 'The lawyer painted an old barn,' there are only two paths to be searched. Since the duration of a search increases with the number of paths to be considered, retrieval will be slower for the 'banker' sentence than for the 'lawyer' one.

An alternative way to think about the retrieval process is in terms of activation. When trying to recognize 'The banker broke the bottle,' for example, the participant activates the representation for 'banker' and the activation then spreads simultaneously along the three paths emanating from 'banker' (see Figure 8.11). When sufficient activation reaches 'broke the bottle,' the sentence can be recognized. Interference arises because the activation from the banker representation must be subdivided among the paths emanating from it. Hence, the more facts associated with 'banker,' the thinner the activation will be on each path and the longer it will take for sufficient activation to reach any particular fact. Thus, thinking of retrieval in terms of spreading activation can also account for why interference slows retrieval (Anderson, 1983).

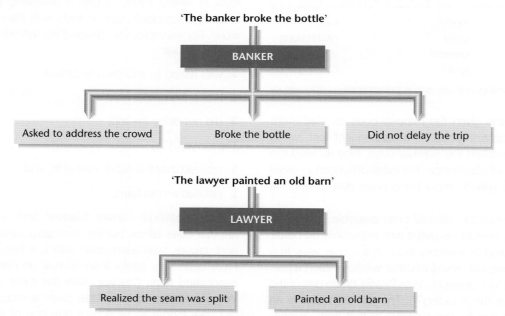

FIGURE 8.11 **Retrieval as a Search Process Versus an Activation Process.** *When the sentence 'The banker broke the bottle' is presented, the term 'banker' accesses the banker representation in long-term memory. Once at this representation, there are three paths to be searched. When the sentence 'The lawyer painted an old barn' is presented, 'lawyer' accesses the lawyer representation, from which there are two paths to be searched. Alternatively, the term 'banker' may activate the banker representation, and this activation then spreads simultaneously along the three paths (and similarly for the 'lawyer' example).*

Forgetting: Loss of information from storage

The fact that some forgetting is due to retrieval failures does not imply that all forgetting is. It seems most unlikely that everything we ever learned is still there in memory waiting for the right retrieval cue. Some information is almost certainly forgotten; that is, lost from storage (Loftus & Loftus, 1980).

Some evidence of storage loss comes from people who receive electroconvulsive therapy to alleviate severe depression (a mild electric current applied to the brain produces a brief epileptic-like seizure and momentary unconsciousness; see Chapter 16). In such cases the patient loses some memory for events that occurred in the months just prior to the shock, but not for earlier events (Squire & Fox, 1980). These memory losses are unlikely to be due to retrieval failures because if the shock disrupted retrieval, all memories should be affected, not just the recent ones. More likely, the shock disrupts storage processes that consolidate new memories over a period of months or longer, and information that is not consolidated is lost from storage.

Most research on storage in long-term memory is done at the biological level. Researchers have made substantial progress in determining the neuroanatomical bases of consolidation. It appears that the critical brain structures involved are the hippocampus and the cortex surrounding the hippocampus (which includes the enthorhinal, perirhinal, and parahippocampal cortices; they are involved in the exchange of information between the hippocampus and much of the cerebral cortex). The hippocampus's role in consolidation seems to be that of a cross-referencing system, linking together aspects of a particular memory that are stored in separate parts of the brain (Squire, 1992). While a global memory loss in humans usually occurs only when the surrounding cortex as well as the hippocampus is impaired, damage to the hippocampus alone can result in severe memory disturbance. This fact was demonstrated by a study that started with an analysis of a particular patient's memory problems (due to complications from coronary bypass surgery) and ended with a detailed autopsy of his brain after his death; the autopsy revealed that the hippocampus was the only brain structure that was damaged (Zola-Morgan et al., 1989).

A study using monkeys provides the best evidence we have that the function of the hippocampus is to consolidate relatively new memories. Monkeys learned to discriminate between items in 100 pairs of objects. For each pair, there was food under one object, which the monkey got only if it chose that object. Twenty of the pairs were learned 16 weeks before the researchers removed some monkeys' hippocampus; additional sets of 20 problems were learned either 12, 8, 4, or 2 weeks before the hippocampal surgery. Two weeks after the surgery, the researchers tested the experimental monkeys' memory and compared it to that of a control group of monkeys whose hippocampus was left intact. The experimental monkeys remembered discriminations that they had learned 8, 12, or 16 weeks before surgery just as well as control monkeys did, but did not remember the discriminations learned 2 or 4 weeks before surgery as well as the control monkeys. Moreover, the experimental monkeys actually remembered less about the discriminations learned 2 to 4 weeks before surgery than about the discriminations learned earlier. These results suggest that memories need to be processed by the hippocampus for a period of a few weeks, for it is only during this period that memory is impaired by removal of the hippocampus. Permanent long-term memory storage is almost certainly localized in the cortex, particularly in the regions where sensory information is interpreted (Squire, 1992; Zola-Morgan & Squire, 1990).

Interactions between encoding and retrieval

In describing the encoding stage, we noted that operations carried out during encoding, such as elaboration, make retrieval easier. Two other encoding factors also increase the chances of successful retrieval: (a) organizing the information at the time of encoding, and (b) ensuring that the context in which information is encoded is similar to that in which it will be retrieved.

Organization

The more we organize the material we encode, the easier it is to retrieve. Suppose that you were at a conference at which you met various professionals – doctors, lawyers, and journalists. When you later try to recall their names, you will do better if you initially organize the information by profession. Then you can ask yourself, 'Who were the doctors I met? Who were the lawyers?' and so forth. A list of names or words is far easier to recall when we encode the information into categories and then retrieve it on a category-by-category basis (e.g., Bower et al., 1969).

Context

It is easier to retrieve a particular fact or episode if you are in the same context in which you encoded it (Estes, 1972). For example, it is a good bet that your ability to retrieve the names of your classmates in the first and second grades would improve if you were to walk through the corridors of your elementary school. Similarly, your ability to retrieve an emotional moment with a close friend – for example, an argument with her in a restaurant – would be greater if you were back in the place where the incident occurred. This may explain why we are sometimes overcome with a torrent of memories when we visit a place where we once lived. The context in which an event was encoded is one of the most powerful retrieval cues (see Figure 8.12).

Context is not always external to the individual. It can include what is happening inside us when we encode information – that is, our internal state. For example, individuals who learned a list

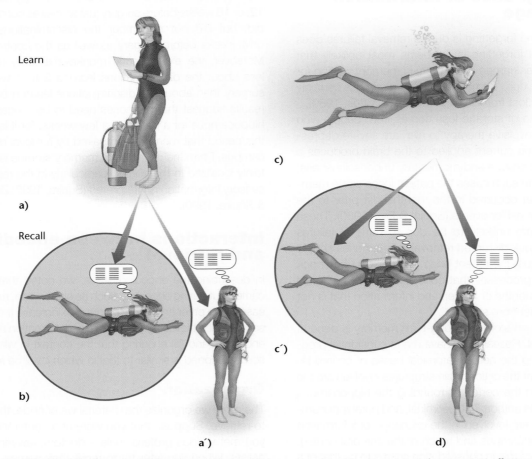

Learn

a)

Recall

b)

c)

c´)

a´)

d)

FIGURE 8.12 **Effects of Environmental Context on Retrieval.** *In an experiment to demonstrate how context affects retrieval, one group of deep-sea divers learned a list of words while they were on the beach (panel a), and another group of divers learned the list while they were beneath 15 feet of water (panel c). Later, each group was divided in half and tried to recall the words either in the same environment in which they had learned them (panels a' and c') or in a different environment (panels b and d).*

of words while under the influence of marijuana recalled more of the words when tested in the same drug-induced state than when tested in a non-drugged state, and individuals who learned the list in a non-drugged state recalled more words when tested in a non-drugged state than when tested in a drug-induced state (Eich, 1980). Such cases are referred to as state-dependent learning because memory is partly dependent on the internal state prevailing during learning. It is thought that feelings evoked by the altered state serve as cues for retrieving information encoded while in that state. The evidence for this phenomenon is controversial, but it does suggest that memory does improve when our internal state during retrieval matches our internal state during encoding (Eich, 1980).

Emotional factors in forgetting

So far we have treated memory as if it were entirely separate from emotion. But don't we sometimes remember or forget

material because of its emotional content? There has been a great deal of research on this question. The results suggest that emotion can influence long-term memory in five distinct ways: rehearsal, flashbulb memories, retrieval interference via anxiety, context effects, and repression.

Rehearsal

The simplest idea is that we tend to think about emotionally charged situations, negative as well as positive, more than we think about neutral ones. We rehearse and organize exciting memories more than we do blander ones. For example, you may forget where you saw this or that movie, but if a fire breaks out while you are in a theater, that incident will dominate your thoughts for a while and you will describe the setting over and over to friends as well as think about the setting over and over to yourself, thereby rehearsing and organizing it. Since we know that rehearsal and organization can improve retrieval from long-term memory, it is not surprising that many researchers have found that memory is better for emotional situations than for unemotional ones (Neisser, 1982; Rapaport, 1942).

Flashbulb memories

The second way emotion can affect memory is via **flashbulb memories**. A flashbulb memory is a vivid and relatively permanent record of the circumstances in which one learned of an emotionally charged, significant event. Many people remember exactly where they were when they learned about the London bombings that took place on July 7th 2005 and who told them about it. Many may also have flashbulb memories of the attacks on the Pentagon and on the World Trade Center in the USA on September 11th 2001. There is a published report indicating that over a century ago Americans had flashbulb memories of the assassination of Abraham Lincoln. When Colegrove (1899) interviewed 179 people, 127 of them were able to give full particulars as to where they were and what they were doing when they heard of Lincoln's assassination.

The problem with early studies of flashbulb memories, such as Colegrove's, is that there was no way of assessing whether they were correct. One man, for example, described detailed memories of a powerful 1960 earthquake in Chile, recalling being woken up early in the morning by the violent shaking of his house and noticing, among other things, that his grandfather clock had stopped at 6:00 a.m. sharp. Many years later, he discovered that the earthquake had actually taken place at 2:11 p.m.: although the earthquake was certainly real, his vivid 'flashbulb' memories of its taking place in the morning were not. Later we discuss the reconstructive processes that lead to such vivid but incorrect memories. For the moment, it is important to point out that when flashbulb memories are carefully studied in conjunction with a record or what actually happened, flashbulb memories turn out to be susceptible to decay and interference just like other kinds of

Many people think they can remember exactly where they were and what they were doing when they heard about the shocking news of the destruction of the Twin Towers.

memories (e.g., Curci *et al.,* 2001; Neisser & Harsch, 1993; Schmolck *et al.,* 2000; Sierra & Berrios, 2000).

Retrieval interference via anxiety

There are also cases in which negative emotions hinder retrieval, which brings us to the third way emotion can affect memory. An experience that many students have at one time or another illustrates this process:

> You are taking an exam about which you are not very confident. You can barely understand the initial question, let alone answer it. Signs of panic appear. Although the second question really isn't hard, the anxiety triggered by the previous question spreads to this one. By the time you look at the third question, it wouldn't matter whether it only asked for your telephone number. There's no way you can answer it. You're in a complete panic.

What is happening to memory here? Failure to deal with the first question produced anxiety. Anxiety is often accompanied by extraneous thoughts, such as 'I'm going to fail' or 'Everybody will think I'm stupid.' These thoughts fill our consciousness and interfere with attempts to retrieve information that is relevant to the question; this may be why memory fails. According to this view, anxiety does not directly cause memory failure; rather, it causes, or is associated with, extraneous thoughts, and these thoughts cause memory failure by interfering with retrieval (Holmes, 1974).

Context effects

Emotion may also affect memory through a context effect. As noted earlier, memory is best when the context at the time of retrieval matches that at the time of encoding. Since our emotional state during learning is part of the context, if the material we are learning makes us feel sad, perhaps we can best retrieve that material when we feel sad again. Experimenters have demonstrated such an emotional-context effect. Participants agreed to keep diaries for a week, recording every emotional incident that occurred and noting whether it was pleasant or unpleasant. One week after they handed in their diaries, the participants returned to the laboratory and were hypnotized. Half the participants were put in a pleasant mood and the other half in an unpleasant mood. All were asked to recall the incidents recorded in their diaries. For participants in a pleasant mood, most of the incidents they recalled had been rated as pleasant at the time that they were experienced; for participants in an unpleasant mood at retrieval, most of the incidents recalled had been rated as unpleasant at the time that they were experienced. As expected, recall was best when the dominant emotion during retrieval matched that during encoding (Bower, 1981).

Repression

Thus far, all of the means by which emotions can influence memory rely on principles already discussed – namely, rehearsal, interference, and context effects. Another view of emotion and memory, Freud's theory of the unconscious, brings up new principles. Freud proposed that some emotional experiences in childhood are so traumatic that allowing them to enter consciousness many years later would cause the individual to be totally overwhelmed by anxiety. Such traumatic experiences are said to be repressed, or stored in the unconscious, and they can be retrieved only when some of the emotion associated with them is defused. Repression, therefore, represents the ultimate retrieval failure: access to the target memories is actively blocked. This notion of active blocking makes the repression hypothesis qualitatively different from the ideas about forgetting discussed earlier. (For a discussion of Freud's theory, see Chapter 13.)

Repression is such a striking phenomenon that we would of course like to study it in the laboratory, but it has proved difficult to do this. To induce true repression in the laboratory, the experimenter must cause the participant to experience something extremely traumatic, but this obviously would be unethical. The studies that have been done have exposed participants to mildly upsetting experiences, and the results have been mixed (Baddeley, 1990; Erdelyi, 1985).

In sum, long-term memory is a system that can hold information for days, years, or decades, typically in a code based on meaning, although other codes are possible. Retrieval of information from this system is sensitive to interference; many apparent 'storage losses' are really retrieval failures. Storage in this system involves consolidation, a process that is mediated by the hippocampal system. Many aspects of long-term memory can be influenced by emotion; such influences may reflect selective rehearsal, retrieval interference, the effects of context, or two special mechanisms: flashbulb memories and repression.

INTERIM SUMMARY

- ➔ Information in long-term memory is usually encoded according to its meaning.
- ➔ Forgetting in long-term memory is due to retrieval failures (the information is there but cannot be found) and to interference by new information.
- ➔ Some forgetting from long-term memory is due to a loss from storage, particularly when there is a disruption of the processes that consolidate new memories. The biological locus of consolidation includes the hippocampus and surrounding cortex. Recent research suggests that consolidation takes a few weeks to be completed.

- ➔ Retrieval failures in long-term memory are less likely when the items are organized during encoding and when the context at the time of retrieval is similar to the context at the time of encoding.
- ➔ Retrieval processes can also be disrupted by emotional factors.

CRITICAL THINKING QUESTION

1 We reviewed various proposals about how emotion affects explicit long-term memory. Some of these proposals imply that emotion helps memory, whereas others suggest that emotion hurts memory. How can you reconcile these apparent differences?

IMPLICIT MEMORY

Thus far, we have been concerned mainly with situations in which people remember personal facts. In such cases memory is a matter of consciously recollecting the past, and is said to be expressed explicitly. But there seems to be another kind of memory, one that is often manifested in skills and shows up as an improvement in the performance of some perceptual, motor, or cognitive task without conscious recollection of the experiences that led to the improvement. For example, with practice we can steadily improve our ability to recognize words in a foreign language, but at the moment that we are recognizing a word, and thereby demonstrating our skill, we need not have any conscious recollection of the lessons that led to our improvement. In such cases, memory is expressed implicitly (Schacter, 1989).

Memory in amnesia

Much of what is known about implicit memory has been learned from people who suffer **amnesia**, or partial loss of memory. Amnesia may result from very different causes, including accidental injuries to the brain, strokes, encephalitis, alcoholism, electroconvulsive shock, and surgical procedures (for example, removal of the hippocampus to reduce epilepsy). Amnesia can be anterograde or retrograde. Anterograde amnesia, which can be extensive, is a profound inability to remember day-to-day events and, hence, to acquire new factual information. Retrograde amnesia is an inability to remember events that occurred prior to the injury or disease. The extent of such retrograde amnesia varies from one patient to another. It is possible for patients to exhibit only anterograde amnesia, only retrograde amnesia, or both.

Memory for skills such as tying one's shoelaces is referred to as implicit memory.

Aside from retrograde and anterograde memory losses, the typical amnesiac appears relatively normal: he or she has a normal vocabulary, the usual knowledge about the world (at least before the onset of the amnesia), and generally no loss of intelligence. An intensively studied patient, identified as N.A., sustained a brain injury when he was struck by a miniature fencing foil that entered the brain through the nose. After the accident, he became unable to participate in a normal conversation because at the least distraction he would lose his train of thought. N.A. suffered from anterograde amnesia as well as some retrograde amnesia covering a period of 2 years prior to his injury, but other cognitive abilities remained intact. Another patient, known as H.M., read the same magazines over and over and continually needed to be reintroduced to doctors who had been treating him for decades.

H.M., who has recently been identified as Henry Gustav Molaison after his passing in December 2008, is the most famous of the brain-damaged patients whose memory functioning has been studied extensively (Milner, 1970; Squire, 1992). At the age of 27, H.M., who suffered from severe epilepsy, underwent surgery to remove portions of the temporal lobe and limbic system on both sides of his brain. The surgery left him unable to form new memories, although he could remember events that had occurred prior to the surgery.

H.M. could retain new information as long as he focused on it, but as soon as he was distracted he would forget the information, and he was unable to recall it later. On one occasion, for example, he kept the number 584 in his mind for 15 minutes, using the following mnemonic system: '5, 8, 4 add to 17. You remember 8, subtract from 17 and it leaves 9. Divide 9 by half and you get 5 and 4, and there you are – 584' (quoted in Milner, 1970). A few minutes later, however, H.M.'s attention shifted and he could no longer remember either the number or his method for remembering it.

Skills and priming

A striking aspect of amnesia is that not all kinds of memory are disrupted. Thus, while amnesiacs generally are unable to either remember old facts about their lives or learn new ones, they have no difficulty remembering and learning perceptual and motor skills. This suggests that there is a different memory for facts than for skills. More generally, it suggests that explicit and implicit memory (which encode facts and skills, respectively) are different systems.

The skills that are preserved in amnesia include motor skills, such as tying one's shoelaces or riding a bike, and perceptual skills, such as normal reading or reading words that are projected into a mirror (and hence reversed). Consider the ability of reading mirror-reversed words. To do this well takes a bit of practice (try holding this book in front of a mirror and reading it). Amnesiacs improve with practice at the same rate as normal participants, although they may have no memory of having participated in earlier practice sessions (Cohen & Squire, 1980). They show normal memory for the skill but virtually no memory for the learning episodes that developed it (the latter being facts).

A similar pattern emerges in situations in which prior exposure to a stimulus facilitates or primes later processing of that stimulus. This pattern is illustrated in the experiment outlined in Table 8.2. In Stage 1 of the experiment, amnesiac and normal participants were given a list of words to study. In Stage 2, stems of words on the list and stems of words not on the list were presented, and the participants tried to complete them (see Table 8.2). The normal participants performed as expected, completing more stems when they were drawn from words on the list than when they were drawn from words not on the list. This difference is referred to as priming because the words presented in Stage 1 facilitated or primed performance on the stem completion problems presented in Stage 2. Significantly, amnesiacs also completed more stems in Stage 2 when they were drawn from words on the list than when they were drawn from words not on the list. In fact, the degree of priming for amnesiacs was exactly the same as for normals. This finding indicates that when memory is manifested implicitly, as in priming, amnesiacs perform normally.

TABLE 8.2 PROCEDURE FOR AN EXPERIMENT TO STUDY IMPLICIT MEMORY IN AMNESIA

Stage 1	Example
Present list of words for study	MOTEL

Stage 2	
Present stems of list words and non-list words for completion. Number of list words completed minus number of non-list words completed = Priming	MOT BLA

Stage 3	
Present original list of words plus new words for recognition	MOTEL STAND

In Stage 3 of the experiment, the original words were presented again along with some novel words, and participants had to recognize which words had appeared on the list. Now amnesiacs remembered far fewer words than normals. Thus, when memory is tested explicitly, as in recognition, amnesiacs perform far below normals.

There is an interesting variation of the preceding study that further strengthens its conclusion. Suppose that in Stage 2 participants are instructed that they will perform better on the stem-completion task if they try to think of the words presented earlier. This instruction makes stem completion into an explicit memory task (because conscious recollection is being emphasized). Now amnesiacs show substantially less priming than normal participants (Graf & Mandler, 1984).

Childhood amnesia

One of the most striking aspects of human memory is that everyone suffers from a particular kind of amnesia: virtually no one can recall events from the first years of life, even though this is the time when experience is at its richest. This curious phenomenon was first discussed by Freud (1905), who called it childhood amnesia.

Freud discovered the phenomenon by observing that his patients were generally unable to recall events from their first 3 to 5 years of life. At first you might think that there is nothing unusual about this, because memory for events declines with time, and for adults there has been a lot of intervening time since early childhood. But childhood amnesia cannot be reduced to normal forgetting. Most 30 year olds can recall a good deal about their high school years, but it is a rare 18 year old who can tell you anything about his or her third

year of life; yet the time interval – about 15 years – is roughly the same in each case.

In some studies, people have been asked to recall and date their childhood memories. For most people, their first memory is of something that occurred when they were age 3 or older; a few individuals will report memories prior to the age of 1. A problem with these reports, however, is that we can never be sure that the 'remembered' event actually occurred (the person may have reconstructed what he or she thought happened). This problem was overcome in an experiment in which participants were asked a total of 20 questions about a childhood event that was known to have occurred – the birth of a younger sibling – the details of which could be verified by another person. The questions asked of each participant dealt with events that occurred when the mother left to go to the hospital (for example, 'What time of day did she leave?'), when the mother was in the hospital ('Did you visit her?'), and when the mother and infant returned home ('What time of day did they come home?'). The participants were college students, and their ages at the time that their siblings were born varied from one to 17 years. The results are shown in Figure 8.13. The number of questions answered is plotted as a function of the participant's age when the sibling was born. If the sibling was born before the participant was three years old, the person could not recall a thing about it. If the birth occurred after that, recall increased with age at the time of the event. These results suggest almost total amnesia for the first 3 years of life. More recent research, however, suggests that such recall may be

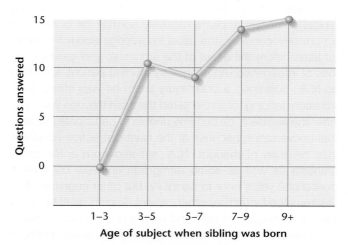

FIGURE 8.13 Recall of an Early Memory. *In an experiment on childhood amnesia, college-age individuals were asked 20 questions about the events surrounding the birth of a younger sibling. The average number of questions answered is plotted as a function of the individual's age when the sibling was born. If the birth occurred before the fourth year of life, no individual could recall a thing about it. If the birth occurred after that, recall increased with age at the time of the event.*

improved if more cues are given and the cues are more specific (Fivush & Hamond, 1991). Still, the bulk of the evidence indicates that we should be skeptical about reports of memory from the first few years of life.

What causes childhood amnesia? A generally accepted explanation is that childhood amnesia is due to a massive difference between how young children encode experience and how adults organize their memories. Adults structure their memories in terms of categories and schemas ('She's that kind of person,' 'It's that kind of situation'), while young children encode their experiences without embellishing them or connecting them to related events. Once a child begins to form associations between events and to categorize those events, early experiences become lost (Schachtel, 1982).

What causes the shift from early childhood to adult forms of memory? One factor is biological development. The hippocampus, which is known to be involved in consolidating memories, is not mature until roughly a year or two after birth. Therefore, events that take place in the first 2 years of life cannot be sufficiently consolidated and consequently cannot be recalled later. Other causes of the shift to adult memory are better understood at the psychological level. These include cognitive factors, particularly the development of language and the beginning of schooling. Both language and the kind of thinking emphasized in school provide new ways of organizing experiences, ways that may be incompatible with the way the young child encodes experiences. Interestingly, language development reaches an early peak at age three, while schooling often begins at age five; and the age span from three to five is the time when childhood amnesia seems to end.

Conceptual implicit memory

There is substantial evidence suggesting that in addition to skills and words, concepts may be implicitly stored and unconsciously activated. For instance, if a person is presented a word (e.g. 'aubergine') and asked to write down words that come to mind, and is later asked to name the vegetables contained in ratatouille, it is more likely that the person will include aubergine in her answer even if she fails to consciously remember the previous presentation (e.g., Blaxton, 1989). The notion of conceptual implicit memory plays an important role in most modern theories of prejudice. The idea is that even a well-intentioned person may store negative implicit conceptual information about a social group based on social experiences such as media presentations. This may lead to prejudiced behaviors in situations where those implicit memories are automatically activated. For example, consider a simple experiment where participants read word pairs as quickly as possible and then press a button to receive the next word pair. Even Caucasian American college students who claim to have positive attitudes towards African Americans are likely to respond more quickly to the word pair *black–lazy* than to the pair *black–smart* (e.g., Kawakami & Dovidio, 2001).

A variety of memory systems

On the basis of work with various brain-damaged patients, researchers have proposed that both explicit and implicit memory come in various forms. One such proposal is presented in the Concept Review Table below. The basic distinction is between explicit and implicit memory. (Recall that explicit memory involves consciously recollecting the past, while implicit memory shows up as improved performance of a skill without conscious recollection of the lessons that led to it.) With regard to implicit memory, a further distinction is made between perceptual-motor skills, such as reading mirror-reversed words, and priming, as occurs in word-stem completions. The reason for assuming that skills and priming may involve different memory stores is that there are patients with brain damage (individuals in the early stages of Alzheimer's disease) who are able to learn motor skills but show less priming than normal. In contrast, there are other brain-damaged patients (individuals with Huntington's disease) who show normal priming but have difficulty learning new motor skills (Schacter, 1989).

The concept review table also distinguishes between two kinds of explicit memory, which are referred to as episodic and semantic. Episodic facts refer to personal episodes and semantic facts to general truths. To illustrate, your memory of your high-school graduation is an episodic fact, and so is your memory of what you had for dinner last night. In each of these cases, the episode is encoded with respect to you, the individual (your graduation, your dinner, and so on), and often with respect to a specific time and place as well. In contrast, semantic facts, such as your memory or knowledge that the word 'bachelor' means an unmarried man and that September has 30 days, is encoded in relation to other knowledge rather than in relation to yourself, and there is no coding of time and place (Tulving, 1985). This distinction between semantic and episodic memory fits with the fact that although amnesiacs have severe difficulty

**CONCEPT REVIEW TABLE
PROPOSED
CLASSIFICATION
OF MEMORY STORES**

Squire *et al.* (1990) propose that there are several different memory systems. The basic distinction is between explicit and implicit memory (which they refer to as *declarative* and *non-declarative*, respectively).

Explicit (Declarative) memory	*Implicit (Non-declarative) memory*
Episodic Semantic	Skills Priming Conditioning Non-associative

CUTTING EDGE RESEARCH HOW METACOGNITION CAN BE USED TO IMPROVE STUDENT PERFORMANCE

Phil Higham, University of Southampton

Good memory is clearly an important part of university success. After all, no student who forgets most of the course material during an exam will perform well. But is that all there is to it? Research in the area of *metacognition* suggests not. Flavell (1979) first described metacognition as thinking about thinking. Sounds complicated right? However, as a student, you make metacognitive decisions all the time, perhaps without thinking about it, and the accuracy of these decisions may be as important to your academic success as having a good memory.

To illustrate, suppose you are revising the course material in preparation for an upcoming test. After studying one topic for some time, you decide that you know it well enough to start revising the next topic. That decision – the assessment that your own state of learning was sufficient to move onto the next topic – is a metacognitive decision (e.g., van Loon *et al.*, in press). It involves knowing about your own state of learning, or more formally, *memory monitoring*.

How might students use metacognition to improve their own performance in university? There are many ways to do this, but here I will focus on three available options. The first is a report option (e.g., Higham, 2007). When asked a question but you are unsure of an answer, you may choose to withhold that response, thus ensuring that you do not report an error. For example, you may be required to provide answers to two of three essay questions for an exam. Students can score very well as long as they can correctly answer two of the questions *and* they know which questions they know the answers to (metacognition). Similarly, to control the problem of inflated scores caused by wild guessing on multiple-choice tests, some instructors implement negative marking or formula scoring (i.e., a fraction of a mark is subtracted for incorrect responses but not for omissions). Deciding which answers to offer and which to omit also involves metacognition (e.g., Higham & Arnold, 2007); that is, students must accurately self-assess their memory and make report/withhold decisions accordingly.

Another option that involves meta-cognition and which students can use to regulate their university performance involves the **grain-size** of the answer. For example, suppose a student is writing an exam essay on Wilhelm Wundt creating the first experimental laboratory in Leipzig, Germany, but she cannot remember the exact date the laboratory was set up (actually 1879). She erroneously believes it was 1875, but she is not confident. To get around this memory failure, she may provide a *coarse-grained* (unspecific) answer rather than a *fine-grained* (specific) one and write that the laboratory was created in the '1870s' rather than '1875.' This decision was a wise one because a (incorrect) fine-grained response would likely be penalized whereas her (correct) coarse-grained response may not. As with the report option, though, to use the grain-size option successfully, she must accurately monitor her memory.

A third option available to students is the *plurality* option (e.g., Higham, in press; Luna *et al.*, 2011; Luna & Martin-Luengo, 2012). This option is similar to the grain-size option in that it entails how specific an answer is. However, rather than adjusting the quantitative boundary around a single answer as in the example above (a decade versus a single year), it involves using metacognition to adjust the *number* of alternative answers to a question. For example, some multiple-choice tests allow students to offer more than one answer, and if the correct answer is included in the answers offered, part marks are assigned. Similarly, students may offer several alternatives on an essay to 'cover all the bases.'

Although all three options can be used to maintain good performance, they must be used with caution. Withholding too many answers, providing ridiculously coarse answers, or offering too many alternatives, can all make an answer uninformative, and poor marks are likely to result (Goldsmith & Koriat, 2008). However, when used judiciously and informed by accurate memory monitoring, these options show that student success is more than just remembering.

---

remembering personal episodes, they seem relatively normal in their general knowledge.

Implicit memory in normal individuals

Studies using normal individuals also suggest that there are separate systems for explicit and implicit memories. There seem to be fundamental differences in how these two kinds of memories are implemented in the brain. The critical evidence comes from brain-scanning experiments (PET). In one experiment (Squire *et al.*, 1992), participants first studied a list of 15 words and then were exposed to three different conditions. The implicit-memory condition was the stem-completion task. Half the stems were drawn from the 15 words originally studied and the other half were new; participants were instructed to complete the stems with the first words that came to mind. The second condition of interest involved explicit memory. Again word stems were presented, but now participants were instructed to use them to recall words from the initial list of 15.

The third condition was a control. Word stems were presented, and participants were instructed to complete them with the first words that came to mind, but now none of the stems were drawn from the words initially studied. The control condition therefore requires no memory. Participants performed all three of these tasks while their brains were being scanned.

Consider first what the brain is doing during the explicit-memory task. From the material presented in the first section of this chapter, we might expect that (1) the hippocampus is involved (remember, this structure is critical in forming long-term memories), and (2) most of the brain activity will be in the right hemisphere (because the task emphasized retrieval, and long-term retrieval involves mainly right-hemisphere processes). This is exactly what was found. More specifically, when brain activity in the explicit-memory condition was compared with that in the control condition, there was increased activation of hippocampal and frontal regions in the right hemisphere.

Now consider the implicit-memory condition. Compared with the control condition, it showed decreases in activation rather than increases. That is, priming is reflected in less-than-usual neural activity, as if there has been a 'greasing of the neural wheels.' Implicit memory, then, has the opposite neural consequences of explicit memory, demonstrating a biological difference between the two kinds of memory.

This evidence points up once again the interconnections between biological and psychological research. In fact, throughout this chapter we have seen instances of the role of biological evidence in explaining psychological phenomena. In many cases the psychological evidence was obtained first and used to direct subsequent biological research. For example, the cognitive distinction between short-term and long-term memory was made in papers published about a century ago, but only relatively recently have biologically oriented researchers been able to demonstrate some of the neural bases for this key distinction. Biological research is contributing to other areas of the study of memory as well. We now know something about the biological basis of storage in explicit long-term memory and about storage in the visual and verbal buffers of short-term memory. Such knowledge is not only useful in its own right but may also prove helpful in combating the ravages of memory brought about by diseases of aging such as stroke and Alzheimer's.

INTERIM SUMMARY

→ Explicit memory refers to the kind of memory manifested in recall or recognition, when we consciously recollect the past. Implicit memory refers to the kind of memory that manifests itself as an improvement on some perceptual, motor, or cognitive task, with no conscious recollection of the experiences that led to the improvement.

→ Although explicit memory – particularly recall and recognition of facts – breaks down in amnesia, implicit memory is usually spared. This suggests that there may be separate storage systems for explicit and implicit memory.

→ Research with normal individuals also indicates that there are separate systems for explicit and implicit memory. Brain-scanning studies with normal individuals show that explicit memory is accompanied by increased neural activity in certain regions, whereas implicit memory is accompanied by a decrease in neural activity in critical regions.

CRITICAL THINKING QUESTIONS

1 On the basis of what you have learned about explicit long-term memory, how would you go about studying for an exam that emphasizes factual recall?

2 We noted that childhood amnesia is related to the development of the hippocampus. What psychological factors might also contribute to childhood amnesia? (Think of things that change dramatically around age three.)

CONSTRUCTIVE MEMORY

Our description of memory processes so far might leave the impression that a good metaphor for creating, maintaining, and using information in long-term store would be creating, maintaining, and using a video tape. Consider these correspondences:

1 Information is acquired and placed into memory via sensation, perception, and attention in the same way as information is acquired and placed onto a video tape via a video camera.

2 Information is forgotten from long-term store in the same way as video tapes gradually become degraded.

3 Information cannot be retrieved from long-term store in the same way as it is difficult to find a particular scene on a home video – particularly if there are a lot of scenes on the video and/or it has been a long time since you last retrieved and viewed the scene.

Despite these apparent similarities, it would be a grave mistake to use a video recorder as the primary metaphor for understanding memory, because there is a very important and fundamental difference between how memory works and how a video tape works. Unlike a video tape, memory is a **constructive** and **reconstructive process**; that is, the memory for an event can and does depart systematically from the objective reality that gave rise to it, both at the time it is formed and then later over time. This crucial difference leads to some of the most interesting and counterintuitive aspects of memory. It almost certainly, for example, underlies Jennifer Thompson's seemingly strange, and certainly catastrophic memory misidentification of the man who raped her. In the subsections that follow, we will first recount a well known personal anecdote that nicely illustrates the reconstructive nature of memory. We will then trace the reconstructive nature of memory from original perception through long-term retrieval. Finally we will briefly discuss the already alluded-to relevance of reconstructive memory to the legal system.

Piaget's childhood memory

The renowned Swiss developmental psychologist Jean Piaget once described a vivid memory from his childhood:

> One of my first memories would date, if it were true, from my second year. I can still see, most clearly, the following scene, in which I believed until I was about 15. I was sitting in my pram, which my nurse was pushing in the Champs Elysees, when a man tried to kidnap me. I was held in by the strap fastened round me while my nurse bravely tried to stand between me and the thief. She received various scratches, and I can still see vaguely those on her face. Then a crowd gathered, a policeman with a short cloak and a white baton came up, and the man took to his heels. I can still see the whole scene, and can even place it near the tube station.

A vivid memory indeed! Why then did Piaget believe in it only 'until I was about 15'? What happened then?

> When I was about 15, my parents received a letter from my former nurse saying that she had been converted to the Salvation Army. She wanted to confess her past faults, and in particular, to return the watch she had been given as a reward [for saving Baby Jean from the kidnapper]. She had made up the whole story, faking the scratches. I, therefore, must have heard, as a child, the account of this story, which my parents believed, and projected into the past in the form of a visual memory.

So as it happened, Piaget discovered that this memory, vivid though it seemed, was not merely incorrect, but fabricated from whole cloth. When you think about it, the implications of this anecdote are far-reaching: at least some of what we firmly believe to be true is probably fiction. As we will discuss below, this implication is not quite as disturbing

as it might seem at first glance, because (1) it takes a special set of circumstances to create a false memory that is this dramatic, and (2) even when such memories are created, they generally do not have any serious real-world consequences. Be that as it may, however, some false memories, like Jennifer Thompson's, can sometimes have devastating consequences.

How do such memories come about? The answer is that they arise from a combination of constructive processes, which can be divided into those occurring at the time of the original encoding of the to-be-remembered event and those occurring after the memory of the remembered event has already been formed.

Constructive processes at the time of memory encoding

Memory **encoding** refers to processes that occur at the time that the long-term memory representation of some event is being established. From the perspective of establishing a long-term representation, encoding has two stages: initial perception (transfer of information into short-term memory), and then whatever processes are entailed in the transfer of information from short-term memory to long-term store. Construction of a false memory can occur at either or both of these stages.

Constructive perception

In Chapter 5, we discussed the systematic ways in which what is perceived does not necessarily correspond to what is objectively out in the world. In many instances, perception is determined not only by the 'bottom-up' processing of raw, objective, sensory data, but also by the 'top-down' influences of history, knowledge, and expectations. It is important to emphasize here what this means for later memory: what is perceived forms the basis for the initial memory; therefore, if what is originally perceived differs systematically from the objective world, the perceiver's initial memory – and, likely, later memories as well – of what happened will likewise be distorted.

To illustrate such constructive perception, we first turn to another personal anecdote, this one from one of the authors of this book (GL). In 1973, GL was visiting a friend who showed him a 'music box,' consisting of a cube, approximately 6 inches each side, with translucent faces. The box was connected to a stereo system, and, as music played, colored lights inside the box lit up in various sequences. With particular light combinations, certain images became clearly visible on the box's translucent sides: for instance, there was a Viet Cong soldier on one side, a picture of Bob Dylan on another side, and a picture of the Beatles on yet a third side. Intrigued by this sequence of images, GL and his friend became curious about how they were formed. They supposed that pictures from news magazines had been clipped and affixed to the inside of the box's translucent sides in such a way that they became visible only with certain combinations of colored lights. At length, they took the box apart to investigate. To their amazement, they discovered that there was nothing but random splatters of paint on the translucent sides: the vivid images they had perceived were not there in the world; rather they had been constructed out of randomness. And, even though GL and his friend discovered that their perceptions were illusory, GL maintains to this day a vivid memory of the music-box images that his perceptual system so artfully constructed.

A good example of how constructive perception can be demonstrated in the scientific laboratory is found in a phenomenon known as **perceptual interference**. Perceptual interference was originally described in a 1964 *Science* article by Jerome Bruner and Mary Potter, who showed observers pictures of common objects (say a rocket) and asked the observers to name the object. The catch was that the objects began by being out of focus – sufficiently out of focus that they were pretty much unrecognizable – and then were gradually brought into focus. There were two main conditions in the experiment. In the very-out-of-focus (VOF) condition, the objects started out very out of focus, while in the moderately out-of-focus (MOF) condition, the objects started out only moderately out of focus. The main finding was that the objects had to eventually be more focused in order that the observers were able to recognize them in the VOF condition rather than in the MOF condition.

Why was this? The hypothesis offered by Bruner and Potter was that, upon seeing any out-of-focus object, an observer would generate hypotheses about what the object was (for instance, an observer might initially hypothesize an out-of-focus rocket to be a pencil). Once a hypothesis was generated, the hypothesis itself largely drove the observer's perception – that is, as the object became more and more focused, the observer would continue to hold the incorrect perception even past the focus level that would allow another observer who *hadn't* generated any incorrect expectations to perceive the object correctly. Because observers in the VOF condition had more opportunity to form incorrect hypotheses than observers in the MOF condition, it would require a greater degree of focus for eventual correct recognition for the VOF than for the MOF observers.

Generation of inferences

As we have pointed out, perception is not sufficient to form a lasting memory of some event. Other processes have to occur that serve to transfer information corresponding to the event from short-term memory to long-term store. Constructive processes can occur here in the form of **inferences**.

Let's illustrate using memory for verbal material. Even when we read something as simple as a sentence we often draw inferences from it and store them along with the sentence in long-term store. This tendency is particularly strong when reading text because inferences are often needed to connect different lines. To illustrate, consider the following story, which was presented to participants in an experiment:

1 Provo is a picturesque kingdom in France.

2 Corman was heir to the throne of Provo.

3 He was so tired of waiting.

4 He thought arsenic would work well.

When reading this story, participants draw inferences at certain points. At line 3, they infer that Corman wanted to be king, which permits them to connect line 3 to the preceding line. But this is not a necessary inference (Corman could have been waiting for the king to receive him). At line 4, participants infer that Corman had decided to poison the king, so they can connect this line to what preceded it. Again, the inference is not a necessary one (there are people other than the king to poison, and there are other uses of arsenic). When participants' memories were later tested for exactly which lines had been presented, they had trouble distinguishing the story lines from the inferences we just described. It is hard to keep what was actually presented separate from what we added to it (Seifert *et al.*, 1985).

Post-event memory reconstruction

Earlier we cautioned against thinking of a video tape as an metaphor for memory. A better metaphor would be a file folder (either a physical, cardboard folder or a computer folder) containing the components of some complex enterprise we're working on – say the material for a novel we're writing, which would include our notes, our chapters-in-progress, our photographs, and so on. Every time we open this folder, the contents of it change in some fashion, as our work progresses. And so it is with our memory for some event: every time we revisit some memory in our minds, the memory changes in some fashion. We may, as we do during memory formation, generate inferences and store these inferences as part of our memory. We may strip away information that doesn't seem to make sense in light of other facts we know or we've learned. We may add new information that is suggested to us by others. All of these kinds of processes fall into the category of **post-event memory reconstruction**.

Internally generated inferences

There are many ways in which people can make inferences which they then incorporate into their memory. A recent example reported by Hannigan and Reinitz (2001) described inference in visual memory. In their experiment, observers viewed a slide sequence depicting some common activity, for example shopping in a supermarket. As part of the sequence they saw scenes depicting some relatively unusual situation (e.g., seeing oranges scattered over the supermarket floor).

Later, the observers confidently asserted that they had seen a picture that reasonably depicted a possible cause of this situation (e.g., a slide of a woman pulling an orange from the bottom of the pile) when in fact they had never seen the slide. These and related results strongly suggest that, in these situations, viewers make inferences about what must have happened, and incorporate the results of such inferences into their memory of the event.

Inferences can also be made based on **schemas**, a term used to refer to a mental representation of a class of people, objects, events, or situations. **Stereotypes**, on which we will focus momentarily, are a kind of schema because they represent classes of people (for example, Italians, women, athletes). Schemas can also be used to describe our knowledge about how to act in certain situations.

For example, most adults have a schema for how to eat in a restaurant (enter the restaurant, find a table, get a menu from the waiter, order food, and so on). Perceiving and thinking in terms of schemas enables us to process large amounts of information swiftly and economically. Instead of having to perceive and remember all the details of each new person, object, or event we encounter, we can simply note that it is like a schema already in our memory and encode and remember only its most distinctive features. The price we pay for such 'cognitive economy,' however, is that an object or event can be distorted if the schema used to encode it does not fit well.

Bartlett (1932) was perhaps the first psychologist to systematically study the effects of schemas on memory. He suggested that memory distortions much like those that occur when we fit people into stereotypes can occur when we attempt to fit stories into schemas. Research has confirmed Bartlett's suggestion. For example, after reading a brief story about a character going to a restaurant, people are likely to recall statements about the character eating and paying for a meal even though those actions were never mentioned in the story (Bower *et al.,* 1979).

Situations in which memory is driven by schemas seem a far cry from the simpler situations discussed earlier in the chapter. Consider, for example, memory for a list of unrelated words: here memory processes appear more bottom-up; that is, they function more to preserve the input than to construct something new. However, there is a constructive aspect even to this simple situation, for techniques such as using imagery add meaning to the input. Similarly, when we read a paragraph about a schema-based activity we must still preserve some of its specifics if we are to recall it correctly. Thus, the two aspects of memory – to preserve and to construct – may always be present, although their relative emphasis may depend on the exact situation.

As noted, one important kind of schema is a **social stereotype**, which concerns personality traits or physical attributes of a whole class of people. We may, for example, have a stereotype of the typical German (intelligent, meticulous,

serious) or of the typical Italian (artistic, carefree, fun-loving). These descriptions rarely apply to many people in the class and can often be misleading guides for social interaction. Our concern here, however, is not with the effects of stereotypes on social interaction (see Chapter 18 for a discussion of this) but with their effects on memory.

When presented with information about a person, we sometimes stereotype that person (for example, 'He's your typical Italian') and combine the information presented with that in our stereotype. Our memory of the person thus is partly constructed from the stereotype. To the extent that our stereotype does not fit the person, our recall can be seriously distorted. A British psychologist provides a first-hand account of such a distortion:

> In the week beginning 23 October, I encountered in the university, a male student of very conspicuously Scandinavian appearance. I recall being very forcibly impressed by the man's Nordic, Viking-like appearance – his fair hair, his blue eyes, and long bones. On several occasions, I recalled his appearance in connection with a Scandinavian correspondence I was then conducting and thought of him as the 'perfect Viking', visualizing him at the helm of a longship crossing the North Sea in quest of adventure. When I again saw the man on 23 November, I did not recognize him, and he had to introduce himself. It was not that I had forgotten what he looked like but that his appearance, as I recalled it, had become grossly distorted. He was very different from my recollection of him. His hair was darker, his eyes less blue, his build less muscular, and he was wearing spectacles (as he always does).

(Hunter, 1974, pp. 265–266)

The psychologist's stereotype of Scandinavians seems to have so overwhelmed any information he actually encoded about the student's appearance that the result was a highly constructed memory. It bore so little resemblance to the student that it could not even serve as a basis for recognition.

Externally provided suggestions

Post-event reconstruction may also occur as a result of information provided by others. A classic experiment, performed by Elizabeth Loftus and John Palmer (1974) illustrates this process. In the Loftus and Palmer experiment, a group of subjects were shown a film of a car accident (one car running into another). After the film, the subjects were asked a series of questions about the accident that they had just seen. The subjects were divided into two subgroups that were treated identically except for a single word in one of the questions. In particular, the 'hit' group was asked the following question

The stereotype of a 'typical rugby player' may interfere with our encoding of information about these people who could have entirely different characteristics from those included in the stereotype.

about speed: 'How fast was the car going when it hit the other car?' The corresponding question asked to the 'smashed' group was, 'How fast was the car going when it smashed into the other car?' Other than that, the 'hit' and 'smashed' groups were treated identically.

The first finding to emerge from this experiment was that the 'smashed' group provided a higher speed estimate than the 'hit' group (roughly 10.5 mph vs 8 mph). This is interesting, in that it demonstrates the effects of leading questions on the answers that are given. More relevant to the issue of post-event reconstruction, however, was the next part of the procedure: all subjects returned approximately a week later and were asked some additional questions about the accident. One of the questions was 'Did you see any broken glass?' In fact, there had been no broken glass, so the correct answer to the question was 'no.' However, the subjects who had originally been asked about speed using the verb 'smashed' were substantially more likely to incorrectly report

In remembering what happened in a traffic accident, we may use general knowledge (such as our knowledge of rules of the road or of the meaning of traffic signals) to construct a more detailed memory.

the presence of broken glass than were subjects who had originally been asked about speed using the verb 'hit.'

The interpretation of this finding is that the verb 'smashed' constituted **post-event information**. Upon hearing this word, the subjects reconstructed their memory for the accident in such a way as to be consistent with a violent accident in which two cars 'smashed' into one another. Integration into their memory of the broken glass was one consequence of such reconstruction. That is how the non-existent broken glass appeared in those subjects' memories a week later.

How powerful is the effect of suggestive information? The Loftus and Palmer study, along with thousands of others that have replicated its basic result over the past three decades, demonstrates the ease of structuring a situation such that a real event is remembered incorrectly with respect to incidental details. Is it possible that, in like fashion, a memory of an entirely fictional event could be created? This seems less likely, based on intuition and common sense; yet intuition and common sense are incorrect in this regard.

To begin with, there are anecdotes of false memories similar to Piaget's described earlier. Even more dramatically, there are occasional reports by people who claim to have experienced events that would be generally considered to be impossible, such as being abducted and experimented on by aliens. Given that these people actually believe that these experiences occurred, they would likely constitute prima facie evidence of false memories for complete events. However, interpretation of such anecdotal reports is problematical. First, implausible though such events are, we cannot completely rule out the possibility that they actually occurred. Second, and of somewhat more concern, we do not know that the witnesses are being truthful. One could argue that a few publicity-seeking members of the population carefully make up, and stick to such stories to gain attention.

More persuasive scientific evidence comes from recent laboratory studies in which memories of entirely fictional events have been shown to be implantable under controlled conditions. For example, Hyman *et al.* (1995) reported a study in which college students were asked whether they remembered a relatively unusual, and entirely fictional event (for example, attending a wedding reception and accidentally spilling a punch bowl on the parents of the bride) that subjects were told occurred when they were relatively young (around five years old). Initially, no one remembered these events. However following two interviews about the 'event' a substantial proportion of the students (20 to 25 percent) reported quite clear 'memories' for parts or all of the events. Indeed, many of the students began 'remembering' details that had never been presented to them (and which, of course, could not have corresponded to objective reality). For example, one subject initially had no recall of the wedding event, but in the second interview, stated, 'It was an outdoor wedding, and I think we were running around and knocked something over like the punch bowl or something and, um, made a big mess and of course got yelled at for it.' Other studies (e.g., Loftus & Pickrell, 1995; Loftus *et al.,* 1996) have reported similar findings, and another study (Garry *et al.,* 1996) has reported that it is possible to induce such memories by merely having people *imagine* fictional renderings of their pasts.

It thus appears that in these studies, subjects are using post-event information provided by the experimenters to create memories of entire events that never occurred. In addition, the process of imagining these events spontaneously led to additional, self-generated post-event information, involving additional details, which then also was incorporated.

As noted, not all subjects in these experiments actually remembered these false events. In general the percentage of people remembering was approximately 25 per cent. The Hyman *et al.* (1995) study reported some personality correlates of false memory creation. The first was scored on the Dissociative Experiences Scale, which measures the extent to which a person has lapses in memory and attention or fails to integrate awareness, thought, and memory. The second correlate was scored on the Creative Imagination Scale, which is a measure of hypnotizability and can also be construed as a self-report measure of the vividness of visual imagery.

Constructive memory and the legal system

As we have suggested in several of our discussions and examples, **constructive memory** is particularly important in the legal system where cases are frequently won or lost – and defendants are or are not meted out punishments ranging from prison sentences to death – on the basis of a witness's memory of what did or did not happen. A dramatic example of the consequences of a false memory is the years spent by Ronald Cotton languishing in prison as a result of Jennifer Thompson's false memory of who raped her. This is by no means an isolated incident but, sadly, is one of many known cases and countless unknown cases of miscarriages of justice caused by false memories. In this section, we will spend some time specifically describing the importance of memory in the legal system.

Confidence and accuracy

A scientist studying memory in the scientific laboratory has the luxury of knowing whether a participant's memory is correct or incorrect. This is because the scientist, having created the event that the witness is trying to remember, is in a position to compare the participant's response to objective reality. In the real world, however – particularly the real world of a witness whose memory is crucial to the outcome of some legal case – no one has the ability to judge objectively whether the witness is correct or incorrect, because there is no objective record of the original event (with a few minor exceptions, such as the discovery that a crime was captured on video as in the infamous Rodney King case). Therefore the main indication of whether a witness is or is not correct is the witness's *confidence* that his or her memory is accurate: a witness who says, 'I'm 100 percent sure that that's the man who raped me,' is judged to be more likely correct than a witness who says, 'I'm 75 percent sure that that's the man who raped me.' This means that a critical question for the legal system is: how good is a witness's confidence as an index of the witness's memory? Common sense says that it's a pretty good indicant. Does scientific evidence back this up?

The answer is that although in both the scientific laboratory and in normal everyday life, high confidence is often predictive of high accuracy, psychologists have also delineated the circumstances in which – contrary to common sense – this normal predictive power vanishes. Such circumstances include (1) some original event that causes poor encoding to begin with (e.g., because of short duration, poor lighting, lack of appropriate attention or any of a number of other factors), (2) some form of post-event reconstruction (e.g., inferences or information suggested by others), and (3) the motivation and opportunity to rehearse the reconstructed memory. (For summaries and specific experiments, see Busey *et al.,* (2000); Deffenbacher (1980); Penrod & Cutler (1995); and Wells *et al.,* (1981).)

For example, Deffenbacher (1980) examined 45 experiments that had measured the relationship between confidence in some memory and the accuracy of that memory. In approximately half of those studies, there was the positive relation between confidence and accuracy that our intuitions would lead us to believe: that is, higher confidence was associated with higher accuracy. In the other half of the experiments, however, there was *no* relation (or, in some instances, even a negative relation) between confidence and accuracy.

Which result was found – that is, whether accuracy was or was not positively related to confidence – depended on the overall circumstances surrounding the formation of the memory. Favorable circumstances (e.g., good lighting, no stress, no post-event information, etc.) lead to the expected positive relation between confidence and accuracy. However, unfavorable circumstances lead to no relation, or a negative relation between confidence and accuracy.

The reason for this is summarized nicely by Leippe (1980). When encoding circumstances are poor, initial memory is filled with gaps. Suppose, for example, that a person experiences a near-accident in a car (say is almost hit by another car). Because of the brevity and stress of the situation, the person probably would not remember many details – for example, he or she might not remember the make or color of the other car, or whether or not there was a passenger in the car. These would be *gaps* in the person's memory. But because the event was salient, the person would rehearse the event in his or her mind. In the process of rehearsing, the memory gaps would tend to be filled in. Such filling in could be random, it could be due to expectations, it could be due to post-event information – it could be due to many things, few of them likely to be accurate. The resulting memory would therefore be generally inaccurate. But the rehearsal of this inaccurate memory would lead to a *strong* memory, in which the person would have relatively high confidence.

An important practical conclusion issue from these studies: when a witness expresses great confidence in some memory (e.g., in the identification of a defendant as the remembered culprit in some crime) the jury would do well to learn of the events that led up to this confident memory. If the circumstances for forming the original memory were good and there was little cause for post-event memory reconstruction, the jury can reasonably accept the high confidence as evidence of the memory's accuracy. If, on the other hand, the circumstances for forming the original memory were poor, and there was ample reason for post-event memory reconstruction, the jury should discount the witness's high confidence as an index of the memory's accuracy.

It is noteworthy that the legal system is finally beginning to take these research findings into account. In April 2001, the state of New Jersey adopted new General Guidelines for identification procedures that were based largely on the kind of research that we have just described. In an accompanying memo, New Jersey Attorney General James Farmer noted that it is important to guard against identification procedures which may invest a witness with a false sense of confidence, and goes on to say, 'Studies have established that the confidence level that witnesses demonstrate regarding their

A very confident eyewitness, while persuasive to a jury, may nevertheless be completely incorrect.

identifications is the primary determinant of whether jurors accept identifications as accurate and reliable.'

Suggestive information and childrens' memories

Young children appear to be particularly susceptible to suggestive information, particularly while they are being interviewed. Ceci and Bruck (1993) describe a variety of studies demonstrating this kind of suggestibility. The problem is particularly acute because children are often interviewed about crimes by interviewers who, wittingly or unwittingly, provide a great deal of suggestive information in the course of the interview.

An example of a recently reported experiment demonstrating the consequences of this sort of confirmatory interview technique worked as follows. First, a trained social worker was given a fact sheet about a particular event in which a child had participated. This fact sheet contained both actual actions that had happened during the event, and false actions – actions that had not actually occurred. The social worker was then asked to interview the child about the event. She was asked specifically not to ask leading questions.

Several results emerged from this procedure. First, the child being interviewed eventually recalled the false actions with a good deal of confidence, thereby indicating that the interviewer had 'infected' the child with her preconceptions about what had happened. Second, other professionals couldn't tell which of the things the child recalled were the real actions, and which were the falsely implanted actions.

So this is a noteworthy example of an instance in which the interview itself – unbiased though the professional interviewer tried to make it – was obviously effective in conveying the interviewer's pre-existing biases to the child *and* actually altering the child's memory about what happened – indeed, altering it in such a fashion that other professionals couldn't tell what in the child's memory was based on actual experience and what was based on after-the-fact suggested information.

Forced confessions

A growing body of work has demonstrated that interrogation techniques carried out by police and other investigators have been able to produce genuinely false memories (and confessions) of crimes that the suspects can be objectively shown not to have committed. Detailed reports and summaries of these general issues are provided by Kassin (1997), Leo (1996) and Ofshe (1992). These writers have demonstrated that false memories can be created in the minds of innocent people by techniques that include, but are not limited to, (a) being told that there is unambiguous evidence (such as fingerprints) proving their culpability, (b) being told that they were drunk or were otherwise impaired so that they wouldn't have remembered the crime, (c) being told that awful crimes are repressed and if they try hard they will be able to 'recover' these repressed memories, and (d) being told that they are suffering from multiple personality disorder and that the crime was committed by another of their personalities.

Richard Ofshe (1992) provides a dramatic, indisputable example of such a sequence of false memories. In a well-known case (described in a series of *New Yorker* articles) Paul Ingram, a high-ranking employee of the Thurston County Sheriff's Department (Washington State, USA), was accused by his two daughters of having raped and abused them over many years as part of a series of satanic cult rituals. Ingram initially claimed innocence, but following a lengthy series of police interrogations began to admit to the crimes and also began to have increasingly vivid 'memories' of the details. Ofshe, a sociologist at the University of California, Berkeley with expertise in cult-related matters, was retained by the prosecution to advise them in the Ingram case. In the course of his investigation, Ofshe concluded that (a) there was zero evidence of the presumed cult activity that constituted the foundation of the accusations against Ingram, and that (b) many of Ingram's 'memories' – detailed though they were, and confident of their validity as Ingram was – could not logically be true, but rather were almost certainly created as a result of the intense suggestion provided during interrogations by police officers and other authority figures. To confirm his false-memory hypothesis, Ofshe carried out an experiment wherein he accused Ingram of a specific event that all other participants agreed did not happen (this fictional event consisted of Ingram successfully demanding that his son and daughter have sex with one another and observing them do so). Ingram initially reported not remembering this event. However, upon intensely thinking about the possibility of it having happened, in conjunction with the accusation by a trusted authority figure (Ofshe), Ingram began to not only 'remember' the fabricated event itself, but also to generate minute details about how the event unfolded. Ingram eventually claimed this memory to be very real to him. Even when stupendous efforts by all parties (Ofshe, the police, and all other interrogators) were eventually made to convince Ingram that the event was not real, but was part of an experiment, Ingram still steadfastly and sincerely refused to cease believing that the incident had actually occurred. Eventually, however, following the cessation of the intense interrogation, Mr Ingram began to question and recant the memories that he had originally formed.

The Ingram case, while probably the most public and dramatic of false memories created by interrogation, is not an isolated anomaly. Kassin (1997, p. 227) follows a description of this same case by remarking that:

> There are other remarkable cases as well that involve coerced-internalized confessions [by which Kassin means confessions based on false memories that are actually believed by the defendant to be true]. The names, places, and dates may change, but they all have two factors in common: (a) a suspect who is 'vulnerable' – that is, one whose memory is vulnerable by virtue of his or her youth, interpersonal trust, naiveté, suggestibility, lack of intelligence, stress, fatigue, alcohol or drug abuse, and (b) the presentation of false evidence such as a rigged polygraph or forensic tests (e.g., bloodstains, semen, hair, fingerprints), statements supposedly made by an accomplice, or a staged eyewitness identification as a way to convince the beleaguered suspect that he or she is guilty.

Jennifer Thompson's memory

We conclude this section by returning to the case of Jennifer Thompson. Why was it that Ms Thompson both misidentified Ronald Cotton and failed to identify the actual rapist? Although we don't know the answers to these questions with absolute certainty, we can, on the basis of what is known about reconstructive memory, certainly offer some reasonable hypotheses.

To begin with, the circumstances surrounding the original event – the rape – were far from optimal from the perspective of Ms Thompson's being able to memorize the rapist's appearance. It was dark, Ms Thompson was terrified, and her attention was likely on what was most important at the moment – trying to avoid being raped and/or to escape – than with what her attacker looked like. Therefore it is likely that her original memory was poor.

Why then did Ms Thompson identify Mr Cotton to begin with? This is unclear; however, based on other evidence the police believed that he was the culprit and may well have suggested this to her during her original identification of him from mug shots. Once she had identified him in this fashion, however, she re-identified him in a live lineup – but one containing Cotton, whose picture she had already seen, along with five other individuals who were completely unfamiliar to her; it is therefore no surprise that she picked out Mr Cotton from the lineup. The important thing, however, is that Mr Cotton's picture that she selected during the original identification, along with Mr Cotton himself whom she selected from the lineup, provided a fertile source of post-event information – information that allowed Ms Thompson to reconstruct her memory for the original event such that her originally hazy memory of the original rapist was transformed into a very vivid memory of Mr Cotton. This reconstruction had three important consequences. First, it formed the basis for Ms Thompson's very confident in-court identification that proved to be the basis for Mr Cotton's conviction. Second, it prevented her from correctly recognizing Bobby Poole as the man who had actually been there. Finally, it evidently formed the basis for Ms Thompson's recollection of how well she had studied him. Notice how she described this process: 'I looked at his hairline; I looked for scars, for tattoos, for anything that would help me identify him.' But did she? If so, why did she recognize the wrong man? The answer is probably that after having constructed an excellent memory of Ronald Cotton as a result of seeing him during the identification procedures, she constructed an accompanying memory of the process by which her image of him got formed.

Memory errors and normal memory

As the previous sections illustrate, memory is often far from accurate. Recently psychologists and neuroscientists have begun an attempt to delineate the various mechanisms that produce memory illusions, which occur when people confidently 'remember' events that did not occur at all. The study of memory illusions is rapidly gaining in popularity because it has obvious real-world applications (for instance, to legal issues involving eyewitness testimony) while at the same time contributing to our understanding of normal memory processes. Many specific memory illusions have been identified. Some have already been described in this text, including the integration of post-event information into memories and mis-remembering inferred information as events that were experienced. One especially heavily studied memory illusion is the DRM effect (the letters refer to James Deese, Henry Roediger, and Kathleen McDermott, who have extensively studied the illusion). Here participants are read lists of words and then immediately asked to recall them. The trick is that the words on each list are all close associates (e.g., sit, table, seat, etc.) of a central 'theme' word (e.g., chair) which is not included on the list. The startling finding is that participants are more likely to 'remember' the never-presented theme word than to remember words that had actually been presented on the list (Roediger & McDermott, 1995). Memory conjunction errors are another popular illusion to study. Here participants are presented with to-be-remembered items (e.g., words, such as someplace and anywhere), and then receive a recognition test including new items constructed from parts of previously studied items (e.g., somewhere). Participants have a very strong tendency to claim that these new items had been presented previously (e.g., Reinitz & Hannigan, 2004).

Although each of these illusions is distinct, they may each be described as a failure to accurately remember the *source* of information in memory. Marcia Johnson and her colleagues (Mitchell & Johnson, 2000; Johnson *et al.,* 1993) have proposed that an important memory process, called source monitoring, involves attributing information in memory to its source. For instance, if you remember having heard that a new film is worth seeing it is helpful to be able to remember who told you this so that you can decide whether you share a taste in films. Source monitoring processes identify the most likely source in an inferential manner – for instance, if you know that you heard about the film very recently then you will consider only sources that you have recently encountered. Because source monitoring is based in inference it sometimes fails, leading to inaccurate memories for the source of information. This may help explain a number of memory illusions. For example, people may misattribute the source of post-event information to the event itself, leading to confident but erroneous memories. Similarly, the presentation of multiple associated words in a DRM experiment may cause the theme word to come to mind; participants may then misattribute the source of their recent memory for the theme word to the lists they had heard. In the case of memory conjunction errors, participants may mis-remember the word parts as arising from the same source word. Thus memory illusions illustrate that memory for information is separate from memory for its source, and show the importance of source monitoring for memory accuracy. Source memory has been shown to decline as a part of normal cognitive aging. For instance, in an experiment by Schacter *et al.* (1991) two different individuals read words out loud to younger and older adult participants. Participants in the two age groups were about the same at distinguishing old from new words on a recognition test; however, the younger group was much more accurate at remembering the source of the words (which of the individuals had originally read each word). Thus older adults are likely to be more susceptible to many memory illusions. This in turn may lead to difficulties for older adults – for instance, some older adults complain that they sometimes have trouble remembering whether they recently took their medicine, or whether they instead recently thought about taking their medicine. In this case they have a recent memory about taking medicine, but have difficulty remembering whether the source was an internal thought or an actual behavior.

INTERIM SUMMARY

➜ Both experimental and anecdotal evidence indicate that, unlike a video tape, a memory is constructed and reconstructed on the basis of expectations and knowledge. In this sense, memory for some event often shows systematic departures from the event's objective reality.

➜ Memory reconstruction can occur at the time the memory is originally formed via perceptual errors of various sorts.

➜ More often, memory reconstruction occurs at varying times after its formation on the basis of various kinds of post-event information.

➜ Memory reconstruction forms the basis for memories that, although systematically incorrect, seem very real and are recounted with a great deal of confidence. This is critical in various practical settings, notably the legal system, which often relies heavily on eyewitness memory.

➡ Like perceptual errors such as those entailed in illusions (see Chapter 5) errors are a normal, and probably a useful characteristic of normal memory. If memories were complete and accurate, they would overwhelm our information-processing systems!

CRITICAL THINKING QUESTIONS

1 Suppose that on their tenth anniversary, Jason and his wife Kate are discussing their wedding. Jason laughingly recounts the story of how Kate's mother accidentally stumbled over the food table and spilled a bottle of champagne. Kate, not so laughingly, claims that it was Jason's mother who had had the embarrassing accident. Use what is known about constructive and reconstructive memories to construct a sequence of events that might have led to this disagreement.

2 It is generally agreed that the accuracy of memory declines over time. Describe two separate reasons for why this occurs. (*Hint*: You learned about one in the previous section and about the other in this section.)

IMPROVING MEMORY

Having considered the basics of working memory and long-term memory, we are ready to tackle the question of how memory can be improved, focusing primarily on explicit memory. First we will consider how to increase the working memory span. Then we will turn to a variety of methods for improving long-term memory; these methods work by increasing the efficiency of encoding and retrieval.

Chunking and memory span

For most of us, the capacity of working memory cannot be increased beyond 7 ± 2 chunks. However, we can enlarge the size of a chunk and thereby increase the number of items in our memory span. We demonstrated this point earlier: given the string 149-2177-619-96, we can recall all 12 digits if we recode the string into three chunks – 1492-1776-1996 – and store them in working memory. Although recoding digits into familiar dates works nicely in this example, it will not work with most digit strings because we have not memorized enough significant dates. But if a recoding system could be developed that worked with virtually any string, working memory span for numbers could be dramatically improved.

Psychologists have studied an individual who discovered such a general-purpose recoding system and used it to increase his memory span from seven to almost 80 random

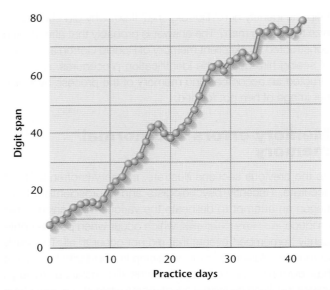

FIGURE 8.14 **Number of Digits Recalled by S.F.** *S.F. greatly increased his memory span for digits by devising a recoding system that used chunking and hierachical organization. Total practice time was about 215 hours.*

digits (see Figure 8.14). This person, referred to as S.F., had average memory abilities and average intelligence for a college student. For a year and a half he engaged in a memory-span task for about 3 to 5 hours per week. During this extensive practice S.F., a good long-distance runner, devised the strategy of recoding sets of 4 digits into running times. For example, S.F. would recode 3492 as '3:49.2 – world class time for the mile,' which for him was a single chunk. Since S.F. was familiar with many running times (that is, he had them stored in long-term memory), he could readily chunk most sets of 4 digits. In cases in which he could not (for example, 1771 cannot be a running time because the third digit is too large), he tried to recode the 4 digits into either a familiar date or the age of some person or object known to him.

Use of these recoding systems enabled S.F. to increase his memory span from 7 to 28 digits (because each of S.F.'s 7 chunks contains 4 digits). He then built up his memory span to nearly 80 digits by organizing the running times in a hierarchy. Thus, one chunk in S.F.'s working memory might have pointed to three running times; at the time of recall, S.F. would go from this chunk to the first running time and produce its 4 digits, then move to the second running time in the chunk and produce its digits, and so on. One chunk was therefore worth 12 digits. In this way S.F. achieved his remarkable memory span. The expansion of his memory capacity was due to increasing the size of a chunk (by relating the items to information in long-term memory), not to increasing the number of chunks that working memory can hold. When he switched from digits to letters, his memory span went back to 7 – that is, 7 letters (Ericsson *et al.*, 1980).

This research on working memory is fairly recent. Interest in expanding long-term memory has a longer history and is the focus of the rest of this section. We will look first at how material can be encoded to make it easier to retrieve and then consider how the act of retrieval itself can be improved.

Imagery and encoding

We mentioned earlier that we can improve the recall of unrelated items by adding meaningful connections between them at the time of encoding, for these connections will facilitate later retrieval. Mental images have been found to be particularly useful for connecting pairs of unrelated items, and for this reason imagery is the major ingredient in many **mnemonic systems**, or systems for aiding memory.

A well-known mnemonic system is the **method of loci** (*loci* is the Latin word for 'places'). This method works especially well with an ordered sequence of arbitrary items such as unrelated words. The first step is to commit to memory an ordered sequence of places – such as the locations you would come upon during a slow walk through your house. You enter through the front door into a hallway, move next to the bookcase in the living room, then to the television in the living room, then to the curtains at the window, and so on. Once you can easily take this mental walk, you are ready to memorize as many unrelated words as there are locations on your walk. You form an image that relates the first word to the first location, another image that relates the second word to the second location, and so on. If the words are items on a shopping list – for example, 'bread,' 'eggs,' 'beer', 'milk', and 'bacon' – you might imagine a slice of bread nailed to your front door, an egg hanging from the light cord in the hallway, a can of beer in the bookcase, a milk commercial playing on your television, and curtains made from giant strips of bacon (see Figure 8.15). Once you have memorized the items in this way, you can easily recall them in order by simply taking your mental walk again. Each location will retrieve an image, and each image will retrieve a word. The method clearly works and is a favorite among people who perform memory feats professionally.

Imagery is also used in the key-word method for learning words in a foreign language (see Table 8.3). Suppose that you had to learn that the Spanish word *caballo* means 'horse,' The key-word method has two steps. The first is to find a part of the foreign word that sounds like an English word. Since *caballo* is pronounced, roughly, 'cob-eye-yo,' 'eye' could serve as the key word. The next step is to form an image that connects the key word and the English equivalent – for example, a giant eye being kicked by a horse (see Figure 8.16). This should establish a meaningful connection between the Spanish and English words. To recall the meaning of *caballo*, you would first retrieve the key word 'eye' and then the stored image that links it to 'horse.' The key-word method may sound complicated, but studies have shown that it is very helpful in learning the vocabulary of a foreign language (Atkinson, 1975; Pressley *et al.*, 1982).

FIGURE 8.15 A Mnemonic System. *The method of loci aids memory by associating items (here, entries on a shopping list) with an ordered sequence of places.*

TABLE 8.3   THE KEY-WORD METHOD

Examples of key words used to link Spanish words to their English translations. For example, when the Spanish word *muleta* is pronounced, part of it sounds like the English word 'mule.' Thus, 'mule' could be used as the key word and linked to the English translation by forming an image of a mule standing erect on a crutch.

Spanish	Key word	English
caballo	(eye)	horse
charco	(charcoal)	puddle
muleta	(mule)	crutch
clavo	(claw)	nail
lagartija	(log)	lizard
payaso	(pie)	clown
hiio	(eel)	thread
tenaza	(tennis)	pliers
jabon	(bone)	soap
carpa	(carp)	tent
pato	(pot)	duck

Elaboration and encoding

We have seen that the more we elaborate items, the more we can subsequently recall or recognize them. This phenomenon arises because the more connections we establish

Caballo ➡ eye ➡ Horse

Pato ➡ pot ➡ Duck

FIGURE 8.16 Foreign Language Learning. *Mental images can be used to associate spoken Spanish words with corresponding English words. Here, possible images for learning the Spanish words for 'horse' and 'duck' are illustrated.*

between items, the larger the number of retrieval possibilities. The practical implications of these findings are straight forward: if you want to remember a particular fact, expand on its meaning. To illustrate, suppose you read a newspaper article about an epidemic in Paris that health officials are trying to contain. To expand on this, you could ask yourself questions about the causes and consequences of the epidemic: was the disease carried by a person or by an animal? Was it transmitted through the water supply? To contain the epidemic, will officials go so far as to stop outsiders from visiting Paris? How long is the epidemic likely to last? Questions about the causes and consequences of an event are especially effective because each question sets up a meaningful connection, or retrieval path, to the event.

Context and retrieval

Since context is a powerful retrieval cue, we can improve our memory by restoring the context in which the learning took place. If your psychology class always meets in a particular room, your recall of the lecture material may be better when you are in that room than when you are in a different building, because the context of the room serves as a cue for retrieving the lecture material. Most often, though, when we have to remember something we cannot physically return to the context in which we learned it. If you are having difficulty remembering the name of a school classmate, you are not about to

go back to your school just to recall it. However, you can try to re-create the context mentally. To retrieve the long-forgotten name, you might think of different classes, clubs, and other activities that you participated in during school to see whether any of these bring to mind the name you are seeking. When participants used these techniques in an actual experiment, they were often able to recall the names of school classmates that they were sure they had forgotten (Williams & Hollan, 1981).

Organization

We know that organization during encoding improves subsequent retrieval. This principle can be put to great practical use: we are capable of storing and retrieving a massive amount of information if we organize it appropriately.

Some experiments have investigated organizational devices that can be used to learn many unrelated items. In one study, participants memorized lists of unrelated words by organizing the words in each list into a story, as illustrated in Figure 8.17. When tested for 12 such lists (a total of 120 words), participants recalled more than 90 per cent of the words. Control participants, who did not use an organizational strategy, recalled only about 10 per cent of the words! The performance of the experimental participants appears to be a remarkable memory feat, but anyone armed with an organizational strategy can do it.

At this point you might concede that psychologists have devised some ingenious techniques for organizing lists of unrelated items. But, you argue, what you have to remember are not lists of unrelated items but stories you were told, lectures you have heard, and readings like the text of this chapter. Isn't this kind of material already organized, and doesn't this mean that the previously mentioned techniques are of limited value? Yes and no. Yes, this chapter is more than a list of unrelated sentences, but – and this is the essential point – there is

---

A LUMBERJACK DARTed out of a forest, SKATEd around a HEDGE past a COLONY of DUCKs. He tripped on some FURNITURE, tearing his STOCKING while hastening toward the PILLOW where his MISTRESS lay.

A VEGETABLE can be a useful INSTRUMENT for a COLLEGE student. A carrot can be a NAIL for your FENCE or BASIN. But a MERCHANT of the QUEEN would SCALE that fence and feed the carrot to a GOAT.

One night at DINNER I had the NERVE to bring my TEACHER. There had been a FLOOD that day, and the rain BARREL was sure to RATTLE. There was, however, a VESSEL in the HARBOR carrying this ARTIST to my CASTLE.

FIGURE 8.17 Organizing Words into a Story. *Three examples in which a list of ten unrelated words is turned into a story. The capitalized items are the words on the list.*

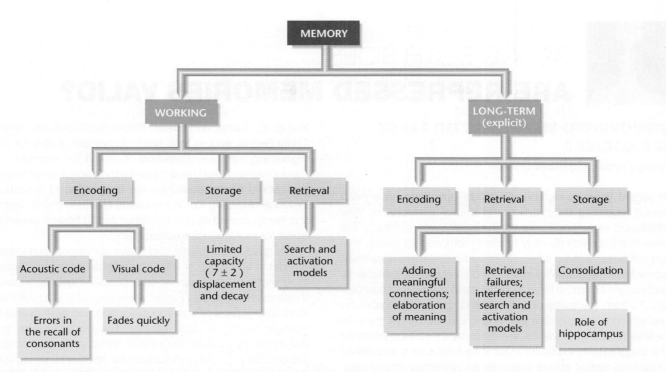

FIGURE 8.18 **A Hierachical Tree.** *Creating hierarchical trees of chapters in textbooks can help students retrieve information about those chapters. This tree represents the organization of part of this chapter.*

always a problem of organization with any lengthy material. Later you may be able to recall that elaborating meaning aids learning, but this may not bring to mind anything about, for example, acoustic coding in short-term memory. The two topics do not seem to be intimately related, but there is a relationship between them: both deal with encoding phenomena. The best way to see that relationship is to note the headings and subheadings in the chapter, because these show how the material in the chapter is organized.

An effective way to study is to keep this organization in mind. You might, for example, try to capture part of the chapter's organization by sketching a hierarchical tree like the one shown in Figure 8.18. You can use this hierarchy to guide your memory search whenever you have to retrieve information about this chapter. It may be even more helpful, though, to make your own hierarchical outline of the chapter. Memory seems to benefit most when the organization is done by the person who needs to remember the material.

Practicing retrieval

Another way to improve retrieval is to practice it – that is, to ask yourself questions about what you are trying to learn. Suppose that you have 2 hours in which to study an assignment that can be read in approximately 30 minutes. Reading and re-reading the assignment four times is generally less effective than reading it once and asking yourself questions about it. You can then re-read selected parts to clear up points that were difficult to retrieve the first time around,

perhaps elaborating these points so that they become well connected to one another and to the rest of the assignment. Attempting retrieval is an efficient use of study time. This was demonstrated long ago by experiments using material similar to that actually learned in courses (see Figure 8.19).

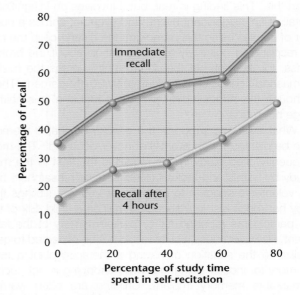

FIGURE 8.19 **Practicing Retrieval.** *Recall can be improved by spending a large proportion of study time attempting retrieval rather than silently studying. Results are shown for tests given immediately and 4 hours after completing study.*

SEEING BOTH SIDES
ARE REPRESSED MEMORIES VALID?

RECOVERED MEMORIES OR FALSE MEMORIES?

Kathy Pezdek, Clairmont College

In recent years, a number of critical questions have been raised regarding the credibility of adults' memory for their childhood experiences. At the heart of these claims is the view that it is relatively easy to plant memories for events that did not occur. Let me say up front that surely there have been some false memories for incest, and surely some therapeutic techniques are more likely to foster false memories than others. Further, it is surely possible to find some individuals who are so highly suggestible that one could readily get them to believe anything. However, the claim by those who promote the suggestibility explanation for long-forgotten memories of childhood sexual abuse assumes an extremely strong construct of memory suggestibility. The truth is that the cognitive research on the suggestibility of memory simply does not support the existence of a suggestibility construct that is sufficiently robust to explain this phenomenon.

How do cognitive psychologists study the suggestibility of memory? This text refers to an experiment by Loftus *et al.* (1985) in which participants were more likely to think that they saw broken glass in the film of a traffic accident (broken glass was not present in the film) if they had been asked a previous question that included the word 'smashed' rather than 'hit.' This finding is real, but it involves an insignificant detail of an insignificant event, and even so, across a number of studies using this paradigm, the difference in the rate of responding positively to the question about the broken glass, for example, in the control ('hit') versus the misled ('smashed') condition is typically only 20–30 percent. Thus, although this suggestibility effect is a real one, it is neither large nor robust.

What evidence supports the conclusion that a memory can be planted for an event that never occurred? The most frequently cited study in this regard is the 'lost in the mall' study by Loftus and Pickrell (1995). These researchers had 24 volunteers suggest to offspring or younger siblings that they had been lost in a shopping mall as a child. Six of the 24 participants reported full or partial memory of the false event. However, these results would not be expected to generalize to the situation of having a therapist plant a false memory for incest. Being lost while shopping is not such a remarkable memory implant. Children are often warned about the dangers of getting lost, have fears about getting lost, are commonly read classic tales about children who get

lost (e.g., Hansel and Gretel, Pinocchio, Goldilocks and the Three Bears), and, in fact, often do get lost, if only for a few frightening minutes. Therefore, it would be expected that most children would have a pre-existing script for getting lost that would be accessed by the suggestion of a particular instance of getting lost in the Loftus study. In sharp contrast, it is hardly likely that most children would have a preexisting script for incestuous sexual contact.

My graduate students and I have conducted a number of studies to test whether Loftus's findings regarding planting a false memory generalize to less plausible events. In one of these studies (Pezdek, Finger, & Hodge, 1997), 20 volunteers read descriptions of one true event and two false events to a younger sibling or close relative. The plausible false event described the relative being lost in a mall while shopping; the implausible false event described the relative receiving a rectal enema. After being read each event, participants were asked what they remembered about the event. Only three of the false events were 'remembered' by any of the participants, and all were the plausible event regarding being lost in the mall. No one believed the implausible false event. Implausible events such as parent–child intercourse or receiving an enema are simply unlikely to be suggestively planted in memory because most children do not have pre-existing scripts for these events.

At a broader level, it is also important to consider that although the 'false memory debate' most often concerns reported memories for childhood sexual abuse, this is only one of the many sources of psychogenic amnesia for which memory recovery has been reported. It is well documented that combat exposure and other violent events can produce psychogenic amnesia (for a review, see Arrigo & Pezdek, 1997). Those who doubt the reality of repressed memory for sexual abuse need to explain psychogenic amnesia for these other types of trauma as well.

In conclusion, cognitive research offers no support for the claim that implausible false events such as childhood sexual abuse are easily planted in memory. Although there are some techniques that can be used to suggestively plant bizarre false memories in some highly suggestive individuals, there is no evidence that this is a widespread phenomenon, and promoting this view is not only misleading, it is not good science.

Kathy Pezdek

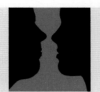

SEEING BOTH SIDES

ARE REPRESSED MEMORIES VALID?

REPRESSED MEMORIES: A DANGEROUS BELIEF?

Elizabeth F. Loftus, University of California, Irvine

In a land transformed by science, pseudoscientific beliefs live on. It was a set of wild, wacky, and dangerous beliefs that led to serious problems for Nadean Cool, a 44-year-old nurse's aide in Appleton, Wisconsin. Nadean had sought therapy in late 1986 to help her cope with her reaction to a traumatic event that her daughter had experienced. During therapy, her psychiatrist used hypnosis and other methods to dig out allegedly buried memories of abuse. In the process his patient became convinced that she had repressed memories of being in a satanic cult, of eating babies, of being raped, of having sex with animals, of being forced to watch the murder of her eight-year-old friend. She came to believe that she had over 120 separate personalities – children, adults, angels, and even a duck – all because, she was told, she had experienced such severe childhood sexual and physical abuse. In addition to hypnosis and other suggestive techniques, the psychiatrist also performed exorcisms on Nadean, one of which lasted 5 hours, replete with the sprinkling of holy water and screams for Satan to leave Nadean's body. When Nadean came to realize that false memories had been planted, she sued for malpractice; her case settled, mid-trial, in early 1997, for $2.4 million dollars (see McHugh *et al.*, 2004 for more cases like Nadean's, and an analysis of what happens to these individuals and their families after this kind of experience).

Hundreds of people, mostly women, have developed memories in therapy of extensive brutalization that they claimed they repressed, and they later retracted these. How do we know that the abuse memories aren't real and the retractions false? One clue is that the women would sometimes develop memories that were psychologically or biologically impossible, such as detailed memories of abuse occurring at the age of 3 months or memories of being forced to abort a baby by a coat hanger when physical evidence confirmed virginity.

How is it possible for people to develop such elaborate and confident false memories? I began studying how false memories take root back in the early 1970s, with a series of experiments on the 'misinformation effect.' When people witness an event and are later exposed to new and misleading information about that event, their recollections often become distorted. The misinformation invades us, like a Trojan horse, precisely because we do not detect its influence. We showed it was relatively easy, with a little bit of suggestion to, for example, make witnesses to an accident believe they saw a car go through a stop sign, when it was actually a yield sign. For a review of 30 years of research on the misinformation effect, see Loftus (2005). Later studies showed that suggestive information not only can alter the details of a recent experience, but also can plant entirely false beliefs and memories in the minds of people. People have been convinced that, as children, they were lost in a shopping mall for an extended time and rescued by an elderly person, that they had an accident at a family wedding, that they nearly drowned and were rescued by a lifeguard, and that they were victims of a vicious animal attack. In some studies as many as half the individuals who underwent suggestive interviewing came to develop either full or partial false childhood memories. (For a review of many of these studies and a comprehensive review of the science of false memory see Brainerd & Reyna, 2005.) Hypnosis, suggestive dream interpretation, and guided imagination – techniques used by some psychotherapists – have all been shown to be successful ways of feeding people erroneous material and getting them to accept it, and develop 'rich false memories.' By this I mean false memories that contain lots of sensory detail, are held with confidence, and expressed with emotion.

Of course, simply because we can plant false childhood memories in subjects in no way implies that memories that arise after suggestion, or imagination, or dream interpretation are all necessarily false. In no way does this invalidate the experiences of the many thousands of individuals who have truly been abused and are later in life reminded of the experience. This happens. But we need to keep in mind the words of Richard McNally from Harvard University who had this to say in his book *Remembering Trauma*: 'The notion that the mind protects itself by repressing or dissociating memories of trauma, rendering them inaccessible to awareness, is a piece of psychiatric folklore devoid of convincing empirical support' (McNally, 2003, pp. 111–112).

Sadly, the mental health professionals who contributed to the problems experienced by patients like Nadean Cool almost never admit that they were wrong (Tavris & Aronson, 2007). They should realize, and we too need to keep in mind, that without corroboration, there is little that even the most experienced evaluator can use to differentiate the true memories from those suggestively planted. Apart from bearing on the controversy about repressed memories that plagued our society for more than a decade, the modern research does reveal important ways in which our memories are malleable, and it reveals much about the rather flimsy curtain that sometimes separates memory and imagination.

Elizabeth F. Loftus

A procedure akin to practicing retrieval may be useful in implicit memory situations. The procedure, referred to as mental practice, consists of imagining the rehearsal of a perceptual motor skill without actually moving any part of the body. For example, you might imagine yourself swinging at a tennis ball, making mental corrections when the imagined swing seems faulty, without moving your arm. Such mental practice can improve performance of the skill, particularly if the mental practice is interspersed with actual physical practice (Swets & Bjork, 1990).

➔ One way to improve encoding and retrieval is to use imagery, which is the basic principle underlying mnemonic systems such as the method of loci and the key-word method.

➔ Other ways to improve encoding (and subsequent retrieval) are to elaborate the meaning of the items and to organize the material during encoding (hierarchical organization seems preferable).

INTERIM SUMMARY

➔ Although we cannot increase the capacity of working memory, we can use recoding schemes to enlarge the size of a chunk and thereby increase the memory span.

CRITICAL THINKING QUESTIONS

1 Suppose that an actor has a very long speech to memorize. How might they best go about such memorization?

2 Given what we know about context and retrieval, what would be the most efficient way to study for a statistics exam?

CHAPTER SUMMARY

1 There are three stages of memory: encoding, storage, and retrieval. Encoding refers to the transformation of information into the kind of code or representation that memory can accept; storage refers to retention of the encoded information; and retrieval refers to the process by which information is recovered from memory. The three stages may operate differently in situations that require us to store material for a matter of seconds (working memory), and in situations that require us to store material for longer intervals (long-term memory). Moreover, different long-term memory systems seem to be involved in storing facts, which are part of explicit memory, and skills, which are part of implicit memory.

2 There is increasing biological evidence for these distinctions. Recent brain-scanning studies of long-term memory indicate that most of the brain regions activated during encoding are in the left hemisphere and that most of the regions activated during retrieval are in the right hemisphere. Evidence from both animal studies and studies of humans with brain damage

indicates that different brain regions may mediate working memory and long-term memory. In particular, in both humans and other mammals, damage to the hippocampal system impairs performance on long-term memory tasks but not on working memory tasks.

3 There are three kinds of memory that differ in terms of their temporal characteristics: sensory memory lasts over a few hundreds of milliseconds; short-term memory (now called working memory) operates over seconds; long-term store operates over times ranging from minutes to years.

4 Sensory memory has a very large capacity but decays in a very short time. Information within sensory memory that is attended to is transferred to the next memory, working memory.

5 Information in working memory may be encoded acoustically or visually depending on the nature of the task at hand. The most striking fact about working memory is that its storage capacity is limited to

7 ± 2 items, or chunks. While we are limited in the number of chunks we can remember, we can increase the size of a chunk by using information in long-term memory to recode incoming material into larger meaningful units. Information can be lost or forgotten from working memory. One cause of forgetting is that information decays with time; another is that new items displace old ones.

6 Retrieval slows down as the number of items in working memory increases. Some have taken this result to indicate that retrieval involves a search process, whereas others have interpreted the result in terms of an activation process.

7 Working memory is used in solving various kinds of problems, such as mental arithmetic, geometric analogies, and answering questions about text. However, working memory does not seem to be involved in the understanding of relatively simple sentences. Working memory may also serve as a way station to permanent memory, in that information may reside in working memory while it is being encoded into long-term memory.

8 Information in long-term memory is usually encoded according to its meaning. If the items to be remembered are meaningful but the connections between them are not, memory can be improved by adding meaningful connections that provide retrieval paths. The more one elaborates the meaning of material, the better the memory of that material will be.

9 Many cases of forgetting in long-term memory are due to retrieval failures (the information is there but cannot be found). Retrieval failures are more likely to occur when there is interference from items associated with the same retrieval cue. Such interference effects suggest that retrieval from long-term memory may be accomplished through a sequential search process or a spreading activation process.

10 Some forgetting from long-term memory is due to a loss from storage, particularly when there is a disruption of the processes that consolidate new memories. The biological locus of consolidation includes the hippocampus and surrounding cortex. Recent research suggests that consolidation takes a few weeks to be completed.

11 Retrieval failures in long-term memory are less likely when the items are organized during encoding and when the context at the time of retrieval is similar to the context at the time of encoding. Retrieval processes can also be disrupted by emotional factors. In some cases, anxious thoughts interfere with retrieval of the target memory; in others, the target memory may be actively blocked (repressed). In still other cases, emotion can enhance memory, as in flashbulb memories.

12 Explicit memory refers to the kind of memory manifested in recall or recognition, in which we consciously recollect the past. Implicit memory refers to the kind of memory that manifests itself as an improvement on some perceptual, motor, or cognitive task, with no conscious recollection of the experiences that led to the improvement. While explicit memory – particularly recall and recognition of facts – breaks down in amnesia, implicit memory is usually spared. This suggests that there may be separate storage systems for explicit and implicit memory.

13 Research with normal individuals also suggests that there may be separate systems for explicit and implicit memory. Much of this research has relied on a measure of implicit memory called priming (for example, the extent to which prior exposure to a list of words later facilitates completing stems of these words). Some studies reveal that an independent variable that affects explicit memory (amount of elaboration during encoding) has no effect on priming, while other studies show that a variable that affects implicit memory has no effect on explicit memory. Brain-scanning studies with normal individuals show that explicit memory is accompanied by increased neural activity in certain regions whereas implicit memory is accompanied by a decrease in neural activity in critical regions.

14 Unlike a video tape, a memory is constructed and reconstructed on the basis of expectations and knowledge: it shows systematic departures from the objective reality that underlies it. This kind of reconstruction can occur at the time the memory is originally formed, or at varying time periods following its formation. This kind of reconstruction forms the basis for memories that, while systematically incorrect, seem very real, and are recounted with a great deal of confidence.

15 Although we cannot increase the capacity of working memory, we can use recoding schemes to enlarge the size of a chunk and thereby increase the memory span. Long-term memory for facts can be improved at the encoding and retrieval stages. One way to improve encoding and retrieval is to use imagery, which is the basic principle underlying mnemonic systems such as the method of loci and the key-word method.

16 Other ways to improve encoding (and subsequent retrieval) are to elaborate the meaning of the items and to organize the material during encoding (hierarchical organization seems preferable). The best ways to improve retrieval are to attempt to restore the encoding context at the time of retrieval and to practice retrieving information while learning it.

CORE CONCEPTS

encoding stage	working memory	perceptual interference
storage stage	phonological loop	inferences
retrieval stage	visual-spatial sketchpad	post-event memory reconstruction
sensory store	memory span	schema
short-term memory	chunking	stereotype
rehearsal	activation models	social stereotype
elaboration	prefrontal lobes	post-event information
long-term store	long-term memory	constructive memory
explicit memory	recall test	memory illusion
implicit memory	flashbulb memory	source monitoring
sensory memory	amnesia	mnemonic system
span of apprehension	grain-size	method of loci
partial-report procedure	constructive and reconstructive	
whole-report performance	processes	
sensory response	encoding	

DIGITAL SUPPORT RESOURCES

Students should use the unique access code included in the front of the book to access the digital support resources which accompany the new edition. These include:

- Multiple Choice Questions and Quizzes
- Critical Thinking Questions
- Practice Essay Questions

- Videos
- Glossary, Flashcards, and More

9 LANGUAGE AND THOUGHT

LEARNING OBJECTIVES:

After reading this chapter you should be able to:

Understand the properties and structure of language.

Understand language comprehension, production, and development.

Recognise the building blocks of thought, and the different forms of reasoning and problem-solving.

Have a good understanding of the neural basis of language and thought.

Define the basic properties of language.

Give examples of specific language deficits and their causes.

Define deductive and inductive reasoning, and recognize known biases in reasoning.

Elucidate the role of prior knowledge and automaticity in solving problems.

The greatest accomplishments of our species stem from our ability to entertain complex thoughts, to communicate them, and to act on them. We might say that the ability to process information, to reason logically and to solve problems sets us apart from other animals. It makes it possible for humans to make discoveries about the world and to develop techniques to change our lives. We have changed almost every aspect of our lives: from the way in which we eat our food to the way we travel, and from the way we live together in very large communities to the way in which we communicate with one another. It is through the use of language that humans can collaborate with one another and make those changes in ways that no other animal species can.

We begin this chapter with a discussion of language, the means by which thoughts are communicated. Then we consider the development or acquisition of language. The remaining sections of this chapter discuss major topics in human thought: reasoning, decision-making, and problem-solving. We will also discuss the role of imagery and automaticity.

CHAPTER OUTLINE

LANGUAGE AND COMMUNICATION
Properties of language
Language structure
Effects of context on comprehension and production
The neural basis of language

THE DEVELOPMENT OF LANGUAGE
Milestones
Language acquisition

CONCEPTS AND CATEGORIZATION: THE BUILDING BLOCKS OF THOUGHT
Functions of concepts
Prototypes
Hierarchies of concepts
Different categorization processes
Acquiring concepts
The neural basis of concepts and categorization

REASONING AND DECISION-MAKING
Deductive reasoning
Inductive reasoning
The neural basis of reasoning

CUTTING EDGE RESEARCH: EVOLUTIONARY RESEARCH INTO THE NATURE OF LANGUAGE

THOUGHT IN ACTION: PROBLEM-SOLVING
Problem-solving strategies
Representing the problem
Imaginal thought
Experts versus novices
Automaticity

SEEING BOTH SIDES: DO PEOPLE WHO SPEAK DIFFERENT LANGUAGES THINK DIFFERENTLY?

LANGUAGE AND COMMUNICATION

Language is our primary means of communicating thought. Moreover, it is universal: every human society has a language, and every human being of normal intelligence acquires his or her native language and uses it effortlessly. The fact that virtually everyone can master and use an enormously complex linguistic system is remarkable. In contrast, even the most sophisticated computers have severe problems in interpreting speech, understanding written text, or speaking in a productive way. Yet most normal children perform these linguistic tasks effortlessly. Why this should be so is among the fundamental puzzles of human psychology.

Properties of language

Language use has two aspects: production and comprehension. In the **production of language**, we start with a thought, somehow translate it into a sentence, and end up with sounds that express the sentence. In the **comprehension of language**, we start by hearing sounds, attach meaning to the sounds in the form of words, and then attach meaning to the combination of the words in the form of sentences. Language use seems to involve moving through various levels, as shown in Figure 9.1. At the highest level are sentence units, including sentences and phrases. The next level is that of words and parts of words that carry meaning (the prefix 'non,' or the suffix 'er,' for example). The lowest level contains speech sounds. The adjacent levels are closely related: the phrases of a sentence are built from words and prefixes and suffixes, which in turn are constructed from speech sounds. **Language** therefore is a multilevel system for relating thoughts to speech by means of word and sentence units (Chomsky, 1965).

The first important property of a language is the fact that language is *symbolic*. Words represent things in an arbitrary way: the word 'book' doesn't look or feel or taste like a book –

it just *represents* it. This symbolic nature of language is a powerful one: it allows humans to refer to and communicate about objects, actions, events, feelings, and even ideas. We can talk about a book which doesn't exist yet (the book you will one day write) as easily as about a book that is sitting in front of us. The second property of language is that it is *structured*. There are rules that govern the way in which symbols can be combined – called the *grammar*. Such rules exist at each level, as we will see below. The third property of language is its *generativity*: rules allow us to combine units at one level into a vastly greater number of units at the next level. This allows us to produce (generate) infinite numbers of messages. This property also applies to all levels. Let's take a look at speech sounds: all languages have only a limited number of speech sounds; English has about 40 of them. But rules for combining these sounds make it possible to produce and understand thousands of words (a vocabulary of 70 000 words is not unusual for an adult; see Bloom, 2000). Similarly, rules for combining words make it possible to produce and understand millions of sentences (if not an infinite number of them). So, the basic properties of language are that it is symbolic, structured at multiple levels, and generative. Every human language has these properties.

Language structure

Let's now consider the units and processes involved at each level of language. We usually take the perspective of a person comprehending language, a listener, though occasionally we switch to that of a language producer, a speaker.

Speech sounds

If you could attend to just the sounds someone makes when talking to you, what would you hear? You would not perceive the person's speech as a continuous stream of sound but rather as a sequence of **phonemes**, or discrete speech sounds. Phonemes are the shortest segment of speech that can be recognized as speech. Our phonemic categories act as filters that convert a continuous stream of speech into a sequence of familiar phonemes. For example, the sound corresponding to the first letter in *boy* is an instance of a phoneme symbolized as /b/. Note that phonemes may correspond to letters, but they are speech sounds, not letters. In English, we divide all speech sounds into about 40 phonemes (see Table 9.1). Although about 200 different phonemes have been documented in human language worldwide, most human languages have no more than 60 phonemes (Ladefoged, 2005). The sounds that make up the phonetic alphabet also vary widely. For example, German and Dutch speakers use certain guttural sounds (produced in the throat) that are never heard in English.

The fact that every language has a different set of phonemes is one reason we often have difficulty learning to pronounce foreign words. Another language may use phonemes that do not appear in ours. It may take us a while even to hear

FIGURE 9.1 **Levels of Language.** *At the highest level are sentence units, including phrases and sentences. The next level is words and parts of words that carry meaning. The lowest level contains speech sounds.*

TABLE 9.1   A PHONETIC ALPHABET FOR ENGLISH PRONUNCIATION

	Consonants							*Vowels*			
p	pill	t	till	k	kill	i	beet	ɪ	bit
b	bill	d	dill	g	gill	e	bait	ɛ	bet
m	mill	n	nil	ŋ	ring	u	boot	U	foot
f	feel	s	seal	h	heal	o	boat	ɔ	bore
v	veal	z	zeal	l	leaf	æ	bat	a	pot/bar
θ	thigh	tʃ	chill	r	reef	ʌ	butt	aw	bout
ð	thy	dʒ	Jill	j	you	aj	bite		
ʃ	shill	ʍ	which	w	witch	ɔj	boy		
ʒ	azure								

the new phonemes, let alone produce them. For example, in Hindi the two different /p/ sounds just described correspond to two different phonemes, so Hindu speakers appreciate differences that others do not. Another language may not make a distinction between two sounds that our language treats as two phonemes. In Japanese, the English sounds corresponding to r and l (/r/ and /l/) are perceived as the same phoneme – which leads to the frequent confusion between words like *rice* and *lice*.

The **phonological rules** of a language dictate which phonemes can follow which other phonemes. When phonemes are combined in the right way, we perceive the combinations as words. In English, for example, /b/ cannot follow /p/ at the beginning of a word (try pronouncing *pbet*). The influence of such rules is revealed when we listen. We are more accurate in perceiving a string of phonemes whose order conforms to the rules of our language than a string whose order violates these rules. The influence of these rules is even more striking when we take the perspective of a speaker. For example, we have no difficulty pronouncing the plurals of nonsense words that we have never heard before. Consider *zuk* and *zug*. In accordance with a simple rule, the plural of *zuk* is formed by adding the phoneme /s/. In English, however, /s/ cannot follow g at the end of a word, so to form the plural of *zug* we must use another rule – one that adds the phoneme /z/, as in *fuzz*. We may not be aware of these rules in forming plurals, but we have no difficulty producing them. We seem to 'know' the rules for combining phonemes in our own language, without always being consciously aware of them.

Word units

We typically perceive words, not phonemes, when we are listening to speech. Unlike phonemes, words carry meaning. However, they are not the only smallish linguistic units that

convey meaning. Suffixes such as *ly* or prefixes such as *un* also carry meaning. They can be added to words to form more complex words with different meanings, as when *un* and *ly* are added to 'time' to form 'untimely.' The term **morpheme** is used to refer to any small linguistic unit that carries meaning. **Morphological rules** state how morphemes can be combined to form words.

Most morphemes are themselves words. Most words denote some specific content, such as *house* or *run*. A few words, however, primarily serve to make sentences grammatical. Such grammatical words, or **grammatical morphemes**, include what are commonly referred to as articles and prepositions, such as *a*, *the*, *in*, *of*, *on*, and *at*. Some prefixes and suffixes also play primarily a grammatical role. These grammatical morphemes include the suffixes *ing* and *ed*.

Grammatical morphemes may be processed differently from content words. One piece of evidence for this is forms of brain damage in which the use of grammatical morphemes is impaired more than the use of content words (Zurif, 1995). Also, as we will see later, grammatical morphemes are acquired in a different way from content words.

The function of language, of course, is to convey meaning. **Semantics** is the study of the meaning of words and sentences. For example: many words carry not only their dictionary meaning, but also some kind of (cultural or emotional) connotation as well. Other words are ambiguous because they name more than one concept. *Club*, for example, names both a social organization and an object used for striking. Sometimes we may be aware of a word's ambiguity, as when we hear the sentence 'He was interested in the club.' In most cases, however, the sentence context makes the meaning of the word sufficiently clear that we do not consciously experience any ambiguity – for example, 'He wanted to join the club.' Even in

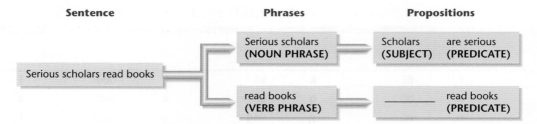

FIGURE 9.2 Phrases and Propositions. *The first step in extracting the proposition from a complex sentence is to decompose the sentence into phrases. This decomposition is based on rules like 'Any sentence can be divided into a noun phrase and a verb phrase.'*

these cases, though, there is evidence that we unconsciously consider both meanings of the ambiguous word for a brief moment. In one experiment, participants were presented a sentence such as 'He wanted to join the club,' followed immediately by a test word that the participant had to read aloud as quickly as possible. Participants read the test word faster if it was related to *either* meaning of club (for example, *group* or *struck*) than if it was unrelated to another meaning (for example, *apple*). This suggests that both meanings of club were activated during comprehension of the sentence and that either meaning could prime, or activate, related words (Swinney, 1979; Tanenhaus *et al.*, 1979).

Sentence units

Usually, we effortlessly combine words into **sentence units**, which include sentences as well as phrases. And, again, rules are at work: the **syntax** of a language (its *syntactical rules*) governs how words can be combined into phrases and sentences. An important property of sentence units is that they can correspond to parts of a statement, or a proposition. Such correspondences allow a listener to 'extract' propositions from sentences.

To understand these correspondences, first you have to appreciate that any **proposition** can be divided into a subject and a predicate (a description). In the proposition 'Audrey has curly hair,' 'Audrey' is the subject and 'has curly hair' is the predicate. In the proposition 'The tailor is asleep,' 'the tailor' is the subject and 'is asleep' is the predicate. And in 'Teachers work too hard' 'teachers' is the subject and 'work too hard' is the predicate. Any sentence can be broken into phrases so that each phrase corresponds either to the subject or the predicate of a proposition or to an entire proposition. For example, intuitively we can divide the simple sentence 'Irene sells insurance' into two phrases, 'Irene' and 'sells insurance.' The first phrase, called a **noun phrase** because it centers on a noun, specifies the subject of an underlying proposition. The second phrase, a **verb phrase**, gives the predicate of the proposition. For a more complex example, consider the sentence 'Serious scholars read books.' This sentence can be divided into two phrases, the noun phrase 'Serious scholars' and the verb phrase 'read books.' The noun phrase expresses an entire proposition,

'scholars are serious'; the verb phrase expresses part (the predicate) of another proposition, 'scholars read books' (see Figure 9.2). Again, sentence units correspond closely to proposition units, which provide a link between language and thought.

When listening to a sentence, people seem to first divide it into noun phrases, verb phrases, and the like, and then to extract propositions from these phrases. In one study, participants listened to sentences such as 'The poor girl stole a warm coat.' Immediately after each sentence was presented, participants were given a probe word from the sentence and asked to say the word that came after it. People responded faster when the probe and the response words came from the same phrase ('poor' and 'girl') than when they came from different phrases ('girl' and 'stole'). So each phrase is regarded as a unit, and when the probe and response are from the same phrase, only one unit needs to be retrieved (Wilkes & Kennedy, 1969).

Analyzing a sentence into noun and verb phrases, and then dividing these phrases into smaller units like nouns, adjectives and verbs, is called syntactic analysis. This serves to structure the parts of a sentence so we can tell what is related to what. For example, in the sentence 'The green bird ate a red snake,' the syntax of English tells us that the bird did the eating and not the snake, that the bird was green but not the snake, that the snake was red but not the bird, and so on. Furthermore, in an example like 'The dogs that the man owned were lazy,' the syntax helps us to identify the man as doing the owning (by word order) and the dogs as being lazy (by word order and number agreement). In identifying the verb and noun phrases of a sentence and how they are related, we are identifying what is what, and who did what to whom.

In the course of understanding a sentence, we usually perform such a syntactic analysis effortlessly and unconsciously. Sometimes, however, our syntactic analysis goes awry, and we become aware of the process. Consider the sentence 'The horse raced past the barn fell.' Many people have difficulty understanding this sentence. Why? Because on first reading, we assume that 'The horse' is the noun phrase and 'raced past the barn' is the verb phrase, which leaves us with no place for the word *fell*. To understand the sentence correctly, we have to repartition it so that the entire phrase 'The horse raced past the barn' is the noun phrase and 'fell' is the verb phrase (that is, the sentence is a shortened version of 'The horse who was raced past the barn fell') (Garrett, 1990; Garrod & Pickering, 1999). The misreading of such sentences is called a *garden path*.

Effects of context on comprehension and production

Figure 9.3 presents an amended version of our levels-based description of language. It suggests that producing a sentence is the inverse of understanding a sentence.

To understand a sentence, we hear phonemes, use them to construct the morphemes and phrases of the sentence, and finally extract the proposition from the sentence unit. We work from the bottom up. To produce a sentence, we move in the opposite direction: we start with a propositional thought, translate it into the phrases and morphemes of a sentence, and finally translate these morphemes into phonemes.

Although this analysis describes some of what occurs in sentence understanding and production, it is oversimplified because it does not consider the context in which language processing occurs. Often the context makes what is about to be said predictable. After comprehending just a few words, we jump to conclusions about what we think the entire sentence means (the propositions behind it) and then use our guess about the propositions to help understand the rest of the sentence. In such cases, understanding proceeds from the highest level down, as well as from the lowest level up (Adams & Collins, 1979). Indeed, sometimes language understanding is nearly impossible without some context (what topic is being talked about). To illustrate, try to follow what is described in the following paragraph:

> **The procedure is actually quite simple. First you arrange things into different groups. Of course, one pile may be sufficient, depending on how much there is to do. If you have to go somewhere else due to lack of facilities, that is the next step; otherwise you are pretty well set. It is important not to overdo things. That is, it is better to do too few things at once than too many. In the short run this**
> **may not seem important, but complications can easily arise. A mistake can be expensive as well. At first the whole procedure will seem complicated. Soon, however, it will become just another facet of life.**
>
> (After Bransford & Johnson, 1973)

In reading the paragraph, you no doubt had difficulty understanding exactly what it was about. But once you know that the topic was 'washing clothes,' it should be easy to follow, using your background knowledge about that topic – try reading it again. The second time around you are making use of the schema that you have for the action 'to wash clothes.'

Another salient part of the context is the person we are communicating with. In understanding a sentence, it is not enough to understand its phonemes, morphemes, and phrases. We must also understand the speaker's intention in uttering that particular sentence. For example, when someone at dinner asks you, 'Can you pass the potatoes?' you usually assume that the speaker's intention was not to find out whether you are physically capable of lifting the potatoes but, rather, to induce you to actually pass the potatoes. However, had your arm's been in a sling, given the identical question, you might assume that the speaker's intention was to determine your physical capability. There is evidence that people determine the speaker's intention as part of the process of comprehension (see Bosco *et al.*, 2004).

There are similar effects in the production of language. If someone asks you 'Where is the Eiffel Tower?' you will say different things depending on the physical context and the assumptions you make about the questioner. If the question is asked of you in London, for example, you might answer, 'In Paris, France.' However, if the question is asked in Quartier Latin (an area in the city of Paris), you might say, 'About 4 kilometers west of here, in the Parc du Champs.' And if the question is asked in the park itself, you might say, 'On the Avenue Gustave Eiffel' – and you'll probably even point in the right direction, assuming the person will want to visit there. In speaking, as in understanding, we must determine how the utterance fits the context.

The neural basis of language

Recall from Chapter 2 that there are two regions of the left hemisphere of the cortex that are critical for language: Broca's area, which lies in the posterior part of the frontal lobes, and Wernicke's area, which lies in the temporal region. Damage to either of these areas – or to some in-between areas – leads to specific kinds of aphasia (a breakdown in language) (Dronkers *et al.*, 2000), so that aphasic patients can teach us a great deal about the neural basis of language.

The disrupted language of a patient with **Broca's aphasia** (a patient with damage to Broca's area) is illustrated by the

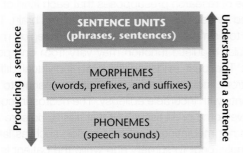

FIGURE 9.3 Levels of Understanding and Producing Sentences.

Language production depends on context. You would probably use different language when giving directions to a tourist than when telling a neighbor where a particular restaurant or store is located.

following interview, in which *E* designates the interviewer (or experimenter) and *P*, the patient:

E: *Were you in the Coast Guard?*

P: *No, er, yes, yes ... ship ... Massachu ... chusetts ... Coast Guard ... years. [Raises hands twice with fingers indicating '19']*

E: *Oh, you were in the Coast Guard for 19 years.*

P: *Oh ... boy ... right ... right.*

E: *Why are you in the hospital?*

P: *Points to paralyzed arm] Arm no good. [Points to mouth] Speech ... can't say ... talk, you see.*

(Gardner, 1975, p. 61)

It is clear that the patient understands the experimenter's questions, but his speech is very disfluent (halting and hesitant). This is in contrast to the fluent speech of a patient with **Wernicke's aphasia** (a patient with damage in Wernicke's area), which preserves syntax but is devoid of content:

Boy, I'm sweating, I'm awful nervous, you know, once in a while I get caught up. I can't mention the tarripoi, a month ago, quite a little, I've done a lot well, I impose a lot, while, on the other hand, you know what I mean, I have to run around, look it over, trebin and all that sort of stuff.

(Gardner, 1975, p. 68)

We see clear problems in finding the right words, and occasionally words are invented (as in *tarripoi* and *trebin*).

One way to summarize these findings is to say that Broca's aphasia is a disorder in language production (and not comprehension), whereas Wernicke's aphasia is a disorder in language comprehension (and not production). This is the classic Geschwind model discussed in Chapter 2, which characterizes Broca's area as the area devoted to speech planning and Wernicke's area devoted to phonology (speech sounds). In this model, the *meaning* of words is stored neither in Broca's, nor in Wernicke's area, but in other areas. A particular type of aphasia, conduction aphasia, is consistent with this model. In this condition, the aphasic seems relatively normal in tests of both syntactic and conceptual abilities but has severe problems when asked to repeat a spoken sentence. A neurological explanation of this curious disorder is that the brain structures mediating basic aspects of comprehension and production are intact but that the neural connections between these structures are damaged. The patient can understand what is said because Wernicke's area is intact, and can produce fluent speech because Broca's area is intact but cannot transmit what was understood to the speech center because the connecting links between the areas are damaged (Geschwind, 1972).

Other findings in aphasic patients are not consistent with the straightforward Geschwind model. In one study, Broca's patients had to listen to sentences and show that they understood it by selecting a picture (from a set) that the sentence described. In the sentence 'The lion that the tiger is chasing is fat,' we must rely on syntax (word order) to determine that it is the lion that is fat and not the tiger. Broca's patients could not do this: they were as likely to select the picture with a fat tiger as the one with the fat lion. On the sentences that did not require much syntactic analysis (for example 'The bicycle the boy is holding is broken'), Broca's aphasics did almost as well as normal participants (Caramazza & Zurif, 1976). This and other studies show quite clearly that Broca's aphasics is not limited to language expression, but that it can also include problems with comprehension.

What we can learn about the neural basis of language through the study of aphasic patients is obviously limited. This type of research presupposes that each kind of aphasia is caused by damage to a specific area of the brain. This idea may be too simple. In reality, the particular region mediating a particular linguistic function may vary from one person to another. The best evidence for such individual differences comes from findings of neurosurgeons preparing to operate on patients with incurable epilepsy. The neurosurgeon needs to remove some brain tissue but first has to be sure that this tissue is not mediating a critical function such as language. Accordingly, prior to surgery and while the patient is awake, the neurosurgeon delivers small electric charges to the area in question and observes their effects on the patient's ability to name things. If electrical stimulation disrupts the patient's naming, the neurosurgeon knows to avoid this location during the operation. One patient's naming may be disrupted by electrical stimulation to locations in the front of the brain but not by stimulation in the back of the brain, whereas another patient might show a different pattern (Ojemann, 1983). If different areas of the brain mediate language in different people, presumably the areas associated with aphasias also vary from one person to another.

Studies using brain imaging techniques such as fMRI to explore the neural basis of language also highlight subject-related differences. For example, Kim *et al.* (1997) showed that the age of acquisition of a second language determines whether or not the representation of that language in Broca's area overlaps with the representation of the native language.

Current models of language-use posit the existence of many different stages, but the neural circuitry involved in each of the stages has yet to be identified in detail (see Sahin *et al.*, 2009). Language production, for example, involves conceptual preparation, lexical retrieval, phonological retrieval, phonetic processing, self-monitoring and articulation (see Indefrey & Levelt, 2004). Each of these processes relies on certain brain areas so that damage to a particular area may result in problems with that particular processing stage as well as in a disruption of subsequent processes. Such models might explain what we saw above, namely that brain damage sometimes causes problems primarily in language production, while in other cases it primarily affects comprehension.

INTERIM SUMMARY

➡ Language is structured at three different levels: (1) sentence units, (2) words and parts of words that carry meaning, and (3) speech sounds.

➡ The three levels of language are interconnected.

➡ Sentence units are built from words (and parts of words), and words are constructed from speech sounds.

➡ A phoneme is a category of speech sounds. Every language has its own set of phonemes – with different sets for different languages – and rules for combining them into words.

➡ A morpheme is the smallest unit of language that carries meaning. Most morphemes are words, but others are prefixes and suffixes that are added to words.

➡ Syntactic rules are used for combining words into phrases and phrases into sentences.

➡ The areas of the brain that mediate language lie in the left hemisphere and include Broca's area and Wernicke's area.

CRITICAL THINKING QUESTIONS

1 Now that you have some idea of the units and levels of language (such as phonemes, words, semantics, and syntax), apply these notions to learning a second language. Which components do you think will be easiest and hardest to learn? What evidence would support your view?

2 As we saw, background knowledge, or knowledge of context, is clearly important for understanding language. Do you think there is a particular region of the brain that mediates such knowledge? What evidence would you use to support your view?

THE DEVELOPMENT OF LANGUAGE

Our discussion thus far makes it clear that understanding language is complex. Yet, by age five virtually all children understand and produce full sentences. How is this learned? In this section, we will first discuss *what* is acquired at each level of language and then *how* it is acquired – specifically, the roles played by learning and innate factors.

Milestones

Development occurs at all three levels of language. It starts at the level of phonemes, proceeds to the level of words and other morphemes, and then moves on to the level of sentence units, or syntax. In what follows, we adopt a chronological perspective, tracing the child's development in both understanding and producing language.

Phonemes and combinations of phonemes

Adult listeners are good at discriminating among different sounds that correspond to different phonemes in their language but poor at discriminating among different sounds that correspond to the same phoneme in their language. Remarkably, children come into the world able to discriminate among different sounds that correspond to different phonemes in any language. What changes over the first year of life is that infants learn which phonemes are relevant to their language and lose their ability to discriminate between sounds that correspond to the same phoneme in their language. In essence, they lose the ability to make distinctions that will be of no use to them in understanding and producing their language. These remarkable facts were determined through experiments in which infants who were sucking on pacifiers were presented with pairs of sounds in succession. Infants tend to suck more in response to a novel stimulus than in response to a familiar one, which means that their rate of sucking can be used to tell whether they perceive two successive sounds as the same or different. Six-month-old infants increase their rate of sucking when the successive sounds correspond to different phonemes in any language, but 1 year olds increase their rate of sucking only when the successive sounds correspond to different phonemes in their own language. Thus, a 6-month-old Japanese child can distinguish /l/ from /r/ but loses this ability by the end of the first year of life (Eimas, 1985).

At every stage of development we see that children can understand language better than they speak it – their passive knowledge of language surpasses their active knowledge. For example: although infants can *distinguish* the different sounds in their languages, they cannot reliably *produce* them yet. By six months of age, they will have begun to *babble*, producing sounds that resemble phonemes, often repeating the same consonant-vowel combination, like 'babababa.'

It takes several years for children to learn how phonemes can be combined to form words. When children first begin to talk, they occasionally produce 'impossible' words like 'dlumber' for lumber. They do not yet know that in English /l/ cannot follow /d/ at the beginning of a word. By age 4, however, children have learned most of what they need to know about phoneme combinations.

Words and concepts

At about one year of age, children begin to speak: the babbling successively sounds more like words in the language spoken in the child's environment. More importantly, the toddlers will use words to refer to concepts. One year olds already have concepts for many things (including family members, household pets, food, toys, and body parts), and when they begin to speak they are mapping these concepts onto words that adults use. The beginning vocabulary is roughly the same for all children. Children one to two years old talk mainly about people ('Dada,' 'Mama,' 'baby'), animals ('dog,' 'cat,' 'duck'), vehicles ('car,' 'truck,' 'boat'), toys ('ball,' 'block,' 'book'), food ('juice,' 'milk,' 'cookie'), body parts ('eye,' 'nose,' 'mouth'), and household implements ('hat,' 'sock,' 'spoon').

Although these words name some of the young child's concepts, they by no means name them all. Consequently, young children often have a gap between the concepts they want to communicate and the words they have at their disposal. To bridge this gap, children aged one to $2\frac{1}{2}$ **overextend** their words – they apply words to neighboring concepts. For example, a child might use the word *doggie* for cats and cows as well as dogs. The child is not unsure of the word's meaning. If presented with pictures of various animals and asked to pick the 'doggie,' the child makes the correct choice. Overextensions begin to disappear at about age $2\frac{1}{2}$, presumably because the child's vocabulary increases so markedly, thereby eliminating many of the gaps.

At some point in time, the child's vocabulary development virtually explodes. Typically, there is a *vocabulary spurt* between ages $1\frac{1}{2}$ and two. A typical 2 year old might learn several new words every day. One way in which this may happen is through a process called **fast mapping**, in which a word is mapped onto the underlying concept after only *one* exposure (Markman *et al.,* 2003). When the child hears a word it does not know, it assumes that it maps onto one of their concepts that was not yet labeled.

From primitive to complex sentences

Between the ages of $1\frac{1}{2}$ and $2\frac{1}{2}$, the acquisition of phrase and sentence units, or syntax, begins. Children start to combine single words into two-word utterances such as 'There cow' (in which the underlying proposition is 'There's the cow'), 'Jimmy bike' ('That's Jimmy's bike'), or 'Towel bed' ('The towel's on the bed'). There is a telegraphic quality about this two-word speech. The child leaves out the grammatical words (such as *a*, *an*, *the*, and *is*), as well as other grammatical morphemes (such as the suffixes *ing*, *ed*, and *s*) and puts in only the words that carry the most important content. Despite their brevity, these utterances express most of the basic intentions of speakers, such as locating objects and describing events and actions.

Children progress rapidly from two-word utterances to more complex sentences that express propositions more precisely. Thus, 'Daddy hat' may become 'Daddy wear hat' and finally 'Daddy is wearing a hat.' Such expansions of the verb phrase appear to be the first complex constructions that occur in children's speech. The next step is the use of conjunctions like *and* and *so* to form compound sentences ('You play with the doll, and I play with the blocks') and the use of grammatical morphemes like the past tense *ed*. The sequence of language development is remarkably similar for all children. By age three, most children will use plurals and past tense. We see that they continue to learn the grammatical rules of their language, for example when they *overregulate*. This means that newly discovered grammatical rules are generalized to irregular cases. In English, for example, a 3 year old might suddenly say 'I *breaked* the cup' (rather than '*broke*'), treating the verb 'break' as a regular verb and thus adding *ed* at the end to produce the past tense. We will discuss these overregularizations more below, when we ask *how* language learning occurs.

Most milestones in language learning are achieved in the first 5 years of a child's life. But the language learning clearly does not end there. At school, most children will be taught the formal rules of their language. Around the same time, most children develop *metalinguistic awareness*, which means that they develop the ability to reflect on the nature of language. For example, between ages six and eight, children start to appreciate irony, because they have learned that statements can have an implied meaning that can differ from its literal meaning ('I really *hate* strawberry ice-cream!') (Creusere, 1999).

Children between 18 and 30 months of age learn to combine words in phrases or sentences.

Language acquisition

How do children acquire language? Clearly, learning processes must play a role, which is why children raised in English-speaking households learn English while children raised in French-speaking households learn French. Innate factors must also play a role, which is why all the children in a household learn language but none of the pets do (Gleitman, 1986).

Learning processes

Behaviorists such as Skinner believed that children learn language through the learning processes we saw described in Chapter 7: conditioning, reinforcement, and imitation. And although these processes are likely to play a role, it quickly becomes clear that they cannot account for many aspects of language development.

Consider conditioning and reinforcement. Adults may reward children when they produce a grammatical sentence and reprimand them when they make mistakes. For this to work, parents would have to respond to every detail in a child's speech. However, Brown *et al.,* (1969) found that parents do not pay attention to how the child says something as long as the statement is comprehensible. When a child says 'Nobody don't like me,' a parent is much more likely to respond by saying 'That's not true, we like you!' than to correct the child's mistake. Moreover, attempts to correct a child (and, hence, apply conditioning) are often futile. In fact, this is how such a conversation might go (McNeill, 1966, p. 49):

CHILD:	Nobody don't like me.
MOTHER:	No, say, 'nobody likes me.'
CHILD:	Nobody don't like me.
MOTHER:	No, now listen carefully; say 'nobody likes me.'
CHILD:	Oh! Nobody don't likes me.

Although imitation plays some role in the learning of words (a parent points to a telephone, says, 'Phone,' and the child tries to repeat the word), it too cannot be the principal means by which children learn to produce and understand sentences. Young children constantly utter sentences that they have never heard an adult say, such as 'All gone milk.' Even when children in the two-word stage of language development try to imitate longer sentences (for example, 'Mr Miller will try'), they produce their usual telegraphic utterances ('Miller try').

The problem with imitation and conditioning is that they focus on specific utterances. However, children often learn something general, such as a rule. They seem to form a hypothesis about a rule of language, test it, and retain it if it works. This is how we explain the overgeneralizations that we saw before. Consider the morpheme *ed*. As a general rule in English, *ed* is added to the present tense of verbs to form the past tense (as in *cook–cooked*). Many common verbs, however, are irregular and do not follow this rule (*go–went, break–broke*). Many of these irregular verbs express concepts that children use from the beginning. So, at an early point, children use the past tense of some irregular verbs correctly (presumably because they learned them by imitation). Then they learn the past tense for some regular verbs and discover the hypothesis 'add *ed* to the present tense to form the past tense.' This hypothesis leads them to add the *ed* ending to many verbs, including irregular ones. They say things like 'Annie goed home' and 'Jackie breaked the cup,' which they have never heard before. Eventually, they learn that some verbs are irregular and stop overgeneralizing their use of *ed* (Pinker, 1994).

How then, do children generate these hypotheses? There are a few operating principles that all children use as a guide to forming hypotheses. One is to pay attention to the ends of words. Another is to look for prefixes and suffixes that indicate a change in meaning. A child armed with these two principles is likely to hit upon the hypothesis that *ed* at the end of verbs signals the past tense, because *ed* is a word ending associated with a change in meaning. A third operating principle is to avoid exceptions, which explains why children initially generalize their *ed*-equals-past-tense hypothesis to irregular verbs. Some of these principles appear in Table 9.2, and they seem to hold for all of the 40 languages studied by Slobin (1985).

Innate factors

To account for the complexity of human language development, Chomsky (1959) developed a theory that criticized Skinner's behaviorist theory. He argued that humans have an innate (or 'native') biological capacity to learn language. According to Chomsky, the human brain is equipped at birth with a *language acquisition device* (LAD), processes that facilitate language learning.

The fact that all children, regardless of their culture and language, seem to go through the same sequence of language development, is consistent with this view. At age one year, the child speaks a few isolated words; at about age

TABLE 9.2 OPERATING PRINCIPLES USED BY YOUNG CHILDREN

Children from many countries seem to follow these principles in learning to talk and to understand speech.

1 Look for systematic changes in the form of words.
2 Look for grammatical markers that clearly indicate changes in meaning.
3 Avoid exceptions.
4 Pay attention to the ends of words.
5 Pay attention to the order of words, prefixes, and suffixes.
6 Avoid interruption or rearrangement of constituents (that is, sentence units).

two, the child speaks two- and three-word sentences; at age three, sentences become more grammatical; and at age four, the child's speech sounds much like that of an adult. Because cultures differ markedly in the opportunities they provide for children to learn from adults – in some cultures parents are constantly speaking to their children, whereas in others parents verbally ignore their children – the fact that this sequence is so consistent across cultures might mean that we are biologically prepared to learn language. Recent research shows that the same milestones in the acquisition of English are seen in internationally adopted children who know no English before they were adopted (Snedeker *et al.*, 2007). The fact that these children were much older ($2\frac{1}{2}$ to $5\frac{1}{2}$ years) when they started to learn English, suggests that these milestones truly reflect language learning, and not general cognitive development in the first years of life.

Indeed, our innate knowledge of language seems to be so rich that children can go through the normal course of language acquisition even when there are no language users around them to serve as models or teachers. A group of researchers studied six deaf children of hearing parents who had decided not to have their children learn sign language. Before the children received any instruction in lip reading and vocalization, they began to use a system of gestures called *home sign*. Initially, their home sign was a kind of simple pantomime, but eventually it took on the properties of a language. For example, it was organized at both the morphemic and syntactic levels, including individual signs and combinations of signs. In addition, these deaf children (who essentially created their own language) went through the same stages of development as normal hearing children. The deaf children initially gestured one sign at a time and later put their pantomimes together into two- and three-concept 'sentences.' These striking results attest to the richness and detail of our innate knowledge (Feldman *et al.*, 1978).

Also consistent with the nativist view are findings showing that language learning has critical periods during which it must

be acquired. This is particularly evident when it comes to acquiring the sound system of a new language – learning new phonemes and the rules for combining them. We have already noted that infants less than one year old can discriminate among phonemes of any language but lose this ability by the end of their first year, so the first months of life are a critical period for homing in on the phonemes of one's native language. This is relevant for second-language learning, discussed below.

Indirect evidence for the existence of a critical period for language acquisition can be seen in cases of children who have experienced extreme isolation. A famous case of social isolation in childhood is that of Genie, a girl whose father was psychotic and whose mother was blind and highly dependent. From birth until she was discovered by child welfare authorities at age 11, Genie was strapped to a potty chair in an isolated room of her parents' home. Before she was discovered, Genie had had almost no contact with other people. She had virtually no language ability. Efforts to teach her to speak had limited results. She was able to learn words, but she could not master the rules of grammar that come naturally to younger children. Although tests showed that she was highly intelligent, her language abilities never progressed beyond those of a third-grader (Curtiss, 1977; Rymer, 1992a, 1992b).

Other research indicates that there is a critical period for learning syntax. The evidence comes from studies of deaf people who know American Sign Language (ASL), which is a full-blown language and not a pantomime system. The studies of interest involved adults who had been using ASL for 30 years or more, but who varied in the age of acquisition. Although all the participants were born to hearing parents, some were native signers who were exposed to ASL from birth, others first learned ASL between ages 4 and 6 when they enrolled in a school for the deaf, and still others did not encounter ASL until after they were 12 (their parents had been reluctant to let them learn a sign language rather than a spoken one). If there is a critical period for learning syntax,

Research has shown that there is a critical period for learning syntax. Deaf people can use American Sign Language more effectively if they learn it at an early age.

the early learners should have shown greater mastery of some aspects of syntax than the later learners, even 30 years after acquisition. This is exactly what the researchers found. With respect to understanding and producing words with multiple morphemes – such as *untimely*, which consists of the morphemes *un*, *time*, and *ly* – native signers did better than those who learned ASL when entering school, who in turn did better than those who learned ASL after age 12 (Meier, 1991; Newport, 1990).

Recent theories of language acquisition state that both biological factors as well as learning play a role in the development of language. Rather than assuming that humans are simply pre-wired for language as Chomsky argued, such theories assume that the neural circuitry required for language processing *emerges* gradually in response to specific experiences (MacWhinney, 1998). The specific learning experiences needed are social interactions involving communication through language. In other words, mere exposure to language is not enough to acquire it; we need a supportive environment as well.

Second-language acquisition

In today's world, many individuals learn a second language later in life. In fact, many of the students reading this textbook are not native speakers of English. What do we know about second-language learning? As with ASL learning, we see a major effect of age of acquisition. Even though adults initially learn quickly because they can be taught the rules of a language (for example, how to conjugate regular verbs), they are ultimately at a disadvantage. Consider phoneme discrimination. We learn to discriminate the sounds of our own language by the end of the first year of life. As a result, it is difficult to acquire the sound system of a second language later in life. After a few years of learning a second language, young children are more likely than adults to speak it without an accent, and they are better able to understand the language when it is spoken in noisy conditions (Lenneberg, 1967; Snow, 1987). Furthermore, when adults learn a second language, they typically retain an accent that they can never unlearn no matter how many years they speak the new language. But the problems in later language acquisition are not limited to phoneme learning and pronunciation.

Johnson and Newport (1989) studied Chinese and Korean speakers who moved to the USA and became immersed in an English-language community (as students and faculty members at a university) at least 5 years prior to testing. Subjects were asked to judge whether or not sentences presented to them were grammatical in English. The researchers found that performance on this task dropped with increasing age of arrival. Subjects who had been between the ages of three and seven when they moved to the USA did just as well as native speakers. However, the older the subjects were when they moved, the lower their score was on this test.

The proficiency of second-language learners does not only depend on their age at the time of acquisition. The more the individual is socially and psychologically integrated into the new culture, the better the learning of the new culture's language will be (Schumann, 1978). Not surprisingly, there is also a positive correlation between motivation and second-language learning (Masgoret & Gardner, 2003).

Can another species learn human language?

Some experts believe that our innate capacity to learn language is unique to our species (Chomsky, 1972; Pinker, 1994). They acknowledge that other species have communication systems but argue that these are qualitatively different from ours. Consider the communication system of the chimpanzee. Chimpanzees' vocalizations and gestures are limited in number, and the generativity of their communication system is very low compared with that of human language, in which a relatively small number of phonemes can be combined to create thousands of words, which in turn can be combined to create an unlimited number of sentences. Another difference is that human language is structured at several levels, whereas chimpanzee communications are not. In particular, in human language there is a clear distinction between the level of words or morphemes, which have meaning, and the level of sounds, which do not. There is no hint of such a duality of structure in chimpanzee communication; every symbol carries meaning. Still another difference is that chimpanzees do not vary the order of their symbols to vary the meaning of their messages as we do. For instance, for us, 'Jonah ate the whale' means something quite different from 'The whale ate Jonah.' There is no evidence for a comparable difference in chimpanzee communications.

The fact that chimpanzee communication is impoverished compared with our own does not prove that chimpanzees lack the capacity for a more complex system. Their system may be adequate for their needs. To determine whether chimpanzees have the same innate capacity we do, we must see whether they can learn our language. In one of the best-known studies of the teaching of language to chimps, Gardner and Gardner (1972) taught a female chimpanzee named Washoe signs adapted from ASL. Sign language was used because chimps lack the vocal equipment to pronounce human sounds. Training began when Washoe was about one year old and continued until she was five. During this time, Washoe's caretakers communicated with her only by means of sign language. They first taught her signs by means of shaping procedures, waiting for her to make a gesture that resembled a sign and then reinforcing her. Later, Washoe learned signs simply by observing and imitating. By age four, Washoe could produce 130 different signs and understand even more. She could also generalize a sign from one situation to another. For example, she first learned the sign for 'more' in connection with 'more tickling' and then

The chimpanzee on the left has learned a kind of sign language and the chimpanzee on the right has been trained to communicate using a keyboard.

generalized it to indicate 'more milk.' Other chimpanzees have acquired comparable vocabularies.

Other animals too, show word-learning ability. One dog in particular drew quite a bit of attention a couple of years ago. Rico, a border collie in Germany showed that he is capable of learning words using the fast-mapping process we see in human toddlers (Kaminski *et al.*, 2004), whereby a new word is learned after one exposure. The researchers approached the dog's owner, after they had seen her appear with Rico in a television show. To everyone's amazement, Rico knows the names of over 200 objects. Rico's owner allowed the researchers to test whether his fast word learning relied on a process of inference, as seen in humans: if you are asked to pick up an object with a name that is new to you (let's say 'wug') and before you is a table with nine familiar objects and one unfamiliar object, you'll pick up the unfamiliar object, inferring that it must be the 'wug.' This was exactly what was seen in Rico, though he was not perfect: Rico would fetch the unfamiliar object on seven out of ten trials.

We saw above that apes can be taught a limited vocabulary and that the concepts behind some of the signs are equivalent to ours. Do these studies support the view that apes can learn human language? Can apes learn syntax and combine signs in the same way that humans combine words into a sentence? For example, not only can we combine the words *man*, *John*, *hurt*, and *the* into the sentence 'The man hurt John,' but we can also combine the same words in a different order to produce a sentence with a different meaning, 'John hurt the man.' Studies by Greenfield and Savage-Rumbaugh (1990) seem to show that it is possible. The researchers worked with a bonobo (pygmy chimpanzee), whose behavior is thought to be more like that of humans than the behavior of the more widely studied common chimpanzee. The bonobo, a 7 year old named Kanzi, communicated by manipulating symbols that stand for words. Unlike previous studies, Kanzi learned to manipulate the symbols in

a relatively natural way, for example by listening to his caretakers as they uttered English words while pointing to the symbols on a keyboard. Most important, after a few years of language training, Kanzi demonstrated some ability to vary word order to communicate changes in meaning. For example, if Kanzi was going to bite his half-sister Mulika, he would signal, 'Bite Mulika,' but if his sister bit him, he would sign, 'Mulika bite.' Kanzi thus seems to have some syntactic knowledge, roughly that of a two-year-old human.

These results are tantalizing, but they need to be interpreted with caution. For one thing, Kanzi is one of very few apes who have shown any syntactic ability, and we might question how general the results are. For another thing, although Kanzi may have a linguistic ability similar to that of a 2 year old, it took him substantially longer to get to that point than it does a human. But perhaps the main reason to be skeptical about the possibility of any ape developing comparable linguistic abilities to a human has been voiced by Chomsky (1991): 'If an animal had a capacity as biologically advantageous as language but somehow hadn't used it until now, it would be an evolutionary miracle, like finding an island of humans who could be taught to fly.'

INTERIM SUMMARY

➔ Infants appear to be preprogrammed to learn phonemes, but they need several years to learn the rules for combining them.

➔ When children begin to speak, they first learn words that name concepts that are familiar in their environment. Then they move on to sentences. They begin with one-word utterances, progress to two-word telegraphic speech, and then elaborate their noun and verb phrases.

➔ Children learn language in part by testing hypotheses (often unconsciously). These hypotheses tend to be guided by a small set of operating principles, which call the children's attention to critical characteristics of utterances, such as word endings.

➔ Innate factors also play a major role in language acquisition. There are numerous findings that support this claim. For one, all children in all cultures seem to go through the same stages in acquiring their language. For another, like other innate behaviors, some language abilities are learned only during a critical period. This partly explains why it is relatively difficult to learn a language later in life.

CRITICAL THINKING QUESTIONS

1 Do you think there is a critical period for learning word meanings? What type of evidence would support your answer? And what type of evidence would refute it?

2 What do you think would happen if parents explicitly taught children language the way that most researchers have taught apes human language? Would it speed up, slow down, or leave unchanged the process of language acquisition?

CONCEPTS AND CATEGORIZATION: THE BUILDING BLOCKS OF THOUGHT

Thought can be conceived of as a 'language of the mind.' Actually, there may be more than one such language. One mode of thought corresponds to the stream of sentences that we seem to 'hear in our mind.' It is referred to as **propositional thought** because it expresses a proposition or claim. Another mode, **imaginal thought**, corresponds to images, which we can 'see' in our minds. Research on thinking in adults has emphasized these two modes, particularly the propositional mode.

We can think of a proposition as a statement that expresses a factual claim. 'Mothers are hard workers' is one proposition. 'Cats are animals' is another. Such statements consists of concepts – such as 'mothers' and 'hard workers' or 'cat' and 'animal' – combined in a particular way. To understand propositional thought, therefore, we first need to understand the concepts that compose it.

Functions of concepts

A **concept** represents an entire class; it is the set of properties that we associate with a particular class. Our concept of 'cat,' for example, includes the properties of having four legs and whiskers. Concepts serve some major functions in mental life. One of those functions is to divide the world into manageable units (cognitive economy). The world is full of so many different objects that if we treated each one as distinct, we would soon be overwhelmed. For example, if we had to refer to every single object we encountered by a different name, our vocabulary would have to be gigantic – so immense that communication might become impossible. (Think what it would be like if we had a separate name for each of the 7 million colors among which we can discriminate!) Fortunately, we do not treat each object as unique. Rather, we see it as an instance of a concept. Many different objects are seen as instances of the concept 'cat,' many others as instances of the concept 'chair,' and so on. By treating different objects as members of the same concept, we reduce the complexity of the world that we have to represent mentally.

Categorization refers to the process of assigning an object to a concept. When we categorize an object, we treat it as if it has many of the properties associated with the concept, including properties that we have not directly perceived. A second major function of concepts is that they allow us to predict information that is not readily perceived (referred to as predictive power). For example, our concept of 'apple' is associated with such hard-to-perceive properties as having seeds and being edible, as well as with readily perceived properties like being round, having a distinctive color, and coming from trees. We may use the visible properties to categorize some object as an 'apple' (the object is red, round, and hangs from a tree) and then infer that the object has the less visible properties as well (it has seeds and is edible). As we will see, concepts enable us to go beyond directly perceived information (Anderson, 1991; Bruner, 1957).

We also have concepts of activities, such as 'eating'; of states, such as 'being old'; and of abstractions, such as 'truth,' 'justice,' or even the number 2. In each case we know something about the properties that are common to all members of the concept. Widely used concepts like these are generally associated with a one-word name. This allows us to communicate quickly about experiences that occur frequently. We can also make up concepts on the spot to serve some specific goal. For example, if you are planning an outing, you might generate the concept 'things to take on a camping trip.' These kinds of goal-driven concepts facilitate planning. Although such concepts are used relatively infrequently, and accordingly have relatively long names, they still provide us with some cognitive economy and predictive power (Barsalou, 1985).

Prototypes

The properties associated with a concept seem to fall into two sets. One set of properties makes up the **prototype** of the concept. They are the properties that describe the best examples of the concept. In the concept 'grandmother,' for example, your prototype might include such properties as a woman who is in her 60s, has gray hair, and loves to spend time with her children. The prototype is what usually comes to mind when we think of the concept. But although the prototype properties may be true of the typical grandmother, they clearly are not true of all instances (think of a woman in her late 30s who, like her daughter, had a child while a teenager). This means that a concept must contain something in addition to a prototype. This additional something is a **core** that comprises the properties that are most important for being a member of a concept. Your core of the concept 'grandmother' would probably include the properties of being a female parent of a parent, the properties that are essential for being a member of the concept (Armstrong *et al.,* 1983).

As another example, consider the concept 'bird.' Your prototype likely includes the properties of flying and chirping – which works for the best examples of 'bird,' such as robins and blue jays, but not for other examples, such as ostriches and penguins. Your core would probably specify something about the biological basis of bird-hood – having certain genes or, at least, having parents that are birds.

Note that in both our examples – 'grandmother' and 'bird'– the prototype properties are salient but not perfect indicators of concept membership, whereas the core properties are more central to concept membership. However, there is an important difference between a concept like 'grandmother' and a concept like 'bird.' The core of 'grandmother' is a definition, and it is easily applied. Anyone who is a female parent of a parent must be a 'grandmother,' and it is relatively easy to determine whether someone has these defining properties. Concepts like this one are said to be well defined. Categorizing a person or object into a well-defined category involves determining whether it has the core or defining properties. In contrast, the core of 'bird' is hardly a definition – we may know only that genes are somehow involved, for example – and the core properties are hidden from view. If we happen upon a small animal, we can hardly inspect its genes or inquire about its parentage. All we can do is check whether it does certain things, such as fly and chirp, and use this information to decide whether it is a bird. Concepts like 'bird'

Do flying and chirping make a bird? Your prototype for 'bird' probably includes these features. However, they do not apply to certain kinds of birds, such as ostriches.

are said to be fuzzy. Deciding whether an object is an instance of a fuzzy concept often involves determining its similarity to the concept's prototype (Smith, 1995). Most natural concepts seem to be fuzzy. They lack true definitions, and categorization of these concepts relies heavily on prototypes.

Some instances of fuzzy concepts have more prototype properties than other instances. Among birds, for example, a robin will have the property of flying, whereas an ostrich will not. The more prototype properties an instance has, the more typical of the concept it is considered to be. In the case of 'bird,' most people rate a robin as more typical than a chicken, and a chicken as more typical than an ostrich; in the case of 'apple,' they rate red apples as more typical than green ones (since red seems to be a property of the concept 'apple'); and so on. The degree to which an instance is typical has a major effect on its categorization. When people are asked whether a pictured animal is a 'bird,' a robin produces an immediate yes, whereas a chicken requires a longer decision time. When young children are asked the same question, a robin will almost inevitably be classified correctly, whereas a chicken will often be declared a non-bird. Typicality also determines what we think of when we encounter the name of the concept. Hearing the sentence 'There is a bird outside your window,' we are far more likely to think of a robin than a vulture, and what comes to mind will obviously influence what we make of the sentence (Rosch, 1978).

Universality of prototypes formation

Are our prototypes determined mainly by our culture, or are they universal? For some concepts, such as 'grandmother,' culture clearly has a major impact on the prototype. But, for more natural concepts, prototypes are surprisingly universal.

Consider color concepts such as 'red.' This is a fuzzy concept (no ordinary person knows its defining properties) and one with a clear prototype: people in our culture agree on which hues are typical reds and which hues are atypical. People in other cultures agree with our choices. Remarkably, this agreement is found even among people whose language does not include a word for 'red.' When speakers of these languages are asked to pick the best example from an array of red hues, they make the same choices we would. Even though the range of hues for what they would call 'red' may differ from ours, their idea of a typical red is the same as ours (Berlin & Kay, 1969).

Other research suggests that the Dani, New Guinea people whose language has terms only for 'black' and 'white,' perceive color variations in exactly the same way as English-speaking people, whose language has terms for many colors. Dani individuals were given a set of red color patches to remember; the patches varied in how typical they were of 'red.' Later the participants were presented with a set of color patches and asked to decide which ones they had seen before. Even though they had no word for 'red,' they

Dani people – although they have no word in their language for red, they can perceive color variations.

recognized more typical red colors better than less typical ones. This is exactly what American participants do when performing a comparable task (Rosch, 1974). Color prototypes thus appear to be universal.

More recent experiments suggest that prototypes for some animal concepts may also be universal. The experiments compared US students and Maya Itza participants. (Maya Itza is a culture of the Guatemalan rainforest that is relatively insulated from Western influences.) The US participants were from southeastern Michigan, which happens to have a number of mammalian species that are comparable to those found in the Guatemalan rainforest. Both groups were presented with the names of these species. They were first asked to group them into sets that go together, then to group those sets into higher-order groups that were related, and so on until all the species were in one group corresponding to 'mammals.' These groupings were determined by the similarity of the prototypes: in the first pass, participants would group together only species that seemed very similar. By making these groupings, each participant created a kind of tree, with the initial groupings at the bottom and 'mammal' at the top; this tree reflects the taxonomy of animals.

The trees or taxonomies created by the Maya Itza were quite similar to those created by the US students; in fact, the correlation between the average Itza and US trees was about +.60. Moreover, both the Itza and US taxonomies were highly correlated with the actual scientific taxonomy. Apparently, all people base their prototypes of animals on properties that they can easily observe (overall shape, or distinctive features like coloring, a bushy tail, or a particular movement pattern). These properties are indicators of the evolutionary history of the species, on which the scientific taxonomy is based (Lopez *et al.*, 1997).

One can also think of cases where the contents of animal concepts differ across cultures. If in some culture ostriches are plentiful but robins are not, that culture may well have a different prototype for 'bird' than does our culture. However, the principles by which prototypes are formed – such as focusing on frequently encountered features of instances of the concept – may well be universal.

Hierarchies of concepts

In addition to knowing the properties of concepts, we also know how concepts are related to one another. For example, 'apples' are members (or a subset) of a larger concept, 'fruit'; 'robins' are a subset of 'birds,' which in turn are a subset of 'animals.' These two types of knowledge (properties of a concept and relationships between concepts) are represented in Figure 9.4 as a hierarchy. An object can be identified at different levels. The same object is at once a 'Golden Delicious apple,' an 'apple,' and a 'fruit.' However, in any hierarchy one level is the **basic level** or preferred one for classification – the level at which we first categorize an object. For the hierarchy in Figure 9.4, the level that contains 'apple' and 'pear' would be the basic one. Evidence for this claim comes from studies in which people are asked to name pictured objects with the first names that come to mind. People are more likely to call a pictured Golden Delicious apple an 'apple' than either a 'Golden Delicious apple,' or a 'fruit.' Basic-level concepts are special in other respects as well. As examples, they are the first ones learned by children, they are used more frequently, and they have shorter names (Mervis & Rosch, 1981).

It seems, then, that we first divide the world into basic-level concepts. What determines which level is basic? The answer appears to be that the basic level has the most distinctive properties. In Figure 9.4, 'apple' has several properties that are distinctive – not shared by other kinds of fruit (for example, red and round are not properties of 'pear'). In contrast, 'Golden Delicious apple' has few distinct properties; most of its properties are shared by 'MacIntosh apple,' for example. And 'fruit,' which is at the highest level of Figure 9.4, has few properties of any kind.

Thus, we first categorize the world at what turns out to be the most informative level (Murphy & Brownell, 1985).

Different categorization processes

We are constantly making categorization decisions. We categorize every time we recognize an object, every time we diagnose a problem ('That's a power failure'), and so on. How do we use concepts to categorize our world? The answer depends on whether the concept is well defined or fuzzy.

For well-defined concepts like 'grandmother,' we may determine how similar a person is to our prototype ('She's sixtyish and has gray hair, so she looks like a grandmother'). But if we are trying to be accurate, we can determine whether the person has the defining properties of the concept ('Is she the female parent of a parent?'). The latter amounts to applying a rule: 'If she's the female parent of a parent, she's a grandmother.' There have been many studies of such rule-based categorization of well-defined concepts, and they show that the more properties there are in the rule, the slower and more error-prone the categorization process becomes (Bourne, 1966). This may be due to processing the properties one at a time.

For fuzzy concepts like 'bird' and 'chair,' we do not know enough defining properties to use rule-based categorization, so we often rely on similarity instead. As already mentioned, one thing we may do is determine the similarity of an object to the prototype of the concept ('Is this object similar enough to my prototype to call it a chair?'). The evidence that people categorize objects in this fashion comes from experiments that involve three steps (Smith, 1995):

1 First the researcher determines the properties of a concept's prototype and of various instances of that concept. (The researcher might ask one group of participants to describe the properties of their prototypical chair and of various pictures of chairs.)

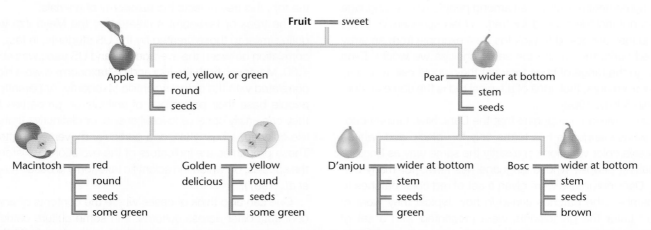

FIGURE 9.4 Hierachy of Concepts. *Words that begin with a capital letter represent concepts; lowercase words depict properties of these concepts. The green lines show relationships between concepts, and the red lines connect properties and concepts.*

2 Then the researcher determines the similarity between each instance (each pictured chair) and the prototype by identifying their shared properties. This results in a similarity-to-prototype score for each instance.

3 Finally, the researcher shows that the similarity-to-prototype score is highly correlated with how accurately and quickly participants can correctly categorize that instance. This shows that similarity-to-prototype plays a role in categorization.

There is another kind of similarity calculation that we can use to categorize objects. We can illustrate it with our chair example. Because we have stored in long-term memory some specific instances or exemplars of chairs, we can determine whether an object is similar to our stored chair exemplars. If it is, we can declare that it is a chair. Thus, we have two means of categorization based on similarity: similarity to prototypes and similarity to stored exemplars.

Acquiring concepts

How do we acquire concepts? Some concepts, such as the concepts of 'time' and 'space,' may be innate. Others have to be learned.

Learning prototypes and cores

We can learn about a concept in different ways. Either we are explicitly taught something about the concept or we learn it through experience. The way we learn depends on what we are learning. Explicit teaching is likely to be the means by which we learn cores of concepts, and experience seems to be the usual means by which we acquire prototypes. Someone explicitly tells a child that a 'robber' is someone who takes another person's possessions with no intention of returning

Parents can teach children to name and classify objects. Later, when the child sees another object, he may determine whether it is in the same category as the stored exemplar.

them (the core), and the child's experiences may lead him or her to expect robbers to be shiftless, disheveled, and dangerous (the prototype).

Children must also learn that the core is a better indicator of concept membership than the prototype, but it takes a while for them to learn this. In one study, children aged five to ten were presented with descriptions of items and asked to decide whether they belonged to particular well-defined concepts. We can illustrate the study with the concept of 'robber.' One description given for 'robber' depicted a person who matched its prototype but not its core:

> A smelly, mean old man with a gun in his pocket who came to your house and takes your TV set because your parents didn't want it anymore and told him he could have it.

Another description given for 'robber' was of a person who matched its core but not its prototype:

> A very friendly and cheerful woman who gave you a hug, but then disconnected your toilet bowl and took it away without permission and no intention to return it.

The younger children often thought that the prototypical description was more likely than the core description to be an instance of the concept. Not until age 10 did children show a clear shift from the prototype to the core as the final arbitrator of concept decisions (Keil & Batterman, 1984).

Learning through experience

There are at least two different ways in which one can learn a concept through experience. The simplest way is called the *exemplar strategy*, and we can illustrate it with a child learning the concept of 'furniture.' When the child encounters a known instance or exemplar – for example, a table – she stores a representation of it. Later, when she has to decide whether a new item – say, a desk – is an instance of 'furniture,' she determines the new object's similarity to stored exemplars of 'furniture,' including tables. This strategy seems to be widely used by children, and it works better with typical instances than with atypical ones. Because the first exemplars a child learns tend to be typical ones, new instances are more likely to be correctly classified to the extent that they are similar to typical instances. Thus, if a young child's concept of 'furniture' consisted of just the most typical instances (say, table and chair), he could correctly classify other instances that looked similar to the learned exemplars, such as desk and sofa, but not instances that looked different from the learned exemplars, such as lamp and bookshelf (Mervis & Pani, 1981). The exemplar strategy remains part of our repertory for acquiring concepts, as there is substantial evidence that adults often use it in acquiring novel concepts (Estes, 1994; Nosofsky & Johansen, 2000).

But as we grow older we start to use another strategy, *hypothesis testing*. We inspect known instances of a concept, searching for properties that are relatively common to them (for example, many pieces of 'furniture' are found in living spaces), and we hypothesize that these common properties are what characterize the concept. We then analyze novel objects for these critical properties, maintaining our hypothesis if it leads to a correct categorization about the novel object and revamping it if it leads us astray. This strategy thus focuses on abstractions – properties that characterize sets of instances rather than just single instances – and is tuned to finding core properties, because they are the ones that are common to most instances (Bruner *et al.,* 1956). What properties we look for, though, may be biased by any specific knowledge we have about the objects themselves. If a child thinks furniture always has a flat surface, this piece of prior knowledge may overly restrict the hypothesis that is generated.

The neural basis of concepts and categorization

The brain seems to store concepts of animals and concepts of artifacts in different neural regions. We mentioned some of the evidence for this in our discussion of perception in Chapter 5. There we noted that there are patients who are impaired in their ability to recognize pictures of animals but who are relatively normal in their recognition of pictured artifacts such as tools, whereas other patients show the reverse pattern. A great number of patients have been described with such category-specific deficits (see Martin & Caramazza, 2003). Research shows that what holds for pictures holds for words as well. Many of the patients who are impaired in naming pictures also cannot tell what the corresponding word means. For example, a patient who cannot name a pictured giraffe also cannot tell you anything about giraffes when presented with the word *giraffe*. The fact that the deficit appears for both words and pictures indicates that it has to do with concepts: the patient has lost part of the concept 'giraffe' (McCarthy & Warrington, 1990). There is an alternative to the idea that concepts of animals and artifacts are stored in different regions of the brain. Concepts of animals may contain more perceptual features (what does it look like?) than functional features (what can it be used for?), whereas concepts of artifacts may have more functional than perceptual features. For example, when brain damage affects perceptual regions more than functional ones, we might expect patients to show more impairment with animal than artifact concepts; when damage affects functional or motor regions of the brain more than perceptual regions, we might expect the opposite pattern (Farah & McClelland, 1991). Such hypotheses generated on the basis of patient data can be tested using functional imaging in a normal population of subjects. Indeed, it was found that specific parts of the brain are active during the naming of tools versus animals (Martin & Chao, 2001). After two decades of research combining the knowledge gained from patient data with functional imaging data in normal subjects, a complex picture is emerging. It appears that different areas in the brain, including perceptual and motor regions, jointly co-ordinate and constrain the organization of category knowledge in the brain (Mahon & Caramazza, 2009).

Other research has focused on processes of categorization. One line of research suggests that determining the similarity between an object and a concept's prototype involves different brain regions than determining the similarity between an object and stored exemplars of the concept. The logic behind these studies is as follows: the exemplar process involves retrieving items from long-term memory. As we saw in Chapter 8, such retrieval depends on brain structures in the medial temporal lobe. It follows that a patient with damage in these regions of the brain will be unable to effectively categorize objects by using a process that involves exemplars, although the patient might be relatively normal in the use of prototypes. This is exactly what researchers have found.

One study tested patients with medial-temporal lobe damage as well as normal individuals on two different tasks. One task required participants to learn to sort dot patterns into two categories (see Figure 9.5 for examples), and the other task required participants to learn to sort paintings into two categories corresponding to two different artists. Independent evidence indicated that only the painting task relied on retrieval of explicit exemplars. The patients learned the dot pattern concepts as easily as the normal participants, but they performed far worse than the normal participants in acquiring the painting concepts (Kolodny, 1994). Thus, use of exemplars depends on the brain structures that mediate long-term memory, but use of prototypes in categorization must depend on other structures. Other research has focused on a patient who is essentially incapable of committing any new information to long-term memory (he cannot learn new exemplars), yet he performs normally on the dot pattern task. Clearly, prototype-based categorization does not depend on the structures that mediate long-term memory (Squire & Knowlton, 1995).

The preceding discussion shows that there are neural differences between categorization based on prototypes and categorization based on stored exemplars. What about categorization based on rules? One study shows that rule use involves different neural circuits than similarity processes. Two groups of participants were taught to categorize imaginary animals into two categories corresponding to whether the animals were from Venus or Saturn. One group learned to categorize the animals on the basis of a complex rule: 'An animal is from Venus if it has antennae ears, curly tail, and hoofed feet; otherwise it's from Saturn.' The second group learned to categorize the animals by relying solely on their

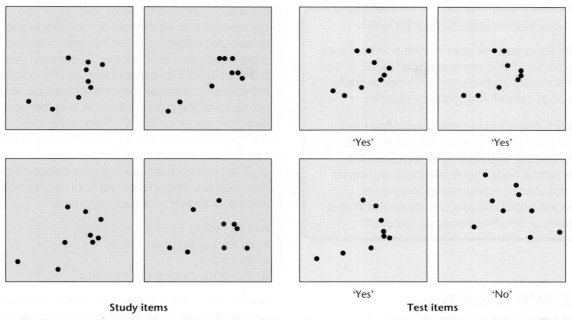

Study items   Test items

FIGURE 9.5 Examples of Dot Patterns Used to Study Categorization in Amnesiac Patients. *Individuals learned that the study items all belonged to one category and then had to decide whether each of the test items belonged in that category. You will see that the test items which belong to the category labelled 'yes' do not match the study items directly. Rather, the test items that belong to the category are sufficiently similar to a prototype of the study items – roughly an average of the dot positions of the study items – to justify a 'yes' response.*

memory. (The first time they saw an animal, they would have to guess, but on subsequent trials they would be able to remember its category.) Then both groups were given novel animals to categorize while having their brains scanned. The rule group continued to categorize by rule, but the memory group had to categorize a novel animal by retrieving the stored exemplar that was most similar to it and then selecting the category associated with that exemplar.

For the memory group, most of the brain areas that were activated were in the visual cortex at the back of the brain. This fits with the idea that these participants were relying on retrieval of visual exemplars. Participants in the rule group also showed activation in the back of the brain, but they showed activation in some frontal regions as well. These regions are often damaged in patients who have trouble doing rule-based tasks. Categorization based on rules therefore relies on different neural circuitry than does categorization based on similarity (Patalano *et al.*, 2002).

This research provides yet another example of the interplay between biological and psychological approaches to a phenomenon. Categorization processes that have been viewed as different at the psychological level – such as using exemplars versus using rules – have now been shown to involve different brain mechanisms. This example follows a pattern that we have encountered several times in earlier chapters: a distinction first made at the psychological level is subsequently shown to hold at the biological level as well.

INTERIM SUMMARY

➔ Thought occurs in both propositional and **imaginal modes**. The key component of a proposition is a concept, the set of properties that we associate with a class.

➔ A concept includes both a prototype (properties that describe a best example) and a core (properties that are most important for being a member of the concept). Core properties play a major role in processing well-defined concepts like 'grandmother,' whereas prototype properties dominate in fuzzy concepts like 'bird.'

➔ Children often learn a new concept by using an exemplar strategy: a novel item is classified as an instance of a concept if it is sufficiently similar to a known exemplar of the concept. As children grow older, they also use hypothesis testing as a strategy for learning concepts.

➔ Different neural regions may mediate different kinds of concepts. For example, perceptual regions of the brain may be more involved in representing animals from artifacts, whereas functional and motor regions of the brain may play a larger role in representing artifacts than animals. Different neural regions may also be involved in different categorization procedures.

REASONING AND DECISION-MAKING

When we think in terms of propositions, our sequence of thoughts is organized. The kind of organization of interest to us here manifests itself when we try to reason. In such cases, our sequence of thoughts often takes the form of an argument, in which one proposition corresponds to a claim, or conclusion, that we are trying to draw. The remaining propositions are reasons for the claim or premises for the conclusion.

Deductive reasoning

Logical rules

According to logicians, the strongest arguments demonstrate **deductive validity**, meaning that it is impossible for the conclusion of the argument to be false if its premises are true (Skyrms, 1986). Consider the following example:

a If it's raining, I'll take an umbrella.
b It's raining.
c Therefore, I'll take an umbrella.

This is an example of a **syllogism**, which contains two premises and a conclusion. Whether or not the conclusion is true or not follows logically from the two premises according to the rules of deductive logic. In this case, the relevant rule is the following:

> **If you have a proposition of the form 'If p then q', and another proposition p, then you can infer the proposition q.**

How does the reasoning of ordinary people line up with that of the logician? When asked to decide whether an argument is deductively valid, people are quite accurate in their assessments of simple arguments like this one. How do we

make such judgments? Some theories of deductive reasoning assume that we operate like intuitive logicians and use logical rules in trying to prove that the conclusion of an argument follows from the premises. Specifically, they identify the first premise ('If it's raining, I'll take an umbrella') with the 'If p then q' part of the rule. They identify the second premise ('It's raining') with the p part of the rule, and then they infer the q part ('I'll take an umbrella'). Presumably then, adults know the rules and use them (perhaps unconsciously) to decide that the previous argument is valid.

Rule following becomes more conscious if we complicate the argument. Presumably, we apply our sample rule twice when evaluating the following argument:

a If it's raining, I'll take an umbrella.
b If I take an umbrella, I'll lose it.
c It's raining.
d Therefore, I'll lose my umbrella.

Applying our rule to propositions a and c allows us to infer 'I'll take an umbrella,' and applying our rule again to proposition b and the inferred proposition allows us to infer 'I'll lose my umbrella,' which is the conclusion.

One of the best pieces of evidence that people are using rules like this is that the number of rules an argument requires is a good predictor of the argument's difficulty. The more rules are needed, the more likely it is that people will make an error and the longer they will take when they do make a correct decision (Rips, 1983, 1994). Moreover, humans are quite likely to make mistakes under specific conditions. For example: contrary to the rules of deductive logic, the great majority of subjects will judge a logically invalid conclusion as valid if it seems *plausible* to them. This finding has been named the **belief bias** in syllogistic reasoning. As an example, consider the following two syllogisms (from Evans *et al.*, 1983):

1 a No addictive things are inexpensive.
   b Some cigarettes are inexpensive.
   c Therefore, some addictive things are cigarettes.

2 a No addictive things are inexpensive.
   b Some cigarettes are inexpensive.
   b Therefore, some cigarettes are not addictive.

The first syllogism is *invalid*: the conclusion does not follow from the two premises. But the plausibility of the conclusion led 92 per cent of the subjects to accept it nevertheless. The second syllogism is *valid*, but was accepted by only 46 per cent of the subjects.

Next, we will look at other effects of content on reasoning.

Effects of content

Logical rules do not capture all aspects of deductive reasoning. Such rules are triggered only by the *logical form* of propositions, yet our ability to evaluate a deductive argument often depends on the *content* of the propositions as well. We can illustrate this point with the following experiment: the Wason selection task (Wason, 1968).

Participants are presented four cards. In one version of the problem, each card has a letter on one side and a digit on the other (see Figure 9.6a). The participant must decide which cards to turn over to determine whether the following claim is correct: 'If a card has a vowel on one side, then it has an even

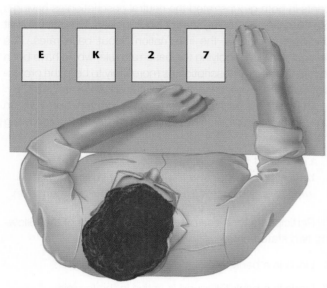

a) Hypothesis: If a card has a vowel on one side, it has an even number on the other side.

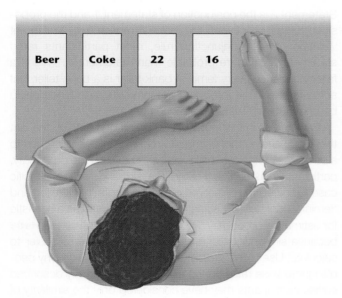

b) Hypothesis: If a person is drinking beer, he or she must be over 19.

FIGURE 9.6 Content Effects in Deductive Reasoning.
(a) An illustration of the problem in which participants decide which two cards could be turned over to test the hypothesis. (b) An illustration of the problem that is logically equivalent to (a) but much easier to solve.

number on the other side.' The correct answer is to turn over the E and the 7. (To see that the '7' card is critical, note that if it has a vowel on its other side, the claim is disconfirmed.) While most participants correctly choose the 'E' card, fewer than 10 per cent of them also choose the '7' card!

Performance improves dramatically, however, in another version of the problem (see Figure 9.6b). Now the claim that participants must evaluate is 'If a person is drinking beer, he or she must be over 19.' Each card has a person's age on one side and what he or she is drinking on the other. This version of the problem is logically equivalent to the preceding version (in particular, 'Beer' corresponds to 'E,' and '16' corresponds to '7'), but now most participants make the correct choices and turn over the 'Beer' and '16' cards (Griggs & Cox, 1982). The content of the propositions clearly affects their reasoning.

Results like these imply that we do not always use logical rules when solving deduction problems. Rather, sometimes we use rules that are less abstract and more relevant to everyday problems – **pragmatic rules**. An example is the permission rule, which states that 'If a particular action is to be taken, often a precondition must be satisfied.' Most people know this rule and use it when presented with the drinking problem in Figure 9.6b; that is, they would think about the problem in terms of permission. Once activated, the rule would lead people to look for failures to meet the relevant precondition (being under age 19), which in turn would lead them to choose the '16' card. In contrast, the permission rule would not be triggered by the letter-number problem in Figure 9.6a, so there is no reason for people to choose the '7' card. Thus, the content of a problem affects whether a pragmatic rule is activated, which in turn affects the correctness of the reasoning (Cheng *et al.*, 1986).

In addition to applying rules, participants may sometimes solve the drinking problem by setting up a concrete representation of the situation – a **mental model**. They may, for example, imagine two people, each with a number on his back and a drink in his hand. They may then inspect this mental model and see what happens, for example, if the drinker with '16' on his back has a beer in his hand. According to this idea, we reason in terms of mental models that are suggested by the content of the problem (Johnson-Laird, 1989).

The two procedures just described – applying pragmatic rules and constructing mental models – have one thing in common. They are determined by the content of the problem, in contrast to the application of logical rules, which should not be affected by problem content. Our sensitivity to content often prevents us from operating as logicians in solving a problem.

Inductive reasoning

Logical rules

Logicians have noted that an argument can be good even if it is not deductively valid. Such arguments are **inductively strong**, meaning that it is improbable that the conclusion is false if the premises are true (Skyrms, 1986). An example of an inductively strong argument is as follows:

a Sam qualified in accounting at college.
b Sam now works for an accounting firm.
c Therefore, Sam is an accountant.

This argument is not deductively valid (Sam may have tired of accounting courses and taken a night watchman's job). Inductive strength, then, is a matter of probabilities, not certainties, and (according to logicians) inductive logic should be based on the theory of probability.

We make and evaluate inductive arguments all the time. In doing so, do we rely on the rules of probability theory as a logician or mathematician would? One relevant probability rule is the **base-rate rule**, which states that the probability of something being a member of a class (such as Sam being a member of the class of accountants) is greater the more class members there are (that is, the higher the base rate of the class). Our sample argument about Sam being an accountant can be strengthened by adding the premise that Sam joined a club in which 90 per cent of the members are accountants.

Another relevant probability rule is the **conjunction rule**: the probability of a proposition cannot be less than the probability of that proposition combined with another proposition. For example, the probability that 'Sam is an accountant' cannot be less than the probability that 'Sam is an accountant and makes more than $60 000 a year.' The base-rate and conjunction rules are rational guides to **inductive reasoning** – they are endorsed by logic – and most people will defer to them when the rules are made explicit. However, in rough-and-tumble everyday reasoning, people frequently violate these rules, as we are about to see.

Heuristics

A **heuristic** is a short-cut procedure that is relatively easy to apply and can often yield the correct answer, but not inevitably so. People often use heuristics in everyday life because they have found them useful. However, as the following discussion shows, they are not always dependable.

In a series of ingenious experiments, Tversky and Kahneman (1973, 1983; Kahneman & Tversky, 1996) have shown that people violate some basic rules of probability theory when making inductive judgments. Violations of the base-rate rule are particularly common. In one experiment, one group of participants was told that a panel of psychologists had interviewed 100 people – 30 engineers and 70 lawyers – and written personality descriptions of them. These participants were then given a few descriptions and asked to indicate the probability that the person described was an engineer. Some descriptions were prototypical of an engineer (for example, 'Jack shows no interest in political issues and spends his free time on home carpentry'), and others were neutral (for example, 'Dick is a man of high ability and promises to be quite successful'). Not

surprisingly, these participants rated the prototypical description as more likely to be that of an engineer.

Another group of participants was given the identical instructions and descriptions, except they were told that the 100 people were 70 engineers and 30 lawyers (the reverse of the first group). The base rate of engineers therefore differed greatly between the two groups. This difference had virtually no effect: participants in the second group gave essentially the same ratings as those in the first group. For example, participants in both groups rated the neutral description as having a 50–50 chance of being that of an engineer. This shows that participants ignored the information about base rates. The rational decision (applying the base-rate rule) would have been to rate the neutral description as more likely to be in the profession with the higher base rate (Tversky & Kahneman, 1973).

People pay no more heed to the conjunction rule. In one study, participants were presented with the following description:

> Linda is 31 years old, single, outspoken, and very bright. In college, she majored in philosophy... and was deeply concerned with issues of discrimination.

Participants then estimated the probabilities of the following two statements:

1 Linda is a bank teller.

2 Linda is a bank teller and is active in the feminist movement.

Statement 2 is the conjunction of statement 1 and the proposition 'Linda is active in the feminist movement.' In flagrant violation of the conjunction rule, most participants rated statement 2 as more probable than statement 1. This is a fallacy because every feminist bank teller is a bank teller, but some female bank tellers are not feminists, and Linda could be one of them (Tversky & Kahneman, 1983).

Participants in this study based their judgments on the fact that Linda seems more similar to a feminist bank teller than to a bank teller. Although they were asked to estimate probability, participants instead estimated the similarity of the specific case (Linda) to the prototype of the concepts 'bank teller' and 'feminist bank teller.' Estimating similarity is used as a heuristic for estimating probability. People use the **similarity heuristic** because similarity often relates to probability yet is easier to calculate. Use of the similarity heuristic also explains why people ignore base rates. In the engineer–lawyer study described earlier, participants may have considered only the similarity of the description to their prototypes of 'engineer' and 'lawyer.' Given a description that matched the prototypes of 'engineer' and 'lawyer' equally well, participants judged that engineer and lawyer were equally probable. Reliance on the similarity heuristic can lead to errors even by experts.

Reasoning by similarity shows up in another common reasoning situation, that in which we know some members of a category have a particular property and have to decide whether other members of the category have that property as well. In one study, participants had to judge which of the following two arguments seemed stronger:

1 a All robins have sesamoid bones.
   b Therefore all sparrows have sesamoid bones.

versus

2 a All robins have sesamoid bones.
   b Therefore all ostriches have sesamoid bones.

Not surprisingly, participants judged the first argument to be stronger, presumably because robins are more similar to sparrows than they are to ostriches. This use of similarity appears rational, inasmuch as it fits with the idea that things that have many known properties in common are likely to share unknown properties as well. But the veneer of rationality fades when we consider participants' judgments on another pair of arguments:

1 a All robins have sesamoid bones.
   b Therefore all ostriches have sesamoid bones (same as the preceding argument).

versus

2 a All robins have sesamoid bones.
   b Therefore all birds have sesamoid bones.

Participants judged the second argument to be stronger, presumably because robins are more similar to the prototype of birds than they are to ostriches. But this judgment is a fallacy. On the basis of the same evidence (that robins have sesamoid bones), it cannot be more likely that all birds have some property than that all ostriches do, because ostriches are in fact birds. Again, our similarity-based intuitions can sometimes lead us astray (Osherson *et al.,* 1990).

Similarity is not our only strong heuristic. Another is the **causality heuristic**. People estimate the probability of a situation by the strength of the causal connections between the events in the situation. In the following example, people judge the second statement to be more probable than the first:

1 Sometime during the year 2010, there will be a massive flood in California in which more than 1000 people will drown.

2 Sometime during the year 2010, there will be an earthquake in California, causing a massive flood in which more than 1000 people will drown.

Judging statement 2 to be more probable than statement 1 is another violation of the conjunction rule (and hence another fallacy). This time, the violation arises because in statement 2 the flood has a strong causal connection to another event, the earthquake, whereas in statement 1 the flood alone is mentioned and has no causal connections.

Other heuristics are used to estimate probabilities and frequencies as well. For example, Kahneman and Tversky (1973) showed that subjects (incorrectly!) estimated the frequency of words starting with the letter *r* (like *rose*) as higher than the frequency of words with the letter *r* in the third position (such as *care*). The reason for this error lies in the ease with which we can retrieve words based on their first letter: the use of an **availability heuristic** leads to an erroneous conclusion in this case.

Another heuristic that can lead us astray is the **representativeness heuristic**: the assumption that each case is representative of its category. As a result, people often extrapolate from a single case, even when such extrapolations are unwarranted. These two heuristics probably explain why subjects overestimate the number of fatalities caused by floods or murder (which get high press coverage, and are easily remembered), while they underestimate the number of fatalities caused by specific diseases (Slovic *et al.,* 1982). The biases resulting from these heuristics are compounded by another aspect of human reasoning, called the **confirmation bias**. We give more credence to evidence that is in line with our previous beliefs than to evidence that contradicts it. To illustrate: once we believe that we live in a dangerous society and that murders are frequent events, we are even more likely to notice and remember news reports about murders – thereby confirming our own beliefs. Gilovich (1983) describes how many compulsive gamblers persist in a belief about their own 'winning game,' even in the face of persistent losses. The confirmation bias determines how the gamblers review their own wins and losses: wins are seen as a confirmation of the 'winning game' and taken at face value, whereas losses are discounted or 'explained away.'

So, our reliance on heuristics often leads us to ignore some basic rational rules, including the base-rate and conjunction rules. But we should not be too pessimistic about our level of rationality. For one thing, heuristics probably lead to correct decisions in most cases. Another point is that under the right circumstances we can appreciate the relevance of certain logical rules to particular problems and use them appropriately (Gigerenzer, 1996; Nisbett *et al.,* 1983). For example, in reading and thinking about this discussion, you were probably able to see the relevance of the base-rate and conjunction rules to the problems at hand.

Framing effects

One last bias in reasoning and decision-making deserves attention here. Imagine that you are given the choice between two options: taking a drug with a 70 per cent effectiveness rate, or a drug with a 30 per cent failure rate. Even though the information given in both cases is actually the same (a 70 percent effectiveness rate means a 30 percent failure rate), most people will choose the first option (Tversky & Kahneman, 1981). This is called a **framing effect**, because the answer given depends on the way the options are described (or framed). In this particular case, it seems that subjects perceive a drug as more risky when their attention is drawn directly to its failure rate. After studying decision-making in great detail, the researchers concluded that people are *risk averse* in a particular way: we avoid risks when we are evaluating potential gains, but we are much more likely to take on risks when we are trying to cut potential losses (Tversky & Kahneman, 1991). In a classic example, subjects are faced with a decision to implement one or another program to combat a disease which will otherwise kill 600 people (Kahneman & Tversky, 1984). In one condition, the emphasis in the phrasing is in terms of 'gains' (the number of people saved):

➔ If program A is adopted, 200 people will be saved.

➔ If program B is adopted, there is a one-third probability that all 600 people will be saved and a two-thirds probability that no people will be saved.

In the second condition, the two programs are phrased with an emphasis on the 'losses' (the number of people who die):

➔ If program C is adopted, 400 people will die.

➔ If program D is adopted, there is a one-third probability that nobody will die and a two-thirds probability that all 600 people will die.

Note that programs A and B are in fact the same as programs C and D, just framed differently. In the first condition most subjects chose the 'sure thing' option A over the 'risky gamble' option B. In the second condition most subjects prefer the risky gamble option D over the certain loss option C. Our risk aversion is likely to affect many of our decisions in everyday life.

The neural basis of reasoning

We noted that many psychologists accept the logicians' distinction between deductive and inductive reasoning, but not all do. Some researchers who believe that mental models underlie deductive reasoning further hold that mental models are used in inductive reasoning and that consequently there is no qualitative difference between deductive and inductive reasoning (for example, see Johnson-Laird, 1997). The question of whether there are two kinds of reasoning or one is a fundamental issue which has been studied at the neural level. For example, researchers have used PET to image peoples' brains while they performed a deductive reasoning or an inductive reasoning task (Osherson *et al.*, 1998). In both tasks, participants had to evaluate arguments like the following:

1 a None of the bakers plays chess.
  b Some of the chess players listen to opera.
  c (Therefore) some of the opera listeners are not bakers.

2 a Some of the computer programmers play the piano.

  b No one who plays the piano watches soccer matches.
  c (Therefore) some computer programmers watch soccer matches.

In the deductive task, participants were asked to distinguish valid arguments (conclusion must be true if the premises are) from invalid arguments (possible for conclusion to be false even if premises are true). Participants were first given some training on this valid–invalid distinction. In these cases, 1 is valid, and 2 is not. The task is not easy, as the researchers wanted to ensure that their participants' reasoning powers were fully engaged. In the induction task, individuals were asked whether the conclusion had a greater chance of being true than false, given that the premises were true. For argument 1, the answer has to be yes – because the argument is deductively valid. For argument 2, the answer is more up for grabs. But what is important is that in both cases participants are reasoning in terms of 'chances of being true'; that is, they're reasoning about probabilities (regardless of how they compute them).

A number of brain areas were active during deductive but not inductive reasoning, and a number of areas showed the reverse pattern. These results are consistent with the hypothesis that deductive and inductive reasoning are mediated by different mechanisms. More specifically, only when reasoning deductively were a number of areas in the right hemisphere activated, some of which were toward the back of the brain. These activations might reflect the participants' use of spatial representations (like Venn diagrams) in trying to answer the difficult validity question. In contrast, when reasoning inductively, some of the major brain activations were in the left hemisphere, in a region of the frontal cortex that is known to be involved in estimation problems (such as 'How many camels are there in North Africa?'). Estimation often involves rough assessments of probabilities (such as 'What's the chance of a medium-sized city having a zoo?').

Recent research has focused on the role of the orbitofrontal cortex in risky decision-making. The orbitofrontal cortex consist of the lower part of the frontal cortex (just behind the eyes). Patients with orbitofrontal damage generally do not have problems with memory, motor behavior, problem-solving, or language. But, compared to undamaged subjects, they seem to evaluate the consequences of their own actions on a different basis – as if they are driven by the desire to be satisfied in the short term, while ignoring long-term consequences. Some researchers have argued that the orbitofrontal cortex is involved in emotional 'gut reactions' that tell us whether our decisions are right or wrong (Damasio *et al.*, 1994). Evidence for this comes from studies in which subjects play a card game that allows them one of two choices: they can either draw from decks of cards that will result in large pay-offs in the short term and losses in the long run, or from decks of cards that will result in smaller pay-offs in the short term, but no losses in the long run. Initially subjects don't know what the long-term

CUTTING EDGE RESEARCH EVOLUTIONARY RESEARCH INTO THE NATURE OF LANGUAGE

Gareth Davies, University of the Highlands and Islands

Chomsky saw language (rightly) as a highly complex phenomenon. Logically, he went on to describe the acquisition of the skills as a highly complex process that could not be adequately explained without the existence of a language acquisition device (LAD) that held the rules of universal grammar (UG). He argued that without the existence of such a device, language would be too complex to learn using the simple learning processes postulated by Skinner. Bandura's Social Learning theory suggested that language was learned by children as a combination of both nature (the LAD) and nurture (operant conditioning). Social Leaning Theory brought nature and nurture together and suggested that they operated less as competing concepts in this domain and more as parallel influences on language development. However, this was still a somewhat simplistic answer. The exploration of language in evolutionary terms seems to offer an additional and promising insight.

Chater & Christiansen (2012) argue that UG amounts to a 'language organ' which is not viable as an evolutionary concept because UG would be an organ with an abstract function. They go on to postulate that language is a cultural product but biological and cognitive influences are crucial because they act as restrictors on language development. Rather than the brain evolving to accommodate language, this suggests that 'language evolves to fit the brain' (Chater & Christiansen, 2012, p. 4).

Evidence from recent research has offered perspectives on the evolutionary dimension to language acquisition with Steel and colleagues (Steel *et al.,* 2012) considering the role of tool use as a stimulant for the evolution of language. They suggest that language might be closely related to manual action (tool use, for example). They point to evidence from neurophysiological research investigating the role of mirror neurons: Iacoboni (2009), and Pulvermüller and Fadiga (2010) found that the same neurons are activated when one individual imitates another (e.g., copying the use of tools or other manual action) and they also play another role in speech comprehension.

Other research strands suggest that community is an important driver of language evolution. Collins (2012) suggests that language is the consequence of our physical world and our interaction with it so it is more than a repository of symbols; it is a repository of understanding the world. This is dependent on our social interactions within it (Collins, 2012). This may also include the use of tools and the communication of the practice of tool use.

Recent research investigating the way in which infants learn words has shown that the social aspect to language acquisition is crucial. Bergelson and Swingley (2012) found that even at very young ages, infants can show that they know the meanings of some common nouns. They found that infants were more likely to fixate upon images that represented common nouns when paired with an auditory stimulus. These included body parts and foods. Parents would say, for example, 'Look at the apple.' They concluded that the visual image of a common noun and the linguistic representation of it influence each other. Bergelson and Swingley (2012) came to the conclusion that because children begin to learn language at a very young age accounting for the seemingly rapid acquisition of language. This rapid and intense language acquisition may account for what Chomsky called universal grammar.

It appears that the evolution of language is the consequence of the use of tools and social interaction. Rather than the brain evolving to accommodate language, current thinking suggests that language has evolved to accommodate the brain (Swingly, 2012).

---

pay-offs for the different decks of cards will be, so they select the decks that result in larger immediate winnings. After a little while, normal subjects show a physiological reaction [an increase in galvanic skin response (GSR)] whenever they select from a 'dangerous' deck of cards – as if their 'gut' tells them that this is a dangerous thing to do. A short while later, these subjects switch to drawing from the other decks. Patients with orbitofrontal damage do not show the GSR response to the dangerous decks of cards, nor do they make the switch to the other, safer, decks (Bechara *et al.*, 1997). Indeed, recent research shows that the prefrontal cortex of healthy subjects is involved: greater activation correlated with better performance in this card game (Lawrence *et al.*, 2009).

INTERIM SUMMARY

➔ In reasoning, some arguments are deductively valid, which means that it is impossible for the conclusion to be false if the premises are true. When evaluating such an argument, we sometimes use logical rules, and other times use heuristics – rules of thumb that operate on the content of propositions, not their logical form.

➔ Other arguments are inductively strong, which means that it is improbable that the conclusion is false if the premises are true. When evaluating such an argument, often we ignore the principles of probability theory and rely on similarity and causality heuristics.

Research on the neural bases of reasoning supports the distinction between deductive and inductive reasoning. When people are presented with the same arguments, different parts of the brain become active when people evaluate deductive validity versus inductive strength.

CRITICAL THINKING QUESTIONS

1 With regard to inductive reasoning, what kind of training might people be given to increase their use of the base-rate and conjunction rules in real-life reasoning situations?

2 How could you use a brain-imaging experiment to see if there is a neural distinction between reasoning by formal procedures (logical rules, probability rules) and reasoning by heuristics?

THOUGHT IN ACTION: PROBLEM-SOLVING

For many people, solving a problem epitomizes thinking itself. When solving a problem, we are striving for a goal but have no ready means of obtaining it. In each case, there is an *initial state* (you need a dress or a suit for a party) and a *goal state* (you have found and bought the clothing you need). Often, we might break down the goal into subgoals (saving enough money and finding the right store) and perhaps divide these subgoals further into smaller subgoals, until we reach a level that we have the means to obtain (Anderson, 1990).

We can illustrate these points with a simple problem. Suppose that you need to figure out the combination of an unfamiliar lock. You know only that the combination has four numbers and that whenever you come across a correct number you will hear a click. Your overall goal is to find the combination. Rather than trying four numbers at random, most people divide the overall goal into four subgoals, each corresponding to finding one of the four numbers in the combination. Your first subgoal is to find the first number, and you have a procedure for accomplishing this – turning the lock slowly while listening for a click. Your second subgoal is to find the second number, for which you can use the same procedure, and so on for the remaining subgoals. In this example, the problem is well-defined: the initial state and the goal state are clearly defined. Many real-world problems, however, are ill-defined. For example, you might think 'I really need to relax a bit this weekend.' Your goal state is rather vague, and doesn't help much in your search for a specific plan. One sensible strategy for solving ill-defined problems is to first make them well-defined.

The strategies people use to solve problems is a major issue in the study of problem-solving. A related issue is how people represent a problem mentally, because it affects how readily we can solve the problem. We will see that experience with the problem at hand also affects how successful we are at solving it. The following discussion considers all of these issues.

Problem-solving strategies

Much of what we know about strategies for breaking down goals derives from the research of Newell and Simon (1972). Typically, the researchers ask participants to think aloud while trying to solve a difficult problem. They then analyze the participants' verbal responses for clues to the underlying strategy. Specifically, the researchers use the verbal responses as a guide in programing a computer to solve the problem. The output can be compared with aspects of people's performance on the problem – for example, the sequence of moves – to see whether they match. If they match, the computer program offers a theory of a problem-solving strategy. A number of general-purpose strategies have been identified in this way.

One strategy is to reduce the difference between our current state in a problem situation and our goal state, in which a solution is obtained. This strategy is called the **difference-reduction method**. Consider again the combination-lock problem. Initially, our current state includes no knowledge of any of the numbers, and our goal state includes knowledge of all four numbers. We therefore set up the subgoal of reducing the difference between these two states, and identifying the first number that accomplishes this subgoal. Our current state now includes knowledge of the first number. There is still a difference between our current state and our goal state. We can reduce this difference identifying the second number, and so on for the third and fourth numbers. The key idea behind difference reduction is that we set up subgoals that, when obtained, put us in a state that is closer to our goal.

A similar but more sophisticated strategy is **means–ends analysis**. We compare our current state to the goal state in order to find the most important difference between them, and eliminating this difference becomes our main subgoal. We then search for a means or procedure to achieve this subgoal. If we find such a procedure but discover that something in our current state prevents us from applying it, we introduce a new subgoal of eliminating this obstacle. Many commonsense problem-solving situations involve this strategy. Here is an example:

I want to take my son to nursery school. What's the [most important] difference between what I have and what I want? One of distance. What [procedure] changes distance? My automobile. My automobile won't work. What is needed to make it work? A new battery. What has new batteries? An auto repair shop.

(After Newell & Simon, 1972, as cited in Anderson, 1990, p. 232)

Means–ends analysis is more sophisticated than difference reduction because it allows us to take action even if it results in a temporary decrease in similarity between our current state and the goal state. In the example just presented, the auto repair shop may be in the opposite direction from the nursery school. Going to the shop temporarily increases the distance from the goal, yet this step is essential for solving the problem. A strict application of the difference-reduction method would never have you drive *away* from the school.

Another strategy is **working backward** from the goal, a particularly useful strategy in solving mathematical problems like the one illustrated in Figure 9.7. The problem is this: given that ABCD is a rectangle, prove that AD and BC are the same length. In working backward, we might proceed as follows:

What could prove that AD and BC are the same length? I could prove this if I could prove that the triangles ACD and BDC are congruent. I can prove that ACD and BDC are congruent if I could prove that two sides and an included angle are equal.

(After Anderson, 1990, p. 238)

We reason from the goal to a subgoal (proving that the triangles are congruent), from that subgoal to another subgoal (proving that the sides and angle equal), and so on, until we reach a subgoal that we have a ready means of obtaining.

The three strategies that we have considered – difference reduction, means–ends analysis, and working backward – are extremely general and can be applied to virtually any problem. These problem-solving strategies, which are often

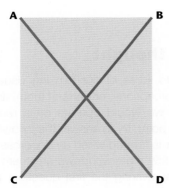

FIGURE 9.7 An Illustrative Geometry Pattern. *Given that ABCD is a rectangle, prove that the line segments AD and BC are the same length.*

TABLE 9.3 STEPS IN PROBLEM-SOLVING

1 Represent the problem as a proposition or in visual form.
2 Determine the goal.
3 Break down the goal into subgoals.
4 Select a problem-solving strategy and apply it to achieve each subgoal.

referred to as weak methods, do not rest on any specific knowledge and may even be innate. People are especially likely to rely on these weak methods when they are first learning about an area and are working on problems whose content is unfamiliar. When people gain expertise in an area, they develop more powerful domain-specific procedures (and representations), which come to dominate the weak methods (Anderson, 1987). The steps in problem-solving by weak methods are listed in Table 9.3.

Representing the problem

Being able to solve a problem depends not only on our strategy for breaking it down but also on how we represent it. Sometimes a propositional representation works best, and at other times a visual representation or image is more effective. Consider the following problem:

One morning, exactly at sunrise, a monk began to climb a mountain. A narrow path, a foot or two wide, spiraled around the mountain to a temple at the summit. The monk ascended at varying rates, stopping many times along the way to rest. He reached the temple shortly before sunset. After several days at the temple, he began his journey back along the same path, starting at sunrise and again walking at variable speeds with many pauses along the way. His average speed descending was, of course, greater than his average climbing speed. Prove that there exists a particular spot along the path that the monk will occupy on both trips at precisely the same time of day.

(Adams, 1974, p. 4)

In trying to solve this problem, many people start with a propositional representation. They may even try to write out a set of equations. The problem is far easier to solve when it is represented visually. All you need do is visualize the upward journey of the monk superimposed on the downward journey. Imagine one monk starting at the bottom and the other at the top. No matter what their speed, at some time and at some point along the path the two monks will meet. Thus, there must be a spot along the path that the monk occupied on both trips at precisely the same time of day. (Note that the problem did not ask you where the spot was.)

Some problems can be readily solved by manipulating either propositions or images. Look at this simple problem: 'Ed runs faster than David but slower than Dan; who's the slowest of the three men?' To solve this problem in terms of propositions, note that we can represent the first part of the problem as a proposition that has 'David' as subject and 'is slower than Ed' as predicate. We can represent the second part of the problem as a proposition with 'Ed' as subject and 'is slower than Dan' as predicate. We can then deduce that David is slower than Dan, which makes David the slowest. To solve the problem by means of imagery, we might imagine the three men's speeds as points on a line, like this:

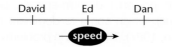

Then we can simply 'read' the answer directly from the image. Apparently some people prefer to represent such problems as propositions, and others tend to represent them visually (Johnson-Laird, 1985).

In addition to the issue of propositions versus images, there are questions about *what* is represented. Often we have difficulty with a problem because we fail to include something important in our representation or because we include something in our representation that is not an important part of the problem. Remember that we often transform an ill-defined problem into a well-defined one. If we make the wrong assumptions in doing so, our **mental set** can create an obstacle on the path to the solution. We can illustrate this point with an experiment. One group of participants was given the problem of supporting a candle on a door, using only the materials depicted in Figure 9.8. The solution was to tack the box to the door and use the box as a platform for the candle. Most participants had difficulty with the problem, presumably because they represented the box as a container (its usual function), not as a platform. This difficulty is often referred to as **functional fixedness**. Another group of participants was given the identical problem except that the contents of the box were removed. These participants had more success in solving the problem, presumably because they were less likely to include the box's container property in their representation and more likely to include its supporter property. It seems that arriving at a useful representation of a problem is half the solution to the problem.

We have seen the importance of **restructuring** a problem: solving a problem is often the result of mentally representing it in a certain way. Once we arrive at the correct mental set ('I can use a box as a supporter') the solution isn't far away.

Another way to solve a problem by thinking about it differently, is to find an appropriate analogy. If two problems

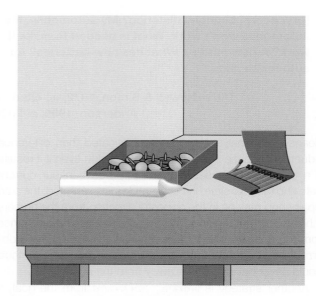

FIGURE 9.8 **Materials for the Candle Problem.** *Given the materials depicted, how can you support a candle on a door? The solution is shown on page 337.*

share the same underlying structure, solving one problem means that you can solve the other by relying on the analogy. In a classic experiment, Gick and Holyoak (1983) showed that subjects were able to solve a complicated 'radiation problem' that way. In this problem, a laser beam should be used to burn away a tumor. The problem is that because the laser beam is very strong, it will also damage the intermediate healthy tissue. Subjects were able to find the solution (to use multiple beams from different directions) if they saw the analogy to a story they were told about small groups of soldiers storming a fortress (which was surrounded by mines) from multiple different directions. The researchers also discovered that it isn't easy to get subjects to compare the underlying structure of two problems. We often overlook an analogy because we tend to focus on the superficial features of a problem rather than on the underlying structure.

Imaginal thought

We seem to do some of our thinking visually. Often we retrieve past perceptions, or parts of them, and operate on them the way we would operate on a real percept. To appreciate this point, try to answer the following questions: what new letter is formed when an uppercase N is rotated 90 degrees? How many windows are there in your living room? When answering the first question, people report first forming an image of a capital N and then mentally 'rotating' it 90 degrees and 'looking' at it to determine its identity. And when answering the second question, people

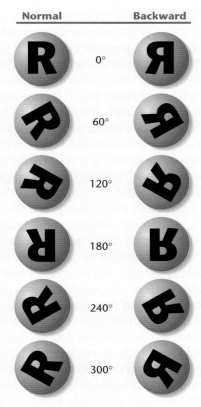

FIGURE 9.9 Study of Mental Rotation. *Examples of the letters presented to participants in studies of mental rotation. On each presentation, participants had to decide whether the letter was normal or backward. Numbers indicate deviation from the vertical in degrees.*

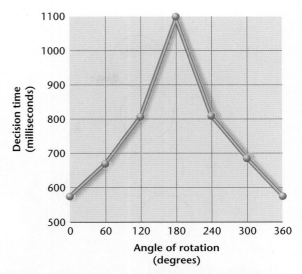

FIGURE 9.10 Decision Times in the Mental Rotation Study. *The time taken to decide whether a letter had normal or reversed orientation was greatest when the rotation was 180 degrees so that the letter was upside down.*

report imagining the room and then 'scanning' the image while counting the windows (Kosslyn, 1983; Shepard & Cooper, 1982).

Evidence suggests that imagery involves the same representations and processes that are used in perception. For this reason, imaginal thought is said to rely on analogical representations. This in contrast with propositional thought, which relies on symbolic representations (consider the word 'room': it does not resemble your parent's living room in any way). One operation that has been studied intensively is **mental rotation**. In a classic experiment, participants saw the capital letter R on each trial. The letter was presented either normally or backward, and either in its usual vertical orientation or rotated by various degrees (see Figure 9.9). The participants had to decide whether the letter was normal or backward. The more the letter had been rotated from its vertical orientation, the longer it took the participants to make the decision (see Figure 9.10). This finding suggests that participants made their decisions by rotating the image of the letter in their minds until it was vertical and then checking to determine whether it was normal or backward.

Another operation that is similar in imagery and perception is that of scanning an object or array. In an experiment on scanning an image, participants first studied the map of a fictional island that contained seven key locations (see Figure 9.11). The map was removed, and participants were asked to form an image of it and fixate on a particular location (for example, the tree in the southern part of the island). Then the experimenter named another location (for example, the tree at the northern tip of the island). Starting at the fixated location, the participants were to scan their images until they found the named location and to push a button upon 'arriving' there. The greater the distance between the fixated location and the named one, the longer the participants took to respond. Indeed, the time people took to scan the image increased linearly with the imagined distance, which suggests that they were scanning their images in much the same way that they scan real objects (Kosslyn *et al.*, 1978).

The neural basis of imagery

Perhaps the most persuasive evidence that imagery is like perception would be demonstrations that the two are mediated by the same brain structures. A substantial amount of evidence of this sort has accumulated.

Some of the evidence comes from studies of brain-damaged patients and shows that any problem the patient has in visual perception is typically accompanied by a parallel problem in visual imagery (Farah *et al.*, 1988). A particularly striking example is patients who suffer damage in the parietal lobe of the right hemisphere and as a result develop

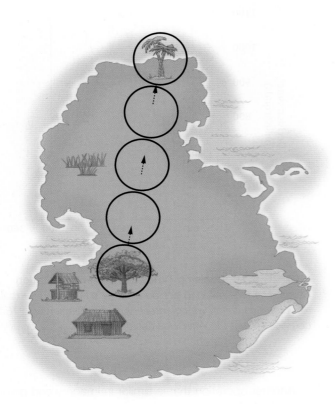

FIGURE 9.11 Scanning Mental Images. *The person scans the image of the island from south to north, looking for the named location. It appears as though the individual's mental image is like a real map and that it takes longer to scan across the mental image if the distance to be scanned is greater.*

visual neglect of the left side of the visual field. Although not blind, these patients ignore everything on the left side of their visual field. A male patient, for example, may neglect to shave the left side of his face. The Italian neurologist Bisiach (Bisiach & Luzzatti, 1978) found that this visual neglect extends to imagery. He asked patients with visual neglect to imagine a familiar square in their native Milan as it looks while standing in the square facing the church. The patients reported most objects on their right but few on their left. When asked to imagine the scene from the opposite perspective, while standing in front of the church and looking out into the square, the patients neglected the objects they had previously reported (which were now on the left side of the image). These patients manifested the same kind of neglect in imagery that they did in perception, which suggests that the damaged brain structures normally mediate imagery as well as perception.

Some studies have used brain-scanning methods to demonstrate that in normal individuals the parts of the brain involved in perception are also involved in imagery. In one

experiment, participants performed both a mental arithmetic task ('Start at 50 and count down, subtracting by 3s') and a visual imagery task ('Visualize a walk through your neighborhood, making alternating right and left turns starting at your door'). While a participant was doing each task, the amount of blood flow in various areas of his or her cortex was measured. There was more blood flow in the visual cortex when participants engaged in the imagery task than when they engaged in the mental arithmetic task. Moreover, the pattern of blood flow during the imagery task was like that normally found in perceptual tasks (Roland & Friberg, 1985).

A PET experiment by Kosslyn and associates (1993) provides a striking comparison of the brain structures involved in perception and imagery. While having their brains scanned, participants performed two different tasks, a perception task and an imagery task. In the perception task, first a block capital letter was presented on a background grid and then an X was presented in one of the grid cells. The participant's task was to decide as quickly as possible whether the X fell on part of the block letter (see Figure 9.12). In the imagery task, the background grid was again presented, but without a block capital letter. Under the grid was a lowercase letter, and participants had been previously instructed to generate an image of the capital version of the lowercase letter and project it onto the grid. Then an X was presented in one of the grid cells, and participants were asked to determine whether the X fell on part of the imagined block letter. Not surprisingly, the perception task resulted in heightened neural activity in parts of the visual cortex, but so did the imagery task. Indeed, the imagery task resulted in increased activity in brain structures that are

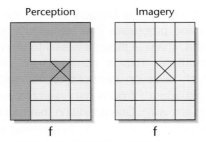

FIGURE 9.12 Imagery and Perception. *Tasks used to determine whether visual imagery involves the same brain structures as visual perception. In the perception task, participants must decide whether the X fell on part of the block letter. In the imagery task, participants generate an image of the block letter and then decide whether the X fell on part of the (image of the) block letter. The person knows which letter to image because the lowercase version of it is presented below the grid. (The lowercase version is also presented in the perception task, just to keep things comparable.)*

among the first regions of the cortex to receive visual information.

We can conclude that imagery is like perception from the early stages of cortical processing, and that imagery and perception are mediated by the same neural mechanisms. It is clear that we can recruit the visual brain to solve certain problems by representing them analogically. Here again, biological research has provided evidence to support a hypothesis that was first proposed at the psychological level.

Experts versus novices

The amount of experience we have in a particular domain influences how we represent a problem. In a given content area (physics, geography, or chess, for instance), experts solve problems qualitatively differently than novices do. These differences are due to differences in the representations and strategies used by experts and novices. Experts have many more specific representations stored in memory that they can bring to bear on a problem. A master chess player, for example, can look for 5 seconds at a configuration of over 20 pieces and reproduce it perfectly; a novice in this situation can reproduce only the usual 7 ± 2 items (see Chapter 8). These discoveries were first made by de Groot (1965, 1966), who wondered what makes expert chess players choose better moves than novices. He found that chess players are not particularly more intelligent in other domains. However, their representation of chess positions is superior and allows them to remember the individual positions. Through years of practice they have developed representations of many possible configurations of chess pieces that permit them to encode a complex configuration in just a few chunks. Further, these representations are presumably what underlies their superior chess game. A master may have stored as many as 50 000 configurations and has learned what to do when each one arises. Master chess players can essentially 'see' possible moves and do not have to think them out the way novices do (Chase & Simon, 1973; Simon & Gilmartin, 1973).

Even when they are confronted with a novel problem, experts represent it differently than novices do. This point is illustrated by studies of problem-solving in physics. An expert (say, a physics professor) represents a problem in terms of the physical principle that is needed for solution: for example, 'This is one of those every-action-has-an-equal-and-opposite-reaction problems.' In contrast, a novice (say, a student taking a first course in physics) tends to represent the same problem in terms of its surface features – for example, 'This is one of those inclined-plane problems' (Chi & Feltovich, 1981).

The tendency to focus on the superficial features of a problem also shows up when novices solve a problem by

Experts solve problems in qualitatively different ways than novices do. For example chess grandmasters, such as Viswanathan Anand, have many more specific representations stored in memory that they can bring to bear on a problem.

using an analogy. When we do not know much about a particular domain and have to solve a problem in it, frequently we think of superficially similar problems that we have encountered to use as analogies. In one illustrative study on this phenomenon (Ross, 1984), people had to learn new ways to edit text on a computer. During the learning phase, people were often reminded by superficial similarities of an earlier text edit and used this to figure out how to do the current edit. For example, people learned two different methods for inserting a word into text, with one method illustrated on a shopping list and the other method illustrated on a restaurant review. Later, they had to insert a word in either another shopping list or restaurant review. People were more likely to use the method they had learned with the similar text (given a shopping list, they tended to insert a word by using the method originally illustrated with a shopping list). Early in learning, we are guided by superficial similarities among problems. Only when we have had training in a given domain, are we able to focus on the structural features of a problem and make effective use of analogies (Novick, 1988).

Experts and novices also differ in the strategies they employ. In studies of physics problem-solving, experts generally try to formulate a plan for attacking the problem before generating equations, whereas novices typically start writing equations with no general plan in mind (Larkin *et al.*, 1980). Another difference is that experts tend to reason from the givens of a problem toward a solution, but novices tend to work in the reverse direction (the working-backward strategy). This difference in the direction of reasoning has also been found in studies of how physicians solve problems. More expert physicians tend to reason in a forward direction – from symptom to possible disease – but the less expert tend to reason in a backward direction – from possible disease to symptom (Patel & Groen, 1986).

The characteristics of expertise just discussed – a multitude of representations, representations based on principles, planning before acting, and working forward – make up some of the domain-specific procedures that come to dominate the weak methods of problem-solving discussed earlier.

Automaticity

With experience comes another advantage: **automaticity**. Automatic processes can be carried out without conscious control, as if on an automatic pilot. Think back to when you first learned to ride a bike or drive a car: the task required all your attention. With more practice it became easier to focus your attention on the traffic – the cycling or driving itself seems to go on effortlessly.

Much of our thinking processes also become automatic with experience. Reading is something that most of us do without paying special attention to it: you see a word and automatically read it, very much unlike when you first learned how to read. The **Stroop effect** (named after John Ridley Stroop, who described it in 1935) demonstrates the automaticity of the reading process. Stroop presented subjects with lists of non-words (such as *suwg*) and real words (such as *blue*) and asked his subjects to name the color that the different items on the lists were printed in. Note that he did not ask them to read the words. Stroop was able to show that his subjects nevertheless read the words automatically, because in one condition he had printed the color words in a non-congruent color (see Figure 9.13). For example, the word *blue* would appear in red ink. This slowed down the color-naming response significantly, compared to the other conditions (the list of non-words, or the list of color words printed in congruent colors). This interference of the automatic reading process with the color-naming task shows that reading is something we do without consciously attending to it (Stroop, 1935).

(a)	(b)	(c)
wopr	blue	red
swrg	green	yellow
zcidb	yellow	blue
zyp	red	green

FIGURE 9.13 An Example of the Stroop Effect.

Unconscious thought for complex decisions

In 2004, Dijksterhuis published results showing that our unconscious can make decisions which are superior to decisions that are made consciously (Dijksterhuis, 2004). In one experiment, subjects were presented with descriptions of a number of apartments (some more desirable than others), and were asked to select the best option. Some subjects had to do so immediately, others were given a few minutes to think about the information (the 'conscious thought' condition), and a third group of subjects was distracted for a few minutes before they decided (the 'unconscious thought' condition). Subjects in the last condition made the best decisions. In subsequent work, the researchers studied how satisfied the subjects were with the choices they had made. They were interviewed about their choice, a few weeks after selecting a poster to take home (Dijksterhuis & van Olden, 2006). Subjects in the 'unconscious thought' condition were more satisfied than the subjects in the other conditions.

These discoveries seem counterintuitive. After all, wouldn't it seem wise to consider your options carefully? When does it help to deliberate your decisions, and when does it not? Research by Dijksterhuis and his co-workers (Dijksterhuis *et al.*, 2006) gives us important clues. In an experiment similar to the one described above, one important variable was added: the complexity of the issues to be discussed was either simple or complex. In this study, subjects were choosing cars. In the 'simple' condition, each car was characterized by four attributes, whereas in the 'complex' condition, each car was characterized by 12 attributes. The researchers reasoned that conscious thought is precise, and should therefore lead to the right choices in simple matters. But since conscious thought requires the use of short-term memory (which has limited capacity), it will lead to inferior decisions on complex matters. And indeed, conscious thinkers were more likely than unconscious thinkers to make the correct choice in the simple condition. But in the complex condition, performance of the unconscious thinkers was superior to that of the conscious thinkers.

Furthermore, it seems that unconscious thought is an active process: first of all, subjects in the unconscious thought condition did better than subjects in the immediate condition (Dijksterhuis, 2004; Dijksterhuis and van Olden,

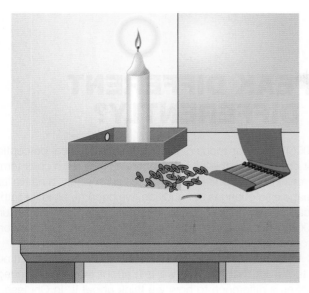

The solution to the candle problem.

2006). Second, unconscious thought is goal-dependent: subjects who are not warned about an upcoming decision do not seem to engage in unconscious thought (Bos *et al.*, 2008). Third, unconscious thought results in a different representation of the information (Dijksterhuis, 2004; Bos *et al.*, 2008). This representation apparently allows for a superior weighing of the many factors that are important in complex decisions.

Throughout this chapter, we have seen that people often use shortcuts in reasoning and solving problems. Which problem-solving strategy or reasoning heuristic is used depends in part on our experience with the problem at hand. Some problems are solved by relying on rules and on conscious and effortful thought. Other problems are solved more automatically. Some theorists argue for a dual-process theory of human reasoning, and have named the 'automatic' processes *intuitive,* in contrast to the rule-based processes (Kahneman, 2003). Social psychologists are especially interested in understanding how we arrive at some of our intuitive knowledge about other human beings. In Chapter 17 you will see that variations on the Stroop task are still used today by social psychologists to study automaticity in social perception.

INTERIM SUMMARY

➲ Problem-solving requires breaking down a goal into subgoals that can be obtained more easily.

➲ Strategies for breaking a goal into subgoals include reducing differences between the current state and the goal state; means–ends analysis (eliminating the most important differences between the current and goal states), and working backward.

➲ Some problems are easier to solve by using a visual representation, and others can be more readily solved by using a propositional representation. Numerous problems can be solved equally well by visual or propositional representations.

➲ Thoughts that are manifested as visual images contain the kind of visual detail found in perception, and mental operations that are performed on images (such as scanning and rotation) are like those carried out on perceptions.

➲ Imagery is like perception because both are mediated by the same parts of the brain. Brain-scanning experiments indicate that the specific regions involved in an imagery task are the same as those involved in a perceptual task.

➲ Expert problem-solvers differ from novices in four ways: they have more representations to bring to bear on the problem, they represent novel problems in terms of solution principles rather than surface features, they form a plan before acting, and they tend to reason forward rather than backward.

➲ Thought processes that do not require effortful attention occur automatically and without conscious control.

CRITICAL THINKING QUESTIONS

1 Think of some activity (an academic subject, game, sport, or hobby) in which you have gained some expertise. How would you describe the changes that you went through in improving your performance? How do these changes line up with those described in the chapter?

2 We discussed visual imagery. By analogy, what type of findings would convince you that auditory imagery also exists?

3 How can the findings about expertise in problem-solving be used in teaching people professional skills, like teaching medical students about a new specialty?

SEEING BOTH SIDES
DO PEOPLE WHO SPEAK DIFFERENT LANGUAGES THINK DIFFERENTLY?

THE ROLE OF LANGUAGE IN MIND

Stephen C. Levinson and Asifa Majid, Max-Planck-Institute for Psycholinguistics, Nijmegen

Imagine you were born among the Pirahã, a remote tribe in the Amazon. You would speak a language with, it seems, no words for color, no words for uncles or cousins, no words for numbers, no easy way to talk about the future or to make complex sentences by embedding (Everett, 2005). What, then, would be the character of your thoughts? Or suppose you parachute into the tribe, and learn to speak their language, do you think you could easily tell them about your world?

Armchair thought-experiments of this kind used to intrigue linguists, laymen, and psychologists, such as Sapir, Whorf and Carroll. Then with the rise of the cognitive science movement in the 1960s they became suddenly unfashionable, because human cognition was viewed as a uniform processing machine, with a structure and content largely built into our genes. It followed that the Pirahã, unbeknownst to themselves, actually had the concepts 'pink,' 'cousin,' '17,' 'next year,' even 'algorithm' and 'symphony' – they simply didn't have the words for them (Fodor, 1975). There was a universal language of thought, 'mentalese,' for which different languages were merely an input-output system (Pinker, 1994). This view is now losing ascendancy, for a number of reasons, one is the rise of alternative computational metaphors (Parallel Distributed Processing, neural networks) that emphasize learning from experience, and another the phenomenal rise of neurocognition and the beginnings of neurogenetics, both of which reveal the importance of human differences.

Another reason why interest is returning to the role of language in cognition is empirical. It turns out for example that the Pirahã can't think '17'; they really don't have elementary number concepts (Gordon, 2004). No experiments have been done on their color discrimination, but in other cultures we find a systematic relation between the kinds of color words and color concepts. For example, speakers of a language like English with a 'blue' vs. 'green' distinction exaggerate the actual distance (in jnd's or just noticeable differences) between blue and green, while speakers of a language (like Taruhumara) with a 'grue' term covering both green and blue, do not (Kay & Kempton, 1984, Davidoff *et al.*, 1999). Recently Kay and colleagues have shown that this effect is due to the right visual field, which projects to the left brain hemisphere where language is processed (Gilbert *et al.*,

2006), and that toddlers switch their categorical perception for color over to the left hemisphere as they learn color terms (Franklin *et al.*, 2008a, 2008b). Less surprisingly, a native language also changes our audition, we become blind (or rather deaf) in early infancy to sounds not in our language (Kuhl, 2000). Thus language alters our very perception of the world around us.

What about more abstract domains like space and time? It turns out that the way we talk about time in a language makes a difference to how we think about it. In Chinese, a vertical spatial metaphor is often used so that earlier events are 'up' and later ones 'down,' whereas in English we prefer to think of the future 'ahead' and the past 'behind.' Chinese speakers, but not English speakers, are faster to respond to a time question when they have previously seen a vertical spatial prime (Boroditsky, 2001). This suggests that for thinking about abstract domains like time we borrow the language we use for the more concrete spatial domain, and so different spatial language makes a difference to temporal thinking.

Spatial language itself differs radically across languages. In some languages there are no terms for 'left' and 'right' (as in 'the knife is left of the fork'). Instead one has to use notions like 'north' and 'south' even for things on the table (Majid *et al.*, 2004)! Systematic experimentation in over a dozen languages and cultures shows how powerful these differences are (Levinson, 2003). Speakers of north/south vs. left/right languages remember and reason in ways consistent with their spatial strategies in language, even when language is not required. An interesting question is, which system is most natural? Experiments with apes and pre-linguistic infants suggest that the north/south one is core, and the left/right emphasis comes from our own culture and language (Haun *et al.*, 2006). So next time you pass the salt, think about how you might be thinking about it differently had you been born in another culture.

Our senses, and arguably our more abstract thoughts too, may be set up innately to deliver veridical information and inference, but rapidly in infancy we imbibe the language and categories of our culture and use these to make the discriminations and inferences that the culture has found useful through historical adaptation to its environment. As psychology enters an era of preoccupation with individual differences, we can be sure that many more ways in which language and culture influence cognition (and, no doubt, constraints on those effects) will be discovered.

SEEING BOTH SIDES

DO PEOPLE WHO SPEAK DIFFERENT LANGUAGES THINK DIFFERENTLY?

HOW IS LANGUAGE RELATED TO THOUGHT?

Anna Papafragou, University of Delaware

How is language related to thought? Do people who speak different languages think differently? According to one theory, language offers the concepts and mechanisms for representing and making sense of our experience, thereby radically shaping the way we think. This strong view, famously associated with the writings of Benjamin Whorf (Whorf, 1956), is certainly wrong. First, people possess many concepts which their language does not directly encode. For instance, the Mundurukú, an Amazonian indigene group, can recognize squares and trapezoids even though their language has no rich geometric terms (Dehaene *et al.*, 2006). Similarly, members of the Pirahã community in Brazil whose language lacks number words can nevertheless perform numerical computations involving large sets (even though they have trouble retaining this information in memory; Frank *et al.*, 2008). Second, there are often broad similarities in the ways different languages carve up domains of experience. For instance, crucial properties of color vocabularies across languages appear to be shaped by universal perceptual constraints (Regier *et al.*, 2007). Also many languages seem to label basic tastes by distinct words (e.g., sweet, salt, sour and bitter; Majid & Levinson, 2008). The presence of constraints on cross-linguistic variation suggests that language categories are shaped by cognitive biases shared across humans.

A weaker version of the Whorfian view maintains that, even though language does not completely determine thought, it still affects people's habitual thought patterns by promoting the salience of some categories and downgrading others. One line of studies set out to examine how English and Japanese speakers draw the conceptual distinction between objects and substances. English distinguishes between count nouns (*a pyramid*) and mass nouns (*cork*), while Japanese does not (all nouns behave like mass nouns). When taught names for novel simple exemplars (e.g., a cork pyramid), which could in principle be considered either objects or substances, English speakers predominantly took the name to refer to the object ('pyramid') but Japanese speakers were at chance between the object or the substance ('cork') construal (Imai & Genter, 1997). These findings have been interpreted as evidence that the linguistic count/mass distinction affects how people draw the conceptual object/substance distinction (at least for indeterminate cases).

Another set of studies focused on speakers of Tseltal Mayan living in Mexico, whose language lacks *left/right* terms for giving directions and locating things in the environment. Tseltal speakers cannot say things such as 'the cup is to my left'; instead they use absolute co-ordinates (e.g., 'north' or 'south') to encode space. In a series of experiments, Tseltal speakers were shown to remember spatial scenes in terms of absolute co-ordinates rather than body-centered (left/right) spatial concepts; speakers of Dutch, a language which, like English, possesses left/right terms, showed the opposite preference (Levinson, 2003).

The precise interpretation of these findings is greatly debated. First, studies such as the above simply show that linguistic behavior and cognitive preferences can co-vary, not that language *causes* cognition to differ across various linguistic populations. Furthermore, some of the reported cognitive differences may have been due to ambiguities in the way instructions to study participants were phrased. When Japanese and English speakers were asked to rate, on a scale from 1 to 7, how likely they were to classify a novel specimen as a kind of object or a kind of substance, their ratings converged (Li *et al.*, in press). Similarly, when Tseltal speakers were given implicit cues about how to solve spatial tasks, they were able to use left/right reasoning; in fact, on some tasks, they were more accurate when using left/right concepts compared to absolute co-ordinates, contrary to what one might expect on the basis of how Tseltal encodes space (Li *et al.*, 2005). These data show that human cognitive mechanisms are flexible rather than streamlined by linguistic terminology.

Other studies have confirmed that cross-linguistic differences do not necessarily lead to cognitive differences. For instance, memory and categorization of motion events, such as an airplane flying over a house, seem to be independent of the way languages encode motion (Papafragou *et al.*, 2002). Relatedly, similarity judgments for containers such as jars, bottles, and cups converge in speakers of different languages despite words for such containers varying cross-linguistically (Malt *et al.*, 1999). In a striking recent demonstration, using eye tracking methods, English and Greek speakers were found to attend to different parts of an event while they were getting ready to describe the event verbally; however, when preparing to memorize the event for a later memory task, speakers of the two languages performed identically in terms of how they allocated attention, presumably because they relied on processes of event perception that are independent of language (Papafragou *et al.*, 2008).

This research suggests that language can be usefully thought of as an additional route for encoding experience. Rather than permanently reshaping the processes supporting perception and cognitive processing, language offers an alternative, often optionally recruited system of encoding, organizing and tracking experience. The precise interplay between linguistic and cognitive functions will continue to be a topic of intense experimentation and theorizing for years to come.

CHAPTER SUMMARY

1 Language, our primary means for communicating thoughts, is structured at three levels. At the highest level are sentence units, including phrases that can be related to thoughts or propositions. The next level is words and parts of words that carry meaning. The lowest level contains speech sounds. The phrases of a sentence are built from words (and parts of words), whereas the words themselves are constructed from speech sounds.

2 A phoneme is a category of speech sounds. Every language has its own set of phonemes and rules for combining them into words. A morpheme is the smallest unit that carries meaning. Most morphemes are words; others are prefixes and suffixes that are added to words. A language also has syntactic rules for combining words into phrases and phrases into sentences. Understanding a sentence requires not only analyzing phonemes, morphemes, and phrases but also using context and understanding the speaker's intention. The areas of the brain that are responsible for language lie in the left hemisphere and include Broca's area (frontal cortex) and Wernicke's area (temporal cortex).

3 Language development occurs at three different levels. Infants come into the world preprogrammed to learn phonemes, but they need several years to learn the rules for combining them. When children begin to speak, they learn words that name familiar concepts. In learning to produce sentences, they begin with one-word utterances, progress to two-word telegraphic speech, and then elaborate their noun and verb phrases.

4 Children learn language at least partly by testing hypotheses. Children's hypotheses appear to be guided by a small set of operating principles, which call their attention to critical characteristics of utterances, such as word endings. Innate factors also play a role in language acquisition.

5 Our innate knowledge of language seems to be very rich and detailed, as suggested by the fact that all children seem to go through the same stages in acquiring a language. Like other innate behaviors, some language abilities are learned only during a critical period. It is a matter of controversy whether our innate capacity to learn language is unique to our species. Many studies suggest that chimpanzees and gorillas can learn signs that are equivalent to our words, but they have difficulty learning to combine these signs in the systematic (or syntactic) way in which humans combine words.

6 Thought occurs in different modes, including propositional and imaginal. The basic component of a proposition is a concept, the set of properties we associate with a class. Concepts provide cognitive economy by allowing us to code many different objects as instances of the same concept, and also permit us to predict information that is not readily perceptible.

7 A concept includes both a prototype (properties that describe the best examples) and a core (properties that are most essential for being a member of the concept). Core properties play a major role in well-defined concepts like 'grandmother'; prototype properties dominate in fuzzy concepts like 'bird.' Most natural concepts are fuzzy. Concepts are sometimes organized into hierarchies; in such cases, one level of the hierarchy is the basic or preferred level for categorization.

8 Children often learn a concept by following an exemplar strategy. With this technique, a novel item is classified as an instance of a concept if it is sufficiently similar to a known exemplar of the concept. As children grow older, they use hypothesis testing as another strategy for learning concepts. Different categorization processes have been shown to involve different brain mechanisms.

9 In reasoning, we organize our propositions into an argument. Some arguments are deductively valid: it is impossible for the conclusion of the argument to be false if its premises are true. When evaluating a deductive argument, we sometimes try to prove that the conclusion follows from the premises by using logical rules. Other times, however, we use heuristics – rules of thumb – that operate on the content of propositions rather than on their logical form.

10 Some arguments are inductively strong: it is improbable for the conclusion to be false if the premises are true. In generating and evaluating such arguments, we often ignore some of the principles of probability theory and rely instead on heuristics that focus on similarity or causality.

11 Not all thoughts are expressed in propositions; some are manifested as visual images. Such images contain the kind of visual detail found in perceptions. The mental operations performed on images (such as scanning and rotation) are like the operations carried out on perceptions. Imagery seems to be like perception because it is mediated by the same parts of the brain. Brain damage that causes the perceptual problem of visual neglect also causes comparable problems in imagery. Experiments using brain-scanning techniques indicate that the specific brain regions involved in an imagery task are the same as those involved in a perceptual task.

 12 Problem-solving requires breaking down a goal into subgoals that are easier to obtain. Strategies for doing this include reducing differences between the current state and the goal state, means–ends analysis (eliminating the most important differences between the current and goal states), and working backward. Some problems are easier to solve by using a propositional representation; for other problems, a visual representation works best.

13 Expert problem-solvers differ from novices in four basic ways: they have more representations to bring to bear on the problem, they represent novel problems in terms of solution principles rather than surface features, they form a plan before acting, and they tend to reason forward rather than working backward.

CORE CONCEPTS

production of language	propositional thought	similarity heuristic
comprehension of language	imaginal thought	causality heuristic
language	concept	availability heuristic
phoneme	categorization	representativeness heuristic
phonological rules	prototype	confirmation bias
morpheme	core	framing effect
morphological rules	basic level	difference-reduction method
grammatical morpheme	imaginal modes	means–ends analysis
semantics	deductive validity	working backward
sentence unit	syllogism	mental set
syntax	belief bias	functional fixedness
proposition	pragmatic rules	restructuring
noun phrase	mental model	mental rotation
verb phrase	inductively strong	visual neglect
Broca's aphasia	base-rate rule	automaticity
Wernicke's aphasia	conjunction rule	Stroop effect
overextend	inductive reasoning	
fast mapping	heuristic	

DIGITAL SUPPORT RESOURCES

Students should use the unique access code included in the front of the book to access the digital support resources which accompany the new edition. These include:

- Multiple Choice Questions and Quizzes
- Critical Thinking Questions
- Practice Essay Questions
- Videos
- Glossary, Flashcards, and More

10 MOTIVATION

LEARNING OBJECTIVES
After reading this chapter you should be able to:

Understand how drives and homeostasis influence motivation.

Discuss incentive motivation relates to drug addiction.

Have learned various causes for hunger, eating, and eating disorders.

Have knowledge of how gender and sexuality are shaped.

Define motivation.

Compare drive to incentive theories of motivation.

Identify the biological bases for 'liking' versus 'wanting.'

Give an example of alliesthesia.

Describe multiple pathways by which genes affect obesity.

Describe objectification theory and how it explains disordered eating.

Discuss different understandings of the causes of sexual orientation.

You're hurrying to get to an important job interview on time. You were running late this morning, so you skipped breakfast. Now you're starving. It seems as if every advertisement you see along your route features food – eggs, sandwiches, and sweet and refreshing juices. Your stomach rumbles and you try to ignore it, but that is next to impossible. Every kilometer you go, you're that much hungrier. You nearly hit the car in front of you as you stare at a sign advertising pizza. In short, you have been overwhelmed by the motivational state known as hunger.

A **motivation** is a condition that energizes behavior and gives it direction. It is experienced subjectively as a conscious desire – the desire for food, for drink, for sex. Most of us can choose whether or not to act on our desires. We can force ourselves to forgo what we desire, and we can make ourselves do what we would rather not do. Perhaps we can even deliberately choose not to think about the desires that we refuse to act on. But it is considerably more difficult – perhaps impossible – to control our motivations directly. When we are hungry, it is hard not to want food. When we are hot and thirsty, we cannot help wanting a cool breeze or a cold drink. Conscious choice appears to be the consequence, rather than the cause, of our motivational states. So what does control motivation, if not deliberate choice?

The causes of motivation range from physiological events within the brain and body to our culture and social interactions with the other individuals who surround us. This chapter will discuss the control of basic motivations such as thirst, hunger, and sex. To a large extent these motivations arise from our biological heritage and reveal general principles about how motivation and reward work to give direction to behavior.

For basic motivations like hunger, thirst, and sex, psychologists have traditionally distinguished between two types of theories of motivation. The difference concerns where the motivation comes from, what causes it, and how the motivation controls behavior. On the one hand are **drive theories**, which emphasize the role of internal factors in motivation. Some internal drives, such as those related to hunger or thirst, have been said to reflect basic physiological needs. For motivations like sex or aggression, drive factors seem less tied to absolute physiological needs. After all, does one ever need to aggressively attack another in the same way that one needs to eat or drink? Still, aggression and sex have been said to have drive aspects, both in the sense that internal factors such as hormonal state often appear important and in the sense that they may have evolved originally to fulfill basic ancestral needs.

On the other hand are **incentive theories** of motivation, which emphasize the motivational role of external events or objects of desire. Food, drink, sexual partners, targets of attack, relationships with others, esteem, money, and the rewards of success – all are incentives. Incentives are the objects of motivation. After all, our motivations don't operate in a vacuum – when we want, we want something. The nature of that something pulls us in one direction or another. The goal might be tasty

CHAPTER OUTLINE

DRIVES AND HOMEOSTASIS

Body temperature and homeostasis

Thirst as a homeostatic process

INCENTIVE MOTIVATION AND REWARD

Drug addiction

CUTTING EDGE RESEARCH: ENVIRONMENT-RELATED HUMAN NEEDS AND URBAN PLANNING

HUNGER, EATING, AND EATING DISORDERS

Interactions between homeostasis and incentives

Physiological hunger cues

Integration of hunger signals

Obesity

Anorexia and bulimia

GENDER AND SEXUALITY

Early sexual development

Hormones versus environment

Adult sexuality

Sexual orientation

SEEING BOTH SIDES: DO THE BRAINS OF ADDICTS REVEAL DISORDERS WITH REWARD OR WITH ANTI-REWARD?

food, water to drink, a partner for interaction, expulsion of an intruder, or possession of a disputed resource. Many incentives also serve as rewards. They can produce pleasure and reinforce behavior that leads to them.

Some incentives are **primary reinforcers**, meaning that they are able to act as rewards independently of prior learning. For example, a sweet taste or a sexual sensation may be pleasant the first time it is experienced. Other incentives are **secondary reinforcers**, meaning that they have gained their status as rewards at least partly through learning about their relationship to other events. For example, money or good grades can be effective incentives, based on our cultural experience with them and with the status and success they represent. For animals, a conditioned stimulus that has been paired with food can serve as an effective reward. In every case, learning is crucial to the formation of secondary reinforcers. Although less important, learning may even play a part in modulating the effectiveness of some primary reinforcers. For example, you may have been hungry when you were born – but you weren't born with any idea of the foods that are now your favorites. Incentive theories of motivation focus especially on the relationship of learning and experience to the control of motivation.

Drive and incentive theories provide different perspectives on the control of motivation. But the difference between the theoretical perspectives is primarily in their points of view, and there actually is no conflict between the two. It is widely acknowledged that both types of processes exist for almost every kind of motivation (Toates, 2011). But it is easier to focus on one type of control and thoroughly understand it before switching to the other. For this reason, we will consider drive processes in the first section and then turn to incentive processes in the second section. In the third section, we will integrate the two perspectives as we discuss eating and eating disorders, because both drive and incentive factors operate together in real life, and they often interact (see Figure 10.1). Consider again the example that opened this chapter. A drive factor (your hunger) enhanced the motivational effect of incentives (the advertisements depicting food). In fact, the taste of food becomes more pleasant to most people when they are hungry and less pleasant when they have eaten enough (Cabanac, 2010). Have you ever skipped lunch to better enjoy an evening feast? Or been scolded for snacking because it would 'ruin your dinner'? Conversely, incentive factors can awaken drive states. Have you ever walked through the delicious aroma from a bakery or restaurant and suddenly realized that you were hungry? Yet even considering drives and incentive factors together leaves the story of motivation incomplete. Social and cultural factors also come into play. We introduce those in our discussion of eating and eating disorders and draw on them again in the fourth and final section on sexuality, a social motive considerably more complex than thirst or hunger.

The causes of motivation range from physiological events such as thirst to social aspirations and cultural influences such as those that create the desire to excel.

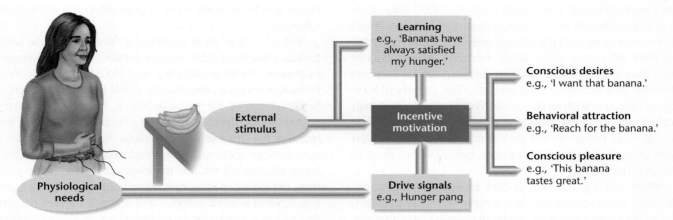

FIGURE 10.1 A Model of Basic Motives. *An external stimulus, such as the sight of food, is compared to the memory of its past reward value. At the same time, physiological signals of hunger and satiety modulate the potential value at the moment. These two types of information are integrated to produce the final incentive motivation for the external stimulus, which is manifested in behavior and conscious experience.*

DRIVES AND HOMEOSTASIS

Our lives depend on keeping certain things the same. If the temperature of your brain changed by more than several degrees, you would quickly become unconscious. If the proportion of water in your body rose or fell by more than a few per cent, your brain and body could not function and you would risk death. Humans and animals walk a tightrope of balance between physiological extremes. Like delicate and finely tuned machines, we cannot work unless our internal environment is in balance. But unlike most machines, we've been designed to maintain this balance ourselves. Even when the outside world changes, our internal states remain relatively stable.

A great deal of basic motivation is directed toward helping to maintain our internal balance. To keep our internal world within the narrow limits of physiological survival, we have active control processes to maintain **homeostasis**, a constant internal state (*homeo* means 'equal,' and *stasis* means 'static' or 'constant'). A homeo-static control process drives a system to actively work to maintain a constant state (that is, homeostasis).

Homeostatic control processes can be psychological, physiological, or mechanical. A familiar example is the thermostat that runs your central heating or cooling system. Thermostats are designed to maintain temperature homeostasis. When you set your thermostat to a particular temperature, that temperature is the goal value or set point. A **set point** is the value that the homeostatic system tries to maintain. If the winter room temperature falls below the value you set, the thermostat is triggered: the discrepancy between its goal and the actual temperature causes it to activate the heating system.

If the summer room temperature rises above the thermostat's set temperature for cooling, the thermostat activates the air conditioner. A thermostat coupled to both heating and cooling systems can be used to keep your room at a stable temperature even as the seasons change. Many physiological processes work like thermostats: they activate motivations that help maintain homeostasis.

Body temperature and homeostasis

With a 10°C drop in brain temperature, you'd lose consciousness. If your brain temperature rose more than 10°C above normal, you would die. Even though you may have been in very hot or cold weather, your brain remained largely protected within a narrow range of several degrees centigrade. Homeostatic control systems, both physiological and psychological, are the reason for this constancy.

Physiological responses such as sweating and shivering are part of the reason your brain temperature remains so constant. These physiological responses provide cooling in the form of evaporation and heating in the form of muscle activity. Psychological reactions also come into play as you begin to feel uncomfortably hot. You may find yourself wanting to shed clothing, have a cool drink, or find shade. But what turns on these physiological and psychological responses?

When you are under the hot sun, your entire body becomes hot. Conversely, if you remain too long unprotected in the cold, your entire body becomes hypothermic (too cold). But only within your brain is the change of temperature actually detected. Neurons at several sites in the brain, especially within the preoptic (front) region of the hypothalamus at the base of the brain, are essentially neural thermostats (Satinoff, 2005). They begin to operate differently as their own temperature changes. These neurons serve as both the thermometer and the homeostatic set point within your body. When their temperatures diverge from their normal levels, their metabolism alters, and this changes their activity or firing patterns. This triggers physiological reactions such as perspiration or shivering, which help correct your body temperature. In addition, it triggers your sensation of being too hot or too cold, which makes you want to seek shade or put on a coat, behavioral solutions to the same problems.

When you are too hot, a cool breeze can feel good. Likewise, when you are too cold, a warm bath feels pleasant. But as your own internal temperature changes, your perception of these outside events also changes. Although ordinarily your entire body changes temperature by a degree or two when you are in situations that make you feel very hot or cold, it is only the slight change in your brain temperature that causes the change in the way you feel. The brain can be fooled into feeling hot or cold by merely changing the temperature of a relatively few neurons in the hypothalamus. For example, cooling of the hypothalamus alone (by painlessly pumping cold liquid through a small loop of tubing that has been surgically implanted into the hypothalamus) motivates a rat to press a bar to turn on a heat lamp that warms its skin – even though its overall body temperature has not been lowered (Satinoff, 2005). The hypothalamic neurons have detected a change in their own temperature away from the normal set point.

Most of us have experienced a temporary change in set point. An illness can temporarily raise brain set points to several degrees above normal. Then the temperature they 'seek' becomes higher, and a fever results. Physiological reactions that elevate body temperature are activated. You shiver, and your body temperature begins to rise above normal. But in spite of the rise in temperature, you may still feel cold – even in a warm room – until your hypothalamic neurons rise all the way to their elevated set point.

Thirst as a homeostatic process

Satisfying thirst is an important homeostatic process. **Thirst** is the psychological manifestation of the need for water, which is essential for survival. What controls this process?

After going without water or exercising intensively, the body begins to deplete two kinds of fluid reservoirs as water is gradually eliminated through perspiration, respiration, or urination. The first type of reservoir is made up of water contained within the cells. This water is mixed with the protein, fat, and carbohydrate molecules that form the structure and contents of the cell. The water inside your cells is your intracellular reservoir. The second type of reservoir is made up of water that is outside the cells. This water is contained in blood and other body fluids and is called the extracellular reservoir.

Extracellular thirst results when our bodies lose water because we have gone without drinking or have exercised intensively. Water is extracted from the body by the kidneys in the form of urine, excreted by sweat glands in the skin, or breathed out of the lungs as vapor, and in each case it comes most directly from the blood supply. The loss reduces the volume of extracellular fluid that remains; in turn, the loss of blood volume produces a reduction in blood pressure. You will not feel this slight change in blood pressure, but pressure receptors within your kidneys, heart, and major blood vessels detect it and activate sensory neurons that relay a signal to the brain. Neurons in the hypothalamus next send an impulse to the pituitary gland, causing it to release antidiuretic hormone (ADH) into the bloodstream. ADH causes the kidneys to retain water from the blood as they filter it. Rather than send this water on to become urine, the kidneys deliver it back to the blood. This happens whenever you go without drinking for more than several hours. For example, you may have noticed that your urine appears more concentrated in color at such times (for instance, when you wake up after a night's sleep). In addition, the brain sends a neural signal to the kidneys that causes them to release the hormone renin. Renin interacts chemically with a substance in the blood to produce yet another hormone, angiotensin, which activates neurons deep within the brain, producing the desire to drink.

You may recall that this entire chain of events is triggered by a drop in blood pressure caused by dehydration. Other events that cause dramatic loss of blood pressure can also produce thirst. For example, soldiers wounded on the battlefield or injured people who have bled extensively may feel intense thirst. The cause of their craving is the activation of pressure receptors, which triggers the same chain of renin and angiotensin production, resulting in the experience of thirst (Fitzsimons, 1990).

Intracellular thirst is caused by osmosis – the tendency of water to move from zones where it is plentiful to zones where it is relatively rare. It is primarily the concentration of 'salt' ions of sodium, chloride, and potassium that determine whether water is plentiful or rare. As the body loses water, these concentrations begin to rise in the bloodstream. In essence, the blood becomes saltier. The higher concentrations within the blood cause water to migrate from the relatively dilute insides of body cells – including neurons – toward the blood. In a process something like sucking up a puddle of water with a paper towel, water is pulled out of the neurons and other cells. Neurons within the hypothalamus become activated when higher salt concentrations in the blood pull water from them, causing them to become dehydrated. Their activation produces 'osmotic' or intracellular thirst, producing the desire to drink. Drinking replaces water in the blood,

Most bar owners know that salty foods trigger osmotic or intracellular thirst and thus induce customers to drink more.

reducing the concentration of salt, which in turn allows water to return to neurons and other cells. That is why people become thirsty after eating salty food – even though they might not have lost water.

INTERIM SUMMARY

→ Motivational states direct and energize behavior. They arise from two sources: internal drive factors, and external incentive factors.

→ Drive factors tend to promote homeostasis: the preservation of a constant internal state.

→ Homeostasis involves (1) a set point, or goal value, for the ideal internal state, (2) a sensory signal that measures the actual internal state, (3) a comparison between the set point and the sensory signal, and (4) a response that brings the actual internal state closer to the set point goal.

→ Temperature regulation is an example of homeostasis. The regulated variable is the temperature of the blood, and sensors for this are located in various parts of the body, including the hypothalamus. Adjustments are either automatic physiological responses (e.g., shivering) or voluntary behavioral ones (e.g., putting on a sweater).

→ Thirst is another homeostatic motive that operates on two regulated variables: extracellular fluid and intracellular fluid. Loss of extracellular fluid is detected by blood-pressure sensors, neurons in major veins and organs that respond to a drop in pressure. Loss of intracellular fluid is detected by osmotic sensors, neurons in the hypothalamus that respond to dehydration.

CRITICAL THINKING QUESTIONS

1 Homeostatic processes can produce both unconscious, automatic responses (e.g., shivering), and conscious, behavioral ones (e.g., getting under a blanket). Compare and contrast each form of motivation. Can you envision one form without the other?

2 Here we've discussed how two internal factors – extracellular thirst, and intracellular thirst – motivate drinking. What other factors might motivate drinking? To what extent do you think social and cultural factors motivate drinking?

INCENTIVE MOTIVATION AND REWARD

Motivation typically directs behavior toward a particular incentive that produces pleasure or alleviates an unpleasant state: food, drink, sex, and so forth. In other words, **incentive motivation** – or wanting something – is typically associated with affect – or liking that same something. Precisely speaking, the term **affect** refers to the entire range of consciously experienced pleasure and displeasure. Yet in discussing motivation and reward, we typically emphasize the pleasure half of the continuum, the part that corresponds with liking. The sheer pervasiveness of affect in our experience of life has led some to suggest that pleasure has evolved to serve a basic psychological role (Cabanac, 2010). That role is to shape behavior by helping to define a psychological 'common currency' that reflects the value of each action we perform. Pleasure tends to be associated with stimuli that increased our ancestors' ability to survive or their offspring's ability to survive. These include tasty food, refreshing drink, and sexual reproduction. Painful or frustrating consequences were associated with events that threatened our ancestors' survival: physical damage, illness, or loss of resources. The rewarding or affective consequences of an action, in other words, generally reflected to our human ancestors whether that action was worth repeating.

But to guide future actions, momentary pleasures and displeasures need to be learned, remembered, and attributed to relevant objects and events, imbuing those objects and events with **incentive salience**, meaning that these objects and events have become linked with anticipated affect, which grabs our attention and steers our seeking behavior. Yet however closely interwoven incentive motivation and pleasurable rewards are in our conscious experiences of the world, this does not mean that 'wanting' something and 'liking' it are the same thing (Berridge, 2007). Indeed, they can diverge under special circumstances. One clear distinction concerns the timing of wanting and liking. **Wanting** is the anticipation of pleasure, as in the cravings that you experience when you think ahead to a delicious meal. **Liking**, by contrast, is the pleasure that you experience in the moment that you begin to eat that meal (Barbano & Cador, 2007). Liking something in the past usually contributes to wanting it in the future. This even occurs in short time spans, such as when the first nibble of food whets your appetite for more. Through such processes, affective rewards (liking) can fuel incentive motivation (wanting).

The biological bases of liking versus wanting were at first difficult for scientists to pinpoint. Indeed, in much earlier work, the two concepts (wanting and liking) were fused together into the simpler notion of rewards. As early as the 1950s, researchers discovered that electrical stimulation of certain areas of the brain served as a powerful reward, evidenced by the fact that animals and people would energetically pursue repeated stimulation to these brain areas (Olds, 1956). This was taken as evidence that brain stimulation was itself a reward, both pleasurable (liked) and desired (wanted). The targeted brain sites were even dubbed 'pleasure centers' by many. And because the dopamine (see Figure 10.2) appeared to be crucial to the so-called pleasure centers (Valenstein, 1976), for many decades scientists linked dopamine with pleasant affect.

The neurons of the **brain's dopamine system** (see Figure 10.2) lie in the upper brain stem, in the ventral tegmental area (VTA), and send their axons through the nucleus accumbens and up to the prefrontal cortex. As their name implies, these neurons use the neurotransmitter dopamine to convey their message. The brain's dopamine system is activated by many kinds of natural rewards, or primary reinforcers, such as tasty food or drink or a desired sexual partner. The same neurons are also activated by many drugs that humans and animals find rewarding, such as cocaine, amphetamines, and heroin.

Yet the only way that scientists can distinguish 'liking' from 'wanting' is to use separate measures for each. Seeking out repeated experiences more closely coincides with the concept of 'wanting.' How could scientists index 'liking' in a way that differentiated it from 'wanting'? Recall that liking – or pleasurable affect – is experienced *during* consumption, not in anticipation of it. Facial and bodily movements often reveal the

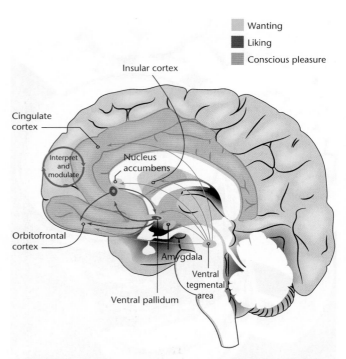

FIGURE 10.2 Dopamine Pathways and Hedonic Hotspots.
The brain's dopamine system (in blue) underlies the experience of 'wanting.' It begins near the brain stem in the ventral tegmental area (VTA) and projects to the amygdala and the nucleus accumbens, as well as up to the prefrontal cortex. The brain's hedonic hotspots (in red) underlie the experience of 'liking.' These small hotspots lie in the medial shell of the nucleus accumbens and in the ventral pallidum, which sits near the amygdala at the base of the forebrain.

experience of pleasure. Consider the case of eating good food. We humans can generally tell when someone else – even an infant – likes the taste of something. When something tastes good, we tend to smile and lick our lips. Likewise, when something tastes bad, we tend to frown with our mouths open and our upper lips raised. It turns out that non-human primates and many other mammals, including rats, share some of these same facial expressions for good- and bad-tasting foods (Steiner *et al.*, 2001)

If rewarding brain stimulation truly induces pleasure, then it should increase seeking as well as expressions of pleasure. Newly armed with separate measures of 'wanting' and 'liking,' researchers tested this proposition. They found that electrically stimulating the brain's dopamine system motivated animals to seek rewards like food, despite the fact that, as they become satiated, they show increasing distaste for the food through their facial expressions (Berridge & Valenstein, 1991). In another study, researchers studied a strand of mice with a genetic mutation that left them with very high concentrations of dopamine in their brains. Compared to typical mice, these mutant mice not only ate and drank more, but also showed faster learning when rewarded with a Froot Loop (a sweet breakfast cereal), suggesting that they

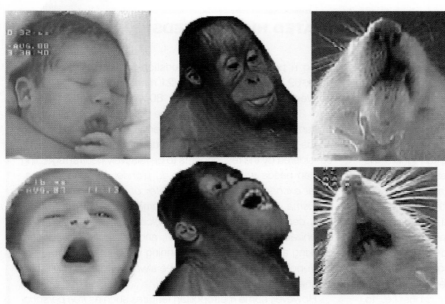

Displays of Liking in Humans and Animals. These photos show human infant, primate and rat affective displays to sweet and bitter tastes. Displays of 'liking' include tongue protusions to a sweet taste (top photographs). Displays of 'disliking' include the gape (bottom photographs).

attributed greater incentive salience to the cereal. Yet when researchers coded facial expressions when mice ate the cereal, mutant mice and typical mice were no different, they liked it just the same (Pecina *et al.,* 2003). The same pattern of results is found when drugs (like amphetamines) are injected into the brain's dopamine system (Wyvell & Berridge, 2000). Each of these experiments demonstrates 'wanting' without 'liking.'

The opposite effect – 'liking' without 'wanting' – has also been demonstrated. Researchers injected a particular chemical neurotoxin into anesthetized rats, which selectively destroyed neurons in the brain's dopamine system but left all other neurons healthy and functioning. Once recovered from their operations, these rats were uninterested in food, water, or any other reward. They even voluntarily starved to death unless fed through a tube. Wanting was thus destroyed along with the dopamine neurons. But not so for liking. If sweet or bitter tastes were infused into the animals' mouths, they showed the same facial and bodily expressions as intact rats (Berridge & Robinson, 1998).

So, paying close attention to laboratory rats' facial expressions of pleasure and displeasure proved to be the key to unlocking the tight association between wanting and liking. From this innovative research, we can conclude that the brain's dopamine system accounts for 'wanting' a diverse array of natural and artificial incentives. Rather than creating sensations of pleasure or liking per se, its activity appears to dispose individuals to want to repeat the event that caused the dopamine infusion, regardless of whether that event produces pleasure or displeasure.

Relying on these same measures to index 'wanting' as distinct from 'liking,' researchers have identified the brain's hedonic hotspots, the actual pleasure centers of the brain that underlie 'liking'. These turned out to be far smaller than originally believed. One of these hedonic hotspots lies in a subregion of the nucleus accumbens called the medial shell. A second lies in the ventral pallidum, which sits near the base of the forebrain (see Figure 10.2). When these areas are electrically stimulated, rats show amplified signs of liking sweet foods. Chemical stimulation of these areas with enkephalin, a natural opioid substance made in the brain, also enhances a rat's liking of sweets. These and other aspects of the brain's opiate system create a chemical chain reaction that intensifies feelings of pleasure (Kringelbach & Berridge, 2012). Under normal circumstances, activity in the brain's hedonic hotspots emerges in concert with the brain's dopamine system, so that we want things that have previously made us feel good, and are indifferent to things that have not. Under certain circumstances, however, wanting and liking become unhinged. Addiction is one such case.

Drug addiction

Addiction is a powerful motivation for some people. The craving for certain drugs, such as opiates (heroin or morphine), psychostimulants (amphetamine or cocaine) or synthetic street versions of these drugs, and certain other drugs (alcohol, nicotine), can become overwhelming. Addicts may crave their drug so strongly that they will sacrifice job, family life and relationships, home, and even freedom to obtain it.

Taking a drug once, or even once in a while, does not constitute addiction. Many people, for instance, have sampled at least one of the drugs just mentioned without becoming addicted. Even regular use (for example, regularly drinking wine with dinner) need not reflect addiction. **Addiction** occurs only when a pattern of compulsive and destructive drug-taking behavior has emerged; often the person compulsively craves the drug. Repeated drug use dramatically alters the incentive salience of the drug – creating pathological 'wanting.' What causes the transformation from trying out a drug, or engaging in social or recreational use, into addiction?

Some drugs are especially powerful in their ability to produce addiction. Three major factors operate together to make psychoactive drugs more addictive than other incentives,

CUTTING EDGE RESEARCH ENVIRONMENT-RELATED HUMAN NEEDS AND URBAN PLANNING

Dr Majken Bieniok, Humbolt University, Berlin

Permanently changing life conditions due to globalization processes and population changes evoke demand for new urban development principles and concepts. However, urban development plans are usually marked by economic elite interests and theoretical models. Therefore, they often ignore the actual needs of the inhabitants, which usually leads to negative social and individual consequences. In order to avoid such consequences, planning should be adapted to the wishes and needs of urban inhabitants. Which needs should be addressed?

Several scholars have addressed the definition of human needs. Altogether, they show that the specific context determines their validity. Kaplan and Kaplan (1982) offered a theory of basic and simultaneous informational needs (to make sense out of the environment and to expand horizons; i.e., to seek involvement). A more recent and environment-related theory (Bieniok, 2012) refers to the following needs:

Physically oriented needs:

→ Physical needs (air, light, water, nutrition, excretion, and sex)

→ Motion and mobility

→ Repose and regeneration

→ Safety and protection

→ Physical and mental health

Socially oriented needs:

→ Social connectedness, relationships, and partnership

→ Various contacts, and communication

→ Love, care, and acceptance

→ Privacy and intimacy

→ Pleasure and emotional expression

Self-oriented needs:

→ Meaning, reasonableness, order, and aesthetics

→ Self-fulfillment, and creativity

→ Self-acceptance, identity, and high self-esteem

→ Knowledge, learning experience, and novelty-seeking

→ Autonomy, and self-determination

→ Control and active shaping of the social, and environmental surrounding

Max-Neef (1992) noted that certain physical and social environmental conditions function as satisfiers or violators of essential human needs. They can also function as synergetic satisfiers or violators if they affect several needs at once.

Using a paper- and pencil questionnaire, 69 subjects (48 women, 21 men) between the ages of 18 and 80 years ($M = 30$, $SD = 13.83$) identified the potential of typical metropolitan features to satisfy essential environment-related human needs (Bieniok, 2012). First, a group of metropolitan features considered by the respondents to be relatively neutral regarding human needs was identified (e.g., *pioneer function*, *international exchange*, *trendsetter*, *center of services*, *fascinating charisma*, *modern infrastructure*, *domicile of many public facilities*, *center of consumption*, *domicile of major international organizations*, *high urban sprawl*, and *characteristic streets*). Looking at widely used city planning concepts, this group of metropolitan features seems to be always enhanced by urban planners in their daily work.

However, some metropolitan features such as *free personal development opportunities*, *friendly and open-minded people*, *various leisure facilities*, and *opportunity to satisfy any conceivable wish* offered a high potential of satisfying environment-related human needs, whereas others such as *being a target of criminal and terror acts*, *psychological and physical stress*, and *high unemployment* were traced as potential violators of need satisfaction. These metropolitan features were shown to have a major effect on human well-being. Therefore, it would be desirable for urban planning experts to bear these crucial features in mind.

Dealing with the positive impact of space, Frances Kuo's research group discovered different effects of green areas in cities:

→ Reduction of fears, aggressiveness, violence, and criminality (2001a, 2001b)

→ Increased sense of safety and mental recovery (1998a, 2001c)

→ Increased interaction between different groups (1997)

→ Increased child play creativity and child social interaction (1998b)

A Dutch research group (Maas *et al.*, 2009) discusses respectively the *social contacts* which are being enabled by certain locations as mediators between the factors *green space* and *health*. Their study could identify *loneliness* and *lack of social support* as risk factors. In the same context, Karmanov and Hamel (2008) have found evidence that a well planed and attractive urban environment like Amsterdam's Eastern Docklands may bear recovering influence. Some scholars (like Sampson & Gifford, 2010) have even found evidence for therapeutic features of one's neighborhood locations in the context of refugee stress relief.

These results offer a new framework for improving the process of neighbourhood structuring, urban planning, and the creation of a green living environment based on satisfying essential environment-related human needs.

although not all of these factors need be present for addiction to occur. The first is the ability of most addictive drugs to over-activate incentive systems in the brain. Because drugs act directly on brain neurons, they can produce levels of activity in the dopamine system that far surpass those produced by natural incentives. Euphoric drugs activate both pleasure (liking) and incentive (wanting) systems, perhaps because they activate both opiate and dopamine neural systems. Once experienced, the memory of such intense pleasure is a potent temptation to regain it again and again.

But the memory of pleasure by itself would not be sufficient to produce addiction, at least for many people, without additional factors. The second factor is the ability of addictive drugs, if taken repeatedly, to produce unpleasant withdrawal syndromes. As a drug is taken again and again, the pleasure systems that it activates may become increasingly resistant to activation in an effort to regain their balanced state. This is, in part, the cause of **tolerance**, the need for a greater amount of a drug to achieve the same euphoria. In addition, after repeated exposure to the drug, the brain may activate processes that have consequences exactly opposite to those of the drug. These processes may help the brain remain in a balanced state when the drug is taken, but by themselves they are experienced as highly unpleasant. If the addict stops using the drug, the lack of activity in resistant pleasure systems and the activation of unpleasant drug-opposite processes can produce **withdrawal**, an intensely aversive reaction to the cessation of drug use. This aversive state presents addicts with another motive to resume taking the drug, at least for as long as the withdrawal state lasts – typically several weeks.

Finally, addictive drugs may produce permanent changes in brain incentive systems that cause cravings even after withdrawal is over. Repeated use of drugs like cocaine, heroin, or amphetamines, which activate the brain's dopamine systems, causes these neurons to become hyperactive or sensitized. **Neural sensitization** may be permanent, and it means that these dopamine neurons will be activated more highly by drugs and drug-related stimuli. Because the brain's dopamine system appears to account for incentive motivation (wanting) more than pleasure (liking), its hyperactivation in addicts may cause exaggerated craving for the drug, even when drug experiences are no longer particularly positive (Robinson & Berridge, 2003). Neural sensitization lasts much longer than withdrawal. This may be why recovered addicts are in danger of relapse into drug use, even after they have completed detoxification programs.

The combination of these factors sheds light on why psychoactive drugs, more than many other incentives, are able to produce addictions. These drugs directly activate brain pleasure and incentive systems to unmatched levels, produce withdrawal syndromes that drive a recovering addict back to the drug, and permanently hyperactivate the brain's dopamine system that causes drugs to be craved. This combination is hard to resist.

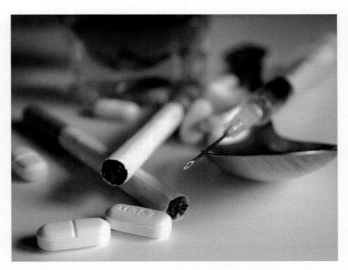

Addictive drugs can permanently change the brain's dopamine system, which creates a hyperactive craving for drugs. This is why objects and events associated with drug use continue to have strong incentive salience and produce cravings, even after recovering addicts have chosen to live drug-free.

People can also become pathologically dependent on things other than drugs – like gambling, food, shopping, work, even the Internet (Chou *et al.*, 2005). When engagement in such activity becomes compulsive and all-consuming, it is often called a behavioral addiction, even though it may not share all the same neurological properties of drug addictions.

INTERIM SUMMARY

→ Incentive motivation (wanting something) is typically associated with pleasurable affect (liking that same something). Although some incentives – such as a sweet food when we are hungry – are powerful motivators by themselves, most incentives are established through learning.

→ The brain's dopamine system appears to underlie incentive motivation, or the experience of 'wanting,' Artificial activation of these neurons by drugs or electrical brain stimulation causes increased motivation for both natural and artificial incentives.

→ The brain's hedonic hotspots orchestrate feelings of pleasure or 'liking.' These include small areas within the nucleus accumbens and the ventral pallidum, which are responsive to enkephalin and other natural opioid substances

→ Drug addiction is a pattern of compulsive and destructive drug-taking behavior. Addictions to psychoactive drugs are difficult to overcome because of changes in drug tolerance, withdrawal symptoms, and neural sensitization.

CRITICAL THINKING QUESTIONS

1   Research suggests that wanting and liking are separable psychological systems. Think of a time in your own life when you experienced wanting without liking (perhaps having to do with food). What caused the two to diverge?

2   Many addictive drugs change the brain's dopamine system, making these neurons hyperactive or sensitized. Because there is no known way to reverse these changes, it's reasonable to conclude that the brains of recovering addicts have been permanently altered. Knowing this, how can recovering addicts avoid relapse? How would you design an effective treatment program to prevent relapse?

Evolutionary psychologists argue that sweet foods, like these pastries, are so compelling to us because 'sweetness' conveyed to our ancestors that a particular food was rich in sugar and calories. Of course, sugars were more rare in our ancestors' environment than they are for us today.

HUNGER, EATING, AND EATING DISORDERS

The control of hunger involves many of the same homeostatic concepts as thirst, but eating is much more complex than drinking. When we're thirsty, we generally need only water, and our thirst is directed toward anything that will provide it. But there are lots of different things to eat. We need to eat a number of different kinds of things (proteins, carbohydrates, fats, minerals) to be healthy. We need to select the proper balance of foods that contain these things. Evolution has given our brains ways of helping us select the foods we need (and avoid eating things that might poison us). Some of these ways involve the basic taste preferences we were born with. Others involve mechanisms for learning preferences for particular foods and aversions to others.

Flavor is the most important factor in food preferences. Flavor contains both taste and odor components, but taste has been relatively more important in human evolution. Humans, like other mammals, are born 'programmed' with likes and dislikes for particular tastes. As we've seen, even infants respond to sweet tastes with lip-smacking movements and facial expressions indicative of pleasure (Steiner, 1979). They respond to bitter tastes by turning away and pulling their faces into expressions of disgust. Food manufacturers capitalize on our natural 'sweet tooth' to devise sweet foods that spur many people to overeat.

Why do we find sweet foods and drinks so attractive? Evolutionary psychologists have suggested that it is because sweetness is an excellent 'label' that told our ancestors, foraging among unknown plants, that a particular food or berry was rich in sugar, a class of digestible carbohydrate. Eating sweet foods is an excellent way to gain calories, and calories were not abundant in our evolutionary past. A similar labeling explanation has been advanced for our dislike of bitterness. The naturally bitter compounds that occur in certain plants can make those plants toxic to humans. Bitterness, in other words, is a label for a natural type of poison that occurs commonly. Ancestors who avoided bitter plants may have been more successful at avoiding such poisons (Rozin *et al.,* 2009).

A second way of developing food preferences is through an array of learning and social learning mechanisms. One of these is a preference based on the consequences of ingesting food with a particular taste. Experience with the nourishing consequences of a food leads to gradual liking for its taste through a process that is essentially a form of classical conditioning (Booth, 1991). Experience with other forms of taste-consequence pairings may also be the basis for developing preferences for tastes that are initially not pleasant, such as alcohol or coffee. In other words, the positive psychological or physical effects of alcohol or caffeinated coffee may cause us to develop preferences for these foods, even if we initially do not like their taste. The same kind of process can work in the opposite direction to produce strong dislike for a particular food. If your first sample of a tasty food or drink is followed sometime later by nausea or vomiting, you may find that the food is not tasty the next time you try it. The food hasn't changed, but you have, because your new associative memories cause the food to subsequently be experienced as unwanted and unpleasant. This process is called **conditioned aversion**.

Interactions between homeostasis and incentives

Whatever particular foods we choose, it is clear that we must eat to maintain energy homeostasis. Body cells burn fuel to produce the energy required for the tasks they perform. Physical exercise causes muscle cells to burn extra fuel to meet the metabolic needs placed on them by energetic movement. By burning more fuel, they draw on stores of calories that have been deposited as body fat or other forms of 'stored energy.' Even as you read this, the neurons of your brain are burning fuel to meet the metabolic needs created as they fire electrical impulses and make and release neurotransmitters. The main fuel used by these brain neurons is glucose, a simple sugar. Without fuel, neurons cannot work. In fact, your brain uses more glucose when you 'exercise it' by thinking hard, such as when you make a difficult decision or otherwise exert self-control (Gailliot *et al.*, 2007).

Glucose is present in many fruits and other foods. It can also be manufactured by the liver out of other sugars or carbohydrates. Once you've eaten a meal, a great deal of glucose will be absorbed into your bloodstream through the process of digestion. Even more will be created by your liver as it converts other forms of nutrients. In this way, a meal replenishes the fuel needed by your brain neurons and your body's other cells.

Because our cells need fuel, we might expect hunger to be solely a homeostatic motivation controlled entirely by the need to keep sufficient sources of energy available. Indeed, homeostasis is the dominant principle operating in the control of hunger. Deficits in available fuels can trigger hunger, and surpluses can inhibit it. But even though homeostasis is crucial to understanding the control of hunger, incentive factors are equally important. That is, we want to eat perhaps as much as we need to eat (Lowe & Butryn, 2007). So we can't fully understand hunger unless we look at the interaction between homeostasis and incentives.

The importance of interactions between homeostatic drive reduction and the taste and other incentive stimuli of food was made clear by a classic experiment by Miller and Kessen (1952). These investigators trained rats to run down a short path for a milk reward. In one case, the rats received milk as a reward in the ordinary way: they drank it. In the other case, the rats received exactly the same amount of milk, but in a more direct way: the milk was gently pumped into their stomachs through a tube passed into an artificial opening, or fistula, that had been implanted weeks before. Both of these rewards provided exactly the same number of calories. Both reduced the rats' fuel deficit to the same degree. But the rats learned to run for the milk reward much better when they were allowed to drink it. The milk was not a powerful motivator when it was pumped directly into the stomach, even though it reduced hunger just as well as when it went into the mouth. The rats needed to *both* taste the reward *and* have it reduce hunger.

The importance of such interactions between oral incentives and drive reduction has been demonstrated in many ways since that original experiment (Toates, 2011). Food that bypasses the normal route of voluntary tasting and swallowing is not strongly motivating for either animals or humans. For example, people who are fed entirely by means of intravenous or intragastric infusions of nutrients often find these 'meals' unsatisfying. They may feel an intense desire to have some food that they can put into their mouths – even if they are required to spit it out again after chewing it. The strong desire for oral stimulation – above and beyond the satisfaction of caloric needs – is also reflected in our widespread use of artificial sweeteners, which provide flavor without calories. Food incentives, in the form of the pleasant sensory experience involved in eating palatable foods and drinks, thus are as crucial to appetite as caloric drive reduction.

Learning is also an important part of the interaction between physiological hunger signals and the incentive stimuli of eating. Dramatic demonstrations can be seen in animals in which the act of eating is uncoupled from the ordinary caloric consequences by the implantation of a stomach fistula, which allows food to leave the stomach as well as to be put into it. If the fistula cap is removed, whatever is eaten will fall out rather than be digested. This is called **sham feeding** because the meal is a sham in the sense that it provides no calories. Sham-fed animals eat normal amounts and then stop. Why do they stop rather than continue eating? The answer becomes clear if one observes food intake during subsequent meals: the animals gradually increase the amount eaten as they learn that the meal conveys fewer calories than it once did (van Vort & Smith, 1987). If the fistula cap is replaced so that everything is digested as it normally would be, the animals eat the 'too large' amount for their next few meals. Gradually, their meal size declines to normal levels as they learn that the food apparently is rich in calories once again. These observations have led to the hypothesis of **conditioned satiety** – that the fullness we feel after a meal is at least in part a product of learning (Booth, 1987).

Humans also are capable of conditioned satiety. In one experiment, people were asked to eat several meals of a distinctive food that was rich in calories and of another food that was low in calories. Later, when the participants were again given the two foods, which were apparently the same as before but with the caloric content made equal, they found the food that had originally been higher in calories more satiating (Booth, 1991). Even imagining eating a big meal leads people to later eat less (Morewedge, Huh, & Vosgerau, 2010).

Typically, ingesting sweets provides calories and therefore energy. But when this association is broken, as it is when foods are prepared with artificial sweeteners, like saccharin, our bodies compensate by gradually increasing caloric intake, leading to increases in body weight and even obesity – hardly the result those who eat 'sugar-free' seek. This ironic effect of consuming artificial sweeteners is thought to occur because their sham incentive value interferes with physiological homeostatic processes (Swithers & Davidson, 2008).

A final form of interaction between food incentives and homeostatic drive is the phenomenon called **alliesthesia** (Cabanac, 2010), in which food (especially sweet and fatty foods) smell and taste better when one is hungry (Plailly *et al.*, 2011). More generally, alliesthesia means that any external stimulus that corrects an internal trouble is experienced as pleasurable. For example, when people are asked to rate the palatability of sweet drinks either after a meal or after several hours without food, they give higher palatability ratings to the same drink when they are hungry than when they have recently eaten.

Physiological hunger cues

You may have noticed that when you are hungry your stomach sometimes growls. At such moments, the stomach walls are engaged in muscular contractions, creating the burbling movements of its contents that you hear. Stomach contractions are most frequent when you are hungry and likely to feel that your stomach is empty. The association of these contractions with feelings of hunger led early investigators to hypothesize that pressure sensors in the stomach detect emptiness and trigger both contractions and the psychological experience of hunger. Later, psychologists and physiologists found that this coincidence is really just that – a coincidence. Stomach sensations from contractions are not the real cause of hunger. In fact, people who have had their stomachs surgically removed for medical reasons, so that food passes directly to the intestines, can still have strong feelings of hunger.

The stomach does have receptors that are important to changes in hunger, but these receptors are primarily chemical in nature. They have more to do with feelings of satiety than with feelings of hunger. They are activated by sugars and other nutrients in stomach contents and send a neural signal to the brain.

The physiological signal for hunger is more directly related to the real source of calories for neurons and other cells: levels of glucose and other nutrients in the body. The brain itself is its own sensor for deficiencies in available calories. You may remember that neurons in the brain use glucose as their principal source of energy. Neurons in particular parts of the brain, especially the brain stem and hypothalamus, are especially sensitive to glucose levels. When the level falls too low, the activity of these neurons is disrupted. This signals the rest of the brain, producing hunger. Such hunger can be produced artificially in laboratory animals even just after a meal. If chemicals that prevent neurons from burning glucose as a fuel are infused into an animal's brain, the animal will suddenly seek out food. Its brain has been fooled into sensing a lack of glucose, even though glucose was actually present, because the neurons have been disrupted in the same way as they are when glucose is low.

Peripheral signals

To some degree, hunger is what we feel when we have no feeling of satiety. As long as caloric food is in our stomach or intestine, or calorie stores are high within our body, we feel relatively sated. When these decline, hunger ensues. The control of hunger is therefore the reverse of the control of satiety.

Many physical systems contribute to the feeling of satiety after a meal. The first system is made up of the parts of the body that process food first: the stomach and intestine. Both the physical expansion of the stomach and the chemicals within the food activate receptors in the stomach's walls. These receptors relay their signal to the brain through the vagus nerve, which carries signals from many other body organs as well. A second kind of satiety message comes from the duodenum, the part of the intestines that receives food directly from the stomach. This signal is sent to the brain as a chemical rather than through a nerve. When food reaches the duodenum, it causes it to release a hormone (cholecystokinin, or CCK) into the bloodstream. CCK helps promote physiological digestion, but it also has a psychological consequence. It travels through the blood until it reaches the brain, where it is detected by special receptors. This produces feelings of satiety. Hungry animals can be fooled into false satiety if microscopic amounts of CCK are infused into their brains shortly after they have begun a meal (Smith & Gibbs, 1994).

Perhaps surprisingly, the brain's most sensitive signal of nutrient availability comes from neuronal receptors that are separate both from the brain and from food: neuronal receptors in the liver (Friedman, 1990). Receptors in the liver are highly sensitive to changes in blood nutrients after digestion. These signals are also sent to the brain through the vagus nerve. A hungry animal will stop eating almost immediately after even a tiny amount of nutrients are infused into the blood supply that goes directly to the liver.

Why should the brain rely on nutrient signals from the liver rather than on its own detectors? The answer may be that the liver can more accurately measure the various types of nutrients used by the body. The brain detects chiefly glucose, but other forms of nutrients, such as complex carbohydrates, proteins, and fats, can be measured, stored, and sometimes converted into other nutrients by the liver. Its role as a general 'currency exchange' for various nutrients may allow the liver to make the best estimate of the total energy stores available to the body.

Integration of hunger signals

Signals for hunger and satiety are processed by the brain in two stages to produce the motivation to eat. First, signals from hunger receptors in the brain itself and satiety signals relayed from the stomach and liver are added together in the brain stem to detect the overall level of need (Grill & Kaplan, 1990). This 'integrated hunger assessment' is also connected in the brain stem to the sensory neural systems that process taste. Taste neurons in the brain stem may change their responsiveness during some forms of hunger and satiety (Scott & Mark, 1986), which may be part of the reason that food tastes more palatable when we are hungry.

To become the conscious experience we know as hunger, and to stimulate the seeking of food, the hunger signal of the

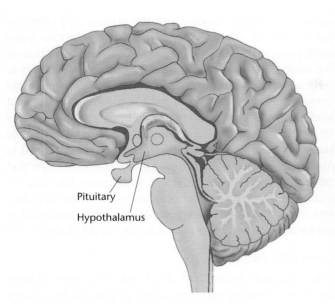

FIGURE 10.3 The Hypothalamus and Pituitary.

Damage to the ventromedial hypothalamus produces overeating and obesity.

brain stem must be processed further in the forebrain. A key site for this processing is the hypothalamus (see Figure 10.3). Hunger is affected in two dramatically different ways by manipulations of two parts of the hypothalamus: the lateral hypothalamus (the parts on each side) and the ventromedial hypothalamus (the lower ['ventral'] and middle ['medial'] portion). Destruction of the lateral hypothalamus produces an apparent total lack of hunger, at least until the rest of the brain recovers and compensates (Teitelbaum & Epstein, 1962). This phenomenon is called the **lateral hypothalamic syndrome**. Animals that have had small lesions made in their lateral hypothalamus may simply ignore food. They may even reject it as though it tasted bad (for example, they may grimace and vigorously spit it out). Unless they are fed artificially, they will starve to death. Nearly the exact opposite pattern of behavior is seen with the **ventromedial hypothalamic syndrome**. Lesions of the ventromedial hypothalamus produce extreme appetites. Animals with such lesions eat voraciously and consume large quantities of food, especially if it is palatable. Not surprisingly, they gain weight until they become quite obese, up to double their normal body weight (King, 2006).

Other manipulations of these brain sites also appear to change hunger. For example, electrical stimulation of the lateral hypothalamus produces overeating: the exact opposite of a lesion of the lateral hypothalamus (and the same effect as a lesion of the ventromedial hypothalamus). An animal with a stimulating electrode in its lateral hypothalamus may begin to look for food and eat as soon as the stimulation begins – and to stop eating once it ends. Conversely, stimulation of the ventromedial hypothalamus will stop a hungry animal's ordinary eating.

Neurochemical stimulation of the hypothalamus works in similar ways. For example, certain compounds such as

neuropeptide Y, or opiate drugs such as morphine, can stimulate feeding when they are injected into the ventromedial hypothalamus. These drugs may temporarily stimulate hunger or make food taste better. Other drugs, such as amphetamines, can halt feeding when injected into parts of the lateral hypothalamus. Many prescription diet drugs are chemically similar to amphetamines. Such drugs might inhibit appetite by acting on neurons in the hypothalamus.

Around 1960, when the importance of the lateral hypothalamus and ventromedial hypothalamus to hunger were discovered, psychologists tended to view these sites simply as hunger or satiety centers. Since then, it has become clear that the concepts of 'hunger center' or 'satiety center' are too simplistic, for a number of reasons. One is that these sites are not the sole centers for hunger or satiety in the brain. They interact with many other brain systems to produce their effects. In fact, some of the same effects can be produced by manipulating related brain systems instead of the hypothalamus. For example, many of the effects of manipulating the lateral hypothalamus can be duplicated by manipulating the brain's dopamine system, which simply passes through the hypothalamus. Like lateral hypothalamic lesions, lesions in this dopamine-containing bundle of axons eliminate feeding. In fact, many early studies of lateral hypothalamic lesions actually destroyed both the dopamine systems and the neurons in the lateral hypothalamus itself. Conversely, the elicitation of feeding by electrical stimulation and by many drugs also depends partly on activation of the brain's dopamine system. Thus, rather than just one or two centers, many neuroanatomical and neurotransmitter systems are involved in appetite and satiety.

One consequence of having many neural systems for appetite is that it is not possible to abolish eating by destroying just one site. Even in animals with lateral hypothalamic lesions, appetite will return eventually. If the rats are artificially fed for several weeks or months after the lesion, they will begin to eat again, but they will eat only enough to maintain their lower body weight. They seem to have reached homeostasis at a lower set point. In fact, rats can be 'protected' from the usual loss of eating that would follow a lateral hypothalamic lesion if they are put on a diet before the lesion that lowers their body weight. This indicates that hypothalamic lesions don't actually destroy hunger. Instead, they may raise or lower the homeostatic set point for body weight that ordinarily controls hunger. Changing the set point is like resetting a thermostat: the system attempts to achieve the new body weight. The effect of ventromedial hypothalamic lesions also conforms to this idea. Animals with those lesions do not gain weight infinitely. Eventually they stop at a new, obese body weight. At that point, they eat only enough to maintain the new set point. But if they are put on a diet and drop below that set point, they will resume overeating in order to regain that body weight when they are finally given the opportunity. Once they regain that level of obesity, they will halt once again.

Obesity

We have emphasized homeostatic processes in hunger, but eating behavior shows several departures from homeostasis. Some people's body weight is not as constant as the homeostatic viewpoint suggests. The most frequent deviation from homeostatic regulation of eating – at least for humans – is obesity. Obese is defined as being 30 per cent or more in excess of one's appropriate body weight. It is well known that certain countries worldwide are experiencing significant increases in obesity levels within populations. One of the highest rates is within the USA, where obesity is considered an epidemic, with roughly 36 per cent of US adults meeting the criteria, a percentage that has more than doubled in the past 20 years. Although the percentage of obese adults in Europe is generally lower (24 per cent of adults in the UK are classed as obese for instance) the link between obesity and health problems makes it a pressing societal concern. The prevalence of obesity also varies among different groups. Physical obesity occurs about equally in both sexes, but the psychological perception of being overweight is more common among women. About 65 per cent of American women, compared with about 47 per cent of men, consider themselves overweight (Burke *et al.,* 2010).

Obesity is a major health hazard. It contributes to a higher incidence of diabetes, high blood pressure, heart disease, and even some forms of cancer. As if this were not bad enough, obesity can also be a social stigma, as obese people are often perceived as being indulgent and lacking in will-power (Crandall *et al.,* 2009). This allegation can be most unfair because, as we will see, in many cases obesity is due to genetic factors rather than overeating. Given the problems associated with obesity, it is not surprising that each year millions of people spend billions of dollars on diets, drugs, and even cosmetic surgery to lose weight.

Most researchers agree that obesity is a complex problem that can involve metabolic, nutritional, psychological, and sociological factors. Obesity probably is not a single disorder but a variety of disorders that all have fatness as their major symptom (Rodin, 1981). Asking how one becomes obese is like asking how one gets to Paris – there are many ways to do it, and which one you 'choose' depends on where you are coming from. In what follows, we will divide the factors that lead to weight gain into two broad classes: (1) genetics, and (2) calorie intake (overeating). Roughly speaking, people may become obese because they are genetically predisposed to metabolize nutrients into fat, even if they don't eat more than other people (metabolic reasons), or because they eat too much (for psychological or sociocultural reasons). Both factors may be involved in some cases of obesity, and in other cases genetics or overeating alone may be the culprit.

Genetic factors

It has long been known that obesity runs in families. In families in which neither parent is obese, only about 10 per cent of the children are obese; if one parent is obese, about 40 per cent of the children are also obese; and if both parents are obese, approximately 70 per cent of the children are also obese (Gurney, 1936). These statistics suggest a biological basis of obesity, but other interpretations are possible – for example, perhaps the children are simply imitating their parents' eating habits. Recent findings, however, strongly support a genetic basis for obesity.

Twin studies

One way to get evidence about the role of genetics in obesity is to study identical twins. Because identical twins have the same genes, and because genes supposedly play a role in weight gain, identical twins should be alike in their patterns of weight gain.

In one experiment, 12 pairs of identical twins (all males) agreed to stay in a college dormitory for 100 days. The intent of the experiment was to get the twins to gain weight. Each man ate a diet that contained 1000 extra calories per day. For men, 1000 extra calories is the rough equivalent of eating four very large meals a day, instead of three regular meals. Also, the men's physical activity was restricted. They were not allowed to exercise and instead spent much of their time reading, playing sedentary games, and watching television. By the end of the 100 days, all of the men had gained weight, but the amount gained ranged from 9 to 30 pounds. However – and this is the key point – there was hardly any variation in the amount gained by the members of each pair of twins (the variation occurred between pairs of twins). In other words, identical twins gained almost identical amounts. Moreover, identical twins tended to gain weight in the same places. If one member of a pair of twins gained weight in his middle, so did the other; if one member of another pair of twins gained weight on his hips and thighs, so did the other (Bouchard *et al.,* 1990).

These results make it clear that both calorie intake and genetics contribute to weight gain. The fact that all the men in the study gained weight shows that increased calories translates into increased weight, which is hardly surprising. The fact that the amount of weight gained varied from one pair of twins to another but did not vary within a pair of twins suggests that genetic factors determine how much we gain when we increase our calorie intake.

The results also make it clear why we should not assume that obese people necessarily eat more than non-obese people. Despite eating roughly the same amount (1000 extra calories), the amount of weight gained by different pairs of twins varied. This difference seems to arise from how their bodies metabolized the extra calories. Some people's bodies tend to convert a larger proportion of calories into fat stores, and others are likely to burn off the same calories through different metabolic processes, regardless of how much is eaten (Ravussin *et al.*, 1988).

A critic might object to making too much of the study just described. Identical twins not only have identical genes but also grow up in very similar environments. Perhaps environmental factors were responsible for the identical twins being alike in weight gain. We need to study identical twins who have been reared apart and see how similar the members of a pair are in weight gain. This was done in a study conducted in Sweden (Stunkard *et al.*, 1990). The researchers studied the weights of 93 pairs of identical twins reared apart, as well as that of 153 pairs of identical twins reared together. Members of a pair of twins reared apart were found to be remarkably similar in weight; indeed, they were as similar in weight as members of pairs of twins reared together. Clearly, genes are a major determinant of weight and weight gain.

Fat cells

Given that genes play a role in weight gain, we want to know some details of that role. In particular, what are the digestive and metabolic processes that are affected by genes and that mediate weight gain? One answer involves fat cells, where all body fat is stored. There are between 30 billion and 40 billion fat cells in the bodies of most normal adults, but the degree of excess weight carried by ordinary American adults varies by more than the 25 to 33 per cent this figure would suggest. The additional variation comes from the size, rather than the mere number, of fat cells: the more calories one eats and fails to burn off, the larger existing fat cells become.

In one study, obese participants were found to have three times as many fat cells as normal participants (Knittle & Hirsch, 1968). In other studies, researchers have shown that rats with double the usual number of fat cells tend to be twice as fat as control rats. And when researchers cut some of the fat cells out of young rats so that they had only half as many fat cells as their littermates, those rats grew up to be only half as fat as their littermates (Faust, 1984; Hirsch & Batchelor, 1976). Because there is a link between genes and the number of fat cells, and another link between the number of fat cells and obesity, through this chain, genes are connected to obesity.

Dieting and set points

When people take diet drugs, a variety of things can happen. The drug might suppress appetite directly, which would reduce the feeling of hunger. Another drug might suppress the set point – the point at which body weight is set and that the body strives to maintain – rather than suppress appetite directly. For example, it has been suggested that some diet drugs have this effect (Stunkard, 1982), such as fenfluramine, no longer on the market due to its link to heart disease. Such an effect would be equivalent to direct appetite suppression as long as body weight was higher than the lowered set point. Once body weight fell to the lower level, appetite would return to just the degree needed to remain at that weight. When a person stopped taking the drug, the set point would return to its higher level, and the person would regain the weight that had been lost. Finally, some drugs, such as nicotine, may help people lose weight by elevating the metabolic rate of cells, causing them to burn more calories than they ordinarily would.

One reason that the set point hypothesis has become popular among psychologists is the strong tendency for obese adults, both humans and animals, to return to their original body weight after ceasing dieting. In contrast to the young rats just described, even surgical removal of fat deposits by liposuction appears not to produce permanent weight loss when it is performed on adult rats: the adults regain the fat elsewhere. This also appears to be true of liposuction performed on obese human adults (Vogt & Belluscio, 1987).

Some investigators have suggested that once adult levels of fat tissue have been reached, they are maintained at that level. The brain may detect changes in the level of body fat and influence hunger accordingly (Weigle, 1994). For example, an 'obesity gene' in mice is thought to control the ability of fat cells to produce a chemical 'satiety signal' (Zhang *et al.*, 1994). Mice that lack this gene become obese. Ordinarily, the more body fat one has, the more a satiety signal is released into the blood. Whether human obesity involves a disruption in this satiety factor or gene is not yet known. But the possibility that the level of fat stores is kept constant may help explain why some obese people find it difficult not to regain weight that they lost through dieting.

In sum, there are various routes by which genes can be responsible for excessive weight gain, including having many and large fat cells, having a high set point, and having a low metabolic rate.

Overeating

Although physiological factors such as fat regulation and metabolic rate are important determinants of body weight, there is no question that overeating can also cause obesity. The psychological factors that contribute to overeating include the breakdown of conscious restraints and emotional arousal.

Breakdown of conscious restraints

Some people stay obese by going on eating binges after dieting. An obese man may break a 2-day diet and then overeat so much that he eventually consumes more calories than he would have, had he not dieted at all. Because the diet was a conscious restraint, the breakdown of control is a factor in increased calorie intake.

To gain a more detailed understanding of the role of conscious restraints, researchers have developed a questionnaire that asks about diet, weight history, and concern with eating (for example, How often do you diet? Do you eat sensibly in front of others, yet overeat when alone?). The results show that almost everyone – whether thin, average, or overweight – can be classified into one of two categories: people who consciously restrain their eating, and people who do not. In addition, regardless of their actual weight, the eating behavior of restrained eaters is closer to that of obese individuals than to that of unrestrained eaters (Herman & Polivy, 1980; Ruderman, 1986).

A laboratory study shows what happens when restraints are dropped. Restrained and unrestrained eaters (both of normal weight) were required to drink either two milkshakes, one milkshake, or none; they then sampled several flavors of ice cream and were encouraged to eat as much as they wanted (Herman & Mack, 1975). The more milkshakes the unrestrained eaters were required to drink, the less ice cream they consumed later. In contrast, the restrained eaters who had been preloaded with two milkshakes ate more ice cream than did those who drank one milkshake or none. Thus, individuals who are trying to restrain their eating by ignoring their ordinary impulse to eat more may also come to ignore the feelings of satiety that would ordinarily halt their desire to eat. Ironically, then, this is why conscious efforts to diet often backfire.

Emotional arousal

Overweight individuals often report that they tend to eat more when they are tense or anxious, and experimental results support these reports. Obese participants eat more in a high-anxiety situation than they do in a low-anxiety situation, but normal-weight participants eat more in situations of low anxiety (McKenna, 1972). Other research indicates that any kind of emotional arousal seems to increase food intake in some obese people. In one study, overweight and normal-weight participants saw a different film in each of four sessions. Three of the films aroused various emotions: one was distressing, one amusing, and one sexually arousing. The fourth film was a boring travelogue. After viewing each of the films, the participants were asked to taste and evaluate different kinds of crackers. The obese participants ate significantly more crackers after viewing any of the arousing films than they did after seeing the travelogue. Normal-weight individuals ate the same amount of crackers regardless of which film they had seen (White, 1977).

The ability of emotional stress to elicit eating has been observed in other animals, too. This may mean that stress can activate basic brain systems that, under some conditions, result in overeating (Rowland & Antelman, 1976).

Dieting and weight control

Although genetic factors may limit the amount of weight we can comfortably lose, overweight people can still lose weight by following a weight-control program. For a program to be successful, though, it must involve something other than just extreme dieting.

Limitations of dieting

Unfortunately, most dieters are not successful, and those who succeed in shedding pounds often gain weight again after ceasing dieting. This state of affairs seems to be partly due to two deep-seated reactions to a temporary deprivation of food (which is what a diet is). The first reaction, as we've seen, is that deprivation per se can lead to subsequent overeating. In some experiments, rats were first deprived of food for 4 days, then allowed to feed until they regained their normal weights, and finally allowed to eat as much food as they wanted. These rats ate more than control rats with no history of deprivation. Thus, prior deprivation leads to subsequent overeating, even after the weight lost as a result of the deprivation has been regained (Coscina & Dixon, 1983).

The second reaction of interest is that deprivation *decreases* metabolic rate, and, as you may recall, the lower one's metabolic rate, the fewer calories expended, and the higher one's weight. Consequently, the calorie reduction during dieting is partly offset by the lowered metabolic rate, making it difficult for dieters to meet their goals. The reduced metabolic rate caused by dieting may also explain why many people find it harder and harder to lose weight with each successive diet: the body responds to each bout of dieting with a reduction in metabolic rate (Brownell, 1988).

Both reactions to dieting – binge-eating and lowered metabolic rate – are understandable in evolutionary terms. Until very recently in human history, whenever people experienced deprivation it was because of a scarcity of food in the environment. One adaptive response to such scarcity is to overeat and store in our bodies as much food as possible whenever it is available. Natural selection may have favored the ability to overeat following deprivation, which explains the overeating reaction. A second adaptive response to a scarcity of food in the environment is for organisms to decrease the rate at which they expend their limited calories, so natural selection may have favored the ability to lower one's metabolic rate during deprivation. This explains the second reaction of interest. Over the millennia, these two reactions have served our species well in times of famine, but once famine is not a concern – as in most economically developed countries today – they prevent obese dieters from losing weight permanently (Polivy & Herman, 1985).

Weight control programs

To lose weight and keep it off, it seems that overweight individuals need to establish a new set of permanent eating habits (as opposed to temporary dieting) and engage in a program of exercise. Some support for this conclusion is provided by the following study, which compared various methods for treating obesity (Craighead *et al.*, 1981; Wadden *et al.*, 1997).

For 6 months, obese individuals followed one of three treatment regimens: (1) lifestyle change through behavior modification of eating and exercise habits, (2) drug therapy using an appetite suppressant, and (3) a combination of behavior modification and drug therapy. Participants in all three treatment groups were given information about exercise and extensive nutritional counseling, including a diet of no more than 1200 calories per day. Participants in the behavior modification groups were taught to become aware of situations that prompted them to overeat, to change the conditions associated with their overeating, to reward themselves for appropriate eating behavior, and to develop a suitable exercise regimen. In addition to the three treatment groups, there were two control groups: one consisted of participants waiting to take part in the study, and the other of participants who saw a physician for traditional treatment of weight problems.

Table 10.1 presents the results of the study. The participants in all three treatment groups lost more weight than the participants in the two control groups, with the group combining behavior modification and drug therapy losing the most weight and the behavior-modification-only group losing the least. However, during the year after treatment, a striking reversal developed. The behavior-modification-only group regained far less weight than the two other treatment groups; these participants maintained an average weight loss of nearly 20 pounds by the end of the year, whereas the weight

losses for the drug-therapy-only group and the combined-treatment group regained roughly two-thirds of the weight they had initially lost.

What caused this reversal? An increased sense of self-efficacy or self-control may have been a factor. Participants who made lifestyle changes as a result of the behavior-modification-only treatment could attribute their weight loss to their own efforts, thereby strengthening their resolve to continue controlling their weight after the treatment ended. Participants who received an appetite suppressant, on the other hand, probably attributed their weight loss to the medication and did not develop a sense of self-control. Another possible factor stems from the fact that the medication had decreased the participants' feelings of hunger, or temporarily lowered their set point, and consequently participants in the drug-therapy-only group and the combined-treatment group may not have been sufficiently prepared to cope with the increase in hunger they felt when the medication was stopped.

Anorexia and bulimia

Although obesity is the most common eating problem, the opposite problem has also surfaced in the form of anorexia nervosa and bulimia. Both of these disorders involve a pathological desire not to gain weight and disproportionately strike women.

Anorexia nervosa is an eating disorder characterized by extreme, self-imposed weight loss, such that an individual weighs less than 85 per cent of his/her expected minimum normal weight. Some anorexics in fact weigh less than 50 per cent of their normal weight. Despite the extreme loss of weight and the resulting problems, the typical anorexic denies that there is a problem and refuses to gain weight. In fact, anorexics frequently think that they look too fat. Anorexics achieve and maintain their pathologically low body weights either by restricting their caloric intake, or by also binge-eating followed by purging, by means of self-induced vomiting or the misuse of laxatives. For females to be diagnosed as anorexic, in addition to the weight loss, they must also have stopped menstruating. The weight loss can lead to a number of dangerous side-effects, including emaciation, susceptibility to infection, and other symptoms of undernourishment. These side-effects can lead to death.

Anorexia is relatively rare. Its prevalence across Western Europe and the USA is about 0.3 per cent. However, this represents more than a doubling since the 1950s, although the frequency seems to have stabilized since the 1970s (Hoek & van Hoeken, 2003). Anorexia is 20 times more likely to occur in women than in men, and the majority of anorexics are young women between their teens and their thirties. Typically, anorexics are entirely focused on food, carefully calculating the amount of calories in anything they might

TABLE 10.1 WEIGHT LOSS FOLLOWING DIFFERENT TREATMENTS

Weight loss in pounds at the end of 6 months of treatment and on a follow-up 1 year later. Participants in the two control groups were not available for the 1-year follow-up.

	Weight loss after treatment	Weight loss 1 year later
Treatment groups		
Behavior modification only	24.0	19.8
Drug therapy only	31.9	13.8
Combined treatment	33.7	10.1
Control groups		
Waiting list	2.9 (gain)	–
Physician office visits	13.2	–

consume. Sometimes this concern reaches the point of obsession, as when one anorexic commented to her therapist, 'Of course I had breakfast; I ate my Cheerio [a single small piece of breakfast cereal],' or when another said, 'I won't lick a postage stamp – one never knows about calories' (Bruch, 1973). The obsession with food and possible weight gains leads some anorexics to become compulsive exercisers as well, sometimes exercising vigorously several hours a day (Logue, 1991).

Bulimia is an eating disorder characterized by recurrent episodes of binge-eating (rapid consumption of a large amount of food in a discrete period of time coupled with a sense of lack of control), followed by attempts to purge the excess by means of vomiting, laxative use, or fasting and excessive exercise. The binges can be frequent and extreme. A survey of bulimic women found that most women binged at least once per day (usually in the evening) and that an average binge involved consuming some 4800 calories (often sweet or salty carbohydrate foods). However, because of the purges that follow the binges, a bulimic person's weight may stay relatively normal, which allows bulimics to keep their eating disorder hidden. But this behavior can have a high physiological cost. Vomiting and use of laxatives can disrupt the balance of potassium in the body, which can result in problems like dehydration, cardiac arrhythmias, and urinary infections.

Like anorexia, bulimia primarily afflicts young women. But bulimia is somewhat more frequent than anorexia, with an estimated 1.1 per cent meriting a full diagnosis in Western Europe and the USA, and up to 5.4 per cent showing at least some symptoms (Hoek & van Hoeken, 2003).

Researchers have suggested a variety of causes for anorexia and bulimia, including social, biological, and personality or family factors. It is probably necessary for several of these factors to occur together for any individual to develop an eating disorder.

Sociocultural causes

Many psychologists have proposed that social and cultural factors play major roles in anorexia and bulimia. In particular, they point to Western society's emphasis on thinness in women. This emphasis has increased markedly in the past 50 years, which fits with the observation that the incidence of eating disorders has also increased during that period. An indication of this trend is the change in what people regard as a 'perfect' woman's figure. The photos place Jayne Mansfield, who was widely thought to have an ideal figure in the 1950s, next to a photo of actress Nicole Kidman, who reflects today's ideal. Kidman is clearly much thinner than Mansfield, especially in the hips and thighs, the region of the body with which most women experience deep dissatisfaction.

But how exactly do media images of the 'ideal' female body sink in and account for high rates of disordered eating?

Jayne Mansfield (left) represented the perfect female figure for the 1950s, whereas Nicole Kidman (right) is framed as the perfect female figure today. However, there has also been something of a cultural backlash in recent years in favour of 'healthy women' (e.g. the 'real women have curves' Dove campaign) and these claims often describe super-skinny models and Hollywood stars as sick or unhealthy.

Insight into this process is offered by **objectification theory**, a sociocultural account of how being raised in a culture that sexually objectifies the female body (both within the visual mass media and within actual interpersonal encounters) fundamentally alters girls' and women's self-views and well-being (Fredrickson & Roberts, 1997; Fredrickson *et al.,* 2011). Sexual objectification occurs any time a person is treated first and foremost as a body valued for its sexual use to (or consumption by) others. Sexual objectification is a dehumanizing form of interpersonal regard. It reduces the targeted person's full humanity to the status of an object for the observer's benefit.

The first psychological consequence of repeated exposure to cultural practices of sexually objectifying female bodies, the theory holds, is that girls and women learn to internalize an objectifying observer's perspective on their own body. This preoccupation with physical appearance is termed **self-objectification** (see the Concept Review Table). In brief, self-objectification means that a person thinks about and values her own body more from a third-person perspective, focusing on observable body attributes ('How do I look?'), rather than from a first-person perspective, focusing on privileged, or unobservable body attributes ('How do I feel?'). Self-objectification has been shown to be both a relatively stable trait – with some girls and women self-objectifying more than others – and a temporary state – with some situations pulling for self-objectification more than others (Breines *et al.,* 2008). Self-objectification has been shown to affect women of various ethnic backgrounds (Hebl *et al.,* 2004) as well as gay men (Martins *et al.,* 2007).

Objectification theory claims that self-objectification causes a range of psychological and emotional reactions. First and foremost, self-objectification leads to a form of self-consciousness characterized by vigilant monitoring of the body's outward appearance. This preoccupation with appearance has been shown to disrupt a person's stream of consciousness and thereby limit the mental resources that she can devote to other activities (Quinn *et al.,* 2006). It also creates a predictable set of emotional reactions, including increased shame and anxiety and diminished positive emotions and sexual pleasure. Over time, these emotional reactions can accumulate and compound, which explains why certain health and mental health problems disproportionately afflict girls and women. Chief among these problems are various forms of disordered eating, which include anorexia and bulimia, as well as restrained eating (dieting) more generally. But the theory doesn't stop there. It accounts for gender differences in depression and sexual dysfunction as well (see the Concept Review Table).

Risks for these three problems – disordered eating, depression, and sexual dysfunction – not only coincide with gender but also coincide with age. Intriguingly, the risks change in

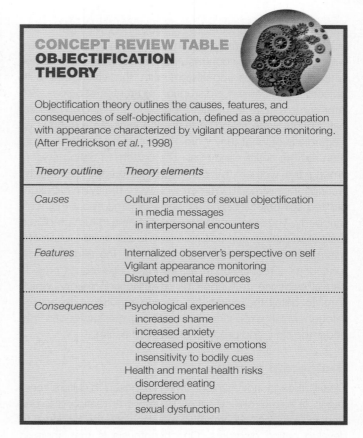

CONCEPT REVIEW TABLE
OBJECTIFICATION THEORY

Objectification theory outlines the causes, features, and consequences of self-objectification, defined as a preoccupation with appearance characterized by vigilant appearance monitoring. (After Fredrickson *et al.*, 1998)

Theory outline	Theory elements

Causes	Cultural practices of sexual objectification
	    in media messages
	    in interpersonal encounters

Features	Internalized observer's perspective on self Vigilant appearance monitoring Disrupted mental resources

Consequences	Psychological experiences
	    increased shame
	    increased anxiety
	    decreased positive emotions
	    insensitivity to bodily cues
	Health and mental health risks
	    disordered eating
	    depression
	    sexual dysfunction

step with observable life-course changes in the female body: they first emerge for girls in early adolescence and lessen for women in late middle age. Objectification theory notes that women are most targeted for sexual objectification during their years of reproductive potential and uses this fact to explain these changing risk patterns over the life course.

Survey studies of college women show that self-objectification, feelings of shame and anxiety about one's body, decreased positive emotions, insensitivity to bodily cues, disordered eating, and depressed mood are all associated with one another (Noll & Fredrickson, 1998; Tiggemann & Williams, 2012). But those are simply correlations. How do we know that self-objectification can be a cause of disordered eating, and not just a consequence or a symptom? A series of clever laboratory experiments provided the necessary evidence. In these studies, participants – male and female college students – believed they were partaking in a study on consumer decisions. Under this guise, they sampled various products and rated how those products made them feel. When it came time to try on and evaluate a garment (in a private 'dressing room'), participants were randomly assigned to try on either a bulky sweater or a swimsuit (each was available in a range of sizes). For both men and women, trying on the swimsuit produced a self-conscious state of self-objectification. But that's where any similarity between men and women ended. Later came a difficult math test (presented as another study altogether). Men performed equally well on the math test regardless of what they were wearing. Women, by contrast, performed worse on the test when wearing less, consistent with the claim that self-objectification causes a disruption of mental resources. Still later came a taste test. After redressing in their own clothes, participants were asked to taste and evaluate a candy bar. Regardless of what they wore – swimsuit or sweater – most men ate the entire candy bar. The pattern of eating evident among the women, by contrast, was greatly affected by wearing the swimsuit. Women who wore the swimsuit experienced self-objectification as well as shame about their current body. The emotional reaction of shame in turn predicted restrained eating, perhaps as a way to correct the shameful mismatch between their own body and the ultra-thin cultural ideals (Fredrickson et al., 1998). These results provide causal evidence in support of objectification theory, which aims to detail the psychological and emotional processes through which exposure of objectifying messages can 'get under the skin' and produce disordered eating.

Biological causes

Clearly, though, not everyone who is exposed to cultural messages of sexual objectification develops an eating disorder. Certain biological vulnerabilities may increase the tendency to develop eating disorders. One hypothesis is that anorexia is caused by malfunctions of the hypothalamus, the part of the brain that helps regulate eating. Anorexic individuals show lowered functioning of the hypothalamus and abnormalities in several of the neuro-chemicals that are important to the functioning of the hypothalamus (Fava et al., 1989). With regard to bulimia, there may be a deficiency in the neurotransmitter serotonin, which plays a role in both mood regulation and appetite (Mitchell & deZwann, 1993) or in executive functioning, which affects decision-making and impulse control (Brand et al., 2007).

Familial causes

Personality and family factors may also play a role in anorexia and bulimia. Many young women with eating disorders come from families that demand 'perfection' and extreme self-control but do not allow expressions of warmth or conflict (Bruch, 1973; Minuchin et al., 1978). Some young women may seek to gain some control over, and expressions of concern from, their parents by controlling their eating habits, eventually developing anorexia. Others may turn to binge-eating when they feel emotionally upset or are painfully aware of their low self-esteem (Polivy & Herman, 1993).

Therapies designed to help people with eating disorders regain healthy eating habits and deal with the emotional issues they face have proven useful (Agras, 1993; Fairburn & Hay, 1992). Drugs that regulate serotonin levels can also be helpful, particularly for people with bulimia (Mitchell &

deZwann, 1993). Anorexia and bulimia are serious disorders, however, and people who have them often continue to have significant problems for several years.

INTERIM SUMMARY

➜ Humans have both innate and learned taste preferences, and aversions that guide choice of foods. Homeostatic hunger signals, which arise when the body is low in calorie-containing fuels such as glucose, produce appetite partly by causing the individual to perceive food incentives as more attractive and pleasant.

➜ Hunger is largely controlled by homeostatic deficit and satiety signals. Certain neurons in the brain, especially in the brain stem and hypothalamus, detect shortages in glucose and trigger hunger. Other nutrient detectors, especially in the liver, detect increasing energy stores and trigger satiety. A satiety signal, in the form of the hormone cholecystokinin, is also released from the intestines to help stop hunger and eating.

➜ Two regions of the brain are critical to hunger: the lateral hypothalamus and the ventromedial hypothalamus. Destruction of the lateral hypothalamus leads to undereating; destruction of the ventromedial hypothalamus leads to overeating.

➜ People become obese primarily because (1) they are genetically predisposed to be overweight, or (2) they overeat (for psychological reasons). The influence of genes is mediated by their effect on fat cells, metabolic rate, and set points. As for overeating and obesity, obese people tend to overeat when they break a diet, eat more when emotionally aroused, and are more responsive to external hunger cues than normal-weight individuals.

➜ In treating obesity, extreme diets appear ineffective because deprivation leads to subsequent overeating and to a lowered metabolic rate. What seems to work best is to establish a lifestyle change characterized by a new set of permanent eating habits and habitual engagement in exercise.

➜ Anorexia nervosa is characterized by extreme, self-imposed weight loss. Bulimia is characterized by recurrent episodes of binge eating, followed by attempts to purge the excess by means of vomiting, laxatives, fasting, or excessive exercise. Possible causes of these eating disorders include personality factors such as low self-esteem, social factors such as a cultural emphasis on thinness and pervasive cultural messages that objectify the female body, and biological factors such as low serotonin levels.

CRITICAL THINKING QUESTIONS

1 A potent negative emotion, such as feeling ashamed of one's body, can contribute to both overeating and obesity, as well as to undereating and various eating disorders. Why is this so? Describe the pathways to each deviation from normal eating. What do you think determines which pathway is followed?

2 The text describes a number of problems associated with dieting, or restrained eating. Why does dieting continue to be very popular? What sociocultural factors come into play?

GENDER AND SEXUALITY

Like thirst and hunger, sexual desire is a powerful motivation. There are, however, some important differences. Sex is a social motive – it typically involves another person – whereas the survival motives concern only the individual. In addition, sex does not involve an internal deficit that needs to be regulated and remedied for the organism to survive. Consequently, social motives do not lend themselves to a homeostatic analysis.

With regard to sex, two critical distinctions should be kept in mind. The first stems from the fact that, although we begin to mature sexually at puberty, the basis for our sexual identity is established in the womb. We therefore distinguish between adult sexuality (that is, beginning with changes at puberty) and early sexual development. The second distinction is between the biological and environmental determinants of sexual behaviors and feelings. For many aspects of sexual development and adult sexuality, a fundamental question is the extent to which the behavior or feeling in question is a product of biology (particularly hormones), environment and learning (early experiences and cultural norms), or interactions between biological and environmental factors.

Early sexual development

To have gratifying social and sexual experiences as adults, most individuals need to develop an appropriate **gender identity**, in which males come to think of themselves as males and females as females. This development is quite complex and actually begins before birth. For the first couple of months after conception, only the chromosomes of a human embryo indicate whether it will develop into a boy or a girl. Up to this stage, both sexes are identical in appearance and have tissues that will eventually develop into either testes or ovaries, as well as a genital tubercle that will become either a penis or a clitoris. But between 2 and 3 months after conception, a primitive sex gland, or gonad, develops into testes if the embryo is genetically male or into ovaries if the embryo is genetically female (see Chapter 2). Once testes or ovaries

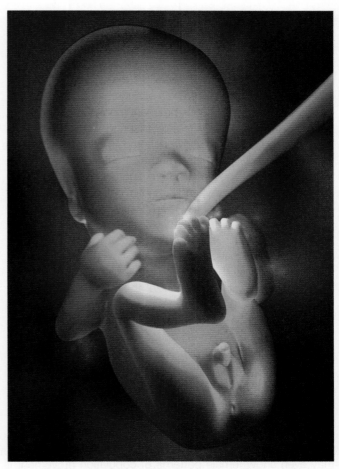

If the embryonic sex glands produce enough androgen, the fetus will develop male genitals. Shown here is a male fetus 11 weeks after conception.

develop, they produce the sex hormones, which then control the development of the internal reproductive structures and the external genitals. The sex hormones are even more important for prenatal development than they will be for the expression of adult sexuality.

The critical hormone in genital development is androgen. If the embryonic sex glands produce enough androgen, the newborn will have male genitals; if there is insufficient androgen, the newborn will have female genitals even if it is genetically male. Conversely, if androgens are added artificially, the newborn will have male genitals even if it is genetically female. In other words, the presence or absence of a male (Y) chromosome normally influences sexual development simply by determining whether the embryo will secrete androgens. The anatomical development of the female embryo does not require female hormones, only the absence of male hormones. In short, nature will produce a female unless androgen intervenes.

The influence of androgen, called **androgenization**, extends far beyond anatomy. After it has molded the genitals, androgen begins to operate on the brain cells. Studies with rats provide evidence that prenatal androgen changes the volume and detailed structure of cells in the fetus's hypothalamus, an organ that regulates motivation in humans as well as in rats (Money, 1987). These effects of androgen essentially masculinize the brain and may be responsible for some masculine traits and behaviors that appear months or years later, such as higher levels of aggressiveness.

In a series of experiments, pregnant monkeys were injected with androgen, and their female offspring were observed in detail. These offspring showed some anatomical changes (penises instead of clitorises) and also acted differently from normal females. They were more aggressive in play, more masculine in sexual play, and less intimidated by approaching peers (Goy, 1968; Phoenix, Goy, & Resko, 1968). These findings indicate that some gender-typical behaviors (such as greater aggression in males) are partly hormonally determined in non-human animals.

Early hormonal abnormalities can also have the opposite consequence. They can 'feminize' the later sexual behavior of males. A striking example is 'maternal stress': a change in the sexual behavior of male rats whose mothers experienced high emotional stress during pregnancy (Ward, 1992). High levels of stress in a pregnant mother rat trigger hormonal events that result in a decrease in the amount of androgens produced by the male embryo's testes. That, in turn, results in a reduction of androgen reaching the developing brain. The hypothalamus and other brain regions appear to develop differently in such embryos. When these male rats become adults, they show less male sexual behavior and may even show female patterns of copulation movement if they are mounted by another male.

It is not known whether similar effects on brain development or behavior occur in humans. Although some believe that these experiments may provide insights into the basis of human heterosexual versus homosexual orientation, there are differences between the results of these animal experiments and human behavior. For example, male rats born to maternally stressed mothers tend to show less sexual behavior of any kind than ordinary male rats, but this is not true of gay men compared with heterosexual men. Nevertheless, these examples illustrate the importance of early hormonal environment for the later sexual behavior of non-human animals, and they raise the possibility that prenatal hormones may be important for human sexual motivation as well.

Hormones versus environment

In humans, much of what is known about the effects of prenatal hormones and early environment has been uncovered by studies of individuals who, for various reasons, were exposed to the prenatal hormones that would ordinarily be experienced by one sex but then were raised in a social role that would ordinarily typify the other sex. In most such cases, the assigned label and the sex role in which the individual is raised have a much greater influence on gender identity than the individual's genes and hormones.

For example, many thousands of women born during the 1950s and 1960s were exposed to an anti-miscarriage drug, diethylstilbestrol, that had unexpected hormone-like effects on brain development. Ordinarily, the testosterone (the major androgen) secreted by a male embryo's testes is converted in the brain into a substance similar to diethylstilbestrol. Pregnant women who took the drug therefore unknowingly exposed their fetus to a chemical environment similar to that experienced by the developing brain of a normal male. For male fetuses, this would have little consequence: Their brains were already exposed to male patterns of chemical stimulation. But the female fetuses were exposed to a male-like chemical stimulation for the period when their mothers took the drug. For the overwhelming majority of these daughters, the prenatal exposure had no detectable effect. Most girls who were exposed prenatally to diethylstilbestrol went on to grow up like other girls and to become indistinguishable from women with normal prenatal experience. Social environment, in other words, appears to have had a much greater influence on the sexual and gender development of these women than prenatal hormones.

But this is not to say that the prenatal chemical environment had absolutely no effect. Researchers have detected several subtle differences that characterize at least some of the women exposed to diethylstilbestrol. For example, a slightly higher proportion of these women appear to be homosexual or bisexual than would ordinarily be expected. Sexual orientation is not identical to gender identity, but in this case a slight effect of prenatal hormones on both may be reflected. (Sexual orientation is discussed in detail later in this section.) Similarly, these women show slightly lower ratings on some measures of 'maternal interest,' such as finding infants attractive, even though they are not different from other women by most other measures of parental, sexual, or social behavior and attitudes (Ehrhardt et al., 1989). Such studies suggest that although prenatal hormonal events may have some subtle consequences for later sexual and social development, their effect is much weaker in humans than in non-human animals. For humans, social and cultural factors appear to be dominant (Money, 1980).

There are, however, some studies that point to the opposite conclusion. The most famous of these occurred in remote villages of the Dominican Republic. It involved 18 XY individuals (genetic males) who, owing to a condition known as androgen insensitivity, were born with internal reproductive organs that were clearly male but with external genitals that were closer to those of females, including a clitoris-like sex organ. In androgen insensitivity, the gonads develop as normal testes and begin to secrete testosterone and other androgens. However, the receptor systems that would be activated by androgens are missing from at least some of the body tissues that would ordinarily be masculinized by the hormones. Even though androgens are secreted and are present in the bloodstream of such a boy, they do not produce the male pattern of genital and physical development. All 18 of the infants studied had been raised as girls, which was at odds with both their genes and their prenatal hormonal environment. When they reached puberty, the surge of male hormones produced the usual bodily changes and turned their clitoris-like sex organs into penis-like organs. The vast majority of these males-reared-as-females rapidly turned into males. They seemed to have little difficulty adjusting to a male gender identity. They went off to work as miners and woodsmen, and some found female sexual partners. In this case, biology triumphed over environment (Imperato-McGinley et al., 1979).

There is controversy, however, about these Dominican boys who appeared to be girls. They do not seem to have been raised as ordinary girls (which is not surprising, in that they had ambiguous genitals). Rather, they seemed to have been treated as half-girl, half-boy, which could have made their subsequent transition to males easier (Money, 1987). A study in the UK compared 22 XY individuals with androgen insensitivity, all reared as girls and identifying as women in adulthood, to typical XX females. No differences were observed in life outcome measures, including quality of life, gender identity, sexual orientation, gender-typical behavior, marital status, and personality traits. This evidence underscores the importance of androgenization, suggesting that two X chromosomes and ovaries are not required for typical feminine development (Hines et al., 2003; see also Mazur, 2005).

In other cases, the results of conflict between prenatal hormones and social rearing are less clear. In the most dramatic example, identical twin boys had a completely normal prenatal environment. But at the age of 8 months, one of the boys had his penis completely severed in what was supposed to be a routine circumcision. Ten months later, the parents authorized surgery to turn their child into a little girl – the testes were removed and a vagina was given preliminary shape. The child was then given female sex hormones and raised as a girl. Within a few years, the child seemed to have assumed a female gender identity: she preferred more feminine clothes, toys, and activities than her twin brother did. Because she appeared to be a normal girl in many ways, most investigators concluded that this was a case in which social environment had won out.

However, studies of the child at the time she reached puberty revealed that the outcome was more complex. As a teenager, she was unhappy and appeared to be confused about her sexuality, even though she had not been told about her original sex or the sex-change operation she had undergone. In interviews, she refused to draw a picture of a woman and instead would draw only a man. Aspects of her body language, such as her walking gait and patterns of posture and movement, were masculine in appearance. Socially, she had considerably more than the usual degree of difficulty in forming relationships with her peers.

A follow-up on this individual found that he eventually rejected the female gender identity and has successfully lived as a male since then (Diamond & Sigmondson, 1997). In the long run, the attempt to control his gender identity through socialization and to raise him as a 'normal girl' was unsuccessful. It is difficult to know the precise source of the difficulty he experienced in emotional and social adjustment at puberty. Explanations include the possibility that his early brain development as a male placed constraints on his later ability to adapt to a female gender identity.

What can we conclude about gender identity? Clearly, prenatal hormones and environment are both major determinants of gender identity and typically work in harmony. When they clash, as they do in some individuals, most experts believe that environment will dominate. But this is a controversial area, and expert opinion may change as additional data are gathered.

Adult sexuality

Changes in body hormone systems occur at puberty, which usually begins between the ages of 11 and 14 (see Figure 10.4). The hypothalamus begins to secrete chemicals called *gonadotropin-releasing factors*; these stimulate the pituitary gland, which lies immediately below the hypothalamus. The pituitary secretes sex hormones, called *gonadotropins*, into the bloodstream. These circulate through the body and reach the gonads – ovaries in females and testes in males – which generate egg or sperm cells. Gonadotropins activate the gonads, causing them to secrete additional sex hormones into the bloodstream.

In women, the hypothalamus releases its gonadotropin-releasing factors on a monthly cycle, rising and falling approximately every 28 days. This stimulates the pituitary to secrete

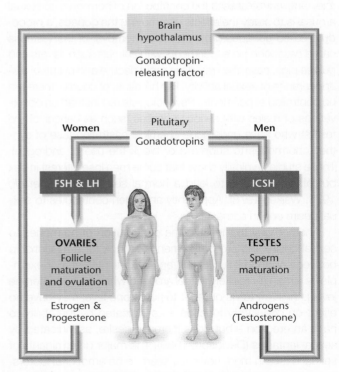

FIGURE 10.4 The Hormonal System Involved in Sex. *By way of hormones, the hypothalamus directs the pituitary, which in turn directs the gonads to secrete the sex hormones.*

two gonadotropins: follicle-stimulating hormone (FSH) and luteinizing hormone (LH), also on a monthly cycle. These hormones activate the ovaries. Follicle-stimulating hormone stimulates the ovaries to generate follicles, clusters of cells in the ovaries that allow fertile eggs to develop. Once a follicle is generated, it begins to secrete the female hormone, estrogen. Estrogen is released into the bloodstream to affect the body's sexual development and, in many species of animals, to activate sexual motivation in the brain. The second gonadotropin, luteinizing hormone, is released from the pituitary slightly later than follicle-stimulating hormone. Luteinizing hormone causes ovulation, the release of a mature fertile egg cell from the follicle. When the follicle releases its egg, it also secretes a second female hormone, progesterone, which prepares the uterus for implantation of a fertilized egg and, in some species of animals, also activates sexual motivation in the brain.

In men, the hypothalamus secretes gonadotropin-releasing factor in a constant fashion rather than in a monthly cycle. This causes the male pituitary to constantly release its gonadotropin, called *interstitial cell stimulating hormone* (ICSH), into the bloodstream. ICSH causes male testes to produce mature sperm cells and dramatically boost secretion of androgens, especially testosterone. Testosterone and other androgens stimulate the development of male physical characteristics and, in most species of animals, act on the brain to activate sexual desire.

Effects of hormones on desire and arousal

In many species, sexual arousal is closely tied to variations in hormonal levels. In humans, however, hormones play less of a role. One way to assess the contribution of hormones to sexual arousal is to study the effects of removing the gonads, a procedure called *gonadectomy*. (In males, removal of the testes is called *castration*.) In experiments with animals such as rats and guinea pigs, castration results in rapid decline and eventual disappearance of sexual activity. For humans, of course, there are no controlled experiments. Psychologists rely instead on observations of males with serious illnesses (such as cancer of the testes) who have undergone chemical castration (use of synthetic hormones to suppress or block the use of androgen). These studies typically show that some men lose interest in sex but others continue to lead a normal sex life (Money *et al.*, 1976; Walker, 1978). Apparently androgen contributes to sexual desire only in some cases.

Another way to measure the contribution of hormones to sexual desire and arousal in men is to look for a relationship between hormonal fluctuation and sexual interest. For example, is a man more likely to feel aroused when his testosterone level is high? It turns out that testosterone level may have no effect on copulatory function – as indicated by the ability to have an erection – but does increase desire, as indicated by sexual fantasies (Davidson, 1989). The major determinants of sexual desire in men, however, seem to be emotional factors. For males as well as females, the most common cause of low desire in couples seeking sex therapy is marital conflict.

Sexual desire is even less dependent on hormones in women. This contrasts with non-primate species, in which female sexual behavior is highly dependent on sexual hormones. In all other animals, removal of the ovaries results in cessation of sexual activity. Such a female ceases to be receptive to the male and usually resists sexual advances. The major exception is the human female. Following menopause (when the ovaries have ceased to function), most women do not experience diminished sexual desire. In fact, some women show increased interest in sex after menopause, possibly because they are no longer concerned about becoming pregnant. There is evidence to indicate that women's sexual desire is facilitated by trace amounts of sex hormones in the bloodstream (Sherwin, 1988) and that the types of men that women find attractive vary with normal monthly hormone fluctuation (Gangestad *et al.*, 2007). However, the level required is so low that it may be exceeded in most women and hence not play a significant role in changes in overall desire.

Studies of the relationship between hormonal fluctuation and sexual arousal in premenopausal females lead to a similar conclusion: normal changes in hormones control arousal in other animals but not in humans. In female mammals, hormones fluctuate cyclically, with accompanying changes in fertility. During the first part of the mammalian cycle (while the egg is being prepared for fertilization), the ovaries secrete estrogen, which prepares the uterus for implantation and also tends to arouse sexual interest. After ovulation occurs, both progesterone and estrogen are secreted. This fertility or estrous cycle is accompanied by a variation in sexual motivation in most mammalian species. Most female animals are receptive to sexual advances by a male only during the period of ovulation, when the estrogen level is at its highest; during this time, the female is said to be 'in heat,' Among primates, however, sexual activity is less strongly influenced by the fertility cycle. Monkey, ape, and chimpanzee females copulate during all phases of the cycle, although ovulation is still the period of most intense sexual activity. In the human female, sexual desire and arousal seem to be affected much more by social and emotional factors.

In sum, the degree of hormonal control over sexual behavior is lower in humans than in other animals. Still, even for humans there may be some hormonal control, as witnessed by the relationship between testosterone levels and sexual desire in men.

Neural control

In one sense, the primary sex organ is the brain. The brain is where sexual desire originates and where sexual behavior is controlled. In humans, the sexual function of the brain extends to the control of sexual thoughts, images, and fantasies. Within the brain, sexual hormones can influence neural function in adult individuals. Next, we discuss how sexual hormones also influence the physical growth and connection patterns of neurons in early life for all mammalian species, including humans, and in adults for at least some species (Breedlove, 1994).

The nervous system is affected by sexual hormones at many levels. At the level of the spinal cord, neural circuits control the movements of copulation. In males, these include erection of the penis, pelvic movements, and ejaculation. All of these actions can be elicited in a reflex fashion in men whose spinal cords have been severed by injury and who have no conscious body sensations. Similarly, clinical studies of women with spinal injury indicate that vaginal secretions in response to genital stimulation and pelvic movements may be controlled by neural reflex circuits within the spinal cord (Offir, 1982).

Higher levels of the brain, especially the hypothalamus, contain the neural systems that are important to more complex aspects of sexual behavior. For example, sexual pursuit and copulation can be elicited in both males and females of many animal species by electrical stimulation of hypothalamic regions. Even in humans, stimulation of brain regions near the hypothalamus has been reported to induce intense sexual feelings and desire (Heath, 1972). Conversely, lesions of the hypothalamus can eliminate sexual behavior in many species, including humans.

Early experiences

The environment also influences adult sexuality. Early experience is a major determinant of the sexual behavior of many mammals and can affect specific sexual responses. For instance, in their play, young monkeys exhibit many of the postures required later for copulation. When wrestling with their peers, infant male monkeys display hindquarter grasping and thrusting responses that are components of adult sexual behavior. Infant female monkeys retreat when threatened by an aggressive male infant and stand steadfastly in a posture similar to the stance required to support the weight of the male during copulation. These presexual responses appear as early as 60 days of age and become more frequent and refined as the monkey matures. Their early appearance suggests that they are innate responses to specific stimuli, and the modification and refinement of these responses through experience indicate that learning plays a role in the development of the adult sexual pattern.

Experience also affects the interpersonal aspect of sex. Monkeys raised in partial isolation (in separate wire cages, where they can see other monkeys but cannot have contact with them) are usually unable to copulate at maturity. The male monkeys are able to perform the mechanics of sex: they masturbate to ejaculation at about the same frequency as normal monkeys. But when confronted with a sexually receptive female, they do not seem to know how to assume the correct posture for copulation. They are aroused, but they aimlessly grope the female or their own bodies. Their problem is not just a deficiency of specific responses. These monkeys have social or affectional problems. Even in

Normal heterosexual behaviour in primates such as these snow monkeys depends on an affectionate bond with a member of the other sex, as well as on hormones and the development of specific sexual responses.

non-sexual situations, they are unable to relate to other monkeys, exhibiting either fear and flight or extreme aggression. Apparently, normal heterosexual behavior in primates depends not only on hormones and the development of specific sexual responses but also on an affectional bond with a member of the other sex. This bond is an outgrowth of earlier interactions with the mother and peers, through which the young monkey learns to trust, to expose its delicate parts without fear of harm, to accept and enjoy physical contact with others, and to be motivated to seek the company of others (Harlow, 1971).

Although we must be cautious about generalizing these findings to human sexual development, clinical observations of human infants suggest certain parallels. Human infants develop their first feelings of trust and affection through a warm and loving relationship with their primary caretaker (see Chapter 3). This basic trust is a prerequisite for satisfactory interactions with peers. And affectionate relationships with other youngsters of both sexes lay the groundwork for the intimacy required for sexual relationships among adults.

Cultural influences

Culture also influences the expression of sexual desire. Unlike that of other primates, human sexual behavior is strongly determined by culture. For example, every society places some restrictions on sexual behavior. Incest (sexual relations within the family) is prohibited in almost all cultures. Other aspects of sexual behavior – sexual activity among children, homosexuality, masturbation, and premarital sex – are permitted in varying degrees by different societies. Among preliterate cultures, acceptable sexual activity varies widely. Some very permissive societies encourage autoerotic activities and sex play among children of both sexes and allow them to observe adult sexual activity. The Chewa of Africa, for example, believe that if children are not allowed to exercise themselves sexually, they will be unable to produce offspring later. The Sambia of New Guinea have institutionalized bisexuality: from prepuberty until marriage, a boy lives with other males and engages in homosexual practices (Herdt, 1984).

In contrast, very restrictive societies try to control pre-adolescent sexual behavior and prevent children from learning about sex. The Cuna of South America believe that children should be totally ignorant about sex until they are married; they do not even permit their children to watch animals give birth.

Although the most obvious way to study cultural differences is to investigate practices in different countries, one can also look at culture changes that occur within a country. One such change occurred in the USA and other Western countries between the 1940s and the 1970s. In the 1940s and 1950s, the USA and most other Western countries would have been classified as sexually restrictive. Traditionally, the existence of prepubertal sexuality had been ignored or denied. Marital sex was considered the only legitimate sexual outlet, and other forms of sexual expression (homosexual activities, premarital and extramarital sex) were generally condemned and often prohibited by law. Of course, many members of these societies engaged in such activities, but often with feelings of shame.

Over the years, sexual activities became less restricted. Premarital intercourse became more acceptable and more frequent. Among American university-educated individuals interviewed in the 1940s, 27 per cent of the women and 49 per cent of the men had engaged in premarital sex by age 21 (Kinsey *et al.,* 1948; Kinsey *et al.,* 1953). In contrast, several surveys of American university students conducted in the 1970s reported percentages ranging from 40 per cent to over 80 per cent for both males and females (Hunt, 1974; Tavris, & Sadd, 1977). Over the past several decades, there has been a gradual trend toward initiating sex at an earlier age. Roughly 50 per cent of 16–17 year olds in the USA report having had sexual intercourse (Centers for Disease Control, 2012). Figure 10.5 gives the reported incidence of premarital intercourse in studies conducted over a 35-year span. Note that the change in sexual behavior was greater among women than among men and that the biggest changes occurred in the late 1960s. These changes led many observers of the social scene in the 1970s to conclude that a 'sexual revolution' had occurred.

Today it seems that the sexual revolution has been stymied by the fear of sexually transmitted diseases, particularly AIDS. Moreover, the 'revolution' may have involved behavior more than feelings. In interviews with young couples in the USA in the 1970s, only 20 per cent thought that sex between casual acquaintances was completely acceptable (Peplau *et al.,* 1977). In a similar vein, although women are becoming more like men with regard to sexual behavior, they continue

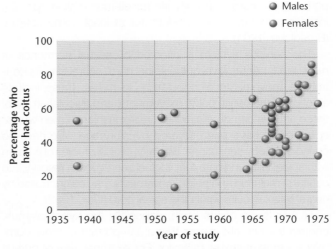

FIGURE 10.5 Reported Incidence of Premarital Coitus. *Each data point represents findings from a study of the incidence of premarital sex among college men and women. Note the marked upward trend starting in the 1960s.*

to differ from men in certain attitudes toward sex before marriage. The majority of women who engage in premarital sex do so with only one or two partners with whom they are emotionally involved. Men, in contrast, are more likely to seek sex with multiple partners (Laumann *et al.,* 1994). However, within a given 5-year period, the majority of both men and women are likely to have no more than one sexual partner (Laumann *et al.,* 1994).

Sex differences

Studies of heterosexuals have shown that young men and women differ in their attitudes about sex: women are more likely than men to view sex as part of a loving relationship. Related to this, differences between women and men have been reported in the nature of the type of event that is most likely to elicit sexual jealousy: emotional infidelity, or sexual infidelity. Whether measured by self-reports or by autonomic reactions such as heart rate, women react more strongly to the prospect of emotional infidelity (the prospect of their partners forming a romantic relationship with someone else), regardless of whether the infidelity involves an actual sexual act. By contrast, men react more strongly to the prospect of sexual infidelity, regardless of whether their partner's sexual liaison involves an emotional commitment (Buss *et al.,* 1992).

Men and women are also sexually responsive to different sorts of stimuli, regardless of their sexual orientation. Heterosexual and homosexual men and women were shown a range of sexual films in a private, laboratory setting, while their genital responses were recorded continuously using psychophysiological sensors. The films depicted men and women engaging in same-sex intercourse, solitary masturbation, or nude exercise, or human heterosexual intercourse or animal copulation. Across all participants, genital responses were weakest to nude exercise and strongest to intercourse. Men's responses, however, depended primarily on the sex of the actors, with heterosexual men responding most to female actors and homosexual men responding most to male actors. By contrast, women's responses depended primarily on the level of sexual activity depicted, and not on the sex of the actors involved (Chivers *et al.,* 2007).

Differences between the sexes apply to behavior as well as to attitudes. Women who engage in premarital sex are likely to have fewer sexual partners than men. Differences between male and female patterns of sexual behavior persist regardless of sexual orientation. For example, lesbian couples are likely to have sex less frequently than heterosexual couples, and gay male couples have sex more often than heterosexual couples. Such differences can be viewed as reflecting a continuum that extends from female-typical characteristics to male-typical characteristics (Buss, 1994a).

Sexual orientation

An individual's **sexual orientation** is the degree to which he or she is sexually attracted to persons of the other sex and/or to persons of the same sex. Like Alfred Kinsey, the pioneering sex researcher of the 1940s, most behavioral scientists conceptualize sexual orientation as a continuum, ranging from exclusive heterosexuality to exclusive homosexuality. For example, on Kinsey's own 7-point scale, individuals who are attracted exclusively to persons of the other sex and who engage in sexual behavior only with such persons are at the heterosexual end of the scale (category 0); those who are attracted exclusively to persons of the same sex and who engage in sexual behavior only with such persons are at the homosexual end of the continuum (category 6). Individuals in categories 2 through 4 are usually defined as bisexual.

This oversimplifies the situation, however, because sexual orientation comprises several distinct components, including erotic attraction or sexual desire, sexual behavior, romantic attraction, and self-identification as a heterosexual, homosexual, or bisexual person. It is not uncommon for an individual to be at different points on the scale for different components. For example, many people who are sexually attracted to persons of the same sex have never participated in any homosexual behaviors, and many who have had frequent homosexual encounters do not identify themselves as homosexual or bisexual persons. To further complicate matters, a subset of people show a complete lack of sexual attraction, termed **asexuality**, estimated at 1 per cent of the population in a UK sample (Bogaert, 2004, 2006).

Frequency of different sexual orientations

In a survey of sexuality in the USA, 10.1 per cent of adult men and 8.6 per cent of adult women in a national random sample reported at least one of the following: (1) They were currently attracted 'mostly' or 'only' to persons of their own sex, (2) they found having sex with someone of the same sex 'somewhat' or 'very' appealing, or (3) they had engaged in sexual behavior with a person of the same sex since age 18. These percentages are similar to the percentage of people who are left-handed (about 8 per cent). In terms of self-identification, 2.8 per cent of the men and 1.4 per cent of the women identified themselves as homosexual (or gay or lesbian) or bisexual – similar to the percentage of people in the USA who identify themselves as Jewish (2–3 per cent).

As the authors of the survey acknowledge, these percentages must be regarded as underestimates because many people are reluctant to report desires or behaviors that are still considered by some to be immoral or pathological. The problem was particularly acute in this survey because the interviews were conducted in the respondents' own homes, and other family members, including children, were also in the home at the time, although not necessarily in the room, during more than 20 per cent of the interviews. And although actual homosexual behavior is somewhat atypical, the potential for homosexual responses – given the right person and the right situation – is rather common, estimated at 33 per cent for men and 65 per cent for women (Santtila *et al.,* 2008).

Causes of sexual orientation

The common question 'What causes homosexuality?' is scientifically misconceived because it implicitly assumes either that heterosexuality needs no explanation or that its causes are self-evident. Those who have thought about it at all are likely to conclude that because only heterosexual behavior results in reproduction, it must be the 'natural' outcome of evolution, so only deviations from heterosexuality (such as homosexuality) pose a scientific puzzle. Freud did not agree: '[heterosexuality] is also a problem that needs elucidation and is not a self-evident fact based upon an attraction that is ultimately of a chemical nature' (1905/1962, pp. 11–12). It is because we agree with Freud that we have called this section of the chapter 'sexual orientation' and not 'homosexuality.'

At issue once again is the nature–nurture question, which we introduced in Chapter 1 and discussed in the chapter on development (Chapter 3) and will discuss again in the chapter on individual differences (Chapter 12): to what extent is an adult's sexual orientation determined by earlier life experiences or to innate biological influences, such as genes or prenatal hormones?

The best data on earlier life experiences comes from an intensive, large-scale interview study of approximately 1000 homosexual and 500 heterosexual men and women living in

DO THE BRAINS OF ADDICTS REVEAL DISORDERS WITH REWARD OR WITH ANTI-REWARD?

THE CASE FOR DISORDERS WITH REWARD

Kent Berridge, University of Michigan

What happens in the brain to create an addiction? Withdrawal and tolerance are famous contributors, described in counterpoint by Koob, but there are others too. One important addiction mechanism may be abnormally intense 'wanting' – specifically a psychological component of motivation called incentive salience – generated by brain systems involving the nucleus accumbens (which sits in the front of the brain just below the cortex) and the neurotransmitter dopamine (Robinson & Berridge, 2003).

Difference between Brain Mechanisms of 'Liking' and 'Wanting'

Brain mechanisms for 'wanting' a reward are different from mechanisms for 'liking' the same reward. That first came as a surprise when discovered in studies with Terry Robinson at the University of Michigan. We were asking whether 'liking' for the pleasure of sweetness reward was mediated by the neurotransmitter dopamine. For many others who had asked that question, the answer generally seemed to be 'yes.' But most studies had used psychological measures of how much the reward was 'wanted' (preferred, pursued, worked for, or consumed) to infer how much the reward was 'liked' (pleasure or hedonic impact). Our approach used a more naturalistic selective window into pleasure to measure 'liking': affective facial expressions, similar to expressions of a human infant who smacks lips when tasting a 'liked' sweet food, but gapes and turns away from 'disliked' bitterness. We were surprised to find that removing brain dopamine from rats left their 'liking' reactions to pleasant sweetness completely normal, though dopamine loss apparently abolished all 'wanting' for the reward. Subsequent brain studies confirmed that raising dopamine also didn't enhance pleasure 'liking,' though extra dopamine boosted 'wanting' (Berridge, 2007). Instead, other brain mechanisms turned out to generate pleasure 'liking' (for example, small hedonic hotspots in nucleus accumbens using heroin-like neurotransmitters) (Kringelbach & Berridge, 2012). Recently, human neuroimaging studies have supported the conclusion that brain dopamine mediates 'wanting' rather than 'liking' in people for addictive drugs, as well as tasty foods and other pleasant rewards (Volkow *et al.*, 2002; Evans *et al.*, 2005; Leyton, 2010; Hardman *et al.*, 2012).

Dopamine 'Wanting' in Addiction

Identifying the difference between 'wanting' and 'liking' led directly to addiction (Robinson & Berridge, 1993, 2008). Addictive drugs (cocaine, amphetamine, heroin, alcohol, nicotine, etc.) can 'sensitize' brain dopamine systems, especially in some vulnerable individuals, especially at high doses, and especially when the drugs are taken in binge-like patterns. Vulnerability to sensitization depends on an individual's genes, hormonal-emotional-stress states, and earlier life experiences.

Neural sensitization means that the system's neurons become changed more or less permanently (for example, neurons change their anatomical sprouting of branches, etc.). Most important, a sensitized brain system becomes hyper-reactive, generating larger than normal responses to drugs. Once sensitized, a brain can release more dopamine, and generate more 'wanting.' As a result, a sensitized addict might experience higher 'wanting' than most people ever do. For example, an ordinary person might have to go hungry for several days to 'want' food as intensely as an addict 'wants' drugs.

Brain sensitization to drugs is nearly the opposite of brain tolerance. Both can happen simultaneously in the same brain or even the same neurons, but sensitization lasts longer – perhaps years (Paulson & Robinson, 1995; Boileau *et al.*, 2007; Vezina & Leyton, 2009). Because sensitization is so enduring, it creates a long-lasting danger for relapse that persists after a person quits. Even after a former addict was drug-abstinent for months or years, and no longer feeling withdrawal symptoms, compulsive 'wanting' might occasionally still be triggered.

Experiments have shown that 'wanting' is amplified to still higher levels when a dopamine-stimulating drug is present in a sensitized brain. Amplification may make it difficult for an addict to restrict consumption to moderate amounts. Although intending to 'take just one' hit or drink and then stop, the 'just one' may turn into many, or even an entire lost weekend. The binge can result from amplification of 'wanting' to a higher peak as the first hit takes hold, rather than diminishing (even if a hit produces a high, it won't be enough to satisfy the addict).

Further, some people with so-called food addiction, or gambling addiction, or shopping addiction, etc., have been suggested to have sensitization-like patterns of hyper-reactivity in their dopamine-accumbens brain system, whether or not they've taken addictive drugs (Davis *et al.*, 2009; O'Sullivan *et al.*, 2011; Hartston, 2012; Linnet *et al.*, 2012; Ray *et al.*, 2012). If so, sensitized-like brain changes might sometimes develop spontaneously in highly vulnerable individuals producing various types of addictions.

Sensitization mechanism can make addicts compulsively 'want' to take drugs, whether or not they actually 'like' their drug very much when it comes, and even when no longer in withdrawal. Amplified 'wanting' due to dopamine-accumbens sensitization is not the only brain mechanism of addiction. But realizing how 'wanting' is generated by these brain mechanisms may help us to understand addiction better.

SEEING BOTH SIDES

DO THE BRAINS OF ADDICTS REVEAL DISORDERS WITH REWARD OR WITH ANTI-REWARD?

THE CASE FOR PROBLEMS WITH ANTI-REWARD

George F. Koob, The Scripps Research Institute, California, USA

My argument is that drug addiction involves a three-stage cycle: *binge/intoxication*, *withdrawal/negative affect*, and *preoccupation/anticipation*. These stages worsen over time, and as one moves from the impulsivity of the early stages of the addiction process, an additional source of motivation, one not engaged by Berridge, is recruited: negative reinforcement which we believe contributes to, or even defines, compulsivity (Koob & Le Moal, 1997). The development of the aversive emotional state that drives the negative reinforcement of addiction is defined here as the 'dark side' of addiction. We have argued that drug addiction progresses from a source of positive reinforcement that may indeed involve a form of sensitization of incentive salience, as argued by Berridge, to sensitization of the brain stress and anti-reward systems that set up a powerful negative reinforcement process. Positive reinforcement is defined as the process by which presentation of a stimulus increases the probability of a response; negative reinforcement is defined as the process by which removal of an aversive stimulus (or aversive state in the case of addiction) increases the probability of a response. These stages are thought to feed into each other, become more intense, and ultimately lead to the pathological state known as *addiction*.

My thesis is that addiction involves a long-term, persistent dysregulation of the activity of neural circuits that mediate motivational systems, deriving from two sources: decreased function of the brain reward systems that normally mediate natural rewards (decrease in reward) and recruitment of anti-reward systems that drive aversive states (increase in stress and dysphoria). Anti-reward is a concept developed by Koob and Le Moal (2008), based on the hypothesis that brain systems are in place to limit reward, employing an opponent process mechanism that forms a general feature of biological systems. Opponent process is a concept in psychology where following euphoria produced by a drug there is an opposing reaction of dysphoria that follows. With repeated exposure to the drug, the euphoria was hypothesized to decline whereas the dysphoria was hypothesized to get larger. Our argument is that there is a neurocircuitry basis for opponent process and the mechanism involves both within- and between-system neuroadaptations to excessive activation of the reward system, or excessive 'incentive sensitization,' if one prefers. Within-system neuroadaptations are decreased function of the reward system itself by circuitry changes within the reward system. A between-system

neuroadaptation is a circuitry change, in which another circuit, an anti-reward circuit, is recruited from the reward system (Koob & Bloom, 1988).

Such within and between system neuroadaptations begin in the *binge/intoxication stage*, are most evident in the *withdrawal/negative affect* stage, and persist into the *preoccupation/anticipation (craving) stage*. The *withdrawal/ negative affect stage* can be defined as the presence of motivational signs of withdrawal in humans, including chronic irritability, physical pain, emotional pain, malaise, dysphoria, and loss of motivation for natural rewards. In animal models where animals increase their drug taking with extended access, there are increases in reward thresholds (dysphoric-like response) that temporally precede and are highly correlated with escalation in drug intake. Such acute withdrawal is associated with decreased activity of the mesocorticolimbic dopamine system (the incentive salience system), reflected by both electrophysiological recordings of dopamine neuron activity and *neurochemical measures of extracellular dopamine with dopamine projections*. Human imaging studies of individuals with addiction during withdrawal or protracted abstinence show decreases in dopamine D_2 receptors (hypothesized to reflect hypo-dopaminergic functioning), hyporesponsiveness to dopamine challenge (Volkow *et al.*, 2003), and hypoactivity of the orbitofrontal-infralimbic cortex system (Volkow *et al.*, 2003). The decreased dopamine function is hypothesized to be within-system neuroadaptations mediated by decreased presynaptic release or post-synaptic receptor plasticity.

More importantly for the present thesis, as dependence and motivational withdrawal develop, brain anti-reward systems, such as corticotropin-releasing factor (CRF), norepinephrine, and dynorphin, are recruited in key motivational and emotional parts of the brain such as the nucleus accumbens and the amygdala. We hypothesize that these brain anti-reward neurotransmitter systems known to be activated during the development of excessive drug taking comprise a between-system opponent process, and this activation is manifest motivationally when the drug is removed, producing dysphoria, anxiety, emotional pain, and irritability symptoms associated with acute and protracted abstinence. Thus, we hypothesize that anti-reward circuits are recruited as between-system neuroadaptations (Koob & Bloom, 1988) during the development of addiction, producing aversive-like or stress-like states when the drug is removed (withdrawal) via two between system mechanisms: direct activation of stress-like, fear-like states in the extended amygdala (CRF-norepinephrine) and reward deficits in the mesocorticolimbic dopamine system by suppressing dopamine function (via the activation of dynorphin, possibly in the nucleus accumbens). In regards to the *preoccupation/anticipation stage*, a residual anti-reward state allows drug priming, drug cues, and acute stressors to acquire even more power to elicit drug-seeking behavior and promote relapse. Indeed, 60–70 per cent of all relapses occur in the context of a negative emotional state, and thus I would argue that long-lasting sensitization of incentive salience (Berridge, 2007) is not the only explanation for relapse; the dark side is also sensitized.

Thus, the combination of decreases in reward neurotransmitter function and recruitment of anti-reward systems provides a powerful source of negative reinforcement that defines compulsive drug-seeking behavior and addiction and contributes to relapse. The development of the aversive emotional state that drives the negative reinforcement in addiction is the 'dark side' of the brain incentive salience system and motivation in general. I have speculated that the brain motivational systems are a limited resource, and proper homeostatic balance that we call reward balance (happiness?) requires a hedonic Calvinist approach (Koob & Le Moal, 1997). Drug addiction is not only failing to manage incentive salience but also failing to manage the anti-reward consequences of too much incentive salience.

---

the San Francisco Bay area (Bell *et al.*, 1981a). The study uncovered one – and only one – major factor that predicted a homosexual orientation in adulthood for both men and women: childhood gender nonconformity. A. P. Bell, M. A. Weinberg, and S. K. Hamerstein's research on the development of sexual preference asked participants what play activities they had or had not enjoyed as children, gay men and lesbians were significantly more likely than heterosexual men and women to report that they had not enjoyed activities typical of their sex and significantly more likely to report that they had enjoyed activities typical of the other sex. Gay men and lesbians were also more likely than their heterosexual counterparts to report that they had not been masculine (for men) or feminine (for women) as children. In addition to this gender nonconformity, gay men and lesbians were more likely to report having had more friends of the other sex. Studies like this rely on retrospections about one's childhood, which makes memory bias a legitimate threat to validity. The same findings about childhood gender nonconformity emerge, however, even with less biased research methods, for instance the study of childhood home videos (Rieger *et al.*, 2008).

Two features of the data found by Bell, Weinberg, and Hamerstein's research on the development of sexual preference are worth noting. First, the findings were quite strong and similar for men and women: 63 per cent of both gay men and lesbians had not enjoyed childhood activities typical of their sex, compared with only 10 to 15 per cent of their heterosexual counterparts. Second, it is clear that women are more likely than men to have enjoyed activities typical of the other sex during childhood and to have had more childhood friends of the other sex. In fact, a majority of both the lesbians and the heterosexual women in this study were 'tomboys' – that is, enjoyed boys' activities as children. It is the non-enjoyment of sex-typical activities that appears to be the best predictor of an adult homosexual orientation for both men and women. The overall finding that childhood gender nonconformity predicts an adult homosexual outcome has now been confirmed in several other studies (Bailey & Zucker, 1995; Rieger *et al.*, 2008), including several that followed gender-nonconforming boys into adolescence and adulthood and assessed their sexual orientations (Green, 1987a, 1987b; Zucker, 1990).

In addition to the gender nonconformity finding, the San Francisco study also yielded many negative findings that were important because they disconfirmed common theories about the antecedents of a homosexual orientation. For example:

→ A person's identification with the other-sex parent while growing up appears to have no significant impact on whether he or she turns out to be homosexual or heterosexual. This fails to confirm Freud's psychoanalytic theory (discussed in Chapter 13), as well as other theories based on the dynamics of the person's childhood family.

→ Gay men and lesbians were no more likely than their heterosexual counterparts to report having their first sexual encounter with a person of the same sex. Moreover, they neither lacked heterosexual experiences during their childhood and adolescent years nor found such experiences unpleasant.

→ A person's sexual orientation is usually determined by adolescence, even though he or she might not yet have become sexually active. Gay men and lesbians typically experienced same-sex attractions about 3 years before they had engaged in any 'advanced' sexual activity with persons of the same sex.

These last two sets of findings indicate that, in general, homosexual feelings, not homosexual behaviors, are the crucial antecedents of an adult homosexual orientation. They thus disconfirm any simple behavioral learning theory of sexual orientation, including the popular, lay-persons' version, which asserts that an individual can become gay by being 'seduced' by a person of the same sex or by having an admired, openly gay teacher, parent, or clergyperson. Cross-cultural data are also consistent with this conclusion. For example, in the Sambian culture of New Guinea, cited earlier, all boys engage in exclusively homosexual behaviors from prepuberty through late adolescence. At that point, virtually all of them marry and become exclusively heterosexual (Herdt, 1984).

Finally, it is clear from all the studies that one's sexual orientation is not something that one simply chooses. Gay men and lesbians do not choose to have erotic feelings toward persons of the same sex any more than heterosexual persons choose to have erotic feelings toward persons of the other sex. Behavioral scientists disagree over the relative contributions of nature versus nurture – the extents to which the major determinants of sexual orientation are rooted in biology or experience – but the public often misconstrues the question to be whether sexual orientation is determined by variables beyond the individual's control or is freely chosen. That is not the same question.

Approaches that combine nature and nurture are becoming more common. The more general point is that just because a behavior might be advantageous from the standpoint of reproduction, it does not follow that evolution has 'hardwired' it into the species (nature only). A similar case for the combined action of nature and nurture can be made for the notion of **imprinting**, which is the early rapid learning that allows a newborn (or newly hatched) animal to develop an attachment to its mother (see Chapter 7). Within the first hours of life, infants of many non-human species are 'programmed' to learn an emotional attachment to the closest social figure. Most often this is the mother, but if the first moving object seen is a human or a mobile toy, the imprinting process can produce attachment beyond species boundaries. Imprinting turns out to have consequences for later sexual behavior as well, because mate choices follow maternal imprinting. The imprinting instinct is genetic (nature), but as long as the environment (nurture) supports or promotes reproductively advantageous behavior often enough, attachment and reproductive behaviors need not necessarily get fully programmed into the genes. And just as ducklings encounter mother ducks most of the time, so, too, human societies see to it that men and women see each other as dissimilar often enough to ensure that the species will not perish from the earth.

INTERIM SUMMARY

Prenatal hormones contribute to sexual development. If the embryonic sex glands produce enough androgen hormones, the embryo will have a male pattern of genital and brain development. If androgens are low or missing, the embryo will have a female pattern of genital and brain development.

For non-human animals, prenatal hormones appear to be powerful determinants of adult sexual behavior. For humans, prenatal hormones appear to be less important than post-natal social gender roles in determining adult sexual behavior.

The female hormones (estrogen and progesterone) and male hormones (androgens) are responsible for the changes in the body that occur at puberty, but, in contrast to other animals, they play a limited role in human sexual arousal. In primates and humans, early social experiences with parents and peers have a large influence on adult sexuality, and, for humans, cultural norms are also influential.

Recent studies have bolstered the claim that biological, genetic, hormonal, or neural factors may partly determine whether an individual will be heterosexual or homosexual, but the evidence is not conclusive. It is also unknown whether biological factors may influence sexual orientation directly, or whether they instead contribute to other traits, such as gender conformity, that indirectly influence the development of sexual orientation.

CRITICAL THINKING QUESTIONS

1 How does sexual identity differ from sexual orientation?

2 Why do you think many people believe that sexual desire and activity in humans is strongly influenced by hormones when the evidence suggests that it is not?

Throughout this chapter, we have seen that psychological and biological causes are so closely intertwined in the control of many motivations that they merge into one stream of events. Not only can biological causes control psychological motivations like hunger and thirst, but psychological processes and experiences control motivation and may feed back to control physiological responses. For example, repeated use of an addictive drug may permanently change particular brain systems. More commonly, the particular foods and drinks we desire are established as objects of choice largely by learning, and even the degree of satiety produced by a stomach full of food is influenced by previous experience. Our social attachments are determined largely by the consequences of earlier social interactions with particular individuals. When it comes to many motivational processes, biology and psychology are not separate domains but, rather, two aspects of control that continually interact to direct motivational processes.

CHAPTER SUMMARY

1 Motivational states direct and activate behavior. They arise from two sources: internal drive factors and external incentive factors.

2 Drive factors tend to promote homeostasis: the preservation of a constant internal state. Homeostasis involves several components: a goal value or set point for the ideal internal state, a sensory signal that measures the actual internal state, a comparison between the goal value and the sensory signal, and finally, a response that brings the actual internal state closer to the goal value.

3 Regulation of temperature is an example of homeostasis. The regulated variable is the temperature of the blood, and sensors for this are located in various parts of the body, including the hypothalamus. Adjustments are either automatic physiological responses (for example, shivering) or voluntary behavioral ones (such as putting on a sweater).

4 Thirst is another homeostatic motive. There are two regulated variables, intracellular fluid and extracellular fluid. Loss of intracellular fluid is detected by osmotic sensors, neurons in the hypothalamus that respond to dehydration. Loss of extracellular fluid is detected by blood-pressure sensors, neurons in major veins and organs that respond to a drop in pressure. Intracellular and extracellular signals act together to produce thirst.

5 Incentive factors are goals in the outside world, such as food, water, sexual partners, and drugs. Incentives are the target of motivated behavior and are typically rewarding. Although some incentives – such as a sweet food when we are hungry – are powerful motivators by themselves, most incentives are established through learning.

6 Many types of natural rewards may activate the brain's dopamine system. Activity in these neurons may constitute the neural basis for all incentives or 'wants.' Artificial activation of these neurons by drugs or electrical brain stimulation causes increased motivation for both natural and artificial incentives. Changes in this system, produced by repeatedly taking drugs that activate it, may partly cause the compulsive craving of addiction.

7 Hunger has evolved to allow us to select an array of nutrients. Humans have innate taste preferences, such as for sweetness, and innate aversions, such as for bitterness, that guide our choice of foods. In addition, we may develop a wide variety of learned preferences and aversions. Homeostatic hunger signals, which arise when the body is low in calorie-containing fuels such as glucose,

produce appetite partly by causing the individual to perceive food incentives as more attractive and pleasant.

8 Hunger is largely controlled by homeostatic deficit and satiety signals. Certain neurons in the brain, especially in the brain stem and hypothalamus, detect shortages in glucose and trigger hunger. Other nutrient detectors, especially in the liver, detect increasing energy stores and trigger satiety. A satiety signal, in the form of the hormone cholecystokinin, is released from the intestines to help stop hunger and eating.

9 Two regions of the brain are critical to hunger: the lateral hypothalamus and the ventromedial hypothalamus. Destruction of the lateral hypothalamus leads to undereating; destruction of the ventromedial hypothalamus leads to overeating. Although these regions were originally thought to be centers for hunger and satiety, hunger is not permanently destroyed by any lesion. Another interpretation of these effects is that the two regions of the hypothalamus exert reciprocal effects on the homeostatic set point for body weight. Damage to the lateral hypothalamus may lower the set point, and damage to the ventromedial hypothalamus may raise the set point. Diet drugs that alter appetite may work partly by affecting neurons in these regions of the hypothalamus.

10 People become obese primarily because: (1) they are genetically predisposed to be overweight, or (2) they overeat (for psychological reasons). The influence of genes is mediated by their effect on fat cells, metabolic rate, and set points. As for overeating and obesity, obese people tend to overeat when they break a diet, eat more when emotionally aroused, and are more responsive to external hunger cues than normal-weight individuals. In treating obesity, extreme diets appear ineffective because the deprivation leads to subsequent overeating and to a lowered metabolic rate. What seems to work best are lifestyle changes that establish a new set of permanent eating and exercise habits.

11 Anorexia nervosa is characterized by extreme, self-imposed weight loss. Bulimia is characterized by recurrent episodes of binge eating, followed by attempts to purge the excess by means of vomiting, laxatives, fasting, or excessive exercise. Possible causes of these eating disorders include personality factors such as low self-esteem, social factors such as a cultural emphasis on thinness and pervasive cultural messages that objectify the female body, and biological factors such as low serotonin levels.

Prenatal hormones contribute to sexual development. If the embryonic sex glands produce enough androgen hormones, the embryo will have a male pattern of genital and brain development. If androgens are low or missing, the embryo will have a female pattern of genital and brain development. For non-human animals, prenatal hormones appear to be powerful determinants of adult sexual behavior. For humans, prenatal hormones appear to be much less important, although they may still play a role in later sexual behavior. In cases in which the hormonal exposure of the embryo is typical of one sex but the social role and gender after birth is more typical of the other sex (due to hormone imbalance, prenatal drugs, or a postnatal accident), the individual's development seems to correspond most closely to the postnatal social gender.

 The female hormones (estrogen and progesterone) and male hormones (androgens) are responsible for the changes in the body that occur at puberty, but they play a limited role in human sexual arousal. In contrast, in other animals there is substantial hormonal control over sex. Early social experiences with parents and peers have a large influence on adult sexuality in primates and humans. For humans, other environmental determinants of adult sexuality include cultural norms. Although Western society has become increasingly flexible regarding female and male sex roles, men and women may still differ in their attitudes toward sex and relationships.

 Recent studies have bolstered the claim that biological, genetic, hormonal, or neural factors may partly determine whether an individual will be heterosexual or homosexual, but the evidence is not conclusive. It is also unknown whether biological factors may influence sexual orientation directly or whether they instead contribute to other traits, such as gender conformity, that indirectly influence the development of sexual orientation.

CORE CONCEPTS

motivation	incentive salience	lateral hypothalamic syndrome
drive theories	wanting	ventromedial hypothalamic syndrome
incentive theory	liking	obese
primary reinforcer	brain's dopamine system	anorexia nervosa
secondary reinforcer	addiction	bulimia
homeostasis	tolerance	objectification theory
set point	withdrawal	self-objectification
thirst	neural sensitization	gender identity
extracellular thirst	conditioned aversion	androgenization
intracellular thirst	sham feeding	sexual orientation
incentive motivation	conditioned satiety	asexuality
affect	alliesthesia	imprinting

DIGITAL SUPPORT RESOURCES

Students should use the unique printed access card included in the front of the book to access the digital support resources which accompany the new edition. These include:

- Multiple Choice Questions and Quizzes
- Critical Thinking Questions
- Practice Essay Questions
- Videos
- Glossary, Flashcards, and More

11 EMOTION

LEARNING OBJECTIVES

After reading this chapter you should be able to:

Describe the components of emotion.

Explore personal meanings and conceptual knowledge shape emotions.

Understand the role of feelings and thought–action tendencies in emotions.

Examine how bodily changes shape or differentiate emotions.

Recognize how facial muscle movements communicate and shape emotions.

Understand to emotion regulation strategies.

Discuss how gender and cultural differences impact emotions.

Understand the role of positive emotions in positive psychology.

List and describe six components of the emotion process.

Describe the relationship between cognitive appraisals and emotions.

Explain how emotions influence people's thoughts and actions.

Describe the James–Lange theory and the evidence for and against it.

Identify how different emotion regulation strategies alter the components of the emotion process.

Describe the reasons why emotion processes vary by gender and culture.

Describe the broaden-and-build theory of positive emotions and why it matters.

In the 1970s, Ted Bundy broke into the apartment of a young female student at the University of Washington, knocked her unconscious, assaulted her sexually, then killed her. He did this again more than 30 times across the USA. His desire was to possess a lifeless female form – comatose or dead – and just before his 1989 execution, he admitted to police detectives that he kept some of his victims in such a state for hours or days before he disposed of their bodies. He even photographed his victims and kept a stash of their skulls in his Seattle apartment. Bundy explained, 'When you work hard to do something right, you don't want to forget it.'

Ted Bundy felt no remorse, guilt, or shame about violating the standards of human decency. On the contrary, he was proud of himself. Later, when facing his own murder trial and probable death sentence, his examining psychiatrist uncovered further unusual emotions. He described Bundy as cheerful and jovial. He stated that although Bundy 'intellectually' understood the charges against him, 'he sure didn't act like a man who was facing a death sentence. He was acting like a man who did not have a care in the world.' Against the strong urgings of his legal advisors, Bundy even chose to serve as counsel in his own defense. As his psychiatrist later explained, '[Bundy] was not motivated by a need to help himself. He was motivated by the need to be the star of the show. ... He was the producer of a play in which he was playing a big role. The defense and his future were of secondary importance to him.' Ted Bundy had no fear for future consequences.

Emotions, it turns out, are so central to human experience and successful social encounters that we consider those who seem to have no emotions – like the serial killer who shows no shame or no fear – to be inhuman. We call such people cold-blooded. This label fits, because although we share basic motives such as hunger and sex with cold-blooded reptiles, we seem to share emotions only with other warm-blooded mammals (Panksepp, 1998).

People like Ted Bundy are, in fact, thought to have specific biological and social-cognitive deficits. They are said to have **antisocial personality disorder** (and are sometimes called *psychopaths* or *sociopaths*), a disorder characterized

CHAPTER OUTLINE

COMPONENTS OF EMOTION

COGNITIVE APPRAISAL AND EMOTION

Discovery of appraisals

Themes and dimensions of appraisals

Conscious and unconscious appraisals

Appraisals in the brain

**SUBJECTIVE EXPERIENCES
AND EMOTION**

Feelings modify attention and learning

Feelings modify evaluations and judgments

**THOUGHT-ACTION TENDENCIES
AND EMOTION**

BODILY CHANGES AND EMOTION

Intensity of emotions

Differentiation of emotions

**CUTTING EDGE RESEARCH:
EMOTIONS CHANGE GENE
EXPRESSION IN IMMUNE CELLS**

FACIAL MUSCLE MOVEMENTS
AND EMOTION

Communication of emotion through facial muscle movements

The facial feedback hypothesis

RESPONSES TO EMOTION:
EMOTION REGULATION

EMOTIONS, GENDER, AND CULTURE

Gender differences

Cultural differences

POSITIVE PSYCHOLOGY

Positive emotions and longevity

Positive emotions build personal resources

SEEING BOTH SIDES: WHAT IS
THE UNDERLYING STRUCTURE OF
EMOTIONS?

by deficits in normal emotional responding – for shame, guilt, and especially fear – as well as deficits in empathy for the emotions of others (Hare, 1999; Marsh *et al.*, 2011). And yet people like Ted Bundy are not completely devoid of emotions. Instead, 'they seem to suffer a kind of emotional poverty that limits the range and depth of their feelings. While at times they appear cold and unemotional, they are prone to shallow and short-lived displays of feeling ... . Many clinicians have commented that the emotions of psychopaths are so shallow as to be of little more than 'proto-emotions' – primitive responses to immediate needs' (Hare, 1999, p. 52). In this chapter we will explore what Ted Bundy seemed to lack – the full array of meaningful human emotions.

Emotions and motives (discussed in Chapter 10) are closely related. Emotions can activate and direct behavior in the same way that basic motives do. They may also accompany motivated behavior: sex, for example, is not only a powerful motive but also a potential source of joy or guilt. Despite their similarities, we need to distinguish between motives and emotions. One distinction is that emotions are typically triggered from the outside, whereas motives are more often activated from within. That is, emotions are usually aroused by a person's current external circumstances, identified as the person–environment relationship in Figure 11.1, and emotional reactions are directed toward these circumstances. Motives, in contrast, are often aroused by internal circumstances (such as a homeostatic imbalance) and are naturally directed toward particular objects in the environment (such as food, water, or a mate). Another distinction between motives and emotions is that a motive is usually elicited by a specific need, but an emotion can be elicited by a wide variety of stimuli (think of all the different things that can make you angry or happy).

These distinctions are not absolute. An external source can sometimes trigger a motive, as when the sight of food triggers hunger. And the discomfort caused by a homeo-static imbalance – severe hunger, for example – can arouse emotions. Nevertheless, emotions and motives are different enough in their sources, subjective experience, and effects on behavior that they merit separate treatment.

COMPONENTS OF EMOTION

An **emotion** is a brief, multicomponent response to some change in the way people interpret – or appraise – their current circumstances. When you appraise your current circumstances as somehow bad for you, a negative emotion arises, and when you register good prospects or good fortune, a positive emotion arises. An intense emotion can involve at least six components (Frijda, 1986; Lazarus, 1991b). Typically, an emotion begins with a **cognitive appraisal**, a person's assessment of the personal meaning of his or her current circumstances (see Figure 11.1). This appraisal process is considered the first component of an emotion. Cognitive appraisals, in turn, trigger a cascade of responses that represent other loosely connected components of an emotion. The component that we most frequently recognize is the **subjective experience** of the emotion – the affective state or feeling tone that colors your private experience. A third and closely related component includes thought–action tendencies – urges to think and act in certain ways. When something sparks your interest, for instance, you want to explore it and learn more about it. When someone angers you, you may be tempted to act aggressively, either physically or verbally. A fourth component includes internal bodily changes, especially those of the **autonomic nervous system**, the division of the peripheral nervous system that controls the heart and other smooth muscles (see Chapter 2). When you are afraid, for example, your heart may pound in your chest, and your palms may sweat. A fifth component of an emotion includes **facial muscle movements**, the muscle actions that move facial landmarks in particular ways that create what is commonly called a facial expression. When you experience disgust, for example, you probably frown while also raising your upper lip and partially closing your eyes, as if to shut out the smell and sight of whatever offends you. The final component includes **responses to emotion**, meaning how people cope with or react to their own emotion or the situation that elicited it. The Concept Review Table reviews these various components

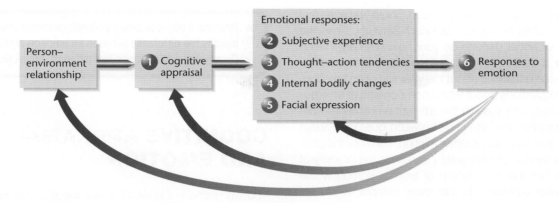

FIGURE 11.1 Schematic Diagram of the Emotion Process. *Six components of emotion are triggered by circumstances described by certain person–environment relationships.*

CONCEPT REVIEW TABLE
SIX COMPONENTS OF THE EMOTION PROCESS

Cognitive appraisal	A person's assessment of the personal meaning of his or her current circumstances
Subjective experience	The affective state or feeling tone that colors private experience
Thought–action tendencies	Urges to think or act in particular ways
Internal bodily changes	Physiological responses, particularly those involving the autonomic nervous system such as changes in heart rate and sweat gland activity
Facial muscle movements	Muscle contractions that move facial landmarks – like cheeks, lips, noses, and brows – into particular configurations
Responses to emotion	How people regulate, react to, or cope with their own emotion or the situation that triggered it

None of these six components by itself is an emotion. Instead, they come together to create a particular emotion. Neither, as we shall see, are any of six components simple or one-dimensional. Each can in fact be viewed as a system in its own right, one that interacts with the other systems to create an emotional episode. Viewing emotion as a complex system involving multiple components helps distinguish emotions from closely related states, like moods. Emotions are distinct from moods in multiple ways. First, emotions typically have a clear cause. They are about something or someone (Beedie *et al.,* 2005; Oatley *et al.,* 2006). You are angry *at* your sister. You are awestruck *by* the Grand Canyon. **Moods**, on the other hand, are often free-floating and diffuse affective states. For unknown reasons, you feel irritable one day, and cheerful the next. This raises a second difference: emotions are typically brief, lasting only seconds or minutes, but moods endure longer, lasting for hours, even days (Beedie *et al.,* 2005). A third difference is that emotions typically implicate the multiple component systems described previously, but moods may be salient only at the level of subjective experience (Rosenberg, 1998). Finally, emotions are often conceptualized as fitting into discrete categories, like fear, anger, joy, and interest. Moods, by contrast, are often conceptualized as varying along the dimensions of pleasantness and arousal level. This last point is still hotly debated, however. An example of this debate is provided in the Seeing Both Sides feature later in this chapter.

Many emotion theorists hold a systems perspective on emotion, in which the components of an emotion are seen as having reciprocal effects on each other. In other words, each component can influence the others. Whereas Figure 11.1 outlines the typical way that an emotion unfolds – through cognitive appraisal (Reisenzein, 1983) – laboratory experiments have shown that introducing another component of an emotion first – like physiological arousal or a facial muscle movements – can jump-start the entire, multicomponent emotion process. Let's say you race up four flights of stairs and arrive at your friend's apartment with your heart pounding. In that aroused state, you may be more likely to appraise an ambiguous remark from your friend (such as 'nice hair') as an insult and lash out. The critical questions in contemporary emotion research concern the detailed nature of each of the components of an emotion and the specific mechanisms by which they influence each other. For example, one set of questions concerns the functions of each component. Why do emotions color subjective experience? Why do they evoke bodily changes? Why do they show up on our faces? Another set of questions concerns how responses of the various components contribute to the intensity of an experienced emotion. Do you feel angrier when you experience more arousal of your autonomic nervous system? Indeed, could you even feel angry if you had no autonomic arousal? Similarly, does the intensity of your anger depend on your having a certain kind of thought or a certain set of facial muscle movements? In contrast to these questions about the intensity of an emotion, there are also questions about which components of an emotion are responsible for making the different emotions feel different. To appreciate the difference between questions about intensity and questions about differentiation, consider the possibility that autonomic arousal greatly increases the intensity of our emotions but that the pattern of arousal is roughly the same for several emotions. In this case, autonomic arousal could not differentiate among emotions.

These questions will guide us in this chapter as we consider cognitive appraisals, subjective experiences, thought–action tendencies, internal bodily changes, and observable facial muscle movements. We will also consider people's responses to their own emotions and their attempts to regulate their emotional experiences. We then discuss gender and cultural variation in emotions. In the final section, we turn to the relatively new subfield of positive psychology, which revolves in part around the science of positive emotions. This burgeoning area of study has enormous practical relevance because it points to ways that you can improve your own happiness and health. Throughout this chapter, we will be concerned primarily with the most intense and prototypical emotions, like anger, fear, and joy. Even so, the ideas and principles that will emerge in our discussion are relevant to a variety of feelings.

INTERIM SUMMARY

➜ An emotion is a complex, multicomponent episode that creates a readiness to act.

➜ There are six components of emotions: cognitive appraisals, the subjective experiences of emotion, thought–action tendencies, internal bodily changes, facial muscle movements, and responses to the emotion.

➜ Emotions are distinct from moods in several ways. For instance, emotions have clear causes, are particularly brief, and implicate multiple components.

CRITICAL THINKING QUESTIONS

1 Reconsider Figure 11.1, which describes the six components of the emotion process. Do you think that all six components need to be present in order to call a given experience an emotion? Why or why not? What might be the rationale for including responses to emotion as the sixth component?

2 Drawing from your own day-to-day experiences, can you identify the difference between an emotion and a mood? Do emotions and moods feel different, subjectively?

COGNITIVE APPRAISAL AND EMOTION

You will notice in Figure 11.1 that the first box in the model mentions the **person–environment relationship**. This refers to the objective situation in which a person finds herself – her current circumstances in the world, or in relation to others. One such circumstance, for instance, is receiving an insult; another is seeing a colorful sunset. These person–environment relationships are not themselves components of emotions because they do not always or directly trigger emotions. For these circumstances to produce an emotion in you, you would need to interpret them as relevant to your personal goals or well-being. This interpretation process is called cognitive appraisal. For instance, you might interpret receiving an insult as a threat to your honor. If so, you'd experience anger. In another instance, you might interpret that same insult as the meaningless ranting of an erratic person and experience no emotion whatsoever. Likewise, if you are a spiritual person, you might interpret the sunset as evidence of God's immense power and artistry, and experience a mixture of awe and gratitude. On another evening, you might be frightened by the impending loss of daylight, because you're on a day hike and worry that you can't make it back to your campsite before dark. It is through this appraisal process, then, that you assess whether the current person–environment relationship impinges on your goals or well-being. If it does, the appraisal process translates the objective circumstance into a personally meaningful one. Personal meaning, in turn, determines the type of emotion we experience, as well as its intensity (Lazarus, 1991b).

Cognitive appraisals are largely responsible for differentiating the emotions. Indeed, we often emphasize cognitive appraisals when we describe the quality of an emotion. We say, 'I was angry because she was so unfair,' or 'I was frightened because I felt abandoned.' Assessments of unfairness and abandonment are clearly abstract beliefs that result from a cognitive process. These observations suggest that cognitive appraisals are often sufficient to determine the quality of emotional experience.

Discovery of appraisals

The importance of this cognitive component within emotions was first spotlighted in a famous study in the early 1960s. Schachter and Singer (1962) suggested that if people could

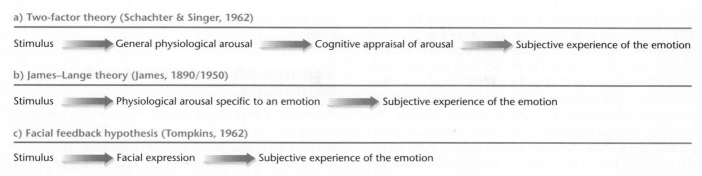

FIGURE 11.2 **Classic Theories of Emotion.** *Early theories of emotion proposed different relationships between the components of emotion.*

be induced to be in a general state of autonomic arousal, the quality of their emotion would be determined solely by their appraisal of the situation (see Figure 11.2a; we will discuss the James–Lange Theory and the facial feedback hypothesis, also included in Figure 11.2, later in this chapter). This was called the **two-factor theory** of emotions. According to this theory, emotions were thought to result from the combination of two factors or ingredients – an initial state of unexplained arousal plus a cognitive explanation (or appraisal) for that arousal.

Participants in Schachter and Singer's study were given an injection of epinephrine, which typically causes autonomic arousal – an increase in heart and respiration rates, muscle tremors, and a jittery feeling. The experimenter then manipulated the information that the participants were given regarding the effects of the injection. Some participants were correctly informed about the arousal consequences of the drug, but others were given no information about the drug's physiological effects. The informed participants therefore had an explanation for their sensations, whereas the uninformed participants did not. Schachter and Singer predicted that how the uninformed participants interpreted their symptoms would depend on the situation in which they were placed. Participants were left in a waiting room with another person, ostensibly another participant but actually a confederate of the experimenter. The confederate created either a happy situation (by making paper airplanes, playing basketball with wads of paper, and so on), or an angry situation (by complaining about the experiment, tearing up a questionnaire, and so on). The uninformed participants placed in the happy situation rated their feelings as happier than did the informed participants in that same situation. Although the data were less clear for the angry situation, Schachter and Singer claimed that the uninformed participants were angrier than the informed participants. In other words, participants who had a physiological explanation for their arousal (i.e., 'that injection I got') appeared to be less influenced by the situation than those who did not have an explanation.

The Schachter and Singer experiment was extremely influential over the next two decades, but scientists have debated whether that influence was justified (Reisenzein, 1983). The pattern of results in the study did not strongly support the experimenters' hypotheses, in that the differences between critical groups did not reach statistical significance and a control group did not react in a manner consistent with the hypotheses. In addition, the autonomic arousal may not have been the same in the happy and angry situations, and it certainly was not neutral. Follow-up experiments have found that participants rate their experiences more negatively (less happy or more angry) than the situation warrants, suggesting that the physiological arousal produced by epinephrine is experienced as somewhat unpleasant. Also, later experimenters had difficulty reproducing the results obtained by Schachter and Singer (Marshall & Zimbardo, 1979; Maslach, 1979; Mezzacappa *et al.,* 1999). We need further evidence that completely neutral arousal may be mistakenly attributed to a particular emotion.

Another study supplied such evidence. Participants first engaged in strenuous physical exercise and then participated in a task, during which they were provoked by a confederate of the experimenter. The exercise created physiological arousal that was neutral and that persisted until the participant was provoked. This arousal should have combined with any arousal elicited by the provocation, resulting in a more intense response of anger. In fact, participants who had just exercised responded more aggressively to the provocation than those who did not (Zillmann & Bryant, 1974). Although these results do not support Schachter and Singer's two-factor theory per se, they do support a more limited effect, called the **misattribution of arousal**. This effect means that lingering physiological arousal – say, from running up four flights of stairs – can be mistakenly attributed to subsequent circumstances – like an ambiguous remark, 'nice hair' – and intensify our emotional reactions to those circumstances. In the case of our earlier example, the lingering arousal could fuel anger. This effect has been replicated in many studies.

Schachter and Singer's famous study, along with the later work on the misattribution of arousal, is important because it created a central role for cognitive appraisals within the emotion process. Even so, the two-factor theory did little to explain how emotions unfold outside the laboratory (Reisenzein, 1983). This is because Schachter and Singer's first factor of unexplained physiological arousal may occur only rarely in real life. Think for a moment of the last time you were really afraid. Where were you? What happened? As you visualize the details of that experience, try to locate the exact moment when you experienced *unexplained* arousal. Suppose, for instance, that you experienced fear while you were snorkeling and saw a shark. Although you did sense a huge adrenalin rush that helped you swim to safety, that arousal was never unexplained. The shark was the explanation! Or more precisely, your appraisal that the shark endangered you was the explanation.

Departing from Schachter and Singer, many contemporary appraisal theorists would place the component of cognitive appraisal *before* the component of physiological arousal, not after it. But, as Schachter and Singer suggested, the perceived arousal and cognitive appraisal are not experienced as independent. Rather, the arousal is attributed to the appraisal – 'My heart is racing because I'm so angry about what Mary said.' So both arousal and appraisal contribute to the intensity of experience – and sometimes appraisal alone can determine the quality of experience.

Schachter and Singer's two-factor theory has been called a psychological constructionist approach to emotions because it describes how emotions arise from recipes that combine more basic psychological ingredients, in this case the two factors of a general physiological arousal and a cognitive explanation (or appraisal) of that arousal (Barrett, 2006b, 2009a). A contemporary psychological constructionist approach that bears some similarity to the two-factor theory is Barrett's conceptual act model (2012). Like the two-factor theory, the conceptual act model suggests that bodily states and cognitive processes combine to produce emotional states. Departing from the two-factor theory, the conceptual act model calls out three basic ingredients that, in various combinations, yield the wide range of experiences that comprise your mental life: sensations from the world beyond your skin, sensations from inside your body, and your prior experiences. During an emotion, according to this view, internal sensations from the body and external sensations from the world become meaningful because your brain automatically and effortlessly categorizes them based on your prior experiences. The knowledge carried by emotions words is especially pivotal in this model. Indeed, a series of experiments by Barrett and colleagues randomly assigned participants to say a given emotion word, like 'anger' or 'fear,' either three times slowly, such that speaking the word primed emotion knowledge, or 30 times quickly, such that the meaning of the word became temporarily less accessible in a process called semantic satiation. Consistent with the conceptual act model, participants who temporarily lost access to their emotion knowledge had a harder time perceiving emotions (Lindquist, Barrett *et al.,* 2006). We will return to the

conceptual act model when we discuss bodily changes and emotions.

Themes and dimensions of appraisals

The model of emotion presented in Figure 11.1 is consistent with various appraisal theories of emotion. All appraisal theories are alike in that they suggest that people's appraisals of their current circumstances (not their appraisals of physiological arousal) lead to the subjective experience of emotion, the arousal associated with it, and other components of the emotional response. Yet various appraisal theories differ in how they conceptualize the appraisal process. These theories can be divided into (1) **minimalist appraisal theories**, which reduce the number of appraisal dimensions to minimum, often based on fundamental themes, and (2) **dimensional appraisal theories**, which identify a range of appraisal dimensions thought to be sufficient to account for differences among emotions.

According to the minimalist appraisal theories, there are certain fundamental human transactions that yield specific emotions. One appraisal theorist, Richard Lazarus (1991b), identifies these fundamental transactions as core relational themes. A **core relational theme** represents the personal meaning that results from a particular pattern of appraisals about a specific person–environment relationship. It distills the appraisal process to its essence. Table 11.1 lists several emotions (such as sadness) and the core relational themes that trigger them (for sadness, irrevocable loss). These fundamental themes and their associated emotions can be found in every human culture. Some circumstances are appraised the same by almost everyone. For example, for most humans and even most animals, being near a large hissing snake tends to be appraised as threatening (Ohman, 2009). Even so, the types of circumstances that elicit the appraisal patterns listed in Table 11.1 may differ across cultures, a point we will return to in a later section.

The dimensional appraisal theories are concerned with specifying the various dimensions of appraisals and the emotional consequences of those dimensions. An example is given in Table 11.2. One dimension is the desirability of an anticipated event, and another is whether the event occurs. When we combine these two dimensions, we get four possible appraisals, each of which seems to produce a distinct emotion. (We are using only four emotions in our example to try to keep things simple.) When a desired event (such as falling in love) occurs, we experience joy; when a desired event does not occur (the person we are in love with does not love us), we experience sorrow; when an undesired event (such as doing poorly on an exam) occurs, we experience distress; and when an undesired event does not occur (not doing poorly on an exam), we experience relief.

TABLE 11.1   EMOTIONS AND THEIR COGNITIVE CAUSES

Fifteen emotions and their associated core relational themes (appraisal patterns).

Emotion	Core relational theme
Anger	A demeaning offense against me and mine
Anxiety	Facing uncertain, existential threat
Fright	Facing an immediate, concrete, and overwhelming physical danger
Guilt	Having transgressed a moral imperative
Shame	Having failed to live up to an ego ideal
Sadness	Having experienced an irrevocable loss
Envy	Wanting what someone else has
Jealousy	Resenting a third party for loss or threat to another's affection
Disgust	Taking in or being too close to an indigestible object or idea (metaphorically speaking)
Happiness	Making reasonable progress toward the realization of a goal
Pride	Enhancing our ego identity by taking credit for a valued object or achievement, either our own or that of some person or group with whom we identify
Relief	A distressing goal-incongruent condition has changed for the better or gone away
Hope	Fearing the worst but yearning for better
Love	Desiring or participating in affection, usually but not necessarily reciprocated
Compassion	Being moved by another's suffering and wanting to help

TABLE 11.2   PRIMARY APPRAISAL DIMENSIONS AND THEIR CONSEQUENCES

Combinations of two appraisal dimensions and their associated emotions. (Based on research conducted by Roseman, 1984.)

	Occur	Not occur
Desirable	Joy	Sorrow
Undesirable	Distress	Relief

The preceding example makes use of only two dimensions, but most dimensional theories of appraisal assume that numerous dimensions are involved. For example, Smith and Ellsworth (1985) found that at least six dimensions were needed to describe 15 different emotions (including, for example, anger, guilt, and sadness). These dimensions were (1) the desirability of the situation (pleasant or unpleasant), (2) the amount of effort the person anticipates spending on the situation, (3) the certainty of the situation, (4) the amount of attention the person wants to devote to the situation, (5) the degree of control the person feels he or she has over the situation, and (6) the degree of control the person attributes to non-human forces in the situation. To illustrate how the last two dimensions operate, anger is associated with an unpleasant situation caused by another person, guilt is associated with an unpleasant situation we brought on ourselves, and sadness is associated with an unpleasant situation controlled by circumstances. So, if you and your friend miss a concert that you had your heart set on hearing, you will feel anger if you missed it because your friend carelessly misplaced the tickets, guilt if you misplaced the tickets, and sadness if the performance is canceled because of a performer's illness. The virtue of this kind of approach is that it specifies the appraisal process in detail and accounts for a wide range of emotional experiences.

Despite the widespread acceptance of appraisal theories of emotion, most of the early evidence for these theories rested on correlations between self-reported appraisals and self-reported emotions. The causal role of appraisals was thus not established (Parkinson & Manstead, 1992). A later experiment supplied this missing evidence. Participants first completed a task in which they attributed a series of neutral events (such as check for the mail, wait for the bus) either to themselves (internal attribution condition) or to someone else (external attribution condition). They did this by generating either 20 sentences like 'I check for the mail' and 'I wait for the bus,' or 20 like 'He checks for the mail' and 'He waits for the bus.' Next, they faced an ambiguous negative situation: they had been told by one experimenter to proceed to the next room to complete the study. When they opened the door to the assigned room, a second experimenter cried out from within, 'Get out! Didn't you read the sign on the door? You disturbed our experiment. Wait outside the door.' How would people respond to this outburst? Would they feel guilty or get angry? Recall that guilt is associated with unpleasant circumstances you bring on yourself and anger is associated with unpleasant circumstances caused by another person. Results of the experiment showed that participants who were earlier primed to make internal attributions were more likely to express guilt and apologize, and those who were earlier primed to make external attributions were more likely to express anger and blame the other experimenter (Neumann, 2000). These findings demonstrate that cognitive appraisals precede and cause the other components of emotion.

Additional evidence for the causal role of appraisals comes from assessments of brain activity. When people evaluate a set of pictures by how pleasant or unpleasant they are, they show more activation in key brain areas associated with emotion than when they evaluate similar pictures along emotion-irrelevant dimensions, such as determining how many people appear in the picture (Hajcak *et al.*, 2006).

Conscious and unconscious appraisals

Much debate among emotion theorists has centered on whether the appraisal process necessarily occurs consciously and deliberately. Some have argued that emotions can occur without any preceding conscious thought (Zajonc, 1984). Experiments on common phobias have tested this idea by presenting pictures of spiders and snakes to participants who (1) fear snakes, (2) fear spiders, or (3) have no phobias (Ohman, 2009). In one condition, the pictures were shown long enough for participants to consciously recognize them. In another condition, a procedure called **backward masking** was used, meaning that pictures were shown for only 30 milliseconds and then masked by a neutral picture so that participants were unaware of the picture's content. Phobics showed nearly identical physiological responses (increased sweat gland activity) to pictures of their phobic object, regardless of whether they consciously saw the spider or snake or not. Other experiments confirm that, even for people without phobias, quick exposure to emotional images using similar backward masking techniques can produce emotion-specific responses (Rohr *et al.*, 2012). These sorts of studies suggest that appraisals can occur at unconscious levels, making people experience emotions for reasons unknown to them.

Most contemporary appraisal theories acknowledge that cognitive appraisals can occur automatically, outside conscious awareness. Debate continues, though, over how much of the appraisal process can occur unconsciously. One suggestion is that only the most rudimentary appraisals of valence ('Are these circumstances good for me or bad for me?'), and urgency ('How quickly must I respond?') are made outside of awareness. By contrast, more complex appraisals, such as agency ('Who is to blame?'), result from conscious information processing (Robinson, 1998).

In short, the cognitive appraisals within emotion processes are similar to other forms of cognition. They result in part from automatic processing, outside conscious awareness, and in part from controlled processing, of which we are aware (see Chapters 6 and 18 for similar dual-process perspectives). To illustrate, if from the corner of your eye you see something shaped like a snake, an automatic and unconscious appraisal process may make you jump before a more controlled and deliberate appraisal process can determine that the object in question is, in fact, a harmless piece of rope.

Appraisals in the brain

Research on the brain circuits involved in emotion processes also supports the view that appraisals occur both consciously and unconsciously. One brain structure that plays a key role within emotion circuits is the **amygdala**, a small, almond-shaped mass that is located in the lower brain and is known to register emotional reactions (Whalen & Phelps, 2009). At one time, it was thought that the amygdala received all its inputs from the cortex and, hence, that those inputs always involved conscious appraisal. But research with rats uncovered connections between sensory channels and the amygdala that do not go through the cortex, and these direct connections may be the biological basis of unconscious appraisals (LeDoux & Phelps, 2000). The amygdala is capable of responding to an alarming situation before the cortex does, which suggests that sometimes we can experience an emotion before we know why.

Although the initial research on the amygdala's role in automatic emotions was based on rats, the neural pathways involved appear similar in humans (Whalen & Phelps, 2009). Brain imaging in humans (see Chapter 2) has also demonstrated a key role for the amygdala within emotions (Figure 11.3). Using the same backward masking technique described earlier, fearful facial expressions were shown to participants for about 30 milliseconds and then masked by neutral expressions on the same faces. Even though participants had no conscious awareness of the fearful faces, imaging data showed activation within the amygdala (Whalen

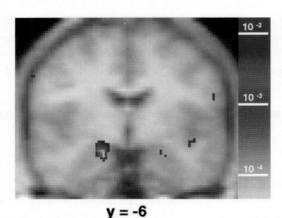

FIGURE 11.3 Amygdala Activation During Unconscious Appraisals. *This image shows a coronal slice of brain. Fearful and happy faces were shown to participants using a backward masking technique that prevented conscious awareness. Portrayed is the activation difference for masked fearful versus masked happy faces. The highlighted area represents greater activation in the amygdala for masked fearful faces. These findings suggest that the amygdala may play a role in the unconscious appraisal of emotionally relevant stimuli.*

et al., 1998). These data suggest that the amygdala monitors emotion-eliciting stimuli at an automatic, non-conscious level. Interestingly, criminals with antisocial personality disorder, like Ted Bundy, described at the start of this chapter, show less activation in the amygdala during emotional processing than normal criminals or normal non-criminals (Kiehl *et al.*, 2001), providing neurological evidence for an emotion-related deficit.

Brain regions beyond the amygdala also contribute to emotions and appraisals. A recent meta-analytic review of neuroimaging studies on human emotion, for instance, finds reliable activation of areas of the prefrontal cortex and other areas consistent with a key role for the conceptualization and language processes that are emphasized by the conceptual act model (Lindquist *et al.*, 2012).

CRITICAL THINKING QUESTIONS

1 What is the relationship between a person–environment relationship and a cognitive appraisal (that is, the first two boxes in Figure 11.1)? Can you think of a specific person–environment relationship that has, at one time, led you to experience an emotion, whereas at another time it did not?

2 If the appraisal process can be outside awareness, sometimes we may experience emotions and not know why. How then, would that sort of an emotion differ from a mood, which also has no known cause?

INTERIM SUMMARY

➡ A cognitive appraisal is an interpretation of the personal meaning of certain circumstances (or person–environment relationships) that results in an emotion. Such appraisals affect both the intensity and the quality of an emotion.

➡ The classic two-factor theory of emotion predicted that when people are induced into a state of undifferentiated arousal, the quality of their emotional experience would be influenced by their appraisal of the situation. This theory, although popular, is not well supported by data. A related effect, known as the misattribution of arousal, has received better empirical support. It states that any lingering physiological arousal can be mistakenly attributed to subsequent circumstances and intensify our emotional reactions to those circumstances.

➡ A contemporary psychological construction view of emotions, which bears some similarities to the two-factor theory, is the conceptual act model. This model holds that emotions result from the combination of more basic ingredients of mind, whereby bodily and external sensations are instantaneously made meaningful by the brain's automatic tendencies to categorize them based on past experiences.

➡ One prominent minimalist appraisal theory emphasizes the importance of emotion-specific core relational themes, like a demeaning offense for anger (see Table 11.1). Dimensional appraisal theories focus on identifying the relevant dimensions of cognitive appraisal of emotion, like degrees of certainty or control.

➡ Cognitive appraisals can occur outside conscious awareness, and brain research identifies the amygdala as involved in automatic appraisals.

SUBJECTIVE EXPERIENCES AND EMOTION

Although the initial appraisal process may occur outside conscious awareness, the subjective experience of emotions – the feeling component – is, by definition, within awareness. Recall the study of phobic people who were shown pictures of their phobic objects (spiders or snakes) via the backward masking technique that prevented conscious awareness. The results showed not only that people experienced bodily responses (increased sweat gland activity) to unseen feared objects but also that they reported feeling aversion, arousal, and lack of control, all consistent with the subjective experience of fear. So, one output of the appraisal process is a change in subjective experience. On the aversive side, we may feel angry, afraid, sad, disgusted, or perhaps some combination of these feelings. On the pleasant side, we may feel elated and joyful, serene and content, interested and engaged, or some other pleasant feeling like awe or gratitude.

To say that subjective experiences are a component of the emotion process does not mean that all emotion experiences come with this component. Researchers have argued persuasively that emotions can occur without any conscious feelings at all (Berridge & Winkielman, 2003). Nonetheless, when present, conscious subjective experiences matter.

What function do these inner feelings serve? A prominent view is that these feelings serve as feedback about the personal relevance of our current circumstances. When we feel a negative emotion, like fear or anger, the unpleasant feeling serves as a cue that something in our environment poses us a threat and that we may need to act fast to protect ourselves. When we feel a positive emotion, like joy or interest, the pleasant feeling signals that we are safe and satiated, and that we can feel free to play or explore. More generally, the feeling component of emotion is thought to guide behavior, decision-making, and information-processing (Schwarz & Clore, 2003).

Feelings modify attention and learning

We tend to pay more attention to events that fit our current feelings than to events that do not. As a consequence, we learn more about the events that fit, or are congruent with, our feelings. One classic experiment that demonstrates these phenomena involved three stages. In the first stage, participants were induced to be either happy or sad. In the second stage, the participants read a brief story about an encounter between two men – a happy character and a sad one. The story vividly described the events of the two men's lives and their emotional reactions. After reading the story, participants were asked who they thought the central character was and with whom they identified. Participants who had been induced to feel happy identified more with the happy character and thought the story contained more statements about him; participants who had been induced to feel sad identified more with the sad character and thought the story contained more statements about him. These results indicate that participants paid more attention to the character and events that were congruent with their feelings than to those that were not (Bower, 1981).

The third stage of this experiment provided evidence that participants also learned more about feeling-congruent events than about feeling-incongruent events. One day, after reading the story, the participants, now in a neutral state, returned to the laboratory, where they were asked to recall the story. Participants recalled more about the character they had identified with: for the previously happy participants, 55 per cent of the facts they recalled were about the happy character; for the previously sad participants, 80 per cent of the facts they recalled were about the sad character (Bower, 1981).

These effects have since been replicated countless times. We now know, for instance, that current feelings guide attention automatically, by producing faster reaction times to feeling-congruent events (Niedenthal, 2008). Exactly how does the congruence between our current feelings and some new material affect the learning of that material? We know that we can learn new material better if we can relate it to information already in memory. We also know that emotions affect our ability to retrieve personal memories (Buchanan, 2007). So our feelings during learning may increase the availability of memories that fit that feeling, and such memories will be easier to relate to new material that also fits that feeling. Suppose that you hear a story about a student failing in school. If you are feeling sad when you hear the story, some of your memories about failure experiences (particularly academic failures) may be easily accessible, and the similarity of these memories to the new fact of someone failing in school will make it easy to relate to them. In contrast, if you are feeling happy when you hear the story, your most accessible memories may be too dissimilar to a school failure to foster a relationship between the old memories and the new fact.

So, our feelings influence what memories are more accessible, and those memories influence what is easy for us to learn at the moment (Bower, 1981).

Feelings modify evaluations and judgments

Our feelings can affect our evaluations of other people. Everyday experiences provide numerous examples of this. When we are feeling happy, a friend's habit of constantly checking his appearance in a mirror may seem just an idiosyncrasy; when we are feeling irritable, we may dwell on how vain he is. Our feelings affect our evaluation of inanimate objects as well. In one experiment, participants were asked to evaluate their major possessions. Participants who had just been made grateful by receiving a small gift rated their televisions and cars more positively than did control participants who were feeling neutral (Isen *et al.,* 1978). Emotions also alter our economic decisions, like how much we'd be willing to pay for some object, or how much we'd be willing to sell that same object for if we already owned it (Lerner *et al.,* 2004).

Our feelings also affect our judgments about the frequency of various risks. Theorists have argued that such influence occurs because emotions activate tendencies to reproduce the same cognitive appraisals that initially produced the emotion, calling this an appraisal tendency framework (Lerner & Keltner, 2001; Han *et al.,* 2007). Feeling fear, for instance, leads us to appraise subsequent circumstances as uncertain and uncontrollable and thus causes us to see future risks as more likely. In contrast, feeling angry or happy, although feelings of different valence, leads us to appraise subsequent circumstances as certain and controllable and thus causes us to see future risks as less likely (Johnson & Tversky, 1983; Lerner & Keltner, 2001). In an experiment testing this idea, participants were first induced to feel anger or fear by vividly recounting circumstances that made them angry or fearful. They were then asked to rate the degree to which the circumstances they described were under their control and how certain or uncertain they were about them. Finally, participants estimated their own chances of experiencing a range of positive and negative life events, like marrying someone wealthy or getting a sexually transmitted disease. The results are shown in Figure 11.4. Fear and anger had opposite effects on cognitive appraisal and on estimates of risk. Those feeling fear appraised their circumstances as uncertain and uncontrollable, and these appraisals in turn predicted more pessimistic risk assessments. Those feeling anger, by contrast, appraised their circumstances as certain and controllable, and these appraisals in turn predicted more optimistic risk assessments (Lerner & Keltner, 2001).

Our feelings influence other types of judgment as well. In another experiment, participants listened to audio clips that left them feeling amused, inspired, or no particular feeling.

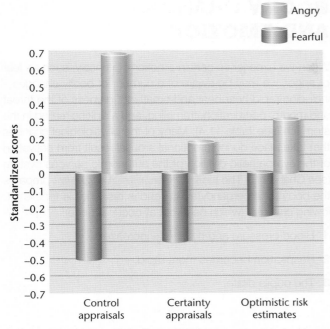

FIGURE 11.4 Fear, Anger, and Risk. *Fear and anger had opposite effects on cognitive appraisals and risk estimates. Effect sizes are represented in standardized scores to put appraisals and risk estimates on the same scale. Compared with angry participants (orange bars), fearful participants (blue bars) rated their circumstances as less under their control (left bars) and less certain (middle bars) and made more pessimistic estimates of future risks (right bars). Subsequent analyses confirmed that appraisals accounted for the effect of emotions on risk estimates.*

They then were asked to evaluate various moral dilemmas. Relative to participants who felt neutral, those who felt amused were more permissive of moral violations, whereas those who felt inspired were less so. These findings also support the appraisal tendency framework: amusement is both triggered by appraisals of irreverence and it led participants to judge moral dilemmas irreverently. By contrast, inspiration arises from appraisals of other people's moral reverence and feeling inspired led participants to judge moral dilemmas reverently (Strohminger *et al.,* 2011).

Feeling afraid, then, makes the world seem more dangerous and such perceptions can reinforce the fearful feelings. By contrast, feeling inspired can elevate moral consciousness in ways that bolster feelings of inspiration. In addition, as noted earlier, our feelings lead us to selectively attend to and learn feeling-congruent facts and memories, which can also reinforce the initial emotion. So, the cognitive consequences of subjective experiences serve to perpetuate emotional states, which can produce downward spirals for negative emotions and upward spirals for positive ones (Garland *et al.,* 2010).

THOUGHT–ACTION TENDENCIES AND EMOTION

One way that feelings guide behavior and information processing is through the urges that accompany them. These urges are called *thought–action tendencies* (Fredrickson, 1998) or sometimes just action tendencies (Frijda, 1986; Lazarus, 1991b). Table 11.3 lists several emotions and the thought–action tendencies they instill. With most negative emotions, people's thought–action tendencies become narrow and specific. In fear, for example, we feel the specific urge to escape the danger. By contrast, with most positive emotions, people's thought–action tendencies become broad and more open to possibilities. In joy, for instance, we feel the urge to be playful in general (Fredrickson & Branigan, 2005). Among the positive emotions, some, like joy and contentment, predominantly produce thought–action tendencies that center on the self, whereas others, like gratitude and inspiration, prompt a focus on other people to a greater extent (Algoe & Haidt, 2009).

Certainly, people do not invariably act on the urges that accompany their emotions. Keep in mind that these are thought–action *tendencies*, not thoughts or actions per se. They merely describe people's ideas about possible courses of action, and whether these ideas narrow to a specific behavioral urge, as for negative emotions, or broaden to encompass a wide range of possibilities, as for positive emotions. Whether urges become actions depends on the complex interplay of

TABLE 11.3 EMOTIONS AND THEIR ASSOCIATED THOUGHT–ACTION TENDENCIES

Twelve emotions and the urges they spark.

Emotion	Thought–action tendency
Anger	Attack
Fear	Escape
Disgust	Expel
Guilt	Make amends
Shame	Disappear
Sadness	Withdraw
Joy	Play
Interest	Explore
Contentment	Savor and integrate
Pride	Dream big
Gratitude	Be prosocial
Inspiration	Become a better person

impulse control, cultural norms, and other factors. Even so, many emotion theorists hold that having particular thought–action tendencies come to mind is what made emotions evolutionarily adaptive: for negative emotions, specific thought–action tendencies are thought to represent those actions that worked best in getting our ancestors out of life-or-death situations (Levenson, 1994; Tooby & Cosmides, 1990). For positive emotions, broadened thought–action tendencies are thought to build enduring personal resources – like health, optimism, and social support – which might have also made the difference between life and death for our ancestors (Fredrickson, 1998, 2001, 2013). We develop this idea later in the chapter, when we turn to positive psychology.

One way researchers have assessed whether specific emotions produce specific action tendencies is to show study participants a range of images selected to induce fear, disgust, sexual attraction, or no emotion whatsoever (e.g., household objects). Participants viewed these images with their hands palms down on an experimental table, and during each picture they were cued to extend their wrists and fingers as quickly as possible, while the electrical signals in the muscles of their forearms were recorded along with the force of their hand movement. Researchers found that, compared to all the other images, the fear-inducing images produced faster withdrawal actions, as indexed by muscle activity in the forearms (Coombes *et al.,* 2007).

INTERIM SUMMARY

➡ Subjective experiences of emotions, or feelings, guide behavior, decision-making, and judgment.

➡ Subjective experiences also steer memory, learning, and risk assessments.

➡ Different emotions carry urges to think and act in certain ways, called *thought–action tendencies*. These are summarized in Table 11.3.

➡ Negative emotions narrow people's momentary thought–action repertoires, promoting quick action in life-threatening circumstances. By contrast, positive emotions broaden people's momentary thought–action repertoires, which, over time, can build lasting resources for survival.

CRITICAL THINKING QUESTIONS

1 What are some of the cognitive processes by which a particular emotion might perpetuate itself?

2 Some theorists argue that the thought–action tendencies listed in Table 11.3 are the result of evolutionary processes. Why might this be the case?

BODILY CHANGES AND EMOTION

When we experience certain emotions intensely, such as fear or anger, we may be aware of a number of bodily changes – including rapid heartbeat and breathing, dryness of the throat and mouth, perspiration, trembling, and a sinking feeling in the stomach (see Table 11.4). Many of the physiological changes that take place during emotional arousal result from activation of the sympathetic division of the autonomic nervous system (see Chapter 2). The **sympathetic nervous system** prepares the body for emergency action and is responsible for the following changes (which need not all occur at once):

1 Blood pressure and heart rate increase.

2 Respiration becomes more rapid.

3 The pupils dilate.

TABLE 11.4 SYMPTOMS OF FEAR IN COMBAT FLYING

Based on reports of combat pilots during World War II.

During combat missions did you feel. . . ?	Sometimes	Often	Total
A pounding heart and rapid pulse	56%	30%	86%
That your muscles were very tense	53	30	83
Easily irritated or angry	58	22	80
Dryness of the throat or mouth	50	30	80
Nervous perspiration or cold sweat	53	26	79
Butterflies in the stomach	53	23	76
A sense of unreality – that this could not be happening to you	49	20	69
A need to urinate frequently	40	25	65
Trembling	53	11	64
Confused or rattled	50	3	53
Weak or faint	37	4	41
That right after a mission you were unable to remember the details of what had happened	34	5	39
Sick to the stomach	33	5	38
Unable to concentrate	32	3	35
That you had wet or soiled your pants	4	1	5

4 Perspiration increases while secretion of saliva and mucus decreases.

5 Blood-sugar level increases to provide more energy.

6 The blood clots more quickly in case of wounds.

7 Blood is diverted from the stomach and intestines to the brain and skeletal muscles.

8 The hairs on the skin become erect, causing goose pimples.

The sympathetic nervous system thus gears up the organism for energy output, often called the 'fight-or-flight' response. As the emotion subsides, the **parasympathetic nervous system** – the energy-conserving system – takes over and returns the organism to its normal state, or what is sometimes called the 'calm-and-connect' response.

These activities of the autonomic nervous system are themselves triggered by activity in certain regions of the brain, including the hypothalamus (which, as we saw in the last chapter, plays a major role in many biological motives) and the amygdala, which, as described earlier in this chapter, is implicated in the appraisal process. Impulses from these areas are transmitted to nuclei in the brain stem that control the functioning of the autonomic nervous system. The autonomic nervous system then acts directly on the muscles and internal organs to initiate some of the bodily changes described here. It also acts indirectly by stimulating the adrenal hormones to produce other bodily changes. Note that the kind of heightened physiological arousal we have described is characteristic of those negative emotions that come with urges for specific actions requiring substantial physical energy (such as attack or flee; the role of this fight-or-flight response in threatening or stressful situations is discussed further in Chapter 14). Indeed, a core idea within many emotion theories is that thought–action tendencies infuse both mind and body. So, for example, when you feel fear and experience the urge to escape, your body simultaneously reacts by mobilizing appropriate autonomic support for the possibility of running. According to this perspective, the function of the physiological changes evident during these potent negative emotions is to prepare the body for specific actions (Levenson, 1994).

Positive emotions, some have argued, produce few bodily changes because their associated thought–action tendencies are broad and not specific. So instead of producing the heightened arousal that supports specific actions, positive emotions may be particularly

suited for helping people recover from any lingering arousal that follows negative emotions, an idea called the **undoing effect of positive emotions**. A laboratory experiment tested this idea. Participants were first asked to prepare a speech on 'Why you are a good friend' under considerable time pressure. They were told that the speech would be video-taped and evaluated by their peers. This speech task produced feelings of anxiety, along with increases in blood pressure, heart rate, and other indices of cardiovascular activity. These physiological changes lingered on even after participants were informed that they would not have to deliver their speech after all. At this point, the participants were shown a randomly selected film clip that induced one of two positive emotions (joy or contentment), a negative emotion (sadness), or no emotion. Results are shown in Figure 11.5. Those who turned their attention to either of the two positive emotion films returned to their own baseline levels of cardiovascular activity faster than those who saw either the neutral or sad films (Fredrickson *et al.*, 2000). Cultivating positive emotions, then, appears to be a particularly good way to combat the lingering physiological aftereffects of negative emotions.

Intensity of emotions

What is the relationship between the heightened physiological arousal experienced with some emotions and the subjective experience of those emotions? In particular, is our perception of our own arousal – called **visceral perception** – part of the experience of the emotion? One way to answer this question is to study the emotional life of individuals with spinal cord injuries. When the spinal cord is severed or lesioned, sensations below the point of injury cannot reach the brain. Because some of these sensations arise from the sympathetic nervous

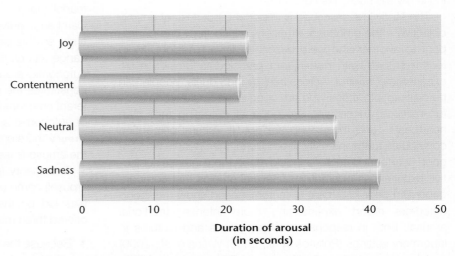

FIGURE 11.5 The Undoing Effect of Positive Emotions. *Joy and contentment produce faster cardiovascular recovery from lingering negative emotional arousal than neutrality and sadness.*

system, the injuries reduce the contributions of autonomic arousal to the experience of emotion.

In one study, US army veterans with spinal cord injuries were divided into five groups according to the location on the spinal cord where the lesion occurred. In one group, the lesions were near the neck (at the cervical level), with no feedback from the sympathetic system to the brain. In another group, the lesions were near the base of the spine (at the sacral level), with at least partial feedback from the sympathetic nerves possible. The other three groups fell between these two extremes. The five groups thus represented a continuum of visceral perception: the higher the lesion on the spinal cord, the less the feedback of the autonomic nervous system to the brain (Hohmann, 1962).

The participants were interviewed to determine their feelings in situations of fear, anger, grief, and sexual excitement. Each person was asked to recall an emotion-arousing incident prior to the injury and a comparable incident following the injury and then to compare the intensity of their emotional experience in each case. The higher the lesion on the individual's spinal cord (that is, the fewer visceral cues), the greater the decrease in emotionality following injury. The same relationship was true for states of sexual excitement and grief. A reduction in autonomic arousal resulted in a reduction in the intensity of experienced emotion.

Comments by veterans with the highest spinal cord lesions suggested that they could react emotionally to arousing situations but that they did not really feel emotional. For example, 'It's sort of a cold anger. Sometimes I act angry when I see some injustice. I yell and cuss and raise hell, because if you don't do it sometimes, I've learned people will take advantage of you; but it doesn't have the heat to it that it used to. It's a mental kind of anger.' Or, 'I say I am afraid, like when I'm going into a real stiff exam at school, but I don't really feel afraid, not all tense and shaky with the hollow feeling in my stomach, like I used to.'

The study just described is important, but it is not entirely objective – the emotional situations varied from one participant to another and were described from hindsight. More recent studies with non-injured participants provide more experimental control. Across healthy individuals, people can be classed into those who are good at visceral perception – for instance, those who are good at detecting their own heartbeat – and those who are not. If visceral perception contributes to the intensity of emotions, then people who are good heartbeat detectors should report more intense subjective experiences of emotions. Several studies that compare good and poor heartbeat detectors indeed show that good detectors report experiencing more intense emotional arousal, both in response to viewing films and pictures in laboratory settings (Pollatos et al., 2005; Wiens et al., 2000) and in response to daily life events (Barrett et al., 2004). Related studies find that good heartbeat detectors show more intense facial expressions (Ferguson & Katkin, 1996)

Physical arousal may intensify feelings of anger.

and more pronounced emotion-related brain activity (Pollatos et al., 2005) in response to emotional pictures. Together with the studies on spinal cord injuries, these studies suggest that visceral perception plays a role in the experience of the intensity of emotions (Schachter, 1964).

Differentiation of emotions

Clearly, autonomic arousal contributes to the intensity of emotional experience. But does it differentiate the emotions? In other words, is there one pattern of physiological activity for excitement, another for anger, still another for fear, and so on? This question dates back to William James, the author of the very first psychology textbook, published in 1890. He proposed that the perception of bodily changes *is* the subjective experience of emotion and that we could not have one without the other: 'We feel sorry because we cry, angry because we strike, afraid because we tremble, and not that we cry, strike, or tremble, because we are sorry, angry, or fearful' (James, 1890/1950, p. 450). The Danish physiologist Carl Lange arrived at a similar conclusion at about the same time, so this view has come to be known as the James–Lange theory. It runs as follows: because the perception of autonomic arousal (and perhaps of other bodily changes) constitutes the experience of an emotion, and because different emotions feel different, there must be a distinct pattern of autonomic activity for each emotion. The **James–Lange theory** therefore holds that autonomic arousal differentiates the emotions (see Figure 11.2b).

This theory (particularly the part dealing with autonomic arousal) came under severe attack in the 1920s. The attack was led by the physiologist Walter Cannon (1927), who offered three major criticisms:

1 Because the internal organs are relatively insensitive structures and are not well supplied with nerves, internal changes occur too slowly to be the primary source of emotional feeling.

2 Artificially inducing the bodily changes associated with an emotion – for example, injecting a drug such as epinephrine – does not produce the experience of a true emotion. At most, it produces 'as if' emotions: injected participants remark, 'I feel as if afraid.'

3 The pattern of autonomic arousal does not seem to differ much from one emotional state to another. For example, anger makes our heart beat faster, but so does the sight of a loved one.

The third argument, then, explicitly denies that autonomic arousal can differentiate the emotions.

Psychologists have tried to rebut Cannon's third point as they develop increasingly accurate measures of the components of autonomic arousal. Although a few experiments in the 1950s reported distinct physiological patterns for different emotions (Ax, 1953; Funkenstein, 1955), until the 1990s most studies had found little evidence for different patterns of arousal being associated with different emotions. A study by Levenson *et al.,* (1990), however, provided evidence of autonomic patterns that are distinct for different emotions. American participants produced the facial muscle movements associated with each of six emotions – surprise, disgust, sadness, anger, fear, and happiness – by following instructions about which particular facial muscles to contract. While they held a given muscle configuration for 10 seconds, the researchers measured their heart rate, skin temperature, and other indicators of autonomic arousal. A number of these measures revealed differences among the emotions (see Figure 11.6). Heart rate was faster for the negative emotions of anger, fear, and sadness than for happiness, surprise, and disgust, and the first three emotions themselves could be partially distinguished by the fact that skin temperature was higher in anger than in fear or sadness. So, even though both anger and the sight of a loved one make our heart beat faster, only anger makes it beat much faster; and although anger and fear have much in common, anger is hot and fear is cold (no wonder people describe their anger as their 'blood boiling' and their fear as 'bone-chilling' or as 'getting cold feet').

Other research suggests that these distinctive arousal patterns may be universal. Levenson, Ekman, and colleagues studied the Minangkabau of Western Sumatra, a culture very different from Western culture. Again, participants produced facial muscle movements for various emotions – fear, anger, sadness, and disgust – while measures were taken of their heart rate, skin temperature, and other

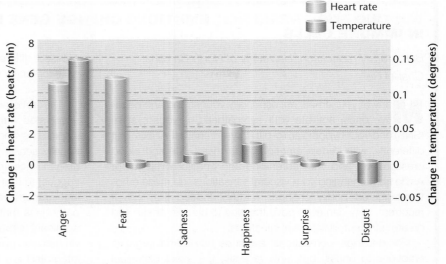

FIGURE 11.6 **Differences in Arousal for Different Emotions.** *Changes in heart rate (orange) and right finger temperature (blue). For heart rate, the changes associated with anger, fear, and sadness were all significantly greater than those for happiness, surprise, and disgust. For finger temperature, the change associated with anger was significantly different from that for all other emotions.*

indicators of arousal. Although the magnitude of the physiological changes was less than that of the changes reported earlier for American individuals, the patterns of arousal for the different emotions were the same: heart rate was faster for anger, fear, and sadness than for disgust, and skin temperature was highest for anger (Levenson *et al.,* 1992).

These results are important, but they do not provide unequivocal support for the James–Lange theory or for the claim that autonomic arousal is the only component that differentiates the emotions. The studies we have described demonstrated that there are some physiological differences between emotions (though some researchers question this; see Cacioppo *et al.,* 2000; Barrett, 2006b), not that those differences are perceived and experienced as qualitative differences between emotions. Even if autonomic arousal does help differentiate some emotions, it is unlikely that it differentiates all emotions. The difference between contentment and gratitude, for example, may not be found in autonomic reactions. Also, Cannon's first two arguments against the James–Lange theory still stand: autonomic arousal is at times too slow to differentiate emotional experiences, and artificial induction of arousal does not yield a true emotion. For these reasons, many emotion theorists still believe that something other than autonomic arousal differentiates the emotions. As we discussed earlier, that something else (or part of it) is usually thought to be the individual's cognitive appraisal of the situation. Pushing further, the conceptual act model integrates appraisal views and visual perception views to suggest that emotions are differentiated by the way the

CUTTING EDGE RESEARCH EMOTIONS CHANGE GENE EXPRESSION IN IMMUNE CELLS

Barbara L. Fredrickson, University of North Carolina, Chapel Hill

Many of your emotions, especially your strong and negative ones, activate your sympathetic nervous system (SNS) and your hypothalamic-pituitary-adrenal (HPA) axis. Put differently, with certain emotions, your heart rate and blood pressure rise and your adrenaline and cortisol levels jump. Aside from changing your visceral sensations, do these emotion-triggered bodily changes matter? Indeed they do. If recurrent, they can even pave the way to chronic illness and greater susceptibility to viral infections.

For decades, correlational evidence has linked negative emotions to illness, but, until recently, the exact biological pathways by which emotions exert a long-term impact on physical health remained a mystery. Breakthroughs came when the human genome was fully sequenced at the turn of the millennium. Psychologists are now able to take a bioinformatics approach to the entire human genome, examining around 22 000 genes at once, to discover emotion-related patterns. Evidence gathered with this approach now suggests how the bodily changes associated with frequent negative emotions – such as those sparked by chronic loneliness, imminent bereavement, stress, or poverty – activate cellular processes that produce sweeping alterations in gene expression, especially in genes that govern the immune system. In particular, recurrent negative emotions appear to up-regulate pro-inflammatory genes and down-regulate anti-viral genes. These changes strongly suggest that your immune system is quite sensitive to your negative emotions, especially if those emotions create a daily diet of certain biochemicals.

Cole's 2009 research on gene expression in human immune cells showed via heat-plots, how genes are expressed differently within white blood cells for lonely versus socially integrated people.

The pattern of changes in gene expression found to be associated with negative emotions is so reliable that it has inspired psychologists to theorize about what value an emotionally sensitive immune system might have held for our human ancestors. Cole and colleagues, for instance, have suggested that our bodies evolved to have a 'forward-thinking' immune response, one that anticipates the kinds of pathogens that we are most likely to encounter if our predominant circumstances continue in the future. Because viruses are spread by social contact, people who are socially integrated are the ones most likely to face viral infection. So, to the extent that people perceive themselves to be well-connected socially, their bodies anticipate viral infections and up-regulate antiviral genes. This is the pattern seen for non-lonely people. By contrast, bacterial infections are arguably more likely for social outcasts. Human ancestors who were cast out of social groups faced increased risks for becoming wounded either by predators or hostile humans. So, to the extent that people perceive themselves to be socially isolated, their bodies anticipate bacterial infections and up-regulate genes associated with innate antibacterial responses. This is the pattern seen for lonely people (Cole *et al.*, 2011). While today's lonely people may not face the same risks for predation and violence, the human immune system still reflects our ancestral history. What this cutting edge research tells us is that the emotions you feel today just might influence capacities of your immune system next season. Just as your daily diet of fruits and vegetables little-by-little influences your long-term health, so does your daily diet of emotions.

---

human brain swiftly categorizes current external and internal sensations based on prior experiences. The Seeing Both Sides feature later in this chapter takes these debated issues further still.

INTERIM SUMMARY

- ➔ Intense negative emotions involve physiological arousal caused by activation of the sympathetic division of the autonomic nervous system.

- ➔ Positive emotions appear to have an undoing effect on lingering negative emotional arousal.

- ➔ People with spinal cord injuries, which limit feedback from the autonomic nervous system, report experiencing less intense emotions. Other studies also suggest that visceral perception contributes to the intensity of emotional experiences.

- ➔ The James–Lange theory states that autonomic arousal also differentiates the emotions, and evidence suggests that, to a degree, the pattern of arousal (for example, heartbeat, skin temperature) differs for different emotions.

FACIAL MUSCLE MOVEMENTS AND EMOTION

The facial movements that sometimes accompany an emotion serve to communicate the sender's emotion, often eliciting emotion in those who make eye contact with the sender (Schrammel et al., 2009). Since the publication of Charles Darwin's 1872 classic, The Expression of Emotion in Man and Animals, psychologists have regarded the communication of emotion as an important function, one that has survival value for the species. Looking frightened may warn others that danger is present, perceiving that someone is angry tells us that he or she may be about to act aggressively, and seeing someone smile genuinely makes us feel safe and drawn to them. Other research suggests that, in addition to their communicative function, facial (and bodily) muscle movements contribute to the subjective experience of emotion, just as appraisals and internal bodily changes do. Facial muscle movements might at times even jump-start the whole emotion process. Although most of the research described below centers on the face, increasingly researchers are extending this work to examine how bodily postures communicate emotions as well (Gross et al., 2012; Stienen & de Gelder, 2011).

Communication of emotion through facial muscle movements

Certain facial muscle movements seem to have a universal meaning, regardless of the culture in which an individual is raised. The universal expression of anger, for example, involves a flushed face, brows lowered and drawn together, flared nostrils, a clenched jaw, and bared teeth. When people from five countries (the USA, Brazil, Chile, Argentina, and Japan) viewed photographs showing facial muscle movements typical of happiness, anger, sadness, disgust, fear, and surprise, they had little difficulty identifying the emotion that each face conveyed. Even members of remote groups that had had virtually no contact with Western cultures (the Fore and Dani peoples in New Guinea) were able to identify the emotions represented by faces of people from Western cultures. Likewise, American college students who viewed videotapes of facial muscle actions of Fore natives identified the associated emotions accurately, although they sometimes confused fear and surprise (Ekman, 1982). Even though facial musculature varies from person to person, the muscles needed to produce these universally recognized emotions appear to be basic and constant across people (Waller et al., 2008), suggesting that the human face has evolved to transmit emotion signals and the human brain has evolved to decode these signals (Smith et al., 2005).

The universality of the facial muscle movements associated with certain emotions supports Darwin's claim that they are innate responses with an evolutionary history. According to Darwin, many of the ways in which we communicate emotion are inherited patterns that originally had some survival value. For example, the expression of disgust or rejection is based on the organism's attempt to rid itself of something unpleasant – perhaps even poisonous – that it has ingested. To quote Darwin (1872):

> The term 'disgust', in its simplest sense, means something offensive to the taste. But as disgust also causes annoyance, it is generally accompanied by a frown, and often by gestures as if to push away or to guard oneself against the offensive object. Extreme disgust is expressed by movements around the mouth identical with those preparatory to the act of vomiting. The mouth is opened widely, with the upper lip strongly retracted. The partial closure of the eyelids, or the turning away of the eyes or of the whole body, are likewise highly expressive of disdain. These actions seem to declare that the despised person is not worth looking at, or is disagreeable to behold. Spitting seems an almost universal sign of contempt or disgust; and spitting obviously represents the rejection of anything offensive from the mouth.

The fact that the facial muscle movements of emotions communicate important information is demonstrated even more powerfully when the facial configuration of one person by itself changes the behavior of another person. Such evidence is provided by studies of infants' interactions with their mothers. In one study, infants who had just started to crawl were placed on an apparatus called a visual cliff (described in Chapter 5, and shown in Figure 5.36). The depth of the apparent cliff was not as deep as that used in studies of depth perception; instead, it was the size of an ordinary step, which made it less clear whether the drop posed a danger or not. When infants approached the edge of the cliff, they would look to their mother. In one condition, mothers had been instructed to move their facial muscles to produce an expression of intense fear. In another, they were instructed

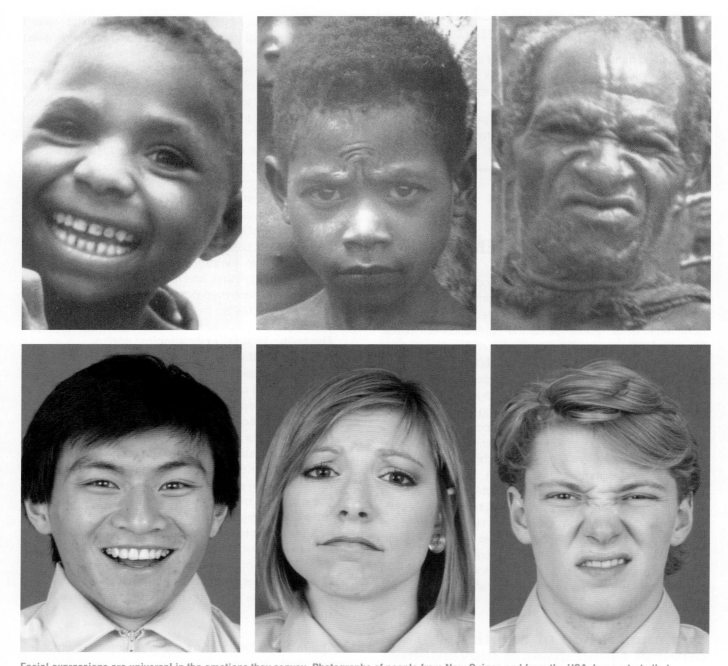

Facial expressions are universal in the emotions they convey. Photographs of people from New Guinea and from the USA demonstrate that specific emotions are conveyed by the same facial expressions. Shown here are, from left to right, happiness, sadness, and disgust.

to smile broadly. The mothers' facial muscle movements resolved the infants' uncertainty about the danger: babies whose mothers showed fear never crossed to the deep side, whereas 74 per cent of those whose mothers smiled did (Sorce *et al.,* 1985).

Although facial muscle movements seem to be innately associated with particular emotions, certain aspects of them are learned. Emotional **display rules**, for instance, vary across cultures and specify the types of emotions people should communicate in certain situations and the behaviors

appropriate for particular emotions. As an example, in some cultures people who lose a loved one are expected to feel sad and to express their sadness by openly crying and wailing for the loved one to return. In other cultures, bereaved people are expected to sing, dance, and be merry. In Europe, two men greeting each other on the street may embrace and kiss, but in the USA such displays of affection are often taboo for men. A laboratory study with participants from Japan and the USA demonstrated cultural similarities in expressions alongside differences in display rules. Participants from both cultures viewed a disgusting film clip either alone or in the presence of an authority figure. Although they showed nearly identical facial muscle movements when alone, when the authority was present, Japanese participants more often masked their disgust with a smile (Ekman, 1972). Superimposed on the basic facial muscle movements of emotion, which appear to be universal, are conventional forms of expressions – a kind of language of emotion that is recognized by other members of the culture but potentially misunderstood by people from other cultures (Elfenbein *et al.,* 2007).

The facial feedback hypothesis

The idea that facial muscle movements, in addition to their communicative function, also contribute to our experience of emotions is called the **facial feedback hypothesis** (Tompkins, 1962). This hypothesis runs parallel to the James–Lange theory: just as we receive feedback about (or perceive) our autonomic arousal, so do we receive feedback about our facial muscles, and this feedback can cause or intensify the experience of emotions. The hypothesis is illustrated in Figure 11.2c. Play around with this idea yourself. Make yourself smile, and hold that smile for several seconds. Did you begin to feel a little happier? Now, make yourself scowl and hold it. Does this make you feel a bit tense or angry?

Testing the facial feedback hypothesis experimentally is trickier than making faces and telling how you feel. Experimenters need to rule out the possibility that participants report their feelings based on common knowledge about which expressions and feelings go together, like the knowledge that smiling and feeling happy go hand-in-hand. The trick is to get participants to smile without knowing it. In one such experiment, participants rated cartoons for funniness while holding a pen either in their teeth or in their lips. Holding a pen in your teeth forces your face into a smile, while holding it in your lips prevents a smile. (Try it!) Consistent with the facial feedback hypothesis, participants who held the pen in their teeth rated the cartoons as funnier than those who held the pen in their lips (Strack *et al.,* 1988). Similar studies show an effect for body postures as well (Flack, 2006).

In addition to these studies, which show a direct connection between facial muscle movements and experienced emotion, other experiments indicate that facial muscle movements may have an indirect effect on experienced emotion by increasing autonomic arousal. Such an effect was demonstrated in the experiment discussed earlier in which producing particular facial muscle movements led to changes in heartbeat and skin temperature (Levenson *et al.,* 1990). We therefore need to add facial muscle movement to our list of factors that can initiate emotions. Even so, knowing that we can jump-start an emotion by moving certain facial muscles does not mean that this is the typical way that emotions unfold. In daily life, appraisals of our current

circumstances are still the most likely trigger of emotions, as described in Figure 11.1. Yet, when facing adversity, knowledge of the facial feedback hypothesis might inspire us to 'grin and bear it,' and studies have shown that doing so is linked with speedy physiological recovery (Kraft & Pressman, in press).

> ### INTERIM SUMMARY
>
> ➔ The facial muscle movements that accompany a subset of emotions have a universal meaning: people from different cultures agree on what emotion a person in a particular photograph is expressing.
>
> ➔ The communicative power of facial muscle movements is evident in parent–infant interactions. Mothers' facial expressions of fear or joy have been shown to dramatically alter their infants' behavior.
>
> ➔ Cultures may differ in the factors that elicit certain emotions and in display rules that specify how emotions should be experienced and expressed.
>
> ➔ In addition to their communicative functions, the facial muscle movements associated with emotions may contribute to the subjective experience of an emotion (the facial feedback hypothesis).

> ### CRITICAL THINKING QUESTIONS
>
> 1 What effect does your smile have on others? What effect does your smile have on you?
>
> 2 How do the facial feedback hypothesis, and Schachter and Singer's classic study relate to the model of emotion illustrated in Figure 11.1?

RESPONSES TO EMOTION: EMOTION REGULATION

Emotion regulation, or people's responses to their own emotions, can be considered a component in the emotion process because people – at least by middle childhood – almost always have reactions to their emotions and goals about what they would like to feel or express, and when. Sometimes people have the goal of maintaining or intensifying an emotion, whether positive or negative. For instance, you might wish to savor and prolong the joy you feel when you're with people you love. In another circumstance, you might want to work up your anger before registering a complaint to a merchant. Other times, people have the goal of minimizing or eliminating an emotion, whether positive or negative. Imagine feeling immensely proud of a personal achievement, perhaps landing a good job. While on that pleasurable high, imagine running into a friend who has recently been turned down for multiple jobs and remains jobless. Might you want to minimize your expressions of pride at that moment? Yet perhaps most commonly, people's goals are to minimize their negative emotions, like sadness or anger. You might pursue this goal to lift your own spirits, to shield another person from your negative expressions, or both.

Emotions and people's efforts to regulate them go hand-in-hand – so much so that we can hardly have one without the other. Indeed, a considerable part of the socialization process is directed toward teaching children how and when to regulate their emotions. Parents teach their children, both directly and by example, when certain emotions are appropriate and when they are not. Take the example of receiving a disappointing gift (say, an ugly sweater) from your grandmother. Can you show your disappointment to your grandmother? Your parents hope that you won't, and eventually you learn not to. Why is this important? Evidence suggests that children's success in learning these lessons about emotion regulation predicts their social success more generally (Eisenberg *et al.*, 2011). For instance, experimenters who have given preschool children disappointing gifts in the lab have learned that kids' abilities to control their expressions of negative emotion are negatively correlated with their risks for later disruptive behavior problems (Cole *et al.*, 1994).

People control or regulate their emotions in many different ways. The timing of people's attempts to regulate their emotions also matters. Table 11.5, for instance, divides different strategies for regulating emotions into antecedent-focused approaches and response-focused approaches.

TABLE 11.5 CLASSIFICATION OF EMOTION REGULATION STRATEGIES

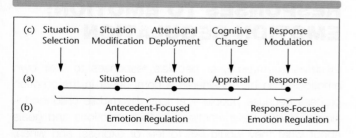

Another study classified the different strategies that people use to improve their negative emotions as either cognitive or behavioral and as either diversion or engagement tactics (Parkinson & Totterdell, 1999). Table 11.5 lists these different kinds of strategies. Suppose you had a fight with a close friend, are angry, but want to feel better. You could disengage from your anger through sheer mental effort, by trying to think of nothing, or by distracting yourself by doing something fun or demanding, like playing your guitar or doing your calculus assignment. Alternatively, you could confront your feelings or the situation with an engagement strategy. Maybe you can reappraise the situation as better than you thought – if there's another reason your friend was so irritable, you need not take it personally. Or you can try to solve the underlying problem, by talking through the issues with your friend. These tactics are not mutually exclusive. You might first use distraction to quell the heat of your anger and then later, when you have a cooler head, you might discuss the underlying problem with your friend. In addition, these tactics are not always deliberately chosen. Like other cognitions and behavior, with repeated use, they can become automatic responses, outside of conscious awareness.

People's responses to their emotions – whether deliberate regulation strategies or automatic responses – can influence the other components of emotion, either directly or indirectly. This is why Figure 11.1 has feedback arrows leading from responses to emotion, on the right, to all the preceding boxes. This influence also underscores that an emotion is a process – one that unfolds and changes over time – and not a simple state that can be captured in a single snapshot. Imagine, for instance, that you are the first to arrive at the scene after a bicyclist is hit by a car. You notice the bicyclist's leg is broken because it's bent in an unnatural position. Here, your initial emotion of disgust might quickly transform into compassion as you reappraise the circumstance as one in which the injured bicyclist needs your help. So your emotions in this situation change over time, in part because of your responses to your own emotions ('I can't show my feelings of disgust to this suffering person'), and in part because the circumstances themselves change over time (e.g., the ambulance arrives, and you feel relieved).

Does it matter which strategy you use to regulate an emotion? Consider that ugly sweater again. One way to convince your grandmother that you appreciate the gift is to focus on what your face shows. You could actively suppress any facial signs of disgust or disappointment and instead make yourself smile and give Grandma a hug. Another strategy would be to focus on how you interpret the situation, reappraising it to be better than you first thought. You might tell yourself (as your parents often did), 'It's the thought that counts' and focus on the care and effort your grandmother invested in selecting or knitting that sweater.

Doing so might naturally yield a smile and hug for Grandma. Although these two strategies for dealing with the ugly sweater might be equally convincing to your grandmother, the strategy of suppressing facial muscle movements has been shown to increase both autonomic nervous system activation (Gross & Levenson, 1997) and amygdala activation (Goldin *et al.,* 2008). Reappraisals, by contrast, don't appear to take a physiological toll and actually reduce amygdala activation (Goldin *et al.*, 2008), because they change emotions, rather than stifle them.

Research has shown that efforts to suppress facial muscle movements take a toll on cognitive functioning, too (Muraven *et al.,* 1998; Richards & Gross, 2000). In one study, participants were shown slides of men with recent or past injuries, many of them quite serious and therefore disgusting to view. During the slide presentation, participants heard each man's name, occupation, and type of accident. In one condition (suppression), participants were instructed to control their facial muscles by looking neutral and keeping still. In another condition (reappraisal), they were told to view the slides 'with the detached interest of a medical professional' and to try to think so objectively that 'you don't feel anything at all.' For comparison, in a third condition, participants were simply told to view the slides carefully. Results showed that people instructed to suppress had poorer memory for the injured men's background information than those who simply watched. Those who reappraised showed no such memory deficit (Richards & Gross, 2000). This finding suggests that efforts to maintain composure by suppressing facial muscle movements associated with emotions may impair people's ability to navigate their social worlds. If, for instance, one person in a heated argument shuts down emotionally and the other doesn't, they may end up with different memories of who said what, which in time could erode the relationship. Indeed, a longitudinal study of first-year university students finds that those who tend to suppress their emotions pay social costs in terms of lower social support, less closeness to others, and lower social satisfaction (Srivastava *et al.,* 2009).

So reappraisal seems a better strategy for regulating emotions than suppressing facial muscle movements. Other research has shown that, at least in the short run, distraction techniques – like playing basketball or reading an absorbing novel – are better strategies than rumination techniques – like thinking over and over again about the causes and consequences of your sadness or anger. Rumination tends to heighten negative emotions, whereas distraction lessens them. Because of the effects of emotions on evaluations and judgments (described earlier), eventual efforts to solve underlying problems tend to be more successful once negative emotions have abated (Hilt *et al.,* 2010). We return to a discussion of rumination and its effects on depression and anxiety in Chapter 14.

INTERIM SUMMARY

➔ People almost always respond to or regulate their emotions, by either exaggerating or minimizing them, and the ability to do so predicts social success.

➔ Emotion regulation strategies have been classified as either cognitive or behavioral and as either diversion or engagement (see Table 11.5).

➔ Responses to emotion can influence other components of the emotion process. This is why Figure 11.1 has feedback arrows leading from 'responses to emotion' to all preceding boxes.

➔ The strategies people use to regulate emotions can have unexpected repercussions. For instance, suppressing facial muscle movements increases autonomic arousal, impairs memory, and takes a social toll.

CRITICAL THINKING QUESTIONS

1 Identify and describe an example from your own life in which you deliberately tried to regulate an emotion. How did you do it? Did your regulation strategy alter the other components of the emotion process? Which ones?

2 Research suggests that if you merely interact with a person who suppresses his own emotions, your own physiological arousal may increase. How might this happen?

EMOTIONS, GENDER, AND CULTURE

So far, in our discussion of the emotion process, we've emphasized how that process is similar for everybody. Yet emotional circumstances often bring out the differences between individuals and across groups. Sometimes those differences reflect personality and individuality (discussed in Chapters 12 and 13), and other times those differences reflect socialization histories, which vary by gender and culture. As we turn to issues of gender and culture in emotion processes, keep in mind that socialized differences and biological similarities both play key roles in the emotion process. As discussed in Chapter 1, it's not 'nature *or* nurture' but rather 'nature *and* nurture.'

Looking back to Figure 11.1, you will notice that the emotion process begins with people's appraisals of their transactions with the environment and ends with their responses to their own emotions. One way to conceptualize the differences in emotion by gender and culture is to situate those differences as 'front-end' or 'back-end' differences. Front-end differences refer to those that begin with, or precede, the appraisal process. For instance, as we saw in our discussion of objectification theory (Chapter 10), to the extent that girls and women face circumstances that emphasize the importance of their weight and appearance, they may experience certain emotions – like shame – and certain emotional consequences – like depression and eating disorders – more frequently than do boys and men. By contrast, back-end differences refer to those linked to responses to emotion. People in some cultures, for instance, express fewer emotions socially, appearing stoic, whereas those in other cultures are very expressive and effusive. Using this perspective, we characterize the middle part of the process – the emotional responses of subjective experience, thought–action tendencies, bodily changes, and, to some extent, facial muscle movements – as relatively less influenced by gender and culture differences. This is clearly an oversimplification. For instance, we just discussed how responses to emotion serve to modify each and every other component of the emotion process. As such, any differences by gender or culture in responses to emotion can also produce differences in these middle components. Indeed, neuroimaging research demonstrates gender differences in brain activation during emotions (Whittle *et al.,* 2011). Even so, those differences in the middle components may be secondary to differences in front-end or back-end processes.

Gender differences

First, note that people – men and women alike – hold strong beliefs about how emotions differ by gender. Women are stereotyped as the more emotional sex, experiencing and expressing emotions more often. The exceptions are anger and pride, which are among the few emotions held to be experienced and expressed more often by men (Plant *et al.,* 2000). How do these stereotypes map onto reality? Consolidating across multiple studies, psychologists have learned that men and women differ more in the *expression* of emotions – both facially and verbally – than in the subjective *experience* of emotions (Fischer, 2000). When gender differences in reports of subjective experience do emerge, they can often be traced back to differences in gender stereotypes. For instance, one study found that endorsement of the gender stereotypes was, for women, associated with reporting high-intensity emotions and, for men, associated with reporting low-intensity emotions (Grossman & Wood, 1993). This suggests that gender stereotypes color people's reports of their own experiences. Men might think, 'I am a man, and men are not emotional, therefore I must not be emotional,' and women might think, 'I am a woman and women are emotional, there-

fore I must be emotional.' Studies have shown that stereotypes most color emotion reports when those reports are made at a global level ('How often do you feel sad or depressed') or from hindsight ('How anxious were you during last week's exam?'). It turns out that gender differences in reported experience vanish when men and women report how they feel in the moment ('How anxious do you feel right now?'), presumably because in the moment, people are more focused on the specifics of their circumstances and feelings and less on how those feelings conform to their gendered beliefs about themselves (Feldman Barrett *et al.,* 1998).

These findings suggest that emotions may be a medium through which men and women (and boys and girls) 'do gender' – behave in gender-appropriate ways. So just as females show femininity by paying attention to their appearance and diet, they may also show femininity by expressing the 'feminine' emotions of sadness, fear, and happiness and avoiding expression of the 'masculine' emotions of anger and pride. Likewise, males may show their masculinity by showing the opposite pattern ('boys don't cry,' 'men show no fear'). Supporting this view, a study demonstrated that people rate photographs of men and women as more or less sexually attractive depending on which emotions their faces convey. Specifically, a happy expression is judged as sexually attractive on a woman's face, but as not sexually attractive on a man's face. The reverse is true for pride. Men are judged as more sexually attractive if they express pride, whereas women are judged as less attractive (Tracy & Beall, 2011).

The link between gender and power has led some psychologists to suggest that a gender hierarchy, in which women have relatively less power and status than men, is responsible for the observed gender differences in emotion. Women, as lower status, express the 'powerless' emotions of sadness, anxiety, and fear (emotions that work to make one appear weak and helpless) and men, as higher status, express the 'powerful' emotions of anger, pride, and contempt (emotions that work to maintain control and dominance) (Fischer, 2000). Again, the distinction here targets emotion *expression*, not emotion experience. In one review of gender and anger, women were found to experience anger just as much as men – and in contexts of interpersonal relationships, even more. Even so, men appear angrier than women because they express their anger in prototypical ways – that is, with physical and verbal assaults. Women, in contrast, express their anger with tears, which may make it easier to dismiss their anger or mislabel it as sadness (Kring, 2000). Women also report being less comfortable than men in expressing their anger. Such gender differences in expressions of anger, then, may be what reinforce men as 'powerful' and women as 'powerless.' Gender stereotypes also come into play: in one study, participants judged how angry or sad a person was who expressed an ambiguous blend of anger and sadness. When the blended expression appeared

Both of these photos show the same blend of two different emotion expressions. The brows are lowered and drawn together as they are for anger, while the lip corners are turned down as they are for sadness. Research has shown that when these and other anger-sadness blends appear on a man's face, people more often see the ambiguous blends as anger, but when the same blends appear on a woman's face, people more often see them as sadness (Plant *et al.* 2000). These findings suggest that gender stereotypes shape perceivers' interpretations of facial expressions.

on a man's face, it was seen as showing more anger; when it appeared on a woman's face, it was seen as showing more sadness (Plant *et al.*, 2000). Can women gain status and power by expressing anger? Not easily. Because showing anger runs counter to gender stereotypes, a woman who expresses anger in a professional context actually loses status, being judged as out of control, a witch, or a shrew, regardless of whether she is the CEO or a trainee. This backlash against women disappears only when an external reason for a woman's anger is obvious (Brescoll & Uhlmann, 2008).

To sum up, gender differences in emotion may stem primarily from the back-end of the emotion process – from the ways in which men and women regulate and express their emotions. These differences, in turn, most likely stem from gender differences in the way males and females are socialized – both by parents and by the culture more generally – to conform to gender stereotypes. Indeed, studies have shown that parents talk to their preschool children differently about emotions – for example, emphasizing sadness more with their daughters than with their sons (Fivush & Buckner, 2000). Such differences may set the stage for the emergence of gender differences in emotion regulation habits in later life. In other words, gender-specific lessons about appropriate emotion regulation are one way that boys and girls learn to be masculine or feminine, powerful or powerless.

Cultural differences

Psychologists studying cultural differences in emotion have mostly focused on how the values associated with collectivism and individualism shape emotional experiences. Recall from Chapter 1 that **collectivism** refers to cultures that emphasize the fundamental connectedness and interdependence among people, and **individualism** refers to cultures that emphasize the fundamental separateness and independence of individuals. Many East Asian, Latin American, and African countries are identified as collectivist cultures, and the USA, Canada, Australia, and many Western European countries are identified as individualist cultures. Of course, not all citizens of these countries can be classified as collectivists or individualists. Variations by gender, social class, and ethnicity are common. Even so, differences along the dimension of collectivism–individualism appear critical to understanding cultural differences in emotions (van Hemert *et al.*, 2007).

To understand why this is so, we can examine how variations in collectivism–individualism affect people's views of self (Markus & Kitayama, 2010). In collectivist contexts, people's sense of self is embedded within relationships, with many personal goals reflecting this, including desires to fit in and create interpersonal harmony. In individualist contexts, by contrast, people's sense of self is bounded, or viewed as separate from close others, with many personal goals reflecting desires to be independent and unique. Continuing with the framework

Happiness is more closely associated with individual achievements in individualist cultures and with good relationships in collectivist cultures.

described earlier, cultural differences in personal goals can produce cultural differences in emotions through 'front-end' differences in the emotion process. That is, if people in different cultures differ in their personal goals, especially regarding interpersonal relationships, so, too, will they differ in their appraisals of the personal meaning of their current circumstances, even when those circumstances are very similar. One study examined people's emotional reactions following errors in shared plans, like missing a scheduled meeting or get-together. In this study, Italians were selected to represent collectivism, and English-speaking Canadians were selected to represent individualism. As expected in collectivist cultures, Italians valued the relationship more than Canadians did. And when plans went wrong, Italians experienced more sorrow, whereas Canadians experienced more anger (Grazzani-Gavazzi & Oatley, 1999). Sorrow reflects collectivism in this circumstance because the error is viewed as a shared loss. Anger, by contrast, reflects individualism because the error is viewed as a something the self deals with individually. So here, because relationships matter differently to people in collectivist and individualist cultures, the same circumstance – a broken plan – yields different emotions.

As another example, researchers have found that the circumstances that yield 'good feelings' vary by culture. In Japan, a more collectivist culture, feeling good most frequently accompanies interpersonal engagement, like feeling friendly, whereas in the USA, a more individualist culture, feeling good most frequently accompanies interpersonal disengagement, like feeling superior or proud (Imada & Ellsworth, 2011; Kitayama et al., 2000). This evidence suggests that people's sources of happiness depend on the ways in which their culture values relationships and social worth – again, presumably because people's self-views and personal goals reflect collectivism or individualism.

From early childhood, cultural messages influence the emotions that people strive to feel. Children's storybooks in the USA, for instance, emphasize excited states, whereas comparably popular books in Taiwan emphasize calm states (Tsai et al., 2007). The persistence of such cultural messages influences the ideals children and adults come to hold for their emotions. Bicultural individuals are in the unique position of identifying with two cultures, often ones with opposing values about emotions. Diary studies have shown that for biculturals, the language spoken most recently influences the ways they experience their own emotions (Perunovic et al., 2007).

So far we've discussed cultural differences in the 'front-end' of the emotional process – that is, differences in the circumstances that yield emotions and differences in the appraisals of personal significance. Yet collectivism and individualism also affect the 'back-end' of the emotional process, by prescribing which emotions can be expressed and when. We encountered one example of this earlier in discussing display rules for facial expressions. Compared with people from the USA, people from Japan more often mask experiences of disgust with smiles when in the presence of another. Relatedly, other studies find that pride is more acceptable to express in individualist cultures than in collectivist cultures (Fischer et al., 1999).

In addition to front-end differences in appraisals and back-end differences in responses to emotion, survey research on culture and emotion suggests that people's fundamental beliefs about emotions may differ in collectivist and individualist contexts (Mesquita, 2001). For instance, in individualist cultures, emotions are taken to reflect the subjective inner worlds of individuals and are thought to 'belong to' a particular person (for instance, 'Mark is angry'). By contrast, in collectivist cultures, emotions are taken to reflect objective reality and are thought to 'belong to' relationships (for instance, 'We are angry'). Studies show, for instance, that judging a target person's emotions from facial muscle movements, Japanese participants look also to the faces of surrounding people, whereas Western participants do not (Masuda et al., 2008). So, just as we said that emotions may be one medium through which people 'do gender' or behave in gender-appropriate ways, emotions may also reinforce and sustain important cultural themes: emotions appear to bind people together in collectivist cultures and to define individual uniqueness in individualist cultures.

INTERIM SUMMARY

 Emotions vary by gender and culture, perhaps most typically at the front-end of the emotion process (such as person–environment relations and cognitive appraisals) and the back-end of the emotion process (such as responses to emotion).

→ Many gender differences can be linked to gender stereotypes about emotions, which assign 'powerless' emotions, like sadness and fear, to women, and 'powerful' emotions, like anger and pride, to men.

→ Cultural differences in individualism versus collectivism also yield differences in emotion, with collectivism's greater focus on relationships affecting both appraisal processes and regulation strategies.

CRITICAL THINKING QUESTIONS

1 Revisit Figure 11.1 and explain the difference between 'front-end' and 'back-end' differences by gender and culture.

2 Are there likely to be aspects of the emotion process that do not vary by gender or culture? Why or why not?

POSITIVE PSYCHOLOGY

After World War II, psychology – especially clinical psychology – became a science devoted to healing. It adopted a disease model of human functioning from the medical sciences and aimed to cure pathologies. Although this focus produced tremendous advances in the field's understanding and treatment of mental illness (see Chapters 15 and 16), it had little to say about what makes life worth living. **Positive psychology** emerged at the turn of the millennium to balance the field's sophisticated scientific understanding of mental illness with an equally sophisticated scientific understanding of

People who describe themselves as 'stuck in a rut' - especially in the workplace - rarely fulfil their real potential.

human flourishing (Seligman, 2002, 2011). Just like any living thing, people can either languish in life, feeling 'stuck in a rut' and falling short of their full potential, or flourish in life, becoming ripe with possibilities and contributions to the greater good as well as remarkably resilient to adversity. Although positive psychology shares with the earlier humanistic psychology a concern with people's development toward their full potential, it departs from humanistic psychology by relying heavily on empirical methods.

Positive psychology targets psychological phenomena at levels ranging from the study of positive subjective experiences, such as positive emotions and optimism, to the study of positive personality traits, such as courage and wisdom, and the study of positive institutions – social structures that might cultivate civility and responsible citizenship (Seligman & Csikszentmihalyi, 2000). In this chapter, to illustrate a positive psychology perspective, we focus on the science of positive emotions. The take-home message is that positive emotions are worth cultivating, not just because they feel good, but also because they trigger upward spirals toward psychological growth and flourishing.

Positive emotions and longevity

What good are positive emotions? This question seems almost silly to ask because at one level the answer is obvious: positive emotions feel good. This fact alone makes them rewarding and valuable experiences. End of story, right?

Unfortunately, for many years, this had been the end of the story. Early reviews of the scientific literature on emotions revealed a near exclusive focus on negative emotions – like fear, anger, disgust, and shame – and only a tiny focus on positive emotions – like joy, contentment, interest, and love. So, although few would argue with the assumption in the US Declaration of Independence that the pursuit of happiness is a worthy goal, until recently, few had pursued positive emotions scientifically.

This situation has changed considerably over the past 15 years, and a landmark study sounded a wake-up call about the profound benefits positive emotions may hold for us. This was a study of 180 Catholic nuns who donated their lives not only to God but also to science. As part of a larger study of aging and Alzheimer's disease, these nuns agreed to give scientists access to their archived work and medical records (and to donate their brains at death). The work archives included autobiographies handwritten in the 1930s and 1940s, when the nuns were in their early 20s and about to take their final vows. Researchers scored these essays for emotional content, recording instances of positive emotion – like happiness, interest, love, and hope – and negative emotions – like sadness, fear, and lack of interest. No association was found between negative emotional content and mortality, perhaps because it was rather rare in these essays. But a strong inverse association was found between positive

There is some evidence to support the idea of an inverse link between positive emotion and mortality in individuals.

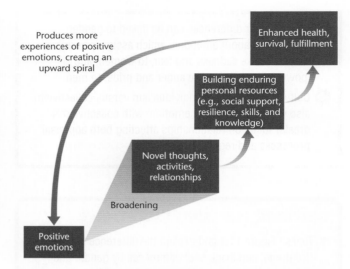

FIGURE 11.7 Broaden and Build. *Positive emotions broaden mindsets.*

emotional content and mortality: those nuns who expressed the most positive emotions lived up to 10 years longer than those who expressed the least positive emotions (Danner *et al.,* 2001). This gain in life expectancy is far larger than the gain you would get from quitting smoking. Imagine how long you would live if you both quit smoking and accentuated the positive?

This study of nuns is not an isolated finding. Several other studies have shown a link between positive emotions and healthy longevity (Moskowitz *et al.,* 2008; Pressman & Cohen, 2012). Plus, a meta-analytic review of nearly 300 published studies, which collectively tested more than 275 000 people, makes a similar conclusion: positive emotions produce success in life as much as they reflect success in life (Lyubomirsky *et al.,* 2005). While these conclusions are compelling, they do not address *how* positive emotions provide benefits.

Insight into the possible pathways is provided by an evolutionary theory that describes the form and function of positive emotions, called the **broaden-and-build theory** of positive emotions (Fredrickson, 1998, 2013). This theory states that pleasant emotional states are psychological adaptations that evolved because they aided the survival of our human ancestors. They did so by creating a form of consciousness marked by a broad scope of awareness that momentarily includes a wider array of thought and action tendencies than is typical. This broadened mindset aided the discovery of new knowledge, new alliances, and new skills, and thereby helped our human ancestors to build their reserves of consequential personal resources that might later make the difference between surviving or succumbing to various threats to life and limb. Resources built through positive emotions also increased the odds that our ancestors would experience subsequent positive emotions, with their additional broaden-and-build benefits, thus creating an upward spiral toward improved odds for survival, health, and flourishing (see Figure 11.7). Evidence to support the broaden-and-build theory is described below.

As mentioned earlier in this chapter, one virtue of negative emotions is that they spark strong urges to act in specific ways: to fight when angry, to flee when afraid, or to spit when disgusted (Lazarus, 1991b). Put differently, negative emotions narrow our mindsets, bringing to mind only a select set of thoughts and actions. Positive emotions have a complementary effect; they broaden our mindsets by expanding our thought–action repertoires. Joy creates the urge to play, interest the urge to explore, contentment the urge to savor, and love a recurring cycle of each of these urges. The virtue here is that positive emotions expand our typical ways of thinking and behaving, and in so doing push us to be more creative, more curious, or more connected to others (Fredrickson, 1998; Isen, 2002). Laboratory experiments support this basic distinction between negative and positive emotions (for a review, see Fredrickson, 2013). In one study, participants were shown one of five emotionally evocative film clips to induce one of two positive emotions (joy or contentment), one of two negative emotions (fear or anger), or no emotion (the control condition). While in these states, participants listed all the things they would like to do right then. Compared with those experiencing no emotion, those experiencing fear or anger listed fewer things they would like to do right then and named things consistent with the specific action tendencies listed in Table 11.3 (for example, those who felt angry felt like being aggressive). By contrast, and again compared with those experiencing no emotion, those experiencing joy or contentment named more things they would like to do right then, consistent with a broadened thought–action repertoire (Fredrickson & Branigan, 2005). Experiments that use eye-tracking technology (Wadlinger & Isaacowitz, 2006) and facial electromyography (Johnson *et al.,* 2010) also support the conclusion that positive emotions expand the scope of people's visual perception, allowing them to see more than they typically do. Seeing the big picture in this way helps people to think more flexibly and come up with creative solutions to difficult problems (Rowe *et al.*, 2007).

Particularly compelling evidence for the broaden effect of positive emotions comes from an elegant brain imaging experiment (Schmitz *et al.*, 2009). The study design rested on well-validated evidence from cognitive neuroscience that one particular brain area, the extrastriate fusiform face area (FFA), reliably responds to human faces, whereas a distinct brain area, the parahippocampal place area (PPA) reliably responds to place processing. The researchers assessed the breadth of participants' field of view by showing them a series of compound images that featured human faces in a central location surrounded by images of houses. Participants were simply asked to indicate whether the face in each compound image was male or female, while ignoring the house that surrounded the face. This task was purposely easy, and nobody made mistakes. Before making these judgments, however, the researchers used pictures to induce positive, negative, or neutral states. The physiological indicator of whether these emotional states influenced the scope of participants' field of view was the changes in blood flow within the PPA, the part of the brain that should be sensitive to the images of houses. Consistent with the broaden hypothesis, results showed greater activation in the PPA following the positive pictures, relative to the neutral pictures, suggesting that when under the influence of positive emotions, you can't help but take in more of the surrounding contextual information. Notably, this study also found decreased activation in the PPA following negative pictures, relative to the neutral pictures, consistent with the hypothesis that negative emotions narrow people's field of view (Schmitz *et al.*, 2009).

Other studies suggest that the broaden effect of positive emotions extends beyond the scope of people's field of view. Positive emotions have also been shown to expand people's circles of trust (Dunn & Schweitzer, 2005), perspective-taking (Waugh & Fredrickson, 2006), and compassion (Nelson, 2009). Plus, examination of the body movements associated with different emotions suggest that positive emotions even expand people's posture (Gross *et al.*, 2012).

Positive emotions build personal resources

Although emotions themselves are short-lived, they can have lasting effects on you. By momentarily broadening your mind-set, positive emotions promote discovery of novel and creative ideas, actions, and social bonds. Playing, for instance, can build your physical and social resources, exploring can generate knowledge, and savoring can set or adjust your life priorities. Importantly, these outcomes often endure long after the initial positive emotion has vanished. In this way, positive emotions build up your store of resources that you can draw on in times of trouble, including physical resources (such as health and effective physical functioning), intellectual resources (such as a cognitive map for finding your way), psychological resources (such as an optimistic outlook), and social resources (such as someone to turn to for help). For instance, longitudinal studies that track friendship formation among university students find that early experiences of positive emotions – especially gratitude – forecast better relationships months later (Algoe *et al.*, 2008; Waugh & Fredrickson, 2006). Daily experiences of positive emotions have also been shown to build resilience and mindfulness, which in turn increase well-being (Catalino & Fredrickson, 2011; Cohn *et al.*, 2009).

Positive emotionality may extend life expectancy.

SEEING BOTH SIDES

WHAT IS THE UNDERLYING STRUCTURE OF EMOTIONS?

PSYCHOLOGICAL CONSTRUCTIONIST APPROACHES TO EMOTION

Kristen A. Lindquist, University of North Carolina, Chapel Hill and Lisa F. Barrett, Northeastern University

What is an emotion? William James (1884) asked this question over a century ago and researchers are still debating about the answer. Of course, we all experience emotions on a daily basis and so the answer seems straightforward and even easy: emotions are states that wash over us, taking control of our bodies and minds, bidding us to engage in certain behaviors. We see emotions in the behavior of infants, children, and animals, so we assume that emotions are inborn, universal, and shared with our mammalian cousins. Emotions are useful, and so it's easy to assume that they evolved as specialized packets of feelings and behaviors to help us cope with life's problems. Accordingly, these packets should be evidenced in the body and brain as consistent and specific facial expressions, bodily expressions, and brain activity.

Yet growing evidence suggests that commonsense experiences of emotion do not reveal the underlying processes that cause emotions. Despite a century of looking, emotions have yet to be revealed as consistent and specific patterns of facial expressions (Barrett, 2006c; Cacioppo *et al.*, 2000; Mauss & Robinson, 2009), bodily expressions (Barrett, 2006c; Cacioppo *et al.*, 2000; Mauss & Robinson, 2009), or brain activity (Lindquist *et al.*, 2012; Vytal & Hamann, 2010). Findings from psychology and neuroscience are instead converging on the idea that emotions are states that are created out of more basic psychological 'ingredients.' Just as flour, salt, and water combine in a variety of recipes to produce breads, pastries, sauces, etc., basic psychological ingredients that are not specific to emotion combine to produce anger, fear, disgust, and sadness, as well as thoughts, plans, memories beliefs, perceptions, and so on. This view is known as a *psychological constructionist approach*. Although not the most intuitive model of emotion, psychological constructionist models are as old as psychology itself, and were put forth by James (1884), Wundt (1897/1998), Schachter and Singer (1962), Mandler (1975), Russell (2003), and most recently, by us (Barrett, 2006a, 2009b, 2012; Lindquist, in press; Lindquist & Barrett, 2012; Lindquist *et al.*, 2012).

Growing evidence shows that the mental events that people refer to as 'emotions' are constructed, in the blink of an eye, from a variety of ever-present psychological ingredients. One ingredient is a psy-

chologically and biologically basic mammalian system that produces states characterized by hedonic *valence* (pleasure or displeasure) and *arousal* (wound up versus tranquil) (Barrett, 2006a, 2006c; Barrett & Bliss-Moreau, 2009; Russell, 2003) (called 'core affect'). Indeed, hundreds of psychological studies of emotion now show that, regardless of how emotion is measured (with facial electromyography, autonomic responses, behavior, self-reports of experience, or self-reports of perceptions of other people's expressions), the underlying ingredient of core affect is observed (Barrett, 2006a; Mauss & Robinson, 2009). Valence and arousal can be thought of as properties that characterize the landscape of affective responses that are possible in an organism. This landscape is actually a formal mathematical model for affect called the *affective circumplex* (Figure 11.8).

A model such as the affective circumplex is often referred to as a 'dimensional approach' to emotion, on the assumption that all emotional states can be described by a combination of the valence and arousal dimensions. Yet the label 'dimensional' is misleading, because most theorists do not believe that dimensions of affect are sufficient to explain experiences and perceptions of discrete emotions such as anger, disgust, fear, etc. (see Lindquist *et al.*, in press). Instead, the proposal is that core affect is transformed into instances of anger, disgust, fear, etc. when a person makes meaning of sensory input using a second basic psychological ingredient called conceptual knowledge. For instance, when people make meaning of an unpleasant, highly aroused feeling of core affect using situation-specific knowledge about the category *fear*, they have the experience of being fearful (Lindquist & Barrett, 2008). Similarly, concept knowledge is important to perceive someone else's unpleasant facial expression (e.g., wide eyes) as an instance of *fear*

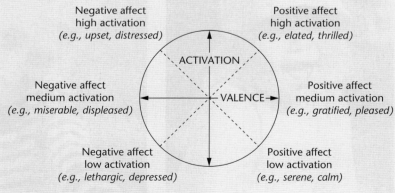

FIGURE 11.8 Affective Circumplex.

v. *anger* (Gendron *et al.,* 2012; Lindquist *et al.,* 2006). Together, core affect and conceptual knowledge (along with several other ingredients, including language and executive function) create instances of emotions as 'situated conceptualizations' in a given context (Barrett, 2009a; Wilson-Mendenhall *et al.,* 2011).

A psychological construction view of emotion, which understands emotions as situated conceptualizations, predicts variation in emotional instances (it does not hypothesize six or seven basic biological types and then treat variance around these types as error). This is because we hypothesize that knowledge about *fear* (and knowledge of all emotion categories, for that matter) consists of a rich cache of situation-specific knowledge that is acquired through prior experience. As a result, there is no one situated conceptualization for *fear,* but many (Wilson-Mendenhall *et al.*, 2011). The result is that a person can have different instances of fear that are perceptually similar in different situations. Furthermore, two people who have different emotion knowledge will have different experiences of fear in the same context (e.g., fear where heart rate goes up, eyes widen, and a person avoids something v. fear where heart rate goes down, a person smiles, and

approaches something). As emotion knowledge changes with development, so too should emotional experiences and perceptions. For instance, prior to knowing the words 'anger,' 'disgust,' and 'fear,' children perceive all facial expressions as merely good (i.e., 'happy') or bad (i.e., 'sad'). But as children acquire emotion knowledge over the course of early childhood, they become reliably able to perceive anger, disgust, fear, happiness and sadness on others' faces (Widen & Russell, 2008, 2010).

Perhaps what's most unique about a psychological constructionist view is that it assumes that the psychological ingredients (e.g., core affect, conceptual knowledge, language, executive function) are not specific to emotional instances, and participate in constructing every moment of psychological life. For example, we hypothesize that core affect plays a role in normal vision (e.g., Anderson *et al.,* 2011; see also Barrett & Bar, 2009), helping people to literally see the world around them. The far-reaching consequence of this idea is that the mental events people call 'emotions,' 'cognitions,' and 'perceptions' differ in how they feel to people, but may not be distinctions that the human brain respects (Barrett, 2009a; Barrett & Bar, 2009; Duncan & Barrett, 2007; Pessoa, 2008).

SEEING BOTH SIDES
WHAT IS THE UNDERLYING STRUCTURE OF EMOTIONS?

AN ARGUMENT FOR DISCRETE EMOTIONS

Robert W. Levenson, University of California–Berkeley

A small set of prototypical challenges and problems that have enormous implications for human survival and thriving undoubtedly played a major role in the evolution of our emotions. Bonding with others, handling threats, dealing with loss, defending what is ours, avoiding noxious substances, and soothing self and others are all integral parts of the human condition. The ubiquity and importance of these problems and challenges would have created enormous selection pressures favoring generalized solutions for each – solutions that have the highest likelihood of producing beneficial outcomes for the individual and for the social group most of the time. Emotions are these solutions, orchestrating configurations of motor behaviors; expressive signals in face and voice; changes in attention, perception, and information processing; and physiological adjustments that can be activated quickly and efficiently, often with little conscious intervention. Viewed in this way, emotions can be seen as time-tested solutions for timeless problems.

This group of problems and challenges and the associated emotional solutions are not distributed evenly across the landscape of human experience. Emotional solutions for dealing with problems of rotting food (disgust), loss of a loved one (sadness), or having a possession taken away (anger) differ more in kind and in configuration than in degree. Because of this, it is virtually impossible to find a single unipolar or bipolar dimensional structure that allows ordinal ranking of the most common emotions (e.g., anger, contempt, disgust, fear, happiness, sadness, surprise). Consider the pervasive 'positive–negative' dimension. Although happiness is clearly more positive than the others in this set, subsequent ranking quickly becomes problematic. Is disgust more negative than fear? Is fear more negative than anger? Or consider another oft-proposed dimension: 'approach–avoidance.' Although disgust can readily be placed at the extreme avoidance end of the scale, the other emotions are not so clear. Sadness, for example, sometimes drives us toward and sometimes away from others (and has a similar bimodal effect on the behavior of others toward us).

The same kinds of problems for the dimensional approach found at these more macro levels of behavior are also found at the more micro levels of individual emotional response systems. Emotional appearance changes in the face poorly fit popular dimensional schemes (Ekman, 1972). Consider trying to map brow changes onto the 'positive–negative' dimension. Lowered and furrowed brows are associated with a negative emotion (anger), but raised brows are not part of the positive emotion (happiness) display. Rather, raised brows are either associated with surprise (if both inner and outer portions are raised), an emotion that is arguably neither positive nor negative, or with sadness (if only the inner portion is raised), an emotion that is clearly negative. Attempting to map lip movements onto this dimension creates similar problems. Lip corners move up bilaterally in a positive emotion (happiness) and move down in a negative emotion (sadness), but they also move up unilaterally in another negative emotion (contempt) and are stretched laterally in yet another negative emotion (fear). Autonomic nervous system responses present comparable difficulties. Heart rate increases are found in two negative emotions (anger, fear) but not in a third (disgust) (Levenson, 1992). These two negative emotions that are alike in heart rate change, diverge in terms of temperature (warming in anger versus cooling in fear), a difference found both in physiological studies of emotion and in common metaphoric parlance (Lakoff, 1987).

These kinds of problems with the dimensional view lead me to conclude that the discrete view is the most parsimonious way to organize emotions (Levenson, 2011). In this view, emotions are seen as having different *configurations* of behavior, expression, and physiology that represent generalized solutions to a small set of common problems and challenges (Levenson, 2003a) . Nonetheless, it is important to note that humans are clearly capable of talking about and thinking about emotions in dimensional ways. We respond to the ubiquitous question of 'How are you feeling today?' by invoking a dimensional structure when we reply with 'good' or 'bad.' However, even in this highly conventional case, a response of 'bad' is likely to engender an additional question probing for more information as to whether we are sad or mad or afraid (or something comparably 'discrete').

What would enable us to resolve the discrete versus dimensional question with greater certainty? It goes without saying that more research evaluating both views, well-designed studies that allow for disconfirmation as well as confirmation, is needed. The traditional approach to evaluating the discrete model has been to elicit a set of discrete emotions under comparable conditions and determine if their expressive and physiological concomitants differ

(Levenson, 2003a, 2003b; Shiota *et al.,* 2011). Other approaches make use of patient populations with particular areas of brain damage (Levenson, 2007) to determine if they impact particular emotions. For example, patients with Huntington's disease may have problems with the recognition and production of disgust but not with other emotions, whereas patients with amygdala damage may have problems recognizing fear (Gray *et al.,* 1997; Hayes *et al.,* 2007; Sprengelmeyer *et al.,* 1996; Sprengelmeyer *et al.,* 1997). Discreteness is also manifest in patients with amyotrophic lateral sclerosis, (a common motor neuron disease) who may manifest spontaneous episodes of laughing and crying (Olney *et al.,* 2011; Wilson, 1924) but do not exhibit behav-

iors related to other emotions such as anger or fear. Many studies have utilized stimulation and blockage of selected brain areas to determine if they affect particular emotions (George *et al.,* 1996; Mosimann *et al.,* 2000). For example, acute brainstem transaction and amygdala stimulation have been shown to produce anger-like behaviors (i.e., 'sham rage') in cats (Reis & Gunne, 1965; Reis *et al.,* 1967). Finally, functional imaging studies have been conducted to determine if the expression and processing of different emotions are associated with different regions of neural activation (Whalen *et al.,* 2001). Application of these and other empirical approaches, while unlikely to quell the controversy completely, can surely enrich the debate.

The more decisive tests of whether positive emotions build personal resources require not only longitudinal approaches, but also random assignment of different groups of people to distinct emotional trajectories. Recent field-based longitudinal experiments offer such tests. In the context of a workplace wellness program, working adults were offered a chance to attend a meditation workshop to 'reduce stress.' They were then randomly assigned to attend a 6-week meditation workshop as part of the experiment, or to attend one later, after the study was completed. Over the next 9 weeks, both groups provided daily reports of their emotional experiences. Before and after the workshop, everyone also completed a set of surveys to assess their life satisfaction, depressive symptoms, and their status on a wide range of personal resources.

Results showed that people can learn new emotional habits to improve their daily diets of positive emotions. Compared to the control group, study participants who learned the meditation techniques reported increasing amounts of positive emotions across the 9 weeks of daily reporting. These participants also showed the largest gains in personal resources, which in turn produced increases in life satisfaction and reductions in depressive symptoms (Fredrickson *et al.,* 2008). Further experiments like this have also shown that when people learn techniques to increase their daily experiences of positive emotions, they show associated improvements on objective indicators of cardiovascular health (Kok *et al.,* 2012).

So, feeling good may do more for you than you may have known. The **broaden-and-build theory** states that positive emotions broaden your typical ways of thinking and acting which, in turn, builds your lasting and consequential personal resources, making you more skilled and resilient than you would be otherwise. The next time you're laughing with friends, pursuing an interest, or enjoying a walk through the park, consider that you may be cultivating more than just fleeting good feelings. You may also be fueling an upward spiral that optimizes your own long-term health and well-being (Fredrickson, 2000, 2013). In this way, daily experiences of positive emotions are psychological nutrients that help you to flourish.

As we've seen, motions, whether pleasant or unpleasant, are complex. Each component of an emotion that we considered – cognitive appraisals, subjective experiences, thought–action tendencies, bodily changes, facial muscle movements, and responses to emotion – is itself a complex event involving multiple factors, both biological and psychological. In fact, each of the perspectives on emotion described in this chapter has addressed how the biological components of emotion (such as physiological arousal and universal facial muscle movements) and the psychological components of emotion (such as cognitive appraisals) interact to produce the experience of emotion. Taken together, the research reviewed in this chapter suggests that in most cases the biological and psychological components of emotion probably have reciprocal influences on each other in a dynamic process that evolves over time. A situation may initially elicit a mild emotion, but as a person evaluates the situation more deeply, the emotion may intensify, and his physiological arousal may increase. The effects of the emotion on his memory for similar events from the past and on his appraisals of this event may further intensify his subjective experience of emotion. Over time, then, feedback loops between the biological and psychological components of an emotion can influence the course of the emotion. We will return to discussions of the feedback between the biological and psychological components of emotion when we discuss stress in Chapter 14 and emotional disorders in Chapters 15 and 16.

Playing can build your physical and social resources.

INTERIM SUMMARY

➡ Positive psychology is the scientific study of human flourishing.

➡ People who experience and express more positive emotions live longer than their less upbeat peers.

➡ The broaden-and-build theory of positive emotions posits that pleasant emotional states are psychological adaptations that aided the survival of human ancestors by broadening their thought–action repertoires and building their consequential personal resources.

→ Brain imaging experiments confirm that people's field of visual awareness expands under the influence of positive emotions.

→ Daily experiences of positive emotions have been shown to function as nutrients that build people's consequential personal resources that promote flourishing.

CRITICAL THINKING QUESTION

1 How are responses to emotion – or attempts to regulate emotion – implicated in the process of human flourishing? Can you steer yourself toward flourishing? Positive emotions predict longevity. What types of evidence suggest that positive emotions play a causal role in extending life?

CHAPTER SUMMARY

1 The components of emotion include cognitive appraisals, the subjective experience of emotion, thought–action tendencies, autonomic arousal, facial muscle movements, and responses to the emotion.

2 A cognitive appraisal is an interpretation of the personal meaning of a situation that results in an emotion. Such appraisals affect both the intensity and the quality of an emotion. When people are induced into a state of undifferentiated arousal, the quality of their emotional experience may be influenced by their appraisal of the situation. Cognitive appraisals can occur outside of conscious awareness, and brain research identifies the amygdala as being involved in automatic appraisals.

3 The conceptual act model is (like the two-factor theory) a psychological constructionist model of emotion. It posits that emotions are constructed through the combination of more basic ingredients of mind, including sensation and language. That is, your internal and external sensations become an emotion only to the extent that your brain automatically categorizes them as such based on your past experiences.

4 Subjective experiences of emotions, or feelings, guide behavior, decision-making, and judgment. Feelings also steer memory, learning, and risk assessments.

5 Different emotions carry urges to think and act in certain ways, called *thought–action tendencies*.

6 Intense negative emotions involve physiological arousal caused by activation of the sympathetic division of the autonomic nervous system. Positive emotions have an undoing effect on lingering negative emotional arousal. People with spinal cord injuries, which limit feedback from the autonomic nervous system, report experiencing less intense emotions. Autonomic arousal may also help differentiate the emotions, because the pattern of arousal (for example, heartbeat, skin temperature) differs for different emotions.

7 The facial muscle movements that accompany a subset of emotions have a universal meaning: people from different cultures agree on what emotion a person in a particular photograph is expressing. Cultures may differ in the factors that elicit certain emotions and in rules for the proper display of emotion. In addition to their communicative functions, the facial muscle movements that accompany emotions may contribute to the subjective experience of an emotion (the facial feedback hypothesis).

8 People almost always respond to or regulate their emotions by either exaggerating or minimizing them, and the ability to do so predicts social success. The strategies people use to regulate emotions can have unexpected repercussions. For instance, suppressing facial muscle movements increases autonomic and amygdala activation and impairs memory.

9 Emotions vary by gender and culture. Many gender differences can be linked to gender stereotypes about emotions, which assign 'powerless' emotions, like sadness and fear, to women, and 'powerful' emotions, like anger and pride, to men. Cultural differences in individualism versus collectivism also yield differences in emotion, with collectivism's greater focus on relationships affecting both appraisal processes and regulation strategies.

10 The broaden-and-build theory of positive emotions holds that pleasant emotional states broaden people's thought–action repertoires and that, over time, such expanded awareness builds people's enduring personal resources. This theory can explain why people who experience and express more positive emotions tend to live longer.

CORE CONCEPTS

antisocial personality disorder	misattribution of arousal	James–Lange theory
emotion	minimalist appraisal theories	display rules
cognitive appraisal	dimensional appraisal theories	facial feedback hypothesis
subjective experience	core relational theme	emotion regulation
autonomic nervous system	backward masking	collectivism
facial muscle movements	amygdala	individualism
responses to emotion	sympathetic nervous system	positive psychology
moods	parasympathetic nervous system	broaden-and-build theory
person–environment relationship	undoing effect of positive emotions	
two-factor theory	visceral perception	

DIGITAL SUPPORT RESOURCES

Students should use the unique access code included in the front of the book to access the digital support resources which accompany the new edition. These include:

- Multiple Choice Questions and Quizzes
- Critical Thinking Questions
- Practice Essay Questions
- Videos
- Glossary, Flashcards, and More

INTELLIGENCE

12

Understand two different meanings of the concept of intelligence.

Be familiar with the development of tests of intellectual ability and the general format of the Stanford–Binet and Wechsler Intelligence Scales. Know how scores on these tests are interpreted.

Be able to describe how factor–analysis was used by Spearman and Thurstone to separate the different abilities that contribute to intelligence.

Understand Gardner's theory of multiple intelligences, including the seven distinct kinds of intelligence in this model.

Be familiar with Anderson's theory of intelligence and development, his concept of a 'basic processing mechanism', and the use of 'modules' to acquire knowledge.

Know the triarchic theory put forth by Sternberg and his three subtheories, in particular the componential theory dealing with thought processes.

Be prepared to contrast these contemporary theories of intelligence in terms of their similarities and differences.

Understand what a heritability estimate does and does not tell us. Be familiar with the twin studies method for genetic contributions to intelligence plus some related evidence. Be able to counter some misunderstandings about heritability.

Tommy was born in December 1856, in Virginia, USA, to Janet Woodrow, the daughter of a Presbyterian minister, and Joseph Ruggles Wilson, himself a Presbyterian minister who became a leader of the Presbyterian Church in the American South. Tommy's parents were educated people who highly valued learning. As a schoolboy, however, Tommy had great difficulty reading. Despite attending special schools, he still was not able to read until late childhood, around age 10 or 11. With a great deal of hard work, he was eventually able to qualify for admission to the College of New Jersey, which later became Princeton University. Even in college, however, Tommy did not excel at coursework.

To this point, you might predict that Tommy's chances for success in life were only moderate. We might say today that 'he didn't look good on paper,' Our modest predictions for Tommy's future would be proven wrong, however. Tommy was Thomas Woodrow Wilson. After graduating from Princeton, he earned a law degree from the University of Virginia and a doctorate in political science from Johns Hopkins University.

During periods as a professor at Bryn Mawr College, Wesleyan University, and Princeton University, Wilson wrote nine books and became a respected essayist. He was named president of Princeton in 1902 and then won the race for governor of New Jersey in a landslide election in 1910. In 1912, he ran for president of the USA against the incumbent, President William Howard Taft, and won, becoming the 28th US president. During his 8 years in office, Wilson led the USA through World War I and worked extensively to establish the post-war armistice and peace in Europe. In 1919, he won the Nobel Peace Prize for his efforts in establishing the League of Nations.

Based on his accomplishments across the course of his life, most people would say that Thomas Woodrow Wilson was an intelligent man. If he had taken an intelligence test or some other kind of aptitude test as a boy, however, he might not have scored in the 'intelligent' range. Wilson's life story raises important questions about what we mean by intelligence.

CHAPTER OUTLINE

ASSESSMENT OF INTELLECTUAL ABILITIES

Early intelligence tests

The Stanford–Binet Intelligence Scale

The Wechsler Intelligence Scales

CONTEMPORARY THEORIES: MANY OR FEW INTELLIGENCES?

Gardner's theory of multiple intelligences

Anderson's theory of intelligence and cognitive development

Sternberg's triarchic theory

CUTTING EDGE RESEARCH: STRENGTHS-BASED APPROACHES TO INTELLECTUAL DIFFICULTIES

GENETICS AND INTELLIGENCE

Heritability

EMOTIONAL INTELLIGENCE

GENERAL LEARNING DISABILITY

Causes of general learning disability

Treatments for general learning disability

SEEING BOTH SIDES: HOW
IMPORTANT IS EMOTIONAL
INTELLIGENCE?

The concept of intelligence has been one of the most contentious across the history of psychology and continues to be so today. Even defining **intelligence** can be difficult because your definition reflects your theory of what it means to be intelligent, and theories of intelligence differ widely, as we will discuss later. Some theorists have argued that intelligence doesn't exist as a real entity, but is simply a label for what intelligence tests measure. Other theorists suggest that intelligence should be considered more broadly and that it involves the ability to learn from experience, think in abstract terms, and deal effectively with one's environment. We will consider various conceptualizations and theories of intelligence in this chapter. First, however, we discuss how intelligence is measured.

ASSESSMENT OF INTELLECTUAL ABILITIES

The earliest record of using a common set of tests to evaluate intellectual abilities comes from China, where applicants for government jobs were given examinations of their knowledge of Confucian philosophy and poetry. The practice finally spread to Europe during the Industrial Revolution, when large numbers of individuals needed to be tested for their ability to do clerical work. Today, many industrialized societies rely heavily on tests in schools and the workplace. Schoolchildren may be placed in instructional groups on the basis of their performances on such tests. Aptitude or ability tests are part of the admissions procedure in some universities, and professional and graduate schools. In addition, many industries and government agencies select job applicants and place or promote employees on the basis of test scores. Although tests of abilities are used worldwide and can have significant consequences for individuals' lives, they rely on having a valid theory of what kind of abilities are important for a given context, and on knowing how to measure those abilities. As we shall see, neither of these tasks are easily accomplished.

Early intelligence tests

Over a century ago, British theorist Sir Francis Galton developed an interest in individual differences after considering the evolutionary theory proposed by his cousin, Charles Darwin. Galton believed that certain families are biologically superior to others – that some people are innately stronger or smarter than others. Intelligence, he reasoned, is a question of exceptional sensory and perceptual skills, which are passed from one generation to the next. Because all information is acquired through the senses, the more sensitive and accurate an individual's perceptual apparatus, the more intelligent the person. (Galton's belief in the heritability of intelligence led him to propose that the human race's mental capacities could be enhanced through eugenics, or selective breeding. Fortunately, he is remembered more for his application of statistics to the study of intelligence than for his espousal of eugenics.)

In 1884, Galton administered a battery of tests (measuring variables such as head size, reaction time, visual acuity, auditory thresholds, and memory for visual forms) to more than 9000 visitors at the London Exhibition. To his disappointment, he discovered that eminent British scientists could not be distinguished from ordinary citizens on the basis of their head size and that measurements such as reaction time were not related to other measures of intelligence.

The first tests resembling modern intelligence tests were devised by the French psychologist Alfred Binet in the late nineteenth century. In 1881, the French government passed a law making school attendance compulsory for all children. Previously, slow learners had usually been kept at home, but now teachers had to cope with a wide range of individual differences. The government asked Binet to create a test that would detect children who were too slow intellectually to benefit from a regular school curriculum.

Binet assumed that intelligence should be measured by tasks that required reasoning and problem-solving abilities rather than perceptual-motor skills. In collaboration with another French psychologist, Théophile Simon, Binet published such a test in 1905 and revised it in 1908 and again in 1911.

Binet reasoned that a slow or dull child was like a normal child whose mental growth was retarded. On tests, the slow child would perform like a younger normal child, whereas the mental abilities of a bright child were characteristic of older children. Binet devised a scale of test items of increasing difficulty that measured the kinds of changes in intelligence ordinarily associated with growing older. The higher a child could go on the scale in answering items correctly, the higher his or her mental age (MA). The concept of mental age was critical to Binet's method. Using this method, the MA of a child could be compared with his or her chronological age (CA) as determined by date of birth.

The Stanford–Binet Intelligence Scale

The test items originally developed by Binet were adapted for American schoolchildren by Lewis Terman at Stanford University. Terman standardized the administration of the test and developed age-level norms by giving the test to thousands of children of various ages. In 1916, he published the Stanford revision of the Binet tests, now referred to as the **Stanford–Binet Intelligence Scale**. It was revised in 1937, 1960, 1972,

1986, and most recently in 2003. Despite its age, the Stanford–Binet is still one of the most frequently used psychological tests.

Terman retained Binet's concept of mental age. Each test item was age-graded at the level at which a substantial majority of the children pass it. A child's mental age could be obtained by summing the number of items passed at each level. In addition, Terman adopted a convenient index of intelligence suggested by the German psychologist William Stern. This index is the **intelligence quotient (IQ)**, which expresses intelligence as a ratio of mental age to chronological age:

$$IQ = MA/CA \times 100$$

The number 100 is used as a multiplier so that the IQ will have a value of 100 when MA is equal to CA. If MA is lower than CA, the IQ will be less than 100; if MA is higher than CA, the IQ will be more than 100.

The most recent revision of the Stanford–Binet uses standard age scores instead of IQ scores. These can be interpreted in terms of percentiles, which show the percentage of individuals in the standardization group falling above or below a given score. And although the concept of IQ is still used in intelligence testing, it is no longer actually calculated by using this equation. Instead, tables are used to convert raw scores on the test into standard scores that are adjusted so that the mean at each age equals 100.

IQ scores tend to fall in the form of a bell-shaped curve, with most people's scores hovering around 100, but with some people's scores much higher or lower than 100. Figure 12.1 provides the percentages of the population who will fall in various ranges of IQ scores.

In line with the current view of intelligence as a composite of different abilities, the current version of the Stanford–Binet

Test materials from the Stanford-Binet Intelligence Scale.

groups its tests into four broad areas: verbal reasoning, abstract/visual reasoning, quantitative reasoning, and short-term memory. A separate score is obtained for each area. Table 12.1 gives some examples of items, grouped by area.

The Wechsler Intelligence Scales

In 1939, David Wechsler developed a new test because he thought the Stanford-Binet depended too heavily on language ability and was not appropriate for adults. The **Wechsler Adult Intelligence Scale**, or WAIS (1939, 1955, 1981), is divided into two parts – a verbal scale and a performance scale – that yield separate scores as well as a full-scale IQ. The test items are described in Table 12.2. Wechsler later developed a similar test for children, the

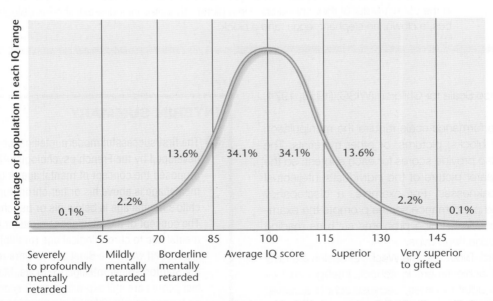

FIGURE 12.1 **The Distribution of IQ Scores.** *IQ scores are designed to fall into a normal distribution, with few scores at either the high or low extremes, and most scores falling around 100.*

TABLE 12.1 ITEMS FROM THE STANFORD-BINET INTELLIGENCE SCALE

Typical examples of items from the 1986 Stanford–Binet Intelligence Scale for a 6- to 8-year-old.

Test	Description
Verbal reasoning	
Vocabulary	Defines words, such as 'dollar' and 'envelope,'
Comprehension	Answers questions, such as 'Where do people buy food?' and 'Why do people comb their hair?'
Absurdities	Identifies the 'funny' aspect of a picture, such as a girl riding a bicycle on a lake or a bald man combing his hair.
Verbal relations	Tells how the first three items in a sequence are alike and how they differ from the fourth: scarf, tie, muffler, shirt.
Quantitative reasoning	
Quantitative	Performs simple arithmetic tasks, such as selecting a die with six spots because the number of spots equals the combination of a two-spot die and a four-spot die.
Number series	Gives the next two numbers in a series, such as 20 16 12 8 ___ ___.
Equation building	Builds an equation from the following array: 2 3 5 + =. One correct response would be $2 + 3 = 5$.
Abstract/visual reasoning	
Pattern analysis	Copies a simple design with blocks.
Copying	Copies a geometrical drawing demonstrated by the examiner, such as a rectangle intersected by two diagonals.
Short-term memory	
Bead memory	Shown a picture of different-shaped beads stacked on a stick. Reproduces the sequence from memory by placing real beads on a stick.
Memory for sentences	Repeats after the examiner sentences such as 'It is time to go to sleep' and 'Ken painted a picture for his mother's birthday.'
Memory for digits	Repeats after examiner a series of digits, such as 5–7–8–3, forward and backward.
Memory for objects	Shown pictures of individual objects, such as a clock and an elephant, one at a time. Identifies the objects in the correct order of their appearance in a picture that also includes extraneous objects; for example, a bus, a clown, an elephant, eggs, and a clock.

Wechsler Intelligence Scale for Children (WISC) (1958, 1974, 1991).

Items on the performance scale require the manipulation or arrangement of blocks, pictures, or other materials. The Wechsler scales also provide scores for each subtest, so the examiner has a clearer picture of the individual's intellectual strengths and weaknesses. For example, a discrepancy between verbal and performance scores prompts the examiner to look for specific learning problems such as reading disabilities or language handicaps.

Both the Stanford–Binet and the Wechsler scales are fairly valid predictors of achievement in school. Intelligence test scores also predict adult incomes, because school achievement leads to better work opportunities (Ceci & Williams, 1997).

INTERIM SUMMARY

→ The first successful modern intelligence tests were developed by the French psychologist Alfred Binet, who proposed the concept of mental age. A bright child's mental age is above his or her chronological age; a slow child's mental age is below his or her chronological age. The concept of the intelligence quotient (IQ), the ratio of mental age to chronological age (multiplied by 100), was introduced when the Binet scales were revised to create the Stanford-Binet Intelligence Scale. Many intelligence test scores are still expressed as IQ scores, but they are no longer actually calculated according to this formula.

TABLE 12.2   TESTS COMPOSING THE WECHSLER ADULT INTELLIGENCE SCALE

The tests of the Wechsler Intelligence Scale for Children are similar to those of the adult scale, with some modifications.

Test	Description
Verbal scale	
Information	Questions tap a general range of information, for example, 'What is the capital of Italy?'
Comprehension	Tests practical information and ability to evaluate past experience, for example, 'Why do we put stamps on a letter to be mailed?'
Arithmetic	Verbal problems testing arithmetic reasoning.
Similarities	Asks in what way two objects or concepts (for example, recipe and map) are similar; assesses abstract thinking.
Digit span	A series of digits presented auditorily (for example, 7–5–6–3–8) is repeated in a forward or backward direction; tests attention and rote memory.
Vocabulary	Assesses word knowledge.
Letter number sequencing	Orally presented letters and numbers in a mixed-up order must be reordered and repeated, first with the numbers in ascending order and then with the letters in alphabetical order; assesses working memory.
Performance scale	
Digit symbol	A timed coding task in which numbers must be associated with marks of various shapes; assesses speed of learning and writing.
Picture completion	The missing part of an incompletely drawn picture must be discovered and named; assesses visual alertness, visual memory, and perceptual organization.
Block design	Pictured designs must be copied with blocks; assesses ability to perceive and analyze patterns.
Picture arrangement	A series of comic-strip pictures must be arranged in the right sequence to tell a story; assesses understanding of social situations.
Matrix reasoning	A geometric shape that is similar in some way to a sample shape must be selected from a set of possible alternatives; assesses perceptual organization.
Object assembly	Puzzle pieces must be assembled to form a complete object; assesses ability to deal with part–whole relationships.
Symbol search	A series of paired groups of symbols are presented, a target group of two symbols and a search group. Examinee must determine if either target symbol appears in the search group; assesses processing speed.

➜ The Wechsler Adult Intelligence Scale (WAIS) assesses many of the same dimensions as the Standord–Binet, but is less reliant on language abilities.

CRITICAL THINKING QUESTIONS

1   In order to determine whether an intelligence test is valid, we have to have some outcome against which performance on the test is measured. What do you think are the right outcomes that any intelligence test should predict?

2   Why do you think some people care so much about measuring intelligence?

CONTEMPORARY THEORIES: MANY OR FEW INTELLIGENCES?

Some psychologists view intelligence as a general capacity for comprehension and reasoning that manifests itself in various ways. This was Binet's assumption. Although his test contained many kinds of items, Binet observed that a bright child tended to score higher than dull children on all of them. He assumed, therefore, that the different tasks sampled a basic underlying ability. Similarly, despite the diverse subscales included in the WAIS, Wechsler also believed that 'intelligence is the aggregate or global capacity of the individual to act purposefully, to think rationally, and to deal effectively with his environment' (Wechsler, 1958).

Other psychologists, however, question whether there is such a thing as 'general intelligence.' They believe that intelligence tests sample a number of mental abilities that are relatively independent of one another. Raymond Cattell subdivided general intelligence into **fluid intelligence**, the ability to think logically and solve problems in novel situations, even without much knowledge of the situation, and **crystallized intelligence**, the ability to use one's acquired knowledge, skills, and experience.

One method of obtaining more precise information about the kinds of abilities that determine performance on intelligence tests is **factor analysis**, a statistical technique that examines the intercorrelations among a number of tests and, by grouping those that are most highly correlated, reduces them to a smaller number of independent dimensions, called factors. The basic idea is that two tests that correlate very highly with each other are probably measuring the same underlying ability. The goal is to discover the minimum number of factors, or abilities, required to explain the observed pattern of correlations among an array of different tests.

It was the originator of factor analysis, Charles Spearman (1904), who first proposed that all individuals possess a general intelligence factor (called **g**) in varying amounts. A person could be described as generally bright or generally dull, depending on the amount of g he or she possessed. According to Spearman, the g factor is the major determinant of performance on intelligence tests. In addition, special factors, each called s, are specific to particular abilities or tests. For example, tests of arithmetic or spatial relationships would each tap a separate s. An individual's tested intelligence would reflect the amount of g plus the magnitude of the various s factors possessed by that individual. Performance in mathematics, for example, would be a function of a person's general intelligence and mathematical aptitude.

A later investigator, Louis Thurstone (1938), objected to Spearman's emphasis on general intelligence, suggesting instead that intelligence can be divided into a number of primary abilities by using factor analysis. After many rounds of administering tests, factor-analyzing the results, purifying the scales, and retesting, Thurstone identified seven factors, which he used to construct his Test of Primary Mental Abilities.

Thurstone's hope of discovering the basic elements of intelligence through factor analysis was not fully realized, for several reasons. For one, his primary abilities are not completely independent. Indeed, the significant intercorrelations among them provide support for the concept of a general intelligence factor underlying the specific abilities. For another, the number of basic abilities identified by factor analysis depends on the nature of the test items. Other investigators, using different test items and alternative methods of factor analysis, have identified from 20 to 150 factors representing the range of intellectual abilities (Ekstrom et al., 1979; Ekstrom et al., 1976; Guilford, 1982).

This lack of consistency in numbers and kinds of factors raises doubts about the value of the factorial approach.

Nevertheless, factor analysis remains an important technique for studying intellectual performance (Lubinski, 2000), and we will encounter it again when we discuss personality traits in Chapter 13.

Gardner's theory of multiple intelligences

Howard Gardner (2004a) developed his theory of multiple intelligences as a direct challenge to what he calls the 'classical' view of intelligence as a general mental capacity for logical reasoning. Gardner was struck by the variety of adult roles in different cultures – roles that depend on a variety of skills and abilities yet are equally important to successful functioning in those cultures. His observations led him to conclude that there is not just one underlying mental capacity or g, but a variety of intelligences that work in combination. He defines an intelligence as the 'ability to solve problems or fashion products that are of consequence in a particular cultural setting or community' (1993b, p. 15). It is these multiple intelligences that enable human beings to take on such diverse roles as physicist, farmer, shaman, and dancer.

Gardner is quick to point out that an intelligence is not a 'thing,' some sort of commodity inside the head, but 'a potential, the presence of which allows an individual access to forms of thinking appropriate to specific kinds of content' (Kornhaber & Gardner, 1991, p. 155). According to **Gardner's theory of multiple intelligences**, there are seven distinct kinds of intelligence that are independent of one another, each operating as a separate system (or module) in the brain according to its own rules. These are (1) linguistic, (2) musical, (3) logical-mathematical, (4) spatial, (5) bodily-kinesthetic, (6) intrapersonal, and (7) interpersonal. These are described more fully in Table 12.3. Gardner adds that this list is by no means exhaustive, and even more intelligences may exist.

Gardner analyzes each kind of intelligence from several viewpoints: the cognitive operations involved, the appearance of prodigies and other exceptional individuals, evidence from cases of brain damage, manifestations in different cultures, and the possible course of evolutionary development. For example, certain kinds of brain damage can impair one type of intelligence and have no effect on the others. He notes that the capacities of adults in different cultures represent different combinations of the various intelligences. Although all normal people can apply all of the intelligences to some extent, each individual is characterized by a unique combination of relatively stronger and weaker intelligences (Gardner, 2004a), which help account for individual differences.

As noted earlier, conventional IQ tests are good predictors of college grades, but they are less valid for predicting later job success or career advancement. Measures of other abilities, such as interpersonal intelligence, may help explain why some people with brilliant college records fail miserably in later life while lesser students become charismatic leaders. Gardner and

TABLE 12.3 GARDNER'S SEVEN INTELLIGENCES

Type of intelligence	Description
1. **Linguistic intelligence**	The capacity for speech, along with mechanisms dedicated to phonology (speech sounds), syntax (grammar), semantics (meaning), and pragmatics (implications and uses of language in various settings).
2. **Musical intelligence**	The ability to create, communicate, and understand meanings made of sound, along with mechanisms dedicated to pitch, rhythm, and timbre (sound quality).
3. **Logical-mathematical intelligence**	The ability to use and appreciate relationships in the absence of action or objects – that is, to engage in abstract thought.
4. **Spatial intelligence**	The ability to perceive visual or spatial information, modify it, and recreate visual images without reference to the original stimulus. Includes the capacity to construct images in three dimensions and to move and rotate those images.
5. **Bodily-kinesthetic intelligence**	The ability to use all or part of the body to solve problems or fashion products; includes control over fine and gross motor actions and the ability to manipulate external objects.
6. **Intrapersonal intelligence**	The ability to distinguish among one's own feelings, intentions, and motivations.
7. **Interpersonal intelligence**	The ability to recognize and make distinctions among other people's feelings, beliefs, and intentions.

colleagues therefore call for 'intelligence-fair' assessments in schools that would allow children to demonstrate their abilities by other means besides paper-and-pencil tests, such as putting together gears to demonstrate spatial skills (Gardner, 2004b).

Anderson's theory of intelligence and cognitive development

One criticism of Gardner's theory is that high levels of ability in any of the various intelligences are usually correlated with high ability in the others; that is, no specific intellectual capacity is

According to Gardner's theory of multiple intelligences, these three individuals are displaying different kinds of intelligence: logical-mathematical, musical, and spatial.

wholly distinct from the others (Messick, 1992; Scarr, 1985). In addition, psychologist Mike Anderson points out that Gardner's multiple intelligences are ill-defined – they are 'sometimes a behavior, sometimes a cognitive process, and sometimes a structure in the brain' (1992, p. 67). Anderson therefore has sought to develop a theory based on the idea of general intelligence proposed by Thurstone and others.

Anderson's theory of intelligence holds that individual differences in intelligence and developmental changes in intellectual competence are explained by different mechanisms. Differences in intelligence result from differences in the 'basic processing mechanism' that implements thinking, which in turn yields knowledge. Individuals vary in the speed at which basic processing occurs. A person with a slower basic processing mechanism is likely to have more difficulty acquiring knowledge than a person with a faster processing mechanism. This is equivalent to saying that a low-speed processing mechanism produces low general intelligence.

Anderson notes, however, that there are some cognitive mechanisms that show no individual differences. For example, people with Down syndrome may not be able to add 2 plus 2 yet can recognize that other people hold beliefs and may act on those beliefs (Anderson, 1992). The mechanisms that provide these universal capacities are 'modules.' Each module functions independently, performing complex computations. Modules are not affected by the basic processing mechanism; they are virtually automatic. According to Anderson, it is the maturation of new modules that explains the increase of cognitive abilities in the course of development. For example, the maturation of a module devoted to language would explain the development of the ability to speak in complete sentences.

In addition to modules, according to Anderson, intelligence includes two 'specific abilities.' One of these deals with propositional thought (language mathematical expression) and the other with visual and spatial functioning. Anderson suggests that the tasks associated with these abilities are carried out by 'specific processors.' Unlike modules, which carry out very particular functions, each of the specific processors handles a broad class of problems or knowledge. Also unlike modules, specific processors are affected by the basic processing mechanism. A high-speed processing mechanism enables a person to make more effective use of the specific processors to score higher on tests and accomplish more in the real world.

Anderson's theory of intelligence thus suggests two different 'routes' to knowledge. The first involves using the basic processing mechanism, which operates through the specific processors, to acquire knowledge. In Anderson's view, this is what we mean by 'thinking,' and it accounts for individual differences in intelligence (which, in his view, are equivalent to differences in knowledge). The second route involves the use of modules to acquire knowledge. Module-based knowledge, such as perception of three-dimensional space, comes automatically if the module has matured sufficiently, and this accounts for the development of intelligence.

Anderson's theory can be illustrated by the case of a 21-year-old man known as MA who suffered convulsions as a child and was diagnosed with autism spectrum disorder (see Chapter 16 for a discussion of autism spectrum disorder). As an adult, he could not talk and achieved very low scores on psychometric tests. However, he was found to have an IQ of 128 and had an extraordinary ability to detect prime numbers, doing so more accurately than a scientist with a degree in mathematics (Anderson, 1992). Anderson concludes that MA had an intact basic processing mechanism, which allowed him to think about abstract symbols, but had suffered damage to his linguistic modules, which hindered acquisition of everyday knowledge and communication.

Sternberg's triarchic theory

Robert Sternberg (2011) agrees that there are multiple types of intelligence, but **Sternberg's triarchic theory** argues that they fall into three categories: analytical intelligence, creative intelligence, and practical intelligence. Analytical intelligence includes the abilities to identify and evaluate a problem, and plan and monitor your progress toward a solution. This is the type of intelligence that tests like the Stanford–Binet and WAIS tend to measure.

Creative intelligence is the ability to handle novel situations or see innovative solutions to problems. For example, if while cooking your big dinner you discover that you do not have a critical ingredient, you would use your creative intelligence to find a way to make the dish without that ingredient. Creative intelligence may be partially innate, but experience also matters greatly. If you have a great deal of experience with a situation, you may be able to solve it with little thought or effort – it becomes automatic. For example, people who have been driving a car for years don't have to think much about applying the break or turning the steering wheel at the appropriate time, but just do it automatically. Creative intelligence comes into play when a person is facing a novel situation and must devise completely solutions that other people might not think of.

Practical intelligence involves the ability to carry out your plan given the situations you confront – what some people call 'street smarts.' For example, if your guests show up late for dinner, you would use your practical intelligence to adjust your cooking times so that the meal would not be ruined. According to Sternberg, individuals using their practical intelligence first look for ways to adapt, or fit into, the environment. If it is not possible to adapt, they try to select a different environment or to shape the existing environment in order to fit into it better. A spouse who is unhappy in a marriage may not be able to adapt to the current circumstances. He or she may therefore select a different environment (for example, through separation or divorce) or try to shape the existing environment (for example, through counseling) (Sternberg, 2011). Analytical, creative, and practical intelligence are intertwined. Each comes into play during the problem-solving process, and none of them can operate independently.

CUTTING EDGE RESEARCH STRENGTHS-BASED APPROACHES TO INTELLECTUAL DIFFICULTIES

Israel Berger, Sydney Medical School,
University of Sydney

Intelligence testing was introduced to select candidates for life courses, namely in the form of selective school entry and military service, and the construct of intelligence has long been used to theorize about gender and sexuality (Hegarty, 2007). Intelligence testing has since become a first line diagnostic tool for intellectual difficulties (e.g., learning disabilities and developmental delays) (see, e.g., American Psychiatric Association, 2000) and placement of children in separate special education classrooms. However, as early as 1989, Siegel found that intelligence tests were not well-correlated with degree of disability, results that have been found in more recent studies as well (e.g., Fletcher *et al.*, 1998). Some clinical standards have begun to follow suit and advise taking a more holistic approach to diagnosis with intelligence testing as just one consideration (e.g., World Health Organization, 2008).

In terms of management of intellectual disabilities, many societies have abandoned the approach of sending people away to institutions and special education classrooms and are recognizing that people with intellectual difficulties are able to make contributions to their peers and society at large. This is the basis of strengths-based approaches and is further developed on the basis that each individual is able to achieve more if strengths and the ability to improve are the foci rather than weaknesses and deficits. Strengths-based approaches have been applied to a variety of contexts, including criminal rehabilitation (Burnett & Maruna, 2006), positive youth development (Silbereisen & Lerner, 2007), substance abuse (Brun & Rapp, 2001), and the study of native peoples (Kana'iaupuni, 2004).

Education and social work have led the movement to applying strengths-based approaches to intellectual difficulties (e.g., Campbell *et al.*, 2001; Mackelprang & Salsgiver, 2009). Many programs have been developed to increase the quality of life and integration into society of people with intellectual difficulties (e.g., Hassink *et al.*, 2010). Some programs have been developed that specifically address the needs of people with intellectual difficulties who have committed crimes or exhibited dangerous behaviors (Ayland & West, 2006), combining the strengths-based approach to rehabilitation with that of intellectual difficulties. Others have addressed the needs of ethnically minoritized students with learning difficulties (Kea *et al.*, 2003). As strengths-based approaches are applied to more areas, other intersections are likely to be reflected in programs and theoretical discussions.

INTERIM SUMMARY

→ Both Binet and Wechsler, the developer of the Wechsler Adult Intelligence Scale (WAIS), assumed that intelligence is a general capacity for reasoning.

→ Similarly, Spearman proposed that a general factor (*g*) underlies performance on different kinds of test items. Factor analysis is a method for determining the kinds of abilities that underlie performance on intelligence tests.

→ Gardner's theory of multiple intelligences suggests that there are seven distinct kinds of intelligence that are independent of one another, each operating as a separate system (or module) in the brain according to its own rules. These are (1) linguistic, (2) musical, (3) logical-mathematical, (4) spatial, (5) bodily-kinesthetic, (6) intrapersonal, and (7) interpersonal.

→ Anderson's theory of intelligence suggests that differences in intelligence result from differences in the 'basic processing mechanism' that implements thinking, which in turn yields knowledge.

→ Sternberg's triarchic theory argues there are three types of intelligence: analytical, creative, and practical.

CRITICAL THINKING QUESTIONS

1 From your observations, what skills or abilities do you think are the most important components of intelligence?

2 What practical skills in your culture are considered key to intelligence?

GENETICS AND INTELLIGENCE

Some of the fiercest debates over intelligence have focused on the contribution of genetics to determining the level of intelligence in individuals or groups. Advocates of particular political positions and social policies frequently argue either

TABLE 12.4   HYPOTHETICAL EXAMINATION SCORES OF TWO GROUPS OF STUDENTS

Group A		Group B	
Alice	100	Greta	89
Bob	95	Harold	88
Carol	89	Ilene	83
Dan	83	John	80
Emily	67	Karen	77
Fred	58	Leon	75
Average	82.0	Average	82.0

for or against the idea that intelligence is inherited (for example, Herrnstein & Murray, 1994). Because these debates reveal widespread public misunderstanding about the empirical issues involved, we will describe in some detail the reasoning and methods that behavioral scientists use to assess how genetic and environmental factors contribute to individual differences, including differences in intelligence.

We begin with Table 12.4, which lists (in descending order) the scores of a hypothetical examination taken by two groups of six students each. As shown in the last row, the average (mean) score of the students within each group is 82.0. But we can also see that the scores from Class A are much more spread out – that is, more variable – than the scores from Class B. In other words, the students in Class A are more different from one another than the students in Class B. The degree to which the scores in a set differ from one another can be expressed mathematically by a quantity called their variance.

Now consider the scores for Class A. Why are they different from one another? Why do some students do better than others? What accounts for the variance we observe? One obvious possibility is that some students studied for the exam longer than other students did. To find out whether and to what extent this is true, we could conduct a hypothetical experiment in which we 'controlled for' the variable of study time by requiring all students to study exactly 3 hours for the exam, no more and no less. If study time really does affect students' scores, what would happen to the variance of those scores?

First, some of the students who would have studied longer than 3 hours and done quite well will now do less well. For example, if Alice – who might have studied for 6 hours to achieve her perfect score of 100 – had been permitted to study for only 3 hours, her score might have been more like Greta's score of 89. Second, some of the students who would have studied less than 3 hours and not done very well will now do better. Fred – who had time to only skim the reading for the exam – might have obtained a score higher than

58 if he had studied for 3 hours. Like Leon, he might at least have obtained a score of 75. In other words, if we controlled the study time of Class A, the students' scores would bunch closer together, looking more like Class B's scores – the variance of their scores would decrease. If we actually did this experiment and observed that the variance in Class A's scores decreased by, say, 60 per cent, we could claim that study time had accounted for 60 per cent of the variance in the original scores for this class. In this hypothetical example, then, a major reason the exam scores differed so much from one another in Class A is that students differed in the amount of time they spent studying.

Theoretically, we could test for other potential sources of variance in the same way. If we think that having a good breakfast might affect students' scores, we could feed all the students the same breakfast (or deny breakfast to all the students) and observe whether the variance of their scores is reduced as a result. In general, holding constant any variable that 'makes a difference' will reduce the variance of the scores. In the extreme case, if we held all the relevant variables constant, the variance would diminish to zero: every student would obtain the same score.

However, we cannot say what will happen to the mean of the scores when we hold a variable constant. For example, if the students in Class A had originally studied for the exam for only 2 hours on average, by requiring them all to study for 3 hours we will raise the class average. If, however, the students had studied for 4 hours on average, we will lower the class average by limiting everybody to only 3 hours of study time.

Heritability

We are now prepared to ask the 'genetics' question: to what extent do some students do better than others on the exam because they are genetically more capable? To put it another way, what percentage of the variance in exam scores is accounted for by genetic differences among the students? In general, the percentage of the variance in any trait that is accounted for by genetic differences among the individuals in a population is the trait's **heritability**. (Heritability is different from heredity, which is the *process* by which parents pass on traits to their offspring.) The more individual differences on a trait are due to genetic differences, the closer the heritability is to 100 per cent. For example, height is heavily influenced by genetics: its heritability ranges from about 85 to 95 per cent across different studies. Note that this does not mean that any one gene accounts for 85 to 95 per cent of the variability in height: most human characteristics are influenced by many genes that each exert a small effect.

Now, however, we face a practical difficulty. We cannot experimentally determine how much of the variance in exam scores is accounted for by genetic differences the way we

Several studies of twins suggest IQ is partly heritable.

did for study time because that would require holding the genetic variable constant – that is, turning all the students into genetic clones. But we can take advantage of the fact that nature sometimes produces genetic clones in the form of identical twins. To the extent that identical twins are more alike on a trait than fraternal twins, we can infer that the trait has a genetic or heritable component (assuming that other factors, such as differential parental treatment, can be ruled out).

Across many twin studies the heritability of intelligence (as measured by intelligence tests) has been estimated to be between 60 per cent and 80 per cent (Lubinski, 2000). One difficulty in interpreting the results of twin studies is that identical twin pairs may be treated more alike than fraternal twin pairs, which may account for the greater similarity of their personalities. This is one reason that researchers at the University of Minnesota decided to study sets of twins who had been reared apart (Bouchard et al., 1990).

The participants in the Minnesota Study of Twins Reared Apart were assessed on a number of ability and personality measures. In addition, they participated in lengthy interviews, during which they were asked questions about such topics as childhood experiences, fears, hobbies, musical tastes, social attitudes, and sexual interests. These studies reveal that twins reared apart are still quite similar to each other across a wide range of abilities although not as much as twins reared together (see Figure 12.2), permitting us to conclude that genetics are important in intelligence, but environment also plays a role (Bouchard et al., 1990; Lykken, 1982; Tellegen et al., 1988).

The recurring public debate over nature–nurture questions reveals widespread misunderstanding about the concept of

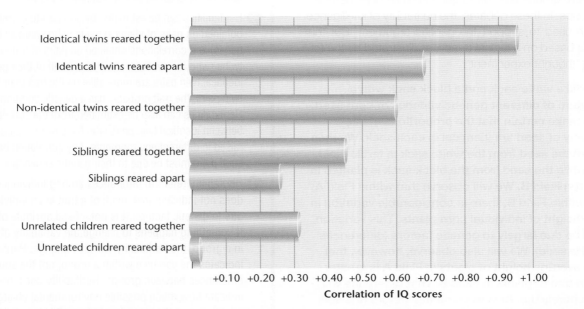

FIGURE 12.2 IQ Data From Twin Studies. *Identical twins tend to have more similar IQs than non-identical twins or other siblings, even when they were reared apart.*

heritability. Therefore, it is important to be clear about the following points:

→ Heritability refers to a population, not to individuals. The heritability of a trait refers to differences among individuals within a population, not to percentages of a trait within an individual. To say that height has a heritability of 90 per cent does not mean that 90 per cent of your height came from your genes and 10 per cent came from the environment. It means that 90 per cent of the differences in height among individuals observed in a particular population is due to genetic differences among those individuals.

→ The heritability of a trait is not a single, fixed number. Heritability refers to an attribute of a trait in a particular population at a particular point in time. If something happens to change the variance of a trait in a population, the heritability of the trait will also change. For example, if everyone in our society were suddenly given equal educational opportunities, the variance of intellectual performance in the society would decrease, and scores on standardized measures of intellectual ability would be more similar. (This is what happened in our hypothetical experiment in which everyone had to study the same length of time for the exam.) And because heritability is the percentage of variance that is due to inherited differences among individuals, the heritability would actually increase because the percentage of the variance due to an important environmental factor, education, would have decreased.

→ Heritability does not tell us about the source of mean differences between groups. One of the most contentious and recurring debates is over the question of whether average differences in the intelligence test scores of different ethnic groups are due to genetic differences between the groups. In these debates, the heritability of intelligence is often used to support the genetic argument. But this claim is based on a logical fallacy, as illustrated by the following 'thought experiment':

> **We fill a white sack and a black sack with a mixture of different genetic varieties of corn seed. We make certain that the proportions of each variety of seed are identical in each sack. We then plant the seed from the white sack in fertile Field A, while the seed from the black sack is planted in barren Field B. We will observe that within Field A, as within Field B, there is considerable variation in the height of individual corn plants. This variation will be due largely to genetic factors (differences in the seed). We will also observe, however, that the average height of plants in Field A is greater than that of plants in Field B. That difference will be entirely due to environmental factors (the soil). The same is true of IQs: Differences in the average IQ of various human populations could be entirely**
>
> **due to environmental differences, even if within each population all variations were due to genetic differences. (Eysenck & Kamin, 1981, p. 97)**

→ Heritability does not tell us about the effects of environmental changes on the average level of a trait. Another incorrect claim about heritability is that a trait with high heritability cannot be changed by a change in the environment. For example, it has been argued that it is futile to use preschool intervention programs to help disadvantaged children enhance their intellectual abilities because those abilities have high levels of heritability. But between 1946 and 1982 the height of young adult males in Japan increased by 3.3 inches, mainly owing to improved nutrition (Angoff, 1988). And yet height is one of the most heritable traits we possess. Then, as now, taller Japanese parents have taller children than do shorter Japanese parents. Similarly, IQ test scores have risen significantly over the past century in many cultures (Flynn, 1987). In sum, heritability is about variances, not average levels.

INTERIM SUMMARY

⊃ Behavioral scientists typically quantify the extent to which a group of people differ from one another on some measure of a trait or ability by computing the variance of the scores obtained. The more the individuals in the group differ from one another, the higher the variance. Researchers can then seek to determine how much of that variance is due to different causes. The proportion of variance in a trait that is accounted for (caused by) genetic differences among the individuals is called the heritability of the trait.

⊃ Heritabilities can be estimated by comparing correlations obtained on pairs of identical twins (who share all their genes) and correlations obtained on pairs of fraternal twins (who, on average, share about half of their genes). If identical twin pairs are more alike on the trait than fraternal twin pairs, the trait probably has a genetic component. Heritabilities can also be estimated from the correlation between identical twin pairs who have been separated and raised in different environments. Any correlation between such pairs must be due to their genetic similarities.

⊃ Heritability refers to differences among individuals; it does not indicate how much of a trait in an individual is due to genetic factors. It is not a fixed attribute of a trait: If something happens to change the variability of a trait in a group, the heritability will also change. Heritability indicates the variance within a group, not the source of differences between groups. Heritability does, however, indicate how much possible environmental changes might change the mean level of a trait in a population.

EMOTIONAL INTELLIGENCE

New York Times writer Daniel Goleman popularized the term **emotional intelligence** in his 1995 book on the subject. He argued that understanding and control of your emotions is one of the most important keys to health and success in life. Goleman's book was based on important empirical work by psychologists such as Peter Salovey, John Mayer, and Reuven Bar-On showing that, indeed, people who are emotionally astute have a leg up on those of us who are not.

Mayer and Salovey (Mayer *et al.*, 2004) suggest there are four critical components to emotional intelligence. The first is *accurate perception and expression* of emotions. Being able to read the emotions of others enables you to anticipate possible threats they might pose. For example, imagine you are in an argument with a co-worker who is known to have a volatile temper. If you can accurately perceive that your co-worker is getting extremely agitated, you will know that it may be time to back off and live to fight another day. If you don't accurately perceive your co-worker's level of anger, you might end up with a bloody nose. Accurately perceiving and expressing others' emotions also helps you empathize with their position. In turn, you can modify your responses to other people, either to be more persuasive in arguing your point or to make them feel that you understand them well. This can make you an effective negotiator and a trusted friend to others.

Accurately perceiving and expressing your own emotions is the first step to responding appropriately to those emotions. People who don't realize they are anxious can have chronic physiological arousal that costs them physical wear and tear and impairs their health (see Chapter 14). People who don't realize they are sad may not take the necessary actions to change the sources of their sadness. People who don't realize they are angry may suddenly and impulsively lash out at others, feeling out of control.

The second component of emotional intelligence is the ability to *access and generate emotions* in the service of thinking and problem-solving. We often ask ourselves, 'How do I feel about this?' in trying to make an important decision, such as what college to attend or what major to pursue. Being able to access our current feelings about an issue or to anticipate our future feelings, should we make a particular decision, gives us important information that should go into many decisions.

The third component of emotional intelligence is *understanding emotions and emotional meanings*. We may accurately perceive we are anxious, but if we don't understand why we are anxious, we can't do much about it. We often make incorrect attributions for our emotions, which can lead us to take unwise steps. For example, imagine you have been staying up late each night for many weeks to complete your college assignments and then getting up for early morning classes. Eventually, you begin to feel sad, lethargic, and unmotivated. You might conclude that you are feeling sad and unmotivated because you are pursuing the wrong major, or even that college is not for you. The true reason for your sadness, however, may well be sleep deprivation, which can cause depression-like symptoms (see Chapter 6). Attributing your sadness incorrectly to your college major rather than correctly to your lack of sleep could cause you to make some very bad decisions.

The final component of emotional intelligence is *emotional regulation* – being able to manage and regulate your emotions appropriately. This does not mean completely controlling the emotions you feel or express. Indeed, such emotional overcontrol is unhealthy. But letting your emotions rage unabated can also be unhealthy. The most obvious example is with anger. We all feel angry at times, but most of us know we can't express our anger at any time and in any way we wish (at least we can't get away with it). How we channel our anger is critical to our relationships to others and to our own health. People who completely suppress their anger can be exploited by others, and people who chronically express their anger in a hostile manner lose friends quickly. In contrast, people who can express the reasons for their anger in ways that others can hear and accept are more likely to both maintain their friendships and avoid being exploited. In addition, research we will review in Chapter 14 clearly shows that people who do not channel their anger appropriately experience

Emotional intelligence is important in volatile situations.

more heart disease, probably because their cardiovascular system is chronically over-aroused and over-reactive.

Can you learn emotional intelligence? Many schools now have programs to teach young people how to recognize and better manage their anger, in hopes of reducing school violence, and some evaluations of these programs suggest they can be effective in teaching young people anger control (see Bar-On *et al.*, 2007). Many a crusty corporate executive has also undergone emotional schooling to learn how to better empathize with employees and manage with a bigger heart, and it appears these programs can be successful (Bar-On *et al.*, 2007). Much of what psychotherapy focuses on is helping people recognize, accurately label, and manage their emotions better, and many studies show psychotherapy to be effective in relieving a variety of psychological disorders (see Chapter 16). These same techniques are sometimes used to help cardiac patients better control anger and stress so as to improve their health (see Chapter 14). Thus, there is increasing evidence that emotional intelligence truly is important to success and well-being, and fortunately, those of us born emotionally challenged can become more intelligent.

INTERIM SUMMARY

➜ Emotional intelligence is thought to have four components: accurate perception and expression of emotions, the ability to access and generate emotions, understanding of emotions and emotional meanings, and good emotional regulation.

➜ People with higher emotional intelligence tend to be healthier psychologically and physically.

CRITICAL THINKING QUESTIONS

1 How might parents encourage high emotional intelligence in their children?

2 Why might emotional intelligence improve performance on the job or in school?

GENERAL LEARNING DISABILITY

Levels of intelligence fall along a continuum. Individuals whose intellectual and practical skills fall far below average are said to suffer from **general learning disability**. The World Health Organization has set criteria for a diagnosis of general learning disability. In order to be diagnosed as such, an individual must have both subaverage scores on an IQ test, and show significant problems in performing the tasks of daily life. For example, individuals must show significant delays or abnormalities in communication, inability to care for themselves, significant deficits in social or interpersonal skills, inability to use community resources (e.g., riding a bus), inability to be self-directed, very low academic or work skills, no leisure activities, or inability to care for their health or personal safety.

The severity of general learning disability varies greatly. Individuals with *mild general learning disability* can feed and dress themselves with minimal help, may have average motor skills, and can learn to talk and write in simple terms. They can get around their own neighborhoods well, although they may not be able to go beyond their neighborhoods without help. If they are placed in special education classes that address their specific deficits, they can achieve a good education and become self-sufficient. As adults, they can shop for specific items and cook simple meals for themselves. They may be employed in unskilled or semiskilled jobs. Their scores on IQ tests tend to be between about 50 and 69.

Individuals with *moderate general learning disability* typically have significant delays in language development, such as using only four to ten words by the age of three. They may be physically clumsy and, thus, have some trouble dressing and feeding themselves. They typically do not achieve more than rudimentary academic skills but, with special education, can learn simple vocational skills. As adults, they may not be able to travel alone or shop or cook for themselves. Their scores on IQ tests tend to be between about 35 and 49.

Individuals with *severe general learning disability* have very limited vocabularies and speak in two- or three-word sentences. They may have significant deficits in motor development and as children may play with toys inappropriately (e.g., banging two dolls together, rather than having them interact symbolically). As adults, they can feed themselves with spoons and dress themselves if the clothing is not complicated with many buttons or zippers. They cannot travel alone for any distance and cannot shop or cook for themselves. They may be able to learn some unskilled manual labor, but many do not.

Children and adults with *profound general learning disability* are severely impaired and require full-time custodial care. They cannot dress themselves completely. They may be able to use spoons, but not knives and forks. They tend not to interact with others socially, although they may respond to simple commands. They may achieve vocabularies of 300 to 400 words as adults. Many persons with profound general learning disability suffer from frequent illnesses, and their life expectancy is shorter than normal. Their IQ scores tend to be under 20.

Causes of general learning disability

A large number of biological factors can cause general learning disability, including chromosomal and gestational disorders, exposure to toxins prenatally and in early childhood, infections, physical trauma, metabolism and nutrition problems, and gross brain disease. In addition, sociocultural factors can influence general learning disability.

As we have already discussed in this chapter, intellectual skills are at least partially inherited. The families of individuals with general learning disability tend to have high rates of intellectual problems, including the different levels of general learning disability and autism spectrum disorder (Camp *et al.*, 1998).

Two metabolic disorders that are genetically transmitted and that cause general learning disability are *phenylketonuria* (PKU) and *Tay-Sachs disease*. PKU is carried by a recessive gene and occurs in about 1 in 20 000 births. Children with PKU are unable to metabolize phenylalanine, an amino acid. As a result, phenylalanine and its derivative, phenyl pyruvic acid, build up in the body and cause permanent brain damage. Fortunately, an effective treatment is available, and children who receive this treatment from an early age can develop an average level of intelligence. If untreated, children with PKU typically have IQs below 50.

Tay-Sachs disease also is carried by a recessive gene and occurs primarily in Jewish populations. Progressive degeneration of the nervous system begins, usually when a child is between 3 and 6 months old, leading to mental and physical deterioration. These children usually die before the age of six years, and there is no effective treatment.

Several types of chromosomal disorders can lead to general learning disability. One of the best-known causes of general learning disability is *Down syndrome*, which is caused when chromosome 21 is present in triplicate rather than in duplicate. (For this reason, Down syndrome is also referred to as *Trisomy 21*.) Down syndrome occurs in about 1 in every 800 children born in the USA. From childhood, almost all people with Down syndrome have general learning disability, although the level of their disability varies from mild to profound. People with Down syndrome have abnormalities in the neurons in their brains that resemble those found in Alzheimer's disease. *Fragile X syndrome*, which is the second most common cause of general learning disability in males after Down syndrome, is caused when a tip of the X chromosome breaks off. This syndrome is characterized by severe to profound general learning disability, speech defects, and severe deficits in interpersonal interaction.

The quality of the prenatal environment for a fetus can profoundly affect intellectual development. When a pregnant woman contracts the rubella (German measles) virus, the herpes virus, or syphilis, there is a risk of physical damage to the fetus that can cause general learning disability. Chronic maternal disorders, such as high blood pressure and diabetes, can interfere with fetal nutrition and brain development and, therefore, can affect the intellectual capacities of the fetus. Fortunately, effective treatment of these disorders during pregnancy can greatly reduce the risk of damage to the fetus.

The drugs a woman takes while pregnant can pass through the placenta, affecting the development of the fetus. In addition, women who take illicit drugs, such as cocaine, during pregnancy tend to be more socially disadvantaged and more likely to use tobacco, alcohol, marijuana, and other illicit drugs (Tronick *et al.*, 1996). These other risk factors, in addition to exposure to cocaine, may severely impair intellectual growth in the children of these mothers.

Alcohol is another drug that, if taken during pregnancy, can affect the intellectual and physical development of a fetus. Children whose mothers ingested substantial amounts of alcohol during pregnancy are at increased risk for general learning disability and a syndrome known as **fetal alcohol syndrome** (FAS) (Fried & Watkinson, 1990). On average, children with FAS have an IQ of about 68, as well as poor judgment, distractibility, difficulty in perceiving social cues, and an inability to learn from experience. Their academic functioning tends to be low throughout their lives. Abel Dorris was a child with FAS (adapted from Dorris, 1989; Lyman, 1997):

Abel Dorris was adopted when he was 3 years old by Michael Dorris. Abel's mother had been a heavy drinker throughout the pregnancy and after Abel was born, and later died at age 35 of alcohol poisoning. Abel had been born almost 7 weeks premature, with low birth weight. He had been abused and malnourished before being removed to a foster home. At age 3, Abel was small for his age, not yet toilet-trained, and could speak only about 20 words. He had been diagnosed as mildly retarded. His adoptive father hoped that, in a positive environment, Abel could catch up.

Children with Down syndrome typically have general learning disability.

Yet, at age 4, Abel was still in diapers and weighed only 27 pounds. He had trouble remembering the names of other children and his activity level was unusually high. When alone, he would rock back and forth rhythmically. At age 4, he suffered the first of several severe seizures, which caused him to lose consciousness for days. No drug treatments seemed to help.

When he entered school, Abel had trouble learning to count, to identify colors, and to tie his shoes. He had a short attention span and difficulty following simple instructions. Despite devoted teachers, when he finished elementary school, Abel still could not add, subtract, or identify his place of residence. His IQ was measured in the mid-60s.

Eventually, at age 20, Abel entered a vocational training program and moved into a supervised home. His main preoccupations were his collections of stuffed animals, paper dolls, newspaper cartoons, family photographs, and old birthday cards. At age 23, he was hit by a car and killed.

It may not be safe for women to drink any amount of alcohol during pregnancy. Studies suggest that even low to moderate levels of drinking during pregnancy are associated with subtle alcohol-related birth defects (Jacobson & Jacobson, 2000; Kelly *et al.,* 2000; Olson *et al.*, 1998). For example, longitudinal studies of children exposed prenatally to alcohol show negative effects on growth at 6 years of age and on learning and memory skills at 10 years of age, even if they do not evidence the full syndrome of FAS (Cornelius *et al.,* 2002).

Children with general learning disability are more likely to come from low socioeconomic groups (Brooks-Gunn *et al.,* 1996; Camp *et al.*, 1998). This may be because their parents also have general learning disability and have not been able to acquire well-paying jobs. The social disadvantages of being poor may also contribute to lower than average intellectual development. Poor mothers are less likely to receive good prenatal care, increasing the risk of damage to the fetus and of their children being born prematurely. Children living in poverty are at increased risk for exposure to lead, because many old, run-down buildings have lead paint, which chips off and is ingested by the children. Ingestion of lead can cause brain damage and impede intellectual development. Poor children are concentrated in the inner city in poorly funded schools, and this is especially true for poor minority children. Thus, they do not receive the kind of education that could improve their intellectual functioning. Poor children who have lower IQs receive even less favorable attention from teachers and fewer learning opportunities, especially if they are also members of minorities (Alexander *et al.*, 1987). Poor children are less likely to have parents who read to them, who encourage academic success, and who are involved in their schooling. These factors may directly affect a child's intellectual development and may exacerbate the biological conditions that interfere with a child's cognitive development (Camp *et al.*, 1998).

Treatments for general learning disability

Ideally, children at risk of general learning disability receive comprehensive interventions from the first days of life. Intensive individualized interventions can enhance individuals' development of basic skills. Drug therapies reduce aggressive and self-destructive behaviors. And social programs ensure that the environment is optimal for the child's development.

Behavioral interventions can help children and adults learn new skills, from identifying colors correctly to using vocational skills. Other adults may model the desired behavior, starting with the simplest steps, then rewarding the child or adult as he or she comes closer and closer to mastering the skill. Behavioral strategies can also help to reduce self-injurious and other maladaptive behaviors, such as head-banging.

When women drink or smoke during pregnancy, their children are at risk of intellectual disabilities.

Medications are used to reduce seizures, which are common among people with general learning disability. Medications can also reduce aggressive, self-destructive, and antisocial behavior. Finally, antidepressant medications can reduce depressive symptoms, improve sleep patterns, and help control self-injurious behavior in mentally impaired individuals.

Comprehensive interventions for children at risk of general learning disability combine all these strategies and more into one package. One such program was the Infant Health and Development Program (Gross *et al.,* 1992). The 985 children enrolled in this program had a birth weight of 2500 grams or less and a gestational age of 37 completed weeks or less. Low birth weight, premature infants were chosen for this program because these are risk factors for general learning disability. Two-thirds of these infants were randomly assigned to receive high-quality pediatric care for high-risk infants. The other third received the same pediatric care plus a comprehensive psychological intervention

The intervention had three components. First, specially trained counselors visited the homes of these children during the first 3 years of the child's life. The children's mothers were taught good parenting practices and strategies for improving their children's cognitive development. For example, counselors gave mothers strategies to calm their babies (who tended to be irritable). The mothers were shown how to provide appropriate levels of stimulation for their child and how to encourage their children to be self-motivated and to explore their environments. The counselors helped the mothers reduce stress in their environments and in their babies' environments. In addition, each day the children in the intervention program attended a child development center with specially trained teachers, who worked to overcome the children's intellectual and physical deficits. Finally, parent support groups were started to help the parents cope with the stresses of parenting.

At 36 months of age, the children in the intervention group were significantly less likely to have IQ scores in the low range than were those in the control group, who received only medical care (The Infant Health and Development Program, 1990). Among the infants with birth weights between 2001 and 2500 grams, the effects of the program were especially strong: at age 36 months, they had IQ scores on average 13 points higher than the infants in the control group with similar birth weights. The infants with birth weights under 2000 grams also benefited from the program, but to a lesser degree: Their 36-month IQ scores were on average 6.6 points higher than the control-group infants with similar birth weights. Both the 'heavier' and 'lighter' birth weight groups who received the intervention condition also showed fewer behavioral and emotional problems at 36 months than did the children in the control groups.

Early intervention can reduce the risk of intellectual difficulties in low birth weight babies.

The 'heavier' birth weight children continued to show benefits in cognitive development from the intervention at 60 months and 96 months of age, compared with the control groups (Brooks-Gunn *et al.,* 1995). Differences between the intervention groups and the control groups in behavior and emotional problems had disappeared by this age, however. Thus, as has been the case with many early intervention programs, benefits are seen in the short term, but without continuation of the intervention, these benefits often diminish with time.

INTERIM SUMMARY

➔ General learning disability is defined as subaverage intellectual functioning, indexed by an IQ score of under 70 and deficits in adaptive behavioral functioning. There are four levels of general learning disability, ranging from mild to profound.

HOW IMPORTANT IS EMOTIONAL INTELLIGENCE?

EMOTIONAL INTELLIGENCE IS IMPORTANT

Marc A. Brackett and Peter Salovey, Yale University

Salovey and Mayer (1990) proposed that some individuals possess greater ability than others to reason about and use their emotions and emotion-laden information to enhance both cognitive activity and social functioning. Their ability model of emotional intelligence (EI) evolved as the concept of general intelligence was expanding to include an array of mental abilities, including social, practical, and creative intelligence, rather than merely a monolithic 'g' (e.g., Gardner, 1993a).

The 'four branch model' of EI is the framework in broad use (Mayer & Salovey, 1997), and it includes the ability to perceive, use, understand, and manage emotions. These four emotion abilities are arranged such that the more basic psychological processes (i.e., perceiving emotions) are at the foundation, and more advanced processes (i.e., regulating emotions) are at the top of the hierarchy. The advanced processes are thought to be dependent, to some extent, upon the lower-level abilities. Within each dimension there is a developmental progression of skills from the more basic to the more sophisticated.

Perceiving emotion pertains to the ability to identify emotions in oneself and others, as well as in other stimuli including stories, music, and works of art. *Using emotion* involves the ability to harness feelings that assist in certain cognitive activities such as reasoning, decision-making, creativity, and interpersonal communication. *Understanding emotion* involves the capacity to analyze emotions, including an understanding of the emotional lexicon and both the antecedent events and outcomes of emotional experiences. *Managing emotion* pertains to the ability to reduce, enhance, or modify an emotional response in oneself and others, as well as the ability to make decisions about the usefulness of emotions in given situations.

According to the ability model of EI, there are individual differences in people's skills on each of the four branches, and such differences can be measured by performance (i.e., ability) tests. Performance tests are preferable to self-report indices in that the latter can be susceptible to social desirability bias and faking (Day & Carroll, 2008). Furthermore, performance tests address the limitation that individuals often are inaccurate when making judgments about their abilities, and emotional abilities in particular (Brackett et al., 2006).

One measure that was developed to assess all four branches of EI is the Mayer-Salovey-Caruso Emotional Intelligence Test (MSCEIT, V. 2.0; Mayer et al., 2002). The MSCEIT is a 141-item test comprising eight tasks; there are two tasks measuring each of the four abilities. A similar test for adolescents, the MSCEIT-Youth Version (MSCEIT-YV; Mayer et al., in press), also has been developed and validated (Rivers et al., 2012). Responses are evaluated by comparing partici-

pants' answers to those made by either experts or a normative sample. For example, the ability to manage emotions is measured with vignettes describing particular emotional challenges. After reading the vignettes, participants rate a number of possible actions for managing emotions on a scale ranging from 'very ineffective' to 'very effective,' which are then compared to the responses made by experts or those in the normative sample. The MSCEIT has been shown to be a valid measure of EI that correlates well with other ability based EI assessments (Mayer et al., 2012).

MSCEIT scores are related to but distinct from general and verbal intelligence scores (correlations range in the 0.3 to 0.4 range); they also are associated with a wide range of criteria. Individuals with higher MSCEIT scores report better quality friendships and are more likely to be nominated by peers as being socially skilled. Dating and married couples with higher MSCEIT scores report more satisfaction and happiness and less conflict in their relationships. College students with higher MSCEIT scores report lower levels of drug and alcohol consumption and fewer deviant acts, including stealing, gambling, and fighting. Higher MSCEIT scores also are associated with decreased levels of anxiety and depression. In the workplace, MSCEIT scores are correlated positively with objective performance indicators including company rank and percent age merit pay increases, and business professionals with high MSCEIT scores are rated by their supervisors as effective at handling stress and skilled at creating an enjoyable work environment (summarized by Mayer et al., 2008). A recent meta-analysis of nearly 50 studies further supports a positive relationship between EI and effective leadership (Mills, 2009), and higher MSCEIT scores also correlate with leadership emergence in groups after controlling for gender, personality, and cognitive ability (Côté et al., 2010). Finally, adolescents with higher scores on the MSCEIT-YV have been rated by their teachers as demonstrating fewer conduct problems and attention or other learning difficulties, as well as less overall problem behavior, aggression, anxiety, depression, and hyperactivity (Rivers et al., 2012).

What we know about EI underscores its importance for outcomes at home, at school, and in the workplace (Mayer et al., 2008). Nevertheless, there is much to be learned about the construct and its measurement. The MSCEIT does not include direct assessment of all emotion abilities captured by the EI framework, especially more fluid skills such as processing speed for identifying facial expressions. Research on EI is only in the beginning stages: the theory was not published until the 1990s, and performance measures like the MSCEIT have been used in scientific investigations since only the early 2000s. A better understanding of the validity of EI is in the hands of future researchers who will investigate the construct in greater detail.

HOW IMPORTANT IS EMOTIONAL INTELLIGENCE?

A CRITIQUE OF EMOTIONAL INTELLIGENCE

Chockalingam Viswesvaran, Florida International University

Emotional intelligence (EI) is an exciting new concept. Nevertheless, scientists and researchers need to critically evaluate it before enthusiastically endorsing its use in high-stakes testing. Let us consider some issues where the current literature is deficient.

Consider the definition of EI. At the beginning of this chapter, you learned how different definitions have been proposed for intelligence, but, nevertheless, a common core (information processing) is discernible. At present, there is a controversy in defining emotional intelligence (EI). It is not merely the presence of definitional variation that is the issue. In fact, in any concept in the social sciences, scientists emphasize different aspects of the concept – with the specific definition of that concept varying accordingly. The problem with the EI literature is that there are at least two distinct models of EI. One model defines EI as a specific intelligence and is called the ability model of EI (Mayer & Salovey, 1997). The second can be referred to as the mixed or trait model of EI and defines EI as a set of personality dispositions (Bar-On, 1997). The average correlation between the measures of these two models across several studies is only 0.12 (van Rooy *et al.,* 2005). This is a low correlation.

Some researchers have tried to address this low correlation by asserting that EI should be defined only as a specific ability. They dismiss the other conceptualization as being an eclectic hodgepodge mix of variables (i.e., the mixed model). However, the average correlation among measures of the mixed models is 0.61, a value that suggests a common core across these 'hodgepodge' measures. More importantly, EI measures using either model have been found to be predictive of important outcomes. van Rooy and Viswesvaran (2004) report a correlation of 0.17 for MEIS (an ability measure of EI) and 0.18 for EQ-I (a mixed model measure).

There are other explanations for the low correlation of 0.12. It is possible that we have two conceptualizations of EI that assess distinct domains of the EI construct. After all, it is likely that to be emotionally intelligent one needs certain skills and also certain dispositions! What we need are factor analytic studies (see definition of factor analysis in the text) that analyze multiple measures from the two models to test for alternate conceptualizations. It took decades for intelligence researchers to delineate the boundaries of intelligence – EI research is nowhere near achieving that clarity.

You have read in this chapter about how test scores should be correlated with important outcomes (i.e., criterion related validity). There are hundreds of studies in the literature that document a relationship between general intelligence and job performance measured as supervisory ratings, production counts, co-worker assessments, and so on. We know unambiguously that general intelligence is related to performance. The literature on EI is in its infancy in attempting to reach this level of certainty. Much more needs to be done here. Further, under construct validity, you read why it is important to test not only relationships between test scores and important outcomes but also why this relationship holds. For example, we know that general intelligence results in higher job knowledge acquisition, which in turn improves performance. There are many empirical studies investigating such processes with general intelligence. We need such explicit articulation of why EI will relate to important outcomes and empirical tests of such propositions. The current EI literature needs to be substantially improved.

Despite these shortcomings, EI is being touted as an important variable on which individuals should be assessed in high-stakes selection situations (e.g., applying for a job). EI is presented as an alternative to general intelligence because (1) there is adverse impact when general intelligence scores are used for selection decisions, and (2) EI helps in explaining performance beyond general intelligence. Adverse impact is where a much larger percentage of one group (e.g., whites) gets selected compared to another group (e.g., blacks). However, there are no systematic evaluations of group differences in EI in applicant settings. Most studies are using student samples in non-selection settings and it is not sure whether these results will generalize to selection settings. Similarly, there is scarce literature on predictive bias of EI or cross-cultural equivalence. Two plus two is four in all cultures but emotion regulation will differ across cultures. In this age of globalization, much more needs to be done before EI is accepted as an important trait on which individuals are to be evaluated and screened.

Consider the claim that EI explains variance in performance beyond that explained by general intelligence (or personality factors). To substantiate this claim the incremental validity of EI over performance beyond general intelligence and personality variables for different criteria needs to be established. That is, general intelligence and Big Five factors of personality have some validity in predicting different criteria. For EI to be a distinct and useful construct, we need to show that EI improves the validity of predictions beyond that of general intelligence and factors of personality. This improvement is referred to as incremental validity. Very few studies have reported the incremental validity of EI over personality and general intelligence which raises the legitimate concern that EI is old wine in a new bottle.

➔ A number of biological factors are implicated in general learning disability, including metabolic disorders (PKU, Tay-Sachs disease); chromosomal disorders (Down syndrome, Fragile X, Trisomy 13, and Trisomy 18); prenatal exposure to rubella, herpes, syphilis, or drugs (especially alcohol).

➔ There is some evidence that intensive and comprehensive educational interventions, administered very early in life, can help to decrease the level of general learning disability.

CRITICAL THINKING QUESTIONS

1 Do you think the cost of comprehensive interventions for individuals with general learning disability does or does not outweigh the benefits? Why?

2 What kinds of interventions might be important for parents of children with general learning disability to reduce their stress and improve their parenting to their child?

CHAPTER SUMMARY

1 There are many different definitions of intelligence. Some theorists view it as simply what intelligence tests measure. Others view it as a set of general abilities, including the ability to learn from experience, think in abstract terms, and deal effectively with one's environment.

2 Modern intelligence tests derive from the work of the French psychologist Alfred Binet, who proposed the concept of mental age. A bright child's mental age is above his or her chronological age; a slow child's mental age is below his or her chronological age. The concept of the intelligence quotient (IQ), the ratio of mental age to chronological age (multiplied by 100), was introduced when the Binet scales were revised to create the Stanford–Binet. Many intelligence test scores are still expressed as IQ scores, but they are no longer actually calculated according to this formula.

3 Both Binet and Wechsler, the developer of the Wechsler Adult Intelligence Scale (WAIS), assumed that intelligence is a general capacity for reasoning.

4 Similarly, Spearman proposed that a general factor (*g*) underlies performance on different kinds of test items. Factor analysis is a method for determining the kinds of abilities that underlie performance on intelligence tests.

5 Gardner's theory of multiple intelligences suggests that there are seven distinct kinds of intelligence that are independent of one another, each operating as a separate system (or module) in the brain according to its own rules. These are (1) linguistic, (2) musical, (3) logical-mathematical, (4) spatial, (5) bodily-kinesthetic, (6) intra-personal, and (7) interpersonal.

6 Sternberg's triarchic theory argues there are three types of intelligence: analytical, creative, and practical.

7 Behavioral scientists typically quantify the extent to which a group of people differ from one another on some measure of a trait or ability by computing the variance of the scores obtained. The more the individuals in the group differ, the higher the variance. Researchers can then seek to determine how much of that variance is due to different causes. The proportion of variance in a trait that is accounted for (caused by) genetic differences among the individuals is called the heritability of the trait.

8 Heritabilities can be estimated by comparing correlations obtained on pairs of identical twins (who share all their genes) and correlations obtained on pairs of fraternal twins (who, on average, share about half of their genes). If identical twin pairs are more alike on the trait than fraternal twin pairs, the trait probably has a genetic component. Heritabilities can also be estimated from the correlation between identical twin pairs who have been separated and raised in different environments. Any correlation between such pairs must be due to their genetic similarities.

9 Heritability refers to differences among individuals; it does not indicate how much of a trait in an individual is due to genetic factors. It is not a fixed attribute of a trait: If something happens to change the variability of a trait in a group, the heritability will also change. Heritability indicates the variance within a group, not the source of differences between groups. Heritability does, however, indicate how much possible environmental changes might change the mean level of a trait in a population.

10 Emotional intelligence is thought to have four components: accurate perception and expression of emotions, the ability to access and generate emotions, understanding of emotions and emotional meanings, and good emotional regulation. People with higher emotional intelligence tend to be healthier psychologically and physically.

11 General learning disability is defined as subaverage intellectual functioning, indexed by an IQ score of under 70 and deficits in adaptive behavioral functioning. A number of biological factors are implicated in this, including metabolic disorders (PKU, Tay-Sachs disease); chromosomal disorders (Down syndrome, Fragile X, Trisomy 13, and Trisomy 18); prenatal exposure to rubella, herpes, syphilis, or drugs (especially alcohol) and premature delivery. Intensive and comprehensive educational interventions, administered very early in life, can help to decrease the level of general learning disability.

CORE CONCEPTS

intelligence	*g*	heritability
Stanford–Binet Intelligence Scale	Gardner's theory of multiple intelligences	emotional intelligence
intelligence quotient (IQ)		general learning disability
Wechsler Adult Intelligence Scale	Anderson's theory of intelligence	fetal alcohol syndrome
factor analysis	Sternberg's triarchic theory	construct validity

DIGITAL SUPPORT RESOURCES

Students should use the unique access code included in the front of the book to access the digital support resources which accompany the new edition. These include:

- Multiple Choice Questions and Quizzes
- Critical Thinking Questions
- Practice Essay Questions
- Videos
- Glossary, Flashcards, and More

13 PERSONALITY

LEARNING OBJECTIVES

After reading this chapter you should be able to:

Know the *Big Five* of the personality factors that have emerged from years of research on personality traits.

Be familiar with methods of personality assessment, including the criterion-keyed method and the MMPI, as well as with the Q-sort method.

Know the key concepts of Freud's psychoanalytic theory, including his assumptions about personality structure, dynamics, and personality development.

Be able to discuss later theories that modified Freud's views and some of the assessment methods in the psychoanalytic approach to personality, including the Rorschach test and the TAT.

Be familiar with evaluations of the psychoanalytic approach in terms of its portrait of human personality and criticisms of the theory.

Understand the basic assumptions of the behavioral approach, some of its key concepts, its portrait of personality, and related contributions and criticisms.

Know the cognitive approach to personality, including Bandura's social-cognitive theory, and the views of Mischel and Kelly. Understand the concepts of schemas and self-schemas. Be familiar with evaluations of the cognitive approach.

Understand how the humanistic approach differs from the psychoanalytic and social-learning approaches. Know the basic assumptions underlying the theories of Carl Rogers, including his notions regarding the self-concept, the theory of Abraham Maslow, and evaluations of the humanistic perspective.

Be able to describe the evolutionary approach to personality, its views on male–female differences, and the various criticisms of this view of the origins of human behavior.

Be familiar with the twin studies evidence for the genetics of personality and the concept of genotype–environment interaction.

Be prepared to define the three dynamic processes of personality–environment interactions (reactive, evocative, and proactive) and to give examples of each. Be able to relate these processes to some puzzling patterns that have emerged in studies of twins.

Oskar Stohr and Jack Yufe are identical twins who were born in Trinidad and separated shortly after birth. Their mother took Oskar to Germany, where he was raised by his grandmother as a Catholic and a Nazi. Jack remained in Trinidad with his Jewish father, was raised as a Jew, and spent part of his youth on an Israeli kibbutz. The two families never corresponded.

When they were in their late forties, Oskar and Jack were brought together by researchers at the University of Minnesota who were studying sets of twins who had been raised apart. Although Oskar and Jack had met only once before, they showed some remarkable similarities. Both showed up for the study wearing mustaches, wire-rimmed glasses, and blue double-breasted suits. Their mannerisms and temperaments were similar, and they shared certain idiosyncrasies: both liked spicy foods and sweet liqueurs, were absentminded, flushed the toilet before using it, liked to dip buttered toast in their coffee, and enjoyed surprising people by sneezing in elevators.

Many other sets of identical twins studied by the Minnesota researchers also displayed similarities. One example was twins who were separated at birth and not reunited until they were 31 years old, by which time both had become firefighters,

CHAPTER OUTLINE

CONCEPTUALIZING AND MEASURING PERSONALITY

How many traits?

Personality inventories

THE PSYCHOANALYTIC APPROACH

Defense mechanisms

Personality development

Modifications of Freud's theories

Projective tests

Problems with projective tests

A psychoanalytic portrait of human nature

An evaluation of the psychoanalytic approach

THE BEHAVIORIST APPROACH

Social learning and conditioning

A behaviorist portrait of human behavior

An evaluation of the behaviorist approach

THE COGNITIVE APPROACH

Social-learning theory

Kelly's personal construct theory

Self-schemas

A cognitive portrait of human nature

An evaluation of the cognitive approach

THE HUMANISTIC APPROACH

Carl Rogers

Abraham Maslow

A humanistic portrait of human nature

An evaluation of the humanistic approach

THE EVOLUTIONARY APPROACH

An evolutionary portrait of human nature

An evaluation of the evolutionary approach

CUTTING EDGE RESEARCH: FINDING

THE SELF IN THE BRAIN

THE GENETICS OF PERSONALITY

Interactions between personality
and environment

SEEING BOTH SIDES: IS FREUD'S

INFLUENCE ON PSYCHOLOGY STILL

ALIVE?

liked the same type of beer, and had married women with the same first name. What causes such similarities? Surely there aren't firefighting genes, or genes for dipping toast, or surprising people in elevators. Such similarities reflect the inherited components of more basic personality characteristics that may then lead to preferences for certain kinds of behaviors.

In many ways, every person is like every other person. The biological and psychological processes discussed in this book – development, consciousness, perception, learning, remembering, thinking, motivation, and emotion – are basically the same for all of us. But in other ways every person is different from every other person. Each of us has a distinctive pattern of abilities, beliefs, attitudes, motivations, emotions, and interpersonal styles that makes us unique. In this chapter we will focus on theories of the distinctions between people that are captured in the notion of personality.

Four theoretical approaches have dominated personality psychology in the past 100 years: the psychoanalytic, behaviorist, humanistic, and cognitive approaches. We will also discuss evolutionary approaches, which have been applied to understand personality only in the past couple of decades. In reviewing these theories, we raise a question that has never been satisfactorily answered: to what degree are our beliefs, emotions, and actions free and in what ways are they determined by causes beyond our control? Are we basically good, neutral, or evil? Fixed or modifiable? Active or passive in controlling our destinies? These are not empirical questions, and theories of personality do not attempt to answer them explicitly. But each theoretical approach contains implicit answers – a set of distinctive underlying assumptions about human nature. Historically, these more philosophical factors have been as important as the empirical data in provoking controversies and in winning converts for the competing accounts of personality.

We also return to a major theme that we introduced in Chapter 3: the interaction between nature and nurture. In Chapter 3 we discussed how innate biological factors interact with events in an individual's environment to determine the course of development, focusing particularly on factors that make us all alike. We considered, for example, how innately determined sequences of maturation cause all children to go through the same stages of development in the same sequence, regardless of differences in their environments. In this chapter we focus on the biological and environmental factors that make us different from one another – in other words, the factors that create individuality. First, however, we discuss what we mean by personality and how we measure it.

Dr Thomas Bouchard of the University of Minnesota conducted personality tests on James Lewis and James Springer, identical twins adopted by separate families. The tests were done about 6 weeks after the twins were reunited (1979).

CONCEPTUALIZING AND MEASURING PERSONALITY

Personality can be defined as the distinctive and characteristic patterns of thought, emotion, and behavior that make up an individual's personal style of interacting with the physical and social environment. When we are asked to describe an individual's personality, we are likely to use terms referring to personality traits – adjectives such as extroverted and conscientious. Personality psychologists have attempted to boil down the huge number of characteristics we might think of as personality traits to a manageable set that will still cover the diversity of human personality.

One way to begin the task of deriving a comprehensive but manageable number of traits is to consult a dictionary. This assumes that a language will encode most, if not all, of the important distinctions among individuals in cultures that use that language. Language embodies the accumulated experience of the culture, and the dictionary is the written record of that experience. In the 1930s Allport and Odbert (1936) recorded approximately 18 000 words in the English dictionary that refer to characteristics of behavior – nearly 5 per cent of all the words in the dictionary! Next, they reduced the list to about 4500 terms that represented the most typical traits.

How many traits?

Still, 4500 traits is an unwieldy number, so researchers have attempted to group these traits into a small number of categories of traits that are typically related to each other. They do this by obtaining ratings of individuals on these traits and then looking at the correlations among these ratings with a statistical procedure called *factor analysis*. Different researchers have reached varying conclusions about the ultimate number of trait categories needed to capture human personality. Raymond Cattell (1943, 1945) condensed traits to 16 factors. British psychologist Hans Eysenck (1953) used psychiatrists' ratings of patients' characteristics to arrive at two personality factors: introversion–extroversion and neuroticism. **Introversion-extroversion** refers to the degree to which a person's basic orientation is turned inward toward the self or outward toward the external world. At the introversion end of the scale are individuals who are shy and prefer to work alone. They tend to withdraw into themselves, particularly in times of emotional stress or conflict. At the extroversion end are individuals who are sociable and prefer occupations that permit them to work directly with other people. In times of stress, they seek company. **Neuroticism** (instability–stability) is a dimension of emotionality, with moody, anxious, temperamental, and maladjusted individuals at the neurotic or unstable end, and calm, well-adjusted individuals at the other. Figure 13.1 shows how these two dimensions combine to organize a number of subtraits that are correlated with the factors.

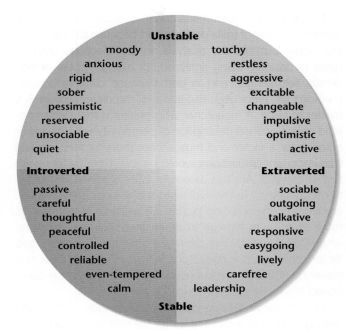

FIGURE 13.1 Eysenck's Personality Factors. *This figure shows the two major factors that emerge from factor-analytic studies of the intercorrelations between traits by Eysenck and others. The Stable–Unstable axis defines the neuroticism factor; the Introverted–Extraverted axis defines the extraversion factor. The other terms around the circle indicate where other traits are placed with respect to these two factors.*

Extraverted people are not afraid to be the center of attention.

Differences between researchers' conclusions about the ultimate number of traits occur in part because different traits are initially put into the analysis, in part because different types of data are being analyzed (for example, peer ratings versus self-ratings), and in part because different analytic methods are employed. But some of the disagreement is a matter of taste. A researcher who prefers a more differentiated or fine-grained description of personality will set a lower criterion for a factor and thus accept more factors, arguing that important distinctions would be lost if the factors were further merged. Another researcher, like Eysenck, will prefer to merge several lower-level factors into more general ones, arguing that the resulting factors will be more stable (that is, more likely to re-emerge in other analyses). For example, when Cattell's 16 factors are factor analyzed, Eysenck's two factors emerge as superfactors. We can therefore think of a hierarchy of traits in which each broad general trait is composed of several subordinate, narrower traits.

Despite these disagreements, a consensus is emerging among many trait researchers that five trait dimensions capture most of what we mean by personality – referred to as the '**Big Five**' (Goldberg, 1981). Although the five factors were originally identified through a factor analysis of the Allport–Odbert trait list, the same five have emerged from a wide variety of personality tests (McCrae & Costa, 1999). There is still disagreement about how best to name and interpret the factors, but frequently used names include Openness to experience, Conscientiousness, Extroversion, Agreeableness, and Neuroticism. Table 13.1 displays some representative examples of the dimensions that characterize each of the five factors. Many personality psychologists consider the discovery and validation of the Big Five to be one of the major breakthroughs of contemporary personality psychology. Proponents of the Big Five argue that these core personality traits organize the myriad of more narrowly focused personality characteristics that have been discussed by other researchers (McCrae & Costa, 2006). In other words, they argue that all aspects of personality are subsumed under the Big Five.

The basic structure of the Big Five has been replicated across many cultures and seems to be consistent across people of various ages (Benet-Martinez & John, 1998; McCrae & Costa, 2006; Yang et al., 2002). The personality traits in the five-factor model appear to be strongly influenced by genetics (Jang et al., 1998).

Personality inventories

Some personality tests ask individuals to rate themselves on personality trait dimensions. On others, individuals are asked a set of questions about how they react in certain situations. For example, they might be asked to indicate how much they agree or disagree with the statement 'I often try new and foreign foods' or 'I really like most people I meet.' Questionnaires

TABLE 13.1 FIVE TRAIT FACTORS

The five trait factors known as the Big Five reliably emerge when a wide variety of assessment instruments are factor-analyzed. The adjective pairs are examples of dimensions that characterize each of the factors.

Big Five factor	Representative dimensions
Openness	Conventional–Original Unadventurous–Daring Conservative–Liberal
Conscientiousness	Careless–Careful Undependable–Reliable Negligent–Conscientious
Extroversion	Retiring–Sociable Quiet–Talkative Inhibited–Spontaneous
Agreeableness	Irritable–Good natured Ruthless–Soft hearted Selfish–Selfless
Neuroticism	Calm–Worrying Hardy–Vulnerable Secure–Insecure

that assess personality – called **personality inventories** – ask the same questions of each person, and the answers are usually given in a form that can be easily scored, often by computer. Each item on a personality inventory is written to tap into a particular personality trait, and subsets of similar items are summed to give the individual a score on each trait scale. For example, the item 'I often try new and foreign foods' is on the Openness to Experience scale of one inventory designed to measure the Big Five; the item 'I really like most people I meet' is on the Extroversion scale.

Items on most personality inventories are initially composed according to the developer's theory of each trait and then retained or discarded from the final inventory, depending on whether they correlate or fail to correlate with other items on the same scale. Often a large number of trial items are placed on a preliminary form of the inventory, which is administered to a large number of people. Their responses are then analyzed to determine which subsets of items intercorrelate and whether these subsets actually belong to the trait scale for which they were originally devised.

Minnesota Multiphasic Personality Inventory (MMPI)

A very different method of test construction, called the *criterion-keyed method*, was used to develop one of the most popular of all personality inventories, the **Minnesota Multiphasic**

Personality Inventory (MMPI). The MMPI has more than 550 statements concerning attitudes, emotional reactions, physical and psychological symptoms, and experiences. The test taker responds to each statement by answering 'true,' 'false,' or 'cannot say.'

Here are four representative items:

→ I have never done anything dangerous for the thrill of it.

→ I daydream very little.

→ My mother or father often made me obey, even when I thought it was unreasonable.

→ At times my thoughts have raced ahead faster than I could speak them.

Instead of formulating items on the basis of a theory, designers of the MMPI gave hundreds of test items like these to groups of individuals. Each group was known to differ from the norm on a particular criterion. For example, to develop a scale of items that distinguish between paranoid and non-paranoid individuals, the same questions were given to two groups. The criterion group consisted of individuals who had been hospitalized with the diagnosis of paranoid disorder; the control group consisted of people who were similar to the criterion group in age, sex, socioeconomic status, and other important variables but had never been diagnosed as having psychiatric problems. Only the questions that discriminated between the psychiatric group and the control group were retained on the inventory. Questions that at face value might seem to distinguish normal from paranoid individuals (for instance, 'I think that most people would lie to get ahead') may or may not do so when put to test. In fact, patients diagnosed as paranoid were significantly less likely to respond 'true' to this statement than were normal individuals. On the final test, the responses to each item are scored according to the extent to which they correspond to answers given by the different criterion groups.

The MMPI includes scales that attempt to determine whether the person has answered the test items carefully and honestly, known as *validity scales*. If an individual's score on any of these scales is too high, his or her scores on the content scales must be interpreted with particular caution or disregarded altogether. These scales have been helpful but not completely successful at detecting invalid scores. Table 13.2 lists the three validity and ten content scales usually scored on the MMPI.

Because the MMPI is derived from differences between criterion and control groups, it does not really matter whether what the person says is true. What is important is

TABLE 13.2   MMPI SCALES

The first three scales are 'validity' scales, which help determine whether the person has answered the test items carefully and honestly. For example, the F (Frequency) scale measures the degree to which infrequent or atypical answers are given. A high score on this scale usually indicates that the individual was careless or confused in responding. (However, high F scores often accompany high scores on the Schizophrenia scale, which measures bizarre thinking.) The remaining 'clinical' scales were originally named for categories of psychiatric disorders, but interpretation now emphasizes personality attributes rather than diagnostic categories.

Scale name	Scale abbreviation	Interpretation of high scores
Lie	L	Denial of common frailties
Frequency	F	Invalidity of profile
Correction	K	Defensive, evasive
Hypochondriasis complaints	Hs	Emphasis on physical sensations
Depression	D	Unhappy, depressed
Hysteria problems	Hy	Reacts to stress by denying
Psychopathic deviancy	Pd	Lack of social conformity; often in trouble with the law
Masculinity–Femininity	Mf	Feminine orientation; masculine orientation
Paranoia	Pa	Suspicious
Psychoasthenia	Pt	Worried, anxious
Schizophrenia	Sc	Withdrawn, bizarre thinking
Hypomania	Ma	Impulsive, excitable
Social Introversion–Extroversion	Si	Introverted, shy

the fact that he or she says it. If people with schizophrenia answer 'true' and control participants answer 'false' to the statement 'My mother never loved me,' their answers distinguish the two groups regardless of how their mothers actually behaved. This is an advantage of a test based on the criterion-keyed method over one based on a test constructor's assumption that certain answers indicate specific personality traits. The disadvantage is that one does not really have a theoretical understanding of the connection between the test responses and the personality characteristics they identify.

There are now more than 10 000 published studies on the MMPI, and it has been translated into at least 150 languages. The MMPI has been most valuable in distinguishing in a general way between abnormal and normal populations and can be used to evaluate the overall severity of a particular individual's disturbance. It is less successful, however, in making finer distinctions among various forms of psychopathology.

The Q-sort

A special method for measuring personality traits is called the **Q-sort** (the Q was chosen arbitrarily and has no particular meaning.) In this method, a rater or sorter describes an individual's personality by sorting a set of approximately 100 cards into piles. Each card contains a personality statement (for example, 'Has a wide range of interests,' and 'Is self-defeating'). The rater sorts the cards into nine piles, placing the cards that are least descriptive of the individual in pile 1 on the left and those that are most descriptive in pile 9 on the right. The other cards are distributed in the intermediate piles, with those that seem neither characteristic nor uncharacteristic of the individual going into the middle pile (pile 5). Each Q item receives a score ranging from 1 to 9, with higher numbers indicating that the item is more characteristic of the person. (Some Q-sorts use fewer or more than nine piles, but the technique is the same.)

At first glance, this would seem no different from asking raters to rate an individual on a set of traits, using a 9-point rating scale. And, in fact, the item scores can be used in this way if the researcher wishes. But there is an important difference. When filling out rating scales, the rater is implicitly comparing the individual with others (for example, a rating of 'very friendly' implies that the individual is very friendly compared with other individuals). When performing a Q-sort, however, the rater is explicitly comparing each trait with other traits within the same individual (for example, placing the item 'friendly' in pile 9 implies that, compared with other traits, friendliness stands out as particularly descriptive of the individual).

Researchers can compare two Q-sorts by computing the correlation between them, thereby assessing the degree to which two individuals are similar in their overall personality configurations. If the two Q-sorts are descriptions of the same individual at two different times, the correlation assesses the test-retest reliability of the Q-sort, or the continuity of the individual's overall personality profile over time. If two Q-sorts are descriptions of a single individual made by two raters, the correlation assesses the **interjudge reliability** of the Q-sort, or the degree to which two people perceive the individual in the same way. (For example, in marital counseling, it could be helpful to assess the degree to which two spouses agree or disagree in their perceptions of each other.) Finally, if one of the Q-sorts is a description of a hypothetical personality type, the correlation between an individual's Q-sort and the hypothetical sort assesses the degree to which the person is similar to that personality type. For example, one researcher asked clinical psychologists to construct Q-sorts of the hypothetical 'optimally adjusted personality.' The correlation between a person's Q-sort and this hypothetical sort can be directly interpreted as an adjustment score (Block 1961/1978).

By itself, the trait approach is not a theory of personality but a general orientation and set of methods for assessing stable characteristics of individuals. By themselves, personality traits do not tell us anything about the dynamic processes of personality functioning, and trait psychologists who have sought to develop theories of personality have had to look to other approaches to address the second major task of personality psychology: synthesizing the many processes that influence an individual's interactions with the physical and social environments – biology, development, learning, thinking, emotion, motivation, and social interaction – into an integrated account of the total person.

INTERIM SUMMARY

➔ To arrive at a comprehensive but manageable number of personality traits on which individuals can be assessed, investigators first collected all the trait terms found in an English dictionary (about 18 000) and then reduced them to a smaller number. Ratings of individuals on these terms were factor-analyzed to determine how many underlying dimensions were needed to account for the correlations among the scales.

➔ Although different investigators arrive at a different numbers of factors, most now believe that five factors provide the best compromise. These have been labeled the 'Big Five' and are: Openness to experience, Conscientiousness, Extroversion, Agreeableness, and Neuroticism.

➔ Personality inventories are questionnaires on which individuals report their reactions or feelings in certain situations. Responses to subsets of items are summed to yield scores on separate scales or factors within the inventory.

➔ Although items on most inventories are composed or selected on the basis of a theory, they can also be selected on the basis of their correlation with an external criterion – the criterion-keyed method of test construction. The best-known example is the Minnesota Multiphasic Personality Inventory (MMPI), which is designed to identify individuals with psychological disorders.

➔ The Q-sort is a method of assessing personality in which raters sort cards with personality adjectives into nine piles, placing the cards that are least descriptive of the individual in pile 1 on the left and those that are most descriptive in pile 9 on the right.

CRITICAL THINKING QUESTIONS

1 There are consistent differences between women and men in scores on some of the 'Big Five' personality traits. On which traits would you expect to find gender differences, and in what direction?

2 How would you rate yourself on the 'Big Five' personality traits? Do you think your personality can be accurately described in this way? What important aspect of your personality seems to be left out of such a description? If you and a close friend (or a family member) were to describe your personality, on which characteristics would you be likely to disagree? Why? Are there traits on which you think this other person might actually be more accurate than you in describing your personality? If so, why?

THE PSYCHOANALYTIC APPROACH

Sigmund Freud, the creator of **psychoanalytic theory**, is a central figure in theories of personality. Freud divided personality into three major systems that interact to govern human behavior: the id, the ego, and the superego.

The id

According to Freud, the **id** is the most primitive part of the personality and the part from which the ego and the superego later develop. It is present in the newborn infant and consists of the most basic biological impulses or drives: the need to eat, to drink, to eliminate wastes, to avoid pain, and to gain sexual (sensual) pleasure. Freud believed that aggression is also a basic biological drive. In fact, he believed that the sexual and aggressive drives were the most important instinctual determinants of personality throughout life. The id seeks immediate gratification of these impulses. Like a young child, it operates on the *pleasure principle*: it continually strives to obtain pleasure and to avoid pain, regardless of the external circumstances.

The ego

Children soon learn that their impulses cannot always be gratified immediately. Hunger will not be alleviated until someone provides food. Relief of bladder or bowel pressure must be delayed until the bathroom is reached. Certain impulses – playing with one's genitals or hitting someone – may be punished. A new part of the personality, the ego, develops as the young child learns to consider the demands of reality. The **ego** obeys the *reality principle*: the gratification of impulses must be delayed until the situation is appropriate. The ego thus is essentially the executive of the personality: it decides which id impulses will be satisfied and in what manner. The ego mediates among the demands of the id, the realities of the world, and the demands of the superego.

The superego

The third part of the personality is the **superego**, which judges whether actions are right or wrong. More generally, the superego is the internalized representation of the values and morals of society. It is the individual's conscience, as well as his or her image of the morally ideal person (called the *ego ideal*).

The superego develops in response to parental rewards and punishments. Initially, parents control children's behavior directly through reward and punishment. By incorporating parental standards into the superego, children bring behavior under their own control. Children no longer need anyone to tell them it is wrong to steal; their superego tells them. Violating the superego's standards, or even the impulse to do so, produces anxiety – beginning with anxiety over loss of parental love. According to Freud, this anxiety is largely unconscious but may be experienced as guilt. If parental standards are overly rigid, the individual may be guilt-ridden and inhibit all aggressive or sexual impulses. In contrast, an individual who fails to incorporate any standards for acceptable social behavior will feel few behavioral constraints and may engage in excessively self-indulgent or criminal behavior. Such a person is said to have a weak superego.

The three components of personality are often in conflict: the ego postpones the gratification that the id wants immediately, and the superego battles with both the id and the ego because behavior often falls short of the moral code it represents. In the well-integrated personality, the ego remains in firm but flexible control; the reality principle governs. Freud

CONCEPT REVIEW TABLE
MAJOR DEFENSE MECHANISMS

Repression	Excluding from conscious awareness impulses or memories that are too frightening or painful.
Rationalization	Assigning logical or socially desirable motives to what we do so that we seem to have acted rationally.
Reaction formation	Concealing a motive from ourselves by giving strong expression to the opposite motive.
Projection	Assigning our own undesirable qualities to others in exaggerated amounts.
Intellectualization	Attempting to gain detachment from a stressful situation by dealing with it in abstract, intellectual terms.
Denial	Denying that an unpleasant reality exists.
Displacement	Directing a motive that cannot be gratified in one form into another channel.

proposed that all of the id and most of the ego and superego are submerged in the **unconscious** and that small parts of the ego and superego are in either the **conscious** or the **preconscious**.

Defense mechanisms

Conservation of energy

Freud argued there is a constant amount of psychic energy for any given individual, which he called **libido** (Latin for 'lust'), reflecting his view that the sexual drive was primary. If a forbidden act or impulse is suppressed, its energy will seek an outlet somewhere else in the system, possibly appearing in a disguised form. The desires of the id contain psychic energy that must be expressed in some way, and preventing the expression of those desires does not eliminate them. Aggressive impulses, for example, may be expressed in disguised form by racing sports cars, playing chess, or making sarcastic remarks. Dreams and neurotic symptoms are also manifestations of psychic energy that cannot be expressed directly.

Individuals with an urge to do something forbidden experience anxiety. One way of reducing this anxiety is to express the impulse in a disguised form that will avoid punishment either by society or by its internal representative, the superego. Freud and his daughter Anna Freud described several additional **defense mechanisms**, or strategies for preventing or reducing anxiety, and several are listed in the Concept Review Table.

We all use defense mechanisms at times. They help us over the rough spots until we can deal with stressful situations more directly. Defense mechanisms are maladaptive only when they become the dominant mode of responding to problems.

Freud considered repression to be the basic, and most important, defense mechanism. In **repression**, impulses or memories that are too frightening or painful are excluded from conscious awareness. Memories that evoke shame,

guilt, or self-deprecation are often repressed. Freud believed that repression of certain childhood impulses is universal. In later life, individuals may repress feelings and memories that could cause anxiety because they are inconsistent with their self-concepts. Feelings of hostility toward a loved one and experiences of failure may be banished from conscious memory.

Repression is different from suppression. **Suppression** is the process of deliberate self-control, keeping impulses and desires in check (perhaps holding them in private while denying them publicly) or temporarily pushing aside painful memories. Individuals are aware of suppressed thoughts but are largely unaware of repressed impulses or memories.

Freud believed that repression is seldom completely successful. The repressed impulses threaten to break through into consciousness; the individual becomes anxious (though unaware of the reason) and employs other defense mechanisms to keep the partially repressed impulses from awareness.

When the fox in Aesop's fable rejected the grapes that he could not reach because they were sour, he illustrated a defense mechanism known as **rationalization**. Rationalization does not mean 'to act rationally,' as we might assume; it refers to the assignment of logical or socially desirable motives to what we do so that we seem to have acted rationally. Rationalization serves two purposes: it eases our disappointment when we fail to reach a goal ('I didn't want it anyway'), and it gives us acceptable motives for our behavior. If we act impulsively or on the basis of motives that we do not wish to acknowledge even to ourselves, we rationalize what we have done in order to place our behavior in a more favorable light.

In searching for the good reason rather than the true reason, individuals make a number of excuses. These excuses are usually plausible; they simply do not tell the whole story. For example, 'My roommate failed to wake me,' or 'I had too many other things to do' may be true, but they may not be the real reasons for the individual's failure to perform the behavior in question. Individuals who are really concerned set an alarm clock or find the time to do what they are expected to do.

Sometimes individuals can conceal a motive from themselves by giving strong expression to the opposite motive. This tendency is called **reaction formation**. A mother who feels guilty about not wanting her child may become overindulgent and overprotective in order to assure the child of her love and assure herself that she is a good mother.

All of us have undesirable traits that we do not acknowledge, even to ourselves. A defense mechanism known as **projection** protects us from recognizing our own undesirable qualities by assigning them to other people in exaggerated amounts. Suppose that you have a tendency to be critical of or unkind to other people, but you would dislike yourself if you admitted this tendency. If you are convinced that the people around you are cruel or unkind, your harsh treatment of them is not based on your bad qualities – you are simply 'giving them what they deserve.' If you can assure yourself that everybody else cheats on college examinations, your unacknowledged tendency to take some academic shortcuts seems not so bad. Projection is really a form of rationalization, but it is so pervasive that it merits discussion in its own right.

Intellectualization is an attempt to gain detachment from a stressful situation by dealing with it in abstract, intellectual terms. This kind of defense may be a necessity for people who must deal with life-and-death matters in their jobs. A doctor who is continually confronted with human suffering cannot afford to become emotionally involved with each patient. In fact, a certain amount of detachment may be essential for the doctor to function competently. This kind of intellectualization is a problem only when it becomes so pervasive that individuals cut themselves off from all emotional experiences.

When an external reality is too unpleasant to face, an individual may engage in **denial**, refusing to acknowledge that the undesired reality exists. The parents of a terminally ill child may refuse to admit that anything is seriously wrong, even though they are fully informed of the diagnosis and the expected outcome. Because they cannot tolerate the pain that acknowledging reality would produce, they resort to

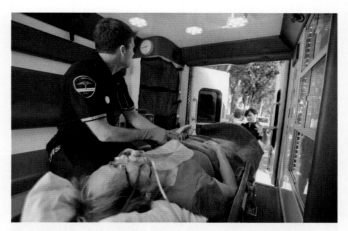

Paramedics may need to develop many defenses to handle their high-stress jobs.

denial. Less extreme forms of denial may be seen in individuals who consistently ignore criticism, fail to perceive that others are angry with them, or disregard all kinds of clues suggesting that their spouse is having an affair.

Sometimes, denying facts may be better than facing them. In a severe crisis, denial may give the person time to face the grim facts at a more gradual pace. For example, victims of a stroke or a spinal cord injury might give up altogether if they were fully aware of the seriousness of their condition. Hope gives them an incentive to keep trying. Soldiers who have faced combat or imprisonment report that denying the possibility of death helped them function. In such situations, denial clearly has an adaptive value. On the other hand, the negative aspects of denial are evident when people postpone seeking medical help. For example, a woman may deny that a lump in her breast may be cancerous and delay going to a physician until the condition has become life-threatening.

Through the mechanism of **displacement**, a motive that cannot be gratified in one form is directed into a new channel. A common example of displacement is when anger that cannot be expressed toward the source of frustration (e.g., one's boss) is redirected toward a less threatening object (e.g., one's dog). Freud felt that displacement was the most satisfactory way of handling aggressive and sexual impulses. The basic drives cannot be changed, but we can change the object toward which a drive is directed. Erotic impulses that cannot be expressed directly may be expressed indirectly in creative activities such as art, poetry, and music. Hostile impulses may find socially acceptable expression through participation in contact sports.

It seems unlikely that displacement actually eliminates the frustrated impulses, but substitute activities do help reduce tension when a basic drive is thwarted. For example, the activities of taking care of others or seeking companionship may help reduce the tension associated with unsatisfied sexual needs.

Some people may displace their aggressive impulses by engaging in aggressive sports.

Personality development

Freud believed that during the first 5 years of life, the individual progresses through several developmental stages that shape his or her personality. Applying a broad definition of sexuality, he called these periods **psychosexual stages**. During each stage, the pleasure-seeking impulses of the id focus on a particular area of the body and on activities connected with that area. If a child is either deprived of the opportunity to gratify these impulses or overindulged in gratifying these impulses, he or she can become *fixated* on the issues typical of that stage.

Freud called the first year of life the **oral stage** of psychosexual development. During this period, infants derive pleasure from nursing and sucking and begin to put anything they can reach into their mouths. Fixation at the oral stage can result in an oral personality, characterized by concerns with 'taking in' from others and the environment. People with an oral personality often lack trust in others, are envious, demanding, and prone to depression. Freud called the second year of life the beginning of the **anal stage** and believed that during this period children find pleasure both in withholding and in expelling feces. These pleasures come into conflict with parents who are attempting toilet training, the child's first experience with imposed control. Individuals fixated at this stage develop an anal personality – they can be rigid and preoccupied with issues of control, possessions, and cleanliness.

In the **phallic stage**, from about age three to age six, children begin to derive pleasure from fondling their genitals. They observe the differences between males and females and begin to direct their awakening sexual impulses toward the parent of the opposite sex. Around the age of five or six, according to Freud, a boy's sexual impulses are

directed toward his mother. This leads him to perceive his father as a rival for his mother's affection. Freud called this situation the **Oedipal conflict**, after the ancient Greek myth in which Oedipus unwittingly kills his father and marries his mother. Freud also believed that the boy fears that his father will retaliate against these sexual impulses by castrating him. He labeled this fear *castration anxiety*. In a normal case of development, the boy simultaneously reduces this anxiety and vicariously gratifies his feelings toward his mother by identifying with his father – that is, by internalizing his father's attitudes and values. The same process in a girl – resulting in her identifying with her mother – is analogous but more complicated. Children who do not resolve the issues of the phallic stage are said to develop personalities that are overly preoccupied with issues of power, authority, seduction, and jealousy.

The phallic stage is followed by the **latency period**, a sexually quiescent time from about age seven to age 12 during which children become less concerned with their bodies and turn their attention to the skills needed for coping with their environment. Finally, adolescence and puberty usher in the **genital stage**, the mature phase of adult sexuality and functioning.

Modifications of Freud's theories

Freud modified his theories throughout his life. Like a good scientist, he remained open to new data, revising his earlier

According to psychoanalytic theory, a child resolves the Oedipal conflict by identifying with the same-sex parent.

Sigmund Freud with his daughter Anna.

positions as new observations accumulated that could not be accommodated by the original theory. For example, quite late in his career he completely revised his theory of anxiety. Freud's theory has been further extended by his daughter Anna, who played a particularly important role in clarifying the defense mechanisms (1946/1967) and applying psychoanalytic theory to the practice of child psychiatry (1958).

Although Freud was open to new data, he was not open to dissenting opinions. He was particularly adamant that his colleagues and followers not question the libido theory and the centrality of sexual motivation in the functioning of personality. This dogmatism forced a break between Freud and many of his most brilliant associates, some of whom went on to develop rival theories that placed more emphasis on motivational processes other than sexuality. These former associates included Carl Jung and Alfred Adler, as well as later theorists such as Karen Horney, Harry Stack Sullivan, and Erich Fromm.

Of those who broke with Freud, perhaps the most famous was Carl Jung. Originally one of Freud's most dedicated followers, Jung eventually came to disagree profoundly with some aspects of Freud's theory and founded his own school of psychology, which he called *analytic psychology*. Jung believed that in addition to the personal unconscious described by Freud, there is a **collective unconscious**, a part of the mind that is common to all humans. The collective unconscious consists of primordial images or archetypes inherited from our ancestors. Among those archetypes are the mother, the father, the sun, the hero, God, and death. To gather evidence for the presence of these archetypes, Jung examined dreams, myths, and other cultural products, noting that certain images, such as that of a vulture, often appear in dreams and also in religious writings and ancient mythologies with which the dreamer is not familiar. Although Jung agreed with Freud on the existence of the unconscious, he believed that Freud's theory failed to explain the presence of common images or archetypes in the unconscious minds of all humans.

One of the most enduring developments in psychodynamic theory since Freud is **object relations theory**, which deals with a person's attachments and relationships to other people throughout life. Object relations theorists have not rejected the concept of the id or the importance of biological drives in motivating behavior, but they have an equal interest in such questions as degree of psychological separateness from parents, degree of attachment to and involvement with other people versus preoccupation with self, and the strength of the individual's feelings of self-esteem and competence.

Although we did not identify it as such, Erik Erikson's stage theory of development (discussed in Chapter 3) is an example of a revised psychoanalytic theory. Erikson himself was trained as a psychoanalyst by Anna Freud, and he perceived his own views as expanding rather than altering Freudian theory. Instead of viewing developmental stages in terms of their psychosexual functions, Erikson saw them as psychosocial stages involving primarily ego processes. For Erikson, the important feature of the first year of life is not that it focuses on oral gratification but that the child is learning to trust (or mistrust) the environment as a satisfier of needs. The important feature of the second year of life is not that it focuses on anal concerns such as toilet training but that the child is learning autonomy. Toilet training just happens to be a frequent arena of conflict in which the child's striving for autonomy clashes with new demands by parents. Erikson's theory also adds more stages in order to encompass the entire life span.

Projective tests

Personality psychologists who follow in Freud's psychoanalytic tradition are particularly interested in assessing unconscious wishes, motivations, and conflicts. Accordingly, they prefer tests that resemble Freud's technique of **free association**, in

Children must develop ways of handling their sometimes mixed feelings about their parents.

FIGURE 13.2 A Rorschach Inkblot. *A person could be asked to tell what he or she sees in this inkblot, which could be viewed from any angle.*

which the individual is free to say whatever comes to mind. For this reason, they developed projective tests. A **projective test** presents an ambiguous stimulus to which the person may respond as he or she wishes. Because the stimulus is ambiguous and does not demand a specific response, it is assumed that the individual projects his or her personality onto the stimulus and thus reveals something about himself or herself. Two of the most widely used projective techniques are the Rorschach Test and the Thematic Apperception Test (TAT).

The Rorschach Test

The **Rorschach Test**, developed by the Swiss psychiatrist Hermann Rorschach in the 1920s, is a series of 10 cards, each of which displays a rather complex inkblot like the one shown in Figure 13.2. Some of the blots are in color; some are black and white. The person is instructed to look at one card at a time and report everything the inkblot resembles. After the person has finished the 10 cards, the examiner usually goes over each response, asking the person to clarify some responses and indicate which features of the blot gave a particular impression.

The individual's responses may be scored in various ways. Three main categories are location (whether the response involves the entire inkblot or a part of it), determinants (whether the individual responds to the shape of the blot, its color, or differences in texture and shading), and content (what the response represents). Most testers also score responses according to frequency of occurrence; for example, a response is 'popular' if many people assign it to the same inkblot.

Several elaborate scoring systems have been devised on the basis of these categories, but most of them have proved to be of limited predictive value. Consequently, many psychologists base their interpretations on an impressionistic evaluation of the response record, as well as on the individual's general reaction to the test situation (for example, whether the person is defensive, open, competitive, co-operative, and so on).

The Thematic Apperception Test

Another popular projective test, the **Thematic Apperception Test (TAT)**, was developed by Henry Murray in the 1930s. The participant is shown as many as 20 ambiguous pictures of persons and scenes, similar to the one in Figure 13.3, and asked to make up a story about each picture. The individual is encouraged to give free rein to his or her imagination and to tell whatever story comes to mind. The test is intended to reveal basic themes that recur in a person's imaginings. (Apperception is a readiness to perceive in certain ways, based on prior experiences.) People interpret ambiguous pictures according to their apperceptions and elaborate stories in terms of preferred plots or themes that reflect personal fantasies. If particular problems are bothering them, those problems may become evident in a number of the stories or in striking deviations from the usual theme in one or two stories. For example, when shown a picture similar to the one in Figure 13.3, a 21-year-old male told the following story:

> **She has prepared this room for someone's arrival and is opening the door for a last general look over the room. She is probably expecting her son home. She tries to place everything as it was when he left. She seems like a very tyrannical character. She led her son's life for him and is going to take over again as soon as he gets back. This is merely the beginning of her rule, and the son is definitely**

FIGURE 13.3 The Thematic Apperception Test. *This picture is similar to the pictures used on the Thematic Apperception Test. The pictures usually have elements of ambiguity so that the individual can 'read into' them something from personal experience or fantasy.*

cowed by this overbearing attitude of hers and will slip back into her well-ordered way of life. He will go through life plodding down the tracks she has laid down for him. All this represents her complete domination of his life until she dies.

(Arnold, 1949, p. 100)

Although the original picture shows only a woman standing in an open doorway looking into a room, the young man's readiness to talk about his relationship with his mother led to this story of a woman's domination of her son. Facts obtained later confirmed the clinician's interpretation that the story reflected the man's own problems.

In analyzing responses to TAT cards, the psychologist looks for recurrent themes that may reveal the individual's needs, motives, or characteristic way of handling interpersonal relationships.

Problems with projective tests

Hundreds of studies have been done to test the validity and reliability of interpretations of the Rorschach Test, and the results are not encouraging (see Lilienfield *et al.*, 2000). Psychologically healthy individuals who take the Rorschach Test are too often misclassified as pathological, particularly individuals who are members of ethnic minority groups, or cultures other than mainstream cultures of the USA or Western Europe. The reliability of results from the Rorschach Test has generally been poor, in large part because the same responses may be evaluated quite differently by two trained examiners. And attempts to demonstrate the Rorschach's ability to predict behavior or discriminate between groups have met with limited success.

The TAT has fared somewhat better (Lilienfield *et al.*, 2000). When specific scoring systems are used (for example, to measure achievement motives or aggressive themes), interscorer reliability is fairly good. TAT measures have also proven useful in predicting some specific behaviors. For example, the need for power, as assessed by TAT responses, significantly predicted important life outcomes, such as the choice of a career that gave one influence over others, in two long-term studies of female college students (Winter *et al.*, 1998).

Many other projective tests have been devised. Some ask the individual to draw pictures of people, houses, trees, and so on. Others involve completing sentences that start with 'I often wish ... ,' 'My mother ... ,' or 'I feel like quitting when they ... ,' In fact, any stimulus to which a person can respond in an individualistic way could be considered the basis for a projective test. But many projective tests have not been subjected to enough research to establish their usefulness in assessing personality, and those that have been researched have not proven to have consistently strong reliability or validity (Lilienfield *et al.*, 2000).

A psychoanalytic portrait of human nature

At the beginning of the chapter, we noted that each approach to personality carries with it a distinctive philosophy of human nature. To what extent are our actions free or determined? Good, neutral, or evil? Fixed or modifiable? Active or passive? Our description of Freud's theory has hinted at many of his views on these matters. Freud is often compared with Copernicus and Darwin. Like them, he was accused of undermining the stature and dignity of humanity. The astronomer Copernicus demoted the earth from its position as the center of the universe to one of several planets moving around a minor star; Darwin demoted the human species to one of numerous animal species. Freud took the next step by emphasizing that human behavior is determined by forces beyond our control, thereby depriving us of free will and psychological freedom. By emphasizing the unconscious status of our motivations, he deprived us of rationality; by stressing the sexual and aggressive nature of those motivations, he dealt the final blow to our dignity.

Psychoanalytic theory also paints a portrait of human nature as basically evil. Without the restraining forces of society and its internalized representative, the superego, humans would destroy themselves. Freud was a deeply pessimistic man. He was forced to flee from Vienna when the Nazis invaded in 1938, and he died in September 1939 just as World War II began. He saw these events as natural consequences of the human aggressive drive when it is not held in check.

According to psychoanalytic theory, our personalities are basically determined by inborn drives and by events in our environment during the first 5 years of life. Only extensive psychoanalysis can undo some of the negative consequences of early experiences, and it can do so only in limited ways. We also emerge from psychoanalytic theory as relatively passive creatures. Although the ego is engaged in an active struggle with the id and superego, we are passive pawns of this drama being played out in our unconscious. Finally, for Freud, psychological health consisted of firm but flexible ego control over the impulses of the id. As he noted, the goal of psychoanalysis was to ensure that 'Where id is, there ego shall be' (1933/1964).

An evaluation of the psychoanalytic approach

Psychoanalytic theory is so broad in scope that it cannot simply be pronounced true or false. However, there can be no doubt of its impact on our culture, or of the value of some of its scientific contributions. For example, Freud's method of free association opened up an entirely new database of observations that had never before been explored systematically. In addition, the recognition that our behavior often reflects a compromise between our wishes and our fears accounts for many of the apparent contradictions in human behavior better than any other theory of personality. And Freud's recognition that unconscious processes play an important role in much of our behavior is almost universally accepted – although these processes are often reinterpreted in learning-theory or information-processing terms (Funder, 2001).

Nevertheless, as a scientific theory, the psychoanalytic account has been persistently criticized. One of the main criticisms is that many of its concepts are ambiguous and difficult to define or measure objectively. Also, psychoanalytic theory assumes that very different behaviors may reflect the same underlying motive. For example, a man who had a hostile and uncaring father may become a hostile parent to his own children or overly protective of them. When opposite behaviors are claimed to result from the same underlying motive, it is difficult to confirm the presence or absence of the motive or to make predictions that can be empirically verified.

A more serious criticism concerns the validity of the observations that Freud obtained through his psychoanalytic procedure. Critics have pointed out that it often is not clear what Freud's patients told him spontaneously about past events in their lives, what he may have 'planted' in their minds, and what he simply inferred. For example, Freud reported that many of his patients recalled being seduced or sexually molested as children. At first he believed them, but then he decided that these reports were not literally true but, rather, reflected the patients' own early sexual fantasies. He regarded this realization as one of his major theoretical insights. But one writer argued that Freud's original assumption about the reality of the seductions was probably more accurate, an argument that seems more reasonable in light of our increased awareness of child sexual abuse (Masson, 1984).

Other critics have gone further and suggested that Freud may have questioned his patients so persistently with leading questions and suggestions that they were led to reconstruct memories of seductions that never occurred – a hypothesis that Freud considered but rejected (Powell & Boer, 1994). Others charge that in many cases Freud simply inferred that seduction had occurred, even though the patient never reported such an incident; he actually substituted his theoretical expectations for data (Esterson, 1993; Scharnberg, 1993).

When Freud's theories have been empirically tested, the results have been mixed (Westen et al., 2007). Efforts to link adult personality characteristics to psychosexually relevant events in childhood have generally met with negative outcomes (Sears et al., 1957; Sewell & Mussen, 1952). When relevant character traits are identified, they appear to be related to similar character traits in the parents (Beloff, 1957; Hetherington & Brackbill, 1963). Thus, even if a relationship were to be found between toilet-training practices and adult personality traits, it could have arisen because both are linked to parental emphasis on cleanliness and order. In such a case, a simple learning-theory explanation – parental reinforcement and the child's imitation of the parents' behavior – would be a more economical explanation of the adult traits than the psychoanalytic hypothesis.

A man who had an uncaring father may, according to Freud, become a doting father . . .

. . . or, he may become a hostile and uncaring father to his own children.

This outcome should also remind us that Freud based his theory on observations of a very narrow range of people – primarily upper-middle-class men and women in Victorian Vienna who suffered from neurotic symptoms. In hindsight, many of Freud's cultural biases are obvious, particularly in his theories about women. For example, his theory that female psychosexual development is shaped largely by 'penis envy' – a girl's feelings of inadequacy because she doesn't have a penis – is almost universally rejected as reflecting the sex bias of Freud and the historical period in which he lived. A little girl's personality development during the Victorian era was surely shaped more decisively by her awareness that she lacked the greater independence, power, and social status of her brother than by her envy of his penis.

Despite these criticisms, the remarkable feature of Freud's theory is how well it managed to transcend its narrow observational base. For example, many experimental studies of the defense mechanisms and reactions to conflict have supported the theory in contexts quite different from those in which Freud developed the theory (Westen *et al.*, 2007). The structural theory (ego, id, and superego), the psychosexual theory, and the energy concept have not fared well over the years. Even some psychoanalytic writers are prepared to abandon them or to modify them substantially (Kline, 1972; Schafer, 1976). On the other hand, Freud's dynamic theory – his theory of anxiety and the mechanisms of defense – has withstood the test of time, research, and observation. A survey of psychoanalytically oriented psychologists and psychiatrists found widespread agreement with a number of ideas that were controversial when Freud first introduced them, including the importance of early childhood experiences in shaping adult personality and the centrality of both conflict and the unconscious in human mental life (Westen, 1998).

INTERIM SUMMARY

- Freud's psychoanalytic theory holds that many behaviors are caused by unconscious motivations. Personality is determined primarily by the biological drives of sex and aggression and by experiences that occur during the first 5 years of life.
- Freud's theory of personality structure views personality as composed of the id, the ego, and the superego. The id operates on the pleasure principle, seeking immediate gratification of biological impulses. The ego obeys the reality principle, postponing gratification until it can be achieved in socially acceptable ways. The superego (conscience) imposes moral standards on the individual. In a well-integrated personality, the ego remains in firm but flexible control over the id and superego, and the reality principle governs.

- Freud's theory of personality dynamics proposes that there is a constant amount of psychic energy (libido) for each individual. If a forbidden act or impulse is suppressed, its energy will seek an outlet in some other form, such as dreams or neurotic symptoms. The theory assumes that unacceptable id impulses cause anxiety, which can be reduced by defense mechanisms.
- Freud's theory of personality development proposes that individuals pass through psychosexual stages and must resolve the Oedipal conflict, in which the young child sees the same-sex parent as a rival for the affection of the opposite-sex parent. Over the years, Freud's theory of anxiety and defense mechanisms has fared better than his structural and developmental theories have.
- Psychoanalytic theory has been modified by later psychologists, notably Carl Jung. Jung proposed that, in addition to the personal unconscious described by Freud, there is a collective unconscious, a part of the mind that is common to all humans.
- Psychologists who take the psychoanalytic approach sometimes use projective tests, such as the Rorschach Test and the Thematic Apperception Test (TAT). Because the test stimuli are ambiguous, it is assumed that the individual projects his or her personality onto the stimulus, thereby revealing unconscious wishes and motives.

CRITICAL THINKING QUESTIONS

1 As this section makes clear, the value of Sigmund Freud's impact on psychology is hotly debated. What is your opinion on the value of Freud's legacy?

2 Can you identify some of your own assumptions about other people that are rooted in Freudian theory, whether you previously realized they were or not?

THE BEHAVIORIST APPROACH

In contrast to the psychoanalytic approach to personality, the **behaviorist approach** emphasizes the importance of environmental, or situational, determinants of behavior. In this view, behavior is the result of a continuous interaction between personal and environmental variables. Environmental conditions shape behavior through learning; a person's behavior, in turn, shapes the environment. Persons and situations influence each other. To predict behavior, we need to know how the characteristics of the individual interact with those of the situation (Bandura, 2006).

Social learning and conditioning

Operant conditioning

The effects of other people's actions – the rewards and punishments they provide – are an important influence on an individual's behavior. Accordingly, one of the most basic principles of behavioral theory is operant conditioning – the type of learning that occurs when we learn the association between our behaviors and certain outcomes. The basic tenet of behaviorist theory is that people behave in ways that are likely to produce reinforcement and that individual differences in behavior result primarily from differences in the kinds of learning experiences a person encounters in the course of growing up.

Although individuals learn many behavior patterns through direct experience – that is, by being rewarded or punished for behaving in a certain manner – they also acquire many responses through observational learning. People can learn by observing the actions of others and noting the consequences of those actions. It would be a slow and inefficient process, indeed, if all of our behavior had to be learned through direct reinforcement of our responses. Similarly, the reinforcement that controls the expression of learned behaviors may be direct (tangible rewards, social approval or disapproval, or alleviation of aversive conditions), vicarious (observation of someone receiving reward or punishment for behavior similar to one's own), or self-administered (evaluation of one's own performance with self-praise or self-reproach).

Because most social behaviors are not uniformly rewarded in all settings, the individual learns to identify the contexts in which certain behavior is appropriate and those in which it is not. To the extent that a person is rewarded for the same response in many different situations, generalization takes place, ensuring that the same behavior will occur in a variety of settings. A boy who is reinforced for physical aggression at home, as well as at school and at play, is likely to develop an aggressive personality. More often, aggressive responses are differentially rewarded, and the individual learns to distinguish between situations in which aggression is appropriate and situations in which it is not (for example, aggression is acceptable on the football field but not in the classroom). For this reason, behaviorists challenge the usefulness of characterizing individuals with trait terms like *aggressive*, arguing that such terms obscure the cross-situational variability of behavior.

Classical conditioning

To account for emotion or affect, behaviorists add classical conditioning – the type of learning that occurs when specific situations become associated with specific outcomes – to their account of personality (see Chapter 7). For example, when a child is punished by a parent for engaging in some

The 'naughty step' or other form of 'time out' is a concept based on behaviorist principles.

forbidden activity, the punishment elicits the physiological responses that we associate with guilt or anxiety. Subsequently, the child's behavior may itself elicit those responses, and the child will feel guilty when engaging in the forbidden behavior. In the terminology of classical conditioning, we would say that the behavior becomes a conditioned stimulus by being paired with the unconditioned stimulus of punishment; the anxiety becomes the conditioned response. For the behaviorist, it is classical conditioning that produces the internalized source of anxiety that Freud labeled the superego.

A behaviorist portrait of human behavior

Like the psychoanalytic approach, the behaviorist approach to personality is deterministic. In contrast to the psychoanalytic approach, however, it pays little attention to biological determinants of behavior and focuses on environmental determinants. People are not inherently good or evil but are readily modified by events and situations in their environment. As we noted in Chapter 3, John Watson, the founder of the behaviorist movement in the USA, claimed that he could raise an infant to be anything, regardless of the infant's 'talents, penchants, tendencies, abilities, vocations, and race of his [or her] ancestors,' Few behaviorists would take such an extreme view today. Nevertheless, behaviorists hold a strong optimism about our ability to change human behavior by changing the environment.

The human personality as described by behavioral theorists may be highly modifiable, but it still has a passive quality. We still seem to be shaped primarily by forces beyond our control. This view changed, however, as social-learning approaches (described later in this chapter) replaced traditional behaviorist theories, increasingly emphasize the individual's active role in selecting and modifying the environment, thereby permitting the person to become a causal force in his or her own life. As we will see, however, this role is not active enough for humanistic theorists. In particular, they do not believe that it is sufficient to define psychological health as merely optimal adaptation to the environment.

An evaluation of the behaviorist approach

Through its emphasis on specifying the environmental variables that evoke particular behaviors, behavioral theory has made a major contribution to both clinical psychology and personality theory. It has led us to see human actions as reactions to specific environments, and it has helped us focus on how environments control our behavior and how they can be changed to modify behavior. As we will see in Chapter 16, the systematic application of learning principles has proved successful in changing many maladaptive behaviors.

Behavioral theorists have been criticized for overemphasizing situational influences on behavior. But evidence that people behave differently across situations have forced other personality psychologists to re-examine their assumptions that internal characteristics of the individual shape all behavior. The result has been a clearer understanding of the interactions between people and situations and an enhanced appreciation of each person's individuality. As we see in the next section, the cognitive theorists built on the work of behavioral theorists to introduce quite a different way of viewing personality.

INTERIM SUMMARY

➜ According to behaviorist theory, individual differences in behavior result primarily from differences in the kinds of learning experiences a person encounters in the course of growing up.

➜ Through operant conditioning, people learn to associate specific behaviors with punishment or reward. They can also learn these associations through observational learning.

➜ Through classical conditioning, people learn to associate specific situations with certain outcomes, such as anxiety.

CRITICAL THINKING QUESTIONS

1 Think about your own tendency to be friendly or unfriendly. To what extent is the situation important in determining your level of friendliness? What are some of the reinforcements and punishments you've had in your life that might have contributed to your tendency to be friendly or unfriendly?

2 Behavioral theorists view all types of human behavior as modifiable. Do you think there are any types of behavior that are not modifiable? Why or why not?

THE COGNITIVE APPROACH

Many contemporary personality theorists have joined psychologists in other subfields in becoming more 'cognitive,' In fact, much contemporary experimental work in personality psychology begins from a cognitive base. The cognitive approach is not actually a 'philosophy' of human nature in the way that the other approaches are. Rather, it is a general empirical approach and a set of topics related to how people process information about themselves and the world. For the cognitive theorist, differences in personality stem from differences in the way individuals mentally represent information.

Social-learning theory

Social-learning theory has its roots in early behavioral theory but was considered a radical departure from behaviorism when it was first introduced. The social-learning perspective is aptly summarized in the following comment by Albert Bandura: 'The prospects for survival would be slim indeed if one could learn only from the consequences of trial and error. One does not teach children to swim, adolescents to drive automobiles, and novice medical students to perform surgery by having them discover the requisite behavior from the consequences of their successes and failures' (1986, p. 20). According to social-learning theorists, internal cognitive processes influence behavior, as well as observation of the behaviors of others and the environment in which behavior occurs.

Bandura, one of the leading contemporary theorists in this area, has taken this approach even further, developing what

Albert Bandura developed social cognitive theory.

he calls **social-cognitive theory** (1986, 2006). His theory emphasizes *reciprocal determinism*, in which external determinants of behavior (such as rewards and punishments) and internal determinants (such as beliefs, thoughts, and expectations) are part of a system of interacting influences that affect both behavior and other parts of the system (Bandura, 1986). In Bandura's model, not only can the environment affect behavior but also behavior can affect the environment. In fact, the relationship between environment and behavior is a reciprocal one: the environment influences our behavior, which then affects the kind of environment we find ourselves in, which may in turn influence our behavior, and so on.

Bandura notes that when people encounter a new problem, they imagine possible outcomes and consider the probability of each. Then they set goals and develop strategies for achieving them. This is quite different from the notion of conditioning through rewards and punishments. Of course, the individual's past experiences with rewards and punishments will influence his or her decisions about future behavior.

Bandura also points out that most behavior occurs in the absence of external rewards or punishments. Most behavior stems from internal processes of self-regulation. As

he expresses it, 'Anyone who attempted to change a pacifist into an aggressor or a devout religionist into an atheist would quickly come to appreciate the existence of personal sources of behavioral control' (1977, pp. 128–129).

How do these internal, personal sources of control develop? According to Bandura and other social-learning theorists, we often learn how to behave by observing the behavior of others or by reading or hearing about it. We do not have to actually perform the behaviors we observe; instead, we can note whether those behaviors were rewarded or punished and store that information in memory. When new situations arise, we can behave according to the expectations we have accumulated on the basis of our observation of models.

Bandura's social-cognitive theory thus goes beyond classical behaviorism. Rather than focusing only on how environment affects behavior, it examines the interactions among environment, behavior, and the individual's cognitions. In addition to considering external influences such as rewards and punishments, it considers internal factors such as expectations. And instead of explaining behavior simply in terms of conditioning, it emphasizes the role of observational learning.

Another prominent social-learning theorist, Walter Mischel, has attempted to incorporate individual differences into social learning theory by introducing the following set of cognitive variables:

1 **Competencies: What can you do? Competencies include intellectual abilities, social and physical skills, and other special abilities.**

2 **Encoding strategies: How do you see it? People differ in the way they selectively attend to information, encode (represent) events, and group the information into meaningful categories. An event that is perceived by one person as threatening may be seen by another as challenging.**

3 **Expectancies: What will happen? Expectations about the consequences of different behaviors will guide the individual's choice of behavior. If you cheat on an examination and are caught, what do you expect the consequences to be? If you tell your friend what you really think of him or her, what will happen to your relationship? Expectations about our own abilities will also influence behavior: we may anticipate the consequences of a certain behavior but fail to act because we are uncertain of our ability to execute the behavior.**

4 **Subjective values: What is it worth? Individuals who have similar expectancies may choose to behave differently because they assign different values to the outcomes. Two students may expect a certain behavior to please their**

professor. However, this outcome is important to one student but not to the other.

5 **Self-regulatory systems and plans: How can you achieve it? People differ in the standards and rules they use to regulate their behavior (including self-imposed rewards for success or punishments for failure), as well as in their ability to make realistic plans for reaching a goal.**

(After Mischel, 1973, 1993)

All of these person variables (sometimes referred to as cognitive social-learning person variables) interact with the conditions of a particular situation to determine what an individual will do in that situation.

Kelly's personal construct theory

George Kelly (1905–1966) was another of the personality psychologists to first suggest that cognitive processes play a central role in an individual's functioning. Kelly noted that personality psychologists typically characterized an individual on dimensions that they themselves had constructed. He proposed instead that the goal should be to discover **personal constructs**, the dimensions that individuals themselves use to interpret themselves and their social worlds. These dimensions constitute the basic units of analysis in Kelly's personal construct theory (1955).

More generally, Kelly believed that individuals should be viewed as intuitive scientists. Like formal scientists, they observe the world, formulate and test hypotheses about it, and make up theories about it. They also categorize, interpret, label, and judge themselves and their world. And, like scientists, individuals can entertain invalid theories, beliefs that hinder them in their daily lives and lead to biased interpretations of events and persons, including themselves.

Like scientists trying to make predictions about events, people want to understand the world so that they can predict what will happen to them. Kelly argued that each individual uses a unique set of personal constructs in interpreting and predicting events. Those constructs tend to take an either–or form: a new acquaintance is either friendly or unfriendly, intelligent or unintelligent, fun or boring, and so on. But two people meeting the same individual may use different constructs in evaluating that individual – someone who seems friendly and intelligent to one person may seem unfriendly and unintelligent to another. These differences lead to differences in behavior – one person will respond positively to the new acquaintance while another may avoid him or her. These differences in behavior produce differences in personality.

Self-schemas

Other cognitive theorists have focused on more complex cognitive structures that with which people perceive, organize,

process, and utilize information; these structures are referred to as **schemas**. Through the use of schemas, each individual develops a system for identifying what is important in his or her environment while ignoring everything else. Schemas also provide a structure within which to organize and process information. For example, most people have developed a mother schema. When asked to describe their mother, it is easy for them because the information is organized into a well-defined cognitive structure. It is easier to describe one's mother than to describe a woman one has heard about but has never met.

Schemas are relatively stable over time and therefore result in stable ways of perceiving and utilizing information. They differ from one individual to another, causing people to process information differently and to behave in different ways. They thus can be used to explain differences in personality.

Perhaps the most important schema is the **self-schema**, which consists of 'cognitive generalizations about the self, derived from past experience, that organize and guide the processing of self-related information' (Markus, 1977, p. 64). From an early age, we all develop a cognitive representation of who we are. The resulting self-schema is made up of the aspects of our behavior that are most important to us, and it plays a central role in the way we process information and interact with the world around us. For example, two people may both enjoy jogging and literature, but for one person exercise may be an important part of the self-schema, yet the other person's self-schema may place greater emphasis on being well-read. The first person is likely to spend more time jogging than reading, and the reverse is likely to be true of the second person.

The core of the self-schema is basic information, such as the person's name, physical appearance, and relationships with significant people. But more important from the standpoint of individual differences are particularistic features of the self-schema (Markus & Sentis, 1982; Markus & Smith, 1981). For the person whose self-schema includes an emphasis on exercise, for example, exercise is part of 'who he or she is' and a part of the daily or weekly routine. For the person who enjoys jogging but does not view it as central, an occasional jog around the park will be sufficient. So, differences in self-schemas produce differences in behavior.

Self-schemas not only guide the perception and processing of information but also provide a framework for organizing and storing it. As with the mother schema mentioned earlier, we would expect people to retrieve information from memory more easily when they have a strong schema for it. This hypothesis was tested in an experiment in which university students were presented with a series of 40 questions on a video screen (Rogers et al., 1977). The participants were asked to respond to each question by pressing a yes or no button as quickly as possible. Thirty of the questions could be answered easily without being processed through the self-schema. They asked whether a word was printed in big letters, rhymed with another word, or had the same meaning as another word. The other ten questions required participants to decide whether a word described them, and the researchers proposed that in these cases the information had to be processed through the self-schema.

The participants were later asked to recall as many of the 40 words as they could. The results showed that when participants answered questions about themselves they were more likely to remember the information later. The researchers concluded that the participants processed this information through their self-schemas. Because information in the self-schema is easy to access, words referring to the self were easier to remember than words processed in other ways. In subsequent studies, when participants were asked whether a word described the experimenter (Kuiper & Rogers, 1979) or a celebrity (Lord, 1980), they did not recall those words as easily as words describing themselves. In sum, it appears that the superior organization and accessibility of information about ourselves makes information that is processed through the self-schema more accessible than information that is processed in other ways (Karylowski, 1990; Klein & Loftus, 1988; Klein *et al.,* 1989).

Self-schemas differ considerably across cultures to the extent that some theorists argue that personality is a product of culture (Cross & Markus, 1999). For example, North Americans assume that the self is autonomous and separate from others and from situations and that people have individual choice over their actions and beliefs. In the North American conception of the self, a person's wishes, desires, interests, and abilities make up the self. People have the power and the responsibility to create the self they want to have, rather than allow external influences to shape their self-concepts. In contrast, in some Asian cultures, the self is not an entity separate from others but is thoroughly intertwined with one's obligations and relationships to others. The core issue in the development of the self is not to discover and express one's own wishes, desires, interests, and abilities, but to determine how one is meant to fit in with the social group and to shape oneself to best serve the social group.

A cognitive portrait of human nature

While the psychoanalytic and behaviorist perspectives are essentially deterministic, the cognitive perspective views humans as actively constructing their world and their place in it. The concept of personal **agency** is central to the cognitive approach to personality and behavior (Bandura, 2006). People's sense of agency, or belief that they can influence important situations in their lives, drives their choices of what situations to approach and what to avoid, their level of motivation and persistence, and their well-being. A sense of agency can be elevated or dampened by the conditions individuals encounter: a boy who grows up in abject poverty, with parents who constantly tell him he will never amount to anything, is less likely to have a strong sense of personal agency than a boy who grows up in a comfortable home with parents who encourage him to achieve his goals. But agency trumps environment in social-cognitive theory: even the boy who grows up in poverty with unsupportive parents can rise above his environment and accomplish great things if he has personal agency.

Although the cognitive perspective gives hope and encouragement to some, it can lead to 'blaming the victim.' It suggests that individuals who do not triumph over adversity are lacking the right attitude – if they would just believe in themselves, they could overcome their circumstances. This may not be true for everyone.

An evaluation of the cognitive approach

The cognitive approach has many strengths as well as some weaknesses. One positive aspect of the approach is that it is based on empirical research. Many cognitive structures have been subjected to extensive study in controlled laboratory experiments. Another strength of cognitive theory is that it goes beyond the trait approach in explaining personality characteristics. Rather than simply identifying traits, cognitive theorists use cognitive structures to explain individual differences in behavior.

On the other hand, a frequent criticism of the cognitive approach is that it employs vague concepts. It is difficult to state specifically what a personal construct is or to be sure when a schema is being used, and it is not entirely clear how a personal construct differs from a schema or how any of these cognitive structures relate to memory and other aspects of information processing. Moreover, behaviorists

People indicate their self-schema based on their relationship with significant people.

might ask whether it is really necessary to use these concepts. Perhaps personality can be explained just as well without referring to cognitions.

INTERIM SUMMARY

➡ The cognitive approach to personality is based on the idea that differences in personality stem from differences in the way individuals mentally represent information.

➡ Albert Bandura developed social cognitive theory, which holds that internal cognitive processes combine with environmental pressures to influence behavior, and that cognitive processes and environment have reciprocal effects on each other.

➡ Walter Mischel has identified a number of cognitive person variables that affect people's reactions to the environment and behaviors in the environment.

➡ George Kelly's personal construct theory focuses on the concepts that individuals use to interpret themselves and their social world.

➡ Much research has focused on the self-schema, which consists of the aspects of a person's behavior that are most important to that person. Experiments have shown that people perceive information more readily and recall it better when it is relevant to their self-schemas.

CRITICAL THINKING QUESTIONS

1 Some theorists argue that our most important schemas for ourselves and others are often non-conscious – we don't even realize we hold them and might deny we hold them if asked explicitly. Can you think of some methods by which you might be able to tap into a person's non-conscious schemas?

2 What do you think are some of the most important developmental processes or events that contribute to the type of self-schema an individual develops?

THE HUMANISTIC APPROACH

During the 1950s and 1960s, a group of psychologists proposed another alternative (in addition to social cognitive theory) to the deterministic perspectives of the psychoanalytic and behaviorist approaches. This perspective, the **humanistic approach**, was based on four principles:

1 The experiencing person is of primary interest. Humans are not simply objects of study. They must be described and understood in terms of their own subjective views of the world, their perceptions of self, and their feelings of self-worth. The central question each person must face is 'Who am I?' In order to learn how the individual attempts to answer this question, the psychologist must become a partner with that person.

2 Human choice, creativity, and self-actualization are the preferred topics of investigation. People are not motivated only by basic drives like sex or aggression or physiological needs like hunger and thirst. They feel a need to develop their potentials and capabilities. Growth and self-actualization should be the criteria of psychological health, not merely ego control or adjustment to the environment.

3 We should study important human and social problems, even if that sometimes means adopting less rigorous methods. And while psychologists should strive to be objective in collecting and interpreting observations, their choice of research topics can and should be guided by values. In this sense, research is not value-free.

4 Ultimate value is placed on the dignity of the person. People are basically good. The objective of psychology is to understand, not to predict or control people.

Psychologists who share these values come from diverse theoretical backgrounds. For example, the trait theorist Gordon Allport was also a humanistic psychologist, and we have already pointed out that several psychoanalysts, such as Carl Jung and Erik Erikson, held humanistic views of motivation that diverged from Freud's views. But it is Carl Rogers and Abraham Maslow whose theoretical views lie at the center of the humanistic movement.

Carl Rogers

Like Freud, Carl Rogers (1902–1987) based his theory on work with patients or clients in a clinic (Rogers, 1951, 1959, 1963, 1970). Rogers was impressed with what he saw as the individual's innate tendency to move toward growth, maturity, and positive change. He came to believe that the basic force motivating the human organism is the **actualizing tendency** – a tendency toward fulfillment or actualization of all the capacities of the organization. A growing organism seeks to fulfill its potential within the limits of its heredity. A person may not always clearly perceive which actions lead to growth and which do not. But once the course is clear, the individual chooses to grow. Rogers did not deny that there are other needs, some of them biological, but he saw them as subservient to the organism's motivation to enhance itself.

Rogers's belief in the primacy of actualization forms the basis of his non-directive or client-centered therapy. This method of psychotherapy assumes that every individual has the motivation and ability to change and that the individual is

Carl Rogers believed that individuals have an innate tendency to move toward growth, maturity, and positive change. He referred to this as the actualizing tendency.

best qualified to decide the direction such change should take. The therapist's role is to act as a sounding board while the client explores and analyzes his or her problems. This approach differs from psychoanalytic therapy, during which the therapist analyzes the patient's history to determine the problem and devise a course of remedial action. (See Chapter 16 for a discussion of various approaches to psychotherapy.)

The self

The central concept in Rogers's theory of personality is the **self**, or self-concept (Rogers uses the terms interchangeably.) The self (or real self) consists of all the ideas, perceptions, and values that characterize 'I' or 'me'; it includes the awareness of 'what I am' and 'what I can do.' This perceived self, in turn, influences both the person's perception of the world and his or her behavior. For example, a woman who perceives herself as strong and competent perceives and acts upon the world quite differently from a woman who considers herself weak and ineffectual. The self-concept does not necessarily reflect reality: a person may be highly successful and respected but still view himself or herself as a failure.

According to Rogers, the individual evaluates every experience in relation to his or her self-concept. People want to behave in ways that are consistent with their self-image, and experiences and feelings that are not consistent are threatening and may be denied entry into consciousness. This is essentially Freud's concept of repression, although Rogers felt that such repression is neither necessary nor permanent. (Freud would say that repression is inevitable and that some aspects of the individual's experiences always remain unconscious.)

The more areas of experience a person denies because they are inconsistent with his or her self-concept, the wider the gap between the self and reality and the greater the potential for maladjustment. Individuals whose self-concepts do not match their feelings and experiences must defend themselves against the truth because the truth will result in anxiety. If the gap becomes too wide, the person's defenses may break down, resulting in severe anxiety or other forms of emotional disturbance. A well-adjusted person, in contrast, has a self-concept that is consistent with his or her thoughts, experiences, and behaviors; the self is not rigid but flexible, and it can change as it assimilates new experiences and ideas.

Rogers also proposed that each of us has an **ideal self**, our conception of the kind of person we would like to be. The closer the ideal self is to the real self, the more fulfilled and happy the individual becomes. A large discrepancy between the ideal self and the real self results in an unhappy, dissatisfied person.

Thus, two kinds of inconsistency can develop: between the self and the experiences of reality and between the real self and the ideal self. Rogers proposed some hypotheses about how these inconsistencies may develop. In particular, Rogers believed that people are likely to function more effectively if they are brought up with **unconditional positive regard** – being given the sense that they are valued by parents and others even when their feelings, attitudes, and behaviors are less than ideal. If parents offer only conditional positive regard – valuing the child only when he or she behaves, thinks, or feels correctly – the child's self-concept is likely to be distorted. For example, feelings of competition and hostility toward a younger sibling are natural, but parents disapprove of hitting a baby brother or sister and usually punish such actions. Children must somehow integrate this experience into their self-concept. They may decide that they are bad and feel ashamed. They may decide that their parents do not like them and feel rejected. Or they may deny their feelings and decide they do not want to hit the baby. Each of these attitudes distorts the truth. The third alternative is the easiest for children to accept, but in so doing they deny their real feelings, which then become unconscious. The more people are forced to deny their own feelings and accept the values of others, the more uncomfortable they will feel about themselves. Rogers suggested that the best approach is for the parents to recognize the child's feelings as valid while explaining the reasons why hitting is not acceptable.

Measuring real–ideal self-congruence

Earlier, we described a method of assessment called the *Q-sort*, in which a rater or sorter is given a set of cards, each containing a personality statement (for example, 'Is cheerful'), and asked to describe an individual's personality by sorting the cards into piles. The rater places statements that are least descriptive of the individual in a pile on the left and those that are most descriptive in a pile on the right. The other statements are distributed in the intermediate piles, thereby assigning each Q item a score corresponding to the pile in which it is placed. Researchers can compare two Q-sorts by computing a correlation between their item scores, thereby assessing the degree to which the two sorts are similar.

Rogers pioneered the use of the Q-sort as a way of examining the self-concept. His Q set contains statements like 'I am satisfied with myself,' 'I have a warm emotional relationship with others,' and 'I don't trust my emotions,' In Rogers's procedure, individuals first sort themselves as they actually are – their real self – and then sort themselves as they would like to be – their ideal self. The correlation between the two sorts reveals the degree of incongruence between the real and ideal selves. A low or negative correlation corresponds to a large discrepancy, implying feelings of low self-esteem and lack of worth.

By repeating this procedure several times during the course of therapy, Rogers could assess the effectiveness of therapy. In one study, correlations between self and ideal Q-sorts of individuals seeking therapy averaged −0.01 before therapy but increased to +0.34 after therapy. Correlations for a matched control group that did not receive therapy did not change (Butler & Haigh, 1954). In other words, the therapy had significantly reduced these individuals' perception of the discrepancy between their real selves and their ideal selves. Note that this could occur in two ways: an individual could change his or her concept of the real self so that it was closer to the ideal self or change his or her concept of the ideal self so that it was more realistic. Therapy can produce both kinds of changes.

More recently, psychologist Tory Higgins (Higgins & Spiegel, 2004) has shown that self-discrepancies such as those described by Rogers are associated with psychopathology. People who see themselves as falling far short of the person they would ideally like to be, or feel they ought to be, and who do not believe they can overcome these discrepancies, are prone to depression and anxiety.

Abraham Maslow

The psychology of Abraham Maslow (1908–1970) overlaps with that of Carl Rogers in many ways. Maslow was first attracted to behaviorism and carried out studies of primate sexuality and dominance. He was already moving away from behaviorism when his first child was born, after which he remarked that anyone who observes a baby cannot be a

FIGURE 13.4 Maslow's Hierarchy of Needs. *Needs that are low in the hierarchy must be at least partially satisfied before needs that are higher in the hierarchy become important sources of motivation.*

behaviorist. He was influenced by psychoanalysis but eventually became critical of its theory of motivation and developed his own theory. Specifically, he proposed that there is a **hierarchy of needs**, ascending from the basic biological needs to the more complex psychological motivations that become important only after the basic needs have been satisfied (see Figure 13.4). The needs at one level must be at least partially satisfied before those at the next level become important motivators of action. When food and safety are difficult to obtain, efforts to satisfy those needs will dominate a person's actions, and higher motives will have little significance. Only when basic needs can be satisfied easily will the individual have the time and energy to devote to aesthetic and intellectual interests. Artistic and scientific endeavors do not flourish in societies in which people must struggle for food, shelter, and safety. The highest motive – self-actualization – can be fulfilled only after all other needs have been satisfied.

Maslow decided to study self-actualizers – men and women who had made extraordinary use of their potential. He began by studying the lives of eminent historical figures such as Spinoza, Thomas Jefferson, Abraham Lincoln, Jane Addams, Albert Einstein, and Eleanor Roosevelt. In this way he was able to create a composite picture of a self-actualizer. Maslow then extended his study to a population of university students. Selecting students who fit his definition of self-actualizers, he found this group to be in the healthiest 1 per cent of the population. These students showed no signs of

Creative children sometimes describe the experience of being creative as a peak experience.

maladjustment and were making effective use of their talents and capabilities (Maslow, 1970).

Many people experience what Maslow called **peak experiences**: transient moments of self-actualization. A peak experience is characterized by happiness and fulfillment – a temporary, non-striving, non-self-centered state of goal attainment. Peak experiences may occur in different intensities and in various contexts, such as creative activities, appreciation of nature, intimate relationships, aesthetic perceptions, or athletic participation. After asking a large number of college students to describe any experience that came close to being a peak experience, Maslow attempted to summarize their responses. They spoke of wholeness, perfection, aliveness, uniqueness, effortlessness, self-sufficiency, and the values of beauty, goodness, and truth.

A humanistic portrait of human nature

As a matter of principle, humanistic psychologists have been quite explicit about the principles underlying their approach to human personality. The four principles we summarized earlier draw sharp contrasts between the humanistic portrait of human personality and the portraits drawn by the psychoanalytic and behaviorist approaches. In addition, while humanistic psychology shares with cognitive perspectives a concern with how the individual views the self, humanistic psychology has a much more expansive view of human experience than cognitive perspectives, which goes far beyond the particular thoughts that go through the individual's mind.

Most humanistic psychologists do not dispute the claim that biological and environmental variables can influence behavior, but they emphasize the individual's own role in defining and creating his or her destiny, and they downplay the determinism that is characteristic of the other approaches. In their view, individuals are basically good, striving for growth and self-actualization. They are also modifiable and active. Humanistic psychologists set a particularly high criterion for psychological health. Mere ego control or adaptation to the environment is not enough. Only an individual who is growing toward self-actualization can be said to be psychologically healthy. In other words, psychological health is a process, not an end state.

Such assumptions have political implications. From the perspective of humanistic psychology, anything that retards the fulfillment of individual potential – that prevents any human being from becoming all he or she can be – should be challenged. For example, if women in the 1950s were happy and well adjusted to traditional sex roles, the criterion of psychological health defined by behaviorism was satisfied. But from the humanistic perspective, consigning all women to the same role is undesirable – no matter how appropriate that role might be for some women – because it prevents many from reaching their maximum potential. It is no accident that the rhetoric of liberation movements – such as women's liberation and gay liberation – echoes the language of humanistic psychology.

An evaluation of the humanistic approach

By focusing on the individual's unique perception and interpretation of events, the humanistic approach brings individual experience back into the study of personality. More than other theories we have discussed, the theories of Rogers and Maslow concentrate on the whole, healthy person and take a positive, optimistic view of human personality. Humanistic psychologists emphasize that they study important problems, even if they do not always have rigorous methods for investigating them. They have a point – investigating trivial problems just because one has a convenient method for doing so does little to advance the science of psychology. Moreover, humanistic psychologists have succeeded in devising new methods for assessing self-concepts and conducting studies that treat the individual as an equal partner in the research enterprise.

Nevertheless, critics question the quality of the evidence in support of the humanists' claims. For example, to what extent are the characteristics of self-actualizers a consequence of a psychological process called *self-actualization* and to what extent are they merely reflections of the particular value systems held by Rogers and Maslow? Where, they ask, is the evidence for Maslow's hierarchy of needs?

Humanistic psychologists are also criticized for building their theories solely on observations of relatively healthy people. Their theories are best suited to well-functioning people whose basic needs have been met, freeing them to concern themselves with higher needs. The applicability of these theories to malfunctioning or disadvantaged individuals is less apparent.

Finally, some have criticized the values espoused by the humanistic theorists. A psychology that raises individual self-fulfillment and actualization to the top of the value hierarchy may provide a 'sanction for selfishness' (Wallach & Wallach, 1983). Although Maslow lists concern for the welfare of humanity among the characteristics of self-actualizers and some of the self-actualizers identified by Maslow – such as Eleanor Roosevelt and Albert Einstein – clearly possessed this characteristic, it is not included in the hierarchy of needs.

Albert Einstein and Eleanor Roosevelt were among the individuals Maslow identified as self-actualizers.

INTERIM SUMMARY

➡ The humanistic approach is concerned with the individual's subjective experience. Humanistic psychology was founded as an alternative to psychoanalytic and behaviorist approaches.

➡ Carl Rogers argued that the basic force motivating the human organism is the actualizing tendency – a tendency toward fulfillment or actualization of all the capacities of the self. When the needs of the self are denied, severe anxiety can result. Children come to develop an actualized self through the experience of unconditional positive regard from their caregivers.

➡ Abraham Maslow proposed that there is a hierarchy of needs, ascending from the basic biological needs to the more complex psychological motivations that become important only after the basic needs have been satisfied. The needs at one level must be at least partially satisfied before those at the next level become important motivators of action.

CRITICAL THINKING QUESTIONS

1 Several studies suggest that people in Asian cultures are not as concerned with individualism as Americans are and instead are more concerned with the collective welfare of their family and community. To what extent do you think this refutes humanistic perspectives on personality?

2 Do you think it's always a good idea to give a child unconditional positive regard? Why or why not?

THE EVOLUTIONARY APPROACH

One of the most controversial theories in personality is really an application of a very old theory. Evolutionary theory, as proposed by Darwin (1859), has played an important role in biology for well over a century. Darwin ventured some ideas about the evolutionary roots of human behavior, but the modern field of evolutionary psychology began with the work of Wilson (1975) on 'sociobiology.' The basic premise of sociobiology and, later, **evolutionary psychology** is that behaviors that increased the organism's chances of surviving and leaving descendants would be selected for over the course of evolutionary history and thus would become aspects of humans' personalities.

Not surprisingly, a good deal of the research on the application of evolutionary psychology to personality has focused on mate selection. Mating involves competition – among heterosexuals, males compete with males and females compete with females. What's being competed for differs between the sexes, however, because males and females have different roles in reproduction. Because females carry their offspring for 9 months and then nurse and care for them after birth, they have a greater investment in each offspring and can produce fewer offspring in their lifetimes than men can. This puts a premium for the female on the quality of the genetic contribution of the males with whom she reproduces, as well as on signs of his ability and willingness to help care for his offspring. In contrast, the optimal reproductive strategy for males is to reproduce as often as possible, and they will primarily be looking for females who are available and fertile.

David Buss, Douglas Kenrick, and other evolutionary psychologists have investigated personality differences between males and females that they hypothesize are the result of these differences in reproductive strategies (Buss, 2007; Kenrick, 2006). They reasoned that women who are interested in mating should emphasize their youth and beauty, because these are signs of their fertility, but should be choosier than men about what partners they mate with. In contrast, men who are interested in mating should emphasize their ability to support their offspring and should be less choosy than women about their mating partners. A variety of findings have supported these hypotheses. When asked what they do to make themselves attractive to the opposite sex, women report enhancing their beauty through make-up, jewelry, clothing, and hairstyles. Women also report playing hard to get. Men report bragging about their accomplishments and earning potential; displaying expensive possessions, and flexing their muscles (Buss, 2007).

Evolutionary theory provides an explanation for why older men often seek women who are much younger than they are.

Other studies have found that men are more interested in casual sex than women are (Buss & Schmitt, 1993) and are less selective in their criteria for one-night stands (Kenrick et al., 1993).

One proxy for fertility is youth, and one proxy for economic resources is older age. Evolutionary theory suggests that men will be interested in mating with younger women, whereas women will be interested in mating with older men. These sex differences in mating preferences have been found across 37 cultures (Buss, 1989). Kenrick and Keefe (1992) even found evidence for these mating preferences in singles ads placed in newspapers. In the ads, the older a man was, the more he expressed a preference for a younger woman. Women tended to express a preference for older men, regardless of the women's age.

Some theorists have extended evolutionary predictions far beyond mating preferences, arguing that men are more individualistic, domineering, and oriented toward problem-solving than women because these personality characteristics increased males' ability to reproduce often over history and thus were selected for (Gray, 1992; Tannen, 1990). In contrast, women are more inclusive, sharing, and communal because these personality characteristics increased the chances of survival of their offspring and thus were selected for.

In some of their more controversial work, evolutionary theorists have argued that because of sex differences in mating strategies there should be sex differences in both sexual infidelity and the sources of jealousy. Whereas men's desire to mate frequently makes them more prone to sexual infidelity than women, their concern that they are not investing their resources in offspring who are not their own makes them more concerned about sexual infidelity of their female partners. This suggests that men will be more likely than women to cheat on their female partners and more jealous than women if their spouse or partner cheats on them. Several studies have found support for these hypotheses (Buss, 2007).

When competition among males for available females becomes fierce, it can lead to violence, particularly among males who have fewer resources to compete with, such as unemployed males. Wilson and Daly (1985; Daly & Wilson, 1990) found that homicides between non-relatives are most likely to be among young males, whom they argued were fighting over 'face' and status. They further found that homicides within families are most often husbands killing wives and argued that these killings represent the male's attempt at controlling the fidelity of the female partner.

An evolutionary portrait of human nature

The evolutionary portrait of human nature would appear to be a rather grim one. We are this way because it has been adaptive for the species to develop in this manner, and everything

CUTTING EDGE RESEARCH FINDING THE SELF IN THE BRAIN

Susan Nolen-Hoeksema, Yale University

The 'self' is a key aspect of personality according to several theories discussed in this chapter. People have schemas for the self and personal constructs that describe and organize their perceptions of themselves. They can have a strong or weak sense of self-agency or self-efficacy. They can be more or less self-actualized.

Modern neuroscientists have been interested in whether information about the self, and the processing of self-relevant information, are centralized in certain areas of the brain. They have used several different kinds of tasks to investigate brain regions associated with self-referential processing. For example, some researchers have people evaluate the self-descriptiveness of adjectives or sentences describing personality traits (e.g., Heatherton *et al.*, 2006) or simply think freely about their own personality (D'Argembeau *et al.*, 2005), and have compared brain activity during these tasks with brain activity when individuals are reflecting on the personality traits of another person or making judgments of factual knowledge. The most consistent finding in this literature is that self-referential thought is associated with increased activity in the medial prefrontal cortex (see Figure 13.5).

Interest in the role of the prefrontal cortex in self-relevant thought and self-regulation dates back to the famous case of Phineas Gage (Damasio *et al.*, 1994). Gage was a 25-year-old construction foreman for a railroad line in the northeast USA in the mid-1800s. Controlled blasting was used to level uneven terrain so that railroad ties could be laid, and Gage was in charge of detonations. On September 13, 1848, an accident sent a fine-pointed, 3-cm-thick, 109-cm-long tamp-ing iron hurling at high speed through Gage's face, skull, and brain, and then into the sky. Unbelievably, Gage was only momentarily stunned, but regained full consciousness and walked away with the help of his men. Following the accident, Gage's intellectual capacities seemed intact, but he underwent a remarkable change in personality. Gage had been a highly responsible, well-liked individual prior to the accident. After the accident, however, he became irresponsible, irreverent, and profane. His control over his emotions and social behavior seemed to be lost. Almost 150 years later, researchers using modern neuroimaging techniques on Gage's preserved skull and a computer simulation of the tamping-iron accident showed that the main damage to Gage's brain was in the prefrontal cortex (see Figure 13.6).

The prefrontal cortex is an area of the brain that is involved in many of our most advanced thinking processes. It takes information from all sensory modalities, from other areas of the brain, and from the outside environment, integrating this information and co-ordinating our responses to it. As such, it has been considered the 'chief executive' of the brain. Thus, it is not surprising that aspects of the self – the characteristics we associate with our self, the emotions that these characteristics arouse, and our ability to regulate the self, involve processing in the prefrontal cortex.

It is too simple to say, however, that the self is in the prefrontal cortex. Researchers are finding that fine distinctions in self-relevant processing, for example, thinking about one's hopes and aspirations, versus thinking about one's duties and obligations, activates different areas of the prefrontal cortex, and other areas of the brain (Johnson *et al.*, 2006).

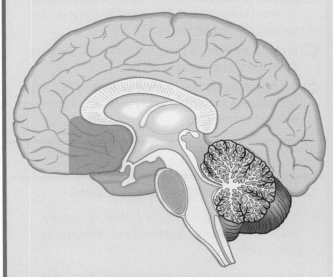

FIGURE 13.5 The Medial Prefrontal Cortex. *Self-referential thought is associated with activity in the medial prefrontal cortex.*

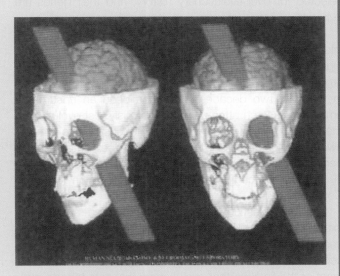

FIGURE 13.6 Phineas Gage's Brain Injury. *Modern neuroimaging techniques have helped identify the precise location of damage to Phineas Gage's brain.*

Further, the ability to regulate one's behaviors and emotions probably has to do with the co-ordination of activity of different areas of the brain, not just whether one area of the brain is active (Ochsner & Gross, 2007). Finally, although activity in different areas of the brain can affect our sense of self, those patterns of activity can be changed by training people to think differently about themselves (e.g., Ray *et al.*, 2005) or through medications (Kennedy *et al.*, 2001).

Thus, modern neuroscience is helping us understand what areas of the brain are active when we think about ourselves. We are still left with the age-old philosophical question, however, What is the self?

about our personalities and social behavior is coded in our genes. This would seem to leave little room for positive change.

Evolutionary theorists are the first to emphasize, however, that evolution is all about change – when the environment changes, only organisms that can adapt to that change will survive and reproduce. This change just happens more slowly than we might like it to.

An evaluation of the evolutionary approach

You should not be surprised that the evolutionary approach has taken a great deal of heat. There are important social and political implications of the arguments and findings of these theorists. Some critics argue that evolutionary psychology simply provides a thinly veiled justification for the unfair social conditions and prejudices in today's world. If women are subordinate to men in economic and political power, it's because this was evolutionarily adaptive for the species. If men beat their wives and have extramarital affairs, they can't help it; it's in their genes. If some ethnic groups have more power and wealth in society, it's because their behaviors have been selected for over-evolutionary history, and their genes are superior.

Evolutionary theorists have also taken heat from the scientific community. The early arguments of sociobiologists were highly speculative and not based on hard data. Some critics argued that their hypotheses were unfalsifiable or untestable. In the past two decades, there has been an upsurge of empirical research attempting to rigorously test evolutionary theories of human behavior. Some theorists have steered away from controversial topics such as sex differences in personality or abilities, to investigate the role of evolution in shaping the cognitive structures of the brain (Tooby & Cosmides, 2002).

Still, the question remains of whether an evolutionary explanation for a given finding – whether a human sex difference or some behavior or structure that all humans share – is necessary. It is easy to develop alternative explanations for most of the findings that evolutionary theorists tend to attribute to reproductive strategies (Wood & Eagly, 2007). For example, sex differences in personality characteristics could be due to sex differences in body size and strength (for instance, men are more dominant than women because their size allows them to be, whereas women are friendlier than men because they are trying not to get beaten up by men). The causes of behavior focused on by most alternative explanations are more proximal than evolutionary causes – the explanations don't rely on claims about what has been true for millions of years and make claims only about what has been true in the relatively recent past. For many findings touted by evolutionary theorists as being consistent with evolutionary history, it is difficult to conceive of experiments that could help us decide between an evolutionary explanation and an alternative explanation that focuses on more proximal causes.

Evolutionary theory is attractive in its power to explain a wide range of behaviors, however. Not since the introduction of behaviorism has psychology had a new explanatory framework that might account for most aspects of human behavior.

> ## INTERIM SUMMARY
>
> ➡ Evolutionary psychology attempts to explain human behavior and personality in terms of the adaptiveness of certain characteristics for survival and reproductive success over human history.
>
> ➡ Evolutionary theory is consistent with some observed sex differences in mate preferences.
>
> ➡ It is a controversial theory, however, both for its social implications and for the difficulty of refuting arguments derived from this theory.

> ## CRITICAL THINKING QUESTIONS
>
> 1 To what extent do you think the political implications of a psychological theory should be of concern to its proponents?
>
> 2 Do you think evolutionary theory can predict anything about how human behavior will change in the next few centuries?

THE GENETICS OF PERSONALITY

We end with another controversial approach to understanding the origins of personality – the argument that personality traits are largely determined by the genes an individual was born with. Some of the best evidence that genes play a role in personality comes from the Minnesota Study of Twins Reared Apart, which we described in Chapter 12 and highlighted at the beginning of this chapter. Recall from Chapter 12 that the participants in this study were assessed on a number of ability and personality measures. In addition, they participated in lengthy interviews during which they were asked questions about such topics as childhood experiences, fears, hobbies, musical tastes, social attitudes, and sexual interests. A number of startling similarities were found. The twins with the most dramatically different backgrounds are Oskar Stohr and Jack Yufe, described at the beginning of the chapter. Another pair of twins with fairly different backgrounds are both British homemakers. They were separated during World War II and raised by families that differed in socioeconomic status. Both twins, who had never met before, arrived for their interviews wearing seven rings on their fingers.

These studies reveal that twins reared apart are just as similar to each other across a wide range of personality characteristics as twins reared together, permitting us to conclude with greater confidence that identical twins are more similar to each other on personality characteristics than fraternal twins because they are more similar genetically (Bouchard, 2004; Tellegen *et al.*, 1988).

For the most part, the correlations found in the Minnesota studies are in accord with results from many other twin studies. In general, the highest levels of heritability are found in measures of abilities and intelligence (60–70 percent), the next highest levels are typically found in measures of personality (about 50 percent); and the lowest levels are found for religious and political beliefs and vocational interests (30–40 percent). For example, one study found that traits such as shyness and the tendency to become easily upset have heritabilities of between 30 percent and 50 percent (Bouchard *et al.*, 1990; Newman *et al.*, 1998).

Interactions between personality and environment

Genotype–environment correlation

In shaping an individual's personality, genetic and environmental influences are intertwined from the moment of birth. First, it may take certain environments to trigger the effects of specific genes (Gottlieb, 2000). For example, a child born with a genetic tendency toward alcoholism may never become alcoholic if never exposed to alcohol. Second, parents give their biological offspring both their genes and

Intelligent parents will both pass their genes on to their children and provide environments that foster intelligence.

a home environment, and both are functions of the parents' own genes. As a result, there is a built-in correlation between the child's inherited characteristics (genotype) and the environment in which he or she is raised. For example, because general intelligence is partially heritable, parents with high intelligence are likely to have children with high intelligence. But parents with high intelligence are also likely to provide an intellectually stimulating environment for their children – both through their interactions with them and through books, music lessons, trips to museums, and other intellectual experiences. Because the child's genotype and environment are positively correlated in this way, he or she will get a double dose of intellectual advantage. Similarly, children born to parents with low intelligence are likely to encounter a home environment that exacerbates whatever intellectual disadvantage they may have inherited directly.

Third, some parents may deliberately construct an environment that is negatively correlated with the child's genotype. For example, introverted parents may encourage participation in social activities to counteract the child's likely introversion: 'We make an effort to have people over because we don't want Chris to grow up to be as shy as we are.' Parents of a very active child may try to provide interesting quiet activities. But whether the correlation is positive or negative, the point is that the child's genotype and environment are not simply independent sources of influence that add together to shape the child's personality. Finally, in addition to being correlated with the environment, a child's genotype shapes the environment in certain ways (Bouchard, 2004). In particular, the environment becomes a function of the child's personality through three forms of interaction: reactive, evocative, and proactive.

Reactive interaction

Different individuals who are exposed to the same environment interpret it, experience it, and react to it differently – a process known as **reactive interaction**. An anxious, sensitive child will experience and react to criticism from his

SEEING BOTH SIDES
IS FREUD'S INFLUENCE ON PSYCHOLOGY STILL ALIVE?

FREUD'S INFLUENCE ON PSYCHOLOGY IS ALIVE AND VIBRANT

Joel Weinberger, Adelphi University, Long Island, New York

Is Freud still alive? Of course Freud is dead. He died on September 23, 1939. No one asks whether Isaac Newton or William James is dead. For some odd reason this is reserved for Freud. If the question is whether psychoanalysis, the branch of psychology he founded, is dead, the answer is clearly no. Psychoanalysis survived Freud and thrives today. The American Psychological Association's division of psychoanalysis is the second largest division in the association. There now exist several schools of psychoanalysis, some of which Freud would probably not recognize. That is just what you would expect from a discipline whose founder is now 70 years dead.

Are Freud's ideas dead? They certainly are not. They have entered our common vernacular. They have entered and forever changed our culture. Think of the terms of *id*, *ego*, *superego*, *Freudian slip*, and so on. There are psychoanalytic writers, historians, psychiatrists, and of course, psychologists. The real question, I suppose, is whether Freud's ideas are still *valid*. The answer is that some are and some are not. A surprising number remain relevant, even central, to modern psychology. So I suppose the charge is to state which of his ideas remain valid. And that is what I will address.

Let's look at some of Freud's central ideas and see how they stack up with today's psychology. Freud said that all human motives could be traced back to biological sources, specifically to sex and aggression. There is a branch of psychology now termed evolutionary psychology (Buss, 1994a, 1994b); there is also sociobiology (Wilson, 1975) and ethology (Hinde, 1982). All champion the importance of biological factors in our behavior. And all have data to back up their claims. This aspect of Freud's thinking is certainly not dead. As for the importance of sex and aggression? Just look at the best-selling books, hit movies, and TV shows around you. What characterizes virtually all of them? Sex and violence. Hollywood and book publishers all seem to be Freudians, and so are the people who sample their wares.

Another idea of Freud's that was very controversial in his time was his notion that children have sexual feelings. Now that is simply commonplace knowledge.

Psychoanalysts have long held that one of the major factors accounting for the effectiveness of psychotherapy is the therapeutic relationship. For many years this was not accepted, particularly by the behaviorist school (Emmelkamp, 1994). We now know that this is a critical factor in therapeutic success (Weinberger, 1996). The related idea that we carry representations of early relationships around in our heads, an idea expanded upon by object relations theory (a school of psychoanalysis) and attachment theory (the creation of a psychoanalyst, John Bowlby), is also now commonly accepted in psychology.

The most central idea usually attributed to Freud is the importance of unconscious processes. According to Freud, we are most often unaware of why we do what we do. For a long while, mainstream academic psychology rejected this notion. Now it seems to have finally caught up to Freud. Modern thinkers now believe that unconscious processes are central and account for most of our behavior. Discussion of unconscious processes permeates research in memory (Graf & Masson, 1993), social psychology (Bargh, 1997), cognitive psychology (Baars, 1988), and so on. In fact, it is now a mainstream belief in psychology. More specific notions of Freud's such as his ideas about defense have also received empirical support (Shedler *et al.*, 1993; Weinberger, 1990). So have some of his ideas about unconscious fantasies (Siegel & Weinberger, 1997). There is even some work afoot to examine Freud's conceptions of transference (Andersen & Glassman, 1996; Crits-Christoph *et al.*, 1990).

Of course, many of the particulars of Freud's thinking have been overtaken by events and have turned out to be incorrect. What thinker who died over 70 years ago has had all of his or her ideas survive intact, without change? In broad outline, however, Freud's ideas are not only alive, they are vibrant. We should probably be testing more of them. Any notion that Freud should be ignored because some of his assertions have been shown to be false is just plain silly. It is throwing out the baby with the bath water. And, he is so much fun to read!

IS FREUD'S INFLUENCE ON PSYCHOLOGY STILL ALIVE?

FREUD IS A DEAD WEIGHT ON PSYCHOLOGY

John F. Kihlstrom, University of California, Berkeley

The twentieth century was the century of Sigmund Freud, because Freud changed our image of ourselves (Roth, 1998). Copernicus showed us that the Earth did not lie at the center of the universe, and Darwin showed us that humans were set apart from other animals, but Freud claimed to show that human experience, thought, and action was determined not by our conscious rationality, but by irrational forces outside our awareness and control – forces which could only be understood and controlled by an extensive therapeutic process called *psychoanalysis*.

Freud also changed the vocabulary with which we understand ourselves and others. Before you ever opened this textbook, you already knew something about the id and the superego, penis envy and phallic symbols, castration anxiety, and the Oedipus complex. In popular culture, psychotherapy is virtually identified with psychoanalysis. Freudian theory, with its focus on the interpretation of ambiguous events, lies at the foundation of 'post-modern' approaches to literary criticism such as deconstruction. More than anyone else, Freud's influence on modern culture has been profound and long-lasting.

Freud's cultural influence is based, at least implicitly, on the premise that his theory is scientifically valid. But from a scientific point of view, classical Freudian psychoanalysis is dead as both a theory of the mind and a mode of therapy (Macmillan, 1991/1997). No empirical evidence supports any specific proposition of psychoanalytic theory, such as the idea that development proceeds through oral, anal, phallic, and genital stages, or that little boys lust after their mothers and hate and fear their fathers. No empirical evidence indicates that psychoanalysis is more effective, or more efficient, than other forms of psychotherapy, such as systematic desensitization or assertiveness training. No empirical evidence indicates that the mechanisms by which psychoanalysis achieves its effects, such as they are, are those specifically predicated on the theory, such as transference and catharsis.

Of course, Freud lived at a particular period of time, and it might be argued that his theories were valid when applied to European culture at that time, even if they are no longer apropos today. However, recent historical analyses show that Freud's construal of his case material was systematically distorted by his theories of unconscious conflict and infantile sexuality, and that he misinterpreted and misrepresented the scientific evidence available to him. Freud's theories were not just a product of his time: they were misleading and incorrect even as he published them.

Of course, some psychologists argue that psychoanalysis has a continuing relevance to twenty-first-century psychology (Reppen, 2006). In an important paper, Drew Westen (Westen, 1998), a psychologist at Emory University, agreed that Freud's theories are archaic and obsolete, but argued that Freud's legacy lives on in a number of theoretical propositions that are widely accepted by scientists: the existence of unconscious mental processes; the importance of conflict and ambivalence in behavior; the childhood origins of adult personality; mental representations as a mediator of social behavior; and stages of psychological development. However, some of these propositions are debatable. For example, there is little evidence that childrearing practices have any lasting impact on personality (Harris, 2006).

More important, this argument skirts the question of whether *Freud's* view of these matters was correct. It is one thing to say that unconscious motives play some role in experience, thought, and action. It is something else to say that our every thought and deed is driven by repressed sexual and aggressive urges; that children harbor erotic feelings toward the parent of the opposite sex; and that young boys are hostile toward their fathers, whom they regard as rivals for their mothers' affections. This is what *Freud* believed, and so far as we can tell *Freud* was wrong in every respect. For example, the unconscious mind revealed in laboratory studies of automaticity and implicit memory bears no resemblance to the unconscious mind of psychoanalytic theory (Kihlstrom, 2008).

Westen also argued that psychoanalytic theory itself had evolved since Freud's time, and that it is therefore unfair to bind psychoanalysis so tightly to the Freudian vision of repressed, infantile, sexual and aggressive instincts. Again, this is true. In both Europe and America, a number of 'neo-Freudian' psychoanalysts such as W. R. D. Fairbairn and D. W. Winnocott in Great Britain, and even Freud's own daughter, Anna, have de-emphasized the sex, aggression, and biology of classical Freudian theory, while retaining Freud's focus on the role of unconscious conflict in personal relationships. But again, this avoids the issue of whether *Freud's* theories are correct. Furthermore, it remains an open question whether these 'neo-Freudian' theories are any more valid than are the classically Freudian views that preceded them. For example, it is not at all clear that Erik Erikson's stage theory of psychosocial development is any more valid than Freud's was.

Some psychoanalysts recognize these problems, and have argued that psychoanalysis must do more to re-connect itself to modern scientific psychology (Bornstein, 2001, 2005). Doubtless, such efforts will help clinical psychoanalysis come up to contemporary standards for scientifically based treatment. But it is not at all clear how this project will benefit scientific psychology. While Freud had an enormous impact on twentieth-century culture, he was a dead weight on twentieth-century psychology – especially with respect to personality and psychotherapy.

parents with tears, but his calm, resilient sister may simply shrug her shoulders at the same criticism. An extroverted child will attend to people and events around her, but her introverted brother will ignore them. A brighter child will get more out of being read to than a less bright child. In other words, each child's personality extracts a subjective psychological environment from the objective surroundings, and it is that subjective environment that shapes personality development. Even if parents provided exactly the same environment for all their children – which they usually do not – it will not be psychologically equivalent for all of them. Reactive interaction occurs throughout life. One person will interpret a hurtful act as the product of deliberate hostility and react to it quite differently from a person who interprets the same act as the result of unintended insensitivity.

Evocative interaction

Every individual's personality evokes distinctive responses from others, which has been referred to as **evocative interaction**. An infant who squirms and fusses when picked up will evoke less nurturance from a parent than one who likes to be cuddled. Docile children will evoke a less controlling style of child rearing from parents than will aggressive children. For this reason, we cannot simply assume that an observed correlation between the child-rearing practices of a child's parents and his or her personality reflects a simple cause-and-effect sequence. Instead, the child's personality can shape the parents' child-rearing style, which, in turn, further shapes the child's personality. Evocative interaction also occurs throughout life: gracious people evoke gracious environments; hostile people evoke hostile environments.

Proactive interaction

As children grow older, they can move beyond the environments provided by their parents and begin to select and construct environments of their own. These environments, in turn, further shape their personalities. This process is referred to as **proactive interaction**. A sociable child will choose to go to the movies with friends rather than stay home alone and watch television because her sociable personality prompts her to select an environment that reinforces her sociability. And what she cannot select she will construct: if nobody invites her to the movies, she will organize the event herself. As the term implies, proactive interaction is a process through which individuals become active agents in the development of their own personalities.

The relative importance of these three kinds of personality-environment interactions shifts over the course of development (Scarr, 1996; Scarr & McCartney, 1983). The built-in correlation between a child's genotype and his or her environment is strongest when the child is young and confined almost exclusively to the home environment. As the child grows older and begins to select and construct his or her own environment, this initial correlation decreases and the influence of proactive interaction

As children grow older, they begin to construct their own environments, independent from their parents.

increases. As we have noted, reactive and evocative interactions remain important throughout life.

Shared versus non-shared environments

Twin studies allow researchers to estimate not only how much of the variation among individuals is due to genetic variation but also how much of the environmentally related variation is due to aspects of the environment that family members share (for example, socioeconomic status) as compared with aspects of the environment that family members do not share (for example, friends outside the family). Surprisingly, some studies suggest that differences due to shared aspects of the environment seem to account for almost none of the environmental variation: after their genetic similarities are subtracted out, two children from the same family seem to be no more alike than two children chosen randomly from the population (Scarr, 1992). This implies that the kinds of variables that psychologists typically study (such as child-rearing practices, socioeconomic status, and parents' education) are contributing virtually nothing to individual differences in personality. How can this be so?

One possible explanation might be that the reactive, evocative, and proactive processes act to diminish the differences between environments as long as those environments permit some flexibility of response. A bright child from a neglecting or impoverished home is more likely than a less bright sibling to absorb information from a television program (reactive interaction), to attract the attention of a sympathetic teacher (evocative interaction), and to go to the library (proactive interaction). This child's genotype acts to counteract the potentially debilitating effects of the home environment, and therefore he or she develops differently from a less bright sibling. Only if the environment is severely restrictive will these personality-driven processes be thwarted (Scarr, 1996; Scarr & McCartney, 1983). This explanation is supported by the finding that the most dissimilar pairs of identical twins reared apart are those in which one twin was reared in a severely restricted environment.

INTERIM SUMMARY

➜ Evidence from twin studies suggests that genetic factors substantially influence personality traits.

➜ In shaping personality, genetic and environmental influences do not act independently but are intertwined from the moment of birth. Because a child's personality and his or her home environment are both a function of the parents' genes, there is a built-in correlation between the child's genotype (inherited personality characteristics) and that environment.

➜ Three dynamic processes of personality–environment interaction are (1) reactive interaction – different individuals exposed to the same environment experience it, interpret it, and react to it differently, (2) evocative interaction – an individual's personality evokes distinctive responses from others, and (3) proactive interaction – individuals select or create environments of their own. As a child grows older, the influence of proactive interaction becomes increasingly important.

➜ After their genetic similarities are subtracted out, children from the same family seem to be no more alike than children chosen randomly from the population. This implies that the kinds of variables that psychologists typically study (such as child-rearing practices and the family's socioeconomic status) contribute virtually nothing to individual differences in personality.

CRITICAL THINKING QUESTIONS

1 What are some ways that reactive, evocative, and proactive interaction might have influenced the development of your personality and abilities?

2 If you have siblings, what do you think are the best explanations for the similarities and differences you see between yourself and your siblings?

CHAPTER SUMMARY

1 Although different investigators arrive at different numbers of factors, most now believe that five factors provide the best compromise. These have been labeled the 'Big Five': Openness to experience, Conscientiousness, Extroversion, Agreeableness, and Neuroticism.

2 Although items on most inventories are composed or selected on the basis of a theory, they can also be selected on the basis of their correlation with an external criterion – the criterion-keyed method of test construction. The best-known example is the Minnesota Multiphasic Personality Inventory (MMPI), which is designed to identify individuals with psychological disorders.

3 The Q-sort is a method of assessing personality in which raters sort cards with personality adjectives into nine piles, placing the cards that are least descriptive of the individual in pile 1 on the left and those that are most descriptive in pile 9 on the right.

4 Freud's psychoanalytic theory holds that many behaviors are caused by unconscious motivations. Personality is determined primarily by the biological drives of sex and aggression and by experiences that occur during the first

5 years of life. Freud's theory of personality structure views personality as composed of the id, the ego, and the superego. The id operates on the pleasure principle, seeking immediate gratification of biological impulses. The ego obeys the reality principle, postponing gratification until it can be achieved in socially acceptable ways. The superego (conscience) imposes moral standards on the individual. In a well-integrated personality, the ego remains in firm but flexible control over the id and superego, and the reality principle governs.

5 Freud's theory of personality development proposes that individuals pass through psychosexual stages and must resolve the Oedipal conflict, in which the young child sees the same-sex parent as a rival for the affection of the opposite-sex parent. Over the years, Freud's theory of anxiety and defense mechanisms has fared better than his structural and developmental theories have.

6 Psychoanalytic theory has been modified by later psychologists, notably Carl Jung. Jung proposed that in addition to the personal unconscious described by Freud, there is a collective unconscious, a part of the mind that is common to all humans.

7 Psychologists who take the psychoanalytic approach sometimes use projective tests, such as the Rorschach Test and the Thematic Apperception Test (TAT). Because the test stimuli are ambiguous, it is assumed that the individual projects his or her personality onto the stimulus, thereby revealing unconscious wishes and motives.

8 Behavioral approaches assume that personality differences result from variations in learning experiences. Through operant conditioning, people learn to associate specific behaviors with punishment or reward. They can also learn these associations through observational learning. Through classical conditioning, people learn to associate specific situations with certain outcomes, such as anxiety.

9 The cognitive approach to personality is based on the idea that differences in personality stem from differences in the way individuals mentally represent information. Albert Bandura developed social cognitive theory, which holds that internal cognitive processes combine with environmental pressures to influence behavior and that cognitive processes and environment have reciprocal effects on each other. Walter Mischel has identified a number of cognitive person variables that affect people's reactions to the environment and behaviors in the environment. George Kelly's personal construct theory focuses on the concepts that individuals use to interpret themselves and their social world. Much research has focused on the self-schema, the aspects of a person's behavior that are most important to that person. Experiments have shown that people perceive information more readily and recall it better when it is relevant to their self-schemas.

10 The humanistic approach is concerned with the individual's subjective experience. Humanistic psychology was founded as an alternative to psychoanalytic and behaviorist approaches. Carl Rogers argued that the basic force motivating the human organism is the actualizing tendency – a tendency toward fulfillment or actualization of all the capacities of the self. When the needs of the self are denied, severe anxiety can result. Children come to develop an actualized self through the experience of unconditional positive regard from their caregivers. Abraham Maslow proposed that there is a hierarchy of needs, ascending from the basic biological needs to the more complex psychological motivations that become important only after the basic needs have been satisfied. The needs at one level must be at least partially satisfied before those at the next level become important motivators of action.

11 Evolutionary psychology attempts to explain human behavior and personality in terms of the adaptiveness of certain characteristics for survival and reproductive success over human history. Evolutionary theory is consistent with some observed sex differences in mate preferences. It is a controversial theory, however, both for its social implications and for the difficulty of refuting arguments derived from this theory.

12 Evidence from twin studies suggests that genetic factors substantially influence personality traits. In shaping personality, genetic and environmental influences do not act independently but are intertwined from the moment of birth. Because a child's personality and his or her home environment are both a function of the parents' genes, there is a built-in correlation between the child's genotype (inherited personality characteristics) and that environment.

13 Three dynamic processes of personality–environment interaction are (1) reactive interaction – different individuals exposed to the same environment experience it, interpret it, and react to it differently, (2) evocative interaction – an individual's personality evokes distinctive responses from others, and (3) proactive interaction – individuals select or create environments of their own. As a child grows older, the influence of proactive interaction becomes increasingly important.

14 After their genetic similarities are subtracted out, children from the same family seem to be no more alike than children chosen randomly from the population. This implies that the kinds of variables that psychologists typically study (such as child-rearing practices and the family's socioeconomic status) contribute virtually nothing to individual differences in personality.

CORE CONCEPTS

personality	reaction formation	classical conditioning
introversion–extroversion	projection	cognitive approach
neuroticism	intellectualization	social-learning theory
'Big Five'	denial	social-cognitive theory
personality inventory	displacement	personal constructs
Minnesota Multiphasic Personality Inventory (MMPI)	psychosexual stages	schema
	oral stage	self-schema
Q-sort	anal stage	agency
interjudge reliability	phallic stage	humanistic approach
psychoanalytic theory	Oedipal conflict	actualizing tendency
id	latency period	self
ego	genital stage	ideal self
superego	collective unconscious	unconditional positive regard
unconscious	object relations theory	hierarchy of needs
conscious	free association	peak experiences
preconscious	projective test	evolutionary psychology
libido	Rorschach Test	reactive interaction
defense mechanisms	Thematic Apperception Test	catharsis
repression	behaviorist approach	evocative interaction
suppression	operant conditioning	proactive interaction
rationalization	observational learning	

DIGITAL SUPPORT RESOURCES

Students should use the unique access code included in the front of the book to access the digital support resources which accompany the new edition. These include:

- Multiple Choice Questions and Quizzes
- Critical Thinking Questions
- Practice Essay Questions
- Videos
- Glossary, Flashcards, and More

14 STRESS, HEALTH, AND COPING

LEARNING OBJECTIVES

After reading this chapter you should be able to:

Give general definitions of stress and stressors. Be able to describe five general characteristics of stressful events and know how predictability and controllability affect the severity of stress.

Describe the fight-or-flight response and the general adaptation syndrome.

Know the physiological reactions of the fight-or-flight response, including the complex responses of the two neuroendocrine systems controlled by the hypothalamus, plus the physiology of post-traumatic stress disorder.

Outline research showing the effects of chronic over-arousal on psychophysiological disorders of the cardiovascular system, and on the body's immune system as studied in the field of psychoneuroimmunology.

Be familiar with the various psychological and related emotional reactions to stressful situations, including post-traumatic stress disorder frustration and aggression, and learned helplessness.

Discuss the differences between primary appraisal and secondary appraisal. Be able to discuss research showing that optimism plays a role in managing stress, the nature of the hardy individual, factors related to finding meaning in trauma and stress, and types of coping that influence stress.

Note the characteristics of the Type A personality and be familiar with the research relating heart disease to Type A behavior and to occupational and social stress.

Summarize two major classes of methods for managing stress, behavioral and cognitive techniques, and several varieties of these methods as well as specific applications.

Janet was feeling near the end of her rope. All day long she had endured one hassle after another. At breakfast, she spilled orange juice on the only clean blouse she had. When she got to work, there were 32 email messages and 15 telephone messages waiting for her. In the afternoon, her boss told her to prepare a financial report for the board meeting that was to occur at 9 a.m. the next morning, but her computer crashed and she could not access the financial records for her division. Tired and overwhelmed, when she got home, she called her mother for support, only to discover that her father had been hospitalized with chest pains. After hanging up, Janet felt disoriented, her heart was racing, and she began to get a migraine.

The kind of stress Janet was experiencing is familiar to many of us – silly mistakes that cause stress, the stress of a demanding boss, the stress in our personal relationships. Exposure to stress can lead to painful emotions like anxiety or depression. It can also lead to physical illnesses, both minor and severe.

Yet, people's reactions to stressful events differ widely: some people faced with stress develop serious psychological or physical problems, whereas other people develop no problems and may even be exhilarated by the challenges they are facing. The study of how stressful circumstances impact physical and psychological health, and how people differ in their reactions to stress, is a major focus of the field of *health psychology* or **behavioral medicine**. In this chapter we discuss the concept of stress and the effects of stress on the mind and body. We also look at the differences between people's ways of thinking about and coping with stressful events, and how these differences contribute to adjustment.

First, however, we need to define what we mean by *stress*. In general terms, **stress** refers to the experience of events that are perceived as endangering one's physical or psychological well-being. These events are usually referred to as **stressors**, and people's reactions to them are termed **stress responses**.

CHAPTER OUTLINE

PHYSIOLOGICAL REACTIONS TO STRESS

STRESS AND PHYSICAL HEALTH
Coronary heart disease
The immune system
Health-related behaviors

STRESS AND PSYCHOLOGICAL HEALTH

APPRAISALS, COPING, AND HEALTH
Appraisals
Coping

CUTTING EDGE RESEARCH: USING NEW MEDIA TO IMPROVE PEOPLE'S HEALTH

MANAGING STRESS

Behavioral techniques

Cognitive techniques

Modifying type A behavior

SEEING BOTH SIDES: ARE THERE

UNIVERSAL OR DISTINCT REACTIONS

TO COPING WITH STRESS?

Almost any type of event, even positive events, can be experienced as stressful, particularly if they require substantial changes or readjustments in our lives. Two pioneering stress researchers, Holmes and Rahe (1967), examined thousands of interviews and medical histories to identify the kinds of events that people found stressful. They then ranked events from most stressful (death of a spouse) to least stressful (minor violations of the law). Because marriage appeared to be a critical event for most people, it was placed in the middle of the scale and assigned an arbitrary value of 50. The investigators then asked approximately 400 men and women of varying ages, backgrounds, and marital status to compare marriage with a number of other life events in terms of how much readjustment the event called for. They were then asked to assign a point value to each event on the basis of their evaluation of its severity and the time required for adjustment. These ratings were used to construct the scale in Table 14.1.

The Holmes and Rahe scale shown in Table 14.1 had a major influence on stress research, but it has also had many critics. Although positive events often require adjustment and hence are sometimes stressful, most research indicates that negative events have a much greater impact on psychological and physical health than positive events. In addition, the Holmes and Rahe scale did not account for the large differences between people in how they are affected by events.

What types of negative events are most likely to be perceived as stressful? Three factors seem to be key: **controllability**, **predictability**, and **duration**. The more uncontrollable an event, the more likely it is to be experienced as stressful. Major uncontrollable events include the death of a loved one, being laid off from work, and

TABLE 14.1   THE LIFE EVENTS SCALE

This scale, also known as the Holmes and Rahe Social Readjustment Rating Scale, measures stress in terms of life changes.

Life event	Value	Life event	Value
Death of spouse	100	Change in responsibilities at work	29
Divorce	73	Son or daughter leaving home	29
Marital separation	65	Trouble with in-laws	29
Jail term	63	Outstanding personal achievement	28
Death of close family member	63	Wife begins or stops work	26
Personal injury or illness	53	Begin or end school	26
Marriage	50	Change in living conditions	25
Fired from job	47	Revision of personal habits	24
Marital reconciliation	45	Trouble with boss	23
Retirement	45	Change in residence	20
Change in health of family member	44	Change in school	20
Pregnancy	40	Change in recreation	19
Sex difficulties	39	Change in church activities	19
Gain of a new family member	39	Change in social activities	18
Business readjustment	39	Change in sleeping habits	16
Change in financial state	38	Change in eating habits	15
Death of a close friend	37	Vacation	13
Change to a different line of work	36	Christmas	12
Foreclosure of mortgage	30	Minor legal violations	11

serious illness. Minor uncontrollable events include such things as having a friend refuse to accept your apology for some misdeed and being bumped off a flight because the airline oversold tickets.

Uncontrollable events can lead to a set phenomenon that's been labeled **learned helplessness** (Seligman, 1975). A classic series of experiments showed that dogs placed in a shuttle box (an apparatus with two compartments separated by a barrier) quickly learn to jump to the opposite compartment to escape a mild electric shock delivered to their feet through a grid on the floor. If a light is turned on a few seconds before the grid is electrified, the dogs can learn to avoid the shock by jumping to the safe compartment when signaled by the light. However, if the dog has previously been confined in another enclosure where shocks were unavoidable and inescapable – so that nothing the animal did terminated the shock – it is very difficult for the dog to learn the avoidance response in a new situation. The animal simply sits and endures the shock in the shuttle box, even though an easy jump to the opposite compartment would eliminate discomfort. Some dogs never learn, even if the experimenter demonstrates the proper procedure by carrying them over the barrier. The experimenters concluded that the animals had learned through prior experience that they were helpless to avoid the shock and therefore gave up trying to do so, even in a new situation. The animals were unable to overcome this learned helplessness (Overmeier & Seligman, 1967).

Although pregnancy is a happy event, it can also be stressful.

Some humans also appear to develop learned helplessness in response to uncontrollable events: after a while they become apathetic, withdrawn, and inactive. They don't seem to take opportunities to regain control over their negative circumstances. The learned helplessness theory is useful in helping us understand why some people seem to give up when they are exposed to difficult events. For example, the theory has been used to explain why prisoners in Nazi concentration camps did not rebel against their captors more often: they had come to believe that they were helpless to do anything about their situation and therefore did not try to escape.

The predictability of an event – the degree to which we know if and when it will occur – also affects its stressfulness. Being able to predict the occurrence of a stressful event – even if the individual cannot control it – usually reduces the severity of the stress. As discussed in Chapter 7, both humans and animals prefer predictable aversive events over unpredictable ones (Abbott *et al.,* 1984). Humans show less emotional arousal and report less distress while waiting for predictable shocks to occur, and they perceive predictable shocks as less aversive than unpredictable ones of the same intensity (Katz & Wykes, 1985). Having a warning signal before an aversive event allows the person or animal to prepare for the event in ways that make them less aversive. For example, a person who hears warnings of an impending hurricane can board up windows in an attempt to prevent damage to the house.

Also, when we know we will have some warning or signal before a negative event will occur, we can relax to some extent until the signal warns that shock is about to occur (Seligman & Binik, 1977). Some jobs, such as firefighting and emergency-room medicine, are filled with unpredictability and are considered very stressful. Even an event as overwhelmingly negative as torture can be affected by the extent to which victims feel that the episodes of torture are predictable. Victims who are able to predict the timing and type of torture they experience while being detained recover better once they are released than victims who perceive the torture as completely unpredictable (Basoglu & Mineka, 1992).

Finally, the duration of a negative event seems to be a strong predictor of its stressfulness, with more chronic events perceived as more stressful than more short-term events. For example, soldiers who are deployed multiple times to the front lines of a war are more likely to experience psychological and physical signs of stress than those who have only one deployment (Iversen *et al.,* 2008). Rape survivors who were repeatedly raped over an extended period are more likely to have mental health problems than those who were raped once (Merrill *et al.,* 2001; Resick, 1993).

People vary greatly in how their minds and bodies respond to stress. Still, there are some physical and emotional reactions to stress that are quite common. We will review these next.

INTERIM SUMMARY

→ Stress refers to experiencing events that are perceived as endangering one's physical or psychological well-being. These events are usually referred to as stressors, and people's reactions to them are termed stress responses.

→ The controllability, unpredictability, and duration or chronicity of a situation affects how stressful it is.

CRITICAL THINKING QUESTIONS

1 Consider the situations in your own life you find stressful. What are the characteristics of these situations that make them so stressful?

2 To what extent do you think the need for control is influenced by culture?

PHYSIOLOGICAL REACTIONS TO STRESS

Whether you fall into an icy river, encounter a knife-wielding assailant, or are terrified by your first parachute jump, your body responds in similar ways (see Concept Review Table). Regardless of the stressor, your body automatically prepares to handle the emergency. This is called the **fight-or-flight response** – the body's mobilization to attack or flee from a threatening situation. Energy is needed right away, so the liver releases extra sugar (glucose) to fuel the muscles, and hormones are released that stimulate the conversion of fats and proteins into sugar. The body's metabolism increases in preparation for expending energy on physical action. Heart rate, blood pressure, and breathing rate increase, and the muscles tense. At the same time, certain unessential activities, such as digestion, are curtailed. Saliva and mucus dry up, thereby increasing the size of the air passages to the lungs, and an early sign of stress is a dry mouth. The body's natural painkillers, endorphins, are secreted,

and the surface blood vessels constrict to reduce bleeding in case of injury. The spleen releases more red blood cells to help carry oxygen, and the bone marrow produces more white corpuscles to fight infection.

CONCEPT REVIEW TABLE

Physiological reactions to stress

Increased metabolic rate
Increased heart rate
Dilation of pupils
Higher blood pressure
Increased breathing rate
Tensing of muscles
Secretion of endorphins and adrenocorticotropic hormone (ACTH)
Release of extra sugar from the liver

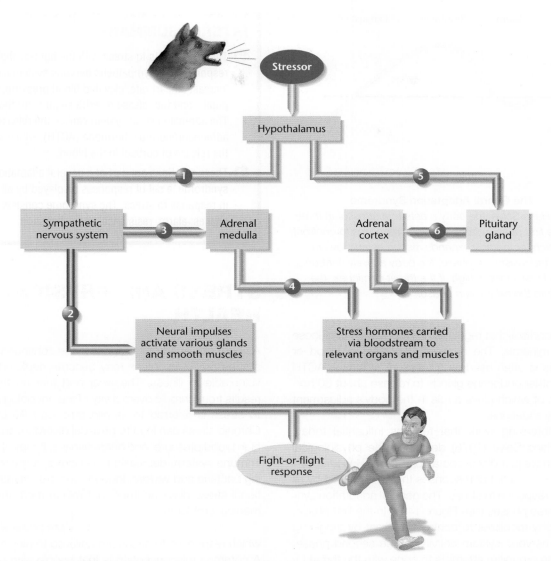

FIGURE 14.1 **The Fight-or-Flight Response.** *A stressful situation activates the hypothalamus, which, in turn, controls two neuroendocrine systems: the sympathetic system (shown in orange) and the adrenal cortical system (shown in green). The sympathetic nervous system, responding to neural impulses from the hypothalamus (1), activates various organs and smooth muscles under its control (2). For example, it increases heart rate and dilates the pupils. The sympathetic nervous system also signals the adrenal medulla (3) to release epinephrine and norepinephrine into the bloodstream (4). The adrenal-cortical system is activated when the hypothalamus secretes CRH (Corticotropin-releasing hormone), a chemical that acts on the pituitary gland, which lies just below the hypothalamus (5). The pituitary gland, in turn, secretes the hormone adrenocorticotropic hormone (ACTH), which is carried via the bloodstream to the adrenal cortex (6), where it stimulates the release of a group of hormones, including cortisol, that regulate blood glucose levels (7). ACTH also signals the other endocrine glands to release some 30 hormones. The combined effects of the various stress hormones carried via the bloodstream plus the neural activity of the sympathetic division of the autonomic nervous system constitute the fight-or-flight response.*

Most of these physiological changes result from activation of two systems controlled by the hypothalamus. The first is the sympathetic division of the autonomic nervous system, which acts directly on muscles and organs to produce increased heart rate, elevated blood pressure, and dilated pupils. The sympathetic system also stimulates the release of the hormones epinephrine (adrenaline) and norepinephrine into the bloodstream to further increase heart rate and blood pressure, and thus serves to perpetuate a state of arousal.

Norepinephrine, through its action on the pituitary gland, is indirectly responsible for the release of extra sugar from the liver (see Figure 14.1).

The hypothalamus carries out its second function, activation of the adrenal-cortical system, by signaling the pituitary gland to secrete adrenocorticotropic hormone (ACTH), the body's 'major stress hormone' (see Chapter 2). ACTH stimulates the outer layer of the adrenal glands (the adrenal cortex), resulting in the release of a group of hormones (the

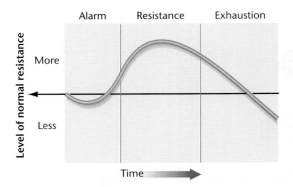

FIGURE 14.2 The Genral Adaptation Syndrome.
According to Hans Selye, the body reacts to a stressor in three phases. In the first phase, alarm, the body mobilizes to confront the threat, which temporarily expends resources and lowers resistance. In the resistance phase, the body actively confronts the threat, and resistance is high. If the threat continues, the body moves into the exhaustion phase.

major one is cortisol) that regulate the blood levels of glucose and certain minerals. The amount of cortisol in blood or urine samples is often used as a measure of stress. ACTH also signals other endocrine glands to release about 30 hormones, each of which plays a role in the body's adjustment to emergency situations.

In groundbreaking work that remains influential today, researcher Hans Selye (1978) described the physiological changes we have just discussed as part of a **general adaptation syndrome**, a set of responses that is displayed by all organisms in response to stress. The general adaptation syndrome has three phases (see Figure 14.2). In the first phase, alarm, the body mobilizes to confront a threat by triggering sympathetic nervous system activity. In the second phase, resistance, the organism attempts to cope with the threat by fleeing it or fighting it. The third phase, exhaustion, occurs if the organism is unable to flee from or fight the threat and depletes its physiological resources in attempting to do so.

Selye argued that a wide variety of physical and psychological stressors can trigger this response pattern. He also argued that repeated or prolonged exhaustion of physiological resources, due to exposure to prolonged stressors that one cannot flee from or fight, is responsible for a wide array of physiological diseases, which he called diseases of adaptation. He conducted laboratory studies in which he exposed animals to several types of prolonged stressors, such as extreme cold and fatigue, and found that, regardless of the nature of the stressor, certain bodily changes inevitably occurred: enlarged adrenal glands, shrunken lymph nodes, and stomach ulcers. These changes decrease the organism's ability to resist other stressors, including infectious and disease-producing agents. As we will see later, chronic arousal can make both animals and people more susceptible to illness.

INTERIM SUMMARY

➔ The body reacts to stress with the fight-or-flight response. The sympathetic nervous system causes increased heart rate, elevated blood pressure, dilated pupils, and the release of extra sugar from the liver. The adrenal-cortical system causes the release of adrenocorticotropic hormone (ACTH), which stimulates the release of cortisol in the blood.

➔ These reactions are part of a general adaptation syndrome, a set of responses displayed by all organisms in response to stress. The syndrome consists of three phases: alarm, resistance, and exhaustion.

STRESS AND PHYSICAL HEALTH

As our body attempts to adapt to the continued presence of a stressor, its resources may become depleted, making us vulnerable to illness. The wear and tear on the body that results from chronic overactivity of the physiological response to stress is referred to as *allostatic load* (McEwen, 2000). Chronic stress can lead to physical disorders such as ulcers, high blood pressure, and heart disease. It may also impair the immune system, decreasing the body's ability to fight invading bacteria and viruses. Indeed, doctors estimate that emotional stress plays an important role in more than half of all medical problems.

Psychophysiological disorders are physical disorders in which responses to stress are believed to play a central role. A common misconception is that people with psychophysiological disorders are not really sick and do not need medical attention. On the contrary, the symptoms of psychophysiological illness reflect physiological disturbances associated with tissue damage and pain. A peptic ulcer caused by stress is indistinguishable from an ulcer caused by a factor unrelated to stress, such as long-term heavy usage of aspirin.

Traditionally, research in psychophysiological disorders focused on such illnesses as asthma, ulcers, colitis, and rheumatoid arthritis. Researchers looked for relationships between specific illnesses and characteristic attitudes toward, or ways of coping with, stressful life events. For example, individuals suffering from colitis were believed to be angry but unable to express their anger. However, most studies that reported characteristic attitudes to be related to specific illnesses have not been replicated (Overmier & Murison, 1998). Thus, the hypothesis that people who react to stress in similar ways will be vulnerable to the same illnesses has generally not been confirmed. An important exception is research on coronary heart disease and Type A behavior patterns.

Coronary heart disease

The over-arousal caused by chronic stressors may contribute to coronary heart disease (CHD). **Coronary heart disease** occurs when the blood vessels that supply the heart muscles are narrowed or closed by the gradual buildup of a hard, fatty substance called plaque, blocking the flow of oxygen and nutrients to the heart. This can lead to pain, called angina pectoris, which radiates across the chest and arm. When the flow of oxygen to the heart is completely blocked, it can cause a myocardial infarction or heart attack.

Coronary heart disease is a leading cause of death and chronic illness across the world. Since 1990, more people have died from coronary heart disease than from any other cause (WHO, 2007). There seems to be a genetic contribution to CHD: people with family histories of CHD are at increased risk for the disease. But 80 to 90 per cent of people dying from CHD have one or more major risk factors that are affected by lifestyle choices, such as high blood pressure, high serum cholesterol, diabetes, smoking, and obesity (WHO, 2007). As we discuss in the Cutting Edge Research feature later in this chapter, new media, such as the Internet, are being used to help people change their behaviors (stop smoking, lose weight, exercise) in ways that will reduce their risk for CHD.

The environments people face can add or subtract to their risk for heart disease as well. A study of 30 000 people in 52 countries found that about a third of the risk for heart disease is connected to the stressfulness of people's environments (Rosengren et al., 2004). People in high-stress jobs are at increased risk for CHD, particularly if their jobs are highly demanding but provide them little control (Hintsanen et al., 2005; Schneiderman et al., 2005). An example of such a job is an assembly line in which rapid, high-quality production is expected and the work is machine-paced rather than self-paced. A longitudinal study conducted in Sweden suggested that the combination of high demand with low control, and high effort with low reward, predicted first heart attacks in a large sample of men and women.

Experimental studies with animals have shown that disrupting their social environment can induce pathology that resembles coronary artery disease (Sapolsky, 2007). Some of these experiments have been conducted with macaque monkeys who live in social groups that have stable hierarchies of dominant and submissive animals. The introduction of unfamiliar monkeys into an established social group is a stressor that leads to increased aggressive behavior as group members attempt to re-establish a social dominance hierarchy (Sapolsky, 2007).

In these studies, some monkey groups were not disrupted, so their dominance hierarchies remained stable; other groups were stressed by the repeated introduction of new members. After about 2 years under these conditions, the high-ranking or dominant males in the unstable social condition showed more extensive atherosclerosis than the subordinate males (Sapolsky, 2007).

Hypertension, or high blood pressure, is a major risk factor for heart disease and attacks. It is a condition in which blood flows through vessels with excessive force, putting pressure on vessel walls. Chronic high blood pressure can cause hardening of the arterial walls and deterioration of the cell tissue, leading to CHD, kidney failure and stroke. Although genetics play a role in hypertension, only about 10 per cent of cases can be traced to genetics or specific organic causes (Klabunde, 2005).

The body's response to stress is to increase blood pressure, so it is not surprising that people who live in chronically stressful environments are more likely to develop hypertension (Schneiderman et al., 2005). For example, people who are members of lower socioeconomic groups, and thus have inadequate financial resources for daily living, poor education, trouble finding good employment, and violent neighborhoods, tend to have higher blood pressure than members of higher socioeconomic groups (Lehman et al., 2009; Marmot, 2004). A Norwegian study showed that workers in a factory in which there were rumors of a possible plant closure showed significant increases in average blood pressure.

The type A pattern

A behavior pattern or personality style that has traditionally been linked to coronoary artery disease is the **type A pattern**. Over the years, physicians had noticed that heart attack victims tend to be hostile, aggressive, impatient individuals who were over-involved in their work. In the 1950s, two cardiologists defined a set of behaviors that seemed to characterize patients with CHD, which were labeled the type A pattern (Friedman & Rosenman, 1974). The three components of the type A pattern were said to be a sense of time urgency, easily aroused hostility, and competitive striving for achievement.

One landmark study followed more than 3000 healthy, middle-aged for eight-and-a-half years (Rosenman et al., 1976). During that period, type A men had twice as many heart attacks or other forms of coronary heart disease as men who were not type A. These results held up even after diet, age, smoking, and other variables were taken into account (Rosenman et al., 1976). Other studies confirmed this twofold risk and linked type A behavior to heart disease in both men and women (see Myrtek, 2007). In addition, type A behavior correlates with severity of coronary artery blockage, as determined at autopsy or in X-ray studies of the inside of coronary blood vessels.

Subsequent research refined the concept of type A behavior, finding that a person's level of hostility is a better predictor of heart disease than his or her overall level of type A behavior. Accordingly, several studies have used personality tests rather than interviews to measure hostility. For example, a 25-year study of 118 male lawyers found that those who scored high in hostility on a personality inventory taken in university were five times more likely to die before age 50 than other classmates (Barefoot *et al.,* 1989). In a similar follow-up study of physicians, hostility scores obtained in medical school predicted the incidence of CHD, as well as mortality from all causes (Barefoot *et al.,* 1983). More recently, a study that followed men for an average of 15 years found that psychological factors including hostility predicted CHD incidence (Boyle *et al.,* 2006). In these studies, the relationship between hostility and CHD was independent of the effects of smoking, age, and high blood pressure.

How does type A behavior or hostility lead to CHD? A possible biological mechanism is the way the sympathetic nervous system responds to stress. When exposed to stressful experimental situations (for example, when faced with the threat of failure, harassment, or competitive task demands), most participants report feeling angry, irritated, and tense. However, participants who score high on hostility as a trait show much larger increases in blood pressure, heart rate, and secretion of stress-related hormones than participants with low hostility scores (Raïkkoenen *et al.,* 1999; Suarez *et al.,* 1998). The same results are found when type A participants are compared with participants who are not type A. The sympathetic nervous systems of hostile and/or type A individuals appear to be hyperresponsive to stressful situations. All of these physiological changes can damage the heart and blood vessels.

Not surprisingly, hostile people also report higher degrees of interpersonal conflict and less social support than other people (e.g., Keltikangas-Javinen & Ravaja, 2002). Reductions in social support have direct negative effects on a number of objective and subjective indices of health (see Uchino *et al.,* 1999). Thus, hostility may have both direct effects on cardiovascular health by increasing chronic arousal and indirect effects by lowering social support.

The good news about the type A behavior pattern is that it can be modified through well-established therapy programs, and people who are able to reduce their type A behavior show lowered risk of CHD. We will discuss this therapy later in the chapter.

The immune system

Psychoneuroimmunology is the study of how the body's immune system is affected by stress and other psychological variables. By means of specialized cells called lymphocytes, the immune system protects the body from disease-causing microorganisms. It affects the individual's susceptibility to infectious diseases, allergies, cancers, and autoimmune disorders (that is, diseases such as rheumatoid arthritis, in which

the immune cells attack the normal tissue of the body). Stress may affect the immune system in several ways. Short-term stress appears to increase the strength of immune responses. Chronic stress, however, decreases immune functioning, in part because some of the biochemical released in the fight-or-flight-response, including cortisol, suppress the immune system if the stress response persists for long periods (Segerstrom & Miller, 2004).

If you've ever developed a cold during a time when you were facing a lot of stress, you have likely experienced the effects of stress on the immune system like the exhausted-looking woman in Figure 14.3. In one study, researchers exposed 400 healthy volunteers to a nasal wash containing one of five cold viruses or an innocuous salt solution (Cohen *et al.,* 1991). The participants answered questions about the number of stressful events they had experienced in the past year, the degree to which they felt able to cope with the demands of daily life, and the frequency with which they experienced negative emotions such as anger and depression. Based on these data, each participant was assigned a stress index ranging from 3 (lowest stress) to 12 (highest stress). The volunteers were examined daily for cold symptoms and for the presence of cold viruses or virus-specific antibodies in their upper respiratory secretions.

The majority of the virus-exposed volunteers showed signs of infection, but only about a third actually developed colds. The rates of viral infection and of actual cold symptoms increased in accordance with the reported stress levels. Compared with the lowest-stress group, volunteers who reported the highest stress were significantly more likely to become infected with the cold virus and almost twice as likely to develop a cold.

FIGURE 14.3 Stress and Colds. *Psychological stress is likely to make people more susceptible to colds and other illnesses because it weakens the immune system.*

Most studies of the effects of stress on the immune system look at individuals undergoing a particularly stressful event – such as academic pressure, bereavement, or marital disruption – and evaluate their immune system functioning (Delahanty *et al.,* 1998; Schneiderman *et al.,* 2005). For example, a study of people who survived Hurricane Andrew in 1992 found that those who experienced more damage to their homes or whose lives were more threatened by the storm showed poorer immune system functioning than people whose homes and lives had been safer (Ironson *et al.,* 1997). Similarly, following the 1994 Northridge earthquake in the Los Angeles area, people whose lives had been more severely disrupted showed more decline in immune system functioning than those who had not experienced as much stress as a result of the earthquake (Solomon *et al.,* 1997). People who worried more about the impact of the earthquake on their lives were especially likely to show detriments in natural killer cells, a type of T-cell that seeks out and destroys cells that have been infected with a virus (Segerstrom *et al.,* 1998).

It doesn't take a natural disaster to affect people's immune systems. Chronic everyday stress can also degrade immune system functioning. People who are caregivers to family members with dementia experience many stressors each day, including having to bathe and dress their loved one, having to answer their loved one's questions over and over, and having to ensure the safety of their loved one, who may wander off or engage in dangerous behavior such as turning the stove on and forgetting it. This stress of caregiving a dementia patient is related to diminished immune system functioning (Gouin *et al.,* 2012).

One factor that appears to be important is the extent to which an individual can control stress. Recall that controllability is one of the variables that determines the severity of stress. A series of animal studies demonstrated that uncontrollable shock has a much greater effect on the immune system than controllable shock (Laudenslager *et al.,* 1982). These experiments subjected rats to the learned helplessness paradigm (see the beginning of this chapter). One group could press a lever to turn off electric shocks. The other animals received an identical sequence of shocks, but their levers were ineffective (see Figure 14.4). In one study using this procedure, the investigators looked at how readily the rats' T-cells multiplied when challenged by an invader. (T-cells are lymphocytes that secrete chemicals that kill harmful cells, such as cancer cells.) They found that the T-cells from rats that could control the shock multiplied as readily as those from rats that were not stressed at all. T-cells from rats exposed to uncontrollable shock, on the other hand, multiplied only weakly. Thus, shock (stress) interfered with the immune response only in rats that could not control it (Laudenslager *et al.,* 1983).

In another study, the investigators implanted tumor cells into rats, gave them shocks, and recorded whether the rats'

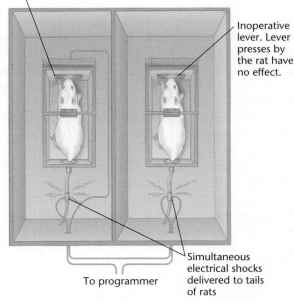

Operative lever. The rat can terminate a shock by pressing the lever in front of him.

Inoperative lever. Lever presses by the rat have no effect.

Simultaneous electrical shocks delivered to tails of rats

To programmer

FIGURE 14.4 Yoked Controls in a Stress Environment.
A series of electrical shocks are pre-programmed to be delivered simultaneously to the tails of the two male rats. The rat on the left can terminate a shock when it occurs by pressing the lever. The rat on the right has no control in the situation (lever is inoperative), but he is yoked to the first rat. That is, when the first rat receives a shock, the yoked rat simultaneously receives the same shock, and the shock remains on until the first rat presses his lever. The lever presses of the yoked rat have no effect on the shock sequence for either animal.

natural defenses rejected the cells or whether they developed into tumors. Only 27 per cent of the rats that were given uncontrollable shocks rejected the tumors, but 63 per cent of the rats that could turn the shocks off rejected the tumors – even though the rats received identical amounts of shock (Visintainer *et al.,* 1982).

Some research suggests that stress can affect the progression of the human immunodeficiency virus (HIV), which causes AIDS (Leserman, 2008). Much of this research has been conducted with gay men, who have disproportionately suffered from the AIDS epidemic. Many men have lost their partners and many close friends to AIDS, particularly before the antiretroviral drugs, which suppress the virus and slow the development of those with AIDS in those infected, were available. One study followed 96 gay men for over 9 years, and found that those who experienced more severe stressors, including deaths of close friends and partners, showed faster progression to AIDS (Leserman *et al.,* 1999, 2000, 2002). For every one-unit increase on an index of stress they experienced, their risk of developing an AIDS-related clinical condition (e.g., pneumocystis pneumonia) tripled. At the end of the study, 74 per cent of the men with high levels of stress developed AIDS, compared with 40 per cent low on stress.

Some gay men feel compelled to conceal their sexual orientation from others to avoid discrimination and rejection, and this can be a chronic stressor. A study of HIV-positive gay men found that those who concealed their identity showed a faster progression of disease than those who did not (Cole *et al.*, 1995). More generally, it shows that HIV-positive men who experienced declines in social support and increases in loneliness showed poorer immune-system control over the virus.

HIV is not just a disease of gay men, of course. World-wide, over 30 million people are infected with HIV (WHO, 2008). A study of 618 HIV-positive young people found those who experienced two or more stressful life events, such as a parent becoming seriously ill, a death in the family, or loss of home, were three times more likely than other participants to show immune system decline over the year they were followed (Howland *et al.*, 2007).

Even stresses experienced long before an individual is infected with HIV seem to increase risk for disease progression. One study followed 490 HIV-positive adult men and women for up to 41 months (Leserman *et al.*, 2007). Those with a history of trauma, including childhood physical or sexual abuse or neglect, or the murder of a family member, showed faster development of opportunistic infections and were more likely to die of AIDS-related causes than those without a history of trauma (Mugavero *et al.*, 2007).

Health-related behaviors

As we have already mentioned, certain health-related behaviors can greatly increase our susceptibility to illness. Smoking is one of the leading causes of cardiovascular disease and emphysema. A high-fat diet contributes to many forms of cancer as well as to cardiovascular disease. People who do not regularly engage in a moderate amount of exercise are at increased risk for heart disease and earlier death. Excessive alcohol consumption can lead to liver disease and cardiovascular disease and may contribute to some cancers. And failure to use condoms during sex significantly increases the risk of contracting HIV. Scientists estimate that most of the diseases people die from in industrialized countries are heavily influenced by health-related behaviors (Schneiderman *et al.*, 2005).

When we are stressed, we may be less likely to engage in healthy behaviors. Students taking exams stay up all night, often for several nights in a row. They may skip meals and snack on junk food. Many men whose wives have died do not know how to cook for themselves and therefore may eat poorly or hardly at all. In their grief, some bereaved individuals

Health-related behaviors, such as smoking, are affected by stress.

increase their rates of alcohol consumption and smoking. People under stress cease normal exercise routines and become sedentary. Thus, stress may indirectly affect health by reducing rates of positive health-related behaviors and increasing rates of negative behaviors.

Engaging in unhealthy behaviors may also increase a person's subjective sense of stress. Drinking too much alcohol on a regular basis can interfere with cognitive functioning; a person who consumes excessive amounts of alcohol cannot think as clearly or quickly as one who does not drink excessively. Excessive drinking can also induce lethargy, fatigue, and a mild or moderate sense of depression that makes it difficult to overcome stressful situations or just keep up with the demands of everyday life.

Similarly, people who do not get enough sleep show impairments in memory, learning, logical reasoning, arithmetic skills, complex verbal processing, and decision making.

Sleeping for only 5 hours per night for just 2 nights significantly reduces performance on math problems and creative thinking tasks. So, staying up late to prepare for an exam can actually decrease performance on the test (Wolfson, 2002).

Among people who already have a serious illness such as cancer or cardiovascular disease, stress can reduce their motivation or ability to engage in behaviors that are critical to their recovery or survival (Schneiderman *et al.*, 2005). For example, they may skip appointments with their physician or fail to take necessary medications. They may not follow diets that are essential for their health; for example, a diabetic may not control sugar intake. One study of people with CHD found that those who had experienced a traumatic stressor were less likely to be exercising and taking their medications, and more likely to be smoking compared to those who had not experienced a traumatic stressor. Studies of persons infected with HIV disease suggest that those under more stress are more likely to engage in unprotected sexual activity or intravenous drug use (Fishbein *et al.*, 1998).

In contrast, people who engage in a healthy lifestyle – eating a low-fat diet, drinking alcohol in moderation, getting enough sleep, and exercising regularly – often report that stressful events seem more manageable and that they feel more in control of their lives. Thus, engaging in healthy behaviors can help reduce the stressfulness of life as well as reducing the risk or progression of a number of serious diseases (Ingledew & McDonough, 1998).

INTERIM SUMMARY

- Psychophysiological disorders are physical disorders in which emotions are believed to play a central role.

- Stress can contribute to coronary heart disease.

- People with the type A behavior pattern tend to be hostile, aggressive, impatient individuals who are over-involved in their work. Studies of men and women show that people who exhibit this pattern – particularly the hostility component – are at increased risk for coronary heart disease.

- Psychoneuroimmunology is the study of how psychological factors can affect the immune system. Stress may impair the functioning of the immune system, increasing the risk of immune-related disorders.

- People under stress also may not engage in positive health-related behaviors, and this may lead to illness.

CRITICAL THINKING QUESTIONS

1 How can we help people with a serious disease like cancer change in ways that might slow the progress of the disease without making them feel that they are being blamed for having the disease?

2 What are some of your unhealthiest behaviors? What prevents you from changing them?

STRESS AND PSYCHOLOGICAL HEALTH

Stressful situations produce psychological reactions ranging from exhilaration (when the event is demanding but manageable) to anxiety, anger, discouragement, and depression. If the stressful situation continues, our emotions may switch back and forth among any of these, depending on the success of our coping efforts.

People who experience events that are beyond the normal range of human suffering (natural disasters, rape, kidnapping) sometimes develop a severe set of symptoms known as **post-traumatic stress disorder** (PTSD). PTSD is no longer classified in the DSM-5 Anxiety Disorders section but has its own section. Following the DSM-5 changes, there are four sets of symptoms of PTSD. The first is a repeated reliving of the trauma. People may dream every night of the trauma and become afraid to go to sleep. Even while awake, they may mentally relive the trauma so vividly that they begin to behave as if they were there. A former combat soldier, when he hears a jet flying low nearby, might hit the ditch, cover his head, and feel as though he is back in combat. A rape survivor might replay scenes from her trauma over and over, and see the face of her attacker in other men.

The second set is characterized by avoidance – people will avoid any situations, people, thoughts, or feelings that remind them of their trauma.

The third set is persistent negative alterations in cognitions and mood. This latter category, which retains most of the DSM-IV numbing symptoms, also includes new or reconceptualized symptoms, such as persistent negative emotional states. They may feel completely numb to the world, as if they have no emotional reactions to anything. People may feel detached and estranged from others and sense of their future is bleak.

The fourth set of symptoms indicates a chronic hyperarousal that retains most of the DSM-IV arousal symptoms such as sleep disturbances, difficulty in concentrating, and over-alertness but also includes irritable or aggressive behavior and reckless or self-destructive behavior.

Other symptoms are not part of the official criteria for diagnosing PTSD, but are common among trauma sufferers.

Some people feel terribly guilty about surviving a trauma when others did not, even if they could not have saved other people, a phenomenon called *survivor guilt*. Some people may alternate between being apathetic and withdrawn and being excessively angry and aggressive. PTSD sufferers may abuse alcohol and psychoactive drugs as a way to 'numb' themselves, and many are diagnosed with depression (see Chapter 15) as well as PTSD.

PTSD may develop immediately after the trauma, or it may be brought on by a minor stress experienced weeks, months, or even years later. It may last a long time. One of the largest natural disasters in recent history was the tsunami that struck south and southeast Asia on December 26 2004. It is estimated that over 280 000 people were killed, 27 000 remain missing and are assumed dead, and 1.2 million people were displaced. In the village of Tamil Nadu, India, 7983 people were killed, and 44 207 people had to be relocated to camps due to damage to their homes. Researchers found that 13 per cent of adults in this area were suffering from PTSD 2 months after the tsunami (Kumar *et al.*, 2007). A study of survivors of the tsunami from the western coastal regions of Phuket, Thailand found that 22 per cent had symptoms of PTSD 2 weeks after the disaster, and 30 per cent had symptoms of PTSD 6 months after the disaster (Tang, 2007).

Other recent natural disasters have also led to PTSD in many survivors. A study of survivors of an earthquake in Turkey found that 23 per cent of those who were at the epicenter had PTSD 14 months later, and 16 per cent had PTSD plus depression (Basoglu *et al.*, 2004). Similar rates of PTSD were found in survivors of a large earthquake in Taiwan (Lai *et al.*, 2004).

Culture and gender appear to interact in interesting ways to influence vulnerability to PTSD. One study compared random community samples of survivors of Hurricane Paulina, which hit Acapulco, Mexico, in 1997 to survivors of Hurricane Andrew, which hit Florida in the USA in 1992

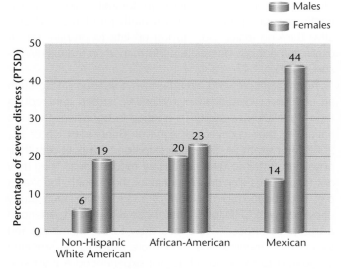

FIGURE 14.5 Cultural and Sex Differences in PTSD.

Sex differences in rates of PTSD were greatest among Mexican Americans, followed by non-Hispanic white Americans, then least among AfricanAmericans in a study of reactions to a hurricane.

(Norris *et al.*, 2001). These two hurricanes were similar in many ways, rated as Category 4 hurricanes and causing widespread property damage, physical injury, and death. Rates of PTSD symptoms were high in both countries. Women had more symptoms than men in both countries (see Figure 14.5), yet the difference in PTSD symptoms between Mexican women and men was much greater than the difference between American women and men. In addition, within the American sample, the difference in PTSD symptoms between non-Hispanic White women and men was significantly greater than the difference between African-American women and men.

The researchers suggest that the relative strength of traditional sex roles across these three cultures (Mexican, non-Hispanic white, and African-American) may have influenced the magnitude of sex differences in PTSD symptoms. (Historically, there has been more social pressure in Mexican culture than in American culture for women to be passive, self-sacrificing, and compliant and for men to be dominant, fearless, and strong (Vazquez-Nuttall *et al.*, 1987. This may have led to Mexican women feeling more helpless following a trauma and to be less able to get the material support they needed, compared with Mexican men.) Within American culture, there is some evidence that sex roles are more egalitarian among African-Americans than among non-Hispanic whites (Davenport & Yurick, 1991). Thus, African-American women did not suffer much more PTSD than African-American men.

Traumas caused by humans, such as sexual or physical assault, terrorist attacks, and war, may be even more likely to cause PTSD than natural disasters, for at least two reasons.

Survivors of wars and natural disasters often experience post-traumatic stress disorder.

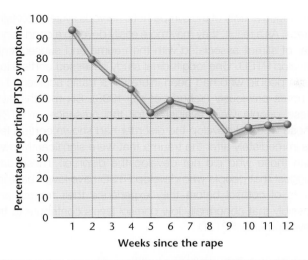

FIGURE 14.6 Post-Traumataic Symptoms in Rape. *Almost all women who have been raped show symptoms of PTSD severe enough to be diagnosed with PTSD in the first or second week following the rape. Over the 3 months following the rape, the percentage of women continuing to show PTSD declines. However, almost 50 per cent of women continue to be diagnosed with PTSD 3 months after a rape.*

First, such traumas challenge our basic beliefs about the goodness of life and other people, and when these beliefs are shattered, PTSD is more likely to occur (Janoff-Bulman, 1992). Second, human-caused disasters often strike individuals rather than whole communities, and suffering through a trauma alone seems to increase a person's risk of experiencing PTSD.

About 95 per cent of rape survivors experience post-traumatic stress symptoms severe enough to qualify for a diagnosis of the disorder in the first 2 weeks following the rape (see Figure 14.6). About 50 per cent still qualify for the diagnosis 3 months after the rape. As many as 25 per cent still suffer from PTSD 4 to 5 years after the rape (Faravelli *et al.*, 2004; Foa & Riggs, 1995; Resnick *et al.*, 1993).

PTSD became widely accepted as a diagnostic category because of difficulties experienced by war veterans. In World War I it was called 'shell shock' and in World War II 'combat fatigue.' Studies of soldiers have found that approximately 15 to 19 per cent of those deployed to Iraq and about 11 per cent of those deployed to Afghanistan could be diagnosed with PTSD (Erbes *et al.*, 2007; Hoge *et al.*, 2004; 2006).

The citizens of countries besieged by war and violence are also at high risk for PTSD. The Afghan people have endured decades of war and occupation, the repressive regime of the Taliban, and then the bombing of their country by the coalition forces after the attacks on the World Trade Center and the Pentagon in the USA. Thousands of Afghanis have been killed, injured, or displaced from their homes. Thousands still live in makeshift tents on a barren landscape without adequate food

and water. Research with Afghani citizens has found that approximately 42 per cent can be diagnosed with PTSD and some level of anxiety symptoms is present in 72 per cent (Cardozo *et al.*, 2004). Afghan women may be especially likely to suffer PTSD because the Taliban deprived them of even the most basic human rights, killed many of their husbands and other male relatives, and then made it impossible for them to survive without these men. A study of women living in Kabul under the Taliban regime found that 84 per cent had lost at least one family member in the war, 69 per cent reported that they or a family member had been detained and abused by Taliban militia, and 68 per cent reported extremely restricted social activities (Rasekh *et al.*, 1998). Forty-two per cent of these women were diagnosed with PTSD, and over 90 per cent of the women reported some symptoms of PTSD (see also Scholte *et al.*, 2004).

The wars in the former Yugoslavia begun in the 1990s were marked by 'ethnic cleansing' – the torture and slaughter of thousands and displacement of millions of former Yugoslavians. This campaign was one of the most brutal in history, with many atrocities, concentration camps, organized mass rapes, and neighbors murdering neighbors. This woman's story is far too common:

Case Study: A woman in her forties worked the family farm in a rural village until the day the siege began, when mortar shells turned most of their house to rubble. A few months before, she and her husband had sent their son away to be with relatives in Slovenia. The morning after the shelling, the Chetniks – Serbian nationalist forces – came and ordered everyone to leave their houses at once. Many neighbors and friends were shot dead before the woman's eyes. She and her husband were forced to sign over the title to their house, car, and bank deposits – and watched as the looting began. Looters included neighbors who were their friends. Over the next few days they traveled back from the Muslim ghetto to their land to feed the animals. One day, as she and her husband stood in the garden, the Chetniks captured them. Her husband was taken away with other men. For the next 6 months she did not know if he was dead or alive. She spent days on transport trains with no food or water, where many suffocated to death beside her. On forced marches she had to step over the dead bodies of friends and relatives. Once her group was forced across a bridge that was lined with Chetnik machine gunners randomly shooting to kill and ordering them to throw all valuables over the edge into nets. She spent weeks in severely deprived conditions in a big tent with many women and children, where constant sobbing could be heard. When she herself could not stop crying she thought that something had broken in her head and that she had gone 'crazy.' Now she says, 'I will never be happy again.' When alone, everything comes back to her. But when she is with others or busy doing chores, she can forget. 'My soul hurts inside, but I'm able to pull it together.' She is able to sleep without nightmares only by using a nightly ritual: 'I lie down and go through every step of the house in Bosnia – the stable, everything they took, the rugs, the horses, the doors. I see it all again.'

(Weine *et al.*, 1995, p. 540)

A study of Bosnian refugees conducted just after they resettled in the USA found that 65 per cent suffered from PTSD, with older refugees more vulnerable to PTSD than younger refugees (Weine *et al.*, 1995; see also Cardozo *et al.*, 2000). A follow-up study of these refugees one year later found that 44 per cent were still suffering from PTSD (Weine *et al.*, 1998).

PTSD sufferers show signs that their physiological responses to stress have become dysregulated. Studies using positron emission tomography (PET) have found some differences between PTSD sufferers and controls in activity levels in parts of the brain involved in the regulation of emotion and the fight-or-flight response (Balenger *et al.*, 2004; Nutt & Malizia, 2004). While imagining combat scenes, combat veterans with PTSD show increased blood flow in the anterior cingulate gyrus and the amygdala – areas of the brain that may play a role in emotion and memory. In contrast, combat veterans without PTSD did not show increases in blood flow in these regions while imagining combat scenes (see Figure 14.7). Some studies also show damage to the hippocampus among PTSD patients. The hippocampus is involved in memory. Damage to it may result in some of the memory problems that PTSD sufferers report.

It is not clear whether these neurobiological abnormalities in PTSD sufferers are a cause or a consequence of their disorder. Deterioration of the hippocampus could be the result of extremely high levels of cortisol at the time of the trauma. Interestingly, however, resting levels of cortisol among PTSD sufferers (when they are not being exposed to reminders of their trauma) tend to be lower than among people without PTSD (Yehuda, 2004). Because cortisol may act to shut down sympathetic nervous system activity after stress, the lower levels of cortisol among PTSD sufferers may result in

prolonged activity of the sympathetic nervous system following stress. As a result, they may more easily develop a conditioned fear of stimuli associated with the trauma and subsequently develop PTSD. One longitudinal study assessed cortisol levels in people who had been injured in a traffic accident 1 to 2 hours previously (Yehuda *et al.*, 1998). Six months later, these people were evaluated for the presence of PTSD. Those who did develop the disorder had shown cortisol levels immediately after the trauma that were significantly lower than those who did not develop the disorder. These data suggest that people who develop PTSD have lower baseline levels of cortisol before they experience their trauma and possibly that abnormally low cortisol levels contribute to the development of PTSD.

INTERIM SUMMARY

➲ Psychological responses to stress can include anxiety, apathy and depression, anger and aggression, and cognitive impairment.

➲ Some people who experience severe stress develop post-traumatic stress disorder (PTSD). The three sets of symptoms of PTSD include reliving the traumatic experience, emotional numbing and detachment, and chronic hyper-arousal.

➲ PTSD sufferers show evidence that their physiological responses to stress have become dysregulated.

CRITICAL THINKING QUESTIONS

1 What kinds of things can family members or friends do to help the survivor of a trauma cope as well as possible with the psychological aftermath of the trauma?

2 Do you think some people are especially prone to develop PTSD following a trauma? If so, why might they be more vulnerable?

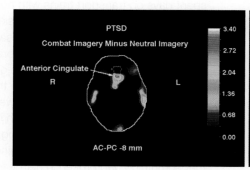
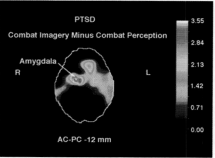

FIGURE 14.7 PTSD and Blood Flow in the Brain. *Studies using positron emission tomography show greater blood flow in the anterior cingulate and amygdala in combat veterans with PTSD than those without PTSD.*

APPRAISALS, COPING, AND HEALTH

Being under stress clearly increases your chances of problems with physical and psychological health. But people vary greatly in how they respond to stress. We all know people who are about to handle even extreme stress quite well. When they are hit with a major stressor, they bounce back quickly. They may even choose to put themselves in stressful circumstances, welcoming the challenge and chance to increase or demonstrate their skills. Others, however, crumble when confronted with even mild stressors, becoming physically ill or psychologically distressed. What accounts for these differences between people? Health psychologists have focused on people's appraisals of stressful circumstances and their coping styles as major contributors to their physical and psychological responses to stress.

Appraisals

When something happens – let's say a professor calls on you in class – you automatically interpret that event as stressful or not. This is known as *primary appraisal* (Lazarus & Folkman, 1984). Circumstances, such as whether you read the assignment for class, can determine whether an event is appraised as stressful. But people also differ in their general tendencies to appraise events as stressful or not. Once you do decide an event is a stressor, you determine if you can handle it or not, a thought process known as *secondary appraisal* (Lazarus & Folkman, 1984). Again, circumstances can play a role in secondary appraisal – if the professor is asking a question about material that isn't even covered in class, it's much harder for you to answer the question correctly. But people also have characteristic ways of thinking about whether they can handle the stressors in their lives as well.

Optimism/Pessimism

People who remain resilient when faced with stress tend to be optimistic – they believe that they can get through this experience and the future will generally be bright. On the other hand, people prone to pessimism, who tend to see negative events as their fault and likely to have wide-ranging future consequences, are more likely to crumble and give up in response to stress (Carver *et al.,* 2010; Rasmussen *et al.,* 2009).

A number of studies have found that pessimists recover more slowly from coronary bypass surgery and have more severe angina than optimists (Rasmussen *et al.,* 2009). One 8-year-long study of over 95 000 women who were healthy at the beginning of the study showed that pessimists were more likely to develop CHD, less likely to die from heart-related causes, and had lower total mortality due to all causes (Tindale *et al.,* 2009). Similarly, a study of Dutch elderly

people showed that those with relatively high levels of pessimism at the beginning of the study were more likely to die over the next 10 years (Giltay *et al.,* 2004).

How does pessimism affect health? People who are pessimistic tend to appraise events as more stressful (Lowe *et al.,* 2003). In turn, this greater sense of stress may contribute to poor health by causing the chronic arousal of the body's fight-or-flight response, resulting in the type of physiological damage discussed earlier. Several studies have found evidence for this. In one, the blood pressure of pessimists and optimists was monitored daily for 3 days. The pessimists had chronically higher blood pressure levels than the optimists across the 3 days (Raïkkonen *et al.,* 1999). Pessimism is also linked to poorer health behaviors. A study of patients with CHD found those who were more pessimistic were more likely to be engaging in risky health behaviors such as smoking and maintaining a poor diet, and in turn were more likely to show risk factors for further heart disease, such as obesity and high cholesterol (Cohen *et al.,* 2010).

The chronic physiological arousal associated with pessimism has also been linked to lowered immune system functioning. For example, a study of older adults found that those who were pessimistic had poorer immune system functioning than those who were optimistic (Kamen-Siegel *et al.,* 1991). In one study of 412 patients with HIV, those who were pessimistic at a baseline assessment had a greater load of the virus 18 months later than those who were less pessimistic (Milam *et al.,* 2004). Similarly, a study of gay men who were HIV-positive found that those who blamed themselves for negative events showed more decline in immune functioning over 18 months than those who engaged in less self-blaming attributions (Segerstrom *et al.,* 1996). Another study of gay men found that among both HIV-positive and HIV-negative men, those who were more pessimistic and fatalistic were less likely to engage in healthy behaviors, such as maintaining a proper diet, getting enough sleep, and

Older adults who are optimistic and upbeat may have better immune systems and engage in healthier behaviors.

exercising (Taylor *et al.,* 1992). This is particularly important for the HIV-positive men, because engaging in these behaviors can reduce the risk of developing AIDS. Thus, a pessimistic outlook may affect health directly, by reducing immune system functioning, or indirectly, by reducing a person's tendency to engage in health-promoting behavior.

Hardiness

Another line of research has focused on people who are most resistant to stress – who do not become physically or emotionally impaired even in the face of major stressful events (Kobasa, 1979; Maddi, 2006). This characteristic is referred to as **hardiness**. There are three components to hardiness: commitment, control, and challenge. Individuals high in commitment believe it is important to remain involved in events and people, no matter how stressful things become. Individuals high in control retain a belief in their ability to influence situations even in the face of obstacles. Individuals high in challenge see stresses as a normal part of living, opportunities to learn, develop, and grow in wisdom.

One longitudinal study followed business executives for 2 years and found that the executives whose attitudes toward life could be rated high on involvement, feelings of control, and positive responses to change remained healthier over time than men who scored low on these dimensions (Kobasa *et al.,* 1982). The most important factors appear to be a sense of control and commitment to goals (Cohen & Edwards, 1989). Other studies of women (Wiebe & McCallum, 1986) and persons symptomatic with HIV disease (Farber *et al.,* 2000) have also found that hardiness predicts better psychological and physical health.

Finding meaning

In a related line of work, researchers have been examining a somewhat surprising but heart-warming phenomenon: many people confronted with a major trauma say that they feel their lives have changed in positive ways as a result of their experiences. Studies of bereaved people, cancer patients, myocardial infarction patients, bone marrow transplant patients, stroke victims and their caregivers, and men testing positive for HIV find that, as a consequence of their experience, they feel their lives have more meaning and they have grown in important ways (for reviews, see Davis & Nolen-Hoeksema, in press; Helgeson *et al.,* 2006). Take, for example, this quote from a woman who recently lost someone she loved very dearly:

> I tend to look at it generally as if all the things that happen in my life are a gift, for whatever reason, or however they happen. It doesn't necessarily have to be only pleasant gifts, but everything that happens ... there's a meaning. I've had a lot of suffering in my life ... and through that I've learned a great deal. While I wouldn't want to go back and

Finding meaning in a loss can help people cope with it.

> relive that, I'm grateful for it because it makes me who I am. There's a lot of joys and sorrows, but they all enrich life.

(Nolen-Hoeksema & Larson, 1999, p. 143)

People often say that they feel they grew in character as a result of their experience, discovering new strengths they didn't know they had. They also say they gained a healthier perspective on what is important in their lives and made major changes in their lives based on this new perspective. Many people report that their relationships with friends and family members are deeper and more meaningful now.

In turn, finding meaning or positive growth in a trauma seems to help people adjust, both physically and psychologically. Several studies have found that people who find meaning or growth in **traumatic events** show less depression and anxiety after the event than others. For example, in a study of recently bereaved people, Davis and colleagues (1998) showed that those who found some meaning in their loss or felt they grew positively showed less depression and fewer symptoms of PTSD than those who did not over the 18 months following their loss. It did not matter to psychological health what type of meaning or growth people found, as long as they found some sort of meaning or growth in their experience.

Some studies also suggest that finding meaning is related to the course of physiological disease. For example, Affleck and colleagues found that men who had had a heart attack and who felt they had grown personally as a result of the heart attack, such as changing their philosophy of life or values, were less likely to have a subsequent heart attack and had less cardiac disease over the next 8 years (Affleck *et al.*, 1987a). In a study of men who were HIV-positive, Bower and colleagues found that those who had found some meaning in the loss of a friend or partner to AIDS maintained healthier immune systems (indexed by CD4 T helper cells) and were less likely to die from AIDS over a 2- to 3-year follow-up period (Bower *et al.*, 1998).

Why are some people able to find meaning or growth in trauma and others do not? Optimism seems to play a role. Optimists are more likely to report positive changes, benefits, or growth following stressful events (see Helgeson *et al.*, 2006). Similarly, hardy people appear to perceive more benefits from their stressful experiences. For example, a study of US soldiers participating in a peacekeeping mission to Bosnia showed that those who scored high on measures of hardiness during their deployment were more likely to believe they had obtained benefits, such as personal growth, from their work in Bosnia than those who were not hardy (Britt *et al.*, 2001).

Coping

When faced with stressful circumstances, people engage in a variety of **coping** behaviors. Coping strategies have been broadly divided into those that focus on changing the stressful situation or its consequences, referred to as **problem-focused coping**, and those that focus on alleviating the emotions associated with the stressful situation, called **emotion-focused coping** (Lazarus & Folkman, 1984). When dealing with a stressful situation, most people use both problem-focused and emotion-focused coping.

Problem-focused coping

There are many strategies for solving problems. First, you must define the problem. Then you can generate alternative solutions and weigh the costs and benefits of the alternatives. Eventually, you must choose between alternative solutions and then act upon your choice. Problem-focused strategies can also be directed inward: you can change something about yourself instead of changing the environment. You can change your goals, find alternative sources of gratification, or learn new skills in inward-directed strategies. How skillfully people employ these strategies depends on their range of experiences and capacity for self-control.

Suppose you receive a warning that you are about to fail a course required for graduation. You might confer with the lecturer, devise a work schedule to fulfill the requirements, and then follow it, or you might decide that you cannot fulfill the requirements in the time remaining and sign up to retake the course. All of these actions are problem-focused methods of coping.

People who tend to use problem-focused coping in stressful situations are less likely to experience depression or anxiety in response to stressful situations (see Aldao *et al.*, 2010; Taylor & Stanton, 2007). Of course, people who are less distressed may find it easier to use problem-focused coping. But longitudinal studies show that problem-focused coping leads to shorter periods of distress, even taking into account people's initial levels of distress. In addition, therapies that teach distressed people to use problem-focused coping can be effective in helping them react more adaptively to stressors (Nezu *et al.*, 1989). Other studies have shown that people who use more problem-focused coping had better health following heart surgery (Scheier *et al.*, 2003).

Emotion-focused coping

People engage in emotion-focused coping to prevent their negative emotions from overwhelming them and making them unable to take action to solve their problems. They also use emotion-focused coping when a problem is uncontrollable (deGroot *et al.*, 1997).

We try to cope with our negative emotions in many ways. Some researchers have divided these into behavioral strategies and cognitive strategies (see Skinner *et al.*, 2003). Behavioral strategies include engaging in physical exercise, seeking emotional support from friends, and using alcohol or other drugs. Cognitive strategies often involve reappraising the situation ('My boss yelled at me because he's tired, not because I did anything wrong'). Obviously, we would expect some behavioral and cognitive strategies to be adaptive and others (such as drinking heavily) to merely cause more stress.

One strategy that appears to help people adjust emotionally and physically to a stressor is seeking emotional support from others (Hallaraker *et al.*, 2001; Pakenham *et al.*, 2007). For example, Taylor *et al.* (2006) found that young adults who had grown up in supportive families showed less activity in certain areas of the brain to emotionally provocative photos, suggesting that they were less physiologically reactive to emotional stress.

The quality of the social support a person receives after experiencing a trauma strongly influences the impact of that support on the individual's health, however (Taylor, 2007; Warwick *et al.*, 2004). Some friends or relatives can be burdens instead of blessings in times of stress. People whose social networks are characterized by a high level of conflict tend to show poorer physical and emotional health after a major stressor such as bereavement (Windholz *et al.*, 1985). Conflicted social relationships may affect physical health through the immune system. Kiecolt-Glaser *et al.*, (1998) found that newlywed couples who became hostile and negative toward each other while discussing a marital problem showed greater decreases in four indicators of immune system functioning than couples who remained calm and non-hostile in discussing marital problems. Couples who became hostile during these discussions also showed elevated blood pressure for a longer period than those who did not become hostile.

On the other hand, talking with supportive others about negative emotions and important issues in one's life appears to have positive effects on health (e.g., Panagopoulou *et al.,* 2006). When we don't have a supportive other to talk with, many of us write about our concerns in diaries or journals, or in blogs or other social media outlets. A series of studies by researcher James Pennebaker (2007) suggests that writing about one's traumas has positive effects on health. In one study, 50 healthy undergraduates were randomly assigned to write either about the most traumatic and upsetting events in their lives or about trivial topics for 20 minutes on 4 consecutive days. Blood samples were taken from the students on the day before they began writing, on the last day of writing, and 6 weeks after writing, and it was tested for several markers of immune system functioning. The number of times the students visited the college health center over the 6 weeks after the

Studies suggest that writing down one's traumas or problems can have a positive effect on health.

writing task was also recorded and compared with the number of health center visits the students had made before the study. Students who revealed their personal traumas in essays showed more positive immune system functioning and visited the health center less frequently than students in the control group (Pennebaker *et al.,* 1988). In contrast, the group who wrote about trivial events experienced a slight increase in health center visits and a decrease in immune response, for unknown reasons.

Expressive writing may also help patients who have had a heart attack. Wilmott *et al.* (2011) randomly assigned individuals who had recently had a heart attack to write about their thoughts and feelings about their attack or in a neutral way about daily events. Over the next 5 months, those who wrote about their heart attack had fewer cardiac symptoms, needed fewer medical appointments, and had lower blood pressure than those who wrote about neutral events had fewer cardiac symptoms, needed fewer medical appointments and had lower blood pressure than those who wrote about neutral events.

Pennebaker (2007) believes that writing is helpful because it assists people in finding meaning in the events that happen to them and helps them understand them. Finding meaning and understanding then reduces the negative emotions people feel about events and may therefore reduce the physiological wear and tear associated with chronic negative emotions.

While some people talk with others or write about their stressful circumstances, others attempt to push thoughts and feelings about their stressors out of conscious awareness, a strategy that is referred to as avoidant coping. Avoidant coping has been linked with several health related problems, such as greater pain (Rosenberger *et al.*, 2004) and compromised recovery of function following surgical procedures (Stephens *et al.,* 2002), lower likelihood of remission in depressed patients (Cronkite *et al.,* 1998), lower adherence to medical regimes and subsequently greater viral load in HIV-positive individuals (Weaver *et al.,* 2005), more risky behaviors in HIV-positive injection drug users (Avants *et al.,* 2001), and increased physical symptoms among AIDS caregivers (Billings *et al.,* 2000). Avoidant coping also predicts chronic disease progression and/or mortality people with cancer (Epping-Jordan *et al.,* 1994), HIV infection (Leserman *et al.,* 2000), congestive heart failure (Murberg *et al.,* 2004), and rheumatoid arthritis (Evers *et al.,* 2003).

The apparent opposite of avoidant coping is rumination, chronically thinking about how bad we feel, worrying about the consequences of the stressful event, or repeatedly talking about how bad things are without taking any action to change them. A number of studies have found that people who ruminate in response to stressors are more likely to develop emotional and physical disorders than those who do not (Nolen-Hoeksema *et al.,* 2008). For example, one longitudinal study of recently bereaved people found that those who ruminated in response to their grief were depressed for longer periods (Nolen-Hoeksema & Larson, 1999). Another

CUTTING EDGE RESEARCH USING NEW MEDIA TO IMPROVE PEOPLE'S HEALTH

Susan Nolen-Hoeksema, Yale University

The explosion of new media in recent decades has led to many innovations in the delivery of interventions designed to improve people's emotional and physical health. Technologies such as personal digital assistants (PDAs) and ambulatory heart rate monitors provide opportunities to gather information about people's behaviors (such as diet, exercise, and medication use) and physiology in real time. This information can then be used by physicians to design more personalized interventions for patients that match both the patient's physiological needs and his or her behavioral habits.

The Internet is probably the new technology with the greatest impact on health. Millions of people around the world get health information from the Internet every day. The quality of this information varies greatly, however. Physicians are increasingly facing questions or beliefs from their patients that come from misinformation gathered from the Internet. For example, a patient may read about an experimental drug on the Internet and ask his or her physician to prescribe it, but that drug may not be appropriate for the patient, or may not be adequately enough tested that the physician is willing to prescribe it.

The Internet can be used to great benefit, however, as a means of delivering high-quality health information and actual interventions to change people's behavior in ways that improve their health. Moreover, Internet-based interventions can be delivered to individuals who might not have access to in-person behavior-change programs, because none are available in their geographic region or because they do not have the means to pay for them. Over half the population of most industrialized countries have access to the Internet, and the majority of Internet users say they get health information off the web (Vandelanotte *et al.*, 2007). Controlled studies of the effectiveness of these interventions give hope that they can be effective in helping people change their behaviors in ways that improve their health.

Many Internet-based behavioral interventions aim to increase people's exercise and improve their diets. Regular physical exercise significantly decreases risk for cardiovascular disease, diabetes, and several forms of cancer. Yet, most people do not engage in regular exercise. Similarly, eating fresh fruits and vegetables every day reduces chances of several major illnesses. Yet, the diets of people around the world are increasingly filled with high fat, high sugar, low nutrition foods (Brownell & Horgen, 2004). As a result, rates of obesity are sky-rocketing, especially in developed countries. Intensive, in-person programs to get people to increase exercise and to improve their diets work, but are expensive, time-consuming, and simply not available to many people. The Internet provides the opportunity to deliver exercise and nutrition programs to large segments of the population at a relatively low cost.

One such program was initially designed by the multinational corporation General Electric, which sought to improve the health of its workforce. Employees were invited by email to participate in the '5-10-25' program, to increase their physical exercise to 10 000 steps per day or 30 minutes of moderate-intensity physical exercise, to eat five servings of fruits and vegetables per day, and to lose weight if they were significantly overweight. Employees who agreed to participate completed an online assessment of their current behaviors and physical needs, and then, based on their profile, received regular emails encouraging their progress in the program and e-newsletters with health tips and case studies of employees who had made major behavioral changes. They were given telephone and email access to nutrition and fitness coaches who could answer their questions and provide personalized advice. Chat rooms were established for employees to discuss fitness and nutrition with each other. The Weight Watchers program was made available online. The company even created a 'video reality series' that followed two employees who participated in the program.

An evaluation of 2498 employees across 53 nations who participated in the program for about 8 months showed that these employees had significant increases in physical activity and the consumption of fruits and vegetables (Pratt *et al.*, 2006). They also lost four to five pounds weight over the period of the program.

Interventions to improve health behaviors are increasingly being delivered over the Internet.

A review of 15 Internet-based programs designed to improve physical activity and diet found that the majority of programs do result in positive outcomes for participants, compared to control groups (Vandelanotte *et al.*, 2007). The gains tend to be relatively modest, and short-term if the programs are not continued. Across thousands or even millions of people, however, the public health impact of these programs is potentially great.

Internet-based programs have been shown to reduce smoking behavior in adults (Japunitch *et al.*, 2006; Munoz *et al.*, 2006) and teens (Woodruf *et al.*, 2007). Recently, the Internet has been used to deliver cognitive-behavioral psychotherapy for depression to adults in developing countries who have no access to psychotherapy, but are given access to the Internet (Christensen *et al.*, 2004; Munoz, personal communication). Other types of media, such as television shows (novellas) designed to positively influence people's health behavior, are showing effects around the world (Bandura, 2006). It seems that health care professionals are learning to harness the power of new media.

found that individuals more prone to ruminate had more symptoms of depression and PTSD after an earthquake than those not prone to ruminate (Nolen-Hoeksema & Morrow, 1991). In contrast, individuals who used pleasant or constructive activities to improve their mood and regain a sense of control experienced short and mild periods of depression and anxiety.

Rumination also may impair physical health. An experimental study found that individuals induced to ruminate after experiencing a stressful event in the lab showed higher blood pressure and a slower return to their baseline blood pressure than individuals not induced to ruminate (Glynn *et al.*, 2002). Studies of breast cancer patients find that women who tend to ruminate waited an average of 2 months longer to contact their physician after finding a breast lump (Lyubomirsky *et al.*, 2006) and report more distressing physical symptoms while being treated for their cancer (Segerstrom *et al.*, 2003).

> ➲ People who take active steps to solve problems are less likely to experience depression and illness following negative life events.
>
> ➲ People who seek social support or write about their traumas tend to adjust better to stress, whereas people who use avoidance or rumination in response to negative events tend to experience more distress and poorer physical health.

CRITICAL THINKING QUESTIONS

1 In what way might the environment in which a child is raised affect the development of his or her coping strategies?

2 How might you differentiate between people who repress or deny that they are distressed and people who really do not experience much distress in the face of difficult events?

INTERIM SUMMARY

➲ Primary appraisal is the determination of whether an event is stressful or not. Secondary appraisal is the determination of whether we can handle an event we've judged to be stressful.

➲ Optimistic people show better immune system functioning and engage in healthier behaviors compared to pessimistic people.

➲ Hardy people tend to see stressful events as challenges and have a strong sense of personal control; these characteristics may protect against the development of illness in the face of stress.

➲ People who are able to find meaning in a traumatic event are less likely to develop emotional problems.

➲ Coping strategies are divided into problem-focused strategies and emotion-focused strategies. In addition, emotion-focused strategies can be divided into behavioral and cognitive strategies.

MANAGING STRESS

People can learn a number of techniques to reduce the negative effects of stress on the body and the mind. In this section, we discuss some behavioral and cognitive techniques that have been shown to help people reduce the effects of stress. We then discuss in detail how these techniques are applied to reduce type A behavior and CHD.

Behavioral techniques

Among the behavioral techniques that help people control their physiological responses to stressful situations are biofeedback, relaxation training, meditation, and aerobic exercise.

Biofeedback

In **biofeedback** training, individuals receive information (feedback) about an aspect of their physiological state and then attempt to alter that state. For example, in a procedure for learning to control tension headaches, electrodes are attached to the participant's forehead so that any movement in the forehead muscle can be electronically detected, amplified, and fed back to the person as an auditory signal. The signal, or tone, increases in pitch when the muscle contracts and decreases when it relaxes. By learning to control the pitch of the tone, the individual learns to keep the muscle relaxed. (Relaxation of the forehead muscle usually ensures relaxation of scalp and neck muscles as well.) After 4 to 8 weeks of biofeedback training, the participant learns to recognize the onset of tension and to reduce it without feedback from the machine. An analysis of 94 studies of biofeedback training found that it is consistently effective in the treatment of migraine and tension headaches (Nestoriuc et al., 2008).

Relaxation training

Relaxation training involves teaching people techniques to deeply relax their muscles and slow down and focus their thoughts. Physiological processes that are controlled by the autonomic nervous system, such as heart rate and blood pressure, have traditionally been assumed to be automatic and not under voluntary control. However, laboratory studies have demonstrated that people can learn to modify heart rate and blood pressure. The results of these studies have led to relaxation procedures for treating patients with high blood pressure (hypertension). One procedure is to show patients a graph of their blood pressure while it is being monitored and to teach them techniques for relaxing different muscle groups. Patients are instructed to tense their muscles (for example, to clench a fist or tighten the abdomen), release the tension, and notice the difference in sensation. By starting with the feet and ankle muscles and progressing through the body to the muscles that control the neck and face, patients learn to modify muscular tension. This combination of biofeedback with relaxation training has proved effective in lowering blood pressure for some individuals (Mukhopadhyay & Turner, 1997; Nestoriuc et al., 2008).

Exercise

Another factor that is important in controlling stress is physical fitness. Individuals who regularly engage in aerobic exercise (any sustained activity that increases heart rate and oxygen consumption, such as jogging, swimming, or cycling) show significantly lower heart rates and blood pressure in response to stressful situations than others (Friedman & Martin, 2007). In turn, physically fit people are less likely to become physically ill following stressful events than people who were not fit. Because of these findings, many stress management programs also emphasize physical fitness.

Exercise is not only good for physical health. People who are physically active and exercise are less likely to develop psychological problems like depression in response to stressful circumstances (Lindwall et al., 2011). Getting people to increase their physical exercise has been shown in multiple studies to be as effective as medication or psychotherapy in preventing and reducing symptoms in people who are already depressed (Mead et al., 2009).

Cognitive techniques

People who are able to control their physiological or emotional responses through biofeedback and relaxation training in the laboratory will have more difficulty doing so in actual stressful situations, particularly if they continue to interact in ways that make them tense. Consequently, an additional approach to stress management focuses on changing the individual's cognitive responses to stressful situations. **Cognitive behavior therapy** attempts to help people identify the kinds of stressful situations that produce their physiological or emotional symptoms and alter the way they cope with these situations. For example, a man who suffers from tension headaches would be asked to keep a record of their occurrence and rate the severity of each headache and the circumstances in which it occurred. Next he would be taught how to monitor his responses to these stressful events and asked to record his feelings, thoughts, and behavior prior to, during, and following the event. After a period of self-monitoring, certain relationships often become evident among situational variables (for example, criticism by a supervisor or co-worker), thoughts ('I can't do anything right'), and emotional, behavioral, and physiological responses (depression, withdrawal, and headache).

The next step is trying to identify the expectations or beliefs that might explain the headache reactions (for example, 'I expect to do everything perfectly, so the slightest criticism upsets me' or 'I judge myself harshly, become depressed, and end up with a headache'). The final and most difficult step is trying to change something about the stressful situation, the individual's way of thinking about it, or the individual's behavior. The options might include finding a less stressful job, recognizing that the need to perform perfectly leads to unnecessary anguish over errors, and learning to behave more assertively in interactions instead of withdrawing.

Biofeedback, relaxation training, exercise, and cognitive therapy have all proved useful in helping people control their physiological and emotional responses to stress. Because the complex demands of everyday life often require flexible coping skills, being able to relax may not be an effective method of coping with some of life's stresses. Programs for stress management frequently employ a combination of biofeedback, relaxation training, exercise, and cognitive modification techniques.

Modifying type A behavior

A combination of cognitive and behavioral techniques has been shown to reduce type A behavior (Friedman et al., 1994). The participants were more than 1000 individuals who

SEEING BOTH SIDES

ARE THERE UNIVERSAL OR DISTINCT REACTIONS TO COPING WITH STRESS?

THERE ARE UNIVERSAL COPING REACTIONS PRESENT ACROSS POPULATIONS

Roslyn Thomas, Webster University, Geneva

So which is it? Are you likely to cope with life's unexpected stressors in *the same way* as your classmates or are you likely to respond *individually* to these challenges? Are there universal coping strategies we all access when stressed or are our reactions unique and based on our personal context?

I argue for the first option by remembering that our brains have not changed fundamentally over the last 10 000 years. Nicholson (1998) applies evolutionary psychology to his proposal: our brains are biologically hardwired to react in a certain way to stress. It's not that we are all identical underneath, but we seem to have inherited inborn and universal aspects of behavior – something like an *a priori* deep structure. Considering these structures may shed light on why we sometimes react to stress in less-than-helpful ways. If our brains are hardwired to respond automatically – that is, involuntarily – to overwhelming stressors, the mobilization of energy can cut us off from rational analysis. This can be fortunate for us as in a do-or-die, survival-focused environment, human beings need to focus on the bad news first. As the body signals a life or death situation, we respond automatically to flee, freeze, or with the impulse to fight. In this light, both ways of dealing with stress – 'avoidance-oriented' and 'approach-oriented' (Weaver, *et al.*, 2005) – are really metaphors for cognitive and emotional activity that is oriented either *toward* or *away from* threatening situations. Again, these are automatic and are intended to be life-preserving.

Developmental psychiatrist, Siegel (2012), describes how these interactions affect us interpersonally – how clusters of neurons in the brain-stem are activated when an event demands a quick mobilization of energy through the brain and body. Working together with the limbic system and the higher cortical regions, the brain-stem determines our state of arousal and regulates our response to perceived stressors. When on high alert, we secrete a hormone that stimulates the adrenal glands to release cortisol and so mobilize us to flee, freeze, or fight in the face of danger. Although highly adaptive in the short term, a chronic presence of cortisol in our system makes it all but impossible to access coping strategies against the stressor.

So our ancestors had a legitimate use for the universal flight, freeze, or fight survival responses. These instinctive responses are virtually identical in all mammals and are not under our conscious control. Rather, they are predictable response patterns that cut across a variety of contexts. In light of this it is crucial to find a way to soothe reactive limbic firing and rebalance emotions originating from the amygdala and the overstimulated hypothalamus. According to Nicholson (1998) our inability to regulate efficiently explains why an evolutionary mechanism of basic survival has become the substance of sleepless nights and anxiety-filled days.

My own research findings (Thomas, 2008) confirm that when caregivers are exposed to critical incidents, emergencies, or wars, they become vulnerable to mental health risks and challenges. My sample of humanitarian workers working in war zones found that exposure to violence led to many feeling as if their identity was being stripped down and shorn away. When hyper-aroused, individuals struggled to regulate affect by soothing the limbic firing through logical thinking and/or social support. They found it difficult to address the existential questions brought on by profoundly disturbing experience. From a mental health perspective, intensely stressful situations can be dangerous times, characterized by an inability to access the executive, decision-making functions of our more developed frontal cortex.

While we know that we have inherited hardwired circuits from our ancestors that turn on our emotional radar in response to stressors, we are not slaves to our biology; and we do well to use another evolutionary ability – what Siegel (2010) refers to as interpersonal neurobiology, or 'mindsight.' This is a kind of focused attention that helps us see the internal workings of our own minds. This subsequent capacity to name events through reflective conversation can lead to an integrated rebalancing of right and left hemisphere brain functioning. Logical cognitive strategies can then intentionally override the limbic states so that we keep our automatic emotional responses within manageable boundaries. We can actually learn how to rewire the brain and establish new neural connections resulting in less hyper-arousal.

In summary, then, people display patterned, predictable biological responses to distressing sights, sounds and situations. We do well to be aware of these so that we do not become wholly overwhelmed by them.

SEEING BOTH SIDES

ARE THERE UNIVERSAL OR DISTINCT REACTIONS TO COPING WITH STRESS?

THERE ARE DISTINCT REACTIONS FOR POPULATIONS UNDER EXTREME STRESS

Erik Mansager, Webster University, Geneva

While I am taking the other side of the argument, I agree that when stresses mount, we can all feel a little anxious. It matters little whether these are good stressors or bad. Your autonomic nervous system is unaware whether you're dreading final exams or are excited about the celebration afterward. It tends to shift into overdrive when we face either extreme. As Dr Thomas points out, this is because our biological basics are set for survival – like keeping ourselves from being eaten ('freezing' in order not to be seen, or 'fleeing' in fear), or from being waylaid by the hunter-gatherers down the road ('fighting' in anger). Still, the evolutionary freeze-flight-fight response needed in life-death situations is not the whole story. We also evolved the ability to express individualized responses. It is this individuality that assists us to respond outside of our instinctual patterns. When we manage to activate the newer structures of our evolved brain – that is, engage our neo-cortex for problem-solving – we do so in ways that may impact our mental and physical health directly.

The way we puzzle individually through stressors, involves trait-like constructs (1) that bias our thinking and behaving, (2) that vary from individual to individual, and (3) that tend to be stable over time (McCrae *et al.,* 1986). We call these characteristics our personality – the means we use to develop patterned ways of responding to the world. This is a give-and-take between ourselves and the stressors we encounter. The stressors we experience form how we make sense of life; our personalities influence precisely how and what we experience as stressors, how we look at the world and make meaning out of it.

We moderate our automatic responses by thinking and reappraising as a healthy alternative to automatically suffering from the stresses we encounter. It takes effort and learning to think clearly. Learning to think about stressors also has some evolutionary pitfalls. Even though we have been using our neo-cortex for millennia, we don't always know when to stop; stop thinking that is. If a little thinking helps, our

compensatory selves (Adler & Brett, 2009) sometimes think that a *lot* of thinking will be better. *Au contraire!* The looping pattern of thought – thinking that emphasizes no way through the negative outcomes of the awful things we face – is a precursor of depression. This looping is called the rumination tendency – a manner of going from negative to negative without relief (Watkins *et al.,* 2007).

It isn't our cognitive abilities alone that settle the matter of stress because a ruminating thinking style can *add* to the stress. Taylor and Stanton's research (2007) indicates that taking a more productive way such as the path of problem-focused coping can actually reduce depression as a response to stress. Another research example on the effectiveness of problem-focused coping is offered by Arthur Nezu and his colleagues (Nezu *et al.,* 2006). They suggest thinking in terms of what it takes to 'adapt' to the stressful situation: ADAPT **A**ttitude – i.e., enhance your problem-solving capacity, **D**efine – i.e., describe your problem and set realistic goals, **A**lternatives – i.e., generate alternative solutions, **P**redict – i.e., consider the consequences and develop a plan for solutions, and **T**ry – i.e., check out the plan and determine if it works.

So, today's investigations focus on specific responses to each stressful context in place of general coping strategies. We no longer seek universal ways to deal with stress. Research considers the individual differences in personality traits that affect ways of coping. Individual coping ability develops with the help of characteristics actively shaped by life experiences (Holmberg *et al.,* 2004). Whether we apply this learning to a successful interaction depends on our creative self-expression or personality.

I conclude that while people display both patterned, predictable biological responses to distressing sights, sounds, and situations, there may be enormous differences in reactions. Both the universal aspect that our biology dictates when we are under stress, and our cultural context and our personal choices – that is our personality dispositions – reciprocally influence our psychological life. Dr Thomas and I agree that a strictly 'either–or' view of how we cope with stress is inconsistent with the facts. Instead by looking more carefully at both the universal and individual responses to stress we can enrich coping styles.

had experienced at least one heart attack. Participants in the treatment group were helped to reduce their sense of time urgency by practicing standing in line (a situation that type A individuals find extremely irritating) and using the opportunity to reflect on things that they do not normally have time to think about, to watch people, or to strike up a conversation with a stranger. Treatment also included helping participants learn to express themselves without exploding at people and to alter certain specific behaviors (such as interrupting others or talking or eating hurriedly). Therapists helped the participants re-evaluate certain beliefs (such as the notion that success depends on the quantity of work produced) that might lead to urgent and hostile behavior. Finally, participants found ways to make their home and work environments less stressful (such as reducing the number of unnecessary social engagements).

The critical dependent variable in this study was the occurrence of another heart attack. By the end of the study four-and-a-half years later, the experimental group had a heart attack recurrence rate almost half that of control participants who were not taught how to alter their lifestyles. Clearly, learning to modify type A behavior was beneficial to these participants' health (Friedman et al., 1994).

Like other research described in this chapter, this study was based on the premise that the mind and the body influence each other. Simple models of how stress affects health are being replaced by complex models that explain how biological, psychological, and social factors intertwine to create disease or health. As we have seen, the body has characteristic physiological reactions to stress. For people with pre-existing biological vulnerabilities, such as a genetic predisposition to heart disease, these physiological reactions to stress can cause deterioration in health. Yet an individual's perception of

stress is determined by characteristics of events in the environment and by his or her personal history, appraisals of the event, and coping styles. Thus, the extent to which the individual experiences psychological distress or ill-health following potentially stressful situations is determined by the biological and psychological vulnerabilities and strengths he or she brings to these situations.

INTERIM SUMMARY

➔ Biofeedback and relaxation training attempt to teach people how to control their physiological responses by learning to recognize tension and reduce it through deep muscle relaxation and concentration.

➔ Exercise can help people cope with stress over the long term.

➔ Cognitive behavior therapy attempts to help people recognize and modify their cognitive and behavioral responses to stress.

➔ Type A behavior can be changed through behavioral and cognitive techniques, resulting in reduced risk of coronary heart disease (CHD).

CRITICAL THINKING QUESTIONS

1 Some people claim to be 'addicted to stress.' If this is possible, what might it mean to be addicted to stress?

2 What do you expect would be the greatest challenges to helping a type A person change his or her behavior?

CHAPTER SUMMARY

① Stress refers to experiencing events that are perceived as endangering one's physical or psychological well-being. These events are usually referred to as stressors, and people's reactions to them are termed stress responses. The controllability, predictability, and duration of events contribute to their being perceived as stressful.

② Some people develop learned helplessness, which is characterized by passivity and inaction, and the inability to see opportunities to control one's environment.

③ The body reacts to stress with the fight-or-flight response. The sympathetic nervous system causes increased heart rate, elevated blood pressure, dilated pupils, and release of extra sugar from the liver. The adrenal-cortical system causes the release of adreno-

corticotropic hormone (ACTH), which stimulates the release of cortisol in the blood.

④ These reactions are part of a general adaptation syndrome, a set of responses displayed by all organisms in response to stress. The syndrome consists of three phases: alarm, resistance, and exhaustion.

⑤ Stress may affect health directly by creating chronic over-arousal of the sympathetic division of the autonomic nervous system or the adrenal-cortical system or by impairing the immune system. People under stress also may not engage in positive health-related behaviors, and this may lead to illness. Psychophysiological disorders are physical disorders in which emotions are believed to play a central role.

6 Stress can contribute to coronary heart disease (CHD). People with the type A behavior pattern tend to be hostile, aggressive, impatient individuals who are over-involved in their work. Studies of men and women show that people who exhibit this pattern are at increased risk for CHD.

7 Psychoneuroimmunology is the study of how psychological factors can affect the immune system. Stress may impair the functioning of the immune system, increasing the risk of immune-related disorders.

8 Some people develop post-traumatic stress disorder (PTSD) following severe stressful events. PTSD is characterized by reliving the trauma, emotional numbing and hyper-arousal.

9 People's appraisals or interpretations of events affect their physical and psychological responses to them. Pessimistic people tend to fare worse than optimistic people physically and psychologically in response to stress. Hardy people tend to see stressful events as challenges and have a strong sense of personal control, characteristics that may protect against the development of illness in the face of stress. People who are able to find meaning in a traumatic event are less likely to develop emotional problems.

10 Coping strategies are divided into problem-focused strategies and emotion-focused strategies. People who take active steps to solve problems are less likely to experience depression and illness following negative life events. Reaching out for social support, and expressive writing, have also been linked to more positive adaptation to stress. People who use rumination or avoidance strategies to cope with negative emotions show more physical and psychological problems after negative events.

11 Biofeedback and relaxation training attempt to teach people how to control their physiological responses by learning to recognize tension and reduce it through deep muscle relaxation and concentration.

12 Exercise can help people cope with stress over the long term.

13 Cognitive behavior therapy attempts to help people recognize and modify their cognitive and behavioral responses to stress.

14 Type A behavior can be changed through behavioral and cognitive techniques, resulting in reduced risk of CHD.

CORE CONCEPTS

behavioral medicine	fight-or-flight response	traumatic events
stress	general adaptation syndrome	coping
stressors	psychophysiological disorders	problem-focused coping
stress responses	coronary heart disease	emotion-focused coping
controllability	type A pattern	biofeedback
predictability	psychoneuroimmunology	relaxation training
duration	post-traumatic stress disorder	cognitive behavior therapy
learned helplessness	hardiness	

DIGITAL SUPPORT RESOURCES

Students should use the unique access code included in the front of the book to access the digital support resources which accompany the new edition. These include:

- Multiple Choice Questions and Quizzes
- Critical Thinking Questions
- Practice Essay Questions
- Videos
- Glossary, Flashcards, and More

15

PSYCHOLOGICAL DISORDERS

Know the four criteria that may be used in defining abnormality as well as the characteristics that are considered indicative of normality.

Understand the advantages and disadvantages of classifying abnormal behavior into categories.

Know the broad perspectives of the biological, psychoanalytic, behavior, cognitive, and sociocultural models.

Describe four types of anxiety disorders. Understand the development of anxiety disorders from the standpoint of biological, cognitive, behavioral, and psychodynamic theories. Know what research on biological factors has contributed thus far to our understanding of these disorders.

Describe the two major mood disorders and to compare cognitive-behavior, psychoanalytic, and interpersonal theories of depression.

Know the defining characteristics of schizophrenia and be able to give examples of each characteristic.

Be familiar with the research on the causes of schizophrenia; be able to discuss the probable contributions of genetic, biochemical, and psychological factors.

Define personality disorders; know the defining characteristics and probable causes of antisocial personalities and borderline personality disorder.

Understand the patterns of behavior that constitute autism spectrum disorders. Describe the biological causes of autism spectrum disorders.

Marc Summers had a lot of worries as a child. These were not the usual worries children have about big dogs or doing well in school, however, as he describes in his autobiography, *Everything in Its Place* (Summers, 2000, p. 42):

> I thought my parents would die if I didn't do everything in exactly the right way. When I took my glasses off at night I'd have to place them on the dresser at a particular angle. Sometimes I'd turn on the light and get out of bed seven times until I felt comfortable with the angle. If the angle wasn't right, I felt that my parents would die. The feeling ate up my insides.
>
> If I didn't grab the molding on the wall just the right way as I entered or exited my room; if I didn't hang a shirt in the closet perfectly; if I didn't read a paragraph a certain way; if my hands and nails weren't perfectly clean, I thought my incorrect behavior would kill my parents.

Most of us have concerns, but Marc Summers' concerns seem extreme. Some people might say they are so extreme as to be abnormal, even mentally 'disordered' or 'ill.' In this chapter, we explore psychological disorders, or more broadly, the concept of abnormal behavior. We will see that sometimes the line between normal and abnormal is clear, but most of the time it is fuzzy. We will investigate in detail several specific types of abnormality and theories of why some people develop psychological disorders and others do not.

CHAPTER OUTLINE

DEFINING ABNORMALITY

Deviation from cultural norms

Unusualness

Maladaptive behavior

Personal distress

Classifying mental health problems

Perspectives on mental health problems

ANXIETY DISORDERS

Panic disorders

Understanding panic disorder and agoraphobia

Phobias

Understanding phobias

Obsessive-compulsive disorder

Understanding obsessive-compulsive disorder

DEPRESSION AND BIPOLAR DISORDERS

Depression

Bipolar disorder

Understanding mood disorders

CUTTING EDGE RESEARCH: UNDERSTANDING SUICIDE

SCHIZOPHRENIA

Characteristics of schizophrenia

Behavioral symptoms and withdrawal from reality

Culture and the progression of schizophrenia

Understanding schizophrenia

PERSONALITY DISORDERS

Antisocial personality disorder

Understanding antisocial personality disorder

Borderline personality disorder

Understanding borderline personality disorder

AUTISM SPECTRUM DISORDER

Diagnosis of autism spectrum disorder

Understanding autism spectrum disorder

SEEING BOTH SIDES: IS ATTENTION DEFICIT HYPERACTIVITY DISORDER (ADHD) OVERDIAGNOSED?

A word of warning may be appropriate before we proceed. It is common for students studying mental disorders for the first time to diagnose these disorders in themselves, just as medical students diagnose themselves as suffering from every new disease they read about. Most of us have had some of the symptoms we will be describing, and that is not cause for alarm. However, if you have been bothered by distressing feelings for a long time, it never hurts to talk to someone about them – perhaps someone in your school's counseling service or student health service.

DEFINING ABNORMALITY

You've no doubt heard other people being referred to as 'crazy,' 'mad,' 'sick,' 'weird,' 'dysfunctional,' or 'abnormal.' What do we mean by '**abnormal**' behavior? By definition, the word means 'away from the norm,' but by what criteria do we distinguish between abnormal and 'normal' behavior? In this age of rapid technological advances, you might think that there would be some objective test – a blood test or brain scan – that could determine whether an individual has a mental disorder. There is no such test currently, however. Instead, we must rely on signs and symptoms, and on subjective criteria for deciding when those symptoms constitute a mental disorder. A number of different types of criteria for defining abnormality have been proposed.

Deviation from cultural norms

Every culture has certain standards, or norms, for acceptable behaviors and ways of thinking, and people who deviate from those norms may be considered abnormal. Proponents of a **cultural relativist perspective** argue that we should respect each culture's definitions of **normality** for the members of that culture. By doing so, we do not impose one culture's standards on another. Opponents of this position point to a number of dangers, however (Szasz, 1971). Throughout history, societies have labeled individuals as abnormal to justify controlling or silencing them, as Hitler branded the Jews abnormal to justify the Holocaust. Even within one culture, the concept of abnormality can change dramatically over time. Fifty years ago, many Europeans would have considered men wearing earrings abnormal, while today it's a fashion statement

Fashions change over time – just as definitions of abnormality do.

violent aggressive outbursts, a paranoid individual who plots to assassinate national leaders). If we use the criterion of maladaptiveness, all of these behaviors would be considered of concern.

Personal distress

A fourth criterion considers abnormality in terms of individuals' subjective feelings of **distress** – their feelings of anxiety, depression, or agitation, or experiences such as insomnia, loss of appetite, or numerous aches and pains. Most people who are diagnosed with a mental disorder feel acutely miserable. Sometimes personal distress may

that is acceptable in most communities. Thus, ideas of normality and abnormality differ from one society to another and over time within the same society.

Unusualness

When people say that another's behaviors or thoughts are weird or abnormal, they often mean that they are unusual or rare – not the way that most people behave or think. What is unusual depends in part, of course, on cultural norms. But within any culture, the *unusualness* or rarity of behavior is often used to define it as abnormal. But according to this definition, a person who is extremely intelligent or extremely happy would be classified as abnormal. Thus, in defining abnormality, we must consider more than what is usual or typical.

Maladaptive behavior

Rather than defining abnormality in terms of either deviance from cultural norms or unusualness, many social scientists believe that the most important criterion is how behaviors, thoughts or feelings affect the functioning of the individual or the social group. According to this criterion, people's behaviors or ways of thinking raise concern if they are **maladaptive** – that is, if they prevent the individual or society from functioning well. Some behaviors or experiences interfere with the individual's ability to function in everyday life (a man who is so fearful of crowds that he cannot ride the bus to work, a woman who drinks alcohol so heavily that she cannot hold a job). Other forms of behavior are harmful to society (an adolescent who has

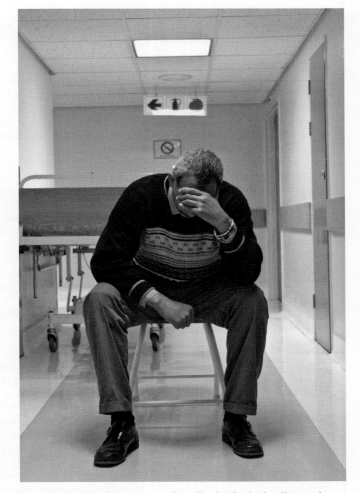

Particularly stressful events, such as the death of a family member, may be the trigger for acute mental health problems for some people.

be the only symptom of the disorder, and the individual's behavior may appear normal to the casual observer.

None of these definitions provides a completely satisfactory description of abnormality. In most instances, all four criteria – social deviation, unusualness, maladaptive behavior, and personal distress – are considered in diagnosing mental health problems.

Classifying mental health problems

Some mental health problems are acute and transitory, resulting from particularly stressful events, whereas others are chronic and lifelong. Each person's behavior and emotional problems are unique, and no two individuals behave in exactly the same manner or share the same life experiences. Still, for the purposes of diagnosis and research, mental health professionals have developed systems to classify maladaptive and distressing symptoms into disorders.

A good classification system has many advantages. By grouping individuals according to similarities in symptoms and then looking for other ways in which they may be similar, we may be able to uncover causes of their symptoms. For example, many people with a particular set of symptoms may also have had certain life experiences, or have biological characteristics in common. A diagnostic label also enables those who work with individuals with mental health problems to communicate information more quickly and concisely. Disadvantages arise, however, if we allow a diagnostic label to carry too much weight. Labeling induces us to overlook the unique features of each person and expect the person to conform to the classification. We may also forget that a label for maladaptive behavior is not an explanation of that behavior. The classification does not tell us how the symptoms originated or what causes

CONCEPT REVIEW TABLE CATEGORIES OF MENTAL DISORDERS

Listed here are the main diagnostic categories of mental disorders in the current (tenth) edition of the ICD. Each category includes numerous subclassifications.

Category	Description
Organic, including symptomatic, mental disorders	Cognitive impairment due to brain disease or injury, such as Alzheimer's disease, delirium, and organic amnesia.
Mental and behavioral disorders due to psychoactive substance use	Misuse of, and dependence on, psychoactive substances, including alcohol, illicit drugs, and prescription drugs.
Schizophrenia, schizotypal and delusional disorders	Disorders characterized by distortions of thought and perception and emotions that are inappropriate or blunted. At some phase, delusions and hallucinations usually occur.
Mood (affective) disorders	Disturbances of normal mood; the individual may be extremely depressed, abnormally elated, or may alternate between periods of elation and depression.
Neurotic, stress-related and somatoform disorders	Disorders characterized by excessive anxiety, extreme and persistent reactions to stress, and alterations in consciousness and identity due to emotional problems, and presentation of physical symptoms that appear to have no medical basis.
Behavioral syndromes associated with physiological disturbances and physical factors	Eating disorders, sleep disorders, sexual disorders, and disorders occurring during the postpartum period.
Disorders of adult personality and behavior	Long-standing patterns of maladaptive behavior that constitute immature and inappropriate ways of coping with stress or solving problems. Examples are antisocial personality disorder and paranoid personality disorder.
General learning disability	Arrested or incomplete development of mind, resulting in impairment of skills.
Disorders of psychological development	Disorders with onset in childhood resulting in impairment or delay of language, visual-spatial, and motor skills.
Behavioral and emotional disorders with onset usually occurring in childhood and adolescence	Hyperkinetic disorders (difficulties in persistence and attention, hyperactivity), conduct disorders (antisocial behavior), emotional disorders, difficulties in attachment, tic disorders, and various other problems first occurring in childhood or adolescence.

them to continue. Finally, being diagnosed with a mental health problem can carry stigma in many societies.

The classification of mental disorders published by the World Health Organization is the **International Classification of Diseases** (known as ICD). It corresponds generally to the system used in the USA, the **Diagnostic and Statistical Manual of Mental Disorders** (DSM for short, and DSM-5 replaced DSM-IV-TR in 2013.). The major categories of mental disorders classified by ICD are listed in the Concept Review Table. ICD provides an extensive list of subcategories under each of these headings, as well as a description of the symptoms that must be present for the diagnosis to be applicable.

A distinction that is traditionally made in classifying mental health problems is between *neuroses* and *psychoses*. **Neuroses** tend to be characterized by anxiety, unhappiness, and maladaptive behavior that are rarely serious enough to require hospitalization. The neurotic individual can usually function in society, though not at full capacity. **Psychoses** are more serious mental disorders. The individual's behavior and thought processes are so disturbed that he or she is out of touch with reality, cannot cope with the demands of daily life, and sometimes has to be hospitalized. Older diagnostic systems used the terms *neuroses* and *psychoses* to refer to a wide range of mental disorders, leading to significant imprecision in diagnosis. The ICD and DSM have defined mental disorders more narrowly, and consequently allow for more precision in diagnosis and agreement between clinicians as to what mental disorder might apply in a given case.

In this chapter, we will examine anxiety disorders, mood disorders, schizophrenia, and different types of personality disorder.

Countries vary in the prevalence of many mental disorders. WHO World Mental Health Consortium (2004) conducted a study entitled 'Prevalence, severity, and unmet need for treatment of mental disorders in the World Health Organization World Mental Health Survey,' which was published in the *Journal of the American Medical Association, 291*, 2581–2590. The data came from interviews with over 60000 people in 14 countries around the world. The variability which arose in the data may be due to cultural norms for the expression of distress and for the use of alcohol and other substances. In addition, many cultures recognize mental health problems that do not correspond to any disorders listed in the ICD or DSM-5 (see Table 15.1). Some of these problems may have the same underlying causes as certain disorders recognized by the ICD and DSM-5 but are manifested by different symptoms in other cultures. Others may be truly unique to the cultures in which they are found. The presence of such culture-bound syndromes suggests that

TABLE 15.1 CULTURE-BOUND SYNDROMES

Some cultures have syndromes or mental disorders that are found only in that culture and that do not correspond to any ICD or DSM-5 categories.

Syndrome	Cultures where found	Symptoms
amok	Malaysia, Laos, Philippines, Papua New Guinea, Puerto Rico, Navajos	Brooding, followed by violent behavior, persecutory ideas, amnesia, exhaustion. More often seen in men than in women.
ataque de nervios	Latin America	Uncontrollable shouting, crying, trembling, heat in the chest rising to the head, verbal or physical aggression, seizures, fainting.
ghost sickness	American Indians	Nightmares, weakness, feelings of danger, loss of appetite, fainting, dizziness, hallucinations, loss of consciousness, sense of suffocation.
koro	Malaysia, China, Thailand	Sudden and intense anxiety that the penis (in males) or the vulva and nipples (in females) will recede into body and cause death.
latah	East Asia	Hypersensitivity to sudden fright, trance-like behavior. Most often seen in middle-aged women.
susto	Mexico, Central America	Appetite disturbances, sleep disturbances, sadness, loss of motivation, feelings of low self-worth following a frightening event. Sufferers believe that their soul has left their body.
taijin kyofusho	Japan	Intense fear that one's body displeases, embarrasses, or is offensive to others.

the diagnoses listed in the ICD and DSM-5 represent only the disorders that occur in mainstream European and American cultures rather than a universal list of disorders to which all humans are susceptible. This supports the views of those who argue that we cannot define abnormality without reference to the norms of a particular culture.

Perspectives on mental health problems

Attempts to understand the causes of mental health problems generally fall under one of the three broad perspectives we have discussed throughout this book. The **biological perspective**, also called the *medical* or *disease* model, suggests that mental health problems are due to brain disorders. Researchers using this approach look for genetic factors that may predispose a person to develop a particular mental health problem by affecting the functioning of the brain. There is no one gene responsible for any of the mental disorders; instead, several genes combine in interactive ways at different stages of development to produce symptoms of a disorder. They also look for abnormalities in specific parts of the brain and dysfunction in neurochemical systems in the brain and other parts of the body, which may be the result of genetic factors. Proponents of this perspective generally favor the use of drugs to treat mental health problems.

There are a number of specific **psychological perspectives** that see mental health problems as problems in the functioning of the mind. The **behavioral perspective** investigates how fears become associated with specific situations and how inappropriate behaviors may be reinforced. The **cognitive perspective** suggests that some mental problems stem from maladaptive cognitive processes and can be alleviated by changing these biased cognitions. The way we think about ourselves, the way we appraise stressful situations, and our strategies for coping with them are all interrelated. The **psychoanalytic perspective** emphasizes unconscious conflicts, usually originating in early childhood, and the use of defense mechanisms to handle the anxiety generated by the repressed impulses and emotions.

Cultural or sociological perspectives take the view that mental health problems are not situated in the brain or mind of the individual but in the social context in which the individual lives. Proponents of this perspective look to stresses in the physical and social environment, such as discrimination and poverty, that can interfere with people's functioning. They also pay attention to how culture shapes the types of mental health problems people are most susceptible to and how they manifest their distress.

The ideas embodied in these brief summaries will become clearer as we discuss them in relation to specific mental health problems. One way of integrating these factors is the **vulnerability-stress model**, which considers the interaction between a predisposition, which makes a person vulnerable for developing a particular mental health problem, and stressful environmental conditions encountered by that person. At the biological level, vulnerability might stem from genetic factors. A substantial percentage of people with mental disorders have a close relative with the same problems perhaps because they each carry a gene that increases the likelihood of developing the problems. At the psychological level, a chronic feeling of hopelessness and inadequacy might make an individual vulnerable to depression. Having a predisposition for a particular mental health problem does not guarantee that the person will develop it. Whether the predisposition leads to an actual problems often depends on the kinds of stressors, including poverty, malnutrition, conflicts, and traumatic life events, that the individual encounters.

The key point of the vulnerability-stress model is that both vulnerability and stress are necessary. It helps explain why some people develop serious psychological problems when confronted with a minimum of stress while others remain healthy regardless of how difficult their lives may become.

INTERIM SUMMARY

➜ The labeling of behaviors, thoughts, and emotions as abnormal is based on social norms, statistical frequency, maladaptiveness of behavior, and personal distress.

➜ The ICD and DSM-5 are the classification systems used for mental health problems. Such classification systems help communicate information and provide a basis for research.

➜ Theories about the causes of mental health problems and proposals for treating them can be grouped according to those that focus on the brain and other biological factors; those that focus on the mind, including psychoanalytic, behavioral, and cognitive perspectives; and those that focus on sociocultural and environmental factors.

➜ The vulnerability-stress model emphasizes the interaction between a predisposition (biological and/or psychological) that makes a person vulnerable to a particular health problem and stressful environmental conditions encountered by the individual.

CRITICAL THINKING QUESTIONS

1 Studying any mental health problem from one theoretical perspective holds the danger that the investigator will be biased to look for particular causes of the problem and to ignore other causes. But is it possible to study mental health problems from a totally theoretical perspective – that is, to approach them with no presumptions about their likely causes? Why or why not?

2 People who are diagnosed with a mental disorder often say it is a relief to have a label for their distress. Why might this be true?

ANXIETY DISORDERS

It's Tuesday afternoon and you are walking to the room where you will take the final examination for an important course. Your heart is beating fast and hard, and your palms are sweating. Your thoughts are racing – Did you study enough? Did you guess correctly what was going to be on the examination? What if you don't do well?

You are experiencing the symptoms of anxiety, a common reaction to stressful or threatening situations. A little anxiety can be adaptive – if you weren't anxious about this exam, you may not have been motivated to study as much as you needed. Anxiety is considered unhealthy when it is out of proportion to the threat you face and goes on even after the threat has passed. **Anxiety disorders** include a group of disorders in which anxiety either is the main symptom (generalized anxiety and panic disorders) or is experienced when the individual attempts to control certain maladaptive behaviors (phobic and obsessive-compulsive disorders). (Post-traumatic stress disorder was discussed in Chapter 14 and it should be noted that it is no longer classified in the Anxiety Disorders section of the DSM-5 but now has its own section). The following passage describes a person suffering from an anxiety disorder:

> **Hazel was walking down a street near her home one day when she suddenly felt flooded with intense and frightening physical symptoms. Her whole body tightened up, she began sweating and her heart was racing, and she felt dizzy and disoriented. She thought, 'I must be having a heart attack! I can't stand this! Something terrible is happening! I'm going to die.' Hazel just stood frozen in the middle of the street until an onlooker stopped to help her.**

There are four types of symptoms of anxiety, and Hazel was experiencing symptoms of each type. First, she had physiological or somatic symptoms similar to those you may feel when facing a tough examination: her heart was racing, she was perspiring, and her muscles tensed. You may recognize these symptoms as part of the fight-or-flight response discussed in Chapter 14. This is the body's natural reaction to a challenging situation – the physiological changes of the fight-or-flight response prepare the body to fight a threat or to flee from it.

Second, Hazel had cognitive symptoms of anxiety: she was sure she was having a heart attack and dying. Third, Hazel had a behavioral symptom of anxiety: she froze, unable to move until help arrived. Fourth, she had the sense of dread and terror that make up the emotional symptoms of anxiety.

All of these symptoms can be highly adaptive when we are facing a real threat, such as a saber-toothed tiger in prehistoric times or a burglar today. They become maladaptive when there is no real threat to fight against or flee from. Hazel's symptoms were not triggered by a dangerous situation but came 'out of the blue.' Even when these symptoms do arise in response to some perceived threat, they can be maladaptive when they are out of proportion to the threat or persist after the threat has passed. Many people with anxiety disorders seem to view situations as highly threatening that most of us would consider benign, and they worry about those situations even when they are highly unlikely to occur. For example, people with social anxiety disorders are terrified of the possibility that they might embarrass themselves in public, and they therefore go to great lengths to avoid social situations.

In one form of anxiety disorder, **generalized anxiety disorder**, people experience a constant sense of tension and dread. They may be unable to relax or sleep well, and experience frequent fatigue, headaches, dizziness, and a rapid heart rate. They may continually worry about potential problems and have difficulty concentrating or making decisions. When they finally make a decision, it becomes a source of further worry ('What if I made the *wrong* decision?'). Other anxiety disorders, such as panic disorder, phobias, and obsessive-compulsive disorder, are characterized by more focused anxiety and are discussed in more detail in the rest of this section.

Panic disorders

Hazel's symptoms suggest that she experienced a **panic attack** – an episode of acute and overwhelming apprehension or terror. During panic attacks, people feel certain that something dreadful is about to happen. This feeling is usually accompanied by such symptoms as heart palpitations, shortness of breath, perspiration, muscle tremors, faintness, and nausea. The symptoms result from excitation of the sympathetic division of the autonomic nervous system (see Chapter 2) and are the same reactions that an individual experiences when extremely frightened. During severe panic attacks, people fear that they will die.

Panic attacks are relatively common during times of stress, with as many as 28 per cent of adults reporting they have occasional attacks (Kessler *et al.*, 2006). For most of these people, the panic attacks are annoying but isolated events that do not change how they live their lives. When panic attacks become a common occurrence and the individual begins to worry about having attacks, he or she may receive a diagnosis of **panic disorder**. Panic disorder is relatively rare: only about 2.1 per cent of European adults will ever develop a panic disorder (Alonso *et al.*, 2004). Usually panic disorder appears sometime between late adolescence and the mid-30s. Without treatment, panic disorder tends to become chronic.

Panic-like symptoms may take a different form across cultures. People from Latino cultures, particularly in the Caribbean, sometimes experience a sudden rush of anxiety symptoms known as *ataque de nervios*. The symptoms of *ataque* include trembling, feelings of out of control, sudden crying, screaming uncontrollably, verbal and physical aggression, and sometimes seizure-like or fainting episodes and suicidal gestures (Lopez & Guarnaccia, 2000). When *ataque de nervios* comes out of the blue, it is often attributed to the stresses of daily living or to spiritual causes. A study of Puerto Ricans after the 1985 floods found that 16 per cent of the victims reported experiencing an *ataque* (Guarnaccia, Canino, Rubio-Stipec, & Bravo, 1993).

About 20 per cent of people with panic disorder also develop agoraphobia (Kessler *et al.*, 2006). People with **agoraphobia** fear any place where they might be trapped or unable to receive help in an emergency. The term *agoraphobia* comes from the ancient Greek words meaning 'fear of the marketplace.' People with agoraphobia fear being in a busy, crowded place such as a shopping mall. They may also fear being in tightly enclosed spaces from which it can be difficult to escape, such as a bus, elevator, or subway, or being alone in wide-open spaces such as a meadow or a deserted beach. All of these places are frightening for people with agoraphobia because if a panic attack or some other emergency occurred, it would be very difficult for them to escape or get help. They may also fear that they will embarrass themselves if others see that they are having a panic attack.

People with agoraphobia significantly curtail their activities, remaining in a few 'safe' places, such as the area within a few blocks of home. Sometimes they can venture into 'unsafe' places if a trusted family member or friend accompanies them. If they attempt to enter 'unsafe' places on their own, however, they may experience a great deal of general anxiety beforehand and have a full panic attack when in the unsafe place. Hazel, whom we met earlier in the chapter, provides an example:

Hazel continued to have panic attacks every few days, sometimes on the same street where she had the first panic attack, but increasingly in places where she'd never had a panic attack before. It seemed she was especially likely to have a panic attack if there were lots of people standing around her, and she became confused about how she would get out of the crowd if she began to panic. The only place Hazel had not had any panic attacks was in her apartment. She began to spend more and more time in her apartment and refused to go anyplace where she had previously had a panic attack. After a few months, she had called in sick to work so often that she was fired. Hazel could not bring herself to leave her apartment at all. She had her groceries delivered to her so she wouldn't have to go out to get them. She would see friends only if they would come to her apartment. Hazel's savings were becoming depleted, however, because she had lost her job. Hazel began looking for a job that she could do from her apartment.

Although people can develop agoraphobia without panic attacks, the vast majority of people with agoraphobia do have panic attacks or panic-like symptoms in social situations (Alonso *et al.*, 2004). Agoraphobia usually develops within a year of the onset of recurrent panic attacks. Obviously, the symptoms of agoraphobia can severely interfere with the ability to function in daily life. People with agoraphobia often turn to alcohol and other drugs to cope with their symptoms. Fortunately, we have learned a great deal about the causes of panic and agoraphobia in recent years.

Understanding panic disorder and agoraphobia

Many people who develop panic disorder probably have a genetic or other biological vulnerability to the disorder. Panic disorder runs in families (Foley *et al.*, 2001; van den Heuvel *et al.*, 2000). This does not mean, of course, that panic disorders are entirely hereditary, in that family members live in the same environment. However, the results of twin studies provide firmer evidence for an inherited predisposition for panic disorder. Recall that identical twins share the same heredity; thus, if a disorder is transmitted entirely genetically, when one identical twin suffers from the disorder, the other twin should be highly likely to suffer from the disorder. In contrast, fraternal twins are no more alike genetically than ordinary siblings, so that when one twin suffers from the disorder, the other twin should not be at greatly increased risk for the disorder. Twin studies have shown that 30 to 40 per cent of the variability in panic disorder is due to genetic factors (Roy-Byrne *et al.*, 2006; Wittchen *et al.*, 2010).

People who are prone to panic attacks may have an overreactive fight-or-flight response. A full panic attack can be induced easily by having such individuals engage in activities that stimulate the initial physiological changes of the fight-or-flight response. For example, when people with panic disorder purposely hyperventilate, breathe into a paper bag, or inhale a small amount of carbon dioxide, they experience an increase in subjective anxiety, and many will experience a full panic attack (see Figure 15.1; Craske & Waters, 2005; Wittchen *et al.*, 2010). In contrast, people without a history of panic attacks may experience some physical discomfort while performing these activities, but they rarely experience a full panic attack.

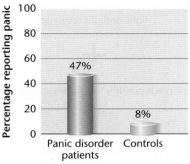

a) After hyperventilating

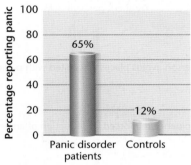

b) After inhaling carbon dioxide

FIGURE 15.1 Panic Attacks of Patients and Controls.
People with panic disorder are much more likely than people without panic disorder to have a panic attack when made to hyperventilate or inhale small amounts of carbon dioxide in laboratory experiments.

This overreactive fight-or-flight response may be the result of abnormal functioning in areas of the brain that regulate this response. Some studies show that people with panic disorder have reduced metabolism in the amygdala, hippocampus, thalamus, and brain-stem area, which are important in regulating responses to fear (Roy-Byrne *et al.,* 2006). People with panic disorder also show functioning in neurotransmitter systems critical to the fear response, including gamma-aminobutyric acid (GABA) and serotonin. These brain and neurotransmitter abnormalities could cause hyper-activation and poor regulation of fear responses.

An overreactive fear response may not be enough to create a full panic disorder, however. Some people who have occasional panic attacks associate slight changes in bodily functioning that occur during a panic attack, such as a change in heart rate, with the full-blown terror of a panic attack, a process known as *interoceptive conditioning* (Bouton *et al.,* 2001). Thus, when these slight bodily changes occur, even if the individual is not consciously aware of them, they elicit conditioned fear and panic because of previous pairings with the terror of panic, and the individual is on his or her way into a full-blown panic attack.

In addition, people who develop panic disorder tend to pay very close attention to their bodily sensations, misinterpret bodily sensations in a negative way, and engage in catastrophic thinking (Clark, 1988; Craske & Waters, 2005). In the case described earlier, when Hazel felt her muscles tightening, she began thinking, 'I'm having a heart attack! I'm going to die!' Not surprisingly, these thoughts increased her emotional symptoms of anxiety, which in turn made her physiological symptoms worse – her heart rate increased even more, and her muscles felt even tighter. Interpreting these physiological changes catastrophically led to a full panic attack. Between attacks, Hazel is hypervigilant, paying close attention to any bodily sensation. Her constant vigilance causes her autonomic nervous system to be chronically aroused, making it more likely that she will have another panic attack.

How does agoraphobia develop out of panic disorder? According to cognitive-behavioral theory, people with panic disorder remember vividly the places where they have had attacks. They greatly fear those places, and that fear generalizes to all similar places. By avoiding those places, they reduce their anxiety, and their avoidance behavior thus is reinforced. They may also find that they experience little anxiety in particular places, such as their own homes, and this reduction of anxiety is also highly reinforcing, leading them to confine themselves to these 'safe' places. Salkovskis (1991) has labeled such avoidance *safety behaviors*. Thus, through classical and operant conditioning, their behaviors are shaped into what we call agoraphobia. As we will see, many of the anxiety disorders are characterized by the kinds of safety behaviors that contribute to agoraphobia.

What evidence is there for this cognitive-behavioral theory of panic and agoraphobia? Several laboratory studies support the contentions that cognitive factors play a strong role in panic attacks and that agoraphobic behaviors may be conditioned through learning experiences (Craske & Waters, 2005). In one study, researchers asked two groups of individuals with panic disorder to wear masks through which they would inhale slight amounts of carbon dioxide. Both groups were told that, although inhaling a slight amount of carbon dioxide was not dangerous to their health, it could induce a panic attack. One group was told that they could not control the amount of carbon dioxide that came through their masks. The other group was told that they could control how much carbon dioxide they inhaled by turning a knob. Actually, neither group had any control over the amount of carbon dioxide they inhaled, and both groups inhaled the same small amount. Eighty per cent of the individuals who believed that they had no control experienced a panic attack, but only 20 per cent of those who believed that they could control the carbon dioxide had an attack. These results clearly suggest that beliefs about control over panic symptoms play a strong role in panic attacks (Sanderson *et al.,* 1989).

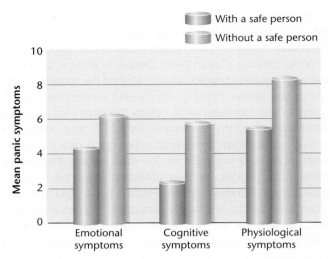

FIGURE 15.2 Panic Symptoms in Panic Patients. *Panic patients were much more likely to show symptoms of panic when a safe person was not with them.*

In a study focusing on agoraphobic behaviors, researchers examined whether people with panic disorder could avoid having a panic attack, even after inhaling carbon dioxide, by having a 'safe person' nearby. Panic patients who were exposed to carbon dioxide with their safe person present were much less likely to experience the emotional, cognitive, and physiological symptoms of panic than panic patients who were exposed to carbon dioxide without their safe person present (see Figure 15.2; Carter *et al.,* 1995). These results show that the symptoms of panic become associated with certain situations and that operant behaviors such as sticking close to a 'safe person' can be reinforced by the reduction of panic symptoms.

The biological and cognitive-behavioral theories of panic disorder and agoraphobia thus can be integrated into a vulnerability-stress model (Roy-Byrne *et al.,* 2006; see Figure 15.3). People who develop panic disorder may have a genetic or biochemical vulnerability to an overreactive fight-or-flight response, so that even with only a slight triggering stimulus, their bodies experience all the physiological symptoms of the response. For a full panic disorder to develop, however, it may be necessary for these individuals to develop a fear of bodily changes, through interoceptive conditioning, and also be prone to catastrophizing these symptoms and worrying excessively about having panic attacks. Interoceptive conditioning and misappraisals further heighten their physiological reactivity, making it even more likely that they will experience a full fight-or-flight response. Agoraphobia develops when they begin to avoid places that they associate with their panic symptoms and confine themselves to places where they experience less anxiety. This vulnerability-stress model has led to exciting breakthroughs in the treatment of panic disorder and agoraphobia, which we will discuss in Chapter 16.

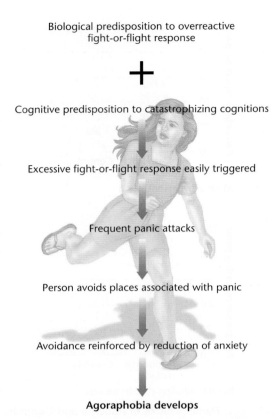

FIGURE 15.3 A Vulnerabilty-Stress Model of Panic and Agoraphobia. *A combination of biological vulnerability to an overreactive fight-or-flight response plus cognitive vulnerability to catastrophizing cognitions may begin a chain of processes leading to panic and agoraphobia.*

Phobias

A **phobia** is an intense fear of a stimulus or situation that most people do not consider particularly dangerous. The individual usually realizes that this is fear greater than what most people experience but still feels anxiety (ranging from strong uneasiness to panic) that can be alleviated only by avoiding the feared object or situation.

Many of us have one or two significant fears – of snakes, insects, and heights, for example. However, a fear is usually not diagnosed as a phobic disorder unless it interferes considerably with the person's daily life. Examples might include a woman whose fear of enclosed places prevents her from entering elevators or a man whose fear of crowds prevents him from attending the theater or walking along congested sidewalks.

The ICD and DSM-5 divide phobic disorders into three broad categories: specific phobias (prior to DSM-5 these were known as *simple phobias*), social anxiety disorders, and agoraphobia. We have already discussed agoraphobia. A **specific phobia** is a fear of a specific object, animal, or situation. Intense fears of

One of the most common phobias is a snake phobia.

snakes, germs, enclosed places, and darkness are examples. Specific phobias are quite common, with nearly 8 per cent of the population in Europe having a diagnosable specific phobia at some time in their lives (Alonso *et al.,* 2004). Most people with specific phobias are healthy in other respects. In more serious cases, individuals have a number of phobias that interfere with many aspects of their lives.

People with **social anxiety disorder** (prior to DSM-5 referred to as *social phobia*) feel extremely insecure in social situations and have an exaggerated fear of embarrassing themselves. Often they are afraid that they will betray their anxiety by such signs as hand tremors, blushing, or a quavering voice. These fears are usually unrealistic: individuals who fear that they might shake do not do so; those who fear that they will stutter or quaver actually speak quite normally. Fear of public speaking or of eating in public are the most common complaints of socially phobic individuals.

People with social anxiety disorders will go to great lengths to avoid situations in which others might evaluate them. They may take jobs that are solitary and isolating to avoid other people. If they find themselves in a feared social situation, they may begin trembling and perspiring, feel confused and dizzy, have heart palpitations, and eventually have a full panic attack. They are sure that others see their nervousness and are judging them as inarticulate, weak, stupid, or 'crazy.'

Social anxiety disorder is less common than specific phobias, with about 2.4 per cent of individuals in Europe qualifying for a diagnosis at some time in their lives (Alonso *et al.,* 2004). Social anxiety disorder typically begins in adolescence and tends to be a chronic problem if it is not treated (Kessler *et al.,* 1998).

Understanding phobias

Historically, phobias have been the subject of a major clash between psychoanalytic theories and behavioral theories. Freud's theory of the development of phobias was one of his most famous and controversial. Freud argued that phobias result when people displace anxiety over unconscious motives or desires onto objects that symbolize those motives or desires. His classic example was the case of Little Hans, a five-year-old who developed an intense fear of horses. Freud interpreted the boy's phobia in terms of Oedipal fears (see Chapter 13) through the following analysis: Hans was in love with his mother, jealously hated his father, and wanted to replace him (the Oedipal conflict); he feared that his father would retaliate by castrating him; the anxiety produced by this conflict was enormous because the wishes were unacceptable to the child's conscious mind; the anxiety was displaced onto an innocent object (a large horse that Hans had seen fall down and thrash about violently in the street).

Freud's evidence for his explanation of Hans's horse phobia consisted of Hans's answers to a series of rather leading questions about what he was 'really' afraid of, along with the fact that Hans appeared to lose his horse phobia after his conversations with Freud. Freud suggested that Hans had gained insight into the true source of his phobia and that this insight had cured the phobia. Critics pointed out, however, that Hans never provided any spontaneous or direct evidence that his real concern was his father rather than the horse. They also noted that Hans's phobia diminished gradually over time rather than abruptly in response to some sudden insight.

Some of the severest critics of Freud's analysis of phobias were behaviorists (Watson & Rayne, 1920). They argued that phobias do not develop from unconscious anxieties but rather from classical and operant conditioning. Many phobias emerge after a traumatic experience – a child nearly drowns and develops a phobia of water, another child is bitten by a dog and develops a phobia of dogs, an adolescent who stumbles through a speech in class is laughed at by peers and develops a phobia of public speaking. In these cases, a previously neutral stimulus (water or dogs or public speaking) is paired with a traumatic event (drowning or biting or embarrassment) that elicits anxiety. Through classical conditioning, the previously neutral stimulus now is able to elicit the anxiety reaction. In addition, many people with such fears avoid the phobic object because avoidance helps reduce their anxiety, and the phobic behavior is maintained through operant conditioning.

Although some phobias appear to result from actual frightening experiences, others may be learned vicariously through observation (Muris *et al.,* 1996). Fearful parents tend to produce children who share their fears. A child who observes parents react with fear to a variety of situations may develop the same reactions to those situations. Indeed, studies find that phobias clearly run in families (Kendler *et al.,* 2001). It is unclear whether this is due largely to children learning phobias from their parents or also partially due to genetic transmission of phobias. The first-degree relatives of people with phobias are

Some people develop phobias of dogs after a frightening encounter with a dog early in their life.

three to four times more likely than others to also have a phobia, and twin studies suggest that this is due, at least in part, to genetics (Hettema *et al.,* 2001). What is likely to be inherited is vulnerability to fear conditioning rather than the phobia per se (Hettema *et al.,* 2003).

Behavioral theories have led to highly successful treatments for phobias, lending further support to these theories. In contrast, treatments based on psychoanalytic theories of phobias tend to be unsuccessful, and current drug treatments tend to relieve phobic symptoms only in the short term.

Obsessive-compulsive disorder

A man gets out of bed several times each night and checks all the doors to make sure they are locked. Upon returning to bed, he is tormented by the thought that he may have missed one. Another man takes three or four showers in succession, scrubbing his body thoroughly with a special

disinfectant each time, fearful that he may be contaminated by germs. A woman has recurrent thoughts about stabbing her infant and feels panic-stricken whenever she has to handle scissors or knives. A teenage girl is always late to school because she feels compelled to repeat many of her actions (replacing her brush on the dresser, arranging the school supplies in her book bag, crossing the threshold to her bedroom) a set number of times, usually some multiple of the number 4.

All of these people have symptoms of **obsessive-compulsive disorder (OCD)**: their lives are dominated by repetitive acts or thoughts. **Obsessions** are persistent intrusions of unwelcome thoughts, images, or impulses that elicit anxiety. **Compulsions** are irresistible urges to carry out certain acts or rituals that reduce anxiety. Obsessive thoughts are often linked with compulsive acts (for example, thoughts of lurking germs, which lead to the compulsion to wash eating utensils many times before using them). Regardless of whether the repetitive element is a thought (obsession) or an act (compulsion), the central feature of the disorder is the subjective experience of loss of control. The victims struggle mightily to rid themselves of the troublesome thoughts or resist performing the repetitive acts but are unable to do so.

At times, all of us have persistently recurring thoughts ('Did I leave the gas on?') and urges to perform ritualistic behavior (arranging items on a desk in a precise order before starting an assignment). But for people with OCDs, such thoughts and acts occupy so much time that they seriously interfere with daily life. These individuals recognize their thoughts as irrational and repugnant but are unable to ignore or suppress them. They realize the senselessness of their compulsive behavior but become anxious when they try to resist their compulsions, and feel a release of tension once the acts are carried out.

Obsessive thoughts cover a variety of topics, but most often they are concerned with causing harm to oneself or others, fear of contamination, and doubt that a completed task has been accomplished satisfactorily (Leckman *et al.,* 2010). Some people with an OCD have intrusive thoughts without engaging in repetitive actions. However, the majority of people with obsessive thoughts also exhibit compulsive behavior. Compulsions take a variety of forms, of which the two most common are washing and checking (Foa & Steketee, 1989). 'Washers' feel contaminated when exposed to certain objects or thoughts and spend hours performing washing and cleaning rituals. 'Checkers' check doors, lights, ovens, or the accuracy of a completed task 10, 20, or 100 times or repeat ritualistic acts over and over again. They believe that their actions will prevent future 'disasters' or punishments. Compulsive acts that are meant to ward off the harm an individual is obsessing about are another example of safety behaviors.

Obsession with germs may lead to compulsive hand washing.

Sometimes these rituals are related to the anxiety-evoking obsessions in a direct way (for example, repeatedly checking to see if the stove has been turned off to avoid a possible fire); other rituals are not rationally related to the obsessions (for example, dressing and undressing in order to prevent one's spouse from having an accident). The common theme behind all of these repetitive behaviors is doubt. Obsessive-compulsive individuals cannot trust their senses or their judgment; they can't trust their eyes, even though they see that the door is locked or that there is no dirt. OCDs are related to phobic disorders in that both involve severe anxiety and both may appear in the same patient. However, there are important differences. Phobic individuals seldom ruminate about their fears, nor do they show ritualistic compulsive behavior. And the two disorders are evoked by different stimuli. Dirt, germs, and harm to others – common obsessive-compulsive preoccupations – seldom cause major problems for phobic individuals.

OCD is receiving increasing attention, as is clear from how DSM-5 now classifies it in its own section instead of simply within the Anxiety Disorders section, and now lists hoarding, skin-picking and hair-pulling as examples of the disorder.

OCD often begins at a young age (Foa & Franklin, 2001). It tends to be chronic if left untreated. Obsessional thoughts are very distressing, and engaging in compulsive behaviors can take a great deal of time and be highly maladaptive (for example, washing one's hands so often that they bleed). People with this disorder thus are quite psychologically impaired. Between 1 per cent and 3 per cent of people develop OCD at some time in their lives (Angst et al., 2004; Kessler et al., 2005). The prevalence of OCD does not seem to differ greatly across countries that have been studied, including the USA, Canada, Mexico, England, Norway, Hong Kong, India, Egypt, Japan, and Korea (Escobar, 1993; Insel, 1984; Kim, 1993).

Understanding obsessive-compulsive disorder

Cognitive and behavioral theorists suggest that people with OCD have more trouble 'turning off' intrusive thoughts because they have a tendency toward rigid, moralistic thinking (Rachman, 1998; Salkovskis, 1999). They tend to feel responsible for preventing harmful things from happening. They are more likely to judge their negative, intrusive thoughts as unacceptable, and they become more anxious and guilty about these thoughts. This anxiety then makes it even harder to dismiss the thought. People with OCD may also believe that they should be able to control all thoughts and have trouble accepting the fact that everyone has negative thoughts occasionally. They tend to believe that having these thoughts means they are going crazy, or they equate having the thought with actually engaging in the behavior ('If I'm thinking about hurting my child, I'm as guilty as if I actually did hurt my child'). Of course, this just makes them even more anxious when they have thoughts, because it's harder to dismiss them.

Compulsions may develop when the obsessional person discovers that some behavior temporarily quells the obsession and the anxiety it arouses. This reduction in anxiety reinforces the behavior, and a compulsion is born: every time the person has the obsession, he or she will feel compelled to engage in the behavior to reduce anxiety. This cognitive-behavioral account of OCD has received a considerable amount of empirical support (Julien et al., 2007). Some of the best evidence in favor of cognitive and behavioral perspectives on OCD can be seen in the fact that therapies based on these perspectives are helpful to people with the disorder, as we will discuss in Chapter 16.

OCD may also have biological causes. Some family research suggests that disordered genes may play a role in determining who is vulnerable to OCD (Mundo et al., 2006). Most of the biological research on OCD, however, has focused on a critical circuit in the brain involved in motor behavior, cognition, and emotion (Milad & Rauch, 2012). This circuit projects from specific areas of the frontal cortex, to areas of the basal ganglia called the striatum, then through the basal ganglia to the thalamus, then loops back to the frontal cortex (see Figure 15.4). People with this disorder may have deficiencies in the neurotransmitter serotonin in the areas of the brain that regulate primitive impulses about sex, violence, and cleanliness – impulses that are often the focus of obsessions (Milad & Rauch, 2012). For people with OCD and related disorders, dysfunction in this circuit may result in the system's inability to turn off the primitive urges (e.g., aggressive urges) or the execution of the stereotyped behaviors. When most of us think our hands are dirty, we engage in a fairly stereotyped form of cleansing: we wash them. People with OCD, however, continue to have the urge to wash their hands because their brains do not shut off their thoughts about dirt or their hand-washing behavior when the behavior is no longer necessary. Proponents of this biological theory point out that many of the obsessions and compulsions of people with OCD have to do with contamination, sex, aggression, and repeated patterns of behavior—all issues with which this brain circuit deals (Milad & Rauch, 2012; Rauch, 2003).

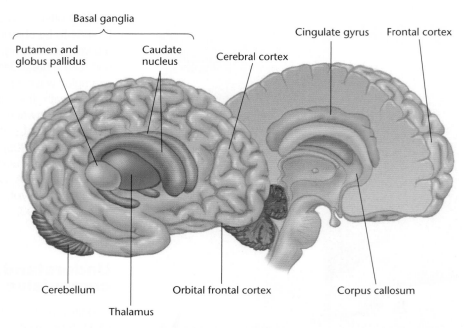

FIGURE 15.4 The Human Brain and OCD. *This three-dimensional view of the human brain shows the locations of the orbital frontal cortex and the basal ganglia – areas implicated in obsessive-compulsive disorder. Among the basal ganglia's structures are the caudate nuclei, which filter powerful impulses that arise in the orbital frontal cortex so that only the most powerful ones reach the thalamus.*

Neuroimaging studies of people with OCD show aberrant activity in the areas of the brain involved in this primitive circuit compared to people without the disorder (Milad & Rauch, 2012). In addition, people with the disorder often get some relief from their symptoms when they take drugs that regulate serotonin levels (Dell'Osso et al., 2006). Finally, patients who respond well to these drugs tend to show greater reductions in the rate of activity in these brain areas than patients who do not respond well to these drugs (Baxter et al., 1992; Swedo et al., 1992). Interestingly, OCD patients who respond to behavior therapies also tend to show decreases in activity in the caudate nucleus and thalamus (Schwartz et al., 1996).

In sum, biological and psychological factors probably combine in creating many of the anxiety disorders. Many people who develop these disorders probably have a genetic, neurological, or biochemical vulnerability to anxiety. But it may be necessary for them also to have a tendency toward catastrophizing and engaging in maladaptive avoidant behaviors that reduce anxiety for a full anxiety disorder to develop.

INTERIM SUMMARY

➤ Anxiety disorders include generalized anxiety (constant worry and tension), panic disorders (sudden attacks of overwhelming apprehension), phobias (irrational fears of specific objects or situations), and obsessive-compulsive disorders (OCDs) (persistent unwanted thoughts, or obsessions, combined with urges, or compulsions, to perform certain acts).

➤ Biological theories of anxiety disorders attribute them to genetic predispositions or to biochemical or neurological abnormalities. Most anxiety disorders run in families, and twin studies strongly suggest that panic disorder and OCD have an inherited component.

➤ People who suffer panic attacks have an overreactive fight-or-flight response, perhaps because of serotonin deficiencies in the limbic system.

➤ People with OCD may have serotonin deficiencies in areas of the brain that regulate primitive impulses.

➜ Cognitive and behavioral theorists suggest that people with anxiety disorders are prone to catastrophizing cognitions and to rigid, moralistic thinking. Maladaptive behaviors such as avoidant behaviors and compulsions arise through operant conditioning when the individual discovers that the behaviors reduce anxiety. Phobias may emerge through classical conditioning.

➜ Psychoanalytic theories attribute anxiety disorders to unconscious conflicts that are disguised as phobias, obsessions, or compulsions.

CRITICAL THINKING QUESTIONS

1 Women are more likely than men to suffer from the anxiety disorders (except for OCD). Can you generate some hypotheses for this gender difference?

2 Humans are much more likely to develop phobias of snakes and spiders than of guns or other modern weapons that are a greater danger to them. Can you generate an evolutionary explanation for this?

DEPRESSION AND BIPOLAR DISORDERS

Mood disorders are characterized by disturbances in mood. There are two basic types of mood disorders: people with **depressive disorders** have periods of sad, depressed, or flat mood; people with **bipolar disorders** alternate between periods of depressed and periods of mania (elated or agitated moods), usually with a return to normal mood between the two extremes. People rarely experience only manic episodes with no history of depression.

Depression

From the time I woke up in the morning until the time I went to bed at night, I was unbearably miserable and seemingly incapable of any kind of joy or enthusiasm. Everything – every thought, word, movement – was an effort. Everything that once was sparkling now was flat. I seemed to myself to be dull, boring, inadequate, thick brained, unlit, unresponsive, chill skinned, bloodless and sparrow drab. I doubted, completely, my ability to do anything well. It seemed as though my mind had slowed down and burned out to the point of being virtually useless. The wretched, convoluted, and pathetically confused mass of gray worked only

well enough to torment me with a dreary litany of my inadequacies and shortcomings in character and to taunt me with the total, the desperate hopelessness of it all.

(Jamison, 1995, p. 110)

Most of us have periods when we feel sad, lethargic, and uninterested in any activities – even pleasurable ones. Mild depressive symptoms are a normal response to many of life's stresses, especially important losses. Depression becomes a disorder when the symptoms become so severe that they interfere with normal functioning, and when they continue for weeks at a time. Depressive disorders are relatively common, with about 13 per cent of people having an episode of severe depression such as Jamison describes at some time in their lives (Alonso *et al.,* 2004; Merikangas *et al.,* 2011). The prevalence of depressive disorders varies considerably across countries, however, ranging from lifetime prevalences of about 6 per cent or less (Japan, Shenzen (China)), Bulgaria, Romania) to lifetime prevalences of near 20 per cent (Brazil, New Zealand, USA) (Merikangas *et al.,* 2011). In most countries, women are more likely than men to develop depression.

Although depression is characterized as a mood disorder, it is truly a disorder of the whole person, affecting bodily functions, behaviors, and thoughts as well as emotions (see Figure 15.5). A person need not have all the symptoms of depression to be diagnosed with a disorder, but the more symptoms he or she has and the more intense they are, the more certain we can be that the individual is suffering from depression.

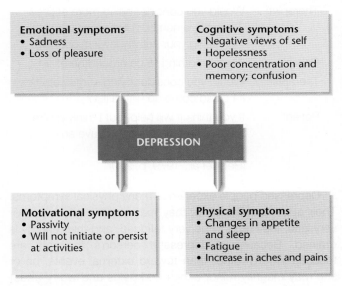

FIGURE 15.5 The Symptoms of Depression. *Depression includes emotional, cognitive, motivational, and physical symptoms.*

The emotional symptoms of depression are not the everyday blues that we all experience from time to time, but an unrelenting pain and despair. People also report that they have lost the ability to experience joy, even in response to the most joyous occasions, a symptom referred to as **anhedonia**. They say that they don't find interacting with family or friends, their work, or their hobbies enjoyable anymore.

The cognitive symptoms consist primarily of negative thoughts, with themes of worthlessness, guilt, hopelessness, and even suicide. Motivation is at a low ebb: The depressed person tends to be passive and has difficulty initiating activities. The following conversation between a patient and his therapist illustrates this passivity. The man, who had been hospitalized after a suicide attempt, spent his days sitting motionless in the lounge. His therapist decided to try to engage him in some activities:

Therapist:	I understand that you spend most of your day in the lounge. Is that true?
Patient:	Yes, being quiet gives me the peace of mind I need.
Therapist:	When you sit here, how's your mood?
Patient:	I feel awful all the time. I just wish I could fall in a hole somewhere and die.
Therapist:	Do you feel better after sitting for two or three hours?
Patient:	No, the same.
Therapist:	So you're sitting in the hope that you'll find peace of mind, but it doesn't sound like your depression improves.
Patient:	I get so bored.
Therapist:	Would you consider being more active? There are a number of reasons why I think increasing your activity level might help.
Patient:	There's nothing to do around here.
Therapist:	Would you consider trying some activities if I could come up with a list?
Patient:	If you think it will help, but I think you're wasting your time. I don't have any interests.
	(Beck *et al.,* 1979, p. 200)

Depressed people experience many physical symptoms. Their appetite may wane, they may sleep a great deal or very little, they tend to be very fatigued, and their energy is drained. Because a depressed person's thoughts are focused inward rather than toward external events, he or she may magnify minor aches and pains and worry about health.

As we see from this description of its symptoms, depression can be a debilitating disorder. Unfortunately, severe

Some people suffer depression for years.

depression can also be long-lasting. One study of people with severe depression found that in a given year they were symptom-free only about 30 per cent of the time (Kessler *et al.,* 2003). Even if they recover from one bout of depression, people remain at high risk for relapses into new episodes. There is some good news, however. Episodes of depression can be greatly shortened – and new episodes prevented – with either drug therapy or psychotherapy, as we discuss in Chapter 16.

Bipolar disorder

The majority of depressions occur without episodes of mania. But some people with a mood disorder will experience both depression and mania and hence can be diagnosed with bipolar disorder, also known as manic-depression. The individual alternates between depression and extreme elation. In some cases the cycle between depressive episodes and manic episodes is swift, with only a brief return to normality in between.

People experiencing **manic episodes** behave in a way that appears on the surface to be the opposite of depression. During mild manic episodes, they are energetic, enthusiastic, and full of self-confidence. They talk continually, rush from one activity to another with little need for sleep, and make grandiose plans, paying little attention to their practicality, as Jamison (1995, pp. 36–37) describes:

> **I was a senior in high school when I had my first attack. At first, everything seemed so easy. I raced about like a crazed weasel, bubbling with plans and enthusiasms, immersed in sports, and staying up all night, night after night, out with friends, reading everything that wasn't nailed down, filling manuscript books with poems and fragments of plays, and making expansive, completely unrealistic plans for my future. The world was filled with pleasure and promise; I felt great. Not just great, I felt *really* great. I felt I could do anything, that no task was too difficult. My mind seemed clear, fabulously focused, and able to make intuitive mathematical leaps that had up to that point entirely eluded me. Indeed, they elude me still. At the time, however, not only did everything make perfect sense, but it all began to fit into a marvelous kind of cosmic relatedness. My sense of enchantment with the laws of the natural world caused me to fizz over, and I found myself buttonholing my friends to tell them how beautiful it all was. They were less than transfixed by my insights into the webbings and beauties of the universe although considerably impressed at how exhausting it was to be around my enthusiastic ramblings: You're talking too fast, Kay. Slow down, Kay. You're wearing me out, Kay. Slow down, Kay. And those times when they didn't actually come out and say it, I still could see it in their eyes: For God's sake, Kay, slow down.**

This kind of energy, self-confidence, and enthusiasm may actually seem quite attractive to you, and, indeed, many people in the midst of a manic episode do not want to get rid of their symptoms. At some point, however, manic symptoms often cross a line from joyful exuberance into hostile agitation. People may become angered by attempts to interfere with their activities and become abusive. Impulses (including sexual ones) are immediately expressed in actions or words. People may become confused and disoriented and may experience delusions of great wealth, accomplishment, or power. Eventually, most manic episodes revert into episodes of depression, sometimes extremely severe.

Bipolar disorders are relatively uncommon, with only about 2 per cent or less of adults across many nations experiencing bipolar disorder sometime in their lives (Alonso *et al.,* 2004; Merikangas *et al.,* 2011). Bipolar disorder, which appears to be equally common in men and women, differs from other mood disorders in that it is more likely to run in families, responds to different medications, and almost always recurs if not treated.

Understanding mood disorders

As with the anxiety disorders, a combined biological and psychological model may best explain the mood disorders. Most people who develop depression – and particularly bipolar disorder – may have a biological vulnerability to these disorders. But the experience of certain types of life events, along with a tendency to think in negative ways, also clearly increases the likelihood of developing these disorders.

The biological perspective

A tendency to develop mood disorders, particularly bipolar disorders, appears to be inherited. Family history studies of people with bipolar disorder find that their first-degree relatives (parents, children, and siblings) have five to ten times higher rates of both bipolar disorder and depressive disorders than relatives of people without bipolar disorder (Farmer *et al.,* 2007). Twin studies of bipolar disorder have also consistently suggested that the disorder has a genetic component. Indeed, the identical twins of individuals with bipolar disorder are 45 to 75 times more likely to develop the disorder than people in the general population (Farmer *et al.,* 2007).

There is some evidence that depression, particularly depression that begins in childhood and recurs across the life span, also is heritable. Family history studies find that first-degree relatives of people with depression have two to four times higher rates of depression than others (Sullivan *et al.,* 2000). Twin studies also suggest that depression is heritable but to a lesser degree than bipolar disorder (Levinson, 2009).

The specific role that genetic factors play in mood disorders is unclear. However, it seems likely that a biochemical abnormality is involved. A group of neurotransmitters called monoamines – norepinephrine, serotonin, and dopamine – are believed to play an important role in the mood disorders. Recall from Chapter 2 that neurotransmitters are synthesized by one neuron and released into the synapse, or gap between neurons. Then the neurotransmitter fits into receptors on the membrane of other neurons like a key in a lock (see Figure 15.6). When a neurotransmitter binds to a receptor, this sets off a cascade of biochemical processes within that neuron that transmits signals down the neuron. This process of neurotransmission can go awry at any stage – there may be an inappropriate amount of neurotransmitter released into the synapse, the number or sensitivity of receptors for the neurotransmitter can be wrong, or the cascade of signals initiated by the binding of the neurotransmitter to the receptor can malfunction. Several studies suggest that people with depression or bipolar disorder may have abnormalities at all the stages of neurotransmission for the monoamines, particularly in areas of the brain that are involved in the regulation of emotion, such as the hypothalamus (Thase, 2009).

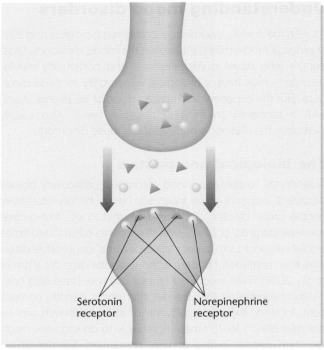

Serotonin

Norepinephrine

FIGURE 15.6 Neurotransmission in Depression. *The neuronal receptors for norepinephrine and serotonin may not work efficiently in depressed people, so that norepinephrine and serotonin released from one neuron cannot bind to receptor sites on other neurons.*

The structure and functioning of the brain also appear to be altered in people with mood disorders. Neuroimaging studies using computed tomography (CT) scans and magnetic resonance imaging (MRI) have found deterioration in the prefrontal cortex of people with severe unipolar depression or bipolar disorder (Thase, 2009). This is associated with abnormalities in metabolism in this area of the brain, according to positron emission tomography (PET) studies. Figure 15.7 shows reduced activity in one area of the prefrontal cortex, the cingulate gyrus, in patients with bipolar disorder, as well as reductions in activity in the thalamus, an area of the brain associated with cognitive functioning and the regulation of emotion. Similarly, people who are depressed show variations in the functioning of the prefrontal cortex, as well as the thalamus, hypothalamus, amygdala, and hippocampus, which are involved in the regulation of responses to stress and in sleep, appetite, sexual drive, motivation, and memory (see Figure 15.8; Southwick *et al.,* 2005). These structural and functional brain abnormalities could be precursors and causes of mood disorders, or they could be the result of biochemical processes in the mood disorders that have a toxic effect on the brain. We do not yet know the precise meaning of these abnormalities, but the rapid advances in neuroimaging technologies are sure to bring exciting new clues in the future.

The cognitive perspective

Cognitive theories focus primarily on depression. According to these theories, people become depressed because they tend to interpret events in their lives in pessimistic, hopeless ways (Abramson *et al.,* 2002). One of the most influential cognitive theorists, Aaron Beck, grouped the negative thoughts of depressed individuals into three categories, which he called the *cognitive triad*: negative thoughts about the self, about present experiences, and about the future (Beck, 1976). Negative thoughts about the self include the depressed person's belief that he or she is worthless and

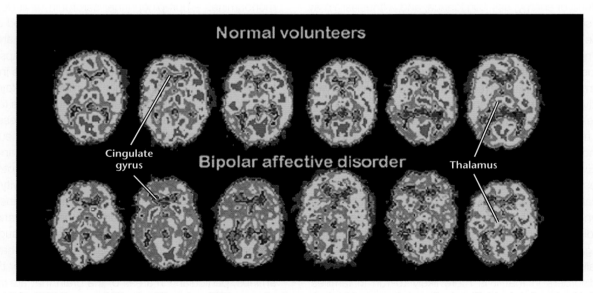

FIGURE 15.7 PET Scans of Bipolar Disorder. *PET scans in six control subjects and six patients with bipolar disorder. Note decreases in relative metabolic rate in the cingulate gyrus and thalamus in bipolar subjects.*

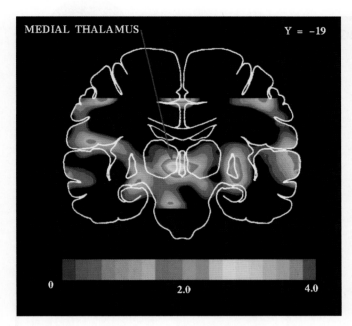

MEDIAL THALAMUS   Y = −19

0   2.0   4.0

FIGURE 15.8 Brain Functioning in Depression. *This brain image shows increased metabolism in the medial thalamus of people with depression compared with those without depression.*

inadequate. The depressed person's negative view of the future is one of hopelessness. Depressed people believe that their inadequacies and defects will prevent them from ever improving their current situation, which they view as bleak.

Beck proposes that the depressed person's negative beliefs about self ('I am worthless,' 'I can't do anything right') are formed during childhood or adolescence through such experiences as loss of a parent, social rejection by peers, criticism by parents or teachers, or a series of tragedies. These negative beliefs are activated whenever a new situation resembles in some way – perhaps only remotely – the conditions in which the beliefs were learned, and depression may result. Moreover, according to Beck, depressed individuals make some systematic errors in thinking that lead them to misperceive reality in a way that contributes to their negative beliefs about themselves. These cognitive distortions are listed in Table 15.2.

Evidence that cognitive factors play a role in depression comes from a study that followed students through their college careers. Researchers measured the students' tendencies toward negative thinking patterns early in their first year of college and followed them for the next few years. Students who evidenced a negative cognitive style were almost seven times more likely to experience episodes of depression during their college years than those who did not, even if they had never been depressed before going to college (Alloy *et al.,* 2006).

Depressed people tend to show biases not only in the content of their thinking but also in their processes of thinking. They tend to *ruminate* – to focus on their problems and feelings in a repetitive, circular manner without moving into problem-solving

TABLE 15.2 COGNITIVE DISTORTIONS IN DEPRESSION

According to Beck's theory, these are the principal errors in thinking that characterize depressed individuals.

Overgeneralization	Drawing a sweeping conclusion on the basis of a single event. For example, a student concludes from his poor performance in one class on a particular day that he is inept and stupid.
Selective abstraction	Focusing on an insignificant detail while ignoring the more important features of a situation. For example, from a conversation in which her boss praises her overall job performance, a secretary remembers the only comment that could be construed as mildly critical.
Magnification and minimization	Magnifying small bad events and minimizing major good events in evaluating performance. For example, a woman gets a small dent in her car fender and views it as a catastrophe (magnification), while the fact that she gave an excellent presentation in class does nothing to raise her self-esteem (minimization).
Personalization	Incorrectly assuming responsibility for bad events in the world. For example, when rain dampens spirits at an outdoor buffet, the host blames himself rather than the weather.
Arbitrary inference	Drawing a conclusion when there is little evidence to support it. For example, a man concludes from his wife's sad expression that she is disappointed in him; if he had checked out the situation, he would have discovered that she was distressed by a friend's illness.

(Nolen-Hoeksema *et al.,* 2008; Watkins, 2008). This tendency to ruminate is not just a symptom of depression – it predisposes people who are not already depressed to develop serious depression (Nolen-Hoeksema, 2000).

Depressed people also show biases toward negative thinking in basic attention and memory processes (Gotlib & Joormann, 2010). They are more likely than non-depressed people to dwell on negative stimuli, such as sad faces, and to have trouble disengaging their attention from negative stimuli. When given a list of words to learn, they will selectively recall the negative words more than the positive words. These biases in attention to, and memory for, negative information could contribute to the

CUTTING EDGE RESEARCH UNDERSTANDING SUICIDE

Susan Nolen-Hoeksema, Yale University

The most disastrous consequence of depression is suicide. Not everyone who attempts or commits suicide is depressed, however, and suicidal thoughts and actions are alarmingly common. Internationally, an estimated 1 million people die by suicide each year, or one person every 40 seconds (WHO, 2008).

Women attempt to commit suicide about three times more often than men do, but men succeed more often than women in killing themselves (see Figure 15.9). The greater number of suicide attempts by women is probably related to the greater incidence of depression among women. The fact that men are more successful in their attempts is related to the choice of method. Women have tended to use less lethal means, such as cutting their wrists or overdosing on sleeping pills; men are more likely to use firearms or carbon monoxide fumes or to hang themselves (CDC, 2007).

There are cross-national differences in suicide rates, with higher rates in Europe, the former Soviet Union, and Australia, and low rates in Latin America and South America (see Figure 15.10; WHO, 2005). The suicide rates in the USA, Canada, and England fall between these two extremes. These differences may have to do with cultural and religious norms against suicide.

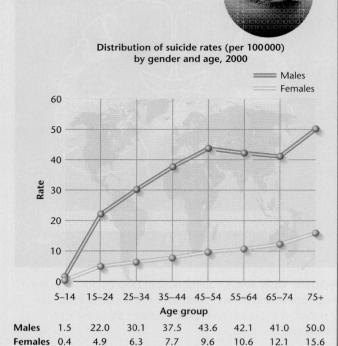

Distribution of suicide rates (per 100 000) by gender and age, 2000

Age group	5–14	15–24	25–34	35–44	45–54	55–64	65–74	75+
Males	1.5	22.0	30.1	37.5	43.6	42.1	41.0	50.0
Females	0.4	4.9	6.3	7.7	9.6	10.6	12.1	15.6

FIGURE 15.9 Gender, Age, and Suicide. *In many nations of the world, men are more likely to commit suicide than women, and the rates of suicide are highest among the elderly.*

>13
6.5-13
<6.5
no data

FIGURE 15.10 Map of Suicide Rates. *There are significant differences across countries in suicide rates. This map shows the rate per 100 000 people in different regions of the world.*

Over 90 per cent of people who commit suicide have probably been suffering from a diagnosable mental disorder, most commonly a mood disorder (Jacobson & Gould, 2009 Fombonne). In addition, drug abuse plays an important role in suicide. The lifetime risk for suicide among people who are dependent on alcohol is seven times greater than the lifetime risk among people not alcohol dependent (Joiner et al., 2005; see also Nock et al., 2008). When alcoholism co-occurs with depression, the risk of suicide is especially high. Alcohol lowers people's inhibitions to engage in impulsive acts, even self-destructive acts like suicide attempts.

Recent research suggests that suicide can be contagious, particularly among people who are already having psychological problems (Jacobson & Gould, 2009). For example, researchers in Taiwan interviewed 438 individuals suffering from depression shortly after massive media coverage of the suicide of a popular television star named M. J. Nee. They found that 38.8 per cent of the depressed individuals reported that the media coverage had increased their own thoughts about suicide, and 5.5 per cent said it had led them to make a suicide attempt (Cheng et al., 2007). Individuals who had themselves made a suicide attempt in the month prior to the media coverage of the celebrity suicide were nearly 12 times more likely to report having made another suicide attempt in response to the media coverage than individuals who had not made a recent suicide attempt.

When a well-known member of the society commits suicide, people who closely identify with that person may see suicide as more acceptable. Among the depressed individuals in the Taiwanese study just described, several said that 'His case showed that suicide is not shameful,' and 'He was a courageous martyr for me to follow elegantly' (Cheng et al., 2007, pp. 72–73). When two or more suicides or attempted suicides are non-randomly bunched in space or time, such as a series of suicide attempts in the same school or a series of completed suicides in response to the suicide of a celebrity, scientists refer to this as a *suicide cluster* (Joiner, 1999). Suicide clusters seem to occur primarily among adolescents (Jacobson & Gould, 2009).

If you suspect that a friend or family member might be contemplating suicide, what should you do? For many of us, this is such a frightening situation that we may not want to deal with it. Or we may think that by asking people about their suicidal feelings, we may suggest something they haven't already thought of. Research shows, however, that it is important to talk directly with people who might be suicidal about their feelings and intentions. Often, they find it a relief that someone notices and is concerned. Then, it is important to get help – to encourage suicidal individuals to seek treatment, and even to help them get emergency care if they are thinking of hurting themselves imminently, by taking them to the emergency room of a hospital or calling a suicide crisis hotline.

development of the negative beliefs depressed people have about themselves, the world and the future, and their tendencies to ruminate (Gotlib & Joormann, 2010).

Interpersonal perspectives

Interpersonal theories of depression suggest that depressed people are often too dependent on the opinions and support of other people (Joiner & Timmons, 2009). Their insecurity about their relationships and their self-image lead them to engage in excessive reassurance seeking – constantly looking for assurances from others that they are accepted and loved. They never quite believe the affirmations other people give, however, and anxiously keep going back for more. After a while, their family members and friends can become weary of this behavior and become frustrated or hostile. The insecure person picks up on these cues of annoyance and becomes even more worried about the relationship, and in turn engages in even more excessive reassurance seeking. Eventually, the person's social support may withdraw altogether, leading him or her to develop even more depression. In support of this theory, studies show that depressed people are more sensitive to rejection and more likely to engage in excessive reassurance seeking than people with other mental disorders, and in turn, community participants with these interpersonal liabilities are more likely to develop depression over time (Joiner & Timmons, 2009).

Depressed people also show a number of other interpersonal difficulties. Their social skills are sometimes lacking and they have more conflictual interpersonal relationships (Joiner & Timmons, 2009). Perhaps surprisingly, depressed people actively seek negative feedback from others, apparently in an attempt to confirm their negative self-views (Swann & Basson, 2010).

Psychosocial factors in bipolar disorder

Although bipolar disorder has strong genetic roots, psychosocial factors play a role in the course of the disorder. Stressful life events can trigger new episodes of bipolar disorder (Johnson et al., 2009). In particular, having an unsupportive family where members are critical, hostile, and exaggerated in emotional responses to each other increases the chances that a person with bipolar disorder will have a relapse of his or her symptoms (Hooley, 2007). In turn, psychotherapy designed to improve a toxic family atmosphere and teach the person with bipolar disorder how to reduce and cope with stress results in a lower risk of relapse of the disorder (Lam & Wong, 2005; Miklowitz & Craighead, 2007).

INTERIM SUMMARY

➔ The mood disorders are divided into depressive disorders, in which individuals experience only depressed mood, and bipolar disorder (or manic-depression), in which individuals experience both depression and mania.

➔ Biological theories attribute mood disorders to genetic factors and to problems in regulation of the neurotransmitters serotonin and norepinephrine.

➔ Cognitive theories attribute depression to pessimistic views of the self, the world, and the future and to maladaptive **attributional styles**.

➔ Psychodynamic theories view depression as a reactivation of loss of parental affection in a person who is dependent on external approval and tends to turn anger inward.

➔ Interpersonal theories view depression as the result of insecurities about relationships and maladaptive patterns of social interaction.

CRITICAL THINKING QUESTIONS

1 There is evidence that depression is much more common among people born in recent generations (since the 1950s) than in people born in earlier generations (around the turn of the twentieth century). Can you generate some hypotheses for this historical trend?

2 Many famous artists and writers have suffered from depression or bipolar disorder, including composer Robert Schumann, writers Sylvia Plath and William Styron, and US comedian Drew Carey. Could there be a link between mood disorders and creativity, and, if so, what might be the nature of that link?

SCHIZOPHRENIA

Things that relate, the town of Antelope, Oregon, Jonestown, Charlie Manson, the Hillside Strangler, the Zodiac Killer, Watergate, King's trial in Los Angeles, and many more. In the last 7 years alone, over 23 Star Wars scientists committed suicide for no apparent reason. The AIDS coverup, the conference in South America in 1987 had over 1000 doctors claim that insects can transmit it. To be able to read one's thoughts and place thoughts in one's own mind without the person knowing it's being done. Realization is a reality of bioelectromagnetic control, which is thought transfer and emotional control, recording individual brain-wave frequencies of thought, sensation and emotions.

(quoted in Nolen-Hoeksema, 2011, p. 232)

This 'announcement' posted by an individual with schizophrenia suggests what many of the unusual symptoms people with this disorder experience, including beliefs that others are conspiring against them, that their thoughts are being controlled, and thoughts are being transmitted into their minds. People with **schizophrenia** have such difficulty in sorting out the real from the unreal and in responding to the everyday events of life that they often become immobilized. Schizophrenia occurs in all cultures, even those that are remote from the stresses of industrialized civilization, and appears to have plagued humanity for at least 200 years. The disorder affects about 1 per cent of the population and occurs equally in men and women (Linscott & van Os, 2010). Schizophrenia exacts heavy costs both on the individual and on his or her family and community. People with schizophrenia must seek psychiatric and medical help frequently, and international studies show that up to 3 per cent of a nation's health care budget can be attributed to the costs of treating schizophrenia (Knapp *et al.,* 2004). The disorder usually begins in late adolescence or early adulthood, just when an individual is beginning a career and starting a family. Unfortunately, schizophrenia is one of the most stigmatized disorders, so individuals with this disorder and their families often carry tremendous shame.

Characteristics of schizophrenia

The symptoms are many and varied. The primary characteristics of schizophrenia can be summarized under the following headings, although not every person diagnosed as having the disorder will exhibit all of these symptoms. It should be noted that a recent change introduced by DSM-5 requires that two Criterion A symptoms is necessary for any diagnosis of schizophrenia and it is also a requirement of Criterion A that the individual must have at least one of these three core positive symptoms: delusions, hallucinations, and disorganized speech.

Disturbances of thought and attention

People with schizophrenia show disturbances in both the process of thinking and the content of their thoughts, as illustrated in the following excerpt from the writings of a person with schizophrenia.

If things turn by rotation of agriculture or levels in regards and timed to everything; I am referring to a previous document when I made some remarks that were facts also tested and there is another that concerns my daughter she has a lobed bottom right ear, her name being Mary Lou. Much of abstraction has been left unsaid and undone in these products milk, weather, trades, government in levels of breakages and fuses in electronics too all formerly states not necessarily factuated.

(Maher, 1966, p. 395)

By themselves, the words and phrases make sense, but they are meaningless in relation to each other. The juxtaposition of unrelated words and phrases and the idiosyncratic word associations (sometimes called **word salad**) are characteristic of the writing and speech of people with schizophrenia. They reflect a **loosening of associations** in which the individual's ideas shift from one topic to another in ways that appear unrelated. Moreover, the train of thought often seems to be influenced by the sound of words rather than by their meaning. The following account by a woman with schizophrenia of her thoughts in response to her doctor's questions illustrates this tendency to form associations by rhyming words, referred to as clang associations:

Doctor:	How about the medication? Are you still taking the Haldol? [an antipsychotic drug]
Patient Thinks:	Foul Wall. (She nods but does not reply.)
Doctor:	What about the vitamins?
Patient Thinks:	Seven sins. Has-beens. (She nods.)
Doctor:	I don't think you're taking all your meds.
Patient Thinks:	Pencil leads.

(North, 1987, p. 261)

The confused thought processes that are the hallmark of schizophrenia seem to stem from a general difficulty in focusing attention and filtering out irrelevant stimuli. Most of us are able to focus our attention selectively. From a mass of incoming sensory information, we are able to select the stimuli that are relevant to the task at hand and ignore the rest. A person who suffers from schizophrenia is receptive to many stimuli at the same time and has trouble making sense of the profusion of inputs, as the following statement by a person with schizophrenia illustrates:

I can't concentrate. It's diversions of attention that trouble me. I am picking up different conversations. It's like being a transmitter. The sounds are coming through to me, but I feel my mind cannot cope with everything. It's difficult to concentrate on any one sound.

(McGhie & Chapman, 1961, p. 104)

A sense of being unable to control one's attention and focus one's thoughts is central to the experience of schizophrenia.

One study of British people with schizophrenic delusions found subjects feared being controlled by television messages.

People with schizophrenia are also subject to **delusions**, beliefs that most people would view as misinterpretations of reality. The most common delusions are beliefs that external forces are trying to control one's thoughts and actions. These delusions of influence include the belief that one's thoughts are being broadcast to the world so that others can hear them, that strange thoughts (not one's own) are being inserted into one's mind, or that feelings and actions are being imposed on one by some external force. Also frequent are beliefs that certain people or certain groups are threatening or plotting against one (delusions of persecution). Less common are beliefs that one is powerful and important (delusions of grandeur).

The term **paranoid** is used to refer to beliefs that focus on persecution. A person with paranoid delusions may become suspicious of friends and relatives, fear being poisoned, or complain of being watched, followed, and talked about. In rare cases, a person who has a paranoid form of schizophrenia may lash out at those he or she thinks are trying to inflict harm. Most people with schizophrenia are not a danger to others, although their confusion may make them a danger to themselves.

The specific content of delusions in schizophrenia may vary across cultures and environments. For example, one study found that many of the delusions of British people with schizophrenia focused on being controlled by televisions, radios and computers, but this was rare among the Pakistani people with schizophrenia, whose delusions were more likely to involve being controlled by black magic (Suhail & Cochrane, 2002). These differences in the content of delusions probably reflect differences in a culture's belief systems as well as differences in the environments the two groups lived in.

Disturbances of perception

People experiencing acute schizophrenic episodes often report that the world appears different (noises seem louder, colors more intense). Their own bodies may no longer appear the same (their hands may seem too large or too small, their legs overly extended, their eyes dislocated in the face). Some people fail to recognize themselves in a mirror, or see their reflection as a triple image. The most dramatic disturbances of perception are **hallucinations**, sensory experiences in the absence of relevant or adequate external stimulation. Auditory hallucinations (usually voices telling one what to do or commenting on one's actions) are the most common. Visual hallucinations (such as seeing strange creatures or heavenly beings) are somewhat less frequent. Other sensory hallucinations (a bad odor emanating from one's body, the taste of poison in food, the feeling of being pricked by needles) occur infrequently. Hallucinations are often frightening, even terrifying, as the following example illustrates:

> At one point, I would look at my co-workers and their faces would become distorted. Their teeth looked like fangs ready to devour me. Most of the time I couldn't trust myself to look at anyone for fear of being swallowed. I had no respite from the illness. Even when I tried to sleep, the demons would keep me awake, and at times I would roam the house searching for them. I was being consumed on all sides whether I was awake or asleep. I felt I was being consumed by demons.

> (Long, 1996)

Auditory hallucinations may have their origin in ordinary thought. We often carry on internal dialogues – for example, commenting on our actions or having an imaginary conversation with another person. We may even occasionally talk aloud to ourselves. The voices that people with schizophrenia hear, calling them names or telling them what to do, are similar to internal dialogues. But a person experiencing an auditory hallucination does not believe that the voices originate within the self or that they can be controlled. The inability to distinguish between external and internal, real and imagined, is central to the experience of schizophrenia.

Disturbances of emotional expression

People suffering from schizophrenia often exhibit unusual emotional responses. They may be withdrawn and unresponsive in situations that should make them sad or happy. For example, a man may show no emotional response when informed that his daughter has cancer. However, this blunting of emotional expression can conceal inner turmoil, and the person may erupt with angry outbursts.

Sometimes individuals with schizophrenia express emotions that are inappropriately linked to the situation or to the thought being expressed, such as smiling while speaking of tragic events. Because our emotions are influenced by cognitive processes, it is not surprising that disorganized thoughts and

perceptions are accompanied by changes in emotional responses. This point is illustrated in the following comments:

> Half the time I am talking about one thing and thinking about half a dozen other things at the same time. It must look queer to people when I laugh about something that has got nothing to do with what I am talking about, but they don't know what's going on inside and how much of it is running around in my head. You see I might be talking about something quite serious to you and other things come into my head at the same time that are funny and this makes me laugh. If I could only concentrate on one thing at the one time I wouldn't look half so silly.

> (McGhie & Chapman, 1961, p. 104)

Behavioral symptoms and withdrawal from reality

People with schizophrenia sometimes exhibit bizarre behaviors. They may grimace, adopt strange facial expressions, or gesture repeatedly using peculiar sequences of finger, hand, and arm movements. Some may become very agitated and move about in continual activity, as in a manic state. Some, at the other extreme, may become totally unresponsive and immobile, adopting an unusual posture and maintaining it for long periods of time. For example, a person may stand like a statue with one foot extended and one arm raised toward the ceiling, maintaining this state of catatonic immobility for hours. Such an individual, who appears to have completely withdrawn from reality, may be responding to inner thoughts and fantasies.

Decreased ability to function

Besides the specific symptoms we have described, people with schizophrenia are impaired in their ability to carry out the daily routines of living. If the disorder occurs in adolescence, the individual shows a decreasing ability to cope with school and has limited social skills and few friends. Adults suffering from schizophrenia are often unsuccessful in obtaining or holding a job. Personal hygiene and grooming deteriorate, and the individual avoids the company of other people. Author Greg Bottoms describes his brother Michael's descent into schizophrenia:

> Michael's decline, both mentally and physically, was astonishingly fast. He had gone from being a decent student and an amazing athlete to failing everything in the space of 4 years; he had gone from being a black belt in karate – lithe, aggressive, handsome – to being a disheveled, Bible-toting one-man show in less than 1 year. The rapidity of

his decline once he hit 20 – particularly the physical decline – caught us all off guard. His poor marks in school had nothing to do with aptitude, but rather with his shifting of focus. He had a mission in life and little time to pursue other things, even if people insisted these things – school, a job, friends – were important.

His body softened dramatically, his hygiene could produce a gag reflex. Where he had once been inordinately handsome, he now had smears of blackheads across his nose, a double chin, greasy hair … . He started smoking three packs of Camels a day, sometimes rocked back and forth uncontrollably in the school smoking section during lunch, looking up through his long bangs at the other dopers to tell them that Jesus loved them … . He never slept – or if he did, it was maybe an hour or two at a time … . Sometimes he'd scream in the middle of the night.

(Bottoms, 2000, pp. 63–64)

The signs of schizophrenia are many and varied. Trying to make sense of the variety of symptoms is complicated by the fact that some may result directly from the disorder, whereas others may be a reaction to the effects of medication.

Culture and the progression of schizophrenia

Generally, schizophrenia is more chronic and debilitating than other psychological disorders. Between 50 and 80 per cent of people who are hospitalized with one episode of schizophrenia are eventually rehospitalized for another episode at some time in their lives (Eaton *et al.,* 1992). Not everyone with schizophrenia shows progressive deterioration in functioning, however. Between 20 and 30 per cent of people treated for schizophrenia recover substantially from the illness within ten to 20 years of its onset (Wiersma *et al.,* 1998).

Culture seems to play a strong role in the course of schizophrenia. People who have schizophrenia in developing countries, such as India, Nigeria, and Colombia, are less likely to remain incapacitated by the disorder for the long term than people who have schizophrenia in developed countries such as Great Britain, Denmark, or the USA (see Figure 15.11; Jablensky, 2000). Why might this be? Differences in how cultures treat their individuals with schizophrenia probably play a strong role. In developing countries, people with schizophrenia are more likely cared for at home by a broad network of family members who share responsibility for the individual (Anders, 2003). In contrast, in developed countries, it is less likely that the person with schizophrenia lives with family or that his or her immediate family has other family members nearby who share in the care. Caring for a family member

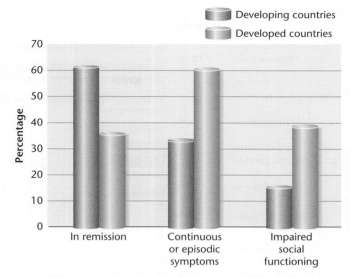

FIGURE 15.11 Cultural Differences in the Course of Schizophrenia. *People with schizophrenia in developing countries show a more positive course of the disorder than people in developed countries.*

with schizophrenia can be a huge burden. When this burden is shouldered by only a few people, there can be tremendous conflict in the family, which may exacerbate the symptoms of the person with schizophrenia.

Understanding schizophrenia

Schizophrenia probably has strong biological roots, but environmental stress may push people who are vulnerable to schizophrenia into more severe forms of the disorder or new episodes of psychosis. According to DSM-5, schizophrenia is now understood along a spectrum which includes the personality disorders identified as schizoid and schizotypal.

The biological perspective

Family studies show that there is a hereditary predisposition for schizophrenia. Relatives of people with schizophrenia are more likely to develop the disorder than people from families that are free of schizophrenia (Gottesman & Reilly, 2003). Figure 15.12 shows the lifetime risk of developing schizophrenia as a function of how closely an individual is genetically related to a person diagnosed with schizophrenia. Note that an identical twin of a schizophrenic is three times more likely than a fraternal twin to develop schizophrenia and 46 times more likely than an unrelated person to develop the disorder. However, fewer than half of identical twins of people with schizophrenia develop schizophrenia themselves, even though they share the same genes.

Genetic abnormalities may lead to abnormal brain structure or functioning in people with schizophrenia. The prefrontal cortex is smaller and shows less activity in some people with

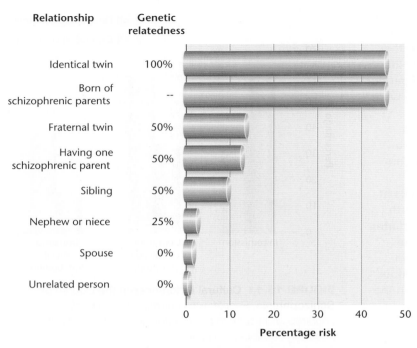

Relationship	Genetic relatedness
Identical twin	100%
Born of schizophrenic parents	--
Fraternal twin	50%
Having one schizophrenic parent	50%
Sibling	50%
Nephew or niece	25%
Spouse	0%
Unrelated person	0%

FIGURE 15.12 Genetic Relationships and Schizophrenia. *The lifetime risk of developing schizophrenia is largely a function of how closely an individual is genetically related to a schizophrenic person and not a function of how much their environment is shared. In the case of an individual with two schizophrenic parents, genetic relatedness cannot be expressed in terms of percentages, but the regression of the individual's 'genetic value' on that of the parents is 100 per cent, the same as it is for identical twins.*

schizophrenia than in people without the disorder (Andreasen, 2001; Barch, 2005; see Figure 15.13). The prefrontal cortex is the largest region of the brain in human beings, nearly 30 per cent of the total cortex, and it has connections to all the other cortical regions, as well as to the limbic system, which is

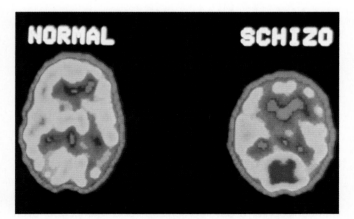

FIGURE 15.13 A Normal Brain Versus a Schizophrenic Brain. *This PET scan shows the metabolic differences between the prefrontal cortex of an individual with schizophrenia and the same areas in the brain of a normal individual.*

involved in emotion and cognition, and the basal ganglia, which is involved in motor movement. The prefrontal cortex plays important roles in language, emotional expression, planning and producing new ideas, and mediating social interactions. Thus, it seems logical that people whose prefrontal cortex is unusually small or inactive would show a wide range of deficits in cognition, emotion, and social interaction, as people with schizophrenia do.

People with schizophrenia also have enlarged ventricles (the fluid-filled spaces in the brain) (see Figure 15.14). The presence of enlarged ventricles suggests atrophy or deterioration in other brain tissue. The specific areas of the brain that have deteriorated, resulting in ventricular enlargement, could lead to different manifestations of schizophrenia.

Although neurochemical theories of mood disorders center on norepinephrine and serotonin, the culprit in schizophrenia is believed to be dopamine (Downar & Kapur, 2008). First, there may be excess dopamine activity in the mesolimbic system, a subcortical part of the brain involved in cognition and emotion, which leads to hallucinations, delusions, and disordered thought. Second, there may be unusually low dopamine activity in the prefrontal area of the brain, which is involved in attention, motivation, and organization of behavior. Low dopamine activity in the prefrontal area may lead to lack of motivation, inability to care for oneself, inappropriate emotional expression.

As we mentioned, these abnormalities in brain structure and neurochemical functioning could be due to genetics, but they also could be the result of insults to the brain of a fetus or young child. Studies have found that people who have schizophrenia are more likely to have a history of birth complications, perinatal brain damage, infections in the central nervous system (such as meningitis) in infancy, and maternal pregnancy complications or influenza in pregnancy (Cannon & Keller, 2006). Each of these might cause permanent damage to the central nervous system of the fetus or young child, perhaps contributing to risk for schizophrenia.

The social and psychological perspective

Psychosocial factors appear to play an important role in determining the eventual severity of the disorder in people with a biological predisposition toward schizophrenia, as well as in triggering new episodes of psychosis. The type of stress that has received the most attention in recent studies is family-related stress. Members of families that are high in expressed emotion are overinvolved with one another, overprotective of the disturbed family member, and, at the same

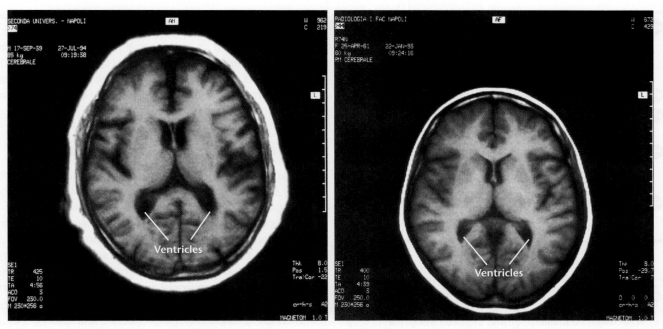

FIGURE 15.14 Brain Functioning in Schizophrenia. *The MRI on the left shows evidence of ventricular enlargement in the brain of a person with schizophrenia compared with that of a person without schizophrenia in the image on the right.*

time, critical, hostile, and resentful toward the disturbed member. People with schizophrenia whose families are high in expressed emotion are three to four times more likely to suffer a new psychotic episode than those whose families are low in expressed emotion (Hooley, 2007). Being in a family with high levels of expressed emotion may create stresses that trigger new episodes of psychosis by overwhelming the schizophrenic person's ability to cope.

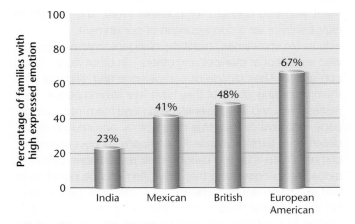

FIGURE 15.15 Cultural Differences in the Prevalence of **Expressed Emotion in Families of Schizophrenics.** *Families of people with schizophrenia from developing countries tend to show lower levels of expressed emotion than do families of schizophrenics from developed countries. This may be one reason that people with schizophrenia from developing countries have fewer relapses than do those from developed countries.*

The link between expressed emotion and relapse in schizophrenia may help to explain the cross-cultural differences in the prognosis of this disorder. One study found that families of people with schizophrenia in Mexico and India scored lower on measures of expressed emotions than did families of people with schizophrenia in Europe and the USA (see Figure 15.15; Karno & Jenkins, 1993).

Critics of the research on expressed emotion argue that the hostility and intrusiveness observed in some families of people with schizophrenia might be the result of the symptoms exhibited by the disturbed member, rather than a factor contributing to the disorder (Parker *et al.*, 1988). Although families are often forgiving of positive symptoms like hallucinations, viewing them as uncontrollable, they can be unforgiving of the negative symptoms like lack of motivation (Hooley, 2007). People with these symptoms may elicit more negative expressed emotion and may be especially prone to relapse. Perhaps the best evidence that expressed emotion actually influences relapse is that treatments that reduce expressed emotion tend to reduce the relapse rate in family members with schizophrenia.

INTERIM SUMMARY

➔ Schizophrenia is characterized by disturbances in thought, including disorganized thought processes, and delusions.

➔ Other symptoms include perceptual disturbances (such as hallucinations), inappropriate emotional expression, bizarre motor activity, withdrawal, and impaired functioning.

➔ Schizophrenia clearly is transmitted genetically.

➔ People with schizophrenia also have problems in dopamine regulation.

➔ Two types of brain abnormalities are consistently seen in schizophrenia: The prefrontal cortex is smaller and less active, and the ventricles are enlarged.

➔ Difficult environments may worsen the disorder and contribute to relapses.

CRITICAL THINKING QUESTIONS

1 What might be the mechanisms by which living in a family with high expressed emotion contributes to relapse in people with schizophrenia?

2 There is evidence that people with schizophrenia are more likely to have been born in the winter or spring of the year than in the summer or fall. Can you generate some hypotheses about why this might be so?

PERSONALITY DISORDERS

Personality disorders are long-standing patterns of maladaptive behavior. In Chapter 13 we described personality traits as enduring ways of perceiving or relating to the environment and thinking about oneself. When personality traits become so inflexible and maladaptive that they significantly impair the individual's ability to function, they are referred to as personality disorders. People with personality disorders experience themselves and the world in ways that are highly distressing to them and/or impair their ability to function in daily life. These experiences begin in childhood or adolescence and persist over time and across situations, affecting most areas of the person's life. The particular emotions, thoughts, and behaviors that an individual experiences vary according to the specific disorder.

The ICD and DSM list several personality disorders. The characteristics of these disorders tend to overlap, making it difficult to agree on how to classify some individuals. Moreover, it is difficult to say when a person's behavior is simply different from other people's behaviors and when the behavior is so severe that it warrants a diagnosis. The personality disorder that has been studied the most and is the most reliably

diagnosed is the antisocial personality disorder (technically labeled dissocial personality disorder in the ICD, but most commonly referred to as antisocial personality disorder, and sometimes referred to as psychopathy or sociopathy). We discuss it in this section, along with borderline personality disorder, a controversial personality disorder that has received much attention in recent years.

Antisocial personality disorder

People who have **antisocial personality disorder** have little sense of responsibility, morality, or concern for others. Their behavior is determined almost entirely by their own needs. In other words, they lack a conscience. Whereas the average person realizes at an early age that some restrictions are placed on behavior and that pleasures must sometimes be postponed in consideration of the needs of others, individuals who have antisocial personalities seldom consider any desires except their own. They behave impulsively, seek immediate gratification of their needs, and cannot tolerate frustration.

Antisocial behavior results from a number of causes, including membership in a delinquent gang or a criminal subculture, the need for attention and status, loss of contact with reality, and inability to control impulses. However, most juvenile delinquents and adult criminals show some concern for others (for example, family or gang members) and adhere to some code of moral conduct (never betray a friend). In contrast, people with antisocial personalities have little feeling for anyone except themselves and seem to experience little guilt or remorse, regardless of how much suffering their behavior may cause. Other characteristics of the antisocial personality include a great facility for lying, a need for thrills and excitement with little concern for possible injury, and inability to alter behavior as a consequence of punishment. Such individuals are sometimes attractive, intelligent, charming people who are adept at manipulating others – in other words, good con artists. Their façade of competence and sincerity wins them promising jobs, but they have little staying power. Their restlessness and impulsiveness soon lead them into an escapade that reveals their true nature; they accumulate debts, desert their families, squander company money, or commit crimes. When they are caught, their declarations of repentance are so convincing that they often escape punishment and are given another chance. But antisocial personalities seldom live up to these declarations; what they say has little relation to what they feel or do. Deceitfulness is one of the defining characteristics of antisocial personality (Kraus & Reynolds, 2001).

Fortunately, the full syndrome of antisocial personality disorder is relatively rare. It is much more common in men than in women, with about 3 per cent of men and 1 per cent of women having this disorder at some time in their lives (Hare & Neumann, 2008).

Understanding antisocial personality disorder

What factors contribute to the development of an antisocial personality? Current research focuses on biological determinants, the quality of the parent–child relationship, and ways of thinking that promote antisocial behaviors.

Biological factors

Genetic factors appear to play a role in the development of antisocial personality. Both twin and adoption studies show that antisocial personality is heritable, perhaps particularly antisocial tendencies that begin early in childhood (Kendler, Jacobson, Myer, & Eaves, 2008).

One of the cardinal features of antisocial personality is impulsivity (Rutter, 1997). Many animal studies and some human studies suggest that impulsive and aggressive behaviors are linked to low levels of the neurotransmitter serotonin (Krakowski, 2003; Mann *et al.,* 2001). Low serotonin levels may contribute to impulsivity in antisocial personality disorder.

People with antisocial personalities also show deficits in the ability to sustain concentration, in abstract reasoning, in formulating and implementing goals, in self-monitoring and self-awareness, and in shifting from maladaptive patterns of behavior to more adaptive ones (Henry & Moffitt, 1997). Collectively, these are known as executive functions, and their control resides largely in the temporal and frontal lobes of the brain. In turn, some studies have found differences between antisocial adults (usually prison inmates) and the general population in the structure or functioning of these areas of the brain (Morgan & Lilienfeld, 2000). These brain anomalies could be the result of medical illnesses and exposure to toxins during infancy and childhood, which are both more common in antisocial people than in controls, or to genetic abnormalities. Whatever their causes, deficits in executive functions could contribute to poor impulse control and difficulty in anticipating the consequences of one's actions.

Other studies have shown that people with antisocial personality disorder have low levels of arousability, measured by relatively low resting heart rates and low skin conductance activity (Sylvers *et al.,* 2008). Low levels of arousal may indicate low levels of fear in response to threatening situations. Fearlesness can be put to good use – for instance, British paratroopers and bomb disposal experts show low levels of arousal (McMillan & Rachman, 1987; O'Connor *et al.,* 1985). However, fearlessness may also allow some people to engage in antisocial and violent behaviors, such as fighting or robbery. In addition, children with low arousal levels may not fear punishment, and thus may not be deterred from antisocial behavior by the threat of punishment.

Chronically low arousal may also be an uncomfortable state that people with antisocial personality disorder relieve

Low levels of arousal sometimes indicates low levels of fear, a useful character trait for bomb disposal officers.

by seeking stimulation (Eysenck, 1994). Again, if an individual seeks stimulation through prosocial or neutral acts, such as skydiving, stimulation seeking may not lead to antisocial behavior. But some individuals may engage in dangerous or impulsive acts to seek stimulation, and they may be more prone to develop antisocial personalities.

Social factors

Even children who have a biological predisposition for antisocial behavior appear unlikely to develop antisocial personality disorder unless they are also exposed to environments that promote antisocial behavior (Dishion & Patterson, 1997; Dodge & Pettit, 2003). The parents of children with antisocial personalities often appear to be simultaneously neglectful and hostile toward their children. The children are frequently unsupervised for long periods. The parents often are not involved in the children's everyday lives, not knowing where they are or who their friends are. But when these parents do interact with their children, the interactions are often characterized by hostility, physical violence, and ridicule (Dishion &

When parents use physical punishment, children are more likely to develop violent tendencies.

Patterson, 1997). This description does not fit all parents of such children, but parental non-involvement and hostility are good predictors of children's vulnerability to antisocial personality disorder.

The biological and family factors that contribute to antisocial personality often coincide. Children who behave in antisocial ways often suffer from neuropsychological problems that are the result of maternal drug use, poor prenatal nutrition, prenatal and postnatal exposure to toxic agents, child abuse, birth complications, and low birth weight (Moffitt, 1993). Children with these neuropsychological problems are more irritable, impulsive, awkward, overreactive, and inattentive, and they learn more slowly than their peers. This makes them difficult to care for, and they are therefore at increased risk for maltreatment and neglect. In turn, the parents of these children are more likely to be teenagers or to have psychological problems of their own that contribute to ineffective, harsh, or inconsistent parenting. Thus, for these children a biological predisposition to disruptive, antisocial behaviors may be combined with a style of parenting that contributes to these behaviors. In a study of 536 boys, Moffitt (1990) found that those who had both neuropsychological deficits and adverse home environments scored four times higher on an aggression scale than those with neither neuropsychological deficits nor adverse home environments.

Cognitive factors

Children with antisocial personalities tend to process information about social interactions in ways that promote aggressive reactions to these interactions (Crick & Dodge, 1994). They assume that other children will be aggressive toward them, and they interpret other children's actions in line with these assumptions rather than using cues from the specific situations they actually face. In addition, they tend to believe that any negative action by a peer – such as taking their favorite pencil – is intentional rather than accidental.

When deciding what action to take in response to a perceived provocation by a peer, children with antisocial personalities tend to think of a narrow range of responses, usually including aggression. When pressed to consider responses other than aggression, they make ineffective or vague responses and often consider responses other than aggression to be useless or unattractive.

Children who think about their social interactions in this way are likely to engage in aggressive behaviors toward others and may therefore suffer retaliation. Other children will hit them, parents and teachers will punish them, and they will be perceived more negatively by others. These actions may feed their assumptions that the world is against them, causing them to misinterpret future actions by others. In this way, a cycle of interactions can be established that maintains and encourages aggressive, antisocial behaviors.

Borderline personality disorder

Borderline personality disorder is a lifelong disorder characterized by extreme variability in mood, relationships, and self-perceptions. It has been the focus of considerable attention in the popular press and in clinical and research writings in psychology in the past couple of decades.

People with borderline personality disorder have unstable moods, self-concept, and relationships with others. They may experience bouts of severe depression, anxiety, or anger seeming to arise frequently, often in response to minor triggers. Their views of themselves may swing from extreme self-doubt and grandiose self-importance. Their relationships with others are often volatile, with switches from idealizing other people to despising them. People with borderline personality disorder often feel desperately empty and will initially cling to a new acquaintance or therapist in the hope that he or she will fill the tremendous void they feel in themselves. At the same time, they may misinterpret other people's innocent actions as signs of abandonment or rejection. Along with instability of mood, self-concept, and interpersonal relationships comes a tendency toward impulsive self-damaging behaviors, including self-mutilation and suicidal behavior. Self-mutilation often takes the form of burning or cutting. Finally, people with borderline personality disorder are prone to transient episodes in which they feel unreal, lose track of time, and may even forget who they are.

In the following passage, a clinician describes a woman who was diagnosed with borderline personality disorder (Linehan *et al.,* pp. 502–504):

At the initial meeting, Cindy was a 30-year-old, white, married woman with no children who was living in a middle-class suburban area with her husband. She had a college education and had successfully completed almost 2 years of medical school. Cindy was referred by her psychiatrist of $1\frac{1}{2}$ years, who was no longer willing to provide more than pharmacotherapy following a recent hospitalization for a near-lethal suicide attempt. In the 2 years prior to referral, Cindy had been hospitalized at least ten times (one lasting 6 months) for psychiatric treatment of suicidal ideation; had engaged in numerous instances of parasuicidal behavior, including at least ten instances of drinking Clorox bleach, multiple deep cuts, and burns; and had had three medically severe or nearly lethal suicide attempts, including cutting an artery in her neck.

Until age 27 Cindy was able to function well in work and school settings, and her marriage was reasonably satisfactory to both partners, although the husband complained of Cindy's excessive anger. When Cindy was in the second year of medical school, a classmate she knew only slightly committed suicide. Cindy stated that when she heard about the suicide, she immediately decided to kill herself also, but had very little insight into what about the situation actually elicited the inclination to kill herself. Within weeks she left medical school and became severely depressed and actively suicidal. Although Cindy presented herself as a person with few psychological problems before the classmate's suicide, further questioning revealed a history of severe anorexia nervosa, bulimia nervosa, and alcohol and prescription medication abuse, originating at the age of 14 years.

Over the course of therapy, a consistent pattern associated with self-harm became apparent. The chain of events would often begin with an interpersonal encounter (almost always with her husband), which culminated in her feeling threatened, criticized, or unloved. These feelings would often be followed by urges either to self-mutilate or to kill herself, depending somewhat on her levels of hopelessness, anger, and sadness. Decisions to self-mutilate and/or to attempt suicide were often accompanied by the thought 'I'll show you.' At other times, hopelessness and a desire to end the pain permanently seemed predominant. Following the conscious decision to self-mutilate or attempt suicide, Cindy would then immediately dissociate and at some later point cut or burn herself, usually while in a state of 'automatic pilot'. Consequently, Cindy often had difficulty remembering specifics of the actual acts. At one point, Cindy burned her leg so badly (and then injected it with dirt to convince the doctor that he should give her more attention) that reconstructive surgery was required.

People with borderline personality disorder also tend to be diagnosed with other disorders, including substance abuse, depression, generalized anxiety disorder, specific phobias, agoraphobia, post-traumatic stress disorder, and panic disorder (Kraus & Reynolds, 2001). Longitudinal studies of people with this disorder indicate that about 10 per cent die by suicide, and perhaps 75 per cent have attempted suicide (Linehan et al., 2001).

About 1 to 4 per cent of the population will develop borderline personality disorder at some time in their lives (Lenzenweger et al., 2007). The disorder is diagnosed much more often in women than in men. People with this disorder tend to have stormy marital relationships, more job difficulties, and a higher rate of physical disability than average.

Understanding borderline personality disorder

Psychoanalytic theorists suggest that individuals with borderline personalities have very poorly developed views of self and others, stemming from poor early relationships with caregivers (Kernberg, 1979). The caregivers of people with borderline personality disorder may have encouraged excessive dependence from them as children, punishing the children's attempts at developing an autonomous self-concept. As a result, people with borderline personality disorder never learn to fully differentiate between their views of self and others. This makes them extremely sensitive to others' opinions of them and to the possibility of being abandoned. When others are perceived as rejecting them, they reject themselves and may engage in self-punishment or self-mutilation.

Psychoanalytic theories also argue that individuals with borderline personalities have never been able to integrate the positive and negative qualities of either their self-concept or their concept of others, because their early caregivers were comforting and rewarding when they remained dependent and compliant toward them but hostile and rejecting when they tried to separate from them. People with borderline personalities therefore tend to see themselves and others as either 'all good' or 'all bad' and vacillate between these two views. This process is referred to as splitting. The instability in these individuals' emotions and interpersonal relationships is caused by splitting – their emotions and their perspectives on their relationships reflect their vacillation between the 'all good' and the 'all bad' self or other.

Research with people with borderline personality disorder are more likely than people without the disorder to report childhoods marked by instability, abuse, neglect, and parental psychopathology (Helgeland & Torgersen, 2004). This is true, however, of the childhoods of people with many different types of psychopathology and does not directly address the psychoanalytic theory of the development of this disorder.

One influential theorist, Marcia Linehan (Linehan et al., 2001), argues that people with borderline personality disorder have fundamental deficits in the ability to regulate emotions. Extreme emotional reactions to situations lead to impulsive actions. In addition, Linehan argues that people with borderline personality disorder have histories of significant others discounting and criticizing their emotional experiences. Such a history makes it even harder for them to learn appropriate emotion-regulation skills and to understand and accept their emotional reactions to events. People with this disorder come to rely on others to help them cope with difficult situations but do not have enough self-confidence to ask for help from others in mature ways. They become manipulative and indirect in trying to gain support from others.

INTERIM SUMMARY

→ Personality disorders are lifelong patterns of maladaptive behavior involving difficulties in coping with stress or solving problems.

→ Individuals with antisocial personality disorder are impulsive, show little guilt, are concerned only with their own needs, and are frequently in trouble with the law.

→ Antisocial personality disorder may have genetic and biological roots. Neglectful and hostile parenting also appear to contribute to the disorder.

→ People with borderline personality disorder show instability in mood, self-concept, and interpersonal relationships.

→ Psychoanalytic theories suggest that the caregivers of people with this disorder required their children to be highly dependent and alternated between extreme expressions of love and hostility. Other theorists argue that people with borderline personality disorder have extreme difficulties in regulating their emotions.

CRITICAL THINKING QUESTIONS

1 Do personality disorders seem to be just the extremes of normal personality traits or distinct entities that are qualitatively different from normal personality traits?

2 What similarities do you see between antisocial personality disorder and borderline personality disorder?

AUTISM SPECTRUM DISORDER

Autism spectrum disorder was recently redefined by DSM-5 to embrace what was formerly referred to as autism, Asperger's disorder, childhood disintegrative disorder, Rett's disorder and pervasive developmental disorder. It is a disor-

der first beginning in childhood and characterized by severe and lasting impairment in several areas of development, including social interactions, communication with others, everyday behaviors, interests, and activities. Many children with an autism spectrum disorder also show at least mild levels of intellectual disability, although some have normal or superior intelligence or special skills.

Diagnosis of autism spectrum disorder

Autism spectrum disorder involves deficits in social interaction, in communication, and in activities. Individuals with an autism spectrum disorder seem unable to make social connections with others. As infants, they may not smile in response to their caregivers as most infants do, or even make eye-to-eye contact. They may not enjoy cuddling, and, when they are older, may not be interested in playing with other children, preferring to remain in solitary play. They also do not seem to react to other people's emotions. Richard is a child with an autism spectrum disorder (adapted from Spitzer *et al.,* 1994, pp. 336–337):

Richard, age 3, appeared to be self-sufficient and aloof from others. He did not greet his mother in the mornings or his father when he returned from work, though, if left with a baby-sitter, he tended to scream much of the time. He had no interest in other children and ignored his younger brother. His babbling had no conversational intonation. At age 3 he could understand simple practical instructions. His speech consisted of echoing some words and phrases he had heard in the past, with the original speaker's accent and intonation; he could use one or two such phrases to indicate his simple needs. For example, if he said, 'Do you want a drink?' he meant he was thirsty. He did not communicate by facial expression or use gesture or mime, except for pulling someone along with him and placing his or her hand on an object he wanted. He was fascinated by bright lights and spinning objects and would stare at them while laughing, flapping his hands, and dancing on tiptoe. He also displayed the same movements while listening to music, which he liked from infancy. He was intensely attached to a miniature car, which he held in his hand, day and night, but he never played imaginatively with this or any other toy. He could assemble jigsaw puzzles rapidly (with one hand because of the car held in the other), whether the picture side was exposed or hidden. From age 2 he had collected kitchen utensils and arranged them in repetitive patterns all over the floors of the house. These pursuits, together with occasional periods of aimless running around, constituted his whole repertoire of spontaneous activities.

Children with an autism spectrum disorder often show no interest in playing with others.

The major management problem was Richard's intense resistance to any attempt to change or extend his interests. Removing his toy car, disturbing his puzzles or patterns, even retrieving, for example, an egg whisk or a spoon for its legitimate use in cooking, or trying to make him look at a picture book precipitated temper tantrums that could last an hour or more, with screaming, kicking, and the biting of himself or others. These tantrums could be cut short by restoring the status quo. Otherwise, playing his favorite music or going for a long car ride were sometimes effective.

His parents had wondered if Richard might be deaf, but his love of music, his accurate echoing, and his sensitivity to some very soft sounds, such as those made by unwrapping chocolate in the next room, convinced them that this was not the cause of his abnormal behavior. Psychological testing gave Richard a mental age of 3 years in non–language-dependent skills (such as assembling objects) but only 18 months in language comprehension.

Children with an autism spectrum disorder show a number of difficulties in communication and speech, as did Richard. Richard echoed what he had just heard, a phenomenon called *echolalia*, rather than responding with his own thoughts. He reversed pronouns, using *you* when he meant *I*. When Richard did speak, he spoke in a monotone almost like a machine.

Finally, children with an autism spectrum disorder show repetitive and stereotyped patterns of activities and interests. Rather than using toys for symbolic play (for example, using dolls to 'have tea'), children with an autism spectrum disorder may be preoccupied with one part of a toy or an object, as Richard was preoccupied with his miniature car. A child with an autism spectrum disorder might take the arm off one doll and simply pass it back and forth between her two hands. Routines and rituals are often extremely important to people with autism spectrum disorder: when any aspect of the daily routine is changed – for example, if a child's mother stops at the bank on the way to school – they may fly into a rage. Some people with autism spectrum disorder use parts of their own body to engage in stereotyped and repetitive behaviors, such as incessantly flapping their hands or banging their heads against walls. These behaviors are sometimes referred to as *self-stimulatory behaviors*, under the assumption that these children engage in these behaviors for self-stimulation. It is not clear, however, that this is their true purpose.

Many children with autism spectrum disorder do poorly on intelligence tests, and 50 to 70 per cent have moderate to severe intellectual impairments (Sigman *et al.,* 2006). Some children, however, only have deficits in skills requiring language and taking the perspectives of others. A very small proportion of children with autism spectrum disorder have special talents, such as the ability to play music without having been taught or to draw extremely well, or exceptional memory and mathematical calculation abilities, as was depicted in the movie *Rain Man*. These persons are sometimes referred to as *savants*. These cases are quite rare, however (Bolte & Poustka, 2004).

In order to be diagnosed with autism spectrum disorder, children must show symptoms before the age of three. There is a wide variation in the severity and outcome of this disorder. Howlin *et al.,* Rutter (2004) followed 68 individuals who had been diagnosed with autism spectrum disorder as children. As adults, one-fifth of them had been able to obtain some sort of academic degree, five had gone on to college, and two had obtained postgraduate degrees. Almost a third were employed and about a quarter had close friendships. The majority, however, remained dependent on their parents or required some form of residential care. Fifty-eight per cent had overall outcomes that were rated as 'poor' or 'very poor.' They were unable to live alone or hold a job, and had persistent problems in communication and social interactions.

The best predictor of the outcome of autism spectrum disorder is a child's IQ and amount of language development before the age of six (Howlin *et al.,* 2004; Nordin & Gillberg, 1998). Children who have IQs above 50 and can speak with others before age six have a much better prognosis than do those with IQs below 50 and no communicative speech.

The prevalence of autism spectrum disorder is about 1 in 500 children, and the prevalence of all forms of **pervasive developmental disorder** is 1 in 160 children (Fombonne, 2003). Boys outnumber girls about three to one.

SEEING BOTH SIDES

IS ATTENTION DEFICIT HYPERACTIVITY DISORDER (ADHD) OVERDIAGNOSED?

ADHD IS OVERDIAGNOSED

Caryn L. Carlson, The University of Texas at Austin

The diagnostic criteria for attention-deficit/hyperactivity disorder (ADHD) in DSM-5 remain very similar to those in DSM-IV. The growing public attention to attention deficit hyperactivity disorder (ADHD) in recent years has increased the detection of legitimate cases and led to much-needed research. We must be cautious, however, that we do not allow the diagnostic pendulum to swing too far, since finding answers about ADHD depends on the rigor and integrity of our classification system.

There is reason to believe that ADHD is currently being overdiagnosed in some areas of the USA. Prescriptions of stimulant medications, which are almost exclusively for ADHD, provide a 'proxy' for diagnostic rates and afford an examination of trends over time and place. Use of methylphenidate in the USA, already high by worldwide standards (International Narcotics Control Board, 1998), skyrocketed in the early 1990s, more than doubling from 1990 through 1995 (Safer *et al.,* 1996) and has continued to increase since then. While rates are up for all age groups, the largest increase is for teenagers and adults; among school-age children in one region, the proportion of high school students using stimulant medication tripled from 1991 through 1995 (Safer *et al.,* 1996). Certainly the true prevalence of ADHD has not increased at this rate, although part of the increase no doubt reflects the detection of previously unrecognized ADHD. While some reports suggest that even now many ADHD children may not be recognized or treated (Wolraich *et al.,* 1998), the average rates are now quite high (Safer *et al.,* 1996).

Part of the dramatic increase probably reflects overdiagnosis, particularly when considered in light of the vast disparities across geographical locales in the USA. The rate of methylphenidate consumption per capita in 1995 was 2.4 times higher in Virginia than in neighboring West Virginia, and nearly 4 times higher than in California (Spanos, 1996). Even more troubling are the high discrepancies across counties within states. For example, although the per capita rate for males of ages 6–12 in 1991 in New York was 4.1 per cent statewide, rates varied by a factor of 10 among counties, ranging up to 14 per cent (Kaufman, 1995).

What factors might lead to overdiagnosis of ADHD? We know from epidemiological research that unreasonable prevalence rates (e.g., up to nearly 23 percent of school-age boys; Wolraich *et al.,* 1998) are obtained when ADHD is identified based merely on simple ratings from one source, but become much lower when full diagnostic criteria – including age of onset by seven, presence across settings, and confirmation of impairment – are imposed. The wide variability in diagnostic rates across locations suggests that clinicians are applying diagnostic criteria inconsistently. Some clinicians diagnose without assessing all criteria, and often they rely only on parent reports. While underdiagnosis may be occurring in some places, overdiagnosis is occurring in others.

When is overdiagnosis most likely? It seems that the diagnosis of ADHD has become fashionable for those who experience some negative life event – such as school failure or job loss – and desire to attribute such problems to a disorder rather than accept personal responsibility. This tendency is apparent even in more mundane arenas, such as feeling bored or unmotivated – 'What a relief: the fact that I find it difficult to pay attention in my "history of Swedish cartographers" class isn't my fault. I have ADHD.'

One safeguard against misdiagnosis is the current criteria that symptoms must appear by age seven. But how early and by what means can we detect ADHD if we agree that it is present from an early age? Since objective measures that can reliably identify ADHD are currently unavailable, we must rely on symptom reports from others. Setting the age of onset at seven years recognizes that normal behavior patterns may be similar to symptoms of ADHD up to about age five, when normally activity decreases and attention increases (but not in children with ADHD). Also, impairment may not occur outside the demands of a classroom environment. But if individuals do not have symptoms early but develop them later for a variety of reasons, including life situations or stress, then diagnosis does not seem warranted. Should such problems be recognized? By all means. Should they be treated? Of course, by teaching people organizational and behavior management strategies, and possibly even with medication. But significant problems in living are not the equivalent of disorders, and to call them that will deter us in the search for etiologies of ADHD.

SEEING BOTH SIDES

IS ATTENTION DEFICIT HYPERACTIVITY DISORDER (ADHD) OVERDIAGNOSED?

ADHD IS NEITHER OVERDIAGNOSED NOR OVERTREATED

William Pelham, SUNY Buffalo

Because ADHD is the most widely diagnosed mental health disorder of childhood and because its frequency of treatment with medication has been increasing exponentially through the 1990s, it has become fashionable in many quarters – particularly among educators – to argue that it is overdiagnosed and consequently overtreated. Histrionic diatribes aside, there is no solid empirical evidence that ADHD is overdiagnosed or overtreated.

First, consider the accusation that ADHD is only a relatively recent phenomenon. To the contrary, the diagnosis was often widely used in the past but played second fiddle to other diagnoses. For example, one of the more important early studies in treatment of conduct disordered children (Patterson, 1974) noted, almost as an aside that more than two-thirds of the boys had hyperkinesis, an early label for ADHD. Thus, while ADHD may well be *diagnosed* more often than in the past 30 years, it is simply being diagnosed more appropriately and given the prominence it deserves.

It is important to note that the major reason for the increasing rate of ADHD identification in the USA since the early 1990s is the 1991 change in the status of ADHD in the Individuals with Disabilities Education Act (IDEA), the federal law that governs special education throughout the USA. This change included ADHD as a handicapping condition. Further, the US Office of Education sent a memorandum to all state officers of education directing them to consider ADHD as a condition eligible for special education. As a result of this directive, school districts throughout the country for the first time were required to establish screening and diagnostic procedures for ADHD. The increase in diagnosis for ADHD is thus not a conspiracy or a fatal flaw in education or an indictment of current parenting practices, but is instead a natural by-product of a change in federal regulations governing education in the USA.

What about the criticism that ADHD is a disorder with diagnostic rates that vary widely both within North America and across the world? The explanation is that local school districts and states vary dramatically in the degree to which they have implemented the mandated changes in the IDEA. Furthermore, ADHD when similar diagnostic criteria are applied, comparable rates to those in North America exist in a diverse collection of countries that include Italy, Spain, South Africa, Israel, Argentina, and Vietnam.

The most important factor in deciding whether a mental health disorder is overdiagnosed is whether the diagnosed individuals have impairments in daily life functioning sufficient to justify the label. ADHD is a particularly compelling example of this issue because the children suffer from dramatic impairment in relationships with peers, parents, teachers, and siblings, as well as in classroom behavior and academic performance. To take a single example, in one classic study of consecutive referrals to a clinic, 96 per cent of ADHD children were rejected by their peers on sociometric nominations at a rate higher than their class averages (Pelham & Bender, 1982). In the field of child psychopathology, the number of negative nominations received on a classroom peer nomination inventory in elementary school is widely thought to be the best indicator of severe impairment in childhood and poor outcome in adulthood, so this elevated rate of negative nominations highlights the impairment that ADHD children suffer in the peer domain.

A corollary of the argument that many children are inappropriately diagnosed with ADHD is the complaint that these children are being inappropriately treated – usually with medication. In fact, the literature shows that only a small minority of diagnosed ADHD children (or all children with mental health disorders for that matter) receive treatment – medication or otherwise. We should be happy that treatment rates for the disorder are increasing. The dramatic rise in the treatment of ADHD – pharmacological or otherwise – clearly results from the increase in the rates of diagnosis, which are secondary to the change in the IDEA noted above. Notably, one of the studies that supports these arguments regarding impairment and treatment was conducted with children identified using only teacher ratings, which have been the main target for complaints of overdiagnosis (Wolraich *et al.,* 1998).

In summary, ADHD is the most common mental health disorder of childhood, and it is one of the most impairing and refractory, and one with poor long-term prognosis. Current diagnostic rates are in line with scientific views of the nature of the disorder. If anything, we need to accurately identify *more* children with ADHD and provide the evidence-based treatments – both behavioral and pharmacological – that they need.

The severity of symptoms of autism spectrum disorder varies widely, and some children only show deficits in social interactions and in activities and interests, but do not show significant delays or deviance in language, a condition widely referred to before DSM-5 as **Asperger's syndrome**. In the first 3 years of life, children with this condition show normal levels of curiosity about the environment and acquire most normal cognitive skills. These children tend to have IQ scores within the average range.

Children with this condition tend to have difficulty in relationships with others and to engage in unusual behaviors (such as memorizing telephone numbers) to the point of being obsessed with arcane facts and issues. They can be rather formal in their speech, and the disorder has sometimes been referred to as the 'little professor syndrome.'

Understanding autism spectrum disorder

Early theorists explained autism spectrum disorder as the result of poor parenting (Bettelheim, 1967; Kanner, 1943). Research over the decades has clearly shown, though, that parenting practisdes play little or no role in the development of autism spectrum disorder. Instead, autism spectrum disorder appears to have strong biological roots.

Biological factors

Genetics clearly play a role in the development of autism spectrum disorder. The siblings of children with autism spectrum disorder are 50 times more likely also to have it than are the siblings of children without it (Sigman *et al.,* 2006). Twin studies find that, if one monozygotic twin has autism spectrum disorder, the co-twin has it 60 to 80 per cent of the time, whereas if one dizygotic twin has it, the co-twin has it only 0 to 10 per cent of the time (Folstein & Rosen-Sheidley, 2001). In addition, about 90 per cent of the MZ co-twins of children with autism have a significant cognitive impairment, compared with 10 per cent of DZ co-twins. Finally, children with autism spectrum disorder have a higher than average rate of other genetic disorders associated with cognitive impairment, including Fragile X syndrome and PKU (Volkmar *et al.,* 2009). Thus, autism spectrum disorder is associated with a genetic risk for several types of cognitive impairment.

The broad array of deficits seen in autism spectrum disorder suggests disruption in the normal development and organization of the brain (DiCicco-Bloom *et al.,* 2006). In addition, approximately 30 per cent of children with autism spectrum disorder develop seizure disorders by adolescence, suggesting a severe neurological dysfunction (Fombonne, 2003).

Neuroimaging studies have been used to assess brain functioning when children with autism spectrum disorder are doing tasks that require perception of facial expressions, joint attention with another person, empathy, and thinking about social situations. These studies suggest that children with

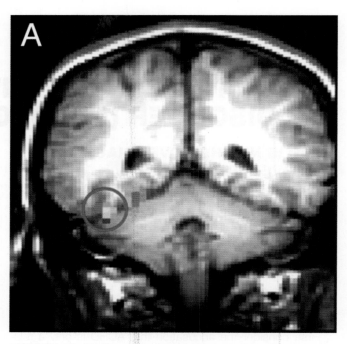

FIGURE 15.16 Functional MRI Abnormalities Observed in ASD (Autism Spectrum Disorders). *Abnormal activation of the fusiform gyrus is seen in autism spectrum disorder.*

autism spectrum disorder show abnormal functioning in areas of the brain that are used in tasks such as these. For example, when shown photos of faces, children with autism spectrum disorder show less activation than healthy children in an area of the brain called the fusiform gyrus, which is involved in facial perception (see Figure 15.16; Schultz, 2005). Difficulties in perceiving and understanding facial expressions could contribute to these children's deficits in social interactions.

One type of task that children with autism spectrum disorder perform more poorly on compared to healthy children taps into *theory of mind,* which is the ability to understand that people – including oneself – have mental states and to use this understanding to interact and communicate with others (Baron-Cohen & Swettenham, 1997). Having a theory of mind is essential to comprehending, explaining, predicting, and manipulating the behavior of others. Children with autism spectrum disorder often fail tasks assessing theory of mind, even when they perform appropriately on other cognitive tasks for their age group (Yirmiya *et al.,* 1998). The absence of a theory of mind may make it impossible for these children to understand and operate in the social world and to communicate appropriately with others. Their strange play behavior – specifically the absence of symbolic play – may also represent an inability to understand anything but the concrete realities before them. When doing tasks that require them to take someone else's perspective, children with autism spectrum disorder show deficits in the medial prefrontal and amygdaloid areas of the brain (Castelli *et al.,* 2002).

INTERIM SUMMARY

➡️ Autism spectrum disorder is characterized by severe and lasting impairment in several areas of development, including social interaction, communication, everyday behaviors, interests, and activities. What was formerly referred to as Asperger's syndrome is a milder variant which includes deficits in social interaction and interests but not in communication.

➡️ There is wide variation in the outcome of autism spectrum disorder, although the majority of autistic children must have continual care as adults. The best predictors of a good outcome in autism are an IQ above 50 and language development before the age of six.

➡️ Biological causes of autism spectrum disorder may include a genetic predisposition and a variety of neurodevelopmental abnormalities.

CRITICAL THINKING QUESTIONS

1 Parents are often very nervous that their child is not developing 'normally.' Do you think that regular screenings for developmental disorders would be a good idea? Why or why not?

2 Intensive behavioral interventions from an early age can help some children with pervasive developmental disorders to develop normal skills. Should this intervention be a right given to all children with these disorders, even though only some will benefit from it?

CHAPTER SUMMARY

1 The diagnosis of abnormal behavior is based on social norms, unusualness, maladaptiveness of behavior, and personal distress. Characteristics of good mental health include efficient perception of reality, control of behavior, self-esteem, ability to form affectionate relationships, and productivity.

2 The ICD and DSM-5 classify mental disorders according to specific behavioral symptoms. Such classification systems help communicate information and provide a basis for research.

3 Theories about the causes of mental disorders and proposals for treating them can be grouped according to those that focus on the brain and other biological factors, those that focus on the mind, including psychoanalytic, behavioral, and cognitive perspectives, and those that focus on sociocultural and environmental factors. The vulnerability-stress model emphasizes the interaction between a predisposition (biological and/or psychological) that makes a person vulnerable to a particular disorder, and stressful environmental conditions encountered by the individual.

4 Anxiety disorders include generalized anxiety (constant worry and tension), panic disorders (sudden attacks of overwhelming apprehension), phobias (irrational fears of specific objects or situations), and obsessive-compulsive disorders (OCDs) (persistent unwanted thoughts, or obsessions, combined with urges, or compulsions, to perform certain acts).

5 Biological theories of anxiety disorders attribute them to genetic predispositions or to biochemical or neurological abnormalities. Most anxiety disorders run in families, and twin studies strongly suggest that panic disorder and OCD have an inherited component. People who suffer panic attacks may have an overreactive fight-or-flight response. People with OCD may have neurotransmitter deficiencies in areas of the brain that regulate primitive impulses.

6 Cognitive and behavioral theorists suggest that people with anxiety disorders are prone to catastrophizing cognitions and to rigid, moralistic thinking. Maladaptive behaviors such as avoidant behaviors and compulsions arise through operant conditioning when the individual discovers that the behaviors reduce anxiety. Phobias may emerge through classical conditioning.

7 Mood disorders are divided into depressive disorders (in which the individual has one or more periods of depression) and bipolar disorders (in which the individual alternates between periods of depression and periods of elation, or mania). Sadness, loss of gratification in life, negative thoughts, and lack of motivation are the main symptoms of depression.

8 Biological theories attribute mood disorders to genetic factors and to problems in regulation of the neurotransmitters serotonin and norepinephrine. Cognitive theories attribute depression to pessimistic views, to rumination, and to negatively biased cognitive processes. Interpersonal theories view depression as the result of deficits in social skills and relationships. Stress, particularly family stress, plays a role in relapse in people with bipolar disorder.

9 Schizophrenia is characterized by disturbances in thought, including disorganized thought processes, and delusions. Other symptoms include perceptual disturbances (such as hallucinations), inappropriate emotional expression, bizarre behaviors, withdrawal, and impaired functioning.

10 Genetic factors appear to be strongly involved in the predisposition to schizophrenia. People with schizophrenia also have problems in dopamine regulation, as well as two types of brain abnormalities: the prefrontal cortex is smaller and less active, and the ventricles are enlarged. Difficult environments probably cannot cause schizophrenia, but they may worsen the disorder and contribute to relapses.

11 Personality disorders are lifelong patterns of maladaptive behavior involving coping with stress or solving problems. Individuals with antisocial personalities are impulsive, show little guilt, are concerned only with their own needs, and are frequently in trouble with the law. Antisocial personality disorder may have genetic and biological roots. Neglectful and hostile parenting may also contribute to the disorder.

12 People with borderline personality disorder show instability in mood, self-concept, and interpersonal relationships. Psychoanalytic theories suggest that the caregivers of people with this disorder required their children to be highly dependent and alternated between extreme expressions of love and hostility. Other theories attribute the disorder to extreme difficulties in emotion regulation.

13 Autism spectrum disorder is characterized by severe and lasting impairment in several areas of development, including social interaction, communication, everyday behaviors, interests, and activities. Genetic and neurodevelopmental factors are involved in this condition.

CORE CONCEPTS

abnormal	vulnerability-stress model	anhedonia
cultural relativist perspective	anxiety disorders	manic episodes
normality	generalized anxiety disorder	attributional styles
maladaptive	panic attack	schizophrenia
distress	panic disorder	word salad
International Classification of Diseases	*ataque de nervios*	loosening of associations
Diagnostic and Statistical Manual of Mental Disorders (DSM-5)	agoraphobia	delusions
	phobia	paranoid
neurosis	specific phobia	hallucinations
psychosis	social anxiety disorder	personality disorders
pervasive developmental disorders	obsessive-compulsive disorder	antisocial personality disorder
biological perspective	obsessions	borderline personality disorder
psychological perspective	compulsions	autism spectrum disorder
behavioral perspective	mood disorders	Asperger's syndrome (pre-DSM-5)
cognitive perspective	depressive disorders	
psychoanalytic perspective	bipolar disorders	

DIGITAL SUPPORT RESOURCES

Students should use the unique access code included in the front of the book to access the digital support resources which accompany the new edition. These include:

- Multiple Choice Questions and Quizzes
- Critical Thinking Questions
- Practice Essay Questions
- Videos
- Glossary, Flashcards, and More

16

TREATMENT OF MENTAL HEALTH PROBLEMS

LEARNING OBJECTIVES

After reading this chapter you should be able to:

Be familiar with the historical background and current trends in the treatment of abnormal behavior, in particular deinstitutionalization and reinstitutionalization.

Be able to describe the following approaches to psychotherapy, including the therapist's techniques and the patient's or client's experiences that are presumed to yield improvement:

a Psychoanalysis and psychodynamic therapies
b Behavior therapies
c Cognitive–behavior therapies
d Humanistic therapies.
e Family and marital therapies.

Be familiar with the techniques, advantages, and disadvantages of the two forms of biological therapy; be able to describe the major classes of psycho-therapeutic drugs, their effects, and their applications to mental disorders.

Be familiar with the suggestions offered for promoting your own emotional well-being.

Steve M. has paranoid schizophrenia. He frequently hears voices berating him and accusing him of having done something wrong. He was convinced that a transmitter had been implanted in his head, through which he was receiving these messages. When he takes his medications, the voices are quieted and the paranoid beliefs begin to recede. Over the past 5 years, Steve has been hospitalized three times. Each time he had stopped his medication, twice believing himself well, and once, just tired of the whole thing. In between hospitalizations, he has spent some time in an outpatient program and some time taking classes at university. He still struggles with determining what is real and what is not, but he has learned through therapy that he can check this out with the people he trusts, principally his stepmother, brother, and father. Steve has developed a long-term relationship with a psychologist from the clinic whom he sees once a week (in addition to his medication checks with the psychiatrist). Together they confront the very real challenges that his illness and the stigma attached to it poses. His parents, through the parent-support group they have joined, are learning to do the same (adapted from Bernheim, 1997, pp. 126–130).

Steve and his family are making use of a variety of types of treatment to control his paranoid schizophrenia. The medications he is taking are one form of biological treatment for psychological problems. He is also seeing a psychotherapist to learn new ways of coping with his problems. His parents are making use of community-based resources to understand Steve's problems.

In this chapter we look at methods for treating abnormal behavior. The most frequently used methods are listed in the Concept Review Table. Each of these treatments is linked to a particular theory of the causes of mental health problems. The types of health systems through which these treatments are delivered will vary from one country to another, but we will focus on the common characteristics of each type of treatment.

CHAPTER OUTLINE

HISTORICAL BACKGROUND

TECHNIQUES OF PSYCHOTHERAPY

Behavior therapies

Systematic desensitization and in vivo exposure

Cognitive-behavior therapies

Psychodynamic therapies

Humanistic therapies

CUTTING EDGE RESEARCH: MINDFULNESS FOR MENTAL HEALTH PROBLEMS

BIOLOGICAL THERAPIES

Psychotherapeutic drugs

Electroconvulsive therapy

Combining biological and psychological therapies

ENHANCING MENTAL HEALTH

SEEING BOTH SIDES: IS ALCOHOLICS ANONYMOUS (AA) AN EFFECTIVE INTERVENTION FOR ALCOHOL MISUSE?

CONCEPT REVIEW TABLE METHODS OF THERAPY

Type of therapy	Example	Description
Behavior therapies	Systematic desensitization	The client is trained to relax and then presented with a hierarchy of anxiety-producing situations and asked to relax while imagining each one.
	In vivo exposure	Similar to systematic desensitization except that the client actually experiences each situation.
	Flooding	A form of in vivo exposure in which a phobic individual is exposed to the most feared object or situation for an extended period without an opportunity to escape.
	Selective reinforcement	Reinforcement of specific behaviors, often through the use of tokens that can be exchanged for rewards.
	Modeling	A process in which the client learns behaviors by observing and imitating others; often combined with behavioral rehearsal (e.g., in assertiveness training).
Cognitive-behavior therapies		Treatment methods that use behavior modification techniques but also incorporate procedures designed to change maladaptive beliefs.
Psychodynamic therapies	Traditional psychoanalysis	Through free association, dream analysis, and transference, attempts to discover the unconscious basis of the client's current problems so as to deal with them in a more rational way.
	Contemporary psychodynamic therapies (e.g., interpersonal therapy)	More structured and short-term than traditional psychoanalysis; emphasize the way the client is currently interacting with others.
Humanistic therapies	Client-centered therapy	In an atmosphere of empathy, warmth, and genuineness, the therapist attempts to facilitate the process through which the client works out solutions to his or her own problems.
Biological therapies	Psychotherapeutic drugs Electroconvulsive therapy (ECT)	Use of drugs to modify mood and behavior. A mild electric current is applied to the brain to produce a seizure.

HISTORICAL BACKGROUND

Throughout history, the treatment of people who appeared to have mental health problems was influenced by beliefs about what the causes of these problems were. Supernatural forces, such as demons, evil spirits, or ghosts, were often blamed for people's abnormal behavior. These forces were removed or exorcised through such techniques as prayer, incantation, and magic. If these techniques were unsuccessful, more extreme measures were taken to ensure that the body would be an unpleasant dwelling place. Flogging, starving, burning, and causing the person to bleed profusely were frequent forms of 'treatment.'

More biological explanations for unusual behavior have also been offered over the centuries. The ancient Chinese viewed the human body as containing both a positive and negative force. If the two forces were not in balance, illness, including insanity, could result. The Greek physician Hippocrates (circa 460–377 BC) is credited with bringing a medical perspective to the study of mental health problems in the Western world. He believed that unusual behaviors were the result of a disturbance in the balance of bodily fluids. Hippocrates, and the Greek and Roman physicians who followed him, stressed the importance of pleasant surroundings, exercise, proper diet, massage, and soothing baths, as well as some less desirable treatments, such as purging and mechanical restraints. Although there were no institutions for the mentally ill, many individuals were cared for with great kindness in temples dedicated to the gods of healing.

This progressive view of mental illness did not continue, however. Primitive superstitions and belief in demon possession were revived during the Middle Ages. The mentally ill were considered to be in league with Satan and to possess supernatural powers with which they could cause floods, pestilence, and injuries to others. Seriously disturbed individuals were treated cruelly: it was believed that beating, starving, and torturing the mentally ill served to punish the devil.

In the late Middle Ages, cities created asylums to cope with the mentally ill. These asylums were simply prisons; the inmates were chained in dark, filthy cells and treated more as animals than as human beings. It was not until 1792, when

Philippe Pinel in the courtyard of the hospital of Salpetriere.

Philippe Pinel was placed in charge of an asylum in Paris, that some improvements were made. As an experiment, Pinel removed the chains that restrained the inmates. Much to the amazement of skeptics who thought Pinel was mad to unchain such 'animals,' the experiment was a success. When released from their restraints, placed in clean, sunny rooms, and treated kindly, many people who for years had been considered hopelessly insane improved enough to leave the asylum.

Psychiatric hospitals have been upgraded markedly in the last century, but there is still much room for improvement. The best psychiatric hospitals are comfortable and well-kept places that provide therapeutic activities: individual and group psychotherapy, recreation, occupational therapy (designed to teach skills as well as provide relaxation), and educational courses to help patients prepare for jobs upon release from the hospital. The worst are primarily custodial institutions where patients lead a boring existence in run-down, overcrowded wards and receive little treatment beyond medication. Most psychiatric hospitals fall somewhere between these extremes.

Beginning in the early 1960s, emphasis shifted from treating individuals with mental health problems in hospitals to treating them in their own communities. This movement toward community treatment was motivated partly by the recognition that hospitalization has some inherent disadvantages, regardless of how good the facilities may be. Hospitals remove people from the social support of family and friends and the familiar patterns of daily life, and they encourage dependence. They are also very expensive.

During the 1950s, psychotherapeutic drugs (discussed later in the chapter) were discovered that could relieve depression and anxiety and reduce psychotic behavior. When these drugs became widely available in the 1960s, many hospitalized patients could be discharged and returned home to be treated as outpatients. By the 1970s, specialized psychiatric hospitals across Europe were closed or reduced in size, with the expectation that patients would be treated in community treatment centers designed to provide outpatient treatment and other services, including short-term and partial hospitalization. In partial hospitalization, individuals may receive treatment at the center during the day and return home in the evening, or they can work during the day and spend nights at the center. The movement toward discharge of institutionalized patients to community-based services became known as **deinstitutionalization**.

As Figures 16.1 and 16.2 show, the number of patients treated in specialized psychiatric hospitals has decreased dramatically in many European countries, but only slightly in some countries recently admitted to the European Union. In Sweden, for example, there are now no psychiatric hospitals and patients who need hospitalization are expected to be treated in general hospitals. Slovakia and Slovenia show little change in the use of psychiatric hospitals for patients, however, and the Russian Federation has the highest number of inpatient psychiatric beds of the countries studied (see Figure 16.2).

For some patients, deinstitutionalization has been successful. The services of mental health centers and private clinicians, along with help from their families and the use of psychotherapeutic drugs, have enabled them to resume satisfactory lives. This is particularly true in countries with good economic resources. For example, one study of 751 patients discharged from two psychiatric hospitals in England found that 5 years later, 90 per cent were living in the community, and very few had come in contact with the criminal justice system or had become homeless (Trieman *et al.*, 1999).

For others, however, deinstitutionalization has had unfortunate consequences, largely because the facilities in their communities are far from adequate. Twenty-eight per cent of European countries have little or no community-based services for people with serious mental health problems (WHO, 2004). Many individuals who improve with hospitalization and

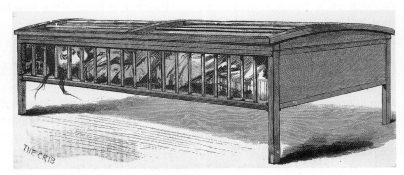

The crib, a restraining device used in a New York mental institution in 1882.

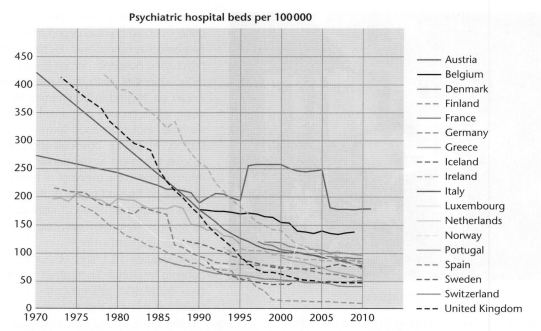

FIGURE 16.1 Trends in the Numbers of Psychiatric Beds in Western Europe 1978–2002. *Reductions in the number of patients treated in specialized psychiatric facilities have occurred in many European nations.*

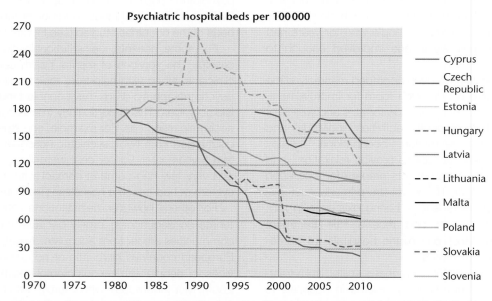

FIGURE 16.2 Trends in the Numbers of Psychiatric Beds in the New EU Member States, 1988–2002. *New EU member states show less reduction in psychiatric hospitalization.*

could manage on their own with assistance do not receive adequate follow-up care in terms of outpatient therapy, monitoring of medication, or help in finding friends, housing, and jobs. As a consequence, they lead a 'revolving-door' existence, going in and out of institutions between unsuccessful attempts to cope on their own.

Some discharged patients are too incapacitated to even attempt to support themselves or function without custodial care. They often live in dirty, overcrowded housing or on the streets. The disheveled man standing on the corner talking to himself and shouting gibberish may be one victim of deinstitutionalization. The woman with all her possessions in a shopping bag who spends one night in the doorway of an office building and the next in a subway station may be another. In some European cities, up to 50 per cent of homeless people have a severe mental health problem (WHO, 2003).

FIGURE 16.3 Likelihood of Violence. *Substance abuse is associated with a heightened likelihood of engaging in violent behavior.*

The increasing visibility of homeless mentally ill individuals, particularly in large cities, has aroused public concern and prompted a move toward reinstitutionalization. However, this raises an important ethical issue. If such people are not readjusting to society, should they be involuntarily committed to a mental hospital? One of the most cherished civil rights in a democratic society is the right to liberty.

Some experts believe that legal action is warranted only if a person is potentially dangerous to others. The rare, but highly publicized, occasions when a person experiencing a psychotic episode attacks an innocent bystander have generated fears for public safety. But such events are rare. One large study found that fewer than 5 per cent of individuals with serious mental health problems committed a violent crime after discharge from a mental health facility (Steadman *et al.,* 1998). That percentage went up to about 22 per cent among people who had both serious mental health problems and a substance misuse problem (such as alcoholism), but this is still clearly a minority of individuals. In general, experts' opinions regarding whether a given individual will commit violent crimes are often incorrect, particularly for the long term (Gardner *et al.,* 1996).

> **INTERIM SUMMARY**
>
> ➡ Treatment of the mentally ill has progressed from the ancient notion that abnormal behavior resulted from possession by evil spirits that needed to be punished, to custodial care in asylums, to modern mental hospitals and community mental health centers.
>
> ➡ The policy of deinstitutionalization was intended to move hospitalized mental patients into the community, where they would receive outpatient services.

> ➡ The deinstitutionalization movement was never adequately funded and, despite its good intentions, has added to the number of homeless mentally ill individuals, causing concern about civil rights and adequate care.

> **CRITICAL THINKING QUESTIONS**
>
> 1 What do you think society's obligations are to people with serious mental health problems? What laws should be enacted to protect the rights of these people?
>
> 2 Does society have any right or obligation to see to it that children with serious mental health problems receive treatment, even if their parents do not agree to the treatment?

TECHNIQUES OF PSYCHOTHERAPY

Psychotherapy refers to the variety of psychological interventions that share the goal of alleviating human problems and facilitating effective functioning in society. Some psychotherapists (such as behavior therapists and cognitive-behavior therapists) focus on changing habitual patterns of thinking and behavior. Others (such as those practicing psychodynamic therapies) believe that modification of behavior is dependent on the individual's understanding of his or her unconscious motives and conflicts. Despite differences in techniques, most methods of psychotherapy have certain basic features in common. They involve a helping relationship between two people: the client (patient) and the therapist. The client is encouraged to discuss intimate concerns, emotions, and experiences freely without fear of being judged by the therapist or having confidences betrayed. The therapist, in turn, offers empathy and understanding, engenders trust, and tries to help the client develop more effective ways of handling problems.

Behavior therapies

The term **behavior therapy** includes a number of therapeutic methods based on the principles of learning and conditioning (see Chapter 7). Behavior therapists assume that maladaptive behaviors are learned ways of coping with stress and that some of the techniques developed in experimental research on learning can be used to substitute more appropriate responses for maladaptive ones.

Behavioral treatments for phobias require people to actually confront the object of their phobia – classes to combat a fear of flying are a good example of this.

Don't people need to gain insight into their behaviors in order to change them? Behavior therapists point out that although the achievement of insight is a worthwhile goal, it does not ensure behavioral change. Often we understand why we behave the way we do in a certain situation but are unable to change our behavior. If you are unusually timid about speaking in class, you may be able to trace this fear to past events (for example, your father criticized your opinions whenever you expressed them). Understanding the reasons behind your fear does not necessarily make it easier for you to contribute to class discussions.

Behavior therapies attempt to modify behaviors that are maladaptive in specific situations. The first step is to define the problem clearly and break it down into a set of specific therapeutic goals. If, for example, the client complains of general feelings of inadequacy, the therapist will try to get the client to describe these feelings more specifically: to pinpoint the kinds of situations in which they occur and the kinds of behaviors associated with them. Once the behaviors that need to be changed have been specified, the therapist and client work out a treatment program, choosing the treatment method that is most appropriate for the particular problem.

Systematic desensitization and in vivo exposure

Systematic desensitization is a method of gradually reducing fearful responses to stimuli and overcoming the maladaptive behaviors that often accompany fear, such as avoidance of feared situations. The client is first trained to relax deeply so that he or she can use relaxation techniques to reduce fearful responses. One way to relax is to progressively tense then relax various muscles, starting, for example, with the feet and ankles and proceeding up the body to the neck and face. The person learns what muscles feel like when they are truly relaxed and how to discriminate among various degrees of tension.

The next step is to create a hierarchy of the anxiety-producing situations. The situations are ranked in order from the one that produces the least anxiety to the one that produces the most. In systematic desensitization, the client is then asked to relax and imagine each situation in the hierarchy, starting with the one that is least anxiety-producing. **In vivo exposure** is a method highly similar to systematic desensitization that requires the client to actually experience the anxiety-producing situations.

An example will make these procedures clearer. Suppose that the client is a woman who suffers from a phobia of spiders. The phobia is so strong that she is afraid to walk in her own back yard, let alone go for a walk in the countryside or on a holiday in a wooded area. Her anxiety hierarchy might begin with a picture of a spider in a book. Somewhere around the middle of the hierarchy might be viewing a spider in a glass cage at the zoo. At the top of the hierarchy would be actually handling a spider. After this woman has learned to relax and has constructed the hierarchy, the therapist begins taking her through her list. In systematic desensitization, she sits with her eyes closed in a comfortable chair while the therapist describes the least anxiety-provoking situation. If she can imagine herself in the situation without any increase in muscle tension, the therapist proceeds to the next item on the list. If the woman reports any anxiety while visualizing a scene, she concentrates on relaxing, and the same scene is visualized until all anxiety has been neutralized. This process continues through a series of sessions until the situation that originally provoked the most anxiety now elicits only relaxation.

During in vivo exposure, the woman would actually experience each of the situations on her list, beginning with the least feared one, with the coaching of the therapist. Before she actually handled a spider herself, the therapist might model handling the spider without being fearful – the therapist would hold the spider in the client's presence, displaying confidence and no anxiety. Eventually the client would handle the spider herself, allowing it to crawl on her while using relaxation to control her anxiety. The term *flooding* is used to refer a type of in vivo therapy in which a phobic individual is exposed to the most feared object or situation for an extended period without an opportunity to escape. In vivo exposure therapy has proven extremely effective in the treatment of phobias and most other anxiety disorders (Rachman, 2009).

Selective reinforcement

Systematic desensitization and in vivo exposure help reduce unwanted behaviors. **Selective reinforcement** is a technique designed to strengthen or increase specific desired behaviors.

Imagine a nine-year-old girl who is inattentive in school, refuses to complete assignments or participate in class, and spends most of her time daydreaming. In addition, her social skills are poor and she has few friends. A teacher may wish to reinforce 'on-task' behavior, such as paying attention to schoolwork or instructions from the teacher, completing reading assignments, and taking part in class discussions. The teacher may give the girl a token (such as a poker chip) whenever she observes the girl performing on-task behaviors. The little girl then could exchange these tokens for special privileges that she values, such as standing first in line (worth three tokens) or being allowed to stay after school to help the teacher with special projects (worth nine tokens).

Reinforcement of desirable responses can be accompanied by withholding reinforcement of undesirable ones. For example, a boy who habitually shouts to get his mother's attention could be ignored whenever he does so and reinforced by her attention only when he comes to her and speaks in a conversational tone.

Operant conditioning procedures involving rewards for desirable responses and no rewards for undesirable ones have been used successfully in dealing with a broad range of childhood problems, including bed-wetting, aggression, tantrums, disruptive classroom behavior, poor school performance, and social withdrawal. Similar procedures have been used in treating autism spectrum disorder, for example, by reinforcing socially appropriate behaviors such as looking other people in the eyes, or reducing inappropriate behavior, such as temper tantrums.

Modeling

Another effective means of changing behavior is modeling. Modeling is the process by which a person learns behaviors by observing and imitating others. Because observing others is a major way in which humans learn, watching people who are displaying adaptive behavior should teach people with maladaptive responses better strategies. Observing the behavior of a model (either live or video taped) has proved effective in reducing fears and teaching new skills. For example, observing a therapist handle a spider can reduce the fears of a person with a spider phobia, making it possible for him or her to eventually handle the spider also.

Modeling is effective in overcoming fears and anxieties because it provides an opportunity to observe someone else go through the anxiety-provoking situation without getting hurt. Watching video tapes of models enjoying a visit to the dentist or going through various hospital procedures has proved successful in helping both children and adults overcome their fears of such experiences (Thorpe & Olson, 1997).

Behavioral rehearsal

In a therapy session, modeling is often combined with **behavioral rehearsal**, or role playing. The therapist helps the client rehearse or practice more adaptive behaviors. In the following excerpt, a therapist helps a young man overcome his anxieties about talking with women. The young man has been pretending to talk to a woman over the telephone and finishes by asking her if she would like to go to the cinema with him.

Client:	Um, I was wondering, you wouldn't want to go to the cinema with me, or anything, would you?
Therapist:	Okay, that's a start. Can you think of another way of asking her out that sounds a bit more positive and confident? For example, 'There's a great new movie showing at the cinema and I'd like very much to take you, if you are free.'
Client:	That's great!
Therapist:	Okay, you try it.
Client:	Um, I've got two free tickets to the movie. If you don't have anything to do, you might want to come along.
Therapist:	That's better. Try it one more time, but this time try to convey to her that you'd really like her to go.
Client:	I've got two tickets for a great new movie. It would be great if you'd go with me, if you're not busy.
Therapist:	Great! Just practise it a couple of more times, and you're ready to pick up the telephone.

This example illustrates the use of behavioral rehearsal in a type of behavior therapy known as assertiveness training. Like the young man in the example, many people have trouble asking for what they want or refusing to allow others to take advantage of them. By practising assertive responses (first in role-playing with the therapist and then in real-life situations), the individual not only reduces anxiety but also develops more effective coping techniques.

Self-regulation

Because the client and therapist seldom meet more than once per week, the client must learn to control or regulate his or her own behavior so that progress can be made outside the therapy hour. Moreover, if people feel that they are responsible for their own improvement, they are more likely to maintain whatever gains they make. **Self-regulation** involves monitoring, or observing, one's own behavior and using various techniques, including self-reinforcement, and exposure to feared situations while practicing relaxation strategies, to change maladaptive behavior. An individual monitors his or her behavior by keeping a careful record of the kinds of situations that elicit the maladaptive behavior and the kinds of responses that are incompatible with it. For example, a person who is concerned with alcohol abuse would note the kinds of situations in which he or she is most tempted to drink and would try to control such situations or devise a response that is incompatible with drinking (see Marlatt's

Seeing Both Sides essay for an application of these techniques). A man who finds it hard not to join his co-workers in a beer at the pub after work might substitute a game of tennis or a jog around the block as a means of relieving tension. This activity would be incompatible with drinking.

Individuals are taught to reward themselves for achieving a specific goal. The reward could be praising yourself, watching a favorite television program, telephoning a friend, or eating a favorite food. They may also be taught to punish themselves for failing to achieve a goal, for example by depriving themselves of something you enjoy (not watching a favorite television program, for instance).

Often, many of the techniques of behavior therapy are used in combination to treat people with serious mental health problems. Behavior therapy has proven effective for several of the anxiety disorders, including panic disorder, phobias, and obsessive-compulsive disorders (OCDs) (Rothbaum & Osalov, 2006; Turner, 2006), for depression (Dimidjian *et al.,* 2006), for problems in sexual functioning (Gambescia & Weeks, 2007), and for several childhood disorders (Kazdin & Weisz, 2003).

Cognitive-behavior therapies

The behavior therapy procedures discussed so far have focused on modifying behavior directly. They devote little attention to the individual's thinking and reasoning processes. Initially, behavior therapists discounted the importance of cognition, preferring a strict stimulus–response approach. However, in response to evidence that cognitive factors – thoughts, expectations, and interpretations of events – are important determinants of behavior, cognitive approaches are now regularly combined with behavioral approaches in what is known as **cognitive-behavior therapy** (Beck *et al.,* 1979; Beck, 1995).

The cognitive component of cognitive-behavior therapy involves helping the client control disturbing emotional reactions, such as anxiety and depression, by teaching more effective ways of interpreting and thinking about experiences. For example, as we noted in discussing Beck's cognitive theory of depression (see Chapter 15), depressed individuals tend to appraise events from a negative and self-critical viewpoint. They expect to fail rather than succeed, and they tend to magnify failures and minimize successes in evaluating their performance. In treating depression, cognitive-behavior therapists help clients recognize the distortions in their thinking and make changes that are more in line with reality. The following dialogue illustrates how a therapist, through carefully directed questioning, makes a client who is suicidal because her marriage is failing aware of the unrealistic nature of her beliefs.

Therapist:	Why do you want to end your life?
Client:	Without Raymond, I am nothing … . I can't be happy without Raymond … . But I can't save our marriage.
Therapist:	What has your marriage been like?
Client:	It has been miserable from the very beginning … . Raymond has always been unfaithful … . I have hardly seen him in the past 5 years.
Therapist:	You say that you can't be happy without Raymond … . Have you found yourself happy when you are with Raymond?
Client:	No, we fight all the time and I feel worse.
Therapist:	You say you are nothing without Raymond. Before you met Raymond, did you feel you were nothing?
Client:	No, I felt I was somebody.
Therapist:	If you were somebody before you knew Raymond, why do you need him [in order] to be somebody now?
Client:	(puzzled) Hmmm … .
Therapist:	If you were free of the marriage, do you think that men might be interested in you – knowing that you were available?
Client:	I guess that maybe they would be.
Therapist:	Is it possible that you might find a man who would be more constant than Raymond?
Client:	I don't know … . I guess it's possible … .
Therapist:	Then what have you actually lost if you break up the marriage?
Client:	I don't know.
Therapist:	Is it possible that you'll get along better if you end the marriage?
Client:	There is no guarantee of that.
Therapist:	Do you have a real marriage?
Client:	I guess not.
Therapist:	If you don't have a real marriage, what do you actually lose if you decide to end the marriage?
Client:	(long pause) Nothing, I guess.

(Beck, 1976, pp. 280–291)

The behavioral component of the treatment comes into play when the therapist encourages the client to formulate alternative ways of viewing her situation and then test the implications of those alternatives. For example, the woman client in the preceding dialogue might be asked to record her moods at regular intervals and then note how her depression and feelings of self-esteem fluctuate as a function of what she is doing. If she finds that she feels worse after interacting with her husband than when she is alone or is interacting with someone else, this information could serve to challenge her belief that she 'can't be happy without Raymond.'

A cognitive-behavioral program to help someone overcome agoraphobia might include training in more adaptive thinking, along with in vivo exposure (accompanied excursions that take the individual progressively farther from home). The therapist teaches the client to replace self-defeating internal dialogues ('I'm so nervous, I know I'll faint as soon as I leave the house') with positive self-instructions ('Be calm; I'm not alone; even if I have a panic attack, I can cope').

Cognitive-behavior therapists agree that it is important to alter a person's beliefs in order to bring about an enduring change in behavior. Most maintain that behavioral procedures are more powerful than strictly verbal ones in affecting cognitive processes. For example, to overcome anxiety about giving a speech in class, it is helpful to think positively: 'I know the material well, and I'm sure I can present my ideas effectively' and 'The topic is interesting, and the other students will enjoy what I have to say.' But first presenting the speech to a roommate and again before a group of friends will probably do more to reduce anxiety. Successful performance increases our feeling of mastery. In fact, it has been suggested that all therapeutic procedures that are effective give the client a sense of mastery or self-efficacy. Observing others cope and succeed, being verbally persuaded that we can handle a difficult situation, and judging from internal cues that we are relaxed and in control contribute to feelings of self-efficacy. But the greatest sense of efficacy comes from actual performance, from the experience of mastery. In essence, nothing succeeds like success (Bandura, 2006).

Cognitive-behavior therapies have proven highly effective in treating an array of non-psychotic conditions, including depression (Hollon & Dimidjian, 2009), anxiety disorders (Clark *et al.,* 2006; van Boeijen *et al.,* 2005), eating disorders (Cooper *et al.,* 2004), drug and alcohol dependence (Koumimtsidis, Reynolds *et al.,* 2007), and sexual dysfunctions (Leiblum & Rosen, 2000). These therapies help people overcome troubling thoughts, feelings, and behaviors and also to prevent relapses after therapy has ended. In addition, cognitive-behavior therapies can help people with psychotic symptoms learn how to manage their symptoms (Beck & Rector, 2005).

Psychodynamic therapies

A key assumption of **psychodynamic therapies** is that people's current problems cannot be resolved successfully without a thorough understanding of their unconscious basis in early relationships with parents and siblings. The goal of these therapies is to bring conflicts (repressed emotions and motives) into awareness so that they can be dealt with in a more rational and realistic way. The psychodynamic therapies include

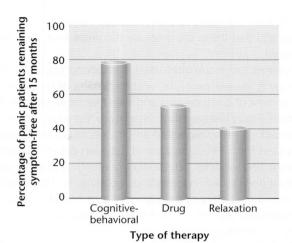

FIGURE 16.4 **Percentage of Panic Patients Remaining Symptom-Free After 15 Months.** *People receiving cognitive-behavioral therapy for panic disorder were more likely to remain symptom-free over 15 months than people receiving only drug therapy or relaxation training.*

traditional Freudian psychoanalysis and more recent therapies based on it (see McWilliams & Weinberger, 2003).

One of the main techniques that psychodynamic therapists use to recover unconscious conflicts is **free association**, in which the client is encouraged to give free rein to thoughts and feelings and to say whatever comes to mind without editing or censoring it. This is not easy to do, however. In conversation, we usually try to keep a connecting thread running through our remarks and exclude irrelevant ideas. With practise, free association becomes easier. But even individuals who conscientiously try to give free rein to their thoughts will occasionally find themselves blocked, unable to recall the details of an event or finish a thought. Freud believed that blocking, or resistance,

"HAVE A COUPLE OF DREAMS, AND CALL ME IN THE MORNING."

results from the individual's unconscious control over sensitive areas and that these are precisely the areas that need to be explored.

Another technique often used in traditional psychoanalytic therapy is **dream analysis**, which consists of talking about the content of one's dreams and then free associating to that content. Freud believed that dreams are 'the royal road to the unconscious'; they represent an unconscious wish or fear in disguised form. He distinguished between dreams' manifest content (the obvious, conscious content) and their latent content (the hidden, unconscious content). By talking about the manifest content of a dream and then free associating to that content, the analyst and client attempt to discover the dream's unconscious meaning.

As the therapist and client interact during therapy, the client will often react to the therapist in ways that seem exaggerated or inappropriate. The client may become enraged when the therapist must reschedule an appointment, or may be excessively deferential to the therapist. The term **transference** refers to the tendency for the client to make the therapist the object of thoughts and emotions: the client expresses attitudes toward the analyst that are actually felt toward other people who are, or were, important in his or her life. By pointing out how their clients are reacting to them, therapists help their clients achieve a better understanding of how they react to others. The following passage illustrates an analyst's use of transference, followed by the use of free association:

Client:	I don't understand why you're holding back on telling me if this step is the right one for me at this time in my life.
Therapist:	This has come up before. You want my approval before taking some action. What seems to be happening here is that one of the conflicts you have with your wife is trying to get her approval of what you have decided you want to do, and that conflict is occurring now between us.
Client:	I suppose so. Other people's approval has always been very important to me.
Therapist:	Let's stay with that for a few minutes. Would you free associate to that idea of getting approval from others. Just let the associations come spontaneously – don't force them.

(Adapted from Woody & Robertson, 1988, p. 129)

Traditional psychoanalysis is a lengthy, intensive, and expensive process. Client and analyst usually meet for 50-minute sessions several times a week for at least a year and often for several years. Many people find self-exploration under traditional psychoanalysis to be of value; however, for some people it is unaffordable. In addition, people suffering from acute depression, anxiety, or psychosis typically cannot tolerate the lack of structure in traditional psychoanalysis and need more immediate relief from their symptoms.

In response to these needs, as well as to changes in psychoanalytic theory since Freud's time, newer therapies that draw upon psychoanalytic theory and practices, but are more structured and short-term than traditional psychoanalysis, have been developed. One such therapy is called **interpersonal therapy** (Weissman & Markowitz, 2002). Sessions are scheduled less frequently, usually once a week. There is less emphasis on complete reconstruction of childhood experiences and more attention to problems arising from the way the individual is currently interacting with others. Free association is often replaced with direct discussion of critical issues, and the therapist may be more direct, raising pertinent topics when appropriate rather than waiting for the client to bring them up. Although transference is still considered an important part of the therapeutic process, the therapist may try to limit the intensity of the transference process. Research has found interpersonal therapy to be helpful in the treatment of depression, anxiety, drug addiction, and eating disorders (Gibbons *et al.,* 2008).

Humanistic therapies

Humanistic therapies are based on the humanistic approach to personality discussed in Chapter 13. They emphasize the individual's natural tendency toward growth and self-actualization. Psychological disorders are assumed to arise when circumstances or other people (parents, teachers, spouses) prevent the individual from achieving his or her potential. When this occurs, people begin to deny their true desires, and their potential for growth is reduced. Humanistic therapies seek to help people get in touch with their real selves and make deliberate choices regarding their lives and behavior rather than being controlled by external events.

Like the psychoanalyst, the humanistic therapist attempts to increase the client's awareness of underlying emotions and motives. But the emphasis is on what the individual is experiencing in the here and now, rather than in the past. The humanistic therapist does not interpret the client's behavior (as a psychoanalyst might) or try to modify it (as a behavior therapist would), because this would amount to imposing the therapist's views on the patient. The goal of the humanistic therapist is to facilitate exploration of the individual's own thoughts and feelings and to assist the individual in arriving at his or her own solutions. This approach will become clearer as we look at client-centered therapy (also called non-directive therapy), one of the first humanistic therapies.

Client-centered therapy, developed in the 1940s by the late Carl Rogers, is based on the assumption that each individual is the best expert on himself or herself and that people are capable of working out solutions to their own problems. The task of the therapist is to facilitate this process – not to ask probing questions, make interpretations, or suggest courses of action. In fact, Rogers preferred the term facilitator to therapist, and he called the people he worked with clients rather than patients because he did not view emotional difficulties as indications of an illness to be cured.

The therapist facilitates the client's progress toward self-insight by restating what the client says about his or her needs and emotions. Rogers believed that the most important qualities for a therapist are empathy, warmth, and genuineness. Rogers

believed that a therapist who possesses these three attributes will facilitate the client's growth and self-exploration (Rogers, 1970).

Client-centered therapy has some limitations, however. Like psychoanalysis, it appears to be successful only with individuals who are fairly verbal and are motivated to discuss their problems. For people who do not voluntarily seek help or are

CUTTING EDGE RESEARCH MINDFULNESS FOR MENTAL HEALTH PROBLEMS

Meg Barker, Senior Lecturer in Psychology, The Open University

Mindfulness is the fastest growing psychological treatment of recent years. It is officially recognized as an effective therapy for a variety of common mental health problems, and an extensive research literature on the topic has appeared since the 1990s, with many best-selling self-help books now bringing mindfulness to a general audience (e.g., Williams & Penman, 2011).

Mindfulness treatments weave Western therapeutic approaches together with practices and ideas from Buddhist philosophy. The modality which has most enthusiastically embraced this has been Cognitive-Behavioral Therapy (CBT), so much so that mindfulness has been termed the 'third wave' of CBT (the first wave being behavioral therapy, and the second the cognitive revolution). Along with the benefits of mindfulness itself, such approaches are popular because they can be taught in a group format over a relatively short period of time (often an 8-week course), so they are also a cost-effective way of treating mental health problems.

The key idea of mindfulness is that some degree of suffering is inevitable in life. It is our attempts to avoid any suffering – to get everything that we want and nothing that we don't want – that causes us to really struggle with experiences like anxiety, depression, and addiction. This is why mindfulness involves things like meditating on the breath, slow walking, or attending to the sensations in our body or the sounds around us. Such practices enable us to shift our habit from trying to change things to being with things as they are (Nhat Hanh, 1991). You can easily try mindfulness for yourself: sit for 5 minutes noticing your breath coming and going. Each time you find yourself distracted, just come back to your breath. You will soon realize how difficult this can be!

When people are depressed they frequently get caught in processes of rumination where they become sad, scared, or self-critical about the fact that they are feeling low. Mindfulness practices can help them to stop getting caught in such spirals: to be with their sad feelings without exacerbating them, and to be in the whole of their experience rather than focusing just on one part of it (Segal *et al.,* 2002). When

people are anxious they generally try to avoid or escape whatever is fearful. Paradoxically this often increases the anxiety (for example, if you put something off till the deadline, or avoid having a difficult conversation). Mindfulness suggests approaching whatever we find fearful in a curious and gentle way (Germer, 2005). For example, instead of trying desperately to escape a confrontation, we might slow down and become more aware of everything that is going on, giving us more options of how we could engage with it (with empathy for both ourself and for any other people involved).

Randomized control trials have found mindfulness therapies – like Mindfulness-Based Stress Reduction (MBSR) (Kabat-Zinn, 1996), Mindfulness-Based Cognitive Therapy (MBCT) (Segal *et al.,* 2002), and Acceptance and Commitment Therapy (ACT) (Hayes, 2005) – to be effective for a number of problems including anxiety and depression (see Chiesa & Serretti, 2010). There has also been great interest in neuroimaging research which has found that mindfulness practice alters brain activity over time (Hölzel *et al.,* 2011). There have been calls for more psychological research drawing together the subjective experiences of mindfulness with further neurological and outcome research (Williams & Kabat-Zinn, 2011).

However, there are challenges in bringing mindfulness to a new, Western, audience. There is a tricky balance to be struck wherein vital aspects of the original Buddhist theories are not diluted or lost, but – at the same time – ways are found to make them accessible and explicable to non-Buddhist audiences. Also, there is a tendency for some mindfulness therapies to neglect the sociocultural situations in which anxiety and depression occur, with the focus on the internal world of the client (Cohen, 2010). As well as helping people with their self-critical thoughts, it is important to recognize the world in which those thoughts arise, for example the commercial culture where people are encouraged to feel bad about themselves in order to buy products. And when helping people to approach fearful situations, it is important to recognize the material reality of things like poverty and discrimination, rather than assuming that fear is just 'in the mind.' If such elements can be integrated then mindfulness has great potential as a fully biopsychosocial approach to mental health (Barker, 2013).

seriously disturbed and unable to discuss their feelings, more directive methods are usually necessary. In addition, by using the client's self-reports as the only measure of psychotherapeutic effectiveness, the client-centered therapist ignores behavior outside the therapy session. Individuals who feel insecure and ineffective in their interpersonal relationships often need more structured help in modifying their behavior.

Marital and family therapy

Problems in communicating feelings, satisfying one's needs, and responding appropriately to the needs and demands of others become intensified in the intimate context of marriage and family life. To the extent that they involve more than one client and focus on interpersonal relationships, **marital therapy** – in which a married or partnered couple undergoes therapy – and **family therapy** – in which the entire family undergoes therapy together – can be considered specialized forms of group therapy.

There are many approaches to family and marital therapy, but most focus on helping individuals with their feelings, develop greater understanding and sensitivity to each other's needs, and work on more effective ways of handling their conflicts (Mirsalimi *et al.*, 2003; Robin, 2003). Sometimes the couple or family members negotiate behavioral contracts, agreeing on the behavior changes each person is willing to make in order to create a more satisfying relationship, and specifying rewards and penalties for making, or not making, the desired changes.

INTERIM SUMMARY

→ Behavior therapies apply methods based on learning principles to modify the client's behavior, including systematic desensitization, in vivo exposure, reinforcement of adaptive behaviors, modeling and rehearsal of appropriate behavior, and techniques for self-regulation of behavior.

→ Cognitive-behavior therapies use behavior modification techniques but also incorporate procedures for changing maladaptive beliefs. The therapist helps the client replace irrational interpretations of events with more realistic ones.

→ Psychoanalysis, which was developed by Freud, uses techniques such as free association, dream analysis, and transference, to help the patient gain insight into problems. Contemporary psychodynamic therapies are briefer than traditional psychoanalysis and place more emphasis on the client's current interpersonal problems.

→ Humanistic therapies help clients become aware of their real selves and solve their problems with a minimum of intervention by the therapist. Carl Rogers, who developed client-centered psychotherapy, believed that the therapist must have three characteristics in order to promote the client's growth and self-exploration: empathy, warmth, and genuineness.

→ Family therapy and marital therapy help members learn to communicate better with each other and resolve conflicts.

CRITICAL THINKING QUESTIONS

1 How might a psychotherapist adapt the therapeutic methods described in this section to help a person with schizophrenia? Which methods do you think would be helpful for a person with schizophrenia? Which methods would not be helpful?

2 If a child is determined to have a significant mental health problem that can be treated, but his or her parents do not want treatment, does the government have a right to require the parents to seek treatment? Why or why not?

BIOLOGICAL THERAPIES

The biological approach to abnormal behavior assumes that mental health problems, like physical illnesses, are caused by biochemical or physiological dysfunctions of the brain.

Psychotherapeutic drugs

By far the most widely used biological therapy is the use of drugs to modify mood and behavior (see the Concept Review Table for a review). Most of these drugs are thought to work by affecting the functioning of neurotransmitters in the brain.

The first **antipsychotic drugs** that were found to relieve the symptoms of schizophrenia belonged to the family called **phenothiazines**. These drugs block receptors for dopamine, and as we discussed in Chapter 15, irregularities in dopamine have been implicated in schizophrenia. These drugs are effective in reducing symptoms such as hallucinations and delusions, but are less effective in reducing the emotional disturbances and loss of motivation in schizophrenia. They also have significant side-effects, including dryness of the mouth, blurred vision, difficulty in concentrating – that prompt many patients to discontinue their medication. One of the most serious side-effects is a neurological

CONCEPT REVIEW TABLE DRUG TREATMENTS FOR MENTAL DISORDERS

These are the major types of drugs used to treat several kinds of mental disorders.

Type of drug	Purpose	Mode of action
Antipsychotic drugs	Reduce symptoms of psychosis (loss of reality testing, hallucinations, delusions)	Block dopamine receptors
Antidepressant drugs	Reduce symptoms of depression	Increase functional levels of serotonin and norepinephrine
Lithium	Reduce symptoms of bipolar disorder (mania and depression)	Regulates levels of serotonin, norepinephrine, and other neurotransmitters
Anticonvulsants	Reduce symptoms of bipolar disorder	Alter ion channels and influence the neurotransmitters GABA and glutamate
Antianxiety drugs	Reduce symptoms of anxiety	Depresses central nervous system
Stimulants	Increase attention and concentration	Possibly by increasing levels of dopamine

disorder known as **tardive dyskinesia**, which involves involuntary movements of the tongue, face, mouth, or jaw.

Newer drugs called **atypical antipsychotics** have been found to reduce symptoms of schizophrenia without causing so many side-effects (Dossenbach *et al.*, 2004). They appear to work by binding to a different type of dopamine receptor than the other drugs, although they also influence several other neurotransmitters, including serotonin.

Antidepressant drugs help elevate the mood of depressed individuals, apparently by regulating two neurotransmitter systems (norepinephrine and serotonin) (see Chapter 15). The most frequently used class of antidepressants is the selective serotonin reuptake inhibitors (SSRIs), which increase serotonin levels by blocking its reuptake. More recent drugs, known as serotonin-norepinephrine reuptake inhibitors (SNRIs) increase the availability of both serotonin and norepinephrine (such as venlafaxine). In addition to relieving depression, these drugs have proved helpful in treating the anxiety disorders, including OCD and panic disorder (Schatzberg, 2000). Common side-effects of these drugs include inhibited orgasm, nausea and diarrhea, dizziness, and nervousness. Older classes of antidepressants include tricyclic antidepressants and **monoamine oxidase (MAO)** inhibitors. These drugs can be highly effective in treating depression and anxiety, but have more side-effects than the newer drugs.

People with bipolar disorder often take an antidepressant medication to control their depression but must take other drugs to control their mania. **Lithium** reduces extreme mood swings and returns the individual to a more normal emotional state, by stabilizing a number of neurotransmitter systems (Thase *et al.*, 2002). Unfortunately, lithium has severe side-effects, including abdominal pain, nausea, vomiting, diarrhea, tremors, twitches, blurred vision, and problems in concentration and attention, and can cause kidney dysfunction, birth defects, and a form of diabetes.

Anticonvulsant medications (such as divalproex sodium, carbamazepine, lamotrigine, gabapentin, and topiramate) are now commonly used to treat bipolar disorder. These drugs can be highly effective in reducing the symptoms of severe and acute mania but do not seem to be as effective as lithium for long-term treatment of bipolar disorder (Ghaemi *et al.*, 2004). The side-effects of the anticonvulsants include dizziness, rash, nausea, and drowsiness. Antipsychotic medications may also be prescribed for people who suffer severe mania.

Several drugs traditionally used to treat anxiety belong to the family known as **benzodiazepines**. These drugs reduce tension and cause drowsiness, and can be addictive. Like alcohol and barbiturates, they depress the action of the central nervous system.

Stimulant drugs are used to treat the attentional problems of children with attention deficit hyperactivity disorder (ADHD). Although it may seem odd to give a stimulant to a hyperactive child, between 70 and 85 per cent of children with ADHD respond to these drugs with decreases in disruptive behavior and increases in attention (Joshi, 2004). Stimulant drugs may work by increasing levels of dopamine in the synapses of the brain.

Electroconvulsive therapy

In **electroconvulsive therapy (ECT)**, also known as electroshock therapy, a mild electric current is applied to the brain to produce a seizure similar to an epileptic convulsion. ECT was

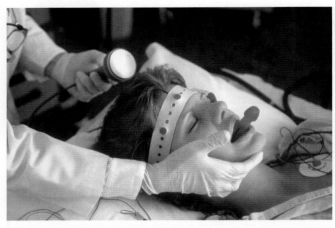

Electroconvulsive therapy is relatively effective in the treatment of depression.

a popular treatment from about 1940 to 1960, before anti-psychotic and antidepressant drugs became readily available. Today it is used primarily in cases of severe depression when the patient has failed to respond to drug therapy.

ECT has been the subject of much controversy, and rates of the use of ECT vary greatly across nations (Eranti & McLouglin, 2003). At one time it was used indiscriminately in mental hospitals to treat such problems as alcoholism and schizophrenia, for which it produced no beneficial results. Before more refined procedures were developed, ECT was a frightening experience for the patient, and often resulted in permanent memory loss and confusion.

Today, ECT is much safer. The patient is given a short-acting anesthesia and injected with a muscle relaxant. A brief, very weak electric current is applied to the brain. It is the seizure itself – not the electricity – that is therapeutic. The muscle relaxant prevents convulsive muscle spasms. The most common side-effect of ECT is memory loss.

Brain seizures cause massive release of norepinephrine and serotonin, and, as noted in Chapter 15, deficiencies of these neurotransmitters may be an important factor in some cases of depression. However it works, ECT is effective in bringing some people out of severe, immobilizing depression, and it does so faster than drug therapy (Sackeim *et al.*, 2007).

Combining biological and psychological therapies

Although in this chapter we divided therapies into psycho-logical and biological therapies, today there is a movement toward combined biological and psychological treatments. In depression and the anxiety disorders, often both the patient's biochemistry and his or her functioning in social and occupa-tional settings are affected by the disorder, and it can be helpful to provide treatment at both the biological and psy-chosocial levels. Even in disorders like schizophrenia, whose primary cause is biological, the patient often experiences

severe losses in social skills and ability to function on a job. Supplementing antipsychotic drugs with psychotherapy designed to help the person cope with the consequences of schizophrenia can be very useful.

The fact that a wide range of both psychotherapies and drugs are effective in the treatment of some problems (especially depression) suggests that intervening at one level of a person's bio-psycho-social system can affect all levels of the system. For example, intervening at the psychological level may cause changes in the patient's bio-chemistry and social behaviors. When this occurs, it is because our biochemistry, our personalities and thought processes, and our social behaviors are so thoroughly inter-twined that each can affect the other in both positive and negative ways.

INTERIM SUMMARY

- Biological therapies include electroconvulsive therapy (ECT) and the use of psychotherapeutic drugs. Of the two, drug therapy is by far the more widely used.

- Antipsychotic drugs, which alter levels of the neurotransmitter dopamine, have proved effective in the treatment of schizophrenia.

- Antidepressants help to elevate the mood of depressed patients by affecting levels of the neurotransmitters serotonin and norepinephrine. Lithium and anticonvulsant medications can be effective in treating bipolar disorders.

- Antianxiety drugs depress the action of the central nervous system and are used to reduce severe anxiety and help clients cope with life crises.

- Stimulant drugs are used to treat attention deficit hyperactivity disorder (ADHD) in children.

CRITICAL THINKING QUESTIONS

1 Many people currently using psychoactive drugs, particularly the serotonin reuptake inhibitors (SSRIs), are not suffering from a severe mood disorder but from the stresses of everyday living. Do you think this is an appropriate use of these drugs? Why or why not?

2 Do you think people with mental health problems should be forced to take drugs to control their symptoms? Would your answer depend on the type of symptoms they suffered?

ENHANCING MENTAL HEALTH

Aside from seeking professional help, there are many ways in which we can positively influence our own psychological well-being. By monitoring our feelings and behavior, we can determine the kinds of actions and situations that cause us pain or get us into difficulty and, conversely, the kinds that benefit us the most. By trying to analyze our motives and abilities, we can enhance our capacity to make active choices in our lives instead of passively accepting whatever happens. The problems that people face vary greatly, and there are no universal guidelines for staying psychologically healthy. However, a few general suggestions have emerged from the experiences of therapists.

Developing interests and hobbies is one key to psychological well-being.

Accept your feelings

Anger, sorrow, fear, and a feeling of having fallen short of ideals or goals are all unpleasant emotions, and we may try to escape anxiety by denying these feelings. Sometimes we try to avoid anxiety by facing situations unemotionally, which leads to a false kind of detachment or 'cool' that may be destructive. We may try to suppress all emotions, thereby losing the ability to accept as normal the joys and sorrows that are part of our involvement with other people.

Unpleasant emotions are a normal reaction to many situations. There is no reason to be ashamed of feeling homesick, being afraid when learning something new, or becoming angry at someone who has disappointed us. These emotions are natural, and it is better to recognize them than to deny them. When emotions cannot be expressed directly (for example, it may not be wise to yell at your boss), it helps to find a way to cope with the stress. Taking a long walk, pounding a tennis ball, or discussing the situation with a friend can help reduce tension and may generate a solution to your problems.

Know your vulnerabilities

Discovering the kinds of situations that upset you or cause you to overreact may help you guard against stress. Perhaps certain people annoy you. You could avoid them, or you could try to understand just what it is about them that disturbs you. Maybe they seem so poised and confident that they make you feel insecure. Trying to pinpoint the cause of your discomfort may help you see the situation in a new light. Perhaps you become very anxious when you have to speak in class or present a paper. Again, you could try to avoid such situations, or you could gain confidence by taking a course in public speaking. You could also reinterpret the situation. Instead of thinking, 'Everyone is waiting to criticize me as soon as I open my mouth,' you could tell yourself, 'The class will be interested in what I have to say, and I'm not going to let it worry me if I make a few mistakes.'

Many people feel especially anxious when they are under pressure. Careful planning and spacing of work can help you avoid feeling overwhelmed at the last minute. The strategy of purposely allowing more time than you think you need to get to classes or appointments can eliminate one source of stress.

Develop your talents and interests

People who are bored and unhappy seldom have many interests. Today's universities offer almost unlimited opportunities for people of all ages to explore their talents in many areas, including sports, academic interests, music, art, drama, and crafts. Often, the more you know about a subject, the more interesting it (and life) becomes. In addition, the feeling of competence gained from developing skills can do a great deal to bolster self-esteem.

Become involved with other people

Feelings of isolation and loneliness are at the core of many emotional health problems. We are social beings, and we need the support, comfort, and reassurance provided by other people. Focusing all your attention on your own problems can lead to an unhealthy preoccupation with yourself. Sharing your concerns with others often helps you view your troubles in a clearer perspective. Also, being concerned for the welfare of other people can reinforce your feelings of self-worth.

Know when to seek help

Although these suggestions can help promote emotional well-being, there are limits to self-understanding and self-help. Some problems are difficult to solve alone. Our tendency toward self-deception makes it hard to view problems objectively, and we may not be aware of all the possible solutions. When you feel that you are making little headway toward gaining control over a problem, it is time to seek professional help. Willingness to seek help is a sign of emotional maturity, not weakness; do not wait until you feel overwhelmed.

SEEING BOTH SIDES

IS ALCOHOLICS ANONYMOUS (AA) AN EFFECTIVE INTERVENTION FOR ALCOHOL MISUSE?

ALCOHOLICS ANONYMOUS: AN EVIDENCE-BASED RESOURCE

Keith Humphreys, Veterans Affairs Palo Alto Health Care System and Department of Psychiatry and Behavioral Sciences, Stanford University

Alcoholics Anonymous (AA) is a worldwide fellowship of over 4 million alcohol-dependent individuals (Humphreys, 2004) who are committed to helping each other permanently abstain from alcohol, as well as become more honest, humble, compassionate and spiritually serene. In over 100 nations, AA members meet in mutual help groups on a regular basis, where they use AA principles (e.g., the 'Twelve Steps'), and their personal 'experience, strength, and hope' to promote sobriety. In many countries, including the USA, AA is the most commonly sought source of help for alcohol problems (Humphreys, 2004; Weisner *et al.,* 1995), outstripping all professional interventions combined.

AA enjoys an excellent reputation among most treatment professionals. At the same time, some clinicians and researchers doubt AA's effectiveness (Humphreys, 2004), noting that the organization offers a loosely monitored and unstandardized program based primarily on the experience and spiritual outlook of its members rather than a standardized professional treatment derived from objective, scientific research.

Cross and colleagues (Cross *et al.,* 1990) followed up a sample of 158 alcohol dependent patients 10 years after treatment to determine what factors (e.g., problem severity, age, sex) predicted long-term abstinence from alcohol. Of all the variables examined, only AA involvement increased the likelihood of abstinence. In randomized clinical trials – the most rigorous design for drawing inferences about the effectiveness of interventions – AA has generally produced levels of abstinence equal or superior to those of comparison conditions (Humphreys, 2006; Timko *et al.,* 2006). Other longitudinal research has linked AA involvement to other benefits, including reducing depression and anxiety, improved social networks, and happier intimate relationships (Humphreys, 2004).

Researchers have also increasingly uncovered 'mediators' of AA's effectiveness. A mediator is an element in the causal chain that connects AA involvement with reduced drinking. Careful longitudinal research have shown that among the mediators of AA's effect on drinking are improved coping with stress, greater self-efficacy, greater desire to abstain, and the replacement of drinking friends with AA members. Changes in these areas are beneficial in themselves, but have the further positive effect of making abstinence easier to attain.

Because AA attendance is free of charge, the organization is probably the most cost-effective way for alcohol dependent individuals to become abstinent. One study of 201 alcohol abusers illustrating this point compared 135 individuals who initially chose to attend AA with 66 individuals who initially chose to seek professional outpatient treatment (Humphreys & Moos, 1996). Despite the fact that individuals were not randomly assigned to each condition, at baseline, there were no significant differences between groups on demographic variables, alcohol problems or psychopathology. By 3-year follow-up, the AA attenders had reduced their daily alcohol intake an average of 75 per cent and had decreased their alcohol dependence symptoms (e.g., blackouts) an average of 71 per cent. Individuals receiving professional treatment improved comparably. However, alcohol-related health care costs over the 3-year study were 45 per cent lower in the AA group than in the treated group. Hence, AA not only promotes abstinence, but does so in a cost-effective fashion that takes a substantial burden off the formal health care system.

AA effectiveness research used to be methodologically weak. But research on the effects of AA participation has improved substantially in the past 15 years, with most studies employing longitudinal designs, comparison groups, and high-quality measures of AA participation and outcome. And as the research has become more rigorous, the case for AA's effectiveness has become stronger rather than weaker, indicating that the organization is genuinely effective. Clinical and scientific skepticism has accordingly waned substantially in recent years. In light of AA's effectiveness, availability and minimal financial cost, it clearly is an important, evidence-based resource for facilitating recovery among alcohol dependent individuals.

SEEING BOTH SIDES

IS ALCOHOLICS ANONYMOUS (AA) AN EFFECTIVE INTERVENTION FOR ALCOHOL MISUSE?

ALCOHOLICS ANONYMOUS IS NOT THE ONLY WAY

G. Alan Marlatt, University of Washington

Although Alcoholics Anonymous (AA) is the most well-known self-help group for many people who are recovering from alcoholism, it is not the only way to help many individuals to stop drinking, and, for some problem drinkers, AA may be a barrier to successful treatment. Studies show that of every two people who attend their first meeting of AA, only one returns for a second or subsequent meeting.

Why does AA appeal to some and not to others? Although AA is described as a 'spiritual fellowship' and is not explicitly identified with any specific religious group, many first-timers are put off by the requirement to admit that one is powerless over one's drinking and that only by turning over personal control to a 'higher power', is recovery possible. Others are discouraged by the AA doctrine that alcoholism is basically a physical disease that cannot be cured, only 'arrested' by total lifelong abstinence from any alcoholic beverages. For those adherents of the disease model, including almost all AA members, there is no possibility of future moderate or controlled drinking. Once an alcoholic, always an alcoholic, according to AA beliefs.

Research has yet to reveal whether it is the specific teachings (theory) associated with AA, or the group support that the meetings provide that is most effective in helping people change their personal habits. Recent evidence indicates the latter is primarily responsible for AA success, which suggests other groups with different theories or beliefs about alcoholism and recovery can also be effective. In recent years, several new self-help groups for alcoholics have become available, including: (1) Rational Recovery, based on rational principles of behavioral change without the need for a 'higher power' in order to maintain abstinence, (2) Self Management and Recovery Training (SMART), based on the principles of cognitive-behavioral therapy such as relapse prevention and social skills training, and (3) Women for Sobriety, for women who have problems relating to the mainly masculine flavor of many AA meetings and who could benefit from addressing alcohol problems shared by many women drinkers.

Another alternative to AA is 'Moderation Management' self-help groups. After several failed attempts at making AA work for her, Audrey Kishline (1994) developed 'Moderation Management,' a program of drinking in moderation, one that has been used in many self-help groups in recent years (including some groups that meet on the Internet rather than in person).

Moderate or controlled drinking programs are also known in the addictions treatment field as examples of a 'harm-reduction' approach. The goal of harm-reduction programs (such as moderation for heavy drinkers, nicotine replacement therapy for smokers who can't fully kick the habit, etc.) is to reduce the harmful consequences to oneself, one's family, and one's community caused by the drug problem. Although abstinence is accepted as an ideal goal for recovery, any steps toward this goal that reduce harm are considered steps in the right direction toward enhanced health and the prevention of disease.

Harm-reduction programs have been successful in teaching high-risk college students to drink more safely. Alcohol harm-reduction programs are designed to teach the novice drinker skills about drinking behavior and corresponding levels of intoxication. A recent study of high-risk, first-year college students found those who attended the program showed a significant drop in binge drinking, blackouts, severe hangovers, and acts of vandalism, and so on compared with students in a control group who did not receive this training program. Thus for students who choose to drink and are at risk for experiencing serious drinking problems, harm reduction offers a viable alternative to abstinence (see my article in the August 1998 issue of the *Journal of Consulting and Clinical Psychology*).

In AA, if someone does not accept the requirement of total abstinence, he or she is likely to be told to go away and not to come back until having 'hit bottom' – in other words, until the person has experienced such profound negative consequences from drinking that he or she sees no other choice but to go back to AA and pursue total abstinence. But what do we do with those drinkers who have not yet 'hit bottom,' even though they may be experiencing serious harmful consequences? Harm reduction offers a variety of helpful strategies for this group to get them started on the road to recovery.

INTERIM SUMMARY

➔ Accepting your feelings is the first step to responding effectively to them.

➔ Knowing your vulnerabilities allows you to avoid triggers for distress and seek help in overcoming certain vulnerabilities.

➔ Developing your talents gives you multiple sources of self-esteem and joy.

➔ Seeking out others is a good strategy for distress. Helping others can increase your self-esteem.

➔ Not all problems can be handled alone; it's important to seek help when you need it.

CRITICAL THINKING QUESTIONS

1 In what circumstances do you think self-help books are helpful, and when might they not be helpful?

2 Some people seem never to be overwhelmed by stress and appear able to handle almost anything. What do you think makes such people super-resilient?

CHAPTER SUMMARY

1 Treatment of people with mental health problems has progressed from the ancient notion that abnormal behavior resulted from possession by evil spirits that needed to be punished, through custodial care in asylums, to modern psychiatric hospitals. The policy of deinstitutionalization, despite its good intentions, has added to the number of homeless people with mental health problems, causing concern about civil rights and adequate care.

2 Psychotherapy is the treatment of mental health problems by psychological means. Behavior therapies apply methods based on learning principles to modify the client's behavior. These methods include systematic desensitization (the individual learns to relax in situations that previously produced anxiety), reinforcement of adaptive behaviors, modeling and rehearsal of appropriate behavior, and techniques for self-regulation of behavior.

3 Cognitive-behavior therapies use behavior modification techniques but also incorporate procedures for changing maladaptive beliefs. The therapist helps the client replace irrational interpretations of events with more realistic ones.

4 Psychoanalysis, which was developed by Freud, uses methods such as free association and dream analysis, to bring repressed thoughts and feelings to the patient's awareness. By interpreting these dreams and associations, the analyst helps the patient gain insight into his or her problems. Transference, the tendency to express feelings toward the analyst that the client has for important people in his or her life, provides another source of interpretation.

5 Contemporary psychodynamic therapies are briefer than traditional psychoanalysis and place more emphasis on the client's current interpersonal problems (as opposed to a complete reconstruction of childhood experiences).

6 Humanistic therapies help clients become aware of their real selves and solve their problems with a minimum of intervention by the therapist. Carl Rogers, who developed client-centered psychotherapy, believed that the therapist must have three characteristics in order to promote the client's growth and self-exploration: empathy, warmth, and genuineness.

7 Marital therapy and family therapy are specialized forms of group therapy that help couples, or parents and children, learn more effective ways of relating to one another and handling their problems

8 Biological therapies include electroconvulsive therapy (ECT) and psychotherapeutic drugs. Of the two, drug therapy is by far the most widely used. Antipsychotic drugs have proved effective in the treatment of schizophrenia, antidepressants help to elevate the mood of depressed patients, and lithium has been effective in treating bipolar disorders. Antianxiety drugs are used to reduce severe anxiety and help clients cope with life crises.

CORE CONCEPTS

deinstitutionalization	free association	tardive dyskinesia
psychotherapy	dream analysis	atypical antipsychotics
behavior therapy	transference	antidepressant drugs
systematic desensitization	interpersonal therapy	monoamine oxidase (MAO)
in vivo exposure	humanistic therapies	lithium
selective reinforcement	client-centered therapy	benzodiazepines
behavioral rehearsal	marital therapy	stimulant drug
self-regulation	family therapy	electroconvulsive therapy (ECT)
cognitive behavior therapy	antipsychotic drubs	
psychodynamic therapies	phenothiazines	

DIGITAL SUPPORT RESOURCES

Students should use the unique access code included in the front of the book to access the digital support resources which accompany the new edition. These include:

- Multiple Choice Questions and Quizzes
- Critical Thinking Questions
- Practice Essay Questions
- Videos
- Glossary, Flashcards, and More

17

SOCIAL INFLUENCE

Explore how the presence of others influences people's behavior.

Cover how deindividuation and bystanders influence social behavior.

Be introduced to classic experiments on compliance and obedience.

Learn how the classic Zimbardo Prison Experiment illustrates the power of situations and institutional norms.

Define the fundamental attribution error and provide an example.

Explain when and why social facilitation vs. social inhibition occurs.

Describe how deindividuation can produce aggression.

Explain pluralistic ignorance and why it matters.

Discuss the differences between informational and normative social influence.

Explain the importance of Milgram's experiments on obedience to authority.

Discuss various explanations for why people change their attitudes to reflect their past behavior.

Explain group polarization and why it happens.

People sometimes do the inexplicable – or what seems inexplicable. Our newspapers and history books provide plenty of examples. From 1933 to 1945, millions of innocent people – mostly Jews – were forced to live in concentration camps in Nazi Germany. Only after World War II did the world community realize that these camps were in fact high-efficiency death 'factories' that systematically slaughtered more than 8 million people. How could this genocide happen? What kind of people could design and operate these death factories? The actions of the Nazi regime seem inexplicable.

On November 18, 1978, US Congressman Leo Ryan was concluding his visit to Jonestown, a settlement of the People's Temple (formerly based in San Francisco) in Guyana, South America. Ryan was investigating Jonestown because reports had come back to the USA that people were being held there against their will. As Ryan boarded his plane to leave Guyana, he and four others were shot and killed by Temple gunmen. Meanwhile, Jim Jones, the leader of the People's Temple, gathered the nearly 1000 residents of Jonestown and asked them to kill themselves by drinking strawberry-flavored poison. They complied. How could this happen? What kind of people would kill themselves at another person's request? The actions of the members of the People's Temple seem inexplicable.

On September 11, 2001, four US planes were hijacked. Two crashed into New York City's twin World Trade Center towers, one crashed into US military headquarters at the Pentagon, outside Washington, D.C., and the fourth crashed in Pennsylvania, missing its intended target. In addition to the hundreds of people killed on board the airplanes and in the Pentagon, nearly 3000 people remained in the World Trade Center towers when they collapsed from the impact. How could this happen? What kind of people could take so many innocent lives, as well as their own? The actions of these suicide hijackers seem inexplicable.

In trying to make sense of these seemingly inexplicable horrors of humanity, our first reaction is often to pin evil (or crazy) actions on evil (or crazy) individuals. 'The suicide hijackers were evil terrorists.' 'Jim Jones's followers were crazy.' 'The Nazis were evil racists.' These sorts of explanations provide some comfort. They distance us 'good' and 'normal' people, from those 'bad' and 'crazy' people. To be sure, there is a grain of truth within explanations that attribute evil actions to evil characters. Osama bin Laden, Jim Jones, and Adolf Hitler, for instance, might well be classified as evil leaders. Even so, social psychologists have argued that explanations that attribute the full cause

CHAPTER OUTLINE

....

THE PRESENCE OF OTHERS

Social facilitation and social inhibition

Deindividuation

Bystander effects

....

CUTTING EDGE RESEARCH:

THE COLLAPSE OF COMPASSION

....

COMPLIANCE AND OBEDIENCE

Conformity to a majority

Minority influence

Obedience to authority

....

INTERNALIZATION

Self-justification

Reference groups and identification

....

GROUP INTERACTIONS

Institutional norms

Group decision making

....

SEEING BOTH SIDES: ARE THE

EFFECTS OF AFFIRMATIVE ACTION

POSITIVE OR NEGATIVE?

....

RECAP: SOCIAL PSYCHOLOGICAL

VIEWS OF THE SEEMINGLY

INEXPLICABLE

....

of an action to someone's personality are often wrong – so often wrong that social psychologists identify these explanations as instances of the fundamental attribution error. The **fundamental attribution error** refers to the tendency to explain other people's actions by overestimating the influence of personality or character and underestimating the influence of situations or circumstances. Moreover, we make this fundamental error not only when trying to make sense of unfathomable horrors but also when making sense of the ordinary, everyday actions of our friends, classmates, and others. Consider, for instance, getting an email message from a new co-worker that contains spelling and grammar errors. Although such errors are at times excused for informal messages, the fundamental attribution error suggests that you may well question the sender's conscientiousness and intelligence. Yet with additional information about the sender's circumstances, like that she's not writing in her native language, you'd be less likely to evaluate her unfavorably (Vignovic & Thompson, 2010).

Social psychology is the scientific study of the ways that people's behavior and mental processes are shaped by the real or imagined presence of others. Social psychologists begin with the basic observation that human behavior is a function of both the person and the situation. Each individual brings a unique set of personal attributes to a situation, leading different people to act in different ways in the same situation. But each situation also brings a unique set of forces to bear on an individual, leading him or her to act in different ways in different situations. Research has repeatedly shown that situations are more powerful determinants of behavior than our intuitions lead us to believe. Thus, one of the foremost contributions of social psychology is an understanding of how powerful situations shape people's behavior and mental processes. Our two-chapter discussion of social psychology begins with this focus on the power of situations.

Yet people do not simply react to the objective features of situations but rather to their subjective interpretations of them. As we learned in Chapter 11 on emotions, the person who interprets an offensive act as the product of hostility reacts differently than the person who construes the same act as the product of mental illness. Accordingly, Chapter 18 examines the power that subjective interpretations and people's modes of thinking have in shaping their thoughts, feelings, and social behavior, a topic known as social cognition. We begin, however, with a focus on social influence and the power of situations themselves.

Horrific world events often seem completely inexplicable. How could people do these things to themselves and to others? Social psychologists argue that answers that appeal only to personality or character traits overlook the powerful influence that social situations can have in shaping human behavior.

THE PRESENCE OF OTHERS

Social facilitation and social inhibition

In 1898, while examining the speed records of bicycle racers, psychologist Norman Triplett noticed that many cyclists achieved better times when they raced against each other than when they raced against the clock. This led him to perform one of social psychology's earliest laboratory experiments. He instructed children to turn a fishing reel as fast as possible for a fixed period. Sometimes two children worked at the same time in the same room, each with his or her own reel. At other times they worked alone. Triplett reported that many children worked faster when someone else doing the same task was present (a situation termed coaction) than when they worked alone.

In the more than 100 years since Triplett conducted his experiment, many other studies have demonstrated the

In 1898 psychologist Norman Triplett noticed that cyclists achieved better times when they raced against other cyclists than when they raced against the clock. This led him to study the phenomenon of social facilitation.

facilitating effects of coaction both in humans and in animals. For example, worker ants in groups dig more than three times as much sand per ant than when alone (Chen, 1937), many animals eat more food if other members of their species are present (Platt et al., 1967), and college students complete more multiplication problems in coaction than when alone (Allport, 1920, 1924).

Soon after Triplett's experiment on coaction, psychologists discovered that the presence of a passive spectator – an audience rather than a coactor – also facilitates performance. For example, the presence of an audience had the same facilitating effect on students' multiplication performance as the presence of coactors in the earlier study (Dashiell, 1930). The term social facilitation is used to refer to the boosting effects of coactors and audiences on performance.

But this simple case of social influence turned out to be more complicated than social psychologists first thought. For example, researchers found that people made more errors on the multiplication problems when in coaction or in the presence of an audience than when they performed alone (Dashiell, 1930). In other words, accuracy decreased even though speed increased. In many other studies, both the speed and accuracy of performance decreased when others were present. The term social inhibition was introduced to refer to the sometimes derailing effects of coactors and audiences on performance.

How can we predict whether the presence of others – either coacting or observing – will improve our performance or impair it? The answer to this question first emerged in the mid-1960s (Zajonc, 1965) and was solidified two decades later in a meta-analysis of 241 studies (Bond & Titus, 1983). The basic finding is that the presence of coactors and audiences improves the speed and accuracy of performance on simple or well-learned tasks but impairs the speed and accuracy of performance on complex or poorly learned tasks.

So social facilitation holds for simple tasks, and social inhibition holds for complex tasks. Despite this useful generalization, this pattern of results still requires explanation. Why does it occur? Social psychologists have offered two competing explanations.

The first explanation, offered by Robert Zajonc (1965), appeals to drive theories of motivation (see Chapter 10). These suggest that high levels of drive or arousal tend to energize the dominant responses of an organism. If the mere presence of another member of the species raises the general arousal or drive level of an organism, the dominant response will be facilitated. For simple or well-learned behaviors, the dominant response is most likely to be the correct response, and performance should be facilitated. For complex behaviors or behaviors that are just being learned, the dominant or most probable response is likely to be incorrect. Consider the multiplication problems discussed earlier. There are many wrong responses but only one correct one. Accurate performance on this complex task should therefore be inhibited.

A number of experiments have confirmed these predictions. For example, people learn simple mazes or easy word lists more quickly but learn complex mazes or difficult word lists more slowly when an audience is present than when it is not (Cottrell *et al.,* 1967; Hunt & Hillery, 1973). A study using cockroaches found that, when attempting to escape light, roaches run an easy route more quickly but a difficult route more slowly if other roaches watch from the sidelines (or run with them) than if they run without other roaches present (Zajonc *et al.,* 1969). More recent experiments conclude that physical presence is not required. Electronic surveillance is sufficient to facilitate the dominant response (Feinberg & Aiello, 2006), as is the presence of a lifelike virtual human, presented by computer screen, who observes via artificial intelligence (Park & Catrambone, 2007).

The second explanation for social facilitation and social inhibition appeals to attention factors (Baron, 1986; Huguet *et al.,* 1999). The core idea is that the presence of others is often distracting, which can produce a mental overload that results in a narrowed focus of attention. This view can also explain the different effects for simple and complex tasks: social facilitation should occur when tasks are simple and require that we focus on only a small number of central cues, and social inhibition should occur when tasks are complex and require our attention to a wide range of cues.

Which explanation is correct? In most circumstances, the two explanations make the same predictions and so cannot be tested against one another. A clever study solved this problem, however, by locating a task for which the two views offer different predictions (Huguet *et al.*, 1999). The Stroop task, introduced in Chapter 9, is a complex, poorly learned task that involves only a few key stimuli (MacLeod, 1991; Stroop, 1935). In this task, a person is asked to identify the ink color in which words or symbols (like '+++') are printed. See Figure17.1 for an example. People perform this task relatively quickly for symbols but are particularly slowed for words that are incongruent (like the word *red* printed in yellow ink).

This phenomenon, called **Stroop interference**, results because word reading is such a dominant and automatic response among skilled readers that it is difficult to follow the instruction to ignore the printed word and name the word's ink color. Because the Stroop task is complex and the automatic response is to name the word (not the ink color), the dominant-response view predicts that social presence should derail performance, producing social inhibition. At the same time, because the Stroop task involves only two key stimuli – the word and the ink color – and a narrowed focus of attention can reduce attention to the irrelevant information (the word), the attention view, by contrast, predicts that social presence should improve performance, producing social facilitation.

The data from several experiments that have manipulated the presence or absence of an audience or coactors during Stroop performance provide clear support for the attention view and fail to support the dominant-response view: people perform *better* on the Stroop task when in the presence of others (Huguet *et al.*, 1999). These and other studies also identify two key limits to social facilitation effects. First, the mere presence of another person does not produce much social facilitation. If the audience member is reading or blindfolded, for example, social facilitation is greatly reduced (Cottrell *et al.,* 1968; Huguet *et al.,* 1999). Second, competition and social comparison with coactors seem to be critical. If coactors perform much worse than participants themselves – that is, if they are no competition – social facilitation is also greatly reduced (Dashiell, 1930; Huguet *et al.*, 1999).

The lineage of studies on social facilitation and social inhibition begins to convey the power of situations. You might have thought that your physical performance (like throwing free throws in basketball) or academic performance (like taking a calculus exam) merely reflected your ability. But the studies described here suggest that whether the performance situation includes real or even virtual others, and what

++++   ####   XXXX

RED YELLOW BLUE

FIGURE 17.1 Items From a Stroop Task. *Say aloud the color of the inks you see in the top row. Now do the same for the bottom row. Notice how much slower you were to name the ink colors for words versus symbols. This is called Stroop interference. Studies show that people perform better on the Stroop task when in the presence of others, a finding that supports the attention explanation for social facilitation.*

Audience effects on performance vary depending on whether the task is easy or difficult for them and on how much the person feels that he or she is being evaluated.

those others are doing (evaluating or providing competition), also critically determine your level of performance. Yet whether the presence of others helps or hurts your performance depends on whether the task at hand is simple or complex for you. A pro basketball player and a student who has mastered the basics of calculus are likely to do better when the situation involves others. For them, the task becomes simple because it is well learned. For a novice basketball player and a student who neglects studying, the situation does not bode so well.

Deindividuation

At about the same time that Triplett was performing his experiment on social facilitation, another observer of human behavior, Gustave Le Bon, was also studying the effects of coaction. In *The Crowd* (1895), Le Bon complained that 'the crowd is always intellectually inferior to the isolated individual'. He believed that the aggressive and immoral behaviors shown by lynch mobs (and, in his view, French revolutionaries) spread through a mob or crowd by contagion, like a disease, breaking down an individual's moral sense and self-control. Such breakdowns, he argued, caused crowds to commit destructive acts that few individuals would commit when acting alone.

Le Bon's early observations of crowd behavior fueled the development of a concept that social psychologists have called **deindividuation**, first introduced in the 1950s (Festinger *et al.,* 1952) but revisited and revised in subsequent decades (in the 1960s by Zimbardo [1969], in the 1970s by Diener [1977, 1980], in the 1980s by Prentice-Dunn & Rogers [1982, 1989], and in the 1990s and beyond by Postmes & Spears [1998]). Although the explanations for the phenomenon have shifted over the decades, the core idea within deindividuation is that certain

FIGURE 17.2 Anonymity Can Increase Aggression. *This was clearly demonstrated during the Ku Klux Klan activities in the USA in the 1930s – prejudice against an outgroup led to aggression that was facilitated by anonymity.*

group situations can minimize the salience of people's personal identities, reduce their sense of public accountability, and in doing so produce aggressive or unusual behavior (for a meta-analysis of 60 studies, see Postmes & Spears, 1998). To illustrate, violent attacks in Northern Ireland during the mid-1990s can be divided into those carried out by identifiable offenders versus offenders who wore disguises to mask their identity. Compared to identifiable offenders, disguised offenders attacked more people at the scene and inflicted more serious injuries (Silke, 2003). Early explanations for the effects of deindividuation suggested that a reduced sense of public accountability weakened the normal restraints against impulsive and unruly behavior (Diener, 1980; Festinger *et al.*, 1952; Zimbardo, 1969).

This was clearly demonstrated during the Ku Klux Klan activities in the USA in the 1930s – prejudice against an outgroup led to aggression that was facilitated by anonymity, see Figure 17.2.

In another famous study of deindividuation, groups of four college women were required to deliver electric shocks to another woman who was supposedly participating in a learning experiment. Half of the groups were deindividuated by making them feel anonymous. They were dressed in bulky laboratory coats and hoods that hid their faces, and the experimenter spoke to them only as a group, never referring to any of them by name. The remaining groups were individuated by having them remain in their own clothes and wear large identification tags. In addition, the women in the latter groups were introduced to one another by name. During the experiment, each woman had a shock button in front of her, which she was to push when the learner made an error. Pushing the button appeared to deliver a shock to the learner (in reality, it did not). The

People often behave differently in a crowd than when alone. Some researchers believe that in a situation like a riot, individuals experience deindividuation – a feeling that they have lost their personal identities and merged anonymously into the group.

results showed that the deindividuated women delivered twice as much shock to the learner as the individuated women (Zimbardo, 1969).

Another study was conducted at several homes on Halloween night in the USA Children out trick-or-treating were greeted at the door by a woman who asked that each child take only one sweet from a large bowl of sweets. The woman then disappeared into the house briefly, giving the children the opportunity to take more sweets. Some of the children had been asked their names, and others remained anonymous. Children who came in groups or who remained anonymous stole more sweets than children who came alone or had given their names to the adult (Diener *et al.,* 1976).

These experiments are not definitive, however. For instance, you can see in Figure 17.2 that the laboratory coats and hoods in the first study resembled the costumes worn by members of the Ku Klux Klan, a historically prominent hate group in the USA Similarly, Halloween costumes often represent witches, monsters, or ghosts. These all carry aggressive or negative connotations. It may be that these costumes did not simply provide anonymity but that they also activated social norms that encouraged aggression. **Social norms** are implicit or explicit rules for acceptable behavior and beliefs. To test whether social norms rather than anonymity produced aggressive behavior, the shock experiment was repeated, but this time each participant wore one of three outfits: a Ku Klux Klan-type costume, a nurse's uniform, or the participant's own clothes. Compared with the group who wore their own clothes, participants wearing Ku Klux Klan-type costumes delivered somewhat more shocks to the learner (but not reliably so). More significantly, participants wearing nurses' uniforms actually gave fewer shocks than participants who wore their own clothes. This study shows that anonymity does not inevitably lead to increased aggression (Johnson & Downing, 1979).

The finding that cues that are specific to the situation (like a nurse's uniform) evoke social norms that guide behavior within anonymous groups led to a later reformulation of the mental processes involved in deindividuation. This view holds that situations that reduce public accountability – like group size and anonymity – do not simply reduce the salience of people's personal identities but also simultaneously enhance the salience of people's group identities (like being a nurse, or a member of the People's Temple). Plus, situations that make group identities salient promote behavior that is normative for the salient group (like being less aggressive if you are role-playing a nurse). So whereas earlier explanations of deindividuation suggested that anonymity produces a breakdown of the normal restraints against unruly behavior, this more recent explanation suggests that these same features of group situations promote greater conformity to situation-specific social norms (Lea *et al.,* 2001; Postmes & Spears, 1998).

Again, the research on deindividuation conveys the power of situations in determining people's behavior. So the next time you find yourself in a large group situation in which you feel anonymous (not uncommon on a university campus), you may notice yourself getting caught up with the group's behavior. If the group is focused on peaceful activities (like a candlelight vigil for victims of terrorist attacks), you may act more patriotic and reverent than you might on your own. Yet if the group is focused on more raucous activities (like looting or harassing others), know that situational forces will exert their pull.

Bystander effects

Earlier we noted that people do not react simply to the objective features of a situation but also respond to their subjective interpretations of it. We have seen that even social facilitation, a primitive kind of social influence, depends in part on the individual's interpretation of what other people are doing or thinking. But as we will now see, defining or interpreting the situation is often the very mechanism through which individuals influence one another.

In 1964 a young woman named Kitty Genovese was attacked outside her New York apartment at around 3 a.m. Two weeks later, the front page of the *New York Times* ran an article headlined, '37 Who Saw Murder Didn't Call the Police: Apathy at Stabbing Shocks Inspector'. The ensuing article claimed that for more than half an hour 38 eyewitnesses watched Kitty Genovese's killer stalk and stab her, but not one called the police during the assault, and only one called after she was dead.

The American public was horrified by this account. Although investigations some 40 years later suggest that far fewer people actually witnessed the Genovese murder (Manning *et al.,* 2007), the powerful image of 38 passive witnesses sparked social psychologists of the time to investigate the causes of what came to be called the **bystander effect**, referring to the finding that people are less likely to help when others are present. You might suppose that if you needed help in an emergency, you'd be more likely to receive it if many people witnessed the event. Simple odds should increase the chances that helpful souls are in the crowd, right? Unfortunately not. Research on bystander effects shows just the reverse: often it is the very presence of other people that prevents us from taking action. In fact, by 1980 more than 50 studies of bystander effects had been conducted, and most of them showed that people reduced helping when others were present (Latané *et al.,* 1981). Latané and Darley (1970) suggest that the presence of others deters an individual from taking action by (1) defining the situation as a non-emergency through the process of pluralistic ignorance, and (2) diffusing the responsibility for acting.

Defining the situation

Many emergencies begin ambiguously. Is that staggering man ill or simply drunk? Is the woman being threatened by a stranger, or is she arguing with her husband? Is that smoke from a fire or just steam pouring out the window? A common way of dealing with such uncertainties is to postpone action, act as if nothing is wrong, and discreetly glance around you to see how other people are reacting. Suppose everyone does the same? What you get is a group of people who all *look* like they know what they are doing, but internally they are each in turmoil, confused and uncertain. This is **pluralistic ignorance**. Everybody – the plurality – is ignorant of everyone else's true feelings and the proper way to behave (Schanck, 1932). Because people often show blank expressions when confronted with ambiguity, especially if trying to maintain their cool, in cases of possible emergency, pluralistic ignorance can mislead everybody in the vicinity to define the situation as a non-emergency. We have all heard about crowds panicking because each person causes everybody else to overreact. The reverse situation – in which a crowd lulls its members into inaction – may be even more common. Several experiments demonstrate this effect.

In one experiment, male college students were invited to an interview. As they sat in a small waiting room completing a questionnaire, what appeared to be smoke began to stream through a wall vent. Some participants were alone in the waiting room when this occurred; others were in groups of three. The experimenters observed them through a one-way window and waited 6 minutes to see if anyone would take action or report the situation. Of the participants who were tested alone, 75 per cent left the room and reported the potential fire. In contrast, less than 13 per cent of the participants who were tested in groups reported the smoke, even though the room was so filled with smoke they had to wave it away to complete their questionnaires. Those who did not report the smoke subsequently reported that they had decided that it must have been steam, air conditioning vapors, or smog – practically anything but a real fire or an emergency. This experiment thus showed that bystanders can define situations as non-emergencies for one another (Latané & Darley, 1968).

But perhaps these participants were simply afraid to appear cowardly. To check on this possibility, a similar study was designed in which the 'emergency' did not involve personal danger. Participants waiting in the testing room heard a female experimenter in the next office climb up on a chair to reach a bookcase, fall to the floor, and yell, 'Oh my God – my foot … . I can't move it. Oh … my ankle … . I can't get this thing off me.' She continued to moan for about a minute longer. The entire incident lasted about 2 minutes. Only a curtain separated the woman's office from the testing room, in which participants waited either alone or in pairs. The results confirmed the findings of the smoke study. Of the participants who were alone, 70 per cent came to the woman's aid, but only 40 per cent of those in two-person groups offered help. Again, those who had not

Although many passers-by noticed the man lying on the street, no one stopped to help – to see if he is asleep, sick, drunk, or dead. Research shows that people are more likely to help if no other bystanders are present.

intervened claimed later that they were unsure of what had happened but had decided that it was not serious (Latané & Rodin, 1969). In these experiments, the presence of others produced pluralistic ignorance; each person, observing the calmness of the others, resolved the ambiguity of the situation by deciding that no emergency existed.

Pluralistic ignorance appeared to govern a more recent and disturbing example of the bystander effect. In 1993, near Liverpool, England, two ten-year-old boys kidnapped two-year-old James Bulger at a local shopping mall. They led the toddler away on a meandering walk, cruelly tortured him along the way, and eventually beat him to death. Over the course of the day, dozens of adults came across the three boys. Later testimony of these bystanders revealed that they had assumed – or were told – that the three boys were brothers (Levine, 1999). Interpreting aggressive actions as 'family squabbles' seemed to define the situation as a non-emergency. This is especially troublesome. If the boys were in fact related, would the frightened and injured toddler be in less need of adult intervention? Similarly, is a woman threatened by her boyfriend or husband in less trouble than one threatened by a stranger? Crime statistics suggest not.

Diffusion of responsibility

Pluralistic ignorance can lead individuals to define a situation as a non-emergency, but this process does not explain incidents like the Genovese murder, in which the emergency is abundantly clear. Moreover, Kitty Genovese's neighbors could not observe one another behind their curtained windows and could not tell whether others were calm or panicked. The crucial process here was **diffusion of responsibility**. When each individual knows that many others are present, the burden of responsibility does not fall solely on him or her. Each can think, 'Someone else must have done something by now; someone else will intervene.'

To test this hypothesis, experimenters placed participants in separate booths and told them that they would take part in a group discussion about personal problems faced by college students. To avoid embarrassment, the discussion would be held through an intercom system. Each person would speak for 2 minutes. The microphone would be turned on only in the booth of the person speaking, and the experimenter would not be listening. In reality, all the voices except the participant's were tape recordings. On the first round, one person mentioned that he had problems with seizures. On the second round, this individual sounded as if he were actually starting to have a seizure and begged for help. The experimenters waited to see if the participant would leave the booth to report the emergency and how long it would take. Note that (1) the emergency is not at all ambiguous, (2) the participant could not tell how the bystanders in the other booths were reacting, and (3) the participant knew that the experimenter could not hear the emergency. Some participants were led to believe that the discussion group consisted only of themselves and the seizure victim. Others were told that they were part of a three-person group, and still others that they were part of a six-person group.

Of the participants who thought that they alone knew of the victim's seizure, 85 per cent reported it; of those who thought they were in a three-person group, 62 per cent reported the seizure; and of those who thought they were part of a six-person group, only 31 per cent reported it (see Figure 17.3). Later interviews confirmed that all the participants perceived the situation to be a real emergency. Most were very upset by

the conflict between letting the victim suffer and rushing for help. In fact, the participants who did not report the seizure appeared more upset than those who did. Clearly, we cannot interpret their non-intervention as apathy or indifference. Instead, the presence of others diffused the responsibility for acting (Darley & Latané, 1968; Latané & Darley, 1968).

Exactly how does the presence of others diffuse responsibility? The answer ties back to deindividuation, or feeling less accountable when you're part of a group. Indeed, recent experiments show that if situations highlight people's accountability, for instance, by making their name or a video camera salient, people are actually more likely to help when bystanders are present (van Brommel *et al.*, 2012). Another experiment shows that even if people simply imagined being in a group a few moments earlier on an unrelated task they experience diffusion of responsibility and become less likely to help (Garcia *et al.*, 2002). Imagining being part of a group, these researchers found, calls to mind ideas related to unaccountability, which derails acting based on a sense of individual responsibility. Deindividuation and loss of accountability help to explain why a city's population size and density are inversely related to the kindness of strangers (Levine *et al.*, 2008).

If pluralistic ignorance and diffusion of responsibility are minimized, will people help one another? To find out, three psychologists used the New York City subway system as their laboratory (Piliavin *et al.*, 1969). Two male and two female experimenters boarded a subway train separately. The female experimenters took seats and recorded the results, while the two men remained standing. As the train moved along, one of the men staggered forward and collapsed, remaining prone and staring at the ceiling until he received help. If no help came, the other man finally helped him to his feet. Several variations of the study were tried: the victim either carried a cane (so he would appear disabled) or smelled of alcohol (so he would appear drunk). Sometimes the victim was white, sometimes black. There was no ambiguity when the person with a cane fell. Clearly the victim needed help, so pluralistic ignorance was minimized in that case. Diffusion of responsibility was also minimized because each bystander could not continue to assume that someone else was intervening. So if pluralistic ignorance and diffusion of responsibility are the main obstacles to helping, people should help the victim with a cane in this situation.

The results supported this optimistic expectation. The victim with the cane received spontaneous help on more than 95 per cent of the trials, within an average of 5 seconds, regardless of the number of bystanders. The 'drunk' victim received help on half of the trials, within an average of 2 minutes. Although in this study on the New York subway both black and white cane victims were aided by black and white bystanders, more recent work suggests that bystanders who share a common group identity with the victim

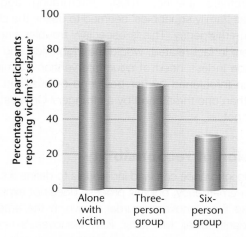

FIGURE 17.3 Diffusion of Responsibility. *The percentage of individuals who reported a victim's apparent seizure declined as the number of other people the individual believed were in his or her discussion group increased.*

(e.g., they're both Manchester United football fans) are especially likely to offer assistance (Levine *et al.*, 2005).

The role of helping models

In the subway study, as soon as one person moved to help, many others followed. This suggests that just as individuals use other people as models to define a situation as a non-emergency (as in pluralistic ignorance), they also use other people as models to indicate when to be helpful. This possibility was tested by counting the number of drivers who would stop to help a woman who was parked at the side of a road with a flat tire. It was found that significantly more drivers would stop to help if they had seen another woman with car trouble receiving help about a quarter of a mile earlier. Similarly, people are more likely to donate to a person soliciting for charity if they observe others doing so (Bryan & Test, 1967; Macaulay, 1970). Even role models on television can promote helping. These experiments indicate that others not only help us decide when not to act in an emergency but also serve as models to show us how and when to be good Samaritans.

The role of information

Now that you have read about the factors that deter bystanders from intervening in an emergency, will you be more likely to act in such a situation? An experiment at the University of Montana suggests that you would. Undergraduates were either given a lecture or shown a film based on the material discussed in this section. Two weeks later, each undergraduate was confronted with a simulated emergency while walking with one other person (a confederate of the experimenters). A person needing aid was sprawled on the floor of a hallway. The confederate was trained to react as if the situation was not an emergency. Those who had heard the lecture or seen the film were significantly more likely than others to offer help (Beaman *et al.*, 1978). This study provides hope: simply learning about social psychological phenomena – as you are doing now – can begin to lessen the power that situations have to produce unwelcome behavior.

INTERIM SUMMARY

➔ Situational forces have tremendous power to shape human behavior, and yet these powerful situational forces are often invisible. People often mistakenly make sense of others' behavior by referring to their personality or character, rather than to situational pressures, called the *fundamental attribution error*.

➔ People perform simple tasks better – and complex tasks worse – when in the presence of coactors or an audience. These social facilitation and social inhibition effects occur because the presence of others narrows people's attention.

➔ The aggressive behavior sometimes shown by mobs and crowds may be the result of a state of deindividuation, in which individuals feel that they have lost their personal identities and merged into the group. Both anonymity and group size contribute to deindividuation. Deindividuation creates increased sensitivity to situation-specific social norms linked with the group. This can increase aggression if the group's norms are aggressive yet can also reduce aggression if the group norms are benign.

➔ A bystander to an emergency is less likely to intervene or help if in a group than if alone. Two factors that deter intervention are pluralistic ignorance and diffusion of responsibility. By attempting to appear calm, bystanders may define the situation for one another as a non-emergency, thereby producing a state of pluralistic ignorance. The presence of other people, even imagined others, also diffuses responsibility so that no one person feels the necessity to act.

CRITICAL THINKING QUESTIONS

1 The presence of others not only alters people's behavior but also alters their mental processes or patterns of thinking. Drawing from studies of (1) social facilitation, (2) deindividuation, and (3) bystander effects, describe three distinct mental processes that are altered by the presence of others in each context.

2 Reconsider the case of the mass suicides at Jonestown described at the opening of this chapter. One thing to know about the members of the People's Temple is that they were devoted to 'the Cause,' a utopian vision of social equality and racial harmony painted by Jim Jones. They moved to the jungle of Guyana for 'the Cause'. They signed over their worldly possessions, gave up legal custody of their children, and lived separately from their spouses, all for 'the Cause'. Imagine being in this crowd of followers when Jim Jones asked them to drink the poison. Describe how deindividuation or pluralistic ignorance might have played a role in people's compliance to Jim Jones's request.

CUTTING EDGE RESEARCH THE COLLAPSE OF COMPASSION

C. Daryl Cameron, University of Iowa

Scholars have long recognized the power of compassion to motivate moral behavior and sustain co-operative communities (Batson, 2011; Goetz *et al.*, 2010). Yet there are many times when people fail to feel compassion for others. People often lack compassion when there are many victims suffering, such as in natural disasters, war, and genocide, and endemic poverty. Joseph Stalin said that one victim is a tragedy, but 1 million is a statistic. And Mother Theresa said that if she thought about the mass of suffering people in the world, that she could not act to save them. Despite their ideological differences, these two agree that it is difficult to feel compassion for many suffering victims. Studies have shown that people feel more compassion for one victim than for many victims, a finding that has been deemed 'the collapse of compassion'. This collapse of compassion may surprise you. People predict that they would, and should, feel more compassion when more people are suffering. Yet when faced with many suffering victims, people ironically feel *less* compassion than they would have if they had just seen one victim.

Why would people respond like this? According to one explanation (Slovic, 2007), people are unable to feel much compassion when many people are suffering. On this view, people have a difficult time attending to the suffering of many different people at once, and so lack a strong emotional response. In collaboration with Keith Payne, I explored a different explanation of the collapse of compassion (Cameron & Payne, 2011). When more victims are suffering, people expect to feel more compassion. This expectation may lead them to become more afraid of the costs of such intense emotions. People may be worried that compassion for many victims would be financially burdensome or just a drop in the bucket. Or they may worry that they would get psychologically overwhelmed and burnt out by such intense emotions. Because people are concerned about the costs of compassion for many victims, they strategically turn off compassion. On this view, the collapse of compassion would not be due to a basic constraint on how much compassion we can feel; instead, it would be the end result of active emotion regulation.

In one experiment, we asked participants to read about either one or eight child war refugees from the Darfur region in

Africa, and gave them the expectation of having to donate money later on in the experiment. We also measured individual differences in emotion regulation skill. Replicating past work, people felt more compassion for one victim than eight victims; but in support of our emotion regulation account, this pattern only emerged for people who could skillfully regulate their emotions. People who were unable to regulate their emotions well did not show the collapse of compassion, suggesting that emotion regulation is necessary for the collapse to emerge. In a follow-up study, we manipulated emotion regulation to provide causal evidence for our account. Some participants were told to freely experience their emotions – without trying to control or regulate them – while viewing information about one or eight Darfur child refugees. Other participants were told to regulate their emotions while reading about the refugees. Those who were told to experience their emotions did not show the collapse of compassion. By encouraging people to accept their emotions without regulating them, we prevented the collapse of compassion from emerging. On the other hand, people who were told to regulate their emotions showed the collapse of compassion, suggesting that emotion regulation causes the collapse of compassion.

These studies indicate that people can control whether they experience compassion for mass suffering. This research also has a promising upshot. If the collapse of compassion results from people choosing to turn off their emotions, then we can persuade people to choose differently. Increasingly, scientists are developing ways to build compassionate feelings and behaviors. For instance, short-term interventions – such as non-conscious similarity cues – can increase compassion for strangers (Valdesolo & DeSteno, 2011). On the other hand, long-term compassion training reduces people's fears of feeling compassion for others (Jazaieri *et al.*, 2012). Such training programs may have direct implications for the collapse of compassion, by enabling people to get past their fears of being overwhelmed by compassion for many victims. As the science of compassion develops, we will begin to learn how to help people feel compassion precisely when it is needed the most.

COMPLIANCE AND OBEDIENCE

Conformity to a majority

When we are in a group, we may find ourselves in the minority on some issue. This is a fact of life to which most of us have become accustomed. We are often too self-focused to absorb

the wisdom of crowds (Mannes *et al.*, 2012), yet, if we do decide that the majority is a more valid source of information than our own experience, we may change our minds and conform to the majority opinion. But imagine yourself in a situation in which you are absolutely sure that your own opinion is correct and that the group is wrong. Would you yield to social pressure and conform under those circumstances? If you're like most people, you don't think you would. While other

In a study of conformity to majority opinion, (top) all of the group members except the man sixth from the left are confederates who have been instructed to give uniformly wrong answers on 12 of the 18 trials. Number 6, who has been told that he is participating in an experiment on visual judgment, therefore finds that he is a lone dissenter when he gives the correct answers. (bottom left) The participant, showing the strain of repeated disagreement with the majority, leans forward anxiously to look at the exhibit in question. (bottom right) This particular participant persists in his opinion, saying that 'he has to call them as he sees them.'

people follow the crowd like sheep, your actions stem from your beliefs and principles (Pronin & Kugler, 2010). But your certainty in your own autonomy most likely provides another instance of the fundamental attribution error, or the underestimation of situational pressures. We know this from a classic series of studies on conformity conducted by social psychologist Solomon Asch (1952, 1955, 1958).

In Asch's standard procedure, a participant was seated at a table with a group of seven to nine others (all confederates of the experimenter). The group was shown a display of three vertical lines of different lengths and asked to judge which line was the same length as a line in another display (see Figure 17.4). Each individual announced his or her decision in turn, and the participant sat in the next-to-last seat. The correct judgments were obvious, and on most trials everyone gave the same response. But on several predetermined trials the confederates had been instructed to each give the wrong answer. Asch then observed the amount of conformity this procedure would elicit from participants.

The results were striking. Even though the correct answer was always obvious, the average participant conformed to the incorrect group consensus about a third of the time; about 75 per cent of the participants conformed at least once.

Moreover, the group did not have to be large to produce such conformity. When Asch varied the size of the group from two to 16, he found that a group of three or four confederates was just as effective at producing conformity as larger groups (Asch, 1958).

Why didn't the obviousness of the correct answer provide support for the participant's independence from the majority? Why isn't a person's confidence in his or her ability to make simple sensory judgments a strong force against conformity? According to one line of argument, it is precisely the obviousness of the correct answer that produces the strong forces toward conformity (Ross *et al.,* 1976). Disagreements in real life typically involve difficult or subjective judgments, such as which economic policy will best create economic recovery or which of two paintings is more aesthetically pleasing. In these cases, we expect to disagree with others occasionally. We even know that being a minority of one in an otherwise unanimous group is a plausible, if uncomfortable, possibility.

The situation in Asch's experiments is much more extreme. Here the participant is confronted with unanimous disagreement about a simple physical fact, a bizarre and unprecedented occurrence that appears to have no rational explanation. Participants are clearly puzzled and tense. They rub their eyes in disbelief and jump up to look more closely at the lines. They squirm, mumble, giggle in embarrassment, and look searchingly at other members of the group for some clue to the mystery. After the experiment, they offer half-hearted hypotheses about optical

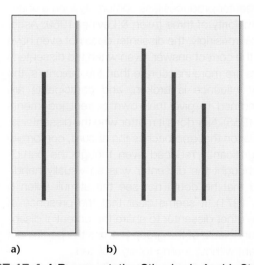

a)   b)

FIGURE 17.4 A Representative Stimulus in Asch's Study. After viewing display (a), participants were told to pick the matching line from display (b). The displays shown here are typical in that the correct decision is obvious.

illusions or suggest that perhaps the first person occasionally made a mistake and each successive person followed suit because of pressure to conform (Asch, 1952).

Consider what it means to dissent from the majority under these circumstances. Just as the judgments of the group seem incomprehensible to the participant, so the participant believes that his or her dissent will be incomprehensible to the group. Group members will surely judge the dissenter to be incompetent, even out of touch with reality. Similarly, if the participant dissents repeatedly, this would seem to constitute a direct challenge to the group's competence, a challenge that requires enormous courage when one's own perceptual abilities are suddenly and inexplicably called into question. Such a challenge violates a strong social norm against insulting others. This fear of 'What will they think of me?' and 'What will they think I think of them?' inhibits dissent and generates the strong pressure to conform in Asch's experiments.

If Asch's conformity situation is unlike most situations in real life, why did he use a task in which the correct answer was obvious? The reason is that he wanted to study **compliance**, pure public conformity, uncontaminated by the possibility that participants were actually changing their minds about the correct answers. Several variations of Asch's study have used more difficult or subjective judgments, and although they may reflect conformity in real life more faithfully, they do not permit us to assess the effects of pure pressure to conform to a majority when we are certain that our own minority judgment is correct (Ross *et al.*, 1976).

One of the most important findings from Asch's and later experiments on conformity is that the pressure to conform is far less strong when the group is not unanimous. If even one confederate breaks with the majority, the amount of conformity drops from 32 per cent of the trials to about 6 per cent. In fact, a group of eight containing only one dissenter produces less conformity than a unanimous majority of three (Allen & Levine, 1969; Asch, 1958). Surprisingly, the dissenter does not even have to give the correct answer. Even when the dissenter's answers are more inaccurate than the majority's, the majority influence is broken, and participants are more inclined to give their own correct judgments (Asch, 1955). Nor does it matter who the dissenter is. In a variation that approaches the absurd, conformity was significantly reduced even though the participants thought the dissenter was so visually handicapped that he could not see the stimuli (Allen & Levine, 1971). It seems clear that the presence of just one other dissenter to share the potential disapproval or ridicule of the group permits the participant to dissent without feeling totally isolated.

Here we see the power of situations to shape behavior yet again. A situation in which we face a unanimous majority creates a strong pull for conformity.

By contrast, a seemingly minor change in that situation – a simple break in the unanimity – allows us to 'be ourselves.' Yet whether or not a situation includes a unanimous majority is a central feature of the situation, so perhaps it is not surprising that rates of conformity depend on it. What about subtler background features of situations? Like what newspaper article you just read, or what's playing on the television in the corner of the room? Recent variations on Asch's experiment have explored the influence of such seemingly trivial situational factors by examining how simple exposure to words and pictures can push us to conform. The key is whether these words and pictures prime – or activate – ideas about conformity or ideas about non-conformity. In one experiment, some participants were exposed to words like *adhere*, *comply*, and *conform*, whereas others were exposed to words like *challenge*, *confront*, and *deviate* (Epley & Gilovich, 1999). In another study, the experimenters primed conformity in some participants by showing them a photo of 'Norman, an accountant', whereas they primed non-conformity in others with a photo of 'Norman, a punk rocker' (Pendry & Carrick, 2001). In both experiments, participants with prior exposure to the mere idea of conformity actually behaved in more conforming ways when later faced with a unanimous majority. This evidence shows how exquisitely responsive to situational factors our behavior can be. Even features of the situation that are in the background – outside our conscious awareness – can exert their power and pull us to conform.

To be sure, we conform to the behavior of others for a number of reasons. Sometimes we find ourselves in ambiguous situations and don't know how to behave. What do you do, for instance, if you don't know which of several forks to use first at a fancy restaurant? You look to see what others do, and conform. This type of conformity is called **informational social**

Simple images can activate the concepts of conformity or non-conformity. Once activated, these concepts can influence people's behavior. Researchers found more conformity among those who saw a picture of 'Norman, an accountant' than among those who saw a picture of 'Norman, a punk rocker'.

influence. In these cases, we conform because we believe that other people's interpretations of an ambiguous situation are more correct than our own. At other times we find ourselves simply wanting to fit in and be accepted by a group. Perhaps you felt this way when you started at a new school or university. This type of conformity is called **normative social influence**. In these cases, we conform to a group's social norms or typical behaviors to become liked and accepted. We go along to get along. Because the correct line length was not ambiguous in Asch's famous study, we know that normative social influence is what pulled Asch's participants to conform. Luckily, it turns out that age plays an important role in conformity. Although informational social influence continues to produce conformity in old age – suggesting that we still value others' expertise in late life – the pressures to fit in and be liked that fuel normative social influence appear to lessen as people grow older (Pasupathi, 1999).

Sometimes it's easy to tell what the group's norms are because it's evident in the group's behavior. Again, this was true in the Asch study. In real life, however, group norms may be more difficult to identify. In these cases, pluralistic ignorance may promote conformity to imagined social norms rather than actual social norms. Recall that pluralistic ignorance occurs when group members mistakenly believe they know what others think. In the case of bystander effects, people mistakenly believe that other bystanders know that the situation is a non-emergency. This group-level phenomenon characterizes many situations beyond bystanders' reactions to emergencies. You and your classmates have probably experienced it countless times in large lecture courses. Your professor, after presenting some new and complex material, asks the class if they have any questions. Do you raise your hand? Probably not. Why would you want to acknowledge your confusion? You don't want to be known as the one who asks stupid questions. Do your classmates raise their hands? No. They obviously understand the material, which is all the more reason to keep your questions to yourself. Do you see the pluralistic ignorance at work? You and all your classmates are behaving identically – you are all sitting quietly, asking no questions. Even faced with this identical behavior, it's common to interpret your own private feelings as being different from those of others: you alone are confused, whereas others are confident. In this case, pluralistic ignorance can make students feel alienated from their classmates. Imagine how much more at ease you'd feel if the person next to you leaned over and whispered, 'I have no idea what she's been saying'. Perhaps you'd even find the courage to raise your hand with your own question.

Pluralistic ignorance often plays a role in normative social influence. An example can be found in binge-drinking on university campuses - defined as heavy consumption of alcohol over a short period of time with the intention of becoming intoxicated. Excessive consumption of alcohol is a major concern for parents and university administrators across the USA.

Alcohol-related accidents are the number one cause of death among university students, and alcohol use is linked to lower academic performance and higher rates of destructive behavior. Ninety per cent of university students, when surveyed, indicate that they've tried alcohol, and about 25 per cent show problems like binge-drinking. We know already that peers exert a big influence on students' drinking. The question is how? Do peers cajole each other into drinking and drinking more? Well, sometimes. Other times, pluralistic ignorance is at work. If 90 per cent of students are drinking, it looks like everyone is comfortable with it. Despite this, surveys show that many students have clear misgivings about drinking. Perhaps you've nursed a sick classmate, heard about a recent death from binge-drinking, or seen that your own hangovers have harmed your academic performance. Even though you have a drink or two at a party, you may not be completely comfortable with the amount of drinking at your university.

Here again is a pattern of pluralistic ignorance: everyone's behavior looks basically the same – they all look comfortable as they drink. And yet, even as they hold that glass full of beer, many students harbor private misgivings about drinking, while assuming that the group norm is to be unconcerned about drinking. What are the consequences for misperceiving this group norm? Conformity with it – an increase in drinking over time! This problematic outcome was first uncovered in a series of studies conducted at Princeton University (Prentice & Miller, 1993).

Yet a little knowledge can be a powerful thing. Sometimes it can even stand up to the power of situational forces and lessen their impact on our behavior. We saw this triumph of knowledge earlier when we discussed the role of information in the bystander effect. Simply learning about the social psychological factors that deter bystanders from helping produced more offers to help (Beaman et al., 1978). Another demonstration of the power of knowledge emerged from the research on pluralistic ignorance in students' binge alcohol consumption. Social psychologists at Princeton University developed and tested a new kind of alcohol education program. First-year students attended a discussion about alcohol use in their residence hall that was either peer-oriented, including information about pluralistic ignorance, or individual-oriented, focusing on decision-making in drinking situations. Four to 6 months later, those who learned about the concept of pluralistic ignorance reported drinking less. Moreover, the study's evidence suggested that knowledge of this social psychological principle did not so much change students' perceptions of the group norm but rather lessened the norm's power to induce conformity (Schroeder & Prentice, 1998). So the next time you find yourself at a party deciding whether you should have a drink (or another drink) and surrounded by nonchalant drinkers, consider basing your choice on your own hunches rather than the apparent beliefs of your companions. Social situations exert powerful pressures toward conformity. But you can fight back with the power of knowledge!

Minority influence

A number of European scholars have been critical of social psychological research in North America because of its pre-occupation with conformity and the influence of the majority on the minority. As they correctly point out, intellectual innovation, social change, and political revolution often occur because an informed and articulate minority begins to convert others to its point of view (Moscovici, 1976). Why not study innovation and the influence that minorities can have on the majority?

To make their point, these European investigators deliberately began their experimental work by setting up a laboratory situation virtually identical to Asch's conformity situation. Participants were asked to make a series of simple perceptual judgments in the face of confederates who consistently gave the incorrect answer. But instead of placing a single participant in the midst of several confederates, these investigators planted two confederates, who consistently gave incorrect responses, in the midst of four real participants. The experimenters found that the minority was able to influence about 32 per cent of the participants to make at least one incorrect judgment. For this to occur, however, the minority had to remain consistent throughout the experiment. If they wavered or showed any inconsistency in their judgments, they were unable to influence the majority (Moscovici *et al.,* 1969).

Since this initial demonstration of minority influence, more than 90 related studies have been conducted in both Europe and North America, including several that required groups to debate social and political issues rather than make simple perceptual judgments (Wood *et al.,* 1994). The general finding of **minority influence** is that minorities can move majorities toward their point of view if they present a consistent position without appearing rigid, dogmatic, or arrogant. Such minorities are perceived to be more confident and, occasionally, more competent than the majority (Maass & Clark, 1984). Minorities are also more effective if they argue a position that is consistent with the developing social norms of the larger society. For example, in two experiments in which feminist issues were discussed, participants were moved significantly more by a minority position that was in line with feminist social norms than by one opposed to feminist norms (Paicheler, 1977).

But the most interesting finding of this research is that the majority members in these studies show a change of private attitude – that is, internalization – not just the public conformity that was found in the Asch experiments. In fact, minorities sometimes provoke private attitude change in majority members even when they fail to obtain public conformity. Typically this attitude change shows up only after a delay (Wood *et al.*, 1994).

One investigator has suggested that minorities are able to produce eventual attitude change because they lead majority individuals to rethink the issues. Even when they fail

Social change – such as the end of apartheid in South Africa – is sometimes brought about because a few people manage to persuade the majority in power to change its attitudes.

to convince the majority, they broaden the range of acceptable opinions. In contrast, unanimous majorities are rarely prompted to think carefully about their position (Nemeth, 1986).

Another view suggests that minority influence occurs in part because majority members believe that they won't be influenced by the minority but simply extend them the courtesy of hearing them out. That is, simply to show their open-mindedness, those in the majority may thoughtfully consider the minority opinion but don't expect this deliberation to change their own views. Ironically, however, it does change people's minds, because thoughtful deliberation unsettles whole sets of related beliefs, which become more likely to change down the road. This process reflects what psychologists have called an **implicit leniency contract** in the treatment of minority group members, meaning that simply to appear fair, majority members let minority members have their say, but by doing so they unwittingly open the door to minority influence (Crano & Sayranian, 2009).

But thoughtful consideration of minority views is not the whole story. We know this because even when a numerical minority presents weak arguments, they can persuade majority members. More recent work suggests that a steadfast minority can change our attitudes because it takes courage to stand up for one's own opinion in the face of disagreement with and even harassment by the majority (Baron & Bellman, 2007). Perceived courage may well be what inspires allegiance.

These findings remind us that majorities typically have the social power to approve and disapprove, to accept or reject, and it is this power that can produce public compliance or conformity. In contrast, minorities rarely have such social power. But if they have credibility and show courage, they have the power to produce genuine attitude change and, hence, innovation, social change, and even revolution.

Obedience to authority

We opened this chapter with some of the most chilling horrors of humanity – perhaps none is more sobering in sheer magnitude than the systematic genocide of more than 8 million people undertaken by Nazi Germany during World War II. The mastermind of that horror, Adolf Hitler, may well have been a psychopath. But he could not have done it alone. What about the people who ran the day-to-day operations, who built the ovens and gas chambers, filled them with human beings, counted bodies, and did the necessary paperwork? Were they all psychopaths, too?

Not according to social philosopher Hannah Arendt (1963), who observed the trial of Adolf Eichmann, a Nazi war criminal who was found guilty and executed for causing the murder of millions of Jews. She described him as a dull, ordinary bureaucrat, who saw himself as a little cog in a big machine. In her book about Eichmann, subtitled *A Report on the Banality of Evil*, Arendt concluded that most of the 'evil men' of the Third Reich were just ordinary people following orders from superiors. Her suggestion was that all of us might be capable of such evil and that Nazi Germany was less wildly alien from the normal human condition than we might like to think. As Arendt put it, 'In certain circumstances the most ordinary decent person can become a criminal.' This is not an easy conclusion to accept because it is more comforting to believe that monstrous evil is done only by monstrous individuals.

The problem of obedience to authority arose again in Vietnam in 1968, when a group of American soldiers, claiming that they were simply following orders, killed civilians in the community of My Lai. Again the international community was forced to ponder the possibility that ordinary citizens are willing to obey authority, even in violation of their own moral consciences.

Arendt's depiction of Adolf Eichmann as an ordinary bureaucrat, just following orders, has been sharply challenged by present day historians (Cesarani, 2004; Lozowick, 2002). They contend that although Eichmann may have begun his Nazi career as a rather ordinary man, his increasing identification with the Nazi movement transformed him into a 'genocidaire' who gained approval and favor for inventing creative new ways to deport and kill Jews. A parallel challenge is growing within social psychology, one that tempers the classic claim that evil situations cause evil behavior with a more nuanced interplay between the ways individuals identify with groups and come to shape and be shaped by powerful situations (Reicher *et al.*, 2012). Exploring the dynamic interactions between, on the one hand, people's identities, goals, and desires, and, on the other hand, the ever-changing situations in which they find themselves, is the topic of much contemporary research and debate within social psychology.

The landmark studies that best represent the power of situations to produce such unthinkable behavior were conducted in the 1960s by Stanley Milgram (1963, 1974)

The 'shock generator' used in Milgram's experiment on obedience (top left). The 'learner' is strapped into the 'electric chair' (top right). A participant receives a sample shock before starting the 'teaching session' (bottom left). Participant refuses to go on with the experiment (bottom right). Most participants became deeply disturbed by the role they were asked to play, whether they remained in the experiment to the end or refused at some point to go on.

at Yale University. A half century later, Milgram's work continues to be a topic of considerable debate and discussion (Burger, 2009; Packer, 2008, Nicholson, 2011; Reicher *et al.*, 2012). Ordinary men and women were recruited through a newspaper ad that offered $4 for 1 hour's participation in a 'study of memory'. When they arrived at the laboratory, each participant met another participant (in actuality, a confederate of the experimenter) and was told that one of them would play the role of teacher in the study, and the other would play the learner. The two participants then drew slips of paper out of a hat, and the real participant discovered that he or she would be the teacher. In that role, the participant was to read a list of word pairs to the learner and then test his memory by reading the first word of each pair and asking him to select the correct second word from four alternatives. Each time the learner made an error, the participant was to press a lever that delivered an electric shock to him.

The participant watched while the learner was strapped into a chair and an electrode was attached to his wrist. The participant was then seated in an adjoining room in front of a shock generator whose front panel contained 30 lever switches in a horizontal line (see photos). Each switch was labeled with a voltage rating, ranging in sequence from 15 to 450 volts, and groups of adjacent switches were labeled descriptively, ranging from 'Slight Shock' through 'Danger: Severe Shock' up to the extreme, labeled simply 'XXX'. When a switch was depressed, an electric buzzer sounded, lights flashed, and the needle on a voltage meter deflected to the right. To illustrate how it worked, the participant was given a sample shock of 45 volts from the generator. As the procedure began, the experimenter instructed the participant to move one level higher on the shock generator after each successive error by the learner (see Figure 17.5).

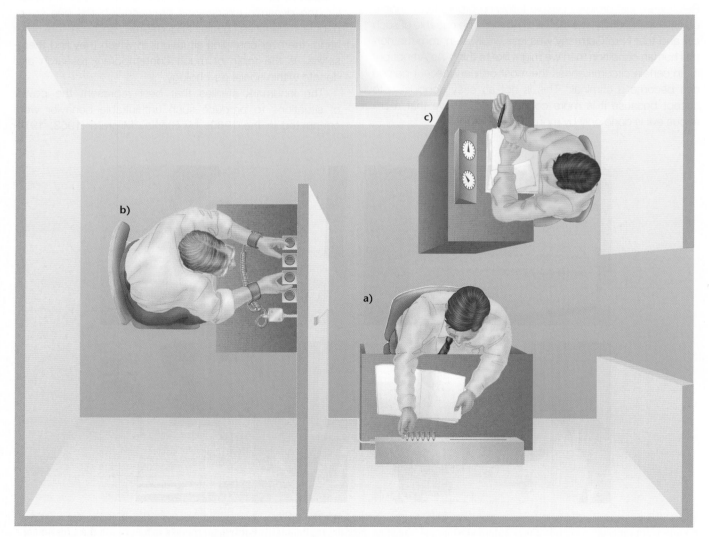

FIGURE 17.5 Milgram's Experiment on Obedience. *The 'teacher' (a) was told to give the 'learner' (b) a more intense shock after each error. If the 'teacher' objected, the experimenter (c) insisted that it was necessary to go on.*

The learner did not actually receive any shocks. He was a mild-mannered 47-year-old man who had been specially trained for his role and his behavior followed a precise script. Starting at 75 volts, his expressions of pain could be heard through the adjoining wall. At 150 volts, his escalating expressions of pain included a request to be released from the study. As the shocks became stronger still, he began to shout and curse. At 300 volts, he began to kick the wall, and at the next shock level (marked 'Extreme Intensity Shock'), he no longer answered the questions or made any noise. As you might expect, many participants began to object to this excruciating procedure, pleading with the experimenter to call a halt. But the experimenter responded with a sequence of calm prods, using as many as necessary to get the participant to go on: 'Please continue,' 'The experiment requires that you continue,' 'It is absolutely essential that you continue,' and 'You have no other choice – you must go on.' Obedience to authority was measured by the maximum amount of shock the participant would administer before refusing to continue.

When college students first learn the details of Milgram's procedure and are asked whether they themselves would continue to administer the shocks after the learner begins to pound on the wall, about 99 per cent say that they would not (Aronson, 1995). Milgram himself surveyed psychiatrists at a leading medical school. They predicted that most participants would refuse to go on after reaching 150 volts, that only about 4 per cent would go beyond 300 volts, and that less than 1 per cent would go all the way to 450 volts.

What did Milgram find? That 65 per cent of the participants continued to obey throughout, going all the way to the end of the shock series (450 volts, labeled 'XXX'). Not one participant stopped before administering 300 volts, the point at which the learner began to kick the wall (see Figure 17.6).

What makes us so unable to fathom the degree of obedience evident in Milgram's work? The answer ties back to the fundamental attribution error, introduced at the start of the chapter. We assume that people's behavior reflects their inner qualities – their wishes and their personalities. We underestimate – even overlook altogether – the power that situations hold over us. So we put Milgram's procedures together with the knowledge that most people would not wish to inflict severe bodily harm to another innocent person and conclude that few would obey. It is true that few *wanted* to obey. Most voiced considerable distress and reservations about delivering the shocks. And yet they continued. Somehow their intentions to 'do no harm' – although voiced – failed to govern their behavior. In assuming that people's intentions guide their behavior, we've failed to see how subtle features of the situation powerfully pulled for obedience.

How do we know that it's the situation at work here? Maybe these were particularly aggressive or spineless people?

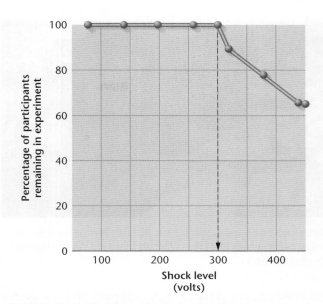

FIGURE 17.6 **Obedience to Authority.** *The percentage of participants who were willing to administer a punishing shock did not begin to decline until the intensity level of the shock reached 300 volts (the danger level).*

Maybe Milgram had unleashed the unconscious aggressive drive that Freud discussed?

We know it's the situation because Milgram conducted many variations on the standard procedure and assigned participants at random to different situations. And each variation in the situation led to drastic changes in the rates of obedience. Four important features of the situation include (1) surveillance, (2) buffers, (3) the presence of role models, and (4) its emerging nature.

Surveillance

One situational comparison varied the degree to which the experimenter supervised the participant. When the experimenter left the room and issued his orders by telephone, the rate of obedience dropped from 65 per cent to 21 per cent (Milgram, 1974). Moreover, several of the participants who continued under these conditions cheated by administering shocks of lower intensity than they were supposed to. So the constant presence or surveillance of the experimenter is one situational factor that pulls for obedience.

Buffers

Another set of situational comparisons varied the proximity of the teacher and learner. In the standard procedure, the learner was in the next room, out of sight and only heard through the wall. When the learner was in the same room as the participant, the rate of obedience dropped from 65 per cent to 40 per cent. When the participant had to personally ensure that the learner held his hand on a shock plate, obedience declined to 30 per cent. By contrast, when

Modern warfare allows individuals to distance themselves from the actual killing, giving them the feeling that they are not responsible for enemy deaths.

the psychological distance was increased and the learner offered no verbal feedback from the next room, the rate of obedience shot up to 100 per cent. So a second situational factor that pulls for obedience is buffers. Milgram's participants believed that they were committing acts of violence, but there were several buffers that obscured this fact or diluted the immediacy of the experience. The more direct the participants' experience with the victim – the fewer buffers between the person and the consequences of his or her act – the less the participant will obey.

The most common buffer found in warlike situations is the remoteness of the person from the final act of violence. Thus, Eichmann argued that he was not directly responsible for killing Jews; he merely arranged for their deaths. Milgram conducted an analog to this 'link-in-the-chain' role by requiring participants only to pull a switch that enabled another teacher (a confederate) to deliver the shocks to the learner. Under these conditions, the rate of obedience soared: a full 93 per cent of the participants continued to the end of the shock series. In this situation, the participant can shift responsibility to the person who actually delivers the shock.

The shock generator itself served as a buffer – an impersonal mechanical agent that actually delivered the shock. Imagine how obedience would have declined if participants were required to hit the learner with their fists. In real life, we have analogous technologies that permit us to destroy distant fellow humans by remote control, thereby removing us from the sight of their suffering. Although we probably would all agree that it is worse to kill thousands of people by pushing a button that releases a guided missile than it is to beat one individual to death with a rock, it is still psychologically easier to push the button. Such are the effects of buffers.

Role models

One reason Milgram's experiment obtained such high levels of obedience is that the social pressures were directed toward a lone individual. If the participant was not alone, would he or she be less obedient? We have already seen some data to support this possibility: a participant in the Asch conformity situation is less likely to go along with the group's incorrect judgments if there is at least one other dissenter.

A similar thing happens in Milgram's obedience situation. In one variation of the procedure, two additional confederates were employed. They were introduced as participants who would also play teacher roles. Teacher 1 would read the list of word pairs, Teacher 2 would tell the learner if he was right or wrong, and Teacher 3 (the participant) would deliver the shocks. The confederates complied with the instructions through the 150-volt shock, at which point Teacher 1 informed the experimenter that he was quitting. Despite the experimenter's insistence that he continue, Teacher 1 got up from his chair and sat in another part of the room. After the 210-volt shock, Teacher 2 also quit. The experimenter then turned to the participant and ordered him to continue alone. Only 10 per cent of the participants were willing to complete the series in this situation. In a second variation, there were two experimenters rather than two additional teachers. After a few shocks, they began to argue. One of them said that they should stop the experiment; the other said that they should continue. Under these circumstances, not a single participant would continue, despite the orders to do so by the second experimenter (Milgram, 1974). So role models who disobeyed allow participants to follow their own conscience. But before we congratulate these participants on their autonomy in the face of social pressure, we should consider the implication of these findings more closely. They suggest participants were not choosing between obedience and autonomy but between obedience and conformity: obey the commanding experimenter or conform to the emerging norm to disobey.

Obeying or conforming may not strike you as a very heroic choice. But these are among the processes that provide the social glue for the human species. One social historian has noted that 'disobedience when it is not criminally but morally, religiously, or politically motivated is always a collective act and it is justified by the values of the collectivity and the mutual engagements of its members' (Walzer, 1970, p. 4).

A recent experiment on obedience explored the effect of following a role model, and quite literally so (Wiltermuth, 2012). Participants were first instructed to follow the experimenter on a walk across campus, remaining a few steps behind him. By random assignment, some participants were directed to walk in synchrony with the experimenter, stepping forward with their own right foot when the experimenter stepped with his right foot, and so on. Other participants were directed to walk out of sync with the experimenter, or given no instructions on how to walk. Later, supposedly as part of another study, the experimenter directed all participants to place as many sow bugs as possible down a funnel that led to a modified coffee grinder called an 'extermination machine'. Those who had previously walked in synchrony with the experimenter 'exterminated' significantly more bugs than others (unbeknownst to the participants, a stopper in the funnel saved the sow bugs from the blades of the coffee grinder). This experiment demonstrates how something as subtle as behavioral synchrony can increase obedience to authority. Maybe this is why marching drills and other synchronized actions persist as military practices.

Emerging situations

So far, when we've discussed the power of situations, we've painted situations in fairly broad brushstrokes. For instance, we've considered how a group with a unanimous opinion exerts more social pressure than a group that includes a single dissenter. These broad brush strokes obscure the fact that the meaning of any given situation unfolds and changes over time. What begins benignly may insidiously evolve into something horrifying. Yet the emerging nature of situations – just like the power of situations more generally – often eludes us.

For instance, many people who hear about the Milgram study wonder why anyone would ever agree to administer the first shock. Most everyone claims that they themselves wouldn't do it. But that's because people tend to focus on the end of the story – how outrageous the situation ends up, with participants delivering shocks so intense they are beyond description ('XXX') to a man who has presumably lost consciousness. What we need to do is focus on how the situation started and, more importantly, how it evolved.

The situation began innocuously enough. Participants replied to an advertisement and agreed to participate in a study at Yale University. By doing so they implicitly agreed to co-operate with the experimenter, follow the directions of the person in charge, and see the job through to completion. This is a very strong social norm, and we tend to underestimate how difficult it is to break such an agreement and go back on our implied word to co-operate. And when participants arrived, they found themselves in a fairly straightforward learning experiment. They might have been thinking, 'How hard could it be to learn these simple word pairs?' 'I bet the threat of shock will speed up the learning process.'

Plus, the first shock was just 15 volts – perhaps not even noticeable. And the shock level increased by a mere 15 volts at a time. Although it's abundantly clear that administering 450 volts is not a good thing, the change from innocuous to unfathomable is not so clear. Once participants gave the first shock, there was no longer a natural stopping point. By the time they wanted to quit, they were trapped. The true character of the situation had emerged only slowly over time.

Making matters worse, in order to break off, participants had to suffer the guilt and embarrassment of acknowledging that they were wrong to begin at all. And the longer they put off quitting, the harder it became to admit their misjudgment in going as far as they had. It is often easier to continue with bad behavior than to admit our mistakes.

Perhaps most significantly, Milgram's participants had no time to reflect. They had no time to think about the strange situation they now found themselves in, and what their own conscience would dictate. This effectively prevented them from accessing their own definition of the situation (as 'horrifying'). Instead, participants were torn apart by two conflicting definitions of the situations: the authority's definition –'The experiment requires that you continue' – and the victim's definition – 'Let me out of here! My heart is starting to bother me!' Most often, in this fast-paced and evolving situation, the participants' behavior reflected other people's definitions of the situation: most participants, following the definition offered by the experimenter, obeyed. Others, following the definitions offered by peers who themselves broke off, disobeyed. Interestingly, among those who did manage to disobey, the vast majority did so at 150 volts, the first time at which the learner requested to be released from the experiment (Packer, 2008). This suggests that, like obedience, disobedience is also very much connected to situational triggers. Participants' own wishes and desires – although voiced – did not steer their behavior. Imagine how much less obedience there would have been if there had been a 15-minute break after 300 volts.

Ideological justification

On top of all the situational factors that pull for obedience (see the Concept Review Table for a review) are societal factors. Milgram suggested that the potential for obedience to authority is such a necessary requirement for communal life that it has probably been built into our species by evolution. The division of labor in a society requires that individuals be willing at times to subordinate their own independent actions to serve the goals of the larger social organization. Parents, school systems, and businesses nurture this willingness by reminding the individual of the importance of following the directives of others who 'know the larger picture'. To understand obedience in a particular situation, then, we need to understand the individual's acceptance of an **ideology** – a set of beliefs and attitudes – that legitimates the authority of the person in charge and justifies following his or her directives. As an example of ideological justification, the Islamic extremists who became suicide hijackers on September 11, 2001, believed that, as martyrs, they would enter infinite paradise if they followed the directives of Osama bin Laden. With eerie similarity, the members of the People's Temple believed that, in drinking the poison, they were 'crossing over' into paradise for the sake of 'the Cause' that Jim Jones illuminated. Ideologies not only guide the bizarre behaviors of religious extremists but also guide the day-to-day activities of military organizations. Nazi officers believed in the primacy of the German state and hence in the legitimacy of orders issued in its name. Similarly, soldiers of any stripe commit themselves to the premise that national or international security requires strict obedience to military commands. Killing

Soldiers follow orders because they believe that national security requires that they do so. This provides an ideological justification for their obedience.

CONCEPT REVIEW TABLE
SITUATIONAL FEATURES OF OBEDIENCE TO AUTHORITY

Feature	Experimental evidence within Milgram's studies
Surveillance	Obedience rate drops when experimenter is not physically present.
Buffers	Obedience rates drop when 'victim' is moved closer to the participant and increase when the 'victim' is never heard.
Role Models	Obedience rates drop when a fellow 'teacher' or a second experimenter stops co-operating.
Emerging Situations	Obedience rates seem to depend on the innocuous start to the study, the small rate of change in shock intensity, and the lack of time for the participant to reflect.

other humans, under a forceful ideology, becomes an honor and a duty.

In the Milgram experiments, 'the importance of science' can be viewed as the ideology that legitimated even extraordinary demands. Some critics have argued that the Milgram experiments were artificial, that the prestige of a scientific experiment led participants to obey without questioning the dubious procedures in which they participated, and that in real life people would never do such a thing (Baumrind, 1964). Indeed, when Milgram repeated his experiment in a rundown set of offices and removed any association with Yale University from the setting, the rate of obedience dropped somewhat from 65 per cent to 48 per cent (Milgram, 1974).

But this criticism misses the major point. The prestige of science is not an irrelevant artificiality but an integral part of Milgram's demonstration. Science serves the same legitimating role in the experiment that the German state served in Nazi Germany and that national security serves in wartime killing. It is precisely their belief in the importance of scientific research that prompts individuals to subordinate their moral autonomy and independence to those who claim to act on behalf of science.

Ethical issues

Milgram's experiments have been criticized on several grounds. First, critics argue that Milgram's procedures created an unacceptable level of stress in the participants during the experiment itself. In support of this claim, they quote Milgram's own description:

> [Participants] were observed to sweat, tremble, stutter, bite their lips, groan, and dig their fingernails into their flesh. These were characteristic rather than exceptional responses to the experiment … . One sign of tension was the regular occurrence of nervous laughing fits … . On one occasion we observed a seizure so violently convulsive that it was necessary to call a halt to the experiment.

> (Milgram, 1963, p. 375)

Second, critics express concern about the long-term psychological effects on participants of having learned that they would be willing to give potentially lethal shocks to a fellow human being. Third, critics argue that participants are likely to feel foolish and 'used' when told the true nature of the experiment, thereby making them less trusting of psychologists in particular and of authority in general.

In response to these and other criticisms, Milgram pointed out that after his experiments he conducted a careful debriefing; that is, he explained the reasons for the procedures and re-established positive rapport with the participant. This included a reassuring chat with the 'victim' who the participant had thought was receiving the shocks. After the completion of an experimental series, participants were sent a detailed report of the purposes and results of the experiment. Milgram then conducted a survey, which revealed that 84 per cent of the participants were glad to have taken part in the study; 15 per cent reported neutral feelings; and 1 per cent stated that they were sorry to have participated. These percentages were about the same for those who had obeyed and those who had defied the experimenter. In addition, 74 per cent indicated that they had learned something of personal importance as a result of being in the study.

Milgram also hired a psychiatrist to interview 40 of the participants to determine whether the study had any injurious effects. This follow-up revealed no indications of long-term distress or traumatic reactions (Milgram, 1964).

In Chapter 1 we noted that research guidelines set forth by the US government and the American Psychological Association emphasize two major principles: informed consent and minimal risk. Milgram's studies were conducted in the early 1960s, before these guidelines were in effect. Despite the importance of the research and the precautions that Milgram took, it seems likely that most of the review boards that must now approve research projects would not permit Milgram's exact study procedures to be carried out today. However, a recent partial replication of Milgram's famous study provided greater protection of the rights and welfare of study participants and thereby allowed an empirical test of whether people today would still obey authority to the same degree as Milgram found. Burger (2009) reasoned that reaching 150 volts on the shock generator in Milgram's original study was a critical turning point. Recall that 150 volts was the first point at which the learner demanded to be released from the study and the point at which the majority of those who disobeyed the experimenter broke off. Put differently, the vast majority of people who shocked the learner at 150 volts (nearly 80 percent) continued to obey the experimenter all the way to 450 volts. Burger thus terminated his replication of Milgram's classic study when shocks reached 150 volts, reasoning that data gathered up until that point would provide sufficient information about obedience rates today. Although Burger's sample was more diverse, and included women as well as men, results were strikingly similar to those obtained more than 50 years earlier. One sobering departure from Milgram's findings, was that Burger (2009) uncovered virtually no effect of seeing a peer role model disobey the experimenter.

Students who first learn the results of Milgram's famous experiments have long questioned whether people today would obey authority as blindly. Apparently so. Situational pressures to obey authority appear as strong today as ever (Burger, 2009).

Obedience in everyday life

Because the Milgram experiments have been criticized for being artificial (Orne & Holland, 1968), it is instructive to look at an example of obedience to authority under more ordinary conditions. Researchers investigated whether nurses in public and private hospitals would obey an order that violated hospital rules and professional practice (Hofling et al., 1966). While on regular duty, the participant (a nurse) received a telephone call from a doctor whom she knew to be on the staff but had not met: 'This is Dr Smith from Psychiatry calling. I was asked to see Mr Jones this morning, and I'm going to have to see him again tonight. I'd like him to have had some medication by the time I get to the ward. Will you please check your medicine cabinet and see if you have some Astroten? That's A-S-T-R-O-T-E-N.' When the nurse checked the medicine cabinet, she saw a pillbox labeled:

ASTROTEN
5 mg capsules
Usual dose: 5 mg
Maximum daily dose: 10 mg

After she reported that she had found it, the doctor continued, 'Now will you please give Mr Jones a dose of 20 milligrams of Astroten. I'll be up within 10 minutes; I'll sign the order then, but I'd like the drug to have started taking effect.' A staff psychiatrist, posted unobtrusively nearby, terminated each trial by disclosing its true nature when the nurse either dispensed the medication (actually a harmless placebo), refused to accept the order, or tried to contact another professional.

This order violated several rules: the dose was clearly excessive. Medication orders may not be given by telephone. The medication was unauthorized – that is, it was not on the ward stock list clearing it for use. Finally, the order was given by an unfamiliar person. Despite all this, 95 per cent of the nurses started to give the medication. Moreover, the telephone calls were all brief, and the nurses put up little or no resistance. None of them insisted on a written order, although several sought reassurance that the doctor would arrive promptly. In interviews after the experiment, all the nurses stated that such orders had been received in the past and that doctors became annoyed if the nurses balked.

Again, these results surprise us. And they surprise professionals as well. When nurses who had not been participants in the study were given a complete description of the situation and asked how they themselves would respond, 83 per cent reported that they would not have given the medication, and most of them thought that a majority of nurses would also refuse. Twenty-one nursing students who were asked the same question all asserted that they would not have given the medication as ordered.

This again portrays the unexpected power of situational forces. We make the mistake of assuming that people's behavior reflects their character and their intentions. We make this fundamental attribution error time and again.

INTERIM SUMMARY

➔ Asch's classic experiments on conformity found that a unanimous group exerts strong pressure on an individual to conform to the group's judgments – even when those judgments are clearly wrong. Much less conformity was observed if even one person dissented from the group.

➔ A minority within a larger group can move the majority toward its point of view if it maintains a consistent dissenting position without appearing to be rigid, dogmatic, or arrogant, a process called *minority influence*. Minorities sometimes even obtain private attitude change from majority members, not just public conformity. This is thought to occur through an implicit leniency contract in which majority members agree to let minority members have their say but don't expect to be influenced by them.

➔ Milgram's classic experiments on obedience to authority demonstrated that ordinary people would obey an experimenter's order to deliver strong electric shocks to an innocent victim. Situational factors conspiring to produce the high obedience rates include (1) surveillance by the experimenter, (2) buffers that distance the person from the consequences of his or her acts, (3) role models, and (4) the emerging properties of situations. Other factors shown to trigger obedience include an ideology about the importance of science and behavioral synchrony with leaders.

CRITICAL THINKING QUESTIONS

1 One account of how individuals are recruited to become suicide terrorists suggests that a charismatic leader indoctrinates a group of people at once, asking them to 'please step forward' if they have any doubts about becoming martyrs for the cause. Although the socialization of suicide terrorists is no doubt complex and multifaceted, describe how this simple tactic exploits the concept of pluralistic ignorance.

2 Consider the unsettling message of Milgram's studies: that if a situation is arranged properly and supported by ideological beliefs, ordinary people – like you – can be pulled to act in ways that you find morally reprehensible. How will you fight against the power of such situations in your own life? Can certain other situations pull you to follow your own conscience?

INTERNALIZATION

Most studies of conformity and obedience focus on whether individuals overtly comply with the social influence wielded within the situation. In everyday life, however, those who attempt to influence us usually seek **internalization**; that is, they want to change our private attitudes, not just our public behaviors, and to obtain changes that will be sustained even after they are no longer on the scene. Certainly the major goal of parents, educators, clergy, politicians, and advertisers is internalization, not just compliance. In this section we begin to examine social influence that persuades rather than coerces.

Self-justification

When discussing the emerging situational predicament that Milgram's participants found themselves in, we concluded that sometimes it's easier to continue with bad behavior than to admit our mistakes. Why is that? Why is it so difficult for us to come clean and say, 'I changed my mind. I no longer think that doing this is right'? Part of the answer is that people don't like to be inconsistent. The pressure to be consistent can be so strong that often people will justify – or rationalize – past behavior by forming or adjusting their private beliefs to support it.

A classic study of social influence tested the power of this pull to be consistent. To get a sense of the study, imagine that you were to knock on the doors of homeowners in your community, identify yourself as belonging to the Community Committee on Public Safety, and ask those who answered: 'Could we install a public service billboard on your front lawn?' Naturally, you'd want to give folks a sense of what the billboard would look like, so you'd show them a photo of an attractive home nearly obscured by a huge, poorly lettered sign that reads 'Drive Carefully'. Would people agree? Not many. In the early 1960s, a research team found that only 17 per cent said yes (Freedman & Fraser, 1966). Although few could argue with the mission of promoting safe driving, the request was simply too large. There is probably no way that people would hand over the use of their front lawn for this or any other cause. Or is there?

Suppose an associate of yours had approached these homeowners a few weeks earlier with a relatively minor request: 'Would you place this sign in your living room window?' Your associate would then show them a small, 3-inch-square sign that reads 'Be a Safe Driver'. The cause is good and the request so small that nearly everyone says yes. And although the actions taken by the homeowner are relatively minor, their effects are powerful and lasting. For the next few weeks, every time these people look at their window, they face a salient reminder that they care about public safety, so much so that they took action. When guests ask about the sign, they will find themselves explaining how important the matter of safe driving is to them and why they had to do something about it. Now, 2 weeks later, you drop by with your large request about the billboard. What happens under these circumstances? The study done in the 1960s found that a full 76 per cent said yes (Freedman & Fraser, 1966). Consider how hard it was for these poor homeowners to say no! After all, they're already known to the community and to themselves as the sort of people who care enough about safe driving to take action on the matter, so be it if that action involves a sacrifice.

This study illustrates the social influence tool called the **foot-in-the-door technique**: to get people to say yes to requests that would ordinarily lead to no, one approach is to start with a small request that few would refuse. Ideally, the small request is a miniature version of the larger request that you already have in mind. Once people have publicly complied with this easy request, they'll start re-examining who they are and what they stand for. The result is that their private attitudes will swing more strongly in line with their public behavior, making it harder for them to say no to the larger request. The original work on the foot-in-the-door technique was conducted in the USA Other experiments suggest that pressures to appear consistent may be especially strong in Western cultures that value individualism (Petrova *et al.,* 2007). The degree to which self-justification tendencies apply universally across cultures continues to be a hotly debated topic (Heine & Lehman, 1997; Imada & Kitayama, 2010; Kitayama *et al.,* 2004).

Cognitive dissonance theory

The foot-in-the-door technique also illustrates that one way to influence people's attitudes is through their behavior. If you can induce people to act in a way that is consistent with the attitude you'd like them to adopt, then they will eventually justify their behavior by adopting the sought-after attitude. The most influential explanation of this sequence of events is Leon Festinger's **cognitive dissonance theory**. This theory assumes that there is a drive toward cognitive consistency, meaning that two cognitions – or thoughts – that are inconsistent will produce discomfort, which will in turn motivate the person to remove the inconsistency and bring the cognitions into harmony. The term *cognitive dissonance* refers to the discomfort produced by inconsistent cognitions (Festinger, 1957).

Although cognitive dissonance theory addresses several kinds of inconsistency, it has been most provocative in predicting the aftermath of behaving in ways that run counter to one's attitudes. One label we have for attitude-behavior discrepancies is hypocrisy. For instance, we call the fundamentalist preacher who frequents strip bars a hypocrite. The sheer negativity of this label offers insight into the discomfort caused by any discrepancies between what we do and what we believe. A core idea within cognitive dissonance theory is that when attitudes and behavior are at odds, we take the

easiest route to ridding ourselves of the unpleasant state of dissonance. That is, we create consonance or consistency by changing our attitudes. Past behavior, after all, cannot be changed. And changing a line of action already undertaken – like stopping the shocks in the Milgram experiment or quitting smoking – can produce even more dissonance because it introduces the idea that your initial judgment was poor, a thought that is inconsistent with your generally favorable view of yourself. So, the behavior is maintained or justified by changing or adding new consonant cognitions. **Rationalization** is another term for this process of self-justification. In the case of the Milgram experiment, some participants were likely to tell themselves, 'At least I'm following orders, unlike that unruly guy who won't learn these word pairs.' If you smoke cigarettes, you may reduce dissonance by telling yourself and others something like, 'I know smoking is bad for my health in the long run, but it relaxes me so much, and that's more important to me.'

One of the earliest and most famous studies of cognitive dissonance examined the effects of induced compliance. University students participated one at a time in an experiment in which they worked on a dull, repetitive task: they were asked to turn wooden pegs on a pegboard, over and over again. After completing the boring task, the experimenter asked participants a favor. They were told that the study was really about how people's expectations influence their performance, and that the guy who normally plays the confederate role and tells people what to expect wasn't available. Under this guise, some participants were offered $1 to tell the next participant that the tasks had been fun and interesting. Others were offered $20 to do this. (This study was conducted in the 1950s. Back then, $1 could buy you dinner at a restaurant, and $20 could buy a week's worth of groceries for you and your family.) Whether paid $1 or $20, all of the participants complied with the request. Later they were asked how much they had enjoyed the tasks. As shown in Figure 17.7, participants who had been paid only $1 stated that they had in fact enjoyed the tasks. But participants who had been paid $20 did not find them significantly more enjoyable than did members of a control group who never spoke to another participant (Festinger & Carlsmith, 1959). The small incentive for complying with the experimenter's request – but not the large incentive – led participants to believe what they had heard themselves say. Why should this be so?

According to cognitive dissonance theory, being paid $20 provides a very clear and consonant reason for complying with the experimenter's request to talk to the waiting participant, and so the person experiences little or no dissonance. The inconsistency between the person's behavior (telling the next person that the task was interesting) and his or her attitude toward the task (the task was boring) is outweighed by the far greater consistency between the compliance and the huge monetary incentive for complying. Accordingly, the participants who were paid $20 did not change their attitudes.

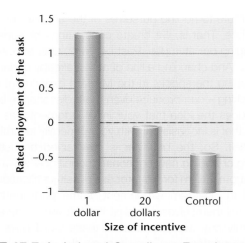

FIGURE 17.7 An Induced-Compliance Experiment.
The smaller incentive for agreeing to say that the tasks were interesting led participants to infer that they had actually enjoyed the tasks. The larger incentive did not.

Those who were paid $1, however, had no clear or consonant reason for complying. Accordingly, they experienced dissonance, which they reduced by coming to believe that they really did enjoy the tasks. The general conclusion is that dissonance-causing behavior will lead to attitude change in induced-compliance situations when the behavior can be induced with a minimum amount of pressure, whether in the form of reward or punishment.

Experiments with children have confirmed the prediction about minimal punishment. If children obey a very mild request not to play with an attractive toy, they come to believe that the toy is not as attractive as they first thought – a belief that is consistent with their observation that they are not playing with it. But if the children refrain from playing with the toy under a strong threat of punishment, they do not change their liking for the toy (Aronson & Carlsmith, 1963; Freedman, 1965).

Other studies within the tradition of cognitive dissonance theory focused on how people justify their past efforts by valuing their chosen paths more strongly. An illustration of this occurs each year on university campuses in the USA: students often go through elaborate rituals – and sometimes painful and dangerous hazings – to join exclusive student social organizations known as campus fraternities and sororities. Experiments on cognitive dissonance provide clues as to why these rituals persist. People who go through more effort to join a group end up valuing that group more than those who join with little effort (Aronson & Mills, 1959). We justify our past decisions similarly (Brehm, 1956). Before a decision is made, a number of alternatives may seem equally attractive. Perhaps you had to decide which of several universities to attend. No doubt they each had their good features, but of course, you could only attend one. After you made your decision, cognitive dissonance theory

predicts that the simple act of choosing one alternative would create dissonance in you, because it is inconsistent with the good features of the alternatives not chosen. To reduce this unpleasant state, the theory predicts that you will justify your choice by downplaying the good features of the paths not taken and exaggerating the good features of the path you took. Does this prediction fit with your own experience?

Self-perception theory

Over the years, alternative explanations have been offered for some of the findings of cognitive dissonance theory. For instance, social psychologist Daryl Bem argued that a simpler theory, which he called *self-perception theory*, could explain all results of the classic dissonance experiments without reference to any inner turmoil or dissonance. In brief, **self-perception theory** proposes that individuals come to know their own attitudes, emotions, and other internal states partially by inferring them from observations of their own behavior and the circumstances in which the behavior occurs. To the extent that internal cues are weak, ambiguous, or uninterpretable, self-perception theory states that the individual is like any outside observer who must rely on external cues to infer the individual's inner states (Bem, 1972). Self-perception theory is illustrated by the common remark, 'This is my second sandwich; I guess I was hungrier than I thought.' Here the speaker has inferred an internal state by observing his or her own behavior. Similarly, the self-observation 'I've been biting my nails all day; something must be bugging me' is based on the same external evidence that might lead a friend to remark, 'You've been biting your nails all day; something must be bugging you.'

With this alternative theory in mind, reconsider the classic peg-turning study (Festinger & Carlsmith, 1959). Recall that participants were induced to tell a waiting participant that a dull peg-turning task had in fact been fun and interesting. Participants who had been paid $20 to do this did not change their attitudes, whereas participants who had been paid only $1 came to believe that the tasks had in fact been enjoyable. Self-perception theory proposes that, just as an observer tries to understand the cause of someone else's behavior, so, too, participants in this experiment looked at their own behavior (telling another participant that the tasks were interesting) and implicitly asked themselves, 'Why did I do this?' Self-perception theory further proposes that they sought an answer the same way an outside observer would, by trying to decide whether to explain the behavior with reference to the person (he did it because he really did enjoy the task) or with reference to the situation (he did it for the money). When the individual is paid only $1, the observer is more likely to credit the person: 'He wouldn't be willing to say it for only $1, so he must have actually enjoyed the tasks.' But if the individual is paid $20, the observer is more likely to credit the situation: 'Anyone would have done it for $20, so I can't judge his attitude toward the tasks on the basis of his statement.' If the individual follows the same inferential process as this hypothetical outside observer, participants who are paid $1 infer their attitude from their own behavior: 'I must think the tasks were enjoyable. Otherwise I would not have said so.' But participants who are paid $20 attribute their behavior to the money and therefore express the same attitudes toward the tasks as the control participants who made no statements to another participant.

Importantly, virtually all the participants in the peg-turning study were willing to tell the next participant that the task was enjoyable – even if they were offered only $1 to do so. But the participants themselves did not know this. Thus, when participants who were paid $1 inferred that they must think the tasks are enjoyable because otherwise they would not have said so, they were wrong. They should have inferred that they talked to the next participant because they were paid $1 to do so. In other words, they committed the fundamental attribution error: they overestimated causes due to the person and underestimated causes due to the situation.

The opposite can also happen: people sometimes overestimate causes due to the situation and underestimate causes due to the person. We saw this back in Chapter 1, when we discussed the unexpected effects of rewarding kids with free pizza for meeting monthly reading goals. Kids do read more if reading earns them pizza. But do they enjoy reading? And do they continue reading once the pizza program ends? Dozens of studies, based on the principles of self-perception theory, suggest that rewards can undermine intrinsic interest and motivation. This happens because when people see that their behavior is caused by some external, situational factor – like a free pizza – they discount the input of any internal, personal factors – like their own enjoyment of the activity. So when kids ask themselves why they read, they'll say it's for the pizza. And when there's no more pizza to be had, they'll see no other compelling reason to read. Even though they might have enjoyed reading, the rewards loomed larger. Recall that this undermining effect of rewards is called the **overjustification effect**, whereby people go overboard and explain their own behavior with too much emphasis on salient situational causes and not enough emphasis on personal causes.

So which theory wins? Does cognitive dissonance theory or self-perception theory best explain our tendencies to justify our actions by changing our attitudes? More recent experiments actually pose a challenge to both theories. A replication of classic self-justification paradigms used participants who were either amnesiac or under cognitive load (that is, multitasking and therefore having impaired attention and working memory). The results showed just as much attitude change, even when participants couldn't even remember the recent behavior that their newly adopted attitude justified! (Lieberman *et al.,* 2001). Another replication, this time with capuchin monkeys, found clear attitude change as

well (Egan *et al.,* 2007). These newer findings suggest that behavior-induced attitude change can happen automatically, without much conscious thought, perhaps through some core innate or otherwise universal knowledge systems that favor consistency. So although both cognitive dissonance theory and self-perception theory hold that people 'rationalize' their past actions by changing their attitudes, this process may not actually involve the deliberate consonance-seeking or sense-making that either theory has presumed.

These various perspectives on self-justification describe the psychological aftermath of potent social influence techniques. Throughout this chapter, we've seen one core lesson within social psychology illustrated time and again: situational forces can be powerful. A related core lesson within social psychology is that these powerful situational forces are often invisible. When some form of social influence pressures us to behave in a certain way, we often fail to recognize it; and when left to make sense of our actions, we wittingly or unwittingly change our inner attitudes to be in line with our outward behavior. From this perspective, the classic experiments on self-justification can be viewed as social influence techniques in action.

Self-justification in Jonestown

Knowing how self-justification processes lead people to rationalize their actions by changing their attitudes, think back to the Jonestown case mentioned at the start of the chapter. When the public first learned of the mass suicide, the fundamental attribution error reigned: Jim Jones's followers must have been crazy or weak-willed. Who else would take their own lives at another's request? Later news reports challenged this view by highlighting the diversity of the People's Temple membership. Although some were poor, uneducated, and perhaps more gullible than most, many were educated professionals. Recall that the lesson within the fundamental attribution error is that we underestimate the power of situations. Taking this to heart, a social psychological analysis of the Jonestown tragedy examines followers' paths to Jonestown and the social influence tactics used by Jim Jones (Osherow, 1984).

Oddly enough, we have a window into daily practices within Jonestown because Jim Jones insisted that most events be audiotaped, including the final act of suicide. Reports from former members of the People's Temple help complete the picture. From this evidence, it becomes clear that Jim Jones was artfully exploiting the foot-in-the-door technique. Jones did not start off by asking would-be members: 'Give me your life savings and your children and move with me to the jungle.' Rather, he first got prospective members to comply with small requests and then gradually stepped up the level of commitment. Recall that Jim Jones had painted a utopian vision of social equality and racial harmony that became known simply as 'the Cause'. At first,

Jim Jones artfully exploited people's tendencies to self-justify.

members were just asked to donate their time to the Cause, later their money, and still later their possessions, legal custody of their children, and so on. Little by little, followers' options became more limited. Step by step, they become motivated to explain or to justify their past behavior in support of the Cause. The easiest way to do that was to become even more committed to the Cause.

Jeanne Mills managed to defect from the People's Temple before the move to Guyana. She became a vocal critic of the group (and was later murdered). In her book, *Six Years With God* (1979), Mills describes the forces of self-justification at work:

> We had to face painful reality. Our life savings were gone. Jim [Jones] had demanded that we sell the life insurance policy and turn the equity over to the church, so that was gone. Our property had all been taken from us…. We thought that we had alienated our parents when we told them we were leaving the country. Even the children whom we had left in the care of [others in the church] were openly hostile toward us. Jim had accomplished all this in such a short time! All we had left now was Jim and the Cause, so we decided to buckle under and give our energies to these two.

> (Mills, 1979, cited in Osherow, 1984)

So, wittingly or unwittingly, Jim Jones used virtually invisible social influence techniques to extract behavioral compliance from his followers. This strategy takes advantage of people's tendencies to self-justify and results in members intensifying their beliefs in Jim Jones and the Cause, while minimizing their assessments of the noxiousness of the costs of membership.

Once in Guyana, Jim Jones continued to escalate the level of commitment he required of members by introducing the idea of the 'final ritual' or 'revolutionary suicide'. He staged events called 'White Nights', which were essentially suicide drills. Jones would pass out wine and then announce later that the wine had been poisoned and that they would all soon die. To test his followers' faith, Jones asked them whether they were ready to die for the Cause. One time, the membership was even asked to vote on its own fate. Later in the evening, Jones would announce, 'Well, it was a good lesson, I see you're not dead.' One ex-member recounted how these White Nights affected him and other followers:

> [Jones] made it sound like we needed the 30 minutes to do very strong, introspective type of thinking. We all felt strongly dedicated, proud of ourselves … [Jones] taught that it was a privilege to die for what you believed in.

> (Winfrey, 1979, cited in Osherow, 1984)

This brief social psychological analysis of the events leading up to the Jonestown mass suicides illustrates social influence in action. It gives a window onto the power that situational forces had to alter the internalized ideologies of Jim Jones's followers.

Reference groups and identification

Nearly every group to which we belong has an implicit or explicit set of beliefs, attitudes, and behaviors that it considers correct. Any member of the group who strays from these social norms risks isolation and social disapproval. Through social rewards and punishments, the groups to which we belong obtain compliance from us. Groups may also pull for **identification**. If we respect or admire other individuals or groups, we may obey their norms and adopt their beliefs, attitudes, and behaviors in order to be like them or to identify with them. We even experience vicarious dissonance and change our own attitudes if we see someone from a group we admire engage in inconsistent behavior (Cooper & Hogg, 2007).

Reference groups are groups with which we identify; we refer to them in order to evaluate and regulate our opinions and actions. Reference groups can also serve as a frame of reference by providing us not only with specific beliefs and attitudes but also with a general perspective from which we view the world – an ideology or set of ready-made interpretations of social issues and events. If we eventually adopt these views and integrate the group's ideology into our own value system, the reference group will have produced internalization. The process of identification, then, can provide a bridge between compliance and internalization.

An individual does not necessarily have to be a member of a reference group to be influenced by its values. For example, lower-middle-class individuals often use the middle class as a reference group. An aspiring athlete may use professional athletes as a reference group.

Life would be simple if each of us identified with only one reference group. But most of us identify with several reference groups, which often leads to conflicting pressures. Perhaps the most enduring example of competing reference groups is the conflict that many young people experience between their family reference group and their university or peer reference group. The most extensive study of this conflict is Theodore Newcomb's classic Bennington Study – an examination of the political attitudes of the entire population of Bennington College, a small, politically liberal college in Vermont. The dates of the study (1935–1939) are a useful reminder that this is not a new phenomenon.

Today Bennington College tends to attract liberal students, but in 1935 most students came from wealthy conservative families. (It is also co-ed today, but in 1935 it was a women's college.) More than two-thirds of the parents of Bennington students were affiliated with the Republican Party. Most people at Bennington College were liberal during the 1930s, but this was not the reason that most of the women selected the college.

Newcomb's main finding was that with each year at Bennington, students moved further away from their parents' attitudes and closer to the attitudes of their academic community. For example, in the 1936 presidential campaign, about 66 per cent of parents favored the Republican candidate, Alf Landon, over the Democratic candidate, Franklin Roosevelt. Landon was supported by 62 per cent of the Bennington freshmen and 43 per cent of the sophomores, but only 15 per cent of the juniors and seniors.

For most of the women, increasing liberalism reflected a deliberate choice between the two competing reference groups. Two women discussed how they made this choice:

> **All my life I've resented the protection of governesses and parents. At college I got away from that, or rather, I guess I should say, I changed it to wanting the intellectual approval of teachers and more advanced students. Then I found that you can't be reactionary and be intellectually respectable.**
>
> **Becoming radical meant thinking for myself and, figuratively, thumbing my nose at my family. It also meant intellectual identification with the faculty and students that I most wanted to be like.**

> (Newcomb, 1943, pp. 134, 131)

Note that the second woman uses the term *identification* in the sense that we have been using it. Note, too, how the women describe a mixture of change produced by social rewards and punishments (compliance) and change produced by attraction to an admired group that they strive to emulate (identification).

From identification to internalization

As mentioned earlier, reference groups also serve as frames of reference by providing their members with new perspectives on the world. The Bennington community, particularly the faculty, gave students a perspective on the Depression of the 1930s and the threat of World War II that their home environments had not, and this began to move them from identification to internalization: listen to how two other Bennington women described the process:

> **It didn't take me long to see that liberal attitudes had prestige value ... . I became liberal at first because of its prestige value; I remain so because the problems around which my liberalism centers are important. What I want now is to be effective in solving problems.**
>
> **Prestige and recognition have always meant everything to me ... . But I've sweat[ed] blood in trying to be honest with myself, and the result is that I really know what I want my attitudes to be, and I see what their consequences will be in my own life.**

> (Newcomb, 1943, pp. 136–137)

Many of our most important beliefs and attitudes are probably based initially on identification. Whenever we start to identify with a new reference group, we engage in a process of 'trying on' a new set of beliefs and attitudes. What we 'really believe' may change from day to day. The first year at a university often has this effect on students, because many of the views they bring from the family reference group are challenged by students and academic staff from very different backgrounds. Students often try on the new beliefs with great intensity and strong conviction, only to discard them for still newer beliefs when the first set does not quite fit. This is a natural process of growth. Although the process never really ends for people who remain open to new experiences, it is greatly accelerated during young adulthood, before the individual has formed a nucleus of permanent beliefs on which to build more slowly and less radically. The real work of young adulthood is to evolve an ideological identity from the numerous beliefs and attitudes that are tested in order to move from identification to internalization.

As noted earlier, one advantage of internalization over compliance is that the changes are self-sustaining. The original source of influence does not have to monitor the individual to maintain the induced changes. The test of internalization, therefore, is the long-term stability of the induced beliefs, attitudes, and behaviors. Was the identification-induced liberalism of Bennington women maintained when the students returned to the 'real world'? The answer is yes. Two follow-up studies conducted 25 and 50 years later found the women had remained liberal. For example, in the 1984 presidential election, 73 per cent of Bennington alumnae preferred the Democratic candidate, Walter Mondale, over the Republican candidate, Ronald Reagan, compared with less than 26 per cent of women of the same age and educational level. Moreover, about 60 per cent of Bennington alumnae were politically active, most (66 per cent) within the Democratic Party (Alwin *et al.,* 1991; Newcomb *et al.,* 1967).

We never outgrow our need for identification with supporting reference groups. The political attitudes of Bennington women remained stable partly because after college they selected new reference groups that supported the attitudes they had developed in college. Those who married more conservative men were more likely to be politically conservative in later life. As Newcomb noted, we often select our reference groups because they share our attitudes, and our reference groups, in turn, help develop and sustain our attitudes. The relationship is bidirectional. The distinction between identification and internalization is a useful one for understanding social influence, but in practice it is not always possible to disentangle them.

Intriguingly, bicultural and bilingual individuals provide yet another example of conflicting reference groups. Contemporary social psychologists have studied these individuals, who navigate their daily life with reference to two distinct sets of cultural values (Hong *et al.,* 2000). Language turns out to be a pivotal situational cue. Studies of Hong Kong biculturals found that when choices are presented in Cantonese, Hong Kong biculturals become motivated to conform to the norms of Chinese culture, like moderation and compromise. But when the same choices are presented in English, norms of decisiveness and risk-taking exert a greater pull (Briley *et al.,* 2005). Here again we see that the situational triggers of social influence can be subtle.

INTERIM SUMMARY

⊖ Cognitive dissonance theory suggests that when people's behavior conflicts with their attitudes it creates an uncomfortable tension that motivates them to change their attitudes to be more in line with their actions. This is one explanation for the process of rationalization, or self-justification.

⊖ Self-perception theory challenged cognitive dissonance theory by stating that inner turmoil does not necessarily occur. To the extent that internal cues are weak, ambiguous, or uninterpretable, people may simply infer their attitudes from their past behavior.

⊖ The phenomenon of self-justification is well-documented and has been shown to exist in non-human animals, suggesting that it does not rely on complex conscious thought, a challenge to both cognitive dissonance theory and self-perception theory.

⊖ In the process of identification, we obey the norms and adopt the beliefs, attitudes, and behaviors of groups that we respect and admire. We use such reference groups to evaluate and regulate our opinions and actions. A reference group can regulate our attitudes and behavior by administering social rewards and punishments or providing a frame of reference, a ready-made interpretation of events and social issues.

⊖ Most people identify with more than one reference group, which can lead to conflicting pressures on beliefs, attitudes, and behaviors. University students frequently move away from the views of their family reference group toward the academic reference group. These new views are usually sustained in later life because (1) they become internalized, and (2) after university we tend to select new reference groups that share our views.

CRITICAL THINKING QUESTIONS

1 Rites of passage or initiation rituals are common in young adulthood across many cultures. Explain how these rituals capitalize on people's tendencies to self-justify. What are the outcomes of the self-justification process? How would cognitive dissonance theory and self-perception theory differ in their explanations of this process? How could you explain the self-justification spawned by initiation rituals using simpler, perhaps unconscious mental habits?

2 Can you identify any changes in your beliefs and attitudes that have come about by being exposed to a new reference group and coming to identify with it?

GROUP INTERACTIONS

So far in our discussions of social influence and the power of situations we have emphasized the effects of these forces on lone individuals. Among the questions we've addressed are: how and why is an individual's performance affected by the presence of others? How and why is an individual's public behavior shaped by a group's unanimity? How and why do an individual's private attitudes change following social influence? In this section, our focus changes from lone individuals to groups of people. We will look at group interactions more generally to understand the dynamics and outcomes of group processes.

Institutional norms

Group interactions are often governed by institutional norms. Institutional norms are like social norms – implicit or explicit rules for acceptable behavior and beliefs – except they are applied to entire institutions, or organizations of the same type, like schools, prisons, governments, or commercial businesses. Group interaction patterns within these settings can often become 'institutionalized', meaning that behavioral expectations are prescribed for people who occupy particular roles – roles like employee or boss, politician, or military officer. Under these circumstances, behavior depends more on particular role expectations than on the individual character of the person who occupies the role. In other words, institutional settings are another potent situation that influences human behavior.

A famous study showing just how potent institutional norms can be is the Stanford Prison Experiment, directed by Philip Zimbardo. Zimbardo and his colleagues were interested in the psychological processes involved in taking the roles of prisoner and prison guard. They created a simulated prison in the basement of the Psychology Department at Stanford University and placed an ad in a local newspaper for participants to take part in a psychological experiment for pay. From the people who responded to the ad, they selected 24 'mature, emotionally stable, normal, intelligent white male college students from middle-class homes throughout the USA and Canada'. None had a prison record, and all seemed very similar in their values. By the flip of a coin, half were assigned to be prison guards and half to be prisoners.

The 'guards' were instructed about their responsibilities and made aware of the potential danger of the situation and their need to protect themselves. The 'prisoners' were unexpectedly picked up at their homes by a mock police car, handcuffed, and taken blindfolded to the improvised jail, where they were searched, deloused, fingerprinted, given numbers, and placed in 'cells' with two other prisoners.

The participants had signed up for the sake of the money, and all expected to be in the experiment for about 2 weeks. But by the end of the sixth day the researchers had to abort the experiment because the results were too frightening to allow them to continue. As Zimbardo (1972, p. 243) explained:

> **It was no longer apparent to most of the [participants] (or to us) where reality ended and their roles began. The majority had indeed become prisoners or guards, no longer able to clearly differentiate between role playing and self. There were dramatic changes in virtually every aspect of their behavior, thinking, and feeling. In less than a week the experience of imprisonment undid (temporarily) a lifetime of learning; human values were suspended, self-concepts were challenged, and the ugliest, most base, pathological side of human nature surfaced. We were horrified because we saw some boys (guards) treat others as if they were despicable animals, taking pleasure in cruelty, while other boys (prisoners) became servile, dehumanized robots who thought only of escape, of their own individual survival, and of their mounting hatred for the guards.**

Far faster and more thoroughly than the researchers thought possible, 'the experiment had become a reality'.

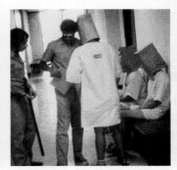
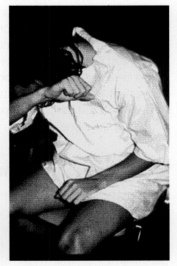

These photos were taken of participants in the now-famous Stanford Prison Experiment. The results demonstrated that group interactions are often shaped by powerful institutional norms. Here we see that prison norms pulled for dehumanizing and violent behavior from guards, and servile and despondent behavior from prisoners.

The Stanford Prison Experiment is a demonstration of the extraordinary power of situations. It also illustrates the power of institutional norms within prison-like settings. Keep in mind that the participants were randomly assigned to the roles of prisoner and guard. Nothing in their character or backgrounds, then, could explain their behavior. Even though those playing the roles of guard and prisoner were essentially free to interact in any way they wished, the group's interactions tended be negative, hostile, and dehumanizing, a pattern remarkably similar to interactions in actual prisons. These findings suggest that the situation itself – the very institution of prison – is so pathological that it can distort and rechannel the behavior of normal individuals.

It's been more than 40 years since the Stanford Prison Experiment was conducted. Has prison policy benefited from it? Have institutional norms and practices within prisons improved? Unfortunately not, at least not in the USA. Indeed, Zimbardo has argued that US criminal justice policies have turned a blind eye to the lessons of this well-known experiment about the power of situations within prisons (Zimbardo, 2007; see also Haney & Zimbardo, 1998). As just one example, Zimbardo (2007) details the chilling parallels between the Stanford Prison Experiment and the cruel, inhumane treatment of prisoners by US military personnel in the Iraqi prison at Abu Ghraib.

The Stanford Prison Experiment remains a lively topic of debate for other reasons as well. Following a trend toward 'reality TV,' the BBC (British Broadcasting Corporation) filmed a replication of Zimbardo's famous study, broadcasting it in 2002 as 'The Experiment' (Reicher & Haslam, 2006, see also Zimbardo, 2006). The results were altogether different from those Zimbardo obtained in the early 1970s. Indeed, in the BBC prison study, the prisoners quickly came to dominate the guards, and it was the guards, not the prisoners, who became depressed, stressed, and paranoid. At one point, the prisoners and guards even joined together to form one harmonious group, akin to a commune. Zimbardo has sharply criticized the BBC project, calling it both irresponsible and unscientific (Zimbardo, 2006). He points out numerous differences between his original work and this made-for-television replication, including the constant and apparent recording by the film crew. Zimbardo contends that surveillance and public accountability alone would eliminate prisoner abuses.

Group decision-making

Many decisions are made not by individuals but by groups. Members of a family jointly decide where to spend their vacation; a jury judges a defendant to be guilty; a city council votes to raise property taxes. How do such decisions compare with those that might have been made by individual decision-makers? Are group decisions better or worse, riskier, or more cautious? These are the kinds of questions that concern us in this section.

Group polarization

In the 1950s, it was widely believed that decisions made by groups were typically cautious and conservative. For example, it was argued that because business decisions were increasingly being made by committees, the bold, innovative risk taking of entrepreneurs like Andrew Carnegie was a thing of the past (Whyte, 1956). James Stoner, then a graduate business student at the prestigious Massachusetts Institute of Technology (MIT), decided to test this assumption (1961).

In Stoner's study, participants were asked to consider a number of hypothetical dilemmas. In one, an electrical engineer must decide whether to stick with his present job at a modest but adequate salary or take a job with a new firm offering more money, a possible partnership in the venture if it succeeds, but no long-term security. In another, a man with a severe heart ailment must seriously curtail his customary way of life or else undergo a medical operation that would either cure him completely or prove fatal. Participants were asked to decide how good the odds of success would have to be before they would advise the person to try the riskier course of action. For example, they could recommend that the engineer take the riskier job if the chances that the new venture would succeed were 5 in 10, 3 in 10, or only 1 in 10. By using numerical odds like these, Stoner was able to compare the riskiness of different decisions quantitatively.

Participants first made their decisions alone, as individuals. They then met in groups and arrived at a group decision for each dilemma. After the group discussion, they again considered the dilemmas privately as individuals. When Stoner compared the group's decisions with the average of the individuals' pregroup decisions, he found that the group's decisions were riskier than the individuals' initial decisions. Moreover, this shift reflected genuine opinion change on the part of group members, not just public conformity to the group decision: the private individual decisions made after the group discussion were significantly riskier than the initial decisions.

These findings were replicated by other researchers, even in situations that presented real rather than hypothetical risks (Bem *et al.,* 1965; Wallach *et al.,* 1962, 1964). The phenomenon was initially called the *risky shift effect*. This turned out not to be an accurate characterization, however. Even in the early studies, group decisions tended to shift slightly but consistently in the cautious direction on one or two of the hypothetical dilemmas (Wallach *et al.,* 1962). The phenomenon is now called the **group polarization effect** because after many more studies it became clear that group discussion leads to decisions that are not necessarily riskier but are more extreme than the individual decisions. If group members are initially inclined to take risks on a particular dilemma, the group's decisions will become riskier; if group members are initially inclined to be cautious, the group will be even more cautious (Myers & Lamm, 1976).

More than 300 studies of the group polarization effect have been conducted, with a dazzling array of variations. For example, in one study, active burglars actually cased houses and then provided individual and group estimates of how easy each would be to burglarize. Compared with the individual estimates, the group estimates were more conservative; that is, they rated the homes to be more difficult to break into successfully (Cromwell *et al.*, 1991).

Group polarization extends beyond issues of risk and caution. For example, group discussion caused French students' initially positive attitudes toward the country's premier to become even more positive and their initially negative attitudes toward Americans to become even more negative (Moscovici & Zavalloni, 1969). Jury decisions can be similarly affected, leading to more extreme verdicts (Isozaki, 1984). Polarization in juries is more likely to occur on judgments concerning values and opinions (such as deciding on an appropriate punishment for a guilty defendant) than on judgments concerning matters of fact (such as the defendant's guilt), and they are most likely to show polarization when they are required to reach unanimous decisions (Kaplan & Miller, 1987).

Many explanations for the group polarization effect have been offered over the years, but the two that have stood up best to intensive testing refer to the concepts of informational social influence and normative social influence that we considered earlier in our discussion of conformity to a majority (Isenberg, 1986). Recall that informational social influence occurs when people see others as valid sources of information. During group discussions, members learn new information and hear novel arguments relevant to the decision under discussion. For example, in discussing whether the electrical engineer should go with the new venture – a decision that almost always shifts in the risky direction – it is quite common for someone in the group to argue that riskiness is warranted because electrical engineers can always find good jobs. A shift in the conservative direction occurred in the burglar

study after one member of the group noted that it was nearly 3 p.m. and children would soon be returning from school and playing nearby.

The more that arguments are raised in support of a position, the more likely it is that the group will move toward that position. And this is where the bias enters: members of a group are most likely to present points in support of the position they initially favor and to discuss information they already share (Stasser *et al.*, 1989; Stasser & Titus, 1985). Accordingly, the discussion will be biased in favor of the group's initial position, and the group will move toward that position as more of the group members become convinced. Interestingly, the polarization effect still occurs, even when all participants are given an extensive list of arguments before the experiment begins – a finding that casts doubt on explanations based solely on informational social influence (Zuber *et al.*, 1992).

Normative social influence, you will recall, occurs when people want to be liked and accepted by a group. Under this type of social influence, people compare their own views with the norms of the group. During the discussion, they may learn that others have similar attitudes or even more extreme views than they themselves do. If they are motivated to be seen positively by the group, they may conform to the group's position or even express a position that is more extreme than the group's. As one researcher noted, 'To be virtuous … is to be different from the mean – in the right direction and to the right degree' (Brown, 1974, p. 469).

But normative social influence is not simply pressure to conform. Often the group provides a frame of reference for its members, a context within which they can re-evaluate their initial positions. This is illustrated by a common and amusing event that frequently occurs in group polarization experiments. For example, in one group a participant began the discussion of the dilemma facing the electrical engineer by confidently announcing, 'I feel this guy should really be willing to take a risk here. He should go with the new job even if it has only a 5 in 10 chance of succeeding.' Other group members were incredulous: 'You think that 5 in 10 is being risky? If he has any guts, he should give it a shot even if there is only 1 chance in 100 of success. I mean, what has he really got to lose?' Eager to re-establish his reputation as a risk taker, the original individual quickly shifted his position further in the risky direction. By redefining 'risky', the group moved both its own decision and its members' postdiscussion attitudes further toward the risky extreme of the scale (Wallach *et al.*, 1962; from the authors' notes).

As this example illustrates, both informational and normative social influence occur simultaneously in group discussions, and several studies have attempted to untangle them. Some studies have shown that the group polarization effect occurs if participants simply hear the arguments of the group, without knowing the actual positions of other members of the group (Burnstein & Vinokur, 1973, 1977). This demonstrates

Group polarization often occurs in juries, especially when they are required to reach unanimous decisions.

that informational social influence by itself is sufficient to produce polarization. Other studies have shown that the polarization effect also occurs when people learn others' positions but do not hear any supporting arguments, demonstrating that normative social influence by itself is sufficient (Goethals & Zanna, 1979; Sanders & Baron, 1977). Typically, however, the effect of informational social influence is greater than the effect of normative social influence (Isenberg, 1986).

Groupthink

'How could we have been so stupid?' This was US President John Kennedy's reaction to the disastrous failure of his administration's attempt to invade Cuba at the Bay of Pigs in 1961 and overthrow the government of Fidel Castro. The plan was badly conceived at many levels. For example, if the initial landing was unsuccessful, the invaders were supposed to retreat into the mountains. But no one in the planning group had studied the map closely enough to realize that no army could have advanced through the 80 miles of swamp that separated the mountains from the landing area. As it turned out, this didn't matter, because other miscalculations caused the invading force to be wiped out long before the retreat would have taken place.

The invasion had been conceived and planned by the president and a small group of advisers. Writing 4 years later, one of these advisers, the historian Arthur Schlesinger Jr (1965, p. 255), blamed himself

for having kept so silent during those crucial discussions in the Cabinet Room, though my feelings of guilt were tempered by the knowledge that a course of objection would have accomplished little save to gain me a name as a nuisance. I can only explain my failure to do more than raise a few timid questions by reporting that one's impulse to blow the whistle on this nonsense was simply undone by the circumstances of the discussion.

What were the 'circumstances of the discussion' that led the group to pursue such a disastrous course of action? After reading Schlesinger's account, social psychologist Irving Janis introduced the term **groupthink** to describe the phenomenon in which members of a group are led to suppress their own dissent in the interests of group consensus (Janis, 1982). After analyzing several other foreign policy decisions, Janis set forth a broad theory to describe the causes and consequences of groupthink.

Groupthink, according to Janis's theory, is caused by (1) a cohesive group of decision-makers, (2) isolation of the group from outside influences, (3) no systematic procedures for considering both the pros and cons of different courses of action, (4) a directive leader who explicitly favors a particular course of action, and (5) high stress, often due to an external threat, recent failures, moral dilemmas, and an apparent lack of viable alternatives. The theory suggests that these conditions foster a strong desire to achieve and maintain group consensus and avoid rocking the boat by dissenting.

Janis argued that the consequences or symptoms of groupthink include (1) shared illusions of invulnerability, morality, and unanimity, (2) direct pressure on dissenters, (3) self-censorship (as Schlesinger's account notes), (4) collective rationalization of a decision rather than realistic examination of its strengths and weaknesses, and (5) self-appointed mind guards, group members who actively attempt to prevent the group from considering information that would challenge the effectiveness or morality of its decisions. For example, the attorney general (President Kennedy's brother Robert) privately warned Schlesinger, 'The President has made his mind up. Don't push it any further.' The secretary of state also withheld information that had been provided by intelligence experts who warned against an invasion of Cuba (Janis, 1982). Janis proposed that these symptoms of groupthink combine to produce damaging flaws in the decision-making process – like incomplete information search and failure to develop contingency plans – which in turn lead to bad decisions.

Janis's theory of groupthink has been extremely influential within social psychology, across the social sciences, and within the culture at large (Turner & Pratkanis, 1998b). Yet it has also received sharp criticism (such as Fuller & Aldag, 1998). First, it is based more on historical analysis of select cases than on laboratory experimentation. Plus, the few dozen experiments that have tested the theory have produced only mixed and limited support. As just one example, Janis's claim that cohesive groups are most likely to succumb to groupthink has not stood up to empirical test. Cohesive groups may, in fact, provide a sense of psychological safety, which has been shown to improve group learning and performance (Nembhard & Edmondson, 2006). One later reformulation of the theory, supported by experimental data, argues that group cohesion yields poor decisions only when combined with threats to the group's positive image of itself. Faced with such threats, group members narrow their focus of attention to the goal of protecting and maintaining their positive group identity, a focus that often comes at the cost of effective decision-making (Turner & Pratkanis, 1998a).

Another reformulation of the theory states that the presence or absence of groupthink depends on the specific content of a group's social norms. Recall that social norms are implicit or explicit rules for acceptable behavior and beliefs. In some cases, group norms favor maintaining consensus, and in these cases, the adverse effects of groupthink should take hold, resulting in poor-quality decisions. In other cases, group norms favor critical thinking, and in these cases, group discussion should actually improve decision quality. An experiment tested these ideas (Postmes *et al.,* 2001). In

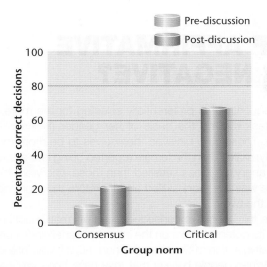

FIGURE 17.8 Group Norms and the Effectiveness of Group Decisions. *Group norms can influence the quality of group decisions. In this experiment, the decisions made by groups with norms for consensus seeking did not benefit from group discussion, whereas those with norms for critical thinking did.*

it, the researchers manipulated group norms by randomly assigning several groups (of four college students each) to engage either in a task that fostered a norm of consensus seeking (making a poster together) or in a task that fostered a norm of critical thinking (discussing an unpopular policy proposal). Next, all groups participated in an unrelated group decision task. The researchers assessed the quality of decisions both before and after the group discussion. Figure 17.8 portrays the results. Inspection of Figure 17.8 shows that when the group norm favored consensus, group discussion did little to improve decision quality, yet when the group norm favored critical thinking, group discussion improved decision quality dramatically. You might notice that this reformulation of groupthink echoes the reformulation of deindividuation described earlier: in both cases, situation-specific social norms guide behavior more than more general features of the group, like group cohesion or personal anonymity.

This study on group norms spotlights one way to minimize the damaging effects of groupthink: fostering norms for critical thinking – as a university education intends – should produce better group decisions. Other ways to improve group decisions include providing groups with trained facilitators who encourage a full sharing of ideas and alternating private idea-generating sessions with group sessions. Another beneficial strategy is to make the group a heterogeneous mix of people. A diverse group is more likely than a homogeneous group to generate a wide range of ideas (Paulus, 1998). Diversity within groups has other benefits as well. Surveys of university students in the USA have found that students of all

ethnic backgrounds – European American, African American, Asian American and Hispanic American – reach higher levels of intellectual engagement and ability when their classrooms reflect ethnic diversity and when they interact informally with diverse peers outside of class. In addition, ethnic diversity on campus fosters perspective-taking and other skills that aid democracy (Gurin *et al.*, 2004). Yet despite the evidence that ethnic diversity produces better individual and group outcomes, the value of affirmative action policies continues to be hotly debated. Two social psychological sides of this debate are featured in the Seeing Both Sides section at the end of this chapter. Many of the ideas raised within these essays – like how we decide what caused our own or someone else's success and the self-fulfilling nature of prejudicial stereotypes – will be addressed further in Chapter 18, our second in this two-chapter series on social psychology.

INTERIM SUMMARY

⊃ Institutions have norms that strongly govern the behavior of people who occupy critical roles within the institution. An example of how institutional norms shape group interactions is provided by the Stanford Prison Experiment, in which ordinary young men were randomly assigned roles of 'prisoner' and 'guard' in a simulated prison.

⊃ When groups make decisions, they often display group polarization: the group decision is in the same direction but is more extreme than the average of the group members' initial positions. This is not just public conformity; group members' private attitudes typically shift in response to the group discussion as well.

⊃ The group polarization effect is due in part to informational social influence, in which group members learn new information and hear novel arguments that are relevant to the decision under discussion. Group polarization is also produced by normative social influence, in which people compare their own initial views with the norms of the group. They may then adjust their position to conform to that of the majority.

⊃ An analysis of disastrous foreign policy decisions led to a proposal that cohesive groups of decision-makers can fall into the trap of groupthink, in which members of the group suppress their own dissenting opinions in the interest of group consensus. Later research suggests that group cohesion is not so much the problem, but rather threats to the group's positive identity and group norms of consensus seeking. Evidence suggests that group outcomes can be improved by fostering norms of critical thinking and promoting group diversity.

SEEING BOTH SIDES

ARE THE EFFECTS OF AFFIRMATIVE ACTION POSITIVE OR NEGATIVE?

NEGATIVE ASPECTS OF AFFIRMATIVE ACTION

Madeline E. Heilman, New York University

Most people would say that rewards should be given according to merit. What happens, then, when people get rewarded not because of their accomplishments but because of who they are or what group they belong to? Many people, perhaps including yourself, react negatively. This is the heart of the affirmative action dilemma. While created to ensure non-discriminatory treatment of women and minorities, affirmative action has come to be seen as little more than preferential selection and treatment without regard to merit (Haynes & Heilman, 2004; Haynes, in press). This, of course, may not depict reality, but it is this perception of affirmative action that is so problematic. There are a number of detrimental consequences.

First, affirmative action (sometimes referred to as 'positive discrimination' in the UK) can stigmatize its intended beneficiaries, causing inferences of incompetence. If you believe that someone has been the beneficiary of preferential selection based on non-merit criteria, then you are likely to 'discount' that individual's qualifications. In fact, you are likely to make the assumption that this person would not have been selected without the help of affirmative action. There has been research linking affirmative action with incompetence inferences (Garcia *et al.,* 1981; Heilman *et al.,* 1992). It has been conducted in the laboratory, where people review employee records, and in the field, where people are asked to evaluate co-workers in their work units. Inferences of incompetence have been found whether the target beneficiary is a woman or a member of a racial minority, and whether the research participants are male or female, or students or working people (Heilman *et al.,* 1997). These inferences of incompetence have been found even when affirmative action is not explicitly indicated, but is assumed, such as when women or blacks have been selected as part of a 'diversity initiative' (Heilman & Welle, 2006). In fact, affirmative action often is assumed – especially when the selection of a woman or minority group member is unusual – and people who have not even benefited from affirmative action are nonetheless victimized by stigmatization (Heilman & Blader, 2001).

A second negative consequence of affirmative action concerns non-beneficiaries. When women and minorities are believed to be preferentially selected, those who traditionally would have been selected for jobs often feel they are really the more deserving, and consequently, they feel unfairly bypassed (Nacoste, 1990). This has been suggested as a major reason for the 'backlash' against affirmative action.

Evidence indicates that there are indeed unfortunate by-products of feeling unfairly bypassed by affirmative action. In one study, male participants were paired with a female who subsequently was preferentially selected for the more desirable task role on the basis of her gender (Heilman *et al.,* 1996). Those who believed themselves to be more (or even equally) skilled than the female reported being less motivated, more angry, and less satisfied than those who were told the female was the more skilled and therefore the more deserving of the two.

The third negative consequence of affirmative action concerns its potential effect on the intended beneficiary. Ironically, affirmative action may sometimes hurt those it was intended to help. When people believe that they have been preferentially selected on the basis of irrelevant criteria there can be a chilling effect on self-view. A series of laboratory experiments in which participants were selected for a desired task role (leader) either on the basis of merit or preferentially on the basis of their gender found strong support for the idea that preferential selection can trigger negative self-regard. In repeated studies, women, but not men, who were preferentially selected were found to rate their performance more negatively, view themselves as more deficient in leadership ability, be more eager to relinquish their desirable leadership role, and shy away from demanding and challenging tasks (see Heilman & Haynes, 2006 for a review of these studies). There is also evidence that the negative self-view prompted by preferential selection can adversely affect task performance, as is demonstrated in research involving problem-solving (Brown *et al.,* 2000). Lastly, intended beneficiaries of affirmative action are burdened with the expectation that others have stigmatized them as incompetent, and this can affect their willingness to take on challenges that involve the risk of failure, but nonetheless are essential for their career progress (Heilman & Alcott, 2001). Thus it is no surprise that the perception of affirmative action status at college entry was found to affect the first year performance of Black and Latino students who were concerned about fulfilling stereotypes (van Laar *et al.,* 2008). Given these consequences, it appears that affirmative action, as it currently is understood, can undermine its own objectives. The stigma associated with affirmative action is apt to fuel rather than discredit stereotypic thinking and prejudiced attitudes. Depriving individuals of the satisfaction and pride that comes from knowing that they have achieved something on their own merits can be corrosive, decreasing self-efficacy and fostering self-views of inferiority. It can also create anxieties about fulfilling others' negative expectations, detrimentally affecting performance. And the frustration resulting from feeling unfairly bypassed for employment opportunities because one does not fit into the correct demographic niche can aggravate workplace tensions and intergroup hostilities. So, paradoxically, despite its success in expanding employment opportunities for women and minorities, affirmative action may contribute to the very conditions that gave rise to the problems it was designed to remedy.

ARE THE EFFECTS OF AFFIRMATIVE ACTION POSITIVE OR NEGATIVE?

THE BENEFITS OF AFFIRMATIVE ACTION

Faye J. Crosby, University of California, Santa Cruz

Few Americans understand how affirmative action operates (Crosby *et al.,* in press). According to the American Psychological Association (APA): 'Affirmative action occurs when an organization expends energy to make sure there is no discrimination in employment or education and, instead, equal opportunity exists' (APA, 1995, p. 5). Affirmative action goes beyond reactive policies that passively endorse justice but wait until a conflict has erupted before enacting corrective measures.

Affirmative action law, in the USA, began in earnest for businesses in 1965, applying to all US government agencies and most organizations that contract work with the federal government. Today one in five employed Americans works for an affirmative action employer. Using well-established methods for making their calculations, affirmative action employers monitor themselves to make sure they employ qualified people from the 'targeted classes' in proportion to their availability.

To see how the system works in the USA, think about your professors as employees of your school. Imagine that 10 per cent of the social science professors in your school are women (utilization 10 per cent) and that 30 per cent of PhDs in the social sciences are women (so that availability is 30 per cent). Detected problems can be corrected using flexible goals (not rigid quotas) and realistic timetables.

Support for affirmative action in US employment is very strong among business leaders. During a set of US Supreme Court cases in 2003, leaders from major corporations submitted a brief in favor of affirmative action (Smith & Crosby, 2008). Their support derived from the fact that the policy has assured business profits while increasing diversity.

Affirmative action remains much debated in educational contexts. Why, people ask, should an applicant with lower scores be admitted to school just because he, or she, is an ethnic minority? Isn't affirmative action just racial profiling in reverse?

While such criticisms of race-sensitive educational policies seem reasonable, they are based on a set of false assumptions. To argue that we should accord rewards strictly according to a set of scores is to assume that the scores are themselves unbiased. In fact, the admissions criteria often privilege some groups over others in subtle ways.

Consider admission to the University of California. One criterion for admissions is the applicant's high school grade point average (GPA) with extra points given to Advanced Placement courses. Thus, an 'A' in a regular course gives the applicant a score of 4, while an 'A' in an AP course gives the applicant a score of 5, and so on. In-depth study has shown how this reasonable-sounding policy gives an undeserved boost to white applicants. High schools serving white neighborhoods offer many more AP courses than do high schools that serve ethnic minority students. Yet, surprisingly, the GPA is equally predictive of college grades when the GPA is calculated without granting the bump as when the GPA is calculated with the bump. From the point of view of predicting who will succeed at the University of California, there is absolutely no reason to give extra points for AP courses. The AP-bump is only one of several practices that have been found to disadvantage minority applicants in non-obvious ways (Crosby *et al.,* 2003).

Some critics argue that affirmative action makes students of color feel stigmatized and irritates whites (Steele, 1991). Nobody likes to be told that he or she is advancing through unjustified preferential treatment, rather than merit (Heilman, 1994). However, a large number of studies have now shown that direct beneficiaries of affirmative action feel no stigma when they are given positive feedback about their performance (Iyer, 2008) or take pride in their group identity. Similarly, research shows that whites generally enjoy working or studying with people from diverse backgrounds who would have been excluded had it not been for affirmative action (Crosby, 2004).

Nor does affirmative action set students of color up for failure, as some have argued (Crosby *et al.,* 2006). A landmark study looked at long-term outcomes for hundreds of black students who had been admitted through affirmative action to 24 elite US colleges in 1951, 1976, and 1989. The black students graduated from school and obtained advanced degrees at rates comparable to white students. And even more than white alumni/ae, black graduates became civic leaders – giving back to the society that had nurtured them (Bowen & Bok, 1998). A provocative study of law-school admissions (Sander, 2004) has challenged the conclusions of Bowen and Bok, but aspects of that study remain contested (Gills *et al.,* 2007). Further studies have shown that white students benefit intellectually from being in diverse college settings (Gurin, 2004).

CRITICAL THINKING QUESTIONS

1 How are institutional norms, like those that operated in the Stanford Prison Experiment, communicated to new institutional members? What roles might informational and normative social influence and pluralistic ignorance play in the process of getting new members to conform to institutional norms?

2 Discuss how informational and normative social influence might produce group polarization in a jury's deliberations. How might groupthink operate to affect such deliberations? Can you think of a specific trial in which some of these phenomena appear to have been present?

RECAP: SOCIAL PSYCHOLOGICAL VIEWS OF THE SEEMINGLY INEXPLICABLE

We opened this chapter with several chilling examples – drawn both from recent world events and from history – that portray seemingly inexplicable and horrifying human behavior. How does a hijacker fly a plane into a world-famous skyscraper, killing himself, his passengers, and the thousands of people working in and visiting that building? How does a religious follower decide to drink lethal poison for 'the Cause'? How does a military official orchestrate and oversee the deaths of millions of innocent people?

Although we may uncover some clues about the origins of these puzzling actions by looking to the character or personality traits of the people involved, one of the foremost lessons of social psychology is that stopping our inquiry at this level is a mistake, one that goes by the name of the fundamental attribution error. To build a more complete understanding of any form of human social behavior – from the extraordinary to the everyday – we need to also search for clues within situational forces. Better yet, we need to look at the complex interplay between people's identities, goals, and desires and the ever-shifting situational landscapes they inhabit.

There is no question that social influence and strong situations can shape people's behavior in surprising and sometimes alarming ways. As you have seen, social psychologists dissect situations to uncover the particular tools of social influence at work. These tools include, among others, situation-specific social norms, pluralistic ignorance, informational and normative social influence, salient role models, internalized ideologies, self-justification, and group polarization. Knowing how these and other social psychological concepts operate can help explain behavior that at first seems inexplicable. Many human actions may in fact be inexplicable from the exclusive perspective of personality psychology, but social psychology illuminates a different vantage point altogether.

In Chapter 18, our second in this two-chapter series on social psychology, we take a closer look at the subjective inner workings of people as they make sense of the social world around them. There you will be introduced to the topics and concepts of social cognition.

CRITICAL THINKING QUESTIONS

1 Now that you are acquainted with several cutting types of social influence that have been used to explain people's behavior from a social psychological perspective, what sorts of clues about particular situations would you look for to explain extreme behavior, like the latest activities of suicide terrorists?

2 Think of an example from your own experience when, while trying to explain what caused an acquaintance to behave in a particular way, you may have committed the fundamental attribution error. What was your initial explanation based on personality or character? What is a possible explanation that makes reference to situational influences?

CHAPTER SUMMARY

1 One of the foremost lessons within social psychology is that situational forces have tremendous power to shape human behavior. A related lesson within social psychology is that these powerful situational forces are often invisible, and we mistakenly make sense of people's behavior by referring to their personality or character. This mistake is so common that social psychologists call it the fundamental attribution error.

2 Both humans and animals respond more quickly when in the presence of other members of their species. This social facilitation occurs whether the others are performing the same task (coactors) or simply watching (an audience). The presence of others appears to narrow people's attention. This facilitates the correct performance of simple responses but hinders the performance of complex ones. For humans, cognitive factors such as concern with evaluation also play a role.

3 The uninhibited aggressive behavior sometimes shown by mobs and crowds may be the result of a state of deindividuation, in which individuals feel that they have lost their personal identities and merged into the group. Both anonymity and group size contribute to deindividuation. A consequence of deindividuation is an increased sensitivity to situation-specific social norms linked with the group. This can increase aggression when the group's norms are aggressive but reduce aggression when the group norms are benign.

4 A bystander to an emergency is generally less likely to intervene or help if in a group than if alone. Two major factors that deter intervention are defining the situation and diffusion of responsibility. By attempting to appear calm, bystanders may define the situation for one another as a non-emergency, thereby producing a state of pluralistic ignorance. The presence of other people also diffuses responsibility so that no one person feels the necessity to act. Bystanders are more likely to intervene when these factors are minimized, particularly if at least one person begins to help.

5 In a series of classic studies on conformity, Solomon Asch found that a unanimous group exerts strong pressure on an individual to conform to the group's judgments – even when those judgments are clearly wrong. Much less conformity is observed if even one person dissents from the group.

6 A minority within a larger group can move the majority toward its point of view if it maintains a consistent dissenting position without appearing to be rigid, dogmatic, or arrogant. Minorities sometimes obtain private attitude change from majority members even when they fail to obtain public conformity.

7 In a series of classic studies on obedience, Stanley Milgram demonstrated that ordinary people would obey an experimenter's order to deliver strong electric shocks to an innocent victim. Factors conspiring to produce the high obedience rates include surveillance by the experimenter, buffers that distance the person from the consequences of his or her acts, the emerging properties of situations, and the legitimating role of science, which leads people to abandon their autonomy to the experimenter.

8 One way that people come to internalize attitudes and beliefs that are consistent with their actions is through the processes of self-justification. Cognitive dissonance theory suggests that when people's behavior conflicts with their attitudes, it creates an uncomfortable tension that motivates them to change their attitudes to be more in line with their actions. Self-perception theory challenged this view by stating that inner turmoil does not necessarily occur. To the extent that internal cues are weak, ambiguous, or uninterpretable, people may simply infer their attitudes from their past behavior. Recent experiments with amnesiacs and monkeys call into question whether complex reasoning is necessary for self-justification processes to unfold.

9 In the process of identification, we obey the norms and adopt the beliefs, attitudes, and behaviors of groups that we respect and admire. We use such reference groups to evaluate and regulate our opinions and actions. A reference group can regulate our attitudes and behavior by administering social rewards and punishments or providing a frame of reference, a ready-made interpretation of events and social issues.

10 Most people identify with more than one reference group, which can lead to conflicting pressures on beliefs, attitudes, and behaviors. University students frequently move away from the views of their family reference group toward their new university reference group. These new views are usually sustained in later life because (1) they become internalized, and (2) after university we tend to select new reference groups that share our views.

11 When groups make decisions, they often display group polarization: the group decision is in the same direction but is more extreme than the average of the group members' initial positions. This is not just public conformity; group members' private attitudes typically shift in response to the group discussion as well. The effect is due in part to informational social influence, in which group members learn new information and hear novel arguments that are relevant to the decision under discussion. Group polarization is also produced by normative social influence, in which people compare their own initial views with the norms of the group. They may then adjust their position to conform to that of the majority.

12 An analysis of disastrous foreign policy decisions led to a proposal that cohesive groups of decision-makers can fall into the trap of groupthink, in which members of the group suppress their own dissenting opinions in the interest of group consensus. Later research suggests that group cohesion is not so much the problem but rather threats to the group's positive identity and group norms of consensus seeking. Evidence suggests that group outcomes can be improved by fostering norms of critical thinking and promoting group diversity.

CORE CONCEPTS

fundamental attribution error	diffusion of responsibility	cognitive dissonance theory
social psychology	compliance	rationalization
coaction	informational social influence	self-perception theory
social facilitation	normative social influence	overjustification effect
social inhibition	minority influence	identification
Stroop interference	implicit leniency contract	reference groups
deindividuation	ideology	institutional norms
social norms	debriefing	group polarization effect
bystander effect	internalization	groupthink
pluralistic ignorance	foot-in-the-door technique	

DIGITAL SUPPORT RESOURCES

Students should use the unique access code included in the front of the book to access the digital support resources which accompany the new edition. These include:

- Multiple Choice Questions and Quizzes
- Critical Thinking Questions
- Practice Essay Questions

- Videos
- Glossary, Flashcards, and More

18 SOCIAL COGNITION

LEARNING OBJECTIVES
After reading this chapter you should be able to:

Explore how stereotypes influence impression formation.

Learn how self-fulfilling prophecies shape social behavior.

See how two different modes of thinking have been used to understand the fundamental attribution error.

Learn how and when persuasive communications change people's attitudes.

Look at the links between attitudes and behavior.

Cover five determinants of interpersonal attraction.

Learn multiple perspectives on love and mating.

Compare System 1 and System 2 effects on social cognition, and give examples of each.

Explain the concept of stereotype threat.

Describe the continuum model of impression formation and explain when and how people individuate others.

Describe the elaboration likelihood model and provide examples of both the central and peripheral routes to persuasion.

List the conditions under which attitudes are most likely to predict behavior.

Use social psychological principles to increase the odds of making a new friend.

Describe evolutionary perspectives on mate selection.

People think about – and judge – other people all the time. For instance, when engaged in casual people-watching at your university, you might surmise that one cluster of people is mostly athletes, another is mostly musicians, and still another an assortment of the most studious types. Another person reminds you of your best friend from school, and you smile. More chilling examples of social cognition can be drawn from recent history: Osama bin Laden said in a 2001 television interview that all Americans were enemies of Islam – or infidels – and so all Americans should be targeted for attack. And after the terrorist attacks on the USA of September 11, 2001, people around the world became more aware of their Arab-born neighbors, wondering if they, too, held the anti-Western attitudes of bin Laden and his followers.

Our thoughts and judgments about others don't simply help us pass the time. They have consequences. How you categorize your university classmates, for instance, determines whether and how you interact with them and whether they become friends or people you avoid. The generalization made by bin Laden and his followers that all Americans are the enemy led to the deaths of thousands of innocent civilians on September 11, 2001, and the subsequent suspicions about Arab-born neighbors has, in some instances, fueled additional prejudice and racially motivated hate crimes.

Recall that social psychology concerns the ways that people's behavior and mental processes are shaped by the real or imagined presence of others. In Chapter 17, we saw one of the foremost lessons of social psychology: that social situations – like the presence of others, unanimous majorities, requests from authorities, social norms, and group interactions – can have enormous power to influence people's behavior, thoughts, and feelings, power that often goes unrecognized. In this chapter,

CHAPTER OUTLINE

IMPRESSION FORMATION
Stereotypes
Individuation
Attributions

CUTTING EDGE RESEARCH:
EMBODIED SOCIAL COGNITION

ATTITUDES
Persuasive communication
Attitudes and behavior

INTERPERSONAL ATTRACTION
Liking and attraction
Loving and mating

SEEING BOTH SIDES: SHOULD WE
TRUST AUTOMATIC THINKING?

RECAP: A TALE OF TWO MODES
OF SOCIAL COGNITION

we will encounter another core lesson of social psychology: that to more fully understand people's social behavior, we need to 'get inside their heads.' The study of **social cognition** does just that. It examines people's subjective interpretations of their social experiences, as well as their modes of thinking about the social world.

As social psychologists have peered inside people's heads, looking for clues that might illuminate social behavior, they have found evidence for two different modes of thinking, one more automatic and unintentional, often very fast and outside conscious awareness, and another more controlled and deliberate, often proceeding more slowly and of which we are fully aware. This idea that there are two different modes of thinking should be familiar to you. In Chapter 11, we saw that people's cognitive appraisals – their interpretations of their current circumstances that trigger emotions – can occur at both unconscious and conscious levels. When appraisals are unconscious, people may feel emotions without knowing why. The same can happen for social cognition more generally. Sometimes thinking is quick, automatic and unintended, and at other times it is slow and under our conscious control. These two modes of thinking are so fundamental that psychologists refer to them in more generic terms, as System 1 and System 2, respectively (Stanovich & West, 2001, see also Kahneman, 2011). **System 1** refers to the quick and automatic mode of thinking, like snap judgments based on prior beliefs, whereas **System 2** refers to the slower and deliberate mode of thinking, like conclusions formed through logical reasoning. Neither mode of thinking is necessarily better or worse than the other. Indeed, the Seeing Both Sides feature at the close of this chapter presents a current debate about the value of System 1. Still, the cleaving of thinking styles into these two modes has been especially valuable both because they are known to be supported by different brain regions (Goel & Dolan, 2003; Houde *et al.*, 2000) and because whether thinking is automatic or controlled turns out to influence how and when the contents of mind influence social behavior and social reactions (Chaiken & Trope, 1999). We will see how these two different modes of thinking work as we consider the processes of impression formation, attitudes, and interpersonal attraction in turn.

IMPRESSION FORMATION

When you come across someone new, how do you come to know him or her? How do you form impressions of others? Does the color or apparent age of their skin matter? Their body size and shape? In other words, do your impressions of new people depend on their ethnicity, age, and gender? How quickly and how accurately can you assess their intelligence or their personality? And do your ulterior motives matter? That is, does it matter whether you simply pass them in the street or whether you are looking for someone to share an apartment? Or whether you expect to collaborate with them on an important project? These and other questions guide our discussion of impression formation.

Stereotypes

Like many others, social psychologists are invested in social justice – fair treatment for all people. This is why considerable energy within the study of social cognition is devoted to the study of stereotypes. If we can understand why, when, and how stereotypes operate, social psychologists argue, we can be better prepared to limit their adverse effects and treat people more fairly.

Several decades of research on stereotypes tell us that, whether we like it or not, our initial impressions of others can be biased by our pre-existing expectations. As we saw in previous chapters, this is true of perception more generally. Whenever we perceive any object or event, we implicitly categorize it, comparing the incoming information with our memories of previous encounters with similar objects and events. In earlier chapters, we saw that memories are not usually photograph-like reproductions of the original stimuli but simplified reconstructions of our original perceptions. As noted in Chapter 8, such representations or memory structures are called **schemas**; they are organized beliefs and knowledge about people, objects, events, and situations. The process of searching in memory for the schema that is most consistent with the incoming data is called **schematic processing**, or top-down thinking. Schemas and schematic processing permit us to organize and process enormous and potentially overwhelming amounts of information very efficiently. Instead of having to perceive and remember all the details of each new object or event, we can simply note that it is like one of our pre-existing schemas and encode or remember only its most prominent features. For instance, schematic processing is what allows us to readily categorize consumables as either food or drink and then put one on a plate and the other in a glass.

As with objects and events, we also use schemas and schematic processing in our encounters with people. For example, within about 100 milliseconds we categorize people into groups based on salient physical attributes – like race, gender, or age – or by their relation to our own social identity – as in 'us versus them' (Ito & Urland, 2003). Schemas can also be more narrowly defined: when someone tells you that you are about to meet someone who is outgoing, you retrieve your 'extrovert' schema in anticipation of the coming encounter. The extrovert schema is a set of interrelated traits such as sociability, warmth, and possibly loudness and impulsiveness. As mentioned in Chapter 8, **stereotypes** are schemas for classes or subtypes of people. The stereotype of an extrovert, the fan of a rival soccer team, or a young black man is a mini-theory about what particular traits or behaviors go with certain other traits or behaviors. We focus on stereotypes in this section because they are a kind of person schema that has far-reaching consequences for impression formation. You should keep in mind, though, that in addition to schemas for classes of people, we also have schemas for particular individuals, such as the president of the USA or our parents. And, as discussed in Chapter 13, we also have a **self-schema** or schema about ourselves – a set of organized self-concepts stored in memory (Markus, 1977). When you see a job advertisement for a peer counselor, for instance, you can evaluate the match between your counselor schema and your self-schema to decide whether you should apply for the job.

Automatic stereotype activation

The associations conveyed within stereotypes – for example, that young black males are hostile, that women are emotional, or that old people are slow – can become overlearned and automatic. We saw in Chapter 6 that, through repeated practice, driving a car becomes so habitual and automatic that we scarcely need to devote any conscious attention to it. A similar process happens with repeated exposure to stereotypes about people: they, too, can become habitual and automatic, operating outside conscious awareness.

Experiments that demonstrate the automaticity of stereotypes rely on priming techniques. You will recall from Chapter 8 that **priming** refers to the incidental activation of schemas by situational contexts. Beyond effects on memory, we saw in Chapter 17 that priming can also influence social behavior:

simply exposing people to words like *adhere*, *comply*, and *conform* increased the likelihood that they would later conform to a unanimous majority.

Priming can also activate stereotypes automatically, outside conscious awareness. In one experiment, university students were asked to imagine a typical professor and list this person's behaviors, lifestyle, and appearance. They did this for either 2 minutes or 9 minutes. Other participants were not primed at all, but instead started on the next task right away. The next task, described as an unrelated pilot study, provided the dependent measure. It was a difficult general knowledge test, based on questions drawn from the popular game *Trivial Pursuit*. The longer participants had visualized the typical professor, the better they performed on the test! Priming the professor stereotype – which includes the idea that professors are people who are intelligent – influenced the test performance of students at a non-conscious level. A second experiment primed the stereotype of a 'soccer hooligan' for either 2 or 9 minutes. Results showed that the longer students pondered the typical soccer hooligan – which includes the attribute 'stupid' – the worse they scored on the test of general knowledge. We know that the effect occurred at a non-conscious level because the students were completely unaware of the connection between the visualization task that primed the stereotypes and the test of their effects (Dijksterhuis & van Knippenberg, 1998).

The connection between stereotype activation and stereotypic behavior is so reliable that simple physical actions can also activate stereotypic thinking. In one experiment, university students subtly induced to move slowly were more likely to apply stereotypes about the elderly, and those subtly induced to move in a portly manner were more likely to apply stereotypes about overweight people, whereas those who moved in an ordinary way didn't apply either stereotype (Mussweiler, 2006).

One major source of primed stereotypes is the visual media – television, movies, billboards, video games, and the like. Exposure to these stereotypes can be damaging. By now you've come to recognize that the people you see in the visual mass media are hardly representative of people in the real world. People on television, for instance, are younger, slimmer, and more attractive than people you come across in your hometown. Portrayals of women are especially stereotyped. Many times women are portrayed simply as sex objects valued only for their physical appearance. Although exposure to media stereotypes of women may seem harmless, it does damage. In Chapter 10, we saw how such media promote eating disorders in girls and women. More generally, people who watch a lot of television endorse more sexist attitudes toward women (Gerbner *et al.*, 1986). But that's simply a correlation. Maybe television does not cause sexism. An experiment that manipulated television exposure provides the necessary causal evidence. The researchers used television advertisements (drawn from regular US prime-time broadcasts) to prime the stereotype of women as sex objects in one group of men. A separate control group watched other, non-sexist TV ads. All the men were later asked to interview a woman for a job as a research assistant. Compared with men in the control group, those primed by TV ads to think of women in stereotypical terms chose more sexist questions when interviewing the female job candidate and behaved in a more sexualized manner toward her (Rudman & Borgida, 1995).

Stereotypes can also be activated through non-conscious priming. We saw in Chapter 11 that very brief, subliminal exposure (less than 30 milliseconds) to pictures of spiders and snakes can produce physiological arousal and aversive feelings, even though people cannot report having seen anything frightening. The same holds for stereotypes. In one experiment, participants (who were not African American) were shown photographs of young, male faces that were either Caucasian American or African American for less than 30 milliseconds, too fast for conscious awareness. These non-conscious, subliminal primes were embedded within a tedious computer task. The computer was rigged

Nonconscious exposure to photographs like these is sufficient to activate stereotypes and influence social behavior.

so that after participants had spent considerable time on the task, it produced an error message: 'F11 error: failure saving data.' It then informed participants that they would need to do the entire computer task over again. Hidden video cameras recorded participants' facial reactions to this news. Those primed with black faces reacted to the computer error with more hostility. Here, priming the young black male stereotype – which includes the idea that young black males are hostile – automatically generated hostile behavior in unsuspecting participants (Bargh *et al.*, 1996). In fact, people don't even have to personally endorse the stereotype to be affected by it: stereotypic behavior was activated equally so for those who scored high and low on questionnaire measures of racist attitudes (see also Devine, 1989; Fazio *et al.,* 1995).

So simply encountering a person can activate a stereotype as we categorize that person by ethnicity, age, or gender, or as 'us versus them.' But when we categorize others, do we also automatically evaluate them? Experiments suggest that we do. Evidence that automatically activated racial categories carry emotional evaluations comes from a series of studies in which black and white university students viewed faces of many ethnic backgrounds, including black and white faces. For black students, white faces represent an outgroup, whereas the reverse is true for white students. The faces were shown briefly (but at more than 300 milliseconds, visibly) and embedded within a word evaluation task in which participants were asked to indicate whether a given adjective (such as *attractive*, *likeable*, *annoying*, or *offensive*) was either 'good' or 'bad' and to make this judgment as quickly and accurately as possible. Participants made these judgments for dozens of words while the experimenters recorded their reaction times. The results of this study are shown in Figure 18.1. For white participants, viewing black faces sped

Many types of advertising can activate stereotypes of women and trigger sexist behavior.

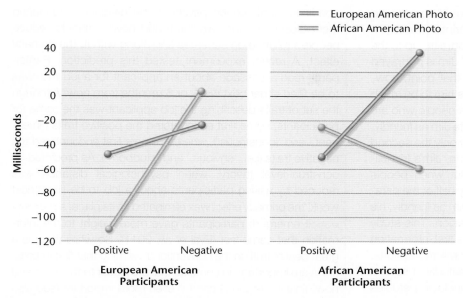

European American Photo
African American Photo

European American Participants

African American Participants

Milliseconds

Positive   Negative

Positive   Negative

FIGURE 18.1 Automatic Stereotype Activation. *These two graphs plot the mean response times for classifying positive and negative adjectives as good or bad when preceded by photos of African American and European American faces. Higher scores indicate faster responses. Notice that for European American participants, the difference in response times for the positive and negative words is greater when preceded by African American faces, with negative judgments made faster. The reverse pattern emerged for African American participants – their negative judgments were facilitated by viewing European American faces. These data indicate that classifying another person as in a racial 'out-group' automatically carries with it negative evaluations.*

responses to negative words. The opposite was true for black participants: viewing white faces sped responses to negative words (Fazio *et al.*, 1995). These findings suggest that when we categorize others as members of an out-group ('them' as opposed to 'us'), we simultaneously and automatically activate negative associations, which facilitates negative responses.

Corroborating evidence comes from a study that used brain imaging (see Chapter 2). Both black and white participants viewed photographs of unfamiliar black and white faces several times for 1 second each. Imaging data showed that initial exposure to all faces produced activation in the amygdala, an area of the brain that is involved in monitoring emotion-eliciting stimuli at a non-conscious level (see Chapter 11). On re-exposure to these same faces, amygdala activation lessened for in-group faces, whereas it remained high for out-group faces (Hart *et al.*, 2000). These data suggest that unfamiliar faces in general, regardless of racial category, are initially perceived as threatening. Over time, however, this threat response abates for those who are 'like us' but not for those who are 'not like us.'

Stereotypes and information processing

Research confirms that stereotypes, like schemas more generally, help us process information. For example, if people

are explicitly instructed to remember as much information as they can about a person, they actually remember less than if they are simply told to try to form an impression (Hamilton, 1979). This is because the instruction to form an impression induces them to search for relevant schemas or stereotypes that help them organize and recall material better.

Without stereotypes, then, we would be overwhelmed by the information that inundates us. If you had no way to organize or access your expectations about different types of people, you would be extraordinarily slow to form impressions of them. But the price we pay for the efficiency that stereotypes bring can be measured in terms of biases in our perceptions and memories of the information given and in the inferences we make. Consider, for example, the impression you form of Jim from the following observations of his behavior:

> **Jim left the house to get some stationery. He walked out into the sun-filled street with two of his friends, basking in the sun as he walked. Jim entered the stationery store, which was full of people. Jim talked with an acquaintance while he waited to catch the clerk's eye. On his way out, he stopped to chat with a school friend who was just coming into the store. Leaving the store, he walked toward the school. On his way he met the girl to whom he had been introduced the night before. They talked for a short while, and then Jim left for school. After school, Jim left the classroom alone. Leaving the school, he started on his long walk home. The street was brilliantly filled with sunshine. Jim walked down the street on the shady side. Coming down the street toward him, he saw the pretty girl whom he had met on the previous evening. Jim crossed the street and entered a candy store. The store was crowded with students, and he noticed a few familiar faces. Jim waited quietly until he caught the counterman's eye and then gave his order. Taking his drink, he sat down at a side table. When he had finished his drink, he went home.**

(Luchins, 1957, pp. 34–35)

What impression do you have of Jim? Do you think of him as friendly and outgoing or as shy and introverted? If you think of him as friendly, you agree with 78 per cent of people who read this description. But examine the description closely; it is actually composed of two very different portraits. Up to the sentence that begins 'After school, Jim left,' Jim is portrayed in several situations as fairly friendly. After that point, however, a nearly identical set of situations shows him to be much more of a loner. Whereas 95 per cent of the people who are shown only the first half of the description rate Jim as friendly, just 3 per cent of the people who are shown only the second half do so. Thus, in the combined description, Jim's friendliness dominates the overall impression. But when people read the same description with the unfriendly half of the paragraph appearing first, only 18 per cent rate Jim as friendly; his unfriendly behavior leaves the major impression. This study illustrates the **primacy effect**: in general, the first information we receive has the greater impact on our overall impressions.

The primacy effect has been found repeatedly in several kinds of studies of impression formation, including studies using real rather than hypothetical individuals (Jones, 1990). For example, people who watched a male student attempt to solve a series of difficult multiple-choice problems were asked to assess his general ability (Jones *et al.,* 1968). Although the student always solved exactly 15 of the 30 problems correctly, he was judged more capable if the successes came mostly at the beginning of the series than if they came near the end. Moreover, when asked to recall how many problems the student had solved, participants who had seen the 15 successes bunched at the beginning estimated an average of 21, but participants who had seen the successes at the end estimated an average of 13.

Although several factors contribute to the primacy effect, it appears to be primarily a consequence of schematic processing or top-down thinking. When we are first attempting to form our impressions of a person, we actively search in memory for the schemas or stereotypes that best match the incoming data. Within a few moments we make a preliminary decision: this person is extroverted, or this person is smart (or some such judgment). We then assimilate any further information to that judgment and dismiss discrepant information as not being representative of the person we have come to know. For example, when asked to reconcile the apparent contradictions in Jim's behavior, participants sometimes say that Jim is really friendly but was probably tired by the end of the day (Luchins, 1957). Our stereotype of extroverts, activated by Jim's initial behaviors, shapes our perception of all subsequent data about Jim. More generally, our subsequent perceptions become schema-driven and therefore relatively impervious to new data.

Supporting the role of schemas in the primacy effect, the **construal-level theory** of psychological distance suggests that greater psychological distance – created, for instance, by transcending your own 'here and now' in time or space – pulls for more abstract and generalized thinking, which is the hallmark of schemas (Trope & Liberman, 2010). If so, then

conditions that reduce psychological distance – rendering them closer to your own 'here and now' – should reduce people's reliance on schemas and along with it, the primacy effect. A recent experiment tested this prediction. Participants read a passage about an applicant for a job that was to be filled either next week or 6 months from now. Although the set of traits describing the job applicant was the same for participants, some first encountered the positive traits ('intelligent,' and 'industrious'), whereas others first encountered the negative traits (i.e., 'envious,' and 'stubborn'). As predicted by construal-level theory, when psychological distance was reduced by asking participants about a job to be filled 'next week' the primacy effect was eliminated. In its place, a **recency effect** emerged: participants gave more weight to the information that came last (Eyal *et al.,* 2011). So while there is a great deal of truth in the conventional warning that first impressions are important, in contexts that are closer to the 'here and now' final impressions can be even more important (see also Fredrickson, 2000b).

Stereotypes also help us make **inferences**, which means to make judgments that go beyond the information given. A classic study by Solomon Asch in 1946 illustrates this effect. To get a sense of the study, form an impression in your mind of Sam, someone described as 'intelligent, skillful, industrious, cold, determined, practical, and cautious.' Based on the impression you have now formed, do you think that Sam is generous? Could you ask him to lend you his car for the day? If you think not, you agree with the participants in Asch's original study: only 9 per cent inferred that a person was generous, given these traits. But what if Sam was described as 'intelligent, skillful, industrious, warm, determined, practical, and cautious'? Only one trait differs: *cold* is replaced by *warm*. Now would you think that Sam is generous? Probably so. A full 91 per cent of those in Asch's original study inferred generosity from the same trait constellation that included *warm* instead of *cold*. So although no information is given

The first information we receive has a greater impact on our overall impressions than later information. This is why people usually wear business suits to interview for a job.

about Sam's likely generosity, we can use our expectations or stereotypes about warm or cold people to go beyond what's given and make an inference. Studies like Asch's have also been done with real rather than hypothetical individuals. For instance, students told that an upcoming guest lecturer was 'rather cold' came to evaluate him quite negatively, whereas other students told that this same guest lecturer was 'rather warm' came to evaluate him quite favorably, even though they observed the same lecturer behaving in the same way (Kelley, 1950). See the Cutting Edge Research box for surprising new extensions of this warm vs. cold effect on personality inferences. The bottom line here is that advance reputations are hard to shake!

Stereotypes about gender and race have also been found to shape our interpretations of other people's behavior. Suppose you learn that someone performed exceptionally well on a math test. Studies show that if that someone is male, most people think he's smart, whereas if she's female, they think she got lucky by studying the right material (Deaux, 1984; Swim et al., 2010). Likewise, when whites hear that a black man punched someone, they tend to conclude that he's aggressive, but if they learn that a white man punched someone, they tend to wonder what provoked him (Hewstone, 1990; Pettigrew, 1979). In these examples, we see that information consistent with a stereotype is taken as diagnostic of that person's underlying ability or personality, whereas information inconsistent with a stereotype is dismissed as not characteristic of them.

Similar evidence comes from the experiment, described earlier, in which one group of men was primed by viewing TV ads with stereotypic images of women. In a later word-recognition task (disguised as a separate study), primed men, compared with men who were not primed, were faster to recognize sexist words (like babe and bimbo) and slower to recognize non-sexist words (like mother and sister) (Rudman & Borgida, 1995). Simply through media exposure, these men were primed to see the world through the lens of the activated sexist stereotype.

The outcomes of stereotypic information processing can be deadly. In 1999, four New York City police officers ordered Amadou Diallo to stop because he matched the description of a crime suspect. When Diallo, an immigrant from Ghana, reached for his pocket, one of the police officers shouted 'Gun!' The rest opened fire. Only after the shooting stopped did it become clear that Diallo had simply reached for his wallet. Diallo's death raised public outrage and sharp criticism of racial bias. Like the tragic death of Kitty Genovese decades earlier (see Chapter 17), Diallo's death also sparked social psychologists into action. A series of clever laboratory experiments confirmed that split-second decisions are especially likely to be shaped by stereotypes. When participants facing a fast-paced computer task are asked to distinguish between images of guns and harmless objects (hand tools), they are more likely to falsely identify harmless objects as guns if those object are preceded by black faces rather than white faces. This split-second weapon bias is so reliable that it shows up even when people actively try to avoid showing any sort of racial bias (Payne, 2006).

To sum up, stereotypes (like top-down, schematic processing more generally) determine how we automatically perceive, recall, and interpret information about people. So, as we form impressions of others, we don't simply take in the available information about them and process it in a thoughtful, unbiased manner. Instead, we filter incoming information through our pre-existing stereotypes and motives and actively yet spontaneously construct our perceptions, memories, and inferences. Making matters worse, the effects of stereotypes on perception and thinking often remain invisible to us: we often take our constructions to be direct and unbiased representations of reality! In other words, we rarely see the role of stereotypes in shaping our interpretations but instead believe that we simply 'call it like it is.' You can begin to see how entrenched and persistent stereotypes can be: even if initially incorrect, people can come to believe that a stereotype is 'true' because they construct – and see – a world in which it is true.

Self-fulfilling stereotypes

Stereotypes can also be like omens – they can predict the future. But this is not because stereotypes are necessarily true. Rather, once activated, stereotypes can set in motion a chain of behavioral processes that serve to draw out from others behavior that confirms the initial stereotype, an effect called the **self-fulfilling prophecy** (Jussim, 1991; Rosenthal & Jacobson, 1968; Snyder et al., 1977). This works because stereotypes don't just reside in our heads. They leak out in our actions. To get a feel for this, suppose that women who attend university in a neighboring city have the reputation for being snobs. In actuality, most are quite friendly, but your sources tell you differently. How will you act toward a student from that university when you cross paths with her before a soccer game? Most likely you'll look away. Why should you bother to smile and say hello to a snob? And how will she act? Now that you've given her the cold shoulder, she'll probably do the same. And now that you see her cold, aloof manner, you'll take that as proof positive that she is a snob and fail to see your own role in producing this evidence! So your stereotype of women from that university, although initially wrongly applied to the woman you met, shaped your own behavior, which in turn shaped her behavior, which in turn provided behavioral confirmation for your initially erroneous stereotype. Beliefs have a way of becoming reality.

In a classic study illustrating this process, investigators first noted that white job interviewers displayed a less friendly manner when interviewing black job applicants than when interviewing white applicants. They hypothesized that this could cause black applicants to come off less well in the interviews. To test this hypothesis, they trained interviewers to reproduce both the less friendly and the more friendly interviewing styles. Applicants (all white) were then video-taped while being interviewed by an interviewer using one of these two styles. Judges who viewed the videotapes rated applicants who had been interviewed in a less friendly manner much lower on their interview performance compared with those who had been interviewed in the friendlier manner (Word *et al.,* 1974). The study thus confirmed the hypothesis that people who hold stereotypes can interact in ways that actually evoke the stereotyped behaviors that sustain their biased beliefs.

Self-fulfilling prophecies can occur completely outside conscious awareness. Earlier we saw that when people's stereotypes about blacks were primed through brief, sub-liminal exposure to young black male faces, they were more likely to act in a hostile manner. Is this hostile behavior potent enough to draw out hostility from others? Another experiment tested this possibility. The same priming proce-dure was used for one person in a pair before the two played a potentially frustrating game with each other. Repli-cating the first study, those who had been primed with black faces showed greater hostility than those primed with white faces. Plus, as the self-fulfilling prophecy predicts, the partners of those primed with black faces (who were *not* themselves primed) also showed greater hostility than those whose partners were primed with white faces. Moreover, the primed participants saw their partners as hostile but did not see their own role in drawing that hostility out (Chen & Bargh, 1997). These data suggest that the mere presence of a stereotyped person can activate stereotypes that soon become self-fulfilling.

Stereotypes that we hold about our own group can also be self-fulfilling. A classic experiment on this topic sheds light on racial differences on standardized tests of intelli-gence. When university students are primed with racial ste-reotypes – which include the idea that blacks are intellectu-ally inferior – black students perform worse than white students on difficult academic tests. But when no racial ste-reotype is activated, blacks perform equal to whites (Steele & Aronson, 1995). The same holds for the stereotype that women are bad at math: when the stereotype is activated, women perform worse than men on difficult math tests. When it is not activated, women perform equal to men (Spencer *et al.,* 1999). These experiments illustrate the self-fulfilling nature of stereotypes that can be applied to one's own group. The phenomenon is called **stereotype threat**, which refers to how the mere threat of being identified with a stereotype can raise an individual's anxiety level, which in turn degrades his or her performance (Steele, 1997). The effect is reliable and is attributed to the added mental load born by targets of stereotypes within testing situations who become highly motivated to disconfirm the negative stereo-type of their group (Jamieson & Harkins, 2012). That is, tar-gets of stereotypes experience undue uncertainty and stress, actively monitor their performance, and try to sup-press negative thoughts and feelings, processes that com-bine to reduce working memory capacity and derail test performance (Schmader, 2010). Fortunately, there's reason for hope. Simply learning about stereotype threat and dis-connecting societal stereotypes from one's own ability and test-taking experience can eliminate the effect altogether (Schmader, 2010).

Individuation

As we've seen, stereotypes can be activated automatically, simply by seeing someone's face. Plus, once activated, ste-reotypes can influence our thinking and behavior in ways that actually draw out stereotype-confirming behaviors from our-selves and from others. (For a review of the various cognitive and behavioral effects of stereotypes, see the Concept Review Table.) If the effects of stereotypes are so automatic and far-reaching, can we ever truly come to know another person accurately? In the 1960s, Martin Luther King Jr expressed a similar yearning to be free from the pernicious effects of stereotypes. In his famous speech entitled 'I Have a Dream,' King voiced his hope that black children might 'one day live in a nation where they will not be judged by the color of their skin, but by the content of their character.' Dr King was actually describing a process that social psychologists call **individuation**, which means assessing an individual's personal qualities on a person-by-person basis. Fortunately, Martin Luther King Jr's dream can come true: we can some-times override the effects of stereotypes and form more accurate and personalized impressions of others through individuation. But typically, this more accurate impression formation requires a more thoughtful and controlled mode of thinking.

CONCEPT REVIEW TABLE
SUMMARY OF THE EFFECTS OF STEREOTYPES

Cognitive effects

1. Automatic evaluation
2. Biased perceptions of incoming information
3. Biased memories
4. Biased inferences and interpretations

Behavioral effects

1. Automatic emotion expression
2. Automatic behavioral tendencies
3. Self-fulfilling prophecies

Triggers of individuation

When and how do we move beyond stereotyping to individuation? One influential model of impression formation, called the **continuum model**, describes the full continuum of processes from stereotyping to individuation (Fiske *et al.,* 1999). The model is described by the flow chart shown in Figure 18.2. You can see in this flow chart that the automatic stereotyping that we've discussed so far is the first psychological process set in motion when we first encounter a person (called 'initial categorization' in Figure 18.2). Within milliseconds of an initial encounter, we have already automatically and non-consciously categorized the person in terms of gender, ethnicity, and age. These categories are used first because they (1) apply to all people, (2) are available immediately and physically, even in suboptimal viewing conditions (Cloutier *et al.,* 2005), and (3) often have important cultural meanings relevant to our interaction goals. Whether we move beyond simple stereotyping depends on whether the person we've encountered has any personal relevance to us. If, for instance, you are deciding whether to share an apartment with this new person, you most certainly will devote more attention to forming your impression.

As Figure 18.2 shows, the first thing that we do once we move into this more thoughtful process of impression formation is try to confirm our initial categorization. Return to that potential housemate. You might want to know whether the young man you've just met is a 'typical 20-year-old guy.' Will he be interested in loud parties, fast cars, and frequent dates? Or is he more of a loner, truly engaged with his studies? You notice that his backpack is overflowing with texts for the most advanced courses, and he tells you that he spends most evenings at the library. So the available information suggests that the initial categorization won't do. Now you find another, narrower category for him: a hardworking student. This is called 'recategorization' in Figure 18.2. Because you are also engaged with your studies most evenings, you suspect that you'd be compatible housemates. You decide to share the apartment.

Over time, and as you learn more about your new housemate, you come to recognize that being a hardworking student is just one facet of his character. He also plays the saxophone, competes in triathlons, and has traveled extensively across South America. Only now do you

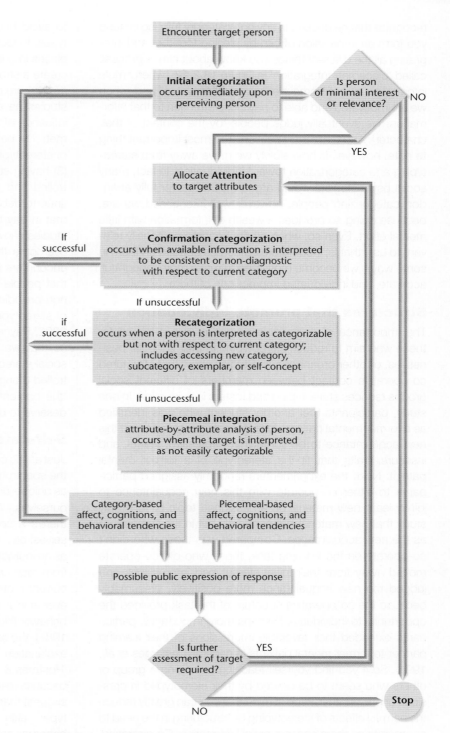

FIGURE 18.2 Impression Formation: From Stereotypes to Individuation.
This flow chart presents Fiske and Neuberg's continuum model of impression formation. It shows the continuum of impression formation processes ranging from stereotyping to individuation as a function of attention and interpretation. Here the most individuating stage is called 'piecemeal integration'. The information available about the person perceived and the perceivers' motivational goals determine how attention and interpretations combine to shape the process of impression formation.

recognize that he doesn't fit any one category fully, so instead you form an impression of him by piecing together and integrating all the different things you know about him, a process called 'piecemeal integration' in Figure 18.2. So, when ample information about someone becomes available, and when we are motivated and able to pay close attention to that information, we eventually judge people 'by the content of their character'. And that's individuation. The most important thing to note, however, is how slowly we move away from stereotyping and categorization toward individuation. In fact, many social psychologists would argue that we never fully abandon categorizing people, however well intentioned we are, because doing so provides a wealth of information with little mental effort. Even so, when others become personally relevant to us – that is, if our future outcomes depend on them in some way – we become motivated to make more thoughtful, accurate, and individuated impressions of them.

Structures that promote individuation

The importance of personal relevance carries a lesson for those who aim to reduce stereotyping in their schools, businesses, or other organizations. Studies show that structured co-operative contact between members of different social groups reduces stereotyping and fosters individuation. In one study, participants met another student who was identified as a former mental patient. At first, participants expected this new acquaintance to be somewhat depressed, fearful, and insecure, traits that fit the stereotype of a former mental patient. Next, the experimenters randomly assigned participants to either co-operate with this new acquaintance to jointly learn new material on an assigned topic or to simply study that new material independently but in the same room as the new acquaintance. Compared with those who didn't co-operate on the learning task, those who did co-operate moved away from their initial stereotyped impressions and judged the new acquaintance more positively, presumably because the co-operative structure of the task provided the opportunity to individuate. Perhaps more importantly, participants extended their favorable impressions of their learning partner to former mental patients in general (Desforges *et al*., 1991). So if you find yourself teaching or leading a group of others who seem to be divided by their stereotyped impressions of one another, keep in mind that you can greatly reduce the harmful effects of stereotyping by structuring in the need to co-operate or share consequential information. Co-operation, of course, has other benefits as well. It can also produce more successful individual and group outcomes (Aronson, 2004).

Controlling stereotypes

As we've seen, sometimes we are drawn toward the individuation end of the impression formation continuum because we are motivated to get to know other people personally and accurately and have ample time to do so. Other times, we may not so much be drawn to individuate as we are motivated to avoid being prejudiced by the biasing effects of stereotypes. In fact, simply knowing that stereotypes can produce biases in our judgments and actions (as you now know) can create a strong desire to override stereotypic responses and apply more egalitarian responses instead. Luckily, laboratory studies have shown that we can consciously override the influence of stereotypes, particularly if certain conditions are met: (1) being aware of the potential negative influence of stereotypes, (2) being motivated to reduce prejudice, and (3) having sufficient attentional resources to engage in controlled and deliberate thinking. Although researchers continue to debate how and how often such conditions can be met in day-to-day life (Bargh, 1999; Monteith *et al.,* 2009), studies show that certain people, through mental effort, can overcome the harmful effects of stereotypes, even in brief encounters (Bodenhausen *et al.,* 1999). Studies even show that people who are highly identified with the goal of being non-prejudiced can also overcome the automatic activation of stereotypes, like that shown in Figure 18.1 (Devine *et al.,* 2002; Payne, 2006). These findings are important. They tell us that we need not be slaves to automatically activated social stereotypes. Instead, with proper motivation and controlled thought, we can learn to treat people justly, based on 'the content of their character', a manner in which we all deserve to be treated.

Self-categorization

Just as the continuum model, depicted Figure 18.2, describes the spectrum from how we stereotype others to seeing them as unique individuals, there's also a spectrum of how we view ourselves. According to the **social identity approach**, there's a spectrum of ways in which we can identify ourselves: as a human being, as a member of a social group, or as an individual. Our identities can shift across this continuum from moment to moment, depending on the situation or our current motives. This is an important point, because whichever social identity is most salient tends to influence our behavior (Hornsey, 2008; Tajfel & Turner, 1986; Turner *et al*., 1987). We saw this effect back in Chapter 17, as a prominent explanation for how people behave when deindividuated (Postmes & Spears, 1998). It becomes relevant again now, because researchers working from a social identity approach suggest that we represent our social groups as mental prototypes, akin to stereotypes. As a particular group identity becomes salient, for instance, being a student at your university or a citizen of your country, your actions and expressed attitudes come to reflect the prototype you hold in mind about that group. Although identifying with a particular social group is often a source of self-esteem, it can also leave you open to negative feelings. For instance, people can feel collective guilt for the past moral shortcomings of groups that are important to them. Consider, for instance, how Germans, even those born after World War II, can feel collective guilt about the Holocaust or how Americans and Europeans alike can feel collective guilt about the enslavement of Africans. Such 'guilt by association' is a product of self-categorization and motivates efforts to compensate outgroup members for the wrongful treatment they experienced in the past (Wohl *et al.,* 2006).

Attributions

Another process through which we form impressions of others – even ourselves – involves understanding the causes of their behavior. Suppose, for example, that a famous athlete endorses a particular brand of athletic shoes on television. Why does he do it? Does he really like those shoes, or is he doing it for the money? You see a woman give a $5 donation to Amnesty International. Why? Is she altruistic? Was she being pressured? Did she need a tax write-off? Does she believe in the work of the organization?

Each of these cases creates an attribution problem. We witness some behavior and must decide to which of many possible causes the action should be attributed. **Attribution** refers to our intuitive attempts to infer the causes of behavior. It has long been a central topic in social psychology and continues to be today (Heider, 1958; Kammrath *et al.,* 2005; Kelley, 1967; Malle, 2011; Nussbaum *et al.,* 2003;).

The fundamental attribution error revisited

As the two preceding examples illustrate, one of the major attribution tasks we face is deciding whether an observed behavior reflects something about the person or something about the situation in which we observed the person. The former option is called an internal or **dispositional attribution**. We infer that something about the person is primarily responsible for the behavior (for instance, the athlete really loves those shoes). Here, *disposition* refers to a person's beliefs, attitudes, and personality characteristics. An alterna-

Is this woman giving money to the Royal British Legion's Poppy Appeal because she supports its work, because she feels pressured, or because she is generally altruistic?

tive choice is called an external or situational attribution. We infer that some external cause is primarily responsible for the behavior (for instance, money, social norms, threats). Although the simple distinction between dispositional and situational attributions has been criticized as being too simplistic (Kammrath *et al.,* 2005; Malle, 2011), this dichotomy has been one of the most influential within social psychology.

Fritz Heider, the founder of attribution theory, noted that an individual's behavior is so compelling to us that we take it as a face-value representation of a person and give insufficient weight to the circumstances surrounding it (1958). Research has confirmed Heider's observation. We underestimate the situational causes of behavior, jumping too easily to conclusions about the person's disposition. If we observe someone behaving aggressively, we too readily assume that he or she has an aggressive personality, rather than concluding that the situation might have provoked similar aggression in anyone. To put it another way, we have a schema of cause and effect for human behavior that gives too much weight to the person and too little to the situation. In Chapter 17, you learned one of the foremost lessons of social psychology: that situations are, in fact, powerful causes of people's social behavior. You also learned a corollary lesson: that in our everyday reasoning, we often overlook the causal power of situations. And you will recall that this corollary lesson has a name of its own: the fundamental attribution error. Formally stated, the **fundamental attribution error** occurs when we underestimate the situational influences on behavior and assume that some personal characteristic of the individual is responsible (Ross, 1977).

In the classic early studies that revealed this bias, participants read a debater's speech that either supported or attacked Cuban leader Fidel Castro. The participants were explicitly told that the debate coach had assigned each debater one side of the issue or the other; the debater had no choice as to which side to argue. Despite this knowledge, when asked to estimate the debater's actual attitude toward Castro, participants inferred a position close to the one argued in the debate. In other words, the participants made a dispositional attribution, even though situational forces were fully sufficient to account for the behavior (Jones & Harris, 1967). This effect is quite powerful. It occurs even if the presentations are deliberately designed to be drab and unenthusiastic and the speaker simply reads a transcribed version of the speech in a monotone and uses no gestures (Schneider & Miller, 1975). Even when the participants themselves designate which side of the issue a speaker is to argue, they still tend to see him or her as actually holding that opinion (Gilbert & Jones, 1986).

An experiment designed as a quiz game illustrates how both participants and observers make the same fundamental attribution error in the same setting. Pairs of university students were recruited to take part in a question-and-answer game testing general knowledge. One member of the pair was randomly assigned to be the questioner and to make up ten difficult questions to which he or she knew the answers (such as 'What is the world's largest glacier?'). The other participant acted as the contestant and attempted to answer the questions. When the contestant was unable to answer a question, the questioner gave the answer. In a re-enactment of the study, observers watched the contest. After the game, both participants and observers were asked to rate the level of general knowledge possessed by the questioner and the contestant, relative to that possessed by the 'average student.' Note that participants and observers all knew that the roles of questioner and contestant had been assigned randomly.

As Figure 18.3 shows, questioners judged both themselves and the contestant to be about average in level of general knowledge. But contestants rated the questioner as superior and themselves as inferior to the average student. They attributed the outcome of the game to their (and the questioner's) level of knowledge rather than taking into account the overwhelming situational advantage enjoyed by the questioner, who was able to decide which questions to ask and to omit any questions to which he or she did not know the answer. Observers, aware that the questioner could ask questions that neither they nor the contestant could answer, rated the questioner's level of knowledge even higher. In other words, both contestants and observers gave too much weight to disposition and

too little to the situation – the fundamental attribution error (Ross *et al.*, 1977).

Causal attributions, like other aspects of impression formation, have also been found to be governed by two different modes of thinking, one more automatic and unintentional, and another more controlled and deliberate. This turns out to influence how frequently the fundamental attribution error occurs. To understand why, it's helpful to break the attribution process down into stages. One framework divides the process of causal attribution into at least two parts. The first step is a dispositional inference (what trait does this action imply?), and the second is situational correction (what situational constraints might have caused that action?). Experiments suggest that the first step of dispositional inference is more automatic than the second step of situational correction (Gilbert & Malone, 1995). This suggests that we make the fundamental attribution error so often because it is an over-learned, automatic process that frequently occurs outside conscious awareness. Only when we have the cognitive resources to think deliberately and carefully do we correct our initial, automatic dispositional attributions with reference to plausible situational causes. Although it may seem encouraging that effortful thinking can override the fundamental attribution error, we need to recognize that most often, as we're forming our impressions of others, we are cognitively busy, thinking about many things at once, like planning our next move, anticipating the other's reaction, and managing the impression that others form of us. All this 'cognitive busyness' means that we will continue to commit the fundamental attribution error time and again (Gilbert & Malone, 1995).

Culture and attributions

For centuries, Western philosophers and psychologists have discussed cognitive processes – or modes of thinking – as if they were the same for all normal adults. In fact, much of the research and thinking on social cognition conveyed within this very chapter has made a similar assumption: that the cognitive processes described are universal, characteristic of humans everywhere. Although it's obvious that different cultures practice different social customs, these were thought to be irrelevant to 'basic' cognitive processes like categorization and causal reasoning.

The first evidence that aspects of social cognition might not be universal after all took aim at the fundamental attribution error itself. Early studies showed that whereas Americans have long been shown to explain other people's behavior in terms of dispositional attributions, Hindu Indians and Chinese people preferred to explain similar behavior in terms of situational attributions (Miller, 1984; Morris & Peng, 1994; Norenzayan & Nisbett, 2000). Researchers initially suggested that the first stage of the two-stage attribution process – that of spontaneous trait inference – is universal, whereas the

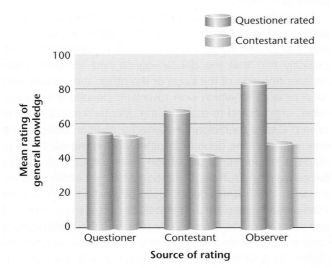

FIGURE 18.3 The Fundamental Attribution Error. *Ratings of questioners and contestants after they had participated in a quiz game. The questioner is rated as superior by both the contestant and observers even though the questioner had an overwhelming situational advantage. Both contestants and observers gave too much weight to dispositional causes and too little to situational causes.*

second stage – that of situational correction is not. Koreans, for example, are more sensitive to situational constraints on behavior (Choi *et al.,* 1999). More recently, however, evidence suggests that spontaneous trait inference may not be universal after all: it shows up for European Americans but not for Asian Americans (Na & Kitayama, 2011). The most recent work in this area uses techniques from neuroscience to examine effects of culture on social cognition, and we can expect to see more work on cultural neuroscience in the years to come.

Evidence continues to mount that East Asians, more than Westerners, pay more attention to contexts and situations (Masuda & Nisbett, 2001), and are more influenced by them (Ji *et al.,* 2000). These and countless other East–West differences in styles of thinking are now taken as evidence that East Asians engage in more holistic thinking, whereas Westerners engage in more analytic thinking (Nisbett *et al.*, 2001). **Holistic thought** is defined as an orientation toward the entire context or field and assigning causality to it, making relatively little use of categories and formal logic, and relying instead on dialectical reasoning, which involves recognizing and transcending apparent contradictions. By contrast, **analytic thought** is defined as an orientation toward objects, detached from their contexts, with much use of categories and formal logic and the avoidance of contradiction.

How did such wide-scale differences in thinking styles emerge? From long-standing different social practices, leading researchers say. In Chapter 1, we introduced the distinction between collectivist and individualist cultures. Collectivist cultures, you will recall, emphasize the fundamental connectedness and interdependence among people, whereas individualist cultures emphasize the fundamental separateness and independence of individuals. Indeed, we saw in Chapter 11 that the very emotions people experience and express reflect their cultural upbringing.

Collectivist tendencies can be traced back to the ancient Chinese focus on social harmony and collective agency, whereas individualist tendencies can be traced back to the ancient Greek focus on personal agency. These quite divergent views of human agency not only infused East–West differences in social practices but also shaped their respective advances in science, mathematics, and philosophy. The legacy of these distinct ancient orientations toward the locus of causality includes the cultural differences in cognition that we find evidence of today: that contemporary East Asians are more holistic in their thinking, whereas contemporary Westerners are more analytical (Nisbett *et al.*, 2001). The ways we use our brains, then, are not universal or dictated by biology. Rather, our styles of thinking are malleable, shaped by those in our culture who came millennia before us, and reinforced by contemporary social practices.

INTERIM SUMMARY

➔ Through schematic processing, we perceive and interpret incoming information in terms of simplified memory structures called *schemas*. Schemas are mini-theories about everyday objects and events that allow us to process information efficiently. Stereotypes are schemas about groups of people.

➔ Through repeated exposure, stereotypes can become habitual and automatic, operating outside conscious awareness.

➔ Because schemas and stereotypes simplify reality, schematic processing produces biases and errors in our processing of social information. In forming impressions of other people, for example, we are prone to the primacy effect: the first information we receive evokes an initial schema and, hence, becomes more powerful in determining our impression than does later information. Schemas and stereotypes also govern our inferences.

➔ Once activated, stereotypes can set in motion a chain of behavioral processes that serve to draw out from ourselves and others behavior that confirms the initial stereotype, an effect called the *self-fulfilling prophecy*. This behavioral sequence can occur completely outside conscious awareness.

➔ Individuation is the process of forming impressions of others by assessing their personal qualities on a person-by-person basis. The continuum model of impression formation, presented in Figure 18.2, details when and how people come to individuate others. Co-operative activities can promote individuation.

➔ Although stereotypes are activated automatically, under the right conditions they can also be controlled through effortful thinking.

➔ Attribution is the process by which we interpret and explain the behavior of other people. One major attribution task is to decide whether someone's action should be attributed to dispositional causes (the person's personality or attitudes) or to situational causes (social forces or other external circumstances). We tend to give too much weight to dispositional factors and too little to situational factors, a bias called the *fundamental attribution error*.

➔ Culture profoundly influence social cognition. East Asians, for instance, engage in more *holistic thought*, reflecting a greater sensitivity to context. By contrast, Westerners engage in more analytic thought, characterized by a detachment of objects from their contexts. By consequence, East Asians are less likely than Westerners to make the fundamental attribution error.

CUTTING EDGE RESEARCH EMBODIED SOCIAL COGNITION

Barbara L. Fredrickson, University of North Carolina, Chapel Hill

One influential new approach to the study of social cognition draws on the view that our minds are profoundly governed by the physical experiences of our bodies. Consider the classic experiment by Asch (1946), discussed earlier, which revealed how the traits *warm* versus *cold* can alter further inferences about another person's dispositions, like whether you can trust this person. More than 60 years later, this experiment was replicated, but instead of exposing participants to the words 'warm' versus 'cold' they were surreptitiously exposed to physical warmth or coldness when the experimenter incidentally asked them to hold a paper cup that contained either hot or iced coffee. Results showed that this brief physical experience produced the same effect on later trait inferences as had Asch's original study (Williams & Bargh, 2008). Further studies show that, at an unconscious level, the concepts of physical warmth and social warmth can substitute for each other. That is, feeling physically cold makes people feel lonely, whereas feeling physically warm can reduce the sting of social rejection, a finding used to explain the surprising association between being chronically lonely and taking more hot baths (Bargh & Shalev, 2012).

What happens when we encounter social indicators of warmth, for instance, when we catch someone smiling at us? Back in Chapter 11 we discussed how certain facial muscle movements are universally recognized as expressing specific emotional states. In daily life, however, the facial signs of emotion can be quite subtle, with meanings that vary substantially from one situation to the next. Why is that new student across the lecture hall smiling at you? Is this a friendly smile? Or is it flirtatious? Or maybe it's a gloating, mocking, or otherwise insincere smile? People smile for all kinds of reasons and scientists estimated that humans may sport at least 50 different kinds of smiles (Niedenthal *et al.,* 2010). With all this nuance, how is it that you can tell what any given smile means?

New evidence under the theme of embodied social cognition suggests that, under the right conditions, we do this instinctually. When you catch someone smiling at you, your own face instantaneously mimics that smile. As it does, your brain begins to simulate the neural state associated with that particular kind of smile. This combination of facial mimicry and neural simulation is what helps you 'know' at an intuitive or 'gut' level, what any given smile means and helps you to decipher the smiler's intentions. Eye contact turns out to be a key gatekeeper. This sort of embodied wisdom does not emerge without it because, studies show, eye contact is needed for facial mimicry to unfold. No eye contact, no mimicry, and therefore no intuitive insight formed by neural simulation (Niedenthal *et al.*, 2010).

One experiment tested the role of facial mimicry in decoding the meaning of sincere or insincere smiles by randomly assigning half the participants to hold a pen sideways between their teeth and lips while viewing the smiles, thereby blocking their ability to mimic them. They were told that by minimizing their own facial movements they could be more objective judges. In fact, the results showed just the opposite. Participants whose faces were free to mimic the target faces, relative to those in whom mimicry was blocked, were significantly better at distinguishing sincere from insincere smiles (Maringer, Krumhuber, Fischer, & Niedenthal, 2011).

So when you meet eyes with someone you figuratively step, not just into their shoes for a moment, but also, to a degree, into their body and brain. As you do, your inferences about their motives become all the more accurate. This line of research helps explain why disembodied forms of social communication, like text messages or email, which lack eye contact and the facial mimicry it triggers, are more likely to yield interpersonal misunderstandings.

So what's a smile for? If it's genuine – and offered in the context of eye contact – it does far more than simply signal one person's positive emotion. It also pulls for the other person – the one who meets this smiling person's gaze – to feel good as well. This now shared positive state, marked by both facial and neural synchrony, creates a micro-moment of connection and mutual understanding, in which positivity resonates between these two people for a moment, like a subtle electric charge. Warm micro-moments of embodied social connection like this may well be what make our social ties with others so life-giving and health-promoting (Fredrickson, 2013b).

CRITICAL THINKING QUESTIONS

1 Suppose you perform badly on an exam. You know it's because you hardly studied at all, but your professor has made the fundamental attribution error and comes to conclude that you're not too bright. Some social psychologists have claimed that the fundamental attribution error is self-erasing – that, over time, it ceases to be an error. Building on the example of your bad test performance, use the concepts of the self-fulfilling prophecy and stereotype threat to explain the logic of this claim.

2 Think of someone you have come to know well over the past few months or years. Did your initial impressions of this person match your current impressions? If not, can you see how stereotypes and categorizations might have influenced your initial impressions? Can you trace your increasing individuation of this person through the continuum model, presented in Figure 18.2.

ATTITUDES

So far our discussion of social cognition has focused on the processes of perceiving, thinking, and impression formation. With the concept of attitude, we take a broader look at how feelings and opinions influence social cognition and social behavior.

Attitudes are likes and dislikes – favorable or unfavorable evaluations of and reactions to objects, people, situations, or other aspects of the world, including abstract ideas and social policies. We often express our attitudes in statements of opinion: 'I love grapefruit,' or 'I can't stand liberals.' But even though attitudes express feelings, they are often linked to cognitions – specifically, to beliefs about the attitude objects ('Grapefruit contain lots of vitamin C,' or 'Liberals just want to tax and spend'). Moreover, attitudes are sometimes linked to the actions we take with respect to the attitude objects ('I eat a grapefruit every morning,' or 'I never vote for liberal candidates').

Accordingly, social psychologists usually conceive of attitudes as comprising a cognitive component, an affective component, and a behavioral component. For example, in studying negative attitudes toward groups, social psychologists often distinguish between negative stereotypes (negative beliefs and perceptions about a group – the cognitive component), prejudice (negative feelings toward the group – the affective component), and discrimination (negative actions against members of the group – the behavioral component). Some theorists prefer to define an attitude as only the cognitive and affective components; others include only the affective component. But despite differing definitions, all share a concern with the interrelationships among the pertinent beliefs, feelings, and behaviors.

Research on attitudes has kept social psychologists busy for decades. As early as the 1950s, attitudes were dubbed 'the primary building stone in the edifice of social psychology' (Allport, 1954). But why exactly are attitudes so important? Two reasons are most critical. The first reason is that, at least in democratic societies, people talk about their attitudes a lot. They also ask about others' attitudes a lot. When we leave the movie theater, for instance, the first thing we ask our companion is 'Did you like it?' After we've introduced our new boyfriend or girlfriend to our friends, we ask, 'What do you think?' Facing a critical election, we ask respected others, 'Who will you vote for?' Marketing and scientific polls turn such queries into formal assessments of public opinion, predicting everything from the box office success of Hollywood movies to the outcomes of presidential elections, and describing everything from month-by-month ratings of public support for a country's elected leader to the public's attitude toward teaching evolutionary theory within elementary schools.

The second reason attitudes have been so central to social psychology and cause for so much talk and polling is a key underlying assumption: that people's attitudes predict their behavior. This assumption is so widely accepted that it has served as the base for psychology's neighboring behavioral science of economics and underlies other rational views of human nature. This assumption can be decomposed into three parts: first, human behavior is intentional and reflects individual preferences. This is the heart of utility theory within economics and the notion of free will within philosophy. Second, attitudes represent preferences. And third, to predict behavior, we can simply look at attitudes. A corollary to this logic is that if we wish to change people's behaviors, we should start by changing their attitudes. As we'll see, though, the core assumption that attitudes predict behavior has been vigorously questioned by social psychologists.

Even so, a long-standing agenda among social psychologists has been to find ways to change people's attitudes. You will recall from Chapter 17 that one way this agenda has been pursued is through social influence techniques. In particular, research on self-justification shows that we can sometimes change people's attitudes by slyly inducing them to engage in some hypocritical (counter-attitudinal) action, like telling another person that a boring task was fun. Reference groups can also play a role in changing people's attitudes, as was illustrated in the study of Bennington College students. Here we take up more direct approaches to attitude change, those undertaken through persuasive communication, like political speeches, advertisements, sermons, and other types of formal or informal lobbying.

Persuasive communication

Just as the practices of Nazi Germany under Hitler created interest in obedience to authority (see Chapter 17), so did wartime propaganda efforts prompt the study of persuasive communication. Intensive research began in the late 1940s at Yale University, where investigators sought to determine the characteristics of successful persuasive communicators, successful communications, and the kinds of people who are most easily persuaded (Hovland et al., 1953). As research on these topics continued over the years, a number of interesting phenomena were discovered, but few general principles emerged. The results became increasingly complex and difficult to summarize, and every conclusion seemed to require several 'it depends' qualifications. Beginning in the 1980s, however, interest in the two modes of cognitive processing that we've been discussing – one more automatic and effortless and the other more controlled and effortful – gave rise to new theories of persuasion that provided a more unified framework for analyzing persuasive communication (Chen & Chaiken, 1999; Petty & Wegener, 1999).

The elaboration likelihood model

The **elaboration likelihood model** has long been one of the more prominent dual-process theories of persuasion (Petty & Wegener, 1999). It aims to predict when certain aspects of a persuasive communication – like argument strength and

Priests and politicians are among those who seek to present persuasive messages that will change the attitudes and behavior of their audiences.

source credibility – will matter and when they won't. A key idea within this model is that people experience a continuum of elaboration likelihood. In simple terms, this means that sometimes we are motivated and able to pay attention, think, and elaborate on the persuasive message, and at other times we are not. Which end of this continuum we're on at any given moment determines the cognitive processes that govern persuasion. So, according to the elaboration likelihood model, if we're at the high end of the continuum – willing and able to think deeply – then persuasion is said to follow a central route, relying on controlled and effortful thinking; if we're at the low end of the continuum – for whatever reasons, not willing or able to think deeply – then persuasion is said to follow a peripheral route, relying on automatic and effortless thinking.

The central route to persuasion

Persuasion is said to follow the **central route** when an individual mentally responds to – and elaborates on – the persuasive communication. The central route to persuasion is taken only when the individual is motivated to generate thoughts in response to the substantive content of a communication and has the ability and opportunity to do so. These thoughts can be about the content of the communication itself or about other aspects of the situation, such as the credibility of the communicator. If the communication evokes thoughts that support the position being advocated, the individual will move toward that position; if the communication evokes unsupportive thoughts (such as counterarguments or disparaging thoughts about the communicator), the individual will remain unconvinced or even shift away from the position being advocated.

A number of studies provide evidence that effortful thought accounts for the central route to persuasion. In one, each participant read a communication containing arguments about a controversial issue and wrote a one-sentence reaction to each argument. One week later, the participants were unexpectedly given a memory test asking them to recall both the arguments in the communication and their written reactions to those arguments. Participants' opinions on the issue were assessed before receiving the communication and again at the time of the memory test. The results showed that the amount of opinion change produced by the communication was significantly correlated with both the supportiveness of participants' reactions to the communication and with their later recall of those reactions, but it was not significantly correlated with their recall of the arguments themselves (Love & Greenwald, 1978). This experiment not only supports the central route to persuasion but also explains what had previously been a puzzling observation: that the persistence of opinion change is often unrelated to an individual's memory of the arguments that produced that change.

In a sense, then, the central route to persuasion can be considered self-persuasion produced by the thoughts that the person generates while reading, listening to, or even just anticipating the communication. Those thoughts turn out to be more influential than the communication itself.

The peripheral route to persuasion

Persuasion is said to follow the **peripheral route** when the individual responds to non-content cues in a communication (such as the sheer number of arguments it contains) or to the context of the communication (such as the credibility of the communicator or the pleasantness of the surroundings). The peripheral route is taken when the individual is – for whatever reason – unable or unwilling to do the cognitive work required to carefully evaluate the content of the communication.

Classical conditioning (which you learned about in Chapter 7) is one of the most primitive means of changing attitudes through the peripheral route. Advertisers use classical conditioning quite a lot, by repeatedly pairing their initially neutral or unknown product with images or ideas that are known to produce positive feelings, like attractive people or beautiful scenery. Through classical conditioning – a peripheral route to persuasion – viewers should come to hold positive attitudes toward the new product as well.

Another peripheral route to persuasion relies on heuristics, or rules of thumb (discussed in Chapter 9) to infer the validity of persuasive messages. Examples of such rules might include 'Messages with many arguments are more likely to be valid than messages with few arguments,' 'Politicians always lie,' and 'University professors know what they are talking about' (Eagly & Chaiken, 1984). Communications that follow these rules of thumb can be persuasive – even if their substantive content is unconvincing – to the extent that listeners are unlikely to elaborate on the information given.

Central or peripheral?

Several factors can influence which route – central or peripheral – will be taken. One such factor is personal involvement. If a communication addresses an issue in which the individual has a personal stake, he or she is more likely to attend carefully to the arguments. In such a case, the individual is also likely to have a rich store of prior information and opinions on the issue. On the other hand, if an issue has no personal relevance for the individual, he or she is not likely to make much of an effort either to support or refute arguments about it. What happens then?

The elaboration likelihood model has been tested in numerous studies. In one rather complex study, university students read an essay allegedly written by the chair of a university committee charged with advising the chancellor on changes in academic policy. The essay proposed that the university institute a comprehensive examination that every student would have to pass before being permitted to graduate. To manipulate the students' involvement in the issue, half of them were told that any policy changes adopted by the chancellor would be instituted the next year (high involvement), and the other half were told that any changes would take effect in 10 years (low involvement). Different forms of the essay were also used. Some contained strong arguments, others weak ones. Some contained only three arguments, others nine.

The post-communication attitudes of students in the high-involvement conditions are shown in Figure 18.4a. It can be seen that strong arguments produced more favorable attitudes overall than did weak arguments. But more important, nine strong arguments produced greater agreement with the

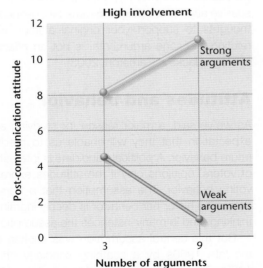

a) **Post-communication attitudes through the central route.** When individuals have high involvement in the issue, nine strong arguments produce more agreement than three strong arguments, but nine weak arguments produce less agreement than three weak arguments.

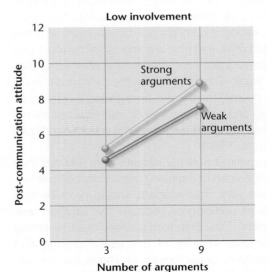

b) **Post-communication attitudes through the peripheral route.** When individuals have low involvement in the issue, nine arguments produce more agreement than three arguments, regardless of whether the arguments are strong or weak.

FIGURE 18.4 A Test of the Elaboration Likelihood Model.

essay than did three strong arguments, whereas nine weak arguments produced less agreement than did three weak arguments. How can we make sense of these patterns?

The elaboration likelihood model predicts that students in the high-involvement conditions will be motivated to process the essay's substantive arguments and thus generate topic-relevant cognitive responses. This is the central route of persuasion, which holds that strong arguments will evoke more supportive cognitive responses and fewer counterarguments than will weak arguments and hence will produce more agreement with the essay – as, indeed, they did. Moreover, nine strong arguments should be more persuasive than three strong arguments because the more strong arguments the individual encounters, the more supportive cognitive responses he or she will generate. In contrast, nine weak arguments should be less persuasive than three weak arguments because the more weak arguments the individual encounters, the more counterarguments he or she will generate. These predictions are in accordance with the findings displayed in Figure 18.4a.

As shown in Figure 18.4b, a different pattern emerges for students in the low-involvement conditions, those who were told that any policy changes would take effect in 10 years. Here the elaboration likelihood model predicts that students with such low-involvement will not be motivated to scrutinize the essay's arguments closely and will instead rely on simple heuristics to evaluate its merits and form their attitudes. This is the peripheral route, which holds that an individual in this setting will not even bother to determine whether the arguments are strong or weak but will simply invoke the heuristic rule: 'Messages with many arguments are more likely to be valid than messages with few arguments.' Thus, strong arguments will be no more effective than weak arguments, and nine arguments will be more persuasive than three arguments – regardless of whether they are strong or weak. This is precisely the pattern shown in Figure 18.4b: overall, there were no significant differences between strong and weak arguments, but nine arguments were more effective than three arguments in both conditions (Petty & Cacioppo, 1984).

In another experiment, all participants were told that their university was considering instituting mandatory comprehensive exams next year. This scenario should produce high involvement in all participants because the situation was personally relevant. They then read a series of either strong or weak arguments in favor of this policy change and offered their opinions. Under typical conditions, the elaboration likelihood model would predict that participants would be more persuaded by strong than weak arguments, as in Figure 18.4a. Yet prior to reviewing arguments half the participants had been randomly assigned to complete a depleting cognitive task for 5 minutes, whereas the other half completed a very simple task. The researchers were testing whether momentary cognitive depletion by itself could push

even those who should be highly involved in an issue to evaluate it through the peripheral route. It did: depleted participants were equally persuaded by strong and weak arguments. An examination of their thoughts in response to the arguments suggested that they simply didn't have the cognitive resources to argue against the weak arguments (Wheeler *et al.,* 2007). These findings offer an important warning: when you're tired or otherwise mentally drained, you're far less able to resist when others try to talk you into a bad idea!

Although much research on persuasion has been conducted in laboratories, there has always been an interest in the practical applications of the findings. An example is an educational program designed to inoculate adolescents against peer pressure to smoke. Older adolescents conducted sessions in which they taught younger adolescents how to generate counterarguments. For example, in role-playing sessions they were taught to respond to being called 'chicken' for not taking a cigarette by saying things like 'I'd be a real chicken if I smoked just to impress you.' They were also taught to respond to advertisements implying that free-thinking people smoke by saying, 'People aren't really free-thinking if they're hooked on tobacco.' Several inoculation sessions were held, and records were kept of how many of the students smoked from the beginning of the study through the next few years. The results showed that inoculated students were half as likely to smoke as students at a matched school that used a more typical smoking education program (McAlister *et al.,* 1980). **Counterarguing**, or directly rebutting the message arguments is indeed the most effective strategy for resisting persuasion. Surprisingly, another common response to persuasive attempts, **attitude bolstering**, defined as generating thoughts to support your original attitude without directly refuting message arguments, is not an effective resistance strategy (Jacks & Cameron, 2003).

Attitudes and behavior

As we've said, a major reason for studying attitudes is the expectation that they will enable us to predict a person's future behavior. A political candidate is interested in a survey of voters' opinions only if the attitudes expressed relate to voting behavior. The assumption that a person's attitudes determine his or her behavior is deeply ingrained in Western thinking, and in many instances the assumption holds.

But this central assumption was shaken to the core in the late 1960s by a scathing scholarly critique (Wicker, 1969). The critique reviewed more than 40 studies that tested the relationship between attitudes and behavior. A classic study conducted during the 1930s illustrated the problem. A white professor traveled across the USA with a young Chinese couple. At that time there was strong prejudice against Asian people, and there were no laws against racial discrimination in public accommodations. The three

According to the elaboration likelihood model, the way we process ads and other persuasive messages depends on the effort we are willing and able to spend. When we have the mental resources to devote to processing persuasive messages and are willing to do so, we tend to engage in controlled thought about the message. Otherwise, we tend to process persuasive messages more automatically.

travelers stopped at more than 200 hotels, motels, and restaurants and were served at all the restaurants and all but one of the hotels and motels without a problem. Later, a letter was sent to all of the restaurants and hotels asking them whether they would accept a Chinese couple as guests. Of the 128 replies received, 92 per cent said that they would not. In other words, these proprietors expressed attitudes that were much more prejudiced than their actual behavior (LaPiere, 1934).

Although the study by LaPiere is not without problems, critics used this and many other studies to raise the question of whether attitudes predict behavior at all. Other critics even recommended that social psychologists abandon the attitude concept altogether and focus instead on the situational determinants of behavior. The logic of this recommendation, you will see, parallels the fundamental attribution error: that even social psychologists had overestimated the causal force of dispositional factors – like attitudes – on determining behavior and underestimated the causal force of situations.

Certainly people's behavior is determined by many factors other than their attitudes. One obvious factor is the degree of constraint in the situation: we must often act in ways that are not consistent with what we feel or believe. As children, we ate vegetables that we detested, and as adults we attend lectures and dinner parties that we consider boring. In Chapter 17, we saw the power of situations time and again. In the Asch study, participants conformed to the majority, even when they knew the majority was wrong. In the Milgram study, participants delivered shocks even when doing so went against their consciences. And in the racial discrimination study just described, the prejudiced proprietors may have found it difficult to act on their prejudices when actually faced with the Chinese couple seeking service.

Peer pressure can exert similar influences on behavior. For example, an adolescent's attitude toward marijuana is moderately correlated with his or her actual use of marijuana, but the number of marijuana-using friends the teenager has is an even better predictor of his or her marijuana use (Andrews & Kandel, 1979). Can you see a similarity here to the classic Asch study?

Far from ending research on attitudes, this critical challenge to the assumption that attitudes predict behavior served to kindle new generations of research on attitudes that aimed to specify the special conditions under which attitudes do in fact predict behavior (Fishbein & Ajzen, 1975; Webb & Sheeran, 2006). In general, attitudes have been found to predict behavior best when (1) they are strong and consistent, (2) they are specifically related to the behavior being predicted, (3) they are based on the person's direct experience, and (4) the individual is aware of his or her attitudes. We will look briefly at each of these factors.

Strong and consistent attitudes

Strong and consistent attitudes predict behavior better than weak or ambivalent ones. Many voters experience ambivalence because they are under pressure from friends and associates who do not agree with one another. For example, a Jewish businessperson belongs to an ethnic group that generally holds liberal political positions, but she also belongs to a business community that frequently holds conservative political positions, particularly on economic issues. When it comes time to vote, she is subjected to conflicting pressures.

Ambivalence and conflict can arise from within the person as well. When the affective and cognitive components of an attitude are not consistent – for example, when we like something that we know is bad for us – it is often difficult to predict behavior (Norman, 1975). In general, when the components of an attitude are clear and consistent, they better predict behavior (Millar & Tesser, 1989).

Attitudes specifically related to behavior

Another finding is that attitudes that are specifically related to the behavior being assessed predict the behavior better than attitudes that are only generally related to it. For example, in one study students in the USA, Britain, and Sweden were asked both about their general attitudes toward nuclear war and about their specific attitudes toward nuclear war, nuclear weapons, and nuclear power plants. Specific attitudes were much better predictors of activist behaviors (such as writing a letter to a newspaper or signing a petition) than more general attitudes (Newcomb *et al.,* 1992).

Attitudes based on direct experience

Attitudes based on direct experience predict behavior better than attitudes formed from reading or hearing about an issue (Fazio, 1990). For example, during a housing shortage at a university, many entering students had to spend the first few weeks of the term in crowded temporary housing. Researchers measured students' attitudes toward the housing crisis and their willingness to sign and distribute petitions or join committees to study it. For students who actually had to live in the temporary housing, there was a high correlation between their attitude toward the crisis and their willingness to take action to solve it. But for students who had not directly experienced the temporary housing, no such correlation existed (Regan & Fazio, 1977). Likewise, researchers have discovered that people who've already decided how to act show a stronger link between their attitudes and behavior compared to those who have held off on making such a decision. Direct experience, then, can also be the mental experience of an implemental or planning mindset (Henderson *et al.,* 2008). Situations that feel like direct experience, for instance, that of being lost in a story, fully transported into the narrative world, can also produce a stronger attitude – behavior link (Williams *et al.,* 2011).

Awareness

Finally, there is evidence that people who are more aware of their attitudes are more likely to behave in ways that are consistent with those attitudes. This is true of people who are generally more focused on their thoughts and feelings as part of their personalities (Scheier *et al.,* 1978), as well as of people who are placed in situations designed to make them more aware, such as in front of a mirror or video camera (Carver & Scheier, 1981; Hutton & Baumeister, 1992).

➲ The elaboration likelihood model states that persuasion can take two routes in producing belief and attitude change: the central route, in which the individual responds to the substantive arguments of a communication, and the peripheral route, in which the individual responds to non-content cues in a communication (such as the number of arguments) or to context cues (such as the credibility of the communicator or the pleasantness of the surroundings).

➲ A communication about an issue of personal relevance is more likely to generate thoughts in response to the communication's substantive arguments. When an issue is of little personal relevance or people are unwilling or unable to respond to the substantive content of a communication, they tend to use simple heuristics – rules of thumb – to judge the merits of the communication.

➲ Attitudes tend to predict behavior best when they are (1) strong and consistent, (2) specifically related to the behavior being predicted, and (3) based on the person's direct experience on planned actions, as well as (4) when the individual is aware of his or her attitudes.

CRITICAL THINKING QUESTIONS

1 Suppose you are running for political office. What sort of advertisements should you design if you suspect that your audience will be distracted? What sort of ads should you design if you suspect that your audience will be motivated to think deeply? Can you appeal to both audiences in the same ad?

2 Many young people are addicted to shopping at the expense of other interests. Based on what you now know about attitude change and the links between attitudes and behavior, identify at least two ways that you could prevent your younger sister from spending all of her time and money shopping for the latest advertised fashions.

INTERIM SUMMARY

➲ Attitudes are likes and dislikes – favorable or unfavorable evaluations of and reactions to objects, people, events, or ideas. Attitudes have a cognitive component, an affective component, and a behavioral component.

INTERPERSONAL ATTRACTION

In our discussion of attitudes, we distinguished between the cognitive and affective components – thinking and feeling. There is, however, no area of human behavior in which cognitions and affects are intertwined in a more complex way than in interpersonal attraction: liking, loving, and sexual desire.

Research in these areas has often confirmed common knowledge, but it has also produced a number of surprises and contradictions. We begin with liking – namely, friendship and the early stages of more intimate relationships.

Liking and attraction

We cannot all be beautiful film stars, but when two such people become a couple, they do illustrate several of the determinants of interpersonal attraction that apply even to us ordinary mortals: physical attractiveness, proximity, familiarity, and similarity. As the high divorce rate among contemporary couples also illustrates, however, these factors are not always sufficient to sustain a long-term relationship.

Physical attractiveness

To most of us, there is something mildly undemocratic about the possibility that a person's physical appearance is a determinant of how well others like him or her. Unlike character and personality, physical appearance is a factor over which we seemingly have little control, and so it seems unfair to use it as a criterion for liking someone. In fact, surveys that have spanned several decades and cultures have shown that people do not rank physical attractiveness as very important in their liking of other people (Buss, 1989; Perrin, 1921).

But research on actual behavior shows otherwise (Brehm, 1992). One group of psychologists set up a 'computer dance' in which college men and women were randomly paired. At intermission, everyone filled out an anonymous questionnaire evaluating his or her date. In addition, the experimenters obtained several personality test scores for each person, as well as an independent estimate of his or her physical attractiveness. The results showed that only physical attractiveness played a role in how much the person was liked by his or her partner. None of the measures of intelligence, social skills, or personality was related to the partners' liking for each other (Walster et al., 1966). This experiment has been replicated many times, and in each case the results have been similar to those just described. Moreover, the importance of physical attractiveness has been found to operate not only on first dates but on subsequent dates (Mathes, 1975) and in marriages (Margolin & White, 1987) as well.

Why is physical attractiveness so important? Part of the reason is that our social standing and self-esteem are enhanced when we are seen with physically attractive companions. Both men and women are rated more favorably when they are with an attractive romantic partner or friend than when they are with an unattractive companion (Sigall & Landy, 1973). But there is an interesting twist to this: both men and women are rated less favorably when they are seen with a stranger who is physically more attractive than they are (Kernis & Wheeler, 1981). Apparently they suffer by comparison with the other person. This effect has been found in other studies. For example, male college students who had just watched a television show starring beautiful young women gave lower attractiveness ratings to a photograph of a more typical-looking woman (Kendrick & Gutierres, 1980).

Fortunately, there is hope for the unbeautiful among us. First of all, physical attractiveness appears to decline in importance when a permanent partner is being chosen (Stroebe et al., 1971). And, as we will see, several other factors can work in our favor.

Proximity

An examination of 5000 marriage license applications in Philadelphia in the 1930s found that one-third of the couples lived within five blocks of each other (Rubin, 1973). Research shows that the best single predictor of whether two people are friends is **proximity**, or how far apart they live. In a study of friendship patterns in apartment houses, residents were asked to name the three people they saw socially most often. Residents mentioned 41 per cent of neighbors who lived in the apartment next door, 22 per cent of those who lived two doors away (about 30 feet), and only 10 per cent of those who lived at the other end of the hall (Festinger et al., 1950). Studies of college dormitories show the same effect. After a full academic year, students who shared an apartment were twice as likely to be friends compared to those who were simply on the same floor, and those on the same floor were more than twice as likely to be friends compared to those simply in the same building (Priest & Sawyer, 1967).

There are cases, of course, in which neighbors and roommates hate one another, and the major exception to the friendship-promoting effect of proximity seems to occur when there are initial antagonisms. In a test of this, a participant waited in a laboratory with a female confederate who treated the participant pleasantly or unpleasantly. When she was pleasant, the closer she sat to the participant, the better she was liked; when she was unpleasant, the closer she sat to the participant, the less she was liked. Proximity simply increased the intensity of the initial reaction (Schiffenbauer &

These neighbors are likely to form a friendship simply because of proximity.

Schiavo, 1976). But because most initial encounters probably range from neutral to pleasant, the most frequent result of sustained proximity is friendship.

Those who believe in miracles when it comes to matters of the heart may believe that there is a perfect mate chosen for each of us waiting to be discovered somewhere in the world. But, if this is true, the far greater miracle is the frequency with which fate conspires to place this person within walking distance.

Familiarity

One of the major reasons that proximity creates liking is that it increases familiarity (Reis *et al.*, 2011). Indeed, abundant evidence supports what is called the **mere exposure effect**, the finding that familiarity all by itself increases liking (Zajonc, 1968). This familiarity-breeds-liking effect is a very general phenomenon. For example, rats repeatedly exposed to the music of either Mozart or Schoenberg enhance their preference for the composer they have heard, and humans repeatedly exposed to selected nonsense syllables or Chinese characters come to prefer those they have seen most often. The effect occurs even when individuals are unaware that they have been previously exposed to the stimuli (Bornstein, 1992; Bornstein & D'Agostino, 1992; Moreland & Zajonc, 1979; Wilson, 1979). More germane to the present discussion is a study in which participants were exposed to pictures of faces and then asked how much they thought they would like the person shown. The more frequently they had seen a particular face, the more they said they liked it and thought they would like the person (Zajonc, 1968) (see Figure 18.5).

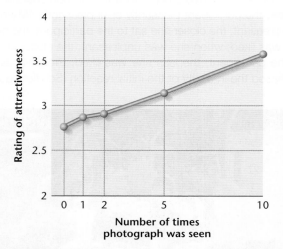

FIGURE 18.5 Familiarity Breeds Liking. *People were asked to rate photographs of unknown faces according to how much they thought they would like the person. The lowest ratings of liking were made by those who had never seen the photograph before; the highest ratings of liking were made by those who had seen the photograph most often. This illustrates the mere exposure effect.*

Similar results are obtained when individuals are exposed to one another in real life (Moreland & Beach, 1992).

In one clever demonstration of the mere exposure effect, the investigators took photographs of college women and then prepared prints of both the original face and its mirror image. These prints were then shown to the women themselves, their female friends, and their lovers. The women themselves preferred the mirror-image prints by a margin of 68 to 32 per cent, but the friends and lovers preferred the non-reversed prints by a margin of 61 to 39 per cent (Mita *et al.*, 1977). Can you guess why?

The take-home message is clear. If you are not beautiful or you find your admiration of someone unreciprocated, simply find ways to be nearby. Proximity and familiarity may just work in your favor.

Similarity

An old saying declares that opposites attract, and lovers are fond of recounting how different they are from each other: 'I love boating, but she prefers mountain climbing.' 'I'm in engineering, but he's a history student.' What such lovers overlook is that they both like outdoor activities; they are both pre-professionals; they are both the same nationality, the same religion, the same social class, and the same educational level; and they are within 3 years of each other in age and within five IQ points of each other in intelligence. In short, the old saying is mostly false.

Research dating all the way back to 1870 supports this conclusion. More than 95 per cent of the married couples in the USA are of the same race, and most are of the same religion. Moreover, statistical surveys show that husbands and wives are significantly similar to each other not only in sociological characteristics – such as age, race, religion, education, and socioeconomic class – but also with respect to psychological characteristics like intelligence and physical characteristics such as height and eye color (Rubin, 1973). A study of dating couples finds the same patterns, in addition to finding that couples were also similar in their attitudes about sexual behavior and sex roles. Moreover, couples who were most similar in background at the beginning of the study were most likely to be together a year later (Hill *et al.*, 1976). Of particular pertinence to our earlier discussion is the finding that couples are closely matched on physical attractiveness as well (Feingold, 1988).

For example, in one study, judges rated photographs of each partner of 99 couples for physical attractiveness without knowing who was paired with whom. The physical attractiveness ratings of the couples matched each other significantly more closely than did the ratings of photographs that were randomly paired into couples (Murstein, 1972). Similar results were obtained in a real-life field study in which separate observers rated the physical attractiveness of members of couples in bars and theater lobbies and at social events (Silverman, 1971).

Partners in successful long-term relationships tend to be similar to each other in characteristics such as age, race, and education, as well as in their interests, personality traits, and even physical attractiveness.

This matching of couples on physical attractiveness appears to come about because we weigh a potential partner's attractiveness against the probability that the person would be willing to pair up with us. Put bluntly, less attractive people seek less attractive partners because they expect to be rejected by someone more attractive than themselves. A study of a video dating service found that both men and women were most likely to pursue a relationship with someone who matched them in physical attractiveness. Only the most attractive people sought dates with the most attractive partners (Folkes, 1982). The overall result of this process is attractiveness similarity: most of us end up with partners who are about as attractive as we are.

But similarities on dimensions other than physical attractiveness are probably even more important over the long-term course of a relationship. A longitudinal study of 135 married couples found that spouses who were more similar to each other in personality also resembled each other more in terms of how much they enjoyed similar daily activities like visiting friends, going out for dinner, and participating in community activities and professional meetings. These couples also reported less marital conflict and greater closeness, friendliness, and marital satisfaction than less similar spouses (Caspi & Herbener, 1990).

Studies show that even arbitrary and trivial points of similarity produce liking. For instance, laboratory experiments show that people like others more when those others have been arbitrarily assigned a numeric code, for example 6-15, that includes the month and date of their own birthday, say June 15. The effect can even happen at subliminal levels, completely outside of conscious awareness (Jones *et al.*, 2004). These surprising findings are interpreted as evidence

for **implicit egotism**. We are non-consciously attracted to people, places, and objects that subtly remind us of ourselves.

Transference

In Chapter 16, you learned about transference, or the tendency for clients to transfer their feelings and assumptions about a particular significant other – like their parent or spouse – onto their therapist. Work from a social cognitive perspective applies the concept of **transference** more generally, arguing that any time we encounter someone new who reminds us of someone who has been important to us in our past, that sense of recognition influences our perceptions – and indeed our liking – of the new person (Chen & Andersen, 1999). The approach follows the tradition of social cognition because it holds that simply being reminded of someone who has been significant to us in the past automatically activates stored knowledge – or schemas – about that significant other. This, in turn, leads us to process information about the newly encountered person in ways consistent with the activated schema.

Laboratory experiments have tested the influence of transference on interpersonal liking. In one study, participants were tested twice. In a pretest session, they identified two of their significant others – one whom they felt good about and one they disliked – and provided several short descriptions of them ('Terry is sincere,' or 'Pat likes to go dancing'). More than 2 weeks later, these same participants were tested again. This time, they learned about a new person – supposedly seated next door – with whom they would soon interact. The descriptions of this new person were rigged to resemble participants' significant others by

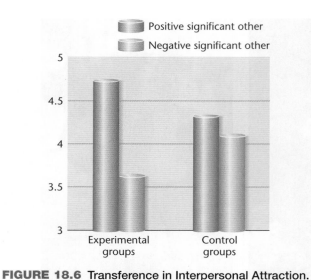

FIGURE 18.6 **Transference in Interpersonal Attraction.** *How much participants liked a new acquaintance depended on whether that new person shared characteristics with the participants' significant others and whether they held positive or negative attitudes about those significant others. Notice that evaluations were more extreme when new acquaintances resembled a participant's own significant other (the experimental groups) than when they resembled someone else's significant other (the control groups).*

mirroring some of the descriptions gathered in the pretest phase. For one experimental group, the new person resembled a liked significant other. For another experimental group, the new person resembled a disliked significant other. To control for the relative pleasantness or unpleasantness of the descriptions used, each was given to another participant as well. For these control groups, the description of the new person resembled somebody else's significant other, not their own. The results are shown in Figure 18.6. When a new person resembled a significant other, he or she is liked or disliked, depending on the participant's attitude toward the significant other – participants even smiled more when the new person resembled their significant other! Additional experiments using this same procedure confirm that this effect of transference on liking is carried by activated schemas. As we learned at the start of this chapter (and in Chapter 8), schemas can be activated (or primed) automatically and, once activated, they influence various aspects of information processing, including memory and inferences. Our schemas for significant others, when triggered by new acquaintances who in some way resemble them, produce all the cognitive and behavioral effects that social psychologists have come to expect (Chen & Andersen, 1999).

The take-home message here is that if you want to forge a new friendship or relationship, and not merely recycle an old one, you need to start with a new acquaintance who is like no other. And you should be cautious when someone approaches you and says, 'You remind me of someone.'

Loving and mating

Love is more than just strong liking. Most of us know people we like very much but do not love, and some of us have felt passionate attraction for someone we did not particularly like. Research confirms these everyday observations. One of the first researchers to study romantic love compiled a number of statements that people thought reflected liking and loving and then constructed separate scales to measure each (Rubin, 1973). Items on the liking scale tap the degree to which the other person is regarded as likable, respected, admired, and having maturity and good judgment. Items on the love scale tap three main themes: a sense of attachment ('It would be hard for me to get along without ___'), a sense of caring for the other person ('I would do almost anything for ___'), and a sense of trust ('I feel that I can confide in ___ about virtually everything'). The two scales are only moderately correlated: 0.56 for men and 0.36 for women.

Love and marriage

The concept of romantic love is an old one, but the belief that it has much to do with marriage is more recent and far from universal. In some non-Western cultures, marriage is still considered to be a contractual or financial arrangement that has nothing to do with love. In the USA, the link between love and marriage has actually become stronger over time. In 1967, US university students were asked, 'If a man (woman) had all the other qualities you desired, would you marry this person if you were not in love with him (her)?' About 65 per cent of the men said no, but only 24 per cent of the women said no (only 4 per cent actually said yes; the majority of the women were undecided) (Kephart, 1967). Feminism was just taking root at that time, and it may be that women were more likely than they are now to consider marriage necessary for financial security. When the survey was repeated in 1984, 85 per cent of both men and women said that they would refuse to marry without being in love (Simpson *et al.,* 1986).

Love and self-expansion

Why do people fall in love? Why do they forge close, loving relationships? At one level, the answer is obvious – because love feels good! But then you could ask, why does love feel good? Some social psychologists have suggested that a primary motivation for falling in love lies in the urge to expand the self (Aron *et al.,* 1998). Close relationships are said to produce **self-expansion** – or increase our potential abilities and resources – in multiple ways. As we become close to another person, we gain access to that person's resources, perspectives, and identities – this might include someone's circle of friends, cooking skills, views on politics or religion, or popularity more generally – each of which can help us to achieve our own goals. People are motivated to expand the self, the reasoning continues, not only to become more able themselves but also because self-expansion, particularly rapid expanding, is exhilarating. So falling in love feels good, this logic suggests, because it produces rapid self-expansion.

The researchers tested the association between falling in love and self-expansion by targeting a large group of beginning university students over the fall semester. Every 2 weeks for 10 weeks, these students answered the question, 'Who are you today?' by listing as many self-descriptive words or phrases as came to mind in a 3-minute period. They also answered a number of other questions, including whether they had fallen in love since the last testing session. Entering university students, it so happens, have a very high chance of falling in love in their first semester – a full one-third of them do (Aron, 2002)! This large sample of those 'lucky in love' enabled the researchers to compare self-descriptions made just prior to falling in love to those made just after. The comparisons provided clear evidence of self-expansion: the diversity of self-descriptions increased significantly after falling in love, an effect that could not be attributed to positive mood. (The self-descriptions of those unlucky in love provided an additional comparison for the degree of change that might be expected in the absence of love; Aron *et al.,* 1998.)

A corollary to the notion that love produces self-expansion is the claim that within close relationships, people tend to think about their beloved in the same manner in which they think of the self. That is, the close other becomes fused – even confused – with the self. One study tested the idea that we 'include the other in the self' by asking married participants to choose as quickly and accurately as possible whether each of a large set of personality traits was 'me' or 'not me'. Based on prior testing, the researchers knew that some of those traits were true of the participant's self but not true of their spouse, or true of the spouse but not true of the self. As expected, participants were slower to respond – and made more errors – for traits on which they and their spouse differed (Aron *et al.,* 1991). So, for instance, if you are not particularly gracious, but your beloved is, when faced with deciding whether the term *gracious* describes you, you get confused. It takes you a moment to sort out that even though you benefit from your beloved's graciousness, you are not actually gracious yourself! But this confusion is a good thing. Other research has shown that the extent to which couples 'include the other in the self' on a simple pictorial measure (see Figure 18.7) predicts how long they will stay together (Aron *et al.,* 1992).

Passionate and companionate love

Several social scientists have attempted to distinguish among different kinds of love. One of the most widely accepted

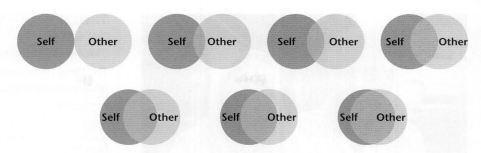

FIGURE 18.7 Including the Other in the Self. *People are asked to circle the picture that best describes their relationship. Research has found that the degree to which people include the other in the self predicts how long a relationship will last.*

distinctions is between passionate and companionate love (Hatfield, 1988).

Passionate love is defined as an intensely emotional state in which 'tender and sexual feelings, elation and pain, anxiety and relief, altruism and jealousy coexist in a confusion of feelings' (Berscheid & Walster, 1974, p. 177). It has been suggested that the experience of passionate love combines physiological arousal with the perception that the arousal is evoked by the beloved (Berscheid & Walster, 1974).

In contrast, **companionate love** is defined as 'the affection we feel for those with whom our lives are deeply intertwined' (Hatfield, 1988, p. 205). The characteristics of companionate love are trust, caring, tolerance of the partner's flaws and idiosyncrasies, and an emotional tone of warmth and affection rather than high-pitched emotional passion. As a relationship continues over time, interdependence grows, and the potential for strong emotion actually increases. This can be seen when long-time partners experience intense feelings of loneliness and desire when temporarily separated or in the emotional devastation typically experienced by someone who loses a long-time partner. But, paradoxically, because companionate couples become so compatible and co-ordinated in their daily routines, the actual frequency of strong emotions is usually fairly low (Berscheid, 1983).

Many of the young men and women in the survey cited earlier stated that if love disappears from a marriage, that is sufficient reason to end it. Those who equate love with passionate love, however, are likely to be disappointed. Although some long-term marriages are characterized by feelings of love that are as intense as those seen among newlyweds (O'Leary *et al.,* 2012), many successful long-term couples emphasize the companionate elements of their relationship, and both theory and research suggest that the intense feelings that characterize passionate love often do not persist over time (Berscheid, 1983). As the sixteenth-century writer Giraldi put it, 'The history of a love affair is in some sense the drama of its fight against time.'

This point is illustrated in a study that compared long-term marriages in the USA – where couples claim to marry for

In later life the passionate component of romantic love tends to become less important than the companionate component.

TABLE 18.1 THE TRIANGULAR THEORY OF LOVE

The three dimensions of love combine to produce eight types of love relationships.

	Intimacy	Passion	Commitment
Non-love	Low	Low	Low
Liking	High	Low	Low
Infatuated love	Low	High	Low
Romantic love	High	High	Low
Empty love	Low	Low	High
Companionate love	High	Low	High
Fatuous love	Low	High	High
Consummate love	High	High	High

love – with marriages in Japan that had been arranged by the couples' parents. As expected, the American marriages started out with a higher level of expressed love and sexual interest than the Japanese marriages. But the amount of love expressed decreased in both groups until after 10 years there were no differences between the two groups. Nevertheless, many couples in this study reported quite gratifying marriages, marriages that had evolved into a deep companionate love characterized by communication between the partners, an equitable division of labor, and equality of decision-making power (Blood, 1967).

The take-home message is that passionate love might be terrific for starters, but the sustaining forces of a good long-term relationship are less exciting, require more work, and have more to do with equality than with passion. In fact, as we will see shortly, there may even be a built-in incompatibility between passionate and companionate love.

The triangular theory of love

Other researchers find the strategy of dichotomizing love into two kinds – passionate and companionate – to be too simplistic. One of the more differentiated classifications offered is the **triangular theory of love**. It divides love into three components: intimacy, passion, and commitment (Sternberg, 1986). **Intimacy** is the emotional component and involves closeness and sharing of feelings. **Passion**, the motivational component, consists of sexual attraction and the romantic feeling of being 'in love.' **Commitment** is the cognitive component; it reflects the intention to remain in the relationship. Combining these three components in different ways yields the eight kinds of relationships shown in Table 18.1. As can be seen, in this scheme passionate love is split into two types: infatuated love and romantic love. Both are characterized by high passion and low commitment, but infatuated love is low in intimacy whereas romantic love is high in inti-

macy. Companionate love is characterized by high intimacy and commitment but low passion.

Pair bonding and mating strategies

Another approach to romantic and sexual attraction draws on Darwin's theory of evolution. As noted in Chapter 1, evolutionary psychology is concerned with the origins of psychological mechanisms. The key idea is that, just like biological mechanisms, psychological mechanisms must have evolved over millions of years through a process of natural selection. They therefore have a genetic basis and have proved useful to the human species in the past for solving problems of survival or increasing the chances of reproducing.

The interest in evolution among social psychologists has led to a (sometimes controversial) re-examination of several behavioral phenomena. Among these are pair bonding in humans and differences between men and women in sexual behavior and mating strategies.

From an evolutionary perspective, men and women mate to produce offspring who will pass their genes along to future generations. To do this, individuals must solve several problems, including (1) winning out over competitors in gaining access to fertile members of the other sex, (2) selecting mates with the greatest reproductive potential, (3) engaging in the necessary social and sexual behavior to achieve conception, (4) preventing the mate from defecting or deserting, and (5) ensuring the survival and reproductive success of one's offspring (Buss, 1994). According to evolutionary psychologists, humans have evolved to form intense, long-term bonds with a partner to ensure that human offspring survive to reproductive age. As noted in Chapter 3, the more complex an organism's nervous system, the longer the time required to reach maturity. A chimpanzee will be a functioning adult member of its species years before a human of the same age is ready to fend for itself. Accordingly, in the history of our species it has been important to have both parents stick around to defend, provide for, and help rear the young. In contrast to humans, both male and female chimpanzees are quite promiscuous, and males have little or no involvement in rearing the young.

Evolutionary psychology further argues that because men and women play different roles in reproduction, the mating tactics and strategies used by the two sexes might also have evolved to be different as well. Because it is theoretically possible for a man to father hundreds of children, it is to his evolutionary advantage to impregnate as many women as possible in order to pass along the greatest number of his own genes. The woman, however, must invest a great deal of time and energy in each birth and can have only a limited number of offspring. It is to her advantage to select a mate who is most willing and best able to assist in protecting and raising her children, thereby maximizing the likelihood of passing her genes along to future generations. This reasoning suggests that evolution would have made men more promiscuous and less discriminating in their choice of sexual partners than women. In fact, it has been documented repeatedly that in most societies men are more promiscuous than women, and societies that permit one man to mate with more than one woman far outnumber those in which one woman may mate with many different men (Wilson, 1978).

Evolutionary psychology also predicts that a man should prefer to mate with the most fertile young women available because they are most likely to bear his children. A woman should prefer to mate with a man of high social status and solid material resources, one who can give the children the best chance of surviving to adulthood and reproducing in their turn. As a result, evolutionary psychologists predict that men will prefer younger women (with many more fertile years ahead of them), whereas women will prefer older men (who have more resources). This sex difference in mate preference has been reported in surveys given in 37 different cultures (Buss, 1989).

Evolutionary psychology has not gone unchallenged. Evidence suggests that when people evaluate real-life potential partners instead of simply stating their general preferences on a survey, the sex differences predicted by evolutionary theory vanish (Eastwick & Finkel, 2008). And some critics argue that even if a behavioral pattern appears across many or all cultures, it does not necessarily follow that it is programmed into the genes. For example, some universal cross-cultural sex differences may have arisen simply because women had less upper body strength than men and – until very recently in technological societies – were pregnant or nursing during most of their adult lives. This created sex-based divisions of labor in virtually all societies, which placed political power and decision-making in the hands of men and confined women to the domestic sphere (Eagly & Wood, 1999). Greater sexual freedom for men could easily emerge from such power differences.

It is often instructive to ask whether evolutionary reasoning could also have predicted a different or opposite outcome. For example, we have seen the argument that a male's ability to produce many hundreds of offspring would create an evolutionary push toward male promiscuity. But the need to ensure that one's offspring survive to reproductive age – the same need that presumably gave rise to human pair bonding in the first place – would provide an opposing evolutionary push toward monogamy. In other words, evolutionary theory could be invoked to explain either male promiscuity or male sexual fidelity.

Despite these criticisms, there is no doubt that evolutionary thinking has reinvigorated both personality and social psychology. There is probably no other single principle in the behavioral sciences with as much potential explanatory power as the principle of evolution. Moreover, the emergence of evolutionary psychology shows once again the important role of biological evidence in contemporary psychology. Even social psychologists who study the processes of social cognition now theorize about how and why our strategies for processing social information might have evolved (Buss & Kenrick, 1998; Schaller & Park, 2011).

INTERIM SUMMARY

- Many factors influence whether we will be attracted to a particular individual. The most important are physical attractiveness, proximity, familiarity, similarity, and transference.

- Theorists have suggested that one reason people fall in love is that doing so expands the self.

- There have been several attempts to classify types of love. Passionate love is characterized by intense and often conflicting emotions, whereas companionate love is characterized by trust, caring, tolerance of the partner's flaws, and an emotional tone of warmth and affection. Another classification of love divides it into the components of intimacy, passion, and commitment.

- Evolutionary psychology suggests that humans have evolved to form long-term bonds with a partner because, over millennia for our ancestors, such pair bonds operated to ensure the survival of offspring to reproductive age. A more controversial hypothesis from evolutionary psychology is that men and women have evolved to pursue different mating strategies, with men evolving to be more promiscuous and seek out younger women.

SEEING BOTH SIDES
SHOULD WE TRUST AUTOMATIC THINKING?

YES, WE SHOULD TRUST AUTOMATIC THINKING

Ap Dijksterhuis, Radboud University Nijmegen

Well, yes. Most of the time. Automatic processes are generally predictable, and indeed reliable. The attitudes we have, our emotional reactions, and the unconscious thought processes underlying decision-making and creativity, all objectively reflect what we have learned, often unconsciously. We all learn to like a sweet taste and avoid a bitter taste. We learn that grass is green and the sky usually blue. We learn that social psychology is fun and that herbology is boring. Our enormous capacity to learn unconsciously and to reproduce and use the learned information at will is at times simply stunning.

In a way, automatic processes behave like computers and in that sense they are highly trustworthy. If you know what information you put in, you can be more or less sure what will come out. If you pair 'sweet' with 'mmm!' and 'bitter' with 'yuck!' ten times, you'll find that your unconscious has developed associations that are highly useful and that prevents you, as a child, from eating the ficus in the living room. However, given that such associations faithfully reflect someone's learning history, things occasionally go astray. If the unconscious is fed inappropriate information, it develops inappropriate associations. If you grow up in front of a TV that generally shows Caucasians while they mow lawns in immaculate suburbs and Africans while they sell drugs in far from immaculate alleyways, you'll end up with an association between 'Black' and 'bad.' Here, again, the unconscious will behave like a computer: garbage in, garbage out.

That being said, such inappropriate associations are really the exception to the rule that the unconscious is, by and large, reliable. One wonderful tool our unconscious gives us is intuition. Sometimes we just know we should buy those shoes, or that we should not buy a car from the somewhat sleazy salesperson. Intuition helps us to make very important decisions such as to buy a house, or to choose a university. In such cases, intuition beats conscious or controlled processes hands down. We can think for a long time about important decisions such as what house to buy, but tempting as this may be, it will most likely not improve your decision. You need your unconscious here. You need to give such major decisions lots of time, and let your unconscious come up with an intuition. Only then you may again bring in consciousness again, for instance to check some details in the contract you have to sign. Einstein once said 'The intellect has little to do on the road to discovery. There comes a leap in consciousness, call it intuition or what you will, and the solution comes to you and you don't know how or why.' True creativity is the domain of the unconscious. In fact, scientific studies show that extraordinary creativity often follows the same process. First, scientists and artists read, think and talk. During this period, the unconscious is fed with useful information. After that, things are left alone for a while. During this period the unconscious crunches the information, and then, suddenly, a solution presents itself. In such cases, the unconscious shows itself in all its majestic magnificence. Conscious thought never leads to great creativity. It really is always the unconscious. If you do not trust your unconscious, or your automatic processes, you'll never be creative.

The bottom line is that you can almost always trust your unconscious as long as you make sure that it uses, or has used, the right information. If this is not the case, such as when your unconscious steers you toward prejudice, you want to use conscious or controlled processes to correct and to prevent damage.

In other cases, you should trust unconscious processes and to some extent distrust conscious processes. It is tempting to think that consciousness should deal with the most important things and that less important matters can be delegated to the unconscious. This is not true. In some domains, such as complex decision-making or creativity, conscious processes can perform abysmally. Very often, the unconscious works are ensuing satisfactorily, and all consciousness can do is throw a wrench in.

Should we trust automatic thinking? Yes, with a few exceptions. Should we trust controlled processes? Sometimes, but only use them when your automatic processes lead you astray.

SEEING BOTH SIDES
SHOULD WE TRUST AUTOMATIC THINKING?

NO, WE SHOULD NOT TRUST AUTOMATIC THINKING

B. Keith Payne, University of North Carolina, Chapel Hill

Should we trust automatic thinking? Not really. To be sure, automatic thought has a lot going for it. It's fast. It's easy. It can keep us alive and solve certain kinds of problems with great skill. But when we rely on automatic thinking, we sometimes act in ways that we would not be proud of.

For example, automatic thought is full of stereotypes and prejudices. When people rely on automatic thinking, they tend to assume that blacks are criminals, immigrants are lazy, and college professors are a bunch of liberals preoccupied with the plight of blacks and immigrants. Some people believe these things consciously, of course, but our automatic reactions are much more biased by stereotypes and prejudices than our conscious and thoughtful responses (Payne, 2006).

Evolutionary theorists argue that automatic thought systems evolved to solve the survival problems that our ancestors faced. As a result, automatic thinking is brilliantly efficient at detecting threats and contaminants, noticing mating opportunities, and so on. But the same tool kit that works so well for passing on genes sometimes causes problems for living in modern democratic societies. Automatic thinking loves hierarchy. It has an *us versus them* mentality, so it is quick to separate our own group from 'outsiders' and 'foreigners.' That might have worked well for our hunter-gatherer ancestors, but it works at the expense of other notions like equality, freedom, and human rights.

But prejudice is not the automatic mind's only trick. On autopilot, we sometimes care about the wrong things and we can get the simplest of judgments wrong. All of us would probably agree that all human life is valuable, and that we should work harder to help two suffering victims than to help one. But when actually asked to help famine victims, people donate more money to help one victim than to help eight victims. There is something about a single victim that elicits

more sympathy than many victims (Cameron & Payne, 2011). This emotional misalignment happens not only for sympathy, but also for fear. People stay away from beaches because they fear outbreaks of shark attacks, despite the fact that distraction from text-messaging kills more people in a day than sharks kill in a year (http://www.cdc.gov). The consequences are not trivial. Automatic thinking leads people to make foolish decisions when a little arithmetic could save their lives. For example, following the September 11, 2001 airplane attacks on the US World Trade Center and Pentagon buildings, Americans became afraid of flying. They shifted instead to driving. Their automatic response did not take into account the fact that the risk of death while driving is about 65 times higher than when flying. As a result, more than 1500 people lost their lives as a direct result of shifting to cars in the months following 9/11 (Gigerenzer, 2006).

Automatic thinking leads people to act impulsively in large and small ways. It beckons people to smoke another cigarette, despite conscious thoughts calmly reminding them that it is unhealthy. Automatic thinking leads people to gamble unwisely, assuming that if they've lost the last six rounds in a row, the next time *just has to be* in their favor. If you look, you can probably find automatic thinking behind the last thing you said that you wish you hadn't said.

So what to do? Simply not thinking automatically is not an option. As far as we know, the human auto-pilot does not have an off-switch. Nor would we want one, as all those automatic survival skills turn out to be quite useful. But that does not mean we ought to simply accept the commands of automatic thought at face value. Trying to decide whether to eat the foul-smelling thing that's been in your refrigerator too long? It's probably best to trust your automatic disgust response. But if you're trying to decide whether you should quit smoking, or whether an immigrant job applicant is qualified, or whether to risk your neck climbing Mount Everest because it's there, do yourself a favor. Think for a few minutes; pay attention, and do the math. Life on automatic pilot can be easy. Sometimes too easy.

RECAP: A TALE OF TWO MODES OF SOCIAL COGNITION

The major lesson of this chapter is that, in addition to understanding the power of social situations (the major lesson of Chapter 17), to more fully understand people's social behavior we also need to 'get inside their heads' and examine how they think about others. The field of social cognition takes on this task. It examines the processes by which stereotypes and other social schemas become activated and affect people's thinking and behavior. It also examines the processes by which people can get beyond stereotypes to more accurately know one another. And it examines the processes by which people are persuaded to change their minds and even fall in love.

Across these many domains of study, social psychologists have repeatedly found that social cognition – or thinking about others – happens in two modes: one mode is more automatic and outside of conscious awareness, and the other is more effortful and deliberate. This recognition has produced a range of 'dual-process theories' within social psychology. Two theories that received the spotlight in this chapter – the continuum model of impression formation (see Figure 18.2) and the elaboration likelihood model of persuasion – illustrate dual-process perspectives, but there are many other renditions (see Chaiken & Trope, 1999). Recognizing these two modes of thinking helps us better understand and even alter social outcomes. To the extent that we are able and willing to engage in effortful thinking, we can curb stereotyping, avert peripheral routes to persuasion, and minimize transference. But when, for whatever reasons, we are unable to engage in effortful thought – perhaps because we're busy carrying on a conversation, trying to manage the impression others form of us, or simply mentally depleted – we are more susceptible to various forms of automatic social cognition and behavior. In the above Seeing Both Sides essays, we see some of the ways our thoughts and behaviors are affected in the absence of effortful thought.

CHAPTER SUMMARY

1 Social cognition is the study of people's subjective interpretations of their social experiences, as well as their modes of thinking about the social world. Two different modes of thinking have been found to be critical within social cognition: one more automatic and unintentional, often fast and outside conscious awareness, and another more controlled, deliberate, and slow, of which we are fully aware.

2 Schematic processing is the perceiving and interpreting of incoming information in terms of simplified memory structures called *schemas*. Schemas are mini-theories about everyday objects and events. They allow us to process social information efficiently by permitting us to encode and remember only the unique or most prominent features of a new object or event. Stereotypes are schemas about groups of people.

3 Through repeated exposure, stereotypes can become habitual and automatic, operating outside conscious awareness.

4 Because schemas and stereotypes simplify reality, schematic processing produces biases and errors in our processing of social information. In forming impressions of other people, for example, we are prone to the primacy effect: the first information we receive evokes an initial schema and, hence, becomes more powerful in determining our impression than does later information. Schemas and stereotypes also govern our inferences.

5 Once activated, stereotypes can set in motion a chain of behavioral processes that serve to draw out from others behavior that confirms the initial stereotype, an effect called the *self-fulfilling prophecy*. This behavioral sequence can occur completely outside conscious awareness.

6 Stereotypes about the self can be self-fulfilling as well. Stereotype threat refers to how the mere threat of being identified with a stereotype can raise a person's anxiety level, reduce working memory capacity, and thereby degrade performance.

7 Individuation is the process of forming impressions of others by assessing their personal qualities on a person-by-person basis. The continuum model of impression formation details when and how people come to individuate others. Co-operative activities can promote individuation.

8 Although stereotypes are activated automatically, under the right conditions they can also be controlled through effortful thinking.

9 Attribution is the process by which we attempt to interpret and explain the behavior of other people – that is, to discern the causes of their actions. One major attribution task is to decide whether someone's action should be attributed to dispositional causes (the person's personality or attitudes) or to situational causes (social forces or other external circumstances). We tend to give too much weight to dispositional factors and too little to situational factors. This bias has been called the *fundamental attribution error*.

10 Ancient cultural practices and beliefs about the locus of causality are believed to have shaped contemporary cultural differences in styles of thinking. Research has shown repeatedly that East Asians think more holistically, whereas Westerners think analytically. This work challenges all claims to universality made about human cognition, both basic and social.

11 Research on embodied social cognition finds that our bodily states – such as those associated with temperature or eye contact – automatically influence our inferences about other people.

12 Attitudes are likes and dislikes – favorable or unfavorable evaluations of and reactions to objects, people, events, or ideas. Attitudes have a cognitive component, an affective component, and a behavioral component.

13 The elaboration likelihood model states that persuasion can take two routes in producing belief and attitude change: the central route, in which the individual responds to the substantive arguments of a communication, and the peripheral route, in which the individual responds to non-content cues in a communication (such as the number of arguments) or to context cues (such as the credibility of the communicator or the pleasantness of the surroundings). A communication about an issue of personal relevance is more likely to generate thoughts in response to the communication's substantive arguments. When an issue is of little personal relevance or people are unwilling or unable to respond to the substantive content of a communication, they tend to use simple heuristics – rules of thumb – to judge the merits of the communication.

14 Attitudes tend to predict behavior best when they are (1) strong and consistent, (2) specifically related to the behavior being predicted, and (3) based on the person's direct experience, as well as (4) when the individual is aware of his or her attitudes.

15 Many factors influence whether we will be attracted to a particular individual. The most important are physical attractiveness, proximity, familiarity, similarity, and transference.

Theorists have suggested that one reason people fall in love is that doing so expands the self.

 There have been several attempts to classify types of love. Passionate love is characterized by intense and often conflicting emotions, whereas companionate love is characterized by trust, caring, tolerance of the partner's flaws, and an emotional tone of warmth and affection. Even though passionate love decreases over time in long-term relationships, the potential for strong emotion actually increases. But, because companionate couples become so compatible in their daily rou-

tines, the actual frequency of strong emotions is fairly low. Another classification of love divides it into the components of intimacy, passion, and commitment.

 Evolutionary psychology suggests that humans have evolved to form long-term bonds with a partner because historically such pair bonds operated to ensure the survival of offspring to reproductive age. A more controversial hypothesis from evolutionary psychology is that men and women have evolved to pursue different mating strategies, with men evolving to be more promiscuous and seek out younger women.

CORE CONCEPTS

social cognition	stereotype threat	counterarguing
System 1	individuation	attitude bolstering
System 2	continuum model	proximity
schema	social identity approach	mere exposure effect
schematic processing	attribution	implicit egotism
stereotype	dispositional attribution	transference
self-schema	fundamental attribution error	self-expansion
priming	holistic thought	passionate love
primacy effect	analytic thought	companionate love
construal-level theory	attitudes	triangular theory of love
recency effect	elaboration likelihood model	intimacy
inferences	central route	passion
self-fulfilling prophecy	peripheral route	commitment

STATISTICAL METHODS AND MEASUREMENT

APPENDIX OUTLINE

DESCRIPTIVE STATISTICS

Frequency distributions

Measures of central tendency

Measures of variation

STATISTICAL INFERENCE

Populations and samples

The normal distribution

Scaling of data

How representative is a mean?

The significance of a difference

THE COEFFICIENT OF CORRELATION

Product-moment correlation

Interpreting a correlation coefficient

Much of the work of psychologists calls for making measurements – either in the laboratory or under field conditions. This work may involve measuring the eye movements of infants when first exposed to a novel stimulus, recording the heart rate of people under stress, counting the number of trials required to condition a monkey to perform a task, determining achievement test scores for students using computer-assisted learning, or counting the number of patients who show improvement following a particular type of psychotherapy. In all these examples, the *measurement operation* yields numbers; the psychologist's problem is to interpret them and to arrive at some general conclusions. Basic to this task is statistics – the discipline that deals with collecting numerical data and with making inferences from such data. The purpose of this appendix is to review certain statistical methods that play an important role in psychology.

This appendix is written on the assumption that the problems students have with statistics are essentially problems of clear thinking about data. An introductory acquaintance with statistics is not beyond the scope of anyone who understands enough algebra to use plus and minus signs and to substitute numbers for letters in equations.

DESCRIPTIVE STATISTICS

Statistics serves, first of all, to provide a shorthand description of large amounts of data. Suppose that we want to study the college entrance examination scores of 5000 students recorded on cards in the registrar's office. These scores are the raw data. Thumbing through the cards will give us some impressions of the students' scores, but it will be impossible for us to keep all of them in mind. So we make some kind of summary of the data, possibly averaging all the scores or finding the highest and lowest scores. These statistical summaries make it easier to remember and to think about the data. Such summarizing statements are called *descriptive statistics*.

Frequency distributions

Items of raw data become understandable when they are grouped in a *frequency distribution*. To group data, we must first divide the scale along which they are measured into intervals and then count the number of items that fall into each interval. An interval in which scores are grouped is called a *class interval*. The decision of how many class intervals the data are to be grouped into is not fixed by any rules but is based on the judgment of the investigator.

Table A1 provides a sample of raw data representing university entrance examination scores for 15 students. The scores are listed in the order in which the students were tested (the first student tested had a score of 84; the second, 61; and so on). Table A2 shows these data arranged in a

TABLE A1   RAW SCORES

Examination scores for 15 students, listed in the order in which they were tested.

84	75	91
61	75	67
72	87	79
75	79	83
77	51	69

TABLE A2   A FREQUENCY DISTRIBUTION

Scores from Table A1, accumulated by class intervals.

Class interval	Number of persons in class
50–59	1
60–69	3
70–79	7
80–89	3
90–99	1

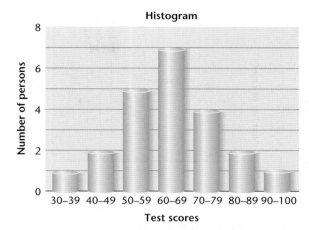

FIGURE A1 **Frequency Diagrams.** *The data from Table A2 are plotted here. A frequency histogram is on the left, a frequency polygon on the right.*

frequency distribution for which the class interval has been set at 10. One score falls in the interval from 50 to 59, three scores fall in the interval from 60 to 69, and so on. Note that most scores fall in the interval from 70 to 79 and that no scores fall below the 50 to 59 interval or above the 90 to 99 interval.

A frequency distribution is often easier to understand if it is presented graphically. The most widely used graph form is the *frequency histogram*; an example is shown in Figure A1. Histograms are constructed by drawing bars, the bases of which are given by the class intervals and the heights of which are determined by the corresponding class frequencies.

In practice, we would obtain a much greater number of items than those plotted in Figure A1, but a minimum amount of data is shown in all of the illustrations in this appendix so that you can easily check the steps in tabulating and plotting.

Measures of central tendency

A *measure of central tendency* is simply a representative point on our scale – a central point that summarizes important information about the data. Three such measures are commonly used: the *mean*, the *median*, and the *mode*.

The mean is the familiar arithmetic average obtained by adding the scores and dividing by the number of scores. The sum of the raw scores in Table A1 is 1125. If we divide this by 15 (the number of students' scores), the mean turns out to be 75.

The median is the score of the middle item, which is obtained by arranging the scores in order and then counting into the middle from either end. When the 15 scores in Table A1 are placed in order from highest to lowest, the eighth score from either end turns out to be 75. If the number of cases is even, we simply average the two cases on each side of the middle. The mode is the most frequent score in a given distribution. In Table A1, the most frequent score is 75; hence, the mode of the distribution is 75.

In a *normal distribution*, in which the scores are distributed evenly on either side of the middle (as in Figure A1), the mean, median, and mode all fall together. This is not true for distributions that are *skewed*, or unbalanced. Suppose we want to analyze the departure times of a morning train. The train usually leaves on time; occasionally it leaves late, but it never leaves early. For a train with a scheduled departure time of 8:00 a.m., 1 week's record might be as follows:

Mon	8:00	Mean =	8:07
Tue	8:04	Median =	8:02
Wed	8:02	Mode =	8:00
Thu	8:19		
Fri	8:22		
Sat	8:00		
Sun	8:00		

The distribution of departure times in this example is skewed because of the two late departures; they raise the mean departure time but do not have much effect on the median or the mode.

Skewness is important because, unless it is understood, the differences between the median and the mean may sometimes be misleading (see Figure A2).

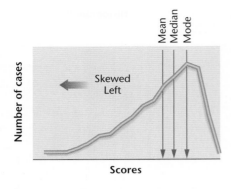

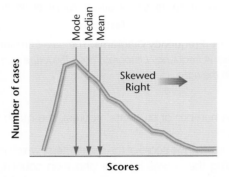

FIGURE A2 Skewed Distribution Curves. *Note that skewed distributions are designated by the direction in which the tail falls. Also note that the mean, median, and mode are not identical for a skewed distribution; the median commonly falls between the mode and the mean.*

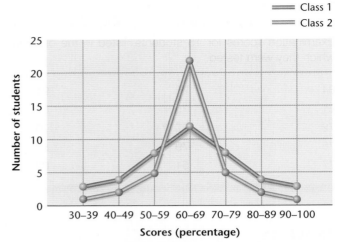

FIGURE A3 Distributions Differing in Variation. *It is easy to see that the scores for Class I cluster closer to the mean than the scores for Class II, even though the means of the two classes are identical (75). For Class I, all the scores fall between 60 and 89, with most of the scores falling in the interval from 70 through 79. For Class II, the scores are distributed fairly uniformly over a wide range from 40 through 109. This difference in variability between the two distributions can be measured using the standard deviation, which is smaller for Class I than for Class II.*

If, for example, company executives and the company's union are arguing about the prosperity of the company's workforce, it is possible for the mean and median incomes to move in opposite directions. Suppose that a company raises the wages of most of its employees, but cuts the wages of its top executives, who were at the extremely high end of the pay scale. The median income of the company might have gone up while the mean went down. The party wanting to show that incomes were getting higher would choose the median, and the party wanting to show that incomes were getting lower would choose the mean.

The mean is the most widely used measure of central tendency, but there are times when the mode or the median is a more meaningful measure.

Measures of variation

Usually more information is needed about a distribution than can be obtained from a measure of central tendency. For example, we need a measure to tell us whether scores cluster closely around their average or whether they scatter widely. A measure of the spread of scores around the average is called a *measure of variation*.

Measures of variation are useful in at least two ways. First, they tell us how representative the average is. If the variation

is small, we know that individual scores are close to the average. If the variation is large, we cannot use the mean as a representative value with as much assurance. Suppose that clothing is being designed for a group of people without the benefit of precise measurements. Knowing their average size would be helpful, but it also would be important to know the spread of sizes. The second measure provides a yardstick that we can use to measure the amount of variability among the sizes.

To illustrate, consider the data in Figure A3, which show frequency distributions of entrance examination scores for two classes of 30 students. Both classes have the same mean of 75, but they exhibit clearly different degrees of variation. The scores of all the students in Class I are clustered close to the mean, whereas the scores of the students in Class II are spread over a wide range. Some measure is required to specify more exactly how these two distributions differ. Three measures of variation frequently used by psychologists are the *range*, the *variance*, and the *standard deviation*.

To simplify computation, we will suppose that five students from each class seek entrance to university and that their entrance examination scores are as follows:

Student scores from Class I:
73, 74, 75, 76, 77 (mean = 75)

Student scores from Class II:
60, 65, 75, 85, 90 (mean = 75)

We will now compute the measures of variation for these two samples. The range is the spread between the highest score and the lowest score. The range of scores for the five students from Class I is 4 (from 73 to 77); the range of scores from Class II is 30 (from 60 to 90).

The range is easy to compute, but the variance and standard deviation are more frequently used. They are more sensitive measures of variation because they account for every score, not just extreme values as the range does. The variance measures how far the scores making up a distribution depart from that distribution's mean. To compute the variance, first compute the deviation d of each score from the mean of the distribution by subtracting each score from the mean (see Table A3). Then, each of the deviations is squared to get rid of negative numbers. Finally, the deviations are added together and divided by the total number of deviations to obtain the average deviation. This average deviation is the variance. When this is done for the data in

Figure A3, we find that the variance for Class I is 2.0 and the variance for Class II is 130. Obviously, Class II has much more variability in its scores than Class I.

One disadvantage of the variance is that it is expressed in squared units of measurement. Thus, to say that Class I has a variance of 2 does not indicate that, on average, scores varied by an average of 2 points from the mean. Instead, it indicates that 2 is the average of the squared number of points that scores varied from the mean. In order to obtain a measure of variability that is expressed in the original units of measurement (in this case, points on an exam), simply take the square root of the variance. This is known as the standard deviation. The standard deviation is denoted by the lowercase Greek letter *sigma, σ*,* which also is used in several other statistical calculations, as we will discuss shortly. The formula for the standard deviation is:

$$\sigma = \sqrt{\frac{\text{sum of } d^2}{N}}$$

The scores for the samples from the two classes are arranged in Table A3 for easy computation of the standard deviation. The first step involves subtracting the mean from each score (the mean is 75 for both classes). This operation yields positive d values for scores above the mean and negative d values for scores below the mean. The minus signs disappear when the d values are squared in the next column. The squared deviations are added and then divided by N, the number of cases in the sample; in our example, $N = 5$. Taking the square root yields the standard deviation.

TABLE A3 COMPUTATION OF THE VARIANCE AND STANDARD DEVIATION

Class I scores (Mean = 75)

	d	d^2
77 − 75 =	2	4
76 − 75 =	1	1
75 − 75 =	0	0
74 − 75 =	−1	1
73 − 75 =	−2	4
		10

Sum of d^2 = 10

Variance = mean of d^2 = 10/5 = 2.0

Standard Deviation (σ) = = 1.4

Class II scores (Mean = 75)

	d	d^2
90 − 75 =	15	225
85 − 75 =	10	100
75 − 75 =	0	0
65 − 75 =	−10	100
60 − 75 =	−15	225
		650

Sum of d^2 = 650

Variance = mean of d^2 = 650/5 = 130

Standard Deviation (σ) = 11.4

STATISTICAL INFERENCE

Now that we have become familiar with statistics as a way of describing data, we are ready to turn to the processes of interpretation – to the making of inferences from data.

Populations and samples

First, it is necessary to distinguish between a *population* and a *sample* drawn from that population. A national census such as that carried out by the UK Office of National Statistics

---

*For this introductory treatment, we will use sigma (σ) throughout. However, in the scientific literature, the lowercase letter s is used to denote the standard deviation of a sample and s is used to denote the standard deviation of the population. Moreover, in computing the standard deviation of a sample s, the sum of d^2 is divided by $N - 1$ rather than by N. For reasonably large samples, however, the actual value of the standard deviation is only slightly affected whether we divide by $N - 1$ or N. To simplify this presentation, we will not distinguish between the standard deviation of a sample and that of a population; instead, we will use the same formula to compute both. For a discussion of this point, see Phillips (1992).

attempts to describe the whole population by obtaining descriptive material on age, marital status, and so on from everyone in the country. The word *population* is appropriate to the census because it represents *all* the people living in the UK.

In statistics, the word 'population' is not limited to people or animals or things. The population may be all of the temperatures registered on a thermometer during the last decade, all of the words in the English language, or all of any other specified supply of data. Often we do not have access to the total population, and so we try to represent it by a sample drawn in a *random* (unbiased) fashion. We may ask some questions of a random fraction of the people, as the UK Office of National Statistics has done as part of recent censuses; we may derive average temperatures by reading the thermometer at specified times, without taking a continuous record; we may estimate the number of words in the encyclopedia by counting the words on random pages. These illustrations all involve the selection of a sample from the population. If any of these processes are repeated, we will obtain slightly different results due to the fact that a sample does not fully represent the whole population and therefore contains *errors of sampling*. This is where statistical inference enters.

A sample of data is collected from a population in order to make inferences about that population. A sample of census data may be examined to see whether the population is getting older, for example, or whether there is a trend of migration to the particular geographical regions. Similarly, experimental results are studied to determine what effects experimental manipulations have had on behavior – whether the threshold for pitch is affected by loudness, whether child-rearing practices have detectable effects later in life. To make *statistical inferences*, we have to evaluate the relationships revealed by the sample data. These inferences are always made under some degree of uncertainty due to sampling errors. If the statistical tests indicate that the magnitude of the effect found in the sample is fairly large (relative to the estimate of the sampling error), then we can be confident that the effect observed in the sample holds for the population at large.

Thus, statistical inference deals with the problem of making an inference or judgment about a feature of a population based solely on information obtained from a sample of that population. As an introduction to statistical inference, we will consider the normal distribution and its use in interpreting standard deviations.

The normal distribution

When large amounts of data are collected, tabulated, and plotted as a histogram, they often fall into a roughly bell-shaped symmetrical distribution known as the *normal distribution*. Most items fall near the mean (the high point of the bell), and the bell tapers off sharply at very high and very low scores. This form of curve is of special interest because

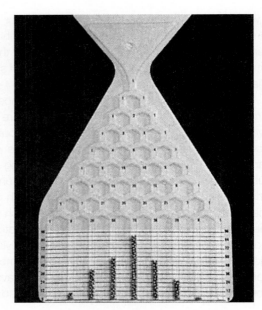

FIGURE A4 **A Device to Demonstrate a Chance Distribution.** *The board is held upside down until all the steel balls fall into the reservoir. Then the board is turned over and held vertically until the balls fall into the nine columns. The precise number of balls falling into each column will vary from one demonstration to the next. On average, however, the heights of the columns of balls will approximate a normal distribution, with the greatest height in the center column and gradually decreasing heights in the outer columns.*

it also arises when the outcome of a process is based on a large number of *chance* events all occurring independently. The demonstration device displayed in Figure A4 illustrates how a sequence of chance events gives rise to a normal distribution. The chance factor of whether a steel ball will fall to the left or right each time it encounters a point where the channel branches results in a symmetrical distribution: More balls fall straight down the middle, but occasionally one reaches one of the end compartments. This is a useful way of visualizing what is meant by a chance distribution closely approximating the normal distribution.

The normal distribution (Figure A5) is the mathematical representation of the idealized distribution approximated by the device shown in Figure A4. The normal distribution represents the likelihood that items within a normally distributed population will depart from the mean by any stated amount. The percentages shown in Figure A5 represent the *percentage of the area* lying under the curve between the indicated scale values; the total area under the curve represents the whole population. Roughly two-thirds of the cases (68%) will fall between plus and minus one standard deviation from the mean ($\pm 1\sigma$); 95% of the cases within $\pm 2\sigma$ and virtually all cases (99.7%) within $\pm 3\sigma$. A more detailed listing of areas under portions of the normal curve is given in Table A4.

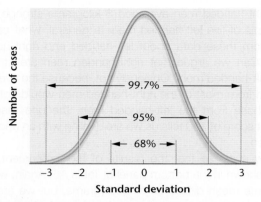

FIGURE A5 The Normal Distribution. *The normal distribution curve can be constructed using the mean and the standard deviation. The area under the curve below -3σ and above $+3\sigma$ is negligible.*

Using Table A4, let us trace how the 68% and 95% values in Figure A5 are derived. We find from Column 3 of Table A4 that between -1σ and the mean lies 0.341 of the total area and between $+1\sigma$ and the mean also lies 0.341 of the area. Adding these values gives us 0.682, which is expressed in Figure A5 as 68%. Similarly, the area between -2σ and $+2\sigma$ is $2 \times 0.477 = 0.954$, which is expressed as 95%.

These percentages have several uses. One is in connection with the interpretation of standard scores, to which we turn next. Another is in connection with tests of significance.

TABLE A4   THE AREA OF THE NORMAL DISTRIBUTION AS A PROPORTION OF TOTAL AREA

Standard deviation	(1) Area to the left of this value	(2) Area to the right of this value	(3) Area between this value and the mean
-3.0σ	0.001	0.999	0.499
-2.5σ	0.006	0.994	0.494
-2.0σ	0.023	0.977	0.477
-1.5σ	0.067	0.933	0.433
-1.0σ	0.159	0.841	0.341
-0.5σ	0.309	0.691	0.191
0.0σ	0.500	0.500	0.000
$+0.5\sigma$	0.691	0.309	0.191
$+1.0\sigma$	0.841	0.159	0.341
$+1.5\sigma$	0.933	0.067	0.433
$+2.0\sigma$	0.977	0.023	0.477
$+2.5\sigma$	0.994	0.006	0.494
$+3.0\sigma$	0.999	0.001	0.499

Scaling of data

In order to interpret a score, we often need to know whether it is high or low in relation to other scores. If a person taking a driver's test requires 0.500 seconds to brake after a danger signal, how can we tell whether the performance is fast or slow? Does a student who scores 60 on a physics examination pass the course? To answer questions of this kind, we have to derive a scale against which the scores can be compared.

Ranked data

By placing scores in rank order from high to low, we derive one kind of scale. An individual score is interpreted on the basis of where it ranks among the group of scores. For example, the graduates of a university may know where they stand in their class – perhaps 35th or 125th in a class of 400.

Standard scores

The standard deviation is a convenient unit to use in scaling because we can interpret how far away 1σ or 2σ is from the mean (see Table A4). A score based on a multiple of the standard deviation is known as a *standard score*. Many scales used in psychological measurement are based on the principle of standard scores.

Table A1 presented college entrance scores for 15 students. Without more information, we do not know whether these scores are representative of the population of all university applicants. On this examination, however, we will assume that the population mean is 75 and the standard deviation is 10.

What, then, is the standard score for a student who had 90 on the examination? We must express how far this score lies above the mean in multiples of the standard deviation.

Standard score for grade of 90:

$$\frac{90 - 75}{10} = \frac{15}{10} = 1.5\sigma$$

As a second example, consider a student with a score of 53.

Standard score for grade of 53:

$$\frac{53 - 75}{10} = \frac{-22}{10} = -2.2\sigma$$

In this case, the minus sign tells us that the student's score is below the mean by 2.2 standard deviations. Thus, the sign of the standard score (+ or −) indicates whether the score is above or below the mean, and its value indicates how far from the mean the score lies in standard deviations.

How representative is a mean?

How useful is the mean of a sample in estimating the population mean? If we measure the height of a random sample of 100 university students, how well does the sample mean predict the true population mean (that is, the mean height of *all* university students)? These questions raise the issue of making an *inference* about a population based on information from a sample.

The accuracy of such inferences depends on *errors of sampling*. Suppose we were to select two random samples from the same population and compute the mean for each sample. What differences between the first and the second mean could be expected to occur by chance? Successive random samples drawn from the same population will have different means, forming a distribution of *sample means* around the *true mean* of the population. These sample means are themselves numbers for which the standard deviation can be computed. We call this standard deviation the standard error of the mean, or σ_M, and can estimate it on the basis of the following formula:

$$\sigma_M = \frac{\sigma}{\sqrt{N}}$$

where σ is the standard deviation of the sample and N is the number of cases from which each sample mean is computed.

According to the formula, the size of the standard error of the mean decreases as the sample size increases; thus, a mean based on a large sample is more trustworthy (more likely to be close to the actual population mean) than a mean based on a smaller sample. Common sense would lead us to expect this. Computations of the standard error of the mean permit us to make clear assertions about the degree of uncertainty in our computed mean. The more cases in the sample, the more uncertainty has been reduced.

The significance of a difference

In many psychological experiments, data are collected on two groups of participants; one group is exposed to certain specified experimental conditions, and the other serves as a control group. The question is whether there is a difference in the mean performance of the two groups, and if such a difference is observed, whether it holds for the population from which these groups of participants have been sampled. Basically, we are asking whether a difference between two sample means reflects a true difference or whether this difference is simply the result of sampling error.

As an example, we will compare the scores on a reading test for a sample of 6-year-old boys with the scores for a sample of 6-year-old girls. The boys score lower than the girls as far as mean performances are concerned, but there is a great deal of overlap; some boys do extremely well, and some girls do very poorly. Thus, we cannot accept the obtained difference in means without making a test of its *statistical significance*. Only then can we decide whether the observed differences in sample means reflect true differences in the population or are due to sampling error. If some of the brighter girls and some of the duller boys are sampled by sheer luck, the difference could be due to sampling error.

As another example, suppose that we have set up an experiment to compare the grip strength of right-handed and left-handed men. The top panel of Table A5 presents hypothetical data from such an experiment. A sample of five right-handed men averaged 8 kilograms stronger than a sample of five left-handed men. In general, what can we infer from these data about left-handed and right-handed men? Can we argue that right-handed men are stronger than left-handed men? Obviously not, because the averages derived from most of the right-handed men would not differ from those from the left-handed men; the one markedly deviant score of 100 tells us we are dealing with an uncertain situation.

Now suppose that the results of the experiment were those shown in the bottom panel of Table A5. Again, we find the same mean difference of 8 kilograms, but we are now inclined to have greater confidence in the results, because the left-handed men scored consistently lower than the right-handed men. Statistics provides a precise way of taking into account the reliability of the mean differences so that we do not have to depend solely on intuition to determine that one difference is more reliable than another.

TABLE A5   THE SIGNIFICANCE OF A DIFFERENCE

Two examples that compare the difference between means are shown. The difference between means is the same (8 kilograms) in both the top and bottom panel. However, the data in the bottom panel indicate a more reliable difference between means than do the data in the top panel.

Strength of grip in kilograms, right-handed men	Strength of grip in kilograms, left-handed men
40	40
45	45
50	50
55	55
100	60
Sum 290	Sum 250
Mean 58	Mean 50

Strength of grip in kilograms, right-handed men	Strength of grip in kilograms, left-handed men
56	48
57	49
58	50
59	51
60	52
Sum 290	Sum 250
Mean 58	Mean 50

These examples suggest that the significance of a difference will depend on both the size of the obtained difference and the variability of the means being compared. From the standard error of the means, we can compute the *standard error of the difference between two means*, $\sigma\Delta_M$. We can then evaluate the obtained difference by using a *critical ratio* – the ratio of the obtained difference between the means D_M to the standard error of the difference:

$$\text{Critical Ratio} = \frac{D_M}{\sigma D_M}$$

This ratio helps us evaluate the significance of the difference between the two means. As a rule of thumb, a critical ratio should be 2.0 or larger for the difference between means to be accepted as significant. Throughout this book, statements that the difference between means is 'statistically significant' indicate that the critical ratio is at least that large.

Why is a critical ratio of 2.0 selected as statistically significant? Simply because a value this large or larger can occur by chance only 5 out of 100 times. Where do we get the 5 out of 100? We can treat the critical ratio as a standard score because it is merely the difference between two means, expressed as a multiple of its standard error. Referring to Column 2 in Table A4, we note that the likelihood is 0.023 that a standard deviation as high as or higher than +2.0 will occur by chance. Because the chance of deviating in the opposite direction is also 0.023, the total probability is 0.046. This means that 46 times out of 1000, or about 5 times out of 100, a critical ratio as large as 2.0 would be found by chance if the population means were identical.

The rule of thumb that says a critical ratio should be at least 2.0 is just that – an arbitrary but convenient rule that defines the '5% level of significance'. Following this rule, we will make fewer than 5 errors in 100 decisions by concluding on the basis of sample data that a difference in means exists when in fact there is none. The 5% level need not always be used; a higher level of significance may be appropriate in certain experiments, depending on how willing we are to make an occasional error in inference.

The computation of the critical ratio calls for finding the *standard error of the difference between two means*, which is given by the following formula:

$$\sigma\Delta_M = \sqrt{(\sigma M_1)^2 + (\sigma M_2)^2}$$

In this formula, σM_1, and σM_2 are the standard errors of the two means being compared.

As an illustration, suppose we wanted to compare reading achievement test scores for 6 year-old boys and girls. A random sample of boys and girls would be identified and given the test. We will assume that the mean score for the boys was 70 with a standard error of 0.40 and that the mean score for the girls was 72 with a standard error of 0.30. On the basis of these samples, we want to decide whether there is a real difference between the reading achievement of boys and girls in the population as a whole. The sample data suggest that girls do achieve better reading scores than boys, but can we infer that this would have been the case if we had tested all the girls and all the boys in the country? The critical ratio helps us make this decision.

$$\sigma D_M = \sqrt{(\sigma M_1)^2 + (\sigma M_2)^2}$$
$$= \sqrt{0.16 + 0.09} = \sqrt{0.25}$$
$$= 0.5$$
$$\text{Critical Ratio} = \frac{D_M}{\sigma D_M} = \frac{72 - 70}{0.5} = \frac{2.0}{0.5} = 4.0$$

Because the critical ratio is well above 2.0, we may assert that the observed mean difference is statistically significant at the 5% level. Thus, we can conclude that there is a reliable difference in performance on the reading test between boys and girls. Note that the sign of the critical ratio could be positive or negative, depending on which mean is subtracted from which; when the critical ratio is interpreted, only its magnitude (not its sign) is considered.

THE COEFFICIENT OF CORRELATION

Correlation refers to the parallel variation of two measures. Suppose that a test is designed to predict success in university. If it is a good test, high scores on it will be related to high performance in university and low scores will be related to poor performance. The *coefficient of correlation* gives us a way of stating the degree of relationship more precisely.

Product-moment correlation

The most frequently used method of determining the coefficient of correlation is the *product-moment method*, which yields the index conventionally designated by the lowercase letter *r*. The product-moment coefficient *r* varies between perfect positive correlation ($r = +1.00$) and perfect negative correlation ($r = -1.00$). Lack of any relationship yields $r = 0.00$.

The formula for computing the product-moment correlation is:

$$r = \frac{Sum\ (dx)\ (dy)}{N\sigma_x\sigma_y}$$

Here, one of the paired measures has been labeled the *x*-score; the other, the *y*-score. The *dx* and *dy* refer to the deviations of each score from its mean, *N* is the number of paired measures, and σ_x and σ_y are the standard deviations of the *x*-scores and the *y*-scores.

The computation of the coefficient of correlation requires the determination of the sum of the (*dx*)(*dy*) products. This sum, in addition to the computed standard deviations for the *x*-scores and *y*-scores, can then be entered into the formula.

TABLE A6 COMPUTATION OF A PRODUCT-MOMENT CORRELATION

Student	Entrance Test (x-score)	Freshman Grades (y-score)	(dx)	(dy)	(dx)(dy)
Adam	71	39	6	9	+54
Bill	67	27	2	−3	−6
Charles	65	33	0	3	0
David	63	30	−2	0	4
Edward	59	21	−6	−9	+54
Sum	325	150	0	0	+102
Mean	65	30			

$$\sigma_x = 4$$
$$\sigma_y = 6$$

$$r = \frac{\text{Sum } (dx)\,(dy)}{N\sigma_x\sigma_y} = \frac{+102}{5 \times 4 \times 6} = +0.85$$

Suppose that we have collected the data shown in Table A6. For each participant, we have obtained two scores – the first being a score on a university entrance test (to be labeled arbitrarily the x-score) and the second being first year grades (the y-score).

Figure A6 is a *scatter diagram* of these data. Each point represents the x-score and y-score for a given participant; for example, the uppermost right-hand point is for Adam (labeled A). Looking at these data, we can easily detect that there is some positive correlation between the x-scores and the y-scores. Adam attained the highest score on the entrance test and also earned the highest first year grades; Edward received the lowest scores on both. The other students' test scores and grades are a little irregular, so we know that the correlation is not perfect; hence, r is less than 1.00.

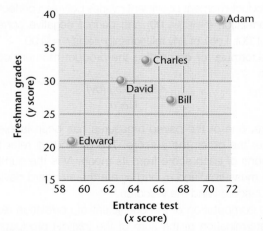

FIGURE A6 A Scatter Design. *Each point represents the x- and y-scores for a particualr student.*

We will compute the correlation to illustrate the method, although no researcher would consent, in practice, to determining a correlation for so few cases. The details are given in Table A6. Following the procedure outlined in Table A3 we compute the standard deviation of the x-scores and then the standard deviation of the y-scores. Next, we compute the (dx)(dy) products for each subject and total the five cases. Entering these results in our equation yields an r of +0.85.

Interpreting a correlation coefficient

We can use correlations in making predictions. For example, if we know from experience that a certain entrance test correlates with first year grades, we can predict the first year grades for beginning university students who have taken the test. If the correlation were perfect, we could predict their grades without error. But r is usually less than 1.00, and some errors in prediction will be made; the closer r is to 0, the greater the sizes of the errors in prediction.

Although we cannot go into the technical problems of predicting first year grades from entrance examinations or of making other similar predictions, we can consider the meanings of correlation coefficients of different sizes. It is evident that with a correlation of 0 between x and y, knowledge of x will not help to predict y. If weight is unrelated to intelligence, it does us no good to know a participant's weight when we are trying to predict his or her intelligence. At the other extreme, a perfect correlation would mean 100% predictive efficiency – knowing x, we can predict y perfectly. What about intermediate values of r? Some appreciation of the meaning of correlations of intermediate sizes can be gained by examining the scatter diagrams in Figure A7.

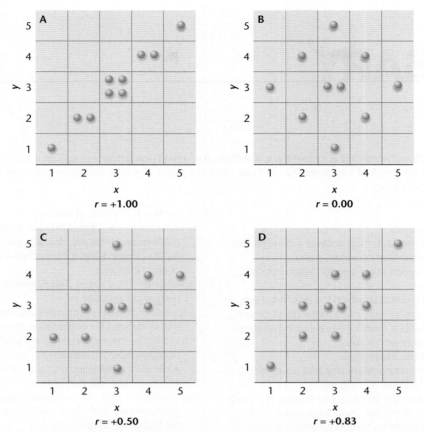

FIGURE A7 Scatter Diagrams Illustrating Correlations of Various Sizes. *Each dot represents one individual's score on two tests, x and y. In A, all cases fall on the diagonal and the correlation is perfect (r = +1.00); if we know a subject's score on x, we know that it will be the same on y. In B, the correlation is 0; knowing a subject's score on x, we cannot predict whether it will be at, above, or below the mean on y. In both C and D, there is a diagonal trend to the scores, so that a high score on x is associated with a high score on y and a low score on x with a low score on y, but the relationship is imperfect.*

In the preceding discussion, we did not emphasize the sign of the correlation coefficient, since this has no bearing on the strength of a relationship. The only distinction between a correlation of $r = +0.70$ and $r = -0.70$ is that increases in x are accompanied by increases in y for the former, and increases in x are accompanied by decreases in y for the latter.

Although the correlation coefficient is one of the most widely used statistics in psychology, it is also one of the most widely misused procedures. Those who use it sometimes overlook the fact that r does not imply a cause-and-effect relationship between x and y. When two sets of scores are correlated, we may suspect that they have some causal factors in common, but we cannot conclude that one of them causes the other.

Correlations sometimes appear paradoxical. For example, the correlation between study time and university grades has been found to be slightly negative (about -0.10). If a causal interpretation were assumed, we might conclude that the best way to raise grades would be to stop studying. The negative correlation arises because some students have advantages over others in grade making (possibly due to better university preparation), so that often those who study the hardest are those who have difficulty earning the best grades.

This example provides sufficient warning against assigning a causal interpretation to a coefficient of correlation. It is possible, however, that when two variables are correlated, one may be the cause of the other. The search for causes is a logical one, and correlations can help us by providing leads to experiments that can verify cause-and-effect relationships.

GLOSSARY

The glossary defines the technical words that appear in the text and some common words that have special meanings when used in psychology. No attempt is made to give the range of meanings beyond those used in the text. For fuller definitions and other shades of meaning, consult any standard dictionary of psychology.

A

abnormal Away from the norm.

absolute threshold The minimum magnitude of a stimulus that can be reliably discriminated from no stimulus at all.

abstraction Loss of information in the transformation from raw physical data to a percept.

accommodation (1) The process by which the lens of the eye varies its focus. (2) In Piaget's theory of cognitive development, the process by which an infant modifies a pre-existing schema in order to include a novel object or event.

acquisition the learning of an association.

action potential An electrochemical impulse that travels from the dendritic area down to the end of the axon.

activation model In memory, the proposal that retrieval of an item depends on the activation of that item reaching a critical level.

actualizing tendency A tendency toward fulfillment or actualization of all the capacities of the organism.

adaptive Adaptive behavior has survival value.

addiction A pattern of compulsive and destructive drug-taking behavior.

adolescence The period of transition from childhood to adulthood.

adolescent growth spurt A period of rapid physical growth that accompanies the onset of puberty.

affect Emotions and feelings.

affective neuroscience The study of how emotional phenomena are executed in the brain.

afferent nerves Nerves that carry signals from the body to the central nervous system.

agency Sense of mastery, control, capability to engage in action.

aggression Behavior that is intended to injure another person (physically or verbally) or to destroy property.

agnosia The general term for breakdowns or disorders in recognition.

agonists A drug that binds to receptors and activates them in much the same way that another drug does.

agoraphobia Fear of places where one might be trapped or unable to receive help in an emergency.

alliesthesia An interaction between incentive and drive theories of motivation which states that any external stimulus that corrects an internal trouble is experienced as pleasurable.

all-or-none law The principle that any neuron propagates its action potential either at full strength, or not at all.

altered states of consciousness A change from an ordinary pattern of mental functioning to a state that seems different to the person experiencing the change.

alternative form reliability The consistency between two or more versions of the same test when given to the same person.

amnesia Partial loss of memory.

amphetamines Central nervous system stimulants that produce restlessness, irritability, anxiety, and rapid heart rate. Dexedrine sulfate ('speed') and methamphetamine ('meth') are two types of amphetamines.

amplitude (of a tone) The difference in pressure between the peak and the trough.

amygdala A brain structure located below the cerebral cortex that is involved in consolidation of emotional memories.

anal stage The second stage in Freud's psychoanalytic theory of psychosexual development, following the oral stage. The sources of gratification and conflict have to do with the expulsion and retention of feces.

analytic thought An orientation toward objects, detached from their contexts, with much use of categories and formal logic and the avoidance of contradiction.

Anderson's theory of intelligence The theory that differences in intelligence result from differences in the 'basic processing mechanism' that implements thinking, which in turn yields knowledge. Individuals vary in the speed at which basic processing occurs.

androgenization Influence of androgen on anatomy and brain development.

anhedonia The loss of the ability to experience joy, even in response to the most joyous occasions.

anorexia nervosa Self-imposed weight loss – at least 15 per cent of the individual's minimum normal weight.

antagonists A drug that locks onto receptors but in a way that does not activate them; the drug serves to 'block' the receptors so that another drug cannot gain access to them.

anterior system (for attention) Designed to control when and how the perceptual features of an object (location in space, shape, color) will be used for selection. See also posterior system (for attention).

antidepressant drugs Drug used to elevate the mood of depressed individuals, presumably by increasing the availability of the neurotransmitters norepinephrine and/or serotonin. Examples are imipramine (Tofranil), isocarboxazid (Marplan), and fluoxetine (Prozac).

antipsychotic drugs A class of medicines used to treat psychosis and other mental and emotional conditions

antisocial personality disorder A disorder characterized by deficits in normal emotional responding – especially for shame, guilt, and fear – as well as deficits in empathy for the emotions of others.

anxiety A state of apprehension, tension, and worry. Synonymous with fear for some theorists, although others view the object of anxiety (such as a vague danger or foreboding) as less specific than the object of a fear (such as a vicious animal).

anxiety disorders A group of mental disorders characterized by intense anxiety or by maladaptive behavior designed to relieve anxiety. Includes generalized anxiety and panic disorders, phobic and obsessive-compulsive disorders. Major category of ICD-10 and DSM-IV covering most of the disorders formerly called neuroses.

aphasia Language deficits caused by brain damage.

apnea The individual stops breathing while asleep. DSM-5 has now identified different types, including obstructive sleep apnea hypopnea and central sleep apnea.

arousal Physiologically, the level of alertness of an organism. Psychologically, the tension that can accompany different levels of arousal, ranging from calmness to anxiety.

asexuality A complete lack of sexual attraction.

Asperger's syndrome No longer classified as such under DSM-5 because it is now part of autism spectrum disorder, this was the term given to a pervasive developmental disorder characterized by deficits in social skills and activities.

association areas Cortical areas responsible for memory, thought, and language.

associationist psychology The view that the mind is filled with ideas that enter by way of the senses and then become associated through principles such as similarity and contrast.

associative agnosia A syndrome in which certain patients cannot recognize visually presented objects.

associative learning Learning that certain contingencies (or relations) exist between events; learning that one event is associated with another.

ataque de nervios Trembling, feelings of out of control, sudden crying, screaming uncontrollably, verbal and physical aggression, and sometimes seizure-like or fainting episodes and suicidal gestures.

Atkinson-Shiffrin theory (of memory) The basis for the distinction between different memories corresponding to different time intervals.

attachment An infant's tendency to seek closeness to particular people and to feel more secure in their presence.

attention The ability to select some information for more detailed inspection, while ignoring other information.

attitude bolstering Generating thoughts to support one's original attitude in the face of persuasion attempts, without directly refuting arguments within the message.

attitudes Favorable or unfavorable evaluations of and reactions to objects, people, situations, or other aspects of the world.

attribution The process by which we attempt to explain the behavior of other people. Attribution theory deals with the rules people use to infer the causes of observed behavior.

attributional styles Styles of making attributions for the events in one's life.

atypical antipsychotics Drugs that reduce symptoms of schizophrenia without causing so many side-effects.

auditory system The ears, parts of the brain, and the various connecting neural pathways.

augmented network A network that includes inhibitory as well as excitatory connections.

autism spectrum disorder A mental disorder, first evident during early childhood, in which the child shows significant deficits in communication, social interaction, and bonding and play activities, and engages in repetitive stereotyped behaviors and self-damaging acts.

automaticity The habituation of responses that initially requires conscious attention.

autonomic nervous system The division of the peripheral nervous system that regulates smooth muscle (organ and glandular) activities. It is divided into the sympathetic and parasympathetic divisions.

autonomic system Connects with the internal organs and glands.

autonomy A child's independence from caretakers.

availability heuristic The assumption that knowledge that is more easily available (for example, because it can more easily be retrieved) is in fact more likely.

available wavelengths The wavelengths of the light that is reflected off the paper reaching your eyes.

avoidance learning The process by which an organism learns to prevent an aversive event from starting (for example, avoiding a certain room if it was associated with a painfully loud noise in the past).

axon That portion of a neuron that transmits impulses to other neurons.

B

back projections Activities that modify the way sensory input is processed.

backward masking A method used in psychological testing. The participant is shown a picture for only 30 milliseconds, which is then masked by a neutral picture so that participants are unaware of the picture's content.

base-rate rule A probability rule which states that the probability of something being a member of a class is greater the more class members there are.

basic level In a hierarchy of concepts, the level at which one first categorizes an object.

basilar membrane A membrane of the ear within the coils of the cochlea supporting the organ of Corti. Movements of the basilar membrane stimulate the hair cells of the organ of Corti, producing the neural effects of auditory stimulation.

behavior genetics Combines the methods of genetics and psychology to study the inheritance of behavioral characteristics.

behavior therapy A method of psychotherapy based on learning principles. It uses such techniques as counterconditioning, reinforcement, and shaping to modify behavior (syn. behavior modification).

behavioral medicine The study of how social, psychological, and biological factors interact to contribute to physical illness (syn. health psychology).

behavioral perspective An approach to psychology that focuses only on observable behavior, and tries to explain it in terms of its relation to environmental events.

behavioral rehearsal Role-playing.

behaviorism A school or system of psychology associated with the name of John B. Watson; it defined psychology as the study of behavior and limited the data of psychology to observable activities. In its classical form it was more restrictive than the contemporary behavioral viewpoint in psychology.

behaviorist approach (to personality) Emphasizes the importance of environmental, or situational, determinants of behavior.

belief bias The finding that, contrary to the rules of deductive logic, humans are quite likely to judge a logically invalid conclusion as valid if it seems plausible to them.

benzodiazepines A class of drugs with similar chemical structures that are effective in reducing anxiety. Examples are diazepam (Valium) and alprazolam (Xanax).

bias A criterion, set by the observer, for making a particular response.

'Big Five' Five trait dimensions capture most of what we mean by personality. They are Openness to experience, Conscientiousness, Extroversion, Agreeableness, and Neuroticism.

binding problem How activity in different parts of the brain, corresponding to different primitives such as color and shape, are combined into a coherent perception of an object.

binocular disparity (as a depth cue) The difference in the views seen by each eye.

biofeedback Receiving information (feedback) about an aspect of one's physiological state and then attempting to alter that state.

biological perspective An approach to psychology that tries to explain behavior in terms of electrical and chemical events taking place inside the body, particularly within the brain and nervous system.

biological psychologist A psychologist concerned with the relationship between biological processes and behavior.

bipolar disorders Alternating between periods of depression and periods of mania (syn. manic-depression).

blocking A phenomenon in classical conditioning: if one conditioned stimulus reliably predicts an unconditioned stimulus, and another conditioned stimulus is added, the relation between the added conditioned stimulus and the unconditioned stimulus will not be learned.

borderline personality disorder A mental disorder in which the individual has manifested unstable moods, relationships with others, and self-perceptions chronically since adolescence or childhood.

bottom-up processes Processes in perception, learning, memory, and comprehension that are driven solely by the information input, and that do not involve the organism's prior knowledge and expectations.

brain The part of the central nervous system encased inside the skull.

brain imaging Techniques such as event-related potentials (ERPs), positron emission tomography (PET), and functional magnetic resonance imaging (fMRI).

brain's dopamine system The neurons of this system lie in the upper brain stem and send their axons through the nucleus accumbens and up to the prefrontal cortex. As their name implies, these neurons use the neurotransmitter dopamine to convey their message.

brightness How much light appears to be reflected from a colored surface.

broaden-and-build theory The theory that positive emotions broaden our typical ways of thinking and acting and, in turn, build our lasting personal resources.

Broca's aphasia Damage to Broca's area leads to difficulties in speech production.

Broca's area That portion of the left cerebral hemisphere involved in the control of speech. Individuals with damage in this area have difficulty enunciating words correctly and speak in a slow and labored way; their speech often makes sense, but it includes only key words.

bulimia Recurrent episodes of binge eating (rapid consumption of a large amount of food in a discrete period of time), followed by attempts to purge the excess by means of vomiting or laxatives.

bystander effect The rule that people are less likely to help when others are present.

C

cannabis The hemp plant from which marijuana is obtained.

case history Biography designed for scientific use.

categorization The process of assigning an object to a concept.

catharsis Purging an emotion by experiencing it intensely.

cathartic effect The hypothesized reduction of aggression that follows the vicarious expression of it.

causality heuristic The use of the strength of the causal connections between the events in a claim to estimate the probability of that claim.

central core The most central portion of the brain, including structures that regulate basic life processes.

central fissure The fissure separating the temporal lobe from the frontal lobe of the brain.

central nervous system All the neurons in the brain and spinal cord.

central route When an individual mentally responds to and elaborates on a persuasive communication.

cerebellum Lobed structure attached to the rear of the brain stem that regulates muscle tone and co-ordination of intricate movements.

cerebral cortex The surface layer of the cerebral hemispheres in higher animals, including humans, commonly called gray matter.

cerebrum The brain's two cerebral hemispheres.

change blindness Not noticing a major change in a visual stimulus that appeared a very short time ago (e.g., a second ago).

childhood amnesia The inability to recall events from the first years of one's life.

chromosomes Structures which carry genes, found in the nucleus of each cell in the body.

chunking Recoding new material into larger, more meaningful units and storing those units in working memory.

circadian rhythms Rhythms of the body that occur approximately every 24 hours.

classical conditioning A learning process in which a previously neutral stimulus becomes associated with another stimulus through repeated pairing with that stimulus.

client-centered therapy A method of psychotherapy developed by Carl Rogers in which the therapist is non-directive and reflective and does not interpret or advise. The operating assumption is that the client is the best expert on his or her problems and can work them out in a non-judgmental, accepting atmosphere (syn. nondirective counseling).

clinical psychologist A psychologist, usually with a Ph.D. or Psy.D. degree, trained in the diagnosis and treatment of emotional or behavioral problems and mental disorders.

clock-dependent alerting process The process in the brain that arouses us at a particular time each day.

coaction The interaction between individuals performing the same task.

cocaine A central nervous system stimulant derived from leaves of the coca plant. Increases energy, produces euphoria, and in large doses causes paranoia.

cochlea The portion of the inner ear containing the receptors for hearing.

cognitive appraisal The interpretation of an event or situation with respect to one's goals and well-being. The cognitive appraisal of an event influences both the quality and intensity of the emotion experienced and the degree of perceived threat.

cognitive approach (to personality) A general empirical approach and a set of topics related to how people process information about themselves and the world.

cognitive behavior therapy A therapy that attempts to help people identify the kinds of stressful situations that produce their physiological or emotional symptoms and alter the way they cope with these situations.

cognitive dissonance theory This theory assumes that there is a drive toward cognitive consistency, meaning that two cognitions – or thoughts – that are inconsistent will produce discomfort, which will in turn motivate the person to remove the inconsistency and bring the cognitions into harmony.

cognitive map A hypothetical structure in memory that preserves and organizes information about the various events that occur in a learning situation; a mental picture of the learning situation.

cognitive neuroscience An interdisciplinary approach that combines aspects of cognitive psychology and neuroscience to study how mental activities are executed in the brain.

cognitive perspective An approach to psychology that focuses on mental processes such as perceiving, remembering, reasoning, deciding, and problem-solving, and tries to explain behavior in terms of these mental processes.

cognitive psychologists Psychologists who take an experimental approach to understanding people's internal mental processes, such as perception and attention, thinking, problem-solving, judgment and decision-making, memory, and language.

collective unconscious A part of the mind that is common to all humans and consists of primordial images or archetypes inherited from our ancestors.

collectivism Refers to cultures that emphasize the fundamental connectedness and interdependence among people.

color constancy The tendency to see a familiar object as of the same color, regardless of changes in illumination on it that alter its stimulus properties.

color-matching experiment An experiment that measures an observer's inclination to see two physically different lights as having the same color.

commitment The cognitive component of love that reflects the intention to remain in the relationship.

companionate love Contrasted with passionate love. The affection we feel for those with whom our lives are deeply intertwined.

complex cell A cell in the visual cortex that responds to a bar of light or straight edge of a particular orientation located anywhere in the visual field.

compliance Going along with the wishes of the influencer without necessarily changing our beliefs or attitudes.

comprehension of language Understanding language by hearing sounds, attaching meanings to the sounds in the form of words, combining the words to create a sentence, and then somehow extracting meaning from it.

compulsion Irresistible urges to carry out certain acts or rituals that reduce anxiety.

computerized axial tomography (CAT or CT) An X-ray technique used to record brain activity.

concept The set of properties that we associate with a particular class.

concrete operational stage Piaget's third stage of cognitive development (ages 7 to 11 years) during which children become capable of logical thought and conservation.

conditioned aversion Learning that occurs when negative associative memories cause something (often food) to subsequently be experienced as unpleasant.

conditioned reinforcer A stimulus that has become reinforcing through prior association with a reinforcing stimulus (syn. secondary reinforcer).

conditioned response (CR) The learned or acquired response to a stimulus that did not evoke the response originally (i.e., a conditioned stimulus).

conditioned satiety The idea that the fullness we feel after a meal is at least in part a product of learning.

conditioned stimulus (CS) A previously neutral stimulus that comes to elicit a conditioned response through association with an unconditioned stimulus.

cones In the eye, specialized cells of the retina found predominantly in the fovea and more sparsely throughout the retina. The cones mediate both chromatic and achromatic sensations.

confirmation bias The tendency to give more credence to evidence that is in line with our previous beliefs than to evidence that contradicts it.

conjunction rule A probability rule which states that the probability of a proposition cannot be less than the probability of that proposition combined with another proposition.

connectionist models Models of cognitive processes (like perception) that incorporate a network of nodes, with excitatory and inhibitory connections between them.

conscious Our current awareness.

consciousness (a) Monitoring ourselves and our environment so that percepts, memories, and thoughts are represented in awareness. (b) Controlling ourselves and our environment so that we are able to initiate and terminate behavioral and cognitive activities.

conservation The understanding that the amount of a substance remains the same even when its form is changed.

constancy The brain's ability to maintain a perception of the underlying physical characteristics of an object, such as shape, size or color, even when the sensory manifestations of these objects change drastically.

construal level theory A theory in social psychology that describes the relation between psychological distance and the extent to which people's thinking (e.g. about objects and events) is abstract or concrete.

construct validity The ability of a test or assessment instrument to confirm predictions of the theory underlying some theoretical concept or construct. Confirming results validate both the concept and the assessment instrument simultaneously.

constructive memory The part of memory that is created after the event that gave rise to the memory is over.

constructive perception What is perceived forms the basis for the initial memory; therefore, if what is originally perceived differs systematically from the objective world, the perceiver's initial memory of what happened will likewise be distorted.

constructive processes The processes by which perception is based on prior knowledge and inference in addition to the objective data from the environment.

contingency Event A is contingent on event B, if A is more likely to occur when B has occurred, than when it has not.

continuum model A model that describes the full continuum of processes from stereotyping to individuation.

contrast acuity The ability to see differences in brightness.

control group In an experiment, the group in which the condition under study is absent.

controllability The degree to which we can stop an event or bring it about.

controlled stimulation Conditions in which the perceptual experiences of an organism are systematically varied in order to determine the effect on subsequent performance. For example, rearing kittens in an environment where they see only vertical stripes for the first few months of life.

conventional level of moral development Level of moral development in which children evaluate actions in terms of other people's opinions.

coping The process by which a person attempts to manage stressful demands.

core The part of a concept that contains the properties that are more essential for determining membership in the concept.

core relational theme The personal meaning that results from a particular pattern of appraisals about a specific person–environment relationship.

coronary heart disease The narrowing or closing of the blood vessels that supply the heart muscles by the gradual buildup of a hard, fatty substance called plaque, blocking the flow of oxygen and nutrients to the heart.

corpus callosum A bundle of nerve fibers connecting the left and right hemispheres of the brain.

correlation coefficient An estimate of the degree to which two variables are related.

counseling psychologist A trained psychologist, usually with a Ph.D. or Psy.D. degree, who deals with personal problems not classified as illness, such as academic, social, or vocational problems of students. He or she has skills similar to those of the clinical psychologist but usually works in a non-medical setting.

counterarguing Directly rebutting the arguments within a message that aims to be persuasive.

critical periods Crucial time periods in a person's life during which specific events occur if development is to proceed normally.

cue A directing stimulus such as a small arrow that directs the subject to attend either to the left or to the right.

cultural perspective (of abnormality) The view that mental disorders are not situated in the brain or mind of the individual but in the social context in which the individual lives.

cultural psychology An interdisciplinary approach involving psychologists, anthropologists, sociologists, and other social scientists that is concerned with how an individual's culture influences his or her mental representations and psychological processes.

cultural relativist perspective (for acceptable behavior) This perspective follows that people should respect each culture's definitions of abnormality for the members of that culture.

D

dark adaptation The increased sensitivity to light when the subject has been continuously in the dark or under conditions of reduced illumination.

dark adaptation curve The absolute threshold decreases with the length of time a person is in darkness.

debriefing The meeting between researcher and participant following a study in which the researcher tells the participant the reasons for keeping them in ignorance – or deceiving them – about the procedures or hypotheses. The researcher also deals with any of the participants' residual emotional reactions so that participants leave with their dignity intact and their appreciation for the research enhanced.

decibel scale A logarithmic scale of loudness. A change of 10 decibels corresponds to a change in sound power of 10 times; 20 decibels, a change of 100 times; and so forth.

deductive validity According to logicians, it is impossible for the conclusion of an argument to be false if its premises are true.

defense mechanisms Strategies that people use to deal with anxiety, which are largely unconscious.

degradation The process in which enzymes in the membrane of a receiving neuron react with a neurotransmitter to break it up chemically and make it inactive; one method (in addition to reuptake) of terminating a neurotransmitter's action.

deindividuation A feeling that one has lost his or her personal identity and merged anonymously into a group.

deinstitutionalization The movement toward discharge of institutionalized mental patients to community-based services.

delusions Beliefs that most people would view as misperceptions of reality.

dendrites Branches projecting from the cell body of a neuron, which receive neural impulses from other neurons.

denial A defense mechanism by which unacceptable impulses or ideas are not perceived or allowed into full awareness.

dependent variable A variable that is hypothesized to depend on the value of the independent variable.

depolarized If the electric potential across the neuron's cell membrane is such that the outside of a neuron is more negatively charged than the inside, the neuron is in a polarized state.

depressants Drugs that depress the central nervous system.

depressive disorders Having one or more periods of depression without a history of manic episodes.

depth cues Different kinds of visual information that, logically or mathematically, provide information about some object's depth.

developmental psychologist A psychologist whose research interest lies in studying the changes that occur as a function of the growth and development of the organism, in particular the relationship between early and later behavior.

Diagnostic and Statistical Manual of Mental Disorders, 5th edition The classification of mental disorders used by most mental health professionals in the USA.

dichromatism Color blindness in which either the red-green or the blue-yellow system is lacking. The red-green form is relatively common; the blue-yellow form is the rarest of all forms of color blindness.

difference-reduction method A problem-solving strategy in which one sets up subgoals that, when obtained, put one in a state closer to the goal.

difference threshold The smallest difference in stimulus intensity that is noticeable.

difficult temperament Term used to describe a child who is irritable, has irregular sleeping and eating patterns, and responds intensely and negatively to new situations.

diffusion of responsibility The tendency for persons in a group situation to fail to take action (as in an emergency) because others are present, thus diffusing the responsibility for acting. A major factor in inhibiting bystanders from intervening in emergencies.

dimensional appraisal theories A group of appraisal theories that identify a range of appraisal dimensions thought to be sufficient to account for differences among emotions.

direct observation The observation of a particular phenomenon under study as it occurs naturally.

discrimination A reaction to differences.

disorganized Term used to describe a child who exhibits contradictory behaviors related to attachment to his or her caretaker.

displacement (a) A defense mechanism whereby a motive that may not be directly expressed (such as sex or aggression) appears in a more acceptable form. (b) The principle of loss of items from short-term memory as too many new items are added.

display rules A culture's rules for the types of emotions people should experience in certain situations, and the behaviors (including facial expressions) appropriate for each emotion.

dispositional attribution Attributing a person's actions to internal dispositions (attitudes, traits, motives), as opposed to situational factors.

dissociation Under certain conditions some thoughts and actions become split off, or dissociated, from the rest of consciousness and function outside of awareness.

dissociative identity disorder The existence in a single individual of two or more distinct identities or personalities that alternate in controlling behavior. Formerly called multiple personality disorder.

distress Feelings of anxiety, depression, or agitation, or experiences such as insomnia, loss of appetite, or numerous aches and pains.

dizygotic Dizygotic (or 'fraternal') twins have developed from different egg cells and are no more alike genetically than ordinary siblings.

dream analysis Talking about the content of one's dreams and then free associating to that content.

dreaming An altered state of consciousness in which remembered images and fantasies are temporarily confused with external reality.

drive theories Theories of motivation that emphasize the role of internal factors.

drug misuse Continued use of a drug by a person who is not dependent on it (that is, shows no signs of tolerance, withdrawal, or compulsive craving), despite serious consequences.

drug dependence A pattern of compulsive drug use usually characterized by tolerance (the need to take more and more of the drug to achieve the same effect), withdrawal (unpleasant physical and psychological reactions if the drug is discontinued), and compulsive use (taking more of the drug than intended, being unable to control drug use, or spending a great deal of time trying to obtain the drug).

drug tolerance The decreased effect of a drug when it is taken repeatedly.

duration The length of time during which an event continues.

dynamic control theory A theory that, instead of an early, hard-wired system sensitive to a small number of visual primitives, there is a malleable system whose components can be quickly reconfigured to perform different tasks at different times.

E

eardrum The membrane at the inner end of the auditory canal, leading to the middle ear.

easy temperament Term used to describe a child who is playful, regular in his or her sleeping and eating patterns, and adapts readily to new situations.

eclectic approach An approach to looking at topics within psychology using multiple psychological perspectives.

educational psychologist A psychologist whose research interest lies in the application of psychological principles to the education of children and adults in schools.

efferent nerves Nerves that carry signals from the central nervous system to the body.

ego The executive of the personality.

egocentrism The condition of being unaware of perspectives other than one's own and believing that everyone perceives the environment in the same way.

elaboration A memory process wherein one expands verbal material so as to increase the number of ways to retrieve the material.

elaboration likelihood model According to this model, if a person is at the high end of the continuum – willing and able to think deeply – then persuasion is said to follow a central route, relying on controlled and effortful thinking; if a person is at the low end of the continuum – for whatever reasons not willing or able to think deeply – then persuasion is said to follow a peripheral route, relying on automatic and effortless thinking.

electroconvulsive therapy (ECT) A mild electric current is applied to the brain to produce a seizure similar to an epileptic convulsion. Also known as electroshock therapy.

emergent features Features that owe their existence to the configuration of other features.

emotion A complex condition that arises in response to certain affectively toned experiences.

emotion-focused coping Ways of reducing anxiety or stress that do not deal directly with the emotion-producing situation; defense mechanisms are a form of emotion-focused coping.

emotion regulation People's responses to their own emotions.

emotional intelligence The ability to perceive, express, understand, use, and manage emotions.

encoding Creating a memory representation of an event.

encoding stage Occurs when environmental information is translated into and stored as a meaningful entity.

endocrine system system of hormone-secreting glands.

engineering psychologist A psychologist who specializes in the relationship between people and machines, seeking, for example, to design machines that minimize human error.

escape learning The process by which an organism learns to terminate an ongoing aversive event (for example, leaving a room if there is a painfully loud noise there).

event-related potentials (ERP) A technique to measure the electrical activity of the brain at the scalp [using electroencephalograms (EEGs)], as it occurs in response to a stimulus or preceding a motor response.

evocative interaction The interaction between individuals and their environments that arises because the behavior of different individuals evokes different responses from others.

evolutionary psychology An area of research that studies how psychological processes have evolved by means of natural selection; those behaviors that aided survival or increased the chance of reproduction have tended to persist through the course of evolutionary history.

excitation threshold If the electric potential is raised above the excitation threshold (for most neurons, around -55 mV) the cell membrane becomes temporarily unstable, resulting in an action potential.

excitatory Synaptic transmission is excitatory if it allows positively charged ions to enter the post-synaptic neuron; this depolarization of the cell makes it more likely to generate an action potential.

excitatory conditioning The ability of a conditioned stimulus to increase the probability or magnitude of a given behavior.

excitatory connections Connections between two nodes in a connectionist network that are positive: An increase in one leads to an increase in the other.

expectation A belief, based on past experience, that something will occur.

experiment The strongest test of hypotheses about cause and effect in which an investigator carefully controls conditions and takes measurements to discover the causal relationships among variables.

experimental group In an experiment, the group of subjects given the treatment whose effect is under investigation.

exploratory behavior The (human) desire to discover and learn new things.

explicit memory The kind of memory that underlies a conscious recollection of something in the past.

exponent (of a power function) A unique number that characterizes the function of each sensory modality.

extinction (a) The experimental procedure, following classical or operant conditioning, of presenting the conditioned stimulus without the usual reinforcement. (b) The reduction in response that results from this procedure.

extracellular thirst The psychological manifestation of the need for water that occurs when our bodies lose water because we have gone without drinking or have exercised intensively.

extrinsic motivation Motivation that derives from external factors, such as (financial) rewards.

eye fixations Periods during which the eyes are stationery and are acquiring information.

F

facial expressions The muscle actions that move facial landmarks in particular ways.

facial feedback hypothesis The hypothesis that people's subjective experience of an emotion is determined by feedback from the physiological arousal caused by engaging in specific facial expressions.

facial muscle movements the muscle actions that move facial landmarks in particular ways

facial preference In infants, an inborn, unlearned preference for faces.

factor analysis A statistical method used in test construction and in interpreting scores from batteries of tests. The method enables the investigator to compute the minimum number of determiners (factors) required to account for the intercorrelations among the scores on the tests making up the battery.

false-alarm rate The proportion of false alarms over all the trials in an experiment.

false alarms The response of incorrectly responding yes when only noise is present.

family therapy Psychotherapy with the family members as a group rather than treatment of the patient alone.

fast mapping A process by which a word is mapped onto the underlying concept after only *one* exposure.

feature-integration theory A cornerstone of understanding object perception that was initially proposed by Anne Treisman.

fetal alcohol syndrome Mental retardation and multiple deformities of the infant's face and mouth due to exposure to alcohol in the womb.

fight-or-flight response A pattern of bodily responses that prepares the organism for an emergency. Includes increases in pupil size, heart rate, blood pressure, respiration, muscle tension, and the secretion of epinephrine, norepinephrine, adrenocorticotropic hormone and other hormones; decreases in saliva, mucous, digestive activity, and the size of blood vessels.

figure The objects of interest, which appear more solid than the ground and appear in front of it. The figure and ground regions are the two most elementary forms of perceptual organization.

fixation In Freud's psychoanalytic theory, arrested development through failure to pass beyond one of the earlier stages of psychosexual development or to change the objects of attachment (such as fixation at the oral stage or fixation on the mother).

fixed interval schedule The organism is reinforced for its first response after a certain amount of time has passed since its last reinforcement.

fixed ratio schedule (FR) The number of responses that has to be made before reinforcement is fixed at a particular value.

flashbulb memory A vivid and relatively permanent record of the circumstances in which one learned of an emotionally charged, significant event.

foot-in-the-door technique To get people to say 'yes' to requests that would ordinarily lead to 'no', this technique suggests beginning with a small request that few would refuse.

forebrain The structures located in the front, or anterior, part of the brain.

formal operational stage Piaget's fourth stage of cognitive development in which the child becomes able to use abstract rules.

fovea In the eye, a small area in the central part of the retina, packed with cones; the most sensitive part of the retina for detail vision and color vision in daylight.

framing effect A cognitive bias that results from the way in which something is framed.

free association A patient is instructed to say everything that comes to mind, regardless of how trivial or embarrassing it may seem.

frequency (of a tone) The number of cycles per second.

Freudian slip In psychoanalytic theory, a mistake or substitution of words in speaking or writing that is contrary to the speaker's conscious intention and presumably expresses wishes or thoughts repressed to the unconscious.

frontal lobe The part of the cerebral cortex in front of the central fissure in the brain.

frustration–aggression hypothesis The hypothesis that frustration (thwarting a person's goal-directed efforts) induces an aggressive drive, which, in turn, motivates aggressive behavior.

functional fixedness When a person has difficulty with a problem, presumably because they represent components of the problem as having a different function than that needed to solve the problem.

functional magnetic resonance imaging (fMRI) A brain imaging technique that measures brain activity by measuring the magnetic changes that result from oxygen consumption.

functionalism Studying how the mind works so that an organism can adapt to and function in its environment.

fundamental attribution error The tendency to underestimate situational influences on behavior and assume that some personal characteristic of the individual is responsible.

G

g General intelligence factor.

ganglia (sing. ganglion) A group of neuronal cell bodies found outside the brain and spinal cord.

Gardner's theory of multiple intelligences The theory that there are seven distinct kinds of intelligence that are independent of one another, each operating as a separate system (or module) in the brain according to its own rules. These are (1) linguistic, (2) musical, (3) logical-mathematical, (4) spatial, (5) bodily-kinesthetic, (6) intrapersonal, and (7) interpersonal.

gate control theory of pain According to this theory, the sensation of pain requires not only that pain receptors be activated, but also that a neural gate in the spinal cord allow these signals to continue to the brain. Pressure stimulation tends to close the gate; this is why rubbing a hurt area can relieve pain. Attitudes, suggestions, and drugs may act to close the gate.

gender identity A firm sense of oneself as either male or female.

gender schema A mental structure that organizes the person's perceptual and conceptual world into gender categories (male–female, masculine–feminine).

genes Segments of DNA molecules that are the basic hereditary units.

general adaptation syndrome A set of responses that is displayed by all organisms in response to stress.

general learning disability Deficits in intellectual and practical skills far below average.

generalization (a) In learning, the detection of a characteristic or principle common to a class of objects or events. (b) In conditioning, the principle that once a conditioned response has been established to a given stimulus, similar stimuli will also evoke that response.

generalized anxiety disorder A constant sense of tension and dread.

genital stage In Freud's psychoanalytic theory, the final stage of psychosexual development, beginning at puberty and culminating in mature adult sexuality.

geons In perception, geometric forms (such as cylinders, cones, blocks, and wedges) that comprise the features of objects. Recognition of an object is good to the extent that the geons of the object can be recovered.

Gestalt A German word meaning 'form' or 'configuration'. Gestalt psychologists are interested primarily in perception and believe that perceptual experiences depend on the patterns formed by stimuli and on the organization of experience.

glial cell A supporting cell (not a neuron); glial cells compose a substantial portion of brain tissue; recent speculation suggests that they may play a role in neural conduction.

grain size A limiting feature in both imaginal and perceptual processing. It can be thought of as our images are occurring in a mental medium whose grain limits the amount of detail we can detect in an image.

grammatical morpheme A morpheme that is not a word, including what are commonly referred to as articles and prepositions.

ground The region that appears to be behind the figure. The figure and ground regions are the two most elementary forms of perceptual organization.

group polarization effect The tendency of groups to arrive at decisions that are in the same direction but are more extreme than the mean of the pre-discussion decisions of the individuals in the group.

group therapy A group discussion or other group activity with a therapeutic purpose participated in by more than one client or patient at a time.

grouping by proximity If the vertical distance between dots is reduced columns will most likely be seen.

grouping by similarity Grouping like with like.

groupthink A phenomenon in which members of a group are led to suppress their own dissent in the interests of group consensus.

H

habit A learned stimulus-response sequence.

habituation The reduction in the strength of a response to a repeated stimulus.

habituation method A technique used to study perception in infants. It is based on the fact that while infants look directly at novel objects they soon tire of doing so (habituation). Hence one can determine the degree to which an infant perceives an object as novel by measuring the time spent looking at it.

hair cells In audition, hairlike receptors in the cochlea that bend due to vibration of the basilar membrane and then send electrical impulses to the brain.

hallucinations Sensory experiences in the absence of relevant or adequate external stimulation.

hallucinogens Drugs whose main effect is to change perceptual experience (syn. psychedelic drugs).

hardiness Resistance to becoming physically or emotionally impaired even in the face of major stressful events.

hashish A form of cannabis commonly used in the Middle East.

Hebbian learning rule The idea that repetition of the same response will lead to permanent changes at the synapses between neurons. In particular, if input from neuron A repeatedly increases the firing rate of neuron B, then the connection between neurons A and B will grow stronger.

hemispheres Structures on the left and right sides of the brain that are connected by the corpus callosum.

heritability The percentage of the variance in any trait that is accounted for by genetic differences among the individuals in a population.

heroin An extremely addictive central nervous system depressant derived from opium.

hertz (Hz) The unit used to measure the frequency of a sound wave, specifically the number of cycles per second.

heuristic A short-cut procedure that is relatively easy to apply and can often yield the correct answer, but not inevitably so.

hierarchy of needs Maslow's way of classifying needs and motives, from the basic biological needs to the more complex psychological motivations that become important only after the basic needs have been satisfied.

hindbrain All the structures located in the hind, or posterior, part of the brain, closest to the spinal cord.

hippocampus A brain structure located below the cerebral cortex that is involved in the consolidation of new memories; its role seems to be that of a cross-referencing system, linking together aspects of a particular memory that are stored in separate parts of the brain.

hit rate The proportion of hits over all the trials in an experiment.

hits The response of correctly responding 'yes' when a signal is present.

holistic thought An orientation toward the entire context or field and assigning causality to it, making relatively little use of categories and formal logic, and relying instead on dialectical reasoning, which involves recognizing and transcending apparent contradictions.

homeostasis The normal level of functioning that is characteristic of the healthy organism (Chapter 2); a constant internal state (Chapter 10).

homeostatic sleep drive A physiological process that strives to obtain the amount of sleep required for a stable level of daytime alertness.

hormones Chemicals secreted by the endocrine glands into the bloodstream and transported to other parts of the body, where they have specific effects on cells that recognize their message.

hue The quality best described by a color's name.

humanistic approach Arising in the 1950s and 1960s, the humanistic approach, most associated with Carl Rogers and Abraham Maslow, offered an alternative to the deterministic perspectives dominant within psychology at the time. The approach centered on individual experience, identity, dignity, and self-actualization.

humanistic therapies A general term for approaches to psychotherapy that emphasize the individual's subjective experiences, free will, and ability to solve his or her own problems. Client-centered therapy and Gestalt therapy are examples.

hypercomplex cell A cell in the visual cortex that responds to a particular orientation and length.

hyperpolarized If the cell is more polarized than it is at rest, it is called hyperpolarized.

hypnosis A willing and co-operative individual relinquishes some control over his or her behavior to the hypnotist and accepts some distortion of reality.

hypothalamus A small but very important structure located just above the brain stem and just below the thalamus. Considered a part of the central core of the brain, it includes centers that govern motivated behavior such as eating, drinking, sex, and emotions; it also regulates endocrine activity and maintains body homeostasis.

hypothesis A statement that can be tested.

I

id The most primitive part of the personality and the part from which the ego and the superego later develop.

ideal self Image of self that represents the best self one can be or aspires to be.

identification Respecting or admiring other individuals or groups and obeying their norms and adopting their beliefs, attitudes, and behaviors in order to be like them and identify with them.

identity confusion Occurs when a person has no consistent sense of self or set of internal standards for evaluating his or her self-worth in major areas of life.

identity crisis In Erikson's theory of psychosocial development, a period of self-doubt and active questioning about one's definition of self ('Who am I?' 'Where am I going?') which typically takes place during adolescence.

ideology A set of beliefs and attitudes.

illicit drugs illegal drugs.

illusion A percept that is false or distorted.

illusory conjunction An incorrect combination of two separate attributes of an object.

imaginal mode A form of thought based in (visual) imagery.

imaginal thought Images, particularly visual ones, that we can 'see' in our mind.

implicit egotism The non-conscious tendency to be attracted to people, places and objects that subtly remind one of oneself.

implicit leniency contract To appear fair, majority members let minority members have their say, but by doing so they unwittingly open the door to minority influence.

implicit memory The kind of memory that underlies perceptual and cognitive skills. It is often expressed as an improvement on some perceptual or cognitive task without any conscious recollection of the experiences that led to the improvement.

imprinting A type of early learning in which a newborn forms an attachment with some kind of model (normally, a parent).

inattentional blindness Not 'seeing' something because one is not paying attention to it.

in vivo exposure A method of therapy highly similar to systematic desensitization that requires the client to actually experience the anxiety-producing situations.

incentive The expected reward of a behavior.

incentive motivation Wanting something.

incentive salience Objects and events that have become linked with anticipated affect, which serves to grab attention and steer seeking behavior.

incentive theory A theory of motivation that emphasizes the importance of negative and positive incentives in determining behavior; internal drives are not the sole instigators of activity.

incus One of three small bones located in the middle ear.

independent variable A variable that is independent of what the participant does.

individualism Refers to cultures that emphasize the fundamental separateness and independence of individuals.

individuation Assessing an individual's personal qualities on a person-by-person basis.

inductive reasoning Reasoning about arguments in which it is improbable that the conclusion is false if the premises are true.

inductive strength It is improbable that the conclusion is false if the premises are true.

inferences (a) A perceptual or memorial process based on what is believed to be true rather than what necessarily is true. (b) Judgments that go beyond the information given.

information-processing model In general, a model based on assumptions regarding the flow of information through a system; usually best realized in the form of a computer program. In cognitive psychology, theories of how the mind functions are often represented in the form of an information-processing model. By simulating the model on a computer, one can study the properties and implications of the theory.

information-processing skills Skills that help one gather and analyze information from the environment.

informational social influence We conform because we believe that other people's interpretations of an ambiguous situation are more correct than our own.

informed consent The participants must enter a study voluntarily and be permitted to withdraw from it at any time without penalty if they so desire.

inhibitory Synaptic transmission is inhibitory if it allows positively charged ions to leave the post-synaptic neuron, or negatively charged ions to enter it; this hyperpolarization of the cell makes it more likely to generate an action potential.

inhibitory conditioning The ability of a conditioned stimulus to decrease the probability or magnitude of a behavioral response.

inhibitory connections Connections between two nodes in a connectionist network that are negative: An increase in one leads to a decrease in the other.

insecurely attached Term used to describe a child who is ambivalent and/or shows resistance to his or her caretaker during a reunion episode.

insight An understanding of a situation, leading to the solution of a problem (contrast with trial-and-error learning).

insomnia Dissatisfaction with the amount or quality of one's sleep.

institutional norms Like social norms – implicit or explicit rules for acceptable behavior and beliefs – except they are applied to entire institutions, or organizations of the same type.

instrumental conditioning Certain responses that are learned because they operate on, or affect, the environment.

intellectualization A defense mechanism whereby a person tries to gain detachment from an emotionally threatening situation by dealing with it in abstract, intellectual terms.

intelligence (a) That which a properly standardized intelligence test measures. (b) The ability to learn from experience, think in abstract terms, and deal effectively with one's environment.

intelligence quotient (IQ) A ratio of mental age to chronological age.

intensity How strong a particular stimulus is.

interference A factor that can impair retrieval from long-term memory. It arises when different items are associated with the same retrieval cue; attempted retrieval of one of these items can be blocked by the inadvertent retrieval of the other item.

interjudge reliability The consistency achieved by two or more observers when assessing or rating some behavior (for example, in rating the aggressiveness of nursery-school children). Also called interrater agreement.

internal consistency A form of test reliability. Specifically, the homogeneity of a set of items on a test, the degree to which they are all measuring the same variable.

internalization influencers seeking to change the private attitudes of an individual not just their public behaviors, to obtain changes that will be sustained even when they themselves will no longer be on the scene.

International Classification of Diseases System to classify mental disorders.

interneuron A neuron that connects sensory and motor neurons.

interpersonal therapy A style of therapy that tends to be more structured and short-term than traditional psychoanalysis.

interposition (as a depth cue) If one object is positioned so that it obstructs the view of the other, the viewer perceives the overlapping object as being nearer.

interval schedules Reinforcement is available only after a certain time interval has elapsed.

intimacy The emotional component of love which involves closeness and sharing of feelings.

intracellular thirst The psychological manifestation of the need for water that is caused by osmosis – the tendency of water to move from zones where it is plentiful to zones where it is relatively rare.

intrinsic motivation Motivation that derives from internal factors, such as feeling satisfaction, pride, and competence.

introspection The observation and recording of one's own perceptions, thoughts, and feelings.

introversion–extroversion The personality dimension first identified by Carl Jung that refers to the degree to which a person's basic orientation is turned inward toward the self or outward toward the external world. At the introversion end are shy individuals who tend to withdraw into themselves; at the extroversion end are sociable individuals who prefer to be with others.

inversion effect The relative difficulty of recognizing upside-down faces compared to other upside-down visual stimuli (such as cars or houses).

in vivo exposure Form of behavior therapy and cognitive behavioral therapy designed to treat post-traumatic stress disorder, characterized by re-experiencing the traumatic event through remembering it and engaging with, rather than avoiding, reminders of the trauma (triggers)

ion Electrically charged molecule.

ion channel A specialized protein molecule that permits specific ions to enter or leave cells. Some ion channels open or close in response to appropriate neurotransmitter molecules; others open or close in response to voltage changes across the cell membrane. This process regulates depolarization and the firing of nerve impulses.

ion pump Protein structure that helps to maintain the uneven distribution of ions across the cell membrane by pumping them into or out of the cell.

J

James–Lange theory A classical theory of emotion, named for the two men who independently proposed it. The theory states that the stimulus first leads to bodily responses, and then the awareness of these responses constitutes the experience of emotion.

Joint attention The ability to share experiences about objects or events with others by following the visual gaze of those other people.

just noticeable difference (jnd) The minimum difference in stimulus magnitude necessary to tell two stimuli apart.

K

knowledge According to knowledge acquisition approaches to development, the child's understanding of how facts in a particular domain are organized.

L

language A multilevel system for relating thoughts to speech by means of word and sentence units.

latency period In Freud's psychoanalytic theory, a period in middle childhood, roughly the years 6–12, when both sexual and aggressive impulses are said to be in a quiescent state.

latent learning Learning that has taken place, but that is not manifesting itself in a change in behavior.

lateral fissure The fissure separating the temporal from the parietal and frontal lobes in the brain.

lateral hypothalamic syndrome An apparent total lack of hunger caused by the destruction of the lateral hypothalamus.

law of effect The principle that any behavior that is followed by reinforcement is strengthened; from the infinite pool of possible responses, those that lead to reinforcement are repeated, whereas those that do not are extinguished.

learned helplessness A condition of apathy or helplessness created experimentally by subjecting an organism to unavoidable trauma (such as shock, heat, or cold). Being unable to avoid or escape an aversive situation produces a feeling of helplessness that generalizes to subsequent situations.

learned taste aversion An aversion to eat a particular food, as a result of an experience in which the food became associated with illness.

learning A relatively permanent change in behavior that occurs as the result of practice.

learning curve a curve representing the increase in learning as a function of experience .

libido (Latin for 'lust'.) In Freud's psychoanalytic theory, the psychic energy of the id.

liking In the study of motivation, liking refers to the pleasure experienced while sought-after rewards are consumed, whereas in the study of interpersonal relationships, liking refers to friendship and the early stages of more intimate relationships.

limbic system A set of structures that are closely interconnected with the hypothalamus and appear to impose additional controls over some of the instinctive behaviors regulated by the hypothalamus and the brain stem.

literature review A scholarly summary of the existing body of research on a given topic.

lithium Drug used to treat mania.

lobes Large regions of the cerebral cortex that perform diverse functions.

localization Determining where objects are in space.

lock-and-key action A model of synaptic transmission based in which a neurotransmitter affects only those receptor sites into which it 'fits' (like a key in a lock).

longitudinal fissure The fissure separating left and right hemispheres in the brain.

long-term depression A long-lasting decrease in synaptic transmission at synapses in the cerebellar cortex.

long-term memory Semi-permanent memory.

long-term potentiation A phenomenon concerning the neural bases of learning. Once stimulated, neurons will show an increase in their rate of activity when subsequently stimulated (at least up to a period of months).

long-term store The large repository of information where we maintain all information that is generally available to us.

loosening of associations Occurs when the individual's ideas shift from one topic to another in ways that appear unrelated.

loudness An intensity dimension of hearing correlated with the amplitude of the sound waves that constitute the stimulus. Greater amplitudes yield greater loudnesses.

LSD A potent drug that produces hallucinations at very low doses. See also hallucinogen.

lucid dream A dream in which events seem so normal (lacking the bizarre and illogical character of most dreams) that the dreamer believes he or she is awake and conscious.

M

magnetic resonance imaging (MRI) A computer-based scanning procedure that uses strong magnetic fields and radio-frequency pulses to generate a picture of a cross section of the brain or body. Provides greater precision than the CT scanner.

maladaptive Having adverse effects on the individual or on society.

malleus One of three small bones located in the middle ear.

manic episode An episode in which an individual is energetic, enthusiastic, full of self-confidence, talks continually, rushes from one activity to another with little need for sleep, and makes grandiose plans, paying little attention to their practicality.

marijuana The dried leaves of the hemp plant (cannabis); also known as hashish, 'pot', or 'grass'. Hashish is actually an extract of the plant material and, hence, is usually stronger than marijuana. Intake may enhance sensory experiences and produce a state of euphoria.

marital therapy Psychotherapy with both members of a couple aimed at resolving problems in their relationship (syn. couples therapy).

maturation An innately determined sequence of growth and change that is relatively independent of external events.

McGurk effect Results from conflicting auditory and visual information.

mean The technical term for an arithmetic average.

meaning The concept named by a word.

means–ends analysis A problem-solving strategy in which one compares one's current state to the goal state in order to find the most important difference between them; eliminating this difference then becomes the main subgoal.

measurement A system for assigning numbers to variables.

meditation Achieving an altered state of consciousness by performing certain rituals and exercises.

medulla The lowest section of the brainstem, a slight enlargement of the spinal cord as it enters the skull; the point at which the major nerve tracts cross over so that the right cerebral hemisphere controls the left side of the body, and the left cerebral hemisphere controls the right side.

MEG This is Magnetoencephalography

melatonin A hormone that induces sleep.

memory illusion Memories for events that never occurred.

memory span the maximum number of items that the participant can recall in perfect order. Typically between five and nine.

menarche The first menstrual period.

mental imagery Mental representations that are picture-like. Not the same as eidetic imagery.

mental model A concrete mental representation of a problem situation that may be useful in solving the problem.

mental rotation The notion that a mental image of an object can be rotated in the mind in fashion analogous to rotating the real object.

mental set A disposition to organize knowledge in a particular way.

mere exposure effect The finding that familiarity all by itself increases liking.

meta-analysis A form of literature review in which authors use statistical techniques to combine and draw conclusions about studies previously conducted.

metacognition Thinking about thinking.

metamers In a color-matching experiment, a pair of two lights with different physical makeups that appear identical.

methadone An agonist drug used in treating heroin-dependent individuals.

method of loci An aid to serial memory. Verbal material is transformed into mental images, which are then located at successive positions along a visualized route, such as an imaged walk through the house or down a familiar street.

midbrain The middle of the brain.

middle ear The part of the ear that transmits sound waves from the eardrum to the oval window of the inner ear by means of three tiny connecting bones (malleus, incus, and stapes).

minimal risk The principle that risks anticipated in the research should be no greater than those ordinarily encountered in daily life.

minimalist appraisal theories A group of appraisal theories that are based on reducing the number of appraisal dimensions to a minimum, often based on fundamental themes.

Minnesota Multiphasic Personality Inventory (MMPI) A pencil-and-paper version of a psychiatric interview that consists of more than 550 statements concerning attitudes, emotional reactions, physical and psychological symptoms, and experiences Test takers respond to each statement by answering, 'True', 'False', or 'Cannot say'.

minority influence Minorities can move majorities toward their point of view if they present a consistent position without appearing rigid, dogmatic, or arrogant.

misattribution of arousal Lingering physiological arousal can be mistakenly attributed to subsequent circumstances and intensify our emotional reactions to those circumstances.

mnemonic system A strategy or set of strategies for efficiently remembering things.

model of the environment A representation of the world within our brains that we use to consciously perceive, make decisions, and behave.

monoamine oxidase (MAO) inhibitors One of the enzymes responsible for the breakdown of a group of neurotransmitters called biogenic amines (norepinephrine, dopamine, and serotonin are examples); believed to be important in the regulation of emotion. Drugs that inhibit the action of this enzyme (MAO inhibitors) are used in treating depression.

monoamine oxidase inhibitor (MAOI) A class of drugs used to treat depression; the drug inhibits the action of an enzyme (monoamine oxidase) that breaks down certain neurotransmitters (such as dopamine, norepinephrine, and serotonin), thereby prolonging the action of these neurotransmitters.

monozygotic Monozygotic (or 'identical') twins have developed from a single fertilized egg cell and share exactly the same genes.

mood disorders Mental disorders characterized by disturbances of mood. Depression, mania (exaggerated excitement), and bipolar disorders in which the individual experiences both extremes of mood are examples.

moods Free-floating and diffuse affective states.

moral judgment Children's understanding of moral rules and social conventions.

morpheme Any small linguistic unit that carries meaning.

morphological rules The rules of a language that dictate how morphemes can be combined into words.

motivation A condition that energizes behavior and gives it direction.

motor neuron A neuron that carries outgoing signals from the central nervous system to muscles and glands.

multivariate experiment A type of experiment that involves the simultaneous manipulation of several independent variables.

Munsell system A scheme for specifying colored surfaces by assigning them one of ten hue names and two numbers, one indicating saturation and the other brightness.

myelin sheath A sheet of glial cells wrapped around the axon.

N

naïve realism People's tendency to take their constructed, subjective realities to be faithful renderings of an objective world.

naltrexone An antagonist drug that blocks the action of heroin because it has a greater affinity for the opioid receptors than does heroin itself.

narcolepsy Recurring, irresistible attacks of drowsiness with the likelihood of falling asleep at any time.

narrative review A form of literature review in which authors use words to describe studies previously conducted and to discuss the strength of the available psychological evidence.

natural selection process by which those variations in (heritable) traits that most contribute to an organism's survival are passed on to the next generation.

nature view The view that human beings enter the world with an inborn store of knowledge and understanding of reality.

nature–nurture debate The problem of determining the relative importance of heredity (nature) and the result of upbringing in a particular environment (nurture) on behavior.

negative hallucinations In a hypnotic state, when a person does not perceive something that normally would be perceived.

negative punishment Decreasing the response frequency by the removal of a pleasant or appetitive stimulus following the response.

negative reinforcement Reinforcing a response by the removal of an aversive stimulus.

negatively correlated As the value of one variable increases, the value of another decreases.

nerve A bundle of elongated axons belonging to hundreds or thousands of neurons.

nervous system The full system of neural tissue.

neural plasticity The ability of the neural system to change in response to experience.

neural sensitization Potentially permanent changes in the brain that follow drug addition whereby dopamine neurons are activated more highly by drugs and drug-related stimuli.

neuron A specialized cell that transmits neural impulses or messages to other neurons, glands, and muscles.

neurosis (pl. neuroses) A mental disorder in which the individual is unable to cope with anxieties and conflicts and develops symptoms that he or she finds distressing, such as obsessions, compulsions, phobias, or anxiety attacks. In Freud's psychoanalytic theory, neurosis results from the use of defense mechanisms to ward off anxiety caused by unconscious conflicts. No longer a diagnostic category of DSM-IV.

neuroplasticity Property that refers to the tendency for experience to change brain structures.

neuroticism The name of the emotional instability–stability dimension in Eysenck's factor-analytic theory of personality. Moody, anxious, and maladjusted individuals are at the neurotic or unstable end; calm, well-adjusted individuals are at the other.

neurotransmitter A chemical that diffuses across the synaptic gap and stimulates the next neuron.

neutral stimulus In classical conditioning, any stimulus that does not naturally elicit the conditioned response.

nodes of Ranvier Small interruptions in the myelin sheath.

noise Anything in the environment irrelevant to what the observer is trying to detect.

non-associative learning Learning about a single stimulus.

non-REM sleep (or NREM sleep) Refers to the other four sleep stages (besides REM) in which eye movements are virtually absent, heart and breathing rates decrease markedly, the muscles are relaxed, and the brain's metabolic rate decreases 25 to 30 per cent compared to wakefulness.

normality Appropriate perception of reality, ability to exercise voluntary control over behavior, self-esteem and acceptance, ability to form affectionate relationships, and productivity.

normative social influence We conform to a group's social norms or typical behaviors to become liked and accepted.

noun phrase A phrase that centers on a noun and specifies the subject of an underlying proposition.

nuclei (sing. nucleus) A collection of nerve cell bodies grouped in the brain or spinal cord.

nurture view The view that human knowledge is acquired through experiences and interactions with the world.

O

obese Being 30 per cent or more above the weight level that would be appropriate for a person's body structure and height.

object recognition Determining what an object is, based on its physical characteristics.

object permanence The awareness that an object continues to exist even when it is not present.

object relations theory An outgrowth of psychoanalytic theory that deals with the person's attachments to others over the course of development. Emphasizes ego functioning more than did classical psychoanalytic theory.

objectification theory A sociocultural account of how being raised in a culture that sexually objectifies the female body fundamentally alters girls' and women's self-views and well-being.

observational learning People can learn by observing the actions of others and noting the consequences of those actions.

obsessions Persistent intrusions of unwelcome thoughts, images, or impulses that elicit anxiety.

obsessive-compulsive disorder An anxiety disorder taking one of three forms: (a) persistent intrusions of unwelcome thoughts, images, or impulses that elicit anxiety (obsessions); (b) irresistible urges to carry out certain acts or rituals that reduce anxiety (compulsions); (c) both of these in combination.

occipital lobe The part of cortex at the back of the brain.

Oedipal conflict In Freud's psychoanalytic theory, the conflict that arises during the phallic stage of psychosexual development in which the individual is sexually attracted to the parent of the opposite sex and perceives the same-sex parent as a rival.

olfaction the sense of smell.

olfactory bulb A region of the brain involved in olfaction (smell); it is a way station between the receptors in the nasal passage and the olfactory cortex.

olfactory cortex The area in the brain responsible for the sense of smell. Located on the inside of the temporal lobes.

olfactory system The receptors in the nasal passage, certain regions of the brain, and interconnecting neural pathways.

operant conditioning Certain responses are learned because they operate on, or affect, the environment.

operation A mental routine for separating, combining, and otherwise transforming information in a logical manner.

opiates Drugs that diminish physical sensation and the capacity to respond to stimuli by depressing the central nervous system.

opponent-color theory A theory of color perception that postulates two types of color-sensitive units that respond in opposite ways to the two colors of an opponent pair. One type of unit responds to red or green, the other to blue or yellow. Since a unit cannot respond in two ways at once, reddish-greens and yellowish-blues cannot occur.

opponent-process model of sleep and wakefulness A theory that states that the brain possesses two opponent processes that govern the tendency to fall asleep or remain awake: the homeostatic sleep drive and the clock-dependent alerting process.

optic chiasm Location where retinal fibers cross over to the other side of the brain.

oral stage In Freud's psychoanalytic theory, the first stage of psychosexual development; pleasure derives from the lips and mouth, as in sucking at the mother's breast.

organizational psychologist A psychologist concerned with selecting people who are most suitable for particular jobs or designing structures that facilitate collaboration and teamwork.

outer ear The external ear and auditory canal, whose purpose is to funnel sound waves towards the inner ear.

oval window A membrane on the cochlea of the inner ear that receives vibrations from the ear drum via three connecting bones (malleus, incus, and stapes). Vibrations at the oval window set up similar vibrations in the internal fluid of the cochlea, ultimately activating the hair cells that serve as auditory receptors.

overextension Tendency to apply a new word too widely.

overjustification effect Explaining one's own behavior with too much emphasis on salient situational causes and not enough emphasis on personal causes, like intrinsic interest.

P

pain threshold The minimum intensity of a stimulus that is perceived as painful.

pain tolerance The maximum intensity of a painful stimulus that can be endured.

panic attack An episode of acute and overwhelming apprehension or terror.

panic disorder An anxiety disorder in which the individual has sudden and inexplicable episodes of terror and feelings of impending doom accompanied by physiological symptoms of fear (such as heart palpitations, shortness of breath, muscle tremors, faintness).

paranoid An individual who has delusions of persecution.

parasympathetic nervous system A division of the automatic nervous system, the nerve fibers of which originate in the cranial and sacral portions of the spinal cord. Active in relaxed or quiescent states of the body and to some extent antagonistic to the sympathetic division, or system.

parietal lobe The part of cortex above the occipital lobe and behind the frontal lobe in the brain.

partial-report procedure An experiment devised by George Sperling in which a varied array of letters is flashed to observers for a brief period.

passion The motivational component of love which consists of sexual attraction and the romantic feeling of being 'in love'.

passionate love Contrasted with companionate love. An intensely emotional state in which tender and sexual feelings, elation and pain, anxiety and relief, altruism and jealousy coexist in a confusion of feelings.

PCP Sold as a hallucinogen (under such street names as 'angel dust', 'Shermans', and 'superacid'), this drug is technically a dissociative anesthetic.

peak experiences Transient moments of self-actualization.

perception Constructing an internal model of the world based on bottom-up sensory processes combined with top-down real-world knowledge.

perceptual constancy An object is perceived as a constant even when the viewer sees a different view of the same object where it may not appear to be the same.

perceptual interference The finding that objects had to eventually be more focused for the observers to recognize them in the very-out-of-focus condition than in the moderately out-of-focus condition.

periaqueductal gray A section of the brain in which neurons are connected to other neurons that inhibit cells that would normally carry the pain signals arising in the pain receptors. This area appears to be the main place where strong painkillers such as morphine affect neural processing.

peripheral nervous system The nerves connecting the brain and spinal cord to other parts of the body.

peripheral route When an individual responds to non-content cues in a communication or to the context of a communication.

personal constructs The dimensions that individuals themselves use to interpret themselves and their social worlds.

personality The distinctive and characteristic patterns of thought, emotion, and behavior that define an individual's personal style of interacting with the physical and social environment.

personality disorders Ingrained habitual, and rigid patterns of behavior or character that severely limit the individual's adaptive potential; often society sees the behavior as maladaptive whereas the individual does not.

personality inventory An inventory for self-appraisal, consisting of many statements or questions about personal characteristics and behavior that the person judges to apply or not to apply to him or her.

personality psychologist A psychologist whose area of interest focuses on classifying individuals and studying the differences between them This specialty overlaps both developmental and social psychologists to some extent.

person–environment relationship The objective situation in which a person finds herself.

perspective (as a depth cue) When parallel lines in a scene appear to converge in the image, they are perceived as vanishing in the distance.

pervasive developmental disorders Disorders characterized by severe and persisting impairment in several areas of development.

phallic stage In Freud's psychoanalytic theory, the third stage of psychosexual development in which gratification is associated with stimulation of the sex organs and sexual attachment is to the parent of the opposite sex.

phasic pain The kind of sharp pain experienced immediately upon suffering an injury; usually brief with a rapid increase in intensity followed by a decrease.

phenothiazines A group of antipsychotic drugs that relieve the symptoms of schizophrenia by blocking the access of the neurotransmitter dopamine to its receptors. Chlorpromazine (Thorazine) and fluphenazine (Prolixin) are examples.

phenotypic plasticity Property that refers to the tendency for experience to change gene expression at cellular levels.

pheromones Chemicals that float through the air to be sniffed by other members of the species.

phobia Intense fear of a stimulus or situation that most people do not consider particularly dangerous.

phoneme Discrete speech categories.

phonological loop The part of working memory in which auditory repetition takes place.

phonological rules The rules of a language that dictate which phonemes can follow which other phonemes.

photon The smallest unit of light energy.

physical description (of an object) A listing of all the information necessary to completely reproduce the object.

physiology The study of the functions of the living organism and its parts.

pitch A sensation based on the frequency of sound.

pituitary gland endocrine gland found just below the hypothalamus.

place theory of pitch perception A theory of hearing that associates pitch with the place on the basilar membrane where activation occurs.

pluralistic ignorance The phenomenon in which everybody in a group misleads everybody else by defining an ambiguous situation as a non-emergency.

polarized If the electric potential across the neuron's cell membrane is such that the inside of a neuron is more negatively charged than the outside, the neuron is in a polarized state.

polygenic Traits determined by a combination of many genes are polygenic.

pons A brain structure (sitting above the medulla) which is important for the control of attentiveness, as well as the timing of sleep

positive hallucinations In a hypnotic state, when a person sees objects or hears voices that are not actually present.

positive psychology The study of how positive experiences, emotions, and personality traits promote human flourishing.

positive punishment Decreasing the response frequency by the delivery of an unpleasant or aversive stimulus following the response.

positive reinforcement Reinforcing a response by the presentation of a positive stimulus.

positively correlated The values of two variables either increase together or decrease together.

positron emission tomography (PET) A computer-based scanning procedure to measure brain activity using a radioactive tracer mixed with glucose.

postconventional level of moral development Level of moral development in which children evaluate actions in terms of higher-order ethical principles.

posterior system (for attention) Represents the perceptual features of an object, such as its location in space, shape, and color, responsible for selecting one object among many on the basis of the features associated with that object.

post-event information Information about an event obtained after the event is over that can be added to memory.

post-event memory reconstruction During memory formation, we may add new information that is suggested to us by others.

posthypnotic amnesia A particular form of post-hypnotic suggestion in which the hypnotized person forgets what has happened during the hypnosis until signaled to remember.

posthypnotic response A response that occurs when a subject who has been roused from hypnosis responds with movement to a prearranged signal by the hypnotist.

post-traumatic stress disorder An anxiety disorder in which a stressful event that is outside the range of usual human experience, such as military combat or a natural disaster, brings in its aftermath such symptoms as a re-experiencing of the trauma and avoidance of stimuli associated with it, a feeling of estrangement, a tendency to be easily startled, nightmares, recurrent dreams, and disturbed sleep.

power function The relation between Y and F, which is (basically) $Y = fr$.

pragmatic rules Rules used in deductive reasoning that are less abstract than logical rules, but still applicable to many different domains of life. An example is the permission rule.

preconscious All the information that is not currently 'on our mind' but that we could bring into consciousness if called upon to do so.

preconscious memories Memories that are accessible to consciousness.

preconventional level of moral development Level of moral development in which children evaluate actions as right or wrong on the basis of anticipated punishment.

predictability The degree to which we know if and when an event will occur.

preferential looking method A method of examining infants' perceptual preferences by presenting them two stimuli simultaneously and noting the amount of time the infants gaze at each object.

prefrontal lobes The lobes just behind the forehead.

preoperational stage Piaget's second stage of cognitive development. The child thinks in terms of symbols, but does not yet comprehend certain rules or operations.

primacy effect The tendency for first information we receive to have a greater impact on our overall impressions.

primary auditory area Cortical area responsible for auditory processing.

primary motor area Cortical area responsible for voluntary movements of the body.

primary reinforcer A reinforcer that is able to act as a reward independently of prior learning.

primary somatosensory area Cortical area responsible for sensory experiences.

primary visual area Cortical area responsible for visual processing.

priming The increased accessibility or retrievability of information stored in memory produced by the prior presentation of relevant cues.

primitive features Qualities such as shape and color.

proactive interaction The interaction between individuals and their environments that arises because different individuals choose to enter different situations and to shape those situations differently after entering them.

problem-focused coping Reducing anxiety or stress by dealing in some way with the anxiety-producing situation. Escaping the situation or finding a way to alter it are examples.

production of language Producing language by starting with a thought that translates into a sentence and ends up with sounds that express the sentence.

projection Repressing one's own unacceptable impulses and expressing hostile attitudes toward others who are perceived to possess those impulses.

projective test Presents an ambiguous stimulus to which the person may respond as he or she wishes.

proposition A statement that expresses a factual claim.

propositional thought Expresses a proposition or claim.

prosopagnosia A loss in the ability to recognize faces that results from brain damage.

prototype The properties that describe the best examples of the concept.

proximate cause Causes of behavior that explain how a behavior was generated.

proximity The physical distance between two people, a key predictor of interpersonal attraction.

psi Processes of information and/or energy exchange that are not currently explicable in terms of known science.

psychoactive drugs Drugs that affect behavior, consciousness, and/or mood.

psychoanalysis (a) The method developed by Freud and extended by his followers for treating mental disorders. (b) The theory of personality which grew out of experiences with the psychoanalytic method of treatment. The theory emphasizes the role of unconscious processes in personality development and in motivation.

psychoanalytic perspective An approach to psychology that tries to explain certain kinds of behaviors in terms of unconscious beliefs, fears, and desires.

psychoanalytic theory The premise that much of what we think and do is driven by unconscious processes.

psychodynamic therapies A style of therapy based on the idea that a person's current problems cannot be resolved successfully without a thorough understanding of their unconscious basis in early relationships with parents and siblings.

psychological perspective A distinct approach or way of looking at topics within psychology.

psychological perspectives (of abnormality) A group of theories that see mental disorders as problems in the functioning of the mind.

psychology The scientific study of behavior and mental processes.

psychoneuroimmunology The study of how the body's immune system is affected by stress and other psychological variables.

psychophysical function Performance as a function of stimulus intensity.

psychophysical procedures Procedures used to determine thresholds of sensory modalities.

psychophysiological disorders Physical disorders in which emotions are believed to play a central role.

psychosexual stages Freud's term for the stages (oral, anal, phallic) during the first 5 years of life in which the individual progresses through developmental periods that affect his or her personality.

psychosis (pl. psychoses) A severe mental disorder in which thinking and emotion are so impaired that the individual is seriously out of contact with reality. No longer a major diagnostic category in DSM-IV.

psychotherapy The treatment of mental disorders by psychological (rather than physical or biological) means.

puberty The period of sexual maturation that transforms a child into a biologically mature adult capable of sexual reproduction.

punishment A procedure used to decrease the strength of a response by presenting an aversive stimulus whenever the response occurs.

pupil In the eye, a circular opening in the iris (the colored part of the eye) that expands and contracts, varying according to the intensity of light present.

Q

Q-sort An assessment technique by which a rater provides a systematic description of an individual's personality by sorting a set of personality statements (for example, 'Has a wide range of interests') into groups, ranging from those that are least descriptive to those that are most descriptive of the individual.

R

random assignment A system for assigning participants to experimental and control groups so that each participant has an equal chance of being assigned to any group.

ratio schedules Reinforcement schedules where reinforcement depends on the number of responses the organism makes.

rationalization A defense mechanism in which self-esteem is maintained by assigning plausible and acceptable reasons for conduct entered on impulsively or for less acceptable reasons.

reaction formation A defense mechanism in which a person denies a disapproved motive through giving strong expressions to its opposite.

reactive interaction The interaction between individuals and their environments that arises because different individuals interpret, experience, and react to situations in different ways.

recall test When a person is asked to produce a memorized item using minimal retrieval cues.

recency effect the phenomenon that when people are asked to recall in any order the items on a list, those that come at the end of the list are more likely to be recalled than the others

receptor A specialized cell sensitive to particular kinds of stimuli and connected to nerves composed of afferent neurons (such as the retina of the eye). Used more loosely, the organ containing these sensitive portions (such as the eye or the ear).

recognition test When a person must decide whether he or she has seen a particular item before.

reconstructive processes The processes by which memory, once formed, is systematically altered based on inference and post-event information.

reductionism Reducing psychological notions to biological ones.

reference groups Groups with which we identify; we refer to them in order to evaluate and regulate our opinions and actions.

reflectance characteristic Property of colored paper that determines how it reflects some wavelengths more than others.

refractory period The brief period (a millisecond or so) after an action potential has been generated, during which another action potential cannot be generated.

rehearsal The conscious repetition of information in short-term memory, usually involving speech. The process facilitates the short-term recall of information and its transfer to long-term memory.

reinforcement (a) In classical conditioning, the experimental procedure of following the conditioned stimulus by the unconditioned stimulus. (b) In operant conditioning, the analogous procedure of following the occurrence of the operant response by the reinforcing stimulus. (c) The process that increases the strength of conditioning as a result of these arrangements.

relative height (as a depth cue) In perception, a monocular cue for depth. Among identical objects, those that are higher in an image are perceived as being farther away.

relative motion (as a depth cue) The different speeds of two objects can be a depth cue.

relative size (as a depth cue) In perception, a monocular cue for depth. If an image contains an array of objects of similar shape, the smaller objects are perceived as being farther away.

relaxation training Training in various techniques for relaxing muscle tension. The procedure is based on Jacobson's progressive relaxation method, in which the person learns how to relax muscle groups one at a time, the assumption being that muscular relaxation is effective in bringing about emotional relaxation.

reliability Yielding reproducible and consistent results.

REM sleep The period of sleep during which rapid eye movements occur.

representativeness heuristic The assumption that each case is representative of its category.

repression The ego pushes a threatening thought or forbidden impulse out of awareness into the unconscious.

resonance The degree to which a sound of a particular frequency reverberates over a mathematically matched distance.

response generalization The more similar stimuli are to the original conditioned stimulus, the more likely they are to evoke the same response.

responses to emotion How people cope with or react to their own emotion or the situation that elicited it.

resting membrane potential The electrical potential across the nerve cell membrane when it is in its resting state (in other words, not responding to other neurons); the inside of the cell membrane is slightly more negative than the outside.

resting potential The electric potential of a neuron at rest; for most neurons the resting potential is around −70 millivolts (mV).

restructuring Reorganizing the mental representation of a situation – often an important step in solving a problem.

reticular formation A system of ill-defined nerve paths and connections within the brain stem, lying outside the well-defined nerve pathways, and important as an arousal mechanism.

retina The portion of the eye sensitive to light, containing the rods and the cones.

retrieval stage Occurs when one attempts to pull from one's memory information that was previously encoded and stored there.

reuptake The process by which a neurotransmitter is 'taken up' again (reabsorbed) by the synaptic terminals from which it had been released.

right to privacy Information about a person acquired during a study must be kept confidential and not made available to others without his or her consent.

rods In the eye, an element of the retina mediating achromatic sensation only; particularly important in peripheral vision and night vision.

Rorschach Test A projective test developed by the Swiss psychiatrist Hermann Rorschach, consisting of a series of ten cards, each of which displays a rather complex inkblot.

S

saccade The quick movement of the eyes between eye fixations.

saltatory conduction Occurs when the nerve impulse jumps from one node of Ranvier to the next.

saturation The purity of a color.

schema (pl. schemas) Theory about how the physical and social worlds operate (Chapter 3); a mental representation of a class of people, objects, events, or situations (Chapter 8); a cognitive structure that helps us perceive, organize, process, and utilize information (Chapter 13); organized beliefs and knowledge about people, objects, events, and situations.

schematic processing The cognitive process of searching for the schema in memory that is most consistent with the incoming information.

schizophrenia A group of disorders characterized by severe personality disorganization, distortion of reality, and inability to function in daily life.

school psychologist A professional psychologist employed by a school or school system, with responsibility for testing, guidance, research, and so on.

scientific Research methods used to collect data are scientific when they are (1) unbiased (do not favor one hypothesis over another) and (2) reliable (other qualified people can repeat the observations and obtain the same results).

second-order conditioning In classical conditioning, a conditioned stimulus (CS) is used as the unconditioned stimiulus (US) in a new conditioning procedure.

secondary reinforcer A reinforcer that gains its status as a reward at least partly through learning about its relationship with other events.

securely attached Term used to describe a child who seeks to interact with his or her caretaker during a reunion episode.

selective adaptation In perception, a loss of sensitivity to motion that occurs when we view motion. The adaptation is selective because we lose sensitivity to the motion viewed, and to similar motions, but not to motion that differs significantly in direction or speed. Presumably the result of fatigued neurons in the cerebral cortex.

selective attention The process of attending to a particular part of the environment while ignoring the rest.

selective breeding A method of studying genetic influences by mating animals that display certain traits and selecting for breeding from among their offspring those that express the trait. If the trait is primarily determined by heredity, continued selection for a number of generations will produce a strain that breeds true for that trait.

selective reinforcement Strengthening of specific desired behaviors.

self All the ideas, perceptions, and values that characterize 'I' or 'me'.

self-concept An individual's fundamental sense of self or beliefs about the self.

self-efficacy An individual's belief in his or her own effectiveness.

self-expansion An increase in our potential abilities and resources.

self-esteem An individual's evaluation of the worthiness of the self.

self-fulfilling prophecy Once activated, stereotypes can set in motion a chain of behavioral processes that serve to draw out from others behavior that confirms the initial stereotype.

self-help groups Groups that are conducted without a professional therapist.

self-objectification When a person thinks about and values her own body more from a third-person perspective, focusing on observable body attributes ('How do I look?'), rather than from a first-person perspective, focusing on privileged, or unobservable body attributes ('How do I feel?').

self-perception theory The theory that attitudes and beliefs are influenced by observations of one's own behavior; sometimes we judge how we feel by observing how we act.

self-regulation Monitoring, or observing, one's own behavior.

self-schema (pl. self-schemas) Cognitive generalizations about the self, derived from past experience, that organize and guide the processing of self-related information.

semantics (the study of) the meaning of words and sentences.

sensations Experiences associated with simple stimuli.

sensitive periods Periods that are optimal for a particular kind of development.

sensitive responsiveness A characteristic of a caretaker who responds promptly when a baby cries and behaves affectionately when they pick up the baby. The caregiver also tailors their response to the baby's needs.

sensitivity The inclination of a sensory system to respond to a stimulus.

sensitization The process by which an organism learns to strengthen its reaction to a stimulus if a threatening or painful stimulus follows.

sensorimotor stage A period in which infants are busy discovering the relationships between their actions and the consequences of those actions.

sensory coding How stimuli are transmitted from the sensory receptors to the brain.

sensory memory A very brief photograph-like memory that outlasts the physical stimulus by a second or less.

sensory neuron A neuron that transmits impulses received by receptors to the central nervous system.

sensory response The magnitude of nervous activity, which rises and then falls.

sensory store The place in the memory where information arriving from the environment is first placed.

sentence unit Grammatical units that can be either a sentence or a phrase.

separation anxiety Distress when a caretaker is not nearby.

serotonin reuptake inhibitors A class of antidepressant drugs that work by increasing levels of the neurotransmitter serotonin in the synapse.

set point The point at which body weight is set and that the body strives to maintain.

sex-linked trait Genetically determined characteristics and disorders that are linked to the 23rd chromosome pair.

sex typing The acquisition of behaviors and characteristics that a culture considers appropriate to one's sex.

sexual orientation The degree to which an individual is sexually attracted to members of the opposite sex and/or to members of the same sex.

sexual selection A special case of natural selection that yields traits that promote reproductive success in the sex with the greater potential reproductive rate.

shading and shadows (as a depth cue) The configuration of shading and shadows provides information about an object's depth.

shadowing Repeating back one auditory message.

sham feeding A result of a surgical procedure so that whenever something is eaten, it will fall out of the body rather than be digested.

shaping Reinforcing only variations in response that deviate in the direction desired by the experimenter.

short-term memory Memory held in consciousness that, if not rehearsed, decays within about 20 seconds.

signal What the observer is trying to detect in an experiment, as opposed to 'noise'.

signal detection theory A theory of the sensory and decision processes involved in psychophysical judgments, with special reference to the problem of detecting weak signals in noise.

similarity heuristic The use of similarity – to a specific case or to a prototype – to estimate the probability of an event.

simple cell A cell in the visual cortex that responds to a bar of light or straight edge of a particular orientation and location in the visual field.

situational attribution Attributing a person's actions to factors in the situation or environment, as opposed to internal attitudes and motives.

sleep disorder When inability to sleep well produces impaired daytime functioning or excessive sleepiness.

slow to warm up temperament Term used to describe a child who is relatively inactive, tends to withdraw from new situations in a mild way, and requires more time than easy infants to adapt to new situations.

Snellen acuity Acuity measured relative to a viewer who does not need to wear glasses.

spatial acuity the ability to see differences in form.

spinal cord The bundle of nerves extending from the brain through the spinal canal, encased in the spinal column (the backbone).

social anxiety disorder (pre-DSM-5 known as social phobia) Extreme insecurity in social situations accompanied by an exaggerated fear of embarrassing oneself.

social cognition The examination of people's subjective interpretations of their social experiences, as well as their modes of thinking about the social world.

social-cognitive theory (of personality) Reciprocal determinism, in which external determinants of behavior (such as rewards and punishments) and internal determinants (such as beliefs, thoughts, and expectations) are part of a system of interacting influences that affect both behavior and other parts of the system.

social desirability effects A particular form of bias that can occur during a survey when some people try to present themselves in a favorable light.

social facilitation The effects of coaction and the presence of an audience.

social identity approach An approach that assumes that people can identify themselves in various ways, for instance, as a human being, as a member of a social group, or as an individual. The most salient social identity in a given situation influences a person's behavior in that situation.

social inhibition The sometimes derailing effects of coactors and audiences on performance.

social-learning theory The application of learning theory to the problems of personal and social behavior (syn. social behavior theory).

social neuroscience The study of how stereotyping, attitudes, person perception, and self-knowledge are executed in the brain.

social norms Implicit rules and expectations that dictate what we ought to think and how we ought to behave.

social psychologist A psychologist who studies social interaction and the ways in which individuals influence one another.

social psychology The study of how people think and feel about their social world and how they interact and influence one another.

social stereotype Personality traits or physical attributes given to a whole class of people.

sociocultural approach An approach to development that characterizes the child not as a physical scientist seeking 'true' knowledge but as a newcomer to a culture who seeks to become a native by learning how to look at social reality through the lens of that culture.

somatic system Carries messages to and from the sense receptors, muscles, and the surface of the body.

sound wave A wave defined by periodically varying air pressure over time.

source monitoring Keeping track of where various components of memory originally came from.

source wavelengths Wavelengths coming from some light source.

span of apprehension The number of immediately recallable items.

specific phobia Excessive fear of a specific object, animal, or situation in the absence of real danger.

spontaneous recovery A phenomenon in classical conditioning discovered by Pavlov. When an organism undergoes execution of a conditioned response and is then moved to a new context, the conditioned response may reappear.

stages of development Developmental periods, usually following a progressive sequence, that appear to represent qualitative changes in either the structure or the function of the organism (such as Freud's psychosexual stages, Piaget's cognitive stages).

standard An arbitrary level of stimulus intensity against which other intensities are judged.

Stanford-Binet Intelligence Scale Stanford revision of the Binet test which measures the kinds of changes in intelligence ordinarily associated with growing older.

stapes One of three small bones located in the middle ear.

statistical significance The trustworthiness of an obtained statistical measure as a statement about reality; for example, the probability that the population mean falls within the limits determined from a sample. The expression refers to the reliability of the statistical finding and not to its importance.

statistics The discipline that deals with sampling data from a population of individuals and then drawing inferences about the population from those data.

stereotype A set of inferences about the personality traits or physical attributes of a whole class of people; schemas of classes of people.

stereotype threat The mere threat of being identified with a stereotype can raise an individual's anxiety level, which in turn degrades his or her performance.

Sternberg's triarchic theory This theory has three parts or subtheories. The componential subtheory, which deals with

thought processes; the experiential subtheory, which deals with the effects of experience on intelligence; and the contextual subtheory, which considers the effects of the individual's environment and culture.

stimulant drugs Drugs used to treat attention deficit hyperativity disorder.

stimulants Drugs that increase alertness and general arousal.

stimulus discrimination The less similar stimuli are to the original conditioned stimulus, the less likely they are to evoke the same response.

storage stage The maintenance of stored information over time.

strange situation An experimental paradigm for assessing children's attachment to adults, in which the adult (usually a parent) leaves the room, and the child's reaction to the adult is observed when the adult returns.

stress Experiencing events that are perceived as endangering one's physical or psychological well-being.

stress responses Reactions to events an individual perceives as endangering his or her well-being. These may include bodily changes that prepare for emergency (the fight-or-flight response) as well as such psychological reactions as anxiety, anger and aggression, apathy and depression, and cognitive impairment.

stressors Events that an individual perceives as endangering his or her physical or psychological well-being.

stroboscopic motion An illusion of motion resulting from the successive presentation of discrete stimulus patterns arranged in a progression corresponding to movement, such as motion pictures.

Stroop effect The Stroop effect or interference results because word reading is such a dominant and automatic response among skilled readers that it is difficult for them to ignore a printed word and name the word's ink color when the word is a color that is different from the color of the ink.

structuralism The analysis of mental structures.

subjective experience The affective state or feeling tone.

subjectivist perspective An orientation toward understanding behavior and mental processes in terms of the subjective realities people actively construct.

substantia nigra A structure in the midbrain that is a crucial part of the dopamine pathway.

superego The part of personality that judges whether actions are right or wrong.

superior and inferior colliculus Areas in the midbrain involved in relaying sensory information to the brain and in the control of movements.

suppression Active attempt to push thoughts or images out of consciousness.

suprathreshold conditions Conditions in which stimulus intensity is above threshold.

survey method A method of obtaining information by questioning a large sample of people.

syllogism In logic, a deductive argument consisting of three propositions: two premises and one conclusion.

symbol Anything that stands for or refers to something other than itself.

sympathetic nervous system A division of the autonomic nervous system, characterized by a chain of ganglia on either side of the spinal cord, with nerve fibers originating in the thoracic and lumbar portions of the spinal cord. Active in emotional excitement and to some extent antagonistic to the parasympathetic division.

synapse The close functional connection between the axon of one neuron and the dendrites or cell body of another neuron.

synaptic gap The slight gap between the terminal button and the cell body or dendrites of the receiving neuron.

synaptic plasticity Changes in the morphology and/or physiology of synapses involved in learning and memory.

syntax A specification of the relationships between words in phrases and sentences.

System 1 and System 2 two modes of thinking. System 1 refers to the quick and automatic mode of thinking, like snap judgements based on prior beliefs, whereas System 2 refers to the slower and deliberate mode of thinking, like conclusions formed through logical reasoning.

systematic desensitization A behavior therapy technique in which hierarchies of anxiety-producing situations are imagined (or sometimes confronted in reality) while the person is in a state of deep relaxation. Gradually the situations become dissociated from the anxiety response.

T

tabula rasa (Latin, meaning 'blank slate'.) The term refers to the view that human beings are born without any innate knowledge or ideas; all knowledge is acquired through learning and experience. Proposed by the seventeenth- and eighteenth-century British empiricists (Locke, Hume, Berkeley, Hartley).

tardive dyskinesia Involuntary movements of the tongue, face, mouth, or jaw.

taste receptors Receptors for taste located in clusters on the tongue and around the mouth. Also called taste buds.

temperament Mood-related personality characteristics.

temporal contiguity Events A and B are temporally continuous if they occur close together in time.

temporal lobe The part of the cortex below the lateral fissure, on each side of the brain.

temporal pattern The spacing sequence of electrical impulses.

temporal theory of sound A theory of pitch perception which assumes that the frequency of neural impulses traveling up the auditory nerve correspond to the frequency of a tone.

terminal buttons The small swellings at the end of the branches of an axon, containing neurotransmitters.

test Presents a uniform situation to a group of people who vary in a particular trait.

thalamus Two groups of nerve cell nuclei located just above the brain stem and inside the cerebral hemispheres. Considered a part of the central core of the brain. One area acts as a sensory relay station, the other plays a role in sleep and waking; this portion is considered part of the limbic system.

Thematic Apperception Test (TAT) A participant is shown up to 20 ambiguous pictures of persons and scenes and asked to make up a story about each picture.

theory An interrelated set of propositions about a particular phenomenon.

theory of ecological optics The information from the environment – or more specifically, its two-dimensional representation on our retina – is all that is really necessary to live a normal life.

theory of mind The child's understanding of basic mental states, such as desires, percepts, beliefs, knowledge, thoughts, intentions, and feelings.

thirst The psychological manifestation of the need for water.

thought-tendencies Urges to think and act in certain ways.

timbre Our experience of the complexity of a sound.

tolerance The need for a greater amount of a drug to achieve the same euphoria.

tonic pain The kind of steady, long-lasting pain experienced after an injury has occurred; usually produced by swelling and tissue damage. In contrast to phasic pain.

top-down feedback connections Connections that go from the higher levels to the lower levels.

top-down processes Processes in perception, learning, memory, and comprehension that are driven by the organism's prior knowledge and expectations, rather than by the input.

transduction Translate physical energy into electrical signals that can make their way to the brain.

transference The tendency for the client to make the therapist the object of emotional responses.

traumatic events Situations of extreme danger that are outside the range of usual human experience.

trial-and-error learning Learning by gradual elimination of ineffective responses (contrast with insight).

trials The 'components' of an experiment, e.g., a repetition of stimulus presentation.

triangular theory of love This theory divides love into three components: intimacy, passion, and commitment.

trichromatic theory A theory of color perception that postulates three basic color receptors (cones), a 'red' receptor, a 'green' receptor, and a 'blue' receptor. The theory explains color blindness by the absence of one or more receptor types (syn. Young-Helmholtz theory).

tricyclic antidepressants A class of antidepressants that relieve the symptoms of depression by preventing the reuptake of the neurotransmitters serotonin and norepinephrine, thereby prolonging their action. Imipramine (brand names, Tofranil and Elavil) is one drug commonly prescribed.

two-factor theory The theory that emotions result from the combination of two factors – an initial state of unexplained arousal plus a cognitive explanation (or appraisal) for that arousal.

type A pattern A behavior pattern discovered in studies of coronary heart disease. Type A's are people who have a sense of time urgency, find it difficult to relax, and become impatient and angry when confronted with delays or with people whom they view as incompetent. Type A's are at risk for heart disease.

U

ultimate cause Causes of behavior that explain why a behavior was generated.

unconditional positive regard Feeling that oneself is valued by parents and others even when their feelings, attitudes, and behaviors are less than ideal.

unconditioned response (UR) In classical conditioning, the response given originally to the unconditioned stimulus used as the basis for establishing a conditioned response to a previously neutral stimulus.

unconditioned stimulus (US) In classical conditioning, a stimulus that automatically elicits a response, typically via a reflex, without prior conditioning.

unconscious The thoughts, attitudes, impulses, wishes, motivations, and emotions of which we are unaware (Chapter 1); contains some memories, impulses, and desires that are not accessible to consciousness (Chapter 6); impulses, wishes, and inaccessible memories that affect our thoughts and behavior (Chapter 13).

undoing effect of positive emotions Positive emotions may be particularly suited for helping people recover from any lingering arousal that follows negative emotions.

V

validity Measuring what is intended to be measured.

variable Something that can occur with different values.

variable interval schedule Reinforcement still depends on a certain interval having elapsed, but the interval's duration varies unpredictably.

variable ratio schedule The organism is reinforced only after making a certain number of responses, but that number varies unpredictably.

ventromedial hypothalamic syndrome Extreme appetites caused by lesions of the ventromedial hypothalamus.

verb phrase The section of a sentence that gives the predicate of the proposition.

vicarious learning Learning by observing the behavior of others and noting the consequences of that behavior (syn. observational learning).

visceral perception Our perception of our own arousal.

visual acuity The eye's ability to resolve details.

visual cortex The part of the brain that is concerned with vision.

visual field The total visual array acting on the eye when it is directed toward a fixation point.

visual neglect A patient who, although not blind, ignores everything on one side of their visual field (usually the left side).

visual search task A task in which the observer is asked to determine whether some target object is present in a cluttered display.

visual-spatial sketchpad One of the two distinct stores of working memory that briefly stores information in a visual or spatial code.

vulnerability-stress model An interactive model of physical or mental disorders that proposes that an individual will develop a disorder only when he or she has both some constitutional vulnerability (predisposition) and experiences stressful circumstances. Same as diathesis-stress model.

W

wanting The anticipation of pleasure, as in cravings.

weapon focus Attention is given to the dangerous weapon and it is therefore more easily remembered than the wielder of the weapon.

Weber fraction The constant of proportionality.

Wechsler Adult Intelligence Scale A verbal scale and a performance scale that yield separate scores as well as a full-scale IQ.

Wernicke's aphasia Damage to Wernicke's area leads to difficulties in speech comprehension.

Wernicke's area That portion of the left cerebral hemisphere involved in language understanding. Individuals with damage in this area are not able to comprehend words; they can hear words, but they do not know their meanings.

whole-report performance After viewing an array of letters for a brief period of time, the observer is asked to report as many letters as possible.

withdrawal The intensely aversive reaction to the cessation of drug use.

withdrawal symptoms Unpleasant physiological and psychological reactions that occur when a person suddenly stops taking an addictive drug; these range from nausea, anxiety, mild tremors, and difficulty sleeping at low levels of dependence to vomiting, cramps, hallucinations, agitation, and severe tremors or seizures at higher levels.

word salad Unrelated words and phrases and idiosyncratic word associations.

working backward A problem-solving strategy in which one works backwards from the goal towards the current state.

working memory Memories that are stored for only a few seconds.

Y

Yerkes-Dodson law This law states that complex tasks are best performed at low levels of arousal, whereas simple tasks are best performed at high levels of arousal.

REFERENCES

ABBOTT, B. B., SCHOEN, L. S., & BADIA, P. (1984) Predictable and unpredictable shock: Behavioral measures of aversion and physiological measures of stress. *Psychological Bulletin*, *96*, 45–71.

ABRAMOVITCH, R., CORTER, C., PEPLER, D. J., & STANHOPE, L. (1986) Sibling and peer interaction: A final follow-up and a comparison. *Child Development*, *57*, 217–229.

ABRAMSON, L. Y., METALSKY, G. I., & ALLOY, L. B. (1989) Hopelessness depression: A theory-based subtype of depression. *Psychological Review*, *96*, 358–372.

ACADEMY FOR MEDICAL ROYAL COLLEGES (2008) *A code of practice for the diagnosis and confirmation of death.* London: The authors. Retrieved from http://www.aomrc.org.uk/ publications/statements/doc_view/42-a-code-of-practice-for-the-diagnosis-and-confirmation-of-death.html.

ADAMS, J. L. (1974) *Conceptual blockbusting.* Stanford, CA: Stanford Alumni Association.

ADAMS, M., & COLLINS, A. (1979) A schema-theoretic view of reading. In R. O. Freedle (Ed.), *New Directions Discourse Processing*, Vol. 12. Norwood, NJ: Ablex.

ADLEMAN, N. E., MENON, V., BLASEY, C. M., WHITE, C. D., WARSOFSKY, I. S., GLOVER, G. H., & REISS, A. L. (2002) A developmental fMRI study of the Stroop color-word task. *Neuroimage*, *16*, 16–75.

ADLER, A., & BRETT, C. (2009) *Understanding human nature: The psychology of personality.* London: One World Publishers. (Original work published 1927.)

AFFLECK, G., TENNEN, H., CROOG, S., & LEVINE, S. (1987a) Causal attribution, perceived benefits and morbidity after a heart attack: An eight-year study. *Journal of Consulting and Clinical Psychology*, *55*, 29–55.

AFFLECK, G., TENNEN, H., CROOG, S., & LEVINE, S. (1987b) Causal attribution, perceived control, and recovery from a heart attack. *Journal of Social and Clinical Psychology*, *5*, 339–355.

AGRAS, W. S. (1993) Short term psychological treatments for binge eating. In C. G. Fairburn & G. T. Wilson (Eds.), *Binge eating: Nature, assessment, and treatment.* New York: Guilford.

AINSWORTH, M. D. S., BLEHAR, M. C., WALTERS, E., & WALL, S. (1978) *Patterns of attachment: A psychological study of the strange situation.* Hillsdale, NJ: Erlbaum.

ALEXANDER, K. L., ENTWISLE, D. R., & THOMPSON, M. S. (1987) School performance, status relations, and the structure of sentiment: Bringing the teacher back in. *American Sociological Review*, *52*, 665–682.

ALEXANDER-BLOCH, A. F., GOGTAY, N., MEUNIER, D., BIRN, R., CLASEN, L., LALONDE, F., LENROOT, R., GIEDD, J., & BULLMORE, E. T. (2010) Disrupted modularity and local connectivity of brain functional networks in childhood-onset schizophrenia. *Frontiers in Systems Neuroscience*, *4*, 1–16.

ALGOE, S. B., & HAIDT, J. (2009) Witnessing excellence in action: The "other-praising" emotions of elevation, gratitude, and admiration. *Journal of Positive Psychology*, *4*, 105–127.

ALGOE, S. B., HAIDT, J., & GABLE, S. L. (2008) Beyond reciprocity: Gratitude and relationships in everyday life. *Emotion*, *8*, 425–429.

ALLEN, N. J., & BARRES, B. A. (2009) Glia – more than just brain glue. *Nature*, *457*, 675–677.

ALLEN, V. L., & LEVINE, J. M. (1969) Consensus and conformity. *Journal of Experimental Social Psychology*, *5*, 389–399.

ALLEN, V. L., & LEVINE, J. M. (1971) Social support and conformity: The role of independent assessment of reality. *Journal of Experimental Social Psychology*, *7*, 48–58.

ALLISON, T., PUCE, A., & MCCARTHY, G. (2000) Social perception from visual cues: Role of the STS region. *Trends in Cognitive Science*, *4*, 267–278.

ALLOY, L. B., & TABACHNIK, N. (1984) Assessment of covariation by animals and humans: Influence of prior expectations and current situational information. *Psychological Review*, *91*, 112–149.

ALLOY, L. B., ABRAMSON, L. Y., WHITEHOUSE, W. G., HOGAN, M. E., PANZARELLA, C., & ROSE, D. T. (2006) Prospective incidence of first onsets and recurrences of depression in individuals at high and low cognitive risk for depression. *Journal of Abnormal Psychology*, *115*, 145–156.

ALLPORT, F. H. (1920) The influence of the group upon association and thought. *Journal of Experimental Psychology*, *3*, 159–182.

ALLPORT, F. H. (1924) *Social psychology.* Boston: Houghton Mifflin.

ALLPORT, G. H. (1954) *The nature of prejudice.* Reading, MA: Addison-Wesley.

ALLPORT, G. W., & ODBERT, H. S. (1936) Trait-names: A psycholexical study. *Psychological Monographs*, *47* (1, Whole No. 211)

ALONSO, J., ANGERMEYER, M. C., BERNERT, S., BRUFFAERTS, R., BRUGHA, T. S., BRYSON, H., DE GIROLAMO, G., DE GRAAF, R., DEMYTTENAERE, K., GASQUET, I., HARO, J. M., KATZ, S. J., KESSLER, R. C., KOVESS, V., LEPINE, J. P., ORMEL, J., POLIDORI, G., RUSSO, L. J., & VILAGUT, G. (2004) 12-month comorbidity patterns and associated factors in Europe: Results from the European Study of the Epidemiology of Mental Disorders (ESEMeD) project. *Acta Psychiatrica Scandinavica*, *109*, 28–37.

ALWIN, D. F., COHEN, R. L., & NEWCOMB, T. M. (1991) *Personality and social change: Attitude persistence and changes over the lifespan.* Madison: University of Wisconsin Press.

American Academy of Neurology (1995) Practice parameters for determining brain death in adults. *Neurology*, *45*, 1012–1014.

AMERICAN MEDICAL ASSOCIATION (1981) Guidelines for the determination of death. Report of the medical consultants on the diagnosis of death to the President's Commission for the Study of Ethical Problems in Medicine and Biomedical and

Behavioural Research. *Journal of the American Medical Association*, 246(19), 2184–2186.

AMERICAN PSYCHIATRIC ASSOCIATION (1994) *Diagnostic and statistical manual of mental disorders* (4th ed.) Washington, DC: American Psychiatric Association.

AMERICAN PSYCHIATRIC ASSOCIATION (2000) *Diagnostic and Statistical Manual of Mental Disorders* (4th ed., text revision) Washington, DC: American Psychiatric Association Press.

AMERICAN PSYCHOLOGICAL ASSOCIATION (1990) Ethical principles of psychologists. *American Psychologist, 45*, 390–395.

ANDERS, S. L. (2003) Improving community-based care for the treatment of schizophrenia: Lessons from native Africa. *Psychiatric Rehabilitation Journal, 27*, 51–58.

ANDERSEN, S. M., & GLASSMAN, N. S. (1996) Responding to significant others when they are not there: Effects on interpersonal inference, motivation, and affect. In R. M. Sorrentino & E. T. Higgins (Eds.), *Handbook of motivation and cognition* (Vol. 3, pp. 262–321). New York: Guilford.

ANDERSON, C. A. (2004) An update on the effects of playing violent video games. *Journal of Adolescence, 27*, 113–122.

ANDERSON, C. A., & BUSHMAN, B. J. (2001) Effects of violent video games on aggressive behavior, aggressive cognition, aggressive affect, physiological arousal, and prosocial behavior: A meta-analytic review of the scientific literature. *Psychological Science, 12*, 353–359.

ANDERSON, C. A., CARNAGEY, N. L., & EUBANKS, J. (2003) Exposure to violent media: the effects of songs with violent lyrics on aggressive thoughts and feelings. *Journal of Personality and Social Psychology, 84*, 960–971.

ANDERSON, C. A., BERKOWITZ, L., DONNERSTEIN, E., HUESMAN, L. R., JOHNSON, J. D., LINZ, D., MALAMUTH, N. M., & WARTELLA, E. (2003) The influence of media violence on youth. *Psychological Science in the Public Interest, 4*, 81–110.

ANDERSON, E., SIEGEL, E. H., & BARRETT, L. F. (2011) What you feel influences what you see: The role of affective feelings in resolving binocular rivalry. *Journal of Experimental Social Psychology, 47*, 856–860.

ANDERSON, J. R. (1983) *The architecture of cognition*. Cambridge, MA: Harvard University Press.

ANDERSON, J. R. (1987) Skill acquisition: Compilation of weak-method problem solutions. *Psychological Review, 94*, 192–210.

ANDERSON, J. R. (1990) *Cognitive psychology and its implications* (3rd ed.) New York: Freeman.

ANDERSON, J. R. (1991) The adaptive nature of human categorization. *Psychological Review, 98*, 409–429.

ANDERSON, M. (1992) *Intelligence and development: A cognitive theory*. Oxford: Blackwell.

ANDREASEN, N. (2001). Neuroimaging and neurobiology of schizophrenia. In K. Miyoshi, C. M. Shapiro, M. Gaviria, & Y. Morita (Eds.), *Contemporary neuropsychiatry* (pp. 265–271). Tokyo: Springer-Verlag.

ANDREWS, K. H., & KANDEL, D. B. (1979) Attitude and behavior. *American Sociological Review, 44*, 298–310.

ANGOFF, W. H. (1988) The nature-nurture debate, aptitudes, and group differences. *American Psychologist, 43*, 713–720.

ANGST, M. D., & CLARK, J. D. (2006) Opioid-induced hyperalgesia. A qualitative systematic review. *Anesthesiology, 104*, 570–587.

APA (AMERICAN PSYCHOLOGICAL ASSOCIATION) (1995) *Affirmative action: Who benefits?* Washington, D. C.: American Psychological Association.

ARCHER, J. (2004). Sex differences in aggression in real-world settings: A meta-analytic review. *Review of General Psychology, 8*, 291–322.

ARENDT, H. (1963) *Eichmann in Jerusalem: A report on the banality of evil*. New York: Viking Press.

ARMSTRONG, S. L., GLEITMAN, L. R., & GLEITMAN, H. (1983) What some concepts might not be. *Cognition, 13*, 263–308.

ARNOLD, M. (1949) A demonstrational analysis of the TAT in a clinical setting. *Journal of Abnormal and Social Psychology, 44*, 97–111.

ARON, A. (2002, January) Self-expansion as a motivational basis for positive psychology. In M. Green & T. McLaughlin-Volpe (Chairs), *Positive Relationships*, Symposium presented at the first annual pre-conference on Positive Psychology, Savannah, GA: Society for Personality and Social Psychology.

ARON, A., ARON, E. N., & SMOLLAN, D. (1992) Inclusion of other in the self scale and the structure of interpersonal closeness. *Journal of Personality and Social Psychology, 63*, 596–612.

ARON, A., NORMAN, C. C., & ARON, E. N. (1998) The self-expansion model and motivation. *Representative Research in Social Psychology, 22*, 1–13.

ARON, A., ARON, E. N., TUDOR, M., & NELSON, G. (1991) Close relationships as including other in the self. *Journal of Personality and Social Psychology, 60*, 241–253.

ARONSON, E. (1995) *The social animal* (7th ed.). San Francisco: Freeman.

ARONSON, E. (2004) Reducing hostility and building compassion: Lessons from the jigsaw classroom. In A. G. Miller (Ed.), *The Social Psychology of Good and Evil* (pp. 469–488). New York: Guildford Press.

ARONSON, E., & CARLSMITH, J. M. (1963) The effect of the severity of threat on the devaluation of forbidden behavior. *Journal of Abnormal and Social Psychology, 66*, 584–588.

ARONSON, E., & MILLS, J. (1959) The effect of severity of initiation on liking for a group. *Journal of Abnormal and Social Psychology, 59*, 177–181.

ARRIGO, J. M., & PEZDEK, K. (1997) Lessons from the study of psychogenic amnesia. *Current Directions in Psychological Science, 6*, 148–152.

ARTMAN, L., & CAHAN, S. (1993) Schooling and the development of transitive inference. *Developmental Psychology, 29*, 753–759.

ASCH, S. E. (1946) Forming impressions of personality. *Journal of Abnormal and Social Psychology, 41*, 258–290.

ASCH, S. E. (1952) *Social psychology*. Englewood Cliffs, NJ: Prentice-Hall.

ASCH, S. E. (1955) Opinions and social pressures. *Scientific American, 193*, 31–35.

ASCH, S. E. (1958) Effects of group pressure upon modification and distortion of judgments. In E. E. Maccoby, T. M. Newcomb, & E. L. Hartley (Eds.), *Readings in social psychology* (3rd ed.). New York: Holt, Rinehart & Winston.

ASLIN, R. N., & BANKS, M. S. (1978) Early visual experience in humans: Evidence for a critical period in the development of binocular vision. In S. Schneider, H. Liebowitz, H. Pick, & H. Stevenson (Eds.), *Psychology: From basic research to practice*. New York: Plenum.

ATKINSON, R. C. (1975) Mnemotechnics in second-language learning. *American Psychologist, 30*, 821–828.

ATKINSON, R. C., & SHIFFRIN, R. M. (1971a) The control of short-term memory. *Scientific American, 225*, 82–90.

ATKINSON, R. C., & SHIFFRIN, R. M. (1971b) Human memory: A proposed system and its control processes. In K. W. Spence (Ed.), *The psychology of learning and motivation: Advances in research and theory* (pp. 89–195). New York: Academic Press.

AVANTS, S. K., WARBURTON, L. A., & MARGOLIN, A. (2001). How injection drug users coped with testing HIV-seropositive: Implications for subsequent health-related behaviors. *AIDS Education and Prevention*, *13*, 207–18.

AWAYA, S., MIYAKE, Y., IMAYUMI, Y., SHIOSE, Y., KNADA, T., & KOMURO, K. (1973) Amblyopia. *Japanese Journal of Ophthalmology*, *17*, 69–82.

AYLAND, L., & WEST, B. (2006) The Good Way model: A strengths-based approach for working with young people, especially those with intellectual difficulties, who have sexually abusive behaviour. *Journal of Sexual Aggression*, *12*(2), 189–201.

AX, A. (1953) The physiological differentiation between fear and anger in humans. *Psychosomatic Medicine*, *15*, 433–442.

BAARS, B. J. (1988) *A cognitive theory of consciousness*. New York: Cambridge University Press.

BADDELEY, A. (2000) The episodic buffer: a new component of working memory? *Trends in Cognitive Sciences*, *4*, 11, 417–423.

BADDELEY, A. D. (1986) *Working memory*. Oxford: Clarendon.

BADDELEY, A. D. (1990) *Human memory: Theory and practice*. Boston: Allyn and Bacon.

BADDELEY, A. D., & ANDRADE, J. (2000) Working memory and the vividness of imagery. *Journal of Experiment Psychology: General*, *129*, 126–145.

BADDELEY, A. D., & HITCH, G. J. (1974) Working memory. In G. H. Bower (Ed.), *The psychology of learning and motivation* (Vol. 8). New York: Academic Press.

BADDELEY, A. D., THOMPSON, N., & BUCHANAN, M. (1975) Word length and the structure of short-term memory. *Journal of Verbal Learning and Verbal Behavior*, *14*, 575–589.

BAER, D. M., PETERSON, R. F., & SHERMAN, J. A. (1967) The development of imitation by reinforcing behavioral similarity to a model. *Journal of the Experimental Analysis of Behavior*, *10*, 405–416.

BAILEY, A., LE COUTEUR, A., GOTTESMAN, I., BOLTON, P., SIMONOFF, E., YUZDA, E., & RUTTER, M. (1995) Autism as a strongly genetic disorder: Evidence from a British twin study. *Psychological Medicine*, *25*, 63–77.

BAILEY, C. H., & KANDEL, E. R. (2004) Synaptic growth and the persistence of long-term memory: A molecular perspective. In M. S. Gazzaniga (Ed.), *The cognitive neurosciences* (3rd ed., pp. 647–663). Cambridge, MA: MIT Press.

BAILEY, J. M. (in press) What is sexual orientation and do women have one? In D. A. Hope (Ed.) *Contemporary perspectives on gay, lesbian, and bisexual identities*.

BAILEY, J. M., & PILLARD, R. C. (1995) Genetics of human sexual orientation. *Annual Review of Sex Research*, *6*, 126–150.

BAILEY, J. M., & ZUCKER, K. J. (1995) Childhood sex-typed behavior and sexual orientation: A conceptual analysis and quantitative review. *Developmental Psychology*, *31* (1), 43–55.

BAILLARGEON, R. (1987) Object permanence in $3\frac{1}{2}$- and $4\frac{1}{2}$-month-old infants. *Developmental Psychology*, *23*, 655–664.

BAILLARGEON, R., & DEVOS, J. (1991) Object permanence in young infants: Further evidence. *Child Development*, *62*, 1227–1246.

BAILLARGEON, R., SPELKE, E. S., & WASSERMAN, S. (1985) Object permanence in five-month-old infants. *Cognition*, *20*, 191–208.

BALLANTYNE, J. C., LAFORGE, K. S. (2007) Opioid dependence and addiction during opioid treatment of chronic pain. *Pain*, *129*, 235–255.

BANDURA, A. (1973) *Aggression: A social learning analysis*. Englewood Cliffs, NJ: Prentice-Hall.

BANDURA, A. (1977) *Social learning theory*. Englewood Cliffs, NJ: Prentice-Hall.

BANDURA, A. (1986) *Social foundations of thought and action: A social cognitive theory*. Englewood Cliffs, NJ: Prentice-Hall.

BANDURA, A. (2001) Social cognitive theory: An agentic perspective. *Annual Review of Psychology*, *52*, 1–26.

BANDURA, A. (2006) Going global with social cognitive theory: From prospect to paydirt. In S. I. Donaldson, D. E. Berger, K. Pezdek (Eds.), *Applied Psychology: New frontiers and rewarding careers* (pp. 53–79). Mahwah, NJ: Lawrence Erlbaum Associates.

BANDURA, A., & WALTERS, R. (1963) *Social learning and personality development*. New York: Holt, Rinehart & Winston.

BANDURA, A., BLANCHARD, E. B., & RITTER, B. (1969) The relative efficacy of desensitization and modeling approaches for inducing behavioral, affective, and attitudinal changes. *Journal of Personality and Social Psychology*, *13*, 173–199.

BANDURA, A., ROSS, D, & ROSS, S. A. (1961) Transmission of aggression through imitation of aggressive models. *Journal of Abnormal and Social Psychology*, *63*, 575–582.

BANDURA, A., ROSS, D., & ROSS, S. A. (1963) Imitation of film-mediated aggressive models. *Journal of Abnormal and Social Psychology*, *66*, 3–11.

BANKS, W. P., & PRINTZMETAL, W. (1976) Configurational effects in visual information processing. *Perception and Psychophysics*, *19*, 361–367.

BARBANO, M. F., & CADOR, M. (2007). Opioids for hedonic experience and dopamine to get ready for it. *Psychopharmacology*, *191*, 497–506.

BARCH, D. M. (2005) The cognitive neuroscience of schizophrenia.n *Annual Review of Clinical Psychology*, *1*, 321–353.

BAREFOOT, J. C., WILLIAMS, R. B., & DAHLSTROM, W. G. (1983) Hostility, CHD incidence and total mortality: A 25-year follow-up study of 255 physicians. *Psychosomatic Medicine*, *45*, 59–63.

BAREFOOT, J. C., DODGE, K. A., PETERSON, B. L., DAHLSTROM, W. G., WILLIAMS, R. B., Jr. (1989) The Cook-Medley Hostility scale: Item content and ability to predict survival. *Psychosomatic Medicine*, *51*, 46–57.

BARGH, J. (2007) Social psychological approaches to consciousness. In P. D. Zelazo, M. Moscovitch, & E. Thompson (Eds.), *The Cambridge handbook of consciousness* (pp. 555–570). New York: Cambridge University Press.

BARGH, J. A. (1997) The automaticity of everyday life. In R. S. Wyer Jr. (Ed.), *Advances in social cognition* (Vol. 10). Mahway, NJ: Erlbaum.

BARGH, J. A. (1999) The cognitive monster: The case against the controllability of automatic stereotype effects. In S. Chaiken & Y. Trope (Eds.), *Dual-process theories in social psychology* (pp. 361–382) New York: Guilford.

BARGH, J. A., & SHALEV, I. (2012) The substitutability of physical and social warmth in daily life. *Emotion*, *12*, 154–162.

BARGH, J. A., CHEN, M., & BURROWS, L. (1996) Automaticity of social behavior: Direct effects of trait construct and stereotype activation on action. *Journal of Personality and Social Psychology, 71*, 230–244.

BARKER, M. (2013) *Mindful counselling & psychotherapy: Practising mindfully across approaches and issues.* London: Sage.

BAR-ON, R. (1997) *Bar-On Emotional Quotient Inventory. Technical Manual*. Toronto, Canada: Multi-Health Systems.

BAR-ON, R., MAREE, J. G., & ELIAS, M. J. (Eds.) (2007) *Educating people to be emotionally intelligent*. Westport, CT: Praeger Publishers.

BARON, R., & BELLMAN, S. (2007) No guts, no glory: Courage, harassment and minority influence. *European Journal of Social Psychology, 37* (1), 101–124.

BARON, R. S. (1986) Distraction-conflict theory: Progress and problems. In L. Berkowitz (Ed.), *Advances in experimental social psychology* (Vol. 19). New York: Academic Press.

BARON, R., & BELLMAN, S. (2007) No guts, no glory: Courage, harassment and minority influence. *European Journal of Social Psychology, 37* (1), 101–124.

BARON-COHEN, S., & STAUNTON, R. (1994) Do children with autism acquire the phonology of their peers? An examination of group identification through the window of bilingualism. *First Language, 14*, 241–248.

BARON-COHEN, S., & SWETTENHAM, J. (1997) Theory of mind in autism: Its relationship to executive function and central coherence. In D. J. Cohen & F. R. Volkmar (Eds.), *Handbook of autism and pervasive developmental disorders* (pp. 880–893). Toronto: Wiley.

BARON-COHEN, S., & WHEELWRIGHT, S. (2004) The empathy quotient: an investigation of adults with Asperger syndrome or high functioning autism, and normal sex differences. *Journal of Autism and Developmental Disorders, 34*, 163–175.

BARON-COHEN, S., BALDWIN, D. A., & CROWSON, M. (1997). Do children with autism use the speaker's direction of gaze strategy to crack the code of language? *Child Development, 68*(1), 48–57.

BARRERA, M. E., & MAURER, D. (1981a) Recognition of mother's photographed face by the three-month-old infant. *Child Development, 52*, 714–716.

BARRERA, M. E., & MAURER, D. (1981b) Discrimination of strangers by the three-month-old. *Child Development, 52*, 558–563.

BARRETT, L. F. (2006a) Solving the emotion paradox: Categorization and the experience of emotion. *Personality and Social Psychology Review, 10*, 20–46.

BARRETT, L. F. (2006b) Valence as a basic building block of emotional life. *Journal of Research in Personality, 40*, 35–55.

BARRETT, L. F. (2006c) Are emotions natural kinds? *Perspectives on Psychological Science, 1*, 28–58.

BARRETT, L. F. (2009a) The future of psychology: Connecting mind to brain. *Perspectives on Psychological Science, 4*, 326–339.

BARRETT, L. F. (2009b) Variety is the spice of life: A psychological construction approach to understanding variability in emotion. *Cognition and Emotion, 23*, 1284–1306.

BARRETT, L. F. (2012) Emotions are real. *Emotion, 12*, 413–429.

BARRETT, L. F., & BAR, M. (2009) See it with feeling: Affective predictions in the human brain. *Philosophical Transactions of the Royal Society of London: Series B. Biological Sciences, 364*, 1325–1334.

BARRETT, L. F., & BLISS-MOREAU, E. (2009) Affect as a psychological primitive. *Advances in Experimental Social Psychology, 41*, 167–218.

BARRETT, L. F., LINDQUIST, K., & GENDRON, M. (2007) Language as a context for emotion perception. *Trends in Cognitive Sciences, 11*, 327–332.

BARRETT, L. F., QUIGLEY, K. S., BLISS-MOREAU, E., & ARONSON, K. R. (2004) Interoceptive sensitivity and self-reports of emotional experience. *Journal of Personality and Social Psychology, 87*, 684–697.

BARSALOU, L. W. (1985) Ideals, central tendency, and frequency of instantiation as determinants of graded structure in categories. *Journal of Experimental Psychology: Learning, Memory, and Cognition, 11*, 629–654.

BARTLETT, F. C. (1932) *Remembering: A study in experimental and social psychology*. Cambridge: Cambridge University Press.

BARTOSHUK, L. M. (1979) Bitter taste of saccharin: Related to the genetic ability to taste the bitter substance propylthiourial (PROP). *Science, 205*, 934–935.

BARTOSHUK, L. M. (1993) Genetic and pathological taste variation: What can we learn from animal models and human disease? *Ciba Foundation Symposium (D7X), 179*, 251–262.

BARTSCH, K., & WELLMAN, H. M. (1995) *Children talk about the mind*. New York: Oxford University Press.

BASOGLU, M., & MINEKA, S. (1992) The role of uncontrollable and unpredictable stress in posttraumatic stress responses in torture survivors. In M. Basoglu (Ed.), *Torture and its consequences: Current treatment approaches* (pp. 182–225). New York: Cambridge University Press.

BASOGLU, M., MINEKA, S., PAKER, M., AKER, T., LIVANOU, M., & GOEK, S. (1997) Psychological preparedness for trauma as a protective factor in survivors of torture. *Psychological Medicine, 27*, 1421–1433.

BASOGLU, M. K., KILIC, C., SALCIOGLU, E., LIVANOU, M. (2004). Prevalence of posttraumatic stress disorder and comorbid depression in earthquake survivors in Turkey: An epidemiological study. *Journal of Traumatic Stress, 17*, 133–141.

BATSON, C. D. (2011) *Altruism in humans*. New York: Oxford University Press.

BAUM, A., & POSLUSZNY, D. M. (1999) Health psychology: Mapping biobehavioral contributions to health and illness. *Annual Reviews of Psychology, 50*, 147–163.

BAUMEISTER, R. F. (2000) Gender differences in erotic plasticity: The female sex drive as socially flexible and responsive. *Psychological Bulletin, 126* (3), 347–374.

BAUMRIND, D. (1964) Some thoughts on ethics of research: After reading Milgram's "Behavioral study of obedience". *American Psychologist, 19*, 421–423.

BAUMRIND, D. (1980) New directions in socialization research. *American Psychologist, 35*, 639–652.

BAXTER, L., SCHWARTZ, J., BERGMAN, K., & SZUBA, M. (1992) Caudate glucose metabolic rate changes with both drug and behavior therapy for obsessive-compulsive disorder. *Archives of General Psychiatry, 49*, 681–689.

BEACH, S. R., & O'LEARY, K. D. (1993) Dysphoria and marital discord: Are dysphoric individuals at risk for marital maladjustment? *Journal of Marital and Family Therapy, 19*, 355–368.

BEAMAN, A. L., BARNES, P. J., KLENTZ, B., & MCQUIRK, B. (1978) Increasing helping rates through information dissemination: Teaching pays. *Personality and Social Psychology Bulletin, 4*, 406–411.

BECHARA, A., DAMASIO, A. R., DAMASIO, H., & ANDERSON, S. W. (1994) Insensitivity to future consequences following damage to human prefrontal cortex. *Cognition, 50*, 7–15.

BECHARA, A., DAMASIO, H., TRANEL, D., & DAMASIO, A. R. (1997) Deciding advantageously before knowing the advantageous strategy. *Science, 275*(5304), 1293–1295.

BECHARA, A., TRANEL, D., DAMASIO, H., ADOLPHS, R., ROCKLAND, C., & DAMASIO, A. R. (1995) Double dissociation of conditioning and declarative knowledge relative to the amygdala and hippocampus in humans. *Science, 269,* 1115–1118.

BECK, A. T. (1976) *Cognitive therapy and the emotional disorder.* New York: International Universities Press.

BECK, A. T., RUSH, A. J., SHAW, B. F., & EMERY, G. (1979) *Cognitive therapy of depression.* New York: Guilford.

BECK, J. S. (1995) *Cognitive therapy: Basics and beyond.* New York: Guilford Press.

BEEDIE, C., TERRY, P., & LANE, A. (2005) Distinctions between emotion and mood. *Cognition & Emotion, 19,* 847–878.

BÉKÉSY, G. VON (1960) *Experiments in hearing* (E. G. Weaver, Trans) New York: McGraw-Hill.

BELL, A. P., WEINBERG, M. S., & HAMMERSMITH, S. K. (1981a) *Sexual preference: Its development in men and women.* Bloomington: Indiana University Press.

BELL, A. P., WEINBERG, M. S., & HAMMERSMITH, S. K. (1981b) *Sexual preference: Its development in men and women. Statistical appendix.* Bloomington: Indiana University Press.

BELL, S. M., & AINSWORTH, M. D. (1972) Infant crying and maternal responsiveness. *Child Development, 43,* 1171–1190.

BELOFF, H. (1957) The structure and origin of the anal character. *Genetic Psychology Monographs, 55,* 141–172.

BELSKY, J., & ROVINE, M. J. (1987) Temperament and attachment security in the strange situation: An empirical rapprochement. *Child Development, 58,* 787–795.

BELSKY, J., FISH, M., & ISABELLA, R. A. (1991) Continuity and discontinuity in infant negative and positive emotionality: Family antecedents and attachment consequences. *Developmental Psychology, 27,* 421–431.

BEM, D. J. (1972) Self-perception theory. In L. Berkowitz (Ed.), *Advances in experimental social psychology* (Vol. 6). New York: Academic Press.

BEM, D. J. (1995) *Exotic becomes erotic: A developmental theory of sexual orientation.* Unpublished manuscript, Cornell University, Ithaca, New York.

BEM, D. J. (2000) Exotic becomes erotic: Interpreting the biological correlates of sexual orientation. *Archives of Sexual Behavior, 29,* 531–548.

BEM, D. J., & HONORTON, C. (1994) Does psi exist? Replicable evidence for an anomalous process if information transfer. *Psychological Bulletin, 115,* 4–18.

BEM, D. J., PALMER, J., & BROUGHTON, R. S. (2001) Updating the ganzfeld database: A victim of its own success? *Journal of Parapsychology, 65,* 207–218.

BEM, D. J., WALLACH, M. A., & KOGAN, N. (1965) Group decision-making under risk of aversive consequences. *Journal of Personality and Social Psychology, 1,* 453–460.

BEM, S. L. (1985) Androgyny and gender schema theory: A conceptual and empirical integration. In T. B. Sonderegger (Ed.), *Nebraska symposium on motivation 1984: Psychology and gender* (pp. 179–226). Lincoln: University of Nebraska Press.

BENJAMIN, J., LI, L., PATTERSON, C., GREENBERG, B. D., MURPHY, D. L., & HAMER, D. H. (1996) Population and familial association between the D4 dopamine receptor gene and measures of novelty seeking. *Nature Genetics, 12,* 81–84.

BENSON, D. F. (1985) Aphasia. In K. M. Heilman & E. Valenstein (Eds.), *Clinical neuropsychology* (2nd ed., pp. 17–47). New York: Oxford University Press.

BERGELSON, E. &, SWINGLEY, D. (2012) At 6–9 Months, human infants know the meanings of many common nouns. *Proceedings of the National Academy of Sciences, 109,* 3253–3258.

BERGER, T. W. (1984) Long-term potentiation of hippocampal synaptic transmission affects rate of behavioral learning. *Science, 224,* 627–630.

BERK, L. E. (1997) *Child development* (4th ed.). Needham Heights, MA: Allyn and Bacon.

BERLIN, B., & KAY, P. (1969) *Basic color terms: Their universality and evolution.* Los Angeles: University of California Press.

BERLYNE, D. E. (1966) Curiosity and exploration. *Science, 153,* 25–33.

BERNAT, J. L. (2013) Controversies in defining and determining death in critical care. *Nature Reviews Neurology, 9,* 164–173.

BERNHEIM, K. F. (1997) *The Lanahan cases and readings in abnormal behavior.* Baltimore: Lanahan.

BERNSTEIN, I. L. (1978) Learned taste aversions in children receiving chemotherapy. *Science, 200,* 1302–1303.

BERNSTEIN, I. L. (1999) Taste aversion learning: A contemporary perspective. *Nutrition, 15,* 229–234.

BERRIDGE, K. C. (1999) Pleasure, pain, desire, and dread: Hidden core processes of emotion. In D. Kahneman, E. Diener, & N. Schwarz (Eds.) *Well-being: The foundations of hedonic psychology* (pp. 525–557). New York: Russell Sage Foundation.

BERRIDGE, K. C. (2003) Pleasures of the brain. *Brain and Cognition, 52,* 106–128.

BERRIDGE, K. C. (2007) The debate over dopamine's role in reward: the case for incentive salience. *Psychopharmacology, 191,* 391–431.

BERRIDGE, K. C., & ROBINSON, T. E. (1998) What is the role of dopamine in reward: Hedonic impact, reward learning, or incentive salience? *Brain Research Reviews, 28,* 309–369.

BERRIDGE, K. C., & VALENSTEIN, E. S. (1991) What psychological process mediates feeding evoked by electrical stimulation of the lateral hypothalamus? *Behavioral Neuroscience, 105,* 3–14.

BERRIDGE, K., & WINKIELMAN, P. (2003) What is an unconscious emotion? (The case for unconscious "liking"). *Cognition & Emotion, 17,* 181–211.

BERSCHEID, E. (1983) Emotion. In H. H. Kelley, E. Berscheid, A. Christensen, J. H. Harvey, T. L. Hutson, G. Levinger, E. McClintock, L. A. Peplau, & D. R. Peterson (Eds.), *Close relationships* (pp. 110–168). New York: Freeman.

BERSCHEID, E., & WALSTER, E. H. (1974) A little bit about love. In T. Huston (Ed.), *Foundation of interpersonal attraction.* New York: Academic Press.

BERSON, I. R., & BERSON, M. J. (2005) Challenging online behaviors of youth: Findings from a comparative analysis of young people in the United States and New Zealand. *Social Science Computer Review, 23,* 29–38.

BETTELHEIM, B. (1967) *The empty fortress: Infantile autism and the birth of the self.* New York: Free Press.

BHATT, R. S., BERTIN, E., HAYDEN, A., & REED, A. (2005) Face processing in infancy: Developmental changes in the use of different kinds of relational information. *Child Development, 76,* 169–181.

BICKART, K. C., WRIGHT, C., DAUTOFF, R., DICKERSON, B. C., & FELDMAN BARRETT, L. (2011) Amygdala volume and social network size in humans. *Nature Neuroscience, 14*, 163–164.

BIEDERMAN, I. (1987) Recognition by components: A theory of human image understanding. *Psychological Review, 94*, 115–1947.

BIEDERMAN, I., & JU, G. (1988) Surface versus edge-based determinants of visual recognition. *Cognitive Psychology, 20*, 38–64.

BIENIOK, M. (2012) *Das Konzept der idealen Metropole in Theorie und Praxis am Beispiel von Berlin.* Berlin: Peter Lang Verlag.

BILLINGS, D. W., FOLKMAN, S., ACREE, M., & MOSKOWITZ, J. T. (2000) Coping and physical health during caregiving: The roles of positive and negative affect. *Journal of Personality and Social Psychology, 79*, 131–142

BINET, A., & SIMON, T. (1905) New methods for the diagnosis of the intellectual level of subnormals. *Annals of Psychology, 11*, 191.

BINNS, K. E., & SALT, T. E. (1997) Post eye-opening maturation of visual receptive field diameters in the superior colliculus of normal- and dark-reared rats. *Brain Research: Developmental Brain Research, 99*, 263–266.

BISIACH, E., & LUZZATI, C. (1978) Unilateral neglect of representational space. *Cortex, 14*, 129–133.

BLAKE, R. (1981) Strategies for assessing visual deficits in animals with selective neural deficits. In R. N. Aslin, J. R. Alberts, & M. R. Petersen (Eds.), *Development of perception:* Vol. 2. *The visual system* (pp. 95–110). New York: Academic Press.

BLANCK, G. (1990) Vygotsky: The man and his cause. In L. C. Moll (Ed.), *Vygotsky and education.* New York: Cambridge University Press.

BLAXTON, T. A. (1989) Investigating dissociations among memory measures: Support for a transfer-appropriate processing framework. *Journal of Experimental Psychology: Learning, Memory, & Cognition, 15*, 657–668.

BLISS, T. V. P., & LØMO, T. (1973) Long-lasting potentiation of synaptic transmission in the dentate area of the anesthetized rabbit following stimulation of the preforant path. *Journal of Physiology, 232*, 331–356.

BLOCK, J. (1961/1978) *The Q-sort method in personality assessment and psychiatric research.* Palo Alto: Consulting Psychologists Press.

BLOOD, R. O. (1967) *Love match and arranged marriage.* New York: Free Press.

BLOOM, P. (2000) *How children learn the meaning of words.* Cambridge, MA: MIT Press.

BLUM, K., CULL, J. G., BRAVERMAN, E. R., & COMINGS, D. E. (1996) Reward deficiency syndrome. *American Scientist, 84*, 132–145.

BODENHAUSEN, G. V., MACRAE, C. N., & SHERMAN, J. W. (1999) On the dialectics of discrimination: Dual processes in social stereotyping. In S. Chaiken & Y. Trope (Eds.), *Dual-process theories in social psychology* (pp. 271–290). New York: Guilford.

BOGAERT, A. F. (2004). Asexuality: prevalence and associated factors in a national probability sample. *The Journal of Sex Research, 41*, 279–288.

BOGAERT, A. F. (2006) Toward a conceptual understanding of asexuality. *Review of General Psychology, 10*, 241.

BOILEAU, I., DAGHER, A., LEYTON, M., WELFELD, K., BOOIJ, L., DIKSIC, M., *et al.* (2007) Conditioned dopamine release in humans: A positron emission tomography [11c] raclopride study with amphetamine. *Journal of Neuroscience, 27*(15), 3998–4003.

BOLLES, R. C. (1970) Species-specific defense reactions and avoidance learning. *Psychological Review, 77*, 32–48.

BOLLES, R. C. (1972) Reinforcement, expectancy, and learning. *Psychological Review, 79*, 394–409.

BOLTE, S., & POUSTKA, F. (2004) Comparing the intelligence profiles of savant and nonsavant individuals with autistic disorder. *Intelligence, 32*, 121–131.

BOND, C. F., & TITUS, L. J. (1983) Social facilitation: A meta-analysis of 241 studies. *Psychological Bulletin, 94*, 265–292.

BOOTH, D. A. (1987) Cognitive experimental psychology of appetite. In R. A. Boakes (Ed.), *Eating habits: Food, physiology, and learned behavior* (pp. 175–209). New York: Wiley.

BOOTH, D. A. (1991) Learned ingestive motivation and the pleasures of the palate. In R. C. Bolles (Ed.), *The hedonics of taste* (pp. 29–58). Hillsdale, NJ: Erlbaum.

BORING, E. G. (1930) A new ambiguous figure. *American Journal of Psychology, 42*, 444–445.

BORNSTEIN, R. F. (2001) The impending death of psychoanalysis. *Psychoanalytic Psychology, 18* (1), 3–20.

BORNSTEIN, R. F. (2005) Reconnecting psychoanalysis to mainstream psychology: Challenges and opportunities. *Psychoanalytic Psychology, 22* (3), 323–340.

BORNSTEIN, R. F., & D'AGOSTINO, P. R. (1992) Stimulus recognition and the mere exposure effect. *Journal of Personality and Social Psychology, 63*, 545–552.

BORODITSKY, L. (2001) Does language shape thought? English and Mandarin speakers' conceptions of time. *Cognitive Psychology, 43*, 1–22.

BOS, M. W., DIJKSTERHUIS, A., & VAN BAAREN, R. B. (2008). On the goal-dependency of unconscious thought. *Journal of Experimental Social Psychology, 44*, 1114–1120.

BOSCO, F. M., BUCCIARELLI, M., & BARA, B. G. (2004) The fundamental context categories in understanding communicative intention. *Journal of Pragmatics, 36*, 467–488.

BOTTOMS, G. (2000) *Angelhead.* New York: Three Rivers Press.

BOUCHARD, C., TREMBLAY, A., DESPRES, J. P., NADEAU, A., LUPIEN, P. J., THERIAULT, G., DUSSAULT, J., MOORJANI, S., PINAULT, S., & FOURNIER, G. (1990) The response to long-term overeating in identical twins. *New England Journal of Medicine, 322*, 1477–1482.

BOUCHARD, T. J., JR. (1984) Twins reared apart and together: What they tell us about human diversity. In S. Fox (Ed.), *The chemical and biological bases of individuality.* New York: Plenum.

BOUCHARD, T. J., JR. (1995) *Nature's twice-told tale: Identical twins reared apart—What they tell us about human individuality.* Paper presented at the annual meeting of the Western Psychological Association, Los Angeles.

BOUCHARD, T. J., JR. (2004) Genetic influence on human psychological traits: A survey. *Current Directions in Psychological Science, 13*, 148–151.

BOUCHARD, T. J., JR., LYKKEN, D. T., MCGUE, M., SEGAL, N. L., & TELLEGEN, A. (1990) Sources of human psychological differences: The Minnesota study of twins reared apart. *Science, 250*, 223–228.

BOUCHARD, T. J., JR., & MCGUE, M. (2003) Genetic and environmental influences on human psychological differences. *Journal of Neurobiology, 54*, 445.

BOURNE, L. E. (1966) *Human conceptual behavior.* Boston: Allyn and Bacon.

BOUTON, M. E., MINEKA, S., & BARLOW, D. H. (2001) A modern learning theory perspective on the etiology of panic disorder. *Psychological Review*, 108, 4–32.

BOWEN, W. G., & BOK, D. (1998) *The shape of the river: Long-term consequences of considering race in college and university admissions*. Princeton, NJ: Princeton University Press.

BOWER, G. H. (1981) Mood and memory. *American Psychologist*, 6, 129–148.

BOWER, G. H., & CLARK, M. C. (1969) Narrative stories as mediators for serial learning. *Psychonomic Science*, 14, 181–182.

BOWER, G. H., & SPRINGSTON, F. (1970) Pauses as recoding points in letter series. *Journal of Experimental Psychology*, 83, 421–430.

BOWER, G. H., BLACK, J. B., & TURNER, T. R. (1979) Scripts in memory for text. *Cognitive Psychology*, 11, 177–220.

BOWER, G. H., CLARK, M. C., WINZENZ, D., & LESGOLD, A. (1969) Hierarchical retrieval schemes in recall of categorized word lists. *Journal of Verbal Learning and Verbal Behavior*, 8, 323–343.

BOWER, J. E., KEMENY, M. E., TAYLOR, S. E., & FAHEY, J. L. (1998) Cognitive processing, discovery of meaning, CD 4 decline, and AIDS-related mortality among bereaved HIV-seropositive men. *Journal of Consulting and Clinical Psychology*, 66, 979–986.

BOWLBY, J. (1973) *Attachment and loss: Separation, anxiety and anger* (Vol. 2). London: Hogarth Press.

BOYDEN, E. S., KATOH, A., & RAYMON, J. L. (2004) Cerebellum-dependent learning: The role of multiple plasticity mechanisms. *Annual Review of Neuroscience*, 27, 581–609.

BOYLE, S. H., MICHALEK, J. E., & SUAREZ, E. C. (2006). Covariation of psychological attributes and incident coronary heart disease in U.S. Air Force veterans of the Vietnam War. *Psychosomatic Medicine*, 68, 844–850.

BRACKETT, M. A., RIVERS, S., SHIFFMAN, S., LERNER, N., & SALOVEY, P. (2006) Relating emotional abilities to social functioning: A comparison of performance and self-report measures of emotional intelligence. *Journal of Personality and Social Psychology*, 91, 780–795.

BRADLEY, S. J., OLIVER, G. D., CHERNICK, A. B., & ZUCKER, K. J. (1998) Ablatio penis at 2 months, sex reassignment at 7 months, and a psychosexual follow-up in young adulthood. *Pediatrics*, 102, E91–E95.

BRADSHAW, G. L., & ANDERSON, J. R. (1982) Elaborative encoding as an explanation of levels of processing. *Journal of Verbal Learning and Verbal Behavior*, 21, 165–174.

BRAINERD, C. J., & REYNA, V. F. (2005) *The science of false memory*. Oxford University Press.

BRAND, M., FRANKE-SIEVERT, C., JACOBY, G. E., MARKOWITSCH, H. J., & TUSCHEN-CAFFIER, B. (2007) Neuropsychological correlates of decision making in patients with bulimia nervosa. *Neuropsychology*, 21, 742–750.

BRANSFORD, J. D., & JOHNSON, M. K. (1973) Considerations of some problems of comprehension. In W. G. Chase (Ed.), *Visual information processing*. New York: Academic Press.

BRAZELTON, T. B. (1978) The remarkable talents of the newborn. *Birth and Family Journal*, 5, 4–10.

BREEDLOVE, S. M. (1994) Sexual differentiation of the human nervous system. *Annual Review of Psychology*, 45, 389–418.

BREFCZYNSKI-LEWIS, J. A., LUTZ, A., & DAVIDSON, R. (2004) A neural correlate of attentional expertise in long-time Buddhist practitioners. (Report no. 715.8.). San Diego: Society for Neuroscience.

BREGMAN, A. S. (1990) *Auditory scene analysis*. Cambridge, MA: MIT Press.

BREHM, J. W. (1956) Postdecision changes in the desirability of alternatives. *Journal of Abnormal and Social Psychology*, 52, 384–389.

BREHM, S. S. (1992) *Intimate relationships* (2nd ed.) New York: McGraw-Hill.

BREINES, J. G., CROCKER, J., & GARCIA, J. A. (2008) Self-objectification and well-being in women's daily lives. *Personality and Social Psychology Bulletin*, 34, 583–595.

BRELAND, K., & BRELAND, M. (1966) *Animal behavior*. New York: Macmillan.

BREMNER, J. D. (1998) Neuroimaging of posttraumatic stress disorder. *Psychiatric Annals*, 28, 445–455.

BRESCOLL, V. L., & UHLMANN, E. L. (2008) Can an angry woman get ahead? Status conferral, gender, and expression of emotion in the workplace. *Psychological Science*, 19, 268–275.

BRIERS, B., PANDELAERE, M., DEWITTE, S., & WARLOP, L. (2006) Hungry for money: the desire for caloric resources increases the desire for financial resources and vice versa. *Psychological Science*, 17, 939–943.

BRILEY, D. A., MORRIS, M. W., & SIMONSON, I. (2005) Cultural chameleons: Biculturals, conformity motives, and decision making. *Journal of Consumer Psychology*, 15 (4), 351–362.

BRITT, T. W., ADLER, A. B., & BARTONE, P. T. (2001) Deriving benefits from stressful events: The role of engagement in meaningful work and hardiness. *Journal of Occupational Health Psychology*, 6, 53–63.

BROADBENT, D. E. (1958) *Perception and communication*. London: Pergamon.

BRODERICK, D. (2007) *Outside the gates of science*. New York: Thunder's Mouth Press.

BROOKS-GUNN, J., KLEBANOV, P. K., & DUNCAN, G. J. (1996) Ethnic differences in children's intelligence test scores: Role of economic deprivation, home environment, and maternal characteristics. *Child Development*, 67, 396–408.

BROOKS-GUNN, J., KLEBANOV, P. K., & LIAW, F. (1995) The learning, physical, and emotional environment of the home in the context of poverty: The Infant Health and Development Program. *Children & Youth Services Review*, 17, 251–276.

BROWN, A. E. (1936) Dreams in which the dreamer knows he is asleep. *Journal of Abnormal Psychology*, 31, 59–66.

BROWN, E. L., & DEFFENBACHER, K. (1979) *Perception and the senses*. Oxford: Oxford University Press.

BROWN, J. (1991) Staying fit and staying well: Physical fitness as a moderator of life stress. *Journal of Personality and Social Psychology*, 60, 555–561.

BROWN, J. M., (1958) Some tests of the decay theory of immediate memory. *Quarterly journal of experimental psychology*, 10, 12–21.

BROWN, R. (1974) Further comment on the risky shift. *American Psychologist*, 29, 468–470.

BROWN, R., CAZDEN, C. B., & BELLUGI, U. (1969) The child's grammar from 1 to 3. In J. P. Hill (Ed.), *Minnesota symposium on child psychology* (Vol. 2). Minneapolis: University of Minnesota Press.

BROWN, R. P., CHARNSANGAVEJ, T., KEOUGH, K. A., NEWMAN, M. L., & RENTFROW, P. J. (2000) Putting the 'affirm' into affirmative action: Preferential selection and academic performance. *Journal of Personality and Social Psychology*, 79, 736–747.

BROWN, R. W., & MCNEILL, D. (1966) The "tip-of-the-tongue" phenomenon. *Journal of Verbal Learning and Verbal Behavior*, *5*, 325–337.

BROWNELL, K. (1988, January) Yo-yo dieting. *Psychology Today*, *22*, 20–23.

BROWNELL, K., & HORGEN, K. B. (2004) *Food fight: The inside story of the food industry, America's obesity crsis, and what we can do about it*. New York: McGraw.

BRUCH, H. (1973) *Eating disorders: Obesity, anorexia nervosa, and the person within*. New York: Basic Books.

BRUN, C., & RAPP, R. C. (2001) Strengths-based case management: Individuals' perspectives on strengths and the case manager relationship. *Social Work*, *46*(3), 278–288.

BRUNER, J. S. (1957) Going beyond the information given. In *Contemporary approaches to cognition: A symposium held at the University of Colorado*. Cambridge, MA: Harvard University Press.

BRUNER, J. S. (1997) Will the cognitive revolutions ever stop? In D. M. Johnson & C. E. Erneling (Eds.), *The future of the cognitive revolution*. New York: Oxford University Press.

BRUNER, J. S., & GOODMAN, C. C. (1947) Value and need as organizing factors in perception. *Journal of Abnormal and Social Psychology*, *42*, 33–44.

BRUNER, J. S., & POTTER, M. C. (1964) Interference in visual search. *Science*, *144*, 424–425.

BRUNER, J. S., GOODNOW, J. J., & AUSTIN, G. A. (1956) *A study of thinking*. New York: Wiley.

BRYAN, J. H., & TEST, M. A. (1967) Models and helping: Naturalistic studies in aiding behavior. *Journal of Personality and Social Psychology*, *6*, 400–407.

BRYDON, K. (2003) AMO array multifocal lens versus monofocal correction in cataract surgery. *Journal of Cataract & Refractive Surgery*, *26*, 96–100.

BUB, D., BLACKS, S., & HOWELL, J. (1989) Word recognition and orthographic context effects in a letter-by-letter reader. *Brain and Language*, *36*, 357–376.

BUCHANAN, C. M., ECCLES, J. S., & BECKER, J. B. (1992) Are adolescents the victims of raging hormones? Evidence for activational effects of hormones on moods and behavior at adolescence. *Psychological Bulletin*, *111*, 62–107.

BUCHANAN, T. W. (2007) Retrieval of emotional memories. *Psychological Bulletin*, *133*, 761–779.

BUCK, L., & AXEL, R. (1991) A novel multigene family may encode odorant receptors: A molecular basis for odor recognition. *Cell*, *65*, 175–187.

BUGGE, J. F. (2009) Brain death and its implications for management of the potential organ donor. *Acta Anaesthesiologica Scandinavica*, *53*, 1239–1250.

BUNDY, C., CARROLL, D., WALLACE, L., & NAGLE, R. (1998) Stress management and exercise training in chronic stable angina pectoris. *Psychology & Health*, *13*, 147–155.

BURGER, J. M. (2009) Replicating Milgram: Would people still obey today? *American Psychologist*, *64*, 1–11.

BURKE, M. A., HEILAND, F. W., & NADLER, C. M. (2010) From "overweight" to "about right": Evidence of a generational shift in body weight norms. *Obesity*, *18*(6), 1226–1234.

BURNETT, R., & MARUNA, S. (2006) The kindness of prisoners: Strengths-based resettlement in theory and in action. *Criminology and Criminal Justice*, *6*(1), 83–106.

BURNSTEIN, E., & VINOKUR, A. (1973) Testing two classes of theories about group-induced shifts in individual choice. *Journal of Experimental Social Psychology*, *9*, 123–137.

BURNSTEIN, E., & VINOKUR, A. (1977) Persuasive arguments and social comparison as determinants of attitude polarization. *Journal of Experimental Social Psychology*, *13*, 315–332.

BUSEY, T. A., & Loftus, G. R. (1994) Sensory and cognitive components of visual information acquisition. *Psychological Review*, *101*, 446–469.

BUSEY, T. A., TUNNICLIFF, J., LOFTUS, G. R., & LOFTUS, E. F. (2000) Accounts of the confidence-accuracy relation in recognition memory. *Psychonomic Bulletin and Review*, *7*, 26–48.

BUSINCK, R. AND KUIKEN, D. (1996). Identifying types of Impactful Dreams: A Replication. *Dreaming*, *6*, 97–120

BUSS, D. M. (1989) Sex differences in human mate preferences: Evolutionary hypotheses testing in 37 cultures. *Behavioral and Brain Sciences*, *12*, 1–49.

BUSS, D. M. (1994a) *The evolution of desire: Strategies of human mating*. New York: Basic Books.

BUSS, D. M. (1994b) Personality evoked: The evolutionary psychology of stability and change. In T. F. Heatherton & J. Weinberger (Eds.), *Can personality change?* Washington, DC: APA Press.

BUSS, D. M. (2007) The evolution of human mating. *Acta Psychological Sinica*, *39*, 502–512.

BUSS, D. M. (2009) The great struggles of life: Darwin and the emergence of evolutionary psychology. *American Psychologist*, *64*, 140–148.

BUSS, D. M., & KENRICK, D. T. (1998) Evolutionary social psychology. In D. T. Gilbert, S. T. Fiske, & G. Lindzey (Eds.), *Handbook of social psychology*, Vol. 2 (4th ed., pp. 982–1026). Boston: McGraw-Hill.

BUSS, D. M., & SCHMIDT, D. P. (1993) Sexual strategies theory: An evolutionary perspective on human mating. *Psychological Review*, *100*, 204–232.

BUSS, D. M., & SHACKELFORD, T. K. (1997) Human aggression in evolutionary psychological perspective. *Clinical Psychology Reviews*, *17*, 605–619.

BUSS, D. M., LARSEN, R. J., WESTERN, D., & SEMMELROTH, J. (1992) Sex differences in jealousy: Evolution, physiology, and psychology. *Psychological Science*, *3*, 251–255.

BUSSEY, K., & BANDURA, A. (2004) Social cognitive theory of gender development and functioning. In A. H. Eagly, A. E. Beall, & R. J. Sternberg (Eds.), *The psychology of gender* (2nd ed.) (pp. 92–119). New York: Guilford.

BUTLER, J. M., & HAIGH, G. V. (1954) Changes in the relation between self-concepts and ideal concepts consequent upon client centered counseling. In C. R. Rogers & R. F. Dymond (Eds.), *Psychotherapy and personality change: Coordinated studies in the client-centered approach* (pp. 55–76). Chicago: University of Chicago Press.

BUTLER, S. F., BUDMAN, S. H., FERNANDEZ, K., BENOIT, C., & JAMISON, R. N. (2008) Validation of the revised Screener and Opioid Assessment for Patients with Pain (SOAPP-R). *Journal of Pain*, *9*, 360–372.

BUTLER, S. F., BUDMAN, S. H., FERNANDEZ, K. C., HOULE, B., BENOIT, C., KATZ, N., & JAMISON, R. N. (2007) Development and validation of the Current Opioid Misuse Measure. *Pain*, *130*, 144–156.

BUTTERFIELD, E. L., & SIPERSTEIN, G. N. (1972) Influence of contingent auditory stimulation on nonnutritional sucking. In J. Bosma (Ed.), *Oral sensation and perception: The mouth of the infant*. Springfield, IL: Charles B. Thomas.

CABANAC, M. (2010) The dialectics of pleasure. In M. L. Kringelbach & K. C. Berridge (Eds.), *Pleasures in the brain* (pp. 113–124). New York: Oxford University Press.

CACIOPPO, J. T., GARDNER, W. L., & BERNTSON, G. G. (1999) The affect system has parallel and integrative processing components: Form follows function. *Journal of Personality and Social Psychology*, *76*, 839–855.

CACIOPPO, J. T., BERNTSON, G. G., LARSEN, J. T., POEHLMANN, K. M., & ITO, T. A. (2000) The psychophysiology of emotion. In M. Lewis & J. M. Haviland-Jones (Eds.), *Handbook of emotions* (2nd ed., pp. 173–191). New York: Guilford.

CAIN, W. S. (1988) Olfaction. In R. C. Atkinson, R. J. Hernstein, G. Lindzey, & R. D. Luce (Eds.), *Stevens' handbook of experimental psychology* (Vol. 1, pp. 409–459). New York: Wiley.

CAMERON, C. D., & PAYNE, B. K. (2011) Escaping affect: How motivated emotion regulation drives insensitivity to mass suffering. *Journal of Personality and Social Psychology*, *100*, 1–15.

CAMP, B. W., BROMAN, S. H., NICHOLS, P. L., & LEFF, M. (1998) Maternal and neonatal risk factors for mental retardation: Defining the "at-risk" child. *Early Human Development*, *50*, 159–173.

CAMPBELL, P. H., MILBOURNE, S. A., & SILVERMAN, C. (2001) Strengths-based child portfolios: A professional development activity to alter perspectives of children with special needs. *Topics in Early Childhood Special Education*, *21*(3), 152–161.

CAMPOS, J. J., BARRETT, K. C., LAMB, M. E., GOLDSMITH, H. H., & STENBERG, C. (1983) Socioemotional development. In P. Mussen (Ed.), *Handbook of child psychology* (Vol. 1, pp. 1–101). New York: Wiley.

CANNON, T., & KELLER, M. C. (2006) Endophenotypes in the genetic analyses of mental disorders. *Annual Review of Clinical Psychology*, *2*, 267–290.

CANNON, W. B. (1927) The James-Lange theory of emotions: A critical examination and an alternative theory. *American Journal of Psychology*, *39*, 106–124.

CARAMAZZA, A., & ZURIF, E. B. (1976) Dissociation of algorithmic and heuristic processes in language comprehension: Evidence from aphasia. *Brain and Language*, *3*, 572–582.

CARDOZO, B. L., VERGARA, A., AGAIN, F., & COTWAY, C. A. (2000) Mental health, social functioning, and attitudes of Kosovar Albanians following the war in Kosovo. *Journal of the American Medical Association*, *284*, 569–577.

CARMICHAEL, L., HOGAN, H. P., & WALTER, A. A (1932) An experimental study of the effect of language on the reproduction of visually perceived form. *Journal of Experimental Psychology*, *15*, 73–86.

CARNEY, P. R., BERRY, R. B., & GEYER, J. D. (2004) *Clinical sleep disorders*. Philadelphia: Lippincott Williams & Wilkins.

CARPENTER, P. A., JUST, M. A., & SHELL, P. (1990) What one intelligence test measures: A theoretical account of the processing in the Raven Progressive Matrices Test. *Psychological Review*, *97*, 404–431.

CARROLL, J. M., YIK, M. S. M., RUSSELL, J. A., & BARRETT, L. F. (1999) On the psychometric principles of affect. *Review of General Psychology*, *3*, 14–22.

CARROLL, M. E., & OVERMIER, J. B. (2001) *Animal research and human health: Advancing human welfare through behavioral science*. Washington, DC: American Psychological Association.

CARTER, M. M., HOLLON, S. D., CARON, R. S., & SHELTON, R. C. (1995) Effects of a safe person on induced distress following a biological challenge in panic disorder with agoraphobia. *Journal of Abnormal Psychology*, *104*, 156–163.

CARVER, C. S., & SCHEIER, M. F. (1981) *Attention and self-regulation: A control-theory approach to human behavior*. New York: Springer-Verlag.

CARVER, C. S., SMITH, R. G., ANTONI, M. H., PETRONIS, V. M., WEISS, S., & DERHAGOPIAN, R. P. (2005) Optimistic personality and psychosocial well-being during treatment predict psychosocial well-being among long-term survivors of breast cancer. *Health Psychology*, *24*, 508–516.

CARVER, C. S., POZO C,. HARRIS, S. D., NORIEGA, V., SCHEIER, M. F., ROBINSON, D. S., KETCHAM, A. S., MOFFAT, F. L., JR., & CLARK, K. C. (1993) How coping mediates the effect of optimism on distress: A study of women with early stage breast cancer. *Journal of Personality and Social Psychology*, *65*, 375–90.

CASE, R., & OKAMOTO, Y. (1996) The role of central conceptual structures in the development of children's thoughts. *Nomographs of the Society for Research in Child Development*, *61*, 1–265.

CASEY, B. J., TOTTENHAM, N., LISTON, C., & DURSTON, S. (2005) Imaging the developing brain: What have we learned about cognitive development? *Trends in Cognitive Science*, *9*, 104–110.

CASPI, A., & HERBENER, E. S. (1990) Continuity and change: Assortative marriage and the consistency of personality in adulthood. *Journal of Personality and Social Psychology*, *58*, 250–258.

CASPI, A., & MOFFIT, T. E. (1991) Individual differences are accentuated during periods of social change: The sample case of girls at puberty. *Journal of Personality and Social Psychology*, *61*, 157–168.

CASPI, A., HARIRI, A. R., HOLMES, A., UHER, R., & MOFFITT, T. E. (2011) Genetic sensitivity to the environment: The case of the serotonin transporter gene and its implications for studying complex diseases and traits. In K. A. Dodge and M. Rutter (Eds.), *Gene-environment interactions in developmental psychopathology* (p. 1858). New York: Guilford Press.

CASTELLI, F., FRITH, C., HAPPE, F., & FRITH, U. (2002) Autism, Asperger's syndrome and brain mechanisms for the attribution of mental states to animated shapes. *Brain*, *125*, 1839–1849.

CATALINO, L. I., & FREDRICKSON, B. L. (2011) A Tuesday in the life of a flourisher: The role of positive emotional reactivity in optimal mental health. *Emotion*, *11*, 938–950.

CATANI, M., JONES, D. K., & FFYTCHE, D. H. (2005) Perisylvian language networks of the human brain. *Annals of Neurology*, *57*(1), 8–16.

CATTEANO, L., & RIZZOLATTI, G. (2009) The mirror neuron system. *Archives of Neurology*, *66*, 557–560.

CATTELL, R. B. (1943) The description of personality: Basic traits resolved into clusters. *Journal of Abnormal and Social Psychology*, *38*, 476–507.

CATTELL, R. B. (1945) The description of personality: Principles and findings in a factor analysis. *American Journal of Psychology*, *58*, 69–90.

CATTERALL, W. A. (2000) From ionic currents to molecular mechanisms: the structure and function of voltage-gated sodium channels. *Neuron*, *26*, 13–25.

CECI, S. J. (1990) *On intelligence … more or less: A bioecological treatise on intellectual development*. Englewood Cliffs, NJ: Prentice-Hall.

CECI, S. J. (1996) *On intelligence: A bioecological treatise.* Cambridge, MA: Harvard University Press.

CECI, S. J., & BRUCK, M. (1993) The suggestibility of the child witness: A historical review and synthesis. *Psychological Bulletin, 113,* 403–409.

CECI, S. J., & ROAZZI, A. (1994) The effect of context on cognition: Postcards from Brazil. In R. J. Sternberg & R. K. Wagner (Eds.), *Mind in context: Interactionist perspectives on human intelligence.* Cambridge: Cambridge University Press.

CENTERS FOR DISEASE CONTROL (2012) Youth risk behavior surveillance – United States. *MMWR, 61* (SS–4).

CERNOCH, J. M., & PORTER, R. H. (1985) Recognition of maternal axillary odors by infants. *Child Development, 56,* 1593–1598.

CESARANI, D. (2004) *Eichmann: His Life and Crimes.* London: Heinemann.

CHAIKEN, S., & TROPE, Y. (1999) *Dual-process theories in social psychology.* New York: Guilford.

CHANG, G., CHEN, L., & MAO, J. (2007) Opioid tolerance and hyperalgesia. *Medical Clinics of North America, 81,* 199–211.

CHAPMAN, L. J., & CHAPMAN, J. P. (1969) Illusory correlation as an obstacle to the use of valid psychodiagnostic signs. *Journal of Abnormal Psychology, 74,* 271–280.

CHASE, W. G., & SIMON, H. A. (1973) The mind's eye in chess. In W. G. Chase (Ed.), *Visual information processing* (pp. 215–281). New York: Academic Press.

CHATER, N., & CHRISTIANSEN, M. H. (2012) *A solution to the logical problem of language evolution: Language as an adaptation to the human brain.* Available at: http://cnl.psych.cornell.edu/pubs/2012-cc-EvoLang-Hbk.pdf (Accessed: January 18, 2013).

CHAUDURI, H. (1965) *Philosophy of meditation.* New York: Philosophical Library.

CHEN, M., & BARGH, J. A. (1997) Nonconscious behavioral confirmation processes: The self-fulfilling consequences of automatic stereotype activation. *Journal of Experimental Social Psychology, 33,* 541–560.

CHEN, S., & ANDERSEN, S. M. (1999) Relationships from the past in the present: Significant-other representations and transference in interpersonal life. *Advances in Experimental Social Psychology, 31,* 123–190.

CHEN, S., & CHAIKEN, S. (1999) The heuristic-systematic model in its broader context. In S. Chaiken & Y. Trope (Eds.), *Dual-process theories in social psychology* (pp. 73–96). New York: Guilford.

CHENG, A. T. A., HAWTON, K., CHEN, T. H. H., YEN, A. M. F., CHANG, J.-C., CHONG, M.-Y., LIU, C.-Y., LEE, C., TEN, P.-R., & CHEN, L.-C. (2007) The influence of media reporting of a celebrity suicide on suicidal behavior in patients with a history of depressive disorder. *Journal of Affective Disorders, 103,* 69–75.

CHEN, S. C. (1937) Social modification of the activity of ants in nest-building. *Physiological Zoology, 10,* 420–436.

CHENG, P. W., HOLYOAK, K. J., NISBETT, R. E., & OLIVER, L. (1986) Pragmatic versus syntactic approaches to training deductive reasoning. *Cognitive Psychology, 18,* 293–328.

CHENG, Y., LIN, C. P., LIU, H. L., HSU, Y. Y., LIM, K. E., HUNG, D., & DECETY, J. (2007) Expertise modulates the perception of pain in others. *Current Biology, 17* (19), 1708–1713.

CHERRY, E. C. (1953) Some experiments on the recognition of speech with one and with two ears. *Journal of the Acoustical Society, 25,* 975–979.

CHESS, S., & THOMAS, A. (1984) *Origins and evolution of behavior disorders: Infancy to early adult life.* New York: Brunner/Mazel.

CHI, M. (1978) Knowledge structures and memory development. In R. S. Siegler (Ed.), *Children's thinking: What develops?* Hillsdale, NJ: Erlbaum.

CHI, M. T. H., & FELTOVISH, R. (1981) Categorization and representation of physics problems by experts and novices. *Cognitive Science, 5,* 121–152.

CHIESA, A., & SERRETTI, A. (2010) A systematic review of neurobiological and clinical features of mindfulness meditation. *Psychological Medicine, 40,* 1239–1252.

CHIVERS, M. L., SETO, M. C., & BLANCHARD, R. (2007) Gender and sexual orientation differences in sexual response to sexual activities versus gender of actors in sexual films. *Journal of Personality and Social Psychology, 93,* 1108–1121.

CHIVERS, M. C., RIEGER, G., LATTY, E. A., & BAILEY, J. M. (2004) A sex difference in the specificity of sexual arousal. *Psychological Science, 15,* 736–744.

COHEN, E. (2010) From the Bhodi tree, to the analyst's couch, then into the MRI scanner: The psychologisation of Buddhism. *Annual Review of Critical Psychology, 8,* 97–119.

CHOI, I., NISBETT, R. E., & NORENZAYAN, A. (1999) Causal attribution across cultures: Variation and universality. *Psychological Bulletin, 125,* 47–63.

CHOMSKY, N. (1957) *Syntactic structures.* Hague: Mouton.

CHOMSKY, N. (1959) A review of B. F. Skinner's 'Verbal Behavior'. *Language, 35,* 26–58.

CHOMSKY, N. (1965) *Aspects of the theory of syntax.* Cambridge, MA: MIT Press.

CHOMSKY, N. (1972) *Language and mind* (2nd ed.). New York: Harcourt Brace Jovanovich.

CHOMSKY, N. (1991, March) Quoted in *Discover.*

CHOU, C., CONDRON, L., & BELLAND, J. C. (2005) A review of the research on internet addiction. *Educational Psychology Review, 17,* 363–388.

CHOU, R., CLARK, E., & HELFAND, M. (2003) Comparative efficacy and safety of long-acting oral opioids for chronic non-cancer pain: A systematic review. *Journal of Pain and Symptom Management, 26,* 1026–1048.

CHOU, R, FANCIULLO, G. J., & FINE, P. G., American Pain Society – American Academy of Pain Medicine Opioid Guidelines Panel (2009) Clinical guideline for the use of chronic opioid therapy in chronic noncancer pain. *Journal of Pain, 10,* 113–130.

CHRISTENSEN, H., GRIFFITHS, K. M., & JORM, A. F. (2004) Delivering interventions for depression using the internet: Randomized controlled trial. *British Medical Journal, 328,* 265.

CHURCHLAND, P. S., & SEJNOWSKI, T. J. (1988) Perspectives on cognitive neuroscience. *Science, 242,* 741–745.

CLARK, D. M. (1988) A cognitive model of panic attacks. In S. Rachman & J. D. Maser (Eds.), *Panic: Psychological perspectives.* Hillsdale, NJ: Erlbaum.

CLARK, D. M., EHLERS, A., HACKMANN, A., MCMANUS, F., *et al.* (2006) Cognitive therapy versus exposure and applied relaxation in social phobia: A randomised controlled trial. *Journal of Consulting and Clinical Psychology, 74,* 568–578.

CLARK, D. M., SALKOVSKIS, P. M., HACKMANN, A., MIDDLETON, H., & collaborators. (1994) A comparison of cognitive therapy, applied, relaxation, and imipramine in the treatment of panic disorder. *British Journal of Psychiatry, 164,* 759–769.

CLARK, E. V. (1983) Meanings and concepts. In P. H. Mussen (Ed.), *Handbook of child psychology* (Vol. 3). New York: Wiley.

CLARKE-STEWART, K. A. (1973) Interactions between mothers and their young children: Characteristics and consequences.

Monographs of the Society for Research in Child Development, *38* (6 & 7, Serial No. 153).

CLOUTIER, J., MASON, M. F., & MACRAE, C. N. (2005) The perceptual determinants of person construal: Reopening the social-cognitive toolbox. *Journal of Personality and Social Psychology*, *88* (6), 885–894.

COBB, J. P., HOTCHKISS, R. S., KARL, I. E., & BUCHMAN, T. G. (1996) Mechanisms of cell injury and death. *British Journal of Anaesthesia*, *77*, 3–10.

COHEN, N. J., & SQUIRE, L. R. (1980) Preserved learning and retention of pattern analyzing skill in amnesia: Dissociation of knowing how and knowing that. *Science*, *210*, 207–209.

COHEN, S., & EDWARDS, J. R. (1989) Personality characteristics as moderators of the relationship between stress and disorder. In R. J. Neufeld (Ed.), *Advances in the investigation of psychological stress* (pp. 235–283). New York: Wiley.

COHEN, S., TYRRELL, D. A. J., & SMITH, A. P. (1991) Psychological stress and susceptibility to the common cold. *New England Journal of Medicine*, *325*, 606–612.

COHN, M. A., FREDRICKSON, B. L., BROWN, S. L., MIKELS, J. A., & CONWAY, A. M. (2009) Happiness unpacked: Positive emotions increase life satisfaction by building resilience. *Emotion*, *9*, 361–368.

COLAPINTO, J. (2000). *As nature made him: The boy who was raised as a girl.* New York: HarperCollins.

COLBY, A., KOHLBERG, L., GIBBS, J., & LIEBERMAN, M. A. (1983) A longitudinal study of moral judgment. *Monographs of the Society for Research in Child Development*, *48*, 1–2.

COLE, M., & COLE, S. R. (2001) *The development of children.* New York: Worth.

COLE, P. M., ZAHN-WAXLER, C., & SMITH, K. D. (1994) Expressive control during a disappointment: Variations related to preschoolers' behavior problems. *Developmental Psychology*, *30*, 835–846.

COLE, S. W. (2009) Social regulation of human gene expression. *Current Directions in Psychological Science*, *18*, 132–137.

COLE, S. W., HAWKLEY, L. C., AREVALO, J. M. G., & CACIOPPO, J. T. (2011) Transcript origin analysis identifies antigen-presenting cells as primary targets of socially-regulated gene expression in leukocytes. *Proceedings of the National Academy of Science*, *108*, 3080–3085.

COLE, S. W., KEMENY, M. E., TAYLOR, S. E., & VISSCHER, B. R. (1996) Elevated physical health risk among gay men who conceal their homosexual identity. *Health Psychology*, *15*, 243–251.

COLE, S. W., KEMENY, M. E., TAYLOR, S. E., VISSCHER, B. R., & FAHEY, J. L. (1995) Accelerated course of human immunodeficiency virus infection in gay men who conceal their homosexual identity. *Psychosomatic Medicine*, *58*, 219–238.

COLEY, R. L., KUO, F. E., & SULLIVAN, W. C. (1997) Where does community grow? The social context created by nature in urban public housing. *Environment & Behavior*, *29*(4), 468–494.

COLEGROVE, F. W. (1899) Individual memories. *American Journal of Psychology*, *10*, 228–255.

COLLINS, H. (2012) Language as a repository for tacit knowledge. In T. Schilhab, F. Stjernfelt & T. Deacon (Eds.), *The symbolic species evolved* (pp.225–239). Netherlands: Springer.

COLLINS, W. A., MACCOBY, E. E., STEINBERG, L., HETHERINGTON, E. M., & BORNSTEIN, M. H. (2000) Contemporary research on parenting: The case for nature and nurture. *American Psychologist*, *55*, 218–232.

COLTHEART, M. (1980) Iconic memory and visible persistence. *Perception and Psychophysics*, *27*, 183–228.

CONKLIN, H. M., & IACONO, W. G. (2002) Schizophrenia: A neurodevelopmental perspective. *Current directions in Psychological Science*, *11*, 33–37.

CONRAD, R. (1964) Acoustic confusions in immediate memory. *British Journal of Psychology*, *55*, 75–84.

COOKE, A. (in press) Readying the head and steadying the heart: A review of cortical and cardiac studies of preparation for action in sport. *International Review of Sport and Exercise Psychology*, DOI:10.1080/1750984X.2012.724438.

COOMBES, S. A., CAURAUGH, J. H., & JANELLE, C. M. (2007) Dissociating motivational direction and affective valence: specific emotions alter central motor processes. *Psychological Science*, *18*, 938–942.

COOPER, J., & HOGG, M. A. (2007) Feeling the anguish of others: A theory of vicarious dissonance. *Advances in Experimental Social Psychology*, *39*, 359–403.

COOPER, L. A., & SHEPARD, R. N. (1973) Chronometric studies of the rotation of mental images. In W. G. Chase (Ed.), *Visual information processing*. New York: Academic Press.

COOPER, L. M. (1979) Hypnotic amnesia. In E. Fromm & R. E. Shor (Eds.), *Hypnosis: Developments in research and new perspectives* (Rev. Ed.). New York: Aldine.

COOPER, R. P., ABRAHAM, J., BERMAN, S., & STASKA, M. (1997) The development of infant preference for motherese. *Infant Behavior and Development*, *20*, 477–488.

COOPER, Z., FAIRBURN, C. G., & HAWKER, D. M. (2004) *Cognitive-behavioral treatment of obesity.* New York: Guilford Press.

CORBETTA, M., MIEZIN, F. M., DOBMEYER, S., SCHULMAN, G. L., & PETERSON, S. E. (1990) Attentional modulation of neural processing of shape, color, and velocity in humans. *Science*, *248*, 1556–1559.

CORBETTA, M., MIEZIN, F. M., SHULMAN, G. L., & PETERSEN, S. E. (1991) Selective attention modulates extrastriate visual regions in humans during visual feature discrimination and recognition In D. J. Chadwick & J. Whelan (Eds.), *Ciba Foundation symposium 163: Exploring brain functional anatomy with positron tomography* (pp. 165–180) Chichester: Wiley.

CORBETTA, M., MIEZIN, F. M., SHULMAN, G. L., & PETERSEN, S. E. (1993) A PET study of visuospatial attention. *Journal of Neuroscience*, *13*, 1202–1226.

COREN, S. (1992) The moon illusion: A different view through the legs. *Perceptual and Motor Skills*, *75*, 827–831.

COREN, S., & GIRGUS, J. S. (1980) Principles of perceptual organization and spatial distortion: The gestalt illusions. *Journal of Experimental Psychology: Human Perception and Performance*, *6*, 404–412.

COREN, S., WARD, L. M., & ENNS, J. T. (1999) *Sensation and perception* (5th ed.). Fort Worth: Harcourt Brace.

CORKUM, V., & MOORE, C. (1998) The origins of joint visual attention in infants. *Developmental Psychology*, *34*(1), 28–38.

CORNELIUS, M. D., GOLDSCHMIDT, L., DAY, N. L., & LARKBY, C. (2002) Alcohol, tobacco, and marijuana use among pregnant teenagers: 6-year follow-up of offspring growth effects. *Neurotoxicology & Teratology*, *24*, 703–710.

CORRELL, J., PARK, B., JUDD, C. M., & WITTENBRINK, B. (2002) The police officer's dilemma: Using ethnicity to disambiguate potentially threatening individuals. *Journal of Personality & Social Psychology*, *83*, 1314–1329.

CORTI, R., BINGGELI, C., SUDANO, I., SPIEKER, L., HÄNSELER, E., RUSCHITZKA, F., CHAPLIN, W. F., LÜSCHER, T. F., & NOLL, G. (2002) Coffee acutely increases sympathetic nerve activity and blood pressure independently of caffeine content: Role of habitual versus nonhabitual drinking. *Circulation, 106,* 2935–2940.

COSCINA, D. V., & DIXON, L. M. (1983) Body weight regulation in anorexia nervosa: Insights from an animal model. In F. L. Darby, P. E. Garfinkel, D. M. Garner, & D. V. Coscina (Eds.), *Anorexia nervosa: Recent developments.* New York: Allan R. Liss.

CÔTÉ, S., LOPES, P. N., SALOVEY, P., & MINERS, C. T. H. (2010) Emotional intelligence and leadership emergence in small groups. *Leadership Quarterly, 21,* 496–508.

COTTRELL, N. B., RITTLE, R. H., & WACK, D. L. (1967) Presence of an audience and list type (competitional or noncompetitional) as joint determinants of performance in paired-associates learning. *Journal of Personality, 25,* 425–434.

COTTRELL, N. B., WACK, D. L., SEKERAK, G. J., & RITTLE, R. H. (1968) Social facilitation of dominant responses by the presence of an audience and the mere presence of others. *Journal of Personality and Social Psychology, 9,* 245–250.

COULL, J. T., FRITH, C. D., FRACKOWIAK, R. S. J., & GRASBY, P. M. (1996) A fronto-parietal network for rapid visual information processing: A PET study of sustained attention and working memory. *Neuropsychologia, 34,* 1085–1095.

COURAGE, M. L., & ADAMS, R. J. (1990a) Visual acuity assessment from birth to three years using the acuity card procedures: Cross-sectional and longitudinal samples. *Optometry and Vision Science, 67,* 713–718.

COURAGE, M. L., & ADAMS, R. J. (1990b) The early development of visual acuity in the binocular and monocular peripheral fields. *Infant Behavioral Development, 13,* 123–128.

CRAIGHEAD, L. W., STUNKARD, A. J., & O'BRIEN, R. M. (1981) Behavior therapy and pharmacotherapy for obesity. *Archives of General Psychiatry, 38,* 763–768.

CRAIK, F. I. M., & TULVING, E. (1975) Depth of processing and the retention of words in episodic memory. *Journal of Experimental Psychology: General, 104,* 268–294.

CRANDALL, C. S., MERMAN, A., & HEBL, A. (2009) Anti-fat prejudice. In T. D. Nelson (Ed.), *Handbook of prejudice, stereotyping, and discrimination* (pp. 469–487). New York: Psychology Press.

CRANO, W. D., & SEYRANIAN, V. (2009) How minorities prevail: The context/comparison-leniency contract model. *Journal of Social Issues, 65,* 335–363.

CRASILNECK, H. B., & HALL, J. A. (1985) *Clinical hypnosis: Principles and applications* (2nd ed.). Orlando, FL: Grune & Stratton.

CRASKE, M. G., & WATERS, A. M. (2005) Panic disorder, phobias, and generalized anxiety disorder. *Annual Review of Clinical Psychology, 1,* 197–226.

CREUSERE, M. A. (1999) Theories of adults' understanding and use of irony and sarcasm: Applications to and evidence from research with children. *Developmental Review, 19,* 213–262.

CRICK, F., & MITCHINSON, G. (1983) The function of dream sleep. *Nature, 304,* 111–114.

CRICK, N. R., & DODGE, K. A. (1994) A review and reformulation of social information-processing mechanisms in children's social adjustment. *Psychological Bulletin, 115,* 74–101.

CRITS-CHRISTOPH, P., COOPER, A., & LUBORSKY, L. (1990) The measurement of accuracy of interpretations. In L. Luborsky & P. Crits-Christoph (Eds.), *Understanding transference: The CCRT method* (pp. 173–188). New York: Basic Books.

CROMWELL, P. F., MARKS, A., OLSON, J. N., & AVARY, D. W. (1991) Group effects on decision-making by burglars. *Psychological Reports, 69,* 579–588.

CRONKITE, R. C., MOOS, R. H., TWOHEY, J., COHEN, C., & SWINDLE, R. (1998) Life circumstances and personal resources as predictors of the ten-year course of depression. *American Journal of Community Psychololgy, 26,* 255–280.

CROSBY, F. J. (2004) *Affirmative action is dead: Long live affirmative action.* New Haven, Ct: Yale University Press.

CROSBY, F. J., IYER, A., & SINCHAROEN, S. (2006) Understanding affirmative action. *Annual Review of Psychology, 57,* 586–611.

CROSBY, F. J., IYER, A., CLAYTON, S., & DOWNING, R. (2003) Affirmative action: Psychological data and the policy debates. *American Psychologist, 58,* 93–115.

CROSBY, F. J., SABATTINI, L., & AIZAWA, M. (in press) Affirmative action and gender equality. In M. K. Ryan & N. R. Branscombe (Eds.), *The Sage handbook of gender and psychology.* London: Sage.

CROSS, G., MORGAN, C., MOONY, A., MARTIN, C., & RAFTER, J. (1990) Alcoholism treatment: A ten-year follow-up study. *Alcoholism Clinical and Experimental Research, 14,* 169–173.

CROSS, S. E., & MARKUS, H. R. (1999) The cultural constitution of personality. In L. A. Pervin & O. P. John (Eds.), *Handbook of personality: theory and research* (pp. 378–398). New York: Guilford Press.

CURCI, A., LUMINET, O., FINKENAUER, C., & GISLE, L. (2001) Flashbulb memories in social groups: A comparative test-retest study of the memory of French President Mitterrand's death in a French and a Belgian group. *Memory, 9,* 81–101.

CURTISS, S. (1977) *Genie: a psycholinguistic study of a modern-day "wild child".* New York: Academic Press.

CUTTING, J. E. (1986) *Perception with an eye for motion.* Cambridge, MA: MIT Press.

CYNADER, M., TIMNEY, B. N., & MITCHELL, D. E. (1980) Period of susceptibility of kitten visual cortex to the effects of monocular deprivation extends beyond 6 months of age. *Brain Research, 191,* 545–550.

DALY, M., & WILSON, M. I. (1990) Killing the competition: Female/female and male/male homicide. *Human Nature, 1,* 81–107.

DAMASIO, A. R. (1985) Disorders of complex visual processing: Agnosia, achromatopsia, Balint's syndrome, and related difficulties of orientation and construction. In M. M. Mesulam (Ed.), *Principles of behavioral neurology* (pp. 259–288). Philadelphia: F. A. Davis.

DAMASIO, A. R. (1990) Category-related recognition defects as a clue to the neural substrates of knowledge. *Trends in Neurosciences, 13,* 95–98.

DAMASIO, A. R. (1994) *Descartes' error.* New York: Putnam.

DAMASIO, H., GRABOWSKI, T., FRANK, R., GALABURDA, A. M., & DAMASIO, A. R. (1994) The return of Phineas Gage: Clues about the brain from the skull of a famous patient. *Science, 264,* 1102–1105.

DANEMAN, M., & CARPENTER, P. A. (1980) Individual differences in working memory and reading. *Journal of Verbal Learning and Verbal Behavior, 19,* 450–466.

DANNER, D. D., SNOWDON, D. A., & FRIESEN, W. V. (2001) Positive emotions in early life and longevity: Findings from the nun study. *Journal of Personality and Social Psychology, 80,* 804–813.

D'ARGEMBEAU, A., COMBLAIN, C., & VAN DER LINDEN, M. (2005) Affective valence and the self-reference effect: Influence of retrieval conditions. *British Journal of Psychology*, *96*, 457–466.

DARLEY, J. M., & LATANÉ, B. (1968) Bystander intervention in emergencies: Diffusion of responsibility. *Journal of Personality and Social Psychology*, *8*, 377–383.

DARWIN, C. (1859) *On the origin of species*. London: Murray.

DARWIN, C. (1872) *The expression of emotion in man and animals*. New York: Philosophical Library.

DASGUPTA, N., MCGHEE, D. E., GREENWALD, A. G., & BANAJI, M. R. (2000) Automatic preference for White Americans: Eliminating the familiarity explanation. *Journal of Experimental Social Psychology*, *36*, 316–328.

DASHIELL, J. F. (1930) An experimental analysis of some group effects. *Journal of Abnormal and Social Psychology*, *25*, 190–199.

DAVENPORT, D. S., & YURICH, J. M. (1991) Multicultural gender issues. *Journal of Counseling and Development*, *70*, 64–71.

DAVIDOFF, J., DAVIES, I., & ROBERSON, D. (1999) Color categories of a stone-age tribe. *Nature*, *398*, 203–204.

DAVIDSON, J. (1989) Sexual emotions, hormones, and behavior. *Advances*, *6*, 56–58.

DAVIDSON, R. J. (1992) Anterior cerebral asymmetry and the nature of emotion. *Brain & Cognition*, *20*, 125–151.

DAVIDSON, R. J., PUTNAM, K. M., & LARSON, C. L. (2000) Dysfunction in the neural circuitry of emotion regulation—A possible prelude to violence. *Science*, *289*, 591–594.

DAVIDSON, R. J., KABAT-ZINN, J., SCHUMACHER, J., ROSENKRANZ, M., MULLER, D., SANTORELLI, S. F., URBANOWSKI, F., HARRINGTON, A., BONUS, K., & SHERIDAN, J. F. (2003) Alterations in brain and immune function produced by mindfulness meditation. *Psychosomatic Medicine*, *65*, 564–570.

DAVIS, C. A., LEVITAN, R. D., REID, C., CARTER, J. C., KAPLAN, A. S., PATTE, K. A., *et al.* (2009) Dopamine for "wanting" and opioids for "liking": A comparison of obese adults with and without binge eating. *Obesity*, 17, 1220–1225.

DAVIS, C. G., & NOLEN-HOEKSEMA, S. (in press) Positive responses to loss. In S. Lopez & R. Snyder (Eds.), *Handbook of Positive Psychology*, Vol. 2. New York: Oxford University Press.

DAVIS, M. (1997) Neurobiology of fear responses: The role of the amygdala. *Journal of Neuropsychiatry and Clinical Neurosciences*, *9*, 382–402.

DAY, A. L., & CARROLL, S. A. (2008) Faking emotional intelligence (EI): Comparing response distortion on ability and trait-based EI measures. *Journal of Organizational Behavior*, *29*, 761–784.

DEAUX, K. (1984) From individual differences to social categories: Analysis of a decade's research on gender. *American Psychologist*, *39*, 105–116.

DECASPER, A. J., & FIFER, W. P. (1980) Of human bonding: Newborns prefer their mothers' voices. *Science*, *208*, 1174–1176.

DECASPER, A. J., & PRESCOTT, P. A. (1984) Human newborns' perception of male voices: Preference, discrimination and reinforcing value. *Developmental Psychobiology*, *17*, 481–491.

DECASPER, A. J., & SPENCE, M. J. (1986) Prenatal maternal speech influences newborns' perception of speech sounds. *Infant Behavior and Development*, *9*, 133–150.

DECASPER, A. J., LECANUET, J. P., BUSNEL, M. C., GRANIER-DEFERRE, C., & MAUGEAIS, R. (1994) Fetal reactions to recurrent maternal speech. *Infant Behavior and Development*, *17*, 159–164.

DECI, E. L., & RYAN, R. M. (1985) *Intrinsic motivation and self-determination in human behavior*. New York: Plenum.

DECI, E. L., RYAN, R. M., & KOESTNER, R. (1999) A meta-analytic review of experiments examining the effects of extrinsic rewards on intrinsic motivation. *Psychological Bulletin*, *125*, 627–668.

DEFFENBACHER, K. (1980) Eyewitness accuracy and confidence: Can we infer anything about their relationship? *Law and Human Behavior*, *4*, 243–260.

DE GROOT, A. D. (1965) *Thought and Choice in Chess*. The Hague, The Netherlands: Mouton.

DE GROOT, A. D. (1966) Perception and memory versus thought. In B. Kleinmuntz (Ed.), *Problem-Solving*. New York: Wiley.

DEGROOT, K. I., BOEKE, S., BONKE, B., & PASSCHIER, J. (1997) A revaluation of the adaptiveness of avoidant and vigilant coping with surgery. *Psychology & Health*, *12*, 711–717.

DEHAENE, S., IZARD, V., PICA, P., & SPELKE, E. S. (2006) Core knowledge of geometry in an Amazonian indigene group. *Science*, *311*, 381–384.

DEHART, G. B., SROUFE, L. A., & COOPER, R. G. (2000) *Child Development: Its Nature and Course*. Boston: McGraw Hill.

DEIKMAN, A. J. (1963) Experimental meditation. *Journal of Nervous and Mental Disease*, *136*, 329–373.

DELAHANTY, D. L., DOUGALL, A. L., BROWNING, L. J., HYMAN, K. B., & BAUM, A. (1998). Duration of stressor and natural killer cell activity. *Psychology & Health*, *13*, 1121–1134.

DELL'OSSO, B., NESTADT, G., ALLEN, A., & HOLLANDER, E. (2006) Serotonin-norepinephrine reuptake inhibitors in the treatment of obsessive compulsive disorder: A critical review. *Journal of Clinical Psychiatry*, *67*, 600–610.

DEMENT, W. C., & WOLPERT, E. (1958) The relation of eye movements, bodily mobility, and external stimuli to dream content. *Journal of Experimental Psychology*, *55*, 543–553.

DE MOOR, J. S., DE MOOR, C. A., BASEN-ENGQUIST, K., KUDELKA, A., BEVERS, M. W., & COHEN, L. (2006) Optimism, distress, health-related quality of life, and changes in cancer antigen 125 among patients with ovarian cancer undergoing chemotherapy. *Psychosomatic Medicine*, *68*, 555–562.

DENNIS, W., & DENNIS, M. (1940) The effects of cradling practices upon the onset of walking in Hopi children. *Journal of Genetic Psychology*, *56*, 77–86.

DESCARTES, R. (1662) *Trait de l'homme*. E. S. Haldane & G. R. T. Ross (Trans.). Cambridge: Cambridge University Press.

DESFORGES, D. M., LORD, C. G., RAMSEY, S. L., MASON, J. A., VAN LEEUWEN, M. D., WEST, S. C., & LEPPER, M. R. (1991) Effects of structured cooperative contact on changing negative attitudes toward stigmatized social groups. *Journal of Personality and Social Psychology*, *60*, 531–544.

DEVALOIS, R. L., & DEVALOIS, K. K. (1980) Spatial vision. *Annual Review of Psychology*, *31*, 309–341.

DEVALOIS, R. L., & JACOBS, G. H. (1984) Neural mechanisms of color vision. In I. Darian-Smith (Ed.), *Handbook of physiology* (Vol. 3). Bethesda, MD: American Physiological Society.

DEVINE, P. G. (1989) Stereotypes and prejudice: Their automatic and controlled components. *Journal of Personality and Social Psychology*, *56*, 5–18.

DEVINE, P. G., PLANT, E. A., AMODIO, D. M., HARMON-JONES, E., & VANCE, S. L. (2002) The regulation of explicit and implicit race bias: The role of motivations to respond without prejudice. *Journal of Personality and Social Psychology*, *82*, 835–848.

DE WAAL, F. B. M. (1996) *Good natured: The origins of right and wrong in humans and other animals*. Cambridge, MA: Harvard University Press.

DEWALL, C. N., & BAUMEISTER, R. F. (2006) Alone but feeling no pain: Effects of social exclusion on physical pain tolerance and pain threshold, affective forecasting, and interpersonal empathy. *Journal of Personality and Social Psychology, 91* (1), 1–15.

DIAMOND, L. M. (2008) *Sexual fluidity: Understanding women's love and desire*. Cambridge, MA: Harvard University Press.

DIAMOND, M., & SIGMONDSON, H. K. (1997) Sex reassignment at birth: Long-term review and clinical implications. *Archives of Pediatrics and Adolescent Medicine, 151,* 298–304.

DIAMOND, M. (1982) Sexual identity, monozygotic twins reared in discordant sex roles and a BBC follow-up. *Archives of Sexual Behavior, 11,* 181–186.

DIAMOND, M., & SIGMUNDSON, K. (1997) Sex reassignment at birth: Long-term review and clinical implications. *Archives of Pediatric Medicine, 151,* 298.

DICICCO-BLOOM, E., LORD, C., ZWAIGENBAUM, L., COURCHESNE, E., DAGER, S. R., SCHMITZ, C., SCHULTZ, R. T., CRAWLEY, J., & YOUNG, L. J. (2006) The developmental neurobiology of autism spectrum disorder. *Journal of Neuroscience, 26,* 6897–6906.

DIENER, E. (1977) Deindividuation: Causes and consequences. *Social Behavior and Personality, 5,* 143–155.

DIENER, E. (1980) Deindividuation: The absence of self-awareness and self-regulation in group members. In P. B. Paulus (Ed.), *The psychology of group influence*. Hillsdale, NJ: Erlbaum.

DIENER, E., FRASER, S. C., BEAMAN, A. L., & KELEM, R. T. (1976) Effects of deindividuation variables on stealing among Halloween trick-or-treaters. *Journal of Personality and Social Psychology, 33,* 178–183.

DIJKSTERHUIS, A. (2004). Think different: The merits of unconscious thought in preference development and decision making. *Journal of Personality and Social Psychology, 87* (5), 586–598.

DIJKSTERHUIS, A., & BARGH, J. A. (2002) The perception-behavior expressway: Automatic effects of social perception on social behavior. In M. Zanna (Ed.), *Advances in Experimental Social Psychology, 33,* 1–40.

DIJKSTERHUIS, A., & VAN KNIPPENBERG, A. (1998) The relation between perception and behavior, or how to win a game of Trivial Pursuit. *Journal of Personality and Social Psychology, 74,* 865–877.

DIJKSTERHUIS, A., & VAN OLDEN, Z. (2006) On the benefits of thinking unconsciously: Unconscious thought can increase post-choice satisfaction. *Journal of Experimental Social Psychology, 42,* 627–631.

DIJKSTERHUIS, A., BOS, M. W., NORDGREN, L. F., & VAN BAAREN, R. B. (2006) On making the right choice: The deliberation-without-attention effect. *Science, 311,* 1005–1007.

DI LOLLO, V. (1980) Temporal Integration in Visual Memory. *Journal of Experimental Psychology: General, 109,* 75–97.

DI LOLLO, V., KAWAHARA J., ZUVIC, S. M., & VISSER, T. A. W. (2001) The preattentive emperor has no clothes: A dynamic redressing. *Journal of Experimental Psychology: General, 130,* 479–492.

DI PELLEGRINO, G., FADIGA, L., FOGASSI, L., GALLESE, V., RIZZOLATTI, G. (1992) Understanding motor events: A neurophysiological study. *Experimental Brain Research, 91,* 176–180.

DIPIETRO, J. A. (2001) Fetal neurobehavioral assessment. In L. T. Singer (Ed.), *Biobehavioral assessment of the infant* (pp. 43–80). New York: Guilford.

DISHION, T. J., & PATTERSON, G. R. (1997) The timing and severity of antisocial behavior: Three hypotheses within an ecological framework. In D. M. Stoff, J. Breiling, & J. D. Maser (Eds.), *Handbook of antisocial personality disorder* (pp. 205–217). New York: Wiley.

DOBB, E. (1989, November–December) The scents around us. *The Sciences, 29,* 46–53.

DODGE, K. A., & PETTIT, G. S. (2003) A biopsychosocial model of the development of chronic conduct problems in adolescence. *Developmental Psychology, 39,* 349–371.

DOLLARD, J., DOOB, L. W., MILLER, N. E., MOWRER, O. H., & SEARS, R. R. (1939) *Frustration and aggression*. New Haven, CT: Yale University Press.

DOMJAN, M. (2005) Pavlovian conditioning: A functional perspective. *Annual Review of Psychology, 56,* 179–206.

DORRIS, M. (1989) *The unbroken cord*. New York: Harper & Row.

DOSSENBACH, M., EROL, A., EL MAHFOUD KESSACI, M., SHAHEEN, M. O., SUNBOL, M. M., BOLAND, J., HODGE, A., O'HALLORAN, R. A., & BITTER, I. (2004) Effectiveness of antipsychotic treatments for schizophrenia: Interim 6-month analysis from a prospective observational study (IC-SOHO) comparing olanzapine, quetiapine, risperidone, and haloperidol. *Journal of Clinical Psychiatry, 65,* 312–321.

DRAGINSKI, B., GASER, C., BUSCH, V. SCHUIERER, G., BOGDAHN, U., & MAY, A. (2004) Neuroplasticity: Changes in grey matter induced by training. *Nature, 427,* 1580–1582.

DRONKERS, N. F., REDFERN, B. B., & KNIGHT, R. T. (2000) The neural architecture of language disorders. In: M. S. Gazzaniga (Ed.), *The new cognitive neuroscience* (2nd ed., pp. 949–958). Cambridge, MA: MIT Press.

DUBOIS, D. L., BULL, C. A., SHERMAN, M. D., & ROBERTS, M. (1998) Self-esteem and adjustment in early adolescence: A social-contextual perspective. *Journal of Youth and Adolescence, 27,* 557–583.

DUCLAUX, R., & KENSHALO, D. R. (1980) Response characteristics of cutaneous warm fibers in the monkey. *Journal of Neurophysiology, 43,* 1–15.

DUNCAN, J., & HUMPHREYS, G. W. (1989) Visual search and stimulus similarity. *Psychological Review, 96,* 433–458.

DUNCAN, S., & BARRETT, L. F. (2007) Affect as a form of cognition: A neurobiological analysis. *Cognition and Emotion, 21,* 1184–1211.

DUNN, J. R., & SCHWEITZER, M. E. (2005) Feeling and believing: The influence of emotion on trust. *Journal of Personality and Social Psychology, 88,* 736–748.

DUNN, K. M., SAUNDERS, K. W., RUTTER, C. M., BANTA-GREEN, C., MERRILL, J. O., et al. (2010) Opioid prescriptions for chronic pain and overdose: A cohort study. *Annals of Internal Medicine, 152,* 85–92.

EAGLY, A. H., & CHAIKEN, S. (1984) Cognitive theories of persuasion. In L. Berkowitz (Ed.), *Advances in experimental social psychology* (Vol. 17, pp. 267–359). New York: Academic Press.

EAGLY, A. H., & WOOD, W. (1999) The origins of sex differences in human behavior: Evolved dispositions versus social roles. *American Psychologist, 54,* 408–423.

EASTWICK, P. W., & FINKEL, E. J. (2008) Sex differences in mate preferences revisited: Do people know what they initially desire in a romantic partner? *Journal of Personality and Social Psychology, 94* (2), 245.

EATON, W. W., MOORTENSENK, P. B., HERRMAN, H., & FREEMAN, H. (1992) Long-term course of hospitalization for schizophrenia: risk for rehospitalization. *Schizophrenia Bulletin, 18,* 217–228.

EBBINGHAUS, H. (1885) *Uber das gedachthis.* Leipzig: Dunckes and Humbolt.

EDGAR, D. M., & DEMENT, W. C. (1992) Evidence for opponent processes in sleep/wake regulation. *Sleep Research, 20A,* 2.

EGAN, L. C., SANTOS, L. R., & BLOOM, P. (2007) The origins of cognitive dissonance: Evidence from children and monkeys. *Psychological Science, 18* (11), 978–983.

EHRHARDT, A. A., MEYER-BAHLBURG, H. F., ROSEN, L. R., FELDMAN, J. F., VERIDIANO, N. P., ELKIN, E. J., & MCEWEN, B. S. (1989) The development of gender-related behavior in females following prenatal exposure to diethylstilbestrol (DES) *Hormones and Behavior, 23,* 526–541.

EIBL-EIBESFELDT, I. (1970) *Ethology: The biology of behavior* (E. Klinghammer, Trans.). New York: Holt, Rinehart & Winston.

EICH, J. E. (1980) The cue-dependent nature of state-dependent retrieval. *Memory and Cognition, 8,* 157–173.

EICHENBAUM, H. (2000) A cortical-hippocampal system for declarative memory. *Nature Reviews Neuroscience, 1,* 41–50.

EIMAS, P. D. (1985) The perception of speech in early infancy. *Scientific American, 252,* 46–52.

EISENBERG, N., SMITH, C. L., & SPINRAD, T. L. (2011) Effortful control: Relations with emotion regulation, adjustment, and socialization in childhood. In K. D. Vohs & R. F. Baumeister (Eds.), *Handbook of self-regulation: Research, theory, and application* (2nd ed., pp. 263–283). New York: Guilford Press.

EISENBERGER, N. I., LIEBERMAN, M. D., & WILLIAMS, K. D. (2003) Does rejection hurt? An fMRI study of social exclusion. *Science, 302,* 290–292.

EKMAN, P., LEVENSON, R. W., & FRIESEN, W. V. (1983). Autonomic nervous system activity distinguishes among emotions. *Science, 221,* 1208–1210.

EKMAN, P. (1972) Universals and cultural differences in facial expressions of emotion. In J. Cole (Ed.), *Nebraska symposium on motivation, 1971* (pp. 207–283). Lincoln: University of Nebraska Press.

EKMAN, P. (1982) *Emotion in the human face* (2nd ed.). New York: Cambridge University Press.

EKSTROM, R. B., FRENCH, J. W., & HARMAN, H. H. (1979) *Cognitive factors: Their identification and replication. Multivariate behavioral research monographs.* Fort Worth: Society for Multivariate Experimental Psychology.

EKSTROM, R. B., FRENCH, J. W., HARMAN, H. H., & DERMAN, D. (1976) *Manual for kit of factor-referenced cognitive tests, 1976.* Princeton, NJ: Educational Testing Service.

ELFENBEIN, H. A., BEAUPRÉ, M., LÉVESQUE, M., & HESS, U. (2007) Toward a dialect theory: Cultural differences in the expression and recognition of posed facial expressions. *Emotion, 7,* 131–146.

EMMELKAMP, P. M. G. (1994) Behavior therapy with adults. In A. E. Bergin & S. L. Garfield (Eds.), *Handbook of psychotherapy and behavior change* (4th ed., pp. 379–427). New York: Wiley.

ENARD, W., PRZEWORSKI, M., FISHER, S. E., LAI, C. S. L., WIEBE, V., KITANO, T., ... PAABO, S. (2002) Molecular evolution of FOXP2, a gene involved in speech and language. *Nature, 418,* 869–872.

ENNS, J. T., & GIRGUS, J. S. (1985) Perceptual grouping and spatial distortion: A developmental study. *Developmental Psychology, 21,* 241–246.

ENNS, J. T., & PRINZMETAL, W. (1984) The role of redundancy in the object-line effect. *Perception and Psychophysics, 35,* 22–32.

ENNS, J. T., & RESNICK, R. A. (1990) Sensitivity to three-dimensional orientation in visual search. *Psychological Science, 1,* 323–326.

EPLEY, N., & GILOVICH, T. (1999) Just going along: Nonconscious priming and conformity to social pressure. *Journal of Experimental Social Psychology, 35,* 578–589.

EPPING-JORDAN, J. E., COMPA, S. B. E., & HOWELL, D. C. (1994) Predictors of cancer progression in young adult men and women: Avoidance, intrusive thoughts, and psychological symptoms. *Health Psychology, 13,* 539–547.

EPSTEIN, S., & MEIER, P. (1989) Constructive thinking: A broad coping variable with specific components. *Journal of Personality and Social Psychology, 57,* 332–350.

ERANTI, S. V., & MCLOUGHLIN, D. M. (2003) Electroconvulsive therapy – state of the art. *British Journal of Psychiatry, 182,* 8–9.

ERBES, C., WESTERMEYER, J., ENGDAHL, B., & JOHNSEN, E. (2007) Post-traumatic stress disorder and service utilization in a sample of service members from Iraq and Afghanistan. *Military Medicine, 172,* 359–363.

ERDELYI, M. H. (1985) *Psychoanalysis: Freud's cognitive psychology.* New York: Freeman.

ERICSSON, K. A., CHASE, W. G., & FALOON, S. (1980) Acquisition of a memory skill. *Science, 208,* 1181–1182.

ERICSSON, K. A., KRAMPE, R. TH., & TESCH-ROEMER, C. (1993) The role of deliberate practice in the acquisition of expert performance. *Psychological Review, 100,* 363–406.

ERIKSON, E. H. (1963) *Childhood and society* (2nd ed.). NewYork: Norton.

ERIKSON, E. H. (1968) *Identity: Youth and crisis.* New York: Norton.

ESCOBAR, J. I. (1993) Psychiatric epidemiology. In A. C. Gaw (Ed.), *Culture, ethnicity and mental illness* (pp. 43–73). Washington, DC: American Psychiatric Press.

ESTERSON, A. (1993) *Seductive mirage: An exploration of the work of Sigmund Freud.* Chicago: Open Court.

ESTES, W. K. (1972) An associative basis for coding and organization in memory. In A. W. Melton & E. Martin (Eds.), *Coding processes in human memory.* Washington, DC: Winston.

ESTES, W. K. (1994) *Classification and cognition.* New York: Oxford University Press.

EVANS, A. H., LAWRENCE, A. D., POTTS, J., APPEL, S., & LEES, A. J. (2005) Factors influencing susceptibility to compulsive dopaminergic drug use in parkinson disease. *Neurology, 65*(10), 1570–1574.

EVANS, C. (1984) *Landscapes of the night: How and why we dream.* New York: Viking.

EVANS, J. ST. B. T., BARSTON, J. L., & POLLARD, P. (1983) On the conflict between logic and belief in syllogistic reasoning. *Memory & Cognition, 11,* 295–306.

EVERETT, D. L. (2005) Cultural constraints on grammar and cognition in Pirahã: Another look at the design features of human language. *Current Anthropology, 46,* 621–645.

EVERS, A. W. M., KRAAIMAAT, F. W., GEENEN, R., JACOBS, J. W. G., & BIJLSMA, J. W. J. (2003) Stress-vulnerability factors as long-term predictors of disease activity in early rheumatoid arthritis. *Journal of Psychosomatic Research, 55,* 293–302

EYAL, T., HOOVER, G. M., FUJITA, K., & NUSSBAUM, S. (2011) The effect of distance-dependent construals on schema-driven impression formation. *Journal of Experimental Social Psychology, 47,* 278–281.

EYSENCK, H. J. (1953) *The structure of human personality.* New York: Wiley.

EYSENCK, H. J. (1994) The biology of morality. In B. Puka (Ed.), *Defining perspectives in moral development* (pp. 212–229). New York: Garland.

EYSENCK, H. J., & KAMIN, L. (1981) *The intelligence controversy.* New York: Wiley.

FADIGA, L., FOGASSI, L., GALLESE, V., & RIZZOLATTI, G. (2000) Visuomotor neurons: Ambiguity of the discharge or 'motor' perception? *International Journal of Psychophysiology, 35* (2–3), 165–177.

FAIRBURN, C. G., & HAY, P. J. (1992) Treatment of bulimia nervosa. *Annals of Medicine, 24,* 297–302.

FAIRBURN, C. G., NORMAN, P. A., WELCH, S. L., O'CONNOR, M. E., DOLL, H. A., & PEVELER, R. C. (1995) A prospective study of outcome in bulimia nervosa and the long-term effects of three psychological treatments. *Archives of General Psychiatry, 52,* 304–312.

FALBO, T. (2012) Only children: An updated review. *Journal of Individual Psychology, 68,* 3849.

FALBO, T., & POLIT, D. F. (1986) Quantitative research of the only child literature: Research evidence and theory development. *Psychological Bulletin,* 100, 176–189.

FAN, J., MCCANDLISS, B. D., SOMMER, T., RAZ, A., & POSNER, M. I. (2002) Testing the efficiency and independence of attentional networks. *Journal of Cognitive Neuroscience, 14,* 340–347.

FANSELOW, M. S. (1994) Neural organization of the defensive behavior system responsible for fear. *Psychonomic Bulletin & Review, 1,* 429–439.

FARAH, M., HAMMOND, K. M., & LEVINE, D. N. (1988) Visual and spatial mental imagery: Dissociable systems of representation. *Cognitive Psychology, 20,* 439–462.

FARAH, M. J. (1990) *Visual agnosia: Disorders of object recognition and what they tell us about normal vision.* Cambridge, MA: MIT Press.

FARAH, M. J., & MCCLELLAND, J. L. (1991) A computational model of semantic memory impairment. *Journal of Experimental Psychology: General, 120,* 339–357.

FARAH, M. J., TANAKA, J. W., & DRAIN, H. M. (1995) What causes the face inversion effect? *Journal of Experimental Psychology: Human Perception and Performance, 21,* 628–634.

FARAVELLI, C., GIUGNI, A., SALVATORI, S., & RICCA, V. (2004) Psychopathology after rape. *American Journal of Psychiatry, 161,* 1483–1485.

FARBER, E. W., SCHWARTZ, J. A. J., SCHAPER, P. E., MOONEN, D. J., & MCDANIEL, J. S. (2000) Resilience factors associated with adaptation to HIV disease. *Psychosomatics, 41,* 140–146.

FARMER, A., ELKIN, A., & MCGUFFIN, P. (2007) The genetics of bipolar affective disorder. *Current Opinion in Psychiatry, 20,* 8–12.

FARRONI, T., MENON, E., RIGATO, S. AND JOHNSON, M. H. (2007) The perception of facial expressions in newborns. *European Journal of Developmental Psychology, 4,* 2–13.

FARTHING, G. W. (1992) *The psychology of consciousness.* Englewood Cliffs, NJ: Prentice Hall.

FAUST, I. M. (1984) Role of the fat cell in energy balance physiology. In A. T. Stunkard & E. Stellar (Eds.), *Eating and its disorders.* New York: Raven Press.

FAVA, M., COPELAND, P. M., SCHWEIGER, U., & HERZOG, D. B. (1989) Neurochemical abnormalities of anorexia nervosa and bulimia nervosa. *American Journal of Psychiatry, 146,* 963–971.

FAZIO, R. H. (1990) Multiple processes by which attitudes guide behavior: The MODE model as an integrative framework. In M. P. Zanna (Ed.), *Advances in experimental social psychology* (Vol. 23). San Diego: Academic Press.

FAZIO, R. H., JACKSON, J. R., DUNTON, B. C., & WILLIAMS, C. J. (1995) Variability in automatic activation as an unobtrusive measure of racial attitudes: A bona fide pipeline? *Journal of Personality and Social Psychology, 69,* 1013–1027.

FECHNER, G. T. (1860/1966) *Elements of psychophysics* (H. E. Adler, Trans.). New York: Holt, Rinehart & Winston.

FEINBERG, J. M., & AIELLO, J. R. (2006) Social facilitation: a test of competing theories. *Journal of Applied Social Psychology, 36* (5), 1087–1109.

FEINGOLD, A. (1988) Cognitive gender differences are disappearing. *American Psychologist, 43,* 95–103.

FELDMAN, H., GOLDIN-MEADOW, S., & GLEITMAN, L. R. (1978) Beyond Herodotus: The creation of language by linguistically deprived children. In A. Lock (Ed.), *Action, gesture, and symbol: The emergence of language.* London: Academic Press.

FELDMAN BARRETT, L., ROBIN, L., PIETROMONACO, P. R., & EYSSELL, K. M. (1998) Are women the "more emotional" sex? Evidence from emotional experiences in social context. *Cognition and Emotion, 12,* 555–578.

FERGUSON, E., MATTHEWS, G., & COX, T. (1999) The appraisal of life events (ALE) scale: Reliability and validity. *British Journal of Health Psychology, 4,* 97–116.

FERGUSON, M. L., & KATKIN, E. S. (1996) Visceral perception, anhedonia, and emotion. *Biological Psychology, 42,* 131–145.

FERNALD, A. (1985). Four-month-old infants prefer to listen to motherese. *Infant Behavior & Development, 8,* 181–195.

FERNALD, A. (1993) Approval and disapproval: Infant responsiveness to vocal affect in familiar and unfamiliar languages. *Child Development, 64,* 657–674.

FESTINGER, L. (1957) *A theory of cognitive dissonance.* Stanford: Stanford University Press.

FESTINGER, L., & CARLSMITH, J. M. (1959) Cognitive consequences of forced compliance. *Journal of Abnormal and Social Psychology, 58,* 203–210.

FESTINGER, L., PEPITONE, A., & NEWCOMB, T. M. (1952) Some consequences of deindividuation in a group. *Journal of Abnormal and Social Psychology, 47,* 383–389.

FESTINGER, L., SCHACHTER, S., & BACK, K. (1950) *Social pressures in informal groups: A study of human factors in housing.* New York: Harper & Row.

FIRKOWSKI, A., OSTROWSKI, A., & SOKOLOWSKI, M., STEIN, Z., & SUSSER, M. (1978) Cognitive development in social policy. *Science,* 200, 1357–1362.

FISCHER, A. H. (2000) *Gender and emotion: Social psychological perspectives.* New York: Cambridge University Press.

FISCHER, A. H., MANSTEAD, A. S. R., & MOSQUERA, P. M. R. (1999) The role of honour-related vs. individualistic values in conceptualizing pride, shame, and anger: Spanish and Dutch cultural prototypes. *Cognition and Emotion, 13,* 149–179.

FISCHER, J., & HAMMERSCHMIDT, K. (2012) Ultrasonic vocalizations in mouse models for speech and socio-cognitive disorders: insights into the evolution of vocal communication. *Genes, Brain and Behavior*, 10, 17–27.

FISHBEIN, M., & AJZEN, I. (1975) *Belief, attitude, intention and behavior: An introduction to theory and research*. Reading, MA: Addison Wesley.

FISHBEIN, M., TRIANDIS, H. C., KANFER, F. H., BECKER, M., MIDDLESTADT, S. E., & EICHLER, A. (1998) Factors influencing behavior and behavior change. *Handbook of Health Psychology*. In press.

FISHER, P. J., TURIC, D., WILLIAMS, N. M., MCGUFFIN, P., ASHERSON, P., BALL, D., CRAIG, I., ELEY, T., HILL, L., CHURNEY, K., CHURNEY, M. J., BENBOW, C. P., LUBINSKI, D., PLUMIN, R., OWEN, M. J. (1999) DNA pooling identifies QTLs on chromosome 4 for general cognitive ability in children. *Human Molecular Genetics*, 8, 915–922.

FISHER, S., & GREENBERG, R. (1977) *The scientific credibility of Freud's theories and therapy*. New York: Basic Books.

FISHER, S., & GREENBERG, R. (1996) *Freud scientifically appraised*. New York: Wiley.

FISKE, S. T., LIN, M., & NEUBERG, S. L. (1999) The continuum model: Ten years later. In S. Chaiken & Y. Trope (Eds.), *Dual-process theories in social psychology* (pp. 231–254). New York: Guilford.

FITCH, W. T. (2010) *The evolution of language*. Cambridge: Cambridge University Press.

FITZSIMONS, J. T. (1990) Thirst and sodium appetite. In E. M. Stricker (Ed.), *Neurobiology of food and fluid intake* (pp. 23–44). New York: Plenum.

FIVUSH, R., & BUCKNER, J. P. (2000) Gender, sadness, and depression: The development of emotional focus through gendered discourse. In A. H. Fischer (Ed.), *Gender and emotion: Social psychological perspectives* (pp. 232–253). New York: Cambridge University Press.

FIVUSH, R., & HAMOND, N. R. (1991) Autobiographical memory across the preschool years: Toward reconceptualizing childhood memory. In R. Fivush & N. R. Hamond (Eds.), *Knowing and remembering in young children*. New York: Cambridge University Press.

FLACK, W. (2006) Peripheral feedback effects of facial expressions, bodily postures, and vocal expressions on emotional feelings. *Cognition & Emotion*, 20, 177–195.

FLAVELL, J. H. (1979) Metacognition and cognitive monitoring: A new area of cognitive-developmental inquiry. *American Psychologist*, 34, 906–911. doi:10.1037//0003-066X.34.10.906

FLAVELL, J. H. (1999) Cognitive development: Children's knowledge about the mind. *Annual Review of Psychology*, 50, 21–45.

FLETCHER, J. M., FRANCIS, D. J., SHAYWITZ, S. E., LYON, G. R., FOORMAN, B. R., STUEBING, K. K., & SHAYWITZ, B. A. (1998) Intelligent testing and the discrepancy model for children with learning disabilities. *Learning Disabilities Research & Practice*, 13(4), 186–203.

FLOR, H., FYDRICH, T., & TURK, D. C. (1992) Efficacy of multidisciplinary pain treatment: A meta-analytic review. *Pain*, 49, 221–230.

FLORES, H. G., HOFFMAN, W., RUSSELL, C. L., HOLMES, I. K., ROBERTS, M. E., POLAK, M. A., SERGHIOU, P., BLAKENEY, D. R., PATTERSON, W. J., MEYER, I. I. I. (2008) Longer, multiple virtual reality pain distraction treatments of Hispanic and Caucasian children with large severe burns. Paper presented at CyberPsychology and Behavior, June 13, 2008, San Diego, CA.

FLYNN, J. R. (1987) Massive IQ gains in 14 nations: What IQ tests really measure. *Psychological Bulletin*, 101, 171–191.

FOA, E., & STEKETEE, G. (1989) Obsessive-compulsive disorder. In C. Lindemann (Ed.), *Handbook of phobia therapy*. Northvale, NJ: Jason Aronson.

FOA, E. B., & FRANKLIN, M. E. (2001) Obsessive-compulsive disorder. *Clinical handbook of psychological disorders: a step-by-step treatment manual* (3rd ed., pp. 209–263). New York: Guilford.

FOA, E. D., & RIGGS, D. S. (1995) Posttraumatic stress disorder following assault: Theoretical considerations and empirical findings. *Current Directions in Psychological Science*, 4, 61–65.

FODOR, J. A. (1975) *The language of thought*. New York: Crowell.

FOLEY, D. L., PICKLES, A., MAES, H. H., SILBERG, J. L., HEWITT, J. K., & EAVES, L. J. (2001) Parental concordance and comorbidity for psychiatric disorder and associate risks for current psychiatric symptoms and disorders in a community sample of juvenile twins. *Journal of Child Psychology and Psychiatry & Allied Disciplines*, 42, 381–394.

FOLKES, V. S. (1982) Forming relationships and the matching hypothesis. *Personality and Social Psychology Bulletin*, 8, 631–636.

FOMBONNE, E. (2003) The epidemiology of autism: A review. *Psychological Medicine*, 29, 769–786.

FORDYCE, W. E. (1976) *Behavioral methods for chronic pain and illness*. St. Louis, MO: C. V. Mosby.

FORDYCE, W. E. (1976) *Behavioral methods for chronic pain and illness*. St. Louis, MO: C. V. Mosby.

FORTUNE, S. A., & HAWTON, K. (2005) Deliberate self-harm in children and adolescents: A research update. *Current Opinions in Psychiatry*, 18, 401–406.

FOSTER, K. R., & KOKKO, H. (2009) The evolution of superstitious and superstition-like behavior. *Proceedings of the Royal Society, Biological Sciences*, 276, 31–37.

FRANK, J. D., & FRANK, J. B. (1991) *Persuasion and healing: A comparative study of psychotherapy* (3rd edition). Baltimore: Johns Hopkins University Press.

FRANK, M. C., EVERETT, D. L., FEDORENKO, E., & GIBSON, E. (2008) Number as a cognitive technology: Evidence from Pirahã language and cognition. *Cognition*, 108, 819–824.

FRANKLIN, A., DRIVONIKOU, G. V., CLIFFORD, A., KAY, P., REGIER, T., & DAVIES, I. R. L. (2008a) Lateralization of categorical perception of color changes with color term acquisition. *Proceedings of the National Academy of Sciences*, 105, 18221–18225.

FRANKLIN, A., DRIVONIKOU, G. V., BEVIS, L., DAVIES, I. R. L., KAY, P., & REGIER, T. (2008b) Categorical perception of color is lateralized to the right hemisphere in infants, but to the left hemisphere in adults. *Proceedings of the National Academy of Sciences*, 105, 3221–3225.

FRANTZ, R. L. (1966) Pattern discrimination and selective attention as determinants of perceptual development from birth. In A. H. Kikk & J. F. Rivoire (Eds.), *Development of perception*: Vol. 2, *The visual system* (pp. 143–173). New York: International University Press.

FREDRICKSON, B. L. (1998) What good are positive emotions? *Review of General Psychology*, 2, 300–319.

FREDRICKSON, B. L. (2000) Cultivating positive emotions to optimize health and well-being. *Prevention and Treatment*. Available on the Internet: http://journals.apa.org/prevention.

FREDRICKSON, B. L. (2000b) Extracting meaning from past affective experiences: The importance of peaks, ends, and specific emotions. *Cognition and Emotion*, 14, 577–606.

FREDRICKSON, B. L. (2001) The role of positive emotions in positive psychology: The broaden-and-build theory of positive emotions. *American Psychologist*, *56*, 218–226.

FREDRICKSON, B. L. (2002) Positive emotions. In C. R. Snyder & S. J. Lopez (Eds.), *Handbook of positive psychology* (pp. 120–134). New York: Oxford University Press.

FREDRICKSON, B. L. (2013) Positive emotions broaden and build. In E. Ashby Plant & P. G. Devine (Eds.), *Advances on experimental social psychology*, Volume 47 (pp. 1–53).

FREDRICKSON, B. L. (2013b) *Love 2.0: How our supreme emotion affects everything we feel, think, do, and become.* New York: Hudson Street Press.

FREDRICKSON, B. L., & BRANIGAN, C. (2001) Positive emotions. In T. J. Mayne & G. A. Bonnano (Eds.), *Emotion: Current issues and future developments* (pp. 123–151). New York: Guilford.

FREDRICKSON, B. L., & BRANIGAN, C. (2005) Positive emotions broaden the scope of attention and thought–action repertoires. *Cognition and Emotion*, *19*, 313–332.

FREDRICKSON, B. L., & COHN, M. A. (in press) Positive emotions. In M. Lewis, J. Haviland-Jones, & L. F. Barrett (Eds.), *Handbook of Emotions, 3rd Edition*. New York: Guilford Press.

FREDRICKSON, B. L., & JOINER, T. (2002) Positive emotions trigger upward spirals toward emotional well-being. *Psychological Science*, *13*, 172–175.

FREDRICKSON, B. L., & LEVENSON, R. W. (1998) Positive emotions speed recovery from the cardiovascular sequelae of negative emotions. *Cognition and Emotion*, *12*, 191–220.

FREDRICKSON, B. L., & ROBERTS, T. (1997) Objectification theory: Toward understanding women's lived experience and mental health risks. *Psychology of Women Quarterly*, *21*, 173–206.

FREDRICKSON, B. L., MANCUSO, R. A., BRANIGAN, C., & TUGADE, M. M. (2000) The undoing effect of positive emotions. *Motivation and Emotion*, *24*, 237–258.

FREDRICKSON, B. L., COHN, M. A., COFFEY, K. A., PEK, J., & FINKEL, S. M. (2008) Open hearts build lives: Positive emotions, induced through loving-kindness meditation, build consequential personal resources. *Journal of Personality and Social Psychology*, *95*, 1045–1062.

FREDRICKSON, B. L., HENDLER, L. M., NILSEN, S., O'BARR, J. F., & ROBERTS, T. (2011) Bringing back the body: A retrospective on the development of objectification theory. *Psychology of Women Quarterly*, *35*, 689–696.

FREDRICKSON, B. L. ROBERTS, T., NOLL, S. M., QUINN, D. M., & TWENGE, J. M. (1998) That swimsuit becomes you: Sex differences in self-objectification, restrained eating and math performance. *Journal of Personality and Social Psychology*, *75*, 269–284.

FREEDMAN, J. L. (1965) Long-term behavioral effects of cognitive dissonance. *Journal of Experimental Social Psychology*, *1*, 145–155.

FREEDMAN, J. L., & FRASER, S. C. (1966) Compliance without pressure: The foot-in-the-door technique. *Journal of Personality and Social Psychology*, *4*, 195–203.

FREUD, A. (1946/1967) *The ego and the mechanisms of defense* (Rev. Ed.). New York: International Universities Press.

FREUD, A. (1958) Adolescence. *The psychoanalytic study of the child*, *13*, 255–278.

FREUD, S. (1885/1974) *Cocaine papers* (edited and introduction by R. Byck; notes by A. Freud). New York: Stonehill.

FREUD, S. (1900/1953) *The interpretation of dreams* (Reprint ed., Vols. 4, 5). London: Hogarth Press.

FREUD, S. (1901/1960) *Psychopathology of everyday life* (Standard ed., Vol. 6). London: Hogarth Press.

FREUD, S. (1905/1962) *Three contributions to theory of sex* (4th ed.; A. A. Brill, Trans.). New York: Nervous and Mental Disease Monograph.

FREUD, S. (1933/1964) *New introductory lectures on psychoanalysis* (J. Strachey, Ed. and Trans.). New York: Norton.

FREUD, S. (1933/1965) Revision of the theory of dreams. In J. Strachey (Ed. and Trans.), *New introductory lectures on psychoanalysis* (Vol. 22, Lect. 29). New York: Norton.

FREY, K. S., & RUBLE, D. N. (1990) Strategies for comparative evaluation: Maintaining a sense of competence across the lifespan. In R. J. Sternberg & J. Kolligian, Jr. (Eds.), *Competence considered* (pp. 167–189). New Haven, CT: Yale University Press

FRIED, P. A., & WATKINSON, B. (1990) 36- and 48-month neurobehavioral follow-up of children prenatally exposed to marijuana, cigarettes, and alcohol. *Journal of Developmental and Behavioral Pediatrics*, *11*, 49–58.

FRIEDERICI, A. D., BRAUER, J., & LOHMANN, G. (2011) Maturation of the language network: From inter- to intrahemispheric connectivities. *PLoS One*, *6*(6), e20726.

FRIEDMAN, H. S., & MARTIN, L. R. A. (2007) Lifespan approach to personality and longevity: The case of conscientiousness. In C. M. Aldwin, C. L. Park, & A. Spiro III (Eds.), *Handbook of health psychology and aging* (pp. 167–185). New York: Guilford Press.

FRIEDMAN, M., & ROSENMAN, R. H. (1974) *Type A behavior*. New York: Knopf.

FRIEDMAN, M., THORESEN, C. E., GILL, J. J., ULMER, D., POWELL, L. H., PRICE, V., BROWN, B., THOMPSON, L., RABIN, D. D., and collaborators. (1994) Alteration of Type A behavior and its effect on cardiac recurrences in post myocardial infarction patients: Summary results of the recurrent coronary prevention project. In A. Steptoe (Ed.), *Psychosocial processes and health: A reader*. Cambridge: Cambridge University Press.

FRIEDMAN, M. I. (1990) Making sense out of calories. In E. M. Stricker (Ed.), *Neurobiology of food and fluid intake* (pp. 513–528). New York: Plenum.

FRIJDA, N. H. (1986) *The emotions*. Cambridge: Cambridge University Press.

FRODI, A., & THOMPSON, R. (1985) Infants' affective responses in the strange situation: Effects of prematurity and of quality of attachment. *Child Development*, *56*, 1280–1290.

FULLER, S. R., & ALDAG, R. J. (1998) Organizational Tonypandy: Lessons from a quarter century of groupthink phenomenon. *Organizational Behavior and Human Decision Processes*, *73*, 163–184.

FUNDER, D. C. (2001) Personality. *Annual Reviews of Psychology*, *52*, 197–221.

FUNK, J. B., BALDACCI, H. B., PASOLD, T., & BAUMGARDNER, J. (2004). Violence exposure in real-life, video games, television, movies, and the internet: is there desensitization? *Journal of Adolescence*, *27*, 23–39.

FUNKENSTEIN, D. (1955) The physiology of fear and anger. *Scientific American*, *192*, 74–80.

FURLAN, A. D., SANDOVAL, J. A., MAILIS-GAGNON, A., & TUNKS, E. (2006) Opioids for chronic noncancer pain: A meta-analysis of effectiveness and side-effects. *Canadian Medical Association Journal*, *174*, 1584–1594.

GAILLIOT, M. T., BAUMEISTER, R. F., DEWALL, N. C., MANER, J. K., PLANT, A. E., TICE, D. M., BREWER, L. E., & SCHMEICHEL, B. J. (2007) Self-control relies on glucose as a limited energy source: Willpower is more than a metaphor. *Journal of Personality and Social Psychology*, 92, 325–336.

GALEF, B. G. (1996) Social enhancement of food preferences in Norway rats: A brief review. In C. M. Heyes, & B. G. Galef (Eds.), *Social Learning in Animals: The Roots of Culture* (pp. 49–64). San Diego: Academic Press.

GALLANT, J. L., SHUOP, R. E., & MAZER, J. A. (2000) A human extrastriate area functionally homologous to macaque V4. *Neuron*, 27, 227–235.

GALLUP, G. G., JR. (1998) Can animals empathize? *Scientific American Presents*, 9, 66–71.

GALVAN, A., HARE, T. A., PARRA, C. E., PENN, J., VOSS, H., GLOVER, G., & CASEY, B. J. (2006) Earlier development of the accumbens relative to orbitofrontal cortex might underlie risk-taking behavior in adolescents. *Journal of Neuroscience*, 26, 6885–6892.

GAMBESCIA, N., & WEEKS, G. (2007) Sexual dysfunction. In N. Kazantzis & L. L'Abate (Eds.), *Handbook of homework assignments in psychotherapy: Research, practice, and prevention* (pp. 351–368). New York: Springer Science & Business Media.

GANGESTAD, S. W., GARVER-APGAR, C. E., SIMPSON, J. A., & COUSINS, A. J. (2007) Changes in women's mate preferences across the ovulatory cycle. *Journal of Personality and Social Psychology*, 92, 151–163.

GARB, F., & STUNKARD, A. (1974) Taste aversions in man. *American Journal of Psychiatry*, 131, 1204–1207.

GARCIA, J., & KOELLING, R. A. (1966) The relation of cue to consequence in avoiding learning. *Psychonomic Science*, 4, 123–124.

GARCIA, L. T., ERSKINE, N., HAWN, K., & CASMAY, S. R. (1981) The effect of affirmative action on attributions about minority group members. *Journal of Personality*, 49, 427–437.

GARCIA, S. M., WEAVER, K., MOSKOWITZ, G. B., & DARLEY, J. M. (2002) Crowded minds: The implicit bystander effect. *Journal of Personality and Social Psychology*, 83 (4), 843–53.

GARDNER, B. T., & GARDNER, R. A. (1972) Two-way communication with an infant chimpanzee. In A. M. Schrier & F. Stollnitz (Eds.), *Behavior of nonhuman primates* (Vol. 4). New York: Academic Press.

GARDNER, E. L. (1992) Brain reward mechanisms. In J. H. Lowinson, P. Ruiz, & R. B. Millman (Eds.), *Substance abuse: A comprehensive textbook* (2nd ed.). Baltimore, MD: Williams & Wilkins.

GARDNER, H. (1975) *The shattered mind*. New York: Knopf.

GARDNER, H. (1993a) *Frames of mind: The theory of multiple intelligences*. New York: Basic Books.

GARDNER, H. (1993a) *Frames of mind: The theory of multiple intelligences (10th Anniversary Edition)*. New York: Basic Books. (Original work published 1983.)

GARDNER, H. (1993b) *Multiple intelligences: The theory in practice*. New York: Basic Books.

GARDNER, H. (2004a) *The unschooled mind: How children think and how schools should teach*. New York: Basic Books.

GARDNER, H. (2004b) *Frames of mind: The theory of multiple intelligences*. New York: Basic Books.

GARDNER, H., KORNHABER, M. L., & WAKE, W. K. (1996) *Intelligence: Multiple perspectives*. Fort Worth: Harcourt Brace.

GARDNER, M. (1981) *Science: Good, bad, and bogus*. New York: Prometheus.

GARDNER, W., LIDZ, C. W., MULVEY, E. P., & SHAW, E. C. (1996) Clinical versus actuarial predictions of violence in patients with mental illnesses. *Journal of Consulting and Clinical Psychology*, 64, 602–609.

GARLAND, E. L., FREDRICKSON, B. L., KRING, A. M., JOHNSON, D. P., MEYER, P. S., & PENN, D. L. (2010) Upward spirals of positive emotions counter downward spirals of negativity: Insights from the broaden-and-build theory and affective neuroscience on the treatment of emotion dysfunctions and deficits psychopathology. *Clinical Psychology Review*, 30, 849–864.

GARRETT, M. F. (1990) Sentence processing. In D. N. Osherson & H. Lasnik (Eds.), *An invitation to cognitive science: Language* (Vol. 1). Cambridge, MA: MIT Press.

GARROD, S. C., & PICKERING, M. J. (1999) *Language processing of words*. Hove: Psychology Press.

GARRY, M., MANNING, C., LOFTUS, E. F., & SHERMAN, S. J. (1996) Imagination inflation. *Psychonomic Bulletin & Review*, 3, 208–214.

GASER, C., & SCHLAUGH, G. (2003) Brain structures differ between musicians and non-musicians. *Journal of Neuroscience*, 23, 9240–9245.

GATES, A. I. (1917) Recitation as a factor in memorizing. *Archives of Psychology*, 40.

GAZZANIGA, M. S. (1985) *The social brain: Discovering the networks of mind*. New York: Basic Books.

GENDRON, M., & BARRETT, L. F. (in press) Reconstructing the past: A century of emotion theorizing in psychology. *Emotion Review*.

GENDRON, M., LINDQUIST, K. A., BARSALOU, L. W., & BARRETT, L. F. (2012) Emotion words shape emotion percepts. *Emotion*, 12, 314–325.

GEORGE, M. S., *et al.* (1996) Changes in mood and hormone levels after rapid-rate transcranial magnetic stimulation (rTMS) of the prefrontal cortex. *Journal of Neuropsychiatry and Clinical Neurosciences*, 8 (2), 172–180.

GEORGE, M. S., NAHAS, Z., KOZEL, F. A., LI, X., YMANAKA, K., MISHORY, A., & BOHNING, D. E. (2003) Mechanisms and current state of transcranial magnetic stimulation. *CNS Spectrums*, 8, 511–514.

GERBNER, G., GROSS, L., MORGAN, M., & SIGNORIELLI, N. (1986) Living with television: The dynamics of the cultivation process. In J. Bryant & D. Zillmann (Eds.), *Perspectives on media effects*. Hillsdale, NJ: Erlbaum.

GERMER, C. K. (2005) Anxiety disorders: Befriending fear. In C. K. Germer, R. D. Siegel & P. R. Fulton (Eds.), *Mindfulness and psychotherapy* (pp. 152–172). New York: Guildford Press.

GESCHWIND, N. (1972) Language and the brain. *Scientific American*, 226, 76–83.

GESCHWIND, N. (1979) Specializations of the human brain. *Scientific American*, 241, 180–199.

GESELL, A., & THOMPSON, H. (1929) Learning and growth in identical twins: An experimental study by the method of co-twin control. *Genetic Psychology Monographs*, 6, 1–123.

GHAEMI, S. N., PARDO, T. B., & HSU, D. J. (2004) Strategies for preventing the recurrence of bipolar disorder. *Journal of Clinical Psychiatry*, 65 (Suppl. 10), 16–23.

GIANOULAKIS, C., KRISHNAN, B., & THAVUNDAYIL, J. (1996) Enhanced sensitivity of pituitary endorphin to ethanol in subjects at high risk of alcoholism. *Archives of General Psychiatry*, 53, 250–257.

GIBSON, E. J., & WALK, R. D. (1960) The "visual cliff". *Scientific American*, *202*, 64–71.

GICK, M. L., & HOLYOAK, K. J. (1983) Schema induction and analogical transfer. *Cognitive Psychology*, *15*, 1–38.

GIGERENZER, G. (1996) The psychology of good judgment: Frequency formats and simple algorithms. *Journal of Medical Decision Making*, *16*, 273–280.

GIGERENZER, G. (2006) Out of the frying pan into the fire: behavioral reactions to terrorist attacks. *Risk Analysis*, *26*, 347–351.

GILBERT, A., REGIER, T., KAY, P., & IVRY, R. (2006) Whorf hypothesis is supported in the right visual field but not the left. *Proceedings of the National Academy of Sciences*, *103*, 489–494.

GILBERT, D. T., & JONES, E. E. (1986) Perceiver-induced constraint: Interpretations of self-generated reality. *Journal of Personality and Social Psychology*, *50*, 269–280.

GILBERT, D. T., & MALONE, P. S. (1995) The correspondence bias. *Psychological Bulletin*, *117*, 21–38.

GILCHRIST, A. L. (1988) Lightness contrast and failures of constancy: A common explanation. *Perception and Psychophysics*, *43*, 415–424.

GILLIGAN, C. (1982) *In a different voice*. Cambridge, MA: Harvard University Press.

GILLS, J., SCHMUKLER, K., AZMITIA, M., & CROSBY, F. J. (2007) Affirmative action and ethnic minority students: Enlarging pipelines to support success. In C. Wainryb, J. G. Smetana, & E. Turiel (Eds.), *Social development, social inequalities, and social justice* (pp. 81–107). New York, New York.: L. E. Erlbaum Associates.

GILOVICH, T. (1983) Biased evaluation and persistence in gambling. *Journal of Personality and Social Psychology*, *44*, 1110–1126.

GILTAY, E. J., GELEIJNSE, J. M., ZITMAN, F. G., BUIJSSE, B., & KROMHOUT, D. (2007) Lifestyle and dietary correlates of dispositional optimism in men: The Zutphen Elderly Study. *Journal of Psychosomatic Research*, *63*, 483–490.

GLASS, D. C., & SINGER, J. E. (1972) *Urban stress: Experiments on noise and social stressors*. New York: Academic Press.

GLASS, G. V., MCGAW, B., & SMITH, M. L. (1981) *Meta-analysis in social research*. Beverly Hills, CA: Sage.

GLASS, R. M. (2001) Electroconvulsive therapy: Time to bring it out of the shadows. *Journal of the American Medical Association*, *285*, 1346–1348.

GLEITMAN, H. (1986) *Psychology* (2nd ed.). New York: Norton.

GLEITMAN, L. R. (1986) Biological predispositions to learn language. In P. Marler & H. S. Terrace (Eds.), *The biology of learning*. New York: Springer-Verlag.

GOETHALS, G. P., & ZANNA, M. P. (1979) The role of social comparison in choice shifts. *Journal of Personality and Social Psychology*, *37*, 1469–1476.

GOETZ, J. L., KELTNER, D., & SIMON-THOMAS, E. (2010) Compassion: An evolutionary analysis and empirical review. *Psychological Bulletin*, *136*, 351–374.

GOLDBERG, L. R. (1981) Language and individual differences: The search for universals in personality lexicons. In L. Wheeler (Ed.), *Review of Personality and Social Psychology* (Vol. 2, pp. 141–165). Beverly Hills, CA: Sage.

GOLDIN, P. R., MCRAE, K., RAMEL, W., & GROSS, J. J. (2008) The neural bases of emotion regulation: Reappraisal and suppression of negative emotion. *Biological Psychiatry*, *63*, 577–586.

GOLDIN-MEADOW, S. (1982) The resilience of recursion: A structure within a conventional model. In E. Wanner & L. R. Gleitman (Eds.), *Language acquisition: The state of the art*. Cambridge: Cambridge University Press.

GOLDMAN-RAKIC, P. S. (1987) Circuitry of primate prefrontal cortex and regulation of behavior by representational memory. In F. Plum (Ed.), *Handbook of physiology: The nervous system*. Bethesda, MD: American Physiology Society.

GOLDSTEIN, E. B. (1989) *Sensation and perception* (3rd ed.). Belmont, CA: Wadsworth.

GOLDSTEIN, M. (1987) Family interaction patterns that antedate the onset of schizophrenia and related disorders: A further analysis of data from a longitudinal prospective study. In K. Hahlweg & M. Goldstein (Eds.), *Understanding major mental disorders: The contribution of family interaction research* (pp. 11–32). New York: Family Process Press.

GOLDSTEIN, M. J., TALOVIC, S. A., NUECHTERLEIN, K. H., & FOGELSON, D. L. (1992) Family interaction versus individual psychopathology: Do they indicate the same processes in the families of schizophrenia? *British Journal of Psychiatry*, *161*, 97–102.

GOLEMAN, D. (1995, May 2) Biologists find the site of working memory. *New York Times*.

GÓMEZ, J.-C. (2008) The evolution of pretence: From intentional availability to intentional non-existence. *Mind and Language*, *23*(5), 586–606.

GOODALL, J. (1978) Chimp killings: Is it the man in them? *Science News*, *113*, 276.

GORDON, P. (2004) Numerical cognition without words: Evidence from Amazonia. *Science*, *306*, 496–499.

GOTTESMAN, I. I., & REILLY, J. L. (2003) Strengthening the evidence for genetic factors in schizophrenia (without abetting genetic discrimination). In M. F. Lenzenweger & J. M. Hooley (Eds.), *Principles of experimental psychopathology: Essays in honor of Brendan A. Maher* (pp. 31–44). Washington, DC: American Psychological Association.

GOTTESMAN, I. I., & SHIELDS, J. (1982) *Schizophrenia, the epigenetic puzzle*. New York: Cambridge University Press.

GOTTLIEB, G. (2000) Environmental and behavioral influences on gene activity. *Current Directions in Psychological Science*, *9*, 93–97.

GOUIN, J., GLASER, R., MALARKEY, W. B., BEVERSDORF, D., & KIECOLT-GLASER, J. (2012). Chronic stress, daily stressors, and circulating inflammatory markers. *Health Psychology*, *31*, 264–268.

GOULD, E., BEYLIN, A., TANAPAT, P., REEVES, A., & SHORS, T. J. (1999) Learning enhances adult neurogenesis in the hippocampal formation. *Nature Neuroscience*, *2*, 260–265.

GOURINE, A. V, KASYMOV, V., MARINA, N., TANG, F., FIGUEIREDO, M. F., LANE, S., TESCHEMACHER, A. G., SPYER, K. M., DEISSEROTH, K., & KASPAROV, S. (2010) Astrocytes control breathing through pH-dependent release of ATP. *Science*, *329*, 571–575.

GOY, R. W. (1968) Organizing effect of androgen on the behavior of rhesus monkeys. In R. F. Michael (Ed.), *Endocrinology of human behaviour*. London: Oxford University Press.

GRADY, C. L., HAXBY, J. V., HORWITZ, B., SCHAPIRO, M. B., RAPOPORT, S. I., UNGERLEIDER, L. G., MISHKIN, M., CARSON, R. E., & HERSCOVITCH, P. (1992) Dissociation of object and spatial vision in human extrastriate cortex: Age-related changes in activation of regional cerebral blood flow measured with [15O] water and positron emission tomography. *Journal of Cognitive Neuroscience, 4*, 23–34.

GRAF, P., & MANDLER, G. (1984) Activation makes words more accessible, but not necessarily more retrievable. *Journal of Verbal Learning and Verbal Behavior, 23*, 553–568.

GRAF, P., & MASSON, M. E. J. (Eds.) (1993) *Implicit memory: New directions in cognition, development, and neuropsychology*. Hillsdale, NJ: Erlbaum.

GRAHAM, S. A., & FISHER, S. E. (2012) Decoding the genetics of speech and language. *Current Opinion in Neurobiology, 23*,1–9.

GRANDIN, T. (1995) *Thinking in pictures and other reports from my life with autism*. New York: Vintage Books.

GRANRUD, C. E. (1986) Binocular vision and spatial perception in 4- and 5-month-old infants. *Journal of Experimental Psychology: Human Perception and Performance, 12*, 36–49.

GRAY, J. (1992) *Men are from Mars, women are from Venus: A practical guide for improving communication and getting what you want in your relationships*. New York: HarperCollins.

GRAY, J. M., YOUNG, A. W., BARKER, W. A., CURTIS, A., & GIBSON, D. (1997) Impaired recognition of disgust in Huntington's disease gene carriers. *Brain, 120*, 2029–2038.

GRAY-LITTLE, B., & HAFDAHL, A. R. (2000) Factors influencing racial comparisons of self-esteem: A quantitative review. *Psychological Bulletin, 126*, 26–54.

GRAZZANI-GAVAZZI, I., & OATLEY, K. (1999) The experience of emotions of interdependence and independence following interpersonal errors in Italy and Anglophone Canada. *Cognition and Emotion, 13*, 49–63.

GREEN, B. L., LINDY, J. D., GRACE, M. C., & LEONARD, A. C. (1992) Chronic post-traumatic stress disorder and diagnostic comorbidity in a disaster sample. *Journal of Nervous and Mental Disease, 180*, 760–766.

GREENE, D., STERNBERG, B., & LEPPER, M. R. (1976) Overjustification in a token economy. *Journal of Personality and Social Psychology, 34*, 1219–1234.

GREEN, D. M., & WIER, C. C. (1984) Auditory perception. In I. Darian-Smith (Ed.), *Handbook of physiology* (Vol. 3). Bethesda, MD: American Physiological Society.

GREEN, J. G., FOX, N. A., & LEWIS, M. (1983) The relationship between neonatal characteristics and three-month mother-infant interaction in high-risk infants. *Child Development, 54*, 1286–1296.

GREEN, R. (1987a) Gender identity in childhood and later sexual orientation: Follow-up of 78 males. In S. Chess & T. Alexander (Eds.) *Annual progress in child psychiatry and child development* (pp. 214–220). Philadelphia, PA: Brunner/Mazel.

GREEN, R. (1987b) *The "sissy boy syndrome" and the development of homosexuality*. New Haven, CT: Yale University Press.

GREENBERG, D. F. (1990) *The construction of homosexuality*. Chicago: University of Chicago Press.

GREENFIELD, P. M., & SAVAGE-RUMBAUGH, S. (1990) Grammatical combination in *Pan Paniscus*: Processes of learning and invention in the evolution and development of language. In S. Parker & K. Gibson (Eds.), *"Language" and intelligence in monkeys and apes: Comparative developmental perspectives*. New York: Cambridge University Press.

GRIFFITHS, M. D. (1993) Fruit machine gambling: The importance of structural characteristics. *Journal of Gambling Studies, 9*, 133–152.

GRIGGS, R. A., & COX, J. R. (1982) The elusive thermatic-materials effect in Watson's selection task. *British Journal of Psychology, 73*, 407–420.

GRILL, H. J., & KAPLAN, J. M. (1990) Caudal brainstem participates in the distributed neural control of feeding. In E. M. Stricker (Eds.), *Neurobiology of food and fluid intake* (pp. 125–149). New York: Plenum Press.

GROSS, E. F. (2004) Adolescent internet use: What we expect, what teens report. *Journal of Applied Developmental Psychology, 25*, 633–649.

GROSS, J. J., & LEVENSON, R. W. (1997) Hiding feelings: The acute effects of inhibiting positive and negative emotions. *Journal of Abnormal Psychology, 106*, 95–103.

GROSS, M. M., CRANE, E., & FREDRICKSON, B. L. (2008) *Methodology for assessing bodily expression of emotion*. Manuscript under review.

GROSS, M. M., CRANE, E. A., & FREDRICKSON, B. L. (2012) Effort-shape and kinematic assessment of bodily expression of emotion during gait. *Human Movement Science, 31*, 202–221.

GROSS, R. T., BROOKS-GUNN, J., & SPIKER, D. (1992) Efficacy of educational interventions for low birth weight infants: The Infant Health and Development Program. In S. L. Friedman & M. D. Sigman (Eds.), *The psychological development of low birth weight children: Advances in applied developmental psychology*. Norwood, NJ: Ablex.

GROSSMAN, M., & WOOD, W. (1993) Sex differences in intensity of emotional experience: A social role interpretation. *Journal of Personality and Social Psychology, 65*, 1010–1022.

GUARNACCIA, P. J., CANINO, G., RUBIO-STIPEC, M., & BRAVO, M. (1993) The prevalence of ataques de nervios in the Puerto Rico Disaster Study: The role of culture in psychiatric epidemiology. *Journal of Nervous and Mental Disease, 181*, 157–165.

GUILFORD, J. P. (1982) Cognitive psychology's ambiguities: Some suggested remedies. *Psychological Review, 89*, 48–49.

GURIN, P. (2004) The educational value of diversity. In P. Gurin, J. S. Lehman, & E. Lewis (Eds.), *Defending diversity: Affirmative action at the University of Michigan* (97–188). Ann Arbor, MI: University of Michigan Press.

GURIN, P., NAGDA, B. A., & LOPEZ, G. E. (2004) The benefits of diversity in education for democratic citizenship. *Journal of Social Issues, 60*, 17–34.

GURNEY, R. (1936) The hereditary factor in obesity. *Archives of Internal Medicine, 57*, 557–561.

HABER, R. N. (1969) Eidetic images. *Scientific American, 220*, 36–55.

HABER, R. N. (1979) Twenty years of haunting edetic imagery: Where's the ghost? *Behavioral and Brain Sciences, 24*, 583–629.

HAITH, M. M. (1998) Who put the cog in infant cognition: Is the rich interpretation too costly? *Infant Behaviour and Development, 21*, 167–180.

HAJCAK, G., MOSER, J. S., & SIMONS, R. F. (2006) Attending to affect: Appraisal strategies modulate the electrocortical response to arousing pictures. *Emotion, 6*, 517–522.

HALL, C. S. (1947) Diagnosing personality by the analysis of dreams. *Journal of Abnormal and Social Psychology, 42*, 68–79.

HALL, C. S. (1953) A cognitive theory of dreams. *Journal of General Psychology, 48*, 169–186.

HALLARAKER, E., AREFJORD, K., HAVIK, O. E., & MAELAND, J. G. (2001) Social support and emotional adjustment during and after a severe life event: A study of wives of myocardial infarction patients. *Psychology & Health, 16*, 343–355.

HAMER, D. H., HU, S., MAGNUSON, V. L., HU, N., & PATTATUCCI, A. M. L. (1993) A linkage between DNA markers on the X chromosome and male sexual orientation. *Science, 261*, 321–327.

HAMILTON, D. L. (1979) A cognitive-attributional analysis of stereotyping. In L. Berkowitz (Ed.), *Advances in experimental social psychology* (Vol. 12). New York: Academic Press.

HAMMERSCHMIDT, K., & FISCHER, J. (2008) Constraints in primate vocal production. In U. Griebel & K. Oller (Eds.), The evolution of communicative creativity: From fixed signals to contextual flexibility (pp. 93–119). Cambridge. MA: The MIT Press.

HAMMERSCHMIDT, K., REISINGER, E., WESTEKÄMPER, K., EHRENREICH, H., STRENZKE, N., & FISCHER, J. (2012) Mice do not require auditory input for the normal development of their ultrasonic vocalizations. *BMC Neuroscience, 13*, 40.

HAN, S., LERNER, J. S., & KELTNER, D. (2007) Feelings and consumer decision making: The Appraisal-Tendency Framework. *Journal of Consumer Psychology, 17*, 158–168.

HANEY, C., & ZIMBARDO, P. (1998) The past and the future of U.S. prison policy: Twenty-five years after the Stanford Prison Experiment. *American Psychologist, 53*, 709–727.

HANNIGAN, S. L., & REINITZ, M. T. (2001) A demonstration and comparison of two types of inference-based memory errors. *Journal of Experimental Psychology: Learning, Memory, and Cognition, 37*, 931–940.

HARDMAN, C. A., HERBERT, V. M., BRUNSTROM, J. M., MUNAFO, M. R., & ROGERS, P. J. (2012) Dopamine and food reward: Effects of acute tyrosine/phenylalanine depletion on appetite. *Physiology & Behavior, 105*(5), 1202–1207.

HARE, R. D. (1999) *Without conscience: The disturbing world of the psychopaths among us*. New York: Guilford.

HARLOW, H. F. (1971) *Learning to love*. San Francisco: Albion.

HARLOW, H. F., & HARLOW, M. K. (1969) Effects of various mother-infant relationships on rhesus monkey behaviors. In B. M. Foss (Ed.), *Determinants of infant behavior* (Vol. 4), London: Methuen.

HARRIS, J. R. (1995) Where is the child's environment? A group socialization theory of development. *Psychological Review, 102*, 458–489.

HARRIS, J. R. (1998) *The nurture assumption*. New York: Free Press.

HARRIS, J. R. (2006) *No two alike: Human nature and human individuality*. New York: Norton.

HARRIS, J. R. (2009) *The nurture assumption* (2nd ed). New York: Free Press.

HARRIS, M. J., & ROSENTHAL, R. (1988) *Interpersonal expectancy effects and human performance research*. Washington, DC: National Academy Press.

HART, A. J., WHALEN, P. J., SHIN, L. M., MCINERNEY, S. C., FISCHER, H., & RAUCH, S. L. (2000) Differential response in the human amygdala to racial outgroup vs. ingroup face stimuli. *Neuroreport, 11*, 2351–2355.

HARTER, S. (1998) The development of self-representation. In N. Eisenberg (Ed.), *Handbook of child psychology* (5th ed.), Vol. 3: Social, emotional, and personality development (pp. 553–617). New York: Wiley.

HARTSTON, H. (2012) The case for compulsive shopping as an addiction. *Journal of Psychoactive Drugs, 44*(1), 64–67.

HARVEY, A., WATKINS, E., MANSELL, W., & SHAFRAN, R. (2004) *Cognitive behavioural processes across psychological disorders: A transdiagnostic approach to research and treatment*. Oxford: Oxford University Press.

HASSINK, J., ELINGS, M., ZWEEKHORST, M., VAN DEN NIEUWENHUIZEN, N., & SMIT, A. (2010) Care farms in the Netherlands: Attractive empowerment-oriented and strengths-based practices in the community. *Health & Place, 16*(3), 423–430.

HATFIELD, E. (1988) Passionate and companionate love. In R. J. Sternberg & M. L. Barnes (Eds.), *The psychology of love* (pp. 191–217). New Haven, CT: Yale University Press.

HATHAWAY, S. R., & MCKINLEY, J. C. (1943) *Manual for the Minnesota Multiphasic Personality Inventory*. New York: Psychological Corporation.

HAUN, D. B. M., RAPOLD, C., CALL, J., JANZEN, G., LEVINSON, S. C. (2006) Cognitive cladistics and cultural override in Hominid spatial cognition. *Proceedings of the National Academy of Sciences, 103*, 17568–17573.

HAWKINS, R. D., & KANDEL, E. R. (1984) Is there a cell-biological alphabet for simple forms of learning? *Psychological Review, 91*, 375–391.

HAXBY, J. V., GRADY, C. L., HORWIZ, B., UNGERLEIDER, L. G., MISHKIN, M., CARSON, R. E., HERSCOVITCH, P., SCHAPIRO, M. B., & RAPOPORT, S. I. (1990) Dissociation of object and spatial visual processing pathways in human extrastriate cortex. *Neurobiology, 88*, 1621–1625.

HAYDON, P. G. (2001) GLIA: listening and talking to the synapse. *Nature Reviews Neuroscience, 2*, 185–193.

HAYES, C. J., STEVENSON, R. J., & COLTHEART, M. (2007) Disgust and Huntington's disease. *Neuropsychologia, 45* (6), 1135–1151.

HAYES, S. (2005) *Get out of your mind and into your life: The new acceptance and commitment therapy*. Oakland, CA: New Harbinger Publications, Inc.

HAYNES, M. C. (in press) In the eye of the beholder: Perceptions of the centrality of merit in affirmative action and its psychological implications. *Journal of Organizational Psychology*.

HAYNES, M. C., & HEILMAN, M. E. (2004, August) Perceptions of affirmative action programs: What are they anyway? Paper presented at the Academy of Management meetings, New Orleans, LA.

HAYNES, S. G., & FEINLEIB, M. (1980) Women, work, and coronary heart disease: Prospective findings from the Framingham heart study. *American Journal of Public Health, 70*, 133–141.

HE, Z. J., & NAKAYAMA, K. (1992) Surfaces versus features in visual search. *Nature, 359*, 231–233.

HEATHERTON, T. F., WYLAND, C. L., MACRAE, N., DEMOS, K. E., DENNY, B. T. & KELLEY, W. M. (2006). Medial prefrontal activity differentiates self from close others. *SCAN, 1*, 18–25.

HEATH, R. G. (1972) Pleasure and brain activity in man. Deep and surface electroencephalograms during orgasm. *Journal of Nervous and Mental Disease, 154*, 3–18.

HEBB, D. O. (1955) Drives and the conceptual nervous system. *Psychological Review, 62*, 243–253.

HEBB, D. O. (1958) *A textbook of psychology* (1st ed). Philadelphia: Saunders.

HEBB, D. O. (1966) *A textbook of psychology* (2nd ed). Philadelphia: Saunders.

HEBB, D. O. (1982) Understanding psychological man: A state-of-the-science report. *Psychology Today, 16*, 52–53.

HEBL, M. R., KING, E. B., & LIN, J. (2004) The swimsuit becomes us all: ethnicity, gender, and vulnerability to self-objectification. *Personality and Social Psychology Bulletin, 30*, 1322.

HECHT, S., SHALER, S., & PIREENE, M. H. (1942) Energy, quanta, and vision. *Journal of General Physiology, 25*, 819–840.

HEGARTY, P. (2007) From genius inverts to gendered intelligence: Lewis Terman and the power of the norm. *History of Psychology, 10*(2), 132–155.

HEIDER, F. (1958) *The psychology of interpersonal relations*. New York: Wiley.

HEILMAN, M. E. (1994) Affirmative action: Some unintended consequences for working women. In B. Staw & L. L. Cummings (Eds.), *Research in organizational behavior* (Vol. 16, pp. 125–169). Greenwich, CT: JAI Press.

HEILMAN, M. E., & ALCOTT, V. B. (2001) What I think you think of me: Women's reactions to being viewed as beneficiaries of preferential selection. *Journal of Applied Psychology, 86*, 574–582.

HEILMAN, M. E., & BLADER, S. (2001) Assuming preferential selection when the admissions policy is unknown: The effects of gender rarity. *Journal of Applied Psychology, 86*, 188–193.

HEILMAN, M. E., & HAYNES, M. C. (2006) Affirmative action: Unintended adverse effects. In M. F. Karsten (Ed.), *Gender, race, and ethnicity in the workplace* (Vol. 2, pp. 1–24). Westport, CT: Greenwood Publishing Co.

HEILMAN, M. E., & WELLE, B. (2006) Disdvantaged by diversity: The effects of diversity goals on competence perception. *Journal of Applied Social Psychology, 36*, 1291–1319.

HEILMAN, M. E., BLOCK, C. J., & LUCAS, J. A. (1992) Presumed incompetent? Stigmatization and affirmative action efforts. *Journal of Applied Psychology, 77*, 536–544.

HEILMAN, M. E., BLOCK, C. J., & STATHATOS, P. (1997) The affirmative action stigma of incompetence: Effects of performance information ambiguity. *Academy of Management Journal, 40*, 603–625.

HEILMAN, M. E., MCCULLOUGH, S. F., & GILBERT, D. (1996) The other side of affirmative action. Reactions of non-beneficiaries to sex-based preferential selection. *Journal of Applied Psychology, 81*, 346–357.

HEINE, S. J., & LEHMAN, D. R. (1997) Culture, dissonance, and self-affirmation. *Personality and Social Psychology Bulletin, 23*, 389–400.

HELD, R. (1965) Plasticity in sensory motor systems. *Scientific American, 21*, 84–94.

HELGELAND, M. I., & TORGERSEN, S. (2004) Developmental antecedents of borderline personality disorder. *Comprehensive Psychiatry, 45*, 138–147.

HELGESON, V. S., REYNOLDS, K. A., & TOMICH, P. L. (2006) Meta-analytic review of benefit finding and growth. *Journal of Consulting and Clinical Psychology, 74*, 797–816.

HELLIGE, J. B. (1990) Hemispheric asymmetry. *Annual Review of Psychology, 41*, 55–80.

HELLIGE, J. B. (1993) Unity of thought and action: Varieties of interaction between left and right hemispheres. *Current Directions in Psychological Science, 2*, 21–25.

HEMMI, T. (1969) How we have handled the problem of drug abuse in Japan. In F. Sjoqvist & M. Tottie (Eds.), *Abuse of central stimulants*. New York: Raven Press.

HENDERSON, M. D., DE LIVER, Y., & GOLLWITZER, P. M. (2008) The effects of an implemental mind-set on attitude strength. *Journal of Personality and Social Psychology, 94* (3), 396–411.

HENRIKSSON, L., KARVONEN, J., SALMINEN-VAPARANTA, N., RAILO, H., & VANNI, S. (2012) Retinotopic maps, spatial tuning, and locations of human visual areas in surface coordinates characterized with multifocal and blocked fMRI designs. *PLoS ONE, 7*(5), e36859. doi:10.1371/journal.pone.0036859.

HENRY, B., & MOFFITT, T. E. (1997) Neuropsychological and neuroimaging studies of juvenile delinquency and adult criminal behavior. In D. M. Stoff, J. Breiling, & J. D. Maser (Eds.), *Handbook of antisocial personality disorder* (pp. 280–288). New York: Wiley.

HENSEL, H. (1973) Cutaneous thermoreceptors. In A. Iggo (Ed.), *Handbook of sensory physiology* (Vol. 2). Berlin: Springer-Verlag.

HERDT, G. H. (Ed.) (1984) *Ritualized homosexuality in Melanesia*. Berkeley: University of California Press.

HERING, E. (1878) *Outlines of a theory of the light sense* (L. M. Hurvich & D. Jameson, Trans.). Cambridge, MA: Harvard University Press.

HERMAN, C. P., & MACK, D. (1975) Restrained and unrestrained eating. *Journal of Personality, 43*, 647–660.

HERMAN, C. P., & POLIVY, J. (1980) Retrained eating. In A. J. Stunkard (Ed.), *Obesity*. Philadelphia: Saunders.

HERRNSTEIN, R. J., & MURRAY, C. (1994) *The bell curve: Intelligence and class structure in American life*. New York: Free Press.

HERZ, R. S. (2003) The effects of verbal context on olfactory perception. *Journal of Experimental Psychology: General, 132*, 595–606.

HETHERINGTON, E. M., & BRACKBILL, Y. (1963) Etiology and covariation of obstinacy, orderliness, and parsimony in young children. *Child Development, 34*, 919–943.

HETTEMA, J. M., NEALE, M. C., & KENDLER, K. S. (2001) A review and meta-analysis of the genetic epidemiology of anxiety disorders. *American Journal of Psychiatry, 158*, 1568–1578.

HEWSTONE, M. (1990) The "ultimate attribution error"? A review of the literature on intergroup causal attribution. *European Journal of Social Psychology, 20*, 311–335.

HEYES, C. M., & DAWSON, G. R. (1990) A demonstration of observational learning in rats using a bidirectional control. *Quarterly Journal of Experimental Psychology, 42B*, 59–71.

HIGGINS, E. T., & SPIEGEL, S. (2004) Promotion and prevention strategies for self-regulation: A motivated cognition perspective. In R. F. Baumeister & K. D. Vohs (Eds.), *Handbook of self-regulation: Research, theory, and applications* (pp. 171–187). New York: Guilford Press.

HIGHAM, P. A. (2007) No special K! A signal-detection framework for the strategic regulation of memory accuracy. *Journal of Experimental Psychology: General, 136*, 1–22. doi:10.1037/0096-3445.136.1.1

HIGHAM, P. A. (in press) Regulating accuracy on university tests with the plurality option. *Learning and Instruction*. doi:10.1016/j.learninstruc.2012.08.001

HIGHAM, P. A., & ARNOLD, M. M. (2007) How many questions should I answer? Using bias profiles to estimate optimal bias and maximum score on formula-scored tests. *European Journal of Cognitive Psychology, 19*, 718–742. doi:10.1080/09541440701326121

HILL, C., RUBIN, Z., & PEPLAU, L. A. (1976) Breakups before marriage: The end of 103 affairs. *Journal of Social Issues, 32*, 147–168.

HILT, L. M., MCLAUGHLIN, K. A., & NOLEN-HOEKSEMA, S. (2010) Examination of the response styles theory in a community sample of young adolescents. *Journal of Abnormal Child Psychology, 38*, 545–556.

HINDE, R. (1982) *Ethology: Its nature and relations with other sciences*. New York: Oxford University Press.

HINES, M., AHMED, S. F., & HUGHES, I. A. (2003) Psychological outcomes and gender-related development in complete androgen insensitivity syndrome. *Archives of Sexual Behavior, 32*, 93–101.

HINTSANEN, M., KIVIMAKI, M., ELOVAINIO, M., PULKKI-RABACK, L., KESKIVAARA, P., JUONALA, M., RAITAKARI, O. T., KELTIKANGAS-JARVINEN, L. (2005). Job strain and early atherosclerosis: The Cardiovascular Risk in Young Finns Study. *Psychosomatic Medicine*, 67, 740–747.

HIRSCH, J., & BATCHELOR, B. R. (1976) Adipose tissue cellularity and human obesity. *Clinical Endocrinology and Metabolism*, 5, 299–311.

HOEK, H. W., & VAN HOEKEN, D. (2003) Review of the prevalence and incidence of eating disorders. *International Journal of Eating Disorders*, 34, 383–396.

HOFFMAN, H. G. (2004) Virtual-reality therapy. *Scientific American*, 291 (2) (August), 58–65. And related video: http://www.sciencentral.com/articles/view.php3? language=english&type=&article_id=218392308.

HOFFMAN, H. G, PATTERSON, D. R., & CARROUGHER, G. J. (2000a) Use of virtual reality for adjunctive treatment of adult burn pain during physical therapy: A controlled study. *Clinical Journal of Pain*, 16, 244–250.

HOFFMAN, H. G., DOCTOR, J. N., PATTERSON, D. R., CARROUGHER, G. J., & FURNESS, T. A. III. (2000b) Use of virtual reality for adjunctive treatment of adolescent burn pain during wound care: A case report. *Pain*, 85, 305–309.

HOFFMAN, H. G., PATTERSON, D. R., SEIBEL, E., SOLTANI, M., JEWETT-LEAHY, L., & SHARAR, S. R. (2008) Virtual reality pain control during burn wound debridement in the hydrotank. *Clinical Journal of Pain*, 24, 299–304.

HOFFMAN, H. G., RICHARDS, T. L., CODA, B., BILLS, A. R., BLOUGH, D., RICHARDS, A. L., & SHARAR, S. R. (2004) Modulation of thermal pain-related brain activity with virtual reality: evidence from fMRI. *Neuroreport*, 15, 1245–1248.

HOFFMAN, H. G,, MEYER, W. J. III, RUSSEL, W. J,, FUCHS, H., COWEN, A,, WIECHMAN, S. A,, & PATTERSON, D. R. A (2012) Randomized, multisite study on virtual reality pain distraction in pediatric burn patients during phhysical therapy. *Supplement to Journal of Burn Care and Research*, 33, 156.

HOFLING, C. K., BROTZMAN, E., DALRYMPLE, S., GRAVES, N., & PIERCE, C. M. (1966) An experimental study in nurse-physician relationships. *Journal of Nervous and Mental Disease*, 143, 171–180.

HOHMANN, G. W. (1962) Some effects of spinal cord lesions on experienced emotional feelings. *Psychophysiology*, 3, 143–156.

HOLMES, D. S. (1974) Investigations of repression: Differential recall of material experimentally or naturally associated with ego threat. *Psychological Bulletin*, 81, 632–653.

HOLMES, D. S. (1984) Meditation and somatic arousal reduction: A review of the experimental evidence. *American Psychologist*, 39, 1–10.

HOLMES, T. H., & RAHE, R. H. (1967) The social readjustment rating scale. *Journal of Psychosomatic Research*, 11, 213–218.

HOLMBERG, S., THELIN, A., & STEIRNSTRÖM, E. L. (2004) Relationship of sense of coherence to other psychocodial indices. *European Journal of Psychological Assessment*, 20, 227–236.

HOLT, E. B. (1931) *Animal drive and the learning process*. New York: Holt.

HÖLZEL, B. K., LAZAR, S. W., GARD, T., SCHUMAN-OLIVIER, Z., VAGO, D. R., & OTT, U. (2011) How does mindfulness meditation work? Proposing mechanisms of action from a conceptual and neural perspective. *Perspectives on Psychological Science*, 6(6), 537–559.

HONG, Y., MORRIS, M. W., CHIU, C., BENET-MARTINEZ, V. (2000) Multicultural minds: A dynamic constructivist approach to culture and cognition. *American Psychologist*, 55, 709–720.

HONORTON, C. (1985) Meta-analysis of psi ganzfeld research: A response to Hyman. *Journal of Parapsychology*, 49, 51–91.

HOOD, B. M. (2009) *SuperSense: Why we believe in the unbelievable*. London: Sonstable & Robinson.

HOOLEY, J. M. (2007) Expressed emotion and relapse of psychopathology. *Annual Review of Clinical Psychology*, 3, 329–352.

HOPKINS, J. R. (1977) Sexual behavior in adolescence. *Journal of Social Issues*, 33, 67–85.

HORNSEY, M. J. (2008) Social identity theory and self categorization theory: A historical review. *Social and Personality Psychology Compass*, 2, 204–222.

HOROWITZ, F. D. (1974) Visual attention, auditory stimulation, and language stimulation in young infants. *Monographs of the Society for Research in Child Development*, 31, Serial No. 158.

HOROWITZ, M. J. (2003) *Treatment of stress response syndromes*. Arlington, VA: American Psychiatric Publishing.

HOVLAND, C., JANIS, I., & KELLEY, H. H. (1953) *Communication and persuasion*. New Haven, CT: Yale University Press.

HOWLAND, L. C., STORM, D. S., CRAWFORD, S. L., MA, Y., GORTMAKER, S. L., & OLESKE, J. M. (2007). Negative life events: Risk to health-related quality of life in children and youth with HIV infection. *JANAC: Journal of the Association of Nurses in AIDS Care, 18*, 3–11.

HOWLIN, P., GOODE, S., HUTTON, J., & RUTTER, M. (2004) Adult outcome for children with autism. *Journal of Child Psychology & Psychiatry*, 45, 212–229.

HSER, Y. I., ANGLIN, D., & POWERS, K. (1993) A 24-year follow-up of California narcotics addicts. *Archives of General Psychiatry*, 50, 577–584.

HU, S., PATTATUCCI, A. M., PATTERSON, C., LI, L., FULKER, D. W., CHERNY, S. S., KRUGLYAK, L., HAMER, D. H. (1995) Linkage between sexual orientation and chromosome Xq28 in males but not in females. *Nature Genetics*, 11, 248–256.

HUBEL, D. H., & WIESEL, T. N. (1968) Receptive fields and functional architecture of monkey striate cortex. *Journal of Physiology*, 195, 215–243.

HUESMANN, L. R., MOISE-TITUS, J., POLOSKI, C. L., & ERON, L. D. (2003) Longitudinal relations between children's exposure to TV violence and their aggressive and violent behavior in young adulthood 1977–1992. *Developmental Psychology*, 39, 2201–2221.

HUGUET, P., GALVAING, M. P., MONTEIL, J. M., & DUMAS, F. (1999) Social presence effects in the Stroop task: Further evidence for an attentional view of social facilitation. *Journal of Personality and Social Psychology*, 77, 1011–1025.

HULL, C. L. (1943) *Principles of behavior*. New York: Appleton-Century-Crofts.

HUMMEL, J. E., & BIEDERMAN, I. (1992) Dynamic binding in a neutral network for shape recognition. *Psychological Review*, 99, 480–517.

HUMPHREYS, K. (2004) *Circles of Recovery: Self-help organisations for addictions*. Cambridge: Cambridge University Press.

HUMPHREYS, K. (2006) The trials of Alcoholics Anonymous. *Addiction*, 101, 617–618.

HUMPHREYS, K., & MOOS, R. H. (1996) Reduced substance abuse-related health care cost among voluntary participants in Alcoholics Anonymous. *Psychiatric Services*, 47, 709–713.

HUMPHREYS, K., MOOS, R. H., & COHEN, C. (1997) Social and community resources and long-term recovery from treated and untreated alcoholism. *J. Studies Alcohol*, 58, 231–238.

HUNT, M. (1974) *Sexual behavior in the 1970's*. Chicago: Playboy Press.

HUNT, P. J., & HILLERY, J. M. (1973) *Social facilitation at different stages in learning*. Paper presented at the Midwestern Psychological Association Meetings, Cleveland.

HUNTER, I. M. L. (1974) *Memory*. Baltimore: Penguin.

HURVICH, L. M., & JAMESON, D. (1974) Opponent processes as a model of neural organizations. *American Psychologist*, 29, 88–102.

HUSELID, R. F., & COOPER, M. L. (1992) Gender roles as mediators of sex difference in adolescent alcohol use and abuse. *Journal of Health and Social Behavior*, 33, 348–362.

HUTTON, D. C., & BAUMEISTER, R. F. (1992) Self-awareness and attitude change: Seeing oneself on the central route to persuasion. *Personality and Social Psychology Bulletin*, 18, 68–75.

HYMAN, I. E., HUSBAND, T. H., & BILLINGS, F. G. (1995) False memories of childhood experiences. *Applied Cognitive Psychology*, 9, 181–197.

HYMAN, R. (1985) The ganzfield psi experiment: A critical appraisal. *Journal of Parapsychology*, 49, 3–49.

HYMAN, R. (1994) Anomaly or Artifact? Comments on Bem and Honorton. *Psychological Bulletin*, 115, 19–24.

HYMAN, R., & HONORTON, C. (1986) A joint communiqué: The psi ganzfeld controversy. *Journal of Parapsychology*, 50, 351–364.

IACOBONI, M. (2009) Imitation, empathy, and mirror neurons. *Annual Review of Psychology*, 60, 653–670.

IMADA, T., & ELLSWORTH, P. C. (2011) Proud Americans and lucky Japanese: Cultural differences in appraisal and corresponding emotion. *Emotion*, 11, 329–345.

IMADA, T., & KITAYAMA, S. (2010) Social eyes and choice justification: Culture and dissonance revisited. *Social Cognition*, 28, 589–608.

IMAI, M., & GENTER, D. (1997) A cross-linguistic study of early word meaning: Universal ontology and linguistic influence. *Cognition*, 62, 169–200.

IMPERATO-MCGINLEY, J., PETERSON, R. E., GAUTIER, T., & STURLA, E. (1979) Androgens and the evolution of male gender identity among male pseudohermaphrodites with 5 alpha reductase deficiency. *New England Journal of Medicine*, 300, 1233–1237.

INDEFREY, P., & LEVELT, W. J. M. (2004) The spatial and temporal signatures of word production components. *Cognition*, 92, 101–144.

INGLEDEW, D. K., & MCDONAGH, G. (1998) What coping functions are served when health behaviours are used as coping strategies. *Journal of Health Psychology*, 3, 195–213.

INGRAM, R. E., HAYES, A., & SCOTT, W. (2000) Empirically supported treatments: A critical analysis. In C. R. Snyder & R. Ingram (Eds.), *Handbook of psychological change* (pp. 40–60). New York: Wiley.

INSEL, T. R. (Ed.) (1984) *New findings in obsessive-compulsive disorder*. Washington, DC: American Psychiatric Press.

INTERNATIONAL NARCOTICS CONTROL BOARD (1998) *Psychotropic substances: Statistics for 1996*. New York: United Nations.

INTRAUB, H, & RICHARDSON, M. (1989) Wide-angle memories of close-up scenes. *Journal of Experimental Psychology: Learning, Memory, and Cognition*, 15, 179–187.

IRONSON, G., BALBIN, E., STUETZLE, R., FLETCHER, M. A., O'CLEIRIGH, C., LEURENCEAU, J. P., SCHNEIDERMAN, N., & SOLOMAN, G. (2005) Dispositional optimism and the mechanisms by which it predicts slower disease progression in HIV: Proactive behavior, avoidant coping, and depression. *International Journal of Behavioral Medicine*, 12, 86–97.

IRONSON, G., WYNINGS, C., SCHNEIDERMAN, N., BAUM, A., RODRIGUEZ, M. GREENWOOD, D., BENIGHT, C., ANTONI, M., LAPERRIER, A., HUANG, H. S., KLIMAS, N., & FLETCHER, M. A. (1997) Posttraumatic stress symptoms, intrusive thoughts, loss and immune function after Hurricane Andrew. *Psychosomatic Medicine*, 59, 128–141.

ISABELLA, R. A., & BELSKY, J. (1991) Interactional synchrony and the origins of infant-mother attachment: A replication study. *Child Development*, 62, 373–384.

ISEN, A. M. (2002) A role for neuropsychology in understanding the facilitating effects of positive affect on social behavior and cognitive processes. In C. R. Snyder & S. J. Lopez (Eds.), *Handbook of positive psychology* (pp. 528–540). Oxford: Oxford University Press.

ISEN, P. M. (1985) The asymmetry of happiness and sadness in effects on memory in normal college students. *Journal of Experimental Psychology: General*, 114, 388–391.

ISEN, P. M., SHALKER, T. E., CLARK, M., & KARP, L. (1978) Affect, accessibility of material in memory, and behavior: A cognitive loop? *Journal of Personality and Social Psychology*, 36, 1–12.

ISENBERG, D. J. (1986) Group polarization: A critical review and meta-analysis. *Journal of Personality and Social Psychology*, 50, 1141–1151.

ISOZAKI, M. (1984) The effect of discussion on polarization of judgments. *Japanese Psychological Research*, 26, 187–193.

ITO, T. A., & URLAND, G. R. (2003) Race and gender on the brain: Electrocortical measures of attention to the race and gender of multiply categorizable individuals. *Journal of Personality and Social Psychology*, 85, 616–626.

IVERSEN, A. C., FEAR, N. T., EHLERS, A., HUGHES, J. H., HULL, L., EARNSHAW, M., GREENBERG, N., RONA, R., WESSELY, S., & HOTOPF, M. (2008). Risk factors for post-traumatic stress disorder among UK Armed Forces personnel. *Psychological Medicine, 38*, 511–522.

IYER, A. (2008) Increasing the representation and status of women in employment: The effectiveness of affirmative action. In M. Barreto, M. Ryan, & M. Schmitt (Eds.), *The glass ceiling in the 21st century: Understanding barriers to gender equality* (pp. 257–276). Washington, DC: American Psychological Association.

JABLENSKY, A. (2000) Epidemiology of schizophrenia: The global burden of disease and disability. *European Archives of Clinical Psychiatry and Neuroscience*, 250, 274–285.

JACKS, J. Z., & CAMERON, K. A. (2003) Strategies for resisting persuasion. *Basic and Applied Social Psychology*, 25, 145–161.

JACKSON, L. A., SAMONA, R., MOOMAW, J., RAMSAY, L., MURRAY, C., SMITH, A., & MURRAY, L. (2007) What children do on the internet: Domains visited and their relationship to socio-demographic characteristics and academic performance. *CyberPsychology and Behavior*, 10, 182–290.

JACKSON, P. L., BRUNET, E., MELTZOFF, A. N., & DECETY, J. (2006) Empathy examined through the neural mechanisms involved in imagining how I feel versus how you feel pain. *Neuropsychologia*, 44 (5), 752–761.

JACOBS, W. J., & NADEL, W. (1985) Stress-induced recovery of fears and phobias. *Psychological Review*, 92, 512–531.

JACOBSON, C. M., & GOULD, M. (2008) Suicide in adolescence. In S. Nolen-Hoeksema & L. M. Hilt (Eds.), *Handbook of depression in adolescents* (pp. 207–236). NewYork: Routledge.

JACOBSON, S. W., & JACOBSON, J. L. (2000) Teratogenic insult and neurobehavioral function in infancy and childhood. In C. A. Nelson (Ed.), *The Minnesota symposia on child psychology*, Vol. 31: The effects of early adversity on neurobehavioral development (pp. 61–112). Mahwah, NJ: Erlbaum.

JAMES, W. (1884) What is an emotion? *Mind*, 188–205.

JAMES, W. (1890/1950) *Principles of psychology*. New York: Dover.

JAMIESON, J. P., & HARKINS, S. G. (2012) Distinguishing between the effects of stereotype priming and stereotype threat on math performance. *Group Processes & Intergroup Relations*, 15, 291–304.

JAMISON, K. R. (1995) *An unquiet mind*. New York: Knopf.

JAMISON, R. N., RAYMOND, S. A., SLAWSBY, E. A. NEDELJKOVIC, S. S., & KATZ, N. P. (1998) Opioid therapy for noncancer back pain: A randomized prospective study. *Spine*, 23, 2591–2600.

JANET, P. (1889) *L'automisme psychologigue*. Paris: Féix Alcan.

JANIS, I. L. (1982) *Groupthink: Psychological studies of policy decisions and fiascoes* (2nd ed.). Boston: Houghton Mifflin.

JANOFF-BULMAN, R. (1992) *Shattered assumptions: Toward a new psychology of trauma*. New York: Maxwell Macmillan International.

JAPUNITCH, S. J., ZEHNER, M. E., SMITH, S. S., JORENBY, D. E., VALDEZ, J. A., FIORE, M. C., BAKER, T. B., & GUSTAFSON, D. H. (2006) Smoking cessation via the Internet: A randomized clinical trial of an Internet intervention as adjuvant treatment in a smoking cessation intervention. *Nicotine and Tobacco Research*, 8, S59–S67.

JAZAIERI, H., JINPA, G. T., MCGONIGAL, K., ROSENBERG, E. L., FINKELSTEIN, J., SIMON-THOMAS, E., CULLEN, M., DOTY, J. R., GROSS, J. J., & GOLDIN, P. R. (2012, in press). Enhancing compassion: A randomized controlled trial of a compassion cultivation training program. *Journal of Happiness Studies*.

JENNET, B., GLEAVE, J., & WILSON, P. (1981) Brain death in three neurosurgical units. *British Medical Journal*, 282(6263), 533–539.

JENNINGS, D., AMABILE, T. M., & ROSS, L. (1982) Informal covariation assessment: Data-based vs. theory-based judgments. In A. Tversky, D. Kahneman, & P. Slovic (Eds.), *Judgment under uncertainty: Heuristics and biases*. New York: Cambridge University Press.

JEVINE COLEY, R., KUO, F. E., & SULLIVAN, W. C. (1997) Where does community grow? – The social context created by nature in urban public housing. *Environment & Behavior*, 31(4), 468–494.

JI, L., PENG, K., & NISBETT, R. E. (2000) Culture, control, and perception of relationship in the environment. *Journal of Personality and Social Psychology*, 78, 943–955.

JIN, S.-H., & CHUNG, C. K. (2012) Messages from the brain connectivity regarding neural correlates of consciousness. *Experimental Neurobiology*, 21, 113–122.

JOCKIN, V., MCGUE, M., & LYKKEN, D. T. (1996) Personality and divorce: A genetic analysis. *Journal of Personality and Social Psychology*, 71, 288–299.

JOHANSSON, G., VON HOFSTEN, C., & JANSON, G. (1980) Event perception. *Annual Review of Psychology*, 31, 27–63.

JOHNSON, E. J., & TVERSKY, A. (1983) Affect, generalization, and the perception of risk. *Journal of Personality and Social Psychology*, 45, 20–31.

JOHNSON, J., & NEWPORT, E. (1989) Critical period effects in second-language learning: The influence of maturational state on the acquisition of English as a second language. *Cognitive Psychology*, 21, 60–99.

JOHNSON, J. G., COHEN, P., DOHREND, D. P., LINK, D. G., & BROOK, J. S. (1990) The longitudinal investigation of social causation and social selection processes involved in association between socioeconomic status and psychiatric disorders. *Journal of Abnormal Psychology*, 108, 490–499.

JOHNSON, K. J., WAUGH, C. E., & FREDRICKSON, B. L. (2010) Smile to see the forest: Facially expressed positive emotions broaden cognition. *Cognition and Emotion*, 24, 299–321.

JOHNSON, M. H. (1997) *Developmental cognitive neuroscience: An introduction*. Oxford: Blackwell.

JOHNSON, M. H., & MORTON, J. (1991) *Biology and Cognitive Development: The Case of Face-Processing*. Oxford: Blackwell.

JOHNSON, M. K., HASHTROUDI, S., & LINDSAY, D. S. (1993) Source monitoring. *Psychological Bulletin*, 114, 3–28.

JOHNSON, M. K., RAYE, C. L., MITCHELL, K. J., TOURYAN, S. R., GREENE, E. J., & NOLENHOEKSEMA, S. (2006) Dissociating medial frontal and posterior cingulate activity during self-reflection. *Social Cognitive and Affective Neuroscience*, 1, 56–64.

JOHNSON, R. D., & DOWNING, L. L. (1979) Deindividuation and valence of cues: Effect on prosocial and antisocial behavior. *Journal of Personality and Social Psychology*, 37, 1532–1538.

JOHNSON-LAIRD, P. N. (1985) The deductive reasoning ability. In R. J. Sternberg (Ed.), *Human abilities: An information processing approach*. New York: Freeman.

JOHNSON-LAIRD, P. N. (1989) Mental models. In M. I. Posner (Ed.), *Foundations of cognitive science*. Cambridge, MA: MIT Press.

JOHNSON-LAIRD, P. N. (1997) Mental modules on the brain. A review of Steven Pinker's How the Mind Works. *Nature*, 389, 557–558.

JOINER, T. E. (1999) The clustering and contagion of suicide. *Current Directions in Psychological Science*, 8, 89–92.

JOINER, T. E., JR. (2002) Depression in its interpersonal context. In I. H. Gotlib & C. L. Hammen (Eds.), *Handbook of depression* (pp. 295–313). New York: Guilford Press.

JOINER, T, E., JR., BROWN, J. S., & WINGATE, L. R. (2005) The psychology and neurobiology of suicidal behavior. *Annual Review of Psychology*, 56, 287–314.

JONES, E. E. (1990) *Interpersonal perception*. New York: Freeman.

JONES, E. E. (1998) Major developments in five decades of social psychology. In D. T. Gilbert, S. T. Fiske, & L. Gardner (Eds.) *The Handbook of Social Psychology*. Vols. 1 and 2 (4th ed., pp. 3–57). New York: McGraw-Hill.

JONES, E. E., & HARRIS, V. A. (1967) The attribution of attitudes. *Journal of Experimental Social Psychology*, 3, 1–24.

JONES, E. E., ROCK, L., SHAVER, K. G., GOETHALS, G. R., & WARD, L. M. (1968) Pattern of performance and ability attribution: An unexpected primacy effect. *Journal of Personality and Social Psychology*, 9, 317–340.

JONES, J. T., PELHAM, B. W., CARVALLO, M., & MIRENBERG, M. C. (2004) How do I love thee? Let me count the Js: Implicit egotism and interpersonal attraction. *Journal of Personality and Social Psychology*, 87 (5), 665–683.

JULIEN, D., O'CONNOR, K. P., & AARDEMA, F. (2007) Intrusive thoughts, obsessions, and appraisals in obsessive-compulsive disorder: A critical review. *Clinical Psychology Review*, *27*, 366–383.

JULIEN, R. M. (1992) *A primer of drug action: A concise, nontechnical guide to the actions, uses, and side effects of psychoactive drugs* (6th ed.) New York: Freeman.

JUSSIM, L. (1991) Social perception and social reality: A reflection-construction model. *Psychological Review*, *98*, 54–73.

JUST, M. A., & CARPENTER, P. A. (1980) A theory of reading: From eye fixations to comprehension. *Psychological Review*, *87*, 329–354.

JUST, M. A., & CARPENTER, P. A. (1992) A capacity theory of comprehension: Individual differences in working memory. *Psychological Review*, *99*, 122.

KABAT-ZINN, J. (1996) *Full catastrophe living: How to cope with stress, pain and illness using mindfulness meditation*. London: Piatkus.

KAGAN, J. (1979) Overview: Perspectives on human infancy. In J. D. Osofsky (Ed.), *Handbook of infant development*. New York: Wiley-Interscience.

KAGAN, J. (1998) *Three seductive ideas*. Cambridge, MA: Harvard University Press.

KAGAN, J., & SNIDMAN, N. (1991) Temperamental factors in human development. *American Psychologist*, *46*, 856–862.

KAGAN, J., KEARSLEY, R. B., & ZELAZO, P. (1978) *Infancy: Its place in human development*. Cambridge, MA: Harvard University Press.

KAGAN, N. (1984) *The nature of the child*. New York: Basic Books.

KAHNEMAN, D. (2003) A perspective on judgment and choice: Mapping bounded rationality. *American Psychologist*, 58, 697–720.

KAHNEMAN, D. (2011) *Thinking, fast and slow*. New York: Farrar, Straus and Giroux.

KAHNEMAN, D., & TVERSKY, A. (1973) On the psychology of prediction. *Psychological Review*, 80, 237–251.

KAHNEMAN, D & AND TVERSKY, A. (1984) Choices, values, and frames. *American Psychologist*, *39*, 341–350.

KAHNEMAN, D., & TVERSKY, A. (1996) On the reality of cognitive illusions. *Psychological Review*, *103*, 582–591.

KALSO, E., EDWARDS, J. E., MOORE, R. A., & MCQUAY, H. J. (2004) Opioids in chronic non-cancer pain: Systematic review of efficacy and Safety. *Pain*, *112*, 372–380.

KAMEN-SIEGEL, L., RODIN, J., SELIGMAN, M. E., & DWYER, J. (1991) Explanatory style and cell-mediated immunity in elderly men and women. *Health Psychology*, *10*, 229–235.

KAMIN, L. J. (1974) *The science and politics of IQ*. Hillsdale, NJ: Erlbaum.

KAMINSKI, J., CALL, J., & FISCHER, J. (2004) Word learning in a domestic dog: Evidence for 'fast mapping'. *Science*, *304*, 1682–1683.

KAMMRATH, L. K., MENDOZA-DENTON, R., & MISCHEL, W. (2005) Incorporating if … then … personality signatures in person perception: Beyond the person–situation dichotomy. *Journal of Personality and Social Psychology*, *88* (4), 605–618.

KANDEL, E. R., SCHWARTZ, J. H., & JESSELL, T. M. (Eds.) (1991) *Principles of neural science* (3rd ed.). New York: Elsevier.

KANDEL, E. R., SCHWARTZ, J. H., & JESSELL, T. M. (2000) *Principles of neuroscience* (4th ed.). New York: McGraw-Hill.

KANNER, L. (1943) Autistic disturbances of affective contact. *Nervous Child*, *21*, 217–250.

KAPLAN, M. R., & MILLER, C. E. (1987) Group decision making and normative versus informational influence: Effects of type of issue and assigned decision rule. *Journal of Personality and Social Psychology*, *53*, 306–313.

KAPLAN, S., & KAPLAN, R. (1982) *Cognition and environment. Functioning in an uncertain world*. New York: Praeger.

KARMANOV, D., & HAMEL, R. (2008) Assessing the restorative potential of contemporary urban environment(s): Beyond the nature versus urban dichotomy. *Landscape and Urban Planning*, *86*, 115–125.

KARNO, M., & JENKINS, J. H. (1993) Cross-cultural issues in the course and treatment of schizophrenia. *Psychiatric Clinics of North America*, *16*, 339–350.

KARYLOWSKI, J. J. (1990) Social reference points and accessibility of trait-related information in self-other similarity judgments. *Journal of Personality and Social Psychology*, *58*, 975–983.

KASSIN, S. M. (1997) The psychology of confession evidence. *American Psychologist*, *52*, 221–233.

KATZ, L. C., & SHATZ, C. J. (1996) Synaptic activity and the construction of cortical circuits. *Science*, *274*, 1133.

KATZ, R., & WYKES, T. (1985) The psychological difference between temporally predictable and unpredictable stressful events: Evidence for information control theories. *Journal of Personality and Social Psychology*, *48*, 781–790.

KAUFMAN, S. B., & STERNBERG, R. J. (2007) Giftedness in the Euro-American Culture. In S. N. Phillipson & M. McCann (Eds.). *Conceptions of giftedness: Sociocultural perspectives*. (pp. 377–412). Mahwah, NJ: Erlbaum.

KAUFMAN, G. (1995, November) *Methylphenidate findings from New York's triplicate prescription data*. Presented at the annual conference of the National Association of State Controlled Substances Authorities.

KAUFMAN, L., & ROCK, I. (1989) The moon illusion thirty years later. In M. Hershenson (Ed.), *The moon illusion* (pp. 193–234). Hillsdale, NJ: Erlbaum.

KAWAKAMI, K., & DOVIDIO, J. F. (2001) The reliability of implicit stereotyping. *Personality and Social Psychology Bulletin*, *27*, 212–225.

KAY, P., & KEMPTON, W. (1984) *What is the Sapir-Whorf hypothesis?* American Anthropologist, *86*, 65–79.

KAZDIN, A. E., & WEISZ, J. R. (2003) *Evidence-based psychotherapies for children and adolescents*. New York: Guilford Press.

KEA, C. D., CAMPBELL-WHATLEY, G. D., & BRATTON, K. (2003) Culturally responsive assessment for African American students with learning and behavioral challenges. *Assessment for Effective Intervention*, *29*(1), 27–38.

KEIL, F. C. (1989) *Concepts, kinds, and cognitive development*. Cambridge, MA: MIT Press.

KEIL, F. C. (in press) *Developmental psychology*. New York: W.W. Norton.

KEIL, F. C., & BATTERMAN, N. A. (1984) Characteristic-to-defining shift in the development of word meaning. *Journal of Verbal Learning and Verbal Behavior*, *23*, 221–236.

KELLEY, H. H. (1950) The warm-cold variable in first impressions of persons. *Journal of Personality*, *18*, 431–439.

KELLEY, H. H. (1967) Attribution theory in social psychology. In D. Levine (Ed.), *Nebraska symposium on motivation* (Vol. 15). Lincoln: University of Nebraska Press.

KELLMAN, P. J. (1984) Perception of three-dimensional form by human infants. *Perception and Psychophysics*, *36*, 353–358.

KELLY, D. J., QUINN, P. C., SLATER, A. M., LEE, K., GIBSON, A., SMITH, M., GE, L., & PASCALIS, O. (2005) Three-month-olds, but not newborns, prefer own-race faces. *Developmental Science, 8*, F31–F36.

KELLY, D. J., LIU, S., GE L., QUINN, P. C., SLATER, A. M., LEE, K., LIU, Q., & PASCALIS, O. (in press) Cross-race preferences for same-race faces extend beyond the African versus Caucasian contrast in 3-month-old infants. *Infancy, 11*.

KELLY, G. A. (1955) *The psychology of personal constructs*. New York: Norton.

KELLY, S. J., DAY, N., & STREISSGUTH, A. P. (2000) Effects of prenatal alcohol exposure on social behavior in humans and other species. *Neurotoxicology & Teratology, 22*, 143–149.

KELTIKANGAS-JARVINEN, L., & RAVAJA, N. (2002) Relationships between hostility and physiological coronary heart disease risk factors in young adults: Moderating influence of perceived social support and sociability. *Psychology & Health, 17*, 173–190.

KENDLER, K. S., JACOBSON, K., MYER, J. M., & EAVES, L. J. (2008) A genetically informative developmental study of the relationship between conduct disorder and peer deviance in males. *Psychological Medicine, 38*, 1001–1071.

KENDLER, K. S., MYERS, J., PRESCOTT, C. A., & NEALE, M. C. (2001) The genetic epidemiology of irrational fears and phobias in men. *Archives of General Psychiatry, 58*, 257–265.

KENNEDY, J. E. (2003) The capricious, actively evasive, unsustainable nature of psi: a summary and hypotheses. *Journal of Parapsychology, 67*, 53–74.

KENNEDY, S. H., EVANS, K. R., KRUGER, S., MAYBERG, H. S., MEYER, J. H., MCCANN, S., ARIFUZZMAN, A. I, HOULE, S., & VACCARINO, F. J (2001) Changes in regional brain glucose metabolism measured with positron emission tomography after paroxetine treatment of major depression. *American Journal of Psychiatry, 158*, 899–905.

KENDRICK, D. T., & GUTIERRES, S. E. (1980) Contrast effects and judgments of physical attractiveness: When beauty becomes a social problem. *Journal of Personality and Social Psychology, 38*, 131–140.

KENRICK, D. T. (2006) Evolutionary psychology: Resistance is futile. *Psychological Inquiry, 17*, 102–109.

KENRICK, D. T., & KEEFE, R. C. (1992) Age preferences in mates reflect sex differences in human reproductive strategies. *Behavioral and Brain Sciences, 15*, 75–91.

KENRICK, D. T., GROTH, G. E., TROST, M. R., & SADALLA, E. K. (1993) Integrating evolutionary and social exchange perspectives on relationships: Effects of gender, self-appraisal, and involvement level on mate selection criteria. *Journal of Personality and Social Psychology, 64*, 951–969.

KENSHALO, D. R., NAFE, J. P., & BROOKS, B. (1961) Variations in thermal sensitivity. *Science, 134*, 104–105.

KEPHART, W. M. (1967) Some correlates of romantic love. *Journal of Marriage and the Family, 29*, 470–474.

KERNBERG, P. F. (1979) Psychoanalytic profile of the borderline adolescent. *Adolescent Psychiatry, 7*, 234–256.

KERNIS, M. H., & WHEELER, L. (1981) Beautiful friends and ugly strangers: Radiation and contrast effects in perception of same-sex pairs. *Journal of Personality and Social Psychology, 7*, 617–620.

KESSLER, R. C., STEIN, M. B., & BERGLUND, P. (1998) Social phobia subtypes in the National Comorbidity Survey. *American Journal of Psychiatry, 155*, 613–619.

KESSLER, R. C., BERGLUND, P., DEMLER, O., JIN, R., KORETZ, D., MERIKANGAS, K. R., RUSH, A. J., WALTERS, E. E., & WANG, P. S. (2003) The epidemiology of major depressive disorder: Results from the National Comorbidity Survey Replication (NCS-R). *Journal of the American Medical Association, 289*, 3095–3105.

KESSLER, R. C., CHIU, W. T., JIN, R., RUSCIO, A. M., SHEAR, K., & WALTERS, E. E. (2006) The epidemiology of panic attacks, panic disorder, and agoraphobia in the National Cormobidity Survey Replication. *Archives of General Psychiatry, 63*, 415–424.

KIECOLT-GLASER, J. K., KENNEDY, S., MALKOFF, S., FISHER, L., SPEICHER, C. E., & GLASER, R. (1988) Marital discord and immunity in males. *Psychosomatic Medicine, 50*, 213–229.

KIECOLT-GLASER, J. K., MCGUIRE, L., ROBLES, T. F., & GLASER, R. (2002) Emotions, morbidity, and mortality: New perspectives from psychoneuroimmunology. *Annual Review of Psychology, 53*, 83–107.

KIEHL, K. A., SMITH, A. M., HARE, R. D., MENDREK, A., FORSTER, B. B., BRINK, J., & LIDDLE, P. F. (2001) Limbic abnormalities in affective processing by criminal psychopaths as revealed by functional magnetic resonance imaging. *Biological Psychiatry, 50*, 677–684.

KIHLSTROM, J. F. (2007) Consciousness in hypnosis. In P. D. Zelazo, M. Moscovitch, & E. Thompson (Eds.), *The Cambridge handbook of consciousness* (pp. 445–479). New York: Cambridge University Press.

KIHLSTROM, J. F. (2008) The psychological unconscious. In O. John, R. Robins & L. A. Pervin (Eds.), *Handbook of Personality: Theory and Research* (3rd ed., pp. in press). New York: Guilford.

KIM, K. H. S., RELKIN, N. R., LEE, K.-M., & HIRSCH, J. (1997) Distinct cortical areas associated with native and second languages. *Nature, 388*, 171–174.

KIM, L. I. C. (1993) Psychiatric care of Korean-Americans. In A. C. Gaw (Ed.) *Culture, ethnicity and mental illness* (pp. 347–345). Washington, DC: Government Printing Office.

KING, B.M. (2006) The rise, fall, and resurrection of the ventromedial hypothalamus in the regulation of feeding behavior and body weight. *Physiology & Behavior, 87*, 221–244.

KINSEY, A. C., POMEROY, W. B., & MARTIN, C. E. (1948) *Sexual behavior in the human male*. Philadelphia: Saunders.

KINSEY, A. C., POMEROY, W. B., MARTIN, C. E., & GEBHARD, P. H. (1953) *Sexual behavior in the human female*. Philadelphia: Saunders.

KIRSCH, I., & LYNN, S. J. (1998) Dissociation theories of hypnosis. *Psychological Bulletin, 123*, 100–115.

KISHLINE, A. (1994) *Moderate drinking*. New York: Three Rivers Press.

KITAYAMA, S., MARKUS, H. R., & KUROKAWA, M. (2000) Culture, emotion, and well-being: Good feelings in Japan and the United States. *Cognition and Emotion, 14*, 93–124.

KITAYAMA, S., MESQUITA, B., & KARASAWA, M. (2006) Cultural affordances and emotional experience: Socially engaging and disengaging emotions in Japan and the United States. *Journal of Personality and Social Psychology, 91*, 890–903.

KITAYAMA, S., SNIBBE, A. C., MARKUS, H. R., SUZUKI, T., & KYOTO, J. (2004) Is there any "free" choice? Self and dissonance in two cultures. *Psychological Science, 15* (8), 527–533.

KLAHR, D. (1982) Nonmonotone assessment of monotone development: An information processing analysis. In S. Strauss (Ed.), *U-shaped behavioral growth*. New York: Academic Press.

KLATZKY, R. L., LEDERMAN, S. J., & METZGER, V. A. (1985) Identifying objects by touch: An expert system. *Perception and Psychophysics, 37,* 299–302.

KLEIN, S. B., & LOFTUS, J. (1988) The nature of self-referent encoding: The contributions of elaborative and organizational processes. *Journal of Personality and Social Psychology, 55,* 5–11.

KLEIN, S. B., LOFTUS, J., & BURTON, H. A. (1989) Two self-reference effects: The importance of distinguishing between self-descriptiveness judgments and autobiographical retrieval in self-referent encoding. *Journal of Personality and Social Psychology, 56,* 853–865.

KLINE, P. (1972) *Fact and fancy in Freudian theory.* London: Methuen.

KLING, K. C., HYDE, J. S., SHOWERS, C. J., & BUSWELL, B. N. (1999) Gender differences in self-esteem: A meta-analysis. *Psychological Bulletin, 125,* 70–500.

KLÜVER, H., & BUCY, P. C. (1937) "Psychic blindness" and other symptoms following temporal lobectomy in rhesus monkeys. *American Journal of Physiology, 119,* 352–353.

KNAPP, M., MANGALORE, R., & SIMON, J. (2004) The global costs of schizophrenia. *Schizophrenia Bulletin, 30,* 279–293.

KNITTLE, J. L., & HIRSCH, J. (1968) Effect of early nutrition on the development of rat epididymal fat pads: Cellularity and metabolism. *Journal of Clinical Investigation, 47,* 2091.

KOBASA, S. C. (1979) Stressful life events, personality, and health: An inquiry into hardiness. *Journal of Personality and Social Psychology, 37,* 1–11.

KOBASA, S. C., MADDI, S. R., & KAHN, S. (1982) Hardiness and health: A prospective study. *Journal of Personality and Social Psychology, 42,* 168–177.

KOENIGS, M., YOUNG, L., ADOLPHS, R., TRANEL, D., CUSHMAN, F., HAUSER, M., DAMASIO, A. (2007) Damage to the prefrontal cortex increases utilitarian moral judgements. *Nature, 446,* 908–911.

KOHLBERG, L. (1996) A cognitive-developmental analysis of children's sex role concepts and attitudes. In E. E. Maccoby (Ed.), *The development of sex differences* (pp. 82–173). Stanford, CA: Stanford University Press.

KOHLBERG, L. (1969) Stage and sequence: The cognitive-developmental approach to socialization. In D. A. Goslin (Ed.), *Handbook of socialization theory and research.* Chicago: Rand McNally.

KOK, B. E., COFFEY, K. A., COHN, M. A., CATALINO, L. I., VACHARKULKSEMSEK, T., ALGOE, S. B., BRANTLEY, M., & FREDRICKSON, B. L. (2012) *Positive emotions drive an upward spiral that links social connections and health.* Manuscript submitted for publication.

KOLATA, G. (2002, May) Runner's high? Endorphins? Fiction, some scientists say. *New York Times.*

KOLODNY, J. A., (1994) Memory processes in classification learning. *Psychological Science, 5,* 164–169.

KOOB, G. F., & BLOOM, F. E. (1988) Cellular and molecular mechanisms of drug dependence. *Science, 242,* 715–723.

KOOB, G. F., & LE MOAL, M. (1997) Drug abuse: Hedonic homeostatic dysregulation. *Science, 278,* 52–58.

KOOB, G. F., LE MOAL, M. (2008) Addiction and the brain antireward system. Annual Review of Psychology, *59,* 29–53.

KORNHABER, M., & GARDNER, H. (1991) Critical thinking across multiple intelligences. In S. Maclure & P. Davies (Eds.), *Learning to think: Thinking to learn.* Oxford: Pergamon.

KOSAMBI, D. D., & KOSAMBI, M. (1967) Living prehistory in India. *Scientific American, 215,* 105.

KOSSLYN, S. M. (1983) *Ghosts in the mind's machine.* New York: Norton.

KOSSLYN, S. M. (1988) Aspects of a cognitive neuroscience of mental imagery: *Science, 240,* 1621–1626.

KOSSLYN, S. M., & KOENIG, O. (1992) *Wet mind: The new cognitive neuroscience.* New York: Free Press.

KOSSLYN, S. M., BALL, T. M., & REISER, B. J. (1978) Visual images preserve metric spatial information: Evidence from studies of image scanning. *J. Exp. Psychol. Hum. Percept. Perform., 4*(1), 47–60.

KOSSLYN, S. M., ALPERT, N. M., THOMPSON, W. L., MALJKOVIC, V., WEISE, S. B., CHABRIS, C. F., HAMILTON, S. E., RAUCH, S. L., & BUONANNO, F. S. (1993) Visual mental imagery activates topographically organized visual cortex. *Journal of Cognitive Neuroscience, 5,* 263–287.

KOUMIMTSIDIS, C., REYNOLDS, M., DRUMMOND, C., DAVIS, P., SELL, L., & TARRIER, N. (2007) *Cognitive-behavioural therapy in the treatment of addiction.* Wiley.

KRAFT, T. L., & PRESSMAN, S. D. (in press) Grin and bear it: The influence of manipulated facial expression on the stress response. *Psychological Science.*

KRAKOWSKI, M. (2003) Violence and serotonin: Influence of impulse control, affect regulation, and social functioning. *Journal of Neuropsychiatry and Clinical Neurosciences, 15,* 294–305.

KRAUS, G., & REYNOLDS, D. J. (2001) The "A-B-C's" of the cluster B's: Identifying, understanding and treating cluster B personality disorders. *Clinical Psychology Review, 21,* 345–373.

KRING, A. (2000) Gender and anger. In A. H. Fischer (Ed.), *Gender and emotion: Social psychological perspectives* (pp. 211–231). New York: Cambridge University Press.

KRINGELBACH, M. L., & BERRIDGE, K. C. (2012) The joyful mind. *Scientific American, 307*(2), 40–45.

KUHL, P. K. (2000) A new view of language acquisition. *Proceedings of the National Academy of Sciences, 97,* 11850–11857.

KUHN, C., SWARTZWELDER, S., & WILSON, W. (1998) *Buzzed: The straight facts about the most used and abused drugs.* New York: Norton.

KUIKEN, D., & SIKORA, S. (1993) The impact of dreams on waking thoughts and feelings. In A. Moffitt, M. Kramer, and Hoffman, R. (Eds.), *The Functions of Dreaming* (pp. 419–476). New York: State University of New York Press.

KUIPER, N. A., & ROGERS, T. B. (1979) Encoding of personal information: Self-other differences. *Journal of Personality and Social Psychology, 37,* 499–514.

KULICK, D. (1998) *Travesti: Sex, gender, and culture among Brazilian transgendered prostitutes.* Chicago: University of Chicago Press.

KUMAR, M. S., MURHEKAR, M. V., HUTIN, Y., SUBRAMANIAN, T., RAMACHANDRAN, V., & GUPTE, M. D. (2007) Prevalence of posttraumatic stress disorder in a coastal fishing village in Tamil Nadu, India, after the December 2004 tsunami. *American Journal of Public Health, 97,* 99–101.

KUMAR, V., ABBAS, A. K., FAUSTO, N., & ASTER, J. C. (2009) *Robbins and Cotran Pathologic Basis of Disease* (8th ed.). Philadelphia, PA: Elsevier Health Sciences Division.

KUMMER, H., & GOODALL, J. (1985) Conditions of innovative behaviour in primates. *Philosophical Transactions of the Royal Society of London. Series B, 308,* 1135.

KUO, F. E. (2001a) Coping with povertry – Impacts of environment and attention in the inner city. *Environment & Behavior, 33*(1), 5–34.

KUO, F. E., & SULLIVAN, W. C. (2001b) Environment and crime in the inner city – Does vegetation reduce crime? *Environment & Behavior, 33*(3), 343–367.

KUO, F. E., & SULLIVAN, W. C. (2001c) Aggression and violence in the city – Effects of environment via mental fatigue. *Environment & Behavior, 33*(4), 543–571.

KUO, F. E., BACAICOA, M., & SULLIVAN, W. C. (1998a) Transforming inner-city landscapes – Trees, sense of safety, and preference, *Environment & Behavior,* Vol. 30 (1), 28–59.

KURTINES, W., & GREIF, E. B. (1974) The development of moral thought: Review and evaluation of Kohlberg's approach. *Psychological Bulletin, 81*, 453–470.

LA BERGE, D. (1995) *Attentional processing: The brain's art of mindfulness.* Cambridge, MA: Harvard University Press.

LABERGE, S. (2007) Lucid dreaming. In D. Barrett & P. McNamara (Eds.), *The new science of dreaming,* Vol. 2: Content, recall, and personality correlates (pp. 307–328). Westport, CT: Praeger Perspectives.

LADEFOGED, P. (2005) *A Course in Phonetics* (5th ed.). Boston: Thomson/Wadsworth.

LAI, T., CHANG, C. CONNOR, K, M., LEE, L., DAVIDSON, J. R. T. (2004). Full and partial PTSD among earthquake survivors in rural Taiwan. *Journal of Psychiatric Research, 38*, 313–322.

LAKOFF, G. (1987) *Women, fire, and dangerous things.* Chicago: University of Chicago Press.

LAM, D., & WONG, G. (2005) Prodromes, coping strategies, and psychological interventions in bipolar disorders. *Clinical Psychology Review, 25*, 1028–1042.

LAMM, C., BATSON, C. D., DECETY, J. (2007) The neural substrate of human empathy: Effects of perspective-taking and cognitive appraisal. *Journal of Cognitive Neuroscience, 19* (1), 42–58.

LAND, E. H. (1986) The retinex theory of color vision. *Scientific American, 237*, 108–128.

LANGER, E. J. (1975) The illusion of control. *Journal of Personality and Social Psychology, 32*, 311–328.

LAPIERE, R. (1934) Attitudes versus actions. *Social Forces, 13*, 230–237.

LARKIN, J. H., MCDERMOTT, J., SIMON, D. P., & SIMON, H. A. (1980) Expert and novice performance in solving physics problems. *Science, 208*, 1335–1342.

LARSON, R., & RICHARDS, M. H. (1991) Daily companionship in late childhood and early adolescence: Changing developmental contexts. *Child Development, 62*, 284–300.

LATANÉ, B., & DARLEY, J. M. (1968) Group inhibition of bystander intervention in emergencies. *Journal of Personality and Social Psychology, 10*, 215–221.

LATANÉ, B., & DARLEY, J. M. (1970) *The unresponsive bystander: Why doesn't he help?* New York: Appleton-Century-Crofts.

LATANÉ, B., NIDA, S. A., & WILSON, D. W. (1981) The effects of group size on helping behavior. In J. P. Rushton & R. M. Sorrentino (Eds.), *Altruism and helping behavior: Social personality, and developmental perspectives.* Hillsdale, NJ: Erlbaum.

LATANÉ, B., & RODIN, J. (1969) A lady in distress: Inhibiting effects of friends and strangers on bystander intervention. *Journal of Experimental and Social Psychology, 5*, 189–202.

LAUDENSLAGER, M. L., RYAN, S. M., DRUGAN, R. C., HYSON, R. L., & MAIER, S. F. (1983) Coping and immunosuppression: Inescapable but not escapable shock suppresses lymphocyte proliferation. *Science, 221*, 568–570.

LAUMANN, E. O., GAGNON, J. H. MICHAEL, R. T., & MICHAELS, S. (1994) *The social organization of sexuality: Sexual practices in the United States.* Chicago: University of Chicago Press.

LAWRENCE, N. S., JOLLANT, F., O'DALY, O., ZELAYA, F., & PHILIPS, M. L. (2009) Distinct roles of prefrontal cortical subregions in the Iowa Gambling Task. *Cerebral Cortex, 19*, 1134–1143.

LAZARUS, R. S. (1991a) Cognition and motivation in emotion. *American Psychologist, 46*, 352–367.

LAZARUS, R. S. (1991b) *Emotion and adaptation.* New York: Oxford University Press.

LAZARUS, R. S., & FOLKMAN, S. (1984) *Stress, appraisal, and coping.* New York: Springer.

LEA, M., SPEARS, R., & DE GROOT, D. (2001) Knowing me knowing you: Anonymity effects on social identity processes within groups. *Personality and Social Psychology Bulletin, 27*, 526–537.

LE BON, G. (1895) *The crowd.* London: Ernest Benn.

LEDOUX, J. E., & PHELPS, E. A. (2000) Emotional networks in the brain. In M. Lewis & J. M. Haviland-Jones (Eds.), *Handbook of emotions* (2nd ed., pp. 157–172). New York: Guilford.

LEE, N., MIKESELL, L., JOAQUIN, A. D. L., MATES, A. W., & SCHUMANN, J. H. (2009) *The interactional instinct: The evolution and acquisition of language.* Oxford: Oxford University Press.

LEHMAN, B. J., TAYLOR, S. E., KIEFE, C. I., SEEMAN, T. E. (2009). Relationship of early life stress and psychological functioning to blood pressure in the CARDIA study. *Health Psychology, 28*, 338–346.

LEIPPE, M. R. (1980) Effects of integrative memorial and cognitive processes on the correspondence of eyewitness accuracy and confidence. *Law and Human Behavior, 4*, 261–274.

LENNEBERG, E. H. (1967) *Biological foundations of language.* New York: Wiley.

LENNON, M. C., & ROSENFIELD, S. (1992) Women and mental health: The interaction of job and family conditions. *Journal of Health and Social Behavior, 33*, 316–327.

LEO, R. (1996) Miranda's revenge: Police interrogation as a confidence game. *Law and Society Review, 30*, 259–288.

LEPPER, M. R., & GREEN, D. (1975) Turning play into work: Effects of adult surveillance and extrinsic rewards on children's intrinsic motivation. *Journal of Personality and Social Psychology, 31*, 479–486.

LERNER, J. S., & KELTNER, D. (2001) Fear, anger, and risk. *Journal of Personality and Social Psychology, 81*, 146–159.

LERNER, J. S., SMALL, D. A., & LOEWENSTEIN, G. (2004) Heart strings and purse strings: Carryover effects of emotions on economic decisions. *Psychological Science, 15*, 337–341.

LESERMAN, J., JACKSON, E. D., PETITTO, J. M., GOLDEN, R. N., SILVA, S. G., PERKINS, D. O., CAI, J., FOLDS, J. D., EVANS, D. L. (1999). Progression to AIDS: The effects of stress, depressive symptoms, and social support. Psychosomatic Medicine, 61, 397–406.

LESERMAN, J., PENCE, B. W., WHETTEN, K., MUGAVERO, M. J., THEILMAN, N. M., SWARTZ, M. S., STANGL, D. (2007). Relation of lifetime trauma and depressive symptoms to mortality in HIV. *The American Journal of Psychiatry, 164*, 1707–1713.

LESERMAN, J., PETITTO, J. M., GU, H., GAYNES, B. N., BARROSO, J. GOLDEN, R. N., PERKINS, D. O., FOLDS, J. D., EVANS, D. L. (2002). Progression to AIDS, a clinical AIDS condition and mortality: Psychosocial and physiological predictors. *Psychological Medicine, 32*, 1059–1073.

LESERMAN, J. (2008). Role of depression, stress, and trauma in HIV disease progression. *Psychosomatic Medicine, 70*, 539–545.

LESERMAN, J., PETITTO, J. M., GOLDEN, R. N., GAYNES, B. N., GU, H., *et al.* (2008) Impact of stressful life events, depression, social support, coping, and cortisol on progression to AIDS. *American Journal of Psychiatry, 157*, 1221–1228.

LEVIN, R., & NIELSEN, T. A. (2007) Disturbed dreaming, posttraumatic stress disorder, and affect distress: A review and neurocognitive model. *Psychological Bulletin, 133*, 482–528.

LEVINE, M., PROSSER, A., EVANS, D.& REICHER, S. (2005) Identity and emergency intervention: How social group membership and inclusiveness of group boundaries shapes non-helping behavior. *Personality and Social Psychology Bulletin, 31* (4), 443–453.

LEVINE, R. V., REYSEN, S., & GANZ, E. (2008) The kindness of strangers revisited: A comparison of 24 U.S. cities. *Social Indicators Research, 85*, 461–481.

LEVENSON, R. W. (1992) Autonomic nervous system differences among emotions. *Psychological Science, 3*, 23–27.

LEVENSON, R. W. (1994) Human emotions: A functional view. In P. Ekman & R. Davidson (Eds.), *The nature of emotion: Fundamental questions* (pp. 123–126). New York: Oxford University Press.

LEVENSON, R. W. (2003a) Autonomic specificity and emotion. In R. J. Davidson, K. R. Scherer, & H. H. Goldsmith (Eds.), *Handbook of affective sciences* (pp. 212–224). New York: Oxford University Press.

LEVENSON, R. W. (2003b) Blow, sweat, and fears: The auotonomic architecture of emotion. In P. Ekman *et al.* (Eds.), *Emotions inside out: 130 years after Darwin's The Expression of the Emotions in Man and Animals* (pp. 348–366). New York: New York Academy of Sciences.

LEVENSON, R. W. (2007) Emotion elicitation with neurological patients. In J. A. Coan and J. J. B. Allen (Eds.), *The handbook of emotion elicitation and assessment* (pp. 158–168). New York: Oxford University Press.

LEVENSON, R. W. (2011) Basic emotion questions. *Emotion Review, 3*, 379–386.

LEVENSON, R. W., EKMAN, P., & FRIESEN, W. V. (1990) Voluntary facial action generates emotion-specific nervous system activity. *Psychophysiology, 27*, 363–384.

LEVENSON, R. W., EKMAN, P., HEIDER, K., & FRIESEN, W. V. (1992) Emotion and autonomic nervous system activity in an Indonesian culture. *Journal of Personality and Social Psychology, 62*, 927–988.

LEVINE, M. (1999) Rethinking bystander nonintervention. Social categorization and the evidence of witnesses at the James Bulger murder trial. *Human Relations, 52*, 1133–1155.

LEVINE, M., PROSSER, A., EVANS, D., & REICHER, S. (2005) Identity and emergency intervenion: How social group membership and inclusiveness of group boundaries shape helping behaviour. *Personality and Social Psychology Bulletin, 31*, 443–453.

LEVINSON, S. C. (2003) *Space in language and cognition: Explorations in cognitive diversity*. Cambridge: Cambridge University Press.

LEVY, J. (1985) Right brain, left brain: Facts and fiction. *Psychology Today, 19*, 38–44.

LEVY, S. M., & HEIDEN, I., (1991) Depression, distress and immunity: Risk factors for infectious disease. *Stress Medicine, 7*, 45–51.

LEWIS, M., ALESSANDRI, S. M., & SULLIVAN, M. W. (1992) Differences in shame and pride as a function of children's gender and task difficulty. *Child Development, 63*, 630–638.

LEYTON, M. (2010) The neurobiology of desire: Dopamine and the regulation of mood and motivational states in humans. In M. L. Kringelbach & K. C. Berridge (Eds.), *Pleasures of the Brain* (pp. 222–243). Oxford: Oxford University Press.

LI, P., ABARBANELLI, L., & PAPAFRAGOU, A. (2005) Spatial reasoning skills in Tenejapan Mayans. *Proceedings from the 27th Annual Meeting of the Cognitive Science Society*. Hillsdale, NJ: Erlbaum.

LI, P., DUNHAM, Y., & CAREY, S. (in press). Of substance: the nature of language effects on entity construal. To appear in *Cognitive Psychology*.

LIBERMAN, A. M., COOPER, F., SHANKWEILER, D., & STUDERT-KENNEDY, M. (1967) Perception of the speech code. *Psychological Review, 74*, 431–459.

LIEBERMAN, M. D., OCHSNER, K. N., GILBERT, D. T., & SCHACTER, D. L. (2001) Attitude change in amnesia and under cognitive load. *Psychological Science, 12*, 135–140.

LEIBLUM, S. R., & ROSEN, R. C. (2000) *Principles and practice of sex therapy*, 3rd ed. New York: Guilford Press.

LILIENFELD, S. O., WOOD, J. W., & GARB, H. N. (2000) The scientific status of projective techniques. *Psychological science in the public interest, 1*, 27–66.

LINDQUIST, K. A. (in press) Emotions emerge from more basic psychological ingredients: A modern psychological constructionist approach. *Emotion Review*.

LINDQUIST, K. A., & BARRETT, L. F. (2008) Constructing emotion: The experience of fear as a conceptual act. *Psychological Science, 19*, 898–898.

LINDQUIST, K. A., & BARRETT, L. F. (2012) A functional architecture of the human brain: Insights from the science of emotion. *Trends in Cognitive Sciences, 16*, 533–540.

LINDQUIST, K. A., BARRETT, L. F., BLISS-MOREAU, E., & RUSSELL, J. A. (2006) Language and the perception of emotion. *Emotion, 6*, 125–138.

LINDQUIST, K. A., SIEGEL, E. H., QUIGLEY, K., & BARRETT, L. F. (in press) The hundred year emotion war: Are emotions natural kinds or psychological constructions? Comment on Lench, Bench and Flores (2011). *Psychological Bulletin*.

LINDQUIST, K. A., WAGER, T. D., KOBER, H., BLISS-MOREAU, E., BARRETT, L. F. (2012) The brain basis of emotion: A meta-analytic review. *Behavioral and Brain Sciences, 35*, 121–202.

LINEHAN, M. M., COCHRAN, B. N., & KEHRER, C. A. (2001) Dialectical behavior therapy for borderline personality disorder. In D. H. Barlow (Ed.), *Clinical Handbook of Psychological Disorders: A Step-by-step Treatment Manual*. New York: Guilford Press.

LINNET, J., MOURIDSEN, K., PETERSON, E., MØLLER, A., DOUDET, D. J., & GJEDDE, A. (2012) Striatal dopamine release codes uncertainty in pathological gambling. *Psychiatry Research: Neuroimaging. 204*(1), 55–60.

LISZKOWSKI, U., CARPENTER, M., HENNING, A., STRIANO, T., & TOMASELLO, M. (2004) Twelve-month-olds point to share attention and interest. *Developmental Science, 7*, 297–07.

LIU, L., & ANCOLI-ISRAEL, S. (2006) Insomnia in the older adult. *Sleep Medicine Clinics, 1*, 409–421.

LIVINGSTONE, M., & HUBEL, D. (1988) Segregation of form, color, movement, and depth: Anatomy, physiology, and perception. *Science, 240*, 740–750.

LOFTUS, E., & KETCHAM, K. (1994) *The myth of repressed memory*. New York: St. Martin's Press.

LOFTUS, E. F. (2005) Planting misinformation in the human mind: A 30-year investigation of the malleability of memory. *Learning and Memory, 12*, 361–366.

LOFTUS, E. F., & LOFTUS, G. R. (1980) On the permanence of stored information in the human brain. *American Psychologist, 35*, 409–420.

LOFTUS, E. F., & PALMER, J. C. (1974) Reconstruction of automobile destruction. *Journal of Verbal Learning and Verbal Behavior, 13*, 585–589.

LOFTUS, E. F., & PICKRELL, J. E. (1995) The formation of false memories. *Psychiatric Annals, 25*, 720–725.

LOFTUS, E. F., COAN, J. A., & PICKRELL, J. E. (1996) Manufacturing false memories using bits of reality. In L. Reder (Ed.), *Implicit memory and metacognition* (pp. 195–220). Mahwah, NJ: Erlbaum.

LOFTUS, E. F., LOFTUS, G. R., & MESSO, J. (1987) Some facts about "weapon focus". *Law and Human Behavior, 11*, 55–62.

LOFTUS, E. F., SCHOOLER, J. W., & WAGENAAR, W. A. (1985) The fate of memory: Comment on McCloskey and Zaragoza. *Journal of Experimental Psychology: General, 114*, 375–380.

LOFTUS, G. R. (1972) Eye fixations and recognition memory for pictures. *Cognitive Psychology, 3*, 525–551.

LOFTUS, G. R. (1985) Size illusion, distance illusion and terrestrial passage. *Journal of Experimental Psychology: General, 114*, 121–123.

LOFTUS, G. R., & HARLEY, E. M. (2005) Why is it easier to recognize someone close than far away? *Psychonomic Bulletin & Review, 12*, 43–65.

LOFTUS, G. R., & MACKWORTH, N. H. (1978) Cognitive determinants of fixation location during picture viewing. *Journal of Experimental Psychology: Human Perception and Performance, 4*, 565–572.

LOGUE, A. W. (1991) *The psychology of eating and drinking: An introduction* (2nd ed.). New York: Freeman.

LONG, P. W. (1996) *Internet mental health*. http://www.mentalhealth.com/.

LOOMIS, A. L., HARVEY, E. N., & HOBART, G. A. (1937) Cerebral states during sleep as studied by human potentials. *Journal of Experimental Psychology, 21*, 127–144.

LOPEZ, A., ATRAN, S., MEDIN, D. L., COOLEY, J., & SMITH, E. E. (1997) The tree of life: Universals of folk biological taxonomies and inductions. *Cognitive Psychology, 32*, 251–295.

LOPEZ, S. R., & GUARNACCIA, P. J. (2000) Cultural psychopathology: Uncovering the social world of mental illness. *Annual Review of Psychology, 51*, 571–598.

LORD, C. G. (1980) Schemas and images as memory aids: Two modes of processing social information. *Journal of Personality and Social Psychology, 38*, 257–269.

LOVE, R. E., & GREENWALD, A. C. (1978) Cognitive responses to persuasion as mediators of opinion change. *Journal of Social Psychology, 104*, 231–241.

LOWE, M. R., & BUTRYN, M. L. (2007) Hedonic hunger: A new dimension of appetite? *Physiology & Behavior, 91*, 432–439.

LOWE, R., VEDHARA, K., BENNETT, P., BROOKES, E., GALE, L., MUNNOCH, K., SCHREIBER-KOUNINE, C., FOWLER, C., RAYTER, Z., SAMMON, A., & FARNDON, J. (2003) Emotion-related primary and secondary appraisals, adjustment and coping: Associations in women awaiting breast disease diagnosis. *British Journal of Health Psychology, 8*, 377–391.

LOZOWICK, Y. (2002) *Hitler's bureaucrats: The Nazi security police and the banality of evil* (H. Walzman, trans). London: Continuum.

LUBINSKI, D. (2000) Scientific and social significance of assessing individual differences: "Sinking shafts at a few critical points". *Annual Reviews of Psychology, 51*, 405–444.

LUCHINS, A. (1957) Primacy-recency in impression formation. In C. L. Hovland (Ed.), *The order of presentation in persuasion*. New Haven: Yale University Press.

LUNA, K., & MARTÍN-LUENGO, B. (2012) Improving the accuracy of eyewitnesses in the presence of misinformation with the plurality option. *Applied Cognitive Psychology, 26*, 387–693. doi:10.1002/acp.2845

LUNA, K., HIGHAM, P. A., & MARTÍN-LUENGO, B. (2011) The regulation of memory accuracy with multiple answers: The plurality option. *Journal of Experimental Psychology: Applied, 17*, 148–158. doi:10.1037/a0023276

LUSTBADER, D., O'HARA, D., WIJDICKS, E. F. M., TAJIK, W., YING, A., BERG, E., & GOLDSTEIN, M. (2011) Second brain death examination may negatively affect organ donation. *Neurology, 76*(2), 119–124.

LUTZ, A., DUNNE, J. D., & DAVIDSON, R. J. (2007) Meditation and the neuroscience of consciousness: An introduction. In P. D. Zelazo, M. Moscovitch, & E. Thompson (Eds.), *The Cambridge handbook of consciousness* (pp. 499–551). New York: Cambridge University Press.

LYKKEN, D. T. (1982) Research with twins: The concept of emergenesis. *The Society for Psychophysiological Research, 19*, 361–373.

LYKKEN, D. T., MCGUE, M., TELLEGEN, A., & BOUCHARD, T. J., JR. (1992) Emergenesis: Genetic traits that may not run in families. *American Psychologist, 47*, 1565–1577.

LYMAN, R. (1997, April 15) Michael Dorris dies at 52: Wrote of his son's suffering. *New York Times*, p. 24.

LYNN, S. J., KIRSCH, I., BARABASZ, A., CARDENA, E., & PATTERSON, D. (2000) Hypnosis as an empirically supported clinical intervention: The state of the evidence and a look to the future. *International Journal of Clinical and Experimental Hypnosis, 48*, 239–259.

LYUBOMIRSKY, S., & NOLEN-HOEKSEMA, S. (1995) Effects of self-focused rumination on negative thinking and interpersonal problem solving. *Journal of Personality and Social Psychology, 69*, 176–190.

LYUBOMIRSKY, S., KING, L., & DIENER, E. (2005) The benefits of frequent positive affect: Does happiness lead to success? *Psychological Bulletin, 131*, 803–855.

MAANI, C., HOFFMAN, H. G., DESOCIO, P. A., MORROW, M., GALIN, C., MAGULA, J., MAIERS, A., & GAYLORD, K. (2008) Pain control during wound care for combat-related burn injuries using custom articulated arm mounted virtual reality goggles. *Journal of CyberTherapy and Rehabilitation, 1*, 193–198. See also, related video: http://www.sciencentral.com/video/2008/11/11/virtual-reality-helps-war-heroes-recover-from-burns/.

Maani, C. V., Hoffman, H. G., Morrow, M., Maiers, A., Gaylord, K., McGhee, L. L., & DeSocio, P. A. (2011) Virtual reality pain control during burn wound debridement of combat-related burn injuries using robot-like arm mounted VR goggles. *Journal of Traumatic Stress, 71*, S125–30.

MAAS, J., DILLEN, S., VERHEIJ, R. A., & GROENEWEGEN, P. P. (2009) Social contacts as a possible mechanism behind the relation between green space and health. *Health & Place, 15,* 586–595.

MAAS, J. B. (1998) *Power sleep: The revolutionary program that prepares your mind for peak performance.* New York: HarperCollins.

MAASS, A., & CLARK, R. D., III (1984) Hidden impact of minorities: Fifteen years of minority influence research. *Psychological Bulletin, 95,* 428–450.

MACAULAY, J. (1970) A shill for charity. In J. Macaulay & L. Berkowitz (Eds.), *Altruism and helping behavior* (pp. 43–59). New York: Academic Press.

MACCHI CASSIA, V., TURATI, C., & SIMION, F. (2004) Can a non-specific bias toward top-heavy patterns explain newborns' face preference? *Psychological Science, 15,* 379–383.

MACCOBY, E. (1998) *The two sexes.* Cambridge, MA: Harvard University Press.

MACCOBY, E. E., & JACKLIN, C. N. (1974) *The psychology of sex differences.* Stanford, CA: Stanford University Press.

MACLEAN, P. D. (1973) *A triune concept of the brain and behavior.* Toronto: Toronto University Press.

MACLEOD, C. M. (1991) Half a century of research on the Stroop effect: An integrative review. *Psychological Bulletin, 109,* 163–203.

MACMILLAN, M. (1991/1997) *Freud evaluated: The completed arc.* Cambridge, MA.: MIT Press.

MACWHINNEY, B. (1998) Models of the emergence of language. *Annual Review of Psychology, 49,* 199–227.

MADDEN, D. R. (2002) The structure and function of glutamate receptor ion channels. *Nature Reviews Neuroscience, 3,* 91–101.

MADDI, S. R. (2006) Hardiness: The courage to grow from stresses. *Journal of Positive Psychology, 3,* 160–168.

MAGUIRE, E. A., WOOLLETT, K., & SPIERS, H. J. (2006) London taxi drivers and bus drivers: A structural MRI and neuropsychological analysis. *Hippocampus, 16,* 1091–1101.

MAGUIRE, E. A., GADIAN, D. G., JOHNSRUDE, I. S., GOOD, C. D., ASHBURNER, J., FRACKOWIAK, R. S. J., & FRITH, C. D. (2000) Navigation-related structural change in the hippocampi of taxi drivers. *Proceedings of the National Academy of Sciences, 97,* 4398–4403.

MAGUIRE, E. A., SPIERS, H. J., GOOD, C. D., HARTLEY, T., FRACKOWIAK, R. S. J., & BURGESS, N. (2003) Navigation expertise and the human hippocampus: A structural brain imaging analysis. *Hippocampus, 13,* 208–217.

MAHER, B. A. (1966) *Principles of psychotherapy: An experimental approach.* New York: McGraw-Hill.

MAIER, S. F., & SELIGMAN, M. E. P. (1976) Learned helplessness: Theory and evidence. *Journal of Experimental Psychology: General, 105,* 3–46.

MAHON, B. Z., & CARAMAZZA, A. (2009) Concepts and categories: A cognitive neuropsychological perspective. *Annual Review of Psychology, 60,* 27–51.

MAIN, M., & CASSIDY, J. (1988) Categories of response to reunion with parents at age 6: Predictable from infant attachment classifications and stable over a 1-month period. *Developmental Psychology, 24,* 415–426.

MAIN, M., & SOLOMON, J. (1986) Discovery of an insecure-disorganized/disoriented attachment pattern: Procedures, findings and implications for the classification of behavior. In T. B. Brazelton, & M. Yogman (Eds.), *Affective development in infancy* (pp. 95–124). Norwood, NJ: Ablex.

MAJID, A., & LEVINSON, S. C. (2008) Language does provide support for basic tastes. *Behavioral and Brain Sciences, 31,* 86–87.

MAJID, A., BOWEMAN, M., KITA, S., HAUN, D., & LEVINSON, S. C. (2004) Can language restructure cognition? The case for space. *Trends in Cognitive Sciences, 8,* 108–114.

MACKELPRANG , R. W., & SALSGIVER, R. O. (2009) Disability: A diversity model approach in human service practice (2nd ed.). Chicago: Lyceaum.

MALINOW, R., OTMAKHOV, N., BLUM, K. I., & LISMAN, J. (1994) Visualizing hippocampal synaptic function by optical detection of Ca2 entry through the N-methyl-Daspartate channel. *Proceedings of the National Academy of Sciences of the United States of America, 91,* 8170–8174.

MALLE, B. F. (2011) Time to give up the dogmas of attribution: An alternative theory of behavior explanation. In J. M. Olson & M. Zanna (Eds.), *Advances in experimental social psychology, Volume 44* (pp. 297–352). San Diego, CA: Academic Press.

MALONE, J. C. (2003) Advances in behaviorism: It's not what it used to be. *Journal of Behavioral Education, 12,* 85–89.

MALONEY, L. T., & WANDELL, B. A. (1986) Color constancy: A method for recovering surface spectral reflectance. *Journal of the Optical Society of America, 3,* 29–33.

MALT, B., SLOMAN, S., GENNARI, S., SHI, M., & WANG, Y. (1999) Knowing versus naming: Similarity and the linguistic categorization of artifacts. *Journal of Memory and Language, 40,* 230–262.

MANDLER, G. (1975) *Mind and emotion.* New York: Wiley.

MANDLER, J. (1983) Representation. In P. H. Mussen (Ed.), *Handbook of child psychology* (Vol. 3). New York: Wiley.

MANN, J. J., BRENT, D. A., & ARANGO, V. (2001) The neurobiology and genetics of suicide and attempted suicide: a focus on the serotonergic system. *Neuropsychopharmacology, 24,* 467–477.

MANNES, A. E., LARRICK, R. P., & SOLL, J. B. (2012) The social psychology of the wisdom of crowds. In J. I. Krueger (Ed.), *Social judgment and decision making* (pp. 227–242). New York: Psychology Press.

MANNING, R., LEVINE, M., & COLLINS, A. (2007) The Kitty Genovese murder and the social psychology of helping: The parable of the 38 witnesses. *American Psychologist, 62* (6), 555–562.

MAQUET, P. (2000) Functional neuroimaging of normal human sleep by positron emission tomography. *Journal of Sleep Research, 9,* 207–231.

MARCIA, J. E. (1966) Development and validation of ego identify status. *Journal of Personality and Social Psychology, 3,* 551–558.

MARCIA, J. E. (1980) Identity in adolescence. In J. Adelson (Ed.), *Handbook of adolescent psychology.* New York: Wiley.

MARCUS, G. F. (1996) Why do children say "breaked"? *Current Directions in Psychological Science, 5,* 81–85.

MAREN, S. (2001) Neurobiology of Pavlovian fear conditioning, *Annual Review of Neuroscience, 24,* 897–931.

MAREN, S. (1999) Neurotoxic basolateral amygdala lesians impair learning and memory but not the performance of conditional fear in rats. *Journal of Neuroscience, 19,* 8696–8703.

MAREN, S., & FANSELOW, M. S. (1996) The amygdala and fear conditioning: Has the nut been cracked? *Neuron, 16,* 237–240.

MARGOLIN, L., & WHITE, L. (1987) The continuing role of physical attractiveness in marriage. *Journal of Marriage and the Family, 49,* 21–27.

MARINGER, M., KRUMHUBER, E. G., FISCHER, A. H., & NIEDENTHAL, P. M. (2011) Beyond smile dynamics: Mimicry and beliefs in judgments of smiles. *Emotion, 11,* 181–187.

MARKMAN, E. M. (1979) Classes and collections: Conceptual organization and numerical abilities. *Cognitive Psychology, 11,* 395–411.

MARKMAN, E. M. (1987) How children constrain the possible meanings of words. In U. Neisser (Ed.), *Concepts and conceptual development: Ecological and intellectual factors in categorizations*. New York: Cambridge University Press.

MARKMAN, E. M., WASOW, J. L., & HANSEN, M. B. (2003) Use of the mutual exclusivity assumption by young word learners. *Cognitive Psychology, 47*, 241–275.

MARKUS, H. (1977) Self-schemata and processing information about the self. *Journal of Personality and Social Psychology, 35*, 63–78.

MARKUS, H., & SENTIS, K. (1982) The self in social information processing. In J. Suls (Ed.), *Psychological perspectives on the self* (Vol. 1). Hillsdale, NJ: Erlbaum.

MARKUS, H., & SMITH, J. (1981) The influence of self-schema on the perception of others. In N. Cantor & J. F. Kihlstrom (Eds.), *Personality, cognition, and social interaction*. Hillsdale, NJ: Erlbaum.

MARKUS, H. R., & KITAYAMA, S. (2010) Cultures and selves: A cycle of mutual constitution. *Perspectives on Psychological Science, 5*, 420–430.

MARLATT, G. A., BAER, J. S., KIVLAHAN, D. R., DIMEFF, L. A., LARIMER, M. E., QUIGLEY, L., SOMERS, J. M., & WILLIAMS, E. (1998) Screening and brief intervention for high-risk college student drinkers: Results from a 2-year follow-up assessment. *Journal of Consulting and Clinical Psychology, 66* (4), 604–615.

MARMOT, M. G. (2004). Tackling health inequalities since the Acheson Inquiry. *Journal of Epidemiological Community Health, 58*, 262–263.

MARSH, A. A., FINGER, E. C., SCHECHTER, J. C. JURKOWITZ, I. T. N., REID, M. E., & BLAIR, R. J. R. (2011) Adolescents with psychopathic traits report reductions in physiological responses to fear. *Journal of Child Psychology and Psychiatry, 52*, 834–841.

MARSHALL, D. A., BLUMER, L., & MOULTON, D. G. (1981) Odor detection curves for n-pentanoic acid in dogs and humans. *Chemical Senses, 6*, 445–453.

MARSHALL, G., & ZIMBARDO, P. G. (1979) Affective consequences of inadequately explained physiological arousal. *Journal of Personality and Social Psychology, 37*, 970–988.

MARTIN, A., & CARAMAZZA, A. (2003) Neuropsychological and neuroimaging perspectives on conceptual knowledge: An introduction. *Cognitive Neuropsychology, 20*, 195–212.

MARTIN, A., & CHAO, L. L. (2001) Semantic memory and the brain: Structure and processes. *Current Opinion in Neurobiology, 11*, 194–201.

MARTIN, N., BOOMSMA, D., & MACHIN, G. (1997) A twin-pronged attack on complex traits. *Nature Genetics, 17*, 387–392.

MARTINS, Y., TIGGEMANN, M., & KIRKBRIDE, A. (2007) Those speedos become them: The role of self-objectification in gay and heterosexual men's body image. *Personality and Social Psychology Bulletin, 33*, 634.

MASGORET, A., & GARDNER, R. (2003) Attitudes, motivation, and second-language learning: A meta-analysis of studies conducted by Gardner and associates. *Language Learning, 53* (1), 123–163.

MASLACH, C. (1979) The emotional consequences of arousal without reason. In Izard, C. E. (Ed.), *Emotion in personality and psychopathology*. New York: Plenum.

MASLOW, A. H. (1970) *Motivation and personality* (2nd ed.). New York: Harper and Row.

MASSACHUSETTS GENERAL HOSPITAL (2011, May 25) *Determination of brain death: Death determination using brain criteria in the adult*. Boston: The Author. Retrieved November 24, 2012 from http://www2.massgeneral.org/stopstroke/protocolbraindeath.aspx.

MASSARO, D., & LOFTUS, G. R. (1996) Sensory storage: Icons and echoes. In E. L. Bjork & R. A. Bjork (Eds.), *Handbook of perception and cognition* (Vol. 10, pp. 68–101). New York: Academic Press.

MASSON, J. M. (1984) *The assault on truth*. New York: Farrar, Straus & Giroux.

MASTERS, W. H., & JOHNSON, V. E. (1966) *Human sexual response*. New York: Little, Brown and Company.

MASUDA, M., & HOLMES, T. H. (1978) Life events: Perceptions and frequencies. *Psychosomatic Medicine, 40*, 236–261.

MASUDA, T., & NISBETT, R. E. (2001) Attending holistically versus analytically: Comparing the context sensitivity of Japanese and Americans. *Journal of Personality and Social Psychology, 81*, 922–934.

MASUDA, T., ELLSWORTH, P. C., MESQUITA, B., LEU, J., TANIDA, S., & VAN DE VEERDONK, E. (2008) Placing the face in context: Cultural differences in the perception of facial emotion. *Journal of Personality and Social Psychology, 94*, 365–381.

MATAS, L., AREND, R. A., & SROUFE, L. A. (1978) Continuity of adaption in the second year: The relationship between quality of attachment and later competence. *Child Development, 49*, 547–556.

MATHES, E. W. (1975) The effects of physical attractiveness and anxiety on heterosexual attraction over a series of five encounters. *Journal of Marriage and the Family, 37*, 769–773.

MATTHEWS, D. F. (1972) Response patterns of single neurons in the tortoise olfactory epithelium and olfactory bulb. *Journal of General Physiology, 60*, 166–180.

MATTILA, M.-L., KIELINEN, M, JUSSILA, K., LINNA, S.-L., BLOIGU, R., EBELING, H., & MOILANEN, I. (2007) An epidemiological and diagnostic study of Asperger syndrome according to four sets of diagnostic criteria. *Journal of the American Academy of Child and Adolescent Psychiatry, 46*, 636–646.

MAUSS, I. B., & ROBINSON, M. D. (2009) Measures of emotion: A review. *Cognition & Emotion, 23*, 209–237.

MAYER, J. D., & SALOVEY, P. (1997a) What is emotional intelligence? In P. Salovey & D. J. Sluyter (Eds.), *Emotional development and emotional intelligence: Educational implications* (pp.4–30). New York: Basic Books.

MAYER, J. D., ROBERTS, R. D., & BARSADE, S. G. (2008a) Human abilities: Emotional intelligence. *Annual Review of Psychology, 59*, 507–536.

MAYER, J. D., SALOVEY, P., & CARUSO, D. (2002a) *The Mayer-Salovey-Caruso Emotional Intelligence Test (MSCEIT), Version 2.0*. Toronto, Canada: Multi Health Systems.

MAYER, J. D., SALOVEY, P., & CARUSO, D. R. (2012) The validity of the MSCEIT: Additional analyses and evidence. *Emotion Review, 4*, 403–408.

MAYER, J. D., SALOVEY, P., & CARUSO, D. R. (in press) *Mayer-Salovey-Caruso Emotional Intelligence Test: Youth version (MSCEIT: YV): Item booklet.* Toronto, Ontario, Canada: Multi-Health Systems.

MAX-NEEF, M. (1992) Development and human needs. In P. Ekins & M. Max-Neef (Eds.), *Real-life economics: Understanding wealth creation* (pp. 197–213). London/New York: Routledge.

MAYER, J. D., & SALOVEY, P. (1997b) What is emotional? In P. Savoley & D. Sluyter (Eds.), *Emotional development and emotional intelligence: Implications for educators* (pp. 3–31). New York: Basic Books.

MAYER, J. D., & SALOVEY, P. (1997c) What is emotional intelligence? In P. Salovey & D. J. Sluyter (Eds.), *Emotional development and emotional intelligence: Educational implications* (pp. 4–30). New York: Basic Books.

MAYER, J. D., ROBERTS, R. D., & BARSADE, S. G. (2008a) Human abilities: Emotional intelligence. *Annual Review of Psychology, 59*, 507–536.

MAYER, J. D., SALOVEY, P., & CARUSO, D. (2002b) *The Mayer-Salovey-Caruso Emotional Intelligence Test (MSCEIT), Version 2.0.* Toronto, Canada: Multi Health Systems.

MAYER, J. D. SALOVEY, P., & CARUSO, D. R. (2004) A further consideration of the issues of emotional intelligence. *Psychological Inquiry, 15*, 249–255.

MAYER, J. D., SALOVEY, P., & CARUSO, D. (2008c) Emotional intelligence: New ability or eclectic traits? *American Psychologist, 65*, 503–517.

MAYR, E (1960) The emergence of evolutionary novelties. In S. Tax (Ed.), *Evolution after Darwin: Vol. 1. The evolution of life* (pp. 349–380). Chicago: University of Chicago Press.

MAZUR, T. (2005) Gender dysphoria and gender change in androgen insensitivity or micropenis. *Archives of Sexual Behavior, 34*, 411–421.

MCALISTER, A., PERRY, C., KILLEN, J., SLINKARD, L. A., & MACCOBY, N. (1980) Pilot study of smoking, alcohol and drug abuse prevention. *American Journal of Public Health, 70*, 719–721.

MCBURNEY, D. H. (1978) Psychological dimensions and the perceptual analysis of taste. In E. C. Carterette & M. P. Friedman (Eds.), *Handbook of perception* (Vol. 6). New York: Academic Press.

MCCARBER, B. H., & BILLINGTON, R. (2006) Consequences of neuropathic pain: Quality-of-life issues and associated costs. *American Journal of Managed Care, 12*, S263–268.

MCCARTHY, R. A., & WARRINGTON, E. K. (1990) *Cognitive neuropsychology: A clinical introduction*. New York: Academic Press.

MCCLELLAND, D. C. (1987) *Human motivation*. New York: Cambridge University Press.

MCCLELLAND, J. L., & RUMELHART, D. E. (1981) An interactive model of context effects in letter perception: Pt. 1. An account of basic findings. *Psychological Review, 88*, 375–407.

MCCLINTOCK, M. K. (1971) Menstrual synchrony and suppression. *Nature, 229*, 244–245.

MCCRAE, R. R., & COSTA, P. T., JR. (1987) Validation of the five-factor model of personality across instruments and observers. *Journal of Personality and Social Psychology, 52*, 81–90.

MCCRAE, R. R., & COSTA, P. T., JR. (1999) A five-factor theory of personality. In L. A. Pervin (Ed.), *Handbook of Personality: Theory and Research*. New York: Guilford.

MCCRAE, R. R., & COSTA, P. T., JR. (2006) Cross-cultural perspectives on adult personality trait development. In D. K. Mroczek & T. D. Little (Eds.), *Handbook of personality development* (pp. 129–145). Mahwah, NJ: Lawrence Erlbaum Associates.

MCCRAE, R. R., COSTA, P. T., & BUSCH, C. M. (1986) Evaluating comprehensiveness in personality systems—the California Q-set and the 5-factor model. *Journal of Personality, 54,* 430–446.

MCELREE, B. DOSHER, B. A. (1989) Serial position and set size in short-term memory. The time course of recognition. *Journal of Experimental Psychology: General, 118*, 346–373.

MCEWEN, B. S. (2000). Allostasis and allostatic load: Implications for neuropsychopharmacology. *Neuropsychopharmacology, 22*, 108–124.

MCGHIE, A., & CHAPMAN, J. (1961) Disorders of attention and perception in early schizophrenia. *British Journal of Medical Psychology, 34*, 103–116.

MCGURK, H., & MACDONALD, J. (1976) Hearing lips and seeing voices. *Nature, 264*, 746–748.

MCHUGH, P., LIEF, H. I., FREYD, P. P., & FETKEWICZ, J. M. (2004) From refusal to reconciliation. *Journal of Nervous and Mental Disease, 192*, 525–531.

MCKENNA, R. J. (1972) Some effects of anxiety level and food cues on the eating behavior of obese and normal subjects. *Journal of Personality and Social Psychology, 22*, 311–319.

MCLELLAN, A. T., & TURNER, B. J. (2010) Chronic noncancer pain management and opioid overdose: Time to change prescribing practices. *Annals of Internal Medicine, 152*, 123–124.

MCMILLAN, T. M., & RACHMAN, S. J. (1987) Fearlessness and courage: A laboratory study of paratrooper veterans of the Falklands War. *British Journal of Psychology, 78*, 375–383.

MCNALLY, R. J. (2003) *Remembering Trauma*. Cambridge, MA: Harvard University Press.

MCNEILL, D. (1966) Developmental psycholinguistics. In F. Smith & G. A. Miller (Eds.), *The genesis of language: A psycholinguistic approach*. Cambridge, MA: MIT Press.

MEHLER, J., JUSCZYK, P., LAMBERTZ, G., HALSTED, N., *et al.* (1988) A precursor of language acquisition in young infants. *Cognition, 29* (2), 143–178.

MEIER, R. P. (1991) Language acquisition by deaf children. *American Scientist, 79*, 60–76.

MELTZOFF, A. N. (1995). Understanding the intentions of others: re-enactment of intended acts by 18th-month-old children. *Developmental Psychology, 31*, 838–850.

MELTZOFF, A. N., & DECETY, J. (2003) What imitation tells us about social cognition. *Philosophical Transactions of the Royal Society, B, 358*, 491–500.

MELZACK, R. (1973) *The puzzle of pain*. New York: Basic Books.

MELZACK, R., & WALL, P. D. (1982, 1988) *The challenge of pain*. New York: Basic Books.

MELZACK, R. (1990) The tragedy of needless pain. *Scientific American, 262*, 27–33.

MERRILL, L. L., THOMSEN, C. J., SINCLAIR, B. B., GOLD, S. R., & MILNER, J. S. (2001). Predicting the impact of child sexual abuse on women: The role of abuse severity, parental support, and coping strategies. *Journal of Consulting and Clinical Psychology, 69*, 992–1006.

MERVIS, C. B., & PANI, J. R. (1981) Acquisition of basic object categories. *Cognitive Psychology, 12*, 496–522.

MERVIS, C. B., & ROSCH, E. (1981) Categorization of natural objects. In M. R. Rosenz & L. W. Porter (Eds.), *Annual review of psychology* (Vol. 21). Palo Alto, CA: Annual Reviews.

MESQUITA, B. (2001) Emotions in collectivist and individualist contexts. *Journal of Personality and Social Psychology, 80*, 68–74.

MESSICK, S. (1992) Multiple intelligences or multilevel intelligence? Selective emphasis on distinctive properties of hierarchy: On Gardner's Frames of Mind and Sternberg's Beyond IQ in the context of theory and research on the structure of human abilities. *Journal of Psychological Inquiry*, 1, 305–384.

MEZZACAPPA, E. S., KATKIN, E. S., & PALMER, S. N. (1999) Epinephrine, arousal, and emotion: A new look at two-factor theory. *Cognition and Emotion*, 13, 181–199.

MIKLOWITZ, D. J., & JOHNSON, S. L. (2006) The psychopathology and treatment of bipolar disorder. *Annual Review of Clinical Psychology*, 2, 199–235.

MIKLOWITZ, D. J., & CRAIGHEAD, W. E. (2007) Psychosocial treatment for bipolar disorder. In P. E. Nathan & J. M. Gorman (Eds.), *A guide to treatments that work* (3rd ed.) (pp. 309–322). Oxford: Oxford University Press.

MILAM, J. E., RICHARDSON, J. L., MARKS, G., KEMPER, C. A., & MCCUTCHAN, A. J. (2004) The roles of dispositional optimism and pessimism in HIV disease progression. *Psychology & Health*, 19, 167–181.

MILGRAM, S. (1963) Behavioral study of obedience. *Journal of Abnormal and Social Psychology*, 67, 371–378.

MILGRAM, S. (1964) Issues in the study of obedience: A reply to Baumrind. *American Psychologist*, 19, 848–852.

MILGRAM, S. (1974) *Obedience to authority: An experimental view*. New York: Harper & Row.

MILLAR, M. G., & TESSER, A. (1989) The effects of affective-cognitive consistency and thought on the attitude–behavior relation. *Journal of Experimental Social Psychology*, 25, 189–202.

MILLER, E. K., & COHEN, J. D. (2001) An integrative theory of prefrontal cortex function. *Annual Review of Neuroscience*, 24, 167–202.

MILLER, F. G. (2009) Death and organ donation: Back to the future. *Journal of Medical Ethics*, 35, 6-6-620.

MILLER, G. A. (1956) The magical number seven plus or minus two: Some limits on our capacity for processing information. *Psychological Review*, 63, 81–97.

MILLER, G. A., & GILDEA, P. M. (1987) How children learn words. *Scientific American*, 257, 94–99.

MILLER, J. G. (1984) Culture and the development of everyday social explanation. *Journal of Personality and Social Psychology*, 46, 961–978.

MILLER, N. E., & DOLLARD, J. (1941) *Social learning and imitation*. New Haven, CT: Yale University Press.

MILLER, N. E., & KESSEN, M. L. (1952) Reward effects of food via stomach fistula compared with those of food via mouth. *Journal of Comparative and Physiological Psychology*, 45, 555–564.

MILLS, J. (1979) *Six years with God*. New York: A & W Publishers.

MILLS, L. B. (2009) A meta-analysis of the relationship between emotional intelligence and effective leadership. *Journal of Curriculum and Instruction*, 3, 22–38.

MILNER, B. (1970) Memory and the medial temporal regions of the brain. In K. H. Pribram & D. E. Broadbent (Eds.), *Biology of memory*. New York: Academic Press.

MILNER, B., CORKIN, S., & TEUBER, H. L. (1968) Further analysis of the hippocampal amnesic syndrome: 14-year follow-up study of H. M. *Neuropsychologia*, 6, 215–234.

MINEKA, S., & COOK, M. (1988) Social learning and the acquisition of snake fear in monkeys. In T. R. Zentall, & B. G. Galef (Eds.), *Social Learning: Psychological and Biological Perspectives* (pp. 3–28). Hillsdale, NJ: Erlbaum.

MINUCHIN, S., ROSMAN, B. L., & BAKER, L. (1978) *Psychosomatic families: Anorexia nervosa in context*. Cambridge, MA: Harvard University Press.

MISCHEL, W. (1973) Toward a cognitive social learning reconceptualization of personality. *Psychological Review*, 80, 272–283.

MISCHEL, W. (1993) *Introduction to personality* (5th ed.). Fort Worth: Harcourt Brace Jovanovich.

MISHKIN, M., UNGERLEIDER, L. G., & MACKO, K. A. (1983) Object vision and spatial vision: Two cortical pathways. *Trends in Neuroscience*, 6, 414–417.

MITA, T. H., DERMER, M., & KNIGHT, J. (1977) Reversed facial images and the mere-exposure hypotheses. *Journal of Personality and Social Psychology*, 35, 597–601.

MITCHELL, C. J., HEYES, C. M., GARDNER, M. R., & DAWSON, G. R. (1999) Limitations of a bidirectional control procedure for the investigation of imitation in rats: Odour cues on the manipulandum. *Quarterly Journal of Experimental Psychology*, 52, 193–202.

MITCHELL, J. E., & DEZWAAN, M. (1993) Pharmacological treatments of binge eating. In C. E. Fairburn & G. T. Wilson (Eds.), *Binge eating: Nature, assessment, and treatment*. New York: Guilford.

MITCHELL, K. J., & JOHNSON, M. K. (2000) Source monitoring: Attributing mental experiences. In E. Tulving & F. I. M. Craik (Eds.), *The Oxford Handbook of Memory* (pp. 179–195). New York: Oxford University Press.

MITCHELL, K. J., YBARRA, M., & FINKELHOR, D. (2007) The relative importance of online victimization in understanding depression, delinquency, and substance use. *Child Maltreatment*, 12, 314–324.

MOFFITT, T. E. (1990) Juvenile delinquency and attention deficit disorder: Boys' development trajectories from age 3 to age 15. *Child Development*, 61, 893–910.

MOFFITT, T. E. (1993) The neuropsychology of conduct disorder. *Development and Psychopathology*, 5, 135–151.

MONEY, J. (1980) Endocrine influences and psychosexual status spanning the life cycle. In H. M. Van Praag (Ed.), *Handbook of biological psychiatry* (Part 3). New York: Marcel Dekker.

MONEY, J. (1987) Sin, sickness, or status? Homosexual gender identity and psychoneuroendocrinology. *American Psychologist*, 42, 384–400.

MONEY, J., WEIDEKING, C., WALKER, P. A., & GAIN, D. (1976) Combined antiandrogenic and counseling programs for treatment for 46 XY and 47 XXY sex offenders. In E. Sacher (Ed.), *Hormones, behavior and psychopathology*. New York: Raven Press.

MONSELL, S. (1979) Recency, immediate recognition memory, and reaction time. *Cognitive Psychology*, 10, 465–501.

MONTEITH, M. J., LYBARGER, J. E., & WOODCOCK, A. (2009) Schooling the cognitive monster: The role of motivation in the regulation and control of prejudice. *Social and Personality Psychology Compass*, 3, 211–226.

MORAN, A. (2012) *Sport and exercise psychology: A critical introduction* (2nd ed.). London: Routledge.

MORAN, J., & DESIMONE, R. (1985) Selective attention gates visual processing in the extrastriate cortex. *Science*, 229, 782–784.

MORAN, A., GUILLOT, A., MACINTYRE, T., & COLLET, C. (2012) Re-imagining motor imagery: Building bridges between cognitive neuroscience and sport psychology. *British Journal of Psychology*, 103, 224–247.

MORAY, N. (1969) *Attention: Selective processes in vision and hearing*. London: Hutchinson.

MORELAND, R. L., & BEACH, S. R. (1992) Exposure effects in the classroom: The development of affinity among students. *Journal of Experimental Social Psychology*, 28, 255–276.

MORELAND, R. L., & ZAJONC, R. B. (1979) Exposure effects may not depend on stimulus recognition. *Journal of Personality and Social Psychology*, 37, 1085–1089.

MOREWEDGE, C. K., HUH, Y. E., & VOSGERAU, J. (2010) Thought for food: Imagined consumption reduces actual consumption. *Science*, 303, 1530–1533.

MORGAN, A. B., & LILIENFELD, S. O. (2000) A meta-analytic review of the relation between antisocial behavior and neuropsychological measures of executive function. *Clinical Psychological Review*, 20, 113–136.

MORRIS, M. W., & PENG, K. (1994) Culture and cause: American and Chinese attributions for social and physical events. *Journal of Personality and Social Psychology*, 67, 949–971.

MOSCOVICI, S. (1976) *Social influence and social change*. London: Academic Press.

MOSCOVICI, S., & ZAVALLONI, M. (1969) The group as a polarizer of attitudes. *Journal of Personality and Social Psychology*, 12, 125–135.

MOSCOVICI, S., LAGE, E., & NAFFRECHOUX, M. (1969) Influence of a consistent minority on the responses of a majority in a color perception task. *Sociometry*, 32, 365–379.

MOSIMANN, U. P., et al. (2000) Mood effects of repetitive transcranial magnetic stimulation of left prefrontal cortex in healthy volunteers. *Psychiatry Research*, 94 (3), 251–256.

MOSKOWITZ, J. T., EPEL, E. S., & ACREE, M. (2008) Positive affect uniquely predicts lower risk of mortality in people with diabetes. *Health Psychology*, 27, S73–S82.

MOSKOWITZ, G. B., SKURNIK, I., & GALINSKY, A. D. (1999) The history of dual-process notions, and the future of preconscious control. In S. Chaiken & Y. Trope (Eds.) *Dual-process theories in social psychology* (pp. 12–36). New York: Guilford Press.

MOSKOWITZ, H. R., KUMRAICH, V., SHARMA, H., JACOBS, L., & SHARMA, S. D. (1975) Cross-cultural difference in simple taste preference. *Science*, 190, 1217–1218.

MOVSHON, J. A., & VAN SLUYTERS, R. C. (1981) Visual neural development. *Annual Review of Psychology*, 32, 477–522.

MOWRER, O. H. (1947) On the dual nature of learning: A reinterpretation of "conditioning" and "problem-solving". *Harvard Educational Review*, 17, 102–148.

MUGAVERO, M. J., PENCE, B. W., WHETEN, K., LESERMAN, J., SWARTZ, M., STANGL, D., & THIELMAN, N. M. (2007). Predictors of AIDS-related morbidity and mortality in a southern US cohort. *AIDS Patient Care and STDs*, 21, 681–690.

MUKHOPADHYAY, P., & TURNER, R. M. (1997) Biofeedback treatment of essential hypertension. *Social Science International*, 13, 1–9.

MÜLLER, S., ABERNETHY, B., EID, M., MCBEAN, R., & ROSE, M. (2010) Expertise and the spatio-temporal characteristics of anticipatory information pick-up from complex movement patterns. *Perception*, 39, 745–760.

MUNDO, E., ZANONI, S., & ALTAMURA, A. C. (2006) Genetic issues in obsessive-compulsive disorder and related disorders. *Psychiatric Annals*, 36, 495–512.

MUNOZ, R. F., LENERT, L. L., DELUCCHI, K., STODDARD, J., PEREZ, J.E., PENILLA, C., & PEREZ-STABLE, E. J. (2006) Toward evidence-based Internet interventions: A Spanish/English Web site for international smoking cessation trials. *Nicotine & Tobacco Research*, 8, 77–87.

MURAVEN, M., TICE, D. M., & BAUMEISTER, R. F. (1998) Self-control as a limited resource: Regulatory depletion patterns. *Journal of Personality and Social Psychology*, 74, 774–789.

MURIS, P., STEERNEMAN, P., MERCKELBACH, H., & MEESTERS, C. (1996) Parental modeling and fearfulness in middle childhood. *Behavioral Research and Therapy*, 28, 263–267.

MURPHY, G. L., & BROWNELL, H. H. (1985) Category differentiation in object recognition: Typicality constraints on the basic category advantage. *Journal of Experimental Psychology*, 11, 70.

MURSTEIN, B. I. (1972) Physical attractiveness and marital choice. *Journal of Personality and Social Psychology*, 22, 8–12.

MUSSWEILER, T. (2006) Doing is for thinking! Stereotype activation by stereotypic movements. *Psychological Science*, 17 (1), 17–21.

MYERS, D. G., & LAMM, H. (1976) The group polarization phenomenon. *Psychological Bulletin*, 83, 602–627.

MYRTEK, M. (2007) Type A behavior and hostility as independent risk factors for coronary heart disease. In J. Jordan, B. Barden, & A. M. Zeiher (Eds.), *Contributions toward evidence-based psychocardiology: A systematic review of the literature* (pp. 159–183). Washington, DC: American Psychological Association.

NA, J., & KITAYAMA, S. (2011) Spontaneous trait inference is culture-specific: Behavioral and neural evidence. *Psychological Science*, 22, 1025–1032.

NACOSTE, R. W. (1990) Sources of stigma: Analyzing the psychology of affirmative action. *Law and Policy*, 12, 175–195

NATHANS, J. (1987) Molecular biology of visual pigments. *Annual Review of Neuroscience*, 10, 163–164.

NATIONAL INSTITUTE ON DRUG ABUSE. (2002) 2001 *Monitoring the future survey released*. www.nida.nih.gov/MedAQdv/00/HHS12-14.html.

NATIONAL SLEEP FOUNDATION (2009) *Sleep in America Poll*. Washington, DC: National Sleep Foundation.

NEISSER, U. (Ed.) (1982) *Memory observed: Remembering in natural contexts*. New York: Freeman.

NEISSER, U. (1988) Five kinds of self-knowledge. *Philosophical Psychology*, 1, 35–59.

NEISSER, U., & HARSCH, N. (1993) Phantom flashbulbs: False recollections of hearing the news about *Challenger*. In E. Winograd & U. Neisser (Eds.), *Affect and accuracy in recall: Studies of "flashbulb" memories* (pp. 9–31). Cambridge: Cambridge University Press.

NELSON, D. W. (2009) Feeling good and open-minded: The impact of positive affect on cross cultural empathic responding. *Journal of Positive Psychology*, 4, 53–63.

NELSON, R. J., & CHIAVEGATTO, S. (2001) Molecular basis of aggression. *Trends in Neurosciences*, 24, 713–719.

NEMBHARD, I. M., & EDMONDSON, A. C. (2006) Making it safe: The effects of leader inclusiveness and professional status on psychological safety and improvement efforts in health care teams. *Journal of Organizational Behavior*, 27, 941–966.

NEMETH, C. (1986) Differential contributions of majority and minority influence. *Psychological Review*, 93, 23–32.

NES, L. S., & SEGERSTROM, S. C. (2006) Dispositional optimism and coping: A meta-analytic review. *Personality and Social Psychology Review*, 10, 235–251.

NEUMANN, R. (2000) The causal influence of attributions on emotions. A procedural priming approach. *Psychological Science*, 11, 179–182.

NEWCOMB, M. D., RABOW, J., & HERNANDEZ, A. C. R. (1992) A cross-national study of nuclear attitudes, normative support, and activist behavior: Additive and interactive effects. *Journal of Applied Social Psychology, 22,* 780–200.

NEWCOMB, T. M. (1943) *Personality and social change.* New York: Dryden Press.

NEWCOMB, T. M., KOENING, K. E., FLACKS, R., & WARWICK, D. P. (1967) *Persistence and change: Bennington College and its students after twenty-five years.* New York: Wiley.

NEWELL, A., & SIMON, H. A. (1972) *Human problem solving.* Englewood Cliffs, NJ: Prentice-Hall.

NEWMAN, D. L., TELLEGEN, A., & BOUCHARD, T. J., Jr. (1998) Individual differences in adult ego development: Sources of influence in twins reared apart. *Journal of Personality and Social Psychology, 74,* 985–995.

NEWPORT, E. L. (1990) Maturational constraints on language learning. *Cognitive Science, 14,* 11–28.

NEW SCIENTIST (2002) Relax: you're not that tempting. *New Scientist, 174,* 25.

NEZU, A. M., NEZU, C. M., & D'ZURILLA, T. J. (2006) *Solving life's problems: A 5-Step guide to enhanced well-being.* New York: Springer.

NEZU, A. M., NEZU, C. M., & PERRI, M. G. (1989) *Problem-solving therapy for depression: Theory, research, and clinical guidelines.* New York: Wiley.

NHAT HANH, T. ([1975] 1991) *The miracle of mindfulness.* London: Rider.

NICHD Early Childcare Research Network (2004) Are child development outcomes related to before-and after-school care arrangements? *Child Development 75,* 280–295.

NICHOLSON, I. (2011) "Torture at Yale": Experimental subjects, laboratory torment, and the "rehabilitation" of Milgram's "Obedience to Authority". *Theory & Psychology, 21,* 737–761.

NICHOLSON, N. (1998) How hardwired is human behavior? *Harvard Business Review,* July–August, 135–147.

NIEDENTHAL, P. (2008) Emotion concepts. In M. Lewis, J. Haviland-Jones, & L. F. Barrett (Eds.), *Handbook of emotions, 3rd edition* (pp. 587–600). New York: Guilford Press.

NIEDENTHAL, P. M., MERMILLOD, M., MARINGER, M., & HESS, U. (2010) The Simulation of Smiles (SIMS) model: Embodied simulation and the meaning of facial expression. *Behavioral and Brain Sciences, 33,* 417–480.

NIELSEN, T. A., & STENSTROM, P. (2005) What are the memory sources of dreaming? *Nature, 437,* 1285–1289.

NISAN, M., & KOHLBERG, L. (1982) Universality and variation in moral judgment: A longitudinal and cross-sectional study in Turkey. *Child Development, 53,* 865–876.

NISBETT, R. E., PENG, K., CHOI, I., & NORENZAYAN, A. (2001) Culture and systems of thought: Holistic versus analytic cognition. *Psychology Review, 108,* 291–310.

NISBETT, R. E., KRANTZ, D. H., JEPSON, C., & KUNDA, Z. (1983) The use of statistical heuristics in everyday inductive reasoning. *Psychological Review, 90*(4), 339–363.

NOBLE, M., TREGEAR, S. J., TREADWELL, J. R., & SCHOELLES, K. (2008) Long-term opioid therapy for chronic non-cancer pain: A systematic review and meta-analysis of efficacy and safety. *Journal of Pain and Symptom Management, 35,* 214–228.

NOCK, M., K., BORGES, G., BROMET, E. J., ALONSO, J., ANGERMEYER, M., BEAUTRAIS, A., BRUFFAERTS, R., CHIU, W. T., DE GIROLAMO, G., GLUZMAN, S., DE GRAAF, R., GUREJE, O., HARO, J. M., HUANG, Y., KARAM, E.,

KESSLER, R. C., LEPINE, J. P., LEVINSON, D., MEDINA-MORA, M. E., ONO, Y., POSADA-VILLA, J., & WILLIAMS, D. (2008) Cross-national prevlance and risk factors for suicidal ideation, plans and attempts. *British Journal of Psychiatry, 192,* 98–105.

NOLEN-HOEKSEMA, S. (2000) The role of rumination in depressive disorders and mixed anxiety/depressive symptoms. *Journal of Abnormal Psychology, 109,* 504–511.

NOLEN-HOEKSEMA, S. (2007) *Abnormal Psychology,* 4th ed. New York: McGraw-Hill.

NOLEN-HOEKSEMA, S., & LARSON, J. (1999) *Coping with loss.* Mahwah, NJ: Erlbaum.

NOLEN-HOEKSEMA, S., & MORROW, J. (1991) A prospective study of depression and distress following a natural disaster: The 1989 Loma Prieta earthquake. *Journal of Personality and Social Psychology, 61,* 105–121.

NOLEN-HOEKSEMA, S., WISCO, B. E., & LYBOMIRSKY, S. (2008) Rethinking rumination. *Perspectives on Psychological Science, 3,* 400–420.

NOLL, S. M., & FREDRICKSON, B. L. (1998) A mediational model linking self-objectification, body shame, and disordered eating. *Psychology of Women Quarterly, 22,* 623–636.

NORDIN, V., & GILLBERG, C. (1998) The long-term course of autistic disorders: Update on follow-up studies. *Acta Psychiatrica Scandinavica, 97,* 99–108.

NORENZAYAN, A., & NISBETT, R. E. (2000) Culture and causal cognition. *Current Directions in Psychological Science, 9,* 132–135.

NORMAN, R. (1975) Affective-cognitive consistency, attitudes, conformity, and behavior. *Journal of Personality and Social Psychology, 32,* 83–91.

NORRIS, F. H., PERILLA, J. L., IBANEZ, G. E., & MURPHY, A. D. (2001) Sex differences in symptoms of posttraumatic stress: Does culture play a role? *Journal of Traumatic Stress, 14,* 7–28.

NORTH, C. (1987) *Welcome silence.* New York: Simon and Schuster.

NOSOFSKY, R. M., & JOHANSEN, M. K. (2000) Exemplar-based accounts of "multiple-system" phenomena in perceptual categorization. *Psychonomic Bulletin and Review, 7,* 375–402.

NOVICK, L. R. (1988) Analogical transfer, problem similarity, and expertise. *Journal of Experimental Psychology: Learning, Memory and Cognition, 14,* 510–520.

NUSSBAUM, S., TROPE, Y., & LIBERMAN, N. (2003) Creeping dispositionalism: The temporal dynamics of behavior prediction. *Journal of Personality and Social Psychology, 84,* 485–497.

NUTT, D. J., & MALIZIA, A. L. (2004) Structural and functional brain changes in posttraumatic stress disorder. *Journal of Clinical Psychiatry, 65* (Suppl. 1), 11–17.

OATLEY, K., KELTNER, D., & JENKINS, J. M. (2006) *Understanding emotions,* 2nd Edition. Cambridge, MA: Wiley-Blackwell.

OCHSNER, K. N., & GROSS, J. J. (2007) The neural architecture of emotion regulation. In J. J. Gross (Ed.), *Handbook of emotion regulation* (pp. 87–109). New York: Guilford Press.

OCHSNER, K. N., & LIEBERMAN, M. D. (2001) The emergence of social cognitive neuroscience. *American Psychologist, 56,* 717–734.

O'CONNOR, K., HALLAM, R., & RACHMAN, S. (1985) Fearlessness and courage: A replication experiment. *British Journal of Psychology, 76,* 187–197.

OFSHE, R. (1992) Inadvertent hypnosis during interrogation: False confessions to dissociative state; misidentified multiple personality and the satanic cult hypothesis. *International Journal of Clinical and Experimental Hypnosis, 40*, 125–156.

OHMAN, A. (2009) Of snakes and faces: An evolutionary perspective on the psychology of fear. *Scandinavian Journal of Psychology, 50*, p. 543–552.

ÖHMAN, A., & MINEKA, S. (2001) Fears, phobias, and preparedness. Toward an evolved module of fear and fear learning. *Psychological Review, 108*, 483–522.

OJEMANN, G. (1983) Brain organization for language from the perspective of electrical stimulation mapping. *Behavioral and Brain Sciences, 6*, 189–230.

OLDS, J. (1956) Pleasure centers in the brain. *Scientific American, 195*, 105–116.

O'LEARY, K. D., ACEVEDO, B. P., ARON, A. HUDDY, L., MASHEK, D. (2012) Is long-term love more than a rare phenomenon? If so, what are its correlates? *Social Psychological and Personality Science, 3*, 241–249.

OFFIR, C. (1982) *Human sexuality*. San Diego: Harcourt Brace Jovanovich.

OLSON, H. C., FELDMAN, J. J., STREISSGUTH, A. P., SAMPSON, P. D, BOOSTEIN, F. L. (1998) Neuropsychological deficits in adolescents with fetal alcohol syndrome: Clinical findings. *Alcoholism: Clinical & Experimental Research, 22*, 1998–2012.

OLNEY, N. T., GOODKIND, M. S., LOMEN-HOERTH, C., WHALEN, P. K., WILLIAMSON, C. A., HOLLEY, D. E., VERSTAEN, A., BROWN, L. M., MILLER, B. L., KORNAK, J., LEVENSON, R. W., & ROSEN, H. J. (2011) Behaviour, physiology and experience of pathological laughing and crying in amyotrophic lateral sclerosis. *Brain, 134*, 3458–3469.

OLSSON, A., & PHELPS, E. A. (2007) Social learning of fear. *Nature Neuroscience. 10*(9), 1095–1102.

ORNE, M. T., & HOLLAND, C. C. (1968) On the ecological validity of laboratory deceptions. *International Journal of Psychiatry, 6*, 282–293.

OSHEROW, N. (1984) Making sense of the nonsensical: An analysis of Jonestown. In E. Aronson (Ed.), *Readings about the social animal* (4th ed., pp. 68–86). New York: Freeman.

OSHERSON, D., PERANI, D., CAPPA, S., SCHNUR, T., GRASSI, F., & FAZIO, F. (1998) Distinct brain loci in deductive versus probabilistic reasoning. *Neuropsychologia, 36*, 369–376.

OSHERSON, D. N., SMITH, E. E., WILKIE, O., LOPEZ, A., & SHAFIR, E. B. (1990) Category based induction. *Psychological Review, 97*, 185–200.

O'SULLIVAN, S. S., WU, K., POLITIS, M., LAWRENCE, A. D., EVANS, A. H., BOSE, S. K., *et al.* (2011) Cue-induced striatal dopamine release in parkinson's disease-associated impulsive-compulsive behaviours. *Brain, 134*(Pt 4), 969–978.

OVERMEIER, J. B., & SELIGMAN, M. E. P. (1967) Effects of inescapable shock upon subsequent escape and avoidance responding. *Journal of Comparative and Physiological Psychology, 63*, 28.

OVERMIER, J. B., & MURISON, R. (1998) Animal models reveal the "psych" in the psychosomatics of peptic ulcers. *Current Directions I Psychological Science, 6*, 180–184.

PACKER, D. J. (2008) Identifying systematic disobedience in Milgram's obedience experiments: A meta-analytic review. *Perspectives in Psychological Science, 3*, 301–304.

PAICHELER, G. (1977) Norms and attitude change: Pt. 1. Polarization and styles of behavior. *European Journal of Social Psychology, 7*, 5–14.

PAKENHAM, K. I., CHIU, J., BURSNALL, S., & CANNON, T. (2007) Relations between social support, appraisal and coping and both positive and negative outcomes in young carers. *Journal of Health Psychology, 12*, 89–102.

PALLIS, C. A. (1955) Impaired identification of faces and places with agnosia for colors. *Journal of Neurology, Neurosurgery, and Psychiatry, 18*, 218–224.

PALMER, S. E. (1975) The effect of contextual scenes on the identification of objects. *Memory and Cognition, 3*, 519–526.

PANAGOPOULOU, E., MAES, S., RIME, B., & MONTGOMERY, A. (2006) Social sharing of emotion in anticipation of cardiac surgery – Effects on preoperative distress. *Journal of Health Psychology, 11*, 809–820.

PANKSEPP, J. (1998) *Affective neuroscience: The foundations of human and animal emotions*. New York: Oxford University Press.

PAPAFRAGOU, A., HULBERT, J., & TRUESWELL, J. (2008) Does language guide event perception? Evidence from eye movements. *Cognition, 108*, 155–184.

PAPAFRAGOU, A., MASSEY, C., & GLEITMAN, L. (2002) Shake, rattle, 'n' roll: The representation of motion in thought and language. *Cognition, 84*, 189–219.

PARÉ, D., COLLINS, D. R., & PELLETIER, J. G. (2002) Amygdala oscillations and the consolidation of emotional memories. *Trends in Cognitive Sciences, 6*, 306–314.

PARK, S., & CATRAMBONE, R. (2007) Social facilitation effects of virtual humans. *Human Factors, 49* (6), 1054–1060.

PARKER, G., JOHNSTON, P., & HAYWARD, L. (1988) Parental "expressed emotion" as a predictor of schizophrenic relapse. *Archives of General Psychiatry, 45*, 806–813.

PARKINSON, B., & MANSTEAD, A. S. R. (1992) Appraisal as the cause of emotion. In M. S. Clark (Ed.), *Review of personality and social psychology* (Vol. 13, pp. 122–149). Newbury Park, CA: Sage.

PARKINSON, B., & TOTTERDELL, P. (1999) Classifying affect-regulation strategies. *Cognition and Emotion, 13*, 277–303.

PASUPATHI, M. (1999) Age differences in responses to conformity pressure for emotional and nonemotional material. *Psychology and Aging, 14*, 170–174.

PATALANO, A. L., SMITH, E. E., JONIDES, J., & KOEPPE, R. A. (2002) PET evidence for multiple strategies of categorization. *Cognitive, Affective, and Behavioral Neuroscience, 1*, 360–370.

PATEL, V. L., & GROEN, G. J. (1986) Knowledge based solution strategies in medical reasoning. *Cognitive Science, 10*, 91.

PATTERSON, F. G. (1978) The gestures of a gorilla: Language acquisition in another pongid. *Brain and Language, 5*, 72–97.

PATTERSON, G. (1974) Intervention for boys with conduct problems: Multiple settings, treatment, and criteria. *Journal of Consulting and Clinical Psychology, 42*, 471–483.

PATTERSON, G. R., LITTMAN, R. A., & BRICKER, W. A. (1967) Assertive behavior in children: A step toward a theory of aggression. *Monographs of the Society for Research in Child Development* (Serial No. 113), 5.

PAULOZZI, L., JONES, C. M., MACK, K. A. (November 1, 2011) Vital signs: Overdoses of prescription opioid pain relievers – United States, 1999–2008. Centers for Disease Control and Prevention. *Morbidity and Mortality Weekly Report, 60*, 1487–1492.

PAULSON, P. E., & ROBINSON, T. E. (1995) Amphetamine-induced time-dependent sensitization of dopamine neurotransmission in the dorsal and ventral striatum: A microdialysis study in behaving rats. *Synapse, 19*(1), 56–65.

PAULUS, M. (2011) How infants relate looker and object: Evidence for a perceptual learning account of gaze following in infancy. *Developmental Science, 14*(6), 1301–1310.

PAULUS, P. B. (1998) Developing consensus about groupthink after all these years. *Organizational Behavior and Human Decision Processes, 73*, 362–374.

PAVLOV, I. P. (1927) *Conditioned reflexes*. New York: Oxford University Press.

PAYNE, B. K. (2006) Weapon bias: split-second decisions and unintended stereotyping. *Current Directions in Psychological Science, 15* (6), 287–291.

PECINA, S., CAGNIARD, B., BERRIDGE, K. C., ALDRIDGE, J. W., & ZHUANG, X. (2003) Hyperdopaminergic mutant mice have higher "wanting" but not "liking" for sweet rewards. *Journal of Neuroscience, 23*, 9395–9402.

PELHAM, W. E., & BENDER, M. E. (1982) Peer relationships in hyperactive children. In K. Gadow & I. Bialer (Eds.), *Advances in learning and behavioral disabilities* (vol. 1, pp. 365–436). Greenwich, CT: JAI Press.

PENDRY, L., & CARRICK, R. (2001) Doing what the mob do: Priming effects on conformity. *European Journal of Social Psychology, 31*, 83–92.

PENFIELD, W., & JASPER, H. (1954) *Epilepsy and the functional anatomy of the human brain*. Boston: Little, Brown.

PENFIELD, W., & RASMUSSEN, T. (1950) *The cerebral cortex of man*. New York: Macmillan.

PENNEBAKER, J. W. (2007) Current issues and new directions in Psychology and Health: Listening to what people say—the value of narrative and computational linguistics in health psychology. *Psychology & Health, 22*, 631–635.

PENNEBAKER, J. W., KIECOLT-GLASER, J. K., & GLASER, R. (1988) Disclosure of traumas and immune function: Health implications for psychotherapy. *Journal of Consulting and Clinical Psychology, 56*, 239–245.

PENROD, S., & CUTLER, B. (1995) Witness confidence and witness accuracy: Assessing their forensic relation. Special Issue: Witness memory and law. *Psychology, Public Policy, & Law, 1*, 817–845.

PEPLAU, L. A., RUBIN, Z., & HILL, C. T. (1977) Sexual intimacy in dating relationships. *Journal of Social Issues, 33*, 86–109.

PERRIN, F. A. C. (1921) Physical attractiveness and repulsiveness. *Journal of Experimental Psychology, 4*, 203–217.

PERUNOVIC, W. Q. E., HELLER, D., & RAFAELI, E. (2007) Within-person changes in the structure of emotion: The role of cultural identification and language. *Psychological Science, 18*, 607–613.

PESSOA, L. (2008) On the relationship between emotion and cognition. *Nature Reviews Neuroscience, 9*, 148–158.

PETERSEN, A. C. (1989) Adolescent development. In M. R. Rosenzweig & L. W. Porter (Eds.), *Annual Review of Psychology* (Vol. 39). Palo Alto, CA: Annual Reviews.

PETERSON, C., SELIGMAN, M. E., & VAILLANT, G. E. (1988) Pessimistic explanatory style is a risk factor for physical illness: A thirty-five-year longitudinal study. *Journal of Personality & Social Psychology, 55*, 23–27.

PETERSON, L. R., & PETERSON, M. J. (1959) Short-term retention of individual verbal items. *Journal of Experimental Psychology, 10*, 12–21.

PETROVA, P. K., CIALDINI, R. B., & SILLS, S. J. (2007) Consistency-based compliance across cultures. *Journal of Experimental Social Psychology, 43* (1), 104–111.

PETTIGREW, T. F. (1979) The ultimate attribution error: Extending Allport's cognitive analysis of prejudice. *Personality and Social Psychology Bulletin, 5*, 461–476.

PETTY, R. E., & CACIOPPO, J. T. (1984) The effects of involvement on responses to argument quantity and quality: Central and peripheral routes to persuasion. *Journal of Personality and Social Psychology, 46*, 69–81.

PETTY, R. E., & WEGENER, D. T. (1999) The elaboration likelihood model: Current status and controversies. In S. Chaiken & Y. Trope (Eds.), *Dual-process theories in social psychology* (pp. 41–72). New York: Guilford.

PEZDEK, K., FINGER, K., & HODGE, D. (1997) Planting false childhood memories: The role of event plausibility. *Psychological Science, 8*, 437–441.

PHAN, M. L., SCHENDEL, K. L., RECANZONE, G. H., & ROBERTSON, L. C. (2000) Auditory and visual spatial localization deficits following bilateral parietal lobe lesions in a patient with Balint's syndrome. *Journal of Cognitive Neuroscience, 12*, 583–600.

PHILLIPS, J. L., JR. (1992) *How to think about statistics* (rev. ed.). New York: Freeman.

PHINNEY, J. S., & ALIPURIA, L. L. (1990) Ethnic identity in college students form four ethnic groups. *Journal of Adolescence, 13*, 171–183.

PHOENIX, C. H., GOY, R. H., & RESKO, J. A. (1968) Psychosexual differentiation as a function of androgenic stimulation. In M. Diamond (Ed.), *Reproduction and sexual behavior*. Bloomington: Indiana University Press.

PIAGET, J. (1932/1965) *The moral judgment of the child*. New York: Free Press.

PIAGET, J. (1950a) *The origins of intelligence in children*. New York: International Universities Press.

PIAGET, J. (1950b) *The psychology of intelligence*. New York: International Universities Press.

PIAGET, J., & INHELDER, B. (1956) *The child's conception of space*. London: Routledge & Kegan Paul. (Originally published 1948.)

PIAGET, J., & INHELDER, B. (1969) *The psychology of the child*. New York: Basic Books.

PILIAVIN, I. M., RODIN, J., & PILIAVIN, J. A. (1969) Good Samaritanism: An underground phenomenon: *Journal of Personality and Social Psychology, 13*, 289–299.

PLASSMANN, H., O'DOHERTY, J., SHIV, B., & RANGEL, A. (2008) Marketing actions can modulate neural representations of experienced pleasantness. *Proceedings of the National Academy of Sciences, 105*, 1050–1054.

PICKERING, T. G., DEVEREUX, R. B., JAMES, G. D., GERIN, W., LANDSBERGIS, P., SCHNALL, P. L., & SCHWARTZ, J. E. (1996) Environmental influences on blood pressure and the role of job strain. *Journal of Hypertension, 14* (Suppl.), S179–S185.

PILIAVIN, I. M., RODIN, J., & PILIAVIN, J. A. (1969) Good Samaritanism: An underground phenomenon: *Journal of Personality and Social Psychology, 13*, 289–299.

PINKER, S. (1991) Rules of language. *Science, 253*, 530–555.

PINKER, S. (1994). *The language instinct: How the mind creates language*. New York: Harper.

PINKER, S. (1997) *How the mind works*. New York: Norton

PINKER, S., & PRINCE, A. (1988) On language and connectionism: Analysis of a parallel distributed processing model of language acquisition. *Cognition, 28*, 71–193.

PINNELL, C. M., & COVINO, N. A. (2000) Empirical findings on the use of hypnosis in medicine: A critical review. *International Journal of Clinical and Experimental Hypnosis*, 48, 170–194.

PLAILLY, J., LUANGRAJ, N., NICKLAUS, S., ISSANCHOU, S., ROYET, J. P., & SOLLMONT-ROSSE, C. (2011) Alliesthesia is greater for odors of fatty foods than of non-fatty foods. *Appetite*, 57, 615–622.

PLANT, A. E., HYDE, J. S., KELTNER, D., & DEVINE, P. G. (2000) The gender stereotyping of emotions. *Psychology of Women Quarterly*, 24, 81–92.

PLANT, E. A., & DEVINE, P. G. (2009) The active control of prejudice: Unpacking the intentions guiding control efforts. *Journal of Personality and Social Psychology*, 96, 640–652.

PLATT, J. J., YAKSH, T., & DARBY, C. L. (1967) Social facilitation of eating behavior in armadillos. *Psychological Reports*, 20, 1136.

PLOEGER, A. (2008) Is evolutionary psychology a metatheory for psychology? A discussion of four major issues in psychology from an evolutionary developmental perspective. *Psychological Inquiry*, 19, 1–18.

PLOMIN, R. (1989) Environment and genes: Determinants of behavior. *American Psychologist*, 44, 105–111.

PLOMIN, R. (1990) *Nature and nurture: An introduction to human behavioral genetics*. Pacific Grove, CA: Brooks/Cole.

PLOMIN, R. (1994) *Genetics and experience*. Thousand Oaks, CA: Sage.

PLOMIN, R., & ASBURY, K. (2005) Nature and nurture: Genetic and environmental influences on behavior. *The ANNALS of the American Academy of Political and Social Science*, 600, 86.

PLOMIN, R., & KOSSLYN, S. M. (2001) Genes, brain and cognition. *Nature Neuroscience*, 4, 1153–1154.

PLOMIN, R., DEFRIES, J. C., & KNOPIK, V. S. (2012) Behavioral genetics (6th ed.). New York: Worth.

PLOMIN, R., OWEN, M. J., & MCGUFFIN, P. (1994) The genetic basis of complex human behaviors. *Science*, 264, 1733–1739.

PLOMIN, R., FULKER, D. W., CORLEY, R., & DEFRIES, J. C. (1997) Nature, nurture, and cognitive development from 1 to 16 years: A parent-offspring adoption study. *Psychological Science*, 8, 442–447.

PLOUS, S. (1996a) Attitudes toward the use of animals in psychological research and education: Results from a national survey of psychologists. *American Psychologist*, 51, 1167–1180.

PLOUS, S. (1996b) Attitudes toward the use of animals in psychological research and education: Results from a national survey of psychology majors. *Psychological Science*, 7, 352–358.

POLIVY, J., & HERMAN, C. P. (1985) Dieting and bingeing: A causal analysis. *American Psychologist*, 40, 193–201.

POLIVY, J., & HERMAN, C. P. (1993) Etiology of binge eating: Psychological mechanisms. In C. E. Fairburn & G. T. Wilson (Eds.), *Binge eating: Nature, assessment, and treatment*. New York: Guilford.

POLLATOS, O., KIRSCH, W., & SCHANDRY, R. (2005) On the relationship between interoceptive awareness, emotional experience, and brain processes. *Cognitive Brain Research*, 25, 948–962.

PORTENOY, R. K., & FOLEY, K. M. (1986) Chronic use of opioid analgesics in non-malignant pain: Report of 38 cases. *Pain*, 25, 171–186.

PORTER, R. H., MAKIN, J. W., DAVIS, L. B., & CHRISTENSEN, K. M. (1992) An assessment of the salient olfactory environment of formula-fed infants. *Physiology and Behavior*, 50, 907–911.

POSNER, M. I. (1988) Structures and functions of selective attention. In T. Boll & B. K. Bryant (Eds.), *Clinical neuropsychology and brain function: Research, measurement, and practice*. Washington, DC: American Psychological Association.

POSNER, M. I., & DEHAENE, S. (1994) Attentional networks. *Trends in Neuroscience*, 17, 75–79.

POSNER, M. I., & RAICHLE, M. E. (1994) *Images of mind*. New York: Scientific American Library.

POSTMES, T., & SPEARS, R. (1998) Deindividuation and antinormative behavior: A meta-analysis. *Psychological Bulletin*, 123, 238–259.

POSTMES, T., SPEARS, R., & CIHANGIR, S. (2001) Quality of decision making and group norms. *Journal of Personality and Social Psychology*, 80, 918–930.

POWELL, R. A., & BOER, D. P. (1994) Did Freud mislead patients to confabulate memories of abuse? *Psychological Reports*, 74, 1283–1298.

PRATT, D. S., JANDZIO, M., TOMLINSON, D., KANG, X., & SMITH, E. (2006) The 5-10-25 challenge: An observational study of a web-based wellness intervention for a global workforce. *Disease Management*, 9, 284–290.

PRENTICE, D. A., & MILLER, D. T. (1993) Pluralistic ignorance and alcohol use on campus: Some consequences of misperceiving the social norm. *Journal of Personality and Social Psychology*, 64, 243–256.

PRENTICE-DUNN, S., & ROGERS, R. W. (1982) Effect of public and private self-awareness on deindividuation and aggression. *Journal of Personality and Social Psychology*, 43, 503–513.

PRENTICE-DUNN, S., & ROGERS, R. W. (1989) Deindividuation and the self-regulation of behavior. In P. B. Paulus (Ed.), *The psychology of group influence* (2nd ed., pp. 86–109). Hillsdale, NJ: Erlbaum.

PRESSLEY, M., LEVIN, J. R., & DELANEY, H. D. (1982) The mnemonic keyword method. *Review of Educational Research*, 52, 61–91.

PRESSMAN, S. D., & COHEN, S. (2012) Positive emotion word use and longevity in famous deceased psychologists. *Health Psychology*, 31, 297–305.

PRESTON, S. D., & DE WAAL, F. B. M. (2002) Empathy: Its ultimate and proximate bases. *Behavioral Brain Science*, 25, 1–20.

PRETI, G., CUTLER, W. B., GARCIA, C. R., HUGGINS, G. R., and collaborators. (1986) Human axillary secretions influence women's menstrual cycles: The role of donor extract of females. *Hormones and Behavior*, 20, 474–482.

PRIEST, R. F., & SAWYER, J. (1967) Proximity and peership: Bases of balance in interpersonal attraction. *American Journal of Sociology*, 72, 633–649.

PRINZMETAL, W. (1981) Principles of feature integration in visual perception. *Perception and Psychophysics*, 30, 330–340.

PROJECT MATCH RESEARCH GROUP (1997) Matching alcoholism treatment to client heterogeneity: Project MATCH posttreatment drinking outcomes. *J. Studies Alcohol*, 58, 7–29.

PRONIN, E., & KUGLER, M. B. (2010) People believe they have more free will than others. *PNAS Proceedings of the National Academy of Sciences of the United States of America*, 107, 22469–22474.

PULVERMÜLLER, F., & FADIGA, L. (2010) Active perception: Sensorymotor circuits as a cortical basis for language. *National Review of Neuroscience*, 11, 351–360.

PUSWELLA, A., DEVITA, M., & ARNOLD, R. (2004) Declaring brain death: The neurologic criteria. *EPERC Fast Facts and Concepts*,

115. Retrieved from http://www.eperc.mcw.edu/fastfact/ff_ 115.htm.

QUINN, D. M., KALLEN, R. W., TWENGE, J. M., & FREDRICKSON, B. L. (2006) The disruptive effect of self-objectification on performance. *Psychology of Women Quarterly*, *30*, 6.

RAAIJMAKERS, J. G., & SHIFFRIN, R. M. (1981) Search of associative memory. *Psychological Review*, *88*, 93–134.

RAAIJMAKERS, J. G., & SHIFFRIN, R. M. (1992) Models for recall and recognition. *Annual Review of Psychology*, *43*, 205–234.

RACHMAN, S. (1998) A cognitive theory of obsessions: Elaborations. *Behaviour Research and Therapy*, *36*, 385–401.

RACHMAN, S. J., & HODGSON, R. J. (1980) *Obsessions and compulsions*. Englewood Cliffs, NJ: Prentice-Hall.

RAIKES, H., PAN, B. A., LUZE, G., TAMIS-LEMONDA, C., BROOKS-GUNN, J., CONSTANTINE, J., TARULLO, L. B., RAIKES, H. A., & RODRIGUEZ, E. T. (2006) Mother–child book-reading in low-income families: Correlates and outcomes during the first three years of life. *Child Development*, *77*, 924–953.

RÄIKKOENEN, K., MATTHEWS, K. A., FLORY, J. D., & OWENS, J. F. (1999) Effects of hostility on ambulatory blood pressure and mood during daily living in healthy adults. *Health Psychology*, *18*, 44–53.

RÄIKKONEN, K., MATTHEWS, K. A., FLORY, J. D., OWENS, J. F., & GUMP, B. B. (1999) Effects of optimism, pessimism, and trait anxiety on ambulatory blood pressure and mood during everyday life. *Journal of Personality and Social Psychology*, *76*, 104–113.

RAMACHANDRAN, V. S., & GREGORY, R. L. (1991) Perceptual filling in of artificially induced scotomas in human vision. *Nature*, *350*, 699–702.

RAMUS, F. (2002) Language discrimination by newborns: teasing apart phonotactic, rhythmic, and intonational cues. *Annual Review of Language Acquisition*, *2*, 851–815.

RAPAPORT, D. (1942) *Emotions and memory*. Baltimore: Williams & Wilkins.

RAPEE, R. M., BROWN, T. A., ANTONY, M. M., & BARLOW, D. H. (1992) Response to hyperventilation and inhalation of 5.5% carbon dioxide-enriched air across the DSM III-R anxiety disorders. *Journal of Abnormal Psychology*, *101*, 538–552.

RASEKH, A., BAUER, H.M., MANOS, M. M., & IACOPINO, V. (1998) Women's health and human rights in Afghanistan. *Journal of the American Medical Association*, *280*, 449–455.

RATHBUN, C., DI VIRGILIO, L., & WALDFOGEL, S. (1958) A restitutive process in children following radical separation from family and culture. *American Journal of Orthopsychiatry*, *28*, 408–415.

RAUCH, S. L. (2003) Neuroimaging and neurocircuitry models pertaining to the neurosurgical treatment of psychiatric disorders. *Neurosurgery Clinics of North America*, *14*, 213–223.

RAUCH, S. L., WEDIG, M. M., WRIGHT, C. I., MARTIS, B., MCMULLIN, K. G., SHIN, L. M., CANNISTRARO, P.A., & WILHELM, S. (2007) Functional magnetic resonance imaging study of regional brain activation during implicit sequence learning in obsessive-compulsive disorder. *Biological Psychiatry*, *61*, 330–336.

RAVENS, J. C. (1965) *Advanced progressive matrices, sets II and II*. London: H. K. Lewis.

RAVUSSIN, E., and collaborators. (1988) Reduced rate of energy expenditure as a risk factor for body-weight gain. *New England Journal of Medicine*, *318*, 467–472.

RAY, N., MIYASAKI, J. M., ZUROWSKI, M., KO, J. H., CHO, S. S., PELLECCHIA, G., *et al.* (2012) Extrastriatal dopaminergic abnormalities of da homeostasis in parkinson's patients with medication-induced pathological gambling: A [11c] flb-457 and pet study. *Neurobiology of Disease*, *48*(3), 519–525.

RAY, R. D., OCHSNER, K. N., COOPER, J. C., ROBERTSON, E. R., GABRIELI, J. D. E., GROSS, J. J. (2005) Individual differences in trait rumination and the neural systems supporting cognitive reappraisal. *Cognitive, Affective & Behavioral Neuroscience*, *5*, 156–168.

RAYNER, K. (1978) Eye movements, reading and information processing. *Psychological Bulletin*, *6*, 618–660.

REED, C. F. (1984) Terrestrial passage theory of the moon illusion. *Journal of Experimental Psychology: General*, *113*, 489–500.

REED, G. M., KEMENY, M. E., TAYLOR, S. E., WANG, H.-Y. J., & VISSCHER, B. R. (1994) "Realistic acceptance" as a predictor of decreased survival time in gay men with AIDS. *Health Psychology*, *13*, 299–307.

REED, P., SKIERA, F., ADAMS, L., & HEYES, C. M. (1996) Effects of isolation rearing and mirror exposure on social and asocial discrimination performance. *Learning and Motivation*, *27*, 113–129.

REGAN, D., BEVERLEY, K. I., & CYNADER, M. (1979) The visual perception of motion depth. *Scientific American*, *241*, 136–151.

REGAN, D. T., & FAZIO, R. (1977) On the consistency between attitudes and behavior: Look to the method of attitude information. *Journal of Experimental Social Psychology*, *13*, 28–45.

REGIER, T., KAY, P., & KHETARPAL, N. (2007) Color naming reflects optimal partitions of color space. *PNAS*, *104*, 1436–1441.

REICHER, G. M. (1969) Perceptual recognition as a function of the meaningfulness of the material. *Journal of Experimental Psychology*, *81*, 275–280.

REICHER, S. D., & HASLAM, S. A. (2006) Rethinking the social psychology of tyranny: The BBC Prison Study. *British Journal of Social Psychology*, *45*, 1–40.

REICHER, S. D., HASLAM, S. A., & SMITH, J. R. (2012) Working toward the experimenter: Reconceptualizing obedience within the Milgram paradigm as identification-based followship. *Perspectives on Psychological Science*, *7*, 315–324.

REINITZ, M. T., & HANNIGAN, S. L. (2004) False memories for compound words: Role of working memory. *Memory & Cognition*, *32*, 463–473.

REINITZ, M. T., WRIGHT, E., & LOFTUS, G. R. (1989) The effects of semantic priming on visual encoding of pictures. *Journal of Experimental Psychology: General*, *118*, 280–297.

REIS, D. J., & GUNNE, L. M. (1965) Brain catecholamines: Relation to the defense reaction evoked by amygdaloid stimulation in cat. *Science*, *149*, 450–451.

REIS, D. J., MIURA, M., WEINBREN, M., & GUNNE, L. M. (1967) Brain catecholamines: Relation to defense reaction evoked by acute brainstem transection in cat. *Science*, *156*, 1768–1770.

REIS, H. T., MANIACI, M. R., CAPRARIELLO, P. A., EASTWICK, P. W., & FINKEL, E. J. (2011) Familiarity does indeed promote attraction in live interaction. *Journal of Personality and Social Psychology*, *101*, 557–570.

REISENZEIN, R. (1983) The Schachter theory of emotion: Two decades later. *Psychological Bulletin*, *94*, 239–264.

REISS, D. (2005) The interplay between genotypes and family relationships: Reframing concepts of development and prevention. *Current Directions in Psychological Science*, *14*, 139–143.

REMINGTON, B., ROBERTS, P., & GLAUTIER, S. (1997) The effect of drink familiarity on tolerance to alcohol. *Addiction Behavior*, *22*, 45–53.

REPPEN, J. (2006) The relevance of Sigmund Freud for the 21st century. *Psychoanalytic Psychology*, *23*, 215–216.

RESCORLA, R. A. (1967) Pavlovian conditioning and its proper control procedures. *Psychological Review*, *74*, 71–80.

RESCORLA, R. A. (1968) Probability of shock in the presence and absence of CS in fear conditioning. *Journal of Comparative and Physiological Psychology*, *66*, 1–55.

RESCORLA, R. A. (1972) Informational variables in Pavlovian conditioning. In G. H. Bower (Ed.), *Psychology of learning and motivation* (Vol. 6). New York: Academic Press.

RESCORLA, R. A. (1980) Overextension in early language development. *Journal of Child Language*, *7*, 321–335.

RESCORLA, R. A. (1987) A Pavlovian analysis of goal-directed behavior. *American Psychologist*, *42*, 119–129.

RESCORLA, R. A., & SOLOMON, R. L. (1967) Two-process learning theory: Relations between Pavlovian conditioning and instrumental learning. *Psychological Review*, *74*, 151–182.

RESICK, P. A. (1993). The psychological impact of rape. *Journal of Interpersonal Violence, 8*, 223–255.

RESNICK, H. S., KILPATRICK, D. G., DANSKY, B. S., & SAUNDERS, B. E. (1993) Prevalence of civilian trauma and posttraumatic stress disorder in a representative national sample of women. *Journal of Consulting and Clinical Psychology*, *61*, 984–991.

RESNICK, H. S., YEHUDA, R., PITMAN, R. K., & FOY, D. W. (1995) Effect of previous trauma on acute plasma cortisol level following rape. *American Journal of Psychiatry*, *152*, 1675–1677.

REUBENS, A. B., & BENSON, D. F. (1971) Associative visual agnosia. *Archives of Neurology*, *24*, 305–316.

REYNOLDS, D. V. (1969) Surgery in the rat during electrical analgesia induced by focal brain stimulation. *Science*, *164*, 444–445.

RICHARDS, J. M., & GROSS, J. J. (2000) Emotion regulation and memory: The cognitive costs of keeping one's cool. *Journal of Personality and Social Psychology*, *79*, 410–424.

RIEGER, G., LINSENMEIER, J. A. W., GYGAX, L., & BAILEY, J. M. (2008) Sexual orientation and childhood gender nonconformity: Evidence from home videos. *Developmental Psychology*, *44*, 46–58.

RIESEN, A. H. (1947) The development of visual perception in man and chimpanzee. *Science*, *106*, 107–108.

RIPS, L. J. (1983) Cognitive processes in propositional reasoning. *Psychological Review*, *90*, 38–71.

RIPS, L. J. (1994) *The psychology of proof*. Cambridge, MA: MIT Press.

RIVERS, S. E., BRACKETT, M. A., REYES, M. R., MAYER, J. D., CARUSO, D. R., & SALOVEY, P. (2012) Measuring emotional intelligence in early adolescence with the MSCEIT-YV: Psychometric properties and relationship with academic performance and psychosocial functioning. *Journal of Psychoeducational Assessment*, *30*, 344–366.

RIZZOLATTI, G., FADIGA, L., GALLESE, V., & FOGASSI, L. (1995) Premotor cortex and the recognition of motor actions. *Cognitive Brain Research*, *3*, 131–141.

ROBINSON, M. D. (1998) Running from William James' bear: A review of preattentive mechanisms and their contributions to emotional experience. *Cognition and Emotion*, *12*, 667–696.

ROBINSON, T. E., & BERRIDGE, K. C. (1993) The neural basis of drug craving: An incentive-sensitization theory of addiction. *Brain Research Reviews*, *18*(3), 247–291.

ROBINSON, T. E., & BERRIDGE, K. C. (2003) Addiction. *Annual Reviews in Psychology*, *54*, 25–53.

ROBINSON, T. E., & BERRIDGE, K. C. (2008) The incentive sensitization theory of addiction: Some current issues. *Philos. Trans. R. Soc. Lond. B. Biol. Sci.*, *363*(1507), 3137–3146.

ROCK, I. (1988) On Thompson's inverted-face phenomenon (Research Note). *Perception*, *17*, 815–817.

RODIN, J. (1981) Current status of the internal-external hypothesis of obesity: What went wrong? *American Psychologist*, *36*, 361–372.

ROEDIGER, H. L., III, & MCDERMOTT, K. B. (1995) Creating false memories: Remembering words not presented in lists. *Journal of Experimental Psychology: Learning, Memory, & Cognition*, *21*, 803–814.

ROGAN, M. T., & LEDOUX, J. E. (1996) Emotion: Systems, cells, synaptic plasticity. *Cell*, *85*, 469–475.

ROGERS, C. R. (1951) *Client-centered therapy*. Boston: Houghton Mifflin.

ROGERS, C. R. (1959) A theory of therapy, personality, and interpersonal relationships as developed in the client-centered framework. In S. Koch (Ed.), *Psychology: A study of a science*: Vol. 3. *Formulations of the person and the social context*. New York: McGraw-Hill.

ROGERS, C. R. (1963) The actualizing tendency in relation to motives and to consciousness. In M. Jones (Ed.), *Nebraska symposium on motivation* (pp. 1–24). Lincoln: University of Nebraska Press.

ROGERS, C. R. (1970) *On becoming a person: A therapist's view of psychotherapy*. Boston: Houghton Mifflin.

ROGERS, T. B., KUIPER, N. A., & KIRKER, W. S. (1977) Self-reference and the encoding of personal information. *Journal of Personality and Social Psychology*, *35*, 677–688.

ROGOFF, B. (2000) *Culture and development*. New York: Oxford University Press.

ROHR, M., DEGNER, J., & WENTURA, D. (2012) Masked emotional priming beyond global valence activations. *Cognition and Emotion*, *26*, 224–244.

ROLAND, P. E., & FRIBERG, L. (1985) Localization of cortical areas activated by thinking. *Journal of Neurophysiology*, *53*, 1219–1243.

ROSCH, E. (1974) Linguistic relativity. In A. Silverstein (Ed.), *Human communication: Theoretical perspectives*. New York: Halsted Press.

ROSCH, E. (1978) Principles of categorization. In E. Rosch & B. L. Lloyd (Eds.), *Cognition and categorization*. Hillsdale, NJ: Erlbaum.

ROSE, J. E., BRUGGE, J. F., ANDERSON, D. J., & HIND, J. E. (1967) Phase-locked response to lower frequency tones in single auditory nerve fibers of the squirrel monkey. *Journal of Neurophysiology*, *390*, 769–793.

ROSEBERGER, P. H., ICKOVICS, J. R., EPEL, E. S., D'ENTREMONT, D., & JOKL, P. (2004) Physical recovery in arthroscopic knee surgery: Unique contributions of coping behaviors to clinical outcomes and stress reactivity. *Psychology and Health*, *19*, 307–320.

ROSEMAN, I. J. (1984) Cognitive determinants of emotion: A structural theory. *Review of Personality and Social Psychology*, *5*, 11–36.

ROSENBERGER, P. H., ICKOVICS, J. R., EPEL, E. S., D'ENTREMONT, D., & JOKL, P. (2004) Physical recovery in arthroscopic knee surgery: Unique contributions of coping behaviors to clinical outcomes and stress reactivity. *Psychology and Health, 19*, 307–320.

ROSENBERG, E. L. (1998) Levels of analysis and the organization of affect. *Review of General Psychology, 2*, 247–270.

ROSENGREN, A., HAWKEN, S., OUNPUU, S., SLIWA, K., ZUBAID, M., ALMAHMEED, W. A., BLACKETT, K., N., SITTHI-AMORN, C., SATO, H., & YUSUF, S. (2004). Association of psychosocial risk factors with the risk of acute myocardial infarction in 11119 cases and 13648 controls from 52 countries (the INTERHEART study): Case-control study. *The Lancet, 364*, 953–962.

ROSENMAN, R. H., BRAND, R. J., JENKINS, C. D., FRIEDMAN, M., STRAUS, R., & WRUM, M. (1976) Coronary heart disease in the Western Collaborative Group Study: Final follow-up experience of 8½ years. *Journal of the American Medical Association, 233*, 878–877.

ROSENTHAL, R. (1984) *Meta-analytic procedures for social research*. Beverly Hills, CA: Sage.

ROSENTHAL, R., & JACOBSON, L. (1968) *Pygmalion in the classroom: Teacher expectation and student intellectual development*. New York: Holt, Rinehart, & Winston.

ROSS, B. H. (1984) Reminders and their effects in learning a cognitive skill. *Cognitive Psychology, 16*, 371–416.

ROSS, L. (1997) The intuitive psychologist and his shortcomings: Distortions in the attribution process. In L. Berkowitz, (Ed.), *Advances in experimental social psychology* (Vol. 10). New York: Academic Press.

ROSS, L., AMABILE, T. M., & STEINMETZ, J. L. (1977) Social roles, social control, and biases in social-perception processes. *Journal of Personality and Social Psychology, 35*, 485–494.

ROSS, L., BIERBRAUER, G., & HOFFMAN, S. (1976) The role of attribution processes in conformity and dissent. Revisiting the Asch situation. *American Psychologist, 31*, 148–157.

ROTH, M. (1998) *Freud: Conflict and culture*. New York: Knopf.

ROTHBART, M., & BATES, J. (1998) Temperament. In W. Damon (Series Ed.) and N. Eisenberg (Vol. Ed.), *Handbook of child psychology*: Vol. 3. *Social, emotional and personality development* (5th ed., pp. 105–176). New York: Wiley.

ROVEE-COLLIER, C. (1999) The development of infant memory. *Current Directions in Psychological Science, 8*, 80–85.

ROWE, G., HIRSH, J. B., & ANDERSON, A. K. (2007) Positive affect increases the breadth of attentional selection. *Proceedings of the National Academy of Sciences of the United States of America, 104*, 383–388.

ROWLAND, N. E., & ANTELMAN, S. M. (1976) Stress-induced hyperphagia and obesity in rats: A possible model for understanding human obesity. *Science, 191*, 310–312.

ROY-BYRNE, P. P., CRASKE, M. G., & STEIN, M. B. (2006) Panic disorder. *Lancet, 368*, 1023–1032..

ROZIN, P., HAIDT, J., & FINCHER, K. (2009). From oral to moral. *Science, 323*, 1179–1180.

ROZIN, P, HAIDT, J., & MCCAULEY, C. R. (2000) Disgust. In M. Lewis & J. M. Haviland-Jones (Eds.), *Handbook of emotions*, 2nd ed. (pp. 637–653). New York: Guilford Press.

RUBIN, Z. (1973) *Liking and loving*. New York: Holt, Rinehart & Winston.

RUBLE, D., & FREY, K. S. (1991) Changing patterns of comparative behavior as skills are acquired: A functional model of self-evaluation. In J. Suls & T. A. Wills (Eds.), *Social comparisons:* *Contemporary theory and research* (pp. 79–113). Hillsdale, NJ: Erlbaum.

RUDERMAN, A. J. (1986). Dietary restraint: A theoretical and empirical review. *Psychological Bulletin, 99*, 247–262.

RUDMAN, L. A., & BORGIDA, E. (1995) The afterglow of construct accessibility: The behavioral consequences of priming men to view women as sexual objects. *Journal of Experimental Social Psychology, 31*, 493–517.

RUMELHART, D. E., & MCCLELLAND, J. L. (1987) Learning the past tenses of English verbs: Implicit rules or parallel distributed processing? In B. MacWhinney (Ed.), *Mechanisms of language acquisition*. Hillsdale, NJ: Erlbaum.

RUSSELL, J. A. (2003) Core affect and the psychological construction of emotion. *Psychological Review, 110*, 145–172.

RUSSELL, M. J. (1976) Human olfactory communication. *Nature, 260*, 520–522.

RUSSELL, M. J., SWITZ, G. M., & THOMPSON, K. (1980) Olfactory influence on the human menstrual cycle. *Pharmacology, Biochemistry and Behavior, 13*, 737–738.

RUTTER, M. (1997) Antisocial behavior: Developmental psychopathology perspectives. In D. M. Stoff, J. Breiling, & J. D. Maser (Eds.), *Handbook of antisocial personality disorder* (pp. 115–124). New York: Wiley.

RUTTER, M., QUINTON, D., & HILL, J. (1990) Adult outcome of institution-reared children: Males and females compared. In L. Robins (Ed.), *Straight and devious pathways from childhood to adulthood* (pp. 135–157). Cambridge: Cambridge University Press.

RYMER, R. (1992a, April 13) A silent childhood. *New Yorker*, pp. 41–53.

RYMER, R. (1992b, April 20) A silent childhood, pt. II. *New Yorker*, pp. 43–47.

SACHS, J. D. S. (1967) Recognition memory for syntactic and semantic aspects of connected discourse. *Perception and Psychophysics, 2*, 437–442.

SACKS, O. (1985) *The man who mistook his wife for a hat and other clinical tales*. New York: Harper Perennial.

SAFER, D. J., ZITO, J. M., & FINE, E. M. (1996) Increased methylphenidate usage for attention deficit disorder in the 1990s. *Pediatrics, 98*, 1084–1088.

SAHIN, N. T., PINKER, S., CASH, S. S., SCHOMER, D, & HALGREN, E. (2009) Sequential processing of lexical, grammatical, and phonological information within Broca's area. *Science, 326*, 445–449.

SALAPATEK, P. (1975) Pattern perception in early infancy. In L. B. Cohen & P. Salapatek (Eds.), *Infant perception: From sensation to cognition* (Vol. 1). New York: Academic Press.

SALKOVSKIS, P. M. (1991) The importance of behaviour in the maintenance of anxiety and panic: A cognitive account. *Behavioural Psychotherapy. Special issue: The changing face of behavioural psychotherapy, 19*, 6–19.

SALKOVISKIS, P. M. (1999) Understanding and treating obsessive-compulsive disorder. *Behaviour Research and Therapy, 37*, S29–S52.

SALOVEY, P., & MAYER, J. D. (1990) Emotional intelligence. *Imagination, Cognition & Personality, 9*, 185–211.

SAMHSA (SUBSTANCE ABUSE AND MENTAL HEALTH SERVICES ADMINISTRATION) (2002) *National survey on drug use and health*. Retrieved November 1, 2004, from http://www.oas.samhsa.gov/nhsda2k2.htm.

SAMHSA (SUBSTANCE ABUSE AND MENTAL HEALTH SERVICES ADMINISTRATION) (2004) *Overview of Findings from the 2003 National Survey on Drug Use and Health* (Office of Applied Studies, NSDUH Series H-24, DHHS Publication No. SMA 04-3963). Rockville, MD.

SAMHSA (SUBSTANCE ABUSE AND MENTAL HEALTH SERVICES ADMINISTRATION) (2010) *Results from the 2009 National Survey on Drug Use and Health: Volume 1: Summary of national findings*. Rockville, MD: US DHHS, SAMHSA, Office of Applied Studies.

SAMS, M., AULANKO, R., HAMALAINEN, M., HARI, R., LOUNASMAA, O. V., LU, S.T., & SIMOLA, J. (1991) Seeing speech: visual information from lip movements modifies activity in the human auditory cortex. *Neuroscience Letters, 127*, 141–145.

SAMPSON, R., & GIFFORD, S. M. (2010) Place-making, settlement and well-being: The therapeutic landscapes of recently arrived youth with refugee background. *Health & Place, 16*, 116–131.

SANDER, R. H. (2004) A systemic analysis of affirmative action in American law schools. *Stanford Law Review, 57*, 367–483.

SANDERS, G. S., & BARON, R. S. (1977) Is social comparison irrelevant for producing choice shifts? *Journal of Experimental Social Psychology, 13*, 303–314.

SANDERSON, W. C., RAPEE, R. M., & BARLOW, D. H. (1989) The influence of illusion of control on panic attacks induced via inhalation of 5.5% carbon dioxide-enriched air. *Archives of General Psychology, 46*, 157–162.

SANOCKI, T. (1993) Time course of object identification: Evidence for a global to local contingency. *Journal of Experimental Psychology: Human Perception & Performance, 19*, 878–898.

SAPOLSKY, R.M.. (2007) Why zebras don't get ulcers: Stress, metabolism, and liquidating your assets. In A. Monat, R. S. Lazarus, & G. Reevy (Eds.), *The Praeger handbook on stress and coping*, Vol. 1 (pp. 181–197). Westport, CT: Praeger.

SANTTILA, P., SANDNABBA, N. K., HARLAAR, N., VARJONEN, M., ALANKO, K., & VON DER PAHLEN, B. (2008) Potential for homosexual response is prevalent and genetic. *Biological Psychology, 77*, 102–105.

SATINOFF, E. (2005) Thermoregulation. In I. Q. Whishaw & B. Kolb (Eds.), *The behavior of the laboratory rat: A handbook with tests* (pp. 226–235). New York: Oxford University Press.

SAUNDERS, D. R. (1985) On Hyman's factor analyses. *Journal of Parapsychology, 49*, 86–88.

SAVAGE, S. R., KIRSH, K. L., PASSIK, S. D. (2008) Challenges in using opioids to treat pain in persons with substance use disorders. *Addiction Science and Clinical Practice, 4*, 4–25.

SAYLER, R. D. (1992) Ecology and evolution of brood parasitism in waterfowl. In B. D. J. Batt, A. D. Afton, M. G. Anderson, C. D. Ankney, D. H. Johnson, J. A. Kadlec, & G. L. Krapu (Eds.), *Ecology and management of breeding waterfowl* (pp. 290–320). Minneapolis, MN: University of Minnesota Press.

SCARR, S. (1985) An author's frame of mind: Review of Frames of Mind, by Howard Gardner. *New Ideas in Psychology, 3*, 95–100.

SCARR, S. (1992) Developmental theories for the 1990s: Development and individual differences. *Child Development, 63*, 1–19.

SCARR, S. (1996) How people make their own environments: Implications for parents and policy makers. *Psychology, Public Policy, and Law, 2*, 204–228.

SCARR, S., & MCCARTNEY, K. (1983) How people make their own environments: A theory of genotype-environment effects. *Child Development, 54*, 424–435.

SCARR, S., WEINBERG, R. A., & LEVINE, A. (1986) *Understanding development*. San Diego: Harcourt Brace Jovanovich.

SCHACHTEL, E. G. (1982) On memory and childhood amnesia. In U. Neisser (Ed.), *Memory observed: Remembering in natural contexts*. San Francisco: Freeman.

SCHACHTER, S. (1964) The interaction of cognitive and physiological determinants of emotional state. In L. Berkowitz (Ed.), *Advances in experimental social psychology* (pp. 49–80). New York: Academic Press.

SCHACHTER, S., & SINGER, J. E. (1962) Cognitive, social and physiological determinants of emotional state. *Psychological Review, 69*, 379–399.

SCHACTER, D. L. (1989) Memory. In M. Posner (Ed.), *Foundations of cognitive science*. Cambridge, MA: MIT Press.

SCHACTER, D. L., KASZNIAK, A. K., KIHLSTROM, J. F., & VALDISERRI, M. (1991) The relation between source memory and aging. *Psychology and Aging, 6*, 559–568.

SCHAFER, R. (1976) *A new language for psychoanalysis*. New Haven, CT: Yale University Press.

SCHALLER, M., & PARK, J. H. (2011) The behavioral immune system (and why it matters). *Current Directions in Psychological Science, 20*, 99–103.

SCHANCK, R. L. (1932) A study of a community and its groups and institutions conceived of as behaviors of individuals. *Psychological Monographs, 43*, 1–133.

SCHARNBERG, M. (1993) *The nonauthentic nature of Freud's observations: Vol. 1. The seduction theory*. Philadelphia: Coronet.

SCHEIER, M. F., BUSS, A. H., & BUSS, D. M. (1978) Self-consciousness, self-reports of aggressiveness, and aggressions. *Journal of Research in Personality, 12*, 133–140.

SCHEIER, M. F., MATTHEWS, K. A., OWENS, J. F., MAGOVERN, G. J., LEFEBYRE, R. C., ABBOTT, R. A., & CARVER, C. S. (1989) Dispositional optimism and recovery from coronary artery bypass surgery: The beneficial effects on physical and psychological well-being. *Journal of Personality and Social Psychology, 57*, 1024–1040. (Reprinted in P. Salovey & A. J. Rothman (Eds.), *Social psychology of health* (pp. 342–361). New York: Psychology Press, 2003.)

SCHIFFENBAUER, A., & SCHIAVO, R. S. (1976) Physical distance and attraction: An intensification effect. *Journal of Experimental Social Psychology, 12*, 274–282.

SCHINDEL, R., & ARNOLD, D. H. (2010, May 11) Visual sensitivity can scale with illusory size changes. *Current Biology, 20*(9), 841–844.

SCHLEIDT, M., HOLD, B., & ATTILI, G. (1981) A cross-cultural study on the attitude toward personal odors. *Journal of Chemical Ecology, 7*, 19–31.

SCHLESINGER, A. M., JR. (1965) *A thousand days*. Boston: Houghton Mifflin.

SCHMADER, T. (2010) Stereotype threat deconstructed. *Current Directions in Psychological Science, 19*, 14–18.

SCHMITZ, T. W., DE ROSA, E., & ANDERSON, A. K. (2009) Opposing influences of affective valence on visual cortical encoding. *Journal of Neuroscience, 29*, 7199–7207.

SCHMOLCK, H., BUFFALO, E. A., & SQUIRE, L. (2000) Memory distortions develop over time: Recollections of the O. J. Simpson trial verdict after 15 and 32 months. *Psychological Science, 11*, 39–45.

SCHNEIDER, D. J., & MILLER, R. S. (1975) The effects of enthusiasm and quality of arguments on attitude attribution. *Journal of Personality, 43*, 693–708.

SCHNEIDERMAN, N., IRONSON, G., & SIEGEL, S. D. (2005). Stress and health: Psychological, behavioral, and biological determinants. *Annual Review of Clinical Psychology, 1*, 607–628.

SCHOLTE, W. F., OLFF, M., VENTEVOGEL, P., DE VRIES, G.-J., JANSVELD, E., CARDOZO, B. L., & CRAWFORD, C. A. G. (2004) Mental health symptoms following war and repression in eastern Afghanistan. *Journal of the American Medical Association, 292*, 585–593.

SCHOU, I., EKEBERG, O., & RULAND, C. M. (2005) The mediating role of appraisal and coping in the relationship between optimism-pessimism and quality of life. *Psychooncology, 14*, 718–727.

SCHRAMMEL, F., PANNASCH, S., GRAUPNER, S., MOJZISCH, A., & VELICHKOVSKY, B. M. (2009) Virtual friend or threat?: The effects of facial expression and gaze interaction on psychophysiological responses and emotional experience. *Psychophysiology, 46*, 922–931.

SCHREDL, M. (2007) Dream recall: Models and empirical data. In D. Barrett & P. McNamara (Eds.), *The new science of dreaming*, Vol. 2: Content, recall, and personality correlates (pp. 79–114). Westport, CT: Praeger Perspectives.

SCHROEDER, C. M., & PRENTICE, D. A. (1998) Exposing pluralistic ignorance to reduce alcohol use among college students. *Journal of Applied Social Psychology, 28*, 2150–2180.

SCHULTZ, R. T. (2005) Developmental deficits in social perception in autism: The role of the amygdala and fusiform face area. *International Journal of Developmental Neuroscience, 23*, 125–141.

SCHULTZ, W. (2002) Getting formal with dopamine and reward. *Neuron, 36*, 241–263.

SCHUMANN, J. (1978) The acculturation model for second-language acquisition. In R. Gringas (Ed.), *Second language acquisition and foreign language teaching* (pp. 27-50). Washington, DC: Center for Applied Linguistics.

SCHUR, E. M. (1971) *Labeling deviant behavior: Its sociological implications*. New York: Harper & Row.

SCHWARTZ, B. (1989) *Psychology of learning and behavior* (3rd ed.). New York: Norton.

SCHWARTZ, B., SNIDMAN, N., & KAGAN, J. (1996) Early childhood temperament as a determinant of externalizing behavior in adolescence. *Development and Psychopathology, 8*, 527–537.

SCHWARTZ, J., STOESSEL, P. W., BAXTER, L. R., MARTIN, K. M., & PHELPS, M. C. (1996) Systemic changes in cerebral glucose metabolic rate after successful behavior modification treatment of obsessive compulsive disorder. *Archives of General Psychiatry, 53*, 109–113.

SCHWARZ, N., & CLORE, G. L. (2003) Mood as information: 20 years later. *Psychological Inquiry, 14*, 296–303.

SCHWARZKOPF, D. S., SONG, C., & REES, G. (2011) The surface area of human V1 predicts the subjective experience of object size. *Nature Neuroscience, 14*(1), 28–30.

SCHYNS, P. G., & OLIVA, A. (1994) From blobs to boundary edges: Evidence for time- and spatial-scale-dependent scene recognition. *Psychological Science, 5*, 195–200.

SCOTT, T. R., & MARK, G. P. (1986) Feeding and taste. *Progress in Neurobiology, 27*, 293–317.

SEARS, R. R., MACCOBY, E. E., & LEVIN, H. (1957) *Patterns of child rearing*. New York: Harper & Row.

SEGAL, Z. V., WILLIAMS, J, M. G., & TEASDALE, J. D. (2002) *Mindfulness-based cognitive therapy for depression: A new approach to preventing relapse*. New York: Guildford press.

SEGERSTROM, S. C., & MILLER, G. E. (2004). Psychological stress and the human immune system: A meta-analytic study of 30 years of inquiry. *Psychological Bulletin, 130*, 601–630.

SEGERSTROM, S. C. (2007) Optimism and resources: Effects on each other and on health over 10 years. *Journal of Research in Personality, 41*, 772–786.

SEGERSTROM, S. C., SOLOMON, G. F., KEMENY, M. E., & FAHEY, J. L. (1998) Relationship of worry to immune sequelae of the Northridge earthquake. *Journal of Behavioral Medicine, 21*, 433–450.

SEGERSTROM, S. C., TAYLOR, S. E., KEMENY, M. E., & FAHEY, J. L. (1998) Optimism is associated with mood, coping, and immune change in response to stress. *Journal of Personality and Social Psychology, 74*, 1646–1655.

SEGERSTROM, S. C., TAYLOR, S. E., KEMENY, M. E., REED, G. M., & VISSCHER, B. R. (1996) Causal attributions predict rate of immune decline in HIV seropositive gay men. *Health Psychology, 15*, 485–493.

SEIFERT, C. M., ROBERTSON, S. P., & BLACK, J. B. (1985) Types of inferences generated during reading. *Journal of Memory and Language, 24*, 405–422.

SEKULER, R. (1975) Visual motion perception. In E. C. Carterette & M. Friedman (Eds.), *Handbook of perception* (Vol. 5, pp. 387–433). New York: Academic Press.

SELIGMAN, M. E. P. (1975) *Helplessness*. San Francisco: Freeman.

SELIGMAN, M. E. P. (2002) Positive psychology, positive prevention, and positive therapy. In C. R. Synder & S. J. Lopez (Eds.) *Handbook of Positive Psychology* (pp. 3–9). New York: Oxford University Press.

SELIGMAN, M. E. P. (2011) *Flourish: A visionary new understanding of happiness and well-being*. New York: Free Press.

SELIGMAN, M. E. P., & BINIK, Y. M. (1977) The safety signal hypothesis. In H. Davis & H. Hurwitz (Eds.), *Pavlovian operant interactions*. Hillsdale, NJ: Erlbaum.

SELIGMAN, M. E. P., & CSIKSZENTMIHALYI, M. (2000) Positive psychology: An introduction. *American Psychologist, 55*, 5–14.

SELLERS, R. M., SMITH, J. A., SHELTON, J. N., ROWLEY, S. A. J., & CHAVOUS, T. M. (1998) Multidimensional model of racial identity: A reconceptualization of African American racial identity. *Personality and Social Psychology Review, 2*, 18–39.

SELYE, H. (1978) *The stress of life*. New York: McGraw-Hill.

SERBIN, L. A., POWLISHTA, K. K., & GULKO, J. (1993) The development of sex typing in middle childhood. *Monographs of the Society for Research in Child Development, 58* (2, Serial No. 232).

SERGENT, J. (1984) Configural processing of faces in the left and the right cerebral hemispheres. *Journal of Experimental Psychology Human Perception and Performance, 10*, 554–572.

SEWELL, W. H., & MUSSEN, P. H. (1952) The effects of feeding, weaning, and scheduling procedures on childhood adjustment and the formation of oral symptoms. *Child Development, 23*, 185–191.

SHALLICE, T. (1988) *From neuropsychology to mental structure*. Cambridge: Cambridge University Press.

SHALLICE, T., FLETCHER, P., FRITH, C. D., GRASBY, P., FRACKOWIAK, R. S. J., & DOLAN, R. J. (1994) Brain regions associated with acquisition and retrieval of verbal episodic memory. *Nature, 368*, 633–635.

SHAPLEY, R., & LENNIE, P. (1985) Spatial frequency analysis in the visual system. *Annual Review of Neurosciences, 8*, 547–583.

SCHATZBERG, A. F. (2000) New indications for antidepressants. *Journal of Clinical Psychiatry, 61*, 9–17.

SHAVLEV, A. Y. (1996) Stress versus traumatic stress. From acute homeostatic reactions to chronic psychopathology. In B. A. Van der Kolk, A. C. McFarlane & L. Weisaeth (Eds.), *Traumatic stress. The effects of overwhelming experience on mind, body, and society.* New York and London: Guildford Press.

SHEDLER, J., MAYMAN, M., & MANIS, M. (1993) The illusion of mental health. *American Psychologist, 48*, 1117–1131.

SHEPARD, R. N., & COOPER, L. A. (1982) *Mental images and their transformations.* Cambridge, MA: MIT Press, Bradford Books.

SHERWIN, B. (1988) A comparative analysis of the role of androgen in human male and female sexual behavior: Behavioral specificity, critical thresholds, and sensitivity. *Psychobiology, 16*, 416–425.

SHEWMON, D. A. (1998) Chronic "brain death:" Meta-analysis and conceptual consequences. *Neurology, 51*, 1538–1545.

SHEWMON, D. A. (2004) The "critical organ" for the organism as a whole: Lessons from the lowly spinal cord. *Advances in Experimental Medicine and Biology, 550*, 23–42.

SHIN, L. M., KOSSLYN, S. M., MCNALLY, R. J., ALPERT, N. M., THOMPSON, W. L., RAUCH, S. L., MACKLIN, M. L., & PITMAN, R. K. (1997) Visual imagery and perception in posttraumatic stress disorder: A positron emission tomographic investigation. *Archives of General Psychiatry, 54*, 233–241.

SHIOTA, M. N., NEUFELD, S. L., YEUNG, W. H., MOSER, S. E., & PEREA, E. F. (2011) Feeling good: autonomic nervous system responding in five positive emotions. *Emotion, 11*, 1368–1378.

SIEGEL, D. J. (2010) *Mindsight: The new science of personal transformation,* New York: Random House.

SIEGEL, L. S. (1989) IQ is irrelevant to the definition of learning disabilities. *Journal of Learning Disability, 22*(8), 469–478.

SIEGEL, P., & WEINBERGER, J. (1998) Capturing the "MOMMY AND I ARE ONE" merger fantasy: The oneness motive. In R. F. Bornstein & J. M. Masling (Eds.), *Empirical perspectives on the psychoanalytic unconscious* (pp. 71–98). Washington, DC: APA Press.

SIEGEL, S. (2001) Pavlovian conditioning and drug overdose: when tolerance fails. *Addiction Research and Theory, 9* (5), 503–513.

SIEGLER, R. S. (1996) *Emerging Minds: The Process of Change in Children's Thinking.* Oxford: Oxford University Press.

SIERRA, M., & BERRIOS, G. (2000) Flashbulb and flashback memories. In G. Berrios & J. R. Hodges (Ed.), *Memory disorders in psychiatric practice* (pp. 369–383). Cambridge: Cambridge University Press.

SIGALL, H., & LANDY, D. (1973) Radiating beauty: The effects of having a physically attractive partner on person perception. *Journal of Personality and Social Psychology, 31*, 410–414.

SIGMAN, M., SPENCE, S. J., & WANG, A. T. (2006) Autism from developmental and neuropsychological perspectives. *Annual Review of Clinical Psychology, 2*, 327–355.

SILBEREISEN, R. K., & LERNER, R. M. (2007) Approaches to positive youth development: A view of the issues. In R. K. Silbereisen & R. M. Lerner (Eds.). *Approaches to positive youth development* (pp. 3–30). London: Sage.

SILKE, A. (2003) Deindividuation, anonymity, and violence: Findings from Northern Ireland. *Journal of Social Psychology, 143* (4), 493–499.

SILVERBERG, S. B., & STEINBERG, L. (1990) Psychological well-being of parents with early adolescent children. *Developmental Psychology, 26*, 658–666.

SILVERMAN, I. (1971) Physical attractiveness and courtship. *Sexual Behavior, 1*, 22–25.

SILVERTHORN, D. E. (2012) *Human physiology: An integrated approach* (6th ed.). San Francisco, CA: Pearson Education.

SIMMONS, J. V. (1981) *Project sea hunt: A report on prototype development and tests.* Technical Report 746, Naval Ocean Systems Center, San Diego.

SIMON, H. A., & GILMARTIN, K. (1973) A simulation of memory for chess positions. *Cognitive Psychology, 5*, 29–46.

SIMONS, D. J., & CHABRIS, C. F. (1999) Gorillas in our midst: sustained inattentional blindness for dynamic events. *Perception, 28*, 1059–1074.

SIMONS, D. J., & LEVIN, D. T. (1998) Failure to detect changes to people during a real-world interaction. *Psychonomic Bulletin and Review, 5*, 644–649.

SIMPSON, J. A., CAMPBELL, B., & BERSCHEID, E. (1986) The association between romantic love and marriage: Kephart (1967) twice revisited. *Personality and Social Psychology Bulletin, 12*, 363–372.

SINGER, J. L., & SINGER, D. G. (1981) *Television, imagination and aggression.* Hillsdale, NJ: Erlbaum.

SINGER, T. (2012) The past, present, and future of social neuroscience: A European perspective. *NeuroImage, 61*, 437–449.

SINGER, T., SEYMOUR, B., O'DOHERTY, J., KAUBE, H., DOLAN, R., & FRITH, C. (2004) Empathy for pain involves the affective but not sensory components of pain. *Science, 303*, 1157–1162.

SINGER, T., SEYMOUR, B., O'DOHERTY, J. STEPHAN, K. E., DOLAN, R. J., & FRITH, C. D. (2006) Empathic neural responses are modulated by the perceived fairness of others. *Nature, 439*, 466–469.

SIQUELAND, E. R., & LIPSITT, J. P. (1966) Conditioned head-turning in human newborns. *Journal of Experimental Child Psychology, 3*, 356–376.

SKINNER, B. F. (1938) *The behavior of organisms.* New York: Appleton-Century-Crofts.

SKINNER, B. F. (1948) "Superstition" in the pigeon. *Journal of Experimental Psychology, 38*, 168–172.

SKINNER, B. F. (1971) *Beyond freedom and dignity.* New York: Knopf.

SKINNER, B. F. (1981) Selection by consequences. *Science, 213*, 501–504.

SKINNER, E. A., EDGE, K., ALTMAN, J., SHERWOOD, H. (2003) Searching for the structure of coping: A review and critique of category systems for classifying ways of coping. *Psychological Bulletin, 129*, 216–269.

SKYRMS, B. (1986) *Choice and chance: An introduction to inductive logic.* Belmont, CA: Dickenson.

SLOBIN, D. I. (Ed.) (1985) *The cross-linguistic study of language acquisition.* Hillsdale, NJ: Erlbaum.

SLOVIC, P. (2007) "If I look at the mass I will never act": Psychic numbing and genocide. *Judgment and Decision Making, 2*, 79–95.

SLOVIC, P., FISCHHOFF, B., & LICHTENSTEIN, S. (1982) Fact versus fears: Understanding perceived risk. In D. Kahneman, P. Slovic, & A. Tversky (Eds.), *Judgment under Uncertainty: Heuristics and Biases.* Cambridge: Cambridge University Press.

SMITH, A. (1759) *The theory of moral sentiments.* London: A. Millar.

SMITH, A. E., & CROSBY, F. J. (2008) From Kansas to Michigan: The path from desegregation to diversity. In G. Adams, M. Biernat, N. Branscombe, C. Crandall, & L. S. Wrightsman (Eds.), *Commemorating Brown: The social psychology of racism and discrimination* (pp. 99–113). Washington, DC: APA Books.

SMITH, C. A., & ELLSWORTH, P. C. (1985) Patterns of cognitive appraisal in emotion. *Journal of Personality and Social Psychology*, *48*, 813–848.

SMITH, D., KING, M., & HOEBEL, B. G. (1970) Lateral hypothalamic control of killing: Evidence for a cholinoceptive mechanism. *Science*, *167*, 900–901.

SMITH, E. E. (1995) Concepts and categorization. In E. E. Smith & D. Osherson (Eds.), *Invitation to cognitive science*, Vol. 3, *Thinking* (2nd ed.), Cambridge, MA: MIT Press.

SMITH, G. P., & GIBBS, J. (1994) Satiating effect of cholecystokinin. *Annals of the New York Academy of Sciences*, *713*, 236–241.

SMITH, M. L., GLASS, G. V., & MILLER, T. I. (1980) *The benefits of psychotherapy*. Baltimore: Johns Hopkins University Press.

SMITH, M. L., COTTRELL, G. W., GOSSELIN, F., & SCHYNS, P. G. (2005) Transmitting and decoding facial expressions. *Psychological Science*, *16*, 184–189.

SMITH, V. C., & POKORNY, J. (1975) Spectral sensitivity of the foveal cones between 400 and 500nm. *Vision Research*, *15*, 161.

SNEDEKER, J., GEREN, J., & SHAFTO, C. (2007) Starting over: International adoption as a natural experiment in language development. *Psychological Science*, *18*, 79–87.

SNOW, C. (1987) Relevance of the notion of a critical period to language acquisition. In M. H. Bornstein (Ed.), *Sensitive periods in development: Interdisciplinary perspectives*. Hillsdale, NJ: Erlbaum.

SNYDER, C. R., ILARDI, S., MICHAEL, S. T., & CHEAVENS, J. (2000) Hope theory: Updating a common process for psychological change. In C. R. Snyder & R. E. Ingram (Eds.), *Handbook of psychological change: Psychotherapy processes and practices for the 21st Century*. New York: Wiley.

SNYDER, M., TANKE, E. D., & BERSCHEID, E. (1977) Social perception and interpersonal behavior: On the self-fulfilling nature of stereotypes. *Journal of Personality and Social Psychology*, *35*, 656–666.

SOLOMON, G. F., SEGERSTROM, S. C., GROHR, P., KEMENY, M., & FAHEY, J., (1997) Shaking up immunity: Psychological and immunologic changes following a natural disaster. *Psychosomatic Medicine*, *59*, 114–127.

SORCE, J. F., EMDE, R. N., CAMPOS, J., & KLINNERT, M. D. (1985) Maternal emotional signaling: Its effect on the visual cliff behavior of 1-year-olds. *Developmental Psychiatry*, *21*, 195–200.

SOUTHWICK, S. M., VYTHILINGAM, M., & CHARNEY, D. S. (2005) The psychobiology of depression and resilience to stress: Implications for prevention and treatment. *Annual Review of Clinical Psychology*, *1*, 255–292.

SOUTHWICK, S. M., YEHUDA, R., & WANG, S. (1998) Neuroendocrine alterations in posttraumatic stress disorder. *Psychiatric Annals*, *28*, 436–442.

SPANOS, B. (1996, December) Quotas, ARCOs, UN report, and statistics. In G. Feussner (Moderator), *Prevalence of ADHD and psychostimulant utilization for treatment*. Symposium conducted at Drug Enforcement Administration meeting on stimulant use in the treatment of ADHD.

SPEARMAN, C. (1904) "General intelligence" objectively determined and measured. *American Journal of Psychology*, *15*, 201–293.

SPELKE, E. S., & KINZLER, K. D. (2007) Core knowledge. *Developmental Science*, *10* (1), 89–96.

SPENCE, C. J., DRIVER, J. (1994) Covert spatial orienting in audition: exogenous and endogenous mechanisms facilitate sound localization. *Journal of Experimental Psychology: Human Perception and Performance*, *20*, 555–574.

SPENCER, H. (1855) *Principles of psychology*. London: Longman, Brown, Green, and Longmans.

SPENCER, S., STEELE, C. M., & QUINN, D. (1999) *Under suspicion of inability: Stereotype threat and women's math performance*. Unpublished manuscript, Stanford University.

SPERLING, G. (1960) The information available in brief visual presentations. *Psychological Monographs*, *74*, 329.

SPERLING, G. (1967) Successive approximations to a model for short term memory. *Acta Psychologica*, *27*, 285–292.

SPERRY, R. W. (1968) Perception in the absence of neocortical commissures. In Association for Research in Nervous and Mental Disease, *Perception and its disorders*. New York: Williams & Wilkins.

SPERRY, R. W. (1970) Perception in the absence of the neocortical commissures. *Research Publications—Association for Research in Nervous and Mental Disease*, *48*, 123–128.

SPIEGEL, D. (1991) Mind matters: Effects of group support on cancer patients. *Journal of NIH Research*, *3*, 61–63.

SPIEGEL, D., BLOOM, J. R., KRAEMER, H. C., & GOTTHEIL, E. (1989) Psychological support for cancer patients. *Lancet*, *2*, 1447.

SPITZER, R. L., GIBBON, M., SKODOL, A. E., WILLIAMS, J. B. W., & FIRST, M. B. (Eds.) (1994) *DSM-IV case book: A learning companion to the Diagnostic and Statistical Manual of Mental Disorders*, fourth edition. Washington, DC: American Psychiatric Association Press.

SPRENGELMEYER, R., *et al.* (1997) Recognition of facial expressions: Selective impairment of specific emotions in Huntington's disease. *Cognitive Neuropsychology*, *14* (6), 839–879.

SPRENGELMEYER, R., YOUNG, A. W., CALDER, A. J., & KARNAT, A. (1996) Loss of disgust: Perception of faces and emotions in Huntington's disease. *Brain*, *119*, 1647–1665.

SPRINGER, S. P., & DEUTSCH, G. (1989) *Left brain, right brain* (3rd ed.). San Francisco: Freeman.

SQUIRE, L. R. (1992) Memory and the hippocampus: A synthesis from findings with rats, monkeys, and humans. *Psychological Review*, *99*, 195–231.

SQUIRE, L. R., & FOX, M. M. (1980) Assessment of remote memory: Validation of the television test by repeated testing during a seven-day period. *Behavioral Research Methods and Instrumentation*, *12*, 583–586.

SQUIRE, L. R., & KANDEL, E. R. (2000) *Memory: From mind to molecules*. New York: Scientific American Library.

SQUIRE, L. R., & KNOWLTON, B. J. (1995) Learning about categories in the absence of memory. *Proceedings of the National Academy of Sciences, USA*, *92*, 12470–12474.

SQUIRE, L. R., & WIXTED, J. T. (2011) The cognitive neuroscience of human memory since H.M. *Annual Reviews of Neuroscience*, *34*, 259–288.

SQUIRE, L. R., OJEMANN, J. G., MIEZIN, F. M., PETERSEN, S. E., VIDEEN, T. O., & RAICHLE, M. E. (1992) Activation of the hippocampus in normal humans: A functional anatomical study of memory. *Proceedings of the National Academy of Science*, *89*, 1837–1841.

SQUIRE, L. R., ZOLA-MORGAN, S., CAVE, C. B., HAIST, F., MUSEN, G., & SUZUKI, W. A. (1990) Memory: Organization of brain systems and cognition. In *Symposium on quantitative* biology, the brain (Vol. 55). Cold Spring Harbor, NY: Cold Spring Harbor Laboratory.

SRIVASTAVA, S., TAMIR, M., MCGONIGAL, K. M., JOHN, O. P., & GROSS, J. J. (2009) The social costs of emotional suppression: A prospective study of the transition to college. Journal of Personality and Social Psychology, 96, 883–897.

STAATS, A. W. (1968) Language, learning, and cognition. New York: Holt, Rinehart & Winston.

STANOVICH, K. E., & WEST, R. F. (2001) Individual differences in reasoning: implications for the rationality debate? Behavioral and Brain Sciences, 23, 645–665.

STASSER, G., & TITUS, W. (1985) Pooling of unshared information in group decision making: Biased information sampling during discussion. Journal of Personality and Social Psychology, 48, 1467–1478.

STASSER, G., TAYLOR, L. A., HANNA, C. (1989) Information sampling in structured and unstructured discussions of three- and six-person groups. Journal of Personality and Social Psychology, 57, 67–78.

STAYTON, D. J. (1973, March) Infant responses to brief everyday separations: Distress, following, and greeting. Paper presented at the meeting of the Society for Research in Child Development.

STEADMAN, H. J., MULVEY, E. P., MONAHAN, J., ROBBINS, P. C., APPLEBAUM, P. S., GRISSO, T., ROTH, L., & SILVER, E. (1998) Violence by people discharged from acute psychiatric inpatient facilities and by others in the same neighborhoods. Archives of General Psychiatry, 55, 393–401.

STEBLAY, N. M (1992) A meta-analytic review of the weapon focus effect. Law and Human Behavior, 16, 413–424.

STEEL, J., FERRARI, F. P., & FOGASSI, L. (2012) From action to language: comparative perspectives on primate tool use, gesture and the evolution of human language. Philosophical Transactions of the Royal Society B, 367, 4–9.

STEELE, C. M. (1997) A threat in the air: How stereotypes shape intellectual identify and performance. American Psychologist, 52, 613–629.

STEELE, C. M., & ARONSON, J. (1995) Stereotype threat and the intellectual test performance of African Americans. Journal of Personality and Social Psychology, 69, 797–811.

STEELE, S. (1991) The content of our character: A new vision of race in America. New York: Harper Collins.

STEINBERG, L., & MORRIS, A. S. (2001) Adolescent development. Annual Reviews of Psychology, 52, 83–110.

STEINER, J. E. (1979) Human facial expressions in response to taste and smell stimulation. Advances in Child Development and Behavior, 13, 257– 295.

STEINER, J. E., GLASER, D., HAWILO, M. E., & BERRIDGE, K. C. (2001) Comparative expression of hedonic impact: Affective reactions to taste by human infants and other primates. Neuroscience and Biobehavioral Reviews, 25, 53–74.

STEPHENS, M. A. P., DRULEY, J. A., ZAUTRA, A. J. (2002) Older adults' recovery from surgery for osteoarthritis of the knee: Psychosocial resources and constraints as predictors of outcomes. Health Psychology, 21, 377–383.

STERNBERG, R., GRIGORENKO, E., CASTEJON, J. L., PRIETO, M. D., & HAUTAMEKI, J. (2001) Confirmatory factor analysis of the Sternberg Triarchic Abilities Test in three international samples: An empirical test of the triarchic theory of intelligence. European Journal of Psychological Assessment, 17, 1–16.

STERNBERG, R. J. (1985) Beyond IQ: A triarchic theory of human intelligence. Cambridge: Cambridge University Press.

STERNBERG, R. J. (1986) Intelligence applied: Understanding and increasing your intellectual skills. San Diego: Harcourt Brace Jovanovich.

STERNBERG, R. J. (2000) The concept of intelligence. In Handbook of intelligence (pp. 3–16). Cambridge: Cambridge University Press.

STERNBERG, R. J. (2007) Foreward. In S. N. Phillipson & M. McCann (Eds.), Conceptions of giftedness: Sociocultural perspectives (pp. xv–xviii). Mahwah, NJ: Erlbaum.

STERNBERG, R. J., & KAUFMAN, J. C. (1998) Human abilities. Annual Reviews of Psychology, 49, 479–502.

STERNBERG, S. (1966) Highspeed scanning in human memory. Science, 153, 652–654.

STERNBERG, S. (1975) Memory scanning: New findings and current controversies. Quarterly Journal of Experimental Psychology, 27, 1–32.

STEWART, W. F., RICCI, J. A., CHEE, E., MORGANSTEIN, D., & LIPTON, R. (2003) Lost productive time and cost due to common pain conditions in the US workforce. Journal of the American Medical Association, 290, 2443–2454.

STIENEN, B. M. C., & DE GELDER, B. (2011) Fear detection and visual awareness in perceiving bodily expressions. Emotion, 11, 1182–1189.

STOERIG, P. (2007) Hunting the ghost: Toward a neuroscience of consciousness. In P. D. Zelazo, M. Moscovitch, & E. Thompson (Eds.), The Cambridge handbook of consciousness (pp. 707–730). New York: Cambridge University Press.

STONER, J. A. F. (1961) A comparison of individual and group decisions involving risk. Unpublished master's thesis, Massachusetts Institute of Technology.

STOWERS, L., HOLY, T. E., MEISTER, M., DULAC, C., & KOENTEGES, G. (2002) Loss of sex discrimination and male-male aggression in mice deficient for TRP2. Science, 295, 1493–1500.

STRACK, F., MARTIN, L. L., & STEPPER, S. (1988) Inhibiting and facilitating conditions of the human smile: A nonobtrusive test of the facial feedback hypothesis. Journal of Personality and Social Psychology, 54, 768–777.

STREISSGUTH, A. P., BARR, H. M., BOOKSTEIN, F. L., SAMPSON, P. D., & OLSON, H. C. (1999) The long-term neurocognitive consequences of prenatal alcohol exposure: A 14-year study. Psychological Science, 10, 186–190.

STROEBE, W., INSKO, C. A., THOMPSON, V. D., & LAYTON, B. D. (1971) Effects of physical attractiveness, attitude similarity and sex on various aspects of interpersonal attraction. Journal of Personality and Social Psychology, 18, 79–91.

STROHMINGER, N., LEWIS, R. L., & MEYER, D. E. (2011) Divergent effects of different positive emotions on moral judgment. Cognition, 119, 295–300.

STROOP, J. R. (1935) Studies of interference in serial-verbal reaction. Journal of Experimental Psychology, 18, 643–662.

STUNKARD, A. J. (1982) Anorectic agents lower a body weight set point. Life Sciences, 30, 2043–2055.

STUNKARD, A. J., HARRIS, J. R., PEDERSEN, N. L., & MCCLEARN, G. E. (1990) A separated twin study of the body mass index. New England Journal of Medicine, 322, 1483–1487.

SUAREZ, E. C., KUHN, C. M., SCHANBERG, S. M., WILLIAMS, R. B., JR., & ZIMMERMAN, E. A. (1998) Neuroendocrine, cardiovascular, and emotional responses of hostile men: The role of interpersonal challenge. Psychosomatic Medicine, 60, 78–88.

SULLIVAN, H. S. (1953) *The interpersonal theory of psychiatry*. New York: Norton.

SULLIVAN, P. F., NEALE, M. C., & KENDLER, K. S. (2000) Genetic epidemiology of major depression: Review and meta-analysis. *American Journal of Psychiatry*, *157*, 1552–1562.

SUMMERS, M. (2000) *Everything in its place*. New York: Putnam.

SWANN, W. B., JR., & SEYLE, C. (2005) Personality psychology's comeback and its emerging symbiosis with social psychology. *Personality and Social Psychology Bulletin*, *31*, 155.

SWANN, W. B., JR. (1990) To be known or to be adored: The interplay of self-enhancement and self-verification. In E. T. Higgins & R. M. Sorrentino (Eds.), *Handbook of motivation and cognition* (Vol. 2, 408–448). New York: Guilford Press.

SWEDO, S. PIETRINI, P., & LEONARD, H. (1992) Cerebral glucose metabolism in childhood-onset obsessive-compulsive disorder. *Archives of General Psychiatry*, *49*, 690–694.

SWETS, J. A., & BJORK, R. A. (1990) Enhancing human performance: An evaluation of "new age" techniques considered by the U.S. Army. *Psychological Science*, *1*, 85–96.

SWIM, J. K., BECKER, J. C., LEE, E., & PRUITT, E. (2010) Sexism reloaded: Worldwide evidence for its endorsement, expression, and emergence in multiple contexts. In H. Landrine & N. F. Russo (Eds.), *Handbook of diversity in feminist psychology* (pp. 137–171). New York: Springer.

SWINGLY, D. (2012) Cognitive development in language acquisition. *Language Learning and Development*, *8*, 1–3.

SWINNEY, D. A. (1979) Lexical access during sentence comprehension: Consideration of context effects. *Journal of Verbal Learning and Verbal Behavior*, *18*, 645–659.

SWITHERS, S. E., & DAVIDSON, T. L. (2008) A role for sweet taste: calorie predictive relations in energy regulation by rats. *Behavioral Neuroscience*, *122*, 161–173.

SYED, M. (2010) *Bounce: How champions are made*. London: Fourth Estate (a Division of Harper-Collins).

SZASZ, T. S. (1971) The sane slave: An historical note on the use of medical diagnosis as justificatory rhetoric. *American Journal of Psychotherapy*, *25*, 228–239.

TAJFEL, H., & TURNER, J. C. (1986) The social identity theory of intergroup conflict. In S. Worchel & W. G. Austin (Eds.), *Psychology of intergroup relations* (pp. 7–24). Chicago: Nelson-Hall.

TANENHAUS, M. G., LEIMAN, J., & SEIDENBERG, M. (1979) Evidence for multiple stages in the processing of ambiguous words in syntactic contexts. *Journal of Verbal Learning and Verbal Behavior*, *18*, 427–441.

TANG, C. S. (2007). Trajectory of traumantic stress symptoms in the aftermath of extreme natural disaster: A study of adult Thai survivors of the 2004 southeast Asian earthquake and tsunami. *Journal of Nervous and Mental Disease, 195*, 54–59.

TANG, S., & HALL, V. C. (1995) The overjustification effect: A meta-analysis. *Applied Cognitive Psychology*, *9*, 365–404.

TANNEN, D. (1990) *You just don't understand: Women and men in conversation*. New York: Ballantine Books.

TVERSKY, A., & KAHNEMAN, D. (1981) The framing of decisions and the psychology of choice. *Science*, *211*, 453–458.

TVERSKY, A., & KAHNEMAN, D. (1991) Loss aversion in riskless choice: A reference-dependent model. *Quarterly Journal of Economics*, *106*, 1039–1061.

TAVRIS, C., & ARONSON, E. (2007) *Mistakes were made (but not by me)*. New York: Harcourt.

TAVRIS, C., & SADD, S. (1977) *The Redbook report on female sexuality*. New York: Dell.

TAYLOR, A. F., WILEY, A., KUO, F., & SULLIVAN, W. C. (1998) Growing up in the inner city – Green spaces as places to grow. *Environment & Behavior*, *30*(1), 3–27.

TAYLOR, S. (1998) The social being in social psychology. In D. T. Gilbert, S. T. Fiske, & L. Gardner (Eds.) *The Handbook of Social Psychology*. Vols. 1 and 2 (4th ed., pp. 58–95). New York: McGraw-Hill.

TAYLOR, S. (1999) *Health psychology* (4th ed.). Boston: McGraw-Hill.

TAYLOR, S., KEMENY, M., ASPINWALL, L., SCHNEIDER, S., RODRIGUEZ, R., & HERBERT, M. (1992) Optimism, coping, psychological distress, and high-risk sexual behavior among men at risk for acquired immunodeficiency syndrome (AIDS). *Journal of Personality and Social Psychology*, *63*, 460–473.

TAYLOR, S. E. (2007) Social support. In H. S. Friedman and R. C. Silver (Eds.), *Foundations of Health Psychology* (pp. 145–171). New York: Oxford University Press.

TAYLOR, S. E., & STANTON, A. L. (2007) Coping resources, coping processes and mental health. *Annual Review of Clinical Psychology*, *3*, 377–401.

TAYLOR, S. E., EISENBERGER, N. I., SAXBE, D., LEHMAN, B. J., & LIEBERMAN, M. D. (2006) Neural responses to emotional stimuli are associated with childhood family stress. *Biological Psychiatry*, *60*, 296–301.

TEASDALE, J. D., SEGAL, Z. V., WILLIAMS, J. M. G., RIDGEWAY, V. A., SOULSBY, J. M., & LAU, M. A. (2000) Prevention of relapse/recurrence in major depression by mindfulness-based cognitive therapy. *Journal of Consulting and Clinical Psychology*, *68*, 615–523.

TEITELBAUM, P., & EPSTEIN, A. N. (1962) The lateral hypothalamic syndrome: Recovery of feeding and drinking after lateral hypothalamic lesions. *Psychological Review*, *69*, 74–90.

TELLEGEN, A., LYKKEN, D. T., BOUCHARD, T. J., JR., WILCOX, K. J., SEGAL, N. L., & RICH, S. (1988) Personality similarity in twins reared apart and together. *Journal of Personality and Social Psychology*, *54*, 1031–1039.

TELLER, D. Y. (1979) The forced-choice preferential looking procedure: A psychophysical technique for use with human infants. *Infant Behavior and Development*, *2*, 135–153.

TELLER, D. Y., & MOVSHON, J. A. (1986) Visual development. *Vision Research*, *26*, 1483–1506.

TERMAN, L. M., & ODEN, M. H. (1959) *Genetic studies of genius*, Vol. IV: *The gifted group at midlife*. Stanford, CA: Stanford University Press.

THASE, M. E., JINDAL, R., & HOWLAND, R. H. (2002) Biological aspects of depression. In I. H. Gotlib & C. L. Hammen (Eds.), *Handbook of depression* (pp. 192–218). New York: Guilford Press.

THIESSEN, E. D., HILL, E. A., SAFFRAN J. R. (2005) Infant-directed speech facilitates word segmentation. *Infancy*, *7*, 53–71.

THOMAS, A., & CHESS, S. (1977) *Temperament and development*. New York: Brunner/Mazel.

THOMAS, A., & CHESS, S. (1986) The New York longitudinal study: From infancy to early adult life. In R. Plomin & J. Dunn (Eds.), *The study of temperament: Changes, continuities and challenges* (pp. 39–52). Hillsdale, NJ: Erlbaum.

THOMAS, A., CHESS, S., BIRCH, H., HERTZIG, M., & KORN, S. (1963) *Behavioral individuality in early childhood*. New York: New York University Press.

THOMAS, R. (2008) *From stress to sense of coherence: Psychological experiences of aid workers in complex humanitarian emergencies.* Oxford University, 2008. Unpublished DPhil Thesis.

THOMPSON, P. M., CANNON, T. D., NARR, K. L., VAN ERP, T., POUTANEN, V. P., HUTTUNEN, M., LONNQVIST, J., STANDERTSKJOLD-NORDENSTAM, C. G., KAPRIO, J., KHALEDY, M., DAIL, R., ZOUMALAN, C. I., & TOGA, A. W. (2001) Genetic influences on brain structure. *Nature Neuroscience, 4,* 1253–1258.

THOMPSON, R. A. (1998) Early sociopersonality development. In W. Damon & N. Eisenberg (Eds.), *Handbook of child psychology,* 5th ed., Vol. 3. Social, emotional, and personality development. (pp. 25–104). Hoboken, NJ: John Wiley & Sons, Inc.

THOMPSON, R. A., LAMB, M., & ESTES, D. (1982) Stability of infant-mother attachment and its relationship to changing life circumstances in an unselected middle-class sample. *Child Development, 53,* 144–148.

THOMPSON, R. F., & KRUPA, D. J. (1994) Organization of memory traces in the mammalilan brain. *Annual Review of Neuroscience, 17,* 519–549.

THOMPSON, S. C. (1999) Illusions of control: How we overestimate our personal influence. *Current Directions in Psychological Science, 8,* 187–190.

THOMPSON, S. K. (1975) Gender labels and early sex role development. *Child Development, 46,* 339–347.

THOMPSON, W. R. (1954) The inheritance and development of intelligence. *Proceedings of the Association for Research on Nervous and Mental Disease, 33,* 209–231.

THORNDIKE, E. L. (1898) Animal intelligence: An experimental study of the associative processes in animals. *Psychological Monographs, 2,* 8.

THORPE, G. L., & OLSON, S. L. (1997) *Behavior therapy: Concepts, procedures, and applications* (2nd ed.). Boston: Allyn and Bacon.

THURSTONE, L. L. (1938) *Primary mental abilities.* Psychometric Monographs, No. 1. Chicago: University of Chicago Press.

TIGGEMANN, M., & WILLIAMS, E. (2012) The role of self-objectification in disordered eating, depressed mood, and sexual functioning among women: A comprehensive test of objectification theory. *Psychology of Women Quarterly, 36,* 66–75.

TIMKO, C., DEBENEDETTI, A., & BILLOW, R. (2006) Intensive referral to 12-Step self-help groups and six-month substance use disorder outcomes. *Addiction, 101,* 678–688.

TINBERGEN, N. (1951) *The study of instinct.* Oxford: Clarendon.

TOATES, F. (2011) *Biological psychology* (3rd ed.). Upper Saddle River, NJ: Prentice Hall/Pearson Education.

TOLMAN, E. C. (1932) *Purpose behavior in animals and men.* New York: Appleton-Century-Crofts. (Reprinted 1967. New York: Irvington.)

TOLMAN, E. C. (1951) *Collected papers in psychology.* Berkeley: University of California Press.

TOLMAN, E. C., & HONZIK, C. H. (1930) Introduction and removal of reward, and maze performance in rats. *University of California Publications in Psychology, 4,* 257–275.

TOMASELLO, M. (1999) *The Cultural Origins of Human Cognition.* Boston, MA: Harvard University Press.

TOMASELLO, M. (2003). *Constructing a language: A usage-based theory of language acquisition.* Boston, MA: Harvard University Press.

TOMASELLO, M., CARPENTER, M., & LISZKOWSKI, U. (2007) A new look at infant pointing. *Child development, 78,* 705–722.

TOMPKINS, S. S. (1962) *Affect, imagery, consciousness: Vol. 1. The positive affects.* New York: Springer.

TOOBY, J., & COSMIDES, L. (1990) The past explains the present: Emotional adaptations and the structure of ancestral environments. *Ethology and Sociobiology, 11,* 375–424.

TOOBY, J., & COSMIDES, L. (2002) Toward mapping of the evolved functional organization of mind and brain. In D. J. Levitin (Ed.), *Foundations of cognitive psychology: Core readings* (pp. 665–681). Cambridge, MA: MIT Press.

TRACY, J. L., & BEALL, A. T. (2011) Happy guys finish last: The impact of emotion expressions on sexual attraction. *Emotion, 11,* 1379–1387.

TREISMAN, A. (1969) Strategies and models of selective attention. *Psychological Review, 76,* 282–299.

TREISMAN, A. (1986) Features and objects in visual processing, *Scientific American, 254,* 114–125.

TREISMAN, A. M. (1986) Features and objects in visual processing. *Scientific American, 255,* 114B–125.

TREISMAN, A. (1992) Perceiving and re-perceiving objects. *American Psychologist, 47,* 862–875.

TRIEMAN, N., LEFF, J., & GLOVER, G. (1999) Outcome of long stay psychiatric patients resettled in the community: Prospective cohort study. *British Medical Journal, 319,* 13–16.

TSAI, J. L., LOUIE, J. Y., CHEN, E. E., & UCHIDA, Y. (2007) Learning what feelings to desire: Socialization of ideal affect through children's storybooks. *Personality and Social Psychology Bulletin, 33,* 17–30.

TULVING, E. (1974) Cue-dependent forgetting. *American Scientist, 62,* 74–82.

TULVING, E. (1985) How many memory systems are there? *American Psychologist, 40,* 385–398.

TULVING, E., KAPUR, S., CRAIK, F. I. M., MOSCOVITCH, M., & HOULE, S. (1994) Hemispheric encoding/retrieval asymmetry in episodic memory: Positron emission tomography findings. *Proceedings of the National Academy of Science of the United States of America, 91,* 2016–2020.

TURK, D. C., & OKIFUJI, A. (1997) What factors affect physicians' decisions to prescribe opioids for chronic non-cancer pain patients? *Clinical Journal of Pain, 13,* 330–336.

TURNER, J. C., HOGG, M. A. OAKES, P. J., REICHER, S. D., & WETHERELL, M. S. (1987) *Rediscovering the social group: A self-categorization theory.* Oxford: Basil Blackwell.

TURNER, M. E., & PRATKANIS, A. R. (1998a) A social identity model of groupthink. *Organizational Behavior and Human Decision Processes, 73,* 210–235.

TURNER, M. E., & PRATKANIS, A. R. (1998b) Twenty-five years of groupthink theory and research: Lessons from the evaluation of a theory. *Organizational Behavior and Human Decision Processes, 73,* 105–115.

TVERSKY, A., & KAHNEMAN, D. (1973) On the psychology of prediction. *Psychological Review, 80,* 237–251.

TVERSKY, A., & KAHNEMAN, D. (1983) Extensional versus intuitive reasoning: The conjunction fallacy in probability judgment. *Psychological Review, 90,* 293–315.

TYLER, H. (1977) The unsinkable Jeane Dixon. *Humanist, 37,* 6–9.

UCHINO, B. N., CACIOPPO, J. T., & KIECOLT-GLASER, J. K. (1996) The relationship between social support and physiological processes: A review with emphasis on underlying mechanisms and implications for health. *Psychological Bulletin, 29,* 1159–1168.

UCHINO, B. N., UNO, D., & HOLT-LUNSTAD, J. (1999) Social support, physiological processes, and health. *Current Directions in Psychological Science*, 8, 145–148.

VALDESOLO, P., & DESTENO, D. A. (2011) Synchrony and the social tuning of compassion. *Emotion*, 11, 262–266.

VALENSTEIN, E. S. (1976) The interpretation of behavior evoked by brain stimulation. In A. Wauquier & E. T. Rolls (Eds.) *Brain-stimulation reward* (pp. 557–575). New York: Elsevier.

VAN BOEIJEN, C. A., VAN OPPEN, P., VAN BALKOM, A. J. L. M., VISSER, S., et al. (2005) Treatment of anxiety disorders in primary care practice: A randomised controlled trial. *British Journal of General Practice*, 55, 763–769.

VAN BROMMEL, M., VAN PROOIJEN, J. W., ELFFERS, H., VAN LANGE, P. A. M. (2012) Be aware to care: Public self-awareness leads to a reversal of the bystander effect. *Journal of Experimental Social Psychology*, 48, 926–930.

VANDELANOTTE, C., SPATHONIS, K. M., EAKIN, E. G., & OWEN, N. (2007) Website-delivered physical activity interventions: A review of the literature. *American Journal of Preventative Medicine*, 33, 54–64.

VAN DEN HEUVEL, M. P., STAM, J. C., KAHN, R. S., & HULSHOFF POL, H. E. (2009) Efficiency of functional brain networks and intellectual performance. *Journal of Neuroscience*, 29, 7619–7624.

VAN DEN HEUVEL, O. A., VAN DE WETERING, B. J. M., VELTMAN, D. J., & PAULS, D. L. (2000) Genetic studies of panic disorder: A review. *Journal of Clinical Psychiatry*, 61, 756–766.

VANDEPUTTE, M., & DE WEERD, A. (2003) Sleep disorders and depressive feelings: A global survey with the Beck Depression Scale. *Sleep Medicine*, 4 (4), 343–345.

VAN HEMERT, D. A., POORTINGA, Y. H., & VAN DE VIJVER, F. J. R. (2007) Emotion and culture: A meta-analysis. *Cognition & Emotion*, 21, 913–943.

VAN LAARI, C., LEVIN, S., & SINCLAIR, S. (2008) Social identity and personal identity stereotype threat: The case of affirmative action. *Basic and Applied Social Psychology*, 30, 295–310.

VAN LOON, M. H., DE BRUIN, A. B. H., VAN GOG, T., & VAN MERRIENBOER, J. J. G. (in press). Activation of inaccurate prior knowledge affects primary-school students' metacognitive judgments and calibration. *Learning and Instruction*. doi:10.1016/j.learninstruc.2012.08.005

VAN NORMAN, G. A. (1999) A matter of life and death: What every anesthesiologist should know about the medical, legal, and ethical aspects of declaring brain death. *Anesthesiology*, 91, 275–287.

VAN PRAAG, H., KEMPERMANN, G., & GAGE, F. H. (1999) Running increases cell proliferation and neurogenesis in the adult mouse dentate gyrus. *Nature Neuroscience*, 2, 266–270.

VAN ROOY, D. L., VISWESVARAN, C., & PLUTA, P. E. (2005). An evaluation of construct validity: What is this thing called emotional intelligence? *Human Performance*, 18 (4), 445–462.

VAN ROOY, D., & VISWESVARAN, C. (2004) Emotional intelligence: A meta-analytic investigation of predictive validity and nomological net. *Journal of Vocational Behavior*, 65, 71–95.

VAN VORT, W., & SMITH, G. P. (1987) Sham feeding experience produces a conditioned increase of meal size. *Appetite*, 9, 21–29.

VARNUM, M. E. E., GROSSMAN, I., KITAYAMA, S., & NISBETT, R. E. (2010) The origin of cultural differences in cognition: The social orientation hypothesis. *Current Directions in Psychological Science*, 19, 9–13.

VAUGHN, B. E., LEFEVER, G. B., SEIFER, R., & BARGLOW, P. (1989) Attachment behavior, attachment security, and temperament during infancy. *Child Development*, 60, 728–737.

VAZQUEZ-NUTTALL, E., ROMERO-GARCIA, I., & DELEON, R. (1987) Sex roles and perceptions of femininity and masculinity of Hispanic women: A review of the literature. *Psychology of Women Quarterly*, 11, 409–425.

VEZINA, P., & LEYTON, M. (2009) Conditioned cues and the expression of stimulant sensitization in animals and humans. *Neuropharmacology*, 56 Suppl. 1, 160–168.

VIGNOVIC, J. A., & THOMPSON, L. F. (2010) Computer-mediated cross-cultural collaboration: Attributing communication errors to the person versus the situation. *Journal of Applied Psychology*, 95, 265–276.

VISINTAINER, M. A., VOLPICELLI, J. R., & SELIGMAN, M. E. P. (1982) Tumor rejection in rats after inescapable or escapable shock. *Science*, 216, 437–439.

VOGT, T., & BELLUSCIO, D. (1987) Controversies in plastic surgery: Suction-assisted lipectomy (SAL) and the HCG (human chorionic gonadotropin) protocol for obesity treatment. *Aesthetic Plastic Surgery*, 11, 131–156.

VOLKOW, N. D., FOWLER, J. S., & WANG, G. J. (2003) The addicted human brain: Insights from imaging studies. *J. Clin. Invest.*, 111, 1444–1451.

VOLKOW, N. D., WANG, G. J., FOWLER, J. S., LOGAN, J., JAYNE, M., FRANCESCHI, D., et al. (2002) "Nonhedonic" food motivation in humans involves dopamine in the dorsal striatum and methylphenidate amplifies this effect. *Synapse*, 44(3), 175–180.

VYGOTSKY, L. S. (1986) *Thought and language* (A. Kozulin, Trans.). Cambridge, MA: MIT Press. (Originally published 1934.)

VYTAL, K., & HAMANN, S. (2010) Neuroimaging support for discrete neural correlates of basic emotions: A voxel-based meta-analysis. *Journal of Cognitive Neuroscience*, 22, 2864–2885.

WADDEN, T. A., BERKOWITZ, R. I., VOGT, R. A., STEEN, S. N., STUNKARD, A. J., & FOSTER, G. D. (1997) Lifestyle modification in the pharmacological treatment of obesity: A pilot investigation of a potential primary care approach. *Obesity Research*, 5, 218–226.

WADLINGER, H. A., & ISAACOWITZ, D. M. (2006) Positive mood broadens visual attention to positive stimuli. *Motivation and Emotion*, 30, 89–101.

WAGNER, W. M., & MONNET, M. (1979) Attitudes of college professors toward extrasensory perception. *Zetetic Scholar*, 5, 7–17.

WALKER, E. (1978) *Explorations in the biology of language*. Montgomery, VT: Bradford.

WALLACH, M. A., & WALLACH, L. (1983) *Psychology's sanction for selfishness*. San Francisco: Freeman.

WALLACH, M. A., KOGAN, N., & BEM, D. J. (1962) Group influence on individual risk taking. *Journal of Abnormal and Social Psychology*, 65, 75–86.

WALLACH, M. A., KOGAN, N., & BEM, D. J. (1964) Diffusion of responsibility and level of risk taking in groups. *Journal of Abnormal and Social Psychology*, 68, 263–274.

WALLACH, M. A., & WALLACH, L. (1983) *Psychology's sanction for selfishness*. San Francisco: Freeman.

WALLER, B. M., CRAY, J. J., & BURROWS, A. M. (2008) Selection for universal facial emotion. *Emotion*, 8, 435–439.

WALLER, S. J., LYONS, J. S., & CONSTANTINIFERRANDO, M. F. (1999) Impact of comorbid affective and alcohol use disorders on suicide ideation and attempts. *Journal of Clinical Psychology*, 55, 585–595.

WALSTER, E., ARONSON, E., ABRAHAMS, D., & ROTTMAN, L. (1966) Importance of physical attractiveness in dating behavior. *Journal of Personality and Social Psychology*, *4*, 508–516.

WALZER, M. (1970) *Obligations*. Cambridge, MA: Harvard University Press.

WAMPOLD, B. E., MONDIN, G. W., MOODY, M., STICH, F., BENSON, K., & AHN, H. (1997) A meta-analysis of outcome studies comparing bona fide psychotherapies: Empirically, "all must have prizes". *Psychological Bulletin*, *122*, 203–215.

WANG, B., FAN, Y., LU, M., LI, S., SONG, Z. et al. (2013) Brain anatomical networks in world class gymnasts: A DTI tractography study. *NeuroImage*, *65* (January 15), 476–487.

WARD, I. L. (1992) Sexual behavior: The products of perinatal hormonal and prepubertal social factors. In A. A. Gerall, H. Motz, & I. L. Ward (Eds.), *Sexual differentiation* (pp. 157–179). New York: Plenum.

WARRINGTON, E. K., & SHALLICE, T. (1969) The selective impairment of auditory verbal short-term memory. *Brain*, *92*, 885–896.

WARRINGTON, E. K., & SHALLICE, T. (1984) Category specific semantic impairments. *Brain*, *107*, 829–853.

WARRINGTON, E. K., & WEISKRANTZ, L. (1978) Further analysis of the prior learning effect in amnesic patients. *Neuropsychologica*, *16*, 169–177.

WARWICK, R., JOSEPH, S., CORDLE, C., & ASHWORTH, P. (2004) Social support for women with chronic pelvic pain: What is helpful from whom? *Psychology & Health*, *19*, 117–134.

WASAN, A., BUTLER, S. F., BUDMAN, S. H., et al. (2007) Psychiatric history and psychologic adjustment as risk factors for aberrant drug-related behavior among patients with chronic pain. *Clinical Journal of Pain*, *23*, 173–179.

WASON, P. C. (1968). Reasoning about a rule. Quarterly Journal of Experimental Psychology, 20, 273–281.

WASON, P. C. (1968) On the failure to eliminate hypotheses – A second look. In P. C. Wason & P. N. Johnson-Laird (Eds.), *Thinking and Reasoning*. Harmondsworth: Penguin.

WASON, P. C., & JOHNSON-LAIRD, P. N. (1972) *Psychology of reasoning: Structure and content*. London: Batsford.

WASSERMAN, E. A. (1990) Detecting response-outcome relations: Toward an understanding of the causal texture of the environment. *Psychology of Learning and Motivation*, *26*, 27–82.

WATKINS, E. (2004) Adaptive and maladaptive ruminative self-focus during emotional processing. *Behaviour Research and Therapy*, *42*, 1037–1052.

WATKINS, E., SCOTT, J., WINGROVE, J., et al. (2007) Rumination-focused cognitive behaviour therapy for residual depression: A case series. *Behaviour Research and Therapy*, *45*, 2144–2154.

WATSON, D., & TELLEGEN, A. (1985) Toward a consensual structure of mood. *Psychological Bulletin*, *98*, 219–23.

WATSON, D., WIESE, D., VAIDYA, J., & TELLEGEN, A. (1999) The two general activation systems of affect: Structural findings, evolutionary considerations, and psychobiological evidence. *Journal of Personality and Social Psychology*, *76*, 820–838.

WATSON, J. B. (1930) *Behaviorism* (rev. ed.). New York: Norton.

WATSON, J. B., & RAYNER, R. (1920) Conditioned emotional reactions. *Journal of Experimental Psychology*, *3*, 1–14.

WATSON, J. S. (1967) Memory and 'contingency analysis' in infant learning. *Merrill-Palmer Quarterly*, *13*, 55–76.

WAUGH, C. E., & FREDRICKSON, B. L. (2006) Nice to know you: Positive emotions, self–other overlap, and complex understanding in the formation of a new relationship. *Journal of Positive Psychology*, *1*, 93–106.

WEAVER, D. E., LLABRE, M. M., DURAN, R. E., ANTONI, M. H., IRONSON, G., et al. (2005) A stress and coping model of medication adherence and viral load in HIV-postive men and women on highly active antitrovival therapy (HAART). *Health Psychology*, *24*, 385–392.

WEAVER, E. G. (1949) *Theory of hearing*. New York: Wiley.

WEAVER, K. E., LLABRE, M. M., DURAN, R. E., ANTONI, M. H., IRONSON, G., et al. (2005) A stress and coping model of medication adherence and viral load in HIV-positive men and women on highly active antiretroviral therapy (HAART). *Health Psychology*, *24*, 385–392.

WEBB, T. L., & SHEERAN, P. (2006) Does changing behavioral intentions engender behavior change? A meta-analysis of the experimental evidence. *Psychological Bulletin*, *132*, 249–268.

WECHSLER, D. (1958) *The measurement and appraisal of adult intelligence*. Baltimore: Williams.

WEIGLE, D. S. (1994) Appetite and the regulation of body composition. *FASEB Journal*, *8*, 302–310.

WEINBERGER, D. (1990) The construct validity of the repressive coping style. In J. L. Singer (Ed.), *Repression and dissociation: Implications for personality theory, psychopathology, and health* (pp. 337–385). Chicago: University of Chicago Press.

WEINBERGER, J. (1996) Common factors aren't so common: The common factors dilemma. *Clinical Psychology: Science and Practice*, *2*, 45–69.

WEINE, S. M., BECKER, D. F., MCGLASHAN, T. H., LAUB, D., LAZROVE, S., VOJVODA, D., & HYMAN, L. (1995) Psychiatric consequences of "ethnic cleansing": Clinical assessments and trauma testimonies of newly resettled Bosnian refugees. *American Journal of Psychiatry*, *152*, 536–542.

WEINE, S. M., VOJVODA, D., BECKER, D. F., MCGLASHAN, T. H., HODZIC, E., LAUB, D., HYMAN, L., SAWYER, M., & LAZROVE, S. (1998) PTSD symptoms in Bosnian refugees 1 year after resettlement in the United States. *American Journal of Psychiatry*, *155*, 562–564.

WEISNER, C., GREENFIELD, T., & ROOM, R. (1995) Trends in the treatment of alcohol problems in the U.S. general population, 1979 through 1990. *American Journal of Public Health*, *85* (1), 55–60.

WEISSMAN, M. M. (1993) Family genetic studies of panic disorder. Conference on panic and anxiety: A decade of progress. *Journal of Psychiatric Research*, *27* (suppl.), 69–78.

WEISSMAN, M. M., & MARKOWITZ, J. C. (2002) Interpersonal psychotherapy for depression. In I. H. Gotlib & C. L. Hammen (Eds.), *Handbook of depression* (pp. 404–421). Guilford Press.

WEISSTEIN, N. A., & WONG, E. (1986) Figure-ground organization and the spatial and temporal responses of the visual system. In E. C. Schwab & H. C. Nusbaum (Eds.), *Pattern recognition by humans and machines*. Vol. 2. *Visual perception* (pp. 31–64). Orlando, FL: Academic Press.

WELLER, L., & WELLER, A. (1993) Human menstrual synchrony: A critical assessment. *Neuroscience and Behavioral Reviews*, *17*, 427–439.

WELLS, G. L., FERGUSON, T. J., & LINDSAY, R. C. L. (1981) The tractability of eyewitness confidence and its implication for triers of fact. *Journal of Applied Psychology*, *66*, 688–696.

WERNER, E. E., & SMITH, R. S. (1982) *Vulnerable but invincible*. New York: McGraw-Hill.

WERTHEIMER, M. (1912/1932) Experimentelle studien uber das sehen von beuegung. *Zeitschrift Für Psychologie, 61*, 161–265.

WESTEN, D. (1998) The scientific legacy of Sigmund Freud: Toward a psychodynamically informed psychological science. *Psychological Bulletin, 124*, 333–371.

WESTEN, D., NOVOTNY, C. M., & THOMPSON-BRENNER, H. (2004) The empirical status of empirically supported psychotherapies: Assumptions, findings, and reporting in controlled clinical trials. *Psychological Bulletin, 130*, 631–663.

WESTEN, D., WEINBERGER, J., & BRADLEY, R. (2007) Motivation, decision making and consciousness: From psychodynamics to subliminal priming and emotional constraint satisfaction. In P. D. Zelazo, M. Moscovitch, & E. Thompson (Eds.), *The Cambridge handbook of consciousness* (pp. 673–702). New York: Cambridge University Press.

WHALEN, P. J., *et al.* (2001) A functional MRI study of human amygdala responses to facial expressions of fear versus anger. *Emotion, 1* (1), 70–83.

WHALEN, P. J., & PHELPS, E. A. (2009) *The human amygdala*. New York: Guilford Press.

WHALEN, P. J., RAUCH, S. L., ETCOFF, N. L., MCINERNEY, S. C., LEE, M. B., & JENIKE, M. A. (1998) Masked presentation of emotional facial expressions modulate amygdala activity without explicit knowledge. *Journal of Neuroscience, 18*, 411–418.

WHEELER, S. C., BRIÑOL, P., & HERMANN, A. D. (2007) Resistance to persuasion as self-regulation: Ego-depletion and its effects on attitude change processes. *Journal of Experimental Social Psychology, 43*, 150–156.

WHITE, C. (1977) Unpublished Ph.D. dissertation, Catholic University, Washington, DC.

WHITEN, A., & HAM, R. (1992) On the nature and evolution of imitation in the animal kingdom: Reappraisal of a century of research. In P. J. B. Slater, J. S. Rosenblatt, & C. Beer (Eds.), *Advances in the Study of Behavior* (pp. 239–283). New York: Academic Press.

WHITLOCK, J. L., POWERS, J. L., & ECKENRODE, J. (2006) The virtual cutting edge: The internet and adolescent self-injury. *Developmental Psychology, 42*, 407–417.

WHITTLE, S., YUCEL, M., YAP, M. B. H., & ALLEN, N. B. (2011) Sex differences in the neural correlates of emotion: Evidence from neuroimaging. *Biological Psychology, 87*, 319–333.

WHO (WORLD HEALTH ORGANIZATION) (2003) Organization of services for mental health (Mental health policy and service guidance package). Geneva, World Health Organization. Downloaded from http://www.who.int/entity/mental_health/resources/en/Organization.pdf on July 1, 2008.

WHO (WORLD HEALTH ORGANIZATION) (2005, January 12–15) Alcohol and mental health. Briefing from the WHO European Ministerial Conference on Mental Health, Helsinki, Finland. Downloaded from http://www.who.int/substance_abuse/facts/psychoactives/en/ on February 18, 2008.

WHO (WORLD HEALTH ORGANIZATION) (2007) Deaths from coronary heart disease. Downloaded from http://www.who.int/cardiovascular_disease/en/cvd_atlas_14_deathHD.pdf on October 31, 2007.

WHO (WORLD HEALTH ORGANIZATION) (2008) *The ICD-10 classification of mental and behavioural disorders: clinical descriptions and diagnostic guidelines*. New York: World Health Organization.

WHO (WORLD HEALTH ORGANIZATION) (2009) Global health risks: Mortality and burden of disease attributable to selected major risks. Downloaded from http://www.who.int/healthinfo/global_burden_disease/GlobalHealthRisks_report_full.pdf on December 15, 2012.

WHORF, B. L. (1956) *Language, thought and reality: Selected writings of Benjamin Lee Whorf*. Edited by J. B. Carroll. Cambridge, MA: MIT Press.

WHYTE, W. H. (1956) *The organization man*. New York: Simon & Schuster.

WICKER, A. W. (1969) Attitudes versus actions: The relationship between verbal and overt behavioral responses to attitude objects. *Journal of Social Issues, 25*, 41–78.

WICKER, B., KEYSERS, C., PLAILLY, J., ROYET, J. P., GALLESE, V., & RIZZOLATTI, G. (2003) Both of us disgusted in my insula: The common neural basis of seeing and feeling disgust. *Neuron, 40*, 655–664.

WIDEN, S. C., & RUSSELL, J. A. (2008) Children acquire emotion categories gradually. *Cognitive Development, 23*, 291–312.

WIDEN, S. C., & RUSSELL, J. A. (2010) Differentiation in preschooler's categories of emotion. *Emotion, 10*, 651–661.

WIEBE, D. J., & MCCALLUM, D. M. (1986) Health practices and hardiness as mediators in the stress–illness relationship. *Health Psychology, 5*, 425–438.

WIENS, S., MEZZACAPPA, E. S., & KATKIN, E. S. (2000) Heartbeat detection and the experience of emotions. *Cognition and Emotion, 14*, 417–427.

WIERSMA, D., NIENHUIS, F. J., SLOOF, C. J., & GIEL, R. (1998) Natural course of schizophrenic disorders: A 15-year followup of a Dutch incidence cohort. *Schizophrenia Bulletin, 24*, 75–85.

WIJDICKS, E. F. (2003) The neurologist and Harvard criteria for brain death. *Neurology, 61*, 970–976.

WIJDICKS, E. F. M. (2012) The transatlantic divide over brain death determination and the debate. *Brain, 135*, 1321–1331.

WILCOXIN, H. C., DRAGOIN, W. B., & KRAL, P. A. (1971) Illness-induced aversions in rat and quail: Relative salience of visual and gustatory cues. *Science, 171*, 823–828.

WILKES, A. L., & KENNEDY, R. A. (1969) Relationship between pausing and retrieval latency in sentences of varying grammatical form. *Journal of Experimental Psychology, 79*, 241–245.

WILLIAMS, A. M., & FORD, P. R. (2008) Expertise and expert performance in sport. *International Review of Sport and Exercise Psychology, 1*, 4–18.

WILLIAMS, D. C. (1959) The elimination of tantrum behavior by extinction procedures. *Journal of Abnormal and Social Psychology, 59*, 269.

WILLIAMS, G. C. (1996) *Plan and purpose in nature*. London: Weidenfeld & Nicolson.

WILLIAMS, J. H., GREEN, M. C., KOHLER, C., ALLISON, J. J., & HOUSTON, T. K. (2011) Stories to communication risks about tobacco: Development of a brief scale to measure transportation into a video story. *Health Education Journal, 70*, 184–191.

WILLIAMS, J. M., & DUNLOP, L. C. (1999) Pubertal timing and self-reported delinquency among male adolescents. *Journal of Adolescence, 22*, 157–171.

WILLIAMS, J. M., & PENMAN, D. (2011) *Mindfulness: A practical guide to finding peace in a frantic world*. London: Piatkus.

WILLIAMS, J. M. G., & KABAT-ZINN, J. (Eds.) (2011) Special issue on mindfulness. *Contemporary Buddhism, 12*(1), 1–306.

WILLIAMS, L. E., & BARGH, J. A. (2008) Experiencing physical warmth promotes interpersonal warmth. *Science, 322*, 606–607.

WILLIAMS, M. D., & HOLLAN, J. D. (1981) The process of retrieval from very long-term memory. *Cognitive Science, 5*, 87–119.

WILLIAMS, R. B. (1995) Somatic consequences of stress. In M. J. Friedman (Ed.), *Neurobiological and clinical consequences of stress: From normal adaptation to post-traumatic stress disorder*. Philadelphia: Lippincott-Raven.

WILLIAMS, R. B. (2003) Psychosocial and biobehavioral factors and their interplay in coronary heart disease. *Annual Review of Clinical Psychology, 4*, 349–365.

WILLIAMSON, D. A., WALDEN, H. M., WHITE, M. A., YORK-CROWE, E., NEWTON, JR., R. L., ALFONSO, A., GORDON, S., & RYAN, D. (2006) Two-year internet-based randomized controlled trial for weight loss in African American girls. *Obesity, 14*, 1231–1243.

WILSON, E. O. (1963) Pheromones. *Scientific American, 208*, 100–114.

WILSON, E. O. (1975) *Sociobiology: The new synthesis*. Cambridge, MA: Harvard University Press.

WILSON, E. O. (1978) *On human nature*. Cambridge, MA: Harvard University Press.

WILSON, M. I., & DALY, M. (1985) Competitiveness, risk-taking and violence: The young male syndrome. *Ethology and Sociobiology, 6*, 59–73.

WILSON, S. A. K. (1924) Some problems in neurology, II: Pathological laughing and crying. *J. Neurol. Psychopathol., 4*, 299–333.

WILSON, W. R. (1979) Feeling more than we can know: Exposure effects without learning. *Journal of Personality and Social Psychology, 37*, 811–821.

WILSON-MENDENHALL, C. D., BARRETT, L. F., SIMMONS, W. K., & BARSALOU, L. W. (2011) Grounding emotion in situated conceptualization. *Neuropsychologia, 49*, 1105–1127.

WILTERMUTH, S. (2012) Synchrony and destructive obedience. *Social Influence, 7*, 78–89.

WINDHOLZ, M. J., MARMAR, C. R., & HOROWITZ, M. J. (1985) A review of the research on conjugal bereavement: Impact on health and efficacy of intervention. *Comprehensive Psychiatry, 26*, 433–447.

WINTER, D. G., STEWART, A. J., JOHN, O. P., KLOHNEN, E. C., & DUNCAN, L. E. (1998) Traits and motives: Toward an integration of two traditions in personality research. *Psychological Review, 105*, 230–250.

WOHL, M. J. A., BRANSCOMBE, N. R., & KLAR, Y. (2006) Collective guilt: Emotional reactions when one's group has done wrong or been wronged. *European Review of Social Psychology, 17*, 1–37.

WOLFSON, A. R. (2001) Bridging the gap between research and practice: What will adolescents' sleep–wake patterns look like in the 21st century? In M. A. Carskadon (Ed.), *Adolescent sleep patterns: Biological, social, and psychological influences* (pp. 198–219). New York: Cambridge University Press.

WOLFSON, A. R., & ARMITAGE, R. (2008) Sleep and its relationship to adolescent depression. In S. Nolen-Hoeksema & L. Hilt (Eds.), *Handbook of depression in adolescents* (pp. 279–302). New York: Taylor & Francis.

WOLFSON, A. R., & CARSKADON, M. A. (1998) Sleep schedules and daytime functioning in adolescents. *Child Development, 69*, 875–887.

WOLRAICH, M., HANNAH, J., BAUMGAERTEL, A., & FEUER, I. (1998) Examination of DSM-IV criteria for attention deficit hyperactivity in a county-wide sample. *Journal of Developmental and Behavioral Pediatrics, 19*, 162–168,

WOOD, W., & EAGLY, A. H. (2007) Social structural origins of sex differences in human mating. In S. W. Gangestad & J. A. Simpson (Eds.), *The evolution of mind: Fundamental questions and controversies* (pp. 383–390). New York: Gilford Press.

WOOD, W., LUNDGREN, S., OUELLETTE, J. A., BUSCEME, S., & BLACKSTONE, T. (1994) Minority influence: A meta-analytic review of social influence processes. *Psychological Bulletin, 115*, 323–345.

WOOD, W., WONG, F. Y., & CHACHERE, J. G. (1991) Effects of media violence on viewers' aggression in unconstrained social situations. *Psychological Bulletin, 109*, 371–383.

WOODRUFF, S. I., CONWAY, T. L., EDWARDS, C. C., ELLIOTT, S. P., & CRITTENDEN, J. (2007) Evaluation of an Internet virtual world chat room for adolescent smoking cessation. *Addictive Behaviors, 32*, 1769–1786.

WOODY, R. H., & ROBERTSON, M. (1988) *Becoming a clinical psychologist*. Madison, CT: International Universities Press.

WORD, C. O., ZANNA, M. P., & COOPER, J. (1974) The nonverbal mediation of self-fulfilling prophecies in interracial interaction. *Journal of Experimental Social Psychology, 10*, 109–120.

WORLD HEALTH ORGANIZATION SURVEY CONSORTIIUM (2004) Prevalence, severity, and unmet need for treatment of mental disorders in the World Health Organization World Mental Health Surveys. *Journal of the American Medical Association, 291*, 2581–2590.

WUNDT, W. (1897/1998). *Outlines of psychology* (C. H. Judd, Trans.). Bristol: Thoemmes Press.

WURTZ, R. H., GOLDBERG, M. E., & ROBINSON, D. L. (1980) Behavioral modulation of visual responses in monkeys. *Progress in Psychobiology and Physiological Psychology, 9*, 42–83.

WYVELL, C. L., & BERRIDGE, K. C. (2000) Intra-accumbens amphetamine increases the pure incentive salience of sucrose reward: Enhancement of reward 'wanting' without 'liking' or response reinforcement. *Journal of Neuroscience, 20*, 8122–8130.

YARROW, K., BROWN, P., & KRAKAUER, J. W. (2009) Inside the brain of an elite athlete: The neural processes that support high achievement in sports. *Nature Reviews: Neuroscience, 10* (August), 585–596.

YEHUDA, R. (2004) Risk and resilience in posttraumatic stress disorder. *Journal of Clinical Psychiatry, 65* (Suppl. 1), 29–36.

YEHUDA, R., MCFARLANE, A. C., & SHALEY, A. Y. (1998) Predicting the development of posttraumatic stress disorder from the acute response to a traumatic event. *Biological Psychiatry, 44*, 1305–1313.

YERKES, R. M., & DODSON, J. D. (1908) The relationship of strength of stimulus to rapidity of habit formation. *Journal of Comparative Neurological Psychology, 18*, 459–482.

YESAVAGE, J. A., LEIER, V. O., DENARI, M., & HOLLISTER, L. E. (1985) Carry-over effect of marijuana intoxication on aircraft pilot performance: A preliminary report. *American Journal of Psychiatry, 142*, 1325–1330.

YIN, R. K. (1969) Looking at upside-down faces. *Journal of Experimental Psychology, 81*, 141–145.

YIN, R. K. (1970) Face recognition by brain-injured patients: A dissociable ability? *Neuropsychologia, 8*, 395–402.

YIRMIYA, N., EREL, O., SHAKED, M., & SOLOMONICA-LEVI, D. (1998). Metaanalysis comparing theory of mind abilities of individuals with autism, individuals with mental retardation, and normally developed individuals. *Psychological Bulletin*, *124*, 283–307.

YOST, W. A., & NIELSON, D. W. (1985) *Fundamentals of hearing* (2nd ed.) New York: Holt, Rinehart & Winston.

YOUNGER, J., ADRIANCE, W., & BERGER, R. J. (1975) Sleep during transcendental meditation. *Perceptual and Motor Skills*, *40*, 953–954.

YU, B., ZHANG, W., JING, Q., PENG, R., ZHANG, G., & SIMON, H. A. (1985) STM capacity for Chinese and English language materials. *Memory and Cognition*, *13*, 202–207.

ZAHN-WAXLER, C., KLIMES-DOUGAN, B., & SLATTERY, M. J. (2000) Internalizing problems of childhood and adolescence: Prospects, pitfalls, and progress in understanding the development of anxiety and depression. *Development and Psychopathology*, *12*, 443–466.

ZAJONC, R. B. (1965) Social facilitation. *Science*, *149*, 269–274.

ZAJONC, R. B. (1968) Attitudinal effects of mere exposure. *Journal of Personality and Social Psychology*, *Monograph Supplement*, *9*, 1–29.

ZAJONC, R. B. (1984) On the primacy of affect. *American Psychologist*, *39*, 117–123.

ZAJONC, R. B., HEINGARTNER, A., & HERMAN, E. M. (1969) Social enhancement and impairment of performance in the cockroach. *Journal of Personality and Social Psychology*, *13*, 83–92.

ZALUTSKY, R. A., & NICOLL, R. A. (1990) Comparison of two forms of longterm potentiation in single hippocampal neurons. *Science*, *248*, 1619–1624.

ZEKI, S. (1993) *A vision of the brain*. Boston: Blackwell Scientific Publications.

ZHANG, Y., PROENCA, R., MAFFEI, M., BARONE, M., LEOPOLD, L., & FRIEDMAN, J. M. (1994) Positional cloning of the mouse obese gene and its human homologue. *Nature*, *372*, 425–431.

ZILLMANN, D., & BRYANT, J. (1974) Effect of residual excitation on the emotional response to provocation and delayed aggressive behavior. *Journal of Personality and Social Psychology*, *30*, 782–791.

ZIMBARDO, P. G. (1969) The human choice: Individuation, reason and order vs. deindividuation, impulse, and chaos. In W. J. Arnold & D. Levine (Eds.), *Nebraska symposium on motivation* (pp. 237–307). Lincoln: University of Nebraska Press.

ZIMBARDO, P. G. (1972) Pathology of imprisonment. *Society*, *9*, 4–8.

ZIMBARDO, P. G. (2006) On rethinking the psychology of tyranny: The BBC prison study. *British Journal of Social Psychology*, *45*, 47–53.

ZIMBARDO, P. G. (2007) *The Lucifer effect: Understanding how good people turn evil*. New York: Random House.

ZOLA-MORGAN, S., & SQUIRE, L. R. (1985) Medial-temporal lesions in monkeys impair memory on a variety of tasks sensitive to human amnesia. *Behavioral Neuroscience*, *99*, 22–34.

ZOLA-MORGAN, S. M., & SQUIRE, L. R. (1990) The primate hippocampal formation: Evidence for a time-limited role in memory storage. *Science*, *250*, 228–290.

ZOLA-MORGAN, S. M., SQUIRE, L. R., & AMARAL, D. G. (1989) Lesions of the hippocampal formation but not lesions of the fornix or the mamalary nuclei produce long-lasting memory impairments in monkeys. *Journal of Neuroscience*, *9*, 898–913.

ZUBER, J. A., CROTT, H. W., & WERNER, J. (1992) Choice shift and group polarization: An analysis of the status of arguments and social decision schemes. *Journal of Personality and Social Psychology*, *62*, 50–61.

ZUCKER, K. J. (1990) Gender identity disorders in children: Clinical description and natural history. In R. Blanchard (Ed.) *Clinical management of gender identity disorders in children and adults* (pp. 3–23). Washington, DC: American Psychiatric Press.

ZUCKERMAN, M. (1995) Good and bad humors: Biochemical bases of personality and its disorders. *Psychological Science*, *6*, 325–332.

ZURIF, E. B. (1995) Brain regions of relevance to syntactic processing. In: D. N. Osherson, L. R. Gleitman, & M. Liberman (Eds.), *An invitation to cognitive science, second edition: Language* (Vol. 1), pp. 381–397. Cambridge, MA: MIT Press.

NAME INDEX

Adler, Alfred 445
Ainsworth, Mary 89–90
Allport, Gordon 455
Anderson, Mike 420
Arendt, Hannah 571
Asch, Solomon 10, 567–8, 602–3
Atkinson, Richard 261

Bandura, Albert 243–4, 451–2
Bar-On, Reuven 425
Baron-Cohen, Simon 83
Baumeister, Roy 34
Békésy, Georg von 127, 129
Biederman, Irving 165
bin Laden, Osama 557, 597
Binet, Alfred 414
Bowlby, John 89
Broca, Paul 48
Bruner, Jerome 226
Bundy, Ted 377–8
Buss, David 460

Cannon, Walter 390–1
Cattell, Raymond 418
Chomsky, Noam 11, 316, 329
Copernicus 447

Darwin, Charles 68, 234, 447, 459
Deese, James 293
Dement, William 202
Descartes, René 8, 34, 196
DeWall, Nathan 34
Duverney, Joseph Guichard 127

Ebbinghaus, Hermann 268
Edgar, Dale 202
Eichmann, Adolf 571, 574
Erikson, Erik 95, 445, 455
Eysenck, Hans 437

Farmer, James 291
Fechner, Gustav 104
Freud, Anna 442, 445
Freud, Sigmund 10–11, 197–8, 205,
    441–5, 447, 464–5, 507
Frisch, Karl von 232
Fromm, Erich 445

Galton, Francis 414
Gardner, Howard 418
Genovese, Kitty 562, 563
Geschwind, Norman 48
Gibson, J.J. 147
Goleman, Daniel 425

Hebb, Donald 246, 251
Heider, Fritz 10, 607
Helmholtz, Hermann von 118, 127
Hering, Ewald 120
Higgins, Tory 457
Hippocrates 7, 538
Hitler, Adolf 557
Horney, Karen 445
James, William 9, 71, 226, 390
Janet, Pierre 199
Johnson, Marcia 293
Johnson, Virginia 23
Jones, Jim 557
Jung, Carl 445, 455

Kandel, Eric 247
Kelly, George 453
Kenrick, Douglas 460
Koffka, Kurt 9
Kohlberg, Lawrence 84–5
Köhler, Wolfgang 9

Lange, Carl 390
Lazarus, Richard 382

Le Bon, Gustave 561
Lewin, Kurt 10
Locke, John 8, 68
Loftus, Elizabeth 288
Lorentz, Konrad 232

MacLean, Paul 42
Maslow, Abraham 455, 457–8
Masters, William 23
Mayer, John 425
Mayr, Ernst 34
McDermott, Kathleen 293
Milgram, Stanley 571–7
Miller, George 268
Molaison, Henry Gustav 281
Müller, Johannes 110
Munsell, Albert 117
Murray, Henry 446

Palmer, John 288
Pavlov, Ivan 9, 226, 227–8
Penfield, Wilder 108–9
Piaget, Jean 75–8, 83–4, 286
Pinel, Philippe 539
Plomin, Robert 55–6

Roediger, Henry 293
Rogers, Carl 455–7
Rorschach, Hermann 446
Rozin, Paul 34
Rundus, Dewey 271–2
Rutherford, Ernest (Lord Rutherford) 126

Sacks, Oliver 33
Salovey, Peter 425
Sanocki, Tom 160
Selye, Hans 476
Shiffrin, Richard 261
Simon, Herbert 11, 227

Simon, Théophile 414
Skinner, B.F. 9, 68, 234
Snellen, Herman 115
Socrates 7
Spearman, Charles 418
Sperling, George 262–3
Sperry, Roger 11, 49–50
Stern, William 415
Sternberg, Robert 420
Stevens, S.S. 105–6
Stroop, John Ridley 336
Sullivan, Harry Stack 445

Terman, Lewis 414–15
Thompson, Jennifer 259,
    286, 290, 292–3
Thorndike, E.L. 234
Thurstone, Louis 418
Tinbergen, Nikolaas 232
Titchener, E.B. 9, 226
Tolman, Edward C. 243
Treisman, Anne 161
Triplett, Norman 559

Vygotsky, Lev 82
Watson, John B. 9, 68, 196, 226,
    242, 451
Weber, Ernst Heinrich 104
Wechsler, David 415
Wernicke, Carl 48
Wertheimer, Max 9
Wilson, (Thomas) Woodrow 413
Wundt, Wilhelm 196, 226

Young, Thomas 118

Zajonc, Robert 559
Zimbardo, Philip 585–6

SUBJECT INDEX

AA (Alcoholics Anonymous) 552–3
abnormality 498–502
absolute thresholds 102–4
    smell 131
    sound intensity 125–6
    taste 132
    vision 115
abstraction 170–3
accommodation 75
acetylcholine 41
action potentials 37–8
active perception 188–9
actualizing tendency 455
adaptive behavior 56
addiction 349–51, 370–2
ADHD (attention deficit hyperactivity
    disorder) 530–1
adolescent development 93–8
affect 347
affective neuroscience 17
afferent nerves 35
affirmative action 590–1
aggression 6, 243
agnosia 169
agonist drugs 216
agoraphobia 504–6
AIDS 479–80
alcohol 212–13, 480
    pregnancy 427–8
Alcoholics Anonymous 552–3
alliesthesia 353–4
all-or-none law 39
ambivalent attachment 90
American Sign Language 314–15
Ames room illusion 177–8
amnesia 280–3
amok 501
amphetamines 217
amplitude 123–4
amygdala 44, 384–5
anal stage of psychosexual develop-
    ment 444
analytic thought 609
Anderson's theory of intelligence
    419–20
androgen insensitivity 364–5
androgenization 363–4, 365
anhedonia 512
animals in research 25
anorexia nervosa 359–62
antagonist drugs 216
anterograde amnesia 280–1
anticonvulsant medications 549
antidepressant drugs 549
antipsychotic drugs 548
antisocial personality disorder 377–8,
    524–6
anxiety, theory of 445
anxiety disorders 503–11
aphasia 48, 309–10
apnea 204
arousal 251
    misattribution of 381

asexuality 369
ASL (American Sign Language) 314–15
Asperger's syndrome 532
assimilation 75
association areas 46
associationist psychology 8
associative agnosia 169
associative learning 226, 247–8
ataque de nervios 501, 504
athletes 52
Atkinson–Shiffrin theory 261
attachment 89–92
attention 148–51
    and memory 150
    neural basis of 179–80
attention deficit hyperactivity disorder
    530–1
attitude bolstering 614
attitudes 611–16
attraction, interpersonal 616–23
attributions 607–9
atypical antipsychotics 549
audition 72–3, 123–9
auditory attention 149–50
auditory canal 125
auditory system 124–5
augmented networks 164
autism spectrum disorder 83, 528–32
automatic stereotype activation
    599–601
automatic thinking 624–5
automaticity 198–9, 336–7
autonomic nervous system 35,
    52–3, 378
availability heuristic 327
available wavelengths 174
aversive conditioning 239–40
avoidance learning 240–1
axons 36

back projections 102
backward masking 384
base-rate rule 326
basilar membrane 125, 127, 129
behavior
    and attitudes 614–16
    evolution of 56
    genetic studies 58–9, 62
    health-related 480–1
    molecular genetics of 59, 62
behavior genetics 55–6
behavior therapy 225, 541–2
behavioral epigenetics 18
behavioral perspective 12, 13, 502
behavioral rehearsal 543
behaviorism 9, 196, 449–51
    evaluation 451
    and human nature 450–1
    and learning 226
belief bias 324
benzodiazepines 549
bias 108
Big Five 438

binding problem 159, 161–2
binocular disparity 155–6
biofeedback 490–1
biological bases of psychology 34–5
biological perspective 12–13, 15–16,
    502, 513–14, 521–2
biological psychology 16
biological therapies 548–50
bipolar disorder 512–13, 517
body temperature 345–6
borderline personality disorder 526–8
brain
    anterior system 179
    asymmetries 48–51
    cortex 42, 43, 45–7
    divisions of labor 179–82
    dopamine system 348
    learning 246–50
    mapping 47–8
    organization of 42–51
    posterior system 179
    self 460–1
    visual cortex 180–1
brain damage 47
brain death 218–19
brain stimulation 47
brightness 117
brightness constancy 175
broaden-and-build theory 402
Broca's aphasia 309–10
Broca's area 48–9
bulimia 360–2
bystander effect 562–5

caffeine 211, 228
cannabis 214–15
case histories 23–4
CAT (computerized axial tomography)
    scans 47
cataracts 150–1
categorization 317
    neural basis 322–3
    processes 320–1
cathartic effects 6
causality heuristic 327
causation 22
central core 42
central fissure 45
central nervous system 35
central route to persuasion 612, 613–14
cerebellum 43
cerebral cortex 42, 43, 45–7
change blindness 150
CHD (coronary heart disease) 477–8
childhood amnesia 5–6, 282–3
childhood memory 286
children
    aggression 243
    cognitive development 75–85
    development 96–7
    discrimination by 183–5
    newborn 71–5
    suggestive information 291

chromosomal disorders 427
chromosomes 56
chronic pain 136–9
chunking 268–9, 294–5
circadian rhythms 202
classical conditioning 227–33, 450
client-centered therapy 546–8
clinical psychology 16
clock-dependent alerting process 202
coaction 559
cocaine 217
cochlea 125
coefficient of correlation 637–9
cognition and learning 242–6
cognitive appraisal 378, 380–5
cognitive approach to personality
    451–5
cognitive behavior therapy
    225, 491
cognitive development in childhood
    75–85
cognitive dissonance theory 579–80
cognitive maps 243
cognitive neuroscience 17
cognitive perspective 12, 13–14,
    226–7, 454, 502, 514–15
cognitive psychology 16
cognitive-behavior therapy 544–5
collective unconscious 445
collectivism 399
color 116–21
    characteristics of 117
    mixing 117–18
color blindness 118
color circle 119
color constancy 116, 174–5
color solid 117
color vision, theories of 118–21
color-matching experiment 118
commitment 622
companionate love 621
comparison stimuli 104
compassion 566
complex cells 163
compliance 566–70
compulsions 508, 509
computerized axial tomography 47
concepts 317
    acquisition 321–2
    hierarchies of 320
    neural basis 322–3
conceptual act model 382
concrete operational stage of cognitive
    development 78
conditioned aversion 352
conditioned reinforcers 236–7
conditioned response
    acquisition 229
    biological constraints 232–3
    cognitive factors 231–2
    extinction 229
    fear 231
    spontaneous recovery 229–30

conditioned satiety 353
conditioned stimulus 228
conditioning
    classical 227–33, 450
    instrumental 234–42
    operant 450
cones 112–14
confessions 291–2
confirmation bias 327
conjunction rule 326
connectionist models 163–4
consciousness 195–220
    altered states of 195
    controlling 197
    definition 196
    monitoring 196–7
conservation 77
constancies 174–6
    and illusions 177
    and sensory modalities 178
construal-level theory 602
constructive memory 285–93
constructive perception 286–7
context 166–8
continuum model 605
contrast acuity 115
control groups 20
controlled stimulation 185–9
conventional morality 84
coping 487–90, 492–3
core relational themes 382
cores 318, 321
cornea 112
coronary heart disease 477–8
corpus callosum 45
correlation 21–2
correlation coefficients 21, 637–9
cortex 42, 43, 45–7
counseling psychology 16
counterarguing 614
CR (conditioned response) 228
critical periods 70
CS (conditioned stimulus) 228
cultural psychology 18
cultural relativist perspective on
        abnormality 498
culture
    and attributions 608–9
    and emotion 399–401

dark adaptation 103–4, 114–15
dark-adaptation curve 115
debriefing 24–5, 577
decision-making 324–9
    group 586–9
deductive reasoning 324–5
deductive validity 324
defense mechanisms 442–3
degradation 40
deindividuation 561–2
deinstitutionalization 539–41
delusions 519
dendrites 36
denial 443
dependent variables 20
depolarization 38
depressants 211–13
depression 511–15, 517
depth cues 155, 176
descriptive statistics 630–3
developmental psychology 16
diabetes 62
Diagnostic and Statistical Manual of
        Mental Disorders 501
dichromats 118

diethylstilbestrol 364
dieting 357–8
difference thresholds 104–5
difference-reduction method of
        problem-solving 330
difficult temperament 86
diffusion of responsibility 563–5
dimensional appraisal theories 382–3
direct observation 23
discrimination, and generalization 237
disgust 34
disorganized attachment 90
displacement 443
display rules 394–5
dispositional attribution 607
dissociation 199
distance perception 155
distress 499–500
dizygotic twins 59
dopamine 41
dopamine system 348
Down syndrome 427
dream analysis 546
dreams 204–6
drives 343, 345–7
DRM effect 293
drug addiction 349–51
drug dependence 211
drug misuse 211
drug tolerance 228–9, 351
drug withdrawal 351
drugs, pregnancy 427–8
DSM-5 (Diagnostic and Statistical
        Manual of Mental Disorders) 501
dynamic control theory 162

eardrums 125
ears 124–5
easy temperament 86
ecological optics 147
ECT (electroconvulsive therapy) 549–50
educational psychology 16
EEGs (electroencephalograms) 47,
        200, 207
effect, law of 3, 234
efferent nerves 35
ego 441
egocentrism 77
eidetic images 266
elaboration 261, 274
    and encoding 295–6
elaboration likelihood model 611–12
electroconvulsive therapy 549–50
electroencephalograms 47, 200, 207
embodied social cognition 610
Emmert's experiment 176
emotion 378–408
    and bodily changes 388–92
    and cognitive appraisal 380–5
    components of 378–80
    and culture 399–401
    differentiation of 390–2
    dimensions of 383
    discrete 406–7
    and facial muscle movements
        393–5
    and gender 397–9
    gene expression 392
    intensity of 389–90
    and motivation 378
    responses to 378, 395–7
    structure of 404–7
    and subjective experiences 385–7
    and thought-action tendencies

387–8
    two-factor theory 381
emotion regulation 395–7
emotional intelligence 425–6, 430–1
emotion-focused coping 487–90
encoding
    and elaboration 295–6
    and imagery 295
    and long-term memory 273–4
    and memory 260–2, 286
    and retrieval 277–8
    and working memory 265–6
endocrine system 54–5
engineering psychology 16–17
enkephalin 349
ERPs (event-related potentials) 47
escape learning 240–1
ethics 24–5
event-related potentials 47
evocative interaction 466
evolution of behavior 56
evolutionary psychology 18, 459–63
    evaluation 462
    and human nature 460, 462
excitation threshold 38
excitatory connections 164
excitatory effects 39–40
exercise 491
expectation 108
experimental groups 20
experiments 19–21
explicit memory 262
exploratory behavior 251
exponents 106
extinction of a conditioned response
        229
extracellular thirst 346
extrinsic motivation 251
extroversion 437
eye fixations 148–9
eyeblink conditioning 248
eyes 111–14
Eysenck's Personality Factors 437

face recognition 5, 168–9
facial feedback hypothesis 395
facial muscle movements 378, 391,
        393–5
facial preference 71–2
factor analysis 418
false alarms 107–8
false memory 259–60, 286, 289–90,
        291–2, 292–3, 298–9
familiarity 618
family therapy 548
FAS (fetal alcohol syndrome) 427–8
fast mapping 312
fear 231, 388–9
fear-conditioning 248
feature detectors 162–3
feature-integration theory 161–2
features
    of natural objects 165–6
    relations among 163
fetal alcohol syndrome 427–8
FI (fixed interval) schedules 238–9
fight-or-flight response 474–6
five functions of perception 147
fixed interval schedules 238–9
fixed ratio schedules 238
flashbulb memories 279
fMRI (functional magnetic resonance
        imaging) scans 47–8, 128, 207
foot-in-the-door technique 579
forced confessions 291–2

forebrain 42
forgetting 269, 277, 278–80
formal operational stage of cognitive
        development 78
fovea 113
FR (fixed ratio) schedules 238
Fragile X syndrome 427
framing effects 327–8
free association 10, 445–6, 545–6
frequency 123
frequency distributions 630–1
Freudian slips 197
frontal lobe 45
functional brain imaging 47–8
functional fixedness 332
functional magnetic resonance imaging
        47–8, 128, 207
functionalism 9
fundamental attribution error 5, 557–8,
        607–8

g (general intelligence factor) 418
GABA (gamma-aminobutyric acid) 41–2
gamma-aminobutyric acid 41–2
ganglions 36
Gardner's theory of multiple intelligences
        418–19
gate control theory of pain 135
gender, and emotion 397–9
gender identity 363–5
general adaptation syndrome 476
general intelligence factor 418
general learning disability 426–9
generalization, discrimination 237
generalized anxiety disorder 503
genes 56–8, 62
genetic studies of behavior 58–9, 62
genetics
    and autism 532
    and intelligence 421–4
    and obesity 356–7
    of personality 463, 466
    and schizophrenia 521–2
genital stage of psychosexual develop-
        ment 444
genotype-environment correlation 463
geons 165–6
Geschwind model 48, 310
Gestalt psychology 9–10
ghost sickness 501
glial cells 36–7
global-to-local processing 159–61
glutamate 41
grammatical morphemes 307
group decision-making 586–9
group interactions 584–9
group polarization effect 586–7
grouping 154–5
groupthink 588–9
gustation 73, 131–2
gustatory system 132

habituation 225, 246–7
habituation method 184
hair cells 125
hallucinations 520
hardiness 486
hashish 214
HD (Huntington's disease) 57–8
health 489–90
hearing *see* audition
Hebbian learning rule 246
hedonic hotspots 349
hemispheres 45
hemispheric specialization 51

heritability of intelligence 422–4
Hermann grid 115–16
heroin 215–16
hertz 123
heuristics 326–7
hierarchy of needs 457–8
hindbrain 42–3
hippocampus 44
hit rate 107
HIV (human immunodeficiency virus) 479–80
Holistic thought 609
holocaust 557
homeostasis 345–7, 352–4
homeostatic sleep drive 202
hormones 54, 364–5
HPA (hypothalamic-pituitary-adrenal axis) 392
hue 117
human immunodeficiency virus 479–80
human nature
    and behaviorism 450–1
    and cognitive approach 454
    and evolutionary psychology 460, 462
    and humanistic approach 458
    and psychoanalytic theory 447
humanistic approach 455–9
humanistic therapies 546
hunger 352–6
Huntington's disease 57–8
hypercomplex cells 163
hyperosmia 33
hyperpolarization 40
hypnosis 208–10
hypothalamic-pituitary-adrenal (HPA) axis 392
hypothalamus 43–4
hypotheses 19

ICD (International Classification of Diseases) 501
iconic memory 263
id 441
ideal self 456–7
identification 582–4
identity confusion 95
identity crisis 95
ideology 575–6
illicit drugs 214–17
illusions 127–8, 176–8
illusory conjunction 161
imaginal thought 317, 332–5
immune cells 392
immune system 478–80
implicit egotism 619
implicit leniency contract 570
implicit memory 262, 280–5
impression formation 598–609
imprinting 373
in vivo exposure 542–4
inattention blindness 150
incentive motivation 347–51
incentive salience 348
incentive theories 343–4
incentives 251
    and homeostasis 352–4
incus 125
independent variables 20
individualism 399
individuation 604–6
inductive reasoning 325–8
inductively strong arguments 325–6
infants see children
inferences 287, 602

inferior colliculus 43
informational social influence 568–9
information-processing models 11
information-processing skills 80
informed consent 24
Ingram, Paul 292
inhibitory neurons 40
insecure attachment 90
insight 234
insomnia 203
Institutional norms 585–6
instrumental conditioning 234–42
    biological constraints 242
    cognitive factors 241–2
    experiments 234–41
intellectual difficulties 421
intellectualization 443
intelligence 413–31
    Anderson's theory 419–20
    emotional intelligence 425–6, 430–1
    Gardner's theory of multiple intelligences 418–19
    and genetics 421–4
    heritability 422–4
    measurement of 414–17
    multiple intelligences 418–19
    prenatal environment 427
    Sternberg's triarchic theory 420
intelligence quotient 415
intelligence tests 414–17, 421
interference 275–6
internalization 578–84
International Classification of Diseases 501
internet 94
interneurons 36
interpersonal attraction 616–23
interpersonal therapy 546
interval schedules 238–9
intimacy 622
intracellular thirst 346–7
intrinsic motivation 251, 254
introspection 8–9
introversion-extroversion 437
inversion effect 169
ion channels 37–8
ion pumps 38
ions 37
IQ (intelligence quotient) 415

James-Lange theory 390–1
jnd (just noticeable differences) 104–5
joint attention 82
Jonestown 557, 581–2
just noticeable differences 104–5

knowledge-acquisition 80–1
koro 501

language
    acquisition 313–16
    brain mechanisms for 48–9, 309–11
    comprehension 306, 309
    context 309
    development 311–16
    evolution of 245
    evolutionary research 329
    morphological rules 307
    neural basis 48–9, 309–11
    non-humans 315–16
    overextensions 312
    phonological rules 307
    production 306, 309
    second language 315

structure 306–9
    and thought 338–9
latah 501
latency stage of psychosexual development 444
latent learning 243
lateral fissure 45
lateral geniculate nucleus 113
lateral hypothalamic syndrome 355
lateral inhibition 115–16
law of effect 3, 234
learned helplessness 241, 473
learned taste aversion 232–3
learning
    and behaviorism 226
    brain 246–50
    cellular basis 248–50
    and cognition 242–6
    cognitive perspective 226–7
    definition 225
    and intrinsic motivation 251, 254
    and memory 73–5
    and motivation 251–4
    observational 243–4, 450
    prior beliefs 244–6
    social 252–3
    structural consequences 250
learning curve 229
learning disability 426–9
legal system and constructive memory 290–3
lesions 47
LGN (lateral geniculate nucleus) 113
libido 442, 445
light 111
liking 348–9
limbic system 42, 44
linguistics 11
literature reviews 24
lithium 549
localization
    of brain function 60–1
    of information 151–9
    and recognition 181–2
lock-and- key action 39
longitudinal fissure 45
long-term depression 248
long-term memory 261, 273–80
    emotion 278–80
    forgetting 277, 278–80
    retrieval 274–6, 277–8
    and working memory 270–2
long-term potentiation 248
loosening of associations 519
loudness 124
love 620–3
LTD (long-term depression) 248
LTP (long-term potentiation) 248
lucid dreams 204

MA (mental age) 414
magnetic resonance imaging 47
maladaptive behavior 499
malleus 125
manic episodes 512
manic-depression 512–13, 517
many-to-one problem 147
marijuana 214
marital therapy 548
marriage 620
mating 622–3
maturation 69
McGurk effect 168
means 20–1, 635–6
means-ends analysis 330–1

measurement 20–1, 630–9
measures of central tendency 631–2
measures of variation 632–3
meditation 206–8
medulla 42
melatonin 202
memory 11, 73–5, 259–300
    and attention 150
    constructive 285–93
    false 259–60, 286, 289–90, 291–2, 292–3, 298–9
    iconic 263
    implicit 262, 280–5
    improvement 294–300
    long-term 261, 273–80
    recovered 298–9
    repressed 298–9
    sensory 261, 262–4
    short-term 261
    stages of 260–1
    stores 261
    working 265–72
memory illusions 293
memory span 268, 294–5
mental age 414
mental asylums 538–9
mental health
    enhancement 551
    problems
        ADHD (attention deficit hyperactivity disorder) 530–1
        anxiety disorders 503–11
        autism 83, 528–32
        biological therapies 548–50
        classification 500–2
        culture-bound 501
        history of 538–41
        mood disorders 511–17
        personality disorders 524–8
        perspectives on 502
        psychotherapy 541–8, 550
        schizophrenia 62, 518–23
        treatments 537–53
mental models 325
mental rotation 333
mental sets 332
mere exposure effect 618
meta-analysis 24
metacognition 82, 284
metamers 118
methadone 216
mice 245
midbrain 42, 43
Milgram's experiment 571–7
mind 82–3 see also thought
mindfulness 547
minimal risk principle 24
minimalist appraisal theories 382
minimum stimuli 103
Minnesota Multiphasic Personality Inventory 438–40
minority influence 570
misattribution of arousal 381
MMPI (Minnesota Multiphasic Personality Inventory) 438–40
mnemonic systems 295
model of the environment 147
modeling 543
molecular genetics of behavior 59, 62
monitoring 196–7
monochromats 118
monocular cues 156–7
monozygotic twins 59
mood disorders (depression and bi-polar disorders) 511–17

moods 379
moon illusion 177
moral disgust 34
moral judgment 83–5
morphemes 307
morphological rules of language 307
motion, perception of 157–9
motivation 343–73
    and emotion 378
    and learning 251–4
motor development 69
motor neurons 36
MRI (magnetic resonance imaging) scans 47
multiple intelligences 418–19
multivariate experiments 20
myelin sheath 38

naïve realism 14
naltrexone 216
narcolepsy 203–4
narrative reviews 24
natural selection 55
nature–nurture debate 8, 68–71
negative correlation 21
negative punishment 235
negative reinforcement 235
nerves 36
nervous system 34, 35
network models 163–5
networks with feedback 164–5
neural coding 39–40
neural plasticity 246
neural sensitization 351
neuroimaging 207
neurons 36–42
neuroplasticity 18
neuropsychology 11
neuroses 501
neuroticism 437
neurotransmitters 36, 41–2
neutral stimulus 227
new media 489–90
nicotine 211, 480
nightmares 204–5
9/11 557
NMDA receptors 250
nodes of Ranvier 38
noise 106
non-associative learning 225–6
non-rapid eye movement sleep 201–2
norepinephrine 41
normal distribution 634–5
normative social influence 569
noun phrases 308–9
NREM sleep 201–2
NS (neutral stimulus) 227
nuclei 36

obedience 571–7
obesity 6, 356–9
object perception 162–3
object permanence 76–7, 78–9
object recognition 165
object relations theory 445
objectification theory 361
observation 23–4
observational learning 243–4, 450
obsessions 508
obsessive-compulsive disorder 508–10
occipital lobe 45
OCD (obsessive-compulsive disorder) 508–10
Oedipal conflict 444
olfaction 33, 73, 129–31

olfactory bulb 130
olfactory cortex 130–1
olfactory system 130–1
omission training 235–6
operant conditioning 450
operations 77
opiates 215–16
opiods 136–9
opioid receptors 216
opponent-color theory 120–1
opponent-process model of sleep and wakefulness 202
optic chiasm 46
oral stage of psychosexual development 444
organizational psychology 16
oval window 125
over justification effect 3
overeating 357
overextensions 312
overjustification effect 254, 581

PAG (periaqueductal gray) 135
pain 133–9
    gate control theory 135
    virtual reality 152–4
pain threshold 34
pain tolerance 34
pair bonding 622–3
panic attacks 225, 503
panic disorder 503–6
paranoid delusions 519
paranoid schizophrenia 537
parasympathetic nervous system 53, 389
parenting styles 90–1
parents and child development 96–7
parietal lobe 45
partial reinforcement 237–8
partial-report procedure 262–3
passion 622
passionate love 621
patterns 115–16
Pavlovian conditioning 227–33
peak experiences 458
perception 102, 145–89
    active 188–9
    bottom-up processes 166
    of depth 185
    of distance 155
    five functions of 147
    of forms 184–5
    of motion 157–9
    and sensation 121–2
    top-down processes 166–8
perceptual constancies 148, 173–8, 185
perceptual development 183–9
perceptual distortions 168
perceptual interference 287
periaqueductal gray 135
peripheral nervous system 35
peripheral route to persuasion 612–14
permission rule 325
personal construct theory 453
personal distress 499–500
personality 86–92, 435–66
    development 444
    genetics of 463, 466
    psychoanalytic approach 441–9
    traits 437–8
personality disorders 524–8
personality inventories 438–40
personality psychology 16
person-environment relationships 380
persuasive communication 611–14

pessimism 485
PET (positron emission tomography) scans 47, 182, 207
phenothiazines 548–9
phenotypic plasticity 18
phenylketonuria 57, 427
pheromones 129
phobias 506–8
phonemes 306–7, 311–12
phonological coding 265
phonological loop 267–8
phonological rules of language 307
photons 104
physiology 7
Piaget's stage theory of development 75–9
pitch 123, 126, 127
pitch perception 126–9
pituitary gland 44
PKU (phenylketonuria) 57, 427
place theory of pitch 127
pluralistic ignorance 563
polarization 25
polygenic characteristics 58
pons 42
populations 633–4
positive correlation 21
positive discrimination 590–1
positive psychology 401–3, 408
positive punishment 235
positive reinforcement 235
positron emission tomography 47, 182, 207
postconventional morality 84
post-event information 289
post-event memory reconstruction 287–90
posthypnotic amnesia 209
posthypnotic response 209
post-traumatic stress disorder 481–4
power functions 106
pragmatic rules 325
pre-adaptation 34
preconscious memories 197
preconventional morality 84
preferential looking method 183
pregnancy 427–8
prenatal hormones 364–5
preoperational stage of cognitive development 76, 77–8
pressure 133
primacy effect 271, 602
primary auditory area 46
primary motor area 46
primary reinforcers 344
primary somatosensory area 46
primary visual area 46
priming 599–601
prior beliefs 244–6
privacy 25
proactive interaction 466
problem-focused coping 487
problem-solving 330–7
    difference-reduction method 330
    experts 335–6
    functional fixedness 332
    means-ends analysis 330–1
    novices 335–6
    restructuring 332
    working backward 331
product-moment correlation 637–8
projection 443
projective tests 445–7
propositional thought 317
propositions 308

prosopagnosia 5, 169, 170
prototypes 318–20, 321
proximate causes 56
proximity 617–18
psychiatric hospitals 539
psychoactive drugs 210–17
psychoanalysis 10–11
psychoanalytic perspective 12, 14, 502
psychoanalytic theory 441–9
psychodynamic therapies 545–6
psycholinguistics 11
psychological constructionism 382, 404–5
psychological disorders 497–532
psychological perspectives 12–17
    on mental health problems 502
psychological research 19–25
psychology
    biological bases of 34–5
    definition 5
    historical origins 7–11
    positive 401–3, 408
    scientific 8–9
    scope of 5–6
    subfields of 16–17
psychoneuroimmunology 478–80
psychopathology 457
psychopaths 377–8
psychophysical procedures 103
psychophysiological disorders 476
psychoses 501
psychosexual stages of personality development 444
psychotherapeutic drugs 539, 548–9
psychotherapy 541–8, 550
PTSD (post-traumatic stress disorder) 481–4
puberty 93
punishment 235
pupil 112
pure alexia 170

Q-sorts 440, 457

radiology 106–7
random assignment 20
rapid eye movement sleep 201–2
ratio schedules 238
rationalization 442–3, 579
reaction formation 443
reactive interaction 463, 466
real motion 157–9
reasoning 324–9
    neural basis 328–30
recency effect 271, 602
receptors 36
recognition 159–70
    failure of 169–70
    and localization 181–2
recognition-by-components 165
recovered memory 298–9
reductionism 15–16
reference groups 582–4
reflectance characteristics 174
refractory periods 38
rehearsed information 261
reinforcement 235–9
reinforcers 344
relaxation training 491
REM sleep 201–2
representativeness heuristic 327
repressed memory 298–9
repression 442
research 19–25
resonance 127

responses to emotion 378, 395–7
resting potential 38
reticular formation 42
retina 111–12
retrieval, modes of 276
retrieval failures 274–5
retrieval stage of memory 260
retrograde amnesia 280–1
reuptake 40
rods 112–14
Rorschach Test 446

saccades 148–9
saltatory conduction 38
samples 633–4
saturation 117
scaling of data 635
schemas 75, 288, 453, 598–9
schematic processing 598–9
schizophrenia 62, 518–23
school psychology 16
scientific psychology 8–9
scientific theories 19
secondary reinforcers 344
second-order conditioning 231
secure attachment 90
selective adaptation 157–8
selective attention 148–51
selective breeding 58
selective lesions 47
selective reinforcement 542–3
self 456–7, 460–1
self-concepts 92, 456–7
self-efficacy 244
self-esteem 92
self-expansion 620–1
self-fulfilling prophecies 603–4
selfishness 26–7
self-justification 578–82
self-objectification 361
self-perception theory 580–1
self-regulation 543–4
self-schemas 453–4, 599
semantics 307–8
sensations 101–2, 121–2
sensitive periods 70–1
sensitive responsiveness 90
sensitivity 108, 113–14
sensitization 225, 246–7
sensorimotor stage of cognitive
     development 76–7
sensory coding 108–10
sensory information 147
sensory memory 261, 262–4
sensory modalities 102–10, 178
sensory neurons 36
sensory response 264
sentence units 308
separation anxiety 88–9
serotonin 41
sex-change 365
sex-linked traits 58
sexual development 363–5
sexual orientation 364, 369, 372–3
sexuality 365–9
shadowing 150
sham feeding 353
shape constancy 175
shaping 236
short-term memory 261
signal detection theory 106–8
signals 106
significance of a difference 636–7
similarity heuristic 326–7

simple cells 162–3
simple networks 163–4
simple phobias 506–7
single-cell recordings 47
situational attribution 607
size constancy 176
sleep 199–204, 480–1
     advice on 203
     -wake disorders 202–4
     non-rapid eye movement 201–2
     rapid eye movement (REM) 201–2
     stages of 200–2
     theory 202
slow to warm up temperament 86
smell see olfaction
smiling 87–8
Snellen chart 115
social anxiety disorder (formerly social
     phobia) 507
social behavior 87–9
social cognition 597–626, 610
social desirability effects 23
social development 86–92
social exclusion 34–5
social facilitation 559–61
social identity 606–7
social influence 557–92
social inhibition 559–61
social learning 252–3, 451–3
social neuroscience 17
social norms 562
social phobia (now social anxiety
     disorder) 507
social psychology 16, 558
social stereotypes 288
social-cognitive theory 452–3
sociocultural approach to development
     81–2
sociopaths 377–8
somatic system 35
sound, characteristics of 117
sound waves 123–4
source monitoring 293
source wavelengths 174
span of apprehension 262
spatial acuity 115
speech 245 see also language
spinal cord 35
spinal cord injuries 389–90
split-brain research 49–50
spontaneous recovery 229–30
stage theory of development 95, 445
stages of development 70–1
standards 104
Stanford Prison Experiment 585–6
Stanford-Binet Intelligence Scale
     414–15
stapes 125
statistical inference 633–7
statistical significance 21, 636–7
statistics 20, 630–9
stereotype threat 604
stereotypes 288, 599–604
Sternberg's triarchic theory 420
Stevens' law 105–6
stimulant drugs 549
stimulants 216–17
stimulation 185–8
storage stage of memory 260
strange situation 90
stress 471–4
     appraisals 485–7
     coping 487–90, 492–3
     managing 490–4
          and physical health 476–81

          and psychological health 481–4
     psychological reactions to 474–6
stress responses 472
stressors 472
stroboscopic motion 157
Stroop effect 336
Stroop interference 560
structural brain imaging 47
structural consequences of learning
     250
structuralism 9
subjective experiences 378, 385–7
subjectivist perspective 12, 14
substantia nigra 43
suicide 516–17
superego 441–2
superior colliculus 43
suppression 442
suprathreshold sensation 105–6
survey methods 23
susto 501
syllogisms 324
symbols 147
sympathetic nervous system 53, 388
synapses 36
synaptic gaps 36
synaptic plasticity 249
synaptic transmission 39–40
syntax 308
System 1 & 2 modes of thinking 598
systematic desensitization 542–4

tabula rasa 8
taijin kyofusho 501
tardive dyskinesia 549
taste see gustation
TAT (Thematic Apperception Test)
     446–7
Tay-Sachs disease 427
temperament 86–7
temperature 133
temporal lobe 45
temporal patterns 110
temporal theory 126–7
terminal buttons 36
tests 21–2
thalamus 43
Thematic Apperception Test 446–7
theories 19
theory of ecological optics 147
theory of mind 82–3
thirst 346–7
thought 317–24 see also mind
     and language 338–9
     and working memory 270
thought-action tendencies 378,
     387–8
threshold sensitivity 102–5
timbre 124
TMS (transcranial magnetic
     stimulation) 47
tolerance 351
tongue maps 132
top-down feedback connections 164
touch 133
transcranial magnetic stimulation 47
transduction 113
transference 546, 619–20
trial-and-error learning 234
trials 103
triangular theory of love 622
trichromatic theory 118–21
Trisomy 21, 427
twins 58–9
type A behavior 477–8, 491, 494

ultimate causes 56
unconditional positive regard 456
unconditioned response 227
unconditioned stimulus 227
unconscious 10, 197–8
     collective 445
undoing effect of positive emotions 389
unusualness 499
UR (unconditioned response) 227
urban planning 350
US (unconditioned stimulus) 227

V1 (visual cortex) 180–1
variable interval schedules 239
variable ratio schedules 238
variables 19–20
ventromedial hypothalamic syndrome
     355
verb phrases 308–9
VI (variable interval) schedules 239
virtual reality and pain 152–4
visceral perception 389–90
vision 71–2, 111–22
visual acuity 115
visual coding 265–6
visual cortex 180–1
visual field 71
visual neglect 334
visual search tasks 161–2
visual system 111–13
visual-spatial sketchpad 267–8
VR (variable ratio) schedules 238
vulnerability-stress model 502

WAIS (Wechsler Adult Intelligence
     Scale) 415–17
wanting 348–9
Wason selection task 325
weapon focus 149
Weber fraction 105
Weber-Fechner law 105
Wechsler Adult Intelligence Scale
     415–17
weight control 358–9
Wernicke-Geschwind model 48–9
Wernicke's aphasia 310
Wernicke's area 48–9
withdrawal 351
word salad 519
working memory 265–72
     buffers 266–8
     forgetting 269
     and long-term memory 270–2
     retrieval 269–70
     storage 268–9
     and thought 270

Yerkes–Dodson law 251
Young–Helmholtz theory 118–21

Photo Credit

All Figures, Tables and artwork *not* listed on this credit page are the authors' own work and so do not require any credit lines, permissions acknowledgements or referencing citations.

The following photographs have all been reproduced with permission of the copyright holders, and the credit-lines are listed below:

p. 4 photo © Shutterstock
p. 6 photo © Shutterstock
p. 7 All photos © Shutterstock
p. 8 photo © Shutterstock
p. 10 All photos © Bettman/Corbis
p. 12 photo © Volker Steoer/Peter Arnold, Inc.
p. 13 1st photo © Shutterstock
p. 13 2nd photo © istockphoto.com
p. 14 photo © NYPL/SCIENCE SOURCE/SCIENCE PHOTO LIBRARY
p. 15 photo © Graham Franks / Alamy
p. 23 photo © MARKA / Alamy
p. 24 photo © istockphoto.com
p. 26 photo No source-line needed
p. 27 photo © Purestock/Alamy
p. 40 photo © SCIENCE VU, VISUALS UNLIMITED /SCIENCE PHOTO LIBRARY
p. 48 1st photo © Shutterstock
p. 48 2nd photo © WELLCOME DEPT. OF COGNITIVE NEUROLOGY/ SCIENCE PHOTO LIBRARY
p. 59 All photos © Shutterstock
p. 70 1st photo © Jorge Saenz/ Associated Press
p. 70 All other photos © Shutterstock
p. 73 photo © Andy Bishop / Alamy
p. 80 photo © istockphoto.com
p. 82 photo © Shutterstock
p. 86 photo © Shutterstock
p. 87 photo © Shutterstock
p. 91 photo © Shutterstock
p. 92 photo © Shutterstock
p. 93 photo © Shutterstock
p. 95 photo © Littleny | Dreamstime.com
p. 96 photo © Judith Rich Harris
p. 97 photo © Jerome Kagan
p. 103 photo © Shutterstock
p. 108 photo © The Natural History Museum, London
p. 117 photo © Shutterstock
p. 124 photo © Shutterstock
p. 123 photo © Kgtoh | Dreamstime.com
p. 127 photo Courtesey of Scott Murray & Huseyin Boyaci
p. 130 photo © Shutterstock
p. 131 1st photo © Everett Collection Historical / Alamy
p. 131 2nd photo © Hemis / Alamy
p. 133 photo © Shutterstock
p. 137 photo © Robert N. Jamison
p. 139 photo © Dennis C. Turk
p. 146 photo © Shutterstock
p. 150 photo © Shutterstock
p. 158 photo © Chris Howes/Wild Places Photography / Alamy
p. 159 photo © Shutterstock
p. 160 photo © Shutterstock
p. 169 photo © World History Archive / Alamy
p. 171 photo © Rex Features
p. 174 photo © Shutterstock
p. 175 photo Edward Adelson
p. 177 photo © Shutterstock

p. 187 photo © Mark Johnson
p. 196 photo © Shutterstock
p. 198 cartoon © Cengage Learning EMEA
p. 202 photo © Shutterstock
p. 204 photo © Louie Psihoyos/Science Faction/Corbis
p. 205 photo © Shutterstock
p. 206 photo © Shutterstock
p. 210 photo © PHILIPPE PLAILLY/SCIENCE PHOTO LIBRARY
p. 212 photo © Shutterstock
p. 227 photo © RIA Novosti / Alamy
p. 234 photo © Everett Collection Historical / Alamy
p. 237 photo © Shutterstock
p. 238 photo © Shutterstock
p. 251 photo © Shutterstock
p. 261 photo © Shutterstock
p. 262 photo © Tim Houghton / Alamy
p. 266 photo © Cengage Learning EMEA
p. 267 1st photo © Shutterstock
p. 267 2nd photo © Cengage Learning EMEA
p. 271 photo © 1995, reprinted courtesey of Bill Host and Parade Magazine
p. 274 photo © Shutterstock
p. 279 photo © Beth Dixson / Alamy
p. 281 photo © Shutterstock
p. 289 1st photo © Ankevanwyk | Dreamstime.com
p. 289 2nd photo © Shutterstock
p. 291 photo © Shutterstock
p. 298 photo © Kathy Pezdek
p. 299 photo © Elizabeth R. Loftus
p. 310 photo © Shutterstock
p. 313 photo © Shutterstock
p. 314 photo © Huntstock, Inc / Alamy
p. 316 1st photo © SUSAN KUKLIN/SCIENCE PHOTO LIBRARY
p. 316 2nd photo © FRANS LANTING/National Geographic Stock
p. 318 photo © istockphoto.com
p. 319 photo © martin westlake / Alamy
p. 321 photo © Shutterstock
p. 335 photo © epa european pressphoto agency b.v. / Alamy
p. 344 1st photo © Shutterstock
p. 344 2nd photo © Action Plus Sports Images / Alamy
p. 347 photo © Shutterstock
p. 349 photo After Berridge, 1999, and Steiner et al., 2001 Photos Courtesy K. C. Berridge.
p. 251 photo © Shutterstock
p. 352 photo © Chuckplace | Dreamstime.com
p. 355 photo © OAK RIDGE NATIONAL LABORATORY/US DEPARTMENT OF ENERGY/SCIENCE PHOTO LIBRARY
p. 360 1st photo © INTERFOTO / Alamy
p. 360 2nd photo © Peter Stroh / Alamy
p. 363 photo © NUCLEUS MEDICAL MEDIA/VISUALS UNLIMITED, INC. / SCIENCE PHOTO LIBRARY
p. 367 photo © Melissa Tse, Getty Images
p. 403 1st photo © Jurgita | Dreamstime.com
p. 403 2nd photo © Shutterstock
p. 390 photo © Jonathan Larsen/Diadem Images / Alamy

Figure and Table Credit

p.6	Figure 1.2 Defining the Boundaries of Childhood Amnesia.	Reprinted with permission from Davis, N., Gross, J., Hayne, H., (2008). Defining the boundaries of childhood amnesia. Memory, 16, 465–474.
p.6	Figure 1.3 The Relationship Between Childhood Viewing of Violent Television and Adult Aggression.	Reprinted with permission from Gentile, D. A. & Bushman, B. J. (2012) Reassessing media violence effects using a risk and resilience approach to understanding aggression. Psychology of Popular Media Culture, 1, 138–151.
p.45	Figure 2.11 Photograph of Human Brain	© Shutterstock
p.72	Figure 3.2 Visual Acuity.	© Shutterstock
p.74	Figure 3.4 A Study of Infant Memory.	Reprinted with permission from Rovee-Collier, C. (1999). The development of infant memory. Current Directions in Psychological Science, 8, 80–85
p.74	Figure 3.5 Preference for Sounds.	© Rich Malkames
p.76	Figure 3.6 Object Permanence.	© DOUG GOODMAN/SCIENCE PHOTO LIBRARY
p.81	Figure 3.10 Early Testing of Conservation.	© Shutterstock
p.88	Figure 3.11 Children's Stress at Mother's Departure.	© Shutterstock
p.89	Figure 3.12 A Monkey's Response to an Artificial Mother.	© PHOTO RESEARCHERS/SCIENCE PHOTO LIBRARY
p.117	Figure 4.18 The Color Solid.	Reprinted courtesey of X-Rite Incorporated Grand Rapids, MI.
p.120	Figure 4.21 The Trichromatic Theory.	Reprinted from 'Spectral Sensitivity of the Foveal Cone Photopigments Between 400 and 500 nm', in Vision Search, 15, pp. 161–171. © 1975, with permission from Elsevier Science.)
p.122	Figure 4.24 Effects of Distance.	© ZUMA Press, Inc. / Alamy
p.149	Figure 5.2 Eye Movements in Viewing a Picture.	Reprinted with permission from D. L. Yarbuss (1967) 'Eye Movements and Vision', Plenum Publishing Corporation. Reproduced by permission of the publisher)
p.152	Figure 5.4 The Slave Market with a Disappearing Bust of Voltaire.	Reprinted with permission from Salvador Dali, Slave Market with Disappearing Bust of Voltaire, 1950, The Salvador Dali Museum, St. Petersburg, Fla
p.156	Figure 5.6 Monocular Distance Cues in a Picture.	© Shutterstock
p.167	Figure 5.20 An Ambiguous Stimulus.	© PARIS PIERCE / Alamy
p.173	Figure 5.24 Boundary Extension and Abstraction.	Reprinted with permission from Intraub, H., & Richardson, M. (1989). Wide-angle memories of close-up scenes. Journal of Experimental Psychology: Learning, Memory, and Cognition, 179–18, the American Psychological Association.
p.180	Figure 5.30 PET Images Reveal Differences in Cortical Activity.	Reprinted with permission from M. Corbetta, F. M. Miezen, S. Dobmeyer, D. L. Shulman, S. E. Persen, "Attentional Modulation of Neural Processing of Shape, Color and Velocity in Humans," Science V. 248 p. 1558, 1990; Reprinted by permission of the American Association for the Advancement of Science.
p.182	Figure 5.33 Recognition and Localization Tasks.	Reprinted with permission from Journal of Cognitive Neruroscience, pp. 23–24, Fig. 5-2, p. 30, vol. 4:1, Winter 1992, by permission of the MIT Press, Cambridge, MA
p.183	Figure 5.34 Testing the Visual Preferences of an infant.	© PHILIPPE PLAILLY/SCIENCE PHOTO LIBRARY
p.184	Figure 5.35 Visual Acuity and Contrast Sensitivity.	Reprinted with permission from Sensations and Perception by E. Bruce Goldstein, © 1989, 1984, 1980 Wadsworth Publishing Co.
p.185	Figure 5.36 The Visual Cliff.	© SCIENCE SOURCE/SCIENCE PHOTO LIBRARY
p.235	Figure 7.5 Apparatus for Instrumental Conditioning.	© Richard Wood/Index Stock
p.244	Figure 7.10 Bandura's 'Bobbo Doll Study'.	© Albert Bandura
p.267	Figure 8.5 Testing for Eidetic Images.	© Shutterstock
p.294	Figure 8.14 Number of Digits Recalled by S.F.	Reprinted with permission from 'Acquisition of a Memory Skill', Science, Vol. 208, 1980, pp. 1181–1182 by I. A. Ericsson, et al. Copyright © 1980 by American Association for the Advancement of Science

p.384	Figure 11.3 Number of Digits Recalled by S.F.	Reprinted with permission from Whalen, Rauch, Etcoff, McInerney, Lee, & Jenike, (1998), 'Masked Presentation of Emotional Facial Expressions Modulate Amygdala Activity Without Explicit Knowledge', *Journal of Neuroscience* 18, 411–418.
p.437	Figure 13.1 Eysenck's Personality Factors.	Reprinted with permission from H.J. Eysenck & S. Rachman (1965), The Causes and Cures of Neurosis, by H.J. Eysenck. Copyright © 1965 by H.J. Eysenck and S. Rachman. Reprinted by permission of EdiTS.
p.446	Figure 13.2 A Rorschach Inkblot.	© Science Photo Library
p.461	Figure 13.6 Phineas Gage's Brain Injury.	Damasio, H., Grabowski, T., Frank, R., Galaburda, A. M., and Damasio, A. R.: The return of Phineas Gage: clues about the brain from the skull of a famous patient. Science, (1994) Vol 264, Issue 5162, Pages 1061–1199. Copyright © 1994 American Association for the Advancement of Science
p.478	Figure 14.3 Stress and Colds.	© Shutterstock
p.484	Figure 14.7 PTSD and Blood Flow in the Brain.	Photos courtesey of Dr. Lisa Shin in relation to her and Kosslyn, Alpert, Rauch, Macklin & Pitman (1997) 'Visual Imagery and Perception in Posttraumatic Stress Disorder: A Positron Emission Tomographic Investigation' Archives of General Psychiatry
p.514	Figure 15.7 PET Scans of Bipolar Disorder.	Reprinted with courtesy of Monte S. Buschbaum, M.D., Mt. Sinai School of Medicine, New York
p.516	Figure 15.9 Gender, Age, and Suicide.	Sourced with permission from World Health Organization (2004). Distribution of suicide rates per (1,000,000) by gender and age, 2000. Retrieved from http://www.who.int/mental_health/prevention/suicide/charts/en/
p.103	Table 4.1 Minimum Stimuli	Reprinted with permission from Galanter, E. (1962). 'Contemporary Psychophysic,' from Roger Brown & collaborators (eds.), New Directions in Psychology, Vol. 1.
p.275	Table 8.1 Examples From a Study of Retrieval Failures	Reprinted with permission from E. Tulving and Z. Pearlstone (1976) 'Availability and Accessibility', from Journal of Memory and Language, 5:381–391. Reprinted by permission of Academic Press
p.282	Table 8.2 Procedure for an Experiment to study implicit memory	Reprinted with permission from Neuropsychologia, Vol. 16. pp. 169–172 by W. K. Warrington and L. Weiskrantz, 'Further Analysis of the Proper Learning Effect in Amnesiac Parents'. Copyright © 1978, with permission from Elsevier Science, Ltd.
p.314	Table 9.2 Operating Principles Used by Young Children	Reprinted with permission from Dan I. Slobin (1971) from 'Developmental Psycholinguistics', in A Survey of Linguistic Science, edited by W. O. Dingwall, pp. 298–400.
p.388	Table 11.4 Symptoms of Fear in Combat Flying	Reprinted with permission from L. F. Shaffer (1947) 'Fear and courage in aerial combat' in Journal of Consulting and Clinical Psychology, 11:137–143
p.396	Table 11.5 The process model of emotion regulation	Reprinted with permission from Sheppes, G. & Gross, J. J. (2011). Is timing everything? Temporal considerations in emotion regulation. Personality and Social Psychology Review, 15, 319-331.
p.472	Table 14.1 The Life Events Scale	Reprinted with permission from T. H. Holmes & R. H. Rahe (1967) "The Social Readjustment Rating Scale," in the Journal of Psychosomatic Research, Vol. 11, No. 2, pp. 213–218. Copyright © 1967 Elsevier Science.)

The following Figures and Tables have all been adapted and changed from the original sources so did not require permission but below are citation references to the research, for referencing purposes:

p.40	Figure 2.8 Release of Neurotransmitters Into a Synaptic Gap.	Referencing 'Search for the Human Mind' by Robert Sternberg © 1994 Harcourt Brace & Company
p.46	Figure 2.13 Visual Pathways	Referencing 'Human Anatomy' by Anthony J. Gaudin and Kenneth C. Jones 1988
p.50	Figure 2.15 Sensory Inputs to the Two Hemispheres.	Referencing Neuropsychologia Vol. 9 by R.D. Nebes and W. Sperry p.247 © 1971, Elsevier Science
p.58	Figure 2.21 Inheritance of Maze Learning in Rats	Referencing Thompson 1954.
p.79	Figure 3.9 Testing Object Permanence.	Referencing Baillargeon, R., 'Object Performance in 3 1/2 and 4 1/2 month old infants' from Development Psychology, © 1987, Academic Press
p.112	Figure 4.10 A Schematic Picture of the Retina.	Referencing J. E. Dowling and B. B. Boycott (1969) 'Organization of the Primate Retina' from Proceedings of the Royal Society of London, Series B, Vol. l66, pp. 80–111.
p.125	Figure 4.27 A Schematic Diagram of the Middle and Inner Ear.	Referencing Sensation and Perception 3/e by S. Coremn and L. Ward © 1989 John Wiley & Sons.
p.134	Figure 4.31 Culture and Pain	Referencing research conducted by D.D. Kosambi & Dr. Meera Kosambi in 1967, 'Living Prehistory in India' Scientific American.
p.165	Figure 5.16 Perception of Letters and Words.	Referencing Reicher, 1969
p.166	Figure 5.18 A Possible Set of Features (Geons) for Natural Objects.	Referencing L. Biederman in 1985, Computer Vision, Graphics & Image Processing, Academic Press
p.167	Figure 5.19 Object Recognition and Geon Recovery.	Referencing by L. Biederman in 1985, *Computer Vision, Graphics & Image Processing*, Academic Press
p.168	Figure 5.21 Effects of Temporal Context.	Referencing Fisher, Perception of Ambiguous Stimulus Materials' study in 1967 in Perception & Psychophysics.
p.178	Figure 5.29 The True Shape of the Ames Room.	Referencing Goldstein, 1984
p.181	Figure 5.31 Two Cortical Visual Systems.	Referencing Mortimer Mishkin, Leslie G. Ungerleider, & Kathleen A. Macko, 'Object Vision and Spatial Vision: Two Cortical Pathways', Trends in Neuroscience, in 1983
p.213	Figure 6.7 Consumption of Pure Alcohol in Various Regions of the World.	Data used referencing research by the World Health Organization in 2005
p.214	Figure 6.8 Differencs in Binge-drinking among 18-24 Year Olds.	Data used referencing research by the World Health Organization in 2004
p.214	Figure 6.9 Percent of Illicit Drug Users Reporting Use of Various Drugs in the Last Year.	Data used referencing research by the World Health Organization in 2008
p.229	Figure 7.2 Acquisition and Extinction of a Conditioned Response.	Referencing 'Conditioned Reflexes' conducted by E. P. Pavlov, 1927, Oxford University Press.
p.230	Figure 7.3 The Gradient of Generalization	Referencing, 'The Sensory Generalization of Conditioned Responses with Varying Frequencies of Tone' conducted by the Helen Dwight Reid Educational Foundation, Journal of General Psychology 1937.
p.230	Figure 7.4 Conditioned Discrimination.	Referencing, 'Differential Classical Conditioning: Verbalization of Stimulus Contingencies' conducted by M. J. Fuhrer & P. E. Baer in 1965, Science Journal 1965, American Association for the Advancement of Science.
p.236	Figure 7.6 Search and Rescue by Pigeons.	Referencing Simmons, 1981
p.239	Figure 7.7 Typical Patterns of Responding on the Four Basic Schedules of Reinforcement.	Referencing Barry Schwartz, 'Psychology of Learning and Behaviour 3/e', W.W. Norton & Co. Inc.
p.260	Figure 8.1 Three Stages of Memory.	Referencing A. W. Melton in 1963, 'Implication of Short-Term Memory for a General Theory of Memory', Journal of Verbal Learning and Verbal Behaviour, Academic Press
p.268	Figure 8.6 An Experiment on Acoustic and Visual Buffers	Referencing Smith, 1995
p.269	Figure 8.7 Retrieval as a Search Process.	Referencing S. Sternberg 'High Speed Scanning in Human Memory', *Science*, 1966, American Association for the Advancement of Science.
p.270	Figure 8.8 Illustration of a Geometric Analogy.	Referencing M.A. Just and P. Shell in 1990 'What one intelligence test measures: a theoretical account of the processing in the Raven Progressive Matrices Test', *Psychological Review*.
p.271	Figure 8.9 Results of a Free Recall Experiment	Referencing B. B. Murdock in 1962, "The Serial Position Effect in Free Recall', *Journal of Experimental Psychology*.
p.278	Figure 8.12 Effects of Environmental Context on Retrieval.	Referencing D. Godden and A. D. Baddeley (1975) 'Context-Dependent Memory in Two Natural Environments: On Land & Under Water', *British Journal of Psychology*.
p.282	Figure 8.13 Recall of an Early Memory.	Referencing Sheingold & Tenney, 1982
p.296	Figure 8.17 Organizing Words into a Story.	Referencing Bower & Clark, 1969

p.297	Figure 8.19 Practicing Retrieval.	Referencing Gates, 1917
p.333	Figure 9.10 Decision Times in the Mental Rotation Study.	Referencing L.A. Cooper & R.N. Shepherd, 1973, 'Chronometric Studies of the Rotation of Mental Images', W.G. Chase, ed.Visual Information Processing
p.334	Figure 9.11 Scanning Mental Images.	Referencing by S. M. Kosslyn, et al., (1978), 'Scanning Mental Images, Visual Images Preserve Metric Spatial Information: Evidence from Studies of Image Scanning', Journal of Experimental Psychology
p.334	Figure 9.12 Imagery and Perception.	Referencing Robert J. Sternberg, Beyond IQ: A Triarchic Theory of Human Intelligence © 1985 Robert J. Sternberg, Cambridge University Press.
p.323	Figure 9.5 Examples of Dot Patterns Used to Study Categorization in Amnesiac Patients	Referencing Squire & Knowlton in 1995.
p.325	Figure 9.6 Content Effects in Deductive Reasoning.	Referencing research by Grigs & Cox (1982) and Wason & Johnson-Laird (1972).
p.333	Figure 9.9 Study of Mental Rotation.	Referencing L.A. Cooper & R.N. Shepherd, 1973, 'Chronometric Studies of the Rotation of Mental Images', W.G. Chase, ed. Visual Information Processing
p.345	Figure 10.1 A Model of Basic Motives.	Referencing Toates, 2011
p.368	Figure 10.5 Reported Incidence of Premarital Coitus.	Referencing J. R. Hopkins (1977) "Sexual Behavior in Adolescence," in Journal of Social Issues, Vol. 33(2):67–85.
p.387	Figure 11.4 Fear, Anger, and Risk.	Referencing Lerner and Keltner in 2001, Journal of Personality and Social Psychology
p.389	Figure 11.5 The Undoing Effect of Positive Emotions.	Referencing by B.L. Fredrickson, R.A. Mancuso, C. Branigan, & M.M Tugade 2000, Motivation & Emotion.
p.391	Figure 11.6 Differences in Arousal for Different Emotions.	Referencing P. Ekman et al's research into this, 1983, Science, American Association for the Advancement of Science.
p.415	Figure 12.1 The Distribution of IQ Scores.	Referencing research conducted by A. Anastasia & S. Urbina, Psychological Testing 7/e, 1997.
p.423	Figure 12.2 IQ Data From Twin Studies.	Referencing "Familiar Studies of Intelligence: A Review,"T. Bouchard, et al., Science, Vol. 212, #4498, p 1055–9, 29 May 1981. Copyright © 1981 American Association for the Advancement of Science.
p.457	Figure 13.4 Maslow's Hierarchy of Needs.	Referencing the academic concept of 'Maslow's Hierarchy of Needs'
p.482	Figure 14.5 Cultural and Sex Differences in PTSD.	Referencing Norris et al 'Sex Differences in Symptoms of Post-traumatic Stress: Does Culture Play a Role?' Journal of Tramatuc Stress
p.483	Figure 14.6 Post-Traumataic Symptoms in Rape.	Referencing Foa & Riggs, 1995.
p.505	Figure 15.1 Panic Attacks of Patients and Controls.	Referencing R.M. Rapee, T.A. Brown, M.M. Anthony & D.H. Barlow 1992, 'Response to hyperventilation and inhalation of 5.5% carbon-dioxide-enriched air across the DSM-III-R anxiety disorders', Journal of Abnormal Psychology.
p.506	Figure 15.2 Panic Symptoms in Panic Patients	Referencing Carter, Hollon, Caron & Shelton's research into this in 1995.
p.515	Figure 15.8 Brain Functioning in Depression.	Referencing W.C. Drevetts,2000, 'Neuroimaging studies of mood disorders', Biological Psychiatry, 48, 813–829
p.521	Figure 15.11 Cultural Differences in the Course of Schizophrenia.	Referencing A. Jablensky in 2000, 'Epidemiology of Schizophrenia: the global burden of disease and disability', European Archives of Psychiatry & Clinical Neuroscience, Volume 50, No. 6, Dec. 2000
p.522	Figure 15.12 Genetic Relationships and Schizophrenia.	Referencing Schizophrenia: The Epigenetic Puzzle, by I. I. Gottesman & J. Shields. Copyright © 1992 Cambridge University Press.
p.545	Figure 16.4 Percentage of Panic Patients Remaining Symptom-Free After 15 Months.	Referencing Clark et al in 1994
p.564	Figure 17.3 Diffusion of Responsibility.	Referencing by M.M. Darley & B. Latane1968 'Bystander Intervention in Emergencies: Diffusion of Resonsibility', Journal of Personality and Social Psychology
p.572	Figure 17.5 Milgram's Experiment on Obedience.	Referencing Stanley Milgram, 1974, 'Obedience to Authority: An Experimental View', 1974
p.573	Figure 17.6 Obedience to Authority.	Referencing S. Milgram (1963), 'Behavioral Study of Obedience', from Journal of Abnormal and Social Psychology, 67, p. 376.
p.580	Figure 17.7 An Induced-Compliance Experiment	Referencing Festinger and Carlsmith in 1959.
p.589	Figure 17.8 Group Norms and the Effectiveness of Group Decisions	Referencing T. Postmes & R. Spears in 2001, 'Quality of decision making and group norms', Journal of Personality and Social Psychology, 80, 918–930.
p.601	Figure 18.1 Automatic Stereotype Activation.	Referencing, R.H. Fazio, J.R. Jackson, B.C. Dunton & C. J. Williams, 1995, 'Variability in automatic activation as an unobtrusive measure of racial attitudes: A bona fide pipeline?' Journal of Personality and Social Psychology, 69, 1013–1027, (c) 1995
p.605	Figure 18.2 Impression Formation: From Stereotypes to Individuation.	Referencing S.T. Friske, M. Lin & S.L. Neuberg, 1999, 'The continuum model: Ten years later', S. Chaiken & Y. Trobe, Dual-process Theories in Social Psychology pp. 231–254, New York, Guildford Press.

p.608	Figure 18.3 The Fundamental Attribution Error.	Referencing Ross, Armabole & Steinmetz, 1977.
p.613	Figure 18.4 A Test of the Elaboration Likelihood Model.	Referencing R.E. Petty & J.T. Cacioppo, 1984, 'The effects of involvement on responses to arguments quantity and quality, central and peripheral routes to persuasion', *Jounral of Personality & Social Psychology 46:6-81*
p.621	Figure 18.7 Including the Other in the Self.	Referencing A. Aron, E. N. Aron, and D. Smollan in 1992 'Inclusion of the self scale and the structure of interpersonal closeness' *Advances in Experimental Social Psychology, 63, 596-612.*
p.92	Table 3.2 The percentages of attachment styles as measured by the Strange Situation	Referencing Thompson,1998
p.232	Table 7.1 An Experiment on Constraints and Taste Aversion	Referencing J. Garcia and R. A. Koelling (1966) 'The Relation of Cue to Consequence in Avoidance Learning,' Psychonomic Science, 4: 123–124, no
p.307	Table 9.1 A phonetic alphabet for English pronunciation	Referencing Fromkin, Rodman & Hyams, *An introduction to Language, 7th edition* (2003), Wadsworth.
p.359	Table 10.1 Weight Loss Following Different Treatments	Referencing research conducted by L. W. Craighead, A. J. Stankard, & R. M. O'Brien (1981) 'Behavior Therapy and Pharmcotherapy for Obesity', in Archives of General Psychiatry, 38:763–768.
p.383	Table 11.1 Emotions and their cognitive causes	Referencing research conducted by Lazarus, 1991b
p.383	Table 11.2 Primary appraisal dimensions	Referencing research conducted by Roseman, 1984
p.387	Table 11.3 Emotions and their associated though-action tendencies	Referencing multiple sources including Fredrickson, 1998, 2002
p.438	Table 13.1 Five trait factors	Referencing research conducted by McCrae & Costa, 1987
p.622	Table 18.1 The Triangular Theory of Love	Referencing Sternberg (1986), 'Triangular Theory of Love', in *Psychological Review,* 93:119–135